Trade Associations and Professional Bodies of United Kingdom & Eire

Trade Associations and Professional Bodies of United Kingdom & Eire

An alphabetical and subject classified guide to 5,000 organisations that promote and foster business, commerce, trade, science, and related activities in United Kingdom and Eire.

Consulting Editor
Tara E. Atterberry

GRAHAM & WHITESIDE™

THOMSON

GALE

London • Detroit • New York • San Diego • San Francisco • Cleveland • New Haven, Conn. • Waterville, Maine • Munich

THOMSON

GALE

TRADE ASSOCIATIONS AND PROFESSIONAL BODIES OF UNITED KINGDOM & EIRE
Consulting Editor: Tara Atterberry

ISBN 1 86099 365 6

CONTENTS

INTRODUCTION

This updated and expanded directory, a co-publication between the Gale Group and Graham & Whiteside, provides essential information on nearly 5,000 trade associations and professional bodies in Eire (Republic of Ireland), England, Northern Ireland, Scotland and Wales in the following sectors: trade, business, and commercial; environmental and agricultural; legal, government, public administration and military; engineering, technological, natural and social sciences; educational; health and medical; public affairs; labour unions associations, and federations.

Typical entries include as available: name, address, phone, fax, e-mail, website, year founded, number of members; number of staff, contact name, fee, description of activities, library type, details of meetings and conventions.

Indexes cover: associations by regions, by subject classification; and by acronym.

In order to keep our information as up-to-date and reliable as possible, we would appreciate hearing about any changes in the entries included in this edition. We would also be grateful to know about any new or existing associations which are not currently included.

Please contact:
The Publisher,
Trade Associations and Professional Bodies of Continental Europe,
Graham & Whiteside,
High Holborn House,
50/51 Bedford Row,
London
WC1R 4LR

We also welcome any comments or suggestions.

EIRE

Action from Ireland
AFrI

134 Phibsboro Rd., Phibsboro, Dublin 7, Eire (Rep. of Ireland)
Tel: 353 1 8827881
Fax: 353 1 8827576
Email: afri@iol.ie
Website: http://www.afri.buz.org
Founded: 1975
Members: 3000
Staff: 3
Contact: Joseph Murray, Coor.
Fee: €20
Description: Non-partisan political organization. Works to increase awareness of the causes of poverty. Believes these causes include: unfair distribution of wealth; misuse of the earth's resources; exploitation of the economically disadvantaged; waste of resources caused by international arms races and debt crises.
Publication: Book
Publication title: Just a Second
Second publication: Newsletter
Publication title: Peacemaker
Meetings/Conventions: - annual conference

Adelaide Hospital Society

c/o Adelaide and Meath Hospital
Tallaght, Dublin 24, Eire (Rep. of Ireland)
Tel: 353 1 4142072
Fax: 353 1 4142070
Email: info@adelaide.ie
Website: http://www.adelaide.ie
Founded: 1839
Members: 1000
Staff: 2
Contact: Dr. Fergus O'Ferrall, Dir.
Description: Promotes the participation of the Protestant community in the Irish health system. Makes available financial support to Adelaide and Meath Hospital. Conducts fundraising activities; sponsors charitable programs.

Admissions Officers' Association
AOA

Office for Academic Affairs, Dublin City University, Dublin 9, Eire (Rep. of Ireland)
Tel: 353 1 7045398
Description: Professional admissions officers in institutions of higher education in Ireland.

Adopted Peoples Association - Ireland
APA

27 Templeview Green, Clare Hall, Dublin 13, Eire (Rep. of Ireland)
Tel: 353 1 4624430
Email: info@adoptionireland.com
Website: http://www.connect.ie/~apa/
Description: Promotes the rights and interests of adopted people in Ireland.

Age Action Ireland

30/31 Lower Camden St., Dublin 2, Eire (Rep. of Ireland)
Tel: 353 1 4756989
Fax: 353 1 4756011
Email: info@ageaction.ie
Website: http://www.ageaction.ie

Founded: 1992
Members: 970
Staff: 73
Contact: Robin Webster, CEO
Description: Works to improve the quality of life of all older people, especially those who are most disadvantaged and vulnerable, by enabling them to live full, independent and satisfying lives for as long as they wish in their own homes. Membership is open to all organizations and individuals concerned with aging and older people. Main activities include information and publishing, library, education and training, U3A, Carer Support Programme, innovative projects, research, policy development and campaigning.
Library Subject: aging, older people
Library Type: open to the public
Publication title: Bulletin
Meetings/Conventions: conference

Agricultural Economics Society of Ireland

Dept. of Agribusiness, UCD, Bellfield, Dublin 4, Eire (Rep. of Ireland)
Tel: 353 1 7067706
Fax: 353 2837328
Email: deidre.oconnor@ucd.ie
Founded: 1967

Agricultural Science Association

Bluebell, Irish Farm Centre, Dublin 12, Eire (Rep. of Ireland)
Tel: 353 1 4501166
Fax: 353 4565415

Alzheimer Society of Ireland
ASI

Alzheimer House, 43 Northumberland Ave., Dublin, Eire (Rep. of Ireland)
Tel: 353 1 2846616
Fax: 353 1 2846030
Email: info@alzheimer.ie
Website: http://www.alzheimer.ie
Founded: 1982
Members: 5000
Staff: 140
Contact: Maurice O'Connell, Chief Exec.
Description: Individuals and organizations. Seeks to improve the quality of life of people with Alzheimer's disease and their families; promotes advancement in the diagnosis and treatment of Alzheimer's disease. Makes available home support and day care service to people with Alzheimer's disease and their families; maintains respite home; serves as a clearinghouse on Alzheimer's disease and services available to people with the disease.
Publication: Newsletter
Publication title: Alheimer Society of Ireland Newsletter

American Chamber of Commerce Ireland
AMCHAM IRELAND

c/o Heritage House
6 Wilton Pl., Dublin 2, Eire (Rep. of Ireland)
Tel: 353 1 6616201
Fax: 353 1 6616217
Email: info@amcham.ie
Website: http://www.amcham.ie
Founded: 1961
Members: 350

Staff: 2
Contact: Bernard Collins, Pres.
Description: Companies and individuals engaged in trading and investing between the United states and Ireland.
Library Subject: Ireland-U.S. trade
Library Type: reference
Publication: Directory
Publication title: American Business Directory: Directory and Year Book of American Business in Ireland. Advertisements.
Second publication: Newsletter
Meetings/Conventions: - monthly

Amnesty International - Ireland
Sean McBride House, 48 Fleet St., Dublin 2, Eire (Rep. of Ireland)
Tel: 353 1 6776361
Fax: 353 1 6776392
Email: info@amnesty.ie
Website: http://www.amnesty.ie
Contact: Mary Lawlor, Dir.
Description: Irish section of Amnesty International. Promotes human rights.

Anatomical Society of Great Britain and Ireland
c/o Prof. J.P. Fraher
Department of Anatomy, University College, Cork, Eire (Rep. of Ireland)
Tel: 353 21 4902115
Fax: 353 21 4902246
Email: j.fraher@ucc.ie
Website: http://www.anatsoc.org.uk
Founded: 1887
Members: 650
Contact: J.P. Fraher, Sec.
Fee: €35
Membership Type: ordinary
Fee: €65
Membership Type: with journal
Description: Individuals involved in anatomical science. Promotes development and advancement in anatomy and related science through research and education. Offers program for graduate students.
Publication: Journal
Publication title: Journal of Anatomy
Meetings/Conventions: - semiannual meeting - Exhibits.

Animal and Plant Health Association
8 Woodbine Park, Blackrock, Dublin, Eire (Rep. of Ireland)
Tel: 353 1 2603050
Fax: 353 1 2603021
Email: info@apha.ie
Website: http://www.apha.ie
Founded: 1994
Members: 31
Staff: 3
Contact: Mr. Declan O'Brien
Description: Promotes awareness of animal and plant health issues.
Publication: Book
Publication title: Veterinary Data Sheet Compendium

Anne Sullivan Foundation for Deafblind
40 Lower Drumcondra Rd., Dublin 9, Eire (Rep. of Ireland)
Tel: 353 1 8300562
Fax: 353 1 8300562

Founded: 1989
Staff: 36
Description: Irish national agency formed to help people who are both deaf and blind, and particularly those who are also low-functioning. Operates a residential center, a home for life, for young congenital deaf and blind people. Provides outreach services to other agencies.

Anthropological Association of Ireland
AAI
c/o Department of Anthropology
National University of Ireland, Maynooth, Kildare, Eire (Rep. of Ireland)
Tel: 353 1 6285222
Email: scoleman@may.ie
Website: http://www.may.ie/academic/anthropology/AAI/
Contact:
Fee: €15
Membership Type: member
Fee: €10
Membership Type: student
Description: Promotes the study of anthropology in Ireland.

Aosdana
70 Merrion Sq., Dublin 2, Eire (Rep. of Ireland)
Tel: 353 1 6180200
Fax: 353 1 6761302
Email: info@artscouncil.ie
Website: http://www.artscouncil.ie
Founded: 1981
Members: 200
Staff: 2
Contact: Patricia Quinn, Dir.
Description: Artists, composers, and writers of Irish birth or residence.
Meetings/Conventions: - annual general assembly

Architectural Association of Ireland
AAI
8 Merrion Sq., Dublin 2, Eire (Rep. of Ireland)
Tel: 353 1 6614100
Fax: 353 1 6614150
Email: aai@archeire.com
Website: http://www.irish-architecture.com/aai/
Founded: 1896
Contact: Peter Cody, Pres.
Description: Architects and those interested in the progress of architecture in Ireland. Promotes and affords facilities for the study of architecture and the allied sciences and arts. Provides a medium of communication between members; sponsors a public lecture series.

Arthritis Society of Ireland
ASI
1 Clanwilliam Sq., Grand Canal Quay, Dublin 2, Eire (Rep. of Ireland)
Tel: 353 1 6618188
Fax: 353 1 6618261
Description: Individuals and organizations with an interest in arthritis. Seeks to improve the quality of life of people with arthritis; promotes advancement in the diagnosis and treatment of arthritis. Serves as a clearinghouse on arthritis, its treatment, and services available to people with arthritis; makes available aids and appliance to make life easier for people with arthritis; conducts educational programs;

sponsors children's services; provides financial support to arthritis research programs.
Publication: Newsletter
Publication title: Arthritis News

Artists Association of Ireland

Arthouse, 43 Temple Bar, Dublin 2, Eire (Rep. of Ireland)
Tel: 353 1 8740529
Fax: 353 1 6771585
Email: info@artistsireland.com
Website: http://www.artistsireland.com
Founded: 1981
Members: 900
Staff: 4
Contact: Stella Coffey, Exec.Dir.
Description: Professional visual artists. Create and sustain an environment where artist can thrive and provide them with the means to develop their careers.
Library Type: by appointment only

Artists' Association of Ireland
AAI

43 Temple Bar, Dublin, Eire (Rep. of Ireland)
Tel: 353 1 8740529
Fax: 353 1 6771585
Email: info@artistsireland.com
Website: http://www.artistsireland.com
Founded: 1981
Members: 1191
Staff: 8
Contact: Stella Coffee, CEO
Description: Information resource for professional visual artists in Ireland.
Publication: Journal
Publication title: Art Bulletin

Arts Council of Ireland
AC

70 Merrion Sq., Dublin 2, Eire (Rep. of Ireland)
Tel: 353 1 6180200
Fax: 353 1 6761302
Email: info@artscouncil.ie
Website: http://www.artscouncil.ie
Founded: 1951
Members: 17
Staff: 22
Contact: Patricia Quinn, Dir.
Description: Independent statutory body assisting and promoting the arts. Assists promoters of musical events and publishers of translations of contemporary Irish literature.
Publication title: Annual Report
Publication title: Art Matters
Meetings/Conventions: - monthly meeting

Asperger Syndrome Association of Ireland
ASPIRE

Carmichael House, North Brunswick St., Dublin 7, Eire (Rep. of Ireland)
Tel: 353 1 2871122
Email: aspire@indigo.ie

Description: People with Asperger's syndrome and their families; health care providers and other individuals providing support and services to people with Asperger's syndrome. Seeks to improve the quality of life of people with Asperger's syndrome. Functions as a support network for people with Asperger's syndrome and their families; facilitates research projects.

Association for Higher Education Access and Disability
AHEAD

Newman House, 86 St., Stephen's Green, Dublin, Dublin 2, Eire (Rep. of Ireland)
Tel: 353 1 4752386
Fax: 353 1 4752387
Email: ahead@iol.ie
Website: http://www.ahead.ie
Founded: 1989
Members: 70
Staff: 5
Contact: Caroline McGrath, Exec.Dir.
Description: Individuals and organizations. Promotes increased access to higher education for people with disabilities. Lobbies for more stringent statutes mandating accessibility of educational institutions; represents the interests of people with disabilities before institutions of higher education.

Association of Advertisers in Ireland
AAI

Rock House, Main St., Blackrock, Dublin, Eire (Rep. of Ireland)
Tel: 353 1 2780499
Fax: 353 1 2780488
Email: info@aai.ie
Website: http://www.aai.ie
Founded: 1951
Members: 100
Staff: 3
Contact: Michael Caraher, Chief Exec.
Description: Commercial organizations supplying advertising goods or services. Encourages greater understanding and confidence in the role advertising plays in society. Fosters self-regulatory practices as a means to higher industry standards. Defends members' interests. Provides advisory services; disseminates information on agencies, media, rates, and services.
Library Type: reference
Publication: Directory
Publication title: MAPS Directory - Media, Advertising, Promotions, Sponsorship. Advertisements.
Meetings/Conventions: lecture

Association of Community and Comprehensive Schools

2 Herbert Ave., Dublin 4, Eire (Rep. of Ireland)
Tel: 353 1 2695375
Fax: 353 1 2695096
Email: acs@acs.iol.ie
Founded: 1982
Members: 89
Staff: 4
Contact: Sean McCann, Gen.Sec.
Description: School boards of education. Seeks to advance education and the concept of broad comprehensive curricula. Promotes the wider community concept of schools.

Publication: Newsletter
Publication title: ACS Newsletter
Meetings/Conventions: - annual convention - Exhibits. Waterford Ireland

Association of Consulting Engineers of Ireland
ACEI

51 Northumberland Rd., Ballsbridge, Dublin 4, Eire (Rep. of Ireland)
Tel: 353 1 6600374
Fax: 353 1 6682595
Email: info@acei.ie
Website: http://www.acei.ie
Founded: 1938
Members: 200
Staff: 2
Contact: A. Pottor, Exec.Dir.
Description: Independent consulting firms and principal engineers within such firms in Republic of Ireland and Northern Ireland; degreed engineers or individuals with equivalent experience. Promotes the practice, profession, and procedures of engineering (particularly consultative); encourages professional advancement of individuals in the field. Works to develop public awareness of the usefulness of engineering. Bestows awards.
Publication title: Annual Report
Second publication: Membership Directory
Meetings/Conventions: - annual convention

Association of Electrical Contractors Ireland
AECI

McKinley House, 16 Main St., Blackrock, Dublin, Eire (Rep. of Ireland)
Tel: 353 1 2886499
Fax: 353 1 2885870
Email: aeci@indigo.ie
Founded: 1960
Members: 351
Staff: 3
Contact: Noel Jameson, Exec. Officer
Description: Association of electrical contractors in Ireland. Promotes economic development of members through training in commercial and physical areas. Represents members' interests in industrial relations. Makes legal services and insurance available to members at group rates.
Library Subject: Wiring rules. Emergency lighting & fire alarm regulations
Library Type: reference
Meetings/Conventions: - annual conference - Exhibits.

Association of Independent Radio Stations
c/o Fleishman-Hillard Saunders
15 Fitzwilliam Query, Dublin 4, Eire (Rep. of Ireland)
Tel: 353 1 6188444
Description: Independent radio stations.

Association of Irish Jurists
Four Courts, Dublin 7, Eire (Rep. of Ireland)
Tel: 353 1 8720622
Fax: 353 8720455
Founded: 1981

Association of Irish Musical Societies
AIMS

25 Harcourt Lodge, Goldenbridge, Dublin 8, Eire (Rep. of Ireland)
Tel: 353 1 4536406
Fax: 353 1 4536406
Email: admin@aims.ie
Website: http://www.aims.ie
Founded: 1965
Members: 130
Contact: Frank Foley, Sec.
Description: Musical society umbrella organisation to improve the standard of presentation and production of amateur musicals. Provides advice,education and information about production and technical personnel, performers, and other aspects of show production to members. Commissions new works. Conducts summer schools and workshops, sponsors festivals, runs annual youth summer school.
Library Subject: musical scores and libretti
Library Type: reference
Publication: Journal
Publication title: Show Times. Advertisements.
Meetings/Conventions: AIMS Seminar - annual convention

Association of Physical Scientists in Medicine
APSM

St. James's Hospital, Dublin, Eire (Rep. of Ireland)
Tel: 353 1 4162645
Fax: 353 1 4103478
Email: nohare@stjames.ie

Association of Secondary Teachers Ireland
AST

ASTI House, Winetavern St., Dublin 8, Eire (Rep. of Ireland)
Tel: 353 1 6719144
Fax: 353 1 6719280
Email: info@asti.ie
Website: http://www.asti.ie
Founded: 1909
Members: 17000
Staff: 22
Contact: Charlie Lennon, Gen.Sec.
Fee: €15.98
Membership Type: second level teachers
Description: Second level school teachers. Promotes effective second level education. Works to enhance the professional status of members. Represents members' interests before government agencies, school administrative bodies, and the public.
Library Subject: education policy, social and economic issues
Library Type: open to the public
Publication: Magazine
Publication title: ASTI Review. Advertisements.
Meetings/Conventions: - annual convention

Association of Town Clerks of Ireland
Dan Breen House, Tipperary Town, Tipperary, Eire (Rep. of Ireland)
Tel: 353 1 90542263
Fax: 353 1 92542689
Email: dcoleman@southtippcoco.ie
Contact: David Coleman, Sec.
Fee: €20
Description: Represents bodies for all town clerks including town local government units in Ireland.

Asthma Society of Ireland
ASI

Eden House, 15-17 Eden Quay, Dublin 1, Eire (Rep. of Ireland)
Tel: 353 1 8788511
Fax: 353 1 8788128
Email: asthma@indigo.ie
Website: http://www.asthmasociety.ie
Founded: 1973
Members: 5000
Staff: 14
Contact: Genie Hennessy, Prog.Mgr.
Fee: €10
Description: Individuals with asthma; health care personnel and other individuals providing support and services to people with asthma. Seeks to improve the quality of life of people with asthma. Serves as a clearinghouse on asthma and its treatment; supports health professionals treating people with asthma.
Library Subject: asthma, allergy, copd, eczema
Library Type: open to the public
Publication: Magazine
Publication title: Asthma Society News. Advertisements.
Meetings/Conventions: Asthma Information Day - annual seminar

Biochemical Society, Irish Area Section

St. James's Gate, Dublin 8, Eire (Rep. of Ireland)
Fax: 353 1 4537804

Biomedical Engineering Association of Ireland
BEAI

c/o Patrick Pentony
St. Vincents University Hospital, Dept. of Clinical Engineering, Elm Park, Dublin 2, Eire (Rep. of Ireland)
Tel: 353 1 2094073
Email: p.pentony@st-vincents.ie
Website: http://www.beai.org/
Founded: 1990
Contact: Patrick Pentony, Chm.
Fee: €30
Membership Type: full
Fee: €20
Membership Type: associate
Description: Promotes biomedical and clinical engineering in Ireland.
Publication title: Spectrum

BirdWatch Ireland

Ruttledge House, 8 Longford Pl., Monkstown, Dublin, Eire (Rep. of Ireland)
Tel: 353 1 2804322
Fax: 353 1 2844407
Email: info@birdwatchireland.org
Website: http://www.birdwatchireland.ie
Founded: 1968
Members: 5000
Staff: 12
Contact: John Peart, Chm.
Description: Conservation and protection of wild birds in their natural habitat in Ireland.
Library Subject: ornithology, bird life, conservation
Library Type: not open to the public

BODYWHYS: Help, Support, Understanding for Anorexia and Bulimia Nervousa

PO Box 105, Blackrock, Dublin, Eire (Rep. of Ireland)
Tel: 353 1 2834963
Fax: 353 1 2834963
Email: info@bodywhys.ie
Website: http://www.bodywhys.ie
Founded: 1995
Staff: 3
Contact: Barbara Doyle, Devel.Dir.
Description: Offers support to people with/affected by eating disorders. Disseminates information to promote a better understanding of eating disorders. Runs self-help and support groups. Operates telephone helpline.
Library Subject: eating disorders, related issues
Library Type: not open to the public

Brainwave The Irish Epilepsy Association
BIEA

249 Crumlin Rd., Dublin 12, Eire (Rep. of Ireland)
Tel: 353 1 4557500
Email: info@epilepsy.ie
Website: http://www.epilepsy.ie
Founded: 1967
Members: 1500
Staff: 30
Contact: Mike Glynn, CEO
Fee: €1270
Membership Type: ordinary
Description: Individuals and organizations. Seeks to improve the quality of life of people with epilepsy; promotes advancement in the diagnosis and treatment of epilepsy. Serves as a clearinghouse on epilepsy; provides support and assistance to people with epilepsy and their families and caregivers working with people with epilepsy.
Publication: Magazine
Publication title: Epilepsy News. Advertisements.
Meetings/Conventions: conference Cork Ireland

Bram Stoker Club
BSC

c/o David Lass
Regent House, Trinity College, Dublin 2, Eire (Rep. of Ireland)
Fax: 3531 671 9003
Email: dlass@tcd.ie
Website: http://benecke.com/stoker.html
Founded: 1986
Members: 20
Contact: David M. Lass, Sec.
Fee: €10
Fee: €10
Description: Affiliated with the Bram Stoker Society, Encourages the study, appreciation, and presentation of the works of Abraham (Bram) Stoker (1847-1912), Irish author noted for his use of Gothic tradition with supernatural themes, as in his book Dracula. Studies works of Irish writers influenced by Stoker; conducts research on the Stoker family; campaigns for plaques to be placed on Irish sites associated with the Stoker family; promotes tourist visits to such locales as well as to sites associated with other Gothic novelists.
Meetings/Conventions: meeting Dublin Ireland

Bram Stoker Society - Ireland
BSS

c/o David Lass
Regent House, Trinity College, Dublin 2, Eire (Rep. of Ireland)
Fax: 3531 671 9003
Email: dlass@tcd.ie
Website: http://benecke.com/stoker.html
Founded: 1980
Members: 120
Contact: David Lass, Hon. Sec.
Fee: €10
Fee: €10
Description: Enthusiasts of the works of Abraham (Bram) Stoker (1847-1912), Irish author noted for his use of Gothic tradition with supernatural themes, as in his book Dracula. Encourages the study and appreciation of the life and works of Bram Stoker and other Irish authors of the Gothic and Supernatural tradition including, Charles Robert Maturin (1780-1824), Joseph Sheridan Le Fanu (1814-1873), and Lord Dunsany (1878-1957). Sponsors film shows and lectures.
Library Subject: gothic, occult, Bram Stoker memorabilia
Library Type: not open to the public
Publication: Journal
Publication title: Bram Stoker Society Journal. Advertisements.
Second publication: Newsletter
Publication title: Bram Stoker Society Newsletter
Meetings/Conventions: Summer School - annual conference - Exhibits. Dublin Ireland

British Society for the Study of Prosthetic Dentistry

University Dental School and Hospital, Wilton, Cork, Eire (Rep. of Ireland)
Tel: 353 21 4901141
Fax: 353 21 4345737
Email: finbarrallen@hotmail.com
Website: http://www.bsspd.org
Founded: 1953
Members: 490
Contact: P.F. Allen, Hon.Sec.
Fee: €20
Description: Ordinary and Honorary Members. Ordinary membership shall be available to those dentists, doctors or scientists who profess an interest in prosthetic dentistry and shall be by election. Established to advance education in prosthetic dentistry for the benefit of the public.
Publication: Proceedings
Publication title: BSSPD Proceedings
Meetings/Conventions: - annual conference - Exhibits. Nottingham UK

Business Spouses Association

c/o IMI Center
Sandyford Rd., Dublin 16, Eire (Rep. of Ireland)
Founded: 1989
Members: 130
Contact: Rosemarie Ashe, Chariman
Description: Helps business spouses handle more successfully the effect of a busy lifestyle on marriage and family life.

Car Rental Council of Ireland

5 Upper Pembroke St., Dublin, Eire (Rep. of Ireland)
Tel: 353 1 6761690
Fax: 353 1 6619213
Email: predmond@simi.ie

Website: http://www.carrentalcouncil.ie
Description: Represents car hire companies operating in the Republic of Ireland.

Carers Association

c/o St. Mary's Community Center
Richmond Hill, Rathmines, Dublin 6, Eire (Rep. of Ireland)
Tel: 353 1 4974498
Fax: 353 1 4976108
Email: carers@tinet.ie
Founded: 1987
Members: 8000
Staff: 106
Contact: Eddie Collins-Hughes, Dir.
Description: Care-givers who provide high levels of care in their own homes for family members and neighbors. Provides home-based respite services. Disseminates information; conducts educational programs.
Library Subject: welfare, home-care
Library Type: reference
Publication: Journal

Cerebral Palsy Ireland
CPI

Kiltartan House, Forster St., Galway, 4, Eire (Rcp. of Ireland)
Tel: 353 91 566686
Fax: 353 1 2694983
Founded: 1951
Staff: 250
Contact: Dermot Ward, Chief Exec.
Description: Works to provide therapy, training, and vocational education programs for children and adults with cerebral palsy and other physical dissabilities.

Chambers of Commerce of Ireland
CCI

17 Merrion Sq., Dublin 2, Eire (Rep. of Ireland)
Tel: 353 1 6612888
Fax: 353 1 6612811
Email: info@chambersireland.ie
Website: http://www.chambersireland.ie
Founded: 1923
Members: 59
Staff: 8
Contact: Simon Nugent, CEO
Description: Local chambers of commerce representing 10000 businesses in the Republic of Ireland. Promotes, develops, and represents Irish industry and commerce. Provides lobbying services for members. Conducts training seminars and programs.
Publication title: Annual Report
Second publication: Magazine
Publication title: Inside Business. Advertisements.
Meetings/Conventions: - annual conference

Cherish

2 Lower Pembroke St., Dublin 2, Eire (Rep. of Ireland)
Tel: 353 1 6629212
Fax: 353 1 6629096
Email: info@cherish.ie
Website: http://www.cherish.ie
Founded: 1972
Members: 400

Staff: 10
Contact: Karen Kiernan, Mgr.
Description: Single parents. Provides a support, advice, information, and counseling to single parent families. Campaigns for legal reform in the areas of single parents' and children's rights. Offers the following services: information service, practical support, parenting support, outreach, unmarried fathers support, single parent counseling, support groups, computer training, personal development, professional training, campaigning and lobbying, and pregnancy counseling.
Library Type: reference
Publication: Newsletter
Publication title: Cherish News. Advertisements.
Meetings/Conventions: - annual conference Dublin Ireland

Cheshire Foundation in Ireland
CFI

1-4 Adelaide Rd., Glasthule, Dublin, Eire (Rep. of Ireland)
Tel: 353 1 2804879
Fax: 353 1 2804954
Email: info@cheshire-foundation.ie
Website: http://www.cheshire-foundation.ie
Description: Individuals and organizations. Seeks to improve the quality of life of people with disabilities. Provides housing and support and services to people with disabilities and their families.

Children at Risk in Ireland

110 Lower Drumcondra Rd., Dublin 9, Eire (Rep. of Ireland)
Tel: 353 1 8308529
Fax: 353 1 8306309
Email: info@cari.ie
Website: http://www.cari.ie
Founded: 1989
Staff: 50
Contact: Mary Flaherty, Dir.
Description: Provides post-assessment therapy services for children (up to 18 years old) who have experienced child sexual abuse. Provides an information service, outreach presentations and workshops. Operates confidential telephone advice and support line.
Library Subject: child sexual abuse, psychology, law, child development
Library Type: reference
Meetings/Conventions: - periodic workshop

Children's Books Ireland

17 Lower Camden St., Dublin 2, Eire (Rep. of Ireland)
Tel: 353 1 8725854
Fax: 353 1 8725854
Email: info@childrensbooksireland.com
Website: http://www.childrensbooksireland.com
Founded: 1997
Members: 800
Staff: 2
Contact: Claire Ranson, Exec.Dir.
Fee: €25
Membership Type: member
Fee: €45
Membership Type: overseas
Description: Parents, teachers, librarians, booksellers, authors, and illustrators. Promotes children's books and reading.
Library Subject: children's books
Library Type: reference
Publication: Magazine
Publication title: Inis. Advertisements.
Meetings/Conventions: - 5/year conference

Clanwilliam Institute
CI

18 Clanwilliam Terrace, Grand Canal Quay, Dublin 2, Eire (Rep. of Ireland)
Tel: 353 1 6761363
Fax: 353 1 6762800
Email: office@clanwilliam.ie
Website: http://www.clanwilliam.ie
Founded: 1982
Members: 24
Staff: 21
Contact: Dr. Edmund McHale, CEO
Description: Psychologists, family therapists, and other mental health and family service providers. Promotes healthy and happy family relations. Provides consulting services, therapy, and mediation to families in crisis; makes individual and family psychological assessments; offers substance abuse, stress management, and adult education programs. Conducts family enrichment activities; sponsors professional training courses for mental health and family service providers. Sponsors public education campaigns to raise awareness of family issues; lobbies government agencies on issues relating to families and family life. Employee assistance programme offers counseling and training programmes for their staff.

Classical Association of Ireland
CAI

Department of Classics, NUI Dublin (UCD), Dublin 4, Eire (Rep. of Ireland)
Email: andrew.smith@ucd.ie
Website: http://www.ucd.ie/~cai
Founded: 1908
Contact: Prof. Andrew Smith, Pres.
Description: Individuals with a general interest in ancient Greek and Roman civilizations and those who teach Classics at the second and third levels. Seeks to cultivate and further an interest in classical studies in Ireland. Provides lectures and field trips; organizes social events; promotes the study of Classics in the curriculum; assists in the development of study aids; raises community awareness.
Publication: Journal
Publication title: Classics Ireland. Advertisements.
Meetings/Conventions: Summer School - annual

Cleft Lip and Palate Association of Ireland
CLAPAI

c/o Ms. Libby O'Brien, Hon.Sec.
Station Rd., Ballyshannon, Donegal, Eire (Rep. of Ireland)
Tel: 353 72 58026
Email: dulaing@cleft.ie
Website: http://www.cleft.ie/
Description: Provides support and information for parents and children affected by cleft lip and palate; provides support to new parents and advice on feeding and ongoing medical care throughout treatment.

Clonmel Chamber of Commerce
8 Sarsfield St., Clonmel, Tipperary, Eire (Rep. of Ireland)
Tel: 353 52 26500
Fax: 353 52 26378
Email: info@clonmel.ie
Website: http://www.clonmel.ie/
Description: Promotes commerce and industry in Ireland.

Coeliac Society of Ireland

4 N Brunswick, Carmichael House, Dublin 7, Eire (Rep. of Ireland)
Tel: 353 1 8721471
Email: coeliac@iol.ie
Website: http://www.coeliac.ie
Founded: 1970
Members: 2500
Staff: 1
Contact: Ann Boland, Hd.Off.
Fee: €10
Membership Type: ordinary
Description: Promotes, safeguards, and protects the interests of our members in relation to coeliac disease. Produces a list of gluten free foods, information leaflets, and cook books.
Publication: Newsletter. Advertisements.

COFORD: National Council for Forest Research and Development

University College of Dublin, Agriculture Bldg., Belfield, Dublin 4, Eire (Rep. of Ireland)
Tel: 353 1 7167700
Fax: 353 1 7161180
Email: info@coford.ie
Website: http://www.coford.ie
Founded: 1993
Staff: 5
Contact: Dr. Eugene Hendrick, Dir.
Description: Harvesters and manufacturers of forest products; forestry researcha and educational programs and institutions. Promotes improved communication and cooperation among forest industries and forestry researchers; seeks to ensure sustainable use of forestry resources. Monitors and evaluates forest research projects; facilitates innovation in the practice of forestry and the harvesting and manufacturing of forest products; sponsors research and educational programs. Represents the Republic of Ireland in international forestry and research organizations; maintains liaison with European Union forestry agencies.
Publication: Directory
Publication title: Directory of Forestry Research in Ireland
Second publication: Annual Report

COMAD - Aviation Heritage Productions

6 Wilfield Park, Ballsbridge, Dublin 4, Eire (Rep. of Ireland)
Tel: 353 1 2696757
Fax: 353 1 2696757
Founded: 1995
Members: 600
Staff: 3
Contact: Madeleine O'Rourke, Dir.
Description: Organizes educational programs for secondary schools in the Republic of Ireland. Is concerned with educational programs in the areas of aerobatics, ballooning, gliding, hang gliding, parachuting, and flying. Researches history of Irish aviation from 1910. Produces historical aviation material on video and CD-ROM.
Formerly: Formed by Merger of, Air Education Group Irish Aviation Council
Publication title: Air Display Program. Advertisements.
Second publication: Video
Publication title: Aviation Newsround

Comhlamh

10 Upper Camden St., Dublin 2, Eire (Rep. of Ireland)
Tel: 353 1 4783490
Fax: 353 1 4783738
Email: info@comhlamh.org
Website: http://www.comhlamh.org
Founded: 1975
Members: 800
Staff: 11
Contact: Colm O'Cuanachain, Coord.
Description: Citizens of the Republic of Ireland who have participated in development work overseas; interested others. Promotes international cooperation in development. Works to increase awareness and understanding of development issues. Offers a support and information service to returning development workers; holds annual series of training seminars. Offers support to volunteers involved in development education.
Library Subject: development and developmental education
Library Type: open to the public
Publication: Magazine
Publication title: Focus on Ireland and the Wider World. Advertisements.
Second publication: Newsletter
Publication title: NODE News: Network Outreach in Development Education
Meetings/Conventions: - semiannual regional meeting

Connemara Pony Breeders Society

The Showgrounds, Galway, Clifden, Eire (Rep. of Ireland)
Tel: 353 9521863
Fax: 353 9521005
Email: enquiries@cpbs.ie
Website: http://www.cpbs.ie
Founded: 1923
Members: 850
Staff: 2
Contact: Michael Ward, Sec.
Fee: €30
Membership Type: ordinary
Description: Breeders of Connemara ponies.
Library Subject: breeding
Library Type: reference
Publication: Newsletter
Publication title: An Capaillin. Advertisements.
Meetings/Conventions: - annual general assembly

Construction Industry Federation
CIF

Construction House, Canal Rd., Dublin 6, Eire (Rep. of Ireland)
Tel: 353 1 4066000
Fax: 353 1 4966953
Email: cif@cif.ie
Website: http://www.cif.ie/
Founded: 1935
Members: 3000
Contact: Gerald Purcell, Sr.VP
Description: General contractors, mechanical and electrical contractors, specialist contractors, and homebuilders. Provides problem-solving expertise for the industry, monitors issues and trends, and initiates proposals.
Publication: Newsletter
Publication title: CIF News Update

Consumers Association of Ireland

45 Upper Mount St., Dublin 2, Eire (Rep. of Ireland)
Tel: 353 1 6612466
Fax: 353 1 6612464

Email: cai@consumerassociation.ie
Website: http://www.consumerassociation.ie
Founded: 1966
Members: 9500
Staff: 9
Contact: Mr. Dermott Jewell, CEO
Description: Works on behalf of the interest of Irish consumers. Also runs a telephone advice and information service to help consumers with complaints.
Publication: Magazine
Publication title: Consumer Choice

Cork Operative Butcher's Society

55 North Main St., Cork, Cork, Eire (Rep. of Ireland)
Tel: 353 21 277151
Fax: 353 21 4251099
Founded: 1916
Members: 120
Staff: 1
Contact: Noel Murphy, Gen.Sec.
Fee: €130
Membership Type: full membership
Description: Butchers in the Cork area.

Creative Activity for Everyone
CAFE

10-11 Earl St. S, Dublin 8, Eire (Rep. of Ireland)
Tel: 353 1 4736600
Fax: 353 1 4736599
Email: cafe@connect.ie
Website: http://www.communityartsireland.com
Founded: 1983
Members: 200
Staff: 5
Contact: Arthur Duignan, Asst.Dir.
Description: Individuals, artists, arts development workers, activists, art centers and other interested parties united to promote collective creative activities. Seeks to achieve social and cultural equality through creative action. Promotes community arts as a collective liberating artform that creates a voice for social and cultural equality. Promotes an environment where community arts is celebrated and valued. Conducts research into key aspects of arts practice, policy, structures and development. Liaises with similar organizations in Ireland and Europe.
Library Subject: community arts, creativity, social change
Library Type: by appointment only
Publication: Newsletter
Publication title: CAFEnews
Second publication: Handbook
Publication title: Irish Funding Handbook 4th Edition

Cuba Support Group - Ireland

15 Merrion Square, Dublin 2, Eire (Rep. of Ireland)
Tel: 353 1 8436448
Fax: 353 1 6611738
Email: cubasupport@eircom.net
Website: http://homepage.eircom.net/~csg
Founded: 1993
Staff: 2
Contact: Declan McKenna, Coord.
Fee: €20
Description: Brings together people across the political spectrum who believe in Cuba's right to trade, develop and self-determination.

Library Type: by appointment only
Publication: Newsletter
Publication title: Cuba Today

Cystic Fibrosis Association of Ireland
CFAI

CF House, 24 Lower Rathmines Rd., Dublin 6, Eire (Rep. of Ireland)
Tel: 353 1 4962433
Fax: 353 1 4962201
Email: info@cfireland.ie
Website: http://www.cfireland.ie
Founded: 1963
Members: 900
Staff: 7
Contact: Ciairin de Buis, Dir.
Description: People with cystic fibrosis and their families; individuals and organizations providing support and services to people with cystic fibrosis. Seeks to improve the quality of life of people with cystic fibrosis. Provides backup services for young people with cystic fibrosis.
Library Type: reference
Publication: Magazine. Advertisements.
Meetings/Conventions: - annual conference

DEBRA Ireland

10 Burgh Quay, Dublin 2, Eire (Rep. of Ireland)
Tel: 353 1 6776855
Fax: 353 1 6776875
Email: info@debraireland.org
Website: http://www.debraireland.org
Founded: 1988
Staff: 5
Contact: Margaret Webb, Mgr.
Fee: €7
Description: Individuals and organizations. Seeks to improve the quality of life of people with EB and their families. Makes available specialist care; conducts educational programs for health care personnel and the public.

Dental Health Foundation

26 Harcourt St., Dublin 2, Eire (Rep. of Ireland)
Tel: 353 1 4780466
Fax: 353 1 4780475
Email: info@dentalhealth.ie
Description: Promotes oral health in Ireland.

Diabetes Federation of Ireland

76 Lower Gardiner St., Dublin 1, Eire (Rep. of Ireland)
Tel: 353 1 8363022
Fax: 353 1 8365182
Email: info@diabetes.ie
Website: http://www.diabetesireland.ie
Founded: 1967
Members: 5000
Staff: 6
Contact: Kieran O'Leary, Admin.
Description: Represents people with diabetes. Provides information, creates awareness encourages research and ongoing support of people with diabetes.
Publication: Magazine
Publication title: Identity. Advertisements.

Disability Federation of Ireland
DFI

2 Sandyford Office Park, Dublin 18, Eire (Rep. of Ireland)
Tel: 353 1 2959344
Fax: 353 1 2959346
Email: info@disability-federation.ie
Website: http://ireland.iol.ie/~dfi/
Founded: 1960
Members: 73
Staff: 7
Contact: John Dolan, CEO
Description: Voluntary and nonstatutory agencies providing support services to people with disabilities. Seeks to increase the availability and quality of services for people with disabilities; promotes development of the full potential of all people. Provides support and assistance to members; facilitates communication and networking among members; develops training programs for people providing services to people with disabilities; serves as a liaison linking members with public agencies responsible for statutes affecting people with disabilities. Makes available resource services; sponsors research and educational programs; conducts lobbying activities.
Publication: Newsletter
Publication title: DFI Newsletter
Second publication: Directory
Publication title: Disability Federation of Ireland Directory

Disabled Drivers' Association of Ireland
DDA, Ballindine, Mayo, Eire (Rep. of Ireland)

Tel: 353 9464054
Fax: 353 9464336
Email: ability@iol.ie
Website: http://www.iol.ie/~ability
Founded: 1970
Members: 4500
Staff: 5
Contact: Derek H. Farrell, CEO
Fee: €5
Membership Type: individual
Description: Individuals and organizations. Promotes improve mobility for people with disabilities. Lobbies to safeguard the right of people with disabilities to obtain drivers' licenses; conducts educational and training programs.
Publication: Magazine
Publication title: Steering Wheel. Advertisements.

DOCHAS, The Irish Association of Non-Governmental Development Organizations

59 Deerpark Rd., Mount Merrion, Dublin, Eire (Rep. of Ireland)
Tel: 353 1 2886141
Fax: 353 1 2780571
Email: dochasaf@iol.ie
Founded: 1974
Members: 24
Staff: 1
Contact: Anna Farrell, Sec.
Description: Brings together 31 Irish NGDO involved in development and relief overseas and/or in the provision of development education. Aims to provide a forum for consultation and cooperation between its members and acts as the Irish Assembly of Development and Relief Organisations in relation to the liaison committee of NGDOs to the European Union.
Library Subject: human rights, gender, debt, refugees
Library Type: not open to the public

Down Syndrome Ireland
DSI

30 Mary St., Dublin 1, Eire (Rep. of Ireland)
Tel: 353 1 8730999
Fax: 353 1 8731064
Email: dsi@eircom.net
Website: http://www.downsyndrome.ie
Founded: 1972
Members: 2650
Staff: 3
Contact: Paul Daly, CEO
Description: People with Down syndrome and their families; health care and service providers working with people with Down syndrome. Seeks to improve the quality of life of people with Down syndrome. Provides support and services to people with Down syndrome and their families; conducts educational programs.
Library Subject: Down syndrome
Publication: Magazine
Second publication: Newsletter

Driving Instructor Register of Ireland

39-41 Glasnevin Hill, Glasnevin, Dublin 9, Eire (Rep. of Ireland)
Tel: 353 1 8570377
Fax: 353 1 8570381
Email: info@dir.ie
Website: http://www.dir.ie
Founded: 1996
Members: 1000
Staff: 3
Contact: Des Cummins, Exec.Chm.
Description: Registered driving instructors. Works to improve the standard of instruction provided to the public. Promotes motor safety through driver education.
Library Type: reference
Publication: Newsletter
Publication title: RDI Update. Advertisements.

Dublin Chamber of Commerce

7 Clare St., Dublin 2, Eire (Rep. of Ireland)
Tel: 353 1 6447200
Fax: 353 1 6765433
Email: info@dubchamber.ie
Website: http://www.dubchamber.ie
Founded: 1783
Members: 2000
Staff: 20
Contact: Jim Miley, Chief Exec.
Description: Promotes commerce and industry in Dublin, Ireland.

Dublin City Centre Business Association

21 Dawson St., Dublin 2, Eire (Rep. of Ireland)
Tel: 353 1 6622995
Fax: 353 1 6622284
Email: info@dcba.ie
Website: http://www.dcba.ie
Founded: 1971
Members: 800
Contact: Mr. Tom Coffey, CEO
Description: Retail Federation in the city of Dublin. Promotes a sustainable city centre that is attractive to live, work, visit, and shop in centre.
Library Subject: cities, Dublin
Library Type: by appointment only
Publication title: Dublin Map & Visitor Guide. Advertisements.

Dyspraxia Association of Ireland

c/o Communications House
Spruce Ave., Unit 58, Stillorgan Industrial Estate, Dublin, Eire (Rep. of Ireland)
Email: dyspraxiaireland@eircom.net
Website: http://www.dyspraxiaireland.com
Founded: 1995
Contact: Aileen Tierney, Chm.
Description: Parents of children with dyspraxia. Seeks to raise awareness of dyspraxia in Ireland and to create a better understanding of the difficulties children and parents face. Ensures adequate professional and medical resources are available to parents; provides information and a support network; works to improve diagnostic services.

EAN Ireland

Confederation House, 84/86 Lower Baggot St., Dublin 2, Eire (Rep. of Ireland)
Tel: 353 1 6051539
Fax: 353 1 6381539
Email: info@ean.ie
Website: http://www.ean.ie
Founded: 1980
Members: 2300
Staff: 5
Contact: Jim Bracken, Dir.
Description: Membership involved in the retail food industry, general merchandise, healthcare and D.I.Y, concerned with article numbering and bar coding.
Formerly: Article Numbering Association of Ireland
Publication: Newsletter
Publication title: EAN Ireland. Advertisements.
Meetings/Conventions: - quarterly workshop

Economic and Social History Society of Ireland

c/o Modern History Department
Trinity College, Dublin 2, Eire (Rep. of Ireland)
Tel: 353 1 8741680
Fax: 353 1 8368920
Website: http://eh.net/eshsi/
Founded: 1967
Members: 650
Staff: 12
Contact:
Fee: €20
Description: Encourages the study of Irish economic and social history at all levels, and brings together those engaged in teaching and research.
Library Subject: history, economics
Library Type: open to the public
Publication: Newsletter
Meetings/Conventions: - annual conference

Economic and Social Research Institute
ESRI

4 Burlington Rd., Dublin 4, Eire (Rep. of Ireland)
Tel: 353 1 6671525
Fax: 353 1 6686231
Email: admin@esri.ie
Website: http://www.esri.ie
Founded: 1960
Members: 500

Staff: 85
Contact: Brendan J. Whelan, Dir.
Description: Applies current thinking in economics and the social sciences to the actual and potential problems of Irish society ESRI. Research is a vital constituent in the national debate on economic and social issues.
Library Subject: economic and social policy
Library Type: reference

Encounter

c/o Irish Secretariat
201 Ardmore Park, Bray, Wicklow, Eire (Rep. of Ireland)
Tel: 353 1 2745397
Fax: 353 1 2745397
Email: encounter@eircom.net
Website: http://www.british-irish-encounter.org
Founded: 1983
Contact: Joyce Timms, Sec.
Description: Individuals and organizations. Promotes improved relations and mutual cultural appreciation between Ireland and the United Kingdom. Sponsors cultural exchanges; facilitates communication between the peoples of Ireland and the United Kingdom.
Publication: Brochure
Publication title: Encounter
Meetings/Conventions: - periodic conference

Energy Action
EA

IDA Unit 14, Newmarket, Dublin 8, Eire (Rep. of Ireland)
Tel: 353 1 4545464
Fax: 353 1 4549797
Email: info@energyaction.ie
Website: http://www.energyaction.ie
Founded: 1988
Members: 14
Staff: 61
Contact: Charles Roarty, Gen.Mgr.
Description: Individuals interested in meeting the energy needs of the elderly. Seeks to improve energy efficiency in the homes of elderly people. Provides home insulation services at no cost to elderly individuals. Trains unemployed people to install insulation in accordance with building codes and safety standards.
Library Subject: energy conservation in the home, job creation
Library Type: open to the public

Energy Research Group
ERG

University College Dublin, Richview, Clonskeagh, Dublin 14, Eire (Rep. of Ireland)
Tel: 353 1 2692750
Fax: 353 1 2838908
Email: erg@erg.ucd.ie
Website: http://erg.ucd.ie/erg_main.html
Founded: 1975
Staff: 700
Contact: J. Owen Lewis
Description: Promotes architectural innovation and technical change in the construction industries leading to more energy-efficient buildings. Conducts research and development activities; makes available consulting services; provides technical support to architects and designers. Current projects focus on application of solar energy technologies to architectural designs. Gathers and disseminates information to raise public awareness of energy efficiency in architecture; sponsors educational programs.

Engineering and Scientific Association of Ireland
13 Mather Rd. South, Mount Merrion, Dublin, Eire (Rep. of Ireland)
Founded: 1903

Erb's Palsy Association of Ireland
Canrawer, Oughterard, Galway, Eire (Rep. of Ireland)
Tel: 353 91 552623
Email: info@erbspalsy.ie
Website: http://www.erbspalsy.ie
Members: 186
Contact: Mary Verbruggen, Chm.
Description: Parents of children born with Erb's Palsy. Seeks to raise awareness of and provide information on Erb's Palsy, a childbirth injury causing temporary and sometimes permanent paralysis in the arm.
Publication: Newsletter
Meetings/Conventions: Family Day - annual

European Health Management Association
EHMA
Vergemount Hall, Clonskeagh, Dublin 6, Eire (Rep. of Ireland)
Tel: 353 1 2839299
Fax: 353 1 2838653
Email: marie@ehma.org
Website: http://www.ehma.org
Founded: 1966
Members: 200
Staff: 4
Contact: Philip C. Berman, Dir.
Description: Policy makers, senior managers, personnel directors, academic institutions, and research organizations in the healthcare sector. Seeks to improve healthcare in Europe by raising standards of managerial performance in the health sector. Fosters cooperation between health service organizations and institutions in the field of healthcare management education and training. Promotes the continuing education and development of healthcare managers. Offers advice and support to national governments in Europe; evaluates members' management development programs.
Formerly: European Association of Programmes in Health Services Studies
Publication: Journal
Publication title: Conference Proceedings
Second publication: Directory
Publication title: Health Services Administration Education and Research
Meetings/Conventions: - annual conference - Exhibits.

European Movement - Ireland
32 Nassau St., Dublin 2, Eire (Rep. of Ireland)
Tel: 353 1 6714300
Fax: 353 1 6798203
Email: info@european.movement.iol.ie
Website: http://www.europeanmovement.ie
Founded: 1954
Members: 800
Staff: 4
Contact: Patricia Lawlor, CEO
Description: Promotes the economic, political and social development of Europe. Plays an active role in shaping Irish attitudes to Europe. Works to influence policy process; promotes public discussion on key issues relating to Europe's development, and their implications for Ireland. Disseminates information on European Union issues.

Publication: Journal
Publication title: Euronewsline
Second publication: Newsletter
Meetings/Conventions: - periodic conference

European Real Estate Society
ERES
11 Churchfield Ln., Skerries, Dublin, Eire (Rep. of Ireland)
Tel: 353 1 7068825
Fax: 353 1 2835482
Email: eres@tinet.ie
Website: http://www.eres.org
Founded: 1994
Contact: Ingo Hupach, Exec.Dir.
Fee: €33
Membership Type: ordinary
Fee: €200
Membership Type: group of ten or more
Description: Real estate academics and professionals. Seeks to advance the study and practice of real estate decision making in areas including real estate finance, economics, appraisal, investment, and asset management. Serves as a forum for mutual exchange between academics and professionals in real estate and related fields; sponsors research and educational programs.
Publication: Newsletter
Meetings/Conventions: - periodic conference

European Society for Cataract and Refractive Surgeons
ESCRS
Temple House, Temple Rd., Black Rock, Dublin 2, Eire (Rep. of Ireland)
Tel: 353 1 2091100
Fax: 353 1 2091112
Email: escrs@agenda-comm.ie
Website: http://www.escrs.com
Founded: 1958
Members: 3000
Contact: Peter Barry, Treas.
Description: Strives to advance scientific knowledge in the field of intraocular lens implantation and in the art and practice of such surgery.
Meetings/Conventions: - annual congress - Exhibits.

European Society for Quality in Health Care
c/o Mary Halpin
Mid-Western Health Board, 31-33 Catherine St., Limerick, Eire (Rep. of Ireland)
Tel: 353 61 483389
Fax: 353 61 483211
Contact: Mary Halpin, Hon.Sec.
Description: Support quality improvement in European healthcare by creating a formal European Network of National Societies. Provides a forum for addressing issues of importance to quality health care.

European Society of Biomechanics
ESB
c/o Dr. P. J. Prendergast
Department of Mechanical Engineering, Trinity College, Dublin 2, Eire (Rep. of Ireland)
Tel: 353 1 6081383
Fax: 353 1 6795554

Email: pprender@tcd.ie
Website: http://www.utc.fr/esb/
Founded: 1976
Members: 250
Contact: Dr. P. J. Prendergast, Gen.Sec.
Fee: €15
Membership Type: student
Fee: €56
Membership Type: ordinary
Description: Engineers, surgeons, and physicians interested in the mechanics (musculoskeletal, cardiovascular, dental, and athletic) of the human body; universities and research institutions. Promotes biomechanics research; organizes courses, symposia, and seminars.
Publication: Proceedings
Meetings/Conventions: Conference of the European Society of Biomechanics - biennial congress - Exhibits.

Experiment in International Living - Ireland
EIL

E.I.L 1 Empress Pl. Summerhill, North Cork, Cork, Eire (Rep. of Ireland)
Tel: 353 21 4551535
Fax: 353 21 4551587
Email: info@eilireland.org
Website: http://www.eilireland.org
Founded: 1932
Members: 2000
Staff: 9
Contact: Kevin Hickey, National Dir.
Description: Member organizations are nonprofit, nonpolitical and nonreligious. Works to establish peace and understanding among different cultures through cooperation with government agencies and schools. Sponsors cultural immersion and volunteer programs.

Farm Tractor and Machinery Trade Association

c/o Michael Moroney
Irish Farm Center, Bluebell, Dublin, Eire (Rep. of Ireland)
Tel: 353 14509954
Fax: 353 14504420
Email: info@ftmta.ie
Website: http://www.ftmta.ie
Founded: 1956
Members: 275
Staff: 2
Contact: Michael Moroney, Ch.Exec.
Description: Provides information, advice and lobbying services for those involved in the farm machinery industry in Ireland.

Federation of Active Retirement Association
FARA

Shamrock Chambers, 59-61 Dame St., Dublin 2, Eire (Rep. of Ireland)
Tel: 353 1 6792142
Fax: 353 1 6792142
Founded: 1995
Members: 110000
Staff: 2
Description: Retired individuals over 55 years of age. Encourages member to lead a full, happy and healthy retirement. Organizes outings, social activities, sports activities, educational programs, and community service activities.
Publication: Bulletin

Federation of Irish Beekeepers Associations
FIBA

Bollinakill, Enfield, Meath, Eire (Rep. of Ireland)
Tel: 353 504 41433
Email: mgglee@eircom.net
Website: http://www.irishbeekeeping.ie
Members: 42
Contact: Michael J. Gleeson, Sec.
Description: Local authorities representing 1500 beekeepers. Promotes growth and development of domestic apiculture; seeks to advance beekeeping techniques and related sciences. Represents members' collective interests; conducts research and educational programs; operates labelling scheme for Irish bee products; maintains speakers' bureau; makes available discounts on insurance and apicultural supplies to members; formulates beekeeping standards and conducts certification examinations; undertakes lobbying campaigns.
Library Subject: apiculture
Library Type: not open to the public
Publication: Journal
Publication title: An Beachaire
Second publication: Booklet
Meetings/Conventions: Irish National Honey Show - annual trade show

Federation of Irish Film Societies

The Studio Bldg., Meeting House Sq., Dublin 2, Eire (Rep. of Ireland)
Tel: 353 1 6794420
Fax: 353 1 6794166
Email: fifs@eircom.net
Founded: 1977
Members: 4000
Staff: 3
Contact: Brenda Gannon, Dir.
Description: Aims to create an awareness and understanding of films as an art form in Ireland; encourage the production, distribution, and exhibition of films in Ireland including the work of Irish film-makers; promote the understanding of other cultures through film. Arranges film seasons, seminars, lectures and special screening's. Imports and distributes films to member societies and others. Organizes and assists in the development of new film societies.
Library Subject: film, cinema
Library Type: reference

Feis Ceoil Association
FCA

37 Molesworth St., Dublin 2, Eire (Rep. of Ireland)
Tel: 353 1 6767365
Fax: 353 1 6767429
Founded: 1896
Members: 600
Contact: Carmel Byrne, Admin.
Description: Individuals interested in the Feis Ceoil, an annual music festival and competition associated with the Gathering of Tara described in the Book of Leinster. Promotes skills development among music teachers and students. Selects Feis Ceoil judges; works to increase public appreciation of amateur musicians and their work.
Library Subject: music
Library Type: reference
Meetings/Conventions: festival - Exhibits.

Fertiliser Association of Ireland

c/o Brendan Barnes
151 Thomas St., Dublin 8, Eire (Rep. of Ireland)
Tel: 353 1 6717131
Website: http://www.fertilizer-assoc.ie
Founded: 1968
Members: 120
Contact: Mr. P. Dreuman, Hon.Sec.
Fee: €100
Membership Type: corporate
Fee: €5
Membership Type: single
Description: Provides a forum for the exchange of scientific and technical information in relation to the production and use of fertilizers. Promotes the efficient use of fertilizers in Ireland.
Library Type: reference

Fianna Fail Women's and Equality Forum

Aras de Valera, 65-66 Lower Mount St., Dublin 2, Eire (Rep. of Ireland)
Tel: 353 1 6761551
Fax: 353 1 6785690
Email: maryw@fiannafail.ie
Founded: 1992
Members: 5000
Staff: 1
Contact: Mary White
Description: Fosters equal rights for women in Ireland.

Finnish Business Club

c/o Embassy of Finland
Russell House, St. Stephen's Green, Dublin 2, Eire (Rep. of Ireland)
Tel: 353 1 4781344
Fax: 353 1 4783727
Founded: 1988
Members: 100
Contact: Tom Eklund, Chm.
Description: Promotes business and trade between Finland and Ireland. Disseminates business and political information to members.

Folk Music Society of Ireland
FMSI

63 Merrion Sq., Dublin 2, Eire (Rep. of Ireland)
Tel: 353 1 6619699
Email: sales@itma.ie
Website: http://homepage.tinet.ie/~shields/fmsi/
Founded: 1971
Members: 250
Staff: 1
Contact: Ellen MacIsaac, Hon.Sec.
Description: Individuals in 10 countries interested in the practice and study of traditional Celtic folk music. Gathers previously unpublished collections of traditional Irish music. Conducts lectures and recitals.
Publication: Newsletter
Publication title: Ceol Tire
Second publication: Journal
Publication title: Irish Folk Music Studies
Meetings/Conventions: - annual convention

Folklore of Ireland Society

Belfield, Dublin 4, Eire (Rep. of Ireland)
Tel: 353 1 2693244
Founded: 1927

Food and Drink Federation

c/o Irish Business and Employers Confederation
Confederation House, 84/86 Lower Baggot St., Dublin 2, Eire (Rep. of Ireland)
Tel: 353 1 6051500
Fax: 353 1 6051500
Email: marie.larby@ibec.ie
Website: http://www.ibec.ie
Members: 29
Contact: Ciaran Fitzgerald, Dir.
Description: Agribusiness, meat, dairy, baby food, sugar, cereals and cold-storage, drinks, brewing and distilling industries, food processors and suppliers, non-food grocery products, including health and beauty and tobacco. Advocates for members in regulatory matters, business representation, and human resources.

Foroige, National Youth Development Organisation

Irish Farm Centre, Bluebell, Dublin 12, Eire (Rep. of Ireland)
Tel: 353 1 4501122
Fax: 353 1 4501941
Email: foroige@eircom.net
Website: http://www.foroige.ie
Founded: 1952
Members: 40000
Staff: 100
Contact: Michael B. Cleary, Dir.
Description: Youth and their volunteer leaders united for self-improvement and the development of the community. Works with youth and volunteer leaders in educational programs in areas including agriculture, horticulture, youth cooperative education, citizenship, culture, family and life skills, health, leadership, and science. Provides support and services to at-risk youth, exchange program and study trips.
Library Subject: personal development, training, educational psychology, voluntary sector management, research
Library Type: reference
Publication: Journal
Publication title: Annual Review
Publication title: Club Committee Resource Pack
Meetings/Conventions: Leaders' Annual Conference - annual conference - Exhibits.

Friedreichs Ataxia Society of Ireland
FASI

San Martino, Mart Ln., Foxrock, Dublin 18, Eire (Rep. of Ireland)
Tel: 353 1 2894788
Fax: 353 1 2898845
Email: fasi@eircom.net
Website: http://www.fasi.ie
Founded: 1980
Members: 250
Staff: 3
Contact: Clare Creedon, Pres.
Description: Individuals and organizations. Seeks to improve the quality of life of people with Friedreich's ataxia and their families. Makes available support and services; conducts educational and advocacy campaigns.
Library Type: reference
Publication: Newsletter
Publication title: FASI Newsletter
Meetings/Conventions: general assembly

Friends of St. Luke's Hospital

c/o St. Luke's Hospital
Highfield Rd., Rathgar, Dublin 6, Eire (Rep. of Ireland)
Tel: 353 1 4065102
Fax: 353 1 4065237
Email: info@friendsofstlukes.ie
Website: http://www.friendsofstlukes.ie
Founded: 1981
Members: 15
Staff: 5
Contact: Fiona Campbell, Office Mgr.
Description: Seeks to enhance the care, comfort and management of cancer patients at Dublin's St. Luke's Hospital. Works to ensure that patients benefit to the fullest extent from the advances in techniques and equipment.

Friends of the Earth - Ireland

7 Upper Camden St., Dublin 2, Eire (Rep. of Ireland)
Tel: 353 1 4785100
Fax: 353 1 4973773
Email: foeeire@iol.ie
Website: http://www.iol.ie/~foeeire
Founded: 1986
Members: 400
Staff: 12
Contact: Gus Worth, Mgr.
Description: Works to increase public awareness of environmental problems. Conducts media and educational campaigns on topics such as air pollution, toxic waste issues, alternative energy, and climate change. Maintains an information service.
Library Subject: environmental
Library Type: reference
Formerly: Earthwatch
Publication: Magazine
Publication title: Earthwatch. Advertisements.
Second publication: Reports
Publication title: Sustainable Waste-Resource Management
Meetings/Conventions: - annual meeting

Galway Chamber of Commerce and Industry

Commerce House, Merchants Rd., Galway, Eire (Rep. of Ireland)
Tel: 353 9 1563536
Fax: 353 9 1561963
Email: info@galwaychamber.com
Website: http://www.galwaychamber.com
Contact: Michael Coyle, CEO
Description: Promotes commerce and industry in County Galway, Ireland.

Gay HIV Strategies

c/o Nexus Research Co-operative
Fumbally Ct., Tower One, Fumbally Ln., Dublin 8, Eire (Rep. of Ireland)
Tel: 353 1 473 0599
Fax: 353 1 473 0597
Email: ghs@nexus.ie
Website: http://www.iol.ie/nexus/ghs.htm
Founded: 1997
Members: 10
Staff: 1
Contact: Kieran Rose, Dir.
Description: Facilitates new programs, resources and linkages between the Statutory, Nongovernmental Organizations, and other agencies and the gay community for HIV prevention strategies for gay men.

Genetic and Inherited Disorders Organization
GIDO

Carmichael House, N Brunswick St., Dublin 7, Eire (Rep. of Ireland)
Tel: 353 1 8721501
Email: inherited.disorders@ireland.com
Founded: 1989
Description: An umbrella organization for voluntary organizations in Ireland involved with genetic disorders.

Geographical Society of Ireland

Geography Department, National University of Ireland, Belfield, Dublin 4, Eire (Rep. of Ireland)
Email: gerald.mills@ucd.ie
Website: http://www.geographical-society-ireland.org/
Founded: 1934
Description: Geographers, geography students and educators, and other individuals with an interest in geography. Promotes geographical studies in Ireland. Serves as forum for the exchange of information among members; functions as a clearinghouse on geography. Conducts field trips and other educational programs.
Publication: Newsletter
Publication title: Geonews
Second publication: Journal
Publication title: Irish Geography
Meetings/Conventions: - annual seminar

Geophysical Association of Ireland

c/o Martin Mollhoff
Geology Department, University College Dublin, Belfield, Dublin 4, Eire (Rep. of Ireland)
Founded: 1999
Contact: Peter O'Conner, Chm.
Description: Acts as a forum for technical discussion and exchange on geophysical topics.

Green Book of Ireland

55 Park Ave., Ballsbridge, Dublin 4, Eire (Rep. of Ireland)
Tel: 353 1 6762555
Fax: 353 1 6762995
Email: ireland@greenbook.ie
Website: http://www.greenbook.ie/
Description: Promotes the hospitality industry in Ireland, including private hotels, castles and country houses.

Guild of Agricultural Journalists - Ireland

c/o Irish Food Publishers
31 Deansgrange Rd., Blackrock, Dublin, Eire (Rep. of Ireland)
Tel: 353 1 2893305
Fax: 353 1 289406
Email: david@ifpmedia.com
Website: http://www.ifaj.org
Contact: David Markey
Description: Promotes agricultural journalism in Ireland.

Headway Ireland - National Association for Acquired Brain Injury
HINHIA

101 Parnell St., Dublin 1, Eire (Rep. of Ireland)
Tel: 353 1 8729222
Fax: 353 1 8729590
Email: services@headwayireland.ie
Website: http://www.headwayireland.ie

Founded: 1993
Members: 800
Staff: 13
Contact: Ms. Bernie Murphy
Description: Individuals and organizations. Seeks to improve the quality of life of people with head injuries and their families. Makes available support and services; conducts educational and advocacy campaigns; sponsors training programs for providers of care and services to people with head injuries.
Library Type: reference

Health Economics Association of Ireland
HEAI

c/o Mr. Brendan McElroy
Department of Economics and General Practice, University College Cork, Cork, Eire (Rep. of Ireland)
Email: c.oneill2@ulst.ac.uk
Contact: Ciaran O'Neill, Chm.
Description: Promotes health economics in Ireland.

Health Research Board
73 Lower Baggot St., Dublin 2, Eire (Rep. of Ireland)
Tel: 353 1 6761176
Fax: 353 1 6612335
Email: hrb@hrb.ie
Website: http://hrb2002.healthnet.ie/
Founded: 1987
Description: Promotes, assists, commissions or conducts medical, epidemiological, health and health services research.

Higher Education and Training Awards Council
26 Mountjoy Sq., Dublin 1, Eire (Rep. of Ireland)
Tel: 353 1 8556526
Fax: 353 1 8554250
Website: http://www.hetac.ie/index.cfm
Founded: 1972
Description: Sets standards for higher education and training awards; validates higher education and training programmes; monitors institutional quality assurance procedures; delegates awarding powers to recognized institutions and ensures that student assessment procedures are fair and consistent.
Formerly: National Council for Educational Awards

Home Birth Association of Ireland
36 Springlawn Ct., Blachardstown, Dublin 15, Eire (Rep. of Ireland)
Tel: 353 1 8206940
Email: homebirth@eircom.net
Website: http://www.homebirth.ie
Founded: 1982
Members: 210
Contact: Padraicin Ni Mhurchu, Coord.
Fee: €15
Membership Type: member
Description: Those interested in homebirthing. Seeks to increase the awareness of birth as a normal physiological process, while incorporating homebirthing into mainstream maternity services. Produces information booklets, midwives' directory, and holds conferences and support group meetings.
Library Subject: birth, pregnancy, breastfeeding, diet, vaccination
Library Type: not open to the public
Publication: Newsletter. Advertisements.
Meetings/Conventions: - annual conference

Home Birth Association of Ireland
36 Springlawn Ct., Blachardstown, Dublin 15, Eire (Rep. of Ireland)
Tel: 353 1 8206940
Email: homebirth@eircom.net
Website: http://www.homebirth.ie
Founded: 1982
Members: 210
Contact: Padraicin Ni Mhurchu, Coord.
Fee: €15
Membership Type: member
Description: Those interested in homebirthing. Seeks to increase the awareness of birth as a normal physiological process, while incorporating homebirthing into mainstream maternity services. Produces information booklets, midwives' directory, and holds conferences and support group meetings.
Library Subject: birth, pregnancy, breastfeeding, diet, vaccination
Library Type: not open to the public
Publication: Newsletter. Advertisements.
Meetings/Conventions: - annual conference

Huntington's Disease Association of Ireland
HDAI

Carmichael House, N. Brunswick St., Dublin 7, Eire (Rep. of Ireland)
Tel: 353 1 8721303
Fax: 353 1 8729931
Email: hdai@indigo.ie
Website: http://indigo.ie/~hdai
Description: Individuals and organizations. Seeks to improve the quality of life of people with Huntington's disease and their families. Makes available support and services; conducts educational and advocacy campaigns; serves as a clearinghouse on Huntington's disease.

Incorporated Law Society of Ireland
Solicitors' Buildings, Blackhall Pl, Dublin 7, Eire (Rep. of Ireland)
Tel: 353 1 6710711
Fax: 353 1 6710704
Founded: 1841

Industrial Heritage Association of Ireland
IHAI

77 Brian Rd., Marino, Dublin 3, Eire (Rep. of Ireland)
Tel: 353 1 4535827
Email: cormac@scally@ntlworld.com
Website: http://www.steam-museum.ie/ihai/
Founded: 1996
Members: 104
Contact: Ron Cox, Chm.
Fee: €10
Membership Type: individual
Fee: €25
Membership Type: heritage enterprise/affiliate association
Description: Individuals, associations, and corporations interested in preserving Ireland's industrial heritage. Seeks to foster a greater understanding and appreciation of the sites, monuments, and machinery which constitute Ireland's industrial heritage. Promotes a nationwide inventory, survey, and record of all industrial sites.
Publication: Newsletter
Meetings/Conventions: - annual tour

Inland Waterways Association of Ireland

c/o Ms. Rosaleen Miller, Hon. Sec.
Rondavel, Owning, Piltown, Kilkenny, Eire (Rep. of Ireland)
Tel: 353 51 643184
Email: duiske@esatclear.ie
Website: http://www.iwai.ie
Founded: 1954
Members: 1500
Contact: Mr. Colin Becker, Pres.
Description: Promotes the development, use, and maintenance of Ireland's navigable rivers and canals. Lobbies and advises national and local governments and other organizations on issues concerning waterways, including pollution and future developments.
Publication: Newsletter
Publication title: Inland Waterways News. Advertisements.
Meetings/Conventions: L. Derg Boat Rally

Institute of Accounting Technicians in Ireland

CA House, 87/89 Pembroke Rd., Ballsbridge, Dublin 4, Eire (Rep. of Ireland)
Tel: 353 1 6377363
Fax: 353 1 6377357
Email: info@iati.ie
Founded: 1983
Members: 4000
Staff: 12
Contact: Ms. Gay Sheehan, Mgr.
Description: Aims to provide a qualification in accounting and information skills for persons working in firms in public practice, in industry and commerce and in public sector, and to provide members services to support them in professional work.
Library Subject: business accounting
Library Type: reference

Institute of Advertising Practitioners in Ireland
IAPI

8 Upper Fitzwilliam St., Dublin 2, Eire (Rep. of Ireland)
Tel: 353 1 6765991
Fax: 353 1 6614589
Email: info@iapi.com
Website: http://www.iapi.ie
Founded: 1964
Members: 37
Staff: 12
Contact: Steve Shanahan, Chief Exec.
Description: Advertising agencies and professionals. Promotes growth and development of the domestic advertising industries. Represents members before industrial organizations and government agencies; sponsors continuing professional development programs for advertisers; conducts promotional activities.
Library Subject: Advertising
Library Type: open to the public

Institute of Chemistry of Ireland

c/o Science Section
RDS, Ballsbridge, Dublin 4, Eire (Rep. of Ireland)
Email: info@instituteofchemistry.org
Website: http://www.instituteofchemistry.org
Founded: 1950
Members: 800
Description: Chemists, Chemical technicians, students of chemistry, and chemical companies. Promotes interest in all branches and applications of chemistry, including industry. Disseminates information.
Publication: Magazine
Publication title: Irish Chemical News
Meetings/Conventions: - annual congress

Institute of Designers in Ireland
IDI

Merrion Square 8, Dublin 2, Eire (Rep. of Ireland)
Tel: 353 1 7167885
Fax: 353 1 7168736
Email: idi@indigo.ie
Founded: 1972
Members: 260
Contact: Rina Whyte, Exec. Officer
Description: Designers of consumer products, interiors, exhibitions, textiles, and fashion; photographers; theater, film, and television set designers; graphic designers; design educators and administrators. Promotes the design industry in the Republic of Ireland. Seeks to: maintain standards of professional practice, conduct, and integrity; further the education in the field; provide a forum for the discussion of design matters. Represents the interests of designers.
Library Type: reference
Formerly: Society of Designers in Ireland
Publication: Booklets
Publication title: Design Directory Ireland
Second publication: Directory
Publication title: SDI Design Directory Ireland
Meetings/Conventions: IDI Design Awards - annual competition

Institute of Geologists of Ireland
IGI

Geology Dept., University College Dublin, Belfield, Dublin 4, Eire (Rep. of Ireland)
Tel: 353 1 7162085
Fax: 353 1 2837733
Email: info@igi.ie
Website: http://www.igi.ie
Founded: 1999
Members: 130
Contact: Susan Pyne
Description: Aims to promote the interests of the geoscience professions and advance the science and practice of the geosciences in Ireland.

Institute of International Trade of Ireland
IITI

28 Merrion Sq., Dublin 2, Eire (Rep. of Ireland)
Tel: 353 1 6612182
Fax: 353 1 6612315
Email: iiti@irishexporters.ie
Website: http://www.irishexporters.ie/index3.html
Founded: 1996
Members: 360
Staff: 3
Contact: John Whelan, Dir.
Description: Professionals engaged in international trade and marketing. Promotes professional development of members; seeks to increase international trade involving the Republic of Ireland. Formulates and maintains professional standards for international trade and marketing practitioners; conducts research and educational programs.
Publication: Newsletter
Publication title: Export Link. Advertisements.

Institute of Management Consultants in Ireland

Harcourt St, Dublin 2, Eire (Rep. of Ireland)
Tel: 353 1 757971

Institute of Numerical Computation and Analysis
INCA

c/o Dr. John Miller
Mathematics Dept., Trinity College, Dublin 2, Eire (Rep. of Ireland)
Tel: 353 1 2804838
Fax: 353 1 2804838
Email: jm@incaireland.org
Website: http://www.maths.tcd.ie/~miller/inca.html
Founded: 1980
Members: 25
Staff: 3
Contact: Dr. John Miller, Dir.
Description: Encourages the development of numerical analysis, computation, and related areas. Fosters exchange among members.

Institute of Public Administration
IPA

57-61 Lansdowne Rd., Dublin 4, Eire (Rep. of Ireland)
Tel: 353 1 2697011
Fax: 353 1 2698644
Email: sales@ipa.ie
Founded: 1957

Institution of Engineers of Ireland

22 Clyde Rd., Ballsbridge, Dublin 4, Eire (Rep. of Ireland)
Tel: 353 1 6684341
Fax: 353 1 6685508
Email: info@iei.ie
Website: http://www.iei.ie/
Members: 16000
Contact: Brian Kearney, Pres.
Description: Engineers and engineering students. Seeks to advance the engineering professions; promotes continuing professional development of members. Facilitates communication and collaboration among members; sponsors educational programs; conducts golf tournaments and other social activities. Conducts qualifying examinations; promulgates standards of competence, ethics, and practice for the engineering professions.
Library Subject: engineering
Library Type: reference
Meetings/Conventions: - annual conference

Insurance Institute of Ireland

Insurance House, 39 Molesworth St., Dublin 2, Eire (Rep. of Ireland)
Tel: 353 1 6772582
Fax: 353 1 6772621
Email: info@insurance-institute.ie
Website: http://www.insurance-institute.ie
Founded: 1885
Members: 5600
Staff: 14
Contact: Denis Hevey, CEO
Description: Brokers, insurance agents, and companies engaged in all aspects of the insurance and financial services professions. Promotes efficiency and improvement in business practice among its members. Provides education, training, and professional development programs, including exams. Encourages a high standard of ethical behavior.
Meetings/Conventions: - annual conference

Interculture

10A Lower Camden St., Dublin 2, Eire (Rep. of Ireland)
Tel: 353 1 4782046
Fax: 353 1 4780614
Email: info-ireland@afs.org
Founded: 1976
Members: 200
Staff: 8
Contact: Kerry Lawless
Description: A program of AFS International. Individuals and organizations with an interest in intercultural understanding. Seeks to promote tolerance and understanding and combat prejudices and injustice through intercultural programs and international exchanges. Provides intercultural learning opportunities to empower individuals to create a more just and peaceful world. Sponsors international and intercultural exchange programs.
Publication: Newsletter
Publication title: Interlink. Advertisements.

International Adoption Association - Ireland
IAA

PO Box 5522, Shankill, Dublin, Eire (Rep. of Ireland)
Email: info@iaaireland.com
Website: http://www.iaaireland.com
Founded: 1990
Members: 750
Description: Provides help and guidance to Irish families who have adopted abroad or are intending to do so.

International Association for the Exchange of Students for Technical Experience
IAESTE

PO Box 6104, Swords, Dublin, Eire (Rep. of Ireland)
Tel: 353 1 8402055
Fax: 353 1 8402055
Email: general.secretary@iaeste.org
Website: http://www.iaeste.org
Founded: 1948
Members: 89
Contact: James Edward Reid
Description: National committees (57) and cooperating institutions (32). Represents academic, industrial, and student interests in the organization of technical exchange programs supplementing university and college education. Promotes international understanding by providing students with technical experience abroad. Maintains placement service.
Publication title: Activity Report
Publication title: Annual Report. Advertisements.
Meetings/Conventions: - annual conference

International Association for the Scientific Study of Intellectual Disabilities
IASSID

Moore Abbey, Monasterevan, Eire (Rep. of Ireland)
Tel: 353 45 525327
Fax: 353 45 525251
Email: 101720.3537@compuserve.com
Website: http://www.iassid.org/
Founded: 1964
Members: 430
Contact: Stephen Kealy, Sec.
Fee: €125

Membership Type: individual & research center
Description: Scientific study of mental deficiency by means of a multidisciplinary approach.
Publication: Newsletter. Advertisements.
Second publication: Journal
Publication title: Journal of Intellectual Disability Research
Meetings/Conventions: meeting Montpelier France

International Association for the Study of Irish Literatures
IASIL

c/o Dr. Christopher Murray, Chair
University College, Dublin National University of Ireland, Belfield, Dublin 4, Eire (Rep. of Ireland)
Email: cmurray@macollamh.vcd.ie
Website: http://www.ulst.ac.uk/faculty/humanities/langlit/iasil/index.htm
Founded: 1969
Description: Supports teaching and study of Irish writing in third-level education throughout the world.

International Association of Young Lawyers
IAYL

c/o Eugene F. Collins
Temple Chambers, 3 Burlington Rd., Dublin 4, Eire (Rep. of Ireland)
Tel: 353 1 6675111
Fax: 353 1 6675200
Email: gcoll@efc.ie
Website: http://www.lawsociety.ie/aija.htm
Founded: 1962
Members: 2500
Staff: 3
Contact: Gerard Coll, Pres.
Description: Lawyers in 55 countries; national or regional law societies and bar associations. Promotes the interests of young lawyers and the entire legal profession, and encourages cooperation among lawyers. Studies problems of law; assists young lawyers facing difficulties in the free exercise of their professional rights and duties. Intervenes when the rights of persons to be legally represented and to receive a fair trial are threatened. Contributes to the development of the legal profession and the harmonization of its professional rules; defends common principles considered to be invincible from the notion of justice and law. Encourages formation of new national associations in countries where such groups do not exist. Fosters international communication and friendship among lawyers. Holds annual courses in law; offers service for placement of young lawyers as trainees with foreign law firms.
Library Type: reference
Publication title: AIJA Gazette. Advertisements.
Publication title: Annuaire AIJA
Meetings/Conventions: - annual congress - Exhibits.

International Geographical Union
IGU

c/o Prof. Anne Buttimer, Pres.
Department of Geography, University College Dublin, Belfield, Dublin 4, Eire (Rep. of Ireland)
Tel: 353 1 7068174
Fax: 353 1 2695597
Email: anne.buttimer@ucd.ie
Website: http://www.igu-net.org
Founded: 1922

Members: 85
Contact: Prof. Anne Buttimer, Pres.
Description: Academies of science, research councils, or similar bodies in 85 countries. Promotes the study of geographical problems; initiates and coordinates geographical research requiring international cooperation and promotes its scientific discussion and publication. Provides for the participation of geographers in the work of similar international organizations. Facilitates the collection and diffusion of geographical data and documentation in and between member countries. Participates in various forms of international cooperation with the goal of advancing the study and application of geography. Maintains 22 commissions and 10 study groups concerned with specific areas of geographic investigations.
Library Subject: Maintained at the Societa Geografica Italiana, Rome, Italy
Library Type: open to the public
Publication: Bulletin
Publication title: IGU Bulletin. Advertisements.
Second publication: Newsletter
Publication title: IGU Newsletter. Advertisements.
Meetings/Conventions: International Geographical Congress - quadrennial congress Glasgow UK

International Law Association, Irish Branch
9 Sylvan Drive, Fairlands, Newcastle, Galway, Eire (Rep. of Ireland)
Fax: 353 91 750506
Founded: 1986

International Songwriters' Association - Ireland
ISA

PO Box 46, Limerick, Limerick, Eire (Rep. of Ireland)
Tel: 353 61 228837
Fax: 352 61 229464
Email: jliddane@songwriter.iol.ie
Website: http://www.songwriter.co.uk/
Founded: 1967
Members: 4800
Staff: 3
Contact: James D. Liddane, Chm.
Description: Songwriters, music publishers, and recording executives in 60 countries. Represents and offers advice to songwriters; provides information on outlets for writers. Compiles statistics.
Library Type: reference
Publication: Magazine
Publication title: Basic Course in Songwriting. Advertisements.
Publication title: Best of the Songwriter
Meetings/Conventions: - periodic competition

Irish Academy of Letters
Merrion Rd., Dublin 4, Eire (Rep. of Ireland)
Founded: 1932

Irish Association for American Studies
IAAA

c/o Dr. Ron Callan, Chair
Dept. of English, University College Dublin, Belfield, Dublin 2, Eire (Rep. of Ireland)
Tel: 353 1 7068158
Website: http://www.ucd.ie/~ire-amer/
Founded: 1972
Members: 43
Contact: Stephen Matterson

Fee: €10
Membership Type: full
Description: Scholars and teachers involved in research or teaching concerning U.S. culture and society.
Publication: Journal
Publication title: Irish Journal of American Studies. Advertisements.
Second publication: Newsletter
Meetings/Conventions: - annual conference

Irish Association for Counselling and Therapy
IACT

8 Cumberland St., Dun Laoghaire, Dublin, Eire (Rep. of Ireland)
Tel: 353 1 2300061
Fax: 353 1 2300064
Email: iact@irish-counseling.ie
Website: http://www.irish-counselling.ie
Description: Professional counselors and therapists in Ireland. Seeks to set, maintain, and regulate standards for the profession of counseling and therapy in order to protect the public. Operates accreditation schemes; operates a complaints procedure.

Irish Association for Economic Geology

c/o Gerry Stanley, Pres.
Beggars Bush, Haddington Rd., Dublin 4, Eire (Rep. of Ireland)
Tel: 353 1 6782863
Email: gerrystanley@gsi.ie
Website: http://www.iaeg.org
Founded: 1973
Members: 320
Description: Economic geologists and other interested individuals. Compiles statistics. Conducts educational programs.
Library Subject: economics, exploration, mine geology
Library Type: reference
Publication title: Annual Review. Advertisements.
Second publication: Newsletter. Advertisements.
Meetings/Conventions: - monthly lecture

Irish Association for European Studies
IAES

National Technological Park, Plassey, Limerick, Eire (Rep. of Ireland)

Irish Association for Nurses in Oncology
IANO

PO Box 1499, Dublin 4, Eire (Rep. of Ireland)
Tel: 353 1 2310529
Email: mkennedy@irishcancer.ie
Website: http://www.iano.ie/
Description: Provides education and information exchange for members of the nursing profession, particularly those caring for people with cancer.

Irish Association for Quaternary Studies
IQUA

c/o Robbie Meehan
Teagasc, Kinsealy Research Center, Malahide Rd., Dublin 17, Eire (Rep. of Ireland)
Tel: 353 1 8460644
Fax: 353 1 8460524
Email: rmeehan@kinsealy.teagasc.ie
Website: http://homepage.eircom.net/~iqua/
Founded: 1975

Members: 150
Contact: Dr. Robbie Meehan, Treas.
Fee: €15
Membership Type: general
Fee: €10
Membership Type: student
Description: Aims to promote quaternary studies in Ireland through publications and the activities of the organization.
Library Subject: quaternary geology, archaeology
Library Type: reference
Publication: Newsletter. Advertisements.

Irish Association for Spina Bifida and Hydrocephalus
IASBH

Old Nangor Rd., Clandalkin, Dublin 22, Eire (Rep. of Ireland)
Tel: 353 1 4572329
Fax: 353 1 4572328
Description: Individuals and organizations. Seeks to improve the quality of life of people with spina bifida or hydrocephalus and their families. Makes available support and services; conducts educational and advocacy campaigns.

Irish Association of Art Historians

PO Box 7189, Churchtown, Dublin 14, Eire (Rep. of Ireland)
Tel: 353 1 7068679
Fax: 353 1 7968453
Founded: 1972
Members: 450
Contact: Dr. Lynda Mulin, Con.
Fee: €15
Membership Type: ordinary, student
Description: Promotes the study and interest in the history of art and architecture.
Formerly: Association of Irish Historians

Irish Association of Distributive Trades

Rock House, Main St., Blackrock, Dublin, Eire (Rep. of Ireland)
Tel: 353 1 2887584
Fax: 353 1 2832206
Contact: Ailish Forde, Dir.Gen.
Description: Promotes the food wholesaler trade in Ireland; works to protect the interests of the independent retail and wholesale sectors and customers in the European Union.

Irish Association of Investment Managers
IAIM

35 Fitzwilliam Pl., Dublin 2, Eire (Rep. of Ireland)
Tel: 353 1 6761919
Fax: 353 1 6761954
Email: iaim@indigo.ie
Website: http://www.iaim.ie
Founded: 1986
Members: 14
Description: Promotes the investment management industry to ensure the best working practices. Represents members' interests to government, regulatory bodies, and other organizations.

Irish Association of Pension Funds
IAPF

Ste.2, Slane House, 25 Lower Mount St., Dublin 2, Eire (Rep. of Ireland)
Tel: 353 1 6612427
Fax: 353 1 6621196
Email: iapf@iol.ie
Website: http://www.iapf.ie
Founded: 1973
Members: 380
Staff: 3
Contact: John Feely, Chm.
Description: Acts a forum for discussion relating to legislative and practical aspects of occupational pension schemes. Liaises with governmental bodies and other professional bodies.
Publication: Newsletter
Publication title: Pensions Voice

Irish Association of Russian and East European Studies
IAREES

Trinity College, Dublin 2, Eire (Rep. of Ireland)
Tel: 353 1 6081651
Fax: 353 1 6770546
Email: rhill@tcd.ie

Irish Association of Social Workers
IASW

114-116 Pearse St., Dublin 2, Eire (Rep. of Ireland)
Tel: 353 1 6774838
Fax: 353 1 6715734
Email: iasw@iol.ie
Website: http://iasw.eire.org
Founded: 1971
Contact: Mary McDevitt
Description: Seeks to improve the standards and equality of social work. Provides support to social workers in the practice of their profession. Represents the views of social workers on matters of social policy at the national and international levels.

Irish Association of Suicidology
IAS

St. Mary's Hospital, Castlebar, Mayo, Eire (Rep. of Ireland)
Tel: 353 94 21333
Fax: 353 94 27904
Email: info@ias.ie
Website: http://www.ias.ie/
Founded: 1996
Description: Works to facilitate communication between clinicians, volunteers, survivors, and researchers in all matters relating to suicide and suicide behavior; promotes public awareness of problems of suicide and suicidal behavior.
Meetings/Conventions: conference

Irish Association of the Sovereign Military Order of Malta
IASMOM

St. John's House, 32 Clyde Rd., Ballsbridge, Dublin 4, Eire (Rep. of Ireland)
Tel: 353 1 6684891
Fax: 353 1 6685288
Email: smom@ordereofmalta.ie
Website: http://www.orderofmalta.ie
Founded: 1934
Members: 4000
Staff: 13
Contact: Comdt. Frank Hearns, CEO
Description: Volunteers committed to serving those in need. Seeks to increase the availability of emergency services. Operates ambulance corps.

Irish Astronomical Association
IAA

c/o John O'Neill, Sec.
PO Box 2547, Dublin 14, Eire (Rep. of Ireland)
Tel: 353 1 2980181
Email: eter@gateway.thegap.com
Founded: 1946
Members: 200
Staff: 6
Contact: Rowan McLaughlin, Hon.Sec.
Fee: €12
Membership Type: ordinary
Description: Individuals in Ireland interested in astronomy and space exploration. Encourages public awareness of astronomy.
Formerly: Irish Astronomical Society
Publication: Newsletter
Publication title: Newssheets. Advertisements.
Second publication: Magazine
Publication title: Stardust. Advertisements.
Meetings/Conventions: - biweekly meeting Belfast Northern Ireland

Irish Bankers Federation
IBF

Nassau House, Nassau St., Dublin 2, Eire (Rep. of Ireland)
Tel: 353 1 6715311
Fax: 353 1 6796680
Email: ibf@ibf.ie
Website: http://www.ibis.ie/
Founded: 1973
Members: 60
Contact: James Bardon, Dir.Gen.
Description: Financial institutions, including licensed domestic and foreign banks and institutions operating in the international Financial Services Centre. Represents and promotes the interests of the Irish banking industry in Ireland and abroad. Liaises with national authorities; disseminates information; represents Irish banking abroad, particularly in the EU.

Irish Book Publishers' Association
IBPA

43/44 Temple Bar, Dublin 2, Eire (Rep. of Ireland)
Tel: 353 1 6706393
Fax: 353 1 6706642
Email: cle@iol.ie

Website: http://www.publishingireland.com
Founded: 1970
Members: 50
Staff: 2
Contact: Orla Martin, Exec.Dir.
Description: Book publishers. Promotes the sale, distribution, and export of books published in the Republic of Ireland. Facilitates communication and cooperation among members; advises members on copyright laws and related issues.

Irish Breakfast Cereals Association

Confederation House, Lower Baggot House 84-86, Dublin, Eire (Rep. of Ireland)
Tel: 353 1 6601011
Fax: 353 1 6381576
Email: frances.mullaney@ibec.ie
Website: http://www.ibec.ie/fdf
Contact: Frances Mullaney
Description: Promotes the Irish breakfast cereals industry; seeks to advance the importance of the oat milling sector in Ireland. Areas of interest include the use of health and nutritional claims for breakfast cereals, the Merchandising Marks Act for breakfast cereals and general market information.

Irish Brokers Association
IBA

87 Merrion Sq., Dublin 2, Eire (Rep. of Ireland)
Tel: 353 1 6613067
Fax: 353 1 6619955
Email: info@irishbrokers.com
Website: http://www.irishbrokers.com/
Founded: 1991
Members: 600
Contact: Paul Carty, Chief Exec.
Description: Representative and regulatory body for insurance brokers in Ireland.
Meetings/Conventions: - annual general assembly

Irish Business and Employers' Confederation
IBEC

Confederation House, 84-86 Lower Baggot St., Dublin 2, Eire (Rep. of Ireland)
Tel: 353 1 6051500
Fax: 353 1 6381500
Email: info@ibec.ie
Website: http://www.ibec.ie
Founded: 1992
Members: 4000
Staff: 150
Contact: Turlough O'Sullivan, Dir.Gen.
Description: Firms. Industrial, commercial, and public sector firms that manufacture products or provide services. Promotes the growth and development of Irish industry and commercial activity. Advises government and represents interests of industry on relevant legislative issues. Maintains the Irish Business Bureau in conjunction with Irish Business and Employers Confederation and the Chambers of Commerce of Ireland. Develops public awareness of the role of industry in national development through press, radio, television, and public meetings. Monitors technological developments; compiles statistics; provides advice and assistance to members; maintains speakers' bureau.
Library Subject: industrial relations, government, training, statistics, and EC O.J.

Library Type: not open to the public
Formerly: Formed by Merger of, Conference of Irish Industry
Publication title: Economic Trends Quarterly
Second publication: Magazine
Publication title: IBEC Economic Trends

Irish Campaign for Nuclear Disarmament
ICND

PO Box 6327, Dublin 6, Eire (Rep. of Ireland)
Tel: 353 87 2364312
Email: irishcnd@ireland.com
Website: http://indigo.ie/~goodwill/icnd.html
Founded: 1959
Members: 150
Contact: Billy Fitzpatrick, Chp.
Fee: €19
Membership Type: individual/household
Description: Coordinates activities in the Republic of Ireland to encourage nuclear disarmament. Conducts demonstrations, campaigns, and lobbying activities. Maintains speakers' bureau.
Publication: Newsletter
Publication title: PeaceWork
Meetings/Conventions: - annual convention

Irish Cancer Society
ICS

5 Northumberland Rd., Dublin 4, Eire (Rep. of Ireland)
Tel: 353 1 2310500
Fax: 353 1 2310555
Email: reception@irishcancer.ie
Website: http://www.irishcancer.ie
Contact: Tom Hudson
Description: National cancer societies. Promotes advancement in the prevention, diagnosis, and treatment of cancer; seeks to improve the quality of life of people with cancer and their families. Facilitates communication and cooperation among members; sponsors research and educational programs; provides support and services to people with cancer.

Irish Cardiac Society

4 Clyde Rd., Ballsbridge, Dublin 4, Eire (Rep. of Ireland)
Tel: 353 1 6685001
Fax: 353 1 6685896
Email: irishcardiac@eircom.net
Website: http://www.irishcardiacsociety.org
Members: 135
Contact: Dr. K.M. Daly, Pres.
Description: Promotes the study of cardiology in Ireland.
Meetings/Conventions: - annual meeting

Irish Cattle and Sheep Farmers Association

Unit 9, Lyster House, Portlaoise, Laoighis, Eire (Rep. of Ireland)
Fax: 353 502 62121
Email: info@icsaireland.com
Website: http://www.icsaireland.com
Founded: 1890
Members: 5000
Staff: 6
Contact: Charlie Reilly, Chair
Description: Livestock producers. Represents the beef and lamb sectors in the political arena.
Formerly: Irish Cattle Traders' and Stockowners Association

Irish Centre for European Law
ICEL

Law School, House 39, Trinity College, Dublin 2, Eire (Rep. of Ireland)
Tel: 353 1 6081845
Fax: 353 1 6794080
Email: icel@tcd.ie
Website: http://www.icel.ie
Founded: 1988
Members: 450
Staff: 2
Contact: Cathryn Costello, Dir.
Fee: €295
Membership Type: corporate
Fee: €118
Membership Type: individual
Description: Promotes the knowledge, study, and discussion of European Community and European Human Rights law in Ireland. Organizes continuing education programs. Disseminates information.
Publication: Book
Publication title: European Initiatives in Intellectual Property
Second publication: Book
Publication title: Irish Social Security Law in a European Context

Irish Chamber of Shipping

Tolka Quay Rd., Dublin Port, Dublin 1, Eire (Rep. of Ireland)
Tel: 353 1 6618211
Fax: 353 1 6618270
Email: bks@iol.ie
Founded: 1972
Contact: Brian W. Kerr, Dir.
Description: National branch of the European Community Shipowners' Associations. Promotes the interests of water freight and passenger shipping concerns in the Republic of Ireland.

Irish Christmas Tree Growers
ICTG

PO Box 8581, Dublin, Glenageary, Eire (Rep. of Ireland)
Tel: 353 1 2304973
Fax: 353 86 2627731
Email: info@ictg.org
Website: http://www.ictg.org/
Founded: 1989
Members: 78
Contact: Dorothea Melvin, Exec.Sec.
Description: Christmas tree growers are full members; individuals and corporations in related fields are associate members. Promotes growth and development in the Christmas tree industry. Represents members' interests before national and international government agencies. Establishes quality standards for Christmas trees; makes available technical support and assistance to members; maintains contact with related associations and agencies worldwide. Facilitates communication among members.
Publication: Catalog
Publication title: Buy & Sell Catalogue. Advertisements.
Second publication: Directory. Advertisements.

Irish Commercial Horticultural Association

Irish Farm Centre, Bluebell, Dublin 12, Eire (Rep. of Ireland)
Tel: 353 1 4500266
Fax: 353 1 4565146
Email: postmaster@ifa.ie
Founded: 1947
Members: 3000
Staff: 2
Contact: Kevin Harrington, Exec.Sec.
Description: Members include the Irish Mushroom Growers Association, Irish Handy Nursery Stock Association, Irish Field Vegetable Producers Association, Irish Bedding Plant Producers Association, Irish Protected Vegetable Producers Association, Irish Apple Growers Association, Irish Soft Fruit Growers Association and Irish Bulb Producers Association. Aims to provide the most professional representative service possible to their members, on a local, national and international level. Activities include lobbying Government at all levels, compiling weekly market reports and analyses, liasing with other representative bodies across Europe and assisting with the promotion of Irish Horticultural produce around the world.

Irish Commission for Justice and Peace
ICJP

169 Booterstown Ave., Blackrock, Dublin, Eire (Rep. of Ireland)
Tel: 353 1 2885021
Fax: 353 1 2834161
Email: icjp@eircom.net
Founded: 1970
Members: 15
Staff: 4
Contact: Jerome Connolly, Exec.Sec
Description: National commission of the Conference of the European Justice and Peace Commissions. Cooperates with other national commissions on human rights, peace, development, and justice issues. Monitors human rights issues in the Republic of Ireland; lobbies for improved relationships between Ireland, the European Union, and the Third World. Advocates peace education at all levels of Irish society; conducts research on peace education curriculum and Third World development; provides in-service peace education training.
Library Subject: Peace, human rights, development, security, social justice, Northern Ireland
Library Type: reference
Publication: Booklet
Publication title: Human Rights Notes

Irish Computer Society, 17-19 Sir John Rogerson's Quay, Dublin 2, Eire (Rep. of Ireland)

Tel: 353 1 6727998
Fax: 353 1 6728003
Email: info@ics.ie
Website: http://www.ics.ie
Founded: 1967
Members: 1065
Staff: 1
Contact: Suki Garvey, Administrator
Description: Information technology professionals, educators, and students. Promotes development and use of computers and computer-related techniques; establishes and maintains standards of practice for computer professionals. Facilitates exchange of information among members; represents members' interests before government agencies and international technical and scientific organizations.
Publication: Newsletter
Publication title: Irish Computer Society Newsletter
Meetings/Conventions: - periodic seminar

Irish Council for Civil Liberties
ICCL

Dominick Ct., 40-41 Lower Dominick St., Dublin 1, Eire (Rep. of Ireland)
Tel: 353 1 8783136
Fax: 353 1 8783109
Email: iccl@iol.ie
Website: http://www.iccl.ie
Founded: 1976
Members: 450
Staff: 2
Contact: Alma Farrell, Admin.
Description: Conducts campaigns in support of civil liberties. Stresses the importance of preserving and extending civil liberties and examines relevant laws and official practices. Sponsors seminars.
Library Subject: human rights, civil liberties
Library Type: by appointment only
Publication title: Journal of Rights
Publication title: Reports
Meetings/Conventions: - annual convention

Irish Deaf Society
IDS

c/o National Association of the Deaf
30 Blessington St., Dublin 7, Eire (Rep. of Ireland)
Tel: 353 1 8601878
Fax: 353 1 8601960
Email: ids@indigo.ie
Founded: 1981
Members: 300
Staff: 14
Contact: John Bosco, Honorary Sec. of the I.D.S.
Description: A representative organization of the Deaf seeks recognition of Irish sign language and conducts various educational and advocacy campaigns.

Irish Dental Association
IDA

Clonskeagh Rd., Dublin 14, Eire (Rep. of Ireland)
Tel: 353 1 2830499
Email: info@irishdentalassoc.ie
Website: http://www.dentist.ie
Founded: 1922

Irish Diabetes Association

76 Lower Gardiner St., Dublin, Eire (Rep. of Ireland)
Tel: 353 1 8363022
Website: http://www.iol.ie/diabetes/
Description: Supports individuals with diabetes and diabetes research.

Irish Draught Horse Society
IDHS

c/o Helen Kelly
Derrynagara, Collinstown, Westmeath, Eire (Rep. of Ireland)
Tel: 353 4461199
Email: idhs@eircom.net
Website: http://www.irishdraught.ie/
Founded: 1976
Contact: Helen Kelly, Sec.
Description: Committed to preserve, promote, protect and improve the Irish Draught Horse in Ireland and throughout the world.

Irish Economic Association, Belfield, Dublin 4, Eire (Rep. of Ireland)

Tel: 353 1 7068618
Fax: 353 1 2830068
Email: john.sheehan@ucd.ie

Irish Ergonomics Society

c/o Manufacturing & Operations Engineering
University of Limerick, Limerick, Eire (Rep. of Ireland)
Tel: 353 61 202900
Fax: 353 61 202913
Website: http://www.ul.ie/~ies/
Description: Professionals involved in the ergonomics field promoting the discovery and exchange of knowledge concerning the characteristics of human beings that are applicable to the design of systems and devices of all kinds.

Irish Exporters Association
IEA

28 Merrion Sq., Dublin 2, Eire (Rep. of Ireland)
Tel: 353 1 6612182
Fax: 353 1 6612315
Email: iea@irishexporters.ie
Website: http://www.irishexporters.ie
Founded: 1951
Members: 400
Staff: 6
Contact: John F. Whelan, Chief Exec.
Description: Facilitates national and international trade by providing companies and industries with information on Irish exports. Conducts education and training programs. Lobbies government, the European Union and the World Trade Organization.
Publication: Magazine
Publication title: Export Link. Advertisements.
Meetings/Conventions: National Export Forum - annual general assembly - Exhibits.

Irish Family History Society

PO Box 36, Naas, Kildare, Eire (Rep. of Ireland)
Tel: 353 1850 203204
Email: ifhs@eircom.net
Website: http://homepage.eircom.net
Founded: 1980
Members: 550
Contact: John C. Heueston, Chm.
Fee: €24
Membership Type: ordinary
Description: Aims to promote the study of Irish Family History and genealogy. Promotes the recording of gravestone inscriptions. Aims to promote the preservation, security and accessibility of archival material. Advises all those interested in seeking their Irish roots. Encourages the repatriation of information from overseas on Irish emigrants. Maintains a reference library for the use of members. Collaborates with and supports other societies with similar aims.
Library Subject: family history
Library Type: not open to the public
Publication: Journal
Publication title: Irish Family History Society

Irish Family Planning Association
IFPA

Solomons House, 42A Pearse St., Dublin 2, Eire (Rep. of Ireland)
Tel: 353 1 4740944
Fax: 353 1 4740945
Email: post@ifpa.ie
Website: http://www.ifpa.ie
Founded: 1969
Contact: Tony O'Brien, Exec.Dir.
Description: Works to improve the quality of life for individuals living in Ireland by promoting family planning and responsible parenthood. Advocates family planning as a basic human right. Offers programs in sex education, family planning, and health. Provides contraceptive and health care services. Conducts research.
Library Subject: sexual and reproductive health in Ireland
Library Type: by appointment only

Irish Federation of University Teachers
IFUT

11 Merrion Sq., Dublin 2, Eire (Rep. of Ireland)
Tel: 353 1 6610910
Fax: 353 1 6610909
Email: ifut@eircom.net
Website: http://www.ifut.ie
Founded: 1965
Members: 1500
Contact: Daltun O'Ceallaigh, Gen.Sec.
Description: Professors and other educators employed at the postsecondary level. Promotes effective postsecondary education. Works to enhance the professional status of members. Represents members' interests before government agencies, college and university administrative bodies, and the public.
Publication title: Equality Issues
Second publication: Newsletter
Publication title: IFUT News. Advertisements.
Meetings/Conventions: - annual conference

Irish Federation of University Women

2 Mount Salus, Dalkey, Dublin, Eire (Rep. of Ireland)
Tel: 353 1 668 5923
Fax: 353 1 668 5923
Email: melissawebb@oceanfree.net
Description: Women university graduates. Advocates women's pursuit of higher education in Ireland.

Irish Fish Processors and Exporters Association

c/o Tom Geoghegan
25 Kincora Ave., Clontarf, Dublin, Eire (Rep. of Ireland)
Tel: 353 18337882
Fax: 353 18337882
Founded: 1963
Contact: Tom Geoghegan, Sec.
Description: Represents the interests of Irish fish processors and exporters at Irish Government and Semi-State Boards levels and also in various consultative forums in the European Economic Community.

Irish Fish Producers Organization
IFPO

11 Elgin Rd., Dublin 4, Eire (Rep. of Ireland)
Tel: 353 1 66857077
Fax: 353 1 66854466
Email: ifpo@eircom.net

Founded: 1975
Members: 83
Staff: 3
Contact: Mark Lochrin
Description: Owners of commercial sea-fishing vessels. Works to make the best use of the available fish stocks to optimize returns.

Irish Fragile X Society

5 Fitzwilliam Pl., Dublin 2, Eire (Rep. of Ireland)
Email: info@fragilex-ireland.org
Website: http://www.fragilex-ireland.org/pages/app.htm
Contact:
Fee: €10
Membership Type: family
Fee: €15
Membership Type: associate
Description: Works to improve the quality of life of all people affected by Fragile X syndrome; provides mutual support and information to families, promotes public awareness of Fragile X syndrome.

Irish Geological Association
IGA

c/o Tom de Brit
Data Relate Software, Unit 2, Hills Complex, Lucan, Dublin, Eire (Rep. of Ireland)
Contact:
Fee: €12
Membership Type: professional
Description: Aims to foster and develop a wider interest in Geology. Activities include regular lecture meetings. Several day excursions to sites of geological interest every year. Weekend excursions take place three times a year. Annual social events include Members' Night in May.

Irish Georgian Society
IGS

74 Merrion Sq., Dublin 2, Eire (Rep. of Ireland)
Tel: 353 1 6767053
Fax: 353 1 6620290
Email: info@irishgeorgiansoc.org
Website: http://www.irish-architecture.com/igs
Founded: 1958
Members: 3500
Staff: 5
Contact: Mary Bryan B. Arch, Exec.Sec.
Description: International society of individuals, firms, and libraries from 23 countries united to preserve Irish art and architecture, especially that of the Georgian period. Conducts rescue, repair and restoration work on buildings in need. Promotes tourism as a means of preserving the Irish heritage. Arranges expeditions to buildings of interest; holds lectures on Irish art and architecture.
Library Subject: conservation
Library Type: not open to the public
Formerly: Irelands Architectural Heritage Society
Publication: Journal
Publication title: Irish Architectural and Decorative Studies
Second publication: Newsletter
Publication title: Newsletter
Meetings/Conventions: - periodic conference

Irish Gerontological Society
IGS

Department Age-Related Healthcare, Adelaide & Health Hospital, Tallaght, Tallaght, Dublin 24, Eire (Rep. of Ireland)
Tel: 353 1 4143215
Email: des.oneill@amnch.ie
Founded: 1952
Members: 300
Staff: 3
Contact: Prof. Desmond O'Neill, Sec.
Fee: €25
Membership Type: full
Description: Health care professionals treating the elderly; scientists and clinicians with an interest in the aging process and diseases of the aged. Promotes gerontological research and increased availability of gerontological care; facilitates training of gerontology specialists. Represents the interests of gerontologists and gerontological organizations.
Meetings/Conventions: - annual conference Dublin Ireland

Irish Girl Guides

27 Pembroke Pk., Dublin 4, Eire (Rep. of Ireland)
Tel: 353 1 6683898
Fax: 353 1 6602779
Email: info@irishgirlguides.ie
Website: http://www.irishgirlguides.ie
Founded: 1911
Members: 12000
Staff: 14
Contact: Linda Peters, CEO
Description: Provides a meeting place for girls from a variety of backgrounds. Works to help girls grow in self confidence and develop leadership skills. Teaches girls practical indoor and outdoor skills. Encourages community service activities.
Library Subject: guiding, nature, games and activities, social affairs, crafts, and songs
Library Type: reference

Irish Guide Dogs for the Blind
IGDB

Model Farm Rd., Cork, Cork, Eire (Rep. of Ireland)
Tel: 353 21 4878200
Fax: 353 21 4874152
Email: info@guidedogs.ie
Website: http://www.guidedogs.ie
Description: Dog trainers and individuals providing support and services to people with impaired vision. Seeks to improve the quality of life of people with impaired vision. Makes available trained guide dogs to people with impaired vision; conducts training programs for people wishing to use guide dogs.

Irish Haemophilia Society
IHS

Iceland House, Arran Ct., Arran Quay, Dublin 7, Eire (Rep. of Ireland)
Tel: 353 1 8724466
Fax: 353 1 8724494
Email: info@haemophilia-society.ie
Website: http://www.haemophilia-society.ie
Founded: 1968
Members: 300
Staff: 6
Contact: Margaret Dunne, Office Mgr.

Description: Individuals and organizations. Seeks to improve the quality of life of people with hemophilia and their families. Makes available support and services; conducts educational and advocacy campaigns; supports hematological research.
Library Subject: all aspects of Haemophilia
Library Type: reference
Publication: Newsletter
Meetings/Conventions: - annual meeting

Irish Hard of Hearing Association

c/o Emma McAuley
35 N Frederick St., Dublin 1, Eire (Rep. of Ireland)
Tel: 353 1 8723800
Fax: 353 1 8723816
Email: info@ihha.ie
Website: http://www.ihha.ie/homepage.html
Founded: 1986
Contact: Emma McAuley, VP
Fee: €10
Description: Hearing impaired persons holding social evenings to share problems and fears and offer support. Offers lip reading courses, family information nights, one-to-one counseling, coping strategies, technical aids, and more.
Publication: Magazine
Publication title: Hearsay
Meetings/Conventions: - annual meeting

Irish Home Builders Association

Construction House, Canal Rd., Dublin 6, Eire (Rep. of Ireland)
Tel: 353 1 4066000
Fax: 353 1 4966953
Email: ihba@cif.ie
Website: http://www.cif.ie
Founded: 1932
Members: 1500
Staff: 5
Contact: Ciaran Ryan, Dir.
Description: Represents and promotes the economic interests of residential building contractors in the Republic of Ireland. Conducts lobbying and advocacy campaigns. Gathers and disseminates industry information.
Publication: Newsletter
Publication title: Homebuilder Magazine
Meetings/Conventions: - annual convention

Irish Hotels Federation
IHF

13 Northbrook Rd., Dublin 6, Eire (Rep. of Ireland)
Tel: 353 1 4976459
Fax: 353 1 4974613
Email: info@ihf.ie
Website: http://www.ihf.ie
Founded: 1937
Members: 650
Staff: 7
Contact: John Power
Description: Hotel and guesthouse proprietors in the Republic of Ireland. Promotes and protects members' interests and represents the industry. Offers advisory services to members on legal, technical, and economic matters including fire precautions, marketing, labor relations, and business promotions. Works with the Irish Tourist Board. Makes recommendations to government agencies on industry

issues. Monitors trends in the European Economic Community and their application to Irish affairs.
Publication title: Annual Report
Second publication: Booklet
Publication title: Be Our Guest - Hotel and Guesthouse Guide
Meetings/Conventions: - annual meeting

Irish Institute of Credit Management
128 La Baggot St., Dublin 2, Eire (Rep. of Ireland)
Tel: 353 1 6767822
Fax: 353 1 6614145
Email: iicm@indigo.ie
Website: http://www.iicm.ie
Founded: 1980
Members: 350
Contact: Declan Flood, Ch.Exec.
Fee: €165
Membership Type: full
Fee: €85
Membership Type: associate
Description: Represents the credit management profession in Ireland by holding conferences and seminars on credit management issues.
Publication: Newsletter. Advertisements.
Meetings/Conventions: seminar

Irish Institute of Purchasing and Materials Management
5 Belvedere Pl., Dublin 1, Eire (Rep. of Ireland)
Tel: 353 1 8559257
Fax: 353 1 8559259
Email: iipmm@iol.ie
Website: http://www.iipmm.ie
Founded: 1971
Members: 1500
Staff: 5
Contact: Des Crowther, CEO
Description: Purchasing and materials managers. Educates, trains, and provides support for the profession.
Library Type: not open to the public

Irish Institute of Training and Development
Leinster Mills, Millennium Business Pk., Osberstown, Naas, Kildare, Eire (Rep. of Ireland)
Tel: 353 45 881166
Fax: 353 45 881192
Email: info@iitd.com
Website: http://www.iitd.com
Founded: 1969
Members: 1550
Staff: 2
Contact: Sinead Heneghan, Off.Dir.
Description: Individuals working in human resource development in Ireland. Fosters communication among members. Conducts educational programs.
Library Subject: training and development
Library Type: open to the public
Publication: Magazine
Publication title: HRD Ireland. Advertisements.
Second publication: Membership Directory
Meetings/Conventions: Training for the Future - annual

Irish Insurance Federation
Insurance House, 39 Molesworth St., Dublin, Eire (Rep. of Ireland)
Email: fed@iif.ie
Website: http://www.iif.ie
Description: Promotes insurance companies in Ireland; works to influence the domestic and international regulatory, legal, political and social environments in order to advance the interests of the insurance industry and consumers.

Irish Internet Association
IIA
43/44 Temple Bar, Dublin 2, Eire (Rep. of Ireland)
Tel: 353 1 6707621
Fax: 353 1 6707623
Email: info@iia.ie
Website: http://www.iia.ie
Founded: 1997
Members: 3400
Staff: 3
Contact: Colm Reilly, CEO
Description: Companies and organizations involved with electronic commerce and Internet-related services. Promotes and represents the Internet industry in Ireland.
Publication: Magazine
Publication title: IIA Members Digest
Publication title: IIA Non-Members Update
Meetings/Conventions: - annual conference Dublin Ireland

Irish Kidney Association
IKA
Donor House, 43A Park W, Dublin 12, Eire (Rep. of Ireland)
Tel: 353 1 6689788
Fax: 353 1 6683820
Email: info@ika.ie
Website: http://www.ika.ie
Founded: 1978
Members: 2200
Staff: 16
Contact: Mark Murphy, Ch.Exec.
Description: Provides support for those with end-stage renal disease and kidney transplants. Prints and distributes Organ Donor Cards. Irish representative of the World Transplant Games; maintains five-apartment Holiday Centre in Tramore for all kidney patients; offers counseling and financial assistance. The Renal Support Centre on the grounds of Beaumont Hospital, the only transplant center in Ireland, provides accommodation and support to family members of inpatients while in hospital.
Publication: Magazine
Publication title: Support

Irish LP Gas Association
c/o Flogas Ireland Ltd.
Dublin Rd., Drogheda, Louth, Eire (Rep. of Ireland)
Tel: 353 41 9831041
Website: http://www.ilpga.ie/
Description: Promotes safe storage, distribution and use of LP gas.

Irish Management Institute International
IMI

National Management Centre, Sandyford Rd., Dublin 16, Eire (Rep. of Ireland)
Tel: 353 1 2078400
Fax: 353 1 2953723
Email: john.mcinerney@imi.ie
Website: http://www.imi-int.ie
Contact: Barry Kenny, Chief Exec.
Description: Works with individuals and organisations to improve the practice of management in Ireland.

Irish Manuscripts Commission
I.M.C.

73 Merrion Sq., Dublin 2, Eire (Rep. of Ireland)
Tel: 353 1 6761610
Founded: 1928

Irish Master Printers Association

Sheridan House, 33 Parkgate St., Dublin 8, Eire (Rep. of Ireland)
Tel: 353 1 6793679
Fax: 353 1 6779144
Email: info@rnan.ie
Website: http://www.tradepartners.gov.uk
Founded: 1917
Members: 52
Staff: 8
Description: Works to advance the science and art of printing.

Irish Mathematical Society

c/o Dr. D. Wraith, Treas.
Department of Mathematics, National University of Ireland, Maynooth, Kildare, Eire (Rep. of Ireland)
Website: http://www.maths.tcd.ie/pub/ims/
Contact: Dr. D. Wraith, Treas.
Description: Aims to further mathematics and mathematical research in Ireland.
Publication: Bulletin
Meetings/Conventions: - annual conference

Irish Medical Association
IMA

10 Fitzwilliam Pl., Dublin 2, Eire (Rep. of Ireland)
Tel: 353 1 6767273
Fax: 353 1 6612758
Email: im@101.ie
Founded: 1936

Irish Medical Organisation
IMO

10 Fitzwilliam Pl., Dublin 2, Eire (Rep. of Ireland)
Tel: 353 1 6767273
Fax: 353 1 6612758
Email: imo@imo.ie
Members: 5000
Description: Physicians and medical students and their families. Seeks to develop a caring, efficient and effective health service. Serves as a professional body representing physicians in Ireland; facilitates exchange of information among members; encourages medical research.
Publication: Journal
Publication title: Irish Medical Journal

Irish Meteorological Society

c/o Met Eireann
Glasnevin Hill, Dublin 9, Eire (Rep. of Ireland)
Tel: 353 1 806426
Email: climat.enquiries@met.ie
Website: http://homepage.tinet.ie/~kcommins/MetSoc/about.html
Founded: 1981
Contact: Met Eireann, Sec.
Fee: €12
Membership Type: adult, Dublin area
Fee: €8
Membership Type: adult, outside Dublin
Description: Promotes interest in all areas of meteorology and dissemination of meteorological knowledge. Member's backgrounds include areas such as meteorology, aviation, marine and agriculture, and the environment.
Publication: Newsletter
Meetings/Conventions: - annual dinner

Irish Mining and Quarrying Society

87-89 Waterloo Rd., Dublin 4, Eire (Rep. of Ireland)
Tel: 353 1 685193

Irish Motor Neurone Disease Association

Coleraine House, Coleraine St., Dublin 7, Eire (Rep. of Ireland)
Tel: 353 1 8730422
Fax: 353 1 8731409
Email: info@imnda.ie
Founded: 1985
Staff: 5
Contact: Eithne Frost
Description: Promotes interest in motor neurone disease (MND) research among medical and scientific communities and the public in Ireland. Offers support services to MND sufferers and their families. Disseminates information about the disease.
Publication: Newsletter
Publication title: IMNDA Newsletter

Irish Music Rights Organisation

Copyright House, Pembroke Row, Lower Baggot St., Dublin 2, Eire (Rep. of Ireland)
Tel: 353 1 6614844
Fax: 353 1 6763125
Email: info@imro.ie
Website: http://www.imro.ie
Contact: Adrian Gaffney, Chief Exec.
Description: Musicians, music publishers, and other individuals, agencies, and organizations with an interest in the intellectual property rights of musicians and composers. Promotes broadening and strengthening of existing intellectual property laws governing music rights. Serves as a clearinghouse on the intellectual property rights of musicians and composers; conducts educational and advocacy programs; provides licensing assistance to musicians and composers.

Irish National Teachers' Organisation
INTO

35 Parnell Sq., Dublin 1, Eire (Rep. of Ireland)
Tel: 353 1 8722533
Fax: 353 1 8722462
Email: info@into.ie
Website: http://www.into.ie
Founded: 1868

Members: 27000
Staff: 38
Contact: John Carr, Gen.Sec.
Description: Union of primary school teachers in the Republic of Ireland and primary and postprimary school teachers in Northern Ireland. Seeks to: express a collective opinion on education and teaching; safeguard and improve employment conditions; advise and assist on professional matters; promote interests and the raising of educational standards. Administers funds for assistance of members.
Library Subject: education and equality
Library Type: not open to the public
Publication: Magazine
Publication title: Intouch. Advertisements.
Meetings/Conventions: - annual congress - Exhibits.

Irish Nutrition and Dietetic Institute
INDI

Ashgrove House, Kill Ave., Dun Laoghaire, Dublin, Eire (Rep. of Ireland)
Tel: 353 1 2804839
Fax: 353 1 2804299
Email: info@indi.ie
Website: http://www.indi.ie
Founded: 1968
Members: 350
Description: Professional dietitians. Promotes growth in the number of dietary and nutrition-related positions in the Republic of Ireland. Represents the interests of members.
Publication: Papers
Meetings/Conventions: Annual Study Day - biennial

Irish Organic Farmers and Growers Association
IOFGA

Harbour Bldg., Harbour Rd., Kilbeggan, Westmeath, Eire (Rep. of Ireland)
Tel: 353 1 50632563
Fax: 353 1 50632063
Email: info@irishorganic.ie
Website: http://www.irishorganic.ie
Founded: 1982
Members: 1050
Staff: 13
Contact: Angela Clarke, Oper.Mgr.
Description: Organic Farmers. Promotes production and consumption of organic food. Maintains a set of rigorous production standards and operates an inspection program.
Library Subject: organic farming, gardening, processing, education, research, and politics
Library Type: reference
Publication: Magazine
Publication title: Organic Matters. Advertisements.
Meetings/Conventions: - annual conference

Irish Peace Council
IPC

37 N. Great Georges St., Dublin 1, Eire (Rep. of Ireland)
Tel: 353 1 8731884
Founded: 1986
Members: 26
Contact: Ken McCue, Gen.Sec.

Description: National peace and solidarity organizations. Created to coordinate activities in the Republic of Ireland for the United Nations (see separate entry) International Year of Peace.

Irish Peatland Conservation Council

119 Capel St., Dublin 1, Eire (Rep. of Ireland)
Tel: 353 1 8722397
Fax: 353 1 8722397
Email: info@ipcc.ie
Website: http://www.ipcc.ie
Founded: 1985
Members: 1500
Staff: 4
Contact: Dr. Peter Foss, Chm.
Fee: €25
Membership Type: standard
Description: Works to conserve living intact Irish bogs and peatlands. Purchases bogland nature reserves and repairs damaged bogs. Encourages a lifestyle in harmony with the environment.
Library Subject: peatlands, nature conservancy
Library Type: by appointment only
Publication: Newsletter
Publication title: Peatland News. Advertisements.

Irish Pharmaceutical Healthcare Association
IPHA

Franklin House, 140 Pembroke Rd., Dublin, Eire (Rep. of Ireland)
Tel: 353 1 6603350
Fax: 353 1 6686672
Email: info@ipha.ie
Website: http://www.ipha.ie/
Description: Promotes the economic and political environment of the pharmaceutical industry in Ireland in order to provide quality medicines and healthcare to patients.

Irish Playwrights and Screenwriters Guild
IPSG

Irish Writers' Centre, 19 Parnell Sq., Dublin 1, Eire (Rep. of Ireland)
Tel: 353 1 8722491
Fax: 353 1 8726282
Email: moffatts@indigo.ie
Website: http://www.writerscentre.ie/IPSG.html
Founded: 1969
Members: 150
Staff: 1
Contact: Sean Moffatt, Chm.
Fee: €50
Membership Type: full
Description: Irish dramatists writing for theatre, radio, and television. Promotes and protects the rights of Irish dramatists and encourages and promotes aspiring writers. Negotiates terms and conditions of employment in TV and radio. Hosts guest speakers who talk about various scriptwriting topics.

Irish Psycho-Analytical Association

89 Grosvenor Sq., Rathmines, Dublin 6, Eire (Rep. of Ireland)
Tel: 353 1 4967288
Fax: 353 1 4978766
Founded: 1942
Members: 21
Contact: Mitch Elliott, Pres.

Description: Practicing psychoanalysts and psychoanalytic psychotherapists. Represents members in dealings with government agencies, both Irish and within the European Union, and maintains standards of psychoanalytic practice in Ireland in conjunction with sister organizations.

Irish Raynaud's and Scleroderma Society
IRSS

PO Box 2958, Foxrock, Dublin 18, Eire (Rep. of Ireland)
Tel: 353 1 2350900
Fax: 353 1 2350900
Email: irss@indigo.ie
Founded: 1988
Members: 400
Staff: 2
Contact: Philippa Quigley, Chief Exec.
Fee: €10
Description: Individuals and organizations. Seeks to improve the quality of life of people with Raynaud's disease or scleroderma and their families. Promotes better physician-patient communication. Makes available support and services; conducts educational and advocacy campaigns.
Publication: Newsletter
Meetings/Conventions: - annual conference

Irish Research Scientists' Association
IRSA

28 Sandyford Hall Park, Kilgobbin Rd., Sandyford, Dublin 18, Eire (Rep. of Ireland)
Tel: 353 1 2950630
Fax: 353 1 2950630
Email: secretary@irsa.ie
Website: http://www.irsa.ie/
Members: 700
Description: Promotes excellence in scientific research in Ireland, as well as a greater awareness of the role of research in lives and Ireland's scientific heritage.

Irish Security Industry Association

21 Waterloo Rd., Dublin 4, Eire (Rep. of Ireland)
Tel: 353 1 8493426
Fax: 353 1 8492402
Email: info@isia.ie
Website: http://www.isia.ie
Founded: 1972
Members: 60
Staff: 1
Contact: Barry Brady, Exec.Dir.
Fee: €1200
Membership Type: full
Fee: €300
Membership Type: associate
Description: Provides security company members. Provides product/services at professional rates. Provides lobby services and quality assurance.

Irish Seed Trade Association

Temple Hall, Temple Rd., Blackrock, Dublin, Eire (Rep. of Ireland)
Tel: 353 1 2831021
Fax: 353 1 2889483
Email: fm@iol.ie
Description: Seed producers in Ireland.

Irish Small and Medium Enterprises Association

17 Kildare St., Dublin 2, Eire (Rep. of Ireland)
Tel: 353 1 6622755
Fax: 353 1 6612157
Email: info@isme.ie
Website: http://www.isme.ie
Founded: 1993
Members: 2000
Staff: 6
Contact: Mark Fiecoinl, CEO
Description: Represents small and medium size business entrepreneurs. Promotes the development of small enterprises. Acts as a liaison with government agencies. Conducts educational and training programs.
Library Type: by appointment only
Publication: Book
Publication title: Irish Employers Obligations Procedures and Practices Guide
Second publication: Membership Directory
Meetings/Conventions: - quarterly conference

Irish Society for Archives
ISA

c/o National Archives
Bishop St., Dublin 8, Eire (Rep. of Ireland)
Tel: 353 1 4072300
Fax: 353 1 4072333
Founded: 1970
Members: 177
Contact: Dr. Kenneth Milne, Chm.
Description: Individuals and institutions with an interest in archives. Promotes preservationa and cataloging of archival materials to facilitate primary historical research. Represents archives before government agencies and lobbies for free access to archival materials; sponsors research and educational programs; serves as a clearinghouse on archival collections in Ireland.
Publication: Journal
Publication title: Irish Archives

Irish Society for Autism
ISA

Unity Bldg., 16 Lower O'Connell St., Dublin 1, Eire (Rep. of Ireland)
Tel: 353 1 8744684
Fax: 353 1 8744224
Email: autism@isa.iol.ie
Website: http://www.iol.ie/~isa1
Founded: 1963
Staff: 100
Contact: Pat Matthews
Description: Individuals and organizations. Seeks to improve the quality of life of people with autism and their families. Makes available support and services; conducts educational and advocacy campaigns.
Publication: Newsletter

Irish Society for Design and Craftwork

112 Ranelagh, Dublin 6, Eire (Rep. of Ireland)
Founded: 1894

Irish Society for Quality in Healthcare
ISQH

PO Box 6448, Dublin 9, Eire (Rep. of Ireland)
Tel: 353 1 8092585
Fax: 353 1 8093318
Email: secretary@isqh.net
Website: http://www.isqh.net/
Founded: 1995
Staff: 4
Contact: Tony Duffy, Dir.
Fee: €32
Membership Type: individual
Description: Promotes quality healthcare in Ireland.

Irish Society for Rheumatology

c/o Dr. Paul O'Connell
Beaumont Hospital, Dublin, Eire (Rep. of Ireland)
Website: http://www.isr.ie/about_isr.htm
Members: 60
Contact: Dr. Paul O'Connell, Sec.
Description: Promotes the specialty medical field of rheumatology in Ireland.

Irish Society for the Prevention of Cruelty to Animals

300 Lower Rathmines Rd., Dublin 6, Eire (Rep. of Ireland)
Tel: 353 1 4977874
Fax: 353 1 4977940
Email: info@ispca.ie
Website: http://www.ispca.ie/
Founded: 1949
Members: 300
Staff: 4
Contact: Mr. Ciaran O'Donovan, CEO
Description: Individuals with an interest in the well-being of animals. Promotes humane treatment of animals and works to uphold and expand the rights of animals.

Irish Society of Arts and Commerce

55 Fairview Strand, Dublin, Eire (Rep. of Ireland)
Founded: 1911

Irish Society of Chartered Physiotherapists

Royal College of Surgeons, St. Stephen's Green, Dublin 2, Eire (Rep. of Ireland)
Tel: 353 1 4022148
Fax: 353 1 4022160
Email: info@iscp.ie
Website: http://www.iscp.ie
Founded: 1983
Members: 1600
Staff: 3
Contact: Barbara Schmidt, Sec./Admin.
Description: Physiotherapists.

Irish Society of Homeopaths
ISHom

Ruxton Ct., 35-37 Dominick St., Galway, Eire (Rep. of Ireland)
Tel: 353 91 565040
Fax: 353 91 565040
Email: ishom@eircom.net
Website: http://www.irishsocietyofhomeopaths.com/

Founded: 1990
Members: 297
Description: Represents lay homeopaths in Ireland. Works to make homeopathy accessible to all, increase awareness and understanding about Homeopathy, regulate standards and ethics of professional practice, provide continuing professional development, and work towards integration of Homeopathy within the Irish health care system.

Irish Society of Human Genetics
ISHG

c/o Dr. David Croke
Department of Biochemistry, Royal College of Surgeons in Ireland, Dublin 2, Eire (Rep. of Ireland)
Email: dtcroke@rcsi.ie
Website: http://www.iol.ie/~ishg/
Contact: Dr. David Croke, Sec.
Fee: €35
Membership Type: regular
Fee: €20
Membership Type: reduced
Description: Geneticists, molecular biologists, medical doctors, laboratory scientists, epidemiologists, ethicists, and lawyers. Promotes study and research in human genetics as it relates to health and disease. Conducts research; disseminates information.
Meetings/Conventions: - annual meeting

Irish Society of Occupational Medicine
ISOM

c/o Dr. Dominick Natin, Hon.Sec.
PO Box 7453, Malahide, Dublin, Eire (Rep. of Ireland)
Email: isom@eircom.net
Website: http://www.iol.ie/~isom/
Members: 270
Contact: Dr. Paul Gueret, Pres.
Description: Occupational physicians and doctors promoting occupational medicine in Ireland.
Meetings/Conventions: meeting

Irish Society of Periodontology

c/o Dr. Anne O'Donoghue
108 Merrion Rd., Ballsbridge, Dublin 4, Eire (Rep. of Ireland)
Tel: 353 1 2692985
Fax: 353 1 2837818
Website: http://www.iol.ie/~perio/
Contact: Dr. P.J. Byrne, Pres.
Description: Works as professional organization that brings together Irish dentists to promote excellence in dentistry and the importance of periodontology in dental health.

Irish Spirits Association

c/o IBEC
Confederation House 84-86, Lower Baggot St., Dublin 2, Eire (Rep. of Ireland)
Tel: 353 1 6051576
Fax: 353 1 6381576
Email: frances.mullaney@ibec.ie
Website: http://www.ibec.ie/fdf
Founded: 1997
Members: 10
Staff: 2
Contact: Rosemary Garth, Dir.

Description: Promotes the interests of the Irish spirits industry nationally and internationally; works to ensure that optimal international trading conditions exist for the Irish spirits industry.

Irish Sports Medicine Association

Trinity College, Dublin 2, Eire (Rep. of Ireland)
Tel: 353 1 6081182
Fax: 353 1 6790119

Irish Stammering Association
ISA

Carmichael House, North Brunswick St., Dublin 7, Eire (Rep. of Ireland)
Tel: 353 1 8735702
Fax: 353 1 5735737
Website: http://www.europe.is/elsa/members/m_ireland.html
Contact: Patrick Kelly
Description: Works to find a cure for stuttering in Ireland.

Irish Sudden Infant Death Association
ISIDA

Carmichael House, 4 N Brunswick St., Dublin 7, Eire (Rep. of Ireland)
Tel: 353 1 8732711
Fax: 353 1 8726056
Email: kibnsidr@iol.ie
Website: http://www.iol.ie/~isidansr/main.htm
Description: Provides information and support to families bereaved by sudden infant death and others affected by it; supports research into the causes and prevention of sudden infant death syndrome. Offers bereavement group therapy, befriending service, annual memorial service, SIDS Model of Care, speakers' bureau.
Publication: Book
Publication title: A Book of Remembrance
Second publication: Handbook
Publication title: A Precious Past, A Hopeful Future
Meetings/Conventions: meeting

Irish Trakehner Horse Society
ITHS

Kilcorney, North Horsemount, Cork, Eire (Rep. of Ireland)
Tel: 353 2958372
Email: info@trakehner.ie
Website: http://www.trakehner.ie/
Description: Breeders and enthusiasts committed to the development and promotion of the Trakehner horse breed in Ireland.

Irish Travel Agents Association
ITAA

Heaton House, 32/34 S William St., Dublin 2, Eire (Rep. of Ireland)
Tel: 353 1 6794179
Fax: 353 1 67199897
Email: info@itaa.ie
Website: http://www.itaa.ie
Founded: 1970
Members: 390
Description: Retail travel agents and tour operators in Ireland. Promotes the travel and tourism industry in Ireland and high standards of excellence and ethics among members.

Irish Tyre Industry Association
ITIA

PO Box 5387, Dublin 13, Eire (Rep. of Ireland)
Tel: 353 1 8324295
Fax: 353 1 8323129
Website: http://www.itia.ie
Founded: 1998
Members: 108
Contact: Jack Farrell, Chief Exec.
Description: Manufacturers, importers, remolders, and retailers of tires; suppliers to the tire industry. Encourages adherence to the highest standards in all aspects of the tire industry in the interest of the consumer; promotes security of investment and employment within the tire industry. Represents members' interests before governmental regulatory and environmental agencies; cooperates with public road and vehicle safety organizations and agencies.

Irish Veterinary Association

53 Lansdowne Rd., Ballsbridge, Dublin 4, Eire (Rep. of Ireland)
Founded: 1888
Contact: John B. Magee, Pres.
Description: Promotes the veterinary profession.

Irish Welding Association

Fitzwilton House, Wilton Pl, Dublin 2, Eire (Rep. of Ireland)
Tel: 353 1 760306

Irish Wheelchair Association
IWA

Aras Chuchulainn, Blackheath Dr., Clontarf, Dublin 3, Eire (Rep. of Ireland)
Tel: 353 1 8186400
Fax: 353 1 8333873
Email: info@iwa.ie
Website: http://www.iwa.ie
Founded: 1960
Members: 11000
Description: Individuals and organizations. Seeks to improve the social, economic, and legal status of people with disabilities. Makes available support and services; conducts educational and advocacy campaigns.
Library Subject: physical disability and community development
Library Type: lending
Publication: Magazine. Advertisements.

Irish Youth Foundation

Glencullen House, Kylemore Rd., Ballyfermot, Dublin 10, Eire (Rep. of Ireland)
Tel: 353 1 6261090
Fax: 353 1 6261072
Email: info@iyf.ie
Website: http://www.iyf.ie
Founded: 1985
Staff: 3
Contact: Liam O'Dwyer, Exec.Dir.
Description: Supports projects and programs that make a positive difference in the lives of less advantage children and young people in Ireland. Raises funds through donations, gifts, and events. Develops facilities and amenities for young people; provides necessary equipment to youth projects.

Irish Youth Hostel Association
IYHA
61 Mountjoy St., Dublin 7, Eire (Rep. of Ireland)
Tel: 353 1 8304555
Fax: 353 1 8305808
Email: mailbox@anoige.ie
Website: http://www.irelandyha.org
Founded: 1931
Members: 11000
Staff: 150
Contact: Ken Kilkenny
Description: Provides inexpensive accommodation for young visitors to Ireland. Conducts educational programs, leader courses, environmental walks, tree plantings and photography club.
Library Subject: tourism literature, Ireland
Library Type: reference
Publication title: Annual Handbook. Advertisements.
Second publication: Newsletter
Publication title: The Hosteller

Killarney Chamber of Commerce
KTI Centre, Deerpark, Killarney, Kerry, Eire (Rep. of Ireland)
Tel: 353 64 37928
Fax: 353 64 37892
Email: contact@killarney-chamber.com
Founded: 1978
Members: 150
Staff: 1
Contact: Anthony Walsh, Pres.
Fee: €110
Membership Type: individual
Fee: €220
Membership Type: corporate
Description: Individuals and businesses wishing to further the economic development of Killarney. Representative body for the business interests of its members at the local, regional, national, and international level.
Library Subject: business, enterprise, export, trade
Library Type: reference

Labour Party - Ireland
17 Ely Pl., Dublin 2, Eire (Rep. of Ireland)
Tel: 353 1 6784700
Fax: 353 1 6612640
Email: head_office@labour.ie
Website: http://www.labour.ie
Founded: 1912
Members: 7000
Staff: 45
Contact: Mike Allen, Gen.Sec.
Fee: €10
Description: Political party advocating democratic socialism in the Republic of Ireland.
Publication: Newsletter
Publication title: Labour News
Meetings/Conventions: - biennial conference - Exhibits. Kilarney County Kerry Ireland

Law Society of Ireland
Blackhall Pl., Dublin 7, Eire (Rep. of Ireland)
Tel: 353 1 6724800
Fax: 353 1 6724801
Email: c.sullivan@lawsociety.ie
Website: http://www.lawsociety.ie/
Founded: 1773
Members: 5000
Contact: Ken Murphy, Dir.Gen.
Description: Solicitors, law students and scholars, and other individuals with an interest in the law. Seeks to improve access to the law. Represents the professional interests of, and provides support and services to, solicitors. Handles public complaints regarding the conduct of members; administers statutory compensation fund. Develops guidelines for legal practice and education. Sponsors continuing professional development courses for solicitors.
Library Subject: law, court proceedings, European Union regulations
Library Type: reference
Publication: Journal
Publication title: Gazette
Second publication: Handbooks
Publication title: Practice Notes
Meetings/Conventions: - periodic seminar

Library Association of Ireland
LAI
53 Upper Mount St., Dublin 2, Eire (Rep. of Ireland)
Tel: 353 1 8452026
Email: marjory.sliney@fingalcoco.ie
Website: http://www.libraryassociation.ie
Founded: 1928
Members: 600
Staff: 1
Contact: Geraldine McHugh, Hon.Sec.
Description: Libraries and individuals employed in libraries and information service industries in the Republic of Ireland. Promotes librarianship and high standards of practice. Represents members' interests. Monitors relevant legislation; conducts research.
Formerly: Absorbed, Online Users' Group/Ireland
Publication: Journal
Publication title: An Leabharlann. Advertisements.
Second publication: Proceedings
Publication title: Conference Proceedings
Meetings/Conventions: - annual conference

Limerick Chamber of Commerce
96 O'Connell St., Limerick, Eire (Rep. of Ireland)
Tel: 353 61 415180
Fax: 353 61 415785
Email: info@limchamber.ie
Website: http://www.limchamber.ie
Contact: J. Brendan Woods, Chief Exec.
Description: omotes commerce andn trade in County Limerick, Ireland.

Local Authorities Solicitors Association
LASA
County Hall, Dun Laoghaire, Dublin, Eire (Rep. of Ireland)
Tel: 353 1 2054700
Fax: 353 1 2801022
Email: bcurtin@dlrcoco.ie
Founded: 1966
Members: 40
Contact: Bryan F. Curtin, Hon.Sec.
Description: Solicitors employed by local government. Promotes professional advancement of members. Facilitates communication and cooperation among members; sponsors continuing professional

development courses. Links with in house local authority solicitors in Northern Ireland, England and Wales.
Library Subject: laws governing municipal government
Library Type: not open to the public

Macra Na Feirme

Irish Farm Centre, Bluebell, Dublin 12, Eire (Rep. of Ireland)
Tel: 353 1 4508000
Fax: 353 1 4514908
Email: macra@macra.ie
Website: http://www.macra.ie
Founded: 1944
Members: 11000
Staff: 25
Contact: Terry Cooke
Description: Youths interested in agriculture and rural development. Promotes the education of members in agriculture and related fields. Offers courses in agriculture, leadership training, public speaking, drama, machinery maintenance, and animal husbandry. Sends delegations and representatives to seminars, courses, and conferences in several countries. Maintains charitable programs; operates placement service.
Publication title: Annual Report
Second publication: Directory
Publication title: Discount Directory
Meetings/Conventions: - periodic competition

Mandate Trade Union

9 Cavendish Row, Dublin, Eire (Rep. of Ireland)
Tel: 353 1 8746321
Fax: 353 1 8729581
Email: mandate@mandate.ie
Website: http://www.mandate.ie
Founded: 1901
Members: 38000
Staff: 40
Contact: Owen Nulty, Gen.Sec.
Description: Represents the interests of individuals working in retail, bar, and administrative positions in the Republic of Ireland. Conducts educational programs.
Formerly: Irish Distributive and Administrative Trade Union
Publication: Magazine
Publication title: Mandate News
Meetings/Conventions: Delegate Conference - biennial

Marketing Society
MS

PO Box 58, Bray, Wicklow, Eire (Rep. of Ireland)
Tel: 353 1 2761995
Fax: 353 1 2761995
Email: info@marketingsociety.ie
Website: http://www.marketingsociety.ie
Founded: 1969
Members: 400
Contact: Mr. Gerard O'Neill
Description: Senior managers and other interested professionals. Advances marketing as the key to successful business growth. Organizes debates and seminars; maintains speakers' bureau. Fosters exchange among members.
Publication: Newsletter
Meetings/Conventions: - annual conference

Mediators Institute Ireland

95 Stillorgan Wood, Stillorgan, Dublin, Eire (Rep. of Ireland)
Tel: 353 1 2884190
Fax: 353 1 2783453
Email: corry@indigo.ie
Website: http://www.mediatorsinstituteireland.ie
Founded: 1992
Members: 120
Staff: 1
Contact: Geoffrey Corry, Ch.
Description: Professional association for business, community and family mediators. Maintains register of accredited practitioner mediators and sets accreditation for professional mediators.
Library Type: by appointment only
Publication: Newsletter
Publication title: Agreement
Meetings/Conventions: - annual conference

Mental Health Association of Ireland
MHAI

Mensana House, 6 Adelaide St., Dun Laoghaire, Dublin, Eire (Rep. of Ireland)
Tel: 353 1 2841166
Fax: 353 1 2841736
Email: info@mensana.org
Contact: Mr. Brian Howard, Chief Exec. Officer
Description: Seeks to help those who are mentally ill and to promote positive mental health in Ireland. Works to provide various types of accommodation outside the hospital, to set-up workshops, to visit and befriend those affected, and to arrange social events.

Migraine Association of Ireland

Senior House, All Hallows College, Gracepark Rd., Drumcondra, Dublin 9, Eire (Rep. of Ireland)
Tel: 353 1 8064121
Fax: 353 1 8064122
Email: info@migraine.ie
Website: http://www.migraine.ie
Founded: 1994
Members: 1700
Staff: 5
Contact: Clare Keegan, CEO
Description: Seeks to share information and provide support for those affected by chronic migraine headaches in Ireland. Encourages medical research; lobbies for a national headache/migraine specialist clinic in Ireland; maintains relationships with other related societies and associations.
Library Subject: migraine
Library Type: not open to the public
Publication: Newsletter
Publication title: Migraine Association of Ireland
Meetings/Conventions: - semiannual meeting

Military History Society of Ireland

c/o Newman House
86 St. Stephen's Green, Dublin 2, Eire (Rep. of Ireland)
Tel: 353 1 2985617
Fax: 353 1 7067422
Founded: 1949
Members: 875
Contact: Col. Patrick G. Kirby
Description: Individuals with an interest in Irish military history. Promotes study and interest in the topics of Irish military history and

the history of the Irish at war. Facilitates exchange of information among members; serves as a clearinghouse on Irish military history; sponsors research and educational programs. Conducts field trips to battle sites.
Publication: Journal
Publication title: Irish Sword
Meetings/Conventions: - monthly lecture

Miscarriage Association of Ireland

Carmichael Centre, N. Brunswick St., Dublin, Eire (Rep. of Ireland)
Tel: 353 1 8735702
Fax: 353 1 8735737
Website: http://www.coombe.ie/mai
Description: Seeks to provide support to women (and men) who are dealing with miscarriage.
Publication: Newsletter

Monaghan Photographic Society

Belbroid Centre, North Rd., Monaghan, Eire (Rep. of Ireland)
Website: http://www.monaghanphotographicsociety.com/index2.html
Founded: 1976
Description: Promotes photography in Ireland.
Library Subject: winning photographs from competitions
Meetings/Conventions: - weekly workshop

Multiple Sclerosis Care Centre

Bushy Park House, 65 Bushy Park Rd., Rathgar, Dublin 6, Eire (Rep. of Ireland)
Tel: 353 1 1906234
Fax: 353 1 4906724
Email: msc@iol.ie
Founded: 1989
Staff: 25
Description: Provides short-term respite care to people with Multiple Sclerosis and other neurological conditions. Assists people in dealing with disability and maintaining independence.
Library Subject: Multiple Sclerosis, disability aids
Library Type: reference

Multiple Sclerosis Society of Ireland
MSSI

Darmouth House, Grand Parade, Dublin 6, Eire (Rep. of Ireland)
Tel: 353 1 2694599
Fax: 353 1 2693746
Email: mscontact@ms-society.ie
Website: http://www.ms-society.ie
Founded: 1961
Members: 5000
Staff: 65
Contact: Monica Collins, Membership Off.
Description: Individuals and organizations. Seeks to improve the quality of life of people with multiple sclerosis and their families. Makes available support and services; conducts educational and advocacy campaigns.
Library Subject: multiple sclerosis
Library Type: reference
Publication: Magazine
Publication title: MS News. Advertisements.
Meetings/Conventions: - annual conference

Muscular Dystrophy Ireland
MDI

c/o Coleraine House
Coleraine St., Dublin 7, Eire (Rep. of Ireland)
Tel: 353 1 8721501
Fax: 353 1 8721501
Email: info@mdi.ie
Website: http://www.mdi.ie
Founded: 1972
Members: 500
Staff: 13
Contact: Joe Mooney
Description: Individuals and organizations. Seeks to improve the quality of life of people with muscular dystrophy and their families. Makes available support and services; conducts educational and advocacy campaigns.
Publication: Newsletter
Publication title: MDI News Update. Advertisements.

Music Association of Ireland

69 South Great George's St., Dublin 2, Eire (Rep. of Ireland)
Tel: 353 1 4785368
Founded: 1948

Music Network

The Coach House, Dublin Castle, Dublin 2, Eire (Rep. of Ireland)
Tel: 353 1 6719429
Fax: 353 1 6719430
Email: info@musicnetwork.ie
Website: http://www.musicnetwork.ie
Founded: 1986
Members: 10
Staff: 9
Contact: John O'Kane, CEO
Description: Aims to make music accessible to all people, regardless of geographic location. Organizes tours for classical, traditional and jazz musicians. Develops and publicizes musical education. Operates information service publishing online directories of music sector and music education in Ireland.
Publication: Directory
Publication title: Directory of Musicians in Ireland
Second publication: Book
Publication title: Irish Music Handbook 2nd edition
Meetings/Conventions: Promoter Forum - annual conference

National Association for Deaf People
NADP

35 N Frederick St., Dublin 1, Eire (Rep. of Ireland)
Tel: 353 1 8723800
Fax: 353 1 8723816
Email: nad@iol.ie
Website: http://www.nadp.ie
Founded: 1963
Staff: 63
Contact: Niall Keane, CEO
Fee: €10
Fee: €50
Membership Type: life
Description: Individuals and organizations. Seeks to improve the quality of life of people with hearing impairments; promotes full recognition of the rights of people with hearing loss. Makes available support and services; conducts educational and advocacy campaigns.

Offers a job coaching service; operates Family Resource Centre; conducts sign language classes.
Library Subject: deaf issues
Library Type: open to the public
Publication: Magazine
Publication title: Link. Advertisements.

National Association for the Mentally Handicapped of Ireland
NAMHI

5 Fitzwilliam Pl., Dublin 2, Eire (Rep. of Ireland)
Tel: 353 1 6766035
Fax: 353 1 6760517
Email: info@namhi.ie
Website: http://www.namhi.ie
Founded: 1961
Members: 160
Staff: 4
Contact: Deirdre Carroll, Gen.Sec.
Description: Voluntary organizations promotes the welfare of people with intellectual disability; works as an umbrella group for organizations working in the field of intellectual disability.
Library Type: reference
Publication: Directory
Publication title: Directory of Services
Meetings/Conventions: - annual meeting

National Association of Adult Education
AONTAS

22 Earlsfort Terr., Dublin 2, Eire (Rep. of Ireland)
Tel: 353 1 4754121
Fax: 353 1 4780084
Email: mail@aontas.com
Website: http://www.aontas.com
Founded: 1969
Members: 378
Staff: 7
Contact: Berni Brady, Dir.
Description: Organizations and individuals interested in adult education. Seeks to develop a system of lifelong learning which is accessible to all adults, particularly those who are considered socially or educationally disadvantaged. Conducts research on education for women, older learners, and adult education and the unemployed. Formulates adult education policies; promotes positive public attitudes toward adult education. Provides information service.
Library Subject: adult education and further education
Library Type: reference
Publication: Journal
Publication title: Adult Learner
Second publication: Report
Publication title: AONTAS Newsheet
Meetings/Conventions: Adult Learning Exhibition - annual - Exhibits.

National Association of Building Cooperatives Society

50 Merrion Sq. E, Dublin 2, Eire (Rep. of Ireland)
Tel: 353 1 6612877
Fax: 353 1 6614462
Email: admin@nabco.ie
Website: http://www.nabco.ie
Founded: 1973
Members: 25

Staff: 7
Contact: Bernard Thompson, Gen. Sec.
Description: Promotes the cooperative housing movement in Ireland.
Library Subject: housing, cooperative housing
Library Type: not open to the public
Publication: Brochure
Publication title: Co-operative Housing Information

National Association of the Ovulation Method of Ireland

16 N Great George's St., Dublin 1, Eire (Rep. of Ireland)
Tel: 353 1 8786156
Fax: 353 1 8788158
Email: enq@naomi.ie
Website: http://www.naomi.ie
Founded: 1972
Members: 50
Staff: 2
Contact: Mavis Keniry
Description: Promotes natural family planning (ovulation method/ Billings) among engaged and married couples. Conducts pre-marriage courses. Offers educational programs on menopause, infertility, subfertility, and natural family planning.
Library Subject: natural family planning
Library Type: reference

National Council for the Blind of Ireland
NCBI

Whitworth Rd., Druncomdra, Dublin 9, Eire (Rep. of Ireland)
Tel: 353 1 8307033
Fax: 353 1 8307787
Email: info@ncbi.ie
Website: http://www.ncbi.ie
Founded: 1931
Members: 6500
Staff: 150
Contact: Niamh Connolly, Info.Off.
Description: Individuals and organizations. Seeks to improve the quality of life of people with visual impairments; promotes increased independence for people with impaired vision. Makes available support and services; conducts educational and advocacy campaigns.
Publication: Magazine
Publication title: NCBI News

National Federation of Arch Clubs
NFAC

74 Meadow Grove, Dublin 16, Eire (Rep. of Ireland)
Tel: 353 1 2951081
Fax: 353 1 2963049
Description: Individuals and organizations. Seeks to improve the quality of life of people with learning disablties and their families. Makes available recreational facilities for people with learning disabilities.

National Federation of Services for Unmarried Parents and Their Children

14 Gandon House, Custom House Sq., Dublin 1, Eire (Rep. of Ireland)
Tel: 353 1 6700120
Fax: 353 1 6700199
Email: info@treoir.ie
Website: http://www.treoir.ie

Founded: 1976
Members: 50
Staff: 3
Contact: Margaret Droney, Dir.
Fee: €50
Membership Type: member agencies
Fee: €5
Membership Type: associate
Description: Aims to improve the standards of care for unmarried parents and their children in Ireland.
Library Subject: unmarried parents
Library Type: reference

National Guild of Master Craftsmen

3 Greenmount Lane, Harold's Cross, Dublin 12, Eire (Rep. of Ireland)
Tel: 353 1 4732543
Fax: 353 1 4732018
Email: info@nationalguild.ie
Website: http://www.nationalguild.ie
Members: 4000
Contact: Pat Doyle, Mng.Dir.
Description: Represents skilled tradesmen. Aims to protect the skills and integrity of its members and clearly define the skilled from the non-skilled thus enabling the general public to choose a National Guild of Master Craftsmen member to facilitate the service they require.

National League of the Blind of Ireland
NLBI

21 Hillstreet, Dublin 1, Eire (Rep. of Ireland)
Tel: 353 1 8742792
Fax: 353 1 8787139
Founded: 1898
Members: 150
Staff: 4
Contact: Larry Carroll, Chm.
Fee: €30
Description: A self-administered organization of blind individuals in the Republic of Ireland. Conducts advocacy activities, negotiating with local authorities and utility companies for better services for blind people. Offers income support programs to provide financial assistance with optical, medical, dental, clothing, and educational expenses. Advises members on their rights regarding entitlement programs; offers free legal aid. Organizes hospital visitations and sporting and social events including debates and lectures.

National Pro-Life Religious Council
RPIFB

6 Belvedere Pl., off Mountjoy Sq., Dublin 1, Eire (Rep. of Ireland)
Tel: 353 1 8559330
Fax: 353 1 8559331
Description: Religious individuals supporting the right to life of the unborn. Seeks to see every denomination or fellowship proclaim and obey the Biblical teaching and religious tradition that affirm the value of all human life. Articulates the historic Judeo-Christian perspective concerning human life issues to the public; supports efforts to discourage and prevent abortion and voluntary euthanasia; ministers to people considering abortion or voluntary euthanasia. Serves as a clearinghouse on right to life issues; facilitates communication and cooperation among right to life organizations.

National Safety Council of Ireland
NSC

4 Northbrook Rd., Ranelagh, Dublin 6, Eire (Rep. of Ireland)
Tel: 353 1 4963422
Fax: 353 1 4963306
Email: info@nsc.ie
Website: http://www.nsc.ie
Founded: 1987
Staff: 12
Contact: Brian Farrell, Commun.Exec.
Description: Promotes fire prevention and road safety through education and publicity campaigns. Offers seminars and training programs to schools and the public On: fire hazards and prevention measures: road safety.
Publication title: Annual Report and Financial Statement
Publication title: Safety Leaflets
Meetings/Conventions: Road Safety Together Working Group Conference - periodic

National Standards Authority of Ireland
NSAI

Glasnevin, Dublin, Eire (Rep. of Ireland)
Tel: 353 1 8073800
Fax: 353 1 8073838
Email: nsai@nsai.ie
Website: http://www.nsai.ie/
Description: Provides a national standards authority in Ireland; supports enterprise, trade and consumers in the areas of standards, legal metrology, and agreements.

National Travellers Women's Forum

c/o Galway City Partnership
Town Park Centre, Tuam Rd., Galway, 1, Eire (Rep. of Ireland)
Tel: 353 191 771509
Fax: 353 191 771235
Founded: 1988
Staff: 2
Contact: Rachel Doyle, Coord.
Description: Brings together traveller women. Develops solidarity and works toward the achievement of equality and self-determination. Conducts training programs; lobbying, seminars, and other events.
Library Subject: community development, gypsies, anti-racism
Library Type: reference

National Trust for Ireland

The Tailor's Hall, Back Ln., Dublin 8, Eire (Rep. of Ireland)
Tel: 353 1 4541786
Fax: 353 1 4533255
Email: info@antaisce.org
Website: http://www.antaisce.org
Founded: 1948
Members: 5000
Staff: 9
Description: Individuals and others interested in conserving and protecting the best of Ireland's natural environment and built heritage. Lobbies politicians and government departments to improve legislation, funding, and other policies to protect the environment. Conducts educational programs.
Library Type: open to the public

National Women's Council of Ireland
NWCI

16-20 Cumberland St. S, Dublin 2, Eire (Rep. of Ireland)
Tel: 353 1 6615268
Fax: 353 1 6760860
Email: info@nwci.ie
Website: http://www.nwci.ie/whoweare.html
Founded: 1995
Members: 152
Staff: 15
Contact: Dr. Joanna McMinn, Dir.
Fee: €64
Description: Works to create a society where women can participate equally in all aspects of social and economic life; addresses important and controversial issues affecting women.
Library Subject: education, training, employment, equality, health, income, politics and decision making, poverty, social policy, violence, women's studies
Library Type: open to the public
Publication: Magazine
Publication title: Womenzone

National Youth Council of Ireland
NYCI

3 Montague St., Dublin 2, Eire (Rep. of Ireland)
Tel: 353 1 4784122
Fax: 353 1 4783974
Email: info@nyci.ie
Website: http://www.youth.ie
Founded: 1967
Staff: 15
Contact: Mary Cunningham
Description: Youth organizations. Promotes healthy physical, social, and spiritual growth among youth. Represents members before government agencies and the public; coordinates members' activities; lobbies for more effective public policies affecting youth. Conducts research and educational programs; makes available children's services; maintains speakers' bureau; compiles statistics.
Library Subject: youth, public policy
Library Type: not open to the public
Publication: Newsletter
Publication title: Clar Na Og
Meetings/Conventions: board meeting

Neurofibromatosis Association of Ireland
NAI

Carmichael Center, North Brunswick St., Dublin 7, Eire (Rep. of Ireland)
Tel: 353 1 8726338
Fax: 353 1 8735737
Email: info@nfaireland.ie
Website: http://www.nfaireland.ie
Founded: 1985
Members: 410
Staff: 1
Contact: Paddy Griffin, Sr.Admin.
Description: Individuals and organizations. Seeks to improve the quality of life of people with neurofibromatosis and their families; promotes increased awareness of neurofibromatosis among health care providers and the public. Makes available support and services; conducts educational and advocacy campaigns; sponsors research.
Publication: Newsletter
Publication title: Neuro News. Advertisements.
Meetings/Conventions: - annual meeting

New Zealand Ireland Association

c/o New Zealand Consulate
37 Leeson Park, Dublin, Eire (Rep. of Ireland)
Tel: 353 1 6604233
Fax: 353 1 6604228
Email: justin.ryan@areamail.it
Website: http://www.nzireland.com
Founded: 1987
Contact: Justin Ryan, Pres.
Description: Promotes the culture of New Zealand for New Zealanders living in Ireland and for Irish people interested in New Zealand.

NIPPA-The Early Years Organisation
NIPPA

6c Wildflower Way, Apollo Rd., Belfast, Eire, UK
Tel: 44 2890 662825
Fax: 44 2890 381270
Email: mail@nippa.org
Founded: 1965
Members: 960
Staff: 70
Contact: Siobhan Fitzpatrick, Dir.
Fee: €60
Membership Type: Organisation
Fee: €36
Membership Type: Group
Description: Promotes the availability of child care facilities for women with children under 5 years of age. Fosters children's educational and physical development.
Library Subject: Child care and family issues.
Library Type: open to the public
Formerly: Formed by Merger of, Northern Ireland Pre-School Playgroups Association (NIPPA)
Publication: Newsletter
Publication title: NIPPA Network. Advertisements.
Second publication: Annual Report
Meetings/Conventions: - annual conference - Exhibits. UK

Nonprofit International Consortium for Eiffel
NICE

c/o Simon Parker
Eiffel Ireland, 45 Hazelwood, Shankill, Dublin, Eire (Rep. of Ireland)
Tel: 353 1 2823487
Email: nice@twr.com
Website: http://www.eiffel-nice.org
Founded: 1991
Members: 20
Contact: Rpger Browne, Sec.
Fee: €1000
Membership Type: corporate
Fee: €300
Membership Type: educational institution
Description: Corporate vendors and users of the Eiffel computer programming language. Promotes the widespread and successful use of Eiffel as a leading language for object-oriented software development. (Eiffel is an advanced language that supports a high degree of software reusibility and includes capabilities for insuring the correctness of software components.) Directs the Eiffel Standards Group, which strictly controls the Eiffel language definition, selected library and interface standards, and advancement of Eiffel; supports the development and use of validation suites and benchmarking programs for testing the correctness and effectiveness of Eiffel tools;

promotes the teaching of Eiffel and advanced object-oriented concepts; represents the interests of Eiffel users in the context of wider object-oriented standards committees. Provides standardization of language and libraries; conducts educational and advocacy programs.
Library Subject: Eiffel software
Library Type: reference
Publication: Brochure
Publication title: Eiffel Success Stories
Meetings/Conventions: meeting - Exhibits.

OutYouth Dublin
c/o Outhouse
6 S Williams St., Dublin 2, Eire (Rep. of Ireland)
Tel: 353 1 8721055
Fax: 353 1 6706377
Email: outhouse@indigo.ie
Founded: 1982
Members: 70
Staff: 5
Description: Social and support group for gay, lesbian, bisexual, and transgendered youth from the ages of 17 to 25. Provide a safe, comfortable and friendly environment for members. Aims to build self-esteem and self-confidence in youth who may experience discrimination and abuse because of their sexuality.

OXFAM - Ireland
9 Burgh Quay, Dublin 2, Eire (Rep. of Ireland)
Tel: 353 1 6727662
Fax: 353 1 6727680
Email: oxireland@oxfam.ie
Website: http://www.oxfamireland.org
Founded: 1998
Staff: 85
Contact: Dr. Brian Scott, Exec.Dir.
Description: Autonomous national branch of international organization. Sponsors development and relief projects. Strives to reduce hunger and poverty. Promotes community development projects that foster self-sufficiency.

Parkinson's Association of Ireland
Carmichael Centre, N. Brunswick St., Dublin, Eire (Rep. of Ireland)
Tel: 353 1 8722234
Fax: 353 1 8735737
Description: Seeks to provide comfort and assistance to those living with Parkinson's Disease in Ireland.

Pax Christi - Ireland
52 Lower Rathmines Rd., Dublin 6, Eire (Rep. of Ireland)
Tel: 353 1 4965293
Fax: 353 1 4965492
Email: paxtdc@indigo.ie
Website: http://www.paxchristi.net
Description: Purposes are to: work for peace while bearing witness to the peace of Christ; contribute to the construction of a more genuinely humane world, with respect for the life of each human being; collaborate with other Christian groups and peace movements; struggle against sources of injustice such as violence, war, hatred, and economic inequality. Condemns the arms race; urges arms control and disarmament. Stresses the importance of detente between the East and West, human rights, the Catholic church's duty to emphasize peace, and the problems of the Third World.

Periodical Publishers Association of Ireland
18 Upper Grand Canal St., Dublin 4, Eire (Rep. of Ireland)
Tel: 353 1 6682056
Email: gaungier@indigo.ie
Website: http://www.ppa.ie/
Description: Publishers of consumer, business, and professional magazines in Ireland. Promotes members' interests.

Pharmaceutical Society of Ireland
18 Shrewsbury Rd., Dublin 4, Eire (Rep. of Ireland)
Tel: 353 1 2184000
Fax: 353 1 2837678
Email: enquiries@pharmaceuticalsociety.ie
Website: http://www.pharmaceuticalsociety.ie/
Members: 2000
Contact: Ann McGee, Sec.
Description: Individuals working in community retail pharmacies, hospital pharmacies, and pharmaceutical industries. Promotes the development of higher standards of practice in the pharmaceutical industries; seeks to safeguard public health. Enforces laws governing the retail sale of medicines; conducts site inspections of premises where medicines are sold or supplied to insure compliance with legal and professional standards. Promulgates and enforces standards of ethics and practice for the pharmaceutical industries. Conducts continuing professional education programs for pharmacists.

Physical Education Association of Ireland
PEAI
University of Limerick, The National Technological Park, Limerick, Eire (Rep. of Ireland)
Tel: 353 61 330442
Email: peai@ul.ie
Website: http://www.ncte.ie/peai
Founded: 1968
Members: 350
Contact: Dr. Ciaran MacDonncha, Pres.
Fee: €5080
Description: Physical education teachers in the Republic of Ireland. Promotes physical education and works in conjunction with education officials to construct effective curriculums and practical teaching techniques; grants honorary lifetime memberships to individuals in the field. Maintains hall of fame.
Publication: Book
Publication title: Girls & Boys Come Out to Play
Second publication: Journal
Publication title: The P.E. Journal
Meetings/Conventions: - annual meeting

Pioneer Total Abstinence Association
27 Upper Sherrard St., Dublin 1, Eire (Rep. of Ireland)
Tel: 353 1 8749464
Fax: 353 1 8748485
Email: pioneer@s-j.ie
Website: http://www.pioneertotal.ie
Founded: 1898
Members: 500000
Staff: 7
Contact: Bernard J. McGuckian, Dir.
Description: Promotes sobriety, principally by prayer and consecrated abstinence from alcohol of members. Encourages members to engage in good works.
Library Subject: religion
Library Type: reference

Publication: Magazine
Publication title: Pioneer. Advertisements.
Meetings/Conventions: - semiannual meeting

Polio Fellowship of Ireland
PFI

Park House Vocational and Residential Training Center, Stillorgan Grove, Dublin, Eire (Rep. of Ireland)
Tel: 353 1 2888366
Fax: 353 1 2836128
Email: parkhouse@rehab.ie
Website: http://www.irishhealth.com/psg/polio.html
Founded: 1949
Staff: 16
Contact: Thomas J. Stephens, Chm.
Description: Seeks to improve the quality of life of people who have physical disabilities, including polio, and mental health learning difficulties. Provides day activities, training, and residential accommodation.

Political Studies Association of Ireland
PSAI

c/o Gary Murphy, Sec.
Dublin City University Business School, Glasnevin, Dublin 9, Eire (Rep. of Ireland)
Tel: 353 1 7005664
Fax: 353 1 7005446
Email: gary.murphy@dcu.ie
Website: http://www.psai.tcd.ie
Founded: 1982
Members: 290
Contact: Dr. Gary Murphy, Sec.
Description: Professional staff of third-level institutions, research organizations, and similar bodies who are engaged in research in the area of politics, and to post-graduate students. Promotes the study and research of political studies in Ireland.
Publication: Bulletin
Meetings/Conventions: - annual conference

Psychiatric Nurses Association of Ireland

2 Gardiner Pl., Dublin 1, Eire (Rep. of Ireland)
Tel: 353 1 8746793
Fax: 353 1 8740315
Founded: 1971
Members: 4700
Staff: 3
Contact: Des Kavanaugh, Gen.Sec.
Description: Psychiatric nurses in Ireland. Seeks to advance the study and practice of psychiatric nursing. Encourages professional advancement for psychiatric nurses. Liaises with the Department of Health, Department of Environment, Health Boards, and Hospitals.
Library Subject: industrial relations
Library Type: not open to the public
Publication: Journal
Publication title: Psychiatric Nursing. Advertisements.
Meetings/Conventions: - annual conference

Psychological Society Ireland

CX House, 2A Corn Exchange Pl., Poolbeg St., Dublin 2, Eire (Rep. of Ireland)
Tel: 353 1 6717122
Fax: 353 1 6717048

Email: psihq@eircom.net
Founded: 1970
Members: 1600
Staff: 3
Contact: Prof. Desmond Swan, Pres.
Fee: €11
Membership Type: student
Fee: €88
Membership Type: member
Description: Strives to advance psychology as a pure and applied science. Maintains a code of ethics and standards of conduct. Provides professional diploma schemes.
Library Type: reference
Meetings/Conventions: conference

Reach Ireland
RI

Fair Stream, Hedge Rd., Garristown, Dublin, Eire (Rep. of Ireland)
Tel: 353 1 8354953
Fax: 353 1 8427788
Email: reachorg@aol.com
Website: http://www.reach.org.uk
Founded: 1990
Members: 230
Contact: Christopher Creamer, Chm.
Fee: €20
Membership Type: family
Description: Individuals and organizations. Seeks to improve the quality of life of children with limb deficiencies and their families. Makes available support and services; conducts educational and advocacy campaigns.
Publication: Magazine
Publication title: Within Reach. Advertisements.
Meetings/Conventions: REACH AGM & Family Weekend - annual general assembly

Regional Newspaper Advertising Network
RNAN

33 Parkgate St., Sheridan House, Dublin 8, Eire (Rep. of Ireland)
Tel: 353 1 6779049
Fax: 353 1 6779144
Email: info@rnan.ie
Website: http://www.rnan.ie
Founded: 1986
Members: 38
Staff: 8
Contact: Neville Galloway, Chief Exec.
Description: Regional newspapers. Promotes use of regional newspapers by advertisers. Serves as a national facility for the placing of advertisements in regional newspapers.

Regional Newspapers Association of Ireland
RNAI

Sheridan House, 33 Parkgate St., Dublin 8, Eire (Rep. of Ireland)
Tel: 353 1 6779049
Fax: 353 1 6779144
Email: info@rnan.ie
Founded: 1918
Members: 38
Staff: 8
Description: Regional newspapers. Promotes the continued existence of local press outlets outside major metropolitan areas.

Facilitates communication and cooperation among members; makes available business services and other support and assistance to regional newspapers.

Restaurants Association of Ireland

11 Bridge Court, City Gate, St. Augustine St., Dublin 8, Eire (Rep. of Ireland)
Tel: 353 1 6779901
Fax: 353 1 6718414
Email: info@rai.ie
Founded: 1970
Members: 500
Staff: 5
Contact: Henry O'Neill, Chief Exec.
Description: Restaurant owners. Develop policies and goals to ensure future legislation that would assist them in the development of the restaurant sector.
Publication: Newsletter
Publication title: Food For Thought
Meetings/Conventions: - annual general assembly

Retail Grocery, Dairy and Allied Trades Association

Rock House, Main St., Blackrock, Dublin, Eire (Rep. of Ireland)
Tel: 353 1 2888274
Fax: 353 1 2832206
Email: rgdata@rgdata.ie
Website: http://www.rgdata.ie
Founded: 1942
Members: 4500
Contact: Ailish Forde, Dir.Gen.
Description: Supports interests of retail, independent grocers in Ireland, including trade to government, media, consumers, and suppliers.

Royal Academy of Medicine in Ireland
RAMI

6 Kildare St., Dublin 2, Eire (Rep. of Ireland)
Tel: 353 1 6767650
Fax: 353 1 6611684
Email: secretary@rami.ie
Website: http://www.iformix.com
Founded: 1882
Members: 2000
Staff: 3
Contact: Arnold D. K. Hill, Gen.Sec.-Treas.
Fee: €121
Membership Type: fellow
Fee: €58
Membership Type: member
Description: Physicians, medical researchers, and other scientists with an interest in medicine. Seeks to advance medical study, teaching, and practice. Serves as a forum for the exchange of information among members; sponsors research and educational programs.
Publication: Journal
Publication title: Irish Journal of Medical Science. Advertisements.
Meetings/Conventions: - periodic lecture

Royal College of Physicians of Ireland

6 Kildare St., Dublin 2, Eire (Rep. of Ireland)
Tel: 353 1 6616677
Fax: 353 1 6762920
Email: info@rcpi.ie

Founded: 1654
Members: 4500
Staff: 45
Description: Makes available post graduate medical education and training.
Library Subject: medical history
Library Type: by appointment only

Royal College of Surgeons in Ireland
RCSI

123 Saint Stephen's Green, Dublin 2, Eire (Rep. of Ireland)
Tel: 353 1 4022100
Fax: 353 1 4022460
Founded: 1784

Royal Dublin Society
RDS

Ballsbridge, Dublin 4, Eire (Rep. of Ireland)
Tel: 353 1 6680866
Fax: 353 1 6604014
Email: marketing@rds.ie
Website: http://www.rds.ie/
Founded: 1731
Description: Individuals with an interest in Irish culture, history, and development. Promotes the advancement of agriculture, arts, science, and industry in Ireland. Assists in the operation of cultural institutions including the National Museum, National Library, and National Botanical Gardens; contributes to the development of Irish social, cultural, and economic life.

Royal Irish Academy
RIA

19 Dawson St., Dublin 2, Eire (Rep. of Ireland)
Tel: 353 1 6762570
Fax: 353 1 6762346
Email: admin@ria.ie
Website: http://www.ria.ie
Founded: 1785
Members: 299
Staff: 40
Contact: Patrick Buckley, Exec.Sec.
Description: Promotes the advancement of science, humanities, and learning. Facilitates cultural exchanges and conducts joint programs with academies in other countries. It is the national affiliating body to international scientific unions and organizations. Advises government agencies on allocation of funds for archaeological research and other projects. Maintains over 30 national committees in the areas of science and humanities.
Library Subject: Irish history, culture, and scientific achievement.
Library Type: reference
Publication title: Conference Proceedings
Publication title: Eriu - A Journal of Irish Philology and Literature
Meetings/Conventions: - periodic conference

Royal Irish Academy - National Committee for Physics

19 Dawson St., Dublin 2, Eire (Rep. of Ireland)
Tel: 353 1 6762570
Fax: 353 1 6762346
Email: admin@ria.ie
Website: http://www.ria.ie

Members: 17
Contact: Prof. J. McInerney, Chm.
Description: Physicists, physics teachers, and others with an interest in the physical sciences. Seeks to improve the quality of physics education, research, and knowledge.

Royal Irish Academy of Music
RIAM

36 Westland Row, Dublin 2, Eire (Rep. of Ireland)
Tel: 353 1 6764412
Fax: 353 1 6622798
Founded: 1856

Royal Irish Automobile Club
RIAC

34 Dawson St., Dublin 2, Eire (Rep. of Ireland)
Tel: 353 1 6775141
Fax: 353 1 6710793
Contact: D.J. Healey, Sec.

Royal National Lifeboat Institution - Ireland

15 Windsor Terrace, Dun Laoghaire, Dublin, Eire (Rep. of Ireland)
Tel: 353 1 2845050
Fax: 353 1 2845052
Email: lifeboatsireland@rnli.org.uk
Website: http://www.rnli.org.uk/Irereg.asp
Founded: 1824
Members: 2000
Staff: 45
Contact: Mary Newman
Description: Works to save lives at sea by ensuring the volunteer staffing and operation of 41 lifeboat stations around the coast and inland of Ireland.
Library Subject: Irish lifeboats
Library Type: by appointment only
Publication: Yearbook
Publication title: Lifeboats Ireland. Advertisements.

Royal Society of Antiquaries of Ireland

63 Merrion Sq., Dublin 2, Eire (Rep. of Ireland)
Tel: 353 1 6761749
Fax: 353 1 6761749
Email: rsai@gofree.indigo.ie
Founded: 1849
Members: 1100
Staff: 2
Contact: Chris Corlett, Joint Hon.Gen.Sec.
Fee: €26
Membership Type: member
Fee: €32
Membership Type: fellow
Description: Aims to preserve, examine and illustrate all Ancient Monuments and Memorials of the arts, manners, and customs of the past.
Library Subject: archaeology Irish history
Library Type: open to the public
Publication title: Journal of the Royal Society of Antiquaries of Ireland

Schizophrenia Ireland
SI

38 Blessington St., Dublin 7, Eire (Rep. of Ireland)
Tel: 353 1 8601620
Fax: 353 1 8601602
Email: info@sirl.ie
Website: http://www.sirl.ie
Contact: John Saunders, Dir.
Description: Individuals and organizations. Seeks to improve the quality of life of people with schizophrenia and their families. Makes available support and services; conducts educational and advocacy campaigns.

Scouting Ireland CSI

26 Dolphins Barn St., Dublin 8, Eire (Rep. of Ireland)
Tel: 353 1 6761598
Fax: 353 1 6768059
Website: http://homepage.eircom.net/~cbsi
Founded: 1927
Members: 30072
Staff: 16
Contact: Eamonn Lynch, CEO
Description: Aims to help young people develop physically, intellectually, socially, spiritually and culturally so that they may take a constructive place in society as mature adults. Trains members to be responsible and active members of their local, national and international communities. Emphasizes international understanding, cooperation, and brotherhood.

Sculptors' Society of Ireland

Corner Halston St./St. Mary's Lane, Dublin 7, Eire (Rep. of Ireland)
Tel: 353 1 8722296
Fax: 353 1 8722364
Email: info@sculptors-society.ie
Website: http://www.sculptors-society.ie
Founded: 1980
Members: 500
Staff: 10
Contact: Paula Campbell, Dir.
Fee: €32
Membership Type: professional/affiliate
Fee: €38
Membership Type: friend
Description: Professional sculptors. Support and promote professional sculptors in Ireland by increasing awareness and interest in sculpture. Organizes symposiums and exhibits, while encourages and manages commissions from corporate and public bodies.
Library Subject: visual arts, art history, art Organizations
Library Type: reference
Publication: Newsletter. Advertisements.

Services, Industrial Professional and Technical Union
SIPTU

Liberty Hall, Dublin 1, Eire (Rep. of Ireland)
Tel: 353 1 8749731
Fax: 353 1 8748642
Email: info@siptu.ie
Website: http://www.siptu.ie
Founded: 1990
Members: 200000

Staff: 280
Contact: Des Geraghty, Gen.Pres.
Description: Workers in Northern Ireland and the Republic of Ireland. Monitors developments in wages, industry, commerce, and society. Reports on economic and social events. Sponsors the Irish Trade Union Trust which asists unemployed people and funds job creation initiatives. Sponsors training courses in industrial relations for union officials and activists.
Library Type: reference
Formerly: Formed by Merger of, Federated Workers Union
Publication title: Equality Review
Second publication: Newsletter
Publication title: Liberty News
Meetings/Conventions: Delegate Conference - annual

Sligo Chamber of Commerce and Industry

16 Quay St., Sligo, Eire (Rep. of Ireland)
Tel: 353 71 61274
Fax: 353 71 60912
Email: sligochamber@eircom.net
Website: http://www.sligochamber.ie
Contact: Pat Clifford, Pres.
Description: Promotes commerce and industry in County Sligo, Ireland.

Social Workers in the Field of Learning Disability

c/o Irish Association of Social Workers
IASW Offices, 114/116 Pearse St., Dublin 2, Eire (Rep. of Ireland)
Tel: 353 1 6774838
Fax: 353 1 6715734
Email: iasw@iol.ie
Website: http://iasw.eire.org
Founded: 1972
Members: 53
Contact: Mary McDevitt, Office Admin.
Description: Social workers working with people with learning disabilities. Seeks to improve the quality of life of people with learning disabilities; works to insure respect for the human rights of people with learning disabilities. Serves as a forum for the exchange of information among members; assists public agencies in devising public policies impacting people with learning disabilities.
Library Subject: social work, learning disabilities
Library Type: not open to the public

Society for Multivariate Experimental Psychology

The Mere, Upton Park, Eire, UK

Society of Archivists - Ireland
SOAI

Guinness Archive, Guinness Storehouse, St. Jame's Gate, Dublin 8, Eire (Rep. of Ireland)
Tel: 353 1 4714557
Fax: 353 1 4084737
Email: clare.hackett@diageo.com
Website: http://www.archives.org.uk/regions/ireland.asp
Founded: 1979
Members: 100
Contact: Colum O'Riordan, Chm.
Description: Archivists and curators. Encourages preservation of archives and works to advance their administration. Fosters development of professional expertise and contributions to the body of professional knowledge. Provides a forum for communication among members.

Publication: Book
Publication title: Standards for the Development of Archives Services in Ireland

Society of Chartered Surveyors in the Republic of Ireland

5 Wilton Pl, Dublin 2, Eire (Rep. of Ireland)
Tel: 353 1 6765500

Society of Irish Foresters

Ballsbridge, Dublin 4, Eire (Rep. of Ireland)
Founded: 1942

Society of Irish Maltsters

c/o Minch Malt Ltd., Athy, Kildare, Eire (Rep. of Ireland)
Tel: 353 50740300
Fax: 353 50731046
Email: mmcccarthy@minchmalt.ie
Founded: 1957
Members: 3
Contact: Michael McCarthy, Sec.
Description: Professional Irish Maltsters located in Ireland and elsewhere.

Society of Irish Playwrights

c/o Irish Writers Center
19 Parnell Sq., Dublin 1, Eire (Rep. of Ireland)
Tel: 353 1 8421302
Fax: 353 1 8426282
Founded: 1969
Members: 120
Contact: John Lynch, Chm.
Description: Promotes contemporary Irish drama. Upholds professional standards among playwrights.

Society of the Irish Motor Industry
SIMI

5 Upper Pembroke St., Dublin 2, Eire (Rep. of Ireland)
Tel: 353 1 6761690
Fax: 353 1 6619213
Email: info@simi.ie
Website: http://www.simi.ie/
Description: Represents the interests of automobile manufacturers in the Republic of Ireland.

Sociological Association of Ireland

PO Box 8775, Rutland Pl., Dublin 1, Eire (Rep. of Ireland)
Tel: 353 1 6083528
Email: sociology.assoc.ireland@tcd.ie
Website: http://www.ucd.ie/~sai
Founded: 1973
Members: 150
Staff: 1
Contact: Dr. Treasa Galvin
Fee: €35
Membership Type: full member
Fee: €10
Membership Type: student
Description: Graduates in sociology; social/cultural anthropology; political science; demography; human/social geography/social psychology; economics/political economy; history; social administration; linguistics and education. Provides a forum.

Publication: Journal
Publication title: Irish Journal of Sociology. Advertisements.
Meetings/Conventions: - annual conference

South Dublin Chamber of Commerce

Tallaght Business Park, Tallaght, Dublin 24, Eire (Rep. of Ireland)
Tel: 353 1 4622107
Fax: 353 1 4599512
Email: info@southdublinchamber.com
Website: http://www.southdublinchamber.com
Founded: 1984
Members: 400
Staff: 20
Contact: Peter Byrne, Chief Exec.
Description: Promotes and encourages investment in the local economy at all levels.
Library Subject: business
Library Type: reference

Spinal Injuries Action Association
SIAA

National Rehabilitation Hospital, Rochestown Ave., Dun Laoghaire, Dublin, Eire (Rep. of Ireland)
Tel: 353 1 2854777
Fax: 353 1 2350955
Email: siaairl@eircom.net
Founded: 1993
Members: 1200
Staff: 9
Contact: Colin Wooley
Description: Individuals and organizations. Seeks to improve the quality of life of people with spinal injuries and their families. Makes available support and services; conducts educational and advocacy campaigns.
Publication: Newsletter
Publication title: Spinal News

St. Pancras Housing Association

26 Upper Sherrard Street, Dublin 1, Eire (Rep. of Ireland)
Tel: 353 1 8553474
Fax: 353 1 8558269
Email: stpancras@tinet.ie
Founded: 1996
Staff: 5
Contact: Brian O'Gorman, General Mgr.
Description: Meets the housing needs of those who are unable to do so with their own resources.

Statistical and Social Inquiry Society of Ireland
SSISI

Dame St., Dublin 2, Eire (Rep. of Ireland)
Tel: 353 1 6716666
Fax: 353 1 6706871
Founded: 1847

Teachers' Union of Ireland
TUI

73 Orwell Rd., Rathgar, Dublin 6, Eire (Rep. of Ireland)
Tel: 353 1 4922588
Fax: 353 1 4922953
Email: tui@tui.ie

Website: http://www.tui.ie
Members: 10159
Contact: James Dorney, Gen.Sec.
Description: Teachers and other educational personnel. Promotes effective primary and secondary education. Works to enhance the professional status of members. Represents members' interests before government agencies, school administrative bodies, and the public.
Meetings/Conventions: - annual congress

Traditional Irish Music, Singing and Dancing Society

32 Belgrave Sq., Monkstown, Dublin, Eire (Rep. of Ireland)
Tel: 353 1 2800295
Fax: 353 1 2803759
Email: enquiries@comhaltas.com
Website: http://www.comhaltas.com
Founded: 1951
Members: 35000
Staff: 14
Contact: Senator Labhras O'Murchu, Dir.
Description: Irish musicians, singers, dancers, and those who wish to promote the Irish tradition in these areas. Fosters friendship among all lovers of Irish music, particularly the music of the Irish harp and the uilleann (elbow) pipes. Conducts research and educational programs. Holds concerts, festivals, and music competitions.
Library Type: reference
Formerly: Traditional Irish Singing and Dancing Society
Publication: Magazine
Publication title: Treoir. Advertisements.
Meetings/Conventions: - annual congress

Tyrone Guthrie Centre
TGC

Annaghmakerrig, Newbliss, Monaghan, Eire (Rep. of Ireland)
Tel: 353 47 54003
Fax: 353 47 54380
Email: thetgc@indigo.ie
Website: http://www.tyroneguthrie.ie
Founded: 1981
Contact: Sheila Pratschke, Dir.
Description: Artists. Promotes development of the artistic talents of members, particularly those of Irish descent. Makes available residences for artists of all disciplines Irish and International. Provides studio space and other assistance to aspiring artists.
Publication: Magazine
Publication title: The Regent
Second publication: Booklet
Publication title: Tyrone Guthrie Center at Annaghmakerrig

Unicode Consortium
FI

Stanhope Green, Dublin 7, Eire (Rep. of Ireland)
Tel: 353 1 6711219
Fax: 353 1 6778563
Email: focushou@tinet.ie
Description: Computer software corporations and researchers. Promotes standardization of international character encoding. Has developed the Unicode Standard, which serves as a subset of the International Standard ISO/IEC 10646-1:1993. Assists corporations wishing to implement the Unicode Standard.

Union of Students in Ireland
USI

Ceann Aras Na Mac Leinn, Grattan St., Dublin 2, Eire (Rep. of Ireland)
Tel: 353 1 4353400
Fax: 353 1 4353450
Email: enquiries@usi.ie
Website: http://www.usi.ie
Founded: 1959
Members: 250000
Staff: 7
Contact: Colm Jordan, Pres.
Description: Students attending postsecondary institutions in the Republic of Ireland and Northern Ireland. Promotes improvements in education and the quality of life of students. Represents members before educational institutions and government agencies regulating education.
Library Subject: Students, education
Library Type: reference
Publication: Magazine
Publication title: The Student Voice. Advertisements.
Meetings/Conventions: - annual - Exhibits.

University Philosophical Society
UPS

Trinity College, Dublin 2, Eire (Rep. of Ireland)
Tel: 353 1 7022089
Fax: 353 1 6778996
Email: phil@csc.tcd.ie
Website: http://www.csc.tcd.ie/~phil
Founded: 1684
Members: 1500
Contact: Roger Middleton, Pres.
Fee: €3
Membership Type: ordinary
Publication: Magazine
Publication title: Philander

Vegetarian Society of Ireland

PO Box 3010, Dublin 4, Eire (Rep. of Ireland)
Email: vegsoc@ireland.com
Website: http://www.vegetarian.ie
Founded: 1978
Members: 300
Contact: Patricia Timoney, Sec.
Fee: €10
Description: Seeks to inform the people of Ireland about vegetarianism and to co-operate with other organizations promoting vegetarianism, animal welfare and animal rights.
Publication: Newsletter
Publication title: The Irish Vegetarian. Advertisements.
Meetings/Conventions: - annual meeting Dublin Ireland

Veterinary Council

53 Lansdowne Rd., Dublin 4, Eire (Rep. of Ireland)
Tel: 353 1 6684402
Fax: 353 1 6604373
Founded: 1931

Voluntary Service International
VSI

30 Mountjoy Sq., Dublin 1, Eire (Rep. of Ireland)
Tel: 353 1 8551011
Fax: 353 1 8551012
Email: vsi@iol.ie
Website: http://www.iol.ie/~vsi
Founded: 1965
Members: 450
Staff: 4
Contact: Tom Ryder, Sec.
Description: Volunteers working for peace and international understanding through voluntary service. Coordinates the activities of Service Civil International in the Republic of Ireland.
Publication title: Newsletter
Publication title: Workcamp Book

Water Colour Society of Ireland

68 Crannagh Rd., Rathfarnham, Dublin 14, Eire (Rep. of Ireland)
Tel: 353 4904248
Founded: 1870
Members: 120
Contact: George A. McCaw, Pres.
Description: Promotes a high standard of water colours. Holds exhibitions and has a permanent collection at the University of Limerick.
Library Type: reference

Waterford Chamber of Commerce

8 Georges St., Waterford, Eire (Rep. of Ireland)
Tel: 353 51 872639
Fax: 353 51 876002
Email: info@waterfordchamber.ie
Website: http://www.waterfordchamber.com
Founded: 1787
Members: 600
Staff: 11
Contact: Frank O'Donoghue
Description: Promotes commerce and trade in County Waterford, Ireland.
Publication: Newsletter

Western Women's Link

19 Kilkerrin Park, Tuam Rd., Liosban, Eire (Rep. of Ireland)
Tel: 353 91 568974
Fax: 353 91 568974
Founded: 1990
Members: 66
Staff: 1
Contact: Breda Cahill, Admin.
Description: Network of over 70 women's groups in the west of Ireland. Provides information, support, workshops and seminars. Encourages new groups. Informs policy makers of the stated needs of women's groups.
Library Subject: women's issues
Library Type: reference

Wexford Chamber of Industry and Commerce

Crescent Quay, The Ballast Office, Wexford, Eire (Rep. of Ireland)
Tel: 353 53 22226
Fax: 353 53 24170
Email: info@wexchamber.iol.ie
Website: http://www.wexchamber.ie
Description: Promotes trade and commerce in County Wexford, Ireland.

Willing Workers on Organic Farms - Ireland
WWOOF

Harpoonstown, Drinagh, Wexford, Eire (Rep. of Ireland)
Tel: 353 53 35395
Email: mumma@insightkenya.com
Founded: 1970
Members: 70
Staff: 1
Contact: Rose O'Brien
Description: Organic farms; individuals with an interest in organic farming. Promotes organic farming; encourages voluntary farm work as an educational and cultural experience. Places volunteer farm workers with organic farms willing to provide room and board in exchange for labor. Conducts educational programs.
Publication: Directory
Publication title: WWOOF Farm List
Meetings/Conventions: - periodic conference

Women in the Home
WITH

11 Wyattvilee Pk., Loughlinstown, Dun Laurie, Dublin, Eire (Rep. of Ireland)
Tel: 353 1 2826460
Fax: 353 1 4906778
Email: womeninthehome@eircom.net
Website: http://homepage.eircom.net/~WITH
Founded: 1981
Members: 400
Contact: Caitriona Lynch, Ch.
Description: Women homemakers. Supports and encourages women who choose to stay at home to care for their families. Works to achieve equality for women working in the home. Establishes friendship groups for homemakers within their communities and functions as a forum for women to express opinions and influence society. Disseminates information. Conducts seminars and meetings.
Library Subject: Equality issues, family affairs, children, European Union documents.
Library Type: not open to the public
Publication: Newsletter
Publication title: Report
Meetings/Conventions: - annual general assembly

Women's Aid - Ireland

Everton House, 47 Old Cabra Rd., Dublin 7, Eire (Rep. of Ireland)
Tel: 353 1 8684721
Fax: 353 1 8684722
Email: info@womensaid.ie
Website: http://www.womensaid.ie
Founded: 1974
Members: 60
Staff: 40
Contact: Denise Charlton, Dir.
Description: Provides information, support and access to accommodations for women experiencing violence; works to eradicate violence against women through political, cultural and social advocacy.
Publication: Book
Publication title: Making the Links
Second publication: Book
Publication title: Safety and Sanctions
Meetings/Conventions: 16 Days of Action Against Violence Against Women - annual meeting

Youghai Chamber of Tourism and Commerce

Market Square, Youghal, Cork, Eire (Rep. of Ireland)
Tel: 353 1 219390
Fax: 353 1 2492447
Email: youghal@tinet.ie
Founded: 1986
Members: 108
Staff: 6
Contact: Anne Murphy
Fee: €300
Membership Type: tourism
Fee: €150
Membership Type: retail
Description: Fosters enterprise and economic growth, while promoting Youghai and the surrounding areas as a major tourist destination.

Young Women's Christian Association - Ireland

40 Main St., Bray, Wicklow, Eire (Rep. of Ireland)
Tel: 353 1 2761648
Fax: 353 1 2761652
Email: ywca@indigo.ie
Website: http://www.worldywca.org/nat_assoc.html
Founded: 1860
Members: 500
Staff: 1
Contact: Daphne Murphy, Head Admin.
Description: Works to promote Christian fellowship and service among young women in Ireland. Advocates justice, peace, and unity.
Publication: Newsletter
Publication title: Y's Link
Meetings/Conventions: - triennial conference - Exhibits. Dublin Ireland

Zoological Society of Ireland
ZSI

Phoenix Park, Dublin 8, Eire (Rep. of Ireland)
Tel: 353 1 4748900
Fax: 353 1 6771660
Email: info@dublinzoo.ie
Website: http://www.dublinzoo.ie
Founded: 1830
Members: 12786
Staff: 60
Contact: Leo Oosterweghel, Dir.
Fee: €100
Publication: Magazine
Publication title: Zoo Matters. Advertisements.

ENGLAND

150 Association

Royal Sun Alliance, Leadenhall Ct., 1 Leadenhall St., London, EC3
V1PP, England, UK
Tel: 44 1603 682701
Fax: 44 171 7024381
Founded: 1921
Members: 250
Contact: Miles Halliwell, Hon.Sec.
Description: Membership consisting of individuals who are involved
or have been involved in the transacting of consequential loss
insurance. To further interest and knowledge in consequential loss
insurance.

300 Group

PO Box 166, Horsham, RH13 9YS, England, UK
Tel: 44 1403 733797
Fax: 44 1403 734432
Email: 300group@horsham.co.uk
Website: http://www.300group.org.uk/
Founded: 1980
Members: 830
Contact: Clare Pettitt, Admin.
Description: Multi-party campaign working for the greater presence
of women in Parliament and the raising of women's status in all levels
of public life. Offers specialist training. Participates in House of
Commons debates. Sponsors fringe meetings at party conferences.
Sends speakers to lecture at schools and colleges. Disseminates
information.
Publication: Newsletter
Meetings/Conventions: - monthly board meeting

A Rocha
ART

3 Hooper St., Cambridge, CB1 2NZ, England, UK
Tel: 44 1387 710286
Fax: 44 1387 710286
Email: international@arocha.org
Website: http://www.arocha.org
Founded: 1983
Members: 2500
Staff: 40
Contact: Barbara Mearns, Admin.
Fee: £30
Fee: £15
Description: International conservation organization working to share
God's love for all creation, Bulgaria, India, the Netherlands, Portugal,
Lebanon, Finland, France, Kenya, the UK, Canada, the USA, and the
Czech Republic.
Publication: Newsletter
Publication title: A Rocha International News
Second publication: Report
Publication title: A Rocha Observatory Report

ABANTU for Development

1 Winchester House, 11 Cranmer Rd., London, SW9 6EJ, England,
UK
Tel: 44 207 8200066
Fax: 44 207 8200088
Email: directorate@abantu.org
Website: http://www.abantu.org
Founded: 1991
Members: 1000

Staff: 50
Contact: Dr. Wanjiru Kihoro
Description: Individuals and organizations with an interest in
international development and related issues. Promotes sustainable
economic and community development suitable to local needs and
capacities. Serves as a clearinghouse on development; provides
support and assistance to selected development projects.
Library Subject: development
Library Type: open to the public
Publication: Magazine
Publication title: Gap Matters. Advertisements.
Meetings/Conventions: Policy Seminar - semiannual

Abortion Law Reform Association - England
ALRA

2-12 Pentonville Rd., London, N1 9FP, England, UK
Tel: 44 20 72785539
Fax: 44 20 72785236
Email: choice@alra.org.uk
Website: http://www.alra.org.uk
Founded: 1936
Members: 1000
Staff: 2
Contact: Jane Roe, Campaign Mgr.
Fee: £15
Description: Individuals and organizations in England united to
liberalize the Abortion Act passed in Parliament in 1967, which
permits a woman to terminate her pregnancy only if she can prove
continuing it would involve a medical risk. Seeks to extend and protect
a women's right to choose to terminate her pregnancy. Distributes
information to schools and the public. Monitors legislation on abortion
and related issues and expresses concerns to the British Parliament,
Department of Health, and National Health Service. Lobbies for
extension of British laws to Northern Ireland.
Publication: Newsletter
Publication title: ALRA Newsletter
Second publication: Report
Publication title: NHS Abortion Services 1997

Academia Europaea

31 Old Burlington St., London, W1S 3A5, England, UK
Tel: 44 20 77345402
Fax: 44 20 72875115
Email: acadeuro@compuserve.com
Website: http://www.acadeuro.org
Founded: 1988
Members: 1995
Staff: 4
Contact: Dr. David Coates, Exec.Sec.
Description: Academics and other individuals with an interest in
European issues. Promotes increased understanding and
appreciation of European science, culture and scholarship. Facilitates
communication and cooperation among members; sponsors research
and educational programs.
Publication: Journal
Publication title: European Review. Advertisements.
Meetings/Conventions: What Makes Us Human? - annual
conference Graz Austria

Academy of Experts

2 South Square, Gray's Inn, London, WC1R 5HT, England, UK
Tel: 44 20 76370333
Fax: 44 20 76371893

Email: admin@academy-experts.org
Website: http://www.academy-experts.org/
Founded: 1987
Members: 2000
Staff: 3
Contact: Nicola Cohen
Description: Professionals from multi disciplines all specialising in their own fields but all practised in the giving, preparing of experts' reports. A professional society and qualifying body for independent experts experienced in a wide range of professional, commercial and industrial disciplines. The Academy provides an expert matching service as well as maintaining a register of qualified mediators.
Library Type: not open to the public
Formerly: The British Academy of Experts
Publication: Journal
Publication title: The Expert. Advertisements.
Publication title: Guidelines to Mediation

Academy of Learned Societies for the Social Sciences

100 Park Village East, London, NW1 3SR, England, UK
Tel: 44 207 4682296
Fax: 44 207 4682296
Email: admin@the-academy.org.uk
Founded: 1982
Members: 40
Contact: Libby Langley, Exec.Sec.
Description: Social science organizations representing more than 35,000 social scientists in the United Kingdom. Seeks to advance the social sciences; promotes the professional interests of members. Facilitates exchange of information among members; sponsors research and educational programs.
Formerly: Association of Learned Societies in the Social Sciences
Publication: Report
Publication title: Target 2000
Second publication: Report
Publication title: Towards and Academy for the Social Sciences
Meetings/Conventions: - periodic meeting

Access Flooring Association

Westminster Tower, 3 Albert Embankment, London, SE1 7SL, England, UK
Tel: 44 207 7933037
Fax: 44 207 7933003
Founded: 1987
Members: 9
Contact: Mr. G. Antonio, Sec.
Description: Manufacturers or installers of and contractors for access flooring. Promotes the manufacture and installation of access flooring to the highest possible standard and represents the industry with any bodies involved in the production of standards.
Publication: Handbook
Publication title: Platform Floor Performance Specifications MOB PF2 PS/SPU

Acronym Institute for Disarmament Diplomacy

288 St. Paul's Rd., London, N1 2LH, England, UK
Tel: 44 207 5038857
Fax: 44 171 5039153
Email: francesconnellyatfc@acronym.org.ac
Website: http://www.acronym.org.uk/
Founded: 1997
Contact: Rebecca Johnson, Exec.Dir.

Description: Works with policymakers and non-governmental organizations to promote non-proliferation and nuclear disarmament; disseminates information. Promotes talks among nuclear weapon states to identify measures for further progress in transparency, arms control and confidence building, focusing on unilateral initiatives.
Publication: Reports
Publication title: ACRONYM Reports
Second publication: Journal
Publication title: Disarmament Diplomacy

Action Against Allergy
AAA

PO Box 278, Twickenham, Twickenham, TW1 4QQ, England, UK
Tel: 44 20 8922711
Fax: 44 20 8924950
Email: aaa@freeserve.co.uk
Founded: 1978
Members: 1200
Contact: Patricia Schooling, Exec.Dir.
Fee: £15
Membership Type: individual living in the United Kingdom
Fee: £20
Membership Type: individual living outside the United Kingdom
Description: Campaigns for diagnosis and treatment of allergies through the British national health service institutions and physicians. Provides information to chronic allergy sufferers. Coordinates medical reference center.
Library Subject: Allergies
Library Type: reference
Publication: Newsletter
Publication title: Allergy Newsletter. Advertisements.
Second publication: Brochures
Meetings/Conventions: - annual convention - Exhibits.

Action for Blind People

14-16 Verney Rd., London, SE16 3DZ, England, UK
Tel: 44 207 6354800
Fax: 44 207 6354900
Email: info@afbp.org
Website: http://www.afbp.org
Founded: 1857
Staff: 400
Contact: Stephen Remington, CEO
Description: Provides services for visually impaired people in the UK, including employment services, hotels and holidays, accommodation and residential care, and information and welfare rights advice.
Library Subject: visual impairment
Library Type: reference

Action for Sick Children

National Children's Bureau, 8 Wakley St., London, EC1V 7QE, England, UK
Tel: 44 20 78436444
Fax: 44 20 85422424
Email: enquiries@acionforsickchildren.org
Website: http://www.actionforsickchildren.org
Founded: 1961
Members: 800
Staff: 4
Contact: Pamela Barnes, Chm.
Fee: £22.5
Description: Individual members (voting rights) and subscribers to library service. Membership categories are individual, family, affiliate,

statutory, CHC, voluntary organisation, overseas. A partnership of parents and professionals working to promote the best health care for children at home or in hospital.
Meetings/Conventions: - annual conference - Exhibits.

Action for Southern Africa
ASA

28 Penton St., London, N1 9SA, England, UK
Tel: 44 20 78333133
Fax: 44 20 78373001
Email: actsa@actsa.org
Website: http://www.actsa.org
Contact: Ben Jackson, Dir.
Description: Development organizations with operations in southern Africa. Promotes sustainable and appropriate development in the region. Coordinates members' activities; provides support and assistance to locally administered agribusinesses and microenterprises; sponsors educational programs.

Action for Victims of Medical Accidents

44 High St., Croydon, CR0 1YB, England, UK
Tel: 44 208 6868333
Contact: Arnold Simanowitz, Exec.Dir.
Description: Provides independent advice and support to anyone who has suffered a medical accident.

Action in International Medicine
AIM

125 High Holborn, London, WC1V 6QA, England, UK
Tel: 44 171 4053090
Fax: 44 171 4053093
Email: actintmed@aol.com
Founded: 1988
Members: 100
Contact: Dr. Christopher Rose
Fee: £25
Membership Type: individual
Fee: £200
Membership Type: institute
Description: Health care institutions and health services. Promotes adoption of of CCI, a self-help health improvement program which empowers local communities to address their health and poverty issues. Works to establish health care infrastructure in developing areas; provides support and assistance to grass roots health services.
Library Subject: Health, poverty
Library Type: not open to the public
Publication: Newsletter
Publication title: AIM Bulletin. Advertisements.
Meetings/Conventions: - annual meeting

Action on Disability and Development
ADD

Vallis House, 57 Vallis Rd., Frome, BA11 3EG, England, UK
Tel: 44 1373 473064
Fax: 44 1373 452075
Email: add@add.org.uk
Website: http://www.add.org.uk
Founded: 1985
Staff: 90
Contact: Barbara Frost, CEO
Description: Development organizations. Seeks to increase participation by people with disabilities in the development process.

Conducts educational and training courses to enhance the income-generation potential of people with disabilities; supports inclusion of people with disabilities in community rehabilitation initiatives.

Action on Smoking and Health - England
ASH

102 Clifton St., London, EC2A 4HW, England, UK
Tel: 44 207 7395902
Fax: 44 207 6130531
Email: enquiries@ash.org.uk
Website: http://www.ash.org.uk
Founded: 1971
Members: 1000
Staff: 6
Contact:
Fee: £8
Fee: £25
Membership Type: Unemployed
Description: Publicizes the dangers of smoking. Campaigns for smoke-free public areas and for tobacco control legislation. Liaises with medical charities, health promotion organizations, and private groups. Disseminates information; monitors media, scientific, and trade publications.
Library Subject: Smoking and health
Library Type: reference
Publication: Bulletin
Publication title: Burning Views

ActionAid

Hamlyn House, Macdonald Rd., Archway, London, N19 5PG, England, UK
Tel: 44 20 75617561
Fax: 44 20 72634613
Email: mail@actionaid.org.uk
Website: http://www.actionaid.org
Contact: Salil Shetty, CEO
Description: Promotes human rights worldwide.

ActionAid - United Kingdom

Hamlyn House, MacDonald Rd., London, N19 5PG, England, UK
Tel: 44 20 75617561
Fax: 44 20 72720899
Email: mail@actionaid.org.uk
Website: http://www.actionaid.org
Founded: 1972
Members: 120000
Staff: 2500
Contact: Salil Shetty, Chief Exec.
Description: Works in more than 30 countries in Africa, Asia, Latin America, and the Caribbean to listen to, learn from, and work in partnership with over 9 million poor people to help them realize their potential and secure their basic rights of food, water, education, health care, and the chance to earn a living. Believes that by fighting poverty together - working with poor local communities, national governments, and international organizations - it can help bring about real and lasting change to the lives of poor people.
Library Subject: development, related issues
Library Type: open to the public
Publication: Magazine
Publication title: Common Cause
Second publication: Magazine
Publication title: Common Cause. Advertisements.

Adhesive Tape Manufacturers Association
ATMA

Sussex House, 8-10 Homesdale Rd., Bromley, Kent, BR2 9LZ, England, UK
Tel: 44 20 84640131
Fax: 44 20 84646018
Email: tradeassn@craneandpartners.com
Website: http://www.atmaadhesivetapes.com
Founded: 1947
Members: 7
Staff: 1
Contact: Mrs. C. Swan
Fee: £1250
Membership Type: full and associate
Description: Pressure sensitive tape manufacturers in the United Kingdom and Ireland. Promotes the sale of self adhesive tape in the United Kingdom. Strives to: unify tape production and marketing methods; determine and maintain quality standards; enhance public awareness of products supplied by the adhesives industry. Negotiates with government authorities on behalf of members. Conducts research on technical developments in the industry; maintains referral service.
Publication: Brochure
Publication title: Aims, Products, Members List
Meetings/Conventions: meeting

Adult Residential Colleges Association

6 Bath Rd., Felixstowe, 2P11 7JW, England, UK
Tel: 44 1394 278161
Fax: 44 1394 271083
Email: pendrell.college@staffordsshire.gov.uk
Website: http://www.aredu.org.uk
Founded: 1983
Members: 30
Staff: 2
Contact: J.M. Dann, Hon.Sec.
Description: Short term residential colleges, mainly for adult education, offering weekend, mid-week and one week courses. Promotes and disseminates knowledge of the work of member adult education organisations, their primary aim being to provide short-term residential liberal adult education.

Adventist Development and Relief Agency - Trans-European Division
ADRAUK

119 St. Peters St., St. Albans, AL1 3EY, England, UK
Tel: 44 1727 860331
Fax: 44 1727 866312
Founded: 1975
Staff: 500
Contact: W. J. Arthur, Dir.
Description: Development and community service programs. Seeks to improve the quality of life of the economically underpriveleged regardless of race, gender, or political viewpoint. Encourages local administration of development initiatives. Provides programs and services in areas including child care, health, environmental protection, vocational training, education, and emergency relief.

Advertising Association
AA

15 Wilton Rd., London, SW1V 1NJ, England, UK
Tel: 44 207 8282771
Fax: 44 207 9310376
Email: aa@adassoc.org.uk
Website: http://www.adassoc.org.uk
Founded: 1926
Members: 25
Staff: 15
Contact: Andrew Brown
Description: Federation of trade associations and trade bodies representing the advertising and promotional marketing industry, including advertisers, agencies, the media, and support services. Campaigns to maintain the freedom to advertise and to improve public attitudes toward advertising. Represents the United Kingdom advertising profession on British and European legislative proposals at national and international levels. Maintains information center on advertising and related topics. Compiles advertising statistics; conducts seminars and courses; coordinates research on advertising issues.
Library Type: by appointment only
Publication: Report
Publication title: Advertising Statistics Yearbook
Publication title: Annual Review

Advertising Film and Videotape Producers Association

26 Noel St., London, W1V 3RD, England, UK
Tel: 44 207 4342651
Fax: 44 207 4349002
Email: michael@a-p-a.net
Website: http://www.a-p-a.net
Founded: 1986
Members: 127
Staff: 3
Contact: John Hackey, Chief Exec.
Description: Production companies who make television commercials. Represents the producers of television commercials.

Advertising Standards Authority

2 Torrington Pl., London, WC1E 7HW, England, UK
Tel: 44 207 5805555
Fax: 44 207 6313051
Email: inquiries@asa.org.uk
Website: http://www.asa.org.uk
Founded: 1962
Contact: Donna Mitchell
Description: Promotes and enforces the highest standards in all non-broadcast advertisements in the UK. Acting independently of both the government and the industry, it ensures compliance with the British Codes of Advertising and Sales Promotion by investigating complaints, issuing pre-publication advice to advertisers and publishers, and conducting extensive research and monitoring programmes.
Publication title: British Codes of Advertising and Sales Promotion
Second publication: Annual Report

Advice UK

New London Bridge House, 12th Fl., 25 London Bridge St., London, SE1 9ST, England, UK
Tel: 44 207 4076611
Fax: 44 207 4076699

Email: london@advice.org.uk
Website: http://www.fiac.org.uk/index.htm
Founded: 1979
Members: 950
Staff: 17
Contact: Steve Johnson, Chief Exec.
Description: An umbrella organization, providing support services to independent advice centres providing direct access and free services to the public in all areas of welfare law. Promotes the availabilty of quality advice and represents the interests of independent advice centres nationally.
Formerly: Federation of Independent Advice Centres
Publication title: FIAC Jobsheet. Advertisements.
Publication title: FIAC Mailing

Advisory Centre for Education
ACE

1C Aberdeen Studios, 22 Highbury Grove, London, N5 2DQ, England, UK
Tel: 44 20 73548321
Fax: 44 20 73549069
Email: ace-ed@easynet.co.uk
Website: http://www.ace-ed.org.uk
Founded: 1960
Staff: 13
Contact: Julia Parnaby, Info.Ofcr.
Description: Independent national advice centre for parents of children aged 5-16 in state education in England and Wales.
Publication: Journal
Publication title: Ace Bulletin. Advertisements.

Advisory Committee on Protection of the Sea
ACOPS

11 Dartmouth St., London, SW1H 9BN, England, UK
Tel: 44 207 7993033
Fax: 44 207 7992933
Email: acopsorg@netcomuk.co.uk
Website: http://www.acops.org
Founded: 1952
Members: 70
Staff: 5
Contact: Dr. Viktor Sebek, Exec.Dir.
Fee: £5000
Membership Type: corporate
Description: Local authority associations, port and fishery associations, industry and tourist organizations, trade unions, and wildlife groups in 18 countries. Promotes preservation and protection of the world's seas from pollution by human activities. Compiles statistics. Sponsors seminars for local authority representatives. Organizes international conferences on sustainable tourism and national and global plans of action to reduce marine pollution from landbased activities.
Formerly: Advisory Committee on Oil Pollution of the Sea
Publication: Report
Publication title: ACOPS Annual UK Oil Pollution Survey
Publication title: ACOPS Yearbook
Meetings/Conventions: conference - Exhibits.

Advisory Council for the Education of Romany and Other Travellers

Moot House, The Stow, Harlow, CM20 3AG, England, UK
Tel: 44 1279 418666
Fax: 44 1279 418666
Founded: 1972
Members: 100
Contact: Bill Forrester
Fee: £15
Fee: £5
Description: Non-political organization working for realistic and practical policies on Gypsy and Traveller matters including equal access to education, safe and secure accommodation, equal access to health and other community services, good community relations and elimination of discrimination, equal opportunities.
Publication title: The Education of Gypsy and Traveller Children
Second publication: Annual Report

Aeroplane Collection

7 Mayfield Ave., Stretford, Manchester, M32 9HL, England, UK
Tel: 44 161 8668255
Founded: 1962
Members: 35
Contact: John Davidson, Hon.Sec.
Description: Restores and preserves aviation artifacts. Displays artifacts and makes exhibit loans to other organizations.
Library Type: reference
Formerly: Northern Aircraft Preservation Society
Publication: Newsletter
Meetings/Conventions: - monthly meeting

Aerosol Society

PO Box 34, Portishead, BS20 9NR, England, UK
Tel: 44 1275 849019
Fax: 44 1275 844877
Email: admin@aerosol-soc.org.uk
Website: http://www.aerosol-soc.org.uk
Founded: 1986
Members: 300
Staff: 1
Description: Promotes aerosol science.

Aerosol Society

PO Box 34, Portishead, Bristol, BS20 7FE, England, UK
Tel: 44 1275 849019
Fax: 44 1275 844877
Email: admin@aeorsol-soc.org.uk
Website: http://www.aerosol-soc.org.uk
Founded: 1986
Description: Promotes all scientific branches of aerosol research.

AFASIC - Overcoming Speech Impairments

50 - 52 Great Sutton St., London, EC1V 0DJ, England, UK
Tel: 44 20 74909410
Fax: 44 20 72512834
Email: info@afasic.org.uk
Website: http://www.afasic.org.uk/
Founded: 1968
Members: 2300
Staff: 15
Contact: Linda Lascelles
Fee: £15
Membership Type: Family

Fee: £30
Membership Type: Insitutional
Description: Promotes the interests of young people with speech and/or language difficulties. Seeks to enhance understanding of speech and language disorders and improve educational and employment opportunities for young adults with such disorders. Offers advice and support for parents of individuals with speech and language disorders. Conducts research on children's language development. Organizes international symposia, national seminars, and workshops. Maintains speakers' bureau; compiles statistics.
Publication title: Annual Review. Advertisements.
Second publication: Newsletter
Publication title: Newsletter. Advertisements.
Meetings/Conventions: Speech and Language Impairments-From Theory to Practice - quadrennial symposium

Affiliation of Honourable Photographers

68 Barcombe Rd., Brighton, BN1 9JR, England, UK
Tel: 44 1273 606067
Fax: 44 1273 606067
Email: ukphotoahp@aol.com
Founded: 1983
Members: 109
Staff: 2
Contact: J.J. Wollaston
Fee: £30
Membership Type: professional photographers and managers
Description: Professional photographers and their managers operating from U.K. All matters affecting members.
Publication: Journal
Publication title: The Communicator
Second publication: Book
Publication title: Photography - The Business

Africa Centre

38 King St., Covent Garden, London, WC2 8JT, England, UK
Tel: 44 207 8361973
Fax: 44 207 8361975
Email: africacentre@gn.apc.org
Website: http://www.africacentre.org.uk
Founded: 1963
Staff: 9
Contact: Dr. Adotey Bing, Dir.
Fee: £5
Membership Type: student or senior citizen
Fee: £10
Membership Type: ordinary
Description: Subscribers are individuals and organizations with an interest in Africa. Promotes increased understanding of, and appreciation for, African current events, culture, and history among the people of the United Kingdom. Presents programs and activities highlighting African cultures; supports and promotes cultural activities of African communities in Britain and Europe. Maintains library conducts educational and charitable programs.
Library Subject: Africa
Library Type: open to the public
Publication: Newsletter
Publication title: Events Sheet. Advertisements.
Meetings/Conventions: - periodic conference

Africa Now
AN

Bovis House, Townmead Rd., London, SW6 2RH, England, UK
Tel: 44 207 3715603
Fax: 44 207 3717104
Founded: 1982
Staff: 6
Contact: Shala Kaussari, Exec.Dir.
Description: Individuals and organizations with an interest in the economic, social, and political development of Africa. Promotes sustainable development appropriate to local needs throughout the Continent. Provides financial and technical assistance to approved development projects; conducts educational and training programs to increase indigenous developmental and administrative capacities.

Africa Resources Trust
ART

219 Huntingdon Rd., Cambridge, CB3 9JH, England, UK
Tel: 44 1223 277314
Fax: 44 1223 277136
Founded: 1991
Staff: 11
Contact: J. M. Hutton, Dir.
Description: Development and environmental organization that supports the rights of rural communities in the south to improve the quality of their livelihoods through sustainable use of natural resources. Activities include supporting community-based natural resources initiatives and public awareness in the international policy arena.

Africa-Europe Group for Interdisciplinary Studies
AEGIS

Russell Sq., Thornhaugh St., London, WC1H 0XG, England, UK
Tel: 44 20 78984370
Fax: 44 20 78984369
Email: cas@soas.ac.uk
Website: http://aegis.eu.org
Founded: 1991
Members: 14
Contact: Prof. Patrick Chabal, Pres.
Description: Aims to create synergies between experts and institutions, particularly on social sciences and humanities in order to improve understanding about contemporary African societies.
Meetings/Conventions: European Conference - biennial conference

African Biomass Users Network
ABUN

Division of Life Sciences, Campden Hill Rd., King's College, University of London, London, W8 7AH, England, UK
Contact: Frank Rosillo-Calle
Description: Users of biomass and other alternative energy sources. Promotes development and use of renewable energy. Sponsors research; trains individuals to make use of emerging alternative energy sources.

African Books Collective
ABC

Jam Factory, 27 Park End St., Oxford, OX1 1HU, England, UK
Tel: 44 1865 726686
Fax: 44 1865 793298
Email: abc@africanbookscollective.com

Website: http://www.africanbookscollective.com
Founded: 1989
Members: 75
Staff: 10
Contact: Mary Jay, Consultant
Description: Owned by African publishers. Marketing and distribution of African published books. Facilitates exchange of information among African book publishers.

African Foundation for Development
AFFORD

54 Camberwell Rd., London, SE5 0EN, England, UK
Tel: 44 207 7030653
Fax: 44 207 7012552
Email: info@aford.dircon.co.uk
Website: http://www.afford-uk.org
Description: Fosters development programs in Africa.

African Network on HIV/AIDS - Europe

Focus Consultancy, 32B Warwick Sq., London, SW1 V2AQ, England, UK
Tel: 44 171 9320072
Fax: 44 171 9320074
Email: london@fcwsq.demon.co.uk
Contact: Dawn Hill
Description: National European AIDS organizations with an interest in the AIDS epidemic in Africa. Seeks to slow the spread of AIDS and increase the availability of AIDS treatment services in African countries. Makes available educational and consulting services.

African Society of International and Comparative Law
ASICL

402 Holloway Rd., London, N7 6PZ, England, UK
Tel: 44 171 6093800
Fax: 44 171 6095400
Founded: 1986
Members: 2000
Staff: 12
Contact: E. Yakpo, Sec.Gen.
Fee: £150
Membership Type: ordinary
Description: Attorneys and international law scholars. Promotes increased public awareness of the law and of individual civil rights and liberties. Serves as a clearinghouse on international law; sponsors educational programs.
Publication: Journal
Publication title: African Journal of International and Comparative Law. Advertisements.
Meetings/Conventions: - annual conference

African Studies Association of the United Kingdom
ASAUK

School of African and Oriental Studies, Thornhaugh St., Russell Sq., London, WC1H 0XG, England, UK
Tel: 44 20 78984390
Fax: 44 20 78984389
Email: asa@soas.ac.ukasauk.net
Founded: 1963
Members: 500

Staff: 1
Contact: Lindsay Allan, Asst.Hon.Sec.
Fee: £34
Membership Type: joint with the Royal African Society
Description: Academics, educators, students, and other individuals with and interest in international studies. Seeks to advance study and teaching in the field. Conducts research and educational programs.
Publication: Journal
Publication title: African Affairs (The Journal of the Royal African Society). Advertisements.
Second publication: Newsletter
Publication title: ASAUK Newsletter
Meetings/Conventions: - biennial conference

African, Caribbean and Asian Lawyers Group
ACA

c/o The Law Society
113 Chancery Ln., London, WC2A 1PL, England, UK
Tel: 44 20 73205873
Fax: 44 20 73205673
Email: jerry.garvey@lawsociety.org.uk
Founded: 1991
Contact: Jerry Garvey
Description: Law professionals. Promotes legal professions to students of African, Caribbean and Asian descent.
Publication: Magazine
Publication title: Futures & Options
Meetings/Conventions: - annual banquet

Afro-Asian Society of Nematologists

c/o Dr. M.R. Siddiqi
Department of Embryology & Neonatology, IACR-Rothamsted, Wallingford, AL5 2JQ, England, UK
Tel: 44 1582 726724
Email: r.siddign@dialstavt.net
Website: http://www.ifns.org/membership/aasn.html
Founded: 1990
Members: 200
Contact: Dr. M.R. Siddign, Pres.
Fee: £5
Membership Type: individual
Fee: £40
Membership Type: int jnl of nematology individuals
Description: Promotes and enhances the science of plant and insect nematology, particularly in the areas of Africa and Asia.
Publication: Journal
Publication title: International Journal of Nematology. Advertisements.
Meetings/Conventions: - biennial meeting

Age Concern England
ACE

Astral House, 1268 London Rd., London, SW16 4ER, England, UK
Tel: 44 20 87657200
Fax: 44 20 87657240
Email: ace@ace.org.uk
Website: http://www.ageconcern.org.uk
Founded: 1940
Members: 98
Contact: Gordon Lishman, Dir.Gen.
Description: Involved in campaigning, parliamentary work, policy analysis, research, specialist information and advice provision and publishing. Raises funds. Member of the federation of over 400 Age

Concern organizations operating in England. Provides both financial and development support to assist the other members in their provision of vital local services.
Library Type: reference
Publication: Journal
Publication title: Information Bulletin
Second publication: Books
Meetings/Conventions: - annual conference

Age Concern Institute of Gerontology

Franklin-Wilkins Bldg., 150 Stamford St., London, SE1 9NN, England, UK
Tel: 44 40 78483035
Fax: 44 20 78483235
Email: aciog@kcl.ac.uk
Website: http://www.kcl.ac.uk/kis/schools/life_sciences/health/gerontology/top.html
Contact: Prof. Janet Askham, Dir.
Description: Health care professionals treating the elderly; scientists and clinicians with an interest in the aging process and diseases of the aged. Works to insure high standards of research and practice in gerontology, and to maximize availability of gerontological services. Conducts research and educational activities.
Formerly: British Society of Gerontology

Agency for Cooperation and Research in Development
ACORD

Dean Bradley House, 52 Horseferry Rd., London, SW1P 2AF, England, UK
Tel: 44 171 2278600
Fax: 44 171 7991868
Contact: Idriss Jazairy
Description: Economic and community development organizations. Promotes sustainable development; seeks to ensure cooperation among members and between members and local government authorities and indigenous peoples in developing areas. Coordinates members' activities; provides technical assistance and administrative support to development projects.

Agents Association of Great Britian

54 Keyes House, Dolphin Sq., London, SW1V 3NA, England, UK
Tel: 44 207 8340515
Fax: 44 207 8210261
Email: association@agents-uk.com
Website: http://www.agents-uk.com
Founded: 1927
Members: 460
Staff: 3
Contact: Ivan Birchall
Fee: £150
Membership Type: full
Description: Theatrical agents. Professional association for theatrical employment agents including in its membership agents dealing with all sections of the industry from legitimate to contemporary artists. A collective voice for negotiations with unions and government and EC legislation.
Library Type: not open to the public
Formerly: Entertainment Agents Association
Publication: Newsletters

Agricultural Economics Society
AES

1 Arun House, River Way, Uckfield, TN22 1SL, England, UK
Tel: 44 1825 765353
Fax: 44 1825 766945
Email: aes@bhm.co.uk
Website: http://www.aes.ac.uk
Founded: 1926
Members: 450
Contact: Mrs. Cecilia Ingram, Admin.
Fee: £48
Fee: £24
Membership Type: Students/retired
Description: Agricultural economists in the UK, students of agricultural economics, and interested individuals. Promotes the study and teaching of all disciplines relevant to agricultural economics. Areas of interest include agricultural industry; food and related industries; rural communities. Conducts studies in fields of economics, statistics, marketing, business management, politics, history, and sociology.
Publication: Journal
Publication title: Journal of Agricultural Economics. Advertisements.
Meetings/Conventions: - annual conference - Exhibits.

Agricultural Engineers' Association
AEA

Samuelson House, Paxton Rd., Orton Centre, Peterborough, PE2 5LT, England, UK
Tel: 44 1733 362925
Fax: 44 1733 370664
Email: dg@aea.uk.com
Website: http://www.aea-farm-machinery.co.uk
Founded: 1875
Members: 250
Staff: 11
Contact: Jake Vowles, Dir. Gen.
Description: Manufacturers and wholesale distributors of tractors, machinery, implements, buildings, equipment and parts thereof used in agriculture, horticulture, forestry, aquaculture, the cultivation of parks and gardens and in the outdoor leisure industry;. providers of parts and services to the above. Aims to safeguard and promote the interests of manufacturers and wholesale distributors. The areas covered are technical - standards and legislation; legal - patents monitor, EC directives, distribution; economics - market information and statistics; export -missions overseas and UK Government funding for export activities; shows and demonstrations, Royal Smithfield Show.
Publication: Journal
Publication title: British Farm and Outdoor Power Equipment Guide. Advertisements.
Second publication: Directory
Publication title: Outdoor Power Equipment Directory and Price Guide
Meetings/Conventions: Outlook Conference - semiannual meeting

Agricultural Law Association
ALA

63 Palmer Ave., Cheam, Sutton, SM3 8EF, England, UK
Tel: 44 208 6448041
Fax: 44 208 6417328
Founded: 1973
Members: 725

Contact: Ms. E. Pinfold
Fee: £150
Membership Type: individual
Description: Members of the Bar, solicitors, chartered surveyors and other professionals and academics interested in agricultural law. Promotes the study, knowledge and understanding of the law relating to forestry and agriculture, and environmental issues.
Publication: Bulletin
Meetings/Conventions: - monthly seminar

Agricultural Manpower Society
AMS

Farm Management Unit, Dept. of Agriculture, Early Gate, University of Reading, Whiteknights Rd., Reading, OX11 9DJ, England, UK
Founded: 1970
Members: 150
Contact: A.W. Hales, Hon.Treas.
Fee: £10
Description: Agricultural practitioners, scientists, researchers, and teachers in 12 countries united to protect the interests of individuals active in agriculture, horticulture, and forestry. Areas of concern include health, welfare, job safety, improved working conditions, performance and development, and education and training. Encourages research in the field; promotes information exchange between research workers, advisers, teachers, and practitioners.
Publication: Magazine
Publication title: Agricultural Manpower
Meetings/Conventions: - semiannual conference

Agricultural Show Exhibitors' Association

7 Nursery Close, Chadwell Heath, Romford, RM6 4LB, England, UK
Tel: 44 208 2200552
Founded: 1948
Contact: Fred Cater, Sec.
Description: Agricultural, industrial and commercial companies and traders who regularly exhibit or take trade stand space at agricultural shows and other outdoor events. Serving the interests of all categories of exhibitors at agricultural shows.
Publication title: Agricultural and Outdoor Show List of Dates and Venues
Second publication: Bulletin

AIDS Care Education and Training
ACET

The Oasis Centre, 115 Southwark Bridge Rd., London, SE1 0AX, England, UK
Tel: 44 207 4509082
Fax: 44 207 4509001
Email: acet@acetuk.org
Website: http://www.oasistrust.org
Founded: 1988
Staff: 10
Contact: Sarah Mabilia
Description: Promotes effective and unconditional care for people with HIV and AIDS worldwide. Conducts educational and training programs for AIDS care providers; works with national and international AIDS care organizations to improve the quality and availability of AIDS care.
Library Subject: AIDS, HIV, drugs
Library Type: not open to the public
Publication: Newsletter
Publication title: ACET Newsletter
Second publication: Booklet
Publication title: HIV - Facts for Life
Meetings/Conventions: - periodic conference

Air League
AL

Broadway House, Tothill St., London, SW1H 9NS, England, UK
Tel: 44 207 2228463
Fax: 44 207 2228462
Email: exec@airleague.co.uk
Website: http://www.airleague.co.uk
Founded: 1909
Members: 1800
Staff: 8
Contact: E.R. Cox, Dir.
Fee: £40
Membership Type: individual
Fee: £500
Membership Type: corporate
Description: Individuals involved in the aerospace industry, civil and military aviation, and government agencies. Supports British aviation and the British aerospace industry. Represents members' interests before government authorities and the press.
Publication: Newsletter
Publication title: Air League Newsletter. Advertisements.
Second publication: Papers
Meetings/Conventions: - annual

Air-Britain Historians
ABH

22 Minsterley Ave., Shepperton, TW17 8QT, England, UK
Tel: 44 1932 783888
Fax: 44 1932 787768
Website: http://www.air-britain.com
Founded: 1948
Members: 4000
Contact: Malcolm Fillmore, Chm.
Fee: £46
Description: Aviation enthusiasts seeking to encourage the preservation of records of aeronautical development and history.
Library Type: reference
Publication: Magazine
Publication title: Aeromilitaria
Second publication: Magazine
Publication title: Air-Britain Digest
Meetings/Conventions: - periodic competition

Aircraft Owners and Pilots Association of the United Kingdom

50a Cambridge St., London, SW1V 4QQ, England, UK
Tel: 44 207 834 5631
Fax: 44 207 834 8623
Email: info@aopa.co.uk
Website: http://www.aopa.co.uk
Founded: 1966
Members: 4646
Staff: 3
Contact: Martin Robinson, Chief Exec.
Description: Aircraft owners - corporate and private - and all pilots in the general aviation sector. To protect and develop the requirements of UK General Aviation, including pilot training and licensing, aircraft certification, airspace and aerodromes. Also provides the co-ordinating office for the UK General Aviation Awareness Council.
Publication: Journal
Publication title: Light Aviation
Second publication: Newsletters

Aircraft Research Association
ARA

Manton Ln., Bedford, MK41 7PF, England, UK
Tel: 44 1234 350681
Fax: 44 1234 328584
Email: ara@ara.co.uk
Website: http://www.ara.co.uk
Founded: 1952
Members: 4
Staff: 160
Contact: Mr. B.R. Timmins, CEO
Description: Conducts research and engineering work to produce both theoretical and practical model designs. Manufactures models and conducts wind tunnel testing for member companies and others.
Library Subject: Aerodynamics
Library Type: reference
Publication: Monograph
Publication title: ARA Technical Memoranda
Second publication: Annual Report
Meetings/Conventions: - periodic convention

Airfields Environment Trust
AET

Sir John Lyon House, 5 High Timber St., London, EC4V 3NS, England, UK
Tel: 44 20 72482223
Fax: 44 20 73298160
Email: info@aet.org.uk
Website: http://www.aet.org.uk
Founded: 1979
Contact: Moyra Logan, Dir.
Description: Undertakes research on aviation's environmental impacts.

Airline Sports and Cultural Association
ASCA

British Airways PLC, Concorde Centre, Crane Lodge Rd., Hounslow, TW5 9PQ, England, UK
Tel: 44 181 5620509
Fax: 44 181 5628611
Contact: Ken Williams
Description: Airline employees. Promotes increased contact between individuals working in aviation. Sponsors athletic, recreational, and social activities.

Airport Operators Association

3 Birdcage Walk, London, SW1H 9JJ, England, UK
Tel: 44 207 2222249
Fax: 44 207 9767405
Email: aoa@aoa.org.uk
Website: http://www.aoa.org.uk
Founded: 1934
Members: 200
Staff: 6
Contact: Keith Jowett, Chief Exec.
Description: Airports and associated companies. Represents interests of UK airport and aerodrome operators.
Publication: Journal
Publication title: Airport Operator. Advertisements.
Meetings/Conventions: - annual conference - Exhibits. Edinburgh UK

Airship Association

6 Kings Rd., Cheriton, Folkestone, CT20 3LG, England, UK
Tel: 44 1303 277650
Email: secretary@airship-association.org
Website: http://www.airship-association.org
Founded: 1971
Members: 740
Contact: Michael E. Rentell, Sec.
Fee: £20
Description: Aeronautical engineers, aircraft and flight professionals, and individuals interested in the development of airships. Provides a forum for the exchange of information among those who believe that there is a future for the use of modern airships as surveillance and coastal patrol craft, freight and passenger transports, ferries, and film and television platforms. Maintains contacts with organizations and individuals who study, build, or promote airships.
Publication: Journal
Publication title: Airship. Advertisements.
Publication title: Airships Today and Tomorrow
Meetings/Conventions: International Airship Convention - biennial convention - Exhibits.

Al-Anon Family Groups - United Kingdom and Eire

61 Great Dover St., London, SE1 4YF, England, UK
Tel: 44 207 4030888
Fax: 44 207 3789910
Email: alanonuk@aol.com
Website: http://www.al-anonuk.org.uk
Founded: 1951
Description: Family and friends of problem drinkers. Offers support and hope for members, whether the alcoholic is still drinking or not. Offers Alateen programs for young people aged 12-20 who have been affected by someone else's drinking, usually that of a parent.
Publication: Brochure
Publication title: Al-Anon - A Community Resource
Second publication: Brochure
Publication title: Facts About Al-Anon and Alateen

Alcoholics Anonymous - England

PO Box 1, Stonebow House, Stonebow, York, YO1 7NJ, England, UK
Tel: 44 1904 644026
Fax: 44 1904 629091
Website: http://www.alcoholics-anonymous.org.uk
Contact: J. Keeney, Gen.Sec.
Description: Individuals recovering from alcoholism in the United Kingdom and the Republic of Ireland. Members believe that they can free themselves from alcohol abuse by following a 12step program that includes sharing of experiences, strength, and hope with fellow members. Refuses alliance with any sect, denomination, political organization, or institution and does not endorse or oppose any cause.
Formerly: Alcoholics Anonymous World Services - United Kingdom and Eire General Services Office

Algerian British Association

12 Glenburne Rd., London, SW17 7PJ, England, UK
Tel: 44 20 86829476
Contact: Mohammed Medani
Description: Strives to unite the Algerian community and share Algerian culture with the British community. Offers assistance to Algerians worldwide.

Alkan Society
AS

42 St. Alban's Hill, Hemel Hempstead, HP3 9NG, England, UK
Website: http://www.alkansociety.org
Founded: 1977
Members: 180
Staff: 6
Contact: Nicholas King, Hon.Sec.
Fee: £10
Membership Type: ordinary and family
Description: Individuals dedicated to the advancement of public knowledge, understanding, and appreciation of the life and works of Charles Valentin Alkan (1813-88), French composer and pianist. Organizes concerts and lectures.
Library Subject: music, mainly that of Alkan, including scores
Library Type: reference
Publication: Bulletin
Publication title: Bulletin
Publication title: Discography
Meetings/Conventions: Alkan Day - annual general assembly

ALL Party Parliamentary Group on Population, Development and Reproductive Health

House of Commons, Norman Shaw S, Rm. 301, London, SW1A 0AA, England, UK
Tel: 44 71 2192492
Fax: 44 71 2192641
Email: trudydavies@easynet.co.uk
Founded: 1979
Members: 90
Staff: 2
Contact: Trudy Davies, Research and Liaison Off.
Fee: £1
Membership Type: mandatory
Description: Members of the British Parliament. Serves as a forum for discussion of reproductive health and population issues. Maintains contact and encourages the formation of parliamentary population groups worldwide. Presses for increase of resources from governments for population and reproductive health programs and projects worldwide.
Library Subject: population, development and reproductive health
Library Type: by appointment only
Formerly: All Party Parliamentary Group on Population and Development
Publication title: Various Reports
Meetings/Conventions: conference

Alliance of Independent Retailers
AIR

Adam House, Waterworks Rd., Worcester, WR1 3E2, England, UK
Tel: 44 1905 612733
Fax: 44 1905 21501
Email: alliance@indretailer.co.uk
Website: http://www.indretailer.co.uk/Pages/air.html
Founded: 1983
Members: 23470
Staff: 12
Contact: Len Griffin D'Orgee, Gen.Mgr.
Fee: £50
Membership Type: small to medium enterprises
Description: Retailers from all trades seeking to: promote information exchanges between consumers, distributors, manufacturers, the media, retailers, and suppliers; unite manufacturing and distributing trades in support of the independent trader; provide professional advice and legal services; ensure a comprehensive and efficient communications platform; help independent retail trade expand and employ more people; initiate and maintain liaison with enterprise agencies, local authorities, and trade groups in the formation and administration of training programs; utilize marketing, merchandising, and promotion for the improvement of independent retailers. Offers confidential business and legal advice and retailer training program. Represents retailers before government on business issues.
Formerly: Alliance of Independent Retailers and Businesses
Publication: Newsletter
Publication title: Air Mail. Advertisements.
Second publication: Magazine
Publication title: The Hotelier
Meetings/Conventions: - annual convention - Exhibits.

Alliance of International Market Research Institutes
AEMRI

26 Granard Ave., London, SW15 6HJ, England, UK
Tel: 44 20 87803343
Fax: 44 20 82466893
Email: rtchilton@aol.com
Website: http://www.aemri.org
Founded: 1991
Members: 100
Staff: 2
Contact: Richard Chilton, Sec.
Fee: £375
Membership Type: corporate
Description: Professional International market research agencies. Represents corporate interests of members. Offers conferences and training courses.
Publication: Newsletter
Publication title: Synergie Plus
Second publication: Directory
Publication title: Worldwide Directory. Advertisements.
Meetings/Conventions: Running Your Agency Better - annual conference

Alliance of Literary Societies

c/o The Secretary
22 Belmont Grove, Rosemary Culley, Haven, PO9 3PU, England, UK
Tel: 44 2392 475855
Fax: 44 870 560330
Email: rosemary@sndc.demon.co.uk
Website: http://www.sndc.demon.co.uk/als.htm
Founded: 1989
Members: 100
Contact: Rosemary Culley, Hon.Sec.
Description: Open to Literary Societies only. Strives to initiate or support action aimed at preserving our literary heritage. Acts as a liaison body between member societies. Maintains an up-to-date directory of Literary Societies. Supports action aimed at preserving buildings, places etc. with literary connections.
Publication: Magazine
Publication title: The Open Book. Advertisements.
Second publication: Newsletter. Advertisements.
Meetings/Conventions: - annual general assembly - Exhibits.

Alliance of Religions and Conservation
ARC

3 Wynnstay Grove, Fallow Field, Manchester, M14 6XG, England, UK
Tel: 44 161 2485731
Fax: 44 161 2485736
Email: arc_info@email.com
Website: http://www.religionsandconservation.org
Founded: 1995
Description: Individuals and organizations. Promotes the development and implementation of practical educational projects designed to further the involvement of religions in environmental protection. Produces and promotes materials exploring the links between religion and environmental protection.
Publication: Newsletter
Publication title: Newsform ARC

Almshouse Association

Billingbear Lodge, Wokingham, RG40 5RU, England, UK
Tel: 44 1344 452922
Fax: 44 1344 862062
Email: naa@almshouses.org
Website: http://www.almshouses.org
Founded: 1946
Members: 1850
Staff: 9
Contact: Anthony Leask, Dir.
Description: Members are almshouse foundations which provide accommodation for the elderly. Advises members on any matters, concerning almshouses and the welfare of the elderly; promotes improvements in almshouses; promotes study and research into all matters affecting almshouses; makes grants or loans to members.
Publication title: The Almshouses Gazette

Alstrom Syndrome International

49 Southfield Ave., Paignton, TQ3 1LH, England, UK
Email: alstrom@syndromeuk.freeserve.co.uk
Website: http://www.jax.org/alstrom/documents/sasf.html
Founded: 1995
Description: Provides support to those affected by Alstrom Syndrome and their families, friends, and professionals worldwide.
Meetings/Conventions: International Family Conference - triennial conference

Alternative Investment Industry Association
AIMAF

Lower Ground Fl., 10 Stanhope Gate, Mayfair, London, W1K 1AL, England, UK
Tel: 44 20 76599920
Email: info@aima.org
Website: http://www.aima.org
Founded: 1990
Members: 340
Staff: 4
Contact: Florence A. Lombard, Exec.Dir.
Fee: £425
Membership Type: corporate
Description: Investment and financial services providers. Promotes increased use of alternative investments among members' clients. Facilitates exchange of information among members; serves as a clearinghouse on alternative investments; sponsors research and educational programs.
Formerly: Alternative Investment Meeting Association
Publication: Newsletter
Publication title: AIMA Newsletter. Advertisements.

Alternative Investment Management Association
AIMA

Lower Ground Fl., 10 Stanhope Gate, Mayfair, London, W1K 1AL, England, UK
Tel: 44 20 76599920
Fax: 44 20 76599921
Email: info@aima.org
Website: http://www.aima.org
Founded: 1990
Members: 355
Staff: 4
Contact: Florence A. Lombard, Exec.Dir.
Description: International trade association representing alternative investment fund managers, banks, brokers, and exchanges. Strives to increase investor education and to ensure the representation and integration of skill-based investments into mainstream investment management. Works with regulators and interested parties in order to promote and control the use of alternative investments.
Formerly: Formed by Merger of, European Managed Futures Association
Publication: Newsletter
Publication title: AIMA Newsletter. Advertisements.
Meetings/Conventions: - periodic conference

Aluminium Extruders Association

Broadway House, Calthorpe Rd., Birmingham, B15 1TN, England, UK
Tel: 44 121 4561103
Fax: 44 121 4562274
Email: alfed@alfed.org.uk
Website: http://www.alfed.org.uk
Members: 8
Contact: Dr. David A. Harris
Description: Represents members' interests.

Aluminium Federation

Broadway House, Calthorpe Rd., Five Ways, Birmingham, B15 1TN, England, UK
Tel: 44 121 4561103
Fax: 44 870 1389714
Email: info@alfed.org.uk
Website: http://www.alfed.org.uk
Founded: 1962
Members: 220
Staff: 12
Contact: Dr. David A. Harris, Sec.Gen.
Description: Member companies represent most sectors of the UK aluminium industry, which has a total workforce of over 30,000. Provides a wide range of services, helping members to improve productivity, operate safe working practices in an environmentally acceptable way. It assists in the search for new markets and increased usage of aluminium. Represents the interests of the industry with the UK government, EC and the European Parliament.
Library Subject: information club
Library Type: not open to the public

Aluminium Finishing Association

Broadway House, Calthorpe Rd., Birmingham, B15 1TN, England, UK
Tel: 44 121 4561103
Fax: 44 121 4562274
Members: 20
Contact: Ron Moult
Description: Coaters and anodisers.

Aluminium Packaging Recycling Organization

1 Brockhill Ct., Brockhill Ln., Redditch, B97 6RB, England, UK
Tel: 44 1527 597757
Fax: 44 1527 594140
Email: info@alupro.org.uk
Website: http://www.alupro.org.uk
Founded: 1989
Members: 350
Staff: 7
Contact: Alex Griffin, Dir.
Description: Recycling centres across the UK which buy aluminium cans from the general public. Promotes the aluminium can package and, mainly, its recyclability. Supports collectors and has a register of over 350 Recycling Centres who buy aluminium cans from the public. Aiming for a 50% recycling rate for aluminium cans by the year 2000.
Publication: Brochure
Publication title: Schools information pack
Meetings/Conventions: - annual seminar Birmingham UK

Aluminium Powder and Paste Association

Broadway House, Calthorpe Rd., Birmingham, B15 1TN, England, UK
Tel: 44 121 4561103
Fax: 44 121 4562274
Email: alfed@alfed.org.uk
Website: http://www.alfed.org.uk
Members: 4
Contact: Dr. David Harris

Aluminium Primary Producers Association

Broadway House, Calthorpe Rd., Birmingham, B15 1TN, England, UK
Tel: 44 121 4561103
Fax: 44 121 4562274
Email: alfed@alfed.org.uk
Website: http://www.alfed.org.uk
Members: 5
Contact: Dr. David Harris

Aluminium Radiator Manufacturers Association

Tropical House, Charlwoods Rd., East Grinstead, RH19 2HJ, England, UK
Tel: 44 1342 317171
Fax: 44 1342 315362
Contact: Alan Symonds
Description: Aluminum radiator distributors.

Aluminium Rolled Products Manufacturers Association

Broadway House, Calthorpe Rd., Edgbaston, Birmingham, B15 1TN, England, UK
Tel: 44 121 4561103
Fax: 44 121 4562274
Email: arpma@alfed.org.uk
Website: http://www.alfed.org.uk
Contact: Richard Mahoney

Aluminium Stockholders Association
ASA

Broadway House, Calthorpe Rd., Five Ways, Birmingham, B15 1TN, England, UK
Tel: 44 121 4564938
Fax: 44 121 4564937
Email: asa@alfed.org.uk

Website: http://www.asauk.co.uk/
Founded: 1962
Members: 37
Contact: Dr. David A. Harris, Sec.
Description: Trade association of companies and independent organizations.
Publication title: Review
Second publication: Handbook
Meetings/Conventions: Dutch Party - annual conference

Alzheimer's Disease International
ADI

45/46 Lower Marsh, London, SE1 7RG, England, UK
Tel: 44 207 6203011
Fax: 44 207 4017351
Email: info@alz.co.uk
Website: http://www.alz.co.uk
Founded: 1984
Members: 60
Staff: 5
Contact: Elizabeth Rimmer, Exec.Dir.
Description: Umbrella organization of 60 national Alzheimer associations worldwide. Main goal is to build and strengthen these associations so that they are better able to meet the needs of people with dementia and their carers.
Publication: Newsletter
Publication title: Global Perspective
Meetings/Conventions: - annual conference

Alzheimer's Society
AS

Gordon House, 10 Greencoat Pl., London, SW1P 1PH, England, UK
Tel: 44 20 73060606
Fax: 44 20 73060808
Email: enquiries@alzheimers.org.uk
Website: http://www.alzheimers.org.uk
Founded: 1979
Members: 22000
Staff: 200
Contact: Harry Cayton, Chief Exec.
Description: Individuals and organizations. Seeks to improve the quality of life of people with Alzheimer's disease and their families. Makes available support and services; facilitates research on Alzheimer's disease and related disorders; conducts educational programs.
Library Subject: health and social care
Library Type: not open to the public
Formerly: Alzheimer's Disease Society

Amalgamated Chimney Engineers

Whiteacre, Metheringham Fen, Lincoln, LN4 3AL, England, UK
Tel: 44 1526 323990
Fax: 44 1526 323181
Founded: 1985
Members: 40
Staff: 4
Contact: N.T. Allen, Chm.
Description: Formulates and implements national vocational qualification standards for chimney engineering.

Amateur Entomologists Society
AES

PO Box 8774, London, SW7 5ZG, England, UK
Founded: 1936
Members: 1500
Description: Works to promote and disseminate entomological knowledge; promotes interest in entomology to youth.
Publication: Journal
Publication title: The Bulletin. Advertisements.
Second publication: Magazine
Publication title: The AES Bug Club Magazine
Meetings/Conventions: meeting

Ambulance Service Association

Friars House, 2nd Fl., 157-168 Blackfriars Rd., London, SE1 8EU, England, UK
Tel: 44 20 79289620
Fax: 44 20 79289502
Email: richard@bizuk.com
Website: http://www.the-asa.org
Founded: 1948
Staff: 5
Contact: Richard Diment, Chief Exec.
Description: Ambulance services in the United Kingdom. Promotes members' interests. Fosters collaboration and sharing of best practices among members.
Formerly: Association of Chief Ambulance Officers
Publication: Magazine
Publication title: ASA News. Advertisements.
Meetings/Conventions: Ambex International - annual conference - Exhibits.

American Academy of Optometry - British Chapter
ACABC

Andrew Field, 2 Doric Pl., Woodbridge, IP12 1BT, England, UK
Tel: 44 1394 380139
Fax: 44 7967 446413
Email: academy@debenlogic.co.uk
Website: http://www.academy.org.uk
Founded: 1952
Members: 110
Contact: Andrew Field, Hon.Sec.
Fee: £25
Membership Type: student
Fee: £215
Membership Type: candidate or fellow
Description: Optometrists. Seeks to advance the study, teaching, and practice of optometry. Maintains standards of training, ethics, and practice for members; conducts continuing professional development courses for optometrists.
Meetings/Conventions: Clinical Conference - biennial conference

American Chamber of Commerce - United Kingdom

c/o Robert E. Brunck
75 Brook St., London, W1Y 2EB, England, UK
Tel: 44 171 4930381
Fax: 44 171 4932394
Email: acc@amcham.co.uk
Founded: 1916
Members: 900
Staff: 13
Contact: Robert E. Brunck, Dir.Gen.

Description: Encourages exchange of information among Anglo-American businesses. Promotes the interests of members in government policy-making. Disseminates information on business trends; holds seminars.
Library Type: reference
Publication title: Amcham News
Second publication: Directory
Publication title: Membership Directory. Advertisements.
Meetings/Conventions: - periodic conference

American Chamber of Commerce in Britain

75 Brook St., London, W1Y 2EB, England, UK
Tel: 44 207 4930381
Fax: 44 207 4933961
Contact: Robert Brunck
Description: Promotes business and commerce.

American Civil War Round Table - United Kingdom
ACWRT-UK

c/o Mrs. M. Ward, Membership
50 Hinckley Close, Harfield, Uxbridge, UB9 6AZ, England, UK
Tel: 44 1747 828719
Website: http://www.americancivilwar.org.uk
Founded: 1953
Members: 200
Contact: Peter Lockwood, Pres.
Fee: £10
Membership Type: In U.K.
Fee: £10
Membership Type: International
Description: Promotes study of the American Civil War (1861-65). Conducts research on purchasing and naval activities in Great Britain and Europe as well as on the post-war careers of Americans remaining in Great Britain.
Library Type: reference
Publication: Newsletter
Publication title: Crossfire. Advertisements.
Meetings/Conventions: - quarterly meeting - Exhibits.

American Dental Society of Europe
ADSE

c/o Lloyd Searon
2 Harcourt House, 19A Cavendish Sq., London, W1M 9AB, England, UK
Tel: 44 207 6374518
Fax: 44 207 6291869
Email: lloydsearson@compuserve.com
Founded: 1873
Members: 250
Contact: Lloyd Searson, Hon.Sec.
Fee: £160
Membership Type: full
Description: Graduates of North American schools of dentistry who practice in Europe. Seeks the interchange of dental information and the advancement of the profession. Offers scholarship for European dentists to study in the United States.
Meetings/Conventions: - annual meeting - Exhibits.

Amnesty International - International Secretariat

99-119 Rosebery, London, EC1R 4RE, England, UK
Tel: 44 207 8146200
Fax: 44 207 8331510

Email: info@amnesty.org
Website: http://www.amnesty.org
Description: Promotes human rights. Works for the release of nonviolent prisoners of conscience.

Amnesty International - United Kingdom
AI

99-119 Rosebery Ave., London, EC1R 4RE, England, UK
Tel: 44 20 78146200
Fax: 44 20 78331510
Email: info@amnesty.org.uk
Website: http://www.amnesty.org.uk
Founded: 1961
Members: 1000000
Staff: 320
Contact: Irene Kahn, Sec.Gen.
Description: A human rights movement working to secure the immediate and unconditional release of all prisoners of conscience (individuals who have not used or advocated violence and have been imprisoned due to their beliefs, color, sex, religion, ethnic origin, or language); urges immediate, fair trials of political prisoners. Seeks an end to torture, executions and disappearances, abuses by opposition groups, hostage taking, arbitrary killing, and other inhuman, cruel, or degrading treatment or punishment. Conducts research and organizes worldwide action by local members on behalf of prisoners held in countries other than their own; initiates national and international campaigns to publicize patterns of human rights abuses; sends delegates to observe trials and visit countries to interview prisoners and meet with government officials.
Library Subject: human rights, international law, general reference
Library Type: not open to the public
Formerly: Amnesty International - England
Publication title: Amnesty International Report
Second publication: Newsletter
Publication title: Newsletter
Meetings/Conventions: - biennial meeting

Anaesthetic Research Society
ARS

Univ. Dept. of Anaesthesia & Intensive Care, Queen's Medical Centre, Nottingham, NG7 2UH, England, UK
Tel: 44 115 9709229
Fax: 44 115 9700739
Email: ravi.mahajan@nottingham.ac.uk
Website: http://www.ars.ac.uk/
Founded: 1958
Members: 660
Contact: Dr. R.P. Mahajan, Hon.Sec.
Fee: £20
Membership Type: Ordinary
Description: Facilitates the presentation of members' research in anesthesiology (clinical or experimental, completed or in progress).
Publication: Journal
Publication title: Proceedings. Advertisements.
Meetings/Conventions: meeting

Ancient Egypt and Middle East Society

2 Seathorne Crescent, Skegness, PE25 1RP, England, UK
Tel: 44 1754 765341
Fax: 44 1754 765724
Email: suek@beset.fsnet.co.uk
Founded: 1987
Members: 85

Contact: Sue Kirk, Hon.Sec.
Fee: £13
Membership Type: single
Fee: £18
Membership Type: family
Description: Promotes and encourages interest in the history, archaeology, and cultures of the ancient civilizations of the Middle East.
Library Subject: history, archaeology, and cultures of the ancient Middle East
Library Type: reference
Publication: Journal
Publication title: AEMES Journal
Meetings/Conventions: - annual conference

Ancient Monuments Society
AMS

St. Ann's Vestry Hall, 2 Church Entry, London, EC4V 5HB, England, UK
Tel: 44 207 2363934
Fax: 44 207 3293677
Email: office@ancientmonumentsociety.org.uk
Website: http://www.ancientmonumentssociety.org.uk
Founded: 1924
Members: 2000
Staff: 3
Contact: Matthew Saunders, Sec.
Fee: £18
Description: Individuals and institutions united for the study and conservation of ancient monuments and historic buildings of all types and ages. Has formed a working partnership with the Friends of Friendless Churches, which owns 31 architecturally important places of worship.
Library Type: reference
Publication: Newsletter
Publication title: Newsletter
Publication title: Transactions of the Ancient Monuments Society
Meetings/Conventions: - annual convention

Anglican Pacifist Fellowship
APF

11 Weavers End, Hanslope, Milton Keynes, MK19 7PA, England, UK
Tel: 44 1908 510642
Fax: 44 1908 511948
Email: ajkempster@aol.com
Founded: 1937
Members: 1250
Contact: Dr. Tony Kempster, Hon.Sec.
Description: Communicant members, from 27 countries, of the Church of England, or of a church in full communion with it, who believe their membership in the Christian Church involves the complete repudiation of modern war and preparation for it. Purpose is to promote Christianity, especially through the study and application of Christian gospel in its relation to war and allied social issues. Works toward the establishment of peace in the world. Propagates the belief that pacifism is inherent in Christianity. Provides members, in times of war and peace, with opportunities to apply the Christian faith by relieving human suffering. Organizes lecture schools.
Publication title: Annual Report
Second publication: Newsletter
Publication title: The Anglican Peacemaker. Advertisements.
Meetings/Conventions: - annual conference

Anglo Danish Society

26 Old Bailey Rd., London, EC4M 7HW, England, UK
Tel: 44 1753 884846
Founded: 1924
Members: 475
Staff: 1
Contact: Mrs. A-M Eastwood, Sec.
Fee: £10
Membership Type: single
Fee: £15
Membership Type: family
Library Type: reference

Anglo-Albanian Association

East Bldg., Unit E209, Westminster Business Sq., Durham St., London, SE11 5JH, England, UK
Tel: 44 20 75826082
Email: caroline@albaction.org
Founded: 1918
Members: 220
Contact: Peter Rennie, Sec.
Fee: £15
Membership Type: ordinary
Fee: £100
Membership Type: life
Description: Acts as a liaison for individuals and organizations interested in Albanian matters. Celebrates Albanian National Day, November 28.
Publication: Newsletter
Publication title: Drita. Advertisements.
Meetings/Conventions: - annual party

Anglo-Arab Association

21 Collingham Rd., London, SW5 0NU, England, UK
Tel: 44 207 3733414
Fax: 44 207 8352088
Founded: 1961
Members: 300
Staff: 2
Contact:
Fee: £10
Membership Type: individual
Fee: £50
Membership Type: corporate
Description: Promotes communication and exchange between English and Arabic people.
Library Subject: Middle East
Library Type: reference

Anglo-Chilean Society
ACS

12 Devonshire St., London, W1N 2DS, England, UK
Tel: 44 207 5801271
Fax: 44 207 5805901
Website: http://www.anglochileansociety.org
Founded: 1944
Members: 350
Staff: 1
Contact: Maria Teresa Lamarca, Sec.
Fee: £15
Membership Type: single
Fee: £30
Membership Type: married

Description: Individuals (350) and corporations (12). Seeks to foster friendly relations between England and Chile and disseminate information in England about Chile and its culture. Organizes art exhibitions, and film shows. Sends prizes to Chilean schools; conducts essay competitions. Provides information on Chile to individuals and institutions.
Publication title: Chilean News
Second publication: Booklets
Meetings/Conventions: - annual meeting

Anglo-European College of Chiropractic
AECC

13-15 Parkwood Rd., Bournemouth, BH5 2DF, England, UK
Tel: 44 1202 436200
Fax: 44 1202 436312
Email: aecc@aecc.ac.uk
Website: http://www.aecc.ac.uk
Founded: 1965
Members: 25
Staff: 100
Contact: Prof. Gabriel Donleavy
Description: Chiropractic practitioners, educators, and students. Seeks to advance the study, teaching, and practice of chiropractic. Facilitates communication among members; sponsors research and educational programs.
Publication: Newsletter. Advertisements.
Meetings/Conventions: conference

Anglo-German Foundation for the Study of Industrial Society
AGF

34 Belgrave Sq., London, SW1X 8DZ, England, UK
Tel: 44 207 8231123
Fax: 44 207 8232324
Email: info@agf.org.uk
Website: http://www.agf.org.uk
Founded: 1973
Staff: 4
Contact: Bryan Rigby, Chm.
Description: Government agencies of Great Britain and Germany. Promotes comparative research in the fields of industrial, economic, and social policy in the United Kingdom and Germany. Provides financial and other support to bilateral research programs; cultivates better understanding and closer relations between the two countries; works to establish practical and durable links between industry, academics, government, and the media in Great Britain and Germany.
Publication: Reports

Animal Care College

Ascot House, High St., Ascot, SL5 7JG, England, UK
Tel: 44 1344 628269
Fax: 44 1344 622771
Email: admin@rtc-associates.freeserve.co.uk
Website: http://www.corsini.co.uk/animalcare/
Founded: 1980
Contact: David Cavill
Description: Open to all those who have gained certification in course recognized by the Animal Care College. To improve the quality of training in and standards of animal care.
Publication: Magazine
Publication title: Dogs Monthly

Animal Health Distributors Association
AHDA

Gable Court, 8 Parsons Hill, Hollesley, Woodbridge, IP12 3RB, England, UK
Tel: 44 1394 410444
Fax: 44 1394 410455
Email: info@ahda.org.uk
Website: http://www.ahda.org.uk
Founded: 1985
Members: 150
Staff: 2
Contact: Dr. R.R. Dawson
Description: Agricultural Merchants who are registered and qualified to distribute animal medicines to farmers and horse owners together with several wholesalers of such products. Aims to prevent the EC legislating members out of business and to ensure an appropriate number of animal medicines are classified for distribution by registered distributors and that new products are so classified.
Publication: Newsletter
Meetings/Conventions: - annual conference - Exhibits.

Animal Health Information Specialists
AHIS

c/o Tom Roper
RCVS Library and Information Service, Belgravia House, 62-64 Horseferry Rd., London, SW1P 2AF, England, UK
Tel: 44 20 72222021
Fax: 44 20 72222004
Email: t.roper@rcvs.org.uk
Website: http://www.ahis.org
Contact: Tom Roper, Chm.
Description: Fosters cooperation and exchange among individuals interested in animal health information.

Animal Health Trust

Lanwades Park, Kentford, Newmarket, CB8 7UU, England, UK
Tel: 44 8700 502424
Fax: 44 8700 502425
Email: info@aht.org.uk
Website: http://www.aht.org.uk
Founded: 1942
Staff: 215
Contact: Keith Reid, Trust Sec.
Description: Aims to push back the frontiers of veterinary science. Develops new technology and knowledge for the better diagnosis, prevention and cure of disease. Provides a referral service for veterinary surgeons in practice.
Library Subject: veterinarian
Library Type: by appointment only
Publication: Newsletter
Publication title: AHT News
Second publication: Annual Report
Publication title: Annual Review

Animal Transportation Association - European Office

PO Box 251, Redhill, RH1 5FU, England, UK
Tel: 44 1737 822249
Fax: 44 1737 822954
Email: 100257.1720@compuserve.com
Website: http://www.aata-animaltransport.org
Founded: 1975

Members: 400
Staff: 2
Contact: Tim Harris, European Sec.
Fee: £450
Membership Type: corporate
Fee: £225
Membership Type: individual
Description: Individuals and organizations concerned with the humane handling and transportation of animals, particularly livestock, pets, and exotic animals. Gathers and disseminates information on the humane transportation of animals; maintains liaison with national and international agencies regulating animal transportation. Encourages research on improved methods of animal transportation.
Library Subject: animal transportation
Library Type: not open to the public
Publication title: AATA Manual for the Transportation of Animals, 2nd Ed.. Advertisements.
Second publication: Journal
Publication title: AATA Quarterly. Advertisements.
Meetings/Conventions: - annual conference Washington District of Columbia United States

Anthroposophical Medical Association

35 Park Rd., London, NW1 6XT, England, UK
Founded: 1968
Description: Acts as a professional association of registered doctors practicing in the field of anthroposophical medicine.

Anti-Counterfeiting Group

PO Box 578, High Wycombe, HP11 1YD, England, UK
Tel: 44 1494 449165
Fax: 44 1494 465052
Email: admin@a-cg.com
Website: http://www.a-cg.com
Founded: 1980
Members: 200
Staff: 4
Contact: John Anderson, Dir.Gen.
Fee: £1300
Membership Type: associate
Fee: £1400
Membership Type: full
Description: Represents nearly 200 manufacturers and distributors of branded products; trade mark and patent agents; and solicitors. Lobbies for improved resources for investigations of counterfeiting and the enforcement of anti-counterfeiting legislation; communicates the message about the damage counterfeiting does to the national economy, business generally and to the consumer; is the hub of a national and international network of information, advice and contacts on anti-counterfeiting activity.
Meetings/Conventions: - semiannual conference

Antiquarian Booksellers' Association (International)
ABAI

Sackville House, 40 Piccadilly, London, W1J 0DR, England, UK
Tel: 44 207 4393118
Fax: 44 207 4393119
Email: admin@aba.org.uk
Website: http://www.abainternational.com
Founded: 1906
Members: 250

Staff: 4
Contact: John Critchley, Office Dir.
Fee: £325
Description: Bookselling firms and dealers in rare books and manuscripts with a minimum of 5 years' trading experience. Seeks to uphold the standards of antiquarian book trade. Serves as a liaison between potential book collectors and members; disseminates information and advice.
Publication: Membership Directory
Publication title: The Handbook
Second publication: Newsletter
Meetings/Conventions: Chelsea Book Fair - annual trade show
London UK

Antiquarian Horological Society
AHS

New House, High St., Ticehurst, Sussex, TN5 7AL, England, UK
Tel: 44 1580 200155
Fax: 44 1580 201323
Email: secretary@ahsoc.demon.co.uk
Website: http://www.ahsoc.demon.co.uk
Founded: 1953
Members: 2000
Staff: 2
Contact: Mrs. Wendy Barr, Sec.
Fee: £37
Membership Type: junior
Fee: £65
Membership Type: ordinary
Description: Practices and promotes the study of antiquarian horology and allied disciplines worldwide. Horology is the study of the measurement of time. Conducts educational programs.
Library Subject: horology
Library Type: reference
Publication: Journal
Publication title: Antiquarian Horology and the Proceedings of the Antiquarian Horological Society. Advertisements.
Publication title: The Planetarium of Giovanni de Dondi, Citizen of Padau

Anti-Slavery International

Thomas Clarkson House, The Stableyard, Broomgrove Rd., London, SW9 9TL, England, UK
Tel: 44 207 5018920
Fax: 44 20 77384110
Email: antislavery@antislavery.org
Website: http://www.antislavery.org
Founded: 1839
Members: 2000
Staff: 19
Contact: Mary Cunneen, Dir.
Fee: £40
Membership Type: Normal
Fee: £8
Membership Type: Student
Description: Committed to eliminating all forms of slavery in the world today. Works to end slavery by exposing current cases of slavery and campaigning for their eradication. Supports the initiatives of local organizations to release people enslaved. Promotes more effective implementation of international laws against slavery and presses governments of countries where there is slavery to develop and implement measures to end it.
Library Subject: traditional and contemporary slavery
Library Type: reference

Formerly: Absorbed, Aborigines' Protection Society
Publication: Newsletter
Publication title: The Reporter
Meetings/Conventions: - annual general assembly - Exhibits.
London UK

Apparel Knitting and Textiles Alliance
5 Portland Pl., London, W1N 3AA, England, UK
Tel: 44 20 76367788
Fax: 44 20 76367515
Founded: 1989
Members: 1
Contact: A. Mansell
Description: Trade associations in textile, clothing and knitting industry. Spokesbody to media, Parliament and government departments on behalf of the textile and clothing industry.

Applied Vision Association
c/o The College of Optometrists
42 Craven St., London, WC2N 5NG, England, UK
Tel: 44 20 78396000
Fax: 44 20 78396800
Email: ndebrunner@college-optometists.org
Website: http://www.dmu.ac.uk/ava/
Founded: 1975
Members: 240
Contact: N. de Brunner
Fee: £20
Membership Type: member
Description: Works to advance, promote, develop and improve the study and knowledge of human vision including medical problems relating to vision.
Publication: Newsletter
Publication title: Bulletin of the Applied Vision Association. Advertisements.
Meetings/Conventions: conference - Exhibits.S

Appropriate Technology ASIA
ATA

Unit F4, London Fashion Centre, 89-93 Fonthill Road, London, N4 3JH, England, UK
Tel: 44 207 2818180
Fax: 44 207 2818280
Email: atachina@hotmail.com
Founded: 1984
Staff: 12
Contact: Alex Jones, Dir.Gen.
Description: Seeks to find marginal and threatened populations in environmentally challenging situations in Asia and help them to meet their basic needs for housing, household energy, safe water, food and good health. Seeking out the poorest and using participatory practice, ATA will apply technology and knowledge that is appropriate and environmentally sustainable while embedding skills in the communities with which it works.

Approved Driving Instructors National Joint Council
41 Edinburgh Rd., Cambridge, CB4 1QR, England, UK
Tel: 44 1223 359079
Fax: 44 1223 359079
Founded: 1971
Members: 26

Staff: 2
Contact: Peter Edwards, Gen.Sec.
Fee: £195
Description: National or local associations of driving instructors. Acts as united voice for members, dealing with government departments and acting as representatives on their behalf.
Publication: Newsletter
Meetings/Conventions: - annual conference - Exhibits.

APT Enterprise Development

29 Northwick Business Centre, Moreton-in-Marsh, GL56 9RF, England, UK
Tel: 44 1386 700130
Fax: 44 1386 701010
Email: apt.enterprise@dial.pipex.com
Website: http://www.aptenterprise.co.uk
Founded: 1983
Staff: 5
Contact: Andy Jeans, Chief Exec.
Description: Dedicated to the elimination of poverty in developing countries and specializes in educating people to help themselves by providing skills training, technology transfer and support for the development of their own small enterprises. Maximizes benefit to those in need by formulating and implementing sustainable projects that address the real roots of the problems in the most appropriate way.

Arab Horse Society
AHS

Windsor House, Marlborough, Ramsbury, Marlborough, SN8 2PE, England, UK
Tel: 44 1672 520782
Fax: 44 1672 520880
Website: http://www.arabhorsesoc-uk.com/
Founded: 1918
Members: 3000
Staff: 7
Contact: Diana Whittome, Registrar
Fee: £40
Description: Promotes the Arabian horse.
Library Subject: Arab horse breeds
Library Type: reference
Publication: Journal
Publication title: Arab Horse Society Journal. Advertisements.
Second publication: Newsletter
Publication title: Arab Horse Society News
Meetings/Conventions: - annual meeting

Arboricultural Association
AA

Ampfield House, Ampfield, Romsey, SO51 9PA, England, UK
Tel: 44 1794 368717
Fax: 44 1794 368978
Email: admin@trees.org.uk
Website: http://www.trees.org.uk
Founded: 1964
Members: 2000
Staff: 5
Contact: N. Eden, Dir.
Description: Arboriculturists and conservationists; forestry experts; representatives of government departments; interested individuals. Promotes the study of arboriculture (the conservation, planting, and care of trees and woodlands). Works to conserve the forests and woodlands of the United Kingdom Great Britain particularly trees and woods grown for amenity. Strives to raise the standards of arboriculture, to advance knowledge of trees, and to foster community interest in conservation. Makes recommendations to government authorities on matters of arboricultural concern. Coordinates training programs; conducts examinations; stimulates research and development. Organizes lectures; conduct competitions and awards prizes.
Library Subject: Arboriculture: Urban Forestry
Library Type: not open to the public
Publication title: A Guide to Tree Pruning
Second publication: Directory
Publication title: Arboricultural Consultants
Meetings/Conventions: National Arboriculture Conference - annual - Exhibits.

Archaeology Abroad
AA

31-34 Gordon Square, London, WC1H 0PY, England, UK
Fax: 44 207 3832572
Email: arch.abroad@ucl.ac.uk
Website: http://www.britarch.ac.uk/archabroad
Founded: 1972
Members: 500
Staff: 4
Contact: Wendy Rix Morton, Hon.Sec.
Fee: £14
Membership Type: individuals
Fee: £17
Membership Type: overseas individuals
Description: Provides lists of opportunities for archaeological fieldwork outside the UK.
Publication: Bulletin
Publication title: Archaeology Abroad

Architects and Engineers for Social Responsibility
AESR

Stanhill Works, Tennyson Ave., Oswaldtwistle, BB5 4QZ, England, UK
Email: r.butterfield@soton.ac.uk
Website: http://www.jakob.demon.co.uk/
Founded: 1991
Contact: Brian Hanson, Sec.
Fee: £15
Membership Type: ordinary
Fee: £3
Membership Type: unwaged, student, or retired
Description: Active and retired architects and engineers; architecture and engineering students. Promotes abolition of nuclear weapons and a socially responsible ethic in the use of technology. Conducts advocacy campaigns on issues of environmental protection and disarmament; cooperates with related professional groups representing scientists and health care professionals. Sponsors educational programs.
Publication: Newsletter

Architects in Industry and Commerce

66 Portland Pl., London, W1N 4AD, England, UK
Tel: 44 171 5805533
Founded: 1959
Members: 85
Contact: Andrew Price, Chm.

Description: Registered architects who work for companies or organizations whose main business is not architecture. Aims to represent every registered architect working in industry and commerce; to encourage the greater use of architects as in-house.
Publication: Proceedings

Architects Registration Board

8 Weymouth St., London, W1W 5BU, England, UK
Tel: 44 207 5805861
Fax: 44 207 4365269
Email: info@arb.org.uk
Website: http://www.arb.org.uk
Founded: 1931
Members: 30860
Staff: 15
Contact: Owen Luder, Chm.
Description: Architects must have obtained recognised qualifications and have passed a professional practice exam. Maintains a register of architects. Concerned with the recognition of examinations qualifying for registration; discipline of the profession; the prosecution of persons unlawfully using the name, style or title 'architect'. Provides scholarships and maintenance grants for students and supports the furtherance of education and research in architecture.
Formerly: Architects Registration Council of the UK
Publication: Directory
Publication title: Register of Architects

Architectural and Specialist Door Manufacturers Association

Burnside House, 3 Coates Lane, High Wycombe, HP13 5EY, England, UK
Tel: 44 1494 447370
Fax: 44 1494 462094
Email: info@asdma.com
Website: http://www.asdma.com
Founded: 1989
Members: 28
Staff: 1
Contact: Mrs. L. Parry
Fee: £1000
Membership Type: full
Fee: £500
Membership Type: associate
Description: Specialist timber door manufacturers and businesses engaged in allied industries. Promotes the benefits of using independently tested and quality assured doors which meet necessary fire, safety and other performance criteria. Offers advice and information to end users.
Publication: Book
Publication title: Best Practice Guide to Timber Fire Doors

Architectural Cladding Association

60 Charles St., Leicester, LE1 1FB, England, UK
Tel: 44 116 2536161
Fax: 44 116 2514568
Email: aca@britishprecast.org
Website: http://www.britishprecast.org/aca
Founded: 1987
Members: 5
Staff: 2
Contact: C.J. Budge, Sec.
Description: Manufacturers of precast concrete architectural cladding.
Publication: Book

Publication title: Cast in Concrete
Publication title: Code of Practice for the Safe Erection of Precast Concrete Cladding

Architecture and Surveying Institute
ASI

St. Mary House, 15 St. Mary St., Chippenham, SN15 3WD, England, UK
Tel: 44 1249 444505
Fax: 44 1249 443602
Email: mail@asi.org.uk
Website: http://www.asi.org.uk
Founded: 1926
Members: 5000
Staff: 13
Contact: Mr. Ian Norris, Ch.Exec.
Fee: £169
Membership Type: corporate
Description: Architects and surveyors in 54 countries. Aim is to maintain a high standard of education and training for architects, engineers, and surveyors, and to provide practical proficiency through qualified membership. Updates members on periodic changes in industrial techniques and facilitates exchange of information through discussions and industrial contact.
Library Subject: architecture and surveying
Library Type: not open to the public
Formerly: Formed by Merger of, Faculty of Architects and Surveyors
Publication: Magazine
Publication title: A & S Magazine. Advertisements.
Meetings/Conventions: - periodic international conference - Exhibits.

Aristotelian Society
AS

Senate House, Rm. 260, Malet St., London, WC1E 7HU, England, UK
Tel: 44 207 2551724
Fax: 44 207 2551724
Email: mail@aristoteliansociety.org.uk
Website: http://www.sas.ac.uk/aristotelian_society/index.html
Founded: 1870
Members: 1210
Staff: 2
Contact: Goergia Testa, Exec.Sec.
Fee: £22
Membership Type: Ordinary
Fee: £11
Membership Type: Student
Description: Academics, students, and amateur philosophers in English-speaking countries. Promotes the study of philosophy; holds biweekly discussions.
Publication: Journal
Publication title: Proceedings of the Aristotelian Society
Publication title: Supplement to the Proceedings of the Aristotelian Society
Meetings/Conventions: - annual conference - Exhibits. Belfast UK

Arkleton Trust
AT

Enstone, Chipping Norton, OX7 4HH, England, UK
Tel: 44 1608 677255
Fax: 44 1608 677276
Email: arkleton@enstoneuk.demon.co.uk
Website: http://www.enstoneuk.demon.co.uk/arkleton

Founded: 1977
Staff: 5
Contact: John Bryden, Dir.
Description: Promotes creation and implementation of sustainable rural development projects. Serves as a clearinghouse on rural development; sponsors development and agricultural research. Serves as a liaison between development organizations and government agencies overseeing development. Conducts seminars for development personnel and administrators.

Army Families Federation
AFF

Trenchard Lines, Upavon, Pewsey, SN9 6BE, England, UK
Tel: 44 1980 615525
Fax: 44 1980 615526
Email: us@aff.org.uk
Website: http://www.army.mod.uk/aff/
Founded: 1982
Staff: 70
Contact: Lizzie Iron, Chm.
Description: Army families. Channels communication between army families and the military. Concerns itself with matters affecting army families, such as: housing; education; employment; health; and special needs of children. Acts as a liaison with other women's organizations.
Formerly: Federation of Army Wives
Publication: Report
Publication title: Accompanied Service Survey 1997. Advertisements.
Second publication: Journal
Publication title: Army Families Journal. Advertisements.
Meetings/Conventions: - biennial conference - Exhibits.

Army Records Society
ARS

Natl. Army Museum, Royal Hospital Rd., Chelsea, London, SW3 4HT, England, UK
Tel: 44 207 7300717
Fax: 44 207 8236573
Email: ars@hall-mccartney.co.uk
Founded: 1984
Members: 525
Contact: Dr. William Philpott, Hon.Sec.
Fee: £25
Membership Type: ordinary
Fee: £35
Membership Type: overseas and institution
Description: Individuals and organizations in the United Kingdom interested in British military history. Publishes official papers and correspondences of military figures and eyewitness accounts of battles and campaigns.
Publication title: The Army and the Curragh Incident, 1914
Publication title: The British Army and Signals Intelligence during the First World War
Meetings/Conventions: - annual convention

Aromatherapy Organisation Council

PO Box 19834, London, SE25 6WF, England, UK
Tel: 44 208 2517912
Fax: 44 208 2517942
Email: secretary@aocuk.net
Website: http://www.aocuk.net
Founded: 1991

Contact: Nina Ashby, Sec.
Description: Voluntary, regulatory body for the aromatherapy profession. Seeks to establish common standards of training. Offers mediation and arbitration services in disputes involving aromatherapy. Sponsors research.
Meetings/Conventions: - periodic conference

Aromatherapy Trade Council
ATC

PO Box 387, Suffolk, Ipswich, IP2 9AN, England, UK
Tel: 44 1473 603630
Email: info@a-t-c.org.uk
Website: http://www.a-t-c.org.uk/
Founded: 1992
Description: Represents the interests of manufacturers and suppliers of essential oils and aromatherapy products. Establishes guidelines for safety, labeling, and packaging for the aromatherapy trade. Promotes responsible use of aromatherapy products.

Art Libraries Society of United Kingdom
ARLIS

18 College Rd., Bromsgrove, B60 2NE, England, UK
Tel: 44 1527 579298
Fax: 44 1527 579298
Email: sfrench@arlis.demon.co.uk
Website: http://www.arlis.org.uk
Founded: 1969
Members: 700
Staff: 1
Contact: Sonia French, Admin.
Fee: £41
Membership Type: enhanced, personal UK and Ireland
Fee: £28
Membership Type: enhanced, retired, student-unwaged
Description: Art library professional, including librarians, archivists, libraries, publishers. Dedicated to the documentation of visual art. Provides training and development courses; offers behind the scenes visits to libraries, archives, museums, and galleries; sponsors national and international study tours.
Publication title: ARLIS/UK & Ireland News-sheet. Advertisements.
Second publication: Journal
Publication title: Art Libraries Journal
Meetings/Conventions: - annual conference Brighton UK

Art Metalware Manufacturers' Association

10 Vyse St., Birmingham, B18 6LT, England, UK
Tel: 44 121 2362657
Fax: 44 121 2371106
Members: 10
Staff: 1
Contact: Isabel Welsh, Assn. Sec.
Description: Membership organization of brassware distributors.

Art Through Touch

41 Westbury Ct., Nightingale Ln., London, SW4 9AB, England, UK
Tel: 44 20 86735389
Website: http://members.aol.com/ATTouch/
Description: Promotes access to art activity for people who are visually impaired. Organizes visits to museums and galleries. Conducts research in the area of educational practice in art and visual impairment.
Meetings/Conventions: - monthly meeting

Arthritis and Muscoskeletal Alliance
ARMA

41 Eagle St., London, WC1R 4AR, England, UK
Tel: 44 20 8415191
Fax: 44 20 72423277
Email: arma@rheumatology.org.uk
Founded: 1972
Members: 26
Staff: 2
Contact: Sophie Edwards, CEO
Description: Umbrella organization of national societies concerned with rheumatic and musculoskeletal diseases. Has developed patient-centered standards for the care of individuals with arthritis. Conducts audits of current levels of support and care. Aims to raise awareness of the need for high quality services for those with rheumatic and musculoskeletal diseases. Promotes the development of prevention, treatment, rehabilitation, and relief from the disease. Fosters cooperation, understanding, and mutual support between individuals and organizations concerned with rheumatic diseases. Provides a forum for the exchange of ideas and information.
Formerly: British League Against Rheumatism
Publication title: BLAR Purchaser's Pack
Second publication: Report
Publication title: Disability & Arthritis
Meetings/Conventions: congress

Arthritis and Rheumatism Natural Therapy Research Association

c/o Ken Wright, Sec.
12 Clive Rd., West Duluich, London, SE21 8BY, England, UK
Tel: 44 208 6703763
Fax: 44 208 6703763
Email: renewnham@aol.com
Founded: 1994
Members: 220
Staff: 4
Contact: Dr. R.E. Newnham
Fee: £15
Membership Type: individual
Description: Seeks to educate people about arthritic diseases. Conducts research into the causes and cures of arthritis.
Library Subject: arthritis - minerals
Library Type: open to the public
Publication: Book
Publication title: Arthritis Without Drugs
Second publication: Newsletter
Publication title: ARNTRA
Meetings/Conventions: - annual conference

Arthritis Care
AC

18 Stephenson Way, London, NW1 2HD, England, UK
Tel: 44 207 3806500
Fax: 44 207 3806505
Email: lizziee@arthritiscare.org.uk
Website: http://www.arthritiscare.org.uk
Founded: 1948
Members: 66000
Staff: 250
Contact: William Butler, Chief Exec.
Fee: £6
Description: Individuals with arthritis and concerned others. Seeks to: increase awareness of the problems associated with rheumatic diseases; disseminate information; establish a nationwide network of branches; improve welfare facilities; provide information, advice and practical aid. Maintains hotels.
Library Subject: arthritis, daily living, equipment, disability issues
Library Type: not open to the public
Formerly: British Rheumatism and Arthritis Association
Publication: Magazine
Publication title: Arthritis News. Advertisements.

Arthritis Research Campaign

Copeman House, St. Mary's Court, St. Mary's Gate, Chesterfield, S41 7TD, England, UK
Tel: 44 1246 558033
Fax: 44 1246 558007
Email: info@arc.org.uk
Website: http://www.arc.org.uk
Founded: 1936
Members: 40000
Staff: 71
Contact: F. Logan, Ch.Exec.
Description: Voluntary helpers, donators and support staff. Conducts research and education to find the cause of rheumatic disease. In pursuit of these objectives mounts a wide ranging research program involving people, projects and centers - usually at university medical schools. Currently running at over 20 million pounds per year. The income raised to meet this commitment comes entirely from voluntary donations.
Formerly: Arthritis and Rheumatism Council for Research
Publication: Booklets
Publication title: Arthritis Today
Second publication: Booklets

Arthur Ransome Society

Registered Office, Abbot Hall Art Gallery & Museum of Lakeland Life, Kirkland, Kendal, LA9 5AL, England, UK
Tel: 44 1539 722464
Fax: 44 1539 445623
Email: tarsinfo@arthur-ransome.org
Website: http://www.arthur-ransome.org/ar
Founded: 1990
Members: 2400
Contact: Dr. W.H. Janes, Bd.Sec.
Fee: £15
Membership Type: adult
Fee: £20
Membership Type: adult overseas
Description: Promotes wider readership of the works of English author Arthur Ransome (1884-1967). Educates the public about Ransome's life, writing, and ideas. Sponsors activities for children that encourage sailing, fishing, or exploring in areas described in Ransome's books. Conducts research; publishes results. Also conducts charitable programs. Supports museum.
Library Subject: sailing, travel, Russia, fishing, poetry, essays, literature reviews
Library Type: not open to the public
Formerly: The Arthur Ransome Society
Publication: Journal
Publication title: Mixed Moss. Advertisements.
Second publication: Journal
Publication title: Outlaw
Meetings/Conventions: Literary Weekend - biennial conference London UK

Article 19 - Global Campaign for Free Expression
A19

33 Islington High St., London, N1 9LH, England, UK
Tel: 44 207 2789292
Fax: 44 207 7131356
Email: info@article19.org
Website: http://www.article19.org
Founded: 1986
Description: Named for Article 19 of the Universal Declaration of Human Rights, organization unites individuals in 32 countries to advocate the right to freedom to hold opinions without interference and to receive and disseminate information through any media. Works to eradicate censorship worldwide. Pressures governments for greater freedom of information and expression; encourages improved national and international standards to protect such freedoms. Maintains a network of contacts and correspondents for information exchange regarding censorship. Campaigns on behalf of censorship victims. Conducts research programs.
Library Type: by appointment only
Publication title: Censorship News
Publication title: Country Reports

Arts and Business

Nutmeg House, 60 Gainsford St., Butlers Wharf, London, SE1 2NY, England, UK
Tel: 44 207 3788143
Fax: 44 207 4077527
Email: info@aandb.org.uk
Website: http://www.aandb.org.uk
Founded: 1976
Members: 361
Staff: 70
Contact: Colin Tweedy, Chief.Exec.
Fee: £700
Membership Type: business member
Fee: £2000
Membership Type: business patron
Description: Promotes and encourages partnerships between the private sector and the arts, to their mutual benefit and to that of the community at large. Provides a wide range of services to its member organizations and businesses as well as to 700 arts professionals through the Arts & Business Development Forum. Aims to enable individual business people to share their skills with the arts, manages the Skills Bank and the Board Bank through its Arts at Work program. Manages, on behalf of the Department of Cultural, Media and Sport, which can make financial awards to new or established sponsors of the arts. Runs programs from London and through a network of offices nationwide. It is the world's foremost organization in the field of business support of the arts.
Library Subject: arts funding, trusts, and grants
Library Type: reference
Formerly: Association for Business Sponsorship of the Arts
Publication title: Annual Report
Meetings/Conventions: Arts Based Training Seminar

Arts Association

227 Goldhawk Rd., London, W12 8ER, England, UK
Tel: 44 20 87434378
Founded: 1953

Arts Centre Group
ACG

ACGinternationalermission, St. Saviours, Walton Palace, London, SW3 1SA, England, UK
Tel: 44 207 5812777
Fax: 44 270 7060964
Email: info@artcentregroup.org.uk
Website: http://www.artscentregroup.org.uk
Founded: 1971
Members: 700
Staff: 1
Contact: Steve Thomason, Ch.
Fee: £35
Membership Type: Full
Fee: £20
Membership Type: Student
Description: Christians in 12 countries working professionally in the arts, the media, and entertainment. Promotes an understanding of the link between members' Christian identities and their artistic expression. Encourages Christian artists to develop their professional abilities and assists them in merging their faith and careers. Evangelizes other artists by encouraging them to express Christian ideals through their work. Organizes events ranging from debates, discussions and performance to an annual lecture, an annual poetry competition, prayer and bible studies and social events.
Publication: Journal
Publication title: AM. Advertisements.
Second publication: Newsletter
Publication title: FAX. Advertisements.
Meetings/Conventions: - periodic lecture

Arts Council of England
ACE

c/o Information Mgr.
14 Great Peter St., London, SW1P 3NQ, England, UK
Tel: 44 207 3330100
Fax: 44 207 9736564
Email: enquiries@artscouncil.org.uk
Website: http://www.artscouncil.org.uk
Founded: 1945
Staff: 200
Description: National strategic policy body for the arts in England. Works in partnership with the Regional Arts Board, which is responsible for funding and development of the arts in England.
Library Subject: arts policy and management
Library Type: reference
Formerly: Arts Council of Great Britain
Publication title: Annual Report
Second publication: Books

Asbestos Removal Contractors Association
ARCA

237 Branston Rd., Burton-On-Trent, DE14 3BT, England, UK
Tel: 44 1283 531126
Fax: 44 1283 568228
Email: info@arca.org.uk
Website: http://www.arca.org.uk
Founded: 1980
Members: 160
Staff: 2
Contact: Terry Jago, Chief Exec.
Fee: £450

Membership Type: associate
Fee: £975
Membership Type: full
Description: Asbestos contracting managers and individuals in 9 countries. Monitors and recommends guidelines for asbestos handling and disposal. Disseminates information on protective clothing, respiratory equipment, and methods of decontamination. Offers residential and in-house training courses for line managers and supervisory staff.
Library Subject: asbestos removal
Library Type: not open to the public
Publication: Booklet
Publication title: ARCA Asbestos Information File and Guidelines
Second publication: Newsletter
Publication title: ARCA News. Advertisements.
Meetings/Conventions: - annual convention - Exhibits.

Ashford Chamber of Commerce and Industry

Ashford Business Point, Waterbrook Ave., Sevington, Ashford, TN24 OLH, England, UK
Contact: Phil Nichols
Description: Promotes business and commerce.

Asian Women's Project
AWP

PO Box 324, Reading, RG1 6AW, England, UK
Contact: Hydeh Nafaiieh
Description: Individuals and organizations. Seeks to improve the social, economic, and legal status of women in Asia. Provides support and assistance to Asian women's organizations.

Associated Society of Locomotive Engineers and Firemen
ASLEF

9 Arkwright Rd., London, NW3 6AB, England, UK
Tel: 44 20 73178600
Email: info@aslef.org.uk
Website: http://www.aslef.org.uk
Founded: 1880
Members: 18612
Contact: M.D. Rix, Gen.Sec.
Description: Train drivers or others on the footplate employed on UK railways, London Underground and Tyne & Wear Metro. Negotiates terms and conditions of employment; provides legal services and representation; political representation; pensions representation.
Publication: Journal
Publication title: Locomotive Journal

Associates for Research into the Science of Enjoyment
ARISE

PO Box 11446, London, SW18 5ZH, England, UK
Tel: 44 208 8745548
Fax: 44 208 8743755
Email: arise@dial.pipex.com
Website: http://www.arise.org
Founded: 1989
Staff: 1
Contact: David Warburton, Coord.
Description: Scientists with an interest in the human senses. Promotes increased understanding of the physiology and biochemistry of pleasure. Serves as a forum for the exchange of information among members; sponsors research and educational programs.
Publication: Book
Publication title: Pleasure and Quality of Life
Meetings/Conventions: - biennial symposium

Association Building Cleaning Direct Service Providers
ABCDS

3 Jalrg Bank Cottages, Wylam Northwyberland, Wylam, NE41 8JT, England, UK
Tel: 44 1661 854423
Fax: 44 1661 854423
Email: penny@adem.denin.co.uk
Founded: 1990
Members: 150
Contact: Penny Harrison, Sec.
Fee: £120
Membership Type: corporate (local Authority)
Fee: £205
Membership Type: associate (supplier/manufacturer)
Description: Promotes building cleaning within the public sector.
Publication: Newsletter
Publication title: Cleanscene. Advertisements.
Meetings/Conventions: - annual conference - Exhibits.

Association for Analytic and Bodymind Therapy and Training

Princes House, 8 Princes Ave., Muswell Hill, London, N10 3LR, England, UK
Tel: 44 181 8835418
Founded: 1974
Members: 4
Contact: G.S. Seaborn-Jones
Description: Qualified and experienced psychotherapists. To extend psychotherapy from quiet, controlled talking therapy to vocal and bodily awareness and participation. To promote experiential therapy.

Association for Astronomy Education

c/o Royal Astronomical Society
Burlington House, Piccadilly, London, W1V 0NL, England, UK
Website: http://www.aae.org.uk
Founded: 1980
Members: 240
Contact: Dr. Francisco Diego, Pres.
Description: Teachers, lecturers, astronomy professionals and amateurs who have links with education via either formal tuition or local or commercial links e.g. planetaria. Aims to promote and support astronomy education at all levels and to provide a forum for discussion and curriculum development in astronomy education. Registered charity no. 1046041.
Publication title: GNOMON. Advertisements.
Meetings/Conventions: - annual lecture

Association for Child Psychology and Psychiatry
ACPP

Child Clinical Psychology Service, Mary Sheridan Centre for, St. Savlors House, 39/41 Union St., London, SE1 1SO, England, UK
Tel: 44 207 4037458
Fax: 44 207 4037081
Email: acpp@acpp.org.uk

Website: http://www.acpp.org.uk/
Founded: 1956
Members: 2750
Staff: 6
Contact: Frederick Wentworth-Bowyer, Chief Exec.
Description: Professionals working in the field of child mental health. Encourages dissemination of scientific research and information.
Publication title: Child Psychology and Psychiatry Review
Second publication: Journal
Publication title: Journal of Child Psychology and Psychiatry. Advertisements.

Association for Common European Nursing Diagnoses, Interventions and Outcomes
ACENDIO

Royal College of Nursing, 20 Cavendish Sq., London, W1M 0AB, England, UK
Email: alex.westbrook@chelwest.nhs.uk
Founded: 1995
Contact: Alex Westbrook, Sec.
Fee: £40
Membership Type: individual
Fee: £400
Membership Type: institution
Description: Nurses and nursing organizations. Network and development of resources towards standards supporting sharing and comparison of data about nursing.
Meetings/Conventions: - biennial conference

Association for Conferences and Events

ACE International, Riverside House, High St., Huntingdon, PE29 3SG, England, UK
Tel: 44 1480 457595
Fax: 44 1480 412863
Email: ace@martex.co.uk
Website: http://www.martex.co.uk/ace
Founded: 1971
Members: 500
Staff: 3
Contact: Peter Worger, Gen.Mgr.
Fee: £250
Membership Type: organization
Description: Corporate companies, charities and associations, hotels and venues, conference and event organisers, service suppliers, tourist bodies. Provides a forum for member organisations involved in all aspects of the meetings business. Services include: monthly newsletter, events calendar, jobspot, discounts, magazine, information sheets, publications, helpline. Activities include seminars, socials, study weekends, inspection visits, networking opportunities. Training programme includes courses on Meetings Planning and on First Aid at Events.
Library Subject: conferences, events, exhibitions, venues, surveys
Library Type: not open to the public
Formerly: Association of Conference Executives
Publication title: ACE Newsletter. Advertisements.
Second publication: Handbook
Publication title: ACE Yearbook - Who's Who in the Meetings and Events Industry. Advertisements.

Association for Continence Advice
ACA

102a Astra House, Arklow Rd., New Cross, London, SE14 6EB, England, UK
Tel: 44 20 86924680
Fax: 44 20 86926217
Email: info@aca.uk.com
Website: http://www.aca.uk.com/mainindex.html
Founded: 1981
Members: 755
Staff: 2
Description: Professionals with an interest in the health and social care of people with continence problems. Aims to provide a means of communication and support between members and other interested groups; to promote educational activities; to produce and distribute a newsletter; to promote research activities and disseminate research findings; to liaise and maintain dialogue with relevant manufacturers; to promote public awareness and positive attitudes within society.
Publication: Journal
Publication title: Continence
Second publication: Pamphlets
Meetings/Conventions: - annual conference Bournemouth UK

Association for Cultural Exchange
CULTUREX

Babraham, Cambridge, CB2 4AP, England, UK
Tel: 44 1223 835055
Fax: 44 1223 837394
Email: ace@study-tours.org
Website: http://www.study-tours.org
Founded: 1958
Staff: 20
Contact: P.B. Barnes, Sec.
Description: Promotes the study of different cultures and lifestyles through study tours and courses in art, architecture, and archaeology history. Offers about 150 educational programs every year, usually lasting from 1 to 3 weeks.

Association for Dance Movement Therapy - United Kingdom
ADMTUK

c/o Quaker Meeting House, Wedmore Vale, Bristol, BS3 5HX, England, UK
Email: query@admt.org.uk
Website: http://www.admt.org.uk
Founded: 1982
Members: 200
Contact: Jeannettee MacDonald, Chm.
Fee: £35
Membership Type: associate
Fee: £20
Membership Type: student
Description: Individuals united to promote dance movement therapy. Monitors and promotes training. Offers professional services. Organizes summer schools, workshops and seminars.
Publication: Newsletter
Publication title: ADMTUK Quartly - E-Motion. Advertisements.
Second publication: Articles
Meetings/Conventions: - annual convention

Association For Education Welfare Management

The Whiskers, 1 The Boundary, Bradford, BD8 0BQ, England, UK
Tel: 44 1924 305519
Fax: 44 1924 305646
Email: jprice@wakefield.gov.uk
Website: http://www.aewm.co.uk
Founded: 1917
Members: 155
Contact: Mrs. J.A. Price
Fee: £55
Description: Staff involved in the management of education welfare staff. Provides support, advice and information to all its members through regional meetings, local training days and an annual training conference.
Publication title: Conference Digest
Second publication: Newsletter
Publication title: Newsletter

Association for Educational and Training Technology
A.E.T.T.

Beavor Ln., Axminster, EX13 5EQ, England, UK
Founded: 1965

Association for Environmental Archaeology

AEA, Department of Archaeology, University of York, The King's Manor, York, Y01 7EP, England, UK

Tel: 44 1904 434950
Fax: 44 1904 433902
Email: biol8@york.ac.uk
Website: http://www.envarch.net
Founded: 1979
Members: 400
Contact:
Fee: £12
Membership Type: student
Fee: £12
Membership Type: unwaged
Description: Seeks to understand past ecology, with emphasis on man's role, and past human economy and living conditions. Analyzes the remains of plants and animals, and the sediments in which they are buried. Interests include anthropology, paleopathology, parasitology, zooarchaeology, paleobotany, and the study of prehistoric economy.
Publication: Journal
Publication title: Environmental Archaeology
Second publication: Newsletter
Meetings/Conventions: - semiannual meeting

Association for European Transport
AET

1 Vernon Mews, Vernon St., W. Kensington, London, W14 0RL, England, UK
Tel: 44 207 3481978
Fax: 44 207 3481989
Email: info@aetransport.co.uk
Website: http://www.aetransport.co.uk/
Contact: Sally Scarlett
Description: Professionals working in the transportation industries; transportations firms; libraries and information centers. Seeks to advance the business and regulatory interests of the European transportation industries. Serves as a clearinghouse on transportation and transportation research. Facilitates communication and cooperation among members; conducts continuing professional development programs; represents members at the European level.
Meetings/Conventions: - annual conference

Association for French Language Studies

c/o Dr. R.A.M. Temple
Department of Language and Linguistic Science, University of York, Heslington, York, YO10 5DD, England, UK
Tel: 44 1904 432671
Email: ramt1@york.ac.uk
Website: http://www.unl.ac.uk/sals//afls/
Founded: 1981
Contact: Dr. R. Temple
Description: Promotes language teaching activities and research in French language and linguistics.
Publication: Journal
Meetings/Conventions: - periodic workshop

Association for Genito Urinary Medicine
AGUM

c/o Dr. I.H. Ahmed-Jusuf, Hon.Sec.
Department of Genito-Urinary Medicine, Nottingham City Hospital NHS Trust, Hucknall Rd., Nottingham, NG5 1PD, England, UK
Tel: 44 115 9627746
Fax: 44 115 9627684
Email: imtyazahmed@hotmail.com
Website: http://www.agum.org.uk/
Founded: 1992
Contact: Dr. I.H. Ahmed-Jusuf, Hon.Sec.
Description: Represents and promotes the medical specialty for genitourinary medicine; developed a set of guidelines for commissioners on genitourinary medicine service specifications and the management of sexually transmitted infections.

Association for Genito-Urinary Medicine

Dept. of Genito-Urinary Medicine, Nottingham City Hospital, Hucknall Rd., Nottingham, CH2 1UL, England, UK
Tel: 44 1244 363091
Fax: 44 1244 636095
Website: http://www.agum.org.uk
Founded: 1992

Association for Geographic Information
AGI

Block C, 4th Fl., Morelands, 5-23 Old St., London, EC1V 9HL, England, UK
Tel: 44 20 72535211
Fax: 44 20 72514505
Email: info@agi.org.uk
Website: http://www.agi.org.uk
Founded: 1988
Members: 1200
Staff: 4
Contact: Mark Linehan, Dir.
Description: Vendors and users of geographic information and geographic information systems (GIS). To spread the benefits of geographic information throughout the community and to help all users and vendors of geographic information and GIS.
Library Subject: geographic

Library Type: not open to the public
Publication: Book
Publication title: AGI Source Book for GIS. Advertisements.
Second publication: Newsletter
Publication title: Geographic Information
Meetings/Conventions: - annual conference - Exhibits. London UK

Association for Glycogen Storage Disease

1 Cridlands, Lydiard St. Lawrence, Taunton, TA4 3RZ, England, UK
Tel: 44 161 9807303
Fax: 44 161 2263813
Email: info@agsd.org.uk
Website: http://www.agsd.org.uk
Members: 150
Contact: Mrs. Ann Phillips, Pres.
Description: Provides contacts and support for all persons with Glycogen Storage Disease. Encourages the provision of Specialist Centres for the diagnosis, monitoring and treatment of GSD affected persons, both children and adults. Provides a focus for scientific, educational and charitable activities concerning GSD. Encourages the formation and interaction of GSD families and professionals around the world.
Library Subject: rare metabolic disorders
Library Type: reference

Association for Group and Individual Psychotherapy

1 Fairbridge Rd., London, N19 3EW, England, UK
Tel: 44 207 2727013

Association for Industrial Archaeology
AIA

c/o Leicester University
School of Archaelogical Studies, University of Leicester, Leicester, LE1 7RH, England, UK
Tel: 44 116 2525337
Fax: 44 116 2525005
Email: aia@le.ac.uk
Website: http://www.industrial-archaeology.org.uk
Founded: 1973
Members: 1000
Staff: 1
Contact: Simon Thomas
Fee: £23
Membership Type: individual
Fee: £45
Membership Type: institution
Description: Individuals and institutions in 7 countries interested in the archaeology of industry. Stresses the importance of the study and preservation of historic industrial sites. Represents the interests of local industrial archaeological societies. Sponsors specialized conferences, discussions, annual training weekends, and workshops.
Publication: Newsletter
Publication title: AIA Bulletin. Advertisements.
Publication title: Conference Guide
Meetings/Conventions: - annual conference

Association for Information Management

Temple Ave., 3-7 Temple Chambers, London, EC4Y OHP, England, UK
Tel: 44 207 5838900
Fax: 44 207 5838401
Email: irc@aslib.com

Website: http://www.aslib.co.uk
Founded: 1924
Members: 2250
Staff: 30
Contact: Roger Bowes, Chief Exec.
Description: Information users and providers in industry, commerce, research, government, education, and the professions in 70 countries. Operates information service. Conducts seminars; offers training courses; provides recruiting and job placement assistance.
Library Type: reference
Publication: Bulletin
Publication title: ASLIB Proceedings
Second publication: Bulletin
Publication title: Current Awareness Abstracts
Meetings/Conventions: - periodic conference - Exhibits.

Association for International Promotion of Gums
AIPG

Chancery House, Chancery Ln., London, WC2A 1SF, England, UK
Contact: Omer El Mubarak
Description: Manufacturers of gums and related products; marketers and promoters of gums. Promotes increased demand for gums and gum products. Facilitates communication and cooperation among members; sponsors promotional campaigns.

Association for Language Learning

150 Railway Terrace, Rugby, CV21 3HN, England, UK
Tel: 44 1788 546443
Fax: 44 1788 544149
Email: info@all-languages.org.uk
Website: http://www.all-languages.org.uk
Founded: 1990
Members: 5000
Staff: 5
Contact: Sheila James, Proj.Asst.
Fee: £42
Membership Type: full
Fee: £30
Membership Type: reduced
Description: Language teachers and lecturers, advisers, teacher trainers, inspectors in all sectors of education from primary to higher, adult education and training. Aims to support language teachers, lecturers and trainers and to promote languages in the education systems of the UK. It offers members advice, publications and in-service training courses.
Publication: Journal
Publication title: Deutsch Lehren und Lernen. Advertisements.
Second publication: Journal
Publication title: Francophonie. Advertisements.
Meetings/Conventions: Language World Conference - annual conference - Exhibits.

Association for Learning Languages en Famille
ALLEF

c/o Sue Percival
2 Greenfield Rd., Middleton on the Wolds, Driffield, YO25 9UL, England, UK
Tel: 44 1377 217452
Fax: 44 1377 217945
Email: philp@allef.org
Website: http://www.allef.org.uk

Description: Exchange program for British and French children, ages 9 to 11. Promotes total culture immersion to achieve English/French bilingualism.

Association for Learning Technology

c/o Oxford Brookes University
Gipsy Ln. Campus, Oxford, OX3 0BP, England, UK
Tel: 44 1865 484125
Fax: 44 1865 484165
Email: alt@brookes.ac.uk
Website: http://www.alt.ac.uk
Founded: 1993
Members: 700
Staff: 4
Contact: Rhonda Riachi, Dir.
Fee: £40
Membership Type: individual
Description: Learning technology practitioners in tertiary education, including researchers, publishers, manufacturers, service providers, librarians and policy makers. Promotes good practice in the use and development of learning technologies in tertiary education; facilitates interchange between practitioners, researchers and policymakers in education and industry; represents the membership in areas of policy (such as infrastructure provision and resource allocation).
Library Subject: learning technology
Library Type: reference
Publication: Journal
Publication title: ALT-J. Advertisements.
Second publication: Newsletter
Publication title: ALT-N. Advertisements.
Meetings/Conventions: - annual conference - Exhibits. Sheffield UK

Association for Literary and Linguistic Computing
ALLC

c/o Antonio Zampolli, Pres.
Faculty of Computer Studies and Mathematics, University of the West of England, Cold Harbour Ln., Bristol, BS16 1QY, England, UK
Tel: 44 117 9656261
Fax: 44 117 9763860
Email: pisa@ilc.pi.cnt.it
Website: http://www.allc.org
Founded: 1973
Members: 360
Contact: Lisa Lena Opas-Hannimien, Sec.
Description: Individuals who are graduates in languages and/or computing (450); universities that process languages by computer and companies that provide language processing services or market-related products and equipment (350). Seeks to further literary and linguistic research by computer and to provide a means of communication for all those concerned with such research.
Library Type: reference
Publication title: Literary and Linguistic Computing
Publication title: Proceedings of Conference
Meetings/Conventions: - annual conference - Exhibits.

Association for Medical Physics Technology
AMPT

30 Burnham Ave., Ickenham, , England, UK
Founded: 1952

Association for Palliative Medicine of Great Britain and Ireland

11 Westwood Rd., Southampton, SO17 1DL, England, UK
Tel: 44 23 80672888
Fax: 44 23 80672888
Email: apmsecretariat@claranet.co.uk
Website: http://www.palliative-medicine.org
Founded: 1985
Members: 760
Staff: 1
Contact: John Wiles, Sec.
Fee: £80
Membership Type: full
Fee: £40
Membership Type: full with reduced subscription
Description: Aims to promote the advancement and development of palliative medicine and is recognized as representing physicians at all grades who work in palliative medicine and those with an interest in the specialty.

Association for Payment Clearing Services
APACS

Mercury House, Triton Court, 14 Finsbury Sq., London, EC2A 1LQ, England, UK
Tel: 44 20 77116200
Fax: 44 20 72565527
Email: corpcomms@apacs.org.uk
Website: http://www.apacs.org.uk
Founded: 1985
Members: 31
Staff: 130
Contact: Chris Pearson, Chief Exec.
Description: Major banks and building societies. Oversees money transmission in the UK; provides the focus for payments industry co-operative activity to combat plastic card fraud; spokesman for payments industry.
Publication: Annual Report
Publication title: Review

Association for Petroleum and Explosives Administration

PO Box 106, Saffron Walden, CB11 3XT, England, UK
Tel: 44 1799 502929
Fax: 44 1799 502929
Email: admin@apea.org.uk
Website: http://www.apea.org.uk
Founded: 1957
Members: 1200
Contact: A. Berry, Sec.
Fee: £25
Description: Petroleum officers, trading standards officers, government officers, equipment suppliers, installation/service contractors, equipment operators environment agency consultants, and users and oil company engineers. Aims to advance scientific, technical and legal knowledge; to facilitate information exchange; to promote uniformity; to focus attention of legislative requirements, within the petroleum and explosives industry.
Publication: Bulletin
Publication title: The Bulletin. Advertisements.
Meetings/Conventions: - annual conference - Exhibits.

Association for Post Natal Illness
APNI

145 Dawes Rd., Fulham, London, SW6 7EB, England, UK
Tel: 44 20 73860868
Email: info@apni.org
Website: http://www.apni.org/
Founded: 1979
Description: Provides support to mothers suffering from post-natal illness; strives to promote public awareness of post-natal illness; encourages research into post-natal illness.
Publication: Brochures
Second publication: Newsletter

Association for Professionals in Services for Adolescents

1 Arun House, River Way, Uckfield, TN22 1SL, England, UK
Tel: 44 1825760886
Fax: 44 1825768864
Email: contact@bhm.co.uk
Founded: 1969
Members: 500
Contact: Mrs. Celilia Ingram, Admin
Fee: £30
Membership Type: full
Description: Aims to promote the study, understanding and care of adolescents, generate new thinking about adolescent care, both residential and community-based and provide a forum for discussion and exchange of ideas and views.

Association for Project Management

150 West Wycombe Rd., High Wycombe, HP12 3AE, England, UK
Tel: 44 1494 440090
Fax: 44 1494 528937
Email: info@apm.org.uk
Website: http://www.apm.org.uk
Founded: 1972
Members: 13000
Staff: 11
Contact:
Fee: £35
Membership Type: student
Fee: £85
Membership Type: associate
Description: Project managers. Aims to be the national authority on project management, to further professionalism and to achieve recognized standards and certification for project managers.
Library Subject: project management
Library Type: not open to the public
Publication: Journal
Publication title: International Journal of Project Management
Publication title: Project. Advertisements.

Association for Public Service Excellence

Washbrook House, 2nd Fl., Lancastrian Office Centre, 32 Talbot Rd., Old Trafford, Manchester, M32 0FP, England, UK
Tel: 44 161 7721810
Fax: 44 161 7721811
Email: enquiries@apse.org.uk
Website: http://www.apse.org.uk
Founded: 1980
Members: 240
Staff: 12
Contact: Paul O'Brien, Dir.

Description: Local authorities and other organisations subscribing to aims and objectives. Advises local authorities on best practice in delivery of public services. It provides a wide range of services for its members which includes comprehensive briefings and publications on latest developments. It also offers advice and research facilities.
Library Type: not open to the public
Publication: Newsletter
Publication title: Direct News. Advertisements.
Second publication: Annual Report
Meetings/Conventions: - annual conference - Exhibits. Belfast UK

Association for Quality in Healthcare

Regents Park House, Regent St., Leeds, LS2 7QJ, England, UK
Tel: 44 113 2237296
Fax: 44 113 2237298
Email: aqh@virgin.net
Founded: 1986
Members: 600
Staff: 4
Contact: Kirstin Tucker
Fee: £55
Membership Type: individual
Fee: £180
Membership Type: group
Description: Anyone interested in promoting measurable and continuous improvement in the quality of healthcare for the benefit of the public. Dedicated solely to all aspects of the subject of measuring and improving the quality of healthcare services.
Library Subject: healthcare quality
Library Type: open to the public
Publication: Journal
Publication title: Journal for the Association for Quality Healthcare. Advertisements.
Second publication: Newsletter
Publication title: Quality Times. Advertisements.
Meetings/Conventions: - annual conference - Exhibits.

Association for Radiation Research
ARR

c/o Gray Laboratory
PO Box 100, Mount Vernon Hospital, Rickmansworth Rd., Northwood, HA6 2JR, England, UK
Tel: 44 1923 828611
Fax: 44 1923 835210
Email: everett@gci.ac.uk
Website: http://www.gci.ac.uk/usr/arr/home.html
Founded: 1958
Members: 350
Contact: Dr. Steven Everett, Hon.Sec.
Description: Scientific, medical, and technical professionals interested in ionizing radiation in 16 countries. Works to increase and disseminate knowledge pertaining to ionizing radiation in the fields of biology, chemistry, and physics. Stimulates research; grants bursaries to students wishing to attend ARR conference.
Library Type: reference
Publication: Membership Directory
Publication title: Membership Newsletter
Meetings/Conventions: - biennial

Association for Recurrent Education
ARE

36 Collegiate Crescent, Sheffield, England, UK
Founded: 1975

Association for Religious Education
ARE

17 Clover Close, Cumnor Hill, OX2 9JH, England, UK
Tel: 44 18676 3030
Founded: 1968

Association for Research in the Voluntary and Community Sector
ARVAC

2d, Aberdeen Studios, 22-24 Highbury Grove, London, N5 2EA, England, UK
Tel: 44 20 77042315
Fax: 44 20 77042315
Email: arvac@arvac.freeserve.co.uk
Website: http://www.charity.org/arvac/
Founded: 1978

Association for Research into Restricted Growth
ARRG

5 Teak Walk, Witham, CM8 2SX, England, UK
Founded: 1970

Association for Residential Care
ARC

ARC House, Marsden, Chesterfield, S40 1JY, England, UK
Tel: 44 1246 555043
Fax: 44 1246 555045
Email: contact.us@arcuk.org.uk
Website: http://www.arcuk.org.uk
Founded: 1976
Members: 300
Staff: 23
Contact: James Churchill, Chief Exec.
Description: Organizations providing care facilities for the learning disabled. Seeks to ensure quality care for people with learning disabilities. Encourages diversity and high standards in day care and residential programs. Offers training programs for working with people with learning disabilities.
Publication: Newsletter
Publication title: Despatch
Publication title: Stamp
Meetings/Conventions: - annual conference - Exhibits.

Association for Road Traffic Safety and Management
ARTSM

Epic House, Office 8, 128 Fulwell Rd., Teddington, TW11 0RQ, England, UK
Tel: 44 208 9776952
Fax: 44 208 9778339
Email: enquiries@artsm.org.uk
Website: http://www.artsm.org.uk
Founded: 1933
Members: 41

Staff: 3
Contact: Stan Wilson, Dir.
Description: Road sign manufacturers in the United Kingdom. Conducts educational programs.
Formerly: Association for Road Traffic Sign Makers
Publication title: List of Traffic Sign Makers and Products
Second publication: Newsletter
Publication title: Newsletter
Meetings/Conventions: - annual general assembly

Association for Sandwich Education and Training
ASET

3 Westbrook Ct., Sharrow Vale Rd., Sheffield, S11 8YZ, England, UK
Tel: 44 114 2212902
Fax: 44 114 2212903
Email: aset@aset.demon.co.uk
Founded: 1982
Members: 50
Staff: 1
Contact: Mrs. Debbie Smith, Admin.
Fee: £40
Membership Type: individual
Fee: £120
Membership Type: corporate
Description: Employers and universities. To encourage and promote the concept of sandwich education.

Association for Science Education

College Ln., Hatfield, AL10 9AA, England, UK
Tel: 44 1707 283000
Fax: 44 1707 266532
Email: davidmoore@ase.org.uk
Website: http://www.ase.org.uk
Founded: 1902
Members: 22052
Staff: 14
Contact: Dr. David S. Moore
Description: Teachers of science in the primary, secondary and tertiary sectors of education. There are some industrial members and members from abroad. Covers the teaching of science in schools and colleges at all levels - the aim being to help teachers in their work and provide a forum for communication between teachers.
Publication title: ASE Primary Science
Publication title: Education in Science

Association for Shared Parenting

PO Box 2000, Dudley, DY1 1YZ, England, UK
Tel: 44 178 9750891
Fax: 44 178 9751081
Email: myspringcott@netscape.net
Website: http://www.sharedparenting.org.uk/
Founded: 1993
Members: 60
Staff: 6
Contact: Jim Rowan, Sec.
Fee: £20
Description: Promotes children's right to the nurture of both parents after separation or divorce. Operates a Contact Centre, with facilities available on Saturdays for children to enjoy contact with their non-residential parent.
Meetings/Conventions: - semimonthly meeting

Association for Specialist Fire Protection

99 West St., Farnham, GU9 7EN, England, UK
Tel: 44 1252 739142
Fax: 44 1252 739140
Email: info@associationhouse.org.uk
Website: http://www.asfp.org.uk
Founded: 1975
Members: 57
Staff: 4
Contact: John G. Fairley, Sec.
Description: Manufacturers, Contractors, Distributors, Regulatory, Certification, Consultant bodies in specialist fire protection for construction industry. Represents the majority of UK structural fire protection companies with associate members representing regulatory certification, testing and consulting bodies.
Publication: Manual
Publication title: Fire Protection for Structural Steel in Building

Association for Spina Bifida and Hydrocephalus ASBAH

ASBAH House, 42 Park Rd., Peterborough, PE1 2UQ, England, UK
Tel: 44 1733 555988
Fax: 44 1733 555985
Email: postmaster@asbah.org
Website: http://www.asbah.org
Founded: 1966
Staff: 100
Contact: Gill Winfield, Information Officer
Description: Provides help and information to individuals/families with spina bifida and/or hydrocephalus in England, Wales and Northern Ireland; trained advisers visit families; team of specialist advisers in continence, education, mobility etc. Organises study days for professionals and families. Produces factsheets and magazines.
Library Type: not open to the public
Publication title: LINK

Association for Standards and Practices in Electronic Trade

10 Maltravers St., London, WC2R 3BX, England, UK
Tel: 44 20 76559000
Fax: 44 20 76812290
Email: info@e-centre.org.uk
Website: http://www.e-centre.org.uk
Founded: 1976
Members: 15500
Staff: 42
Description: Promotes EAN UCC business data standards (product identification and bar coding) and electronic business.
Library Subject: electronic commerce
Library Type: open to the public
Publication: Magazine
Publication title: ECQ. Advertisements.
Meetings/Conventions: - periodic conference

Association for Studies in the Conservation of Historic Buildings

Institute of Archaeology, 31-34 Gordon Sq., London, WC1H OPY, England, UK
Tel: 44 207 9733326
Fax: 44 207 9733090
Website: http://www.buildingconservation.com/directory/ad030.htm
Founded: 1972
Members: 500

Contact: Margaret Davies, Hon.Sec.
Description: Professionals engaged in the conservation of historic buildings. Membership by invitation only. Provides a forum for the dissemination of knowledge generated by the members in the course of their work on historic buildings.
Publication: Newsletter
Second publication: Proceedings

Association for Teaching Psychology

c/o British Psychological Society
48 Princess Rd., E, Leicester, LE1 7DR, England, UK
Tel: 44 116 2549568
Website: http://www.theatp.org
Members: 1000
Contact:
Fee: £15
Description: Teachers of psychology in Secondary Schools, Further Education Colleges and Colleges of Higher Education. Supports teachers of psychology at pre-degree level. Provides help and advice. Organizes an annual updating conference for members and distributes resources produced by teachers for teachers.
Publication: Journal
Publication title: Psychology Teaching Journal

Association for the Conservation of Energy

Westgate House, Prebend St., London, N1 8PT, England, UK
Tel: 44 207 3598000
Fax: 44 207 3590863
Email: info@ukace.org
Website: http://www.ukace.org
Founded: 1981
Members: 14
Staff: 9
Contact: Andrew Warren, Dir.
Description: UK-based companies which have substantial interests in energy conservation equipment and services. Current members include controls manufacturers, energy service companies, manufacturers and distributors of insulation materials. Acts as a lobby group which carries out policy research on energy conservation. Its remit is to promote wider awareness of the need for and the benefits of using energy more efficiently in buildings, and to help establish a sensible and consistent national energy efficiency policy and programme.
Publication: Newsletter
Publication title: Fifth Fuel

Association for the History of the Northern Seas AHNS

c/o Adrian Jarvis
Centre for Port and Maritime History, GWR Bldg., Meyerside Maritime Museum, Liverpool, L3 1DG, England, UK
Fax: 44 151 4784098
Email: adrian.jarvis@nmgmporthist.demon.co.uk
Website: http://www.swgc.mun.ca/ahns/
Founded: 1974
Members: 100
Contact: Adrian Jarvis, VP
Description: Provides a forum for the free exchange among scholars of North Atlantic and Baltic maritime history in Europe. Fosters research.

Association for the Reduction of Aircraft Noise

11 First St., London, SW3 2LB, England, UK
Tel: 44 171 5841848
Founded: 1964
Contact: S. Eustace, Sec.
Description: Those residing under the east-wide glide path to Heathrow. Formerly the Association for the Re-Siting of London's Airport. The abatement of noise from aeroplanes chiefly but not only those going to or coming from Heathrow; keen to see a new airport on Foulness Island.
Publication: Pamphlets

Association for the Scientific Study of Anomalous Phenomena

Saint Aldhelm, 20 Paul St., Frome, BA1 1DX, England, UK
Tel: 44 1373 451777
Fax: 44 1373 452888
Email: hugh@assap.org
Website: http://www.assap.org
Founded: 1981
Members: 350
Contact: Dr. Hugh Pincott
Description: Open to anyone interested in the aims of the organisation. Research into all paranormal, anomalous and related phenomena.
Library Subject: paranormal, anomalous
Library Type: not open to the public
Publication: Journal
Publication title: Anomaly
Second publication: Newsletter
Publication title: ASSAP News
Meetings/Conventions: Investigators' Training Days

Association for the Study and Preservation of Roman Mosaics
ASPROM

38 Oaklea, Ash Vale, Aldershot, GU12 5HP, England, UK
Tel: 44 1252 316018
Email: honsec@asprom.org
Website: http://www.asprom.org
Founded: 1978
Members: 200
Contact: S.R. Cosh, Sec.
Fee: £12.5
Membership Type: ordinary
Description: Academics, mosaic specialists, conservators, students, institutional members, lay people interested in Romano-British mosaic art. Aims to advance education amongst the general public by fostering the study and preservation of Roman mosaics and related material.
Publication: Newsletter
Publication title: ASPROM Newsletter
Second publication: Journal
Publication title: Mosaic
Meetings/Conventions: - semiannual symposium

Association for the Study of Animal Behaviour
ASAB, 82A High St., Sawston, Cambridge, CB2 4HJ, England, UK

Tel: 44 1223 830665
Fax: 44 1223 839804
Email: asab@grantais.demon.co.uk

Website: http://www.asab.org
Founded: 1936
Members: 1900
Contact: Jenny Levitt
Description: Professionals and students in 20 countries engaged in the scientific study of animal behavior. Promotes the study of animal behavior.
Publication: Journal
Publication title: Animal Behaviour
Second publication: Newsletter
Publication title: Newsletter
Meetings/Conventions: - periodic meeting

Association for the Study of German Politics
ASGP

European Industrial Relations Review, 18-20 Highbury Pl., London, N5 1QP, England, UK
Tel: 44 207 3546790
Email: beatrice.harper@butterworths.com
Website: http://www.bham.ac.uk/ASGP
Founded: 1974
Members: 200
Contact: Beatrice Harper, Sec.
Fee: £14
Membership Type: postgraduate student
Description: Scholars with an interest in the politics and societies of German-speaking countries. Promotes study and teaching in the field of German studies in the widest possible context. Facilitates exchange of information among members; maintains liaison network of graduate students engaged in German studies.
Publication: Journal
Publication title: German Politics
Second publication: Newsletter
Meetings/Conventions: - annual conference

Association for the Study of Modern and Contemporary France
ASMCF

c/o Katharine Kaiserman
Dept. of French, Trinity and All Saints College, Brownberry Ln., Horsforth, LS18 5HD, England, UK
Founded: 1979

Association for the Study of Obesity
ASO

20 Brook Meadow Close, Woodford Green, IG8 9NR, England, UK
Tel: 44 20 85032042
Fax: 44 20 85032042
Email: chris@aso.ndo.co.uk
Website: http://www.aso.org.uk
Founded: 1967
Members: 420
Staff: 1
Contact: Mrs. C. Hawkins, Admin.Off.
Description: Scientists, researchers, dieticians, health education workers, and students in England. Promotes information exchange between members; promotes research into the causes, prevention and treatment of obesity; seeks to encourage action to reduce the prevalence of obesity and to enhance treatment.

Association for the Study of Travel in Egypt and the Near East

South Rd., Durham, DH1 3TG, England, UK
Email: p.g.starkey@atsdurham.ac.uk
Founded: 1997

Association for the Teaching of the Social Sciences

PO Box 6079, Leicester, LE2 4DW, England, UK
Tel: 44 207 6126589
Email: txl@le.ac.uk
Website: http://www.atss.org.uk
Founded: 1965
Members: 1100
Contact: Tony Lawson, Pres.
Description: Individual teachers of social science in schools and in further and higher education; educational institutions concerned with the delivery of the social science curriculum; those involved in teacher training, publishing and academic research relating. to the social sciences. Supports the class teacher and promotes the social sciences in schools and colleges. It organises national and regional conferences for teachers and students annually and works closely with other social science organisations. It has assisted in the development of good classroom practice and been influential in syllabus and resource development.
Publication: Bulletin
Publication title: Events Bulletin
Publication title: Social Science Teacher

Association for Therapeutic Philosophy
ATP

33 Marlborough Rd., Swindon, SN3 1PH, England, UK
Tel: 44 1793 538586
Fax: 44 1793 538586
Email: psycountrg@aol.com
Website: http://members.aol.com/psycountrg
Founded: 1983
Members: 450
Staff: 6
Contact: Dr. Andreas Sofroniou
Description: Seeks to develop therapeutic philosophy concepts and treatment type.
Library Type: reference
Formerly: Association of Psychological Counselling and Training

Association for Veterinary Clinical Pharmacology and Therapeutics

Pfizer Central Research, Sandwich, CT13 9NJ, England, UK
Tel: 44 1304 646160
Fax: 44 1304 651251
Email: avcpt@avcpt.org
Website: http://www.avcpt.org

Association for Vocational Colleges International

c/o W. Bonney Rust
178 Highfield Way, Chorley Wood, WD3 7PJ, England, UK
Tel: 44 1923 776590
Fax: 44 1923 350930
Email: william.rust@ukonline.co.uk
Founded: 1987
Staff: 2
Contact: Dr. W. Bonney Rust, Dir. of Res.

Description: Vocational education and training colleges. Promotes vocational education programs. Monitors developments in vocational education in other countries.
Library Subject: vocational education and training
Library Type: by appointment only
Meetings/Conventions: - semiannual conference

Association for Women in Science and Engineering
AWISE

59 Portland Pl., London, W1N 3AJ, England, UK
Tel: 44 1264 860010
Fax: 44 1264 860042
Email: awise@wellcome.ac.uk
Website: http://www.awise.org/
Contact: Jean Richards, Adm.
Description: Women in the sciences and engineering are members; men supporting the aims of the association are associate members. Promotes increased participation by women and girls in the sciences, engineering, and technological fields. Acts as a clearinghouse on women in the sciences; represents the collective interests of women in the sciences.

Association of Accounting Technicians
AAT

154 Clerkenwell Rd., London, EC1R 5AD, England, UK
Tel: 44 20 78378600
Fax: 44 20 7410906
Email: aat@aat.org.uk
Website: http://www.aat.co.uk
Founded: 1981
Members: 29000
Staff: 90
Contact: Ms. Jane Scott Paul, Exec.
Fee: £56
Membership Type: regular member
Fee: £61
Membership Type: fellow member
Description: Skilled support staff working in accounting and finance across all employment sectors industry and commerce, accountancy practice, and the public sector. Accredited by the UK National Council for Vocational Qualifications (QCA) to provide NVQs (National Vocational Qualifications) in accounting. Provides NVQs in Accounting at levels 2 (Foundation Stage), 3 (Intermediate Stage) and 4 (Technician Stage).
Library Subject: accountancy and related areas
Library Type: not open to the public
Formerly: Formed by Merger of, Accounting Technicians in Finance and Accounting
Publication: Magazine
Publication title: Accounting Technician. Advertisements.
Publication title: Annual Report and Accounts
Meetings/Conventions: Presidential Conference - quarterly conference - Exhibits.

Association of Advisers in Design and Technical Studies
AADTS

33 Foxhill Crescent, Camberley, GU15 1PR, England, UK
Tel: 44 1276 23846

Association of American Correspondents in London
AACL
c/o Time Magazine
Brettenham House, Lancaster Pl., London, WC2E 7TL, England, UK
Tel: 44 20 73221084
Fax: 44 20 73221230
Founded: 1919
Members: 43
Contact: Elizabeth Lea, Exec. Officer
Fee: £90
Description: News organizations, such as newspapers, magazines, and television-radio networks, with headquarters in the U.S. and permanent full-time editorial bureaus and staffs or representatives in London, England. Serves the professional interests of members, promote social cooperation among them, and maintain ethical standards of their profession.
Publication: Directory
Meetings/Conventions: - annual meeting

Association of Anaesthetists of Great Britain and Ireland
21 Portland Pl., London, W1B 1PY, England, UK
Tel: 44 207 6318801
Fax: 44 207 6314352
Email: members@aagbi.org
Website: http://www.aagbi.org
Founded: 1932
Members: 7000
Staff: 9
Contact: Lelsey Murphy, Gen.Mgr.
Description: Ordinary Members, Trainee Members and Associate Members. Aims to promote education and research in anaesthesia and to bring together as many members as is possible at the three annual meetings to disseminate relevant information both at home and abroad. Fosters research in anaesthesia and allied subjects; encourages collaborative ventures involving members; represents members' interests.
Publication: Journal
Publication title: Anaesthesia
Meetings/Conventions: Annual Scientific Meeting - Exhibits.

Association of Applied Biologists
AAB
Horticulture Research International, Wellesbourne, Warwick, CV35 9EF, England, UK
Tel: 44 1789 472020
Fax: 44 1789 470234
Email: carol.aab@hri.ac.uk
Website: http://www.aab.org.uk
Founded: 1904
Members: 1050
Staff: 5
Contact: Mrs. Carol Millman, Exec.Off.
Fee: £76.5
Membership Type: Ordinary
Fee: £44
Membership Type: Student
Description: Research scientists in private and state applied biology institutes and universities in 60 countries interested in furthering development in the field of applied biology.
Publication: Journal
Publication title: Annals of Applied Biology. Advertisements.
Publication title: Aspects of Applied Biology
Meetings/Conventions: - periodic meeting - Exhibits.

Association of Art and Antique Dealers
LAPADA
535 Kings Rd., Chelsea, London, SW10 0SZ, England, UK
Tel: 44 207 8233511
Fax: 44 207 8233522
Email: lapada@lapada.co.uk
Website: http://www.lapada.co.uk
Founded: 1974
Members: 750
Staff: 5
Contact: John Newgas, Chief Exec.
Fee: £812
Description: Dealers in art, antiques and works of art, all VAT registered. Representation of members politically, provision of professional services for members including specialist insurance cover, legal advice and promotion. Free advice service for the public when seeking information on where specialist dealers can be found. Members subject to code of practice governing trading standards with the public and the trade. Conciliation service offered in any case of dispute between members and the public.
Formerly: London & Provincial Antique Dealers Association
Publication: Magazine
Publication title: LAPADA Views. Advertisements.

Association of Art Historians
AAH
Cowcross Court, 70 Cowcross St., London, EC1M 6EJ, England, UK
Tel: 44 207 4903211
Fax: 44 207 4903277
Email: admin@aah.org.uk
Website: http://www.aah.org.uk
Founded: 1974
Members: 1100
Staff: 3
Contact: Claire Davies
Description: Formed to promote the study of art history and ensure wider public recognition of the field. It is the only U.K. organization for professional art historians and researchers including all those who are working in education, museums and galleries. For independent art historians and for all who are studying the subject.
Publication: Magazine
Publication title: The Art Book. Advertisements.
Second publication: Journal
Publication title: Art History
Meetings/Conventions: Articulations - annual conference London UK

Association of Art Institutions
AAI
24 Widemarsh St., Hereford, HR4 9EP, England, UK
Tel: 44 1432 66653
Founded: 1942

Association of Authorised Public Accountants
AAPA
10 Lincoln's Inn Fields, London, WC2A 3BP, England, UK
Tel: 44 207 3965913
Website: http://www.aapa.co.uk
Founded: 1978
Members: 608

Staff: 8
Contact: Anthony Booth, Exec.Sec.
Description: Auditors in 20 countries. Seeks to improve and advance the professional and ethical status and the technical standards of statutory authorized auditors. Represents members' interests. Maintains close liaison with government ministry responsible for trade and industry. Conducts research and educational programs. Compiles statistics.
Library Type: reference
Publication: Newsletter
Publication title: In Practice
Second publication: Papers
Meetings/Conventions: Continuing Professional Development - periodic conference

Association of Authors' Agents
AAA

Haymarkethouse, 28/29 Haymarket, London, SW1Y 4SP, England, UK
Tel: 44 207 3966600
Fax: 44 207 3960110
Email: jlloyd@curtisbrown.co.uk
Website: http://agentsassoc.co.uk
Founded: 1974
Members: 75
Contact: Jonathan Lloyd, Pres.
Fee: £50
Description: British literary agencies and individual agents. Promotes discussion and cooperation between members; encourages high standards of professional conduct; represents members' interests before other professional organizations.
Meetings/Conventions: - quarterly meeting

Association of Average Adjusters

c/o The Baltic Exchange
38 St. Mary Axe, London, EC3A 8BH, England, UK
Tel: 44 207 6235501
Fax: 44 207 3691623
Email: aaa@balticexchange.com
Website: http://www.average-adjusters.com
Founded: 1869
Members: 560
Staff: 2
Contact: Mr. D. Taylor, Hon.Sec.
Description: To prepare marine insurance claims and general average statements on an independent and impartial basis.
Meetings/Conventions: - annual

Association of Blind and Partially Sighted Teachers and Students

BM Box 6727, London, WC1N 3XX, England, UK
Founded: 1970
Members: 350
Contact: Lindsay Armstrong, Sec.
Fee: £12
Membership Type: employed
Description: Visually impaired teachers, trainers, students, people looking for work or who have an interest in education. Provides mutual support through the exchange of ideas and experience of education and employment, promotes the needs and strengths of visually impaired teachers and students, and campaigns on relevant issues.
Publication: Bulletin
Publication title: ABAPSTS Bulletin
Meetings/Conventions: - annual conference

Association of Blind Piano Tuners
ABPT

31 Wyre Cres., Lynwood, Darwen, BB3 0JG, England, UK
Tel: 44 1254 776148
Fax: 44 1254 773158
Email: info@uk-piano.org
Website: http://www.uk-piano.org
Founded: 1954
Members: 110
Contact: Barrie Heaton, Sec.
Fee: £50
Membership Type: full
Description: Serves the professional and particular needs of blind and partially sighted piano tuners.
Publication: Newsletter. Advertisements.

Association of Breastfeeding Mothers
ABM

PO Box 207, Bridgwater, TA6 7YT, England, UK
Tel: 44 207 78131481
Email: abm@clara.net
Website: http://home.clara.net/abm/
Founded: 1980
Members: 400
Contact: Helen Shepperd, Chair
Fee: £10
Membership Type: ordinary
Fee: £5
Membership Type: unwaged
Description: Mothers who have breastfed their babies and are trained as counselors. Believes that breast milk is the perfect food for infants because it promotes the health of infant and mother and is inexpensive, convenient, and allows a mother time to relax with her baby. Offers support and encouragement to mothers who wish to breastfeed. Operates support groups; fosters exchange of information and friendly contact among nursing mothers; provides solutions to non-medical problems of breast-feeding. Offers services such as 24-hour counseling; arranges for speakers to tour schools and clinics.
Library Type: reference
Publication: Magazine
Publication title: ABM Magazine. Advertisements.
Meetings/Conventions: ABM Study Day - annual convention - Exhibits.

Association of British Certification Bodies

c/o SIRA
South Hill, Chislehurst, BR7 5EH, England, UK
Tel: 44 20 82951128
Fax: 44 20 84678091
Email: tinman@abcb.demon.co.uk
Website: http://www.abcb.demon.co.uk
Founded: 1984
Members: 30
Staff: 2
Contact: T.M.V. Inman, Chief Exec.
Fee: £1500
Membership Type: full or associate
Description: Independent accredited certification bodies who undertake impartial certification of quality and environmental management systems, products, and personnel. The objectives of the Association are to provide a forum for the discussion and formulation of policy on matters of common concern; to represent the collective interests of members and, where consistent with such interests, those

of individual members, in appropriate quarters; and to adopt, if thought fit, a code of professional practice in certification matters.
Publication: Newsletter
Publication title: ABCB News
Second publication: Membership Directory

Association of British Chambers of Commerce

9 Tufton St., London, SW1P 3QB, England, UK
Tel: 44 171 5652000
Fax: 44 171 7992202
Contact: Ronald Taylor, Dir.Gen.
Description: Chambers of commerce and related business and trade organizations. Promotes increased international trade and tourism. Gathers and disseminates information; conducts promotional activities; represents members' interests.

Association of British Choral Directors

c/o Rachel Greaves, Gen.Sec.
15 Granville Way, Sherborne, DT9 4AS, England, UK
Tel: 44 1935 389482
Fax: 44 870 1284085
Email: rachel.greaves@abcd.org.uk
Website: http://www.abcd.org.uk
Founded: 1986
Members: 650
Staff: 1
Contact: Rachel Greaves, Gen.Sec.
Fee: £17
Membership Type: student
Fee: £32
Membership Type: individual
Description: Amateur and professional choral conductors and choral trainers, individual, Music publishers and music services organisations, corporate members. Aims to promote, improve and maintain the education, training and development of choral directors with a view to improving standards in all sectors of choral activity within the United Kingdom by organising regional and national training courses. ABCD is a registered charity.
Publication: Journal
Publication title: Mastersinger. Advertisements.
Meetings/Conventions: - annual convention - Exhibits.

Association of British Climatologists
ABC

School of Environmental Science, University College Northampton, Park Campus, Northampton, NN2 7AL, England, UK
Tel: 44 1604 735500
Fax: 44 1604 720636
Email: chris.holt@northampton.ac.uk
Website: http://www.royal-met-soc.org.uk/
Founded: 1971
Members: 125
Contact: Dr. C. Holt, Sec.
Fee: £6
Membership Type: inside United Kingdom
Fee: £7
Membership Type: outside United Kingdom
Description: Specialist group of the Royal Meteorological Society. Individuals working in climatology and related fields. Encourages research and information exchange in all aspects of climatology. Areas of concern include climatology of the British Isles, atmospheric pollution, and climatic change and variability. Sponsors annual

competition for the best undergraduate dissertation on a climatological subject.
Publication: Newsletter
Publication title: Climate News
Publication title: Directory of British Climatologists
Meetings/Conventions: meeting - Exhibits.

Association of British Correspondence Colleges
ABCC

PO Box 17926, London, SW19 3WB, England, UK
Tel: 44 208 5449559
Fax: 44 208 5407657
Email: info@homestudy.org.uk
Website: http://www.homestudy.org.uk
Founded: 1955
Members: 21
Staff: 1
Contact: Heather Owen, Sec.
Description: Correspondence colleges in the United Kingdom. Aims to ensure tuition and service standards, safeguard students' interests, and enhance the prestige of correspondence education. Provides information on correspondence education offered by member schools.
Publication title: Broadsheet
Meetings/Conventions: - annual meeting

Association of British Dispensing Opticians
ABDO

College of Education, Godmersham Park Mansion, Godmersham, Kent, CT4 7DT, England, UK
Tel: 44 122 7738829
Fax: 44 122 7733900
Email: general@abdo.org.uk
Website: http://www.abdo.org.uk
Founded: 1986
Members: 7350
Staff: 30
Contact: Sir Anthony Garrett, Sec.Gen.
Fee: £195
Membership Type: fellowship
Description: By professional examination. Aims to support, protect and advance the character, status and interests of dispensing opticians; to promote the better education and training of dispensing opticians.
Publication: Journal
Publication title: Dispensing Optics. Advertisements.
Meetings/Conventions: - annual conference - Exhibits.

Association of British Drivers
ABD

PO Box 2228, Kenley, CR8 5ZT, England, UK
Tel: 44 7000 781544
Fax: 44 870 1362370
Email: enquiries@abd.org.uk
Website: http://www.abd.org.uk/
Founded: 1992
Description: Automobile drivers in the United Kingdom. Seeks to provide an active, responsible voice to lobby for the beleaguered British car driver. Promotes recognition of the fact that roads are an essential part of the UK transport system. Conducts lobbying activities to secure: improved standards of drivers' training; more realistic speed limits; improvements in road and vehicle safety; and the abolition of toll roads and Gatso cameras.
Publication: Newsletter
Publication title: On the Road

Association of British Fire Trades

Neville House, 4th Fl., 55 Eden St., Kingston Upon Thames, KT1 1BW, England, UK
Tel: 44 20 85498839
Fax: 44 20 85471564
Email: info@abft.org.uk
Founded: 1979
Staff: 13
Contact: B. Gately
Description: Represents members' interests.

Association of British Healthcare Industries

195-203 Waterloo Rd., St. George's House, London, SE1 8WD, England, UK
Tel: 44 20 77873060
Fax: 44 20 77873061
Email: enquiries@abhi.org.uk
Website: http://www.abhi.org.uk
Founded: 1968
Members: 15
Contact: Gordon Aylward, Dir.Gen.
Description: Sterilizing equipment manufacturers in England. Provides a forum for the exchange of information on market conditions. Prepares industry standards in conjunction with other organizations.
Formerly: Association of Sterilizer and Disinfector Equipment Manufacturers Association
Publication: Membership Directory
Meetings/Conventions: Council Meeting - quarterly

Association of British Insurers
ABI

51 Gresham St., London, EC2V 7HQ, England, UK
Tel: 44 207 6003333
Fax: 44 207 6968999
Email: info@abi.org.uk
Website: http://www.abi.org.uk
Founded: 1985
Members: 420
Staff: 150
Contact: Msry Francis, Dir.Gen.
Description: Trade association representing 420 insurance companies in the United Kingdom. Promotes and protects the interests of members. Monitors government actions which may affect members. Cooperates with other associations having similar objectives. Conducts educational programs.
Library Subject: Statistics and financial services.
Library Type: not open to the public
Publication title: Annual Report
Publication title: Insurance Facts, Figures and Trends

Association of British Investigators
ABI

48 Queens Rd., Basingstoke, RG21 7RE, England, UK
Tel: 44 1256 816390
Fax: 44 1256 479547
Email: abi@globelnet.co.uk
Website: http://www.assoc-britishinvestigators.org.uk
Founded: 1913
Members: 400
Staff: 1
Contact: George Rivers, Gen.Sec.

Fee: £127
Membership Type: individual
Fee: £150
Membership Type: outside UK
Description: Private investigators in Britain with more than 2 years of experience. Promotes adherence to ABI code of ethics. Conducts seminars.
Formerly: Formed by Merger of, British Detectives Association
Publication: Directory
Publication title: Directory of Registered Members
Publication title: The New Investigator. Advertisements.
Meetings/Conventions: - annual convention

Association of British Jazz Musicians

c/o Jazz Services Ltd.
132 Southwark St., 1st Fl., London, SE1 0SW, England, UK
Tel: 44 20 79289089
Fax: 44 20 74016870
Email: jazz@dial.pipex.com
Contact: Chris Hodgkins
Description: Jazz musicians.

Association of British Mining Equipment Companies
ABMEC

Unit 1, Thornes Office Park, Monckton Rd., Wakefield, WF2 7AN, England, UK
Tel: 44 1924 360200
Fax: 44 1924 380553
Email: deakin@abmec.org.uk
Website: http://www.abmec.org.uk
Founded: 1978
Members: 40
Staff: 6
Contact: Mr. Beverley Webster, Pres.
Description: Companies in the United Kingdom involved in the manufacture of mining equipment. Promotes the sale of British-made mining equipment in Great Britain and abroad. Disseminates information on mining equipment to customers.

Association of British Neurologists

Ormond House, 4th Fl., 27 Boswell St., London, WC1N 3JZ, England, UK
Tel: 44 207 4054060
Fax: 44 207 4054070
Email: abn@abnoffice.demon.co.uk
Website: http://www.theabn.org
Founded: 1933
Members: 1000
Staff: 2
Contact: Prof. David Miller
Fee: £100
Description: Trainee and consultant in the neurological sciences. To promote the advancement of the neurological sciences, including the practice of neurology in the British Isles.
Publication: Newsletter
Meetings/Conventions: - semiannual meeting

Association of British Oil Industries

30 Great Guildford St., 4th Fl., London, SE1 0HS, England, UK
Tel: 44 207 9289199
Fax: 44 207 9286599
Email: aboi@maritimeindustries.org

Website: http://www.maritimeindustries.org
Founded: 1974
Members: 124
Staff: 12
Contact: Ken Gibbons, Dir.
Description: Companies engaged in the provision of equipment, materials and services to the offshore oil and gas, petroleum, petrochemical and process industries. The exploitation of the sea and the sea-bed.
Formerly: Association of British Offshore Industries
Publication: Membership Directory

Association of British Orchestras

8 Gerrard St., London, W1D 5PJ, England, UK
Tel: 44 20 72870333
Fax: 44 20 72870444
Email: info@abo.org.uk
Website: http://www.abo.org.uk
Founded: 1947
Members: 150
Staff: 4
Contact: Russell Jones, Dir.
Description: All the major symphony orchestras in the UK, chamber orchestras, small and specialist orchestras and ensembles.
Represents the collective interests of professional orchestras working to provide an environment in which they can flourish, artistically and financially.
Publication: Newsletter
Second publication: Yearbook
Meetings/Conventions: - annual conference

Association of British Pewter Craftsmen

Light Trade House, 3 Melbourne Ave., Sheffield, S10 2QJ, England, UK
Tel: 44 114 2663084
Fax: 44 114 2670910
Contact: Cathy Steele
Description: Supported by the Worshipful Company of Pewterers, which has for 600 years striven to promote pewter products. Aims to promote highest standards in pewter manufacture, undertake research into pewter alloy and advance training and professional competence in industry.

Association of British Professional Conference Organisers
ABPCO

6th Fl., Charles House, 148-149 Great Charles St., Birmingham, B3 3HT, England, UK
Tel: 44 121 2121400
Fax: 44 121 2123131
Email: tony@abpco.org
Website: http://www.abpco.org
Founded: 1981
Members: 45
Staff: 1
Contact: Tony Rogers, Exec.Dir.
Fee: £295
Membership Type: & VAT individual, full
Fee: £95
Membership Type: & VAT individual, associate
Description: Professional conference organisers who are proprietors/directors of their own conference organising companies or the conference directors/managers of professional associations. Members

meet for discussion on matters of common interest to professional conference organisers; to train personnel directly or indirectly involved with the conference industry; and to be available for consultation with the management of conference venues and other suppliers to the conference industry.
Meetings/Conventions: Think Tank Weekend - annual Paphos Cyprus

Association of British Sailmakers
ABS

2 Orchard Rd., Locks Heath, Southampton, SO31 6PR, England, UK
Tel: 44 1489 601517
Fax: 44 1489 601518
Email: thesecretariat@theabs.org
Website: http://www.a-b-s.8m.com
Founded: 1960
Members: 51
Staff: 2
Contact: Mrs. C.A. Olden, Exec. Admin.
Fee: £150
Membership Type: corporate
Description: Bona fide sailmakers in full time business of manufacturing sails and related items who operate from proper business premises and have been in business, prior to application, for a minimum period of five years. Sail repairers may join. as associate members. Founded to exchange technical expertise and information relevant to the manufacture of sails and related items. Also to further training for future generations and to bring the suppliers to the trade into closer liaison with the sailmakers in order to improve materials, etc. which are constantly changing to meet the higher-tech boats and racing challenges. Provides a corporate or collective communications network among classes and international ruling bodies.
Library Subject: marine catalogues, technical journals, export and business publications and reference books, yachting periodicals, national and international racing and class rules, club data, and boat specifications
Library Type: not open to the public
Publication: Journal
Publication title: Main Sheet. Advertisements.
Meetings/Conventions: - annual meeting Southampton, Hants UK

Association of British Science Writers

23 Savile Row, London, W1S 2EZ, England, UK
Tel: 44 207 4391205
Fax: 44 207 9733051
Email: absw@absw.org.uk
Website: http://www.absw.org.uk
Founded: 1926
Members: 500
Staff: 1
Contact: Barbara Drillsma
Description: Members are medical and scientific journalists. To increase the standard of science journalism in the UK, written and broadcast media.
Publication: Report
Publication title: Science Reporter

Association of British Steriliser Manufacturers

Walworth Rd., Andover, SP10 5AA, England, UK
Tel: 44 1264 62111
Fax: 44 1264 56452
Description: Steriliser manufacturers.

Association of British Theatre Technicians
47 Bermondsey St., London, SE1 3XT, England, UK
Tel: 44 207 4033778
Fax: 44 207 3786170
Email: office@abtt.org.uk
Website: http://www.abtt.org.uk
Founded: 1963
Members: 2000
Staff: 3
Contact: Jenny Straker, Admin.
Description: Anyone concerned with the technical side of theatre. Covering theatre planning and all technical aspects of theatrical presentation.
Library Type: not open to the public
Publication title: Codes of Practice for the Theatre Industry
Second publication: Magazine
Publication title: Update

Association of British Theological and Philosophical Libraries
ABTAPL
Dr. William's Library, 14 Gordon Sq., London, WC1H 0AR, England, UK
Founded: 1954
Members: 200
Contact: Andrew Lacey, Hon.Sec.
Fee: £12
Membership Type: UK
Fee: £25
Membership Type: outside UK
Description: Librarians, philosophers, and theologians; philosophy and theology libraries; divinity schools. Promotes discussion and exchange of information among librarians working with theological, philosophical, and related materials. Organizes visits to a variety of libraries to encourage familiarity with modern library practice. Provides members with an informal network for consultation, advice, and support.
Publication title: A Guide to the Theological Libraries of Great Britain and Ireland
Publication title: ABTAPL Union List of Periodicals
Meetings/Conventions: - annual

Association of British Travel Agents
ABTA
68-71 Newman St., London, W1T 3AH, England, UK
Tel: 44 207 6372444
Fax: 44 207 6370713
Email: information@abta.co.uk
Website: http://www.abta.com
Founded: 1950
Members: 7531
Staff: 75
Contact: Ian Reynolds, Ch.Exec.
Fee: £515
Membership Type: travel agent, tour operator
Description: Travel agents and tour operators working to create a favorable business environment and ensure high standards of service and accountability to the traveling public. Mandates the use of precise financial parameters for travel and tour services. Offers complaint conciliation and arbitration services. Liaises and negotiates with trade and governmental regulatory bodies.
Library Subject: travel
Library Type: not open to the public
Publication: Newsletter
Publication title: ABTA Magazine. Advertisements.
Publication title: ABTA Members Handbook. Advertisements.
Meetings/Conventions: Overseas Convention - annual convention - Exhibits.

Association of British Veterinary Acupuncture
c/o Bishopton Veterinary Group
Moor Farm, Morchard Bishop, Crediton, EX17 6RX, England, UK
Tel: 44 1363 877636
Fax: 44 1363 877471
Email: robert.vere@farmline.com
Founded: 1987
Members: 70
Contact: Wendy Vere, Sec.
Description: Ordinary members are veterinary surgeons. To further advancement of veterinary acupuncture in the UK.
Publication: Newsletter
Publication title: Newsletter

Association of British Wild Animal Keepers
c/o Chester Zoo, Caughall Rd., Upton, Chester, CH2 1LH, England, UK
Email: r.barnett@chesterzoo.co.uk
Website: http://www.abwak.co.uk
Founded: 1974
Members: 400
Contact: Dr. Miranda Stevenson, Pres.
Fee: £16
Membership Type: professional
Fee: £14
Membership Type: associate
Description: Wild animal keepers in England. Promotes communication and exchange among members.

Association of Broadcasting Doctors
PO Box 15, Sindalthorpe House, Ely, CB7 4SG, England, UK
Tel: 44 1353 688456
Fax: 44 1353 688451
Email: jackiepetts@aol.com
Website: http://www.broadcasting-doctor.org
Founded: 1988
Members: 859
Staff: 3
Contact: Peter Petts
Description: Practicing clinicians - consultants and GPs - who also broadcast in local, regional and national radio and television. Provides training and support for members with the aim of improving the standards of medical broadcasting; acts as a clearing house for broadcasting organizations seeking medical contributors; updates members on medical advances which might attract public attention; acts on behalf of members in their relationships with broadcasting organizations.
Publication: Newsletter
Publication title: Broadcasting Doctor
Meetings/Conventions: Radio Training Session - quarterly workshop

Association of Brokers and Yacht Agents
ABYA
Wheel House, Petersfield Rd., Whitehill, Bordon, GU35 9BU, England, UK
Tel: 44 845 0900162
Fax: 44 845 0900163

Email: info@ybdsa.co.uk
Website: http://www.ybdsa.co.uk
Founded: 1912
Members: 103
Staff: 4
Contact: Mrs. J. Gentry, Ch.Exec.
Fee: £250
Membership Type: professional
Description: Professional association for small craft brokers and agents. Promotes membership of the association, use of standard documentation and maintenance of knowledge through training. Members operate to an industry code of practice.
Library Subject: surveying, brokerage
Library Type: reference
Publication title: Codes of Practice
Second publication: Membership Directory
Publication title: Handbook
Meetings/Conventions: - annual conference

Association of Building Component Manufacturers
ABCM

Clark House, 3 Brassey Dr., Aylesford, ME20 7QL, England, UK
Tel: 44 1622 715577
Fax: 44 870 0543915
Email: abcm@building-components.org
Website: http://www.building-components.org
Founded: 1965
Members: 26
Staff: 2
Contact: Ing. Peter B. Caplin, Dir.
Fee: £1200
Membership Type: manufacturers
Fee: £400
Membership Type: non manufacturers
Description: Organisations and individuals involved in manufacturing and/or interest in building materials and components. Conducts events to provide commercial and technical intelligence for members. Operates an information service about members and their products and services. Represents interests of members to government authorities and international organizations, and standards bodies.
Publication title: List of Members
Second publication: Brochure
Meetings/Conventions: - annual conference - Exhibits.

Association of Building Engineers

Lutyens House, Billing Brook Rd., Northampton, NN3 8NW, England, UK
Tel: 44 1604 404121
Fax: 44 1604 784220
Email: building.engineers@abe.org.uk
Website: http://www.abe.org.uk
Founded: 1925
Members: 5500
Staff: 10
Contact: D.R. Gibson, Ch.Exec.
Fee: £30
Membership Type: student
Library Subject: building engineering
Library Type: not open to the public
Formerly: Incorporated Association of Architects and Surveyors
Publication: Journal
Publication title: Building Engineer. Advertisements.
Meetings/Conventions: - annual conference - Exhibits.

Association of Building Hardware Manufacturers
ABHM

42 Heath St., Tamworth, B79 7JH, England, UK
Tel: 44 1827 52337
Fax: 44 1827 310827
Email: info@abhm.org.uk
Website: http://www.abhm.org.uk
Founded: 1898
Members: 36
Contact: David Whitworth, Chm.
Description: Builders, hardware manufacturers of architectural ironmongery, and sliding door components. Provides advice on research, technical, and marketing matters. Represents members' interests before government departments and private organizations concerned with builders hardwares issues. Commissions and supports many research projects aimed at advancing test methods to prove compliance with, as well as improving, existing performance standards.
Meetings/Conventions: - periodic meeting

Association of Burial Authorities
ABA

155 Upper St., London, N1 1RA, England, UK
Tel: 44 20 72882522
Fax: 44 20 72882533
Email: aba@swa-pr.co.uk
Founded: 1993
Members: 300
Contact: Sam Weller, Chm.
Fee: £250
Membership Type: city, borough, district, unitary council
Fee: £275
Membership Type: proprietary company
Description: Cemetery managers, friends of cemeteries, the Church of England, other churches with burial grounds, memorial masons, landscape architects, service and product suppliers. Coordinates the activities of burial grounds. Seeks to raise awareness and appreciation of cemeteries and churchyards as places of commemoration, heritage, and amenity value. Monitors legislation and regulations affecting burial grounds nationally and within the European Union. Offers a design and planning service for burial ground development. Conducts safety audit surveys and guidance for inspection regimes. Implements proactive public relations campaign.
Library Subject: management of burial grounds, funerals, memorials
Library Type: reference
Publication: Newsletter
Publication title: ABA Information Newsletter. Advertisements.
Meetings/Conventions: - periodic conference - Exhibits.

Association of Business Executives

William House, 14 Worple Rd., Wimbledon, SW19 4DD, England, UK
Tel: 44 20 88791973
Fax: 44 20 89467153
Email: info@abeuk.com
Website: http://www.abeuk.com
Founded: 1973
Members: 22000
Staff: 20
Contact: Christine Gill, Exec.Sec.
Description: Student membership sitting examinations.
Publication title: Business Executive

Association of Business Recovery Professionals
R3

Halton House, 20-23 Holborn, London, EC1N 2JE, England, UK
Tel: 44 207 8316563
Fax: 44 207 4057047
Email: mstancombe@r3.org.uk
Website: http://www.r3.org.uk
Founded: 1990
Members: 3000
Staff: 12
Contact: Mike Stancombe, COO
Fee: £190
Membership Type: subscriber
Description: Business recovery professionals including licensed insolvency practitioners, turnaround managers, students and subscribers. Represents members' interests. Aims to improve standards in the professional performance, theory and practice of insolvency administration; recruit and train skilled insolvency practitioners; and facilitate exchanges of views.
Library Subject: insolvency, turnaround
Library Type: reference
Formerly: Society of Practioners of Insolvency
Publication: Journal
Publication title: Recovery. Advertisements.
Meetings/Conventions: - annual conference

Association of Business Schools
ABS

344/354 Gray's Inn Rd., London, WC1X 8BP, England, UK
Tel: 44 207 8371899
Fax: 44 207 8378189
Email: abs@the-abs.org.uk
Founded: 1992
Members: 100
Staff: 4
Contact: Prof. Stephen Watson, Chair
Description: Educational institutions offering business and management education programs in the United Kingdom. Seeks to advance the study, teaching, and practice of business, management, and related disciplines. Facilitates exchange of information among members; sponsors research and educational programs
Meetings/Conventions: - periodic conference

Association of Button Merchants
ABM

78-80 Borough High St., London, SE1 1XG, England, UK
Tel: 44 207 9289944
Founded: 1928
Members: 30
Description: Button merchants in the United Kingdom. Promotes and represents members' interests.

Association of C and C Users

9 Sparrow Close, Bradwell, NR31 8SG, England, UK
Tel: 44 798 9938758
Email: chair@accu.org
Website: http://accu.org
Founded: 1987
Members: 1000
Contact: Allan Griffiths, Chm.
Fee: £15
Membership Type: student

Fee: £25
Membership Type: individual
Description: Developers, trainers and implementers of C, C, and Java products (compilers, libraries) and programmers using these products. Aims to support good programming practice in C, C, and Java. It also represents the views of C, C, and Java users at national and international level on committees concerned with standards for these languages.
Publication title: CVU. Advertisements.
Publication title: Overload. Advertisements.
Meetings/Conventions: - semiannual conference - Exhibits.

Association of Camphill Communities
ACC

Gawain House, 56 Welham Rd., Norton, Malton, YO17 9DP, England, UK
Tel: 44 1653 694197
Fax: 44 1653 600001
Email: info@camphill.org.uk
Website: http://www.camphill.org.uk
Founded: 1940
Members: 75000
Contact: Andy Paton
Description: Individuals interested in the development of children and adults with learning disabilities. Promotes full cultural, social, and economic integration of all people, particularly those with learning disabilities or other vulnerabilities. Maintains egalitarian communities in which individuals can improve their self-esteem and social and economic skills in a supportive environment. Conducts educational programs; provides support and services to people with learning disabilities and other vulnerable individuals.
Publication: Brochure
Publication title: An Introduction to Camphill Communities
Second publication: Newsletter

Association of Canoe Trades

85 Edgedale Rd., Sheffield, S72 BR, England, UK
Tel: 44 7050 645272
Fax: 44 7974 359468
Email: act@bmif.co.uk
Founded: 1970
Members: 20
Staff: 1
Contact: Dean Maragh, Chief Exec.
Description: Manufacturers and retailers of canoes and all associated equipment. Promotes good standards and safety in canoeing.
Formerly: British Association of Canoe Trades
Meetings/Conventions: - quarterly meeting

Association of Car Rental Industry Systems Standards
ACRISS

PO Box 2807, Eastbourne, BN20, England, UK
Tel: 44 1323 472369
Fax: 44 1323 472369
Email: acrisseeig@aol.com
Description: Aims to facilitate the use of computerized reservations systems for car rental services in Europe; formulates and recommends standards for use in the design, installation, and use of computerized systems used by travel agents, car rental reservations, including systems using ticketing and invoicing facilities.

Association of Cardiothoracic Anaesthetists

21 Portland Pl., London, W1B 1PY, England, UK
Tel: 44 20 76311650
Fax: 44 20 7614352
Email: info@aagbi.org
Website: http://www.acta.org.uk
Founded: 1984
Members: 326
Contact: Dr. Fiona Gibson, Sec.
Fee: £25
Membership Type: full
Description: Consultants who are currently engaged in the practice of cardiothoracic anaesthesia. To further the development of the art and science of caring for patients undergoing heart and chest surgery.
Publication: Articles

Association of Careers Advisers in Colleges Offering Higher Education

c/o Colin Rigg
4 Blake Close, Lawford Dale, Manningtree, CO11 2JR, England, UK
Tel: 44 1206 392161
Fax: 44 1206 392161
Email: colin.rigg@tinyworld.co.uk
Founded: 1977
Members: 50
Staff: 1
Contact: Colin Rigg, Sec.
Description: Career advisers in small advisory units in colleges of higher education. Acts as a network of contact for careers advisers and provides information and training.
Publication: Newsletter. Advertisements.
Meetings/Conventions: - annual conference

Association of Cereal Food Manufacturers - England
ACFM

6 Catherine St., London, WC2B 5JJ, England, UK
Tel: 44 207 8362460
Fax: 44 207 8360580
Founded: 1955
Members: 7
Staff: 1
Contact: David de Menezes
Description: British manufacturers of ready-to-eat breakfast cereals. Works to protect and promote members' interests.
Meetings/Conventions: - quarterly executive committee meeting London UK

Association of Certified Book-Keepers

Akhtar House, 2, Shepherd's Bush Rd., London, W6 7PS, England, UK
Tel: 44 207 2723925
Fax: 44 207 2815723
Founded: 1981
Members: 1350
Staff: 2
Contact: Ms. Angela Clerke
Description: Fellows: FACB; Associate: AACB; Certified Book-Keeper. Professional society mainly for book-keepers and accountants, financial directors, financial controllers and commercial consultants.
Publication title: Certified Book-Keeper

Association of Charitable Foundations

2 Plough Yard, Shoreditch High St., London, EC2A 3LP, England, UK
Tel: 44 20 74228600
Fax: 44 20 74228606
Email: anja@acf.org.uk
Website: http://www.acf.org.uk/foundations
Founded: 1989
Members: 300
Staff: 5
Contact: Nigel Siederer, Ch.Exec.
Fee: £2700
Description: Grant-making trusts and foundations. Supports the work of grant-making charitable trusts and foundations in the U.K.
Library Subject: charitable grant-making
Library Type: not open to the public
Publication: Magazine
Publication title: Trust & Foundation News
Meetings/Conventions: Better Giving - biennial conference

Association of Charity Officers
ACO

Unicorn House, Station Close, Potters Bar, EN6 3JW, England, UK
Tel: 44 1707 651777
Fax: 44 1707 660477
Email: info@aco.uk.net
Website: http://www.aco.uk.net
Founded: 1946
Members: 225
Staff: 5
Contact: Valerie J. Barrow, Dir.
Fee: £280
Membership Type: registered UK charities
Description: Executive officers or secretaries of benevolent funds and registered exempt charities giving non-contributory relief to individuals in need. Seeks to: encourage and improve liaison and cooperation between charities; represent charities on legislative issues; discover those in need and solicit help from members' funds. Informs and advises individuals, governmental and statutory bodies, and voluntary organizations; sponsors discussion groups; disseminates information and provides training classes.
Library Type: not open to the public
Publication title: Individuals in Need: Guidelines for Grantmakers
Second publication: Directory
Meetings/Conventions: - annual convention London UK

Association of Chartered Certified Accountants
ACCA

29 Lincoln's Inn Fields, London, WC2A 3EE, England, UK
Tel: 44 20 73967000
Fax: 44 20 73967070
Email: info@accaglobal.com
Website: http://www.accaglobal.com
Founded: 1904
Members: 87000
Staff: 400
Contact: Anthea Rose, Ch.Exec.
Fee: £5
Description: Accountants (87,000) and accounting students (186,000). Professional and examining organization for those in the accounting field.
Library Subject: accounting, business
Library Type: reference
Publication: Journal
Publication title: Accounting and Business. Advertisements.
Publication title: List of Members

Association of Cheese Processors
19 Cornwall Terrace, London, NW1 4QP, England, UK
Tel: 44 171 4867244
Fax: 44 171 4874734
Founded: 1976
Members: 5
Staff: 1
Contact: P.F. Dawson
Description: Manufacturers and suppliers of processed cheese. Concerned with the manufacture and distribution of processed cheese.

Association of Chief Archivists in Local Government
E Sussex Record Office, The Maltings, Castle Precincts, Lewes, BN7 1YT, England, UK
Tel: 44 1273 482349
Fax: 44 1273 482341
Founded: 1980
Members: 86
Contact: Elizabeth Hughes
Fee: £20
Description: Heads of local government archive services in England and Wales. Speaks on behalf of those archives services on issues of urgency or importance; provides a forum for the exchange of views and a means of collecting and circulating information; produces policy statements and guidelines.
Meetings/Conventions: - biennial seminar

Association of Chief Estate Surveyors and Property Managers in Local Government
23 Athol Rd., Bramhall, Stockport, SK7 1BR, England, UK
Tel: 44 161 4399589
Fax: 44 161 4407383
Email: fostertim@msn.com
Website: http://www.aces.org.uk
Founded: 1986
Members: 352
Contact: T. Foster
Description: Serving and former local government valuers and estate surveyors. To co-ordinate the application of the principles and practice of valuation and estate management in the interest of Local Authorities. To provide a forum for discussion and dissemination of information. To encourage an exchange of views with other Associations and bodies dealing with matters of valuation and estate management.
Publication: Magazine
Publication title: The Terrier. Advertisements.
Meetings/Conventions: - 3/year meeting

Association of Chief Executives of Voluntary Organisations
83 Victoria St., London, SW1H 0HW, England, UK
Tel: 44 845 3458481
Fax: 44 845 3458482
Email: info@acevo.org.uk
Website: http://www.acevo.org.uk
Founded: 1987
Members: 1200
Staff: 9
Contact: Stephen Bubb, Chief Exec.
Fee: £160
Membership Type: full

Description: Chief executives of voluntary organizations. Aims to improve standards within the voluntary sector by improving the professionalism and effectiveness of chief executives of voluntary organizations.
Publication title: Appraising the Chief Executive: A Guide
Publication title: Planning for Partnership: The Relationship Between Chair and Chief Executive
Meetings/Conventions: - semiannual conference

Association of Chief Police Officers of England, Wales and Northern Ireland
25 Victoria St., 7th Fl., London, SW1H 0EX, England, UK
Tel: 44 20 72273434
Fax: 44 20 72273400
Email: info@ccpo.police.uk
Website: http://www.acpo.police.uk
Founded: 1948
Members: 280
Staff: 20
Description: Chief police officers in England, Wales and Northern Ireland.
Publication: Journal
Publication title: Policing Today. Advertisements.

Association of Child Psychotherapists
ACP
120 West Heath Rd., London, NW3 7TU, England, UK
Tel: 44 208 4581609
Email: acp@dial.pipex.com
Founded: 1949
Members: 597
Staff: 1
Contact: Mrs. Judy Shuttleworth, Ch.
Description: Safeguards the interests of psychotherapists and fosters the exchange of information on the treatments of psychological disturbances of behavior, thinking, and feeling. Provides a forum for discussion.
Publication: Journal
Publication title: Journal of Child Psychotherapy. Advertisements.
Second publication: Bulletin
Meetings/Conventions: - annual conference - Exhibits.

Association of Christian Teachers
ACT
94A London Rd., St. Albans, AL1 1NX, England, UK
Tel: 44 1727 840298
Fax: 44 1727 848966
Email: act@christian-teachers.org
Website: http://www.christian-teachers.org
Founded: 1971
Members: 2450
Staff: 3
Contact: Rupert Kaye, Ch.Exec.
Fee: £15
Description: Works to serve, support and unite Christian teachers in England and around the world.
Publication: Journal
Publication title: Act Now. Advertisements.

Association of Circulation Executives
17 James Lee Square, Eufield, EN3 6GR, England, UK
Email: nicki.walsh@newsint.co.uk

Founded: 1951
Members: 415
Staff: 1
Contact: Lindsey J. White, Sec.
Description: Circulation executives of publishing companies selling and distributing paid for, national, regional or international newspapers, magazines or periodicals. Creates a unique forum within the publishing industry for contacting those senior executives concerned with the circulation, marketing and distribution of newspapers (national and regional) and magazines and periodicals.
Publication: Newsletter
Publication title: Sisyphus. Advertisements.

Association of Circus Proprietors of Great Britain

PO Box 131, Blackburn, BB1 9DT, England, UK
Tel: 44 1254 672222
Fax: 44 1254 681723
Founded: 1932
Members: 15
Contact: M. Clay, Sec.
Description: Proprietors of touring or resident circuses within Great Britain who are prepared to abide by the Association's standards relating to both training and animal welfare. An employers association concerned with the continuous improvement of standards of animal welfare and the general control of the British circus industry.
Publication: Brochure
Publication title: Say Yes to the Highest Standards of Animal Welfare

Association of Clinical Biochemists

130-132 Tooley St., London, SE1 2TU, England, UK
Tel: 44 207 4038001
Fax: 44 207 4038006
Email: admin@acb.org.uk
Website: http://www.acb.org.uk
Founded: 1953
Members: 2321
Staff: 3
Contact: Dr. G.V. Groom, Sr.Adm.
Fee: £120
Description: University graduates in science or medicine occupied in the practice of clinical biochemistry, mainly in district, general and teaching hospitals. Associate members from related disciplines, such as cytogenetics, microbiology and immunology. To promote the advancement of clinical biochemistry. Government health departments and many consult it other organisations. Has an education committee, primarily concerned with postgraduate education, a scientific committee and a publications committee.
Publication: Handbook
Publication title: ACB Members Handbook. Advertisements.
Second publication: Newsletter
Publication title: ACB News. Advertisements.
Meetings/Conventions: - annual conference - Exhibits. Manchester UK

Association of Clinical Pathologists
ACP

189 Dyke Rd., Hove, BN3 1TL, England, UK
Tel: 44 1273 775700
Fax: 44 1273 773303
Website: http://www.pathologists.org.uk
Founded: 1927
Members: 2000

Contact: Alison Martin, Admin.
Description: Promotes the study and practice of clinical pathology. Offers courses.
Publication: Newsletter
Publication title: ACP News. Advertisements.
Second publication: Directory
Publication title: ACP Yearbook. Advertisements.
Meetings/Conventions: - annual convention

Association of College Registrars and Administrators

North Kingston Centre, Richomd Rd. Annex, 55 Richmond Rd., Kingston Upon Thames, KT2 5PE, England, UK
Tel: 44 208 5414940
Fax: 44 208 5476745
Founded: 1958
Members: 1000
Contact: Mrs. J. Gould
Description: Administrators in institutions of education. To promote efficiency and higher professional standards while maintaining quality in the administration and management of education establishments by bringing forward proposals for and examples of best practice; to promote the professional development of its members and their work and to contribute to the public debate on all matters relating to education and the provision of a comprehensive training programme relevant to education administrators.
Publication: Newsletter

Association of Colleges

Centre Point, 5th Fl., 103 New Oxford St., London, WC1A 1RG, England, UK
Tel: 44 20 78274600
Fax: 44 20 78274650
Email: enquiries@aoc.co.uk
Website: http://www.aoc.co.uk
Founded: 1992
Members: 400
Staff: 4
Contact: David Gibson
Description: FE colleges throughout the UK.

Association of Coloprociology of Great Britain and Ireland

c/o The Royal College of Surgeons of England
35-43 Lincoln's Inn Fields, London, WC2A 3PE, England, UK
Tel: 44 20 79730307
Fax: 44 20 74309235
Email: acpgbi@asgbi.org.uk
Website: http://www.acpgbi.org.uk
Founded: 1990
Members: 1300
Staff: 2
Contact: Mr. Paul Finan, Hon.Sec.
Fee: £195
Membership Type: ordinary surgical
Fee: £45
Membership Type: associate
Description: A multidisciplinary association to promote standards and training in coloproctology.
Publication: Journal
Publication title: Colorectal Disease. Advertisements.
Second publication: Handbook
Publication title: Guidelines for the Management of Colorectal Cancer
Meetings/Conventions: - annual meeting - Exhibits. Edinburgh UK

Association of Commonwealth Archivists and Records Managers
ACARM

c/o International Record Management Trust
12 John St., London, WC1N 2EB, England, UK
Tel: 44 207 8314101
Fax: 44 207 8317404
Email: newsletter@acarm.org
Website: http://www.acarm.org
Founded: 1984
Members: 120
Contact: Jenny Leijten, Admin.
Fee: £15
Membership Type: Individual
Fee: £100
Membership Type: Institutional
Description: Individual archivists and others representing 57 archives institutions or other specialized repositories in 32 Commonwealth countries. Facilitates exchange of information and experience among archivists and records managers with a common archival heritage, and promotes better understanding of the Commonwealth through the use of records. Works to reaffirm the importance of archives in the national heritage of member countries. Encourages the dissemination of archival material among member institutions. Seeks to establish professional training programs and set high standards in an effort to further the development of archival knowledge and skill.
Formerly: Commonwealth Archivists Association
Publication: Newsletter
Publication title: ACARM Newsletter. Advertisements.
Meetings/Conventions: - quadrennial conference

Association of Commonwealth Universities
ACU

John Foster House, 36 Gordon Sq., London, WC1H 0PF, England, UK
Tel: 44 20 73806700
Fax: 44 20 73872655
Email: info@acu.ac.uk
Website: http://www.acu.ac.uk
Founded: 1913
Members: 500
Staff: 43
Contact: Prof. M. Gibbons, Sec.Gen.
Description: Voluntary association of 500 universities in 35 Commonwealth countries or regions. Promotes contact and cooperation among universities of the Commonwealth. Provides information about universities. Administers scholarship and fellowship programs (including the Commonwealth Scholarship and Fellowship Plan (CSFP)). Also publicizes vacancies in member universities and certain other institutions through its advertising and publicity services section. Policy and research unit coordinates and disseminates research on higher education.
Library Subject: higher education
Library Type: reference
Formerly: Universities Bureau of the British Empire
Publication: Magazine
Publication title: ACU Bulletin. Advertisements.
Second publication: Directory
Publication title: Commonwealth Universities Yearbook. Advertisements.
Meetings/Conventions: Conference of Executive Heads - periodic conference

Association of Community Health Councils for England and Wales
ACHCEW

Earlsmead House, 30 Drayton Park, London, N5 1PB, England, UK
Tel: 44 20 76098405
Fax: 44 207 7001152
Email: mailbox@achcew.org.uk
Website: http://www.achcew.org.uk
Founded: 1977
Members: 204
Staff: 15
Contact: Peter Walsh, Dir.
Description: Community Health Councils set up to monitor the National Health Service. Provides forum for member CHCs, provides information and advisory services to CHCs and represents the user of health services at a national level.
Library Type: by appointment only
Publication title: CHC News
Publication title: Factsheets for the Public
Meetings/Conventions: - annual general assembly - Exhibits.

Association of Community Technical Aid Centres - England
ACTAC

64 Mount Pleasant, Liverpool, L3 5SD, England, UK
Tel: 44 151 7087607
Fax: 44 151 7087606
Founded: 1983
Members: 72
Staff: 3
Contact: Lynn McCann, Admin.
Fee: £85
Membership Type: general
Description: Network of community technical aid centers in England, Northern Ireland, Scotland, and Wales. Assists community organizations and resident groups wishing to develop or improve their natural or manmade environment. Provides the technical expertise of architects, planners, surveyors, interior and graphic designers, and environmental educationalists. Works closely with related organizations. Encourages participation in design, planning, and decision-making. Conducts feasibility studies; conducts training programs; organizes conferences, and co-ordinates publications.
Library Subject: Organization projects.
Library Type: reference
Publication: Newsletter
Publication title: Contact. Advertisements.
Second publication: Directory
Publication title: Directory of Community Technical Aid
Meetings/Conventions: - annual conference - Exhibits.

Association of Community Workers

Stephenson Bldg., Elswick Rd., Newcastle upon Tyne, NE12 8QP, England, UK
Tel: 44 191 2151880
Email: lesleyleach@acw1.fsbusiness.co.uk
Website: http://www.acu.uk.com
Founded: 1968
Members: 400
Staff: 1
Contact: Lesley Leach
Description: Community workers, paid or unpaid, activists and trainers, or those who have an interest in community work. Seeks to

actively encourage good community work practice and support workers and activists.
Publication: Manual
Publication title: Community Work Skills Manual 2001
Second publication: Newsletter
Publication title: Community Work & Talking Point

Association of Company Registration Agents

20 Holywell Row, London, EC2A 4XN, England, UK
Tel: 44 207 3770381
Fax: 44 207 3776646
Email: mc@chettleburghs.co.uk
Founded: 1976
Members: 13
Contact: M.R. Chettleburgh
Description: Company registration agents. To promote and protect the interests of company registration agents in their dealings with the civil service and government over company law.

Association of Computer Professionals

204 Barnett Wood Ln., Ashtead, KT21 2DB, England, UK
Tel: 44 1372 273442
Fax: 44 1372 277778
Email: acp@btinternet.com
Founded: 1984
Members: 4000
Staff: 13
Contact: Mrs. N. Keats, Sec.Gen.
Description: Mainly student membership. To prepare candidates through examination for a successful career in computing up to Higher National Diploma Standard.
Publication: Newsletter. Advertisements.

Association of Consultant Architects
ACA

98 Hayes Rd., Bromley, BR2 9AB, England, UK
Tel: 44 208 3251402
Fax: 44 208 4669079
Email: office@acarchitects.co.uk
Website: http://www.acarchitects.co.uk
Founded: 1973
Members: 200
Staff: 2
Contact: Fiona Griffiths
Description: Architectural consultants in the U.K. Represents members' interests; disseminates information.
Publication title: ACA Form of Building Agreement
Publication title: ACA Form of Sub-Contract
Meetings/Conventions: - annual conference

Association of Consulting Actuaries
ACA

1 Wardrobe Pl., London, EC4V 5AG, England, UK
Tel: 44 20 72361889
Fax: 44 20 72481889
Email: acahelp@aca.org.uk
Website: http://www.aca.org.uk
Founded: 1951
Members: 1400
Contact: David Robertson
Fee: £110
Membership Type: individual

Description: Independent actuaries engaged in private practice. Facilitates the exchange of views and information between consulting trustees, actuaries and the organizations they represent. Advises pension scheme trustee companies, life and general insurance companies in the United Kingdom and overseas.
Publication title: Annual Report
Second publication: Membership Directory
Meetings/Conventions: - monthly meeting

Association of Consulting Engineers
ACE

Alliance House, 12 Caxton St., London, SW1H 0QL, England, UK
Tel: 44 207 2226557
Fax: 44 207 2220750
Email: consult@acenet.co.uk
Website: http://www.acenet.co.uk
Members: 650
Contact: Nicholas Bennett, Chief Exec. and Sec.
Description: National associations of independent consulting engineers. Promotes the interests of independent consulting engineers; represents electrical, civil, environmental, geotechnical, metallurgical, cultural, and other engineering fields. Standardizes forms of agreement, contracts, and guidelines for consulting engineers; acts as clearinghouse.

Association of Consulting Scientists

c/o Dr. D. Simpson
PO Box 4040, High St., Thorpe-le-soken, Clacton-on-Sea, CO16 0EL, England, UK
Tel: 44 1255 861714
Fax: 44 1255 862111
Website: http://www.consultsci.uku.co.uk/
Founded: 1958
Members: 25
Description: Firms engaged in scientific consultancy, the provision of analytical and testing services, the undertaking of contract research.
Publication: Directory

Association of Contact Lens Manufacturers
ACLM

PO Box 735, Devizes, SN10 3TQ, England, UK
Tel: 44 1380 860418
Fax: 44 1380 860121
Email: secgen@aclm.org.uk
Website: http://www.aclm.org.uk/
Founded: 1962
Contact: Simon Rodwell, Sec.Gen.
Description: Manufacturers of contact lenses. Promotes the growth and development of the domestic contact lense industry. Facilitates communication and cooperation among members; represents members before government agencies, labor, professional, medical, and industrial organizations, and the public.

Association of Control Manufacturers
TACMA

Westminster Tower, 3 Albert Embankment, London, SE1 7SL, England, UK
Tel: 44 171 7933008
Fax: 44 171 7939730
Email: pearsonv_beama@compuserve.com
Contact: Dr. H W Porter

Description: Manufacturers of automatic controls and switches. Represents the commercial and technical interests of members in respect of the domestic, commercial and industrial use of switches and automatic time and temperature controls.

Association of Convenience Stores
ACS

17 Farnborough St., Federation House, Farnborough, GU14 8AG, England, UK
Tel: 44 1252 515001
Fax: 44 1252 515002
Email: acs@acs.org.uk
Website: http://www.thelocalshop.com
Founded: 1891
Members: 25000
Staff: 9
Contact: David Rae, Ch.Exec.
Fee: £100
Membership Type: full
Fee: £1000
Membership Type: associate
Description: Is a national trade association representing the interest of over 25,000 convenience and small store operators. ACS represents members interests in matters relating to National and EU legislation and also provides a number of retail services.
Publication title: ACS Yearbook
Second publication: Newsletter
Publication title: thelocalshop.com. Advertisements.
Meetings/Conventions: - annual conference - Exhibits.

Association of Corporate Treasurers
ACT

Ocean House, 10/12 Little Trinity Lane, London, EC4V 2DJ, England, UK
Tel: 44 207 2139728
Fax: 44 207 2482591
Email: enquiries@treasurers.co.uk
Website: http://www.treasurers.org
Founded: 1979
Members: 3000
Staff: 35
Contact: David Creed, Chief Exec.
Fee: £190
Membership Type: Individual
Description: Promotes the study and practice of corporate treasury management (involving the handling of financial markets, the generation of funds for business, the management of currencies and cash flows, and a knowledge of the policies and procedures of corporate finance). Offers correspondence courses for certification; sponsors conferences, seminars, and training weekends.
Library Subject: Finance and treasury
Library Type: reference
Publication title: Corporate Finance and Treasury Management. Advertisements.
Second publication: Journal
Publication title: The Treasurer. Advertisements.
Meetings/Conventions: conference

Association of Corporate Trustees
TACT

The Glen House, 43 Surrey Rd., Westbourne, Bournemouth, BH4 9HR, England, UK
Tel: 44 1202 765559
Fax: 44 1202 761112
Founded: 1974
Members: 71
Staff: 1
Contact: R.J. Payne, Sec.
Fee: £700
Membership Type: full
Fee: £100
Membership Type: associate
Description: Trust companies, and related organizations. Established to ensure high standards of operation in corporate trustee services. Acts as a forum for the exchange of technical information. Assesses technical training programs and offers critical evaluations. Conducts educational programs.
Publication: Directory
Publication title: Directory of Members
Publication title: Tact Review
Meetings/Conventions: - annual meeting London UK

Association of Cost Engineers

Lea House, 5 Middlewich Rd., Sandbach, CW11 1XL, England, UK
Tel: 44 1270 764798
Fax: 44 1270 766180
Email: enquiries@acoste.org.uk
Website: http://www.acoste.org.uk
Founded: 1961
Members: 2140
Staff: 4
Contact: Anne Fairless, Admin.Sec.
Fee: £80
Membership Type: fellow
Fee: £70
Membership Type: regular member
Description: Membership is from the client, contracting and professional areas of industry. Covers planning, project management and cost control. Different grades: fellows, members, associates, graduates, students. Cost engineering embraces activities such as estimating, cost control, construction management, investment appraisal and risk analysis.
Library Subject: cost engineering
Library Type: not open to the public
Publication: Journal
Publication title: Cost Engineer

Association of Council Secretaries and Solicitors

Trafalgar Wharf, 150 Mountbatten Close, Ashton on Ribble, Preston, PR2 2XE, England, UK
Tel: 44 1772 739073
Fax: 44 1772 739073
Email: acsesny@cybase.co.uk
Website: http://www.acses.org.uk
Founded: 1974
Members: 515
Staff: 1
Contact: N. Yates, Exec.Dir.
Description: Chief officers or officers of comparable status and deputies wholly or substantially responsible for the management of the administrative, secretarial and legal functions of local, police and fire authorities England and Wales. Confers on all matters affecting

local government, promotes and develops professional knowledge and talent, and gives advice to any association of local authorities or any other body.
Formerly: Formed by Merger of, Society of County Secretaries
Meetings/Conventions: - annual conference

Association of County Chief Executives
ACCE

County Hall, Trowbridge, BA14 8JF, England, UK
Tel: 44 1225 713101
Fax: 44 1225 713092
Email: jeanpotter@wiltshire.gov.uk
Founded: 1974
Members: 39
Contact: Keith Robinson, Hon.Sec.
Fee: £88
Membership Type: ordinary
Description: Provides information and advice to the Association of County Councils.
Meetings/Conventions: - semiannual meeting

Association of Cycle Traders
ACT

31 A High St., Tunbridge Wells, TN1 1XN, England, UK
Tel: 44 1892 526081
Fax: 44 1892 544278
Email: enquiries@act-bicycles.com
Website: http://www.cyclesource.co.uk
Founded: 1986
Members: 1000
Staff: 3
Contact: Anne Killick, Natl.Sec.
Fee: £175
Membership Type: retailers
Description: Cycle retailers and individuals in related fields united to improve the safety standards of cycles. Negotiates with government departments, the media, and manufacturers to provide a safe environment for cyclists.
Formerly: National Association of Cycle and Motorcycle Traders
Publication: Newsletter
Publication title: The Independent
Meetings/Conventions: - annual conference - Exhibits.

Association of Dental Hospitals of the UK

Birmingham Dental Hospital, St. Chad's Queensway, Birmingham, B4 6NN, England, UK
Tel: 44 121 2368611
Fax: 44 121 2372750
Founded: 1952
Members: 32
Contact: Pauline Harrington, Hon.Sec.
Description: Open only to representatives of Dental Hospitals and Schools.

Association of Directors of European Centres for Plastics
ADECP

Rapra Technology Ltd., Shawbury, Shrewsbury, SY4 4NR, England, UK
Tel: 44 1939 250383
Fax: 44 1939 251118

Email: info@rapra.net
Founded: 1919
Members: 150
Staff: 120
Contact: Andrew Ward, Ch.Exec.
Description: Directors of plastics centers in the European Union. Promotes growth and development of the European plastics industries; seeks to insure environmentally sustainable production and use of plastics. Serves as a clearinghouse on plastics production; provides technical consulting and information services to members.
Library Subject: plastics, rubber
Library Type: reference

Association of Directors of Social Services
ADSS

Social Services Dept., 145 King St., London, W6 9XY, England, UK
Tel: 44 208 7418147
Fax: 44 208 7488054
Email: contact@cpiag.org.uk
Founded: 1971
Members: 147
Staff: 2
Contact: A.G. Williamson
Description: Directors of social service departments and agencies in England. Strives to: increase awareness of organization, policy, and social problems; establish equitable and comprehensive social services for individuals, families, and communities; assist the underprivileged, the elderly, the ill, and the disabled; improve childcare systems. Communicates with government authorities. Cooperates with professional bodies and voluntary organizations.
Publication title: ADSS News
Second publication: Directory
Publication title: Directory of Local Authority Social Services Departments

Association of Disabled Professionals
ADP

BCM ADP, London, WC1N 3XX, England, UK
Tel: 44 208 7785008
Fax: 44 208 92241420
Email: assdisprof@aol.com
Website: http://www.adp.org.uk
Founded: 1971
Members: 230
Contact: Hank Hunt, Ch.
Fee: £25
Membership Type: student, full, sustaining
Description: Professionals and students with disabilities. Offers advice and information especially on employment issues. Provides means to disabled professionals and those in managerial positions to network and offer advice and support. Maintains liaisons with government authorities.
Publication title: ADP Quarterly
Meetings/Conventions: - annual convention

Association of Domestic Management

c/o Watson Associates
C4 Kingfisher House, Kingsway TVTE, Gateshead, NE11 0QJ, England, UK
Tel: 44 1661 853097
Fax: 44 1661 853097
Email: adm@adom.demon.co.uk
Website: http://www.adom.demon.co.uk

Founded: 1965
Members: 300
Contact: Penny Harrison, Business Manager
Fee: £35
Fee: £45
Description: Managers in cleaning and support services. Supplies, maintains and encourages an efficient domestic service to support the principal business operated in any building. Provides a national code of practice to complement professional and occupational training.
Library Subject: standards for environmental cleanliness in hospitals
Library Type: reference
Publication: Proceedings
Publication title: Annual Conference Report
Second publication: Newsletter
Publication title: Excel
Meetings/Conventions: - annual conference - Exhibits.

Association of Drainage Authorities
The Mews, Royal Oak Passage, High St., Huntingdon, PE29 3EA, England, UK
Tel: 44 1480 411123
Fax: 44 1480 431107
Email: drainage@ada.org.uk
Website: http://www.ada.org.uk
Founded: 1937
Members: 300
Contact: David Noble, Ch.Exec.
Fee: £90
Membership Type: associate
Description: Flood defence and drainage authorities in England and Wales with associate membership extended to local authorities, manufacturers, suppliers and other bodies interested in flood defence and land drainage. Represents the interests of flood defence and land drainage in consultation with government departments and other national bodies and to provide an advisory service to the membership. Interests are served through Finance and Administration, Technical and Environmental and Publicity Committees.
Publication title: ADA Gazette. Advertisements.
Meetings/Conventions: - annual meeting - Exhibits.

Association of Drum Manufacturers
St. Johns House, 4 London Rd., Crowborough, TN6 2TT, England, UK
Tel: 44 1842 654414
Fax: 44 1892 654981
Email: adm@kellys.uk.co
Website: http://www.the.adm.co.uk
Founded: 1896
Members: 14
Contact: C.G. Stebbing
Description: UK manufacturers of steel, plastic and fibre drums.
Publication title: Membership and Products Guide

Association of Education Committees
15-17 Cumberland Place, Southampton, SO15 2UY, England, UK
Founded: 1978
Members: 5
Description: Promotes education of persons under the age of 25 years. Meets the lost of pensions for retired staff of the farmer associatens of education committees.
Library Subject: education
Library Type: reference

Association of Educational Psychologists
AEP
26 The Avenue, Durham, DH1 4ED, England, UK
Tel: 44 191 3849512
Fax: 44 191 3865287
Website: http://www.aep.org.uk
Founded: 1963
Members: 2600
Staff: 6
Contact: Mary Jenkin, Sec.
Fee: £159
Membership Type: full
Description: Professional association and trade union for educational psychologists in the United Kingdom.
Publication: Journal
Publication title: Educational Psychology in Practice
Meetings/Conventions: - annual meeting - Exhibits.

Association of Electoral Administrators
PO Box 201, South Eastern, Liverpool, L16 5HH, England, UK
Tel: 44 151 2818246
Fax: 44 151 2818246
Email: gma.aeaadmin@blueyonder.co.uk
Website: http://www.aea-elections.co.uk
Contact: Gina Armstrong, Natl.Admin.
Description: Electoral administrators in Scotland.

Association of Electricity Producers
17 Waterloo Pl., 1st Fl., London, SW1Y 4AR, England, UK
Tel: 44 20 79309390
Fax: 44 20 79309391
Email: enquiries@aepuk.com
Website: http://www.aepuk.com
Founded: 1987
Members: 106
Staff: 7
Contact: David Porter, Chief Exec.
Description: Companies using nearly all types of generating technology and all scales of production. A trade association for companies generating and selling electricity.
Library Type: not open to the public
Formerly: Formed by Merger of, Association of Independent Electricity Producers
Meetings/Conventions: - annual meeting

Association of English Singers and Speakers
Paddocks-Park Lane, Ashtead, KT21 1HD, England, UK
Tel: 44 1372 275430
Fax: 44 1372 275430
Email: nivnmiller@aol.com
Website: http://www.aess.org.uk
Founded: 1913
Members: 75
Contact: Niven Miller, Chm.
Fee: £18
Description: Full membership is open to any person professionally engaged in some aspect of singing and speaking; Associate membership is available for those not necessarily qualified for full membership but who support the aims of the Association and who will benefit from participation in its activities (students included). To encourage the communication of English words in speech and song with clarity, understanding and imagination.
Library Type: open to the public

Formerly: AESS
Publication title: A Century of English Song
Second publication: Annual Report
Meetings/Conventions: Master Classes

Association of European Assay Offices
AEAO

Secretariat Office - The London Assay Office, Goldsmiths' Company, Goldsmiths' Hall, Gutter Lane, London, EC2V 8AQ, England, UK
Tel: 44 20 76068971
Fax: 44 20 78149353
Email: admin@londonassayoffice.co.uk
Website: http://www.thegoldsmiths.co.uk
Founded: 1991
Members: 30
Staff: 2
Contact: David W. Evans, Sec.
Description: National mineral assay offices. Promotes international standardization of assay procedures. Serves as a forum for the discussion of international assay standards.
Meetings/Conventions: - semiannual meeting

Association of European Cooperative and Mutual Insurers

c/o Brigitta Lindstrom
PO Box 21, Altrincham, WA14 4DP, England, UK
Tel: 44 161 9295090
Fax: 44 161 9295090
Email: birgitta.acme@icmif.org
Founded: 1978
Members: 23
Staff: 4
Contact: Ms. Brigitta Lindstrom
Description: A regional section of the International Cooperative and Mutual Insurance Federation. Mutual & cooperative insurance societies and groups of societies in 17 countries. Encourages cooperative and mutual insurance companies in common fields to work together and with other divisions of the cooperative movement; works to strengthen members' position in the market. Assists in the development of policies of international bodies in Europe, the European Union, and related fields that affect insurance mutuals and cooperatives. Promotes well-being and higher living standards in Europe; seeks to contribute to both economic and social development through solidarity. Helps developing nations to set up insurance cooperatives or mutuals. Compiles statistics; provides documentation service.
Publication: Brochure
Publication title: Europe, Our Future
Second publication: Newsletter
Publication title: Together / Ensemble
Meetings/Conventions: Ordinary Plenary Conference - biennial conference

Association of European Document Exchanges
AEDE

DX House, Ridgeway, Iver, SL0 9JQ, England, UK
Tel: 44 181 7719062
Fax: 44 181 7719063
Contact: Henry Seymour
Description: Document exchanges. Promotes free flow of information throughout Europe. Represents members' interests before labor and industrial organizations; government agencies, and the public.

Association of European Manufacturers of Fire and Intruder Alarm Systems
EURALARM

c/o Brendan Gately
c/o Fire Industry Confederation, Neville House, 55 Eden St., Kingston Upon Thames, KT1 1BW, England, UK
Tel: 44 208 5495855
Fax: 44 208 5471564
Founded: 1970
Members: 254
Contact: Brendan Gately
Description: National associations of fire and security alarm system manufacturers and individual manufacturers representing 14 countries. Acts as a forum for the exchange of information and collaboration with other industry-related associations. Assists national and international organizations in the development of standards, rules, and recommendations; helps in the planning, testing, and approval of regulations; supports independent research and testing organizations. Works to eliminate technical trade barriers and to develop the international market. Promotes technological development in order to improve product reliability.
Publication: Bulletin
Publication title: Euralarm Information Bulletin
Meetings/Conventions: - annual general assembly

Association of European Trade Mark Owners
MARQUES

840 Melton Rd., Thurmaston, Leicester, LE4 8BN, England, UK
Tel: 44 116 2640080
Fax: 44 116 2640141
Website: http://www.marques.org
Description: Works to educate and promote the professional development of brand owners in the selection, management and protection of trade marks within a global economy.

Association of Exhibition Organisers

Red and White House, 113 High St., Berkhamsted, HP4 2DJ, England, UK
Tel: 44 1442 873331
Fax: 44 1442 875551
Email: info@aeo.org.uk
Website: http://www.aeo.org.uk
Founded: 1924
Members: 206
Staff: 10
Contact: Trevor Foley, Dir.
Fee: £720
Membership Type: organizer/associate
Description: Cross section of exhibition organizing companies and companies which provide a service to exhibition organizers. The focal point for firms and people who organize exhibitions in the UK, Europe and worldwide. Its aim is to safeguard and promote the interests of its members and to ensure that exhibitors and visitors to shows are guaranteed the highest quality service.
Publication: Newsletter
Publication title: Exhibition Issues. Advertisements.
Meetings/Conventions: - annual conference

Association of Financial Controllers and Administrators
2 Shepher's Bush Rd., London, W6 7PJ, England, UK
Tel: 44 209 7497126
Fax: 44 209 7497127
Email: icea@enta.net
Website: http://www.icea.enta.net
Founded: 1990
Members: 2000
Staff: 3
Contact:
Fee: £40
Membership Type: fellow, associate
Description: Financial controllers and administrators.
Library Subject: accounting, finance, administration
Library Type: reference

Association of First Division Civil Servants
FDA
2 Caxton St., London, SW1H 0QH, England, UK
Tel: 44 20 73431111
Fax: 44 20 73431105
Email: head-office@fda.org.uk
Website: http://www.fda.org.uk
Founded: 1919
Members: 10905
Staff: 16
Contact: Jonathan Baume, Gen.Sec.
Description: Senior civil servants, public sector and NHS managers.
Publication: Magazine
Publication title: Public Service Magazine. Advertisements.

Association of Football Statisticians
AFS
18 St. Philip Sq., London, SW8 3RS, England, UK
Tel: 44 207 7205079
Fax: 44 207 6278346
Email: enquiries@11v11.com
Website: http://www.11v11.co.uk
Founded: 1968
Members: 1200
Staff: 12
Contact: Mark Baber, Man.Dir.
Fee: £18
Membership Type: ordinary
Description: Soccer statisticians in 38 countries. Promotes increased interest in the sport of soccer and its history. Compiles statistics; develops and distributes educational materials.
Publication: Book
Publication title: Who's Who 1888-1915
Second publication: Book
Publication title: Who's Who 1919-1939

Association of Foreign Banks
1 Bengal Ct., London, EC3V 9DD, England, UK
Tel: 44 207 2838300
Fax: 44 207 2838302
Email: secretariat@foreignbanks.org.uk
Website: http://www.fbsa.org.uk
Founded: 1947
Members: 180
Staff: 3
Contact: James Tree, Sec.
Description: Foreign banks and securities houses.
Formerly: Foreign Banks and Securities Houses Association

Association of Franchised Distributors of Electronic Components
The Manor House, High St., Buntingford, SG9 9AB, England, UK
Tel: 44 1763 274768
Fax: 44 1763 273255
Email: afdec@owles.demon.co.uk
Founded: 1970
Members: 100
Contact: Jill Waite, Sec.
Description: Franchised distributors and sustaining members - manufacturers of components. To promote franchised distribution.

Association of Geotechnical and Geoenvironmental Specialists
c/o Forum Court
83 Copers Cope Rd., Beckenham, BR3 1NR, England, UK
Tel: 44 20 86588212
Fax: 44 20 86630949
Email: ags@ags.org.uk
Website: http://www.ags.org.uk
Founded: 1988
Members: 120
Staff: 2
Contact: D. Jennings, Admin.
Description: Consultants and contractors offering specialist services in site investigation, geotechnics, engineering geology, foundation design and construction, geoenvironmental engineering, geochemistry and hydrogeology. Promote and enhance the quality of professional practice in geotechnical engineering; to facilitate liaison between all organizations operating in the field of geotechnics. Agree and publish guidelines on good practice and on ethical or professional matters.

Association of Golf Writers
AGW
c/o Andrew Farrell
1 Pilgrims Bungalow, Mulberry Hill, Chilham, CT4 8AH, England, UK
Tel: 44 1227 732496
Fax: 44 1707 654112
Founded: 1938
Members: 130
Contact: Andrew Farrell, Sec.
Description: Journalists covering golf. Seeks to ensure good working conditions at events; gives advice on proper press facilities.

Association of Governing Bodies of Independent Schools
Brigadier Shane Rutter-Jerome, Field House, Newton Tony, Salisbury, SP4 0HF, England, UK
Website: http://www.agbis.org.uk
Founded: 1941
Members: 333
Staff: 2
Contact: Frank Morgan, Sec.
Description: Membership is restricted to the Governing Bodies of independent secondary schools for boys (and co-educational schools) in the United Kingdom which are constituted as educational charities. There are minimum requirements as to the number of pupils. and academic achievement. Aims to advance education in independent

schools; to discuss matters concerning the policy and administration of independent schools, and to encourage co-operation between their governing bodies; to consider the relationship of such schools to the general educational interests of the community; to express the views of governing bodies on the foregoing matters, and to take such action as may be expedient.
Formerly: Governing Bodies Association

Association of Graduate Careers Advisory Services

c/o Careers Service
University of Sheffield, 8-10 Favell Rd., Sheffield, S3 7QX, England, UK
Tel: 44 870 7703310
Fax: 44 870 7703310
Email: sally.west@agcas.org.uk
Website: http://www.agcas.org.uk
Founded: 1967
Members: 1200
Staff: 5
Contact: Margaret Dane, Chief Exec.
Description: Careers services and advisers in all UK and Irish universities and most Colleges of Higher Education. Acts as the organisation through which those involved in careers advisory work in higher education exchange information and organise collaborative activities.
Publication: Booklets
Publication title: Career Information
Second publication: Magazine
Publication title: Phoenix magazine

Association of Graduate Recruiters
AGR

The Innovation Centre, Warwick Technology Park, Gallows Hill, Warwick, CV34 6UW, England, UK
Tel: 44 1926 623236
Fax: 44 1926 623237
Email: info@agr.org.uk
Website: http://www.agr.org.uk
Founded: 1968
Members: 610
Staff: 4
Contact: Sonia Reeeves, Ch.
Fee: £464
Membership Type: fun/associate
Description: Dedicated to supporting employers in all aspects of graduate recruitment.
Publication title: A Newcomer's Guide to Graduate Recruitment
Second publication: Survey
Publication title: Graduate Salaries and Vacancies Survey
Meetings/Conventions: - annual conference - Exhibits.

Association of Guilds of Weavers, Spinners and Dyers

3, Gatchell Meadow, Trull, Taunton, TA3 7HY, England, UK
Tel: 44 18 233 25345
Email: paddybakker@onetel.net.uk
Website: http://www.wsd.org.uk
Founded: 1955
Members: 5000
Contact: Paddy Bakker, Hon.Sec.
Description: Members belong to one of the country wide 103 affiliated guilds. Concerned with the preservation and improvement of craftsmanship in handweaving, spinning and dying for the benefit of

the members and the promotion of public awareness in such craftsmanship. It provides opportunities for the exchange of information and widening of knowledge through specific schools, courses, conferences and exhibitions, lectures and library facilities.
Library Subject: weaving, spinning, dyeing, textiles
Library Type: not open to the public
Publication: Journal
Publication title: The Journal for Weavers, Spinners and Dyers. Advertisements.
Meetings/Conventions: - biennial conference - Exhibits.

Association of Heads of Outdoor Education Centres

Benrigg Lodge, Old Hutton, Kendall, Cumbria, LA8 0NR, England, UK
Tel: 44 1539 723766
Founded: 1963
Members: 150
Contact: Bill Taylor, Sec.
Description: LEA and Private Centres, Outdoor Pursuits/Outward Bound/Environmental Study. Full time Heads or Deputy Heads in the UK. Concerned with promotion of all-round personal development through outdoor education and residential provision; to develop, establish and maintain good and safe practice in outdoor education. Provides a regional and national forum for members, encourages awareness of, and active respect for environment. Speaks publicly as a national authoritative body.
Publication title: Adventure Education
Second publication: Newsletter

Association of Hispanists of Great Britain and Ireland

Trinity Hall, Cambridge, CB2 1TJ, England, UK
Tel: 44 1223 332522
Email: lmh37@cam.ac.uk
Website: http://www.hispanists.org.uk
Members: 600
Contact: Dr. Louise Haywood, Assoc.Sec.
Fee: £20
Description: Lecturers in Hispanic Studies (including Catalan, Galician, Basque, Portuguese and Latin American) in universities in the UK and Ireland.
Meetings/Conventions: - annual conference

Association of History and Computing (UK Branch)
AHC

Centre for Lifelong Learning, University of Teaside, Bourign Rd., Middlesborough, Cleveland, TS1 3BA, England, UK
Email: matthew@essex.ac.uk
Website: http://www.ahc.ac.uk
Founded: 1987
Description: Promotes the use of applied information science in historical research.

Association of Humanistic Psychology Practitioners
AHPP

c/o Ian Doucet, Admin.
BCM AHPP, London, WC1N 3XX, England, UK
Tel: 44 8457 660326
Email: admin.ahpp@btinternet.com
Website: http://ahpp.org/
Founded: 1980

Contact: Ian Doucet, Admin.
Description: Works as the national accrediting organization for individuals applying the theories of humanistic psychology in their work.

Association of Humanistic Psychology Practitioners
AHPP

BCM AHPP, London, WC1N 3XX, England, UK
Tel: 44 8457 660326
Email: admin.ahpp@btinternet.com
Website: http://www.ahpp.org/
Founded: 1980
Members: 250
Staff: 1
Contact: June Green, Admin.
Description: Provides accreditation of humanistic psychotherapists as member organization of the U.K. Council for Psychotherapy and for other therapists and counsellors; makes available referral services; conducts training and professional development programs. Disseminates information to members.

Association of Illustrators

81 Leonard St., London, EC2A 4QS, England, UK
Tel: 44 20 76134328
Fax: 44 20 76134417
Email: info@-o-illustrators.demon.co.uk
Website: http://www.theaoi.com
Founded: 1973
Members: 1000
Staff: 2
Contact:
Fee: £145
Membership Type: full
Description: Illustrators and those with an interest in illustration. To support illustrators and promote British illustration.
Publication: Journal
Publication title: AOI Journal. Advertisements.

Association of Independent Care Advisors

6 West Mount Close, Southwick, Brighton, BN42 4SR, England, UK
Tel: 44 1483 203066
Fax: 44 1483 202535
Website: http://www.aica.org.uk
Founded: 1994
Members: 8
Contact: Mr. Chris Cain, Chp.
Fee: £50
Membership Type: professional
Description: Members provide advice to individuals about their care options, either in their own homes or in residential homes.
Meetings/Conventions: - annual general assembly

Association of Independent Computer Specialists
AICS

Freepost GL15, Stroud, GL6 7ZZ, England, UK
Tel: 44 701 701118
Email: admin@aics.org.uk
Website: http://www.aics.org.uk
Founded: 1972
Members: 100
Contact: R.K. Brooks, Sec.

Fee: £60
Membership Type: ordinary
Fee: £120
Membership Type: corporate
Description: Consultants, computer programmers, software designers, and training, communications, and documentation specialists. Promotes high professional standards of conduct in independent computer services. Provides technical updates to members.
Publication: Directory
Meetings/Conventions: - periodic convention

Association of Independent Crop Consultants

Agriculture House, Station Rd., Liss, GU33 7AR, England, UK
Tel: 44 1730 895354
Fax: 44 1730 895535
Email: aicc@farmline.com
Website: http://www.aicc.org.uk
Founded: 1980
Members: 125
Contact: Sarah Cowlrick, Exec. Administrator
Description: Independent crop consultants and specialists connected with arable farming. Acts as a professional organization for the truly independent crop consultant. It aims to maintain professional standards and reinforce the independence of its members who provide all aspects of advice in agronomy, covering production, protection, planning and marketing. Full consideration is always given to the technical and practical implications, together with the importance of conservation and the environment, in the decision making process.
Publication: Membership Directory

Association of Independent European Lawyers
AIEL

9 Old Queen St., Westminster, London, SW1H 9JA, England, UK
Tel: 44 207 2222299
Email: lg@legra.co.uk
Website: http://www.aiel.com/
Contact: Barbara Dufrene
Description: Independent attorneys. Promotes adherence to high standards of ethics and practice by members. Represents members' professional interests; sponsors continuing professional development courses.

Association of Independent Financial Advisers
AIFA

Austin Friars House, 2/6 Austin Friars, London, EC2N 2HD, England, UK
Tel: 44 20 76281287
Fax: 44 20 76281678
Email: info@aifa.net
Website: http://www.aifa.net
Founded: 1999
Members: 17000
Staff: 8
Contact: Paul Smee, Dir.Gen.
Description: Trade association. Represents full time IFAs to government, EEC and regulators.
Formerly: IFA Association
Publication title: Selling Financial Services. Advertisements.

Association of Independent Libraries

Leeds Library, 18 Commercial St., Leeds, LS1 6AL, England, UK
Tel: 44 113 2453071
Founded: 1989
Members: 30
Contact: Geoffrey Forster, Chm.
Description: Historic and independent libraries, currently active and providing a general collection for a general readership. Helps to maintain contact within the body of independent libraries, and to seek to enhance public awareness of the location and role of independent libraries as a vital part of our national heritage and an important educational resource.
Publication: Newsletter
Publication title: AIL Newsletter
Meetings/Conventions: - annual conference

Association of Independent Museums
AIM

Park Cottage, W. Dean, Chichester, PO18 0RX, England, UK
Tel: 44 1243 811364
Fax: 44 1243 811364
Email: leavyhorse@mistral.co.uk
Website: http://www.museums.org.uk/aim
Founded: 1976
Members: 900
Contact: Diana Zeuner, Editor
Fee: £30
Description: Individuals, museums, associations, and commercial organizations. Unites museums not directly administered by government. Encourages exchange of experience and advice; represents members' interests. Organizes seminars and study visits.
Publication: Bulletin
Publication title: AIM Bulletin. Advertisements.
Publication title: AIM Focus
Meetings/Conventions: - annual conference

Association of Independent Research and Technology Organizations

PO Box 85, Leatherhead, KT22 7YG, England, UK
Tel: 44 1372 802260
Fax: 44 1372 360835
Email: airto@pira.co.uk
Founded: 1984
Members: 40
Contact: John Bennett, Sec.Gen.
Description: Research and technology organizations.
Meetings/Conventions: - periodic meeting

Association of Independent Tour Operators

133A St Margaret's Rd., Twickenham, TW1 1RG, England, UK
Tel: 44 208 7449280
Fax: 44 208 7443187
Email: info@aito.co.uk
Website: http://www.aito.co.uk
Founded: 1976
Members: 154
Staff: 8
Description: Smaller specialist tour operators, all fully bonded for client protection, who offer the widest choice possible of quality products to their clients. Lobbies on behalf of small specialist tour operators. Helps them to market their products, arranges press functions, helps keep them up-to-date on industry issues which affect them and uses their joint purchasing power to buy a variety of products and services at good rates, particularly training courses and insurance. AITO members all abide by a Quality Charter and Code of Business Practice, and promote environmentally responsible tourism.
Publication: Directory
Publication title: Directory of Real Holidays. Advertisements.
Second publication: Directory
Publication title: Directory of Ski Holidays
Meetings/Conventions: - annual conference

Association of Industrial Laser Users
AILU

100 Ock St., Abingdon, OX14 5DH, England, UK
Tel: 44 1235 539595
Fax: 44 1235 550499
Email: admin@ailu.org.uk
Website: http://www.ailu.org.uk
Founded: 1995
Members: 270
Staff: 2
Contact: Mike Green, Con.
Fee: £210
Membership Type: full corporate
Fee: £60
Membership Type: individual
Description: Aims to foster co-operation and collaboration on non-competitive technical matters and provide a forum and mechanisms for sharing experience and expertise. Represents and promotes the interests of industrial laser users. Disseminates professional and other information to members. Promotes the best practice in the industrial applications of lasers in materials processing and allied technologies. Supports the maintenance and improvement of standards of safety and performance in the industrial user of lasers.

Association of Industrial Road Safety Officers

508 Chiswick High Rd., London, W4 5RG, England, UK
Tel: 44 20 89879459
Fax: 44 20 89879578
Email: airso@talk21.com
Website: http://www.airso.co.uk
Founded: 1965
Members: 400
Contact: Graham Feest
Fee: £25
Description: Open to individuals whose work is or has been connected with the promotion of road safety particularly in the areas of education, training and publicity. Acts as a professional organisation for road safety in industry and represents the views of the Association's membership when in consultation with government bodies and agencies. Keeps members informed of current road safety policies and practices.
Meetings/Conventions: conference - Exhibits.

Association of Information Officers in the Pharmaceutical Industry
AIOPI

PO Box 297, Slough, SL1 7XT, England, UK
Email: aiopi@aiopi.org.uk
Website: http://www.aiopi.org.uk

Association of Insurance and Risk Managers
AIRMIC
6 Lloyd's Ave., London, EC3N 3AX, England, UK
Tel: 44 20 74807610
Fax: 44 20 77023752
Email: enquiries@airmic.co.uk
Website: http://www.airmic.com
Founded: 1963
Members: 950
Staff: 6
Contact: David Gamble
Description: Managers or senior members of risk management or insurance departments in industry, commerce, or government are members; junior members of risk management or insurance departments are associate members; instructors in risk management and other interested individuals are affiliate members. Serves as a forum for the exchange of ideas and information among members; disseminates information on technical matters and new practices in risk management and insurance. Represents members' interests before trade and market associations and government bodies; promotes public understanding of the nature and purposes of risk management; provides educational programs.
Meetings/Conventions: - annual conference

Association of Insurance and Risk Managers
6 Lloyds Ave., London, EC3N 3AX, England, UK
Tel: 44 207 4807610
Fax: 44 207 7023752
Email: enquiries@airmic.co.uk
Website: http://www.airmic.com
Founded: 1963
Members: 860
Staff: 6
Contact: Ina Barker
Description: Professionals practising or responsible for insurance and risk management. Corporate members represent most of the UK's top 200 companies and over 300 individual members whose key roles are risk management and/or insurance. Aims to widen the understanding of risk management and its importance; to develop the professional expertise of risk managers helping them to be pro-active on all relevant issues. Represents the views of insurance and risk managers to key decision makers and organizes an annual conference, seminars, and meetings for exchange of views.
Publication title: Business Risk
Second publication: Newsletter

Association of Interior Specialists
Olton Bridge, 245 Warwick Rd., Solihull, B92 7AH, England, UK
Tel: 44 121 7070077
Fax: 44 121 7061949
Email: info@ais-interiors.org.uk
Website: http://ais-interiors.org.uk
Founded: 1997
Members: 350
Staff: 7
Contact: Jean Birch, Chief Exec.
Description: Represents companies involved in the manufacture, supply and installation of all aspects of interior fit-outs and refurbishment, from main interior contractors to specialist fit-out contractors, interior systems manufacturers to distributors. Maintains and works to improve the standards, quality of workmanship, training and technical expertise to benefit members and clients.
Formerly: Formed by Merger of, Partitioning and Interiors Association
Publication title: AIS Site Guide for Partitioning
Second publication: Magazine
Publication title: Interiors Focus. Advertisements.

Association of International Accountants
AIA
South Bank Bldg., Kingsway, Team Valley, Newcastle upon Tyne, NE11 0JS, England, UK
Tel: 44 191 4824409
Fax: 44 191 4825578
Email: aia@aia.org.uk
Website: http://www.aia.org.uk
Founded: 1928
Members: 11500
Staff: 20
Contact: Nicola Perry, Devel.Mgr.
Description: Accountants (4500) and accounting students (7000). Objectives are: to provide a forum for closer cooperation between accountants; to foster interest in the international aspects of all branches of accountancy; to promote international standards and impose an international code of professional conduct. Holds semiannual examinations and issue practicing certificates.
Publication: Journal
Publication title: International Accountant. Advertisements.
Meetings/Conventions: - annual meeting

Association of International Courier and Express Services
AICES
Global House, Poyle Rd., Colnbrook, Slough, SL3 0AY, England, UK
Tel: 44 1753 680550
Fax: 44 1753 681710
Email: aices@btinternet.com
Founded: 1977
Members: 43
Staff: 2
Contact: Anne De Courcy
Description: International courier and express services companies. Seeks to: represent and promote the industry; improve and maintain professional standards; serve as a negotiating body; promote development of similar overseas associations.
Formerly: Association of International Air Courier Services

Association of International Marketing
AIM
PO Box 70, London, E13 8BQ, England, UK
Tel: 44 208 9867539
Fax: 44 208 9867539
Founded: 1983
Members: 600
Staff: 2
Contact: C. Oham, Dir. & Gen.Sec.
Description: Executives in 10 countries who have at least 3 years experience in international marketing or have completed a specified course offered by the organization. Promotes the advancement and exchange of information and ideas in international marketing. Offers certification courses in international marketing.
Library Subject: international marketing
Library Type: not open to the public
Publication title: A guide to Marketing in Europe
Second publication: Handbook
Publication title: AIM Membership Handbook

Association of Investment Trust Companies - England

Durrant House, 3rd Fl., 8-13 Chiswell St., London, EC1Y 4YY, England, UK
Tel: 44 20 72825555
Fax: 44 20 72825556
Email: enquiries@aitc.co.uk
Website: http://www.itsonline.co.uk
Founded: 1932
Members: 300
Staff: 25
Contact: Daniel Godfrey, Dir.Gen.
Description: Investment trust companies which are approved by the Inland Revenue under s842 ICTA 1988, or under S842AA ICTA and also certain closed-end funds which are not so approved but nonetheless satisfy all the tests in S842. Eligible companies must be closed-end, listed on the London Stock Exchange and whose business is primarily the management of a portfolio consisting mainly of shares and securities. Concerned with the promotion, protection and advancement of the interests of closed-ended investment trust companies and their shareholders by influencing developments in legislation and practice affecting investors, companies and the stock market, by political lobbying and by promotion of their merits, in particular to private investors and independent financial advisers.
Publication: Book
Publication title: Put Not Your Trust in Money

Association of Language Excellence Centres

PO Box 178, Manchester, M60 1LL, England, UK
Tel: 44 161 2281366
Founded: 1990
Members: 50
Contact: Gwen Rhys, Mgr.
Description: Public and private sector providers of language training and related services for business who have achieved recognised Language Excellence (LX) Centre status and entitlement to use the LX logo, the stamp of quality language provision. Promotes high quality language training for business and vocational purposes. It constitutes a unique and influential grouping of language providers specialised in providing training and consultancy to British industry.
Publication: Directory
Publication title: Directory of Materials
Publication title: Guidelines on Good Practice in the Management and Delivery of Foreign Language Training for Business

Association of Language Testers in Europe
ALTE

1 Hills Rd., Cambridge, CB1 2EU, England, UK
Tel: 44 1223 553925
Fax: 44 1223 3036
Email: alte@ucles.org.uk
Website: http://www.alte.org
Description: Works to establish common standards for all stages of the language testing process, including test development, test administration, marking and grading, reporting of test results, test analysis, and reports of findings.

Association of Larger Local Councils

PO Box 528, Staffordshire, ST10 3AT, England, UK
Tel: 44 191 5868210
Email: allc@co-net.com
Founded: 1981
Contact: John Dixon-Dawson, Sec.

Description: Larger parish and town councils in England and Wales, usually with a population of approximately 10,000 or more, or with an appropriate level of service delivery. Established on the basis that larger local councils among the several thousand parish and community councils should seek a wider range of functions than the average local council permitted under the local government reorganisation of 1974. Its objectives are to seek a regular exchange of information between member councils for action to be taken on policy issues to enhance community services at a local level.

Association of Law Costs Draftsmen

Church Cottage, Church Ln., Stuston, Diss, IP21 4AG, England, UK
Tel: 44 1379 741404
Fax: 44 1379 742702
Email: enquiries@alcd.org.uk
Website: http://www.alcd.org.uk
Founded: 1977
Members: 800
Contact: Ms. S. Chapman, Admin.Sec.
Fee: £40
Membership Type: student
Fee: £100
Membership Type: associate
Description: Voluntary membership to a professional body of Law Costs Draftsmen which enables members to take examinations to Associate/Fellowship level.
Publication: Journal
Publication title: ALCD Journal. Advertisements.
Second publication: Book
Publication title: Practice Directions and Hourly Rates Register of the District Registeries

Association of Law Teachers

c/o Alison Bone
University of Brighton, Lewes Rd., Brighton, BN2 4AT, England, UK
Tel: 44 1273 642174
Fax: 44 1273 642980
Email: a.bone@bton.ac.uk
Website: http://www.lawteacher.ac.uk
Founded: 1965
Members: 850
Contact: Alison Bone
Fee: £20
Membership Type: for UK
Fee: £25
Membership Type: for non UK
Description: Law teachers from higher and further education. Furtherance of the study, understanding and reform of educational aspects of law and its teaching, the representation of members' views on the teaching of law and the general support and encouragement of activities of benefit to law teachers.
Publication: Journal
Publication title: The Law Teacher. Advertisements.
Second publication: Bulletin. Advertisements.
Meetings/Conventions: - annual conference - Exhibits.

Association of Lawyer and Legal Advisors

14 Bowling Green Ln., London, EC1R 0NE, England, UK
Tel: 44 1745 584414
Fax: 44 1745 582006
Website: http://www.lawyerassoc.com
Founded: 1995
Members: 3000

Staff: 5
Contact: Carol Baird
Fee: £150
Membership Type: fellow, member
Fee: £50
Membership Type: associate
Description: Persons independently accredited as being competent to provide legal advice and services in their specialized area of law. Offers C.P.D. in conjunction with Knighsbridge University.

Association of Lawyers for Children
PO Box 283, East Molesey, Surrey, KT8 0WH, England, UK
Tel: 44 208 2247071
Fax: 44 208 2247071
Email: admin@alc.org.uk
Website: http://www.alc.org.uk
Founded: 1992
Members: 900
Contact: Julia Higgins, Admin.
Fee: £50
Membership Type: full
Fee: £25
Membership Type: associate
Description: Lawyers, social workers, guardians ad litem, doctors, and others who work with or for children. Offers training, consultation and research, to improve knowledge, furthering best practice, and encouraging inter-agency understanding in work with and for children. Upholds the welfare of children, and raises awareness of children's rights and needs.
Publication: Newsletter
Publication title: ALC Newsletter. Advertisements.
Meetings/Conventions: - annual conference - Exhibits. Bristol UK

Association of Lawyers for the Defence of the Unborn
ALDU
40 Bedford Street, London, WC2E 9EN, England, UK
Email: mail.jlj@lr.dk
Founded: 1978
Members: 3250
Contact: Mr. R.M. Haig, Chmn.
Description: Judges, barristers, law professors and students, solicitors, and legal executives in 25 countries united to oppose abortion and to persuade lawyers of their duty to oppose abortion. Advocates full statutory protection of young human beings against being deliberately attacked and killed from the moment of fertilization onwards. Convention/Meeting: none.
Publication: Newsletter

Association of Learned and Professional Society Publishers
ALPSP
South House, The Street, Clapham, Worthing, BN13 3UU, England, UK
Tel: 44 1903 871686
Fax: 44 1903 871457
Email: sec-gen@alpsp.org
Website: http://www.alpsp.org
Founded: 1972
Members: 236
Staff: 5
Contact: Sally Morris, Sec.Gen.

Description: Represents not-for profit publishers of learned and professional information in all media.
Publication: Journal
Publication title: Learned Publishing. Advertisements.
Meetings/Conventions: International Learned Journals Seminar - annual conference - Exhibits. London UK

Association of Licensed Aircraft Engineers
8 Park St., Bagshot, GU19 5AQ, England, UK
Tel: 44 1276 474888
Fax: 44 1276 452767
Email: alae@bagshot.sagehost.co.uk
Website: http://www.lae.mcmail.com
Founded: 1970
Members: 2000
Staff: 2
Contact: Mark Harris
Fee: £52
Description: Licensed Aircraft Engineers. Non-political, non-partisan organisation aiming to maintain the professional status of the licensed aircraft engineer; represent the licensed aircraft engineer within the aviation industry; promote the advancement of technical knowledge, safety and skills of those engaged in civil aviation.
Publication: Newsletter
Publication title: LPRA News. Advertisements.
Publication title: LPRA Yearbook and Buyers Guide
Meetings/Conventions: - annual general assembly UK

Association of Lighting Designers
PO Box 89, Welwyn Garden City, AL7 1ZW, England, UK
Tel: 44 170 7891848
Fax: 44 170 7891848
Email: office@ald.org.uk
Website: http://www.ald.org.uk
Founded: 1963
Members: 700
Contact: Geoff Spain, Admin.Sec.
Fee: £25
Description: Professional lighting designers in theatre, performance arts and architecture. Associate membership for any interested persons. Provides a resource and forum for discussion and development of artistic and creative aims.
Publication: Magazine
Publication title: Focus. Advertisements.
Publication title: Professional Members Directory
Meetings/Conventions: - monthly meeting

Association of Lightweight Aggregate Manufacturers
c/o LYTAG
Hazel Old Ln., Goole, DN14 0QD, England, UK
Contact: J.M. Hanson
Description: Represents members' interests.

Association of Little Presses
111 Branbury Rd., Oxford, OX2 6JX, England, UK
Tel: 44 1865 718266
Email: alp@melloworld.com
Website: http://www.melloworld.com/alp/index.html
Founded: 1966
Members: 320
Contact: Chris Jones, Coord.
Fee: £12.5

Description: Small publishers and individuals and organizations interested in small press publications. An information exchange, advice centre and general promoter of the benefits of small publishing. It organizes bookfairs, exhibitions and gatherings around the country and gives advice and information on how you can publish it yourself.
Publication title: Getting Your Poetry Published
Second publication: Catalog
Publication title: Little Press Books in Print

Association of Loading and Elevating Equipment Manufacturers
ALEM

Orbital House, 85 Croydon Rd., Caterham, CR3 6PD, England, UK
Tel: 44 1883 334494
Fax: 44 1883 334490
Email: alem@admin.co.uk
Website: http://www.alem.org.uk
Founded: 1973
Members: 26
Contact: Tim Faithfull, Sec.
Fee: £800
Membership Type: full
Description: Manufacturers of loading and elevating equipment in the United Kingdom. Represents members' interests.
Publication: Membership Directory
Publication title: Product Guide

Association of Local Authority Chief Executives

c/o Chief Executive's Office
Three Rivers DC, Three Rivers House, Northway, Rickmansworth, WD3 1RL, England, UK
Tel: 44 1923 727282
Fax: 44 1923 727282
Email: alastair.robertson@threerivers.gov.uk
Website: http://alace.org
Founded: 1974
Members: 400
Contact: A. Robertson, Hon.Sec.
Fee: £110
Membership Type: closed (trade union status)
Description: Local authority chief executives.

Association of Local Bus Company Managers

Halton Borough Transport Ltd., Moor Ln., Widnes, WA8 7AF, England, UK
Tel: 44 151 4233333
Founded: 1985
Members: 90
Staff: 1
Contact: David Cunningham, Sec.
Fee: £5
Membership Type: executive directors
Description: Executive directors of local bus companies. Aims to protect the interests of the local bus operations by representing this part of the industry in discussions with government departments and, through quarterly area and technical panel meetings create a talking shop such as to keep all members fully informed and try to achieve individual company performance improvements. Consults government on industry proposed changes.
Publication: Newsletter
Publication title: Album Update. Advertisements.
Meetings/Conventions: - annual conference - Exhibits.

Association of Logic Programming
ALP

180 Queen's Gate, London, SW7 2BZ, England, UK
Tel: 44 20 75948227
Fax: 44 20 75891552
Email: alp@doc.ic.ac.uk
Website: http://www.cwi.nl/projects/alp/
Founded: 1986

Association of London Chief Librarians

St Nicholas Way, Sutton, Surrey, SM1 1EA, England, UK
Tel: 44 181 8881292
Fax: 44 181 8890110
Founded: 1965
Members: 33
Contact: Trevor Knight, Hon.Sec.
Fee: £50
Description: Chief librarians in London.

Association of London Clubs

c/o Farmers Club
3 Whitehall Court, London, SW1A 2EL, England, UK
Tel: 44 171 930 3751
Contact: Ms. H.J.C. McCulloch
Description: All London membership clubs. Confers on matters of common interest to clubs forming the Association, and, where it is deemed desirable, to take united action.

Association of London Government

59 1/2 Southwark St., London, SE1 OAL, England, UK
Tel: 44 20 79349999
Fax: 44 20 79349991
Email: info@alg.gov.uk
Website: http://www.alg.gov.uk
Founded: 1995
Members: 33
Staff: 160
Contact: Martin Pilgrim, Ch.Exec.
Description: Open to all London boroughs and City of London. Acts as a voice for London boroughs in negotiations and consultations with central government. Central government consults member authorities through the ALG on a wide range of issues. Also coordinates a number of London wide initiatives and projects on behalf of London borough.
Publication: Annual Report
Publication title: ALG Annual Report
Second publication: Magazine
Publication title: ALG London Bulletin. Advertisements.

Association of Magistrates' Courts

79 New Cavendish St., London, W1M 7RB, England, UK
Tel: 44 171 4368524
Fax: 44 171 6367869
Members: 96
Staff: 1
Contact: Mrs. S. Matthews
Description: Concerned with the recruitment of trainee court clerks to the magistrates' courts service of England and Wales.

Association of Makers of Printings and Writings
c/o Richard Sexton, Sec.
Papermakers House, Rivenhall Rd., Westlea, Swindon, SN5 7BD,
England, UK
Tel: 44 1793 889616
Fax: 44 1793 878700
Email: rsexton@paper.org.uk
Members: 12
Contact: Richard Sexton
Description: Companies operating in paper and board manufacture.
The products produced include general home, educational and office
stationery, security papers and wallpaper base. To debate and inform
on issues affecting the sector. To collect and circulate statistics and
other information on specific issues affecting the trade and
manufacture of products produced.

Association of Makers of Soft Tissue Papers
1 Rivenhall Rd., Westlea, Swindon, SN5 7BD, England, UK
Tel: 44 1793 889616
Fax: 44 1793 878700
Email: rsexton@paper.org.uk
Founded: 1975
Members: 10
Contact: R.G. Sexton, Sec.
Description: Makers of soft tissue paper.

Association of Malt Products Manufacturers
1 Surrey Rd., Felixstone, 1PA1 7SB, England, UK
Tel: 44 1394 271713
Fax: 44 1394 271713
Contact: R.E.A. Holt
Description: Malt products manufacturers.

Association of Management and Professional Staffs
AEEU House, Borough Rd., Wakefield, WF1 3AZ, England, UK
Tel: 44 1924 371765
Fax: 44 1924 290327
Email: sec@amps.demon.co.uk
Website: http://www.amps.demon.co.uk
Members: 150000
Contact: Gordon H. Hopwood, Exec.Sec.
Fee: £100
Membership Type: associations
Description: Represents the interests of management personnel and
professionals.
Formerly: Council of Managerial and Professional Staffs

Association of Manufacturers Allied to the Electrical and Electronic Industry
AMA
Westminster Tower, 3 Albert Embankment, London, SE1 7SL,
England, UK
Tel: 44 207 7933038
Fax: 44 207 7933054
Contact: A. Willman, Sec.
Description: Manufacturers of products not included in other
associations run under the auspices of the BEAMA Director General.

Association of Manufacturers of Domestic Appliances
Rapier House, 40-46 Lamb's Conduit St., London, WC1N 3NW,
England, UK
Tel: 44 171 4050666
Fax: 44 171 4056609
Email: peter.carver@amdea.org.uk
Founded: 1959
Members: 60
Staff: 5
Contact: Peter Carver, Dir.Gen.
Description: National trade association representing domestic
appliance manufacturers.
Meetings/Conventions: - semiannual conference

Association of Manufacturers of Power Generating Systems
PO Box 1714, Andover, SP11 6SL, England, UK
Tel: 44 1264 365367
Fax: 44 1264 362304
Email: mail@amps.org.uk
Website: http://www.amps.org.uk
Members: 65
Staff: 4
Contact: G.H. Parkinson, Dir.Gen.
Fee: £850
Membership Type: full
Fee: £425
Membership Type: affiliate
Description: Companies specializing in the design, manufacture,
supply, installation, commission, and maintenance of reciprocating
diesel and gas engine and gas turbine driven electrical generating
systems for prime power and emergency standby applications.
Publication title: The Amps Guide to ISO 8528
Meetings/Conventions: - quarterly general assembly

Association of MBA's
15 Duncan Terr., London, N1 8BZ, England, UK
Tel: 44 20 78373375
Fax: 44 20 72783634
Email: info@mba.org.uk
Website: http://www.mba.org.uk
Founded: 1967
Members: 14000
Staff: 16
Contact: Pauline North, Sec.
Fee: £95
Description: Individual membership is open to students and
graduates of Association of MBAs-approved MBA programmes.
Corporate membership is encouraged for business schools appearing
on the Association's approved list and for companies and other
organisations who share the. objectives of the Association and who
wish to contribute towards them. Committed to enhancing quality in
management and to providing a unique network of contacts for
members. Services and activities include: a membership book; circa
70 networking/educational events pa; career opportunities;
accreditation of MBA programmes; salary research; administration of
a preferential rate MBA loan scheme for students of accredited
programmes; an MBA information service.
Publication: Magazine
Publication title: Ambassador. Advertisements.
Second publication: Book
Publication title: Guide to Business Schools. Advertisements.
Meetings/Conventions: Accredited MBA Fair - semiannual
convention - Exhibits. London UK

Association of Media and Communications Specialists

163 High St., Rickmansworth, WD3 1AY, England, UK
Tel: 44 1923 711981
Founded: 1982
Members: 15
Staff: 3
Contact: Vic Davies
Description: Companies responsible for the planning and buying of advertising media. Responsible for promoting the interests of its members in the field of advertising media.

Association of Medical Microbiologists

c/o Dr. Beryl Oppenheim
Public Health Laboratory, Birmingham Heartlands Hospital, Bordesley Green East, Birmingham, B9 5SS, England, UK
Tel: 44 121 4243240
Fax: 44 121 7726229
Website: http://www.amm.co.uk
Founded: 1983
Members: 500
Contact: Dr. Beryl Oppenheim, Hon.Sec.
Fee: £50
Membership Type: full
Fee: £30
Membership Type: associate
Description: Scientists, academics, consultants, and others interested in medical microbiology. Professional body concerned with all aspects of medical microbiology. Promotes high quality training in medical microbiology.

Association of Medical Research Charities
AMRC

61 Gray's Inn Rd., London, WC1X 8TL, England, UK
Tel: 44 20 72698820
Fax: 44 20 72698821
Email: info@amrc.org.uk
Website: http://www.amrc.org.uk
Founded: 1987
Members: 111
Staff: 7
Contact: Diana A. Garnham, CEO
Description: Represents medical research charities. Furthers the advancement of medical research in the United Kingdom. Focuses attention on the collective effectiveness of members. Provides information, advice and guidance to members and others.
Publication: Booklet
Publication title: Handbook
Second publication: Newsletter
Meetings/Conventions: - periodic meeting

Association of Medical Secretaries, Practice Managers, Administrators and Receptionists
AMSPAR

Tavistock House North, Tavistock Sq., London, WC1H 9LN, England, UK
Tel: 44 207 3876005
Fax: 44 207 3882648
Email: info@amspar.co.uk
Website: http://www.amspar.co.uk
Founded: 1964
Members: 1886

Staff: 7
Contact: Michael Fiennes, Commun.Mgr.
Fee: £50
Membership Type: full, associate, affiliate
Description: Those who have successfully completed AMSPAR examinations or qualify by the experience gained through working in the medical field. An organization formed to encourage high standards among persons engaged in medical administrative employment.
Formerly: Formed by Merger of, Association of Medical Secretaries, Practice Administration and Receptionists
Publication: Magazine
Publication title: AMSPAR. Advertisements.
Meetings/Conventions: - annual conference - Exhibits.

Association of Motion Picture Sound

28 Knox St., London, W1H 1FS, England, UK
Tel: 44 20 77236727
Fax: 44 171 7236727
Email: admin@amps.net
Website: http://www.amps.net
Founded: 1989
Members: 250
Staff: 1
Contact: Brian Hickin
Fee: £50
Description: Persons employed in the production of sound tracks associated with moving images, recording the original dialogue music and sound effects, editing these sounds and rerecording them to accompany the moving picture images. To promote and encourage the science technology and creative application of all aspects of motion picture sound recording and reproduction and seek to promote and enhance the status and recognition of the contribution of those engaged therein.
Publication: Newsletter
Publication title: AMPS Newsletter

Association of Mouth and Foot Painting Artists
AMFPA

9 Inverness Pl., London, W2 3JG, England, UK
Tel: 44 171 2294491
Website: http://www.amfpa.com
Founded: 1956
Members: 500
Description: Works to ensure that physically disabled artists can achieve self-fulfillment. Organizes exhibitions, sales, distribution, and reproduction of artists' works.

Association of Municipal Engineers

c/o The Institution of Civil Engineers
1 Great George St., London, SW1P 3AA, England, UK
Tel: 44 207 2227722
Fax: 44 207 2227500
Email: www@ice.org.uk
Website: http://www.ice.org.uk
Founded: 1984
Members: 11500
Staff: 4
Contact: R. Huxford, Asst.Dir.
Description: Members of the Institution of Civil Engineers employed in public services. Provides a focus for the development of technical and management excellence of municipal and public sector civil engineers and the promotion of professional competence for the

benefit of the community Seeks to promote and enhance the identity, contribution and influence of members within and outside the profession.
Library Subject: engineering
Library Type: by appointment only
Publication: Journal
Publication title: Municipal Engineer
Meetings/Conventions: - annual conference - Exhibits.

Association of National Tourist in the UK
37 Peter Ave., London, NW10 2DD, England, UK
Tel: 44 20 84594052
Fax: 44 20 84594052
Website: http://www.tourist-offices.org.uk
Founded: 1950
Members: 92
Contact: Pierre J. Claus, Exec.Sec.
Description: Representatives of overseas national tourist offices in UK. Co-ordinates and aims to improve the services that government tourist offices representing foreign countries offer to the British travel industry.
Publication title: Guide to ANTOR's Role
Second publication: Membership Directory

Association of Nature Reserve Burial Grounds
6 Blackstock Mews, Blackstock Rd, London, N4 2BT, England, UK
Tel: 44 20 73598391
Fax: 44 20 73543831
Email: rhino@dial.pipex.com
Website: http://www.naturaldeath.org.uk
Founded: 1994
Members: 60
Staff: 3
Contact: Stephanie Wienrich
Fee: £20
Membership Type: full, provisional
Description: Assists woodland or nature reserve burial grounds in the UK by putting forward a code of practice for its members, referral service, information service, and promotion of the concept/publicity.
Library Subject: natural death, dying, caring, green issues
Library Type: by appointment only
Publication: Book
Publication title: The New Natural Death Handbook

Association of Newspaper and Magazine Wholesalers
8-14 Vine Hill, 3rd Fl., London, EC1R 5DX, England, UK
Tel: 44 20 75200480
Fax: 44 20 72786853
Email: enquiries@anmw.co.uk
Website: http://www.anmw.co.uk
Founded: 1907
Members: 26
Staff: 5
Contact: Terry Perry, Managing Dir.
Description: Wholesalers of newspapers, periodicals and magazines situated within the United Kingdom. Represents the wholesale newspaper trade and provides a forum for its membership.
Publication: Membership Directory

Association of Noise Consultants
6 Trap Rd., Guilden Morden, Royston, SG8 0JE, England, UK
Tel: 44 1763 852958
Fax: 44 1763 853252
Email: anc@ukgateway.net
Website: http://www.association-of-noise-consultants.co.uk
Founded: 1973
Members: 56
Contact: Mrs. G. Rhein, Sec.
Description: Consultancy practices. Aims to provide a corporate organisation for independent firms of consultants offering professional services in the field of noise and also vibration.
Publication: Book
Publication title: ANC Guidelines - Measurement and Assessment of Groundborne Noise and Vibration

Association of Nursery Training Colleges
Montessori Centre International, 18 Balderton St., London, W1K 6TJ, England, UK
Tel: 44 118 9471847
Fax: 44 118 9463218
Email: info@chilterncollege.com
Founded: 1931
Members: 5
Contact: Tina Drew, Sec.
Fee: £250
Membership Type: corporate
Description: Private colleges providing nursery nurse training. Aims to foster co-operation between like minded organizations, to exchange information and promote interest in the training of a nursery nurse.
Library Subject: child care
Library Type: reference
Meetings/Conventions: - annual meeting

Association of Operating Department Practitioners AODP
Lewes Enterprise Centre, 112 Malling St., Lewes, BN7 2RJ, England, UK
Tel: 44 870 7460984
Fax: 44 870 7460985
Email: office@aodp.org
Website: http://www.aodp.org
Founded: 1945
Members: 7500
Contact: Roger King, Chm.
Fee: £50
Membership Type: overseas
Fee: £35
Membership Type: member
Description: Seeks to maintain quality standards among operating department practitioners.
Publication: Journal
Publication title: Technic. Advertisements.
Meetings/Conventions: - annual conference - Exhibits.

Association of Optometrists
61 Southwark St., London, SE1 0HL, England, UK
Tel: 44 20 72619661
Fax: 44 20 72610228
Email: postbox@assoc-optometrists.org
Website: http://www.assoc-optometrists.org
Founded: 1946

Members: 7000
Staff: 20
Contact: Ian Hunter, Chief Exec.
Fee: £372
Membership Type: professional
Description: Optometrists and dispensing opticians and students. Aims to support, promote and protect interests of members individually and corporately; to encourage high standards of practice; to make suitable arrangements for the defence of members in disciplinary and professional matters. Advises on commercial, legal and administrative aspects of practice.
Publication: Journal
Publication title: Optometry Today. Advertisements.

Association of Paediatric Anaesthetists of Great Britain and Ireland
APA

c/o Dr. G. H. Meakin
University Department of Anaesthesia, Royal Manchester Childrens Hospital, Manchester, M30 9HF, England, UK
Tel: 44 161 7272291
Fax: 44 161 7272291
Email: george.meakin@man.ac.uk
Website: http://www.apagbi.org.uk
Founded: 1973
Members: 550
Contact: Dr. G.H. Meakin, Hon.Sec.
Description: Pediatric anesthetists practicing in Great Britain and Ireland and outside the British Isles. Promotes the study of pediatric anesthesiology. Collects and disseminates information; conducts research; advises other professional bodies on matters pertaining to pediatric anesthesiology.
Publication title: Paediatric Anaesthesia
Publication title: Yearbook
Meetings/Conventions: - periodic seminar

Association of Painting Craft Teachers

50 Northfield Rd., Kings Norton, Birmingham, B30 1JH, England, UK
Tel: 44 121 4596838
Fax: 44 121 6089335
Website: http://www.apct.co.uk
Founded: 1921
Members: 250
Contact: Mrs. A. Cook
Description: For all engaged in education and training throughout the painting and decorating industry including technology and related skills associated with interior and exterior decoration, vehicle painting, industrial finishing and signwork. Advances education and training in the craft skills throughout the painting and decorating industry; furthers the interests of all who teach these skills; acts as a representative body in consultation with awarding bodies on all matters connected with the teaching of painting and decorating and allied subjects.

Association of Pension Lawyers

c/o Kris Weber, Sec.
PMI House, Rm. 10, 4-10 Artillery Ln., London, E1 7LS, England, UK
Tel: 44 870 2406036
Email: pensionlawyers@runbox.com
Website: http://www.apl.org.uk
Founded: 1984
Members: 770
Contact: David Pollard, Chm.

Description: Lawyers satisfying certain criteria, specialising in pensions law. To promote awareness of the importance of the rule of law in the provision of pensions and in regulating and defining the relationships between pension scheme trustees, employers and beneficiaries.
Publication: Journal
Publication title: Pensions Lawyer

Association of Photographers

81 Lenoard St., London, EC2A 4QS, England, UK
Tel: 44 20 77396669
Fax: 44 20 77398707
Email: general@aophoto.co.uk
Website: http://www.the-aop.org
Founded: 1969
Members: 1700
Staff: 12
Contact: Gwen Thomas, Chief Exec.
Description: Professional photographers working in advertising, editorial, or fashion photography. Conducts monthly workshops and organizes exhibitions. Maintains gallery. Provides education programs and membership legal assistance and awards competitions.
Library Subject: photography
Library Type: reference
Formerly: Association of Fashion, Advertising, and Editorial Photographers
Publication title: ABCD of Copyright
Publication title: Assistant's Catalogue
Meetings/Conventions: Careers Talk - monthly lecture

Association of Plumbing and Heating Contractors
APHC

Ensign House, Ensign Business Centre, Westwood Way, Coventry, CV4 8JA, England, UK
Tel: 44 800 5426060
Fax: 44 2476 470942
Email: enquiries@aphc.co.uk
Website: http://www.aphc.co.uk
Description: Promotes plumbing and heating contractors; provides licensing to plumbing and heating businesses to ensure business practices.

Association of Plumbing and Heating Contractors

Ensign House, Ensign Business Centre, Westwood Way, Coventry, CV4 8JA, England, UK
Tel: 44 2476 470626
Fax: 44 2476 470942
Email: enquiries@aphc.co.uk
Website: http://www.licensedplumber.co.uk
Founded: 1895
Members: 2200
Staff: 22
Contact: Steve Muscroft, CEO
Fee: £178
Membership Type: ordinary
Fee: £390
Membership Type: manufacturer
Description: All employers in plumbing heating and mechanical services contractors. To improve the recognition of the professional plumber/domestic engineer by the public at large and the main contractors in the building industry in particular. To ensure that members and their employees are protected by insurance/pensions/

healthcare schemes and that wage negotiations with Trades Unions are properly carried out.
Library Type: reference
Formerly: National Association of Plumbing, Heating and Mechanical Services Contractors
Publication: Book. Advertisements.
Second publication: Bulletin
Meetings/Conventions: - annual general assembly - Exhibits.

Association of Port Health Authorities
Dutton House, 46 Church St., Runcorn, WA7 1LL, England, UK
Tel: 44 8707 444505
Fax: 44 1928 581596
Email: apha@cieh.org.uk
Website: http://www.apha.org.uk
Founded: 1899
Members: 65
Staff: 2
Contact: Peter Rotheram
Fee: £850
Membership Type: corporate
Description: Local authorities, port health authorities in the United Kingdom, Ireland and the Channel Islands. Promoting the health and safety of seafarers, discussing issues on imported food, environmental health, etc. with central government, EU organisations, etc.
Publication: Newsletter
Publication title: Lookout Newsletter
Second publication: Handbook
Publication title: Port Health Handbook
Meetings/Conventions: - annual meeting

Association of Private Client Investment Managers and Stockbrokers
112 Middlesex St., London, E1 7HY, England, UK
Tel: 44 20 72477080
Fax: 44 20 73770939
Email: info@apcims.co.uk
Website: http://www.apcims.co.uk
Founded: 1990
Members: 200
Staff: 9
Contact: Brian Mairs, Head of Information
Description: Trade association for investment managers and stockbrokers serving the UK's 12 million private investors.
Publication: Directory
Publication title: APCIMS Directory of Members
Meetings/Conventions: - annual conference

Association of Private Market Operators
4 Worrygoose Ln., Rotherham, S60 4AD, England, UK
Tel: 44 1709 700072
Fax: 44 1709 703648
Email: marketsman@lineone.net
Website: http://www.apmomarkets.co.uk
Founded: 1990
Members: 20
Staff: 2
Contact: Mr. D.J. Glasby, Gen.Sec.
Fee: £300
Membership Type: scale A
Fee: £500
Membership Type: scale B

Description: Owners/operators of indoor and outdoor private retail markets. Encourages high standards of professionalism, promotes or opposes Bills in Parliament, affecting private market operators. Arbitrates on trade disputes. Achieves advantages for members by unified action, unlikely to be achieved by members individually.
Publication: Handbook
Publication title: APMO Handbook. Advertisements.
Meetings/Conventions: - quarterly executive committee meeting London UK

Association of Professional Composers
34 Hanway St., 4 Brook St., London, W1P 9DE, England, UK
Tel: 44 207 4360919
Fax: 44 207 4361913
Email: apc@dial.pipex.com
Founded: 1982
Members: 260
Staff: 1
Contact: Rosemary Dixson, Admin.
Description: Composers working in the field of film and tv, concert music, library music, theatre, ballet, jazz, jingles. Seeks to further the collective interests of its members and to inform and advise them on professional and artistic matters.
Publication: Newsletter

Association of Professional Music Therapists
26 Hamlyn Rd., Glastonbury, BA6 8HT, England, UK
Tel: 44 1458 834919
Fax: 44 1458 834919
Email: apmtoffice@aol.com
Website: http://www.apmt.org.uk
Founded: 1976
Members: 500
Staff: 1
Contact: D. Asbridge, Admin.
Description: Professional music therapists and music therapy students. To fulfill the needs of qualified music therapists in Great Britain. Focuses on employment and sharing of information. Works to protect music therapists already in work and to assist in the creation of new posts. Sets standards of practice and training.
Publication: Newsletter
Publication title: APMT Newsletter
Second publication: Journal
Publication title: British Journal of Music Therapy. Advertisements.

Association of Professional Recording Services APRS
PO Box 22, Totnes, TQ9 7YZ, England, UK
Tel: 44 1803 868600
Fax: 44 1803 868444
Email: info@aprs.co.uk
Website: http://www.aprs.co.uk
Founded: 1947
Members: 380
Staff: 1
Contact: Peter Filleul, Exec.Dir.
Description: Companies and people working in the professional audio industry who meet APRS entrance criteria. Acts as the trade association for firms and persons professionally/commercially involved in sound recording and post production in the UK.
Publication: Newsletter
Publication title: APRS Bulletin
Second publication: Directory
Publication title: APRS Handbook 2003. Advertisements.
Meetings/Conventions: - annual trade show - Exhibits.

Association of Public Analysts

Burlington House, Piccadilly, London, W1V 0BN, England, UK
Tel: 44 114 2431016
Fax: 44 114 2448432
Email: ronennion@eurofins.com
Website: http://www.the-apa.co.uk
Founded: 1953
Members: 250
Contact: Norman Michie, SAC Chm.
Description: Public analysts and staff. Assists in upholding and maintaining the character and position of public analysts, and promotes co-operation between them.
Publication: Annual Report
Second publication: Journal

Association of Publishing Agencies
APA

Queens House, 55/56 Lincolns Inn Fields, London, WC2A 3LJ, England, UK
Tel: 44 20 74044166
Fax: 44 20 74044167
Email: hilary.weaver@apa.co.uk
Website: http://www.apa.co.uk
Founded: 1993
Members: 27
Staff: 2
Contact: Hilary Weaver, Dir.
Description: Members must be financially sound, and must have the resources to provide three or more of the following services: editorial, design, advertising, sales, production and distribution management. Members. must abide by the Code of Practice. They must deal fairly and honestly with clients, employees, suppliers, intermediaries and readers. Aims to promote awareness of the effectiveness of a customer magazine as a marketing medium; to maintain high standards of work and business practice; and to act as a central source of information.
Publication title: A to Z of Customer Publishing, Showcase, Research Guide
Meetings/Conventions: Relationship Marketing - annual conference

Association of Qualified Curative Hypnotherapists
AQCH

PO Box 9989, Birmingham, B14 4WA, England, UK
Tel: 44 121 6931223
Email: info@aqch.org
Website: http://www.aqch.org
Founded: 1985
Members: 60
Contact: Michael Harris
Fee: £175
Membership Type: full, associate, licentiate
Fee: £46
Membership Type: overseas
Description: Curative hypnotherapists. Maintains and advances the standards of hypnotherapy. Promotes professional development and training programs. Registered charity.
Library Subject: curative hypnotherapy
Library Type: open to the public
Publication: Journal
Publication title: Hypnotherapy Journal
Meetings/Conventions: - semiannual meeting

Association of Qualitative Research

Davey House, 31 St. Neots Rd., Eaton Ford, St. Neots, PE19 7BA, England, UK
Tel: 44 1480 407227
Fax: 44 1480 211267
Email: info@aqr.org.uk
Website: http://www.aqrp.co.uk/
Founded: 1982
Members: 1150
Contact: Rose Molloy, Sec.
Fee: £50
Membership Type: personal
Description: Practitioners of qualitative market research including those in research agencies, freelancers, field managers and purchasers of market research. AQRP is the UK's specialist professional study for qualitative researchers and all those interested in the discipline. It provides a forum for debate, promotes good practice and helps to train/educate at all levels.
Publication: Directory
Publication title: Directory & Handbook. Advertisements.
Second publication: Magazine
Publication title: In Brief
Meetings/Conventions: Trends Conference - annual London

Association of Radical Midwives
ARM

62 Greetby Hill, Ormskirk, L39 2DT, England, UK
Tel: 44 1695 572776
Fax: 44 1695 572776
Email: arm@radmid.demon.co.uk
Website: http://www.radmid.demon.co.uk
Founded: 1976
Members: 1700
Staff: 1
Contact: Ishbel Kargar, Admin.Sec.
Fee: £25
Membership Type: UK
Fee: £30
Membership Type: Outside UK
Description: Midwives, mothers, health professionals, and interested individuals. Supports the interests of midwives. Provides supportive services and information to women experiencing difficulty in securing adequate and sympathetic maternity care.
Publication: Booklet
Publication title: Choices in Childbirth
Second publication: Magazine
Publication title: Midwifery Matters. Advertisements.
Meetings/Conventions: - quarterly meeting - Exhibits.

Association of Recognised English Language Services

56 Buckingham Gate, London, SWIE 6AG, England, UK
Tel: 44 20 7802 9200
Fax: 44 20 7802 9201
Email: enquiries@arels.org.uk
Website: http://www.arels.org.uk
Founded: 1960
Members: 212
Staff: 11
Contact: Tony Millns, Chief.Exec.
Description: English language teaching centres, recognised by the British Council. Ensures the maintenance of high academic standards,

promotes the learning of English in Britain and acts as a corporate voice for the industry.
Publication: Booklet
Publication title: A Foreign Student in Your Home
Second publication: Magazine
Publication title: Arena
Meetings/Conventions: Arels Fair - annual conference

Association of Reflexologists

27 Old Gloucester St., London, WC1N 3XX, England, UK
Tel: 44 870 5673320
Fax: 44 1989 567676
Email: aor@assocmanagement.co.uk
Website: http://www.aor.org.uk
Founded: 1984
Members: 6700
Staff: 4
Contact: Simon Duncan, Exec.Ofc.
Fee: £50
Membership Type: full and associate
Fee: £26
Membership Type: friend and student
Description: Promotes reflexology to the public.
Publication: Journal
Publication title: Reflexions. Advertisements.
Meetings/Conventions: - 5/year seminar

Association of Regional City Editors

1 Fern Dene, Ealing, London, W13 8AN, England, UK
Tel: 44 208 9976868
Founded: 1975
Members: 20
Contact: John Heffernan, Hon.Sec.
Description: Promotes regional city editors.

Association of Relocation Agents

PO Box 189, Diss, IP22 1PE, England, UK
Tel: 44 8700 737475
Fax: 44 8700 718719
Email: info@relocationagents.com
Website: http://www.relocationagents.com
Founded: 1986
Members: 200
Staff: 2
Contact: Tad Zurlinden
Fee: £250
Membership Type: full or associate
Fee: £400
Membership Type: affiliate
Description: Companies, partnerships, individuals offering relocation services to companies, their employees and individuals moving within the UK and overseas; affiliate members, those offering products or services that may be of use to those relocating. Formed to encourage and promote companies offering relocation services, ensure the professional integrity of its members and high standards of service, to both the private and corporate sectors.
Publication: Book
Publication title: ARA Guide to the UK, 4th Ed.. Advertisements.
Publication title: The Guide to Homesearch
Meetings/Conventions: - annual conference

Association of Researchers in Medicine and Science
ARMS

c/o Dunhill Research Laboratories
Thomas Guy House, 5th Fl., Guy's Hospital, London Bridge, London, SE1 9RT, England, UK
Tel: 44 207 9552438
Fax: 44 161 9554015
Email: arms@fs1.ho.man.ac.uk
Website: http://www.hop.man.ac.uk/arms/
Founded: 1978
Contact: Dr. Steve Hopkins, Chm.
Fee: £10
Membership Type: ordinary
Description: Academic and allied institutions in the United Kingdom. Promotes a higher degree of professional competence in research. Supports the professional and scientific interests of researcher; works to establish a satisfactory career structure for researchers in medicine and science; conducts educational programs to raise public awareness of research and the role of the researcher in society. Conducts surveys; maintains lobbying body at the national level.
Publication: Newsletter
Publication title: ARMS Newsletter

Association of Residential Letting Agents

Maple House, 53-55 Woodside Rd., Amersham, HP6 6AA, England, UK
Tel: 44 8453 455752
Fax: 44 1494 431530
Email: info@arla.co.uk
Website: http://www.arla.co.uk
Founded: 1981
Members: 1009
Contact: Tony Meaden, Chief Exec.
Description: Membership is limited to firms meeting defined criteria and complying with a code of practice. Provides training courses, holds seminars, conducts surveys and promotes the profession through the media. Consulted prior to legislation and always available for comment on rented housing throughout the UK.
Publication: Report
Publication title: Agreement. Advertisements.

Association of Residential Managing Agents
ARMA

178 Battersea Park Rd., London, SW11 4NDD, England, UK
Tel: 44 20 79782607
Fax: 44 20 74986153
Email: info@arma.org.uk
Website: http://www.arma.org.uk
Founded: 1990
Members: 130
Description: Corporate members must hold professional indemnity insurance and provide an annual audit certificate; members must be involved in the management of blocks of flats.
Publication: Newsletter
Meetings/Conventions: - annual conference - Exhibits.

Association of Roman Archaeology
ARA

75 York Rd., Swindon, SN1 2JU, England, UK
Tel: 44 1793 534008
Email: PtWllms@aol.com

Website: http://www.zyworld.com/zarriba/ara.htm
Founded: 1996
Members: 3000
Staff: 6
Contact: B. Walters, Dir.
Fee: £15
Membership Type: single
Fee: £20
Membership Type: double
Description: Promotes Roman studies and archaeology.
Publication: Magazine
Publication title: Bulletin on Roman Discoveries. Advertisements.
Meetings/Conventions: - bimonthly

Association of Rooflight Manufacturers

1 Gadsden Close, Cranfield, Bedford, MK43 0HF, England, UK
Tel: 44 1234 752248
Fax: 44 1234 752647
Email: arm.uk@btinternet.com
Website: http://www.arm.uk.net
Founded: 1965
Members: 13
Staff: 1
Contact: Lorraine Cookham
Fee: £800
Membership Type: full
Fee: £300
Membership Type: associate
Description: Ensures contact and communication between manufactureres, material suppliers, industry and regulatory bodies. Promotes bestworking practices and to generally influence and maintain standards within the Roofling Industry.
Library Subject: rooflights
Library Type: open to the public
Publication title: Technical Guide For the Use of Rooflights Fitted to or Upstands

Association of Sea Fisheries Committees of England and Wales

24 Wykeham, Scarborough, YO13 9QP, England, UK
Tel: 44 1723 863169
Fax: 44 1723 863169
Founded: 1919
Members: 12
Staff: 1
Contact: R. Bradley, Chief Exec.
Description: Concerned with the enforcement of fisheries regulations, byelaws and fisheries management.

Association of Sealant Applicators

c/o Rowland Hall
Grovedell House, 15 Knightswick Rd., Canvey Island, SS8 9PA, England, UK
Tel: 44 1268 696878
Fax: 44 1268 511247
Email: arichardson@rowlandhall.co.uk
Founded: 1984
Members: 50
Staff: 2
Contact: A.E. Richardson
Fee: £525
Membership Type: full applicator, manufacturer, affiliated
Description: Full members are applicating companies; associate members are manufacturers of materials or invited because of

industry knowledge. To promote the highest standards of building design, specifications of material, and applicators workmanship.
Meetings/Conventions: - quarterly meeting

Association of Secretaries General of Parliaments ASGP

Table Office, House of Commons, London, SW1A 0AA, England, UK
Tel: 44 207 2193303
Fax: 44 207 2195568
Email: phillipsris@parliament.uk
Website: http://www.ipu.org/english/asgp.htm
Founded: 1938
Members: 225
Contact: Roger Phillips, Sec.
Description: Secretaries general from parliamentary assemblies in 95 countries, and/or their deputies. Facilitates contacts between secretaries general for the purposes of studying the law, procedure, practice and working methods of different parliaments; proposes measures for improving those methods and for securing cooperation between the services of different parliaments.
Publication: Journal
Publication title: Constitutional and Parliamentary Information
Meetings/Conventions: - semiannual meeting

Association of Security Consultants

PO Box 22, Hampton, TW12 3HL, England, UK
Tel: 44 7071 224865
Fax: 44 208 9795323
Email: info@securityconsultants.org.uk
Website: http://www.securityconsultants.org.uk
Founded: 1991
Members: 60
Staff: 1
Contact: Maurice Parsons, Sec.
Fee: £75
Membership Type: affiliate
Fee: £200
Membership Type: full
Description: Members must be independent consultants bearing no allegiance to specific suppliers of products or services. Founded as the professional organization for independent security consultants. In representing and promoting their specific interests, it aims to set and maintain the highest standards of quality in all its undertakings through adherence to its code of conduct.
Library Subject: British and European security standards
Library Type: reference
Publication: Directory
Publication title: Consultants Resources Directory
Meetings/Conventions: - annual convention - Exhibits. London UK

Association of Show and Agricultural Organisations

PO Box 4575, Sherbourne, DT9 4XA, England, UK
Tel: 44 7711 205833
Fax: 44 1749 823169
Email: asaosecretary@asao.co.uk
Website: http://www.asao.co.uk
Founded: 1923
Members: 190
Contact: P.J. Hooper
Fee: £130
Publication: Directory
Publication title: List of Shows and Sales. Advertisements.
Meetings/Conventions: - semiannual congress - Exhibits.

Association of Social Anthropologists of the UK and the Commonwealth
ASA

c/o RAI
3 Tudor Well Close, Stanmore, HA7 2SD, England, UK
Tel: 44 207 3870455
Fax: 44 207 3834235
Email: admin@theasa.org
Website: http://les1.man.ac.uk/asa
Founded: 1946
Members: 580
Contact: Dr. John Eade, Hon.Sec.
Description: Professional social anthropologists in 42 countries. Promotes study and teaching of social anthropology. Sponsors seminars on professional training and current advances in the field.
Publication: Report
Publication title: Annals of the ASA
Second publication: Newsletter
Publication title: Newsletter
Meetings/Conventions: Indigenious Knowledge - annual conference UK

Association of Solicitor Investment Managers

Baldocks Barn, Chiddingstone Causeway, Tonbridge, TN11 8JX, England, UK
Tel: 44 1892 870065
Fax: 44 1892 870160
Email: admin@asim.org.uk
Website: http://www.asim.org.uk
Founded: 1993
Members: 88
Contact: Mrs. Heather Martin, Chief Exec.
Fee: £700
Membership Type: by firm
Description: Solicitors' firms conducting investment management, usually for private clients. To encourage provision of portfolio investment services by solicitors' firms subject to appropriate expertise and high standards; to increase awareness of such firms among the general public; to lobby the government and self-regulatory or professional bodies on behalf of members; to provide a forum for the exchange of information and experience.
Publication: Membership Directory
Publication title: ASIM Directory of Members. Advertisements.
Second publication: Newsletter
Publication title: ASIM Newsletter
Meetings/Conventions: - annual conference - Exhibits.

Association of South East Asian Studies in the UK

University of Hull, Hull, HU6 7RX, England, UK
Tel: 44 1482 465758
Fax: 44 1482 465758
Email: p.khng@pol-as.hull.ac.uk
Website: http://www.hull.ac.uk/aseasuk/

Association of Speakers Clubs

152 Aylesbury Rd., Hockley Heath, Solihull, B94 6PP, England, UK
Tel: 44 1564 774907
Email: info@the-asc.org.uk
Website: http://www.the-asc.org.uk
Founded: 1978
Members: 3000
Contact: Lilian Watts
Fee: £8

Description: Covers training in public speaking.
Publication: Newsletter. Advertisements.
Meetings/Conventions: - annual conference - Exhibits.

Association of Stress Consultants

BSY Group, Stanhope Sq., Holsworthy, EX22 6DF, England, UK
Tel: 44 1409 259214
Fax: 44 1409 259215
Email: info@bsygroup.co.uk
Website: http://www.bsygroup.co.uk
Founded: 1946
Contact: Ann Williams
Description: Stress consultants.

Association of Stress Therapists

8 Greenriggs, Wigmore, Luton, LU29 TQ, England, UK
Tel: 44 1582 452964
Email: associationofstresstherapists@groups.msn.com
Website: http://uk.msnusers.com/AssociationofStressTherapists
Founded: 1991
Members: 30
Staff: 1
Contact: Ms. N.M Yeoman, Con.
Fee: £25
Membership Type: associate
Fee: £25
Membership Type: full
Description: Promotes stress therapy as a complementary therapy used to alleviate the physical and mental symptoms caused by stress.

Association of Subscription Agents and Intermediaries

10 Lime Ave., High Wycombe, HP11 1DP, England, UK
Tel: 44 1494 534778
Fax: 44 1494 534778
Email: rollo.turner@onet.co.uk
Website: http://www.subscription-agents.org
Founded: 1934
Members: 49
Staff: 1
Contact: Rollo Turner, Sec.Gen.
Description: Open to any company whose main occupation, or a substantial part of it, is that of a subscription agent or an electronic intermediary. Membership may be initiated by invitation or direct application to the Secretary. Exists to ensure that members achieve the highest standards of service for the customers and improve relationships, service and terms with the publishers.
Publication: Newsletter
Publication title: ASA News
Publication title: The Work of Subscription Agents
Meetings/Conventions: - annual conference

Association of Supervisors of Midwives

c/o James Paget Hospital
Corporate Services, Lowestoft Rd., Gorleston, Great Yarmouth, NR31 6LA, England, UK
Tel: 44 1493 452269
Fax: 44 1493 452078
Email: elayne.guest@jpaget.nhs.uk
Founded: 1910
Members: 350
Contact: Elayne Guest
Fee: £10

Description: Qualified midwives nominated as Supervisors of Midwives. Promotes a high standard of Supervision of Midwives in the practice and teaching of midwifery. Offers support to members and represents the interests of Supervisors of Midwives at national and international levels.
Library Type: not open to the public
Publication title: Risk Management in Midwifery Practice
Meetings/Conventions: - annual conference - Exhibits.

Association of Suppliers to the British Clothing Industry

Unit 5, 25 Square Rd., Halifax, HX1 1QG, England, UK
Tel: 44 1422 354666
Fax: 44 1422 381184
Email: info@asbci.co.uk
Website: http://www.asbci.co.uk
Founded: 1992
Members: 125
Staff: 2
Contact: Stephanie Ingham
Fee: £95
Description: Companies that are suppliers to the BCI -retail, manufacturing, chemical, finishers, fabric manufacturers, interlinings, drycleaners, universities. Aims to raise profitability of member companies by effective use of modern technology; to enhance continuously the quality of goods delivered by ASBCI members; to provide exchange of information between the sectors; to continue to improve consumer satisfaction with goods before and after cleaning and laundering.
Library Subject: clothing manufacture
Library Type: by appointment only
Formerly: British Interlining Manufacturers Association
Publication: Bulletins
Publication title: Technical Bulletins
Meetings/Conventions: - annual conference

Association of Surgeons of Great Britain and Ireland

c/o The Royal College of Surgeons of England
35-43 Lincoln's Inn Fields, London, WC2A 3PN, England, UK
Tel: 44 20 79730303
Fax: 44 20 74309235
Email: admin@asgbi.org.uk
Website: http://www.asgbi.org.uk
Founded: 1920
Members: 2000
Staff: 8
Contact: Dr. Nicholas P. Gair, Chief Exec.
Fee: £260
Membership Type: full fellow
Description: General surgeons. Concerned with the advancement of the science and art of surgery and the promoting of friendship amongst surgeons. The Association is the specialty association for general surgery and is recognized as such by Government as well as by the profession.
Publication: Journal
Publication title: British Journal of Surgery
Meetings/Conventions: - annual conference - Exhibits. Manchester UK

Association of Systematic Kinesiology
ASK

19 Westfield Ln., Saint Leonards-on-Sea, TN37 7NE, England, UK
Tel: 44 1424 753375
Email: marie.cheshire@hotmail.com
Website: http://www.kinesiology-uk.com
Founded: 1988
Members: 250
Contact: Marie Cheshire, Sec./Admin.
Fee: £150
Membership Type: professional
Publication: Newsletter
Meetings/Conventions: Open Day - annual London UK

Association of Teachers and Lecturers
ATL

7 Northumberland St., London, WC2N 5RD, England, UK
Tel: 44 207 9306441
Fax: 44 207 9301359
Email: info@atl.org.uk
Website: http://www.askatl.org.uk
Founded: 1978
Members: 140000
Staff: 70
Contact: John Puckrin
Description: Teachers and lecturers In England, Wales, and Northern Ireland. Protects and improves the status of teachers. Offers professional advisory and legal services. Represents members' interests on issues such as training and staffing, salary, superannuation, and probation. Maintains Benevolent Fund to aid members and their dependents in times of illness or financial hardship. Offers courses, conferences, and seminars on educational developments.
Formerly: Formed by Merger of, Association of Assistant Mistresses
Publication: Magazine
Publication title: Report. Advertisements.
Second publication: Booklet
Publication title: Retirement and You
Meetings/Conventions: - annual assembly - Exhibits.

Association of Teachers of Lipreading to Adults

PO Box 506, Hanley, Stoke-On-Trent, ST2 9RE, England, UK
Fax: 44 870 7062916
Email: atla@lipreading.org.uk
Website: http://www.lipreading.org.uk
Founded: 1975
Members: 340
Staff: 6
Contact: Mary Hall, Sec.
Description: To promote understanding of the needs of people with an acquired hearing loss. To advance the awareness of the benefits of lipreading and other communication skills in the rehabilitation of people with an acquired hearing loss.
Publication: Magazine
Publication title: Catchword

Association of Teachers of Mathematics
ATM

7 Shaftesbury St., Derby, DE23 8YB, England, UK
Tel: 44 1332 346599
Fax: 44 1332 204357
Email: admin@atm.org.uk

Website: http://www.atm.org.uk
Founded: 1952
Members: 4000
Staff: 7
Contact: Su Strange, Sr.Admin.Off.
Fee: £49
Membership Type: Personal
Fee: £67
Membership Type: Institution
Description: Teachers, students, colleges, schools, libraries, advisers, inspectors, and educational publishers interested in mathematics in 30 countries. Encourages changes in mathematical education relevant to the needs of students. Organizes working groups to address mathematical issues.
Formerly: Association for Teaching Aids in Mathematics
Publication: Journal
Publication title: Mathematics Teaching. Advertisements.
Second publication: Magazine
Publication title: Micromath
Meetings/Conventions: - annual conference

Association of Teachers of Printing and Allied Subjects

110 Stonnall Rd., Aldridge, Walsall, WS9 8JZ, England, UK
Tel: 44 1922 451983
Founded: 1938
Members: 200
Contact: Leon Symonds
Description: Printing and graphic design lecturers. Concerned with the educational needs of the visual communications industry.
Publication: Journal
Publication title: ATPAS
Meetings/Conventions: - annual conference

Association of Teachers of Singing

Coral Gould, Weir House, 108 Newton Rd., Burton-On-Trent, DE15 0TT, England, UK
Tel: 44 1283 542198
Fax: 44 1283 542198
Email: coralgould7@aol.com
Website: http://www.aotos.co.uk
Founded: 1975
Members: 453
Contact: Coral Gould
Fee: £35
Fee: £80
Membership Type: corporate
Description: Teachers of singing, private and college/institution orientated. Aims to promote, for the benefit of its members and for wider dissemination, understanding of the matters connected with the teaching of singing and to bring together people who are occupied in this work.
Publication: Magazine
Publication title: Singing-Voice of AOTOS
Meetings/Conventions: - annual conference

Association of the British Pharmaceutical Industry

12 Whitehall, London, SW1A 2DY, England, UK
Tel: 44 20 79303477
Fax: 44 20 77471411
Email: abpi@abpi.org.uk
Website: http://www.abpi.org.uk
Founded: 1930
Members: 72

Staff: 65
Contact: Alan W. Hunter, Sec.
Description: Pharmaceutical companies conducting business in the United Kingdom involved in research and development, or those companies interested in pharmaceutical matters. Represents manufacturers of medicines not advertised to the public.
Library Subject: pharmaceutical industry, medicine, health economics
Library Type: not open to the public

Association of the International Rubber Trade

606 The Chanderly, 50 Westminster Bridge Rd., London, SE1 7QY, England, UK
Tel: 44 207 7217440
Fax: 44 207 7217459
Email: airt@dircon.co.uk
Website: http://www.airt.dircon.co.uk/
Founded: 1913
Members: 10
Staff: 1
Contact: Howard A. Evans, Sec.Gen.
Description: Producers, traders, and consumers of natural rubber. Also have 48 trade associate members, and 14 non-trade associates. All types of membership are available to companies worldwide. The declared object of the Association is to provide an efficient and dependable marketing service to producers and consumers of rubber. This includes the formulation of agreed contract terms, and the provision of arbitration and appeal facilities for the settling of commercial disputes involving rubber.
Formerly: The Rubber Trade Association of London
Publication title: Official Prices for Natural Rubber Grades in London Market

Association of Therapeutic Communities
ATC

Bams Centre, Church Ln., Toddington, Cheltenham, EC1R 0JG, England, UK
Tel: 44 1242 620077
Fax: 44 1242 620077
Email: post@therapeuticcommunities.org
Website: http://www.therapeuticcommunities.org
Founded: 1972
Members: 200
Description: Nurses, social workers, researchers, psychologists, creative therapists, managers, residential care staff, teachers, psychotherapists, psychiatrists, and academics. Conducts training and education programs.
Publication: Journal
Publication title: Therapeutic Communities Journal. Advertisements.
Meetings/Conventions: - annual conference

Association of Town Centre Management

1 Queen Anne's Gate, London, SW1H 9BT, England, UK
Tel: 44 207 2220120
Fax: 44 207 2224440
Email: info@atcm.org
Website: http://www.atcm.org
Founded: 1989
Members: 520
Staff: 13
Contact: Alan Tallentire, Chmn.
Fee: £380
Membership Type: individual

Fee: £190
Membership Type: affiliate
Description: Aims to promote town and city centers as environmentally sustainable, socially inclusive and economically vital and viable.
Library Subject: town centre management
Library Type: reference

Association of Translation Companies

Kent House, Stes. 10-11, 87 Regent St., London, W1B 4EH, England, UK
Tel: 44 20 74370007
Fax: 44 20 74397701
Email: info@atc.org.uk
Website: http://www.atc.org.uk
Founded: 1976
Members: 85
Contact: Geoffrey Eowden, Gen.Sec.
Description: Promotes the use of professionally produced translation by exporters. Seeks to raise standards and encourage the adoption of quality systems.

Association of United Kingdom Media Librarians

c/o Sara Margetts
Reference Library, Financial Times, One Southwark Bridge, London, SE1 9HL, England, UK
Tel: 44 207 8733920
Email: info@aukml.org.uk
Website: http://www.aukml.org.uk
Founded: 1986
Members: 120
Contact: Sara Margetts
Description: Librarians working in UK newspaper and broadcasting companies. Exists to keep members informed of developments in text and picture librarianship which directly affect their industry.
Publication: Newsletter
Publication title: Deadline
Second publication: Membership Directory

Association of University Administrators

c/o University of Manchester
Oxford Rd., Manchester, M13 9PL, England, UK
Tel: 44 161 2752063
Fax: 44 161 2752036
Email: aua@man.ac.uk
Website: http://www.aua.ac.uk
Founded: 1993
Members: 4100
Staff: 7
Contact: Lynn Rawlinson, Exec.Sec.
Fee: £53
Membership Type: full
Fee: £47
Membership Type: associate
Description: Administrators and managers in virtually all Higher Education institutions in the UK and Republic of Ireland drawn from all areas of administration including secretariat, registration, estates, and student services. Concerned with the development of sound methods of administration in higher education and encouragement of the professional development of individual administrators and managers in all areas of administration by providing courses, seminars, conferences and opportunities for the exchange of ideas and discussion of current problems in higher education including study visits abroad.

Publication: Newsletter
Publication title: Newslink. Advertisements.
Second publication: Journal
Publication title: Perspectives
Meetings/Conventions: Supporting Success - annual conference - Exhibits. Derby UK

Association of University Professors of French and Heads of French Departments in the UK and Ireland

c/o University of Bristol
Department of French, 17/19 Woodland Rd, Bristol, BS8 ITE, England, UK
Tel: 44 117 9287913
Fax: 44 117 9288922
Email: t.a.unwin@bristol.ac.uk
Website: http://www.bris.ac.uk/auphf
Founded: 1945
Members: 185
Contact: Prof. T. Unwin, Pres.
Fee: £30
Description: Professors of French and Heads of French Depts in UK Universities. Aims to keep members informed of the latest developments in educational policy affecting the discipline and organization of French studies and to make representations on members' behalf on these matters to Government and Funding Councils.
Formerly: Association of University Professors of French and Heads of French Departments
Publication: Proceedings
Publication title: French in the '90s
Meetings/Conventions: - periodic conference

Association of University Research and Industry Links
AURIL

3rd Floor, 10 Fleet Pl., Limeburner Ln., London, EC4M 7SB, England, UK
Tel: 44 20 75751693
Fax: 44 20 75751694
Email: secretariat@auril.org.uk
Website: http://www.auril.org.uk/
Founded: 1994

Association of University Teachers - London

Egmont House, 25-31 Tavistock Pl., London, WC1H 9UT, England, UK
Tel: 44 207 6709700
Fax: 44 207 6709799
Email: hq@aut.org.uk
Website: http://www.aut.org.uk
Founded: 1919
Members: 45000
Staff: 60
Contact: Sally Hunt, Gen.Sec.
Fee: £114
Membership Type: full
Description: Academic and related research staff in university and similar higher education and research organisations. Concerned with the advancement of university education and research, the regulation of relations between academic and related staff and their employers. Also promotes common action by those staff and safeguards the interests of members.
Library Subject: education, industrial relations

Library Type: not open to the public
Formerly: Supersedes, Association of University and College Lecturers
Publication title: AUT Update
Second publication: Journal
Publication title: AUTLOOK. Advertisements.
Meetings/Conventions: - semiannual meeting - Exhibits.

Association of Valuers of Licensed Property

c/o Fleurets
18 Bloomsbury Sq., London, WC1A 2NS, England, UK
Tel: 44 207 6368992
Fax: 44 207 6367490
Email: avlp@btinternet.com
Website: http://www.avlp.net
Founded: 1894
Members: 125
Contact: David Germaney
Description: Experts in valuation of public houses and licensed premises. Promotes professional and proper understanding of value of licensed premises.

Association of Veterinary Anaesthetists

Animal Health Trust, Landvades Park, Newmarket, CB8 7UU, England, UK
Tel: 44 1638 555651
Email: dave.brodbelt@aht.org.uk
Website: http://www.aveta.org.uk
Founded: 1964
Members: 400
Staff: 1
Contact: Mr. D. Brodbelt, Sec.
Fee: £50
Membership Type: ordinary
Fee: £50
Membership Type: corresponding
Description: Veterinary surgeons; medics, anaesthetists, those with medical university qualifications and scientists, Animal technicians and veterinary nurses. Furthers teaching and research in veterinary anaesthetics.
Formerly: Association of Veterinary Anaesthetists of Great Britian and Ireland
Publication: Journal
Publication title: Journal of Veterinary Anaesthesia and Analgesia. Advertisements.
Meetings/Conventions: World Congress - semiannual congress - Exhibits.

Association of Visually Impaired Chartered Physiotherapists

c/o Guildford Physiotherapy and Sports Clinic
Matthews House, 85 Epsom Rd., Guildford, GU1 3PA, England, UK
Tel: 44 1483 575876
Fax: 44 1483 302691
Founded: 1919
Members: 125
Contact: Mr. D. Wood
Description: Visually impaired chartered physiotherapists. To supply support and encouragement and benefits to its members.
Publication: Audiotapes
Publication title: Physiotherapist

Association of Welding Distributors

Stafford Park 1, Enterprise House, Telford, TF3 3BD, England, UK
Tel: 44 1952 290036
Fax: 44 1952 290037
Email: info@awd.org.uk
Website: http://www.awd.org.uk
Founded: 1974
Members: 160
Staff: 2
Contact: Mike Vacher, Dir.
Fee: £1000
Membership Type: corporate
Description: Distributors, manufacturers and importers of welding equipment and consumables. Aims to enhance the status of members and encourage end users to deal only with AWD approved suppliers; improve tangible benefits available to members; develop communications by offering a regular newsletter service to membership. Continues to liaise more closely with METCOM and take full advantage of facilities available to AWD.
Library Subject: welding science, application, finance, administration, trade publications
Library Type: not open to the public
Publication: Newsletter
Publication title: AWD Business Bulletin
Second publication: Magazine
Publication title: Business Bulletin. Advertisements.
Meetings/Conventions: - annual conference Stratford UK

Association of Wholesale Electrical Bulk Buyers

2 Kensington Works, Hallam Fields Rd., Derbyshire, DE7 8EF, England, UK
Tel: 44 115 9441088
Fax: 44 115 9301036
Email: info@awebb.org.uk
Founded: 1976
Members: 59
Staff: 8
Contact: David Dunning, Chief Exec.
Description: Wholesale electrical bulk buyers.

Association of Wholesale Woollen Merchants

Green Acres, Chaddesley Corbett, Kidderminster, DY10 4QD, England, UK
Tel: 44 1562 777141
Fax: 44 1562 777141
Founded: 1934
Members: 10
Contact: David R. Mills
Description: Merchants involved in the sale and distribution of fine woollen and worsted cloth. Promotes the interests of woollen and worsted cloth merchants; protects the public from false descriptions of such goods; liaises with government departments on points of relevant interest to merchants and provides a forum for the exchange of views and ideas amongst members.

Association of Women Barristers
AWB

c/o General Council of the Bar
2-3 Cursitor St., London, WC2A 3RX, England, UK
Tel: 44 20 72421289
Fax: 44 20 72421107
Email: jbradley@barcouncil.org.uk
Founded: 1991

Members: 500
Staff: 1
Contact: Julian Bradley, Admin.
Fee: £10
Membership Type: student
Fee: £35
Membership Type: barrister
Description: Women barristers and law students. Seeks to guarantee fair treatment for women in legal practice, employment, and judicial appointment. Promotes professional advancement of members. Facilitates exchange of information among members; monitors the status of women barristers and publicizes cases of gender discrimination in the legal profession.
Publication: Newsletter
Publication title: AWB Newsletter
Meetings/Conventions: - annual seminar

Association of Women Solicitors

The Law Society, 114 Chancery Ln., London, WC2A 1PL, England, UK
Tel: 44 207 3205793
Email: enquiries@womensolicitors.org.uk
Website: http://www.womensolicitors.org.uk
Founded: 1976
Members: 10000
Contact: Judith McDermott
Description: Promotes the professional and business interests of women attorneys.

Association of Woodturners of Great Britain

c/o Derek Phillips
15 Greens Rd., Cambridge, CB4 3EF, England, UK
Tel: 44 1223 312134
Email: derek.phillips@virgin.net
Website: http://www.woodturners.co.uk
Founded: 1984
Members: 2000
Contact: Derek Phillips, Sec.
Description: Anyone interested in woodturning, most professionals are members but 90% of membership are hobbyists. To foster greater awareness of art and craft of woodturning, provide a forum for exchange of information on turning and turners; encourages training and development and acts as the national body and voice of woodturning in the UK.
Library Subject: woodturning-various aspects
Library Type: not open to the public
Publication: Newsletter
Publication title: Revolutions. Advertisements.
Publication title: Wonders in Wood-The Art of The Woodturner
Meetings/Conventions: - biennial seminar - Exhibits.

Association of Woodwind Teachers

26 Gouge Ave., Northfleet, Kent, DA11 8DP, England, UK
Tel: 44 1474 745524
Email: normanblow1@activemail.co.uk
Website: http://www.awt.org.uk/
Founded: 1960
Members: 190
Contact: Norman Blow, Treas., Membership Sec.
Fee: £15
Description: Teachers of woodwind instruments. Acts as a support group for woodwind teachers; provides opportunities for discussion and exchange of ideas; promotes and encourages high standards of woodwind teaching.

Publication: Magazine
Publication title: Wood Notes. Advertisements.
Second publication: Membership Directory
Meetings/Conventions: Browse and Play Weekend - annual workshop Yorkshire UK

Association of Workers for Children with Emotional and Behavioural Difficulties

Charlton Ct., East Sutton, Maidstone, ME17 3DQ, England, UK
Tel: 44 1622 843104
Fax: 44 1622 844220
Email: awcebd@mistral.co.uk
Website: http://www.awcebd.co.uk
Founded: 1953
Members: 1000
Contact: Allan Rimmer, Admin. Officer
Fee: £48
Membership Type: individual and corporate and outside UK
Description: All professions involved in work with children and young people with emotional and behavioural difficulties and those who are involved in training. Promotes meeting the needs of children and young people with emotional and/or behavioural difficulties, in a variety of settings including education.
Publication: Journal
Publication title: Emotional and Behavioral Difficulties
Second publication: Newsletter
Meetings/Conventions: conference - Exhibits.

Association of X-ray Equipment Manufacturers

St. George's House, 195-203 Waterloo Rd., London, SE1 8WB, England, UK
Tel: 44 207 6428083
Fax: 44 207 6428096
Founded: 1974
Members: 11
Contact: G.L. Fraser
Description: Trade association for U.K. suppliers of diagnostic imaging and radio therapy equipment.

Ataxia - UK

10 Winchester House, Kennington Park, Cranmer Rd., London, SW9 6EJ, England, UK
Tel: 44 207 5821444
Fax: 44 207 5829444
Email: office@ataxia.org.uk
Website: http://www.ataxia.org.uk
Founded: 1965
Members: 2700
Staff: 6
Contact: Julia Willmott
Fee: £15
Membership Type: individual
Fee: £20
Membership Type: individual outside England
Description: Fundraising organization supporting research into Friedreich's, Cerebellar, and other ataxias (hereditary spinal diseases which cause the loss of muscular coordination). Offers support services for ataxia sufferers and their families.
Publication: Magazine
Publication title: Ataxian. Advertisements.
Meetings/Conventions: - annual conference

Ataxia-Telangiectasia Society

IACR - Rothamsted, Harpenden, AL5 2JQ, England, UK
Tel: 44 582 760733
Fax: 44 582 760162
Email: atcharity@aol.com
Website: http://www.atsociety.org.uk
Founded: 1989
Members: 110
Staff: 2
Contact: Mrs. M. Poupard
Description: Seeks to alleviate the suffering caused by Ataxia-Telangiectasia by supporting families, raising awareness of the disease and funding research. Conducts fund-raising activities.
Publication: Newsletter
Publication title: A-T Society News. Advertisements.
Meetings/Conventions: Family Meeting - annual conference

Audio Engineering Society - British Section

PO Box 645, Slough, SL1 8BJ, England, UK
Tel: 44 1628 663725
Fax: 44 1628 667002
Email: uk@aes.org
Website: http://www.aes.org/sections/uk
Founded: 1948
Members: 700
Staff: 2
Contact: Mrs. H. Lane
Description: Members are involved in various areas of audio engineering. Acts as a subsidiary of parent body which has its headquarters in New York, USA
Publication: Journal
Publication title: Journal of the Audio Engineering Society

Audio Visual Association

Fox Talbot House, 2 Amwell End, Ware, SG12 9HN, England, UK
Tel: 44 208 9505959
Fax: 44 208 9507560
Email: bipp@compuserve.com
Founded: 1977
Contact: Mike Simpson
Description: Producers in sub broadcast professional AV and all specialists on whom they rely - equipment manufacturers, hirers, writers, cameramen, electronic images, riggers, sound studios etc. A Specialist Interest Group of the British Institute of Professional Photography.

Australia and New Zealand Chamber of Commerce (UK)

ANZCC (UK)

393 Strand, London, WC2R 0JQ, England, UK
Tel: 44 207 3790720
Fax: 44 207 3790721
Email: enquiries@anzcc.org.uk
Website: http://www.anzcc.org.uk
Founded: 1914
Members: 400
Staff: 4
Contact: Alexandra Reynolds, Dir.
Description: Encourages bilateral trade between Australia, New Zealand and the United Kingdom; promotes business and networking for membership base.
Formerly: Australian-British Chamber of Commerce
Publication: Magazine
Publication title: Up and Under. Advertisements.
Meetings/Conventions: board meeting

Authors' Licensing and Collecting Society

Marlborough Court, 14-18 Holborn, London, EC1N 2LE, England, UK
Tel: 44 207 3950600
Fax: 44 207 3950660
Email: alcs@alcs.co.uk
Website: http://www.alcs.co.uk
Founded: 1977
Members: 18000
Staff: 34
Contact: Dafydd Wyn Phillips, Ch.Exec.
Fee: £8
Membership Type: full or associate
Description: Open to all writers and their successors. Concerned with the collection and distribution of royalties to writers.
Publication: Newsletter
Publication title: ALCS News

Autism Independent UK

199-205 Blandford Ave., Kettering, NN16 9AT, England, UK
Tel: 44 1536 523274
Fax: 44 1536 523274
Email: autism@rmplc.co.uk
Website: http://www.autismuk.com/
Founded: 1987
Members: 4000
Staff: 7
Contact: Keith Lovett
Description: Individuals with autism and their families. Seeks to increase awareness of autism; promotes development of improved diagnosis and treatment of people with autism. Works to improve the quality of life of people with autism. Serves as a nonmedical information center on autism and its treatment; sponsors research and educational programs; provides support and services to people with autism and their families. Maintains Diagnosis and Assessment Resource Centre, where interested individuals can access information on autism and its treatment. Collaborates with county agencies in the development of public health policies impacting people with autism.
Library Subject: autism
Library Type: reference
Formerly: Society of the Austically Handicapped
Meetings/Conventions: - periodic seminar

Autism Initiatives

7 Chesterfield Rd., Crosby, Liverpool, L23 9XL, England, UK
Website: http://www.autisminitiatives.org/
Description: Provides information on autism from behavior management to diagnosis.

Automated Material Handling Systems Association

AMHSA

PO Box 7113, Leicester, LE7 9XX, England, UK
Tel: 44 116 2598518
Fax: 44 870 7877439
Email: secretary@amhsa.co.uk
Website: http://www.amhsa.co.uk
Founded: 1986
Members: 28
Staff: 1
Contact: John Malarkey, Assn.Sec.
Description: UK companies which have designed, installed and commissioned at least one automated material handling system and UK suppliers of unit load conveying equipment and systems. Provides a forum for members to discuss matters of mutual interest and to work

together to promote ever-improving standards of quality, safety and commercial practice.
Publication title: Seven Codes of Practice

Automatic Door Suppliers Association

411 Limpsfield Rd., The Green, Warlingham, CR6 9HA, England, UK
Tel: 44 1883 624961
Fax: 44 1883 626841
Email: nas@clara.net
Website: http://adsa.org.uk
Founded: 1985
Members: 20
Staff: 1
Contact: G.F. Elliott, Dir.
Description: Suppliers of automatic doors: swing, sliding and revolving. To promote standards of safety in the installation and use of automatic doors

Automatic Identification Manufacturers - United Kingdom

The Old Vicarage, Haley Hill, Halifax, HX3 6DR, England, UK
Tel: 44 1422 368368
Fax: 44 1422 355604
Email: ian@aimuk.org
Founded: 1984
Members: 105
Contact: Ian Smith, Chief Exec.
Description: Manufacturers, suppliers, systems integrators and consultants in the field of automatic identification/data capture (bar coding, RF tags, RF data communication, portable terminals, magnetic stripe, OCR, smart cards, vision systems, voice recognition,. etc). To educate the marketplace in automatic identification/data capture technologies and thereby to increase the market for the products and services of its members. To participate in the standardization process to ensure the best use can be made of these technologies.
Publication title: Update and Focus Europe

Automatic Vending Association
AVA

1 Villiers Ct., 40 Upper Mulgrave Rd., Cheam, Sutton, SM2 7AJ, England, UK
Tel: 44 20 86611112
Fax: 44 20 86612224
Email: info@ava-vending.org
Website: http://www.ava-vending.org
Founded: 1929
Members: 300
Staff: 8
Contact: Janette Gledhill, Dir./CEO
Description: Producers, suppliers, importers, exporters, and distributors involved in the vending machine industry in the United Kingdom. Represents members' interests; promotes the vending industry.
Formerly: Automatic Vending Association of Britain
Publication: Directory
Publication title: Handbook and List of Members. Advertisements.
Publication title: Vend Inform Census
Meetings/Conventions: - biennial trade show - Exhibits. London UK

Automotive Distribution Federation

68-70 Coleshill Rd., Hodge Hill, Birmingham, B36 8AB, England, UK
Tel: 44 121 7843535
Fax: 44 12 1 7844411
Email: admin@adf.org.uk
Website: http://www.adf.org.uk
Founded: 1930
Members: 350
Staff: 3
Contact: Brian Spratt, Ch.Exec.
Fee: £1500
Membership Type: ordinary
Fee: £505
Membership Type: service
Description: Members are wholesale distributors and manufacturers of motor components and accessories for the independent automotive aftermarket. Aims to serve, promote and strengthen the independent automotive aftermarket and improve the quality of products and services available to the ultimate benefit of the consumer. Also represents the interests of members, by forging links with Government, European Community, all authoritative bodies and other organizations both nationally and internationally.
Library Type: reference
Formerly: Motor Factors Association (MFA)
Publication: Magazine
Publication title: Eyes and Ears. Advertisements.
Meetings/Conventions: Aftermarket Workout - annual conference

Automotive Manufacturers Racing Association

The Nook, 27 Topside, Grenoside, Sheffield, DA3 8NG, England, UK
Tel: 44 114 2464878
Fax: 44 114 2464858
Email: info@amrauk.com
Website: http://www.amrauk.com
Founded: 1948
Members: 130
Staff: 1
Contact: Mr. Stuart Barnes, Coord.
Fee: £300
Membership Type: full
Fee: £135
Membership Type: associate
Description: Provides collective representation for the automotive manufacturing industry by liaison with motor sports governing bodies, event organizers, and circuit owners in the UK.

AVERT

4 Brighton Rd., Horsham, RH13 5BA, England, UK
Tel: 44 1403 210202
Fax: 44 1403 211001
Email: info@avert.org
Website: http://www.avert.org
Founded: 1986
Staff: 7
Contact: Annabel Kanabus, Dir.
Description: Seeks to improve the quality of life for persons with AIDS. Conducts research and educational programs. Provides free information on AIDS, both within the U.K. and overseas.
Library Subject: AIDS and related subjects
Library Type: reference
Formerly: AIDS Education and Research Trust
Publication: Booklets

Aviation Environment Federation
AEF

Sir John Lyon House, 5 High Timber St., London, EC4V 3NS, England, UK
Tel: 44 207 2482223
Fax: 44 207 3298160
Email: info@aef.org.uk
Website: http://www.aef.org.uk
Founded: 1975
Members: 150
Staff: 3
Contact: Tim Johnson, Dir.
Fee: £18.5
Membership Type: individual
Fee: £24
Membership Type: association
Description: Local authorities, parish councils, and amenity societies; environmentally-aware aviation interests, airfield managements, and pilots; individuals concerned with the protection of the environment. Seeks to see aviation develop in a way which allows reasonable protection of people and the environment from its adverse effects. Was founded largely in response to disturbances created by the increasing use of airfields in Britain. Explores consequences of aviation policies by taking part in public enquiries, evaluating noise and environmental impact, and studying community response. Offers technical and legal information to concerned environmentalists. Encourages good consultative practices and represents environmental interests before civil aviation authorities. Makes recommendations on such issues as environmental protection factors, technical and operational methods of noise reduction, good relations between airfields and neighbors, and careful planning of the use and siting of airfields. Undertakes research; collects data; organizes seminars.
Library Subject: aviation and environmental matters
Library Type: reference
Formerly: Airfields Environment Federation
Publication: Newsletter
Publication title: Flying Green
Second publication: Reports
Meetings/Conventions: - annual conference - Exhibits.

Aviation Insurance Offices' Association

c/o IUA
3 Minster Ct., Mincing Ln., London, EC3R 7DD, England, UK
Founded: 1948
Members: 6
Contact: D. Matchan, Sec.
Description: Insurance companies transacting aviation and/or aerospace insurance or reinsurance business in the United Kingdom. To constitute a body representative of companies transacting aviation insurance in the United Kingdom; to promote the principles and practice of aviation insurance and to provide a forum for discussion and a medium for the circulation of information between members.
Publication: Annual Report

Avicultural Society

Bristol Zoological Gardens, Bristol, BS8 3HA, England, UK
Tel: 44 117 9706176
Email: lee.palm@virgin.net
Founded: 1896
Members: 1000
Contact: Ruth Ezra, Pres.
Fee: £21

Description: Studies British and foreign birds in freedom and captivity. The society has members throughout the world.
Publication: Magazine
Publication title: Avicultural Magazine
Meetings/Conventions: meeting

BA

23 Savile Row, London, W1S 2EZ, England, UK
Tel: 44 207 9733506
Fax: 44 207 9733051
Email: samantha.burge@the-ba.net
Website: http://www.britassoc.org.uk
Founded: 1831
Members: 3000
Staff: 30
Contact: Dr. Peter Briggs, Chief Exec.
Fee: £25
Membership Type: ordinary
Fee: £500
Membership Type: corporate
Description: Scientists; corporations; individuals interested in science. Seeks to enhance public understanding and awareness of science and technology and their impact on society. Maintains 16 subject sections.
Formerly: British Association for the Advancement of Science
Publication: Newsletter
Publication title: Scan
Second publication: Magazine
Publication title: Science and the Public Affairs
Meetings/Conventions: Festival of Science - annual meeting - Exhibits.

Babraham Institute

Babraham Hall, Babraham, Cambridge, CB2 4AT, England, UK
Tel: 44 1223 496000
Fax: 44 1223 496002
Email: babraham.contact@bbsrc.ac.uk
Website: http://www.babraham.ac.uk
Founded: 1948
Staff: 450
Contact: Dr. Caroline Edmonds, Hd.
Description: Focuses on life science research with biotechnological, pharmaceutical and biomedical applications.
Library Subject: biological science
Library Type: not open to the public
Formerly: Institute of Animal Physiology
Publication title: The Babraham Institute Corporate Plan
Publication title: The Babraham Review
Meetings/Conventions: Babraham Bioenterprise Award Lecture - annual lecture

Baby Milk Action

23 St. Andrew's St., Cambridge, CB2 3AX, England, UK
Tel: 44 1223 464420
Fax: 44 1223 464417
Email: info@babymilkaction.org
Website: http://www.babymilkaction.org
Founded: 1985
Members: 2000
Staff: 4
Contact: Patti Rundall, Policy Dir.
Fee: £15
Membership Type: waged
Fee: £7

Membership Type: unwaged
Description: Works to protect mothers and their babies worldwide. Promotes breastfeeding and promotes awareness of the potential for health damage inherent in artificial infant feeding. Seeks to strengthen national and international controls on the marketing of baby foods and formulae; monitors promotional campaigns for baby formulae and challenges companies that violate the World Health Organization's International Code of Marketing of Breastmilk Substitutes. Works with other international organizations to protect and support local breastfeeding initiatives worldwide. Lobbies British government agencies and the European Union on behalf of increased protection of breasfeeding and maternity benefits. Maintains information network.
Library Subject: infant health, nutrition, breastfeeding, and boycott companies
Library Type: not open to the public
Publication: Newsletter
Publication title: Update
Meetings/Conventions: - annual general assembly

Baby Products Association
c/o The Coach House
Erlegh Manor, Vicarage Rd., Pitstone, Leighton Buzzard, LU7 9EY, England, UK
Tel: 44 1296 662789
Fax: 44 1296 660433
Email: bpa@erlegh-manor.demon.co.uk
Website: http://www.britishcompanies.co.uk/babygoods.htm
Founded: 1946
Members: 90
Staff: 3
Contact: Robert Chantry-Price, Sec.
Fee: £500
Membership Type: full
Fee: £500
Membership Type: associate
Description: Membership is open to all companies who manufacture or import children's wheeled goods, nursery furniture or other items for use primarily in the nursery or by babies or infants. Manufacturers of components for use in these products may also join. Promotes the industry to the general public and the trade as being professional and responsible; provides support to member organizations; represents the industry to government departments (in the UK, the EC and elsewhere), to local authorities and other organizations that have an interest in this field.
Library Subject: British and European standards relating to baby products
Library Type: not open to the public
Publication: Yearbook. Advertisements.
Meetings/Conventions: Baby and Child International Fair - annual - Exhibits. London UK

BackCare, The Charity for Healthy Backs
16 Elmtree Rd., Teddington, TW11 8ST, England, UK
Tel: 44 208 9775474
Fax: 44 208 9435318
Email: website@backcare.org.uk
Website: http://www.backcare.org.uk
Founded: 1968
Members: 6000
Staff: 13
Contact: Ms. Allison Mills, Dir.
Fee: £18
Membership Type: ordinary
Fee: £30

Membership Type: professional
Description: Back pain sufferers, osteopaths, chiropractors, medical doctors, and safety and training officers in 12 countries. Sponsors research on the causes and treatment of back pain. Teaches individuals to use their bodies sensibly in order to prevent spinal damage. Promotes the formation of local branches. Keeps back pain sufferers informed on current developments in research, education, treatment and equipment.
Formerly: National Back Pain Association
Publication: Manual
Publication title: A Carer's Guide to Moving and Handling Patients
Publication title: Guide to the Handling of Patients
Meetings/Conventions: - annual meeting

Bagpipe Society
13 The Terrace, Kent, Rochester, ME1 1XN, England, UK
Tel: 44 1634 843663
Fax: 44 1634 829136
Email: bagpipe@bagpipesociety.org.uk
Website: http://www.bagpipesociety.org.uk
Contact: Richard Reader
Description: Promotes bagpipes.

Bakers, Food and Allied Workers' Union BFAWU
Stanborough House, Great North Rd., Stanborough, Welwyn Garden City, AL8 7TA, England, UK
Tel: 44 1707 260150
Fax: 44 1707 261570
Email: bfawu@aol.com
Website: http://www.bfawu.org.uk
Founded: 1849
Members: 36000
Staff: 16
Contact: Joe Marino, Gen.Sec.
Fee: £1.4
Membership Type: general
Description: Individuals employed in the field of baking and related industries. Works to eliminate night work, to set the minimum wage rate, and to nationalize the baking industry. Provides legal assistance to members; offers financial support to members in the case of death, sickness, or unemployment. Organizes biennial apprentice competition; sponsors educational programs.
Library Type: reference
Publication: Manual
Publication title: Book of Rules, Health, and Safety
Second publication: Report
Meetings/Conventions: - annual conference

Ball and Roller Bearing Manufacturers Association
136 Hagley Rd., Birmingham, B16 9PN, England, UK
Tel: 44 121 4544141
Fax: 44 121 4544949
Email: info@brbma.org
Description: Ball and roller bearing manufacturers.

Ballroom Dancers Federation
9 Hazelwood Rd., Cudham, Sevenoaks, TN14 7QU, England, UK
Tel: 44 1689 855143
Fax: 44 1689 855143
Email: sec@bdf.org
Members: 500
Contact: David Sycamore, Hon.Sec.

Fee: £18
Description: Members are professional ballroom dancers concerned with competitions, demonstrations, cabaret, coaching and adjudicating. Protects the interests of members worldwide. Also undertakes the running of European and world events when either are allotted to the UK by the world body of dancing.
Publication: Journal
Publication title: Members' Journal

Baltic Exchange

St Mary Axe, London, EC3A 8BH, England, UK
Tel: 44 20 76235501
Fax: 44 20 73691622
Email: enquiries@balticexchange.co.uk
Website: http://www.balticexchange.co.uk
Founded: 1744
Members: 670
Staff: 25
Contact: Jim Buckley, Chief Exec./Sec.
Description: International shipping exchange.
Publication: Magazine
Publication title: The Baltic. Advertisements.

Banana Link

38-40 Exchange St., Norwich, NR2 1AX, England, UK
Tel: 44 1603 756670
Fax: 44 1603 7611645
Email: blink@gn.apc.org
Website: http://www.bananalink.org.uk
Description: Aims to alleviate poverty and prevent environment degradation in banana exporting communities. Works toward a sustainable banana economy. Facilitates fair trade.

Bangladesh-British Chamber of Commerce

55-59 Hanbury St., London, E1 5JP, England, UK
Contact: Kabir Choudbury
Description: Promotes business and commerce.

Banking, Insurance and Finance Union
BIFU

Sheffield House, 1B Amity Grove, Raynes Park, London, SW20 0LG, England, UK
Tel: 44 181 9469151
Fax: 44 181 8797916
Members: 134012
Description: Banking, insurance, building societies and financial institutions.

Bankruptcy Association of England and Wales
BAGBI

4 Johnson Close, Abraham Heights, Lancaster, LA1 5EU, England, UK
Tel: 44 1524 64305
Fax: 44 1524 389717
Email: bankruptcyassociation@gbandi.freeserve.co.uk
Website: http://www.theba.org.uk
Founded: 1983
Members: 1500
Staff: 3
Contact: John McQueen, CEO
Fee: £15

Description: Campaigns for reform of the United Kingdom's insolvency laws; advises and assists debtors and bankrupts.
Formerly: Association of Bankrupts
Publication: Book
Publication title: Bankruptcy Explained
Second publication: Book
Publication title: Boom To Bust The Great 1990s Slump
Meetings/Conventions: meeting

Bantock Society
BS

St. Barnabas Vicarage, Daventry Rd., Knowle, Bristol, BS4 1DQ, England, UK
Tel: 44 117 9664139
Email: bantock_society@hotmail.com
Website: http://www.musicweb.uk.net/bantock
Founded: 1946
Members: 105
Contact: Ronald Bleach, Chm.
Fee: £15
Description: Musicians and music publishers. Promotes performances, recordings, and broadcasts of the works of Sir Granville Bantock (1868-1946), English operatic conductor, director, and composer of operas, symphonic poems, overtures, choral songs, dances, and other musical works.
Publication: Journal
Publication title: Bamtock Society
Second publication: Brochure
Meetings/Conventions: - periodic meeting

Bar Association for Local Government and the Public Service

c/o Mirza F.N. Ahmad, Chairman
Ingleby House, 11-14 Cannon St., Birmingham, B2 5EN, England, UK
Tel: 44 121 3039991
Fax: 44 121 3031312
Email: chairman@balgps.freeserve.co.uk
Website: http://www.balgps.freeserve.co.uk
Founded: 1945
Members: 100
Contact: Mirza Ahmad, Chm.
Fee: £12
Membership Type: full
Fee: £6
Membership Type: associate
Description: Barristers in local, government and the public sector. Concerned with the protection, and promotion of the professional rights and interests of barristers employed in local government and public sector by giving advice to barristers seeking a career in the public sector, making representations to the Bar Council and elsewhere relating to training, rights of audience and direct access to counsel and by promoting professional knowledge.
Publication: Booklet
Publication title: A Career in Local Government for Barristers
Second publication: Booklets
Publication title: Careers for Barristers in Local Government and the Public Service
Meetings/Conventions: - annual meeting

BARA: The Association for Robotics and Automation

c/o Dr. Ken Young
International Manufacturing Centre, Univ. of Warwick, Coventry, CV4 7AL, England, UK
Tel: 44 24 76573742
Fax: 44 24 76573743
Email: info@bara.org.uk
Website: http://www.bra-automation.co.uk
Founded: 1976
Members: 150
Staff: 1
Contact: Dr. Ken Young
Description: Promotes robotics and automation; facilitates the exchange of information and experience. Conducts research events. Compiles statistics.
Library Subject: robotics and automation
Library Type: not open to the public
Formerly: British Association for Robotics and Automation
Publication title: Data-File of Robot Specifications
Second publication: Newsletter
Publication title: News Summary. Advertisements.

BAREMA

The Stables, Sugworth Ln., Radley, Oxford, OX14 2HX, England, UK
Tel: 44 1865 736393
Fax: 44 1865 736393
Email: barema@btinternet.com
Website: http://www.barema.org.uk
Founded: 1976
Members: 27
Staff: 2
Contact: H. Cooke, Sec.
Description: Maintains close links with government departments, Standards Organisation and professional bodies within its specialty, while actively supporting ABHI in all matters of general interest.
Formerly: British Anaesthetic and Respiratory Equipment Manufacturers Association
Meetings/Conventions: workshop

Barnsley Chamber of Commerce and Industry

Innovation Way, Barnsley, S75 IJL, England, UK
Tel: 44 1226 217770
Fax: 44 1226 215729
Email: info@barnsleychamber.co.uk
Website: http://www.barnsleychamber.co.uk
Members: 874
Staff: 13
Contact: Roger Nunns, Chief Exec.
Description: Promotes business and commerce.

Basketware Importers Association

Wilcox House, 140-148 Borough High St., London, SE1 1LB, England, UK
Tel: 44 207 4070942
Fax: 44 207 4075942
Founded: 1955
Members: 43
Contact: Roger Gross, Chair
Description: Members are importers of basketware and wicker furniture. Supports and protects the import of basketware etc from overseas countries, mainly the Far East.

Bat Conservation Trust - UK
BCT

15 Cloisters House, 8 Battersea Park Rd., London, SW8 4BG, England, UK
Tel: 44 207 6272629
Fax: 44 207 6272628
Email: enquiries@bats.org.uk
Website: http://www.bats.org.uk
Founded: 1990
Members: 4000
Staff: 7
Contact: David Bellamy, Pres.
Fee: £16
Membership Type: standard
Fee: £20
Membership Type: outside UK
Description: Coordinates bat conservation and research in the United Kingdom. Sponsors public education programs to encourage protection of the animals and their roosting sites.
Formerly: Bat Conservation Trust - England
Publication title: Action Plan for the Conservation of Bats in the U.K.
Second publication: Newsletter
Publication title: Bat News. Advertisements.
Meetings/Conventions: National Bat Conference - annual conference - Exhibits.

Bates Association for Vision Education

Savoy Court Hotel, 11-15 Cavendish Pl., Eastbourne, BN1 3EJ, England, UK
Fax: 44 870 2417458
Email: info@seeing.org
Website: http://www.seeing.org
Founded: 1954
Members: 28
Contact: Julia Galvin, Sec.
Fee: £100
Membership Type: professional
Description: Teachers of Bates Method vision education. To advance the knowledge and practice of vision education.
Library Type: not open to the public
Formerly: London Association of Eyesight Training
Publication: Newsletter
Publication title: Vision Education News
Meetings/Conventions: - semiannual meeting

Bath Institute for Rheumatic Diseases

Trim Bridge, Bath, BA1 1HD, England, UK
Tel: 44 1225 448444
Fax: 44 1225 336809
Contact: Fiona Davies, Admin.Mgr.
Description: Promotes the study of rheumatic diseases.

Bathroom Manufacturers Association
BMA

Federation House, Station Rd., Stoke-On-Trent, ST4 2RT, England, UK
Tel: 44 1782 747123
Fax: 44 1782 747161
Email: info@bathroom-association.org.uk
Website: http://www.bathroom-association.org/
Founded: 2001
Members: 20

Staff: 4
Contact: Yvonne Orgill
Description: Promotes the bathroom industry through representation; provides continuous dialogue between members and the industry.

BEAMA Capacitor Manufacturers' Association
BCMA

Westminster Tower, 3 Albert Embankment, London, SE1 7SL, England, UK
Tel: 44 20 77933000
Fax: 44 20 77933030
Email: info@beama.org.uk
Website: http://www.beama.org.uk
Contact: David Possett, CEO
Description: Wound capacitors of film, paper, or mixed dielectric construction.

BEAMA Electrical Cable and Conductor Accessory Manufacturers' Association
BECCAMA

Westminster Tower, 3 Albert Embankment, London, SE1 7SL, England, UK
Tel: 44 207 7933000
Fax: 44 207 7933003
Email: info@beama.org.uk
Website: http://www.beama.org.uk/beccama/beccama.htm
Founded: 1992
Members: 21
Staff: 2
Contact: Mr. David Dossett, CEO
Description: Manufacturers of equipment used in the transmission and distribution of electricity, for fitting, earthing, connecting and terminating electricity cables and conductors.

BEAMA Metering and Communications Association
BEMCA

Westminster Tower, 3 Albert Embankment, London, SE1 7SI, England, UK
Tel: 44 20 77933008
Fax: 44 20 77939730
Email: bemca@beama.org.uk
Contact: Dr. Howard Porter, Dir.
Description: AC integrating electricity meters and all matters affecting the design, manufacture, supply, and operation of electricity metering equipment for the supply utilities.

BEAMA Transmission and Distribution Association
BTDA

Westminster Tower, 3 Albert Embankment, London, SE1 7SL, England, UK
Tel: 44 20 77933039
Fax: 44 20 75828020
Email: btda@beama.org.uk
Members: 30
Staff: 2
Contact: N. Grant, Director
Description: Manufacturers of high voltage, transmission and distribution equipment.

Beaumont Society
BS

27 Old Gloucester St., London, WC1N 3XX, England, UK
Tel: 44 1582 412220
Email: heljones@aol.com
Website: http://www.beaumontsociety.org.uk
Founded: 1966
Description: Transvestites and transsexuals. Promotes improved public understanding of transvestism and gender dysphoria. Seeks to assist members in becoming functional members of society. Serves as a support group for members; conducts educational programs for health care and social workers and other individuals working with people with gender dysphoria. Maintains national information line.
Publication: Magazine
Publication title: Beaumont Magazine. Advertisements.
Meetings/Conventions: - periodic lecture

Bedfordshire and Luton Chamber of Commerce, Training and Enterprise

Kimpton Rd., Luton, Luton, LU2 0LB, England, UK
Tel: 44 845 3570357
Email: infow@beds-and-luton-chamber.co.uk
Members: 1255
Staff: 34
Contact: Ken Lewis, Pres.
Description: Promotes business and commerce.

Bee Improvement and Bee Breeders' Association

50 Station Rd., Cogenhoe, Northampton, NN7 1LU, England, UK
Tel: 44 1604 890117
Fax: 44 1773 570461
Email: info@bibba.com
Website: http://www.bibba.com
Founded: 1964
Members: 357
Contact: David Allen, Sec.
Fee: £15
Membership Type: ordinary
Description: Concerned with the conservation, restoration, study, selection and improvement of the native and near native honeybees of Britain and Ireland.
Formerly: Village Bee Breeders Association
Publication: Magazine
Publication title: Bee Improvement. Advertisements.
Meetings/Conventions: - annual meeting - Exhibits.

Befrienders International
BI

c/o The Samaratins
26-27 Market Pl., Kingston Rd., Ewell, KT1 1JH, England, UK
Tel: 44 208 5414949
Fax: 44 208 5411544
Email: jo@samaritans.org
Website: http://www.befrienders.org
Founded: 1974
Members: 30000
Staff: 5
Contact: Mrs. Rosemary Guilbert, Dir.
Fee: £25
Membership Type: individual
Fee: £50
Membership Type: full

Description: Mission is to build effective suicide prevention services resourced by volunteers throughout the world.
Formerly: Befrienders International Samaritans Worldwide
Publication: Newsletter
Publication title: Befriending Worldwide

Belgian Luxembourg Chamber of Commerce in Great Britain

Riverside House, 27-29 Vauxhall Grove, London, SW8 1SY, England, UK
Tel: 44 207 7931623
Fax: 44 207 7931628
Email: info@blcc.co.uk
Website: http://www.blcc.co.uk
Contact: Dominique Maeremans
Description: Promotes business and commerce.

Benesh Institute

36 Battersea Sq., London, SW11 3RA, England, UK
Tel: 44 207 3268031
Fax: 44 207 3268033
Email: info@rad.org.uk
Website: http://www.benesh.org
Founded: 1962
Members: 110
Staff: 5
Contact: Liz Cunliffe
Description: Full membership available to holders of advanced level certificate (dance course), advanced diploma (clinicians' course) and associates of the Institute. Founded to meet the need for an international centre to train students; functions as an examining body, co-ordinates technical developments; protects copyright in choreographic works. Sub-scheme membership is available to anyone.
Library Subject: dance, notation, music
Library Type: reference
Publication: Newsletter
Publication title: Benesh News
Second publication: Journal
Publication title: Dance Gazette
Meetings/Conventions: Benesh Institute Congress - biennial

Benevolent Fund of the College of Optometrists

42 Craven St., London, WC2N 5NG, England, UK
Tel: 44 171 8396000
Fax: 44 171 8396800
Founded: 1980
Staff: 1
Description: Members/former members of the optical profession and their dependents.

BHR Group

The Fluid Engineering Centre, Cranfield, Bedford, MK43 0AJ, England, UK
Tel: 44 1234 750422
Fax: 44 1234 750074
Email: fluid@bhrgroup.com
Website: http://www.bhrgroup.com
Founded: 1947
Members: 25
Staff: 80
Contact: Nick Guy, Mgr.
Fee: £2500

Membership Type: corporate
Description: Individuals and companies interested in developments in fluid engineering technology. Disseminates technical information to the industry. Represents members' interests. Conducts research programs.
Library Subject: Fluid engineering.
Library Type: reference
Formerly: British Hydromechanics Research Association
Publication: Newsletter
Publication title: BHR Group News
Second publication: Newsletter
Publication title: Industry Focus and Focus on Membership
Meetings/Conventions: - periodic conference

Bibliographical Society - United Kingdom

c/o Margaret Ford, Hon.Sec.
Institute of English Studies, Senate House, Rm. 305, Malet St., London, WC1E 7HU, England, UK
Tel: 44 207 3892150
Fax: 44 207 9762832
Email: jm93@dial.pipex.com
Website: http://www.bibsoc.org.uk
Founded: 1892
Members: 1050
Contact: M. Ford, Hon.Sec.
Fee: £37
Description: Bibliographers, book-sellers, book collectors, academics of all kinds; everyone interested in historical and critical bibliography. Promotes and encourages study and research in the fields of historical, analytical, descriptive and textual bibliography and the history of printing, publishing, bookselling, bookbinding and collecting. Holds meetings at which papers are read and discussed and publishes works concerned with bibliography.
Library Subject: bibliography
Library Type: not open to the public
Publication: Journal
Publication title: The Library. Advertisements.
Second publication: Monographs
Meetings/Conventions: - monthly meeting London

BIBRA International

Woodmansterne Rd., Carshalton, SM5 4DS, England, UK
Tel: 44 208 6521000
Fax: 44 208 6617029
Email: help@bibra.co.uk
Website: http://www.bibra.co.uk
Founded: 1963
Members: 100
Staff: 80
Contact: Dr. Paul G. Brantom
Description: Manufacturing companies in all sectors of industry. To deliver high quality, independent scientific support for industry and government in assessing the health effects of food and chemicals in man.
Library Subject: All aspects of chemical (eco) toxicology and nutrition
Library Type: not open to the public
Formerly: British Industrial Biological Research Association
Publication title: BIBRA Bulletin
Publication title: Food and Chemical Toxicology

Bicycle Association of Great Britain
BAGB

Starley House, Eaton Rd., Coventry, CV1 2FH, England, UK
Tel: 44 2476 553838
Fax: 44 2476 228366
Email: patricia@bicycle-association.org.uk
Founded: 1971
Members: 50
Staff: 2
Contact: Mrs. P. Morris, Sec.
Description: Represents and promotes manufacturers and suppliers of bicycles, bicycle accessories, and parts in Great Britain. Promotes the bicycle industry; represents members' interests.
Publication title: Export Portfolio. Advertisements.
Meetings/Conventions: International Cycle - annual trade show

Biochemical Society - England
BS

59 Portland Pl., London, W1B 1QW, England, UK
Tel: 44 207 5805530
Fax: 44 207 6373626
Email: genadmin@biochemistry.org
Website: http://www.biochemistry.org
Founded: 1911
Members: 7000
Staff: 56
Contact: G.D. Jones, Exec.Sec.
Fee: £47
Membership Type: full
Fee: £14
Membership Type: student
Description: Objectives are to promote biochemistry and to provide a forum for information exchange and discussion of teaching and research in biochemistry. Maintains 7 specialized theme panel.
Publication title: Biochemical Society Transactions
Meetings/Conventions: - annual meeting

Bio-Dynamic Agricultural Association

c/o The Painswick Inn Project
Gloucester St., Stroud, GL5 1QG, England, UK
Tel: 44 1453 759501
Fax: 44 1453 759501
Email: bdaa@biodynamic.freeserve.co.uk
Website: http://www.anth.org.uk/biodynamic
Founded: 1929
Members: 700
Staff: 4
Contact: Bernard Jarman, Exec.Dir.
Fee: £12
Description: Farmers, growers, gardeners consumers/supporters, interested in promoting and supporting the bio-dynamic approach to agriculture. Membership is open to anyone interested whether or not they are practising farmers or gardeners. Main objectives are to foster and promote the agricultural impulse started by Rudolf Steiner in 1924 and to help and support those wishing to put into practice the bio-dynamic method.
Publication title: Bio-Dynamic Farming Practice
Publication title: The Bio-Dynamic Spray and Compost Preparations-Production Methods

BioIndustry Association
BIA

14/15 Belgrave Sq., London, SW1X 8PS, England, UK
Tel: 44 207 5657190
Fax: 44 207 5657191
Email: admin@bioindustry.org
Website: http://www.bioindustry.org
Founded: 1985
Members: 280
Staff: 8
Contact: Mr. Crispin Kirkman, CEO
Description: Individuals interested in contributing to the development of biotechnology in the United Kingdom. Represents members' interests concerning regulatory affairs, policy, and funding. Maintains liaison with trade associations and biotechnology organizations to provide a forum for idea and information exchange. Sponsors exhibitions.
Library Subject: business, bioscience, and related topics
Library Type: reference
Formerly: Association for the Advancement of British Biotechnology
Publication: Book
Publication title: Biotechnologists Book of Abbreviations and Acronyms
Second publication: Newsletter
Publication title: Evolution. Advertisements.

Bipaver

Elsinore House, Buckingham St., Aylesbury, HP20 2NQ, England, UK
Tel: 44 1296 399837
Fax: 44 870 9000610
Email: bipaver@ntda.co.uk
Founded: 1956
Members: 12
Staff: 5
Contact: R. Edy, Sec.Gen.
Description: National associations of tire distributors and retreaders.
Publication: Newsletter
Publication title: Bipaver Newsletter
Second publication: Directory
Publication title: Directory of Trade Associations in Europe

Bird Life International - United Kingdom

Wellbrook Ct., Girton Rd., Cambridge, CB3 0NA, England, UK
Tel: 44 1223 277318
Fax: 44 1223 277200
Email: birdlife@birdlife.org.uk
Website: http://www.birdlife.net
Founded: 1922
Members: 101
Staff: 55
Contact: Dr. Michael Rands, Dir. & Chief Exec.
Description: A partnership of natural conservation organisations. The mission is to conserve all bird species on earth and their habitats, and through this, to work for the world's biological diversity and the sustainability of human use of natural resources. Advises governments and private bodies on significant national and international bird conservation issues.
Library Subject: Ornithology
Library Type: reference
Publication: Annual Report
Publication title: Birdlife International Annual Review
Second publication: Magazine
Publication title: World Birdwatch. Advertisements.

Birmingham Chamber of Commerce and Industry, 75 Harborne Rd., Birmingham, B15 3DH, England, UK

Tel: 44 121 60708090
Fax: 44 121 4558670
Email: info@birmingham-chamber.com
Website: http://www.birmingham-chamber.com
Founded: 1813
Members: 4000
Description: Promotes and supports business and commerce.
Publication: Journal
Publication title: Chamberlink
Second publication: Directory
Publication title: West Midlands Chambers of Commerce Directory

Birmingham Natural History Society

80 Middle Park Rd., Birmingham, B29 4BS, England, UK
Tel: 44 121 477 7550
Email: d_antrobus@hotmail.com
Website: http://freespace.virgin.net/clare.h/bnhs.htm
Founded: 1858
Members: 120
Contact: Dr. David Antrobus, Pres.
Fee: £6
Membership Type: family
Description: Promotes an understanding of general natural history and conservation topics.
Library Subject: general natural history, country floras
Library Type: not open to the public
Publication: Journal
Publication title: Proceedings of BNHS

Biscuit, Cake, Chocolate, and Confectionery Alliance
BCCCA

37-41 Bedford Row, London, WC1R 4JH, England, UK
Tel: 44 20 74049111
Fax: 40 20 74049110
Email: office@bccca.org.uk
Website: http://www.bccca.org.uk
Founded: 1987
Members: 120
Staff: 9
Contact: Mike Webber, Dir.
Description: Bakers and confectioners in the United Kingdom. Promotes and represents members' interests.
Publication title: Annual Review
Meetings/Conventions: - annual conference

Bitumen Waterproofing Association

19 Regina Crescent, Ravenshead, Nottingham, NG15 9AE, England, UK
Tel: 44 1623 430574
Fax: 44 1623 798098
Email: info@bwa-europe.com
Website: http://www.bwa-europe.com
Founded: 1968
Members: 35
Staff: 2
Contact: Paul K. Newman, Chief Exec.
Description: National waterproofing contractors' associations and waterproofing materials manufacturers in 21 countries. Coordinates and undertakes research on rain waterproofing and sealing against underground water of construction or civil engineering works; establishes centers for documentation, information, and research; disseminates information on waterproofing to aid in the advancement of its application. Maintains contact with governments and bodies representing the construction industry and the civil engineering profession in order to inform them of decisions reached at international congresses. Organizes special projects, courses, and exhibitions.
Library Type: open to the public
Formerly: International Asphalt Association

Bitumen Waterproofing Association - England

19 Regina Crescent, Ravenshead, Nottingham, NG15 9AE, England, UK
Tel: 44 1623 430574
Fax: 44 1623 798098
Email: info@bwa-europe.com
Website: http://www.bwa-europe.com
Founded: 1968
Members: 40
Staff: 3
Contact: Paul K. Newman, Chief Exec.
Description: National associations, organizations or other official groups active in the field of waterproofing in their respective countries. Endeavors to co-ordinate studies on waterproofing related matters and to facilitate the dissemination of information on waterproofing and their applications, with a view to improving and developing their applications. The dissemination is assured through the medium of International Congresses by the Association.
Library Subject: waterproofing
Library Type: reference
Formerly: International Waterproofing Association
Meetings/Conventions: conference - Exhibits.

Black and Asian Studies Association
BASA

28 Russell Sq., London, WC1B 5DS, England, UK
Tel: 44 20 78628844
Fax: 44 20 78628820
Email: marika.sherwood@sas.ac.uk
Website: http://www.sas.ac.uk
Founded: 1991
Members: 200
Contact: Marika Sherwood
Fee: £10
Membership Type: subscription
Description: Encourages and disseminates information on the history of Black peoples in Butani.
Publication: Newsletter

Black Country Chamber

Chamber House, Churchill Precinct, Dudley, DY2 7BL, England, UK
Tel: 44 1384 343534
Fax: 44 1384 821405
Email: enquiries@chamber2000.co.uk
Members: 499
Staff: 16
Contact: Ian Brough, Chief Exec.
Description: Promotes business and commerce.

BLC Leather Technology Centre

Leather Trade House, Kings Park Rd., Moulton Park, Northampton, NN3 6JD, England, UK
Tel: 44 1604 679999
Fax: 44 1604 679998
Email: info@blcleathertech.com
Website: http://www.blcleathertech.com
Founded: 1920
Members: 400
Staff: 60
Contact: Adam Hughes, Sales Dir.
Library Subject: leather technology, management, health and safety, environment
Library Type: not open to the public
Publication: Journal
Publication title: BLC Journal
Meetings/Conventions: Panel Meetings seminar

Bliss Classification Association
BCA

c/o The Library
Sidney Sussex College, Cambridge, CB2 3HU, England, UK
Tel: 44 1223 338852
Fax: 44 1223 38884
Email: librarian@sid.cam.ac.uk
Website: http://www.sid.cam.ac.uk/bca/bcahome.htm
Founded: 1967
Members: 95
Contact: Ms. Angela Haselton, Hon.Treas.
Fee: £15
Membership Type: institutional
Fee: £12
Membership Type: personal
Description: Individuals and institutions around the world seeking to promote the use and development of the Bliss Bibliographic Classification System. It provides a detailed classification for use in libraries and information centers of all kinds, maintains a fully faceted notation allowing very specific classification and is highly flexible. Offers training courses on the scheme's application, provides updates to the scheme, and organizes lectures.
Publication: Bulletin
Publication title: Bliss Bibliographic Classification. Advertisements.
Second publication: Bulletin
Publication title: Bliss Classification Bulletin
Meetings/Conventions: - annual meeting

Bloucestershire Chamber of Commerce

Chargrove House, Main Rd., Shurdington, Cheltenham, GL51 5AG, England, UK
Contact: J Cripps
Description: Promotes business and commerce.

BLWA - Association of the Laboratory Supply Industry

St. George's House, 195-203 Waterloo Rd., London, SE1 8WB, England, UK
Tel: 44 207 2079666
Fax: 44 207 2079659
Email: blwa@blwa.co.uk
Website: http://www.martex.co.uk/blwa
Founded: 1915
Members: 200

Staff: 10
Contact: Nicci Pearce
Description: Manufacturers and suppliers of laboratory instrumentation, equipment and supplies. National trade association for the laboratory supply industry and represents nearly 200 manufacturers and distributors of laboratory equipment, clinical instrumentation and diagnostic reagents in the UK. It speaks for its members on all levels and negotiates with Government departments concerning new regulations and legislation.
Publication: Directory
Second publication: Newsletter

Boarding Schools Association

Grosvenor Gardens House, 35-37, Grosvenor Gardens, London, SW1W 0BS, England, UK
Tel: 44 207 7981580
Fax: 44 207 7981581
Email: bsa@iscis.uk.net
Website: http://www.boarding.org.uk
Founded: 1965
Members: 509
Staff: 4
Contact: Adrian Underwood, Dir.
Description: Independent and maintained boarding schools, associations which have an active interest in boarding education. Covers schools, both maintained and independent, with boarding facilities. Ten conferences annually are arranged, to include INSET Training for boarding pastoral work. Research projects commissioned.
Publication: Magazine
Publication title: Boarding School. Advertisements.
Meetings/Conventions: - weekly conference

Bolton and Bury Chamber of Commerce

Commerce House, Bridgeman Pl., Bolton, BL2 1DW, England, UK
Tel: 44 845 6016010
Fax: 44 1204 363212
Email: aratcliff@chamberhelp.co.uk
Website: http://www.chamberhelp.co.uk
Members: 1000
Staff: 200
Contact: David Arkwright, Pres.
Description: Promotes business and commerce.

Book Aid International
BAI

39/41 Coldharbour Ln., Camberwell, London, SE5 9NR, England, UK
Tel: 44 20 77333577
Fax: 44 20 79788006
Email: info@bookaid.org
Website: http://www.bookaid.org
Founded: 1954
Staff: 34
Contact: Nicola Cadbury, Hd. of PR
Description: Works in conjunction with organizations in developing countries to support their work in literacy, education, training, and publishing by providing books and journals at their request. Over 750,000 selected books and journals each year are targeted to enable learning and skills development in around 50 developing countries throughout the world.
Formerly: Ranfurly Library Service
Publication: Newsletter
Publication title: Interchange
Meetings/Conventions: - annual convention

Book Packagers Association

8 St. John's Rd., Saxmundham, IP17 1BE, England, UK
Tel: 44 1728 604204
Fax: 44 1728 604209
Founded: 1985
Members: 26
Contact: Charles Perkins
Fee: £150
Membership Type: full
Fee: £100
Membership Type: associate
Description: Book packagers, freelance suppliers. Provides book packagers with a forum for the exchange of ideas and information; to improve the image of packaging; and to represent its members. It holds open meetings and seminars and takes a stand at the London Book Fair. Standard contracts are available.
Meetings/Conventions: seminar

Bookmakers' Association

13 Commerce House, Vicarage Lane, Water Orton, Birmingham, B46 1RR, England, UK
Tel: 44 121 7484285
Fax: 44 121 7484285
Description: Bookmakers.

Books for Keeps

6 Brightfield Rd., London, SE12 8QF, England, UK
Tel: 44 208 8524953
Fax: 44 208 3187580
Email: booksforkeeps@btinternet.com
Founded: 1976
Members: 8500
Staff: 3
Contact: Richard Hill, Man.Dir.
Description: Membership covers schools, libraries, bookshops, publishers, authors and parents concerned with the importance of book use and availability.
Formerly: School Bookshop Association
Publication: Books
Publication title: Books for Keeps. Advertisements.

Booksellers Association of the United Kingdom and Ireland
BA

Minster House, 272 Vauxhall Bridge Rd., London, SW1V 1BA, England, UK
Tel: 44 207 8345477
Fax: 44 207 8348812
Email: mail@booksellers.org.uk
Website: http://www.booksellers.org.uk
Founded: 1895
Members: 3200
Staff: 40
Contact: Tim Godfray, Chief Exec.
Description: Companies engaged in bookselling. Promotes and protects members' interests; researches methods to increase efficiency and profitability while reducing costs; disseminates information and advice. Organizes marketing programs.
Publication: Newsletter
Publication title: Bookselling
Second publication: Directory
Publication title: Directory of Members
Meetings/Conventions: - annual conference

Boot and Shoe Manufacturers' Association

24-26 Bloomsbury Sq., London, WC1A 2PL, England, UK
Tel: 44 20 76127757
Fax: 44 20 74364663
Email: basma@basma.com
Website: http://www.basma.com
Founded: 1882
Members: 500
Staff: 6
Contact: Michael Gilbert, Chief Exec.
Fee: £25
Description: Provides commercial credit information and debt recovery.
Publication: Newsletter
Publication title: BASMA News

Boston Chamber of Commerce and Industry

Boston Business Centre, Norfolk St., Boston, PE21 9HH, England, UK
Tel: 44 1205 358800
Fax: 44 1205 359388
Email: bcci@brclick.com
Contact: David Cubberley
Description: Promotes business and commerce.

Botanical Society of the British Isles
BSBI

68 Outwoods Rd., Loughborough, LE11 3LY, England, UK
Tel: 44 1283 568136
Email: ailsaburns@cwcom.net
Website: http://www.bsbi.org.uk
Founded: 1836
Members: 2700
Contact: Mr. Ailsa Burns, Hon.Gen.Sec.
Fee: £20
Membership Type: ordinary
Description: Amateur and professional botanists in Great Britain and Ireland. Promotes the study of British and Irish flowering plants and ferns. Organizes field visits and symposia; conducts surveys.
Formerly: Botanical Society of London
Publication title: BSBI Abstracts
Second publication: Newsletter
Publication title: BSBI News
Meetings/Conventions: - annual meeting

Box Culvert Association

60 Charles St., Leicester, LE1 1FB, England, UK
Tel: 44 116 2536161
Fax: 44 116 2514568
Email: boxca@britishprecast.org
Website: http://www.boxculvert.org.uk
Founded: 1975
Members: 4
Staff: 2
Contact: C.J. Budge, Sec.
Description: Manufacturers of precast concrete box culverts.
Publication title: Applications Guide
Publication title: Site Use Guide

Boys' Brigade
BB

Felden Lodge, Hemel Hempstead, HP3 0BL, England, UK
Tel: 44 1442 231681
Fax: 44 1442 235391
Email: enquiries@boys-brigade.org.uk
Website: http://www.boys-brigade.org.uk
Founded: 1883
Members: 400000
Contact: Don McLaren, Sec.
Description: Boys between the ages of 6 and 18; male and female leaders. Promotes Christian ideals among boys in 66 countries. Organizes community projects; offers training for officers and full-time staff. Sponsors competitions; bestows awards. Compiles statistics.
Publication: Magazine
Publication title: Boys' Brigade Gazette. Advertisements.
Second publication: Handbooks
Meetings/Conventions: Brigade Council - annual meeting

Bradford Chamber of Commerce

Devere House, Vicar Ln., Bradford, BD1 5AH, England, UK
Tel: 44 1274 772777
Fax: 44 1274 771081
Email: info@bradfordchamber.co.uk
Website: http://www.bradfordchamber.co.uk
Members: 1100
Staff: 46
Contact: John Pennington, Pres.
Description: Promotes business and commerce.

Brazilian Chamber of Commerce in Great Britain

32 Green St., London, W1K 7AT, England, UK
Tel: 44 20 73999281
Fax: 44 20 74990186
Email: pavlova@brazilianchamber.org.uk
Website: http://www.brazilianchamber.org.uk
Founded: 1942
Members: 208
Staff: 3
Contact: Sir Dionisio de Castro Cerqueira, Sec.
Fee: £387
Membership Type: corporate
Fee: £228
Membership Type: company
Description: Promotes business and commerce.
Publication: Magazine
Publication title: Brazilian Business Brief
Meetings/Conventions: - annual dinner

Breast Cancer Care

Kiln House, 210 New Kings Rd., London, SW6 4NZ, England, UK
Tel: 44 207 3842984
Fax: 44 207 3843387
Email: info@breastcancercare.org.uk
Website: http://www.breastcancercare.org.uk
Founded: 1973
Staff: 50
Contact: Christine Fogg, Ch.Exec.
Description: Provides information and support to those affected by breast cancer. Operates advice line, one-to-one volunteer support, and aftercare services, including prosthesis fitting.
Formerly: Breast Care and Masectomy Association
Publication: Books
Second publication: Newsletter

Brent and Harrow Chamber of Commerce

Kirkfield House, 118-120 Station Rd, Harrow, HA1 2RL, England, UK
Tel: 44 20 89015100
Contact: Liz Mackenzie
Description: Promotes business and commerce.

Bretton Woods Project
BWP

Hamlyn House, Macdonald Rd., London, N19 5PG, England, UK
Tel: 44 20 75617546
Fax: 44 20 72720899
Email: info@brettonwoodproject.org
Website: http://www.brettonwoodsproject.org
Founded: 1995
Staff: 3
Contact: Alex Wilks, Coord.
Description: Serves as a clearinghouse and advocacy organisation on World Bank and International Monetary Fund issues. Works with a range of non-government organisations and researchers. Produces bimonthly Bretton Woods Update newsletter.
Publication: Newsletter
Publication title: Bretton Woods Update
Second publication: Report
Publication title: Blinding with Science: How World Bank analysis determines PRSP policies

Brewing, Food and Beverage Industry Suppliers Association
BFBI

85 Tettenhall Rd., Wolverhampton, WV3 9NE, England, UK
Tel: 44 1902 422303
Fax: 44 1902 795744
Email: info@bfbi.org.uk
Website: http://www.bfbi.org.uk
Founded: 1907
Members: 450
Staff: 4
Contact: MJ Rayner, Ch.Exec.
Fee: £360
Description: Full membership available to companies engaged in supplying the brewing, and food and beverage and distilling industries. Associate Membership is available to individuals or sole traders. Applicants must have been trading within the industry for minimum of 12. months and have to be proposed by an existing Full member. To enable its members to act together in all matters appertaining to their trade or professional interests: to monitor legislative proposals, to form a centre for obtaining and diffusing information: to offer members the opportunity to explore overseas markets: to create a social forum to maintain customer contact.
Formerly: Allied Brewery Traders Association
Publication: Directory
Publication title: ABTA Directory

Brick Development Association

Woodside House, Winkfield, Windsor, SL4 2DX, England, UK
Tel: 44 1344 885651
Fax: 44 1344 890129
Email: brick@brick.org.uk
Website: http://www.brick.org.uk
Founded: 1969
Members: 21

Staff: 10
Contact: Mr. M. Hayward
Description: UK clay and calcium silicate brick manufacturers. Promotes the use of brick. Works to establish and maintain British and European Standards.
Publication: Bulletin
Publication title: Brick Bulletin
Meetings/Conventions: - periodic seminar

Bridge Deck Waterproofing Association

Century House, Telford Ave., Crowthorne, RG45 6YS, England, UK
Tel: 44 1344 725727
Fax: 44 1344 772426
Founded: 1990
Members: 4
Staff: 1
Contact: C.T. Cleverly, Sec.
Fee: £900
Membership Type: company
Description: Companies involved in the supply and/or application of materials for the waterproofing of bridge decks. To encourage the correct use of properly evaluated bridge deck waterproofing materials under safe working conditions; to act as a representative body for members especially in relation to standards, specifications and contact with regulatory bodies.
Publication: Directory
Publication title: BWA
Meetings/Conventions: mccting

Bridge Joint Association

Century House, Telford Ave., Crowthorne, RG45 6YS, England, UK
Tel: 44 1344 725727
Fax: 44 1344 772426
Founded: 1990
Members: 10
Staff: 1
Contact: C.T. Cleverly, Sec.
Fee: £1100
Description: Companies supplying and installing bridge expansion joints. To maintain and improve standards of design, manufacture and installation of bridge expansion joints, to co-operate with purchasers and specifiers, and to represent the interests of members.
Library Type: open to the public
Publication title: Joint Data Sheets
Second publication: Directory

Bristol Chamber of Commerce and Initiative

16 Clifton Park, Bristol, BS8 3BY, England, UK
Tel: 44 117 9737373
Fax: 44 117 9238024
Email: info@businesswest.co.uk
Website: http://www.businesswest.co.uk
Members: 2500
Staff: 50
Contact: Doug Claisse, Pres.
Fee: £1025
Description: Promotes business and commerce.

Bristol Industrial Archaeological Society
BIAS

c/o Bristol Industrial Museum
Princess Wharf, City Docks, Bristol, BS1 4RN, England, UK
Tel: 44 117 9251470
Email: kenneth.andrews@btinternet.com
Founded: 1967

Britain - Nepal Medical Trust
BNMT

c/o Export House
130 Yale Rd., Tonbridge, TN9 1SP, England, UK
Tel: 44 1732 360284
Fax: 44 1732 363876
Founded: 1968
Staff: 135
Contact: Dr. N. Padfield, Chm.
Description: Health care professionals and health organizations. Seeks to improve the health of the people of Nepal. Works with Nepalese government agencies to increase delivery of health services in underserved areas. Evaluates health programs and makes recommendations for their improvement; distributes medical equipment, medications, and other supplies.

Britain and Ireland Association of Aquatic Sciences Libraries and Information Centres
BIASLIC

c/o Information and Library Sciences
Centre for the Environment, Fisheries and Aquaculture Science, Lowestoft, NR33 0HT, England, UK
Email: s.l.carter@cefas.co.uk
Contact: Sarah Carter, Sec.
Description: Libraries, government agencies, and university research institutes. Provides a forum for the exchange of information related to issues of aquatic science librarianship and librarianship as a whole. Provides input for the Aquatic Sciences and Fisheries Abstracts database.
Publication: Directory
Publication title: Directory of Marine and Freshwater Scientists and Research Engineers in the United Kingdom
Meetings/Conventions: - annual meeting

Britain-Nepal Chamber of Commerce

Tamesis House, 35 St. Philips Ave., Worcester Park, KT4 8JS, England, UK
Tel: 44 20 83306446
Fax: 44 20 83307447
Email: bncc@tamgroup.co.uk
Contact: Barry Jaynes, Sec.
Description: Promotes trade and commerce between Nepal and Great Britain.

British Abrasives Federation
BAF

28 Dukes Wood, Crowthorne, RG45 6NF, England, UK
Tel: 44 1344 762968
Fax: 44 1344 762968
Email: intoabrasives@the-british-abrasives-federation.org.uk
Website: http://www.the-british-abrasives-federation.org.uk
Founded: 1923
Members: 35
Staff: 1
Contact: P.E. McAllister, Sec.
Description: Coated abrasive, bonded abrasive, superabrasive, and suppliers.
Library Subject: International standards for abrasives
Library Type: reference
Meetings/Conventions: - annual convention

British Academy
10 Carlton House Terrace, London, SW1Y 5AH, England, UK
Tel: 44 207 9695200
Fax: 44 207 6965300
Email: secretary@britac.ac.uk
Website: http://www.britac.ac.uk/
Founded: 1902
Contact: P.W.H. Brown, Sec.
Description: Scholars in the social sciences and the humanities. Promotes research and scholarship in the social sciences and humanities. Represents members at the national and international levels; supports research programs; facilitates international cooperation and exchange among social sciences and humanities scholars. Provides advice to government and other public bodies on questions affecting social science and humanities research; conducts academic competitions.
Publication: Proceedings
Second publication: Reports
Meetings/Conventions: - periodic conference

British Academy of Composers and Songwriters
British Music House, 2nd Fl., 26 Berners St., London, W1T 3LR, England, UK
Tel: 44 20 76362929
Fax: 44 20 76362212
Email: info@britishacademy.com
Website: http://www.britishacademy.com
Founded: 1947
Members: 3000
Staff: 7
Contact: Chris Green, CEO
Description: Trade association of songwriters and composers. Lobbies for developments in legislation. Presents the Ivors and administers the Song for Europe competition. The Academy is represented on all the major music industry boards.
Formerly: British Academy of Songwriters, Composers and Authors
Publication: Magazine
Publication title: The Works

British Academy of Dramatic Combat
3 Castle View, Hemsley, Y062 5AU, England, UK
Email: enquiries@badc.co.uk
Website: http://www.badc.co.uk
Founded: 1969
Members: 36
Contact: Ian Stapleton
Description: Fight directors for film, theatre and television. Covers the teaching of stage combat within drama schools and training of theatre fight directors.
Formerly: Society of British Fight Directors
Publication: Magazine
Publication title: The Fight Director. Advertisements.

British Academy of Film and Television Arts
195 Piccadilly, London, W1J 9LN, England, UK
Tel: 44 207 7340022
Fax: 44 207 7341792
Email: ruthg@bafta.org
Website: http://www.bafta.org
Founded: 1947
Members: 2057
Staff: 24
Description: Those who work actively within the film and/or television industries and have worked for not less than three years in either of the two industries. Foundation and Corporate Membership available to companies who wish to demonstrate an exceptional. level of support for the Academy and its work. To promote, maintain, improve, and advance original and creative work among persons engaged in film and television production; to create and maintain a high standard of qualification and performance in such persons; and to encourage and promote experiment and research in the arts, sciences, and techniques of film and television production.
Publication title: BAFTA News

British Academy of Forensic Sciences
BAFS
c/o Dr. Patritica Flynn, Sec. Gen.
Whitechapel, Anaesthetic Unit, Royal London Hospital, London, E1 1BB, England, UK
Tel: 44 20 73779201
Email: pjflynn@mds.qmw.ac.uk
Website: http://www.bafs.org.uk/links.htm
Founded: 1959

British Activity Holiday Association
22 Green Ln., Hersham, Walton-On-Thames, KT12 5HD, England, UK
Tel: 44 1932 252994
Fax: 44 1932 252994
Email: les@baha119@snet.co.uk
Website: http://www.baha.org.uk
Founded: 1986
Members: 31
Contact: Les Sharp, Sec.
Description: Members are organisations which provide activity holidays within the United Kingdom. Trade association for organisations which provide activity holidays. It inspects members' establishments annually to ensure set standards are maintained, offers a consumers' advice service and represents and advises members on specific areas of interest.
Publication title: Consumer Guide
Second publication: Newsletter

British Acupuncture Association and Register
BAAR
34 Aldernay St., London, SW1V 4EU, England, UK
Tel: 44 171 8346229
Founded: 1962
Members: 320
Contact: E. Welton Johnson, Exec. Officer
Description: British acupuncturists.
Publication: Journal
Publication title: BAAR Journal
Second publication: Directory
Publication title: Directory
Meetings/Conventions: - annual congress

British Acupuncture Council
63 Jeddo Rd., London, W12 9HQ, England, UK
Tel: 44 208 7350400
Fax: 44 208 7350404
Email: info@acupuncture.org.uk
Website: http://www.acupuncture.org.uk
Founded: 1995
Members: 2000

Description: Practitioners of acupuncture who have completed at least three year's training in traditional acupuncture and western medical sciences appropriate to the practice of acupuncture. Promotes the use of traditional Chinese acupuncture. Maintains standards of education, ethics, discipline, and practice to ensure the health and safety of the public. Encourages exchange of ideas among members. Disseminates information local practitioner members and accredited training courses.
Formerly: Traditional Acupuncture Society
Publication: Newsletter
Publication title: BAcC News
Second publication: Membership Directory
Publication title: Register of Members
Meetings/Conventions: - annual meeting

British Adhesives and Sealants Association
BASA
33 Fellowes Way, Stevenage, SG2 8BW, England, UK
Tel: 44 1438 358514
Email: secretary@basaonline.org
Website: http://www.basa.uk.com
Founded: 1983
Members: 80
Staff: 1
Contact: D.G. Williams, Sec.
Description: Manufacturers and suppliers of adhesives and sealants in Great Britain. Promotes the development of industry and trade.
Publication title: Yearbook and Directory. Advertisements.

British Aerobiology Federation
National Pollen Research Unit, Univ. College, Worcester, WR2 6AJ, England, UK
Tel: 44 1905 748066
Fax: 44 1905 855234
Email: j.emberlin@worc.ac.uk
Website: http://pollenuk.worc.ac.uk
Founded: 1991
Description: Promotes awareness and scientific research in Aerobiology; provides a channel of communication between aerobiologists.

British Aerosol Manufacturers' Association
BAMA
Kings Bldgs., Smith Sq., London, SW1P 3JJ, England, UK
Tel: 44 20 78285111
Fax: 44 20 78348436
Email: enquiries@bama.co.uk
Website: http://www.bama.co.uk
Founded: 1961
Members: 76
Staff: 4
Contact: Sue Rogers
Description: Aerosol manufacturers in the United Kingdom. Promotes and protects members' interests.
Publication title: Air Quality and Aerosols
Publication title: Annual Report

British Agencies for Adoption and Fostering
Skyline House, 200 Union St., London, SE1 0LX, England, UK
Tel: 44 20 75932000
Fax: 44 20 75932001
Email: mail@baaf.org.uk
Website: http://www.baaf.org.uk
Founded: 1980
Members: 1900

Staff: 71
Contact: Felicity Collier, Chief Exec.
Fee: £62
Membership Type: individual
Description: Members include local authority and voluntary adoption agencies and professionals working in adoption, fostering and social work with children. Aims to extend the opportunities for family life for all children being looked after away from their families; to become the major inter-disciplinary and educational force for professionals working with these children; to promote high standards of practice in adoption, fostering and child care social work and increase public understanding of the issues involved.
Library Subject: adoption, fostering, child care
Library Type: open to the public
Formerly: BAAF
Publication: Journal
Publication title: Adoption and Fostering Journal. Advertisements.
Publication title: Adoption and Fostering News

British Agricultural and Garden Machinery Association
14-16 Church St., Rickmansworth, WD3 1RQ, England, UK
Tel: 44 1923 720241
Fax: 44 207 6812983
Email: info@bagma.com
Website: http://www.bagma.com
Founded: 1917
Staff: 3
Contact: Ian Jones
Description: Full members are specialist dealers and service engineers for agricultural machinery; associate members are repairers and service engineers; affiliate members are manufacturers and wholesalers. Exists to promote the interests of specialists in agricultural and garden machinery; to maintain high standards in the trade so that their customers receive professional attention at all times.
Publication title: Garden Machinery Price Guide
Publication title: Market Guide to Used Farm Tractors and Machinery

British Agricultural History Society
c/o University of Exeter
Department of History, Amory Building, Rennes Dr., Exeter, EX4 4RJ, England, UK
Tel: 44 1392 263286
Fax: 44 1392 263305
Email: bahs@exeter.ac.uk
Website: http://www.bahs.org.uk
Founded: 1953
Members: 850
Staff: 1
Contact: Prof. M. Overton, Treas.
Fee: £15
Membership Type: ordinary
Fee: £35
Membership Type: library
Description: Scholars, persons concerned with agriculture and the rural sector, and local historians. Covers all aspects of rural and agricultural history - technical, social, economic, ethnographical, environmental - in Britain and overseas.
Publication: Journal
Publication title: Agricultural History Review. Advertisements.
Meetings/Conventions: - 3/year conference

British Air Line Pilots Association
BALPA

81 New Rd., Harlington, Hayes, UB3 5BG, England, UK
Tel: 44 20 84764000
Fax: 44 20 84764077
Email: balpa@balpa.org
Website: http://www.balpa.org
Founded: 1937
Members: 8000
Staff: 30
Contact: Mr. C. Darke, Gen.Sec.
Description: British civil airline pilots and flight engineers. Concerned with the representation of professional pilots and flight engineers with their employers. Also matters involving regulatory bodies and government departments, both in the UK and within the European Commission.
Publication: Journal
Publication title: The Log. Advertisements.

British American Security Information Council

Lafone House, 11-13 Leathermarket St., London, SE1 3HN, England, UK
Tel: 44 20 74072977
Fax: 44 20 74072988
Email: basicuk@basicint.org
Website: http://www.basicint.org
Founded: 1987
Staff: 10
Contact: Ian Davis, Dir.
Description: Promotes public awareness of defense disarmament, military strategy, and nuclear policies in order to foster informed debate on these issues.
Library Subject: international security
Library Type: reference

British Amusement Catering Trades Association
BACTA

BACTA House, Regent Wharf, 6 All Saints St., London, N1 9RQ, England, UK
Tel: 44 207 7137144
Fax: 44 207 7130446
Email: info@bacta.org.uk
Website: http://www.bacta.org.uk
Founded: 1974
Members: 1200
Staff: 7
Contact: Stuart Greenman, Head of PR & Govt. Affairs
Description: Manufacturers, distributors and operators of coin-operated amusement equipment together with owners of inland and seaside amusement centers and arcades. To promote and protect the interests of members.
Publication: Brochure
Publication title: Annual Review. Advertisements.
Second publication: Newsletter
Publication title: Coinslot. Advertisements.
Meetings/Conventions: - annual convention

British and International Golf Greenkeepers' Association

BIGGA House, Aldwark, Alne, York, YO61 1UF, England, UK
Tel: 44 1347 833800
Fax: 44 1347 833801

Email: admin@bigga.co.uk
Website: http://www.bigga.org.uk
Founded: 1987
Members: 7300
Staff: 21
Contact: Neil Thomas, Exec. Dir.
Description: Golf Greenkeepers, together with those working or interested in the fine turf industries. Promotes and advances all aspects of greenkeeping and assists and encourages the proficiency of members. The Association arranges conferences, seminars and competitions. It collaborates with other bodies or organisations with which there may be a common interest.
Library Subject: greenkeeping and related subjects
Library Type: not open to the public
Publication: Magazine
Publication title: Greenkeeper International. Advertisements.
Meetings/Conventions: BIGGA Turf Management Exhibition - annual trade show - Exhibits.

British and International Sailors Society

3 Orchard Pl., Southampton, SO14 3AT, England, UK
Tel: 44 23 80337333
Fax: 44 23 80338333
Email: events@biss.org.uk
Website: http://www.biss.org.uk
Founded: 1818
Staff: 65
Contact: Donna Mayall
Description: Promotes the interests of sailors and seafarers.

British and Irish Association of Law Librarians
BIALL

26 Myton Crescent, Warwick, CV34 6QA, England, UK
Tel: 44 1926 491717
Fax: 44 1926 491717
Email: susanfrost@compuserve.com
Website: http://www.biall.org.uk
Founded: 1969
Members: 800
Staff: 1
Contact: Mrs. Susan Frost, Admin.
Fee: £54
Membership Type: personal
Fee: £90
Membership Type: institutional
Description: Unites and coordinates the interests, opinions and activities of law library professionals into a single, influential voice, ensuring that members' views are fully taken into account by decision-makers at all levels. Seeks to achieve aims through a variety of activities: represents members' interests in informal discussions with the government and other organizations on relevant policy issues; interacts with other organizations worldwide to exchange views and information; regularly contacts legal profesionals, publishers, data providers, and academics; offers traiing on a range of professional topics and skills and educational support, including bibliographical study and research in law and librarianship; provides informal advice and support through a network of professional contacts and colleagues.
Publication: Newsletter
Publication title: BIALL Newsletter. Advertisements.
Second publication: Directory
Publication title: Directory of Law Libraries
Meetings/Conventions: - annual conference - Exhibits.

British and Irish Law, Education and Technology Association
BILETA

c/o Secretariat
UK Centre for Legal Education, Warwick University, Coventry, CV4 7AL, England, UK
Tel: 44 24 76523117
Fax: 44 24 76523290
Email: s.bloxham@warwick.ac.uk
Website: http://www.bileta.ac.uk
Founded: 1986
Members: 100
Contact: Prof. Abdul Paliwala, Sec.
Fee: £100
Membership Type: institution
Fee: £100
Membership Type: associate membership for law firms
Description: Law teaching institutions in the United Kingdom and overseas. Promotes the use of technology in legal education. Promotes research; supports the development and distribution of legal software; provides information on technology in legal developments; liaises with other related organizations.
Meetings/Conventions: - annual conference

British and Irish Ombudsman Association

24 Paget Gardens, Chislehurst, BR7 5RX, England, UK
Tel: 44 208 4677455
Fax: 44 208 4677455
Email: bioa@btinternet.com
Website: http://www.bioa.org.uk
Founded: 1993
Members: 170
Staff: 2
Contact: Gordon D. Adams, Sec.
Description: Ombudsman and complaint handling organizations.
Publication: Newsletter
Publication title: The Ombudsman
Meetings/Conventions: BIOA Conference - biennial conference Coventry, UK

British Andrology Society

Reproductive & Dev. Med., Sheffield University, Level 4, Jessop Wing, Tree Root Walk, Sheffield, S10 2SF, England, UK
Tel: 44 114 2268195
Fax: 44 114 2268538
Email: a.fazeli@sheffield.ac.uk
Website: http://www.britishandrology.org.uk
Founded: 1977
Contact: Dr. Alireza Fazeli, Sec.
Fee: £15
Membership Type: full member
Fee: £5
Membership Type: student
Description: Scientists and clinicians working in the fields of human and mammalian reproduction with an interest in the male. Promotes the interests of members. Research is an important activity in the organization.

British Angora Goat Society

5 The Langlands, Hampton Lucy, Warwick, CV35 8BN, England, UK
Tel: 44 1789 841219
Email: secretary@angoragoat.fsnet.uk
Members: 350

Contact: Mrs. E. Graham
Fee: £30
Description: Owners and breeders of angora goats.
Publication: Journal
Second publication: Newsletter

British Antique Dealers' Association
BADA

20 Rutland Gate, London, SW7 1BD, England, UK
Tel: 44 20 75894128
Fax: 44 20 75819083
Email: info@bada.org
Website: http://www.bada.org
Founded: 1918
Members: 400
Staff: 5
Contact: Mrs. Elaine Dean, Sec.Gen.
Fee: £495
Description: Members comprise the top 400 antiques dealers in the United Kingdom. Represents the interests of the top antiques dealers in Britain. Its bylaws provide protection for the consumer as does the free arbitration service for disputes.
Publication: Handbook
Publication title: The British Antique Dealers' Association Handbook. Advertisements.
Meetings/Conventions: The BADA Antiques & Fine Art Fair - annual trade show - Exhibits. Chelsea UK

British Antique Furniture Restorers Association

The Old Rectory, Warmwell, Dorchester, DT2 8HQ, England, UK
Tel: 44 1305 854822
Fax: 44 1305 854822
Email: headoffice@bafra.org.uk
Website: http://www.bafra.org.uk
Founded: 1979
Members: 390
Staff: 1
Contact: Michael Barrington, Chmn.
Fee: £250
Membership Type: full
Fee: £75
Membership Type: associate
Description: Promotes the highest standards in furniture conservation and restoration; provides support to members; and educates members and the public in matters of furniture conservation, restoration, and historical aspects.
Library Subject: furniture conservation, restoration, history, and design
Library Type: not open to the public
Publication: Directory. Advertisements.

British Appaloosa Society

78 Military Rd., Gosport, Hampshire, PO12 3AS, England, UK
Tel: 44 23 92528069
Fax: 44 23 92528069
Email: secretary@appaloosa.org.uk
Website: http://www.appaloosa.org.uk/
Founded: 1976
Members: 500
Contact: Laura Ellis-Jones, Sec.
Description: Seeks to improve the quality of the Appaloosa breed.

British Apparel and Textile Confederation

5 Portland Pl., London, W1B 1PW, England, UK
Tel: 44 207 6367788
Fax: 44 207 6367515
Email: batc@dial.pipex.co.uk
Founded: 1992
Contact: A. Mansell
Description: Spinners, weavers, and finishers of cotton, wool, and other textiles. Promotes and defends members' interests in domestic and international legislative and technical matters.
Publication title: Newsletter
Publication title: Statistical Review

British Approvals Board for Telecommunications BABT

Claremont House, 34 Molesey Rd., Hersham, Walton-On-Thames, KT12 4RQ, England, UK
Tel: 44 1932 251200
Fax: 44 1932 251201
Email: customer.services@babt.com
Website: http://www.babt.com
Founded: 1982
Staff: 30
Contact: Mr. J. Wood, Mng.Dir.
Description: Assessment evaluation and approval for telecommunications apparatus intended for connection to the UK public networks. UK notified body for approval of terminal equipment in EEC; UK notified body for electromagnetic compatibility for radio communications terminal equipment in EEC; UK notified body under the Low Voltage Directive. Approval of metering/billing systems for UK public networks.
Publication: Newsletter
Publication title: BABT Newsletter
Meetings/Conventions: - annual workshop - Exhibits.

British Approvals for Fire Equipment

55 Eden St., Neville House, Kingston Upon Thames, KT1 1BW, England, UK
Tel: 44 20 85411950
Fax: 44 20 85471564
Email: bafe@abft.org.uk
Website: http://www.bafe.org.uk
Founded: 1984
Staff: 5
Contact: B. Gately
Description: Promotes the quality assurance of fire protection equipment and services.
Publication: Brochure

British Arachnological Society

c/o Ian K. Dawson, Sec.
100 Hayling Ave., Little Paxton, St. Neots, PE19 6HQ, England, UK
Email: secretary@britishspiders.org.uk
Website: http://www.britishspiders.org.uk
Founded: 1963
Contact: Shaun H. Hexter, Membership Treas.
Description: Promotes the study of arachnida, especially spiders, pseudoscorpions and harvestmen.
Library Subject: arachnology
Library Type: reference
Publication: Bulletin
Publication title: Bulletin of the British Arachnological Society
Second publication: Newsletter

British Art Medal Society

c/o Dept of Coins and Medals
British Museum, Great Russell St., London, WC1B 3DG, England, UK
Tel: 44 207 3238260
Fax: 44 207 3238171
Email: pattwood@thebritishmuseum.ac.uk
Website: http://www.bams.org.uk/
Founded: 1982
Contact: P. Attwood, Sec.
Fee: £20
Description: Encourages, develops and supports the practice and study of medallic art.
Publication title: The Medal. Advertisements.
Meetings/Conventions: - annual conference - Exhibits.

British Arts Festivals Association

The Library, 3rd Fl., 77 Whitechapel High St., London, E1 7QX, England, UK
Tel: 44 20 72474667
Fax: 44 20 72475010
Email: info@artsfestivals.co.uk
Website: http://www.artsfestivals.co.uk
Founded: 1970
Members: 110
Staff: 1
Contact: Gwyn Rhydderch, Coor.
Description: Wide range of arts festivals in the United Kingdom. Provides a forum for exchange of experience between festivals, a representative voice and a source of central information for press and public.
Publication: Brochure
Meetings/Conventions: Annual Conference of Festivals - annual conference

British Association and College of Occupational Therapists

106-114 Borough High St., London, SE1 1HL, England, UK
Tel: 44 207 3576480
Fax: 44 207 4502299
Email: beryl.steeden@cot.co.uk
Website: http://www.cot.org.uk
Founded: 1932
Members: 23000
Staff: 60
Contact: Sheelagh Richards, Chief Exec./Sec.
Description: State registered Occupational Therapists, Occupational Therapy Helpers and Technical Instructors. Acts as a professional association in the field of rehabilitative medicine; promotion of occupational therapy education; honourable practice, repression of malpractice and to provide the facilities for the advancement of the science of occupational therapy. BAOT is also the Trade Union for the members.
Library Subject: occupational therapy and related topics
Library Type: not open to the public
Publication: Journal
Publication title: British Journal of Occupational Therapy. Advertisements.
Second publication: Magazine
Publication title: Occupational Therapy News
Meetings/Conventions: Broadeninct Horizons - annual conference - Exhibits.

British Association for Accident and Emergency Medicine

c/o Royal College of Surgeons of England
35-43 Lincoln's Inn Fields, London, WC2A 3PE, England, UK
Tel: 44 207 8319405
Fax: 44 207 4050318
Email: baem@emergencymedicine.uk.net
Website: http://www.baem.org.uk
Founded: 1967
Members: 1500
Staff: 2
Contact: Mr. SE McCabe, Honorary Sec.
Description: Membership of the British Association for Accident and Emergency Medicine is available to any registered medical practitioner who has an interest in Accident and Emergency Medicine. Concerned with the development of the specialty of Accident and Emergency Medicine and, in particular, to achieve a minimum of one Accident and Emergency Consultant in every major Accident and Emergency Department. It has a network of Regional Representatives who are available to advise Districts on the establishment of Accident and Emergency Consultant posts, staffing issues, design of Accident and Emergency Departments, etc.
Publication: Journal
Publication title: Emergency Medicine

British Association for American Studies
BAAS

c/o Dr. Heidi Macpherson
Department of Cultural Studies, University of Central Lancashire, Preston, PR1 2HE, England, UK
Tel: 44 1772 893039
Fax: 44 1772 892924
Email: hrsmacpherson@uclan.ac.uk
Website: http://www.baas.ac.uk
Founded: 1955
Members: 500
Contact: Dr. Heidi Macpherson, Sec.
Fee: £26
Membership Type: individual
Description: Professional organization concerned with university level conferences.
Publication: Newsletter
Publication title: American Studies in Britain. Advertisements.
Second publication: Books
Publication title: BAAS American Studies
Meetings/Conventions: - annual conference - Exhibits. UK

British Association for Applied Linguistics

c/o Dovetail Mgmt. Consultancy
PO Box 6688, London, SE15 3WB, England, UK
Tel: 44 207 6390090
Fax: 44 207 6356014
Email: admin@baal.org.uk
Website: http://www.baal.org.uk
Founded: 1967
Members: 650
Contact: Jeanie Taylor, Admin.
Fee: £35
Membership Type: individual
Fee: £15
Membership Type: concessionary
Description: Language teachers, lexicologists, teachers, speech therapists, and forensic linguists. Promotes research into language use. Seeks to foster the understanding of languages among nonlinguists.
Publication: Newsletter
Publication title: BAAL Newsletter. Advertisements.
Second publication: Proceedings
Meetings/Conventions: Applied Linguistics at the Interface - annual meeting - Exhibits. Leeds UK

British Association for Behavioural and Cognitive Psychotherapies

Globe Centre, PO Box 9, Accrington, BB5 2GD, England, UK
Tel: 44 1254 875277
Fax: 44 1254 239114
Email: babcp@babcp.com
Website: http://www.babcp.org.uk
Founded: 1972
Members: 2000
Contact: Howard Lomas
Fee: £25
Description: Health, Social Service, education staff and therapists in private practice; individuals interested in psychotherapies and accredited/registered psychotherapists. Promotion of behavioural and cognitive therapy approaches in health, educational and social problem areas.
Publication: Newsletter
Publication title: BABCP Newsletter
Second publication: Journal
Publication title: Behavioural & Cognitive Psychotherapy Journal. Advertisements.
Meetings/Conventions: - annual conference - Exhibits.

British Association for Cancer Research
BACR

Institute of Cancer Research, 15 Cotswold Rd., Sutton, SM2 5NG, England, UK
Tel: 44 208 7224208
Fax: 44 208 7701395
Email: bacr@icr.ac.uk
Website: http://www.icr.ac.uk/bacr
Founded: 1960
Members: 1300
Staff: 1
Contact: Ms. B.J. Cavilla, Admin.
Fee: £40
Membership Type: Full member
Fee: £20
Membership Type: Student
Description: Laboratory and clinical cancer research workers. Conducts and promotes research into the prevention, causes, treatment, and cure of cancer.
Publication: Journal
Publication title: British Journal of Cancer. Advertisements.
Meetings/Conventions: British Cancer Research Meeting - annual conference - Exhibits.

British Association for Cemeteries in South Asia
BACSA

c/o T.C. Wilkinson, MBE
76 1/2 Chartfield Ave., London, SW15 6HQ, England, UK
Tel: 44 208 7886953
Website: http://members.ozemail.com.au/~clday/bacsa.htm
Founded: 1976

Members: 1950
Contact: T.C. Wilkinson, Hon.Sec.
Fee: £7.5
Membership Type: individual
Fee: £10
Membership Type: couple
Description: Historians, genealogists, and individuals interested in the preservation of cemeteries in South Asia that hold bodies of Europeans.
Library Type: reference
Publication: Journal
Publication title: Chowkidar
Meetings/Conventions: - semiannual meeting - Exhibits.

British Association for Chemical Specialities

The Gatehouse, White Cross, Lancaster, LA1 4XQ, England, UK
Tel: 44 1524 849606
Fax: 44 1524 849194
Email: enquiries@bacsnet.org
Website: http://www.bacsnet.org
Founded: 1913
Members: 160
Staff: 3
Contact: Richard J. Farn, Dir.
Description: Trade association representing manufacturers of specialty and performance chemicals, including: maintenance products for institutional, industrial, and consumer use; biocides; disinfectants; specialty surfactants and water treatment. Promotes high standards for health, safety, and environmental impact in the chemical industry. Addresses legislative and regulatory issues at the national and international levels. Provides technical and legal guidance to members. Creates opportunities for members to share ideas and experience. Promotes the prosperity of its members.
Formerly: Formed by Merger of, British Disinfectant Manufacturers Association
Publication title: BACS Annual Review
Publication title: BACS Guide to the Choice of Disinfectants
Meetings/Conventions: meeting

British Association for Chinese Studies
BACS

c/o Carol Rennie
33 Beechwood Park, London, E18 2EH, England, UK
Tel: 44 20 85307401
Fax: 44 20 79695414
Email: secretary@bacsuk.org.uk
Website: http://www.bacsuk.org.uk
Members: 200
Contact:
Fee: £20
Description: Students, faculty, museum and library staff, journalists, and others with an interest in Chinese studies.
Meetings/Conventions: - annual conference

British Association for Counselling and Psychotherapy
BACP

1 Regent Pl., Rugby, CV21 2PJ, England, UK
Tel: 44 870 4 435252
Fax: 44 870 4 435160
Email: bacp@bacp.co.uk
Website: http://www.counselling.co.uk

Founded: 1977
Members: 17000
Staff: 45
Contact: Shirley Mills
Fee: £104
Membership Type: open
Description: Individual or organisational membership for those working as counsellors or those using counselling skills as part of their role. Aims to promote awareness of counselling internationally and raise standards of training and practice through its Ethical Framework for Good Practice in Counselling and Psychotherapy. It provides support for members including an information service for members and the public, divisions for special interest groups and local affiliated groups.
Formerly: British Association for Counselling

British Association for Dramatherapists

41 Broomhouse Ln., London, SW6 3DP, England, UK
Tel: 44 207 7310160
Email: gllian@demon.co.uk
Founded: 1976
Members: 630
Staff: 2
Contact: Gillian Eckley, Admin.
Fee: £143
Membership Type: full
Fee: £60
Membership Type: associate
Description: Aims to: educate the public about dramatherapy, support dramatherapists wherever they work and increase the availability of properly-trained and supervised dramatherapists. Also aims to ensure that high standards are maintained and to implement Equal Opportunities policies. It responds to increasing demands for information and represents dramatherapy at a national and international level.
Publication: Newsletter
Publication title: Dramatherapy
Second publication: Journal
Publication title: The Journal of Dramatherapy. Advertisements.
Meetings/Conventions: - annual general assembly - Exhibits.

British Association for Early Childhood Education

136 Cavell St., London, E1 2JA, England, UK
Tel: 44 20 75395400
Fax: 44 20 75395409
Email: office@early-education.org.uk
Website: http://www.early-education.org.uk
Founded: 1923
Members: 6500
Staff: 6
Contact: Jenny Rabin
Fee: £28
Description: Teachers, parents, nursery nurses, day nursery and family centre staff, playgroup workers, social workers, Local Authority administrators, University and College lecturers, health visitors, doctors and psychologists. Concerned with all aspects of children's learning between 0-9 years. Organises national conferences, publishes a journal and literature, carries out research and through 55 branches arranges meetings, seminars and conferences.
Publication: Newsletter
Publication title: Early Education. Advertisements.
Meetings/Conventions: - annual conference

British Association for Immediate Care
BASICS

Turret House, Turret Ln., Ipswich, IP4 1DL, England, UK
Tel: 44 870 1654999
Fax: 44 870 1654949
Email: admin@basics.org.uk
Website: http://www.basics.org.uk
Founded: 1977
Members: 2500
Staff: 3
Contact: Mrs. J. Clarke, Chief Exec.
Fee: £80
Description: Medical practitioners and non-medical practitioners (e.g., ambulance, nurse, emergency planning personnel) involved in pre-hospital immediate medical care. Aims to foster co-operation between existing Immediate Care Schemes and to encourage and aid the formation and extension of schemes in the UK; to develop and strengthen co-operation between all services in dealing with emergencies and to encourage and assist research into all aspects of pre-hospital immediate medical care and accident prevention.
Publication: Newsletter
Meetings/Conventions: - annual conference - Exhibits.

British Association for Information and Library Education

Liverpool Business School, Liverpool John Morres University, 98 Mount Pleasant, Liverpool, LS16 3QS, England, UK
Tel: 44 113 2832600
Fax: 44 113 2833182
Founded: 1962

British Association for Irish Studies
BAIS

Oxford Rd, Geography Dept., University of Manchester, Manchester, M13 9PL, England, UK
Tel: 44 161 2753623
Fax: 44 161 2757878
Founded: 1985

British Association for Japanese Studies
BAJS

c/o Lynn Baird
University of Essex, Colchester, C04 3SQ, England, UK
Tel: 44 1206 872543
Fax: 44 1206 873408
Email: bajs@bajs.org.uk
Website: http://www.bajs.org.uk
Founded: 1974
Members: 230
Contact: Lynn Baird, Sec.
Description: Seeks to further interest in Japanese studies.
Publication: Journal
Publication title: Japan Forum. Advertisements.
Meetings/Conventions: - annual conference Sheffield UK

British Association for Local History

PO Box 1576, Salisbury, SP1 8SY, England, UK
Tel: 44 1722 322158
Fax: 44 1722 413242
Email: mail@balh.co.uk
Website: http://www.balh.co.uk

Members: 2500
Staff: 5
Contact: Michael Cowan, Gen.Sec.
Fee: £38
Membership Type: individual or institution in the United Kingdom
Fee: £41
Membership Type: individual or institution outside the United Kingdom
Description: People working, individually or in a group, on the history of their house, family, village or town; searching in the archives at a local record office; attending evening classes on local history or the local environment; or visiting buildings and. sites of historical interest. Concerned with promotion of local history for the complementary purpose of academic study and leisure activity.
Publication: Journal
Publication title: The Local Historian. Advertisements.
Second publication: Magazine
Publication title: Local History News
Meetings/Conventions: - annual conference - Exhibits.

British Association for Lung Research
BALR

St. Thomas' Hospital, London, SE1 7EH, England, UK
Tel: 44 20 79228155
Fax: 44 20 79280658
Founded: 1982

British Association for Open Learning

Ste. 12, Pixmore Centre, Pixmore Ave., Letchworth, SG6 1JG, England, UK
Tel: 44 1462 485588
Fax: 44 1462 485633
Email: info@baol.co.uk
Website: http://www.baol.co.uk
Founded: 1990
Members: 285
Staff: 3
Contact: Brian Merison, Gen.Mgr.
Fee: £475
Membership Type: corporate, vat
Fee: £360
Membership Type: full, vat
Description: Seeks to build a dynamic community, with global reach, committed to innovation, excellence and best practice in learning.
Publication: Journal
Publication title: Open Learning Today. Advertisements.

British Association for Paediatric Nephrology

c/o Dr. Lesley Rees
Renal Office, St. Ormond St. Hospital fo Children, London, WC1N 3JH, England, UK
Tel: 44 207 8138346
Fax: 44 207 8298841
Email: reesl@gosh.nhs.uk
Website: http://www.uwcm.ac.uk/uwcm/ch/bapn
Founded: 1973
Members: 60
Contact: Dr. Lesley Rees, Hon.Sec.
Description: Paediatricians participating in the care of children with kidney diseases. Aims to promote policies concerning the care of children with renal disease, to conduct scientific meetings, to consider manpower and training issues and to conduct multicentre trials and other collaborative research.

British Association for Psychopharmacology
BAP

c/o Susan Chandler
36 Cambridge Pl., Hills Rd., Cambridge, CB2 1NS, England, UK
Tel: 44 1223 358395
Fax: 44 1223 321268
Email: susan@bap.org.uk
Website: http://www.bap.org.uk
Founded: 1974
Members: 1200
Staff: 2
Contact: Susan Chandler, Admin.
Fee: £80
Membership Type: Full
Fee: £20
Membership Type: Training
Description: Psychopharmacologists, psychiatrists, neuropharmacologists, psychologists, and neurochemists. Brings together scientists working in academic, clinical, and industrial applications of psychopharmacology. Arranges scientific meetings, study groups, and seminars; encourages basic research and pharmaceutical development. Offers professional guidance to the public on matters related to psychopharmacology.
Publication: Journal
Publication title: Journal of Psychopharmacology. Advertisements.
Second publication: Monographs
Meetings/Conventions: - annual conference - Exhibits.

British Association for Research Quality Assurance
BARQA

3 Wherry Ln., Ipswich, IP4 1LG, England, UK
Tel: 44 1473 221411
Fax: 44 1473 221412
Email: info@barqa.com
Website: http://www.barqa.com
Members: 1450
Staff: 5
Contact: David Weller, Mgr.
Description: Promotes members' interests.
Publication: Magazine
Publication title: QUASAR. Advertisements.
Meetings/Conventions: - annual conference - Exhibits. Nottingham UK

British Association for Sexual and Relationship Therapy

PO Box 13686, London, SW20 9ZH, England, UK
Email: info@basrt.org.uk
Website: http://www.basrt.org.uk
Founded: 1975
Members: 700
Staff: 2
Contact:
Fee: £116
Membership Type: general
Fee: £150
Membership Type: accredited
Description: Professional psychosexual therapists/clinicians/medics working in the field of sexual and marital therapy. Aims to advance the education and training of persons engaged in sexual, marital and relationship therapy; to promote research in this field; to advance public education about sexual, marital and relationship therapy.

Formerly: British Association for Sexual and Marital Therapy
Publication: Journal
Publication title: Sexual and Marital Therapy
Meetings/Conventions: conference

British Association for Slavonic and East European Studies
BASEES

Edgbaston, Birmingham, B15 2TT, England, UK
Tel: 44 121 4146346
Email: P.A.Carr@bham.ac.uk
Founded: 1953
Description: Advances education for the public benefit in the humanities and social sciences as they relate to the former soviet union and the countries of Eastern Europe.

British Association for South Asian Studies
BASAS

University of Lancaster, Department of Geography, Lancaster, LA1 4YW, England, UK
Tel: 44 1524 65201
Email: g.chapman@lancaster.ac.uk
Website: http://www.basas.ac.uk
Founded: 1985
Members: 250
Contact: G. Chapman
Description: Individuals interested in the art, culture, economies, history, religion, sociology and/or politics of India, Pakistan, Bangladesh, Sri Lanka, Nepal, Bhutan, and the Maldives. Seeks to advance scholarship and teaching in the field of south Asian studies. Facilitates exchange of information among members; sponsors research and educational programs.
Publication: Newsletter
Publication title: BASAS Bulletin
Meetings/Conventions: - annual conference

British Association for the Study of Religions

University of Leeds, Dept. of Religious Studies, Arts Faculty, Open University, Walton Hall, Milton Keyes, MK7 6AA, England, UK
Founded: 1954

British Association in Forensic Medicine

Department of Forensic Pathology, University of Sheffield, Sheffield, S3 7ES, England, UK
Tel: 44 141 3304574
Fax: 44 141 3304602
Email: p.d.lumb@sheffield.ac.uk
Website: http://www.shef.ac.uk/~bafm
Founded: 1950
Members: 200
Contact: Dr. C.M. Milroy, Hon.Sec.
Description: Promotes the specialty of forensic pathology. Represents members' interests.
Meetings/Conventions: - periodic meeting

British Association of Advisers and Lecturers in Physical Education

20 The Rise, Hempstead, Gillingham, ME7 3SS, England, UK
Tel: 44 1634 376420
Fax: 44 1634 651824
Email: jenny.newman@kent.gov.uk
Website: http://www.baalpe.org

Founded: 1920
Members: 450
Staff: 3
Contact: Mr. P. Whitlam, Gen.Sec.
Fee: £80
Membership Type: ordinary
Description: Advisors with local authority education departments, advisory teachers with local authority education departments, consultants in physical education and national governing body technical officers/commercial groups, and teachers in schools. Concerned with promoting and maintaining high standards in all aspects and at all levels of physical education. It aims to propagate awareness of the subject, as part of a well balanced curriculum and seeks to offer advice, support and information to those involved in the development of physical education.
Library Subject: Physical education
Library Type: not open to the public
Publication: Bulletin
Publication title: Bulletin of Physical Education. Advertisements.
Publication title: Physical Education for Pupils with Special Education Needs
Meetings/Conventions: Physical Education, Sport and Dance - annual conference

British Association of Aesthetic Plastic Surgeons
BAAPS

Royal College of Surgeons of England, 35-43 Lincoln's Inn Fields, London, WC2A 3PE, England, UK
Tel: 44 207 4052234
Fax: 44 207 4301840
Email: info@baaps.org.uk
Website: http://www.baaps.org.uk
Founded: 1980
Members: 140
Staff: 1
Contact: Mr. C. Orton, Pres.
Fee: £200
Membership Type: full
Description: Fosters exchange of information among surgeons for the advancement of aesthetic plastic surgery. Encourages specialized training among plastic surgeons. Develops and advocates high standards of professional conduct; advises, promotes, and disseminates information on aesthetic plastic surgery. Provides educational programs for general practitioners and the press; conducts semiannual educational program for trainees and consultants.

British Association of Art Therapists

c/o Mary Ward House
5 Tavistock Pl., London, WC1H 9SN, England, UK
Tel: 44 207 3833774
Fax: 44 207 3875513
Email: baat@ukgateway.net
Website: http://www.baat.org
Founded: 1964
Contact: S. Grandison
Description: Art therapists.
Publication: Brochure
Publication title: Art Therapy in Education
Publication title: Code of Ethics

British Association of Audiological Physicians

c/o Dr. Ewa Raglan
St. George's Hospital, Blackshaw Rd., London, SW17 0QT, England, UK
Tel: 44 208 7251988
Fax: 44 208 7251874
Email: info@baap.org.uk
Website: http://www.baap.org.uk/
Founded: 1977
Members: 100
Contact: Ms. Catherine Brown, Admin.Sec.
Fee: £115
Membership Type: full, associate, honorary
Description: Consultant physicians practising in audiology. Concerned with the diagnosis and care/management of adults and children suffering from disorders of balance and hearing; the promotion of education (postgraduate) and standards of medical practice; also concerned with training and educational issues of junior doctors.
Library Subject: policy, careers, curriculum
Library Type: reference
Publication title: Policy Document 2002: Audiological Medicine in a Modern NHS
Meetings/Conventions: - annual conference

British Association of Aviation Consultants

Carlyle House, 285 Vauxhall Bridge Rd., London, SW1V 1EJ, England, UK
Tel: 44 207 6305358
Fax: 44 207 8280667
Email: mail@baac.org.uk
Website: http://www.baac.org.uk
Founded: 1972
Members: 70
Staff: 1
Contact: John W. Marshall, Sec.
Fee: £100
Description: An authoritative body formed to represent the views and further the interest of members, and to advance the status of the profession of registered aviation consultants.
Publication title: Register of Members
Second publication: Newsletter

British Association of Barbershop Singers
BABS

16 Wessex Rd., Horndean, Waterlooville, PO8 0HS, England, UK
Tel: 44 1705 593558
Fax: 44 1705 593558
Email: ask@babscco.co.uk
Website: http://www.singbarbershop.com
Founded: 1974
Members: 1950
Contact: Eddie Kidby, Admin.Dir.
Description: Fosters barbershop harmony singing in the United Kingdom; coordinates the activities of barbershop clubs. Offers Young Men in Harmony educational program and judge training program. Sponsors competitions.
Publication: Directory
Publication title: Directory. Advertisements.
Second publication: Newsletter
Publication title: Harmony Express
Meetings/Conventions: - annual convention - Exhibits.

British Association of Beauty Therapy and Cosmetology

BABTAC House, 70 Eastgate St., Gloucester, GL1 1QN, England, UK
Tel: 44 1452 421114
Fax: 44 1452 421110
Email: enquiries@babtac.com
Website: http://www.babtac.com
Founded: 1976
Members: 8500
Staff: 6
Contact: Lorraine Walker
Description: Qualified and student beauty therapists. Aims to inject a new enthusiasm and dedication to the work; to present a strong united front to increase respect from the general public and press; to maintain and raise the standard of training; to publicise and streamline the Confederation education system; to encourage pride in the presentation and rendering of service to clients.
Publication title: In Touch
Meetings/Conventions: Beauty Therapy Exhibition and Congress - annual - Exhibits.

British Association of Behavioral Optometrists

Greygarth, Littleworth, Winchcombe, Cheltenham, GL54 5BT, England, UK
Tel: 44 1242 602689
Fax: 44 1242 602689
Email: greygarth@compuserve.com
Website: http://www.babo.co.uk
Founded: 1990
Members: 93
Contact: Christine Manser, Sec.
Fee: £95
Membership Type: full
Description: Seeks to improve understanding of Behavioral Optometry, through continuing education and training and by providing an accredited list of trained optometrists.
Library Subject: behavioral optometry
Library Type: reference

British Association of Clinical Anatomists
BACA

School of Biomedical Sciences, University of Leeds, Leeds, LS2 9JT, England, UK
Tel: 44 113 2334296
Founded: 1977

British Association of Colliery Management
BACM

17 South Parade, Doncaster, DN1 2DR, England, UK
Tel: 44 1302 815551
Fax: 44 1302 815552
Email: enquiries@bacmteam.org.uk
Website: http://www.bacmteam.org.uk
Founded: 1947
Members: 6078
Staff: 15
Contact: P.M. Carragher, Gen.Sec.
Description: Union of individuals in the mining and associated industries in Great Britain. Promotes and protects the interests of members. Regulates relations between members, their employers, and other employees in the mining industry. Disseminates information concerning legislation affecting members. Provides legal advice and assistance.

Formerly: British Association of Colliery Management
Publication: Newsletter
Publication title: Newsletter
Meetings/Conventions: - annual conference

British Association of Communicators in Business
CIB

Fluriga Bldg., 1st Fl., Ste. A, Davey Ave., Milton Keyes, MK5 8ND, England, UK
Tel: 44 870 1217606
Fax: 44 870 1217601
Email: enquiries@cib.uk.com
Website: http://www.cib.uk.com
Founded: 1949
Members: 1000
Staff: 1
Contact: Alan Peaford, Pres.
Fee: £155
Membership Type: associate/fellow/member/student/retired
Description: Directors, managers, editors, and assistants involved in the management, editing, and production of corporate communication media. Represents members' interests; fosters information exchange among members. Conducts educational courses.
Formerly: British Association of Industrial Editors
Publication: Newsletter
Publication title: CIB News
Second publication: Magazine
Publication title: Communicators in Business
Meetings/Conventions: - annual convention - Exhibits.

British Association of Conference Destinations

Charles House, 6th Fl., 148-149 Great Charles St., Birmingham, B3 3HT, England, UK
Tel: 44 121 2121400
Fax: 44 121 2123131
Email: info@bacd.org.uk
Website: http://www.bacd.org.uk
Founded: 1969
Members: 80
Staff: 5
Contact: Tony Rogers, Exec.Dir.
Description: Members comprise local authority conference offices, convention bureaus and area tourist boards. The Association has formal links with the British Tourist Authority and the National Tourist Boards of England, Scotland, Wales and N Ireland. Primary aim is to promote British conference, meetings, exhibition and incentive travel facilities. It offers a free and impartial venue finding service covering several thousand venues of every description. It organizes an annual exhibition, 'CONFER', and also runs education courses. Other activities include information services, research, and liaison with government agencies.
Library Subject: conference and exhibition industry
Library Type: reference
Publication: Directory
Publication title: British Conference Destinations Directory. Advertisements.
Meetings/Conventions: - annual convention - Exhibits. Liverpool UK

British Association of Cosmetic Surgeons

17 Harley St., London, W1N 1DA, England, UK
Tel: 44 207 3235728
Founded: 1980
Members: 20

Contact: Anthony Mitra
Description: All members are cosmetic surgeons, carrying out cosmetic surgery in private practice. Maintains and improves the standards of cosmetic surgery in Britain and interchanges information between members. Informs the public.
Publication: Booklet
Publication title: Basic Account of Cosmetic Surgery

British Association of Crystal Growth
BACG

PO Box 217, Millbrook, Southampton, SO15 0EG, England, UK
Tel: 44 2380 702300
Fax: 44 2380 316777
Email: pete.capper@baesystems.com
Website: http://bacg.newi.ac.uk
Founded: 1969

British Association of Day Surgery

35-43 Lincoln's Inn Fields, London, WC2A 3PN, England, UK
Tel: 44 207 9730308
Fax: 44 207 9730314
Email: bads@bads.co.uk
Website: http://www.bads.co.uk
Founded: 1990
Members: 720
Staff: 1
Contact: Mrs. Gee Hugget, Admin. Officer
Fee: £30
Membership Type: ordinary
Description: Nurses, managers, surgeons and anaesthetists. To encourage the expansion of day surgery and to promote education, research and high-quality treatment in this field. Organizes seminars, meetings and holds an annual conference. Advice is provided to Royal Colleges, NHS Executive, regional commissions and trusts including private health organizations.
Publication: Journal
Publication title: Journal of One Day Surgery. Advertisements.
Meetings/Conventions: - annual convention - Exhibits.

British Association of Dental Nurses

11 Pharos St., Fleetwood, FY7 6BG, England, UK
Tel: 44 1253 778631
Fax: 44 1253 773266
Email: admin@badn.org.uk
Website: http://www.badn.org.uk
Founded: 1940
Staff: 5
Contact: Pamela A. Swain, Ch.Exec.
Fee: £30
Membership Type: full
Fee: £22
Membership Type: associate
Description: Professional association representing dental nurses in the UK and overseas as well as other members of the dental industry. Represents members working in specialist areas such as training, orthodontics, special care, and the armed forces. Aims to support, encourage, and provide advice to dental nurses; to develop and maintain nationally recognised standards; to protect the professional status of the dental nurse; and to maintain contact with the necessary bodies to achieve the above.
Library Subject: dental nursing, dentistry
Library Type: not open to the public
Formerly: ABDSA

Publication: Journal
Publication title: The British Dental Nurses Journal. Advertisements.
Meetings/Conventions: - annual conference - Exhibits.

British Association of Dermatologists
BAD

19 Fitzroy Sq., London, W1T 6EH, England, UK
Tel: 44 207 3830266
Fax: 44 207 3885263
Email: admin@bad.org.uk
Website: http://www.bad.org.uk
Founded: 1921
Members: 946
Staff: 16
Contact: Dr. M.J.D. Goodfield, Hon.Sec.
Description: Medical professionals united to further the knowledge and teaching of dermatology. Promotes the interests of members and their patients. Conducts medical and scientific research; disseminates information.
Library Type: reference
Publication: Journal
Publication title: British Journal of Dermatology
Meetings/Conventions: - annual conference - Exhibits.

British Association of Feed Supplement and Additive Manufacturers

238 Chester Rd., Hartford, Northwich, Cheshire, CW8 1LW, England, UK
Tel: 44 1606 783314
Fax: 44 1606 783314
Email: hwebafsam@onetel.net.uk
Founded: 1968
Contact: Mr. H.W. Evans
Description: Feed supplement and additive manufacturers.

British Association of Former United Nations Civil Servants
BAFUNCS

c/o United Nations Association
3 Whitehall Ct., London, SW1A 2EL, England, UK
Email: bafuncs@globalnet.co.uk
Website: http://www.un.org/other/afics
Founded: 1973
Members: 940
Contact: David N. Axford, Chm.
Fee: £10
Membership Type: single
Fee: £15
Membership Type: double
Description: Encourages members to keep in touch with former colleagues through social, cultural and sporting activities. Extends welfare to former employees of the United Nations Civil Service and spouses in need. Represents members' interests in relations with the United Nations and lists Specialized Agencies and British Government authorities. Protects the value of UN pensions through representation on Federation of Associations of Former International Civil Servants.
Publication: Newsletter. Advertisements.
Meetings/Conventions: general assembly

British Association of Golf Course Constructors

The Dormy House, Cooden Beach Golf Club, Bexhill-on-Sea, TN39 4TR, England, UK
Tel: 44 1424 842380
Fax: 44 1424 843375
Email: mightyspyder@aol.com
Website: http://www.bagcc.org.uk
Founded: 1983
Members: 33
Staff: 1
Contact: David White, Sec.
Description: Trade members. Promotes and develop golf course constructions in the UK and overseas, and adoption of policy that will ensure high quality workmanship.
Publication: Handbook
Publication title: Membership Folder

British Association of Green Crop Driers
BAGCD

Silverwood, Stone St., Westenhanger, Hythe, CT21 4HT, England, UK
Tel: 44 1303 267317
Fax: 44 1303 267344
Email: info@bagcd.org
Website: http://www.bagcd.org
Members: 25
Staff: 1
Contact: Roger Earl, Sec.
Description: Producers of dried green crops. The dehydration and processing of forage crops.

British Association of Hair Transplant Surgeons

125 Worlds End Land, Quinton, Birmingham, B32 1JX, England, UK
Description: Promotes the science of hair transplantation.

British Association of Head and Neck Oncologists
BAHNO

Queen Victoria Hospital, Maxillofacial Head & Neck Unit, East Grinstead, RH19 3DZ, England, UK
Tel: 44 1342 410210
Fax: 44 1342 328339
Email: andrew.brown@qvh-tr.sthames.nhs.uk
Founded: 1968

British Association of Homoeopathic Pharmacists
BAHP

c/o Ainsworth Homeopathic Pharmacy
36 New Cavendish St., London, W1G 8UF, England, UK
Tel: 44 20 79355330
Fax: 44 20 74864313
Founded: 1980

British Association of Homoeopathic Veterinary Surgeons
BAHVS

Chinham House, Stanford-in-the-Vale, SN7 8NQ, England, UK
Tel: 44 1367 718115
Fax: 44 1367 718243
Email: enquiries@bahvs.com
Website: http://www.bahvs.com
Founded: 1981

British Association of Hospitality Accountants

c/o Jackie Best
PO Box 384, Harrogate, HG3 4W2, England, UK
Tel: 44 1423 781498
Fax: 44 1423 781488
Email: jbest@thebaha.demon.co.uk
Website: http://www.baha-uk.org
Founded: 1969
Members: 700
Staff: 2
Contact: Jackie Best
Description: Financial directors, financial controllers, accountants and consultants in the hospitality sector. To promote the highest professional standards in financial management in the hospitality industry and to underwrite and develop those standards by the provision of education programmes.
Formerly: British Association of Hotel Accountants
Publication title: Recommended Practice for the Valuation of Hotels
Second publication: Newsletter
Meetings/Conventions: - monthly meeting

British Association of Hotel Representatives
BAHREP

127 New House Pk., St. Albans, AL1 1UT, England, UK
Tel: 44 1727 862327
Fax: 44 1727 812722
Members: 25
Staff: 1
Contact: David Arscott, Pres.
Fee: £150
Description: Hotel sales and reservations employees. Represents members' interests.
Meetings/Conventions: - monthly meeting

British Association of Landscape Industries
BALI

Landscape House, Stoneleigh Park, Coventry, CV8 2LG, England, UK
Tel: 44 2476 690333
Fax: 44 2476 690077
Email: contact@bali.org.uk
Website: http://www.bali.org.uk
Founded: 1972
Members: 700
Staff: 8
Contact: Paul Kerr, Ch.Exec.
Description: Landscapers in the United Kingdom. Promotes practice of professional landscaping. Defends industry interests.
Publication: Membership Directory
Publication title: British Association of Landscape Industries
Second publication: Newsletter
Publication title: Landscape News
Meetings/Conventions: BALI Annual Landscape Conference - Exhibits.

British Association of Leisure Parks, Piers and Attractions

c/o BALPPA House
57-61 Newington Causeway, London, SE1 6BD, England, UK
Tel: 44 207 4034455
Fax: 44 207 4034022
Email: info@balppa.org
Website: http://www.balppa.org

Founded: 1936
Members: 200
Staff: 3
Contact: Stan Bollom, Pres.
Description: Park membership, UK private sector leisure parks, piers and attractions; Trade associate membership, suppliers of goods and services to the parks sector. Aims to promote and defend the interests of the industry; to represent the needs and concerns of the industry to HM Government departments and elsewhere at national level; to provide advice, information and other services to its members, to provide forums for discussion of their interests and concerns and to promote best practice in the industry.
Publication: Directory
Publication title: BALPPA Directory of Members. Advertisements.
Publication title: BALPPA Group Travel Guide

British Association of Medical Managers

Petersgate House, 3rd Fl., St. Petersgate, Stockport, SK1 1HE, England, UK
Tel: 44 161 4741141
Fax: 44 161 4747167
Email: bamm@bamm.co.uk
Website: http://www.bamm.co.uk
Founded: 1991
Members: 1800
Staff: 10
Contact: Prof. Jenny Simpson, Chief Exec.
Fee: £120
Description: Doctors from all specialties and at all levels of interest in management are invited to apply for membership. Junior doctors are warmly welcomed and non medical managers are welcome to apply for associate membership. Concerned with the promotion of quality healthcare by improving and supporting the contribution of doctors in management. Unites doctors with an interest in healthcare management. Members are keen to learn from, and work with each other to ensure a meaningful and effective contribution to the management of organisations.
Publication title: Clinician in Management
Second publication: Newsletter
Meetings/Conventions: - annual conference - Exhibits.

British Association of Neuroscience Nurses

c/o Neuro ICU
Radcliff Infirmary, Woodstock Rd., Oxford, OX2 6HE, England, UK
Tel: 44 28 94461203
Email: admin@bann.org.uk
Website: http://www.bann.org.uk
Founded: 1971
Members: 310
Contact: Anne Murdoch, Exec.Sec.
Fee: £20
Membership Type: full,associate, honorary
Description: Promotes the highest standards of patient care in the Neurosciences field. Provides opportunities for knowledge transfer between neuroscience nurses. Encourages clinical research and promotes interest in the neuroscience area.

British Association of Occupational Therapists

106-114 Borough High St., Southwark, London, SE1 1LB, England, UK
Tel: 44 207 3576480
Fax: 44 207 4502299
Email: cot@cot.co.uk
Website: http://www.cot.co.uk

Founded: 1974
Members: 21000
Staff: 50
Contact: Sheelagh Richards, CEO
Description: Promotes high standards among occupational therapists. Supports the provision of efficient, reliable, and effective services that benefit all users of occupational therapy. Encourages personal and intellectual development of occupational therapists and support staff.

British Association of Oral and Maxillofacial Surgeons of England

c/o Royal College of Surgeons
35-43 Lincoln's Inn Fields, London, WC2A 3PN, England, UK
Tel: 44 20 74058074
Fax: 44 20 74309997
Email: office@baoms.org.uk
Website: http://www.baoms.org.uk
Founded: 1962
Members: 1200
Description: Aims to promote the advancement of education and research into the development of oral and maxillofacial surgery in the British Isles; to encourage, and assist postgraduate education, study and research in oral and maxillofacial surgery. Arranges regular meetings at which lectures and demonstrations will be given.
Publication: Journal
Publication title: British Journal of Oral & Maxillofacial Surgery

British Association of Orthodontists
BAO

16 Castle Hill, Maidenhead, SL6 4JJ, England, UK
Tel: 44 1628 23279
Founded: 1965

British Association of Otorhinolaryngologists - Head and Neck Surgeons

c/o Royal College of Surgeons
35-43 Lincoln's Inn Fields, London, WC2A 3PE, England, UK
Tel: 44 20 74048373
Fax: 44 20 74044200
Email: orl@bao-hns.demon.co.uk
Website: http://www.orl-baohns.org
Founded: 1943
Members: 1111
Staff: 3
Contact: Barbara Komoniewska, Admin.Sec.
Fee: £195
Membership Type: full
Fee: £85
Membership Type: trainee
Description: Consultant ENT and head and neck surgeons, consultant audiological physicians as well as medical practitioners engaged in the practice of otorhinolaryngology and head and neck surgery in grades other than that of consultant. Aims to support and encourage education, research, development, and audit in otorhinolaryngology, head and neck surgery. Promotes the highest standards or medical and surgical practice within otorhinolarynglogy, head and neck surgery, for the benefit of patients.
Publication title: Clinical Otolaryngology
Second publication: Newsletter
Meetings/Conventions: - annual conference

British Association of Paediatric Surgeons
BAPS

c/o Royal College of Surgeons of England
35-43 Lincoln's Inn Fields, London, WC2A 3PH, England, UK
Tel: 44 207 8696915
Fax: 44 171 8696919
Email: adminsec@baps.org.uk
Website: http://www.baps.org.uk
Founded: 1953
Members: 700
Staff: 1
Contact: Prof. D. Lloyd, Pres.
Description: Pedriatric surgeons, consultants, and trainees. Works to improve the techniques of study, practice, and research in pediatric surgery; fosters professional relations among pediatric surgeons. Sponsors training program.
Publication title: Journal of Pediatric Surgery
Meetings/Conventions: - annual congress - Exhibits.

British Association of Paintings Conservator-Restorers

PO Box 32, Hayling Island, PO11 9WE, England, UK
Tel: 44 23 92465115
Fax: 44 23 92465115
Email: carolcarter@lineone.net
Website: http://www.abpr.co.uk
Founded: 1943
Members: 400
Staff: 1
Contact: Jan Robinson
Fee: £48
Membership Type: fellowship
Fee: £30
Membership Type: associate
Description: Membership is limited to those who are engaged full-time in the study or practice of picture conservation and restoration. There are two types of membership - Associate and Fellowship. Fellowship of the Association of British Picture Restorers is the professional qualification. Aims to sustain and improve high standards of excellence in the practice of picture conservation and restoration, encourage the investigation of new methods and materials, protect the interests of the public and the profession in relevant matters. To promote a high standard of conduct by members of the profession.
Formerly: Association of British Picture Restorers
Publication title: The Picture Restorer. Advertisements.
Meetings/Conventions: - triennial conference

British Association of Paper Historians

47 Ellesmere Rd., Chiswick, W4 3EA, England, UK
Tel: 44 1865 378316
Email: baph@freeserve.co.uk
Founded: 1989

British Association of Perinatal Medicine
BAPM

c/o Prof. David Field, Hon.Sec.
Leicester Royal Infirmary, Leicester, LE1 5WW, England, UK
Tel: 44 1162 587707
Fax: 44 1162 585502
Website: http://www.bapm-london.org/
Contact: Prof. David Field, Hon.Sec.
Description: Works to improve the standard of perinatal care in the British Isles.

British Association of Pharmaceutical Physicians

Royal Station Ct., Station Rd., Twyford, Reading, RG10 9NF, England, UK
Tel: 44 118 9341943
Fax: 44 118 9320981
Email: chairman@brapp.org
Website: http://www.brapp.org.uk
Founded: 1957
Members: 700
Staff: 3
Contact: Liz Langley, Assoc.Mgr.
Description: Fully registered medical practitioners practising pharmaceutical medicine in, or on behalf of, the pharmaceutical industry or in the statutory regulatory authority. Assists and advises members in all matters pertaining to the execution of their professional duties relating to the pharmaceutical industry.
Publication title: Pharmaceutical Physician

British Association of Pharmaceutical Wholesalers

19a South St., Farnham, GU9 7QU, England, UK
Tel: 44 1252 711412
Fax: 44 1252 726561
Email: bapwuk@aol.com
Website: http://www.bapw.co.uk
Founded: 1967
Members: 65
Staff: 3
Contact: Mike Rudin, Exec.Dir.
Description: Membership open to all full-time pharmaceutical wholesalers who are able to comply with the Association's Code of Practice. There is also an Associate Membership category open to manufacturers and providers of services to the industry. Representative body for all full-time pharmaceutical wholesalers in discussion with Department of Health, manufacturers and other pharmaceutical industry bodies.
Publication: Directory
Publication title: Members Directory
Second publication: Newsletters

British Association of Picture Libraries and Agencies
BAPLA

18 Vine Hill, London, EC1R 5DZ, England, UK
Tel: 44 20 77131780
Fax: 44 20 77131211
Email: enquiries@bapla.org.uk
Website: http://www.bapla.org
Founded: 1975
Members: 400
Staff: 4
Contact: Linda Royles, Chief Exec.
Description: Works in diverse areas of marketing, industry surveys, industry statistics, lobbying, and setting standards in business practice and technology. Operates referral service to assist picture researchers to locate the best source of photographic images.
Publication: Directory
Publication title: BAPLA Directory. Advertisements.
Second publication: Magazine
Publication title: Light Box
Meetings/Conventions: Picture Buyer's Fair - annual conference - Exhibits.

British Association of Plastic Surgeons

The Royal College of Surgeons, 35-43 Lincoln's Inn Fields, London, WC2A 3PE, England, UK
Tel: 44 20 78315161
Fax: 44 20 78314041
Email: secretariat@baps.co.uk
Website: http://www.baps.co.uk
Founded: 1946
Members: 650
Staff: 5
Contact: C.M. Caddy, Hon.Sec.
Fee: £50
Membership Type: professional, outside UK
Fee: £80
Membership Type: allied
Description: Plastic Surgeons. Promotes and directs the development of plastic surgery and aims to foster and co-ordinate education, study and research in plastic surgery.
Publication: Journal
Publication title: British Journal of Plastic Surgery
Meetings/Conventions: Scientific Meeting - semiannual conference Cardiff UK

British Association of Psychotherapists
BAP

37 Mapesbury Rd., London, NW2 4HJ, England, UK
Tel: 44 20 84529823
Fax: 44 20 84525182
Email: mail@bap-psychotherapy.org
Website: http://www.bap-psychotherapy.org
Founded: 1951
Members: 500
Staff: 6
Contact: Mrs. Elise Ormerod, Chief Exec.
Description: Full, Associate and Student Members, trained and qualified by BAP in either adult or child psychotherapy. Aims to promote the knowledge and application of psychotherapy and the training of both Adult and Child Psychotherapists. External courses were begun in 1989 for the benefit of interested members of the helping professions. A clinical service is also operated to help people find a qualified psychotherapist. An Msc. Training is also available.
Library Subject: psychoanalytical psychotherapy, analytical psychology, and child psychotherapy
Library Type: not open to the public
Publication: Journal
Meetings/Conventions: conference

British Association of Removers

3 Churchill Ct., 58 Station Rd., Harrow, HA2 7SA, England, UK
Tel: 44 20 88613331
Fax: 44 20 88613332
Email: info@bar.co.uk
Website: http://www.bar.co.uk
Founded: 1900
Members: 900
Staff: 12
Contact: Robert D. Syers, Gen.Sec.
Description: Trade association representing approved, professional companies in the furniture removal and associated industries. Provides a customer conciliation service. Acts as a forum for the exchange of information concerning the industry. Conducts research and educational programs.
Formerly: British Association of Removers

Publication: Magazine
Publication title: Removals and Storage. Advertisements.
Meetings/Conventions: - annual meeting

British Association of Seed Analysts

21 Arlington St., London, SW1A 1RN, England, UK
Tel: 44 207 4959100
Fax: 44 207 4959150
Email: paul.rooke@ukasta.org.uk
Website: http://www.ukasta.org.uk
Founded: 1958
Members: 120
Contact: Paul Rooke
Description: Open to all practising or former seed analysts. Concerned with liaison with official organizations and ministries and the dissemination of technical information to its members relating to seeds and seed testing
Publication: Newsletter

British Association of Settlements and Social Action Centres
BASSAC

c/o Winchester House, 1st Fl.
11 Cranmer, London, SW9 6EJ, England, UK
Tel: 44 20 77351075
Fax: 44 20 77350840
Email: info@bassac.org.uk
Website: http://www.bassac.org.uk
Founded: 1920
Members: 75
Staff: 10
Contact: Ben Hughes, Ch.Exec.
Description: National network of multi-purpose organisations seeking to tackle the causes and effects of poverty and social exclusion, primarily in inner city and urban areas. Provides a range of services to members of the local communities in which these organisations are located.
Library Subject: social policy, regeneration
Library Type: not open to the public
Publication: Directory
Publication title: BASSAC Directory
Publication title: BASSAC Mailing

British Association of Skin Camouflage

c/o Resources for Business
South Park Rd., Macclesfield, SK11 6SH, England, UK
Tel: 44 1625 267880
Fax: 44 1625 267879
Email: thorpm@resources.demon.co.uk
Website: http://www.skin-camouflage.net
Founded: 1986
Members: 100
Staff: 1
Contact: Mary Thorp, Exec.Sec.
Fee: £15
Membership Type: full
Fee: £10
Membership Type: associate
Description: Trains professionals. Encourages and supports members. Informs and provides remedial camouflage service for patients.
Publication: Newsletter
Meetings/Conventions: Training Initiatives - semiannual

British Association of Social Workers

16 Kent St., Birmingham, B5 6RD, England, UK
Tel: 44 121 6223911
Fax: 44 121 6224860
Email: info@basw.co.uk
Website: http://www.basw.co.uk
Founded: 1970
Members: 10000
Staff: 20
Contact: Ian Johnston, Dir.
Description: Social workers in the UK. Concerned to promote the social work profession in UK on issues of social work policy and practice. Services to members include advice and representation, publications and the association's journal Professional Social Work.
Publication: Journals

British Association of Sport and Medicine
BASM

67 Springfield Lane, Eccleston, WA10 5HB, England, UK
Tel: 44 1744 28198
Fax: 44 1744 28198
Founded: 1952

British Association of State English Language Teaching
BASELT

c/o BASELT Secretariat
University of Gloucestershire, Cornerways, The Park Campus, The Park, Cheltenham, GL50 2QF, England, UK
Tel: 44 1242 227099
Fax: 44 1242 227055
Email: baselt@glos.ac.uk
Website: http://www.baselt.org.uk
Founded: 1982
Members: 112
Staff: 3
Contact: Nicola Dean, Admin.Asst.
Description: Committed to quality English teaching for international students. All are accredited by the British Council and regularly inspected to assure students of a quality education experience.
Publication: Brochure
Publication title: Study English in the UK
Meetings/Conventions: - semiannual conference

British Association of Surgical Oncology
BASO

c/o Royal College of Surgeons
35-43 Lincoln's Inn Fields, London, WC2A 3PE, England, UK
Tel: 44 20 74055612
Fax: 44 20 74046574
Founded: 1973

British Association of Symphonic Bands and Wind Ensembles
BASBWE

Wayfaring, Smither's Ln., East Peckham, Tonbridge, TN12 5HT, England, UK
Tel: 44 1977 733739
Fax: 44 1622 872758
Email: editor@winds.org.uk
Website: http://www.winds.org.uk
Founded: 1981
Members: 850
Contact: Martin Cope, Exec. Officer
Fee: £20
Membership Type: individual
Description: Organizations, companies, and individuals in the U.K. dedicated to advancing symphonic bands and wind ensembles. Fosters contact between members and encourages information exchange. Organizes clinics on topics including the administrative aspects of running a band or ensemble, conducting, programming, fundraising, and specialist and non-specialist skills; sponsors workshops on instrument maintenance, jazz orchestras, wind ensembles, chamber groups, and arranging for ensembles.
Library Type: reference
Publication: Directory
Publication title: Directory
Second publication: Magazine
Publication title: Winds. Advertisements.
Meetings/Conventions: - periodic competition

British Association of Teachers of the Deaf

21 The Haystacks, High Wycombe, Buckinghamshire, HP13 6PY, England, UK
Tel: 44 1494 464190
Fax: 44 1494 464190
Email: secretary@batod.org.uk
Website: http://www.batod.org.uk
Founded: 1976
Members: 1750
Staff: 4
Contact: Mr. Paul A. Simpson
Fee: £51
Membership Type: associate
Fee: £51
Membership Type: full
Description: Qualified teachers of the deaf; Associate membership available to persons not qualified as teachers of the deaf. Represents the interests of all teachers of the hearing-impaired in Britain. It exists to promote the education of all hearing impaired persons and to promote and safeguard the interests and status of all teachers of the hearing-impaired
Publication: Magazine
Publication title: Association Magazine. Advertisements.
Second publication: Journal
Publication title: The Journal of the British Association of Teachers of the Deaf-Deafness and Education International
Meetings/Conventions: AGM and Conference - annual conference - Exhibits. Cardiff UK

British Association of Toy Retailers

PO Box 13, High Wycombe, HP13 5WT, England, UK
Tel: 44 1494 474762
Fax: 44 1494 474769
Email: anewbold@batr.co.uk
Website: http://www.batr.co.uk
Founded: 1950
Contact: Alison Newbold
Description: Multiples and independents retailing toys.
Publication title: BATR News
Publication title: Toy Trader

British Association of Urological Surgeons of England

c/o Royal College of Surgeons
35-43 Lincoln's Inn Fields, London, WC2A 3PE, England, UK
Tel: 44 20 78696950
Fax: 44 20 74045048
Email: pneville@baus.org.uk
Website: http://www.baus.org.uk
Founded: 1945
Members: 1400
Staff: 4
Contact: Mrs. P.M. Neville
Description: Urological surgeons from the UK and overseas. Medical practitioners in other specialties with an interest in urology. Aims to promote a high standard in the practice of urology.
Publication: Handbook
Publication title: Members Handbook
Meetings/Conventions: - annual meeting - Exhibits.

British Astronomical Association

BAA

Burlington House, Piccadilly, London, W1J 0DU, England, UK
Tel: 44 207 7344145
Fax: 44 207 4394629
Email: office@britastro.com
Website: http://www.britastro.org/main/index.html
Founded: 1890
Members: 3000
Contact: Guy Hurst, Pres.
Description: Astronomical societies and amateur astronomers. Supports modern techniques for observation, data handling, and scientific presentation of results. Facilitates information exchange. Organizes residential weekend courses. Provides information service. Loans instruments to members.
Library Type: reference
Publication title: Circular
Second publication: Book
Publication title: Handbook. Advertisements.
Meetings/Conventions: Exhibition Meeting - annual - Exhibits.

British Audio Dealers Association

PO Box 229, Redhill, RH1 1YG, England, UK
Tel: 44 1737 760008
Fax: 44 1737 760450
Email: info@bada.co.uk
Website: http://www.bada.co.uk
Founded: 1982
Members: 75
Staff: 1
Contact: Robert Hay, Operations Mgr.
Fee: £600
Membership Type: full, associate, affiliate
Description: Specialist hi-fi retailers. Associate members are manufacturers and distributors of real hi-fi and specialist press. Has a Professional Standards of Conduct Charter which members are obliged to display in their shops. Members help customers identify, clarify and satisfy their needs through demonstration of selected (often British) Hi-Fi products. Information and advice to Media available.

British Automatic Sprinkler Association

BASA

Richmond House, Broad St., Ely, CB7 4AH, England, UK
Tel: 44 1353 659187
Fax: 44 1353 666619
Email: info@basa.org.uk
Website: http://www.basa.org.uk
Founded: 1974
Members: 80
Contact: Steward Kidd, Sec.Gen.
Description: Concerned with the promotion of the greater and more efficient use of automatic sprinkler and other systems using water as a means for the control and extinguishing of fires.
Publication: Newsletter

British Aviation Archaeological Council

Carlyle House, 235 Vauxhall Bridge Rd., London, SW1V 1ES, England, UK
Tel: 44 1502 585421
Founded: 1978
Members: 49
Contact: R.J. Collis
Fee: £10
Membership Type: full, associate, research
Description: Voluntary, part-time aviation enthusiasts, historians and researchers. Aims to establish and maintain ethical standards, to provide a forum for discussion, to provide advice for member groups and to promote the preservation of aircraft relics and relevant historical documents.
Publication: Newsletter
Publication title: Wrecksearch. Advertisements.
Meetings/Conventions: - semiannual meeting

British Ballet Organization

Woolborough House, 39 Lonsdale Rd., Barnes, London, SW13 9JP, England, UK
Tel: 44 20 87481241
Fax: 44 20 87481301
Email: info@bbo.org.uk
Website: http://www.bbo.org.uk
Founded: 1930
Members: 806
Staff: 5
Contact: John Travis, Dir
Fee: £27
Membership Type: executant
Fee: £12
Membership Type: student
Description: Teachers, executants, and students. Offers exams in ballet, tap, jazz, and modern dance. Validated by the Council for Dance Education and Training. Teaching examinations in ballet, tap, and jazz.
Library Subject: includes archives of the Espinosa family (founders), dance
Library Type: not open to the public
Publication: Magazine
Publication title: Dancer. Advertisements.
Meetings/Conventions: BBO Concourse - annual seminar London UK

British Bankers' Association
BBA

Pinners Hall, 105-108 Old Broad St., London, EC2N 1EX, England, UK
Tel: 44 207 2168800
Fax: 44 207 2168811
Website: http://www.bba.org.uk
Founded: 1918
Members: 295
Staff: 60
Contact: Ian Mullen, Ch.Exec.
Description: Trade association representing banks conducting business in the United Kingdom.
Meetings/Conventions: - periodic conference

British Battery Manufacturers Association

26 Grosvenor Gardens, London, SW1W 0GT, England, UK
Tel: 44 207 8384800
Fax: 44 207 8384801
Email: info@bbma.co.uk
Website: http://www.bbma.co.uk
Founded: 1987
Members: 7
Staff: 2
Contact: Paul Duke
Description: Manufacturers of batteries. Representing the portable primary dry-cell, and rechargeable battery manufacturers, including environmental and safety aspects.
Publication title: Batteries & the Environment
Publication title: Battery Compartment Guidelines

British Bedding and Pot Plant Association

164 Shaftesbury Ave., London, WC2H 8HL, England, UK
Tel: 44 207 3317281
Fax: 44 207 3317410
Email: bbpa@nfu.org.uk
Members: 200
Contact: Diane McKay, Associations Administrator
Description: Those involved with production (growing) bedding, pot and ornamental plants. Also those in associated trades. Promotes bedding and pot plants through generic promotion of industry and participation in gardening events; Technical advice and discussion and representation through National Farmers' Union.
Publication: Newsletter
Publication title: News and Views
Meetings/Conventions: EUROGRO - biennial conference

British Bee-Keepers' Association

c/o National Beekeeper Centre
National Agricultural Centre, Stoneleigh, Warwickshire, CV8 2LG, England, UK
Tel: 44 2476 696679
Fax: 44 2476 690682
Email: information@bbka.org.uk
Website: http://www.bbka.org.uk
Founded: 1874
Members: 9000
Staff: 3
Contact: Mr. P.B. Spencer
Fee: £25
Membership Type: individual
Fee: £15
Membership Type: outside UK

Description: Nearly all county and district associations in England (as well as a few outside England) are Area Member Associations of the BBKA and joining one of those associations automatically makes you an Indirect Member of the BBKA. Aims to promote and further the craft of beekeeping. Its activities thus serve the interests of all beekeepers, but members of the BBKA also benefit from a number of specific services which are provided, including insurance.
Publication: Newsletter
Publication title: BBKA News. Advertisements.
Meetings/Conventions: - annual convention - Exhibits.

British Beer and Pub Association

Market Towers, 1 Nine Elm Lane, London, SW8 5NQ, England, UK
Tel: 44 207 6279191
Fax: 44 207 6279123
Email: enquiries@beerandpub.com
Website: http://www.beerandpub.com
Founded: 1904
Members: 75
Staff: 22
Contact: W.S. Bridgens
Description: Members are brewery companies and multiple licensed retailers in the United Kingdom.
Formerly: Brewers and Licensed Retailers Association
Publication title: Beer and Pubs Facts
Second publication: Handbook
Publication title: Statistical Handbook

British Biomagnetic Association
BBA

31 St. Marychurch Rd., Torquay, TQ1 3JF, England, UK
Tel: 44 1803 293346
Fax: 44 1803 293346
Description: Promotes research in the application to acupuncture points.

British Biophysical Society

Gunnels Wood Rd., Stevenage, SG1 2NY, England, UK
Tel: 44 1438 763367
Fax: 44 1438 764865
Email: rc8817@glaxowellcome.co.uk
Website: http://www.cryst.bbk.ac.uk/BBS/bbs.html
Founded: 1960

British Blind and Shutter Association

42 Heath St., Tamworth, B79 7JH, England, UK
Tel: 44 1827 52337
Fax: 44 1827 310827
Email: info@bbsa.org.uk
Website: http://www.bbsa.org.uk
Founded: 1919
Members: 358
Staff: 6
Contact: A.D. Skelding
Description: Manufacturers and suppliers of internal and external blinds, awnings and shutters. Represents around 358 member companies involved in the manufacture of blinds and/or shutters in the UK. Representation on BSI and CEN committees regarding standards work. The Association organizes a trade exhibition.
Publication: Magazine
Publication title: Blinds and Shutters
Second publication: Journal
Publication title: Openings

British Blood Transfusion Society
BBTS

Plymouth Grove, Manchester, M13 9LL, England, UK
Tel: 44 161 2514300
Fax: 44 161 2514331
Email: bbts@bbts.org.uk
Website: http://www.bbts.org.uk
Founded: 1983
Members: 1520
Staff: 3
Contact:
Fee: £50
Publication: Journal
Publication title: Transfusion Medicine
Meetings/Conventions: - annual meeting Manchester UK

British Bluegrass Music Association

Ivy Cottage, Back Rowarth, Glossop, SK13 6ED, England, UK
Tel: 44 145 7861789
Fax: 44 145 7861789
Email: tombluegrass@aol.com
Website: http://www.britishbluegrass.com
Founded: 1990
Members: 600
Staff: 8
Contact: Tom Travis, Chm.
Fee: £18
Membership Type: individual
Fee: £24
Membership Type: family
Description: Promotes Bluegrass music in Britain. Encourages new markets for Bluegrass music. Co-ordinates efforts to improve the public image and awareness of Bluegrass music. Establishes and maintains a Bluegrass Directory. Encourages existing festivals, show promoters, radio and media outlets to increase their exposure of Bluegrass music. Acts as a communications resource, assisting members in their activities.
Publication title: British Bluegrass News. Advertisements.
Meetings/Conventions: - annual show

British Board of Film Classification
BBFC

3 Soho Sq., London, W1D 3HD, England, UK
Tel: 44 207 4401570
Fax: 44 207 2870141
Email: webmaster@bbfc.co.uk
Website: http://www.bbfc.co.uk
Founded: 1912
Staff: 50
Contact: Robin Duval, Dir.
Description: Recommends and formulates regulations for films, videos, and some computer games produced or marketed in the United Kingdom. Conducts research programs.
Publication: Annual Report
Second publication: Reports
Meetings/Conventions: International Standards on Screen Entertainment - triennial conference

British Branded Hosiery Group

c/o Charnos pl.
Corporation Rd., Ilkeston, DE7 4BP, England, UK
Tel: 44 115 9322191
Contact: John Roskalns, Mng. Dir.

British Brands Group

8 Henrietta Pl., London, W1G 0NB, England, UK
Tel: 44 7020 934250
Fax: 44 7020 934252
Email: info@britishbrandsgroup.org.uk
Website: http://www.britishbrandsgroup.org.uk
Founded: 1994
Members: 25
Staff: 1
Contact: John Noble, Dir.
Description: Branded product manufacturers. Represents members' interests.
Publication title: British Brands

British Bryological Society
BBS

91 Warbro Rd., Torquay, TQ1 3PS, England, UK
Email: mark.pool@care4free.net
Website: http://www.britishbryologicalsociety.org.uk
Founded: 1896
Members: 600
Contact: Mark Pool, Membership Sec.
Fee: £10
Membership Type: concessionary
Fee: £20
Membership Type: ordinary
Description: Individuals interested in bryology, the study of mosses and liverworts. Promotes a wider interest in all aspects of bryology. Serves as a clearinghouse on bryology; facilitates exchange of information among members; conducts research and educational programs; keeps records of bryophyte distribution and endangered bryophyte species. Maintains panel of referees to assist in the identification of bryophytes; operates herbarium of voucher specimens for consultation by members.
Library Subject: bryology
Library Type: reference
Publication: Newsletter
Publication title: Bulletin
Second publication: Journal
Publication title: Journal of Bryology
Meetings/Conventions: Field Work Week - annual

British Burn Association

BBA Secretariat, Burn Centre, Acute Block, Wythenshawe Hospital, Southmoor Rd., Manchester, M23 9LT, England, UK
Tel: 44 161 2916323
Fax: 44 161 2916823
Email: bba@smuth.nwest.nhs.uk

British Butterfly Conservation Society
BBCS

Dedham, Colchester, CO7 6EY, England, UK
Tel: 44 1206 322342
Fax: 44 1206 322739
Email: butterfly@cix.compulink.co.uk
Founded: 1968

British Cables Association

37A Walton Rd., East Molesey, KT8 0DH, England, UK
Tel: 44 20 89444079
Fax: 44 20 87830104
Email: admin@bcauk.org

Founded: 1899
Members: 15
Staff: 12
Contact: P.M.A. Smeeth
Description: UK manufacturers of metallic and optical fibre cables and wires for transmission/distribution of electric power, and for communications, including telephones, electronic/data control and broadcasting. Represents and promotes the interests of British cablemakers representing industry viewpoint to HM Government/ European Union; it acts as the industry voice to the media, other trade bodies etc; participates in international industry and standards making bodies; provides members with services and new information.
Library Type: not open to the public
Formerly: British Cable Makers Confederation

British Cactus and Succulent Society

49 Chestnut Glen, Hornchurch, RM12 4HL, England, UK
Tel: 44 1708 447778
Fax: 44 1444 454061
Email: bcss@cactus-mall.com
Website: http://www.bcss.org.uk
Founded: 1983
Members: 3500
Contact: E.A. Harris, Sec.
Fee: £30
Membership Type: full
Description: Advances the education of the public by the study, culture and preparation of succulent plants and to promote the conservation of such plants.
Library Subject: all aspects of growing succulent plants
Library Type: reference
Publication: Journal
Publication title: BCSS Journal. Advertisements.
Meetings/Conventions: convention

British Cardiac Society

Unit D1, 2 Station Rd., Swave Sey, CB4 5QJ, England, UK
Email: admin@bcpa.co.uk
Founded: 1937

British Carpet Manufacturers Association
BCMA

PO Box 1155, MFC Complex, 60 New Rd., Kidderminster, DY10 1WW, England, UK
Tel: 44 1562 747351
Fax: 44 1562 747359
Email: bcma@clara.net
Founded: 1936
Members: 20
Staff: 5
Contact: H. G. W. Wilson, Exec.Dir.
Fee: £500
Membership Type: ordinary
Description: Manufacturers of textile floor coverings in the United Kingdom. Represents the interests of members. Provides a forum for the exchange of information.
Publication: Directory
Publication title: Index of Quality Names
Second publication: Annual Report
Meetings/Conventions: - annual meeting

British Cartographic Society

c/o Royal Geographical Society
1 Kensington Gore, London, SW7 2AR, England, UK
Tel: 44 1823 665775
Fax: 44 1823 665775
Email: admin@cartography.org.uk
Website: http://www.cartography.org.uk
Founded: 1963
Members: 700
Contact: Ken Atherton, Admin.
Fee: £35
Membership Type: fellow
Fee: £25
Membership Type: member
Description: Membership is open to all cartographers and others with a professional, vocational, academic or general interest in cartography in its widest sense. Promotes the development of cartography. Within this very broad remit the society facilitates the coming together of all the many different interests in the field of cartography to pool information, exchange ideas and stimulate the discussion which so often lead to technical developments and advances, principally at an annual symposium and in the Cartographic Journal.
Publication: Journal
Publication title: The Cartographic Journal. Advertisements.
Second publication: Newsletter
Publication title: Maplines. Advertisements.
Meetings/Conventions: - annual symposium - Exhibits.

British Carton Association

c/o British Printing Industries Federation
Farringdon Point, 29-35 Farringdon Rd., London, EC1M 3JF, England, UK
Tel: 44 207 9158334
Fax: 44 207 4057784
Email: sue.bridger@bpif.org.uk
Website: http://www.britishprint.com/sigs/bcagroup.asp
Founded: 1935
Members: 100
Staff: 3
Contact: Andy Brown, Mgr.
Fee: £250
Description: Carton manufacturers and suppliers. Covering the folding carton and paperboard packaging industry. Provides information and guidance and represents members to outside organizations and government.
Publication: Booklet
Publication title: Customs of the Trade for the Manufacture of Cartons
Publication title: Dictionary of Carton Imprints

British Casino Association

38 Grosvenor Gardens, London, SW1W 0EB, England, UK
Tel: 44 20 7730 1055
Fax: 44 20 7730 1050
Email: enquiries@britishcasinoassociation.org.uk
Website: http://www.britishcasinoassociation.org.uk/
Founded: 1973
Members: 117
Contact: Air Commodore B.J. Lemon, Gen.Sec.
Description: All licensed casinos in the UK. To provide a national trade association for holders of UK casino licenses.
Publication: Newsletter

British Cattle Veterinary Association
c/o BCVA Office
The Green, Frampton-on-Severn, Gloucester, GL2 7EP, England, UK
Tel: 44 1452 740816
Fax: 44 1452 741117
Email: office@cattlevet.co.uk
Website: http://www.bcva.org.uk
Founded: 1967
Members: 1500
Staff: 4
Contact: D. Rogers, Office Admin.
Fee: £100
Membership Type: U.K.
Fee: £110
Membership Type: outside UK
Description: Veterinary surgeons, research workers; mostly professional veterinary surgeons in practice. Concerned with education; promotion; research into cattle topics; promotion of cattle veterinarian; political opinion on cattle matters; source of information and reference on cattle topics.
Publication: Journal
Publication title: Cattle Practice
Second publication: Newsletters
Meetings/Conventions: Scientific Congress - quarterly - Exhibits.

British Cave Research Association
The Old Methodist Chapel, Great Hucklow, Buxton, SK17 8RG, England, UK
Tel: 44 1298 873800
Fax: 44 1298 873801
Email: enquiries@bcra.org.uk
Website: http://www.bcra.org.uk
Founded: 1973
Members: 1350
Contact: John Wilcock, Hon.Sec.
Fee: £25
Membership Type: individual
Description: Scientists and sporting cavers interested in the scientific aspects of caves and karst. Aims to promote the study of caves and associated phenomena, and to publish the results of the researches carried out in the furtherance of these objects, for the benefit of the public.
Library Subject: caves, caving and karst
Library Type: reference
Publication: Journal
Publication title: Cave & Karst Science
Second publication: Magazine
Publication title: Speleology
Meetings/Conventions: British National Caving Conference - annual conference - Exhibits.

British Cement Association
BCA
Century House, Telford Ave., Crowthorne, RG45 6YS, England, UK
Tel: 44 1344 762676
Fax: 44 1344 761214
Email: library@bca.org.uk
Website: http://www.bca.org.uk
Founded: 1987
Members: 4
Staff: 32
Contact: Mike Gilbert, CEO

Description: Represents producers of Portland cement. Sets standards for concrete materials, design, construction, and testing. Encourages innovative techniques of production and high professional standards. Promotes exchange of information and ideas.
Library Subject: concrete materials and technology
Library Type: reference
Formerly: Formed by Merger of, Cement and Concrete Association
Publication: Journal
Publication title: Concrete Quarterly
Second publication: Catalogs

British Ceramic Confederation
Federation House, Station Rd., Stoke-On-Trent, ST4 2SA, England, UK
Tel: 44 1782 744631
Fax: 44 1782 744102
Email: bcc@ceramfed.co.uk
Website: http://www.ceramfed.co.uk
Founded: 1919
Members: 225
Staff: 12
Contact: Kevin Farrell, Chief Exec.
Description: Manufacturers of ceramic products in the United Kingdom. Representative body for manufacturers of ceramic products in the United Kingdom, providing representation and services in the areas of industrial relations, health and safety, environment, energy, trade etc.

British Ceramic Plant and Machinery Manufacturers Association
BCPMMA
PO Box 28, Biddulph, Stoke-On-Trent, ST8 7AZ, England, UK
Tel: 44 1782 513010
Fax: 44 1782 513020
Email: sales@bcpmma.com
Website: http://www.bcpmma.com
Founded: 1962
Members: 90
Contact: Mr. R. Adams, Sec.Gen.
Description: Manufacturers of ceramics and ceramic-producing machinery in Great Britain. Promotes and protects members' interests.
Publication: Directory
Publication title: Ceramic Production Equipment from Britain
Publication title: Global Ceramic Review
Meetings/Conventions: Technical Meeting - triennial - Exhibits.

British Ceramic Research
Federation House, Station Rd., Stoke-On-Trent, ST4 2SA, England, UK
Tel: 44 1782 845431
Fax: 44 1782 412331
Email: bcc@cerafed.co.uk
Founded: 1948

British Chain Manufacturers Association
Churt Ct., Stourbridge Rd., Halesowen, B63 3TT, England, UK
Tel: 44 121 5509916
Fax: 44 121 5019390
Founded: 1981
Members: 10
Contact: D. Williams-Allden

Description: Limited company manufacturing chain in the U.K. (members).
Meetings/Conventions: - annual meeting

British Chambers of Commerce
BCC

65 Petty France, 1st Fl., St. James Park, London, SW1H 9EU, England, UK
Tel: 44 20 76545800
Fax: 44 20 76545819
Email: info@britishchambers.org.uk
Website: http://www.britishchambers.org.uk
Founded: 1890
Members: 61
Staff: 20
Contact: David Frosl, Acting Dir. General
Description: British Chambers of Commerce.
Publication: Catalog
Publication title: Bookline
Publication title: Economic Survey
Meetings/Conventions: World of Business - annual conference - Exhibits. Glasgow UK

British Chelonia Group
BCG

PO Box 1176, Chippenham, SNI5 1XB, England, UK
Email: bcgonweb@rmplc.co.uk
Website: http://www.britishcheloniagroup.org.uk
Founded: 1976
Description: Promotes research on tortoises, terrapins and turtles.

British Chemical Distributors and Traders Association

Suffolk House, George St., Croydon, CR0 0YN, England, UK
Tel: 44 208 6864545
Fax: 44 208 6887768
Email: bcdta@bcdta.org.uk
Website: http://www.bcdta.org.uk
Founded: 1923
Members: 120
Staff: 5
Contact: Peter J. Newport
Description: Chemical distributors, traders and merchants. To promote and protect the interests of chemical distributors, traders and merchants in the UK.
Publication: Magazine
Publication title: BCDTA

British Chemical Engineering Contractors Association

1 Regent St., London, SW1Y 4NR, England, UK
Tel: 44 20 78396514
Fax: 44 20 79303466
Email: laurie.hickman@bceca.org.uk
Website: http://www.bceca.org.uk
Founded: 1965
Members: 18
Staff: 2
Contact: L.C. Hickman, Dir.
Description: Principal companies in the UK which provide engineering, procurement, construction and project management services to all the process industries, i.e. oil, gas, chemical, pharmaceutical, power, water etc. To improve public understanding of members' activities and to provide a focal point for representation of members' interests to clients, the UK Government, European Community and international institutions and other interested parties.
Publication: Magazine
Publication title: Industrial Statistics

British Cheque Cashers Association

Swan House, Rd. Lynchborough, Passfield, Liphook, GU30 7SB, England, UK
Tel: 44 1428 751123
Fax: 44 1428 751055
Email: info@bcca.co.uk
Website: http://www.bcca.co.uk
Founded: 1996
Members: 350
Staff: 2
Contact: Geoffrey Cooke, Chf.Exec.
Description: Provides representation of its members' interests to government whether in London or Brussels - and its regulatory bodies. Also seeks to enhance understanding of the industry and to promote the interests of check cashers generally by helping to shape a climate of opinion which enables members to conduct their business profitably.
Publication: Newsletter
Publication title: Members Extra. Advertisements.
Meetings/Conventions: - annual conference

British China and Porcelain Artists Association

c/o Joanne Sharp
136 Heath Lane, Childer Thornton, Cheshire, CH66 5NY, England, UK
Tel: 44 151 3393286
Email: jscelebchina@aol.com
Website: http://www.bcpaa-2000.co.uk
Founded: 1979
Members: 1000
Contact: Joanne Sharp, Mem.Sec.
Description: Encourages china painters throughout the UK to share their talents and ideas creating a broader appreciation of this beautiful art. It now attracts members from European and overseas countries.
Publication: Magazine
Publication title: The British China Painter. Advertisements.
Meetings/Conventions: - annual convention - Exhibits. UK

British Chiropractic Association

Blagrave House, 17 Blagrave St., Reading, RG1 1QB, England, UK
Tel: 44 118 9505950
Fax: 44 118 9588946
Email: enquiries@chiropractic-uk.co.uk
Website: http://www.chiropractic-uk.co.uk
Founded: 1925
Members: 860
Staff: 4
Contact: Susan Wakefield, Exec.Dir.
Description: Complementary medicine practitioners/chiropractors. Concerned with treatment of spinal disorders by specialised manipulative techniques.
Publication title: Contact
Second publication: Newsletter
Publication title: In Touch

British Civil Engineering Test Equipment Manufacturers Association

28 Wing Rd., Linsdale, Leighton Buzzard, LU7 7NJ, England, UK
Tel: 44 1525 854819
Fax: 44 1525 854819
Founded: 1968
Members: 7
Contact: Jim Turner
Description: Manufacturers of civil engineering and food testing equipment. To constitute a central national organization for protection of the interests of manufacturers of civil engineering and food testing equipment.

British Cleaning Council

PO Box 1328, Kidderminster, DY11 5ZJ, England, UK
Tel: 44 1562 851129
Fax: 44 1562 851129
Email: bcc@stint.demon.co.ukwww.britishcleaningcouncil.org
Founded: 1982
Members: 15
Contact: J.A. Stinton, Gen.Sec.
Description: Any recognized trade association or research or educational body or institution concerned with industrial, commercial or institutional cleaning. Provides a forum for all constituent bodies to meet together to further the aims of their industry as a whole and takes responsibility for external relations at home and abroad on matters of common interest to members.
Publication: Newsletter
Publication title: Clean City Interchange
Meetings/Conventions: - biennial conference - Exhibits.

British Clothing Industry Association
BCIA

5 Portland Pl., London, W1B 1P4, England, UK
Tel: 44 207 6367788
Fax: 44 207 6367515
Email: bcia@dial.pipex.com
Founded: 1982
Contact: J.R. Wilson, Dir.
Description: Clothing industry corporations. Represents members' interests.

British Coalition for East Timor
BCET

PO Box 2349, London, E1 3HX, England, UK
Tel: 44 181 9851127
Fax: 44 181 9851127
Email: bcet@gn.apc.org
Founded: 1991
Contact: Jackie Hoskins
Description: Individuals united to promote cultural exchange between England and East Timor. Assists in East Timor's social and economic development. Disseminates information. Campaigns for the inalienable right to self-determination of the people of East Timor and the withdrawal of Indonesian troops from the territory.
Publication: Newsletter
Publication title: East Timor: It's Time to Talk

British Coatings Federation

James House, Bridge St., Leatherhead, KT22 7EP, England, UK
Tel: 44 1372 360660
Fax: 44 1372 376069
Email: enquiry@bc.co.uk
Website: http://www.coatings.org.uk
Founded: 1963
Members: 150
Staff: 12
Contact: Mrs. M. McMillan
Description: Full - paint and printing ink manufacturers within UK. Promotes the interests of the UK coatings manufacturing industry. Provides a forum for discussing environmental health safety and technical and commercial issues. Provides legislative advice and information.
Formerly: Formed by Merger of, Paintmakers Association

British Colostomy Association

15 Station Rd., Reading, RG1 1LG, England, UK
Tel: 44 118 9391537
Fax: 44 118 9569095
Email: sue@bcass.org.uk
Website: http://www.bcass.org.uk
Founded: 1967
Members: 16000
Staff: 8
Contact: Olivia Reed, Sec.
Description: Anyone who has a colostomy and/or their carer. Exists to offer help and encouragement to anyone who has had or is about to have a colostomy. Home and hospital visits by arrangement.
Library Type: open to the public
Publication: Booklet
Publication title: Living With a Colostomy
Second publication: Newsletter
Publication title: Tidings

British Colour Makers' Association

12 Heald Dr., Shawclough, Rochdale, OL12 7HH, England, UK
Tel: 44 1706 643462
Fax: 44 1706 643462
Email: info@bcma.org.uk
Website: http://www.bcma.org.uk
Founded: 1919
Members: 20
Staff: 1
Contact: E. Taylor
Description: Major UK pigment manufacturers. Aims to maintain contact with legislative bodies; to ensure that the pigment industry is fully up to date with current government and EC policy. Also responsible for ensuring that the industry acts in a responsible manner.

British Combustion Equipment Manufacturers Association

50 London Rd., Market Pl., Leicester, LE2 0QD, England, UK
Tel: 44 116 2757111
Fax: 44 116 2757222
Email: bcema@btconnect.com
Founded: 1933
Members: 50
Staff: 2
Contact: Mr. A.J. Silvester, Dir.
Description: Manufacturers and suppliers of commercial and industrial combustion equipment. To promote and assist in the preparation of British, European and international standards in order to ensure optimum levels of equipment and performance and safety. Seeks to provide other technical and commercial support to members as required.

British Commercial Rabbit Association

Fairfield House, Sound, Nantwich, CW5 8BG, England, UK
Tel: 44 1270 780248
Founded: 1960
Members: 200
Contact: Mrs. S. McGeoch
Fee: £40
Description: Rabbit farmers and trade suppliers. Provides an advisory service for commercial meat and Angora rabbit farmers. Advice on breeding stock, management and equipment.
Publication title: The Rabbit Farmer
Meetings/Conventions: - annual meeting - Exhibits. Worchestershire UK

British Compressed Air Society

33/34 Devonshire St., London, W1G 6PY, England, UK
Tel: 44 20 79352464
Fax: 44 20 79353077
Email: chriss.dee@virgin.net
Website: http://www.britishcompressedair.co.uk
Founded: 1930
Members: 86
Staff: 3
Contact: Chris Dee, Exec.Dir.
Fee: £992
Membership Type: full
Fee: £495
Membership Type: associate
Description: Manufacturers and distributors of compressed air, gas, vacuum, and related equipment in the UK. Seeks to help members develop their professional competence.
Library Subject: compressors, vacuum pumps
Library Type: open to the public
Publication title: BCAS Technical Guidance, 5th Ed.

British Compressed Gases Association
BCGA

6 St. Mary's St., Wallingford, OX10 0EL, England, UK
Tel: 44 1491 825533
Fax: 44 1491 826689
Email: mhmoye@bcga.co.uk
Website: http://www.bcga.co.uk
Founded: 1971
Members: 60
Staff: 3
Contact: M.H. Moye, Dir.
Description: Trade association representing companies engaged in the manufacture, containment, distribution and application of industrial, food and medical gases. Promotes the advancement of technology and safe practice in the manufacture, containment, distribution and application of industrial, food and medical gases; to participate and provide advice in UK and European Standards-making and legislative processes; to offer practical guidance to users of industrial gases and equipment.
Library Subject: Codes of practice, guidance notes
Library Type: open to the public
Publication title: Codes of Practice
Publication title: Guidance Notes
Meetings/Conventions: - annual conference - Exhibits.

British Computer Association of the Blind
BDS

c/o RNIB
58-72 John Bright St., Birmingham, B1 1BN, England, UK
Tel: 44 121 6654256
Email: info@bcab.org.uk
Website: http://www.bcab.org.uk
Founded: 1969
Members: 230
Contact:
Fee: £21
Membership Type: full
Fee: £10.5
Membership Type: associate
Description: Provides general assistance and advice on information technology issues for blind and visually impaired persons. Organizes training courses. Engages in lobbying.
Publication: Newsletter
Meetings/Conventions: - quarterly workshop

British Computer Society
BCS

c/o Anna Duckworth
1 Sanford St., Swindon, SN1 1HJ, England, UK
Tel: 44 1793 417417
Fax: 44 1793 480270
Email: bcshq@hq.bcs.org.uk
Website: http://www.bcs.org.uk/
Founded: 1957
Members: 39000
Staff: 120
Contact: Anna Duckworth
Description: Information technology professionals accredited by the society or by society-approved courses. Purpose is to compile and keep members abreast of technical developments so as to influence computing in their professions. Strives to further information exchange and to inspire high technical and ethical standards. Acts as a professional qualifying body by accrediting degree and diploma courses; offers accreditation exams. Disseminates expert advice to European Economic Community and British government and industry representatives on issues such as computer misuse, safety-critical systems, computers for the disabled, and quality control of software engineering.
Publication: Bulletin
Publication title: Computer Bulletin
Second publication: Journal
Publication title: Computer Journal
Meetings/Conventions: - periodic conference

British Concrete Masonry Association

Grove Crescent House, 18 Grove Pl., Bedford, MK40 3JJ, England, UK
Tel: 44 1234 353745
Fax: 44 1234 357160
Founded: 1967
Members: 30
Staff: 4
Contact: B.E. Howard, Hon.Sec.Gen.
Fee: £200
Membership Type: full and associate
Description: Aggregate block manufacturers and distributors and suppliers to the precast concrete industry. Brings together manufacturers with the common interest of furthering the use and

improving methods of manufacture of aggregate concrete blocks. Represents the block producing industry in the UK. Incorporates the Aggregate Block Producers Association.
Library Subject: concrete production, design, marketing
Library Type: not open to the public
Publication: Newsletter
Publication title: Blockmedia. Advertisements.
Meetings/Conventions: - annual general assembly

British Confectioners Association
Unit 4, Home Farm Business Centre, Brighton, BN1 9HU, England, UK
Founded: 1905
Members: 60
Contact: J.D. Copeman, Hon. Sec.
Description: To promote the study of the art of flour confectionery and baking; to promote lectures and arrange demonstrations and discussions; to provide opportunities of social intercourse amongst the members; and, generally, to take what steps members may consider desirable to protect and promote the interests of the flour confectionery trade.

British Constructional Steelwork Association
4 Whitehall Ct., Westminster, London, SW1A 2ES, England, UK
Tel: 44 20 78398566
Fax: 44 20 79761634
Email: gillian.mitchell@steelconstruction.org
Website: http://www.steelconstruction.org
Founded: 1906
Members: 200
Staff: 10
Contact: Dr. Derek Tordoff, Dir.Gen.
Description: Represents the steel construction industry.
Publication: Directory
Publication title: Directory for Specifiers and Buyers
Publication title: New Steel Construction

British Consultants and Construction Bureau
BCCB
1 Westminster Palace Gardens, Artillery Row, London, SW1P 1RJ, England, UK
Tel: 44 207 2223651
Fax: 44 207 2223664
Email: mail@bccb.org.uk
Website: http://www.bccb.org.uk
Founded: 1965
Members: 280
Staff: 11
Contact: Colin Adams, Chief Exec.
Description: Marketing association that promotes British consultancy and construction companies worldwide. These companies and individual members cover a wide range of expertise and BCCB will facilitate contact with their members for anyone seeking consultancy or contractor contacts and advice. Also maintains contact with governments and international institutions on behalf of members and provides a variety of networking opportunities.
Publication: Directory
Publication title: BCB Directory
Second publication: Report
Publication title: Guidance for the Exporting Consultant

British Contract Furnishing Association
BCFA
Project House, 25 West Wycombe Rd., High Wycomb, HP11 2LQ, England, UK
Tel: 44 870 7523672
Fax: 44 1494 896799
Email: enquiries@bcfa.org.uk
Website: http://www.bcfa.org.uk
Members: 390
Contact: Martyn Lincoln, Chief Exec.
Description: Trade association of manufacturers and suppliers of contract furnishings, including carpets, lighting, furniture, bedding, blinds, wallcoverings, and floor coverings. Promotes and protects members' interests.
Publication: Membership Directory
Publication title: Contract Furnishing Directory. Advertisements.
Second publication: Magazine
Publication title: Contract Furnishing Magazine

British Contract Packers Association
BCPA
Syonsby Lodge, Nottingham Rd., Melton Mowbray, LE13 0NU, England, UK
Tel: 44 1664 500055
Fax: 44 1664 564164
Email: pamcreed@iop.co.uk
Founded: 2000
Members: 40
Contact: Pam Creed, Sec.
Description: Promotes the technical, trade, and commercial interests of British contract manufacturers and packers.

British Copyright Council
29-33 Berners St., London, W1T 3AB, England, UK
Tel: 44 1986 788122
Fax: 44 1986 788847
Email: copyright@bcc2.demon.co.uk
Website: http://www.editor.net/bcc/
Founded: 1965
Members: 34
Staff: 1
Contact: Janet Ibbotson, Sec.
Description: A forum for the bodies speaking for those who create or hold interests or copyright in literary, dramatic, musical or artistic works and those who perform them.
Publication: Booklet
Publication title: Guide to the Law of Copyright and Rights in Performances
Second publication: Booklet
Meetings/Conventions: - bimonthly meeting

British Council
10 Spring Gardens, London, SW1A 2BN, England, UK
Tel: 44 20 79308466
Fax: 44 20 73896347
Email: general.enquiries@britishcouncil.org
Website: http://www.britishcouncil.org
Founded: 1934
Staff: 7500
Description: Promotes increased understanding of the United Kingdom and the English language worldwide. Facilitates educational, technological, cultural, and scientific cooperation between the United Kingdom and other countries.
Library Subject: all
Library Type: open to the public

British Council of Disabled People
BCODP

Litchurch Plaza, Litchurch Ln., Derby, DE24 8AA, England, UK
Tel: 44 1332 295551
Fax: 44 1332 295580
Email: info@bcodp.org.uk
Website: http://www.bcodp.org.uk
Founded: 1981
Members: 140
Staff: 10
Contact: Andy Ricken, Ch.Exec.
Fee: £25
Membership Type: regional group
Fee: £50
Membership Type: national group
Description: Organizations controlled by disabled people and individual membership is now available to all disabled people and their supporters. The national umbrella organisation representing groups controlled by disabled people. Current concern is to secure anti-discrimination legislation. Has begun a 3-year group development programme to actively support the growth of regional organisations controlled by disabled people.
Library Subject: disability and civil rights
Library Type: not open to the public
Formerly: British Council of Organisations of Disabled People
Publication: Newsletter
Publication title: Activate
Second publication: Newsletter
Publication title: Personal Assistance Users Newsletter
Meetings/Conventions: - annual conference - Exhibits.

British Council of Maintenance Associations

c/o The Old Barn
Barber Booth, Edale, Hope Valley, S33 7ZL, England, UK
Tel: 44 1433 670391
Founded: 1968
Members: 1200
Contact: D. Baird, Gen.Sec.
Fee: £500
Description: Membership is open to maintenance associations in the British Isles and companies who relate to maintenance. Represents maintenance interests nationally/European/internationally by acting as the representative body in connection with maintenance activities and acting as the liaison with public and private bodies (e.g. Government Departments, Universities, Institutions etc).
Library Subject: Maintenance
Library Type: not open to the public
Meetings/Conventions: Maintenance Conference - annual - Exhibits.

British Council of Shopping Centres

1 Queen Anne's Gate, Westminster, London, SW1H 9BT, England, UK
Tel: 44 207 2273458
Fax: 44 207 2224440
Email: info@bcsc.org.uk
Website: http://www.bcsc.org.uk
Founded: 1983
Members: 1200
Contact: M.D. Taplin, Sec.
Description: All those involved in the shopping center industry i.e. funding institutions, managing agents, designers, retailers, architects, lawyers, construction/engineering. Concerned with the development and improvement of shopping facilities.
Publication: Journal

Publication title: Beyond the Horizon
Second publication: Papers
Meetings/Conventions: - annual conference - Exhibits.

British Crop Protection Council

49 Downing St., Farnham, GU9 7PH, England, UK
Tel: 44 1252 733072
Fax: 44 1252 727194
Email: gensec@bcpc.org
Website: http://www.bcpc.org
Founded: 1968
Members: 43
Staff: 1
Contact: John Fisher
Description: Organisations concerned with crop protection. Promotes the knowledge and understanding of crop protection through conferences, publications, teaching resources for schools, training manuals, identifying R&D needs for policy makers. Actively developing its overseas/international links.
Publication: Book
Publication title: Pesticide Manual
Meetings/Conventions: Trade Services Exhibition - annual trade show Brighton UK

British Cryoengineering Society
BCS

33 Badingham Drive, Leatherhead, KT22 9EU, England, UK
Tel: 44 1372 376544
Fax: 44 1372 376544
Email: phil.cook2@btopenworld.com
Founded: 1997
Members: 100
Staff: 1
Contact: Phil Cook, Hon.Sec.
Fee: £16
Description: Promotes knowledge in low temperature science and technology.
Publication: Newsletter
Publication title: Low Temperature News

British Cutlery and Silverware Association
BCSA

Light Trades House, 3 Melbourne Ave., Sheffield, S10 2QJ, England, UK
Tel: 44 114 2769736
Fax: 44 114 2722151
Contact: Cathy Steele, Chief Executive
Description: Manufacturers and suppliers of knives, spoons, forks, and other silverware and cutlery in Great Britain. Promotes the silverware and cutlery industry.
Publication: Directory
Publication title: Buyers Guide

British Dam Society

c/o Institute of Civil Engineers Institution
1-7 Great George St., London, SW1P 3AA, England, UK
Tel: 44 207 6652234
Fax: 44 207 7991325
Email: bds@ice.org.uk
Website: http://www.britishdams.org
Founded: 1967
Members: 500

Contact: Tim Fuller, Sec.
Fee: £33
Membership Type: individual
Fee: £16
Membership Type: retired
Description: Aims to give access to world-wide experience and knowledge in the field of dam and reservoir engineering.
Formerly: British National Committee on Large Dams
Publication: Journal. Advertisements.

British Dance Council

Terpsichore House, 240 Merton Rd., South Wimbledon, London, SW19 1EQ, England, UK
Tel: 44 20 85450085
Fax: 44 20 85450225
Email: secretary@british-dance-council.org
Website: http://www.british-dance-council.org
Founded: 1929
Members: 18
Staff: 2
Contact: Margaret Harris, Office Mgr.
Description: Amateur and professional dancers' associations; dance teaching associations; companies with a professional interest in the ballroom dancing world; honorary members elected by virtue of a lifetime commitment to dancing. Enables teachers to work together on uniform lines. It formulates and administers the rules for competition dancing and co-ordinates the promotion of schemes to publicise the social styles of ballroom dancing.
Formerly: British Council of Ballroom Dancing
Publication title: Modern and Latin Sequence Dances
Second publication: Booklets
Publication title: Rule Book & Dance Teachers Handbook

British Deaf Association

1-3 Worship St., London, EC2A 2AB, England, UK
Tel: 44 207 5883520
Fax: 44 207 5883527
Email: helpline@bda.org.uk
Website: http://www.bda.org.uk
Founded: 1890
Members: 6500
Staff: 50
Contact: J. McWhinney, Chief Exec.
Description: Mainly profoundly deaf people who use sign language as their means of communication. Aims to serve and protect the deaf community.
Publication title: British Deaf News. Advertisements.
Meetings/Conventions: - annual conference - Exhibits.

British Deer Society

Burgate Manor, Fordingbridge, SP6 1EF, England, UK
Tel: 44 1425 655434
Fax: 44 1425 655433
Email: h.q@bds.org.uk
Website: http://www.bds.org.uk
Founded: 1963
Members: 5600
Staff: 5
Contact: Mrs. S.J. Stride, General Mgr.
Description: Concerned with the study and the dissemination of the knowledge of deer, the promotion of proper and humane methods of management of deer and the provision of advice on all matters related to deer.
Publication: Journal
Publication title: Deer Journal

British Dental Association
BDA

64 Wimpole St., London, W1G 8YS, England, UK
Tel: 44 207 9350875
Fax: 44 207 4875232
Email: enquiries@bda-dentistry.org.uk
Website: http://www.bda-dentistry.org.uk
Founded: 1880
Members: 20000
Staff: 70
Contact: Ian Wylie, CEO
Description: Professional association and trade union for dental surgeons in the United Kingdom. Promotes dentistry and the provision of dental services to the public. Represents members' interests individually and collectively before the government.
Library Subject: Dentistry
Library Type: reference
Publication: Newsletter
Publication title: BDA News. Advertisements.
Second publication: Journal
Publication title: British Dental Journal
Meetings/Conventions: - annual conference

British Dental Hygienists Association
BDHA

13 Yatton Ridge, Yatton, Bristol, BS49 4DG, England, UK
Tel: 44 1934 876389
Fax: 44 1934 876389
Founded: 1949

British Dental Practice Managers Association

Osprey House, Primett Rd., Stevenage, SGI 3EE, England, UK
Tel: 44 870 8400341
Fax: 44 870 8400342
Email: info@bdpma.org.uk
Website: http://www.bdpma.org.uk
Founded: 1992
Members: 400
Staff: 1
Contact: Bridget Crump, Chm.
Fee: £49
Membership Type: full, associate, friend, life
Description: Promote co-operation and provide a way to communicate and support those actively involved in Dental Practice Management.
Publication: Newsletter
Publication title: Networking. Advertisements.
Meetings/Conventions: Bright People, Bright Futures - annual conference Bath UK

British Dental Trade Association
BDTA

Mineral Ln., Chesham, HP5 1NL, England, UK
Tel: 44 1494 782873
Fax: 44 1494 786659
Email: admin@bdta.org.uk
Website: http://www.bdta.org.uk
Founded: 1923
Members: 116
Staff: 4
Contact: Tony Reed, Exec.Dir.

Description: Companies manufacturing dental equipment and supplies. Establishes international standards and technical harmonization for dental equipment. Represents members' interests before government bodies, international agencies, and the public. Maintains liaison with organizations representing dentists, dental technicians, and dental supply dealers and distributors. Compiles statistics.
Library Type: not open to the public
Publication: Journal
Publication title: Dental Trader. Advertisements.
Meetings/Conventions: Dental Showcase - annual - Exhibits.

British Design and Art Direction
D&AD

9 Graphite Sq., Vauxhall Walk, London, SE11 5EE, England, UK
Tel: 44 20 78401111
Fax: 44 20 78400840
Email: info@dandad.co.uk
Website: http://www.dandad.org
Founded: 1962
Members: 2300
Staff: 22
Contact: Kathryn Palter, Commun.Dir.
Fee: £170
Membership Type: full
Fee: £140
Membership Type: associate
Description: Leading creatives from design and advertising communities are full members; non creatives who are recognized as encouraging and supporting D&AD's aims are associate members. Professional association and charity working on behalf of the advertising and design communities. Sets standards of creative excellence, promotes this concept in the business arena and educates and inspires the next creative generation.
Formerly: Designers and Art Directors Association of the U.K.
Publication: Book
Publication title: The Copy Book
Publication title: British Design & Art Direction. Advertisements.
Meetings/Conventions: - annual show London UK

British Dietetic Association
BDA

Charles House, 5th Fl., 148/9 Great Charles St. Queensway, Birmingham, B3 3HT, England, UK
Tel: 44 121 2008080
Fax: 44 121 2008081
Email: info@bda.uk.com
Website: http://www.bda.uk.com
Founded: 1936
Members: 4000
Staff: 16
Contact: John Grigg, Chief Exec.
Fee: £144
Membership Type: professional
Description: Professional registered dietitians. Promotes advancement of the science and practice of dietetics and related subjects. Sponsors training and educational programs. Arranges meetings, refresher courses, and study conferences. Provides liaison between dietitians in the United Kingdom and other countries.
Publication title: Adviser Magazine
Publication title: Journal of Human Nutrition and Dietetics
Meetings/Conventions: - annual conference - Exhibits.

British Display Society

146 Welling Way, Welling, Kent, DA16 2RS, England, UK
Tel: 44 208 8562030
Fax: 44 208 8569394
Website: http://www.messiterdesign.co.uk/bds/
Founded: 1940
Staff: 2
Contact: S.P. Simpson, Sec.
Description: Practitioners in display - retail, point of sale, exhibition design -tutors and students of display design. Concerned with the education and promotion of display standards.
Publication: Newsletter
Publication title: BDS Newsletter

British Doll Artists Association

26 Foxholes, Rudgwick, RH12 30X, England, UK
Tel: 44 1403 823596
Fax: 44 1403 823596
Email: mahar.likha@virgin.net
Founded: 1979
Members: 34
Contact: Marian Paiso-Ironmonger, Sec.
Fee: £35
Fee: £40
Membership Type: associate member outside UK
Description: Artists who make totally original dolls. Promotes the work of members via annual exhibitions, slide presentations and the illustrated BDA Directory.
Meetings/Conventions: - annual general assembly - Exhibits.

British Dragonfly Society

The Haywain, Hollywater Rd., Bordon, GU35 0AD, England, UK
Tel: 44 153 8724130
Email: thewains@ukonline.co.uk
Website: http://www.dragonflysoc.org.uk
Founded: 1983
Members: 1507
Staff: 1
Contact: Dr. W.H. Wain
Fee: £50
Membership Type: international
Description: Amateur and professional naturalists and conservation enthusiasts. Aims to promote and encourage the study and conservation of dragonflies and their natural habitats, especially in the United Kingdom. Their habitat are threatened and the aim is to halt the dangerous downward trend.
Publication: Journal
Publication title: British Dragonfly Society Journal
Publication title: Dig a Pond for Dragonflies
Meetings/Conventions: Members Day - annual general assembly

British Dried Flowers Association

c/o Vernon Hurst
Stonedge, Manor Rd., Staverton, North Daventry, Northants, NN11 6JD, England, UK
Tel: 44 1327 702565
Website: http://www.flowergrowers.co.uk
Contact: Vernon Hurst, Sec.
Description: Flower growers interested in dried flower design and arrangement.

British Drilling Association
BDA

55 London End, Upper Boddington, Daventry, NN11 6DP, England, UK
Tel: 44 1327 264622
Fax: 44 1377 264623
Email: info@britishdrillingassociation.co.uk
Website: http://www.britishdrillingassociation.co.uk
Founded: 1975
Members: 836
Staff: 1
Contact: B.J. Stringer
Fee: £336
Membership Type: corporate
Fee: £63
Membership Type: associate
Description: Companies engaged in all aspects of ground drilling. To improve efficiency and raise standards for the non-gas and oil drilling industry, through the dissemination of information and contact with government departments and organizations.
Publication title: Geodrilling International
Meetings/Conventions: - quarterly conference

British Driving Society

27 Dugard Pl., Barford, CV35 8DX, England, UK
Tel: 44 1926 624420
Fax: 44 1926 624633
Email: email@britishdrivingsociety.co.uk
Website: http://www.britishdrivingsociety.co.uk
Founded: 1957
Members: 5000
Staff: 2
Contact: Jenny Dillon
Fee: £22
Membership Type: adult
Fee: £35
Membership Type: dual
Description: To encourage and assist those interested in the driving of all equines.
Publication: Yearbook
Publication title: Annual Shows Almanac. Advertisements.
Second publication: Newsletters
Publication title: BDS Newsletter
Meetings/Conventions: - periodic conference

British Dyslexia Association

98 London Rd., Reading, RG1 5AU, England, UK
Tel: 44 118 9668271
Fax: 44 118 9351927
Email: admin@bda-dyslexia.demon.co.uk
Website: http://www.bda-dyslexia.org.uk/
Founded: 1972
Members: 10000
Staff: 27
Contact: Steve Alexander, Chief Exec.
Description: Acts as an umbrella organization for dyslexia in the UK.
Publication: Magazine
Publication title: Contact
Second publication: Journal
Publication title: Dyslexia
Meetings/Conventions: Dyslexia: The Dividends from Research to Policy & Practice - triennial international conference Warwick UK

British Ecological Society
BES

26 Blades Ct., Putney, London, SW15 2NU, England, UK
Tel: 44 208 8719797
Fax: 44 208 8719779
Email: info@britishecdogicalsociety.org
Website: http://www.britishecologicalsociety.org
Founded: 1913
Members: 5000
Staff: 3
Contact: Dr. Hazel J. Norman, Exec.Sec.
Fee: £40
Membership Type: individuals with a genuine interest in ecology
Description: Teachers, local authority ecologists, research scientists, conservationists, environmental consultants, and others with an interest in ecology, natural history, or the environment. Promotes the science of ecology through research, publications and conferences and uses findings of such research to educate the public and influence policy decisions which involve ecological matters.
Publication: Booklet
Publication title: The Bulletin
Second publication: Journal
Publication title: Journal of Animal Ecology

British Educational Communications and Technology Agency
BECTA

Science Park, Milburn Hill Rd., Coventry, CV4 7JJ, England, UK
Tel: 44 24 76416994
Fax: 44 24 76411418
Email: becta@becta.org.uk
Website: http://www.becta.org.uk
Description: Government's lead agency for ICT in education. Supports the UK government and national organisations in the use and development of ICT in education to raise standards, widen access, improve skills and encourage effective management. Works in partnership to develop the National Grid for Learning strategy.
Formerly: National Council for Educational Technology

British Educational Management and Administration Society

Collegiate Crescent Campus, Sheffield, S10 2BP, England, UK
Tel: 44 114 2252328
Fax: 44 114 2255649
Email: belmas@shu.ac.uk
Website: http://www.belmas.org.uk
Founded: 1971
Members: 550
Contact: K.A. Dungey, Admin.
Publication: Journal
Publication title: Educational Management & Administration
Second publication: Journal
Publication title: Management in Education

British Educational Research Association

c/o Commercial House
King Street, Southwell, NG25 0EH, England, UK
Tel: 44 1636 819090
Fax: 44 1636 813064
Email: admin.bera@btclick.com
Website: http://www.bera.ac.uk
Founded: 1974

Members: 1450
Contact: Mrs. W.M. Strerch, Admin.Sec.
Fee: £55
Description: Educational researchers in UK and abroad. Encourages the pursuit of educational research and its applications for the improvement of educational practice and the general benefit of the community.
Publication: Journal
Publication title: British Educational Research Journal
Publication title: Creating Education through Research
Meetings/Conventions: - annual conference - Exhibits. Edinburgh UK

British Educational Suppliers Association

20 Beaufort Ct., Admirals Way, London, E14 9XL, England, UK
Tel: 44 207 5374997
Fax: 44 207 5374846
Email: besa@besanet.org.uk
Website: http://www.besanet.org.uk
Founded: 1933
Members: 240
Staff: 10
Contact: Dominic Savage, Dir.Gen.
Description: Manufacturers and distributors of equipment, materials, consumables, furniture, technology, ICT hardware and software related services.
Publication: Catalog
Publication title: British Educational Suppliers
Meetings/Conventions: The Education Show - annual trade show

British Educational Suppliers Association
BESA

20 Beaufort Ct., Admirals Way, London, E14 9XL, England, UK
Tel: 44 207 5374997
Fax: 44 207 5374846
Email: besa@besanet.org.uk
Website: http://www.besanet.org.uk
Founded: 1970
Members: 16
Contact: Dominic Savage, Dir.Gen.
Description: All of the member companies within the association employ highly qualified staff with academic backgrounds and maintain contacts with engineering teaching establishments throughout the world. Represents member companies dedicated to the design and manufacture of equipment to meet the world-wide need for technology training at all levels from vocational training to postgraduate research. Disciplines include all fields of engineering, electronics, telecommunications, material sciences, food technology, environmental sciences etc.
Formerly: Engineering Teaching Equipment Manufacturers Association
Publication title: BESAbook - UK Education and Training Products and Suppliers Directory

British Egg Industry Council

Second Fl., 89 Charterhouse St., London, EC1M 6HR, England, UK
Tel: 44 207 76083760
Fax: 44 207 76083860
Email: info@britegg.co.uk
Website: http://www.britegg.co.uk
Founded: 1986
Members: 75

Staff: 4
Contact: Mark Williams, Chief Exec.
Description: Represents the interests of the egg industry. Lobbies government and the European Commission. Fosters research.

British Electrical Systems Association

Westminster Tower, 3 Albert Embankment, London, SE1 7SL, England, UK
Tel: 44 207 7933068
Fax: 44 207 7933003
Email: peter@buisnessserve.co.uk
Website: http://www.besalimited.org.uk/
Founded: 1920
Members: 30
Staff: 2
Contact: Peter Downham, Dir.
Description: Manufacturers in Britain of cable management system in conduit, trunking, tray, ladder, channel - bus fittings, cable ties, cable cleats. Represents members' interests with government and industrial organizations Europe, UK. Standard writing in Europe and UK.
Publication title: Buyers' Guide

British Electrophoresis Society

Ashton St., Liverpool, L69 3GE, England, UK
Tel: 44 151 7945509
Fax: 44 151 7945452
Email: stpen@liv.ac.uk
Website: http://www.harefield.nthames.nhs.uk/nhli/bes
Founded: 1982

British Electrostatic Control Association
BECA

Heathcote House, 136 Hagley Road, Edgbaston, Birmingham, B16 9PN, England, UK
Tel: 44 121 454 4141
Fax: 44 121 454 4949
Email: infoheath@btinternet.com
Website: http://www.beca.co.uk
Members: 24
Contact: Peter Ashburner, Ch.
Fee: £365
Membership Type: full
Description: Works to advance the theory and practice of electrical overstress avoidance, with emphasis on electrostatic discharge phenomena. Focuses on the effects of both material and manmade electromagnetic threats on eletronic components, subsystems, and systems. Promotes exchange of technical information and cooperation among members. Develops standards; conducts educational programs.
Meetings/Conventions: - semiannual seminar

British Electro-Static Manufacturers Association

Croxteth Hall, Ripley, GU23 6EX, England, UK
Tel: 44 1483 225435
Fax: 44 1784 469868
Email: info@besma.org.uk
Website: http://www.besma.org.uk
Founded: 1980
Members: 25
Staff: 3
Contact: D.A. White, External Relations Off.
Fee: £100
Membership Type: corporate

Description: Manufacturers of British made static control products or agents for British produced equipment and anti-static materials. To promote the specification and use of British-made static elimination equipment, anti-static materials and associated products.
Publication: Newsletter
Meetings/Conventions: - annual conference

British Electrotechnical and Allied Manufacturers Associations
BEAMA

Westminster Tower, 3 Albert Embankment, London, SE1 7SL, England, UK
Tel: 44 20 77933000
Fax: 44 20 77933003
Email: info@beama.org.uk
Website: http://www.beama.org.uk
Founded: 1902
Members: 500
Contact: D. Dossett, Dir.Gen.
Description: Represents members' interests.
Publication: Annual Report
Publication title: Annual Report
Second publication: Bulletin
Publication title: Bulletin

British Electrotechnical Approvals Board

1 Station View, Guildford, GU1 4JY, England, UK
Tel: 44 1483 455466
Fax: 44 1483 455477
Email: info@beab.co.uk
Website: http://www.beab.co.uk
Members: 1250
Staff: 35
Contact: M. J. Vint, Mng.Dir.
Description: Manufacturers of electrical and electrotechnical safety approval equipment. Carries out independent third party testing and certification of electrical and electro-technical products to international standards for safety approval.
Publication title: Buyers Guide. Advertisements.

British Endodontic Society
BES

PO Box 707, Gerrards Cross, SL9 0DR, England, UK
Tel: 44 1494 581542
Fax: 44 1494 581542
Founded: 1963

British Engineers' Cutting Tools Association

c/o Institute of Spring Technology
Henry St., Sheffield, S3 7, England, UK
Tel: EQ
Fax: 44 114 2789143
Email: 44 114 2726344
Founded: Industrial Equipment
Contact: Mr. J.R., Markham
Fee: £Contact
Library Subject: A trade association of manufacturers of engineers cutting tools including twist drills, reamers, milling cutters, tool bits and thread cutting tools.

British Entomological and Natural History Society
BENHS

c/o The Pelham-Clinton Bldg.
Dinton Pastures Country Park, Davis St., Hurst, Reading, RG10 0TH, England, UK
Email: secretary@benhs.org.uk
Website: http://www.benhs.org.uk
Founded: 1872
Contact:
Fee: £15
Membership Type: ordinary or corporate
Fee: £5
Membership Type: junior, under 18 years
Description: Promotes amateur and professional entomologists, and those interested in other branches of natural history; works for advancement of research in entomology, particularly the conservation of fauna and flora of the U.K and protection of wildlife worldwide.
Publication: Journal
Meetings/Conventions: Field Meetings meeting

British Epilepsy Association

New Anstey House, Gate Way Dr., Yeadon, Leeds, LS19 7XY, England, UK
Tel: 44 113 2108800
Fax: 44 113 3910300
Email: epilepsy@epilepsy.org.uk
Website: http://www.epilepsy.org.uk
Founded: 1950
Members: 20000
Staff: 36
Contact: Sharon Hudson, Public Relations
Fee: £12
Membership Type: ordinary
Fee: £24
Membership Type: professional
Description: Association is owned by its members. Provides care in the community for the country's estimated 420,000 people with epilepsy. Publications on all aspects of epilepsy counselling, advice, information and support and the National Epilepsy Helpline. Around 140 regional groups and branch - regional office in Belfast. National information centre provides extensive service to public and professionals.
Publication: Magazine
Publication title: Epilepsy Today
Second publication: Journal
Publication title: Seizure

British Equestrian Trade Association
BETA

Stockeld Pk., Wetherby, LS22 4AW, England, UK
Tel: 44 1937 587062
Fax: 44 1937 582728
Email: claire@beta-uk.org
Website: http://www.beta-uk.org
Founded: 1979
Members: 700
Staff: 11
Contact: Claire Williams, Chief Exec./Sec.
Fee: £436
Description: Members are equestrian retailers and manufacturers. Represents and promotes the British equestrian trade, nationally and internationally; promotes safer riding through better equipment and

protection; promotes riding generally and offers the riding public improving standards of service.
Publication: Magazine
Publication title: Equestrian Trade News
Second publication: Newsletter
Publication title: The Beta Event
Meetings/Conventions: - annual trade show - Exhibits. Birmingham UK

British Equine Veterinary Association

Wakefield House, 46 High St., Sawston, CB2 4BG, England, UK
Tel: 44 1223 836970
Fax: 44 1223 835287
Email: info@beva.org.uk
Website: http://www.beva.org.uk
Founded: 1961
Members: 1400
Contact: Miss S. Majendie, Adm.Sec.
Description: Practising equine vets, members of academia, Veterinary universities and members of pharmaceutical companies, home and overseas. Promotes the cultural, scientific and professional activities of veterinary surgeons and others interested in equine practice, welfare, teaching and research.
Publication: Journal
Publication title: Equine Veterinary Education. Advertisements.
Second publication: Journal
Publication title: Equine Veterinary Journal
Meetings/Conventions: - annual congress - Exhibits.

British Essential Oils Association

Exeter Rd., 15 Exeter Mansions, London, NW2 3UG, England, UK
Tel: 44 208 4503713
Fax: 44 208 4503197
Email: beoalondon@mcmail.com
Founded: 1978
Members: 56
Staff: 2
Contact: Malcolm Irvine
Fee: £275
Description: To provide a forum for the industry in dealing with government. Provides essential information on a regular basis to members and promotes the essential oil industry.
Publication: Handbook
Meetings/Conventions: meeting

British European Potato Association

Bldg. 5, Bentwaters Parks, Rendlesham, Woosbridge, 1P12 2TW, England, UK
Tel: 44 1394 460075
Fax: 44 1394 461117
Email: dfradd@naspm.org.uk
Founded: 1992
Members: 17
Staff: 1
Contact: Mr. C.D. Fradd, Sec.
Fee: £400
Description: Represents and promotes the interests of potato growers. Disseminates information. Administers RUCIP Rules in the UK.

British Executive Service Overseas

c/o Gael Ramsey, Ch.Exec.
164 Vauxhall Bridge Rd., London, SW1V 2RB, England, UK
Tel: 44 20 76300644
Fax: 44 20 76300624
Email: team@beso.org
Website: http://www.beso.org
Contact: Gael Ramsey, Ch.Exec.
Description: Works to provide advice and training to organizations unable to afford commercial consultants through qualified volunteers.

British Exhibition Venues Association

c/o Mallards
Five Ashes, Mayfield, TN20 6NN, England, UK
Tel: 44 1435 872244
Fax: 44 1435 872696
Founded: 1979
Members: 20
Staff: 2
Contact: F. Lloyd McLean, Exec. Sec.
Description: Venues where exhibitions, conferences and product launches are held. Provides an awareness of venues available in Britain for potential clients and acts as a free advisory service.
Publication: Newsletter

British Export Accessory and Design Association BEADA

Old Sandwell House, Sandwell St., Walsall, WS1 3DR, England, UK
Tel: 44 1922 624081
Fax: 44 1922 611755
Email: export@beada.com
Founded: 1977
Members: 1500
Staff: 6
Contact: Norman Morison
Description: Promotes the export of British home, office, and hotel products. Offers legal and technical assistance to members.
Library Subject: home and garden
Library Type: reference
Publication: Newsletter
Meetings/Conventions: trade show

British Exporters Association

Broadway House, Tothill St., London, SW1H 9NQ, England, UK
Tel: 44 207 2225419
Fax: 44 207 7992468
Email: bexamail@aol.com
Website: http://www.bexa.co.uk
Founded: 1940
Description: Capital goods manufacturers; international trading/export houses; banks interested in international trade finance; export credit insurers. Lobbying on behalf of export houses, and larger manufacturing exporters and banks involved in international trade finance; puts manufacturers in touch with export houses.
Publication: Directory
Publication title: Directory of Export Buyers in the UK

British False Memory Society, Bradford-on-Avon, BA15 1NF, England, UK

Tel: 44 1225 868682
Fax: 44 1225 862251
Email: bfms@bfms.org.uk
Website: http://www.bfms.org.uk

Founded: 1993
Members: 1200
Staff: 4
Contact: Madeline Greenhalgh, Dir.
Fee: £30
Description: Seeks to raise awareness of the dangers of recovered memory therapy. Collaborates with associated organizations. Offers telephone support to family members falsely accused of childhood sexual abuse. Fosters research.
Library Subject: childhood sexual abuse, recovered memory therapy
Library Type: reference
Publication: Newsletter
Publication title: BFMS Newsletter
Meetings/Conventions: - periodic conference

British Fashion Council

5 Portland Pl., London, W1B 1PW, England, UK
Tel: 44 20 76367788
Fax: 44 20 76367515
Email: bfc@dial.pipex.com
Founded: 1983
Contact: Simon Ward, Admin.
Description: Represents members' interests.
Meetings/Conventions: London Fashion Week - semiannual - Exhibits.

British Federation of Audio

PO Box 365, Farnham, GU10 2BD, England, UK
Tel: 44 1428 714616
Fax: 44 1428 717599
Email: info@british-audio.org.uk
Website: http://www.british-audio.org.uk
Members: 44
Contact: C.I.C. Cowan
Description: Manufacturers and distributors of branded hi-fi/audio goods. Promotion of the audio industry through collective action. Collection of statistical and other data relating to the trade and be a forum for communications between manufacturers, distributors and dealers.

British Federation of Brass Bands

National Office Unit 10, Maple Estate, Stocks Lane, Barnsley, S75 2BL, England, UK
Tel: 44 1274 511280
Fax: 44 1274 511281
Email: bfbb@clara.net
Website: http://www.bfbb.clara.net
Founded: 1969
Members: 320
Staff: 3
Contact: Hayley Granger, Dev. Officer
Fee: £50
Membership Type: brass bands
Description: National body representing the interests of brass bands in the United Kingdom.
Library Subject: music scores, brass band music
Library Type: open to the public
Publication: Directory
Publication title: Directory of Brass Bands. Advertisements.
Meetings/Conventions: - biennial convention - Exhibits.

British Federation of Women Graduates
BFWG

4 Mandeville Courtyard, 142 Battersea Park Rd., London, SW11 4NB, England, UK
Tel: 44 20 74988037
Fax: 44 20 74985213
Email: bfwg@bfwg.demon.co.uk
Website: http://www.bfwg.org.uk
Founded: 1907
Members: 180000
Staff: 3
Contact:
Fee: £40
Description: Promotes women's opportunities in education and public life. Works as part of an international organization to improve the lives of women and girls. Fosters local, national and international friendship.
Library Subject: academic
Library Type: by appointment only
Formerly: British Federation of University Women
Publication: Newsletter. Advertisements.
Meetings/Conventions: - annual conference

British Federation of Young Choirs

Devonshire Square, Devonshire House, Loughborough, LE11 3DW, England, UK
Tel: 44 1509 211664
Fax: 44 1509 260630
Email: admin@youngchoirs.net
Website: http://www.youngchoirs.net
Founded: 1983
Members: 450
Staff: 4
Contact: Malcolm Goldring, Chief Exec.
Fee: £22
Membership Type: individual
Fee: £40
Membership Type: choir
Description: Offers choral events for young people in this country and abroad, a training program for teachers, conductors and youth workers, and advice and financial support.
Library Subject: scores, chorale music
Library Type: reference
Publication: Newsletter
Publication title: Newsletter
Meetings/Conventions: - periodic conference - Exhibits.

British Fertility Society

c/o Helen Gregson
16 The Courtyard, Woodlands, Bradley Stoke, BS32 4NQ, England, UK
Tel: 45 1454 642217
Fax: 45 1454 642222
Email: bfs@bioscientifica.com
Website: http://www.britishfertilitysociety.org.uk
Founded: 1973
Members: 800
Contact: Ian Cooke, Pres.
Fee: £30
Membership Type: full
Description: Promotes the practice, training, education and research in the field of infertility and reproductive medicine.
Library Subject: reproductive medicine, infertility
Library Type: reference

British Film Institute

21 Stephen St., London, W1T 1LN, England, UK
Tel: 44 207 255 1444
Email: discover@bfi.org.uk
Website: http://www.bfi.org.uk
Founded: 1933
Staff: 500
Description: Promotes access to, and appreciation of film culture.
Publication: Catalog

British Fire Protection Systems Association
BFPSA

c/o Neville House
55 Eden St., Kingston-upon-Thames, Kingston Upon Thames, KT1 1BW, England, UK
Tel: 44 208 5495855
Fax: 44 208 5471564
Email: bfpsa@abft.org.uk
Website: http://www.bfpsa.org.uk
Founded: 1966
Members: 108
Staff: 12
Contact: B. Gately, Gen.Mgr.
Description: Manufacturers and installers of fire detection and alarms and fire extinguishing systems. To uphold and enhance the professional status of the Fire Protection Industry by encouraging the adoption of improved standards for personnel training, systems design, equipment quality and after sales service.
Publication title: Annual Review
Second publication: Membership Directory
Meetings/Conventions: - annual general assembly

British Flat Roofing Council

186 Beardall St., Hucknall, Nottingham, NG15 7JU, England, UK
Tel: 44 115 9566666
Fax: 44 115 9633444
Email: postmaster@bfrc.demon.co.uk
Founded: 1982
Members: 3
Staff: 7
Contact: Paul K. Newman, Dir. General
Description: Trade associations of manufacturers/contractors for the flat and low pitched roofing industry. Provides a conference and seminar service; telephone technical advisory service and technical information packs. It also conducts research projects into flat roofing systems.
Publication title: Flat Roofing, Design and Good Practice
Publication title: The Householders Guide to Flat Roofing

British Flue and Chimney Manufacturers Association

Henley Rd., Medmenham, Marlow, SL7 2ER, England, UK
Tel: 44 1491 578674
Fax: 44 1491 575024
Email: info@feta.co.uk
Website: http://www.feta.co.uk
Founded: 1978
Members: 15
Staff: 6
Contact: T. Seward, Commun.Mgr.
Description: Members are manufacturers of factory-made chimneys and flue products. Promotes the advantages and proper use of factory-made conventional natural draught flue and chimney systems.

Also aims to influence building regulations, standards and codes of practice relevant to flue and chimney systems.
Publication title: Guide to Flues & Chimneys
Second publication: Newsletter

British Fluid Power Association
BFPA

Cheriton House, Cromwell Park, Chipping Norton, OX7 5SR, England, UK
Tel: 44 1608 647900
Fax: 44 1608 647919
Email: enquiries@bfpa.co.uk
Website: http://www.bfpa.co.uk
Founded: 1986
Members: 100
Staff: 9
Contact: Roman Russocki, Ch.Exec.
Description: Hydraulic and pneumatic equipment suppliers and manufacturers; individuals involved or interested in the fluid power industries. Promotes cooperation in the field; sets technical standards and guidelines. Represents members' interests. Operates educational programs; conducts research; maintains advisory and information service; disseminates marketing data, statistics, and exporting information.
Formerly: Association of Hydraulic Equipment Manufacturers
Publication title: Annual Review
Second publication: Directory
Publication title: Directory
Meetings/Conventions: - periodic convention

British Fluid Power Distributors Association

Cheriton House, Cromwell Park, Chipping Norton, OX7 5SR, England, UK
Tel: 44 1608 647900
Fax: 44 1608 647919
Email: bfpda@bfpa.co.uk
Website: http://www.bfpa.co.uk/
Founded: 1989
Members: 100
Staff: 4
Contact: Sarah Edington, Mem.Sec.
Description: Quality assurance; support of manufacturers, forum for discussion; code of professional conduct; promotion of training and education, marketing information; technical guidelines; liaison with government and other organisations.
Publication: Newsletter

British Fluoridation Society

5th Fl., Dental School, University of Liverpool, PO Box 147, Pembroke Pl., Liverpool, L69 3GN, England, UK
Tel: 44 151 7065216
Fax: 44 151 7065845
Email: bfs@liv.ac.uk
Website: http://www.liv.ac.uk/bfs
Founded: 1969
Contact: Sheila Jones, Info. Officer
Description: Promotes fluoridation of the water supplies to improve dental health and reduce health inequalities.

British Flute Society

41 Devon St., Twickenham, TW2 6PN, England, UK
Tel: 44 20 82417572
Fax: 44 20 88097436

Email: secretary@bfs.org.uk
Website: http://www.bfs.org.uk
Founded: 1982
Members: 2000
Contact: Sarah Richfield-Wyatt, Sec.
Fee: £20
Description: Professional players, teachers, amateur players. Promotes flute playing at all levels. Events held throughout the country for flute players.
Publication: Journal
Publication title: PAN

British Footwear Association

3 Burystead Pl., Wellingborough, NN8 1AH, England, UK
Tel: 44 1933 229005
Fax: 44 1933 225009
Email: bfa@easynet.co.uk
Website: http://www.britfoot.com
Founded: 1890
Members: 80
Staff: 5
Contact: Niall Campbell
Description: UK footwear manufacturers; associate members are suppliers of mainly British made footwear. To encourage a long term profitable trading environment for footwear manufacturers in the UK.
Publication: Booklet
Publication title: Footwear for Special Needs. Advertisements.
Publication title: Statistical Review

British Fragrance Association

6 Catherine St., London, WC2B 5JJ, England, UK
Tel: 44 207 8362460
Fax: 44 207 8360580
Email: julie.young@fdf.org.uk
Website: http://www.ifraorg.org
Founded: 1942
Members: 29
Staff: 1
Contact: Julie Young, Exec.Sec.
Description: Manufacturers of fragrance ingredients, producers and companies marketing fragrance compounds and aroma chemicals. To promote and protect the interests of the industry, to encourage members to maintain high standards and to appropriately promote, support or oppose legislation affecting the industry or its members. Co-operates with government departments and other bodies interested in or having association with the industry. Collects and disseminates technical, statistical and other information.

British Franchise Association
BFA

Thames View, Newtown Rd., Henley-On-Thames, RG9 1HG, England, UK
Tel: 44 1491 578050
Fax: 44 1491 573517
Email: mailroom@british-franchise.org.uk
Website: http://www.british-franchise.org
Founded: 1977
Members: 279
Staff: 7
Contact: Mr. B. Smart
Description: Members are engaged in the distribution of goods and services through independent outlets under franchise agreements.
Publication: Handbook

Publication title: Franchisee Pack
Second publication: Manual
Publication title: Franchiser Manual
Meetings/Conventions: - annual conference

British Friction Manufacturers Council
BFMC

Brazennose House, Lincoln Sq., Manchester, M2 5BL, England, UK
Tel: 44 161 8345777
Fax: 44 161 8353242
Members: 4
Contact: Susan Murphy
Description: Manufacturers of covering brake linings and clutch facings. Promotes increased awareness of technical and legal issues affecting members. Maintains referencing system linking members.
Library Subject: technical drawings, friction materials
Library Type: not open to the public
Meetings/Conventions: Council Meeting - quarterly meeting

British Frozen Food Federation
BFFF

3rd Fl., Springfield House, Springfield Rd., Grantham, NG31 7BG, England, UK
Tel: 44 147 6515300
Fax: 44 147 6515309
Website: http://www.bfff.co.uk
Contact: A.A. Carr, Sec.Gen.
Description: Encourages development of the British frozen food industry, while maintaining high standards.

British Fruit Juice Importers Association

Unit 5, Gooses Foot Estate, Kingstone, Hereford, HR2 9HY, England, UK
Tel: 44 1432 250086
Fax: 44 1432 840517
Email: bfjia@ashurstassoc.demon.co.uk
Founded: 1942
Members: 57
Contact: Dr. P.R. Ashurst, Sec.
Fee: £200
Membership Type: full, associate
Description: Importers of fruit juices. To co-ordinate and promote interests of importers of fruit juices including contacts with the Ministry of Agriculture, Fishery and Food, and HM Customs & Excise.
Meetings/Conventions: - annual meeting

British Furniture Manufacturers

30 Harcourt St., London, W1H 2AA, England, UK
Tel: 44 207 7240851
Fax: 44 207 7061924
Email: info@bfm.org.uk
Website: http://www.bfm.org.uk/
Founded: 1949
Members: 383
Staff: 12
Contact: Roger Mason
Description: British furniture manufacturers including exhibition, and export division. Acts as the trade association for British furniture manufacturers. Organizes exhibitions, home and overseas, plus supporting export promotions. Acts as the public voice for the industry on all matters from safety to the environment and as industry training body.
Meetings/Conventions: BFM Summer Furniture Show - annual - Exhibits.

British Geological Survey

c/o Kingsley Dunham Centre
Keyworth, Nottingham, NG12 5GG, England, UK
Tel: 44 115 9363100
Fax: 44 115 9363200
Email: libuser@bgs.ac.uk
Website: http://www.bgs.ac.uk
Founded: 1835
Staff: 780
Contact: Dr. D.A. Falvey, Dir.
Description: Approximately 507 of the staff are scientists, the rest is made up of administration and technical support. Contributes to the economic competitiveness of the UK, the effectiveness of public services and policy (including international policy) and the quality of life by providing the best, most relevant and most up-to-date geoscience information and advice for the UK both onshore, offshore and internationally.
Library Subject: earth sciences
Library Type: reference
Publication: Survey
Publication title: British Geological Survey Annual Report
Publication title: Geological Maps

British Geophysical Association
BGA

c/o Prof. R. Paul Young
Department of Earth Sciences, Jane Herdman Laboratories, Brownlow St., Liverpool, L69 3BX, England, UK
Tel: 44 151 7945178
Email: r.p.young@liverpool.ac.uk
Website: http://www.geophysics.org.uk/
Contact: Prof. R. Paul Young, Pres.
Description: Promotes the subject of geophysics in order to strengthen the relationship between geology and geophysics in the U.K. Offers courses.
Meetings/Conventions: meeting

British Geotechnical Society

c/o Institution of Civil Engineers
1-7 Great George St., London, SW1P 3AA, England, UK
Tel: 44 207 6652233
Fax: 44 207 7991325
Email: bga@ice.org.uk
Website: http://www.ice.org.uk/navigation/index_know.asp?page=../know/assoc_bga.asp
Founded: 1949
Members: 1392
Staff: 1
Contact: Gavin Bowyer, Sec.
Fee: £27
Membership Type: student
Description: Individuals, corporate and student members who are geotechnical engineers or otherwise engaged or interested in geotechnics. Concerned with the advancement of public education in the subject of soil and rock mechanics and engineering geology and in their application to engineering.
Meetings/Conventions: - monthly meeting

British Geriatrics Society

Marjory Warren House, 31 St. John's Sq., London, EC1M 4DN, England, UK
Tel: 44 20 76081369
Fax: 44 20 76081041

Email: info@bgs.org.uk
Website: http://www.bgs.org.uk
Founded: 1947
Members: 2500
Staff: 5
Contact: Dr. Jeremy Playfer, Pres. Elect
Description: Consultant geriatricians and other doctors, scientists, and professionals with an interest in geriatric medicine and care of older individuals. To promote scientific developments of geriatric medicine, improve medical and social services for older individuals and promote measures which will improve health throughout adult life to ensure better fitness on achieving old age.
Publication: Journal
Publication title: Age and Ageing. Advertisements.
Meetings/Conventions: - semiannual conference - Exhibits. London UK

British Glass

Northumberland Rd., Sheffield, S10 2UA, England, UK
Tel: 44 114 2686201
Fax: 44 114 2681073
Email: info@britglass.co.uk
Website: http://www.britglass.co.uk/
Founded: 1988
Members: 109
Staff: 42
Contact: Dr. W.G.A. Cook, Dir.Gen.
Description: Trade federation with research arm. Conducts research programs. Compiles statistics on sales of glass containers. Offers consultancy services and technical support.
Library Subject: Glass technology
Library Type: reference
Formerly: Formed by Merger of, Bristish Glass Industry Research Association
Publication: Magazine
Publication title: Digest of Information and Patent Review. Advertisements.
Meetings/Conventions: - periodic conference

British Glove Association
BGA

Sussex House, 8-10 Homesdale Rd., Bromley, Kent, BR2 9LZ, England, UK
Tel: 44 20 84640131
Fax: 44 20 84646018
Email: tradeassn@craneandpartners.com
Website: http://www.gloveassociation.org
Founded: 1941
Members: 40
Staff: 1
Contact: Mrs. C. Swan, Sec.
Description: Glove manufacturers, traders, and suppliers of leather and fabrics to the industry. Promotes glove manufacturing and trading in the United Kingdom.
Formerly: Formed by Merger of, National Association of Glove Manufacturers
Publication title: List of Members

British Goat Society

34-36 Fore St., Bovey Tracey, Newton Abbot, TQ13 9AD, England, UK
Tel: 44 1626 833168
Fax: 44 1626 834536

Email: secretary@allgoats.com
Website: http://www.allgoats.com
Founded: 1879
Members: 2000
Staff: 2
Contact: Peter Coy, Sec.
Description: Aims to circulate knowledge and general information upon goats, to extend and encourage the keeping of goats, so as to increase the production and use of their products. Also to improve the various breeds of goats, and especially to develop those qualities which are generally recognized and valued and to safeguard against cruelty from whatever source.
Publication: Book
Publication title: Herdbook
Second publication: Journal

British Grassland Society

c/o Department of Agriculture
PO Box 237, University of Reading, Reading, RG6 6AR, England, UK
Tel: 44 118 9318189
Fax: 44 118 9666941
Email: bgs@patrol.i-way.co.uk
Website: http://www.britishgrassland.com
Founded: 1945
Members: 1000
Staff: 2
Contact: J.M. Crichton, CEO
Fee: £30
Membership Type: ordinary, junior, retired, honorary life
Description: Farmers, research scientists, and other individuals in 35 countries involved in agricultural education and advisory services. Seeks to advance methods of production and use of grass and forage crops in agriculture through research and education. Conducts educational and summer tours.
Publication: Journal
Publication title: Grass and Forage Science. Advertisements.
Second publication: Newsletter
Publication title: Grass Farmer
Meetings/Conventions: - periodic conference

British Guild of Travel Writers

178 Battersea Park Rd., London, SW11 4ND, England, UK
Tel: 44 207 7209009
Fax: 44 207 4986153
Email: bgtw@garlandintl.co.uk
Website: http://www.bgtw.org
Founded: 1960
Members: 220
Contact: Melissa Shales, Sec.
Description: Professional travel journalists (including writers, photographers and broadcasters). Holds regular meetings (about once a month) on subjects of interest to members.
Publication: Yearbook
Publication title: British Guild of Travel Writers Yearbook. Advertisements.
Second publication: Newsletter
Publication title: Globetrotter

British Hacksaw and Bandsaw Association

Light Trades House, 3 Melbourne Ave., Sheffield, S10 2QJ, England, UK
Tel: 44 114 2663084
Fax: 44 114 2670910
Email: info@lighttradeshouse.co.uk

Contact: M.A. Ponikowski, Sec.Gen.
Description: A trade association of manufacturers of hacksaw and bandsaw blades and associated products.
Publication: Directory
Publication title: British Tools Directory

British Hallmarking Council

St. Philips House, St. Philips Pl., Birmingham, B3 2PP, England, UK
Tel: 44 121 2003300
Fax: 44 121 6337433
Founded: 1975
Members: 16
Contact: D.J. Gwyther, Sec.
Description: Members are individuals appointed by the Government and assay officers of Great Britain. Oversees the activities of the assay offices of Great Britain, to advise HM Government on legislation and to fix maximum price for assaying and hallmarking articles of precious metal.
Publication: Annual Report
Meetings/Conventions: meeting

British Hand Knitting Confederation

c/o NWTEC
Lloyds Bank Chambers, Bradford, BD1 1PH, England, UK
Tel: 44 1274 724235
Website: http://www.ukhandknitting.com
Founded: 1945
Members: 8
Contact: Ann Thomson-Krol, Sec.
Description: Manufacturers of hand knitting yarns, distributing to retail outlets. To promote the craft of hand knitting and encourage the exchange of information between members; teaching knitting and crochet to beginners. Acting in a consultative capacity to government.

British Hardmetal Association

c/o Institute of Spring Technology
Henry St., Sheffield, S3 7EQ, England, UK
Tel: 44 114 2789143
Fax: 44 114 2726344
Email: info@britishtools.com
Website: http://www.britishtools.com
Contact: Mr. J.R. Markham
Description: Manufacturers of hardmetal products. A trade association of manufacturers of hardmetal products.

British Hardware and Housewares Manufacturers' Association

4 The Lakes, Bedford Rd., Northampton, NN4 7YD, England, UK
Tel: 44 1604 622023
Fax: 44 1604 631252
Email: bhhma@brookehouse.co.uk
Website: http://www.bhhma.co.uk
Founded: 1957
Members: 360
Staff: 9
Contact: Mr. A.G. Johnson
Description: Manufacturers or suppliers of hardware and housewares to the UK consumer market. A trade association dedicated to the needs of manufacturers of hardware and housewares in the United Kingdom. Offers a wide range of membership and consultancy services including export assistance, parliamentary and legal and market information.
Formerly: BHHMA

Publication: Newsletter
Publication title: BHHMA Newsletter
Meetings/Conventions: - annual conference

British Hardware Federation

225 Bristol Rd., Edgbaston, Birmingham, B5 7UB, England, UK
Tel: 44 121 4466688
Fax: 44 121 4465215
Email: jonathanswift@bhfgroup.co.uk
Website: http://www.bhfgroup.co.uk
Founded: 1899
Members: 5000
Staff: 64
Contact: Jonathan Swift, Mng.Dir.
Fee: £125
Membership Type: full
Description: Hardware retailers including d-i-y, gardening, tools, ironmongers, housewares, electrical, plumbing. To identify and promote the interests of hardware retailers in the UK.
Library Subject: hardware, housewares, garden products
Library Type: not open to the public
Publication: Catalog
Publication title: Architects and Builders Ironmongery Catalogue
Publication title: BHF Yearbook and List of Members
Meetings/Conventions: - annual conference - Exhibits.

British Hat Guild

c/o The Business Centre
Kimpton Rd., Luton, LU2 0LB, England, UK
Tel: 44 1582 522333
Fax: 44 1582 705088
Email: info@hat-guild.org.uk
Founded: 1977
Members: 70
Staff: 1
Contact: Mrs. Jayne Jackson
Description: Members are manufacturers, milliners, wholesalers and retailers. Dedicated to the design, manufacture, and promotion of hats.
Library Type: open to the public
Publication title: The Guide to a Career in Hat Manufacturing
Publication title: Millinery - Luton's Most Fashionable Heritage

British Hay and Straw Merchants Association

c/o C.J. Trower
The Old Station, Farringdon, Alton, GU34 3DP, England, UK
Tel: 44 1420 587356
Fax: 44 1420 588445
Founded: 1916
Members: 50
Staff: 1
Contact: Mr. C.J. Trower
Description: Hay and straw merchants.
Meetings/Conventions: meeting

British Health Care Association

24A Main St., Garforth, Leeds, LS25 1AA, England, UK
Tel: 44 113 2320903
Fax: 44 113 2320904
Email: cbell@bhca.org.uk
Website: http://www.bhca.org.uk
Founded: 1948
Members: 30

Staff: 2
Contact: Carolyn Bell, Chief Exec.
Description: Professional organization representing hospital cashplan insurance programs, health benefits providers, and health maintenance organizations in the United Kingdom. Promotes effective hospitalization coverage for the public and other health care benefits.
Formerly: British Hospitals Contributory Schemes Association
Publication: Brochure
Publication title: Caring for the Nation's Health
Second publication: Newsletter
Meetings/Conventions: - annual conference - Exhibits.

British Health Food Trade Association

c/o Angel Court
High St., Godalming, GU7 1DT, England, UK
Tel: 44 1483 426450
Fax: 44 1483 426921
Founded: 1973
Members: 2
Staff: 4
Contact: Mr. Rusby
Description: Health Food Manufacturers' Association, The National Association of Health Stores. A bridging association of manufacturers, distributors, suppliers and retailers operating within the health food trade.

British Healthcare Business Intelligence Association
BHBIA

c/o Steven Gibson
Merck Sharp & Dohme Pharmaceuticals, Hertford Rd., Hoddesdon, EN11 9BU, England, UK
Tel: 44 1992 467272
Fax: 44 1992 470191
Email: admin@bhbia.org.uk
Website: http://www.bhbia.org.uk/
Contact: Steven Gibson, Chm.
Fee: £384
Membership Type: corporate
Fee: £125
Membership Type: personal
Publication: Journal
Second publication: Handbook
Meetings/Conventions: - annual conference

British Heart Foundation
BHF

14 Fitzhardinge St., London, W1H 6DH, England, UK
Tel: 44 207 9350185
Fax: 44 207 4865820
Email: internet@bhf.org.uk
Website: http://www.bhf.org.uk
Founded: 1961
Staff: 190
Contact: Maj.Gen. L.F.H. Busk, Dir.Gen.
Description: Funds research into the causes and prevention diagnosis and treatment of cardiovascular disease. Sponsors postgraduate medical education; distributes fellowships and research funds. Organizes symposia, and workshops for health care and research professionals. Provides cardiac equipment for hospitals and ambulance services. Supports heart patients through rehabilitation programmes, heart support groups and BHF nurses. Conducts fundraising events. Compiles statistics.

Publication: Newsletter
Publication title: BHF Heart News
Meetings/Conventions: - biennial convention

British Hedgehog Preservation Society
BHPS

Hedgehog House, Dhustone, Ludlow, 5Y8 3PL, England, UK
Tel: 44 1584 890801
Email: bhps@dhustone.fsbusiness.co.uk
Website: http://www.software-technics.com/bhps
Founded: 1982
Members: 11200
Staff: 4
Contact: Fay Vass, Ch.Exec.
Fee: £8
Membership Type: ordinary
Fee: £13
Membership Type: family
Description: Membership categories are Ordinary, Family, Life and Overseas. Advises on the care of hedgehogs and has a network of carers nationwide; supplies education packs to schools, libraries, wildlife groups etc; arranges talks to interested groups; funds research on the behavioural habits of hedgehogs.
Publication: Catalog
Publication title: Hogalogue. Advertisements.
Second publication: Newsletter

British Helicopter Advisory Board

Graham Suite, Fairoaks Airport, Chobham, Woking, GU24 8HX, England, UK
Tel: 44 1276 856100
Fax: 44 1276 856126
Email: info@bhab.org
Website: http://www.bhab.org
Founded: 1969
Staff: 3
Contact: C.A. Warrington
Description: Membership covers the majority of helicopter operating companies, manufacturers, equipment manufacturers, sales and service companies, corporate and private owners, the Helicopter Club of Great Britain, together with a wide variety of companies with. an interest in helicopter operations including heliport and helipad operators. Represents the British civil helicopter industry and advises on all aspects of civil helicopter operation.
Publication: Handbook. Advertisements.

British Herb Trade Association

c/o NFU
164 Shaftesbury Ave., London, WC2H 8HL, England, UK
Tel: 44 207 3317439
Fax: 44 207 3317410
Email: info@bhta.org.uk
Website: http://www.bhta.org.uk
Founded: 1976
Members: 112
Staff: 1
Contact: Elizabeth Hinde, Sec.
Description: Individuals, firms and organizations who are commercially or professionally involved in the business of herbs in the UK. Aims to encourage improvement and maintenance of standards of product, presentation and business methods within the industry; to assist members in the development of their skills and with the profitable growth of their enterprises; to promote knowledge of and

the increased use and cultivation of herbs in Great Britain; to foster co-operation between all actively involved in, or with an interest in, the herb industry.
Library Subject: herb production and uses
Library Type: reference
Publication: Proceedings
Publication title: Conference Proceedings
Publication title: Herb News
Meetings/Conventions: - annual conference

British Herbal Medicine Association

1 Wickham Rd., Boscombe, Bournemouth, BH7 6JX, England, UK
Tel: 44 1202 433691
Fax: 44 1202 417079
Founded: 1964
Contact: Diana Foreman
Description: Members are importers, manufacturers, herbal practitioners, herbal retailers, wholesalers and health food shops. Ensures herbal medicine is available to all who seek it and fosters herbal research.
Publication title: British Herbal Compendium 1992
Publication title: British Herbal Pharmacopoeia

British Herpetological Society

c/o Zoological Society of London
Regent's Park, London, NW1 4RY, England, UK
Tel: 44 208 4529578
Email: info@thebhs.org
Website: http://www.thebhs.org
Founded: 1948
Members: 1100
Contact: Mrs. M. Green
Fee: £25
Membership Type: full
Fee: £40
Membership Type: institutional
Description: Private individuals, university libraries. Conservation, captive breeding, scientific group and junior sections all very active. Meetings held regularly and a library is available.
Publication: Bulletin
Publication title: BHS Bulletin. Advertisements.
Second publication: Journal
Publication title: The Herpetological Journal

British Holiday and Home Parks Association
BHHPA

Chichester House, 6 Pullman Ct., Great Western Rd., Gloucester, GL1 3ND, England, UK
Tel: 44 1452 526911
Fax: 44 1452 508508
Email: enquiries@bhhpa.org.uk
Website: http://www.bhhpa.org.uk
Founded: 1950
Members: 2200
Staff: 11
Contact: Mike Brumage, Dir. of Operations
Description: Owners and managers of residential, caravan, chalet, tent and self-catering parks. Representation to national, european and local authorities; information and advice to members through, journal, handbook, convention, telephone advice line; marketing and promotions - generic promotions campaign; commercial services - special offer/discount schemes.
Publication: Journal
Publication title: BH & HPA

British Holistic Medical Association
59 Landsdowne Place, East Sussex, Hove, BN3 1FL, England, UK
Tel: 44 1273 725951
Fax: 44 1273 725951
Email: admin@bhma.org
Website: http://www.bhma.org
Founded: 1983
Members: 900
Staff: 3
Contact: Miranda Wilson
Description: Professional corporate/associate membership (for the lay public) nurse/student membership and overseas membership. To educate doctors and other healthcare professionals in the principles and practice of holistic medicine, to encourage research studies and publication of work carried out in the field of holistic medicine and to bring together holistic healthcare practitioners for mutual support and further personal and professional development.
Publication: Newsletter

British Homeopathic Association
15 Clerkenwell Close, London, EC1R 0AA, England, UK
Tel: 44 207 5667800
Fax: 44 207 5667815
Email: info@trusthomeopathy.org
Website: http://www.homeopathy.org
Founded: 1902
Members: 3000
Staff: 3
Contact: Sally Penrose, CEO
Fee: £23
Description: The Association is a registered charity supported by a membership of people who, being convinced of the efficacy of the homoeopathic system of medicine, give regular subscriptions or donations for its maintenance. Aims to support, extend and develop homoeopathy. Puts the general public in touch with homoeopathic doctors, veterinary surgeons and pharmacies. Also book publishers, maintaining in print a number of books on various aspects of homoeopathy as well as the magazine.
Library Subject: homoeopathy
Library Type: not open to the public
Publication: Journal
Publication title: Health & Homoeopathy
Second publication: Books

British Horn Society
c/o CAF Administration Service
Kings Hill, Kent, West Malling, ME19 4TA, England, UK
Tel: 44 171 2403642
Email: mike@british-horn.org
Website: http://www.british-horn.org
Founded: 1978
Members: 500
Contact: Hugh Seenan, Chm.
Description: Professional musicians, amateur musicians and students.
Publication: Magazine
Publication title: Horn Magazine

British Horological Federation
Upton Hall, Upton, Newark, NG23 5TE, England, UK
Tel: 44 1636 813795
Fax: 44 1636 812258
Email: gevansbhf@aol.com
Website: http://www.bhi.co.uk/bhfabout.htm

Members: 50
Contact: W.M.G. Evans, Sec.Gen.
Description: Horological companies. Concerned with high standards from member company, and the promotion of those companies. Represents the British Industry on the Horological Industries Committee of Europe. Also on British and International Standards Committees.
Publication: Journal
Publication title: Horological Journal

British Horological Institute
Upton Hall, Upton, Newark, NG23 5TE, England, UK
Tel: 44 1636 813795
Fax: 44 1636 812258
Email: info@bhi.co.uk
Website: http://www.bhi.co.uk
Founded: 1898
Description: The professional body for individuals.
Publication: Journal
Publication title: Horological Journal. Advertisements.

British Horse Society
Stoneleigh Deer Park, Kenilworth, CV8 2XZ, England, UK
Tel: 44 8701 202244
Fax: 44 1926 707800
Email: enquiry@bhs.org.uk
Website: http://www.bhs.org.uk
Founded: 1947
Members: 56000
Staff: 75
Contact: Nichola Gregory
Fee: £42
Membership Type: gold
Description: Any person with an interest in the equine world - from the horse's welfare, through to road safety and training. Promoting the welfare, care and use of the horse and pony. Encouraging horsemanship and the improvement of horse management and breeding. Represents all equine interests.
Publication: Yearbook
Publication title: BHS Yearbook. Advertisements.
Second publication: Magazine
Publication title: British Horse

British Hospitality Association
Queens House, 55-56 Lincoln's Inn Fields, London, WC2A 3BH, England, UK
Tel: 44 20 74047744
Fax: 44 20 74047799
Email: bha@bha.org.uk
Website: http://www.bha-online.org.uk
Founded: 1910
Members: 23000
Staff: 11
Contact: Bob Cotton, Chief Exec.
Description: Proprietors of group and individually owned hotels, restaurants and catering businesses. Also trade membership open to suppliers to the hospitality industry. Represents the British hospitality industry -hotels, restaurants, contract caterers and Motorway Service Areas. Provides a wide range of advisory and other services for members and puts forward their views to UK and European policymakers.
Publication: Magazine
Publication title: Hospitality Matters

British Humanist Association
BHA

1 Gower St., London, WC1E 6HD, England, UK
Tel: 44 207 4300908
Fax: 44 207 4301271
Email: info@humanism.org.uk
Website: http://www.humanism.org.uk
Founded: 1896
Members: 4100
Staff: 7
Contact: Hanne Stinson, Exec.Dir.
Fee: £30
Description: Thoughtful people from all walks of life, who are concerned with fairness and freedom. To promote Humanism as a valid ethical life stance and an alternative to religion. The BHA provides non religious ceremonies across Great Britain and also seeks to promote Humanism particularly in education and the media.
Library Subject: ethics, humanism, religion
Library Type: not open to the public
Publication: Book
Publication title: Funerals Without God
Second publication: Magazine
Publication title: Humanist News Magazine
Meetings/Conventions: Humanist Conference - annual conference - Exhibits.

British Hydrological Society
BHS

1-7 Great George St., London, SW1P 3AA, England, UK
Tel: 44 207 6652234
Fax: 44 207 7991325
Email: bhs@ice.org.uk
Website: http://www.hydrology.org.uk
Founded: 1983
Contact: Tim Fuller
Fee: £22
Membership Type: individual
Fee: £11
Membership Type: retired or under age 25
Description: Aims to promote interest and scholarship in scientific and applied aspect of hydrology.
Publication: Handbook
Publication title: Membership Handbook
Second publication: Newsletter
Meetings/Conventions: international conference

British Hydropower Association

Unit 12 Riverside Pk., Station Rd., Wimbonbe, Dorset, BH21 1QU, England, UK
Tel: 44 1202 886622
Fax: 44 1202 886609
Email: info@british-hydro.org
Website: http://www.british-hydro.org/
Founded: 1975
Members: 220
Contact: Ms. Charmain Larke, Sec.
Description: Water Power Users, (i.e. millers, weavers, electricity generators), consultants and manufacturers of hydro power equipment. Protection of water power users (from the depredation of Government etc) and promotion of the use of water power.
Publication: Newsletter

British Hypertension Society
BHS

127 High St, Teddington, TW11 8HH, England, UK
Tel: 44 20 89770011
Fax: 44 20 89770055
Email: hmc@hamptonmedical.com
Website: http://www.bhsoc.org
Founded: 1981
Members: 250
Staff: 1
Contact: Gerry McCarthy, Sec.
Fee: £50
Membership Type: ordinary, senior, honorary
Description: Investigates all aspects of research in hypertension and related vascular disease.
Meetings/Conventions: - annual conference Cambridge UK

British In Vitro Diagnostics Association
BIVDA

1 Queen Anne's Gate, London, SW1H 9BT, England, UK
Tel: 44 20 79574633
Fax: 44 20 79574644
Email: enquiries@bivda.co.uk
Website: http://www.bivda.co.uk
Contact: Doris-Ann Williams, Dir.Gen.
Description: Individuals and organizations in the IVD industry in the UK. Promotes the awareness of the value of diagnostics in the wider theatre of healthcare. Represents members' interests to the government, professional bodies, the public, and the European Diagnostic Manufacturers Association.

British Incoming Tour Operators Association
BITOA

Vigilant House, 120 Wilton Rd., London, SW1V 1JZ, England, UK
Tel: 44 207 9310601
Fax: 44 207 8280531
Email: info@bitoa.co.uk
Website: http://www.bitoa.co.uk
Founded: 1977
Members: 330
Staff: 5
Contact: Richard Tobias, Chf.Exec.
Fee: £695
Membership Type: full members
Fee: £895
Membership Type: associate members
Description: Tour operators, hotels, restaurants, tourist attractions, transportation companies, heritage sites, restaurant and catering companies. To promote business between and on behalf of members, to lobby central Government on behalf of the industry and to pass on to member's commercial advantages gained through bulk purchase of goods and services.
Publication: Handbook
Publication title: BITOA Operators Handbook. Advertisements.
Meetings/Conventions: - annual convention

British Independent Plastic Extruders' Association
BIPEA

89 Cornwall St., Birmingham, B3 3BY, England, UK
Tel: 44 121 2361866
Fax: 44 121 2001389

Founded: 1981
Members: 25
Contact: G.C. Saunders
Description: Members manufacture extrusions in nearly all plastic materials and carry out a wide range of finishing and fabrication operations. Distributes information to members.
Publication: Brochure

British Industrial Furnace Constructors Association
BIFCA

The McLaren Bldg., 6th Fl., 35 Dale End, Birmingham, B4 7LN, England, UK
Tel: 44 121 2002100
Fax: 44 121 2001306
Email: enquiry@bifca.org.uk
Website: http://www.bifca.org.uk
Members: 20
Contact: David Corns, Sec.
Description: Industrial furnace constructors and ancillary equipment suppliers.
Meetings/Conventions: Advances in Furnace Technology - annual conference

British Industrial Truck Association
BITA

5-7 High St., Sunninghill, Ascot, SL5 9NQ, England, UK
Tel: 44 1344 623800
Fax: 44 1344 291197
Email: james.clark@bita.org.uk
Website: http://www.bita.org.uk
Founded: 1942
Members: 81
Staff: 5
Contact: James Clark, Sec.Gen.
Description: Industrial truck manufacturers, suppliers, and importers in the United Kingdom. Promotes the interests of the industrial truck industry in the United Kingdom.
Publication: Booklet
Publication title: British Industrial Truck Association
Second publication: Brochure
Publication title: Operator Safety Code Books
Meetings/Conventions: International Materials Handling Exhibition - annual meeting Birmingham UK

British Infection Society

Infectious Disease Unit, Ward 38, Leicester Royal Infirmary, Infirmary Sq., Leicester, LE1 5WW, England, UK
Tel: 44 116 2586952
Fax: 44 116 2585067
Email: martin.wiselka@uhl-tr.nhs.uk
Website: http://www.britishinfectionsociety.org
Founded: 1997
Members: 900
Contact: Dr. CP Conlon
Fee: £40
Membership Type: inside Europe
Fee: £45
Membership Type: outside Europe
Description: Members of the medical profession and others working in related spheres which are relevant to the society's objectives.

Established to relieve sickness by the study of all aspects of infection and to promote the wide dissemination of relevant knowledge.
Formerly: British Society for the Study of Infection
Publication: Journal
Publication title: The Journal of Infection. Advertisements.
Meetings/Conventions: - annual meeting London UK

British Institute of Agricultural Consultants

c/o The Estate Office
Torry Hill, Milstead, Sittingbourne, ME9 0SP, England, UK
Tel: 44 1795 830100
Fax: 44 1795 830243
Email: info@biac.co.uk
Website: http://www.biac.co.uk
Founded: 1957
Members: 305
Staff: 3
Contact: C.A. Hyde, Chief Exec.
Fee: £150
Description: Professionals giving advice and consultancy services in agriculture, horticulture, forestry, amenity, rural planning, etc. Also expert witnesses. Aims to advance the profession of agricultural consultancy and promote and publicize the services of members.
Publication: Directory
Publication title: Directory of Members
Second publication: Newsletter
Publication title: Expert Witness Directory

British Institute of Architectural Technologists
BIAT

397 City Rd., Islington, London, EC1V 1NH, England, UK
Tel: 44 207 2782206
Fax: 44 207 8373194
Email: info@biat.org.uk
Website: http://www.biat.org.uk
Founded: 1965
Members: 6500
Staff: 12
Contact: Francesca Berriman, Ch.Exec.
Description: Objectives are to: enhance the professional status and role of architectural technologists; provide educational programs for trainees and administer qualifying examinations; act as liaison between the profession of architectural technology and governmental and other agencies. Conducts short courses and seminars.
Formerly: Society of Architectural and Associated Technicians
Publication: Magazine
Publication title: Architectural Technology. Advertisements.
Second publication: Brochure
Publication title: Careers Handbook
Meetings/Conventions: - annual conference - Exhibits.

British Institute of Cleaning Science

3 Moulton Ct., Anglia Way, Moulton Park, Northampton, NN3 6JA, England, UK
Tel: 44 1604 678710
Fax: 44 1604 645988
Email: info@bics.org.uk
Website: http://www.bics.org.uk
Founded: 1961
Members: 3600
Staff: 5
Contact: Mike Sweeney, Exec.Dir.

Description: Open to those qualified within the cleaning industry. Professional body promoting training and education in the cleaning industry.

British Institute of Dental and Surgical Technologists

c/o Prof. A.C. Roberts, Pres.
4 Thompson Green, Shipley, BD17 7PR, England, UK
Tel: 44 1274 532303
Website: http://www.bidst.mmu.ac.uk
Founded: 1935
Members: 300
Contact: Mr. Colin Dean, Treas.
Fee: £44
Membership Type: fellow
Description: Maintains standards as a professional institute for dental and surgical technicians.
Formerly: British Institute of Surgical Technologists
Publication: Journal
Publication title: Journal of the British Institute of Surgical Technologists

British Institute of Energy Economics
BIEE

37 Woodville Gardens, London, W5 2LL, England, UK
Tel: 44 20 89973707
Fax: 44 20 85667674
Email: mailbox@biee.demon.co.uk
Founded: 1976

British Institute of Facilities Management

67 High St., Essex, Saffron Walden, CB10 1AA, England, UK
Tel: 44 1799 508606
Fax: 44 1799 513237
Email: admin@bifm.org.uk
Website: http://www.bifm.org.uk
Founded: 1993
Members: 6000
Staff: 15
Contact: Stan Mitchell, Chm.
Fee: £45.5
Membership Type: student
Fee: £98
Membership Type: associate
Description: Professional practising facilities managers and those in related professions with an interest in facilities management. Represents the interests of professional facilities managers, whom it supports through education, training and research in facilities management; a regional based CPD programme and monthly meetings.
Publication title: Guides on FM issues
Second publication: Bulletin
Meetings/Conventions: - annual conference

British Institute of Graphologists
BIG

24-26 High St., Hampton Hill, TW12 1PD, England, UK
Tel: 44 1753 891241
Email: contact@britishgraphology.org
Website: http://www.britishgraphology.org
Founded: 1983

British Institute of Human Rights
BIHR

King's College London, 8th Fl., 75-79 York Rd., London, SE1 7AW, England, UK
Tel: 44 207 4012712
Fax: 44 207 4012695
Email: admin@bihr.org
Website: http://www.bihr.org
Founded: 1970
Members: 170
Staff: 3
Contact: Sarah Cooke, Co-Dir.
Fee: £25
Membership Type: individual
Fee: £300
Membership Type: corporate
Description: Strives to develop and improve human rights protection at home and abroad. Promotes public awareness of human rights through developing community outreach programs to help those socially or economically isolated. Provides specialized human rights education and training and undertakes effective research with a view to contributing to the development of policy from a human rights perspective.
Library Subject: collection includes decisions, reports, and publications of the European Court and Commission of Human Rights (see separate entry)
Library Type: reference
Publication: Newsletter
Publication title: BIHR Brief
Publication title: Human Rights Case Digest
Meetings/Conventions: - monthly lecture

British Institute of Industrial Therapy

243 Shelley Rd., Wellingborough, NN8 3EN, England, UK
Tel: 44 1933 675327
Fax: 44 1933 675327
Founded: 1970
Members: 59
Staff: 1
Contact: Phil Arnold
Description: Directors and managers of services and units providing industrial therapy for those working in the mental health field. Provides information regarding developments in industrial therapy and work schemes as appropriate to those working in the field of training people who are suffering or recovering from mental illness so that they may remain in sheltered or open employment.
Publication title: Focus

British Institute of Innkeeping

Wessex House, 80 Park St., Camberley, GU15 3PT, England, UK
Tel: 44 1276 684449
Fax: 44 1276 23045
Email: reception@bii.org
Website: http://www.bii.org
Founded: 1981
Members: 15500
Staff: 50
Contact: John McNamara, Chief Exec.
Description: Those directly involved in supervising the day-to-day running of public houses. Promotes nationally recognized levels of professional competence amongst the membership and develops business skills. The Institute has an awarding body, BIIAB, which produces nationally recognized qualifications for the licensed retail sector.

Publication: Magazine
Publication title: The New Innkeeper. Advertisements.
Second publication: Book
Publication title: The Pub Industry Handbook
Meetings/Conventions: - annual luncheon London UK

British Institute of International and Comparative Law

Charles Clore House, 17 Russell Sq., London, WC1B 5JP, England, UK
Tel: 44 20 8625151
Fax: 44 20 8625152
Email: info@biicl.org.uk
Website: http://www.biicl.org
Founded: 1958
Members: 560
Staff: 15
Contact: Dr. Mads Andenas, Dir.
Fee: £85
Membership Type: individual
Description: Academic, student, practising lawyers throughout the world. Through its meetings, publications and research and training programmes, it serves to familiarize lawyers with legal systems other than their own (particularly within the EU) and to provide opportunities to contribute by widened experience, comparison and analysis of these systems to the development of national, international and regional law.
Library Subject: international law, comparative law
Library Type: reference
Publication: Bulletin
Publication title: Bulletin of Legal Developments. Advertisements.
Publication title: International & Comparative Law
Meetings/Conventions: conference

British Institute of Learning Disabilities
BILD

Campion House, Green St., Kidderminster, DY10 1JL, England, UK
Tel: 44 1562 723010
Fax: 44 1562 723029
Email: enquiries@bild.org.uk
Website: http://www.bild.org.uk
Founded: 1972
Members: 2000
Staff: 31
Contact: Dr. J. Harris
Fee: £42
Membership Type: individual
Description: Works towards improving the quality of life of people with learning disabilities, by the promotion and provision of education and training; information; research; books and journals. Provides consultancy.
Library Subject: Intellectual disability
Library Type: by appointment only
Publication: Journal
Publication title: British Journal of Learning Disabilities. Advertisements.
Publication title: Current Awareness Service
Meetings/Conventions: conference - Exhibits.

British Institute of Musculoskeletal Medicine

34 The Avenue, Watford, WD17 4AH, England, UK
Tel: 44 1923 220999
Fax: 44 1923 249037

Email: info@bimm.org.uk
Website: http://www.bimm.org.uk
Founded: 1992
Members: 360
Contact: Ms. D. Harris
Fee: £120
Description: Doctors involved in musculoskeletal medicine. Concerned with the furtherance of knowledge and expertise in musculoskeletal medicine which includes treatment of sports injuries, backpain and other conditions of the locomotor system. By osteopathy, injections and other physical modalities.
Publication: Journal
Publication title: Journal of Orthopaedic Medicine

British Institute of Non-Destructive Testing
BInst NDT

1 Spencer Parade, Northampton, NN1 5AA, England, UK
Tel: 44 1604 630124
Fax: 44 1604 231489
Email: info@bindt.org
Website: http://www.bindt.org
Founded: 1954
Members: 2200
Staff: 16
Contact: M.E. Gallagher, Sec.
Fee: £62
Membership Type: member
Description: Engineers, industrial organizations, students, and other interested organizations and individuals. Advances the science and practice of non-destructive testing and condition monitoring in the UK and worldwide. Sets national industry standards and issues certificates of competence to qualified engineers practising non-destructive testing.
Formerly: Formed by Merger of, NDT Society of Great Britain
Publication: Journal
Publication title: Insight, The Journal of the British Institute of Non-Destructive Testing. Advertisements.
Second publication: Newsletter
Publication title: NDT Logbook. Advertisements.
Meetings/Conventions: - annual conference - Exhibits.

British Institute of Organ Studies

c/o Mrs. J Hopkins
39 Church St., Haslingfield, Cambridge, CB3 7JE, England, UK
Tel: 44 1223 872190
Fax: 44 1223 872190
Email: limetree@csma-netlink.co.uk
Website: http://www.bios.org.uk
Founded: 1976
Members: 676
Contact: Prof. Peter Williams, Chm.
Fee: £25
Membership Type: individual
Fee: £18
Membership Type: retired
Description: Amenity society for the British pipe organ. Works for the faithful restoration of historic organs, particularly in Britain. Promotes scholarly research into the history of the organ and its music. Conserves sources and materials related to the history of the organ and makes them accessible to scholars. Encourages exchange of information with similar bodies and individuals outside Britain.
Library Subject: British organ archive, organ builders
Library Type: open to the public
Publication: Journal

Publication title: Journal of the BIOS
Second publication: Report
Publication title: Reporter of the BIOS

British Institute of Persian Studies

c/o British Academy
10 Carlton House Terrace, London, SW1Y 5AH, England, UK
Tel: 44 20 79695203
Founded: 1961

British Institute of Professional Photography

Fox Talbot House, Amwell End, Ware, SG12 9HN, England, UK
Tel: 44 1920 464011
Fax: 44 1920 487056
Email: bippware@aol.com
Website: http://www.bipp.com
Founded: 1901
Members: 3500
Staff: 5
Contact: Mr. Alex Mair, Exec.Sec.
Fee: £103
Description: Professional photographers, photographic technicians and others involved in professional photography. Represents the professional photography industry to the Government and aims to improve the technical knowledge and professional status of people in the photography industry. It also aims to achieve and maintain standards in professional practice and conduct.
Publication: Directory
Publication title: Directory of Professional Photography. Advertisements.
Publication title: The Photographer

British Institute of Radiology
BIR

c/o Mary-Anne Piggott
36 Portland Pl., London, W1B 1AT, England, UK
Tel: 44 207 3071400
Fax: 44 207 3071414
Email: admin@bir.org.uk
Website: http://www.bir.org.uk
Founded: 1897
Members: 2000
Staff: 16
Contact: Peter Sharpe, Pres.
Fee: £115
Membership Type: full
Fee: £59
Membership Type: young Member
Description: Medical radiologists, scientists, and allied professionals in 55 countries. Conducts seminars; bestows awards.
Library Subject: Diagnostic radiology, radiotherapy/oncology, magnetic resonance imaging, etc.
Library Type: reference
Publication: Journal
Publication title: British Journal of Radiology. Advertisements.
Second publication: Membership Directory
Meetings/Conventions: Scientific Congress - annual congress - Exhibits.

British Institute of Traffic Education Research

Kent House, Kent St., Birmingham, B5 6QF, England, UK
Tel: 44 121 6222402
Fax: 44 121 6223450

Founded: 1977
Members: 8
Staff: 10
Contact: Andrew Clayton
Description: Concerned with research and development in road safety and road safety education.

British Insurance Broker's Association

BIBA House, 14 Bevis Marks, London, EC3A 7NT, England, UK
Tel: 44 207 6239043
Fax: 44 207 6269676
Email: enquiries@biba.org.uk
Website: http://www.biba.org.uk
Founded: 1978
Members: 2000
Staff: 20
Contact: Mr. M. Williams, CEO
Description: Insurance brokers in the United Kingdom. Promotes the interests of members.
Formerly: British Insurnace and Investment Brokers' Association
Publication: Magazine
Publication title: The Broker. Advertisements.
Second publication: Directory
Publication title: Membership List. Advertisements.
Meetings/Conventions: - annual conference - Exhibits.

British Insurance Law Association
BILA

c/o London Metropolitan University
84 Mooregate, London, EC2M 6SQ, England, UK
Tel: 44 207 3201490
Fax: 44 207 3201497
Email: bila@londonmet.ac.uk
Website: http://www.bila.org.uk
Founded: 1964

British Interactive Media Association

Briarlea House, Southend Rd., South Green, Billericay, CM11 2PR, England, UK
Tel: 44 1277 658107
Fax: 44 8700 517842
Email: info@bima.co.uk
Website: http://www.bima.co.uk
Founded: 1985
Members: 200
Staff: 2
Contact: Janice Cable
Fee: £150
Membership Type: individual
Fee: £300
Membership Type: institutional
Description: Open to any person or organization with an interest in multimedia. Members come from fields of application development, hardware manufacturing, publishing, distribution, disc pressing, programming and consultancy. Promotes wider understanding of the benefits of multimedia to industry, government and education. Provides a forum for the exchange of views amongst members.
Publication title: BIMA News

British Interior Textiles Association

5 Portland Pl., London, W1B 1PW, England, UK
Tel: 44 20 76367788
Fax: 44 20 76367515

Email: enquiries@interiortextiles.co.uk
Website: http://www.interiortextiles.co.uk
Founded: 1993
Members: 105
Contact: Diane Harding, Chair
Description: Manufacturers, converters and major distributors of furnishing fabrics and household textiles. Promotes, safeguards and protects the interests of members. Provides meeting points for members.
Publication title: Export/Technical Bulletin

British Interlingua Society

14 Ventnor Court, Wostenholm Rd., Sheffield, S7 1LB, England, UK
Tel: 44 114 2582931
Founded: 1954
Members: 71
Contact: B.C. Sexton
Description: Persons interested in using and/or promoting the international language Interlingua. Promoting the international language Interlingua, publishing books in and about Interlingua, including textbooks and dictionaries.
Publication title: Contacto
Publication title: Lingua e Vita

British International Federation of Festivals

198 Park Ln., Macclesfield, SK11 6UD, England, UK
Tel: 44 1625 428297
Fax: 44 1625 503229
Email: info@festivals.demon.co.uk
Website: http://www.festivals.demon.co.uk
Founded: 1921
Members: 1075
Staff: 4
Contact: Ms. E. Whitehead, Gen.Sec.
Description: Amateur festivals of music, dance and speech, professional adjudicator and accompanist members. Concerned with the advancement of the amateur performing arts by providing a platform for performance combined with the teaching of an expert adjudicator.
Publication: Newsletter
Second publication: Yearbook

British International Freight Association
BIFA

Redfern House, Browells Ln., Feltham, TW13 7EP, England, UK
Tel: 44 20 88442266
Fax: 44 20 88905546
Email: bifa@bifa.org
Website: http://www.bifa.org/
Founded: 1944
Members: 1300
Staff: 18
Contact: Colin Beaumont, Dir.Gen.
Description: Companies involved in the freight industry in the United Kingdom. Represents members' interest.
Library Subject: multi-modal international freight transport
Library Type: reference
Publication: Handbook
Publication title: Understanding the Freight Business. Advertisements.
Publication title: BIFA Freight Services Directory. Advertisements.
Meetings/Conventions: - annual conference - Exhibits. York UK

British International Studies Association
BISA

c/o Pauline Kelly
16 Ridge Crift Stone, Stafford, ST15 8PN, England, UK
Email: pkellyBISA@compuserve.com
Website: http://www.bisa.ac.uk
Founded: 1975
Members: 900
Contact: Pauline Kelly, Admin.
Description: Promotes the study of international relations and related subjects through teaching, research and the facilitation of contact between scholars.
Publication: Journal
Publication title: Review of International Studies
Second publication: Newsletter

British Interplanetary Society
BIS

27/29 S. Lambeth Rd., London, SW8 1SZ, England, UK
Tel: 44 20 77353160
Fax: 44 20 78201504
Email: mail@bis-spaceflight.com
Website: http://bis-spaceflight.com
Founded: 1933
Members: 4000
Staff: 6
Contact: S.A. Jones, Exec.Sec.
Fee: £80
Membership Type: Regular
Fee: £120
Membership Type: Fellowship
Description: Academic, scientific, and technical professionals involved in space research, exploration, and technology. Disseminates information to members on current research.
Publication title: Journal of the British Interplanetary Society
Publication title: Space Chronicle
Meetings/Conventions: - 3/year seminar

British In-Vitro Diagnostics Association
BIVDA

1 Queen Anne's Gate, London, SW1H 9BT, England, UK
Tel: 44 207 9574633
Fax: 44 207 9574644
Email: enquiries@bivda.co.uk
Website: http://www.bivda.co.uk
Founded: 1992
Members: 107
Staff: 3
Contact: Doris-Ann Williams, Gen.Dir.
Description: National trade association for companies with major involvement and interest in the In-Vitro Diagnostics industry.

British Jewellers' Association

Federation House, 10 Vyse St., Birmingham, B18 6LT, England, UK
Tel: 44 121 2371112
Fax: 44 121 2371113
Email: enquiries@bja.org.uk
Website: http://www.bja.org.uk
Founded: 1887
Members: 569
Staff: 4
Contact: Diane Thomas, Mem.Coor.

Description: Manufacturing jewellers, silversmiths, designer craftsmen, bullion dealers and companies offering service to the trade. Aims to be the voice of the industry representing members' interests in the media and government; provision of certain benefits and services for members. Close liaison with trade fairs for and with members. Acts for members, individually and collectively on issues of importance.
Publication: Newsletter
Publication title: Jewellery in Britain. Advertisements.
Second publication: Magazine
Publication title: RJ Magazine. Advertisements.

British Jewellery and Giftware Federation
Federation House, 10 Vyse St., Birmingham, B18 6LT, England, UK
Tel: 44 121 2362657
Fax: 44 121 2363921
Website: http://www.bjgf.org.uk
Founded: 1970
Members: 2000
Staff: 31
Contact: Marie Brennan, General Mgr.
Description: Manufacturers and distributors of jewellery, silverware, giftware, art metalware, luggage, leather goods; also metal finishers. An employers' federation comprising six trade associations, namely British Jewellers' Association, Jewellery Distributors' Association, The Giftware Association, Art Metalware Manufacturers' Association, British Luggage and Leathergoods Association and Metal Finishing Association. Activities include trade promotion by exhibiting at trade fairs in UK and overseas; trade protection; trade training and publishing.
Publication title: British Jeweller
Second publication: Book
Publication title: British Jeweller Yearbook

British Laminated Fabricators Association
6 Bath Pl., Rivington St., London, EC2A 3JE, England, UK
Tel: 44 171 4575000
Fax: 44 171 4575038
Email: sluck@bpf.com.uk
Founded: 1960
Members: 54
Contact: Mrs. S. Luck, Group Exec.
Description: Members are actively engaged in the production of laminate, the working of laminate or the provision of necessary chemicals therefor. The only trade association of the decorative laminate industry whose member companies are dedicated to maintaining the highest standards of fabrication of high pressure decorative laminates to the association code of practice. They are qualified to undertake work of all types, from flat planel to sophisticated postforming techniques.
Formerly: British Laminated Plastic Fabricators Association
Publication: Newsletter
Publication title: Face It
Meetings/Conventions: - quarterly meeting

British Leprosy Relief Association
LEPRA
Fairfax House, 3rd Fl., Causton Rd., Colchester, CO1 1PU, England, UK
Tel: 44 1206 562286
Fax: 44 1206 762151
Email: lepra@lepra.org.uk
Website: http://www.lepra.org.uk

Description: Seeks to restore health, hope and dignity to people affected by leprosy. Offers social and economic rehabilitation programs. Sponsors research into the causes, prevention, and treatment of leprosy and allied diseases.

British Lichen Society
BLS
Department of Botany, Natural History Museum, Cromwell Rd., London, SW7 5BD, England, UK
Tel: 44 207 9425617
Fax: 44 207 9425529
Email: bls@nhm.ac.uk
Website: http://www.theBLS.org.uk
Founded: 1958
Members: 526
Contact: P.A. Wolseley, Sec.
Description: International society for all persons interested in taxonomy, ecology, physiology, or environmental issues relating to lichens. Organises field and lecture meetings. Presents awards.
Library Subject: Lichenology.
Library Type: reference
Publication: Bulletin
Publication title: BLS Bulletin
Second publication: Journal
Publication title: The Lichenologist
Meetings/Conventions: - annual convention

British Llama and Alpaca Association
Banks Way House, Effingham Common, Leatherhead, KT24 5JB, England, UK
Tel: 44 1372 458350
Fax: 44 1372 451131
Email: info@alpaca.co.uk
Website: http://www.llama.co.uk
Founded: 1987
Members: 350
Staff: 10
Contact: Mrs. Candia Midworth, Assoc.Sec.
Fee: £30
Membership Type: single
Fee: £45
Membership Type: family
Description: Breeders, owners and general enthusiasts from farmers to surgeons -ages 20s to 70s who own or are interested in South American camelids, ie llamas, alpacas, vicunas, guanacoes. Works to promote good husbandry practices, and the establishment of sound breeding programs for the continued improvement and increase of British stock. Membership offers owners and enthusiasts the opportunity to swap information at our numerous organized social events, seminars, lectures and conferences.
Library Subject: llamas, alpacas, guanacos, vicunas, camels
Library Type: not open to the public
Publication: Magazine
Publication title: The Camelids Chronicle. Advertisements.
Second publication: Newsletter. Advertisements.
Meetings/Conventions: British Camelids Conference - biennial conference - Exhibits.

British Lubricants Federation
Berkhamsted House, 121 High St., Berkhamsted, HP4 2DJ, England, UK
Tel: 44 1442 230589
Fax: 44 1442 259232

Email: enquiries@blf.org.uk
Website: http://www.blf.org.uk
Founded: 1968
Members: 110
Staff: 3
Contact: R.G. Parker, Exec.Dir.
Description: 4 Companies, proprietors or partnerships who are principally involved in refining, importing, blending, manufacturing, distributing or marketing of lubricants, process oils and allied raw material. Establishes and maintains contact with government departments and provides information and advice on current legislation. Disseminates information to members and obtains representation on government and other committees dealing with matters of interest to the industry.
Publication: Journal
Publication title: Lube. Advertisements.

British Luggage and Leathergoods Association
BLLA

Federation House, 10 Vyse St., Hockley, Birmingham, B18 6LT, England, UK
Tel: 44 121 2362657
Fax: 44 121 2363921
Email: diana.fiveash@blla.org.uk
Website: http://www.blla.org.uk
Founded: 1917
Members: 59
Staff: 1
Contact: Diana Fiveash, CEO
Description: Manufacturers and importers of luggage, belts, small leathergoods, handbags. Aims to provide services which will benefit the commercial interests of members; to promote the interests of members; to represent the industry to government and other legislative bodies; to represent the industry in UK affiliated and overseas affiliated organizations; to look at education and training matters; to facilitate export activities; to negotiate minimum terms and conditions of employment., BLLA
Publication: Newsletter
Publication title: BLLA News. Advertisements.
Meetings/Conventions: - annual general assembly

British Lung Foundation
BLF

78 Hatton Garden, London, EC1n 8LD, England, UK
Tel: 44 20 78315831
Email: general@britishlungfoundation.com
Website: http://www.lunguk.org/
Founded: 1984
Members: 75000
Staff: 35
Contact: Helena Shovelton, CEO
Description: Individuals and organizations. Seeks to advance the prevention, diagnosis, and treatment of lung diseases. Maintains support groups for people with lung disease; provides financial and other assistance to lung disease research; conducts educational programs; participates in charitable activities; compiles statistics.
Publication: Newsletter
Publication title: Breathe Easy
Meetings/Conventions: - annual conference

British Marine Federation
BMIF

Marine House, Thorpe Lea Rd., Egham, TW20 8BF, England, UK
Tel: 44 1784 473377
Fax: 44 1784 439678
Email: info@britishmarine.co.uk
Website: http://www.bmif.co.uk
Members: 1500
Staff: 49
Contact: Howard Pridding, Exec.Dir.
Description: Companies engaged in all sectors of the United Kingdom's marine industry. Promotes and protects members' interests.
Publication: Directory
Publication title: Handbook. Advertisements.

British Marine Life Study Society
BMLSS

Glaucus House, 14 Corbyn Crescent, Shoreham-by-Sea, BN43 6PQ, England, UK
Tel: 44 1273 465433
Email: glaucus@hotmail.com
Website: http://ourworld.compuserve.com/homepages/BMLSS/home-page.htm
Founded: 1990
Members: 97
Staff: 1
Contact: Andy Horton, Exec.Dir.
Fee: £20
Membership Type: standard or corporate
Description: Public aquaria, zoos, ecologists, marine biologists, museums. Marine laboratories, education, libraries, general public, local authorities, rockpoolers, fishermen, divers, biological recorders. The study of marine fauna and flora of the shore and seas surrounding the British Isles. Publication and distribution of knowledge of marine fauna and flora and the promotion of ideas and projects concerning the conservation of the British marine environment.
Library Subject: marine wildlife, related subjects: oceanography, marine biology, geology, aquariology
Library Type: reference
Publication: Journal
Publication title: Glaucus. Advertisements.
Second publication: Newsletter
Publication title: Shorewatch
Meetings/Conventions: - periodic workshop - Exhibits.

British Maritime Law Association

c/o Ince & Co.
Knollys House, 11 Byward St., London, EC3R 5EN, England, UK
Tel: 44 207 6232011
Fax: 44 207 623225
Email: patrick.griggs@ince.co.uk
Website: http://www.bmla.org.uk
Founded: 1908
Members: 280
Staff: 2
Contact: Patrick Griggs, Sec.Treas.
Fee: £30
Membership Type: individuals
Fee: £1600
Membership Type: corporate
Description: Association of Average Adjusters; British Insurance Brokers Association; The Chamber of Shipping; Institute of London

Underwriters; Lloyd's Underwriters Association; Protection and Indemnity Clubs; university law departments, solicitors, barristers and loss adjusters. To promote uniformity of maritime law (private rather than public). Co-ordinates contributions to international and national maritime legislation and informs members of latest developments in maritime law.
Meetings/Conventions: - annual lecture

British Market Research Association
BMRA

Devonshire House, 60 Goswell Rd., London, EC1M 7AD, England, UK
Tel: 44 20 75663636
Fax: 44 20 76896220
Email: admin@bmra.org.uk
Website: http://www.bmra.org.uk
Founded: 1998
Members: 210
Staff: 3
Contact: Stephen Hughes
Description: Members are marketing research companies accounting for 80% of all market research conducted in the UK. To promote and represent the practice of market research to the highest quality standards for clients, respondents and employees.
Formerly: Association of Market Survey Organisations
Publication: Handbook
Publication title: Buying Research 2002. Advertisements.
Meetings/Conventions: - annual conference

British Masonry Drill Bit Association

c/o Institute of Spring Technology
Henry St., Sheffield, S3 7EQ, England, UK
Tel: 44 114 2789143
Fax: 44 114 2726344
Email: jrm@britishtools.com
Contact: J.R. Markham, Sec.
Description: Manufacturers of masonry drill bits.
Publication: Directory
Publication title: British Tools Directory

British Masonry Society
BMS

Church Rd., Whyteleafe, CR3 0AR, England, UK
Tel: 44 20 86603633
Fax: 44 20 86686983
Website: http://www.masonry.org.uk
Founded: 1986
Contact: Dr. K. Fisher, Sec.
Publication: Journal
Publication title: Masonry International

British Materials Handling Federation

The McLaren Bldg., 6th Fl., Birmingham, B4 7LN, England, UK
Tel: 44 121 2002100
Fax: 44 121 2001306
Email: enquiry@bmhf.org.uk
Website: http://www.bmhf.org.uk
Contact: David Corns
Description: British Associations of materials handling equipment manufacturers.
Publication: Journal
Publication title: BMHF Yearbook & Directory. Advertisements.
Meetings/Conventions: - triennial conference - Exhibits.

British Measurement and Testing Association

PO Box 101, Teddington, TW11 0NQ, England, UK
Tel: 44 208 9435524
Fax: 44 208 9439712
Email: rw@bmta.co.uk
Website: http://www.bmta.co.uk
Founded: 1990
Members: 90
Staff: 2
Contact: Ray Wilson
Fee: £195
Fee: £320
Description: Organisations and individuals who have an interest in measurement or testing. A focus for measurement and testing in the UK. It keeps its members informed on activities affecting measurement going on at home, in Europe and internationally, and represents the UK interests in the European scene.
Publication: Newsletter
Publication title: BMTA News
Meetings/Conventions: - annual workshop

British Meat Federation

12 Cock Ln., London, EC1A 9BU, England, UK
Tel: 44 207 3290776
Fax: 44 207 3290653
Email: sec@britmf.com
Website: http://www.britmf.com
Founded: 1934
Members: 150
Staff: 4
Contact: P.G. Scott, Dir.
Description: Slaughterers and wholesalers of red meat within England and Wales. To provide a timely and relevant information service and to represent the membership at meetings of local and national government level. To liaise on matters of mutual interest and concern with other trade associations both in the UK and within Europe.
Formerly: Federation of Fresh Meat Wholesalers
Publication: Newsletter
Meetings/Conventions: - annual conference

British Mechanical Power Transmission Association
BMPTA

IMEX Business Park, Ste. 43/45, Shobnall Rd., Burton-On-Trent, DE14 2AU, England, UK
Tel: 44 1283 515521
Fax: 44 1283 515841
Email: admin@bga.org.uk
Website: http://www.bga.org.uk
Founded: 1986
Members: 105
Staff: 4
Contact: Thomas H. Lynch, Ch.Exec.
Description: Membership is open to manufacturers of gears and power transmission products; suppliers to the power transmission industry; users of gears and related power transmission products; academic, educational and research establishments actively involved in. research, design, development etc of the industry; those providing specialised services that advance the use of gearing. Promotes the competitive position of the UK gear and power transmission industry; promotes such technical research, educational and training activities as deemed necessary in the overall interest of the industry;

cooperates with government and other industries on matters of urgency and interest to the industry.
Formerly: British Gear Association
Publication: Handbook
Publication title: Buyers Guide & Members Handbook. Advertisements.
Publication title: Gear Technology Teaching Pack

British Medical Acupuncture Society

12 Marbury House, Higher Whitley, Warrington, WA4 4QW, England, UK
Tel: 44 1925 730727
Fax: 44 1925 730492
Email: admin@medical-acupuncture.org.uk
Website: http://www.medical-acupuncture.co.uk
Founded: 1980
Members: 2000
Staff: 9
Contact: Vanessa Edgerley, Admin.
Fee: £95
Membership Type: medical practitioner
Description: Medically qualified practitioners. Concerned with the training of medical practitioners in acupuncture. Geographic listings of medically qualified practitioners of acupuncture.
Library Subject: acupuncture in medicine
Library Type: not open to the public
Publication: Journal
Publication title: Acupuncture in Medicine. Advertisements.
Meetings/Conventions: - semiannual conference - Exhibits. London UK

British Medical Association
BMA

Tavistock Sq., London, WC1H 9JP, England, UK
Tel: 44 20 73874499
Fax: 44 20 73836400
Email: info.web@bma.org.uk
Website: http://www.bma.org.uk
Founded: 1832
Members: 124000
Staff: 700
Contact:
Fee: £288
Membership Type: standard
Description: Doctors' trade union. A scientific and educational body and a publishing house.
Library Subject: clinical medicine
Library Type: reference
Publication: Magazine
Publication title: BMA News Review. Advertisements.
Second publication: Journal
Publication title: BMJ Specialist Journals
Meetings/Conventions: Annual Representative Meeting - annual meeting - Exhibits.

British Medical Ultrasound Society
BMUS

36 Portland Pl., London, W1N 3DG, England, UK
Tel: 44 207 6363714
Fax: 44 207 3232175
Email: secretariat@bmus.org
Website: http://www.bmus.org

Founded: 1969
Members: 2230
Staff: 3
Contact: Ms. E. Brown, Gen.Sec.
Fee: £30
Membership Type: UK
Fee: £40
Membership Type: Outside UK
Description: Medical practitioners, physicists/scientists, sonographers radiographers, veterinarians, and manufacturers of sonographic equipment. Seeks to advance the science and technology of ultrasound and to improve education in the field.
Formerly: British Medical Ultrasound Group
Publication: Newsletter
Publication title: BMUS Bulletin. Advertisements.
Publication title: BMUS Membership Register
Meetings/Conventions: Annual Scientific Meeting & Exhibition - annual convention - Exhibits.

British Menopause Society
BMS

36 West St., Marlow, SL7 2NB, England, UK
Tel: 44 1628 890199
Fax: 44 1628 474042
Founded: 1989

British Menswear Guild

5 Portland Pl., London, W1B 1PW, England, UK
Tel: 44 207 5808783
Fax: 44 207 4368833
Email: director@british-menswear-guild.co.uk
Website: http://www.british-menswear-guild.co.uk
Founded: 1959
Members: 32
Staff: 2
Contact: Nancy Rose-Pagani, Chair
Description: Top quality manufacturers of men's clothing and accessories. Aims to promote the export of top quality British menswear to leading shops and stores throughout the world.
Publication: Videos
Publication title: Guild Promotion
Second publication: Videos
Publication title: Member Companies Factories and Merchandise
Meetings/Conventions: - annual meeting

British Metals Recycling Association

16 High St., Brampton, Huntingdon, PE28 4TU, England, UK
Tel: 44 1480 455249
Fax: 44 1480 453680
Email: admin@recyclemetals.org
Website: http://www.britmetrec.org.uk
Founded: 1919
Members: 330
Staff: 5
Contact: D.S. Hulse, Dir.Gen.
Description: Promotes and maintains a high standard of conduct between members; promote the welfare and prosperity of the ferrous and non-ferrous scrap industry; promote by research and exchange of information, improvements in processing the products of the industry; represent the common interests of the industry with suppliers, consumers and government.

British Microcirculation Society
BMS

c/o Dr. David Bates
Microvascular Research Laboratories, Department of Physiology,
Preclinical Veterinary School, University of Bristol, Bristol, BS2 8EJ,
England, UK
Tel: 44 171 9289818
Fax: 44 171 9288151
Email: Dave.Bates@bris.ac.uk
Website: http://www.microcirculation.org.uk
Founded: 1963
Members: 220
Contact: Dr. M.J. Lever, Hon.Sec.
Fee: £5
Membership Type: student
Fee: £20
Membership Type: ordinary
Description: Individuals interested in the study of microcirculation
and endothelium. Conducts clinical and scientific research.
Library Subject: annual proceedings and abstracts on microcirculation
Library Type: not open to the public
Meetings/Conventions: Scientific Meeting - annual - Exhibits.

British Mule Society
BMS

2 Boscombe Rd., Swindon, SN25 3EY, England, UK
Tel: 44 179 3615478
Email: anndyer57@aol.com
Website: http://www.hamill.co.uk/british_mule_soc/
Founded: 1978
Members: 150
Contact: Ann Dyer, Sec.
Description: Individuals interested in mules, hinnies, or mule-
breeding donkeys. Encourages the breeding of good quality mules
through selection of parents; promotes appreciation and well-being of
mules. Provides advice and assistance to mule owners and admirers;
maintains mule registry. Produces mule-related memorabilia;
facilitates communication among members.
Publication: Journal
Publication title: The Mule. Advertisements.
Meetings/Conventions: - annual meeting

British Music Hall Society
BMHS

Thurston Lodge, Thurston Park, Whitstable, CT5 1RE, England, UK
Tel: 44 1227 275959
Fax: 44 1227 275959
Email: actorlee@bigwig.net
Website: http://www.music-hall-society.com
Founded: 1963
Members: 1000
Contact: Howard Lee, Hon. Membership Sec.
Fee: £15
Membership Type: UK and worldwide
Fee: £20
Membership Type: outside UK
Description: Anyone interested in light entertainment, past and
present who are united in encouraging interest in music hall and
variety. Aims to preserve the history of music hall and variety, to recall
the artistes who were part of the scene and support entertainers of
the present day. Annual weekend seminar; a monthly study group

meeting; show first Tuesday each month at Central Conference
Theatre, Islington.
Library Type: open to the public
Publication: Journal
Publication title: Call Boy Journal. Advertisements.
Meetings/Conventions: BMHS Semina Weekend - annual retreat -
Exhibits.

British Music Information Centre

10 Stratford Pl., London, W1C 1BA, England, UK
Tel: 44 207 4998567
Fax: 44 207 4994795
Email: info@bmic.co.uk
Website: http://www.bmic.co.uk
Founded: 1967
Members: 120000
Staff: 6
Contact: Matthew Greenall, Dir.
Fee: £15
Description: Over 31,000 scores and 15,000 recordings available in
reference collection of 20th century British music, including much
unpublished and out-of-print material. Regular concerts, talks and
exhibitions of 20th century British music.
Library Subject: British 29th Century music
Library Type: open to the public
Publication: Newsletter
Publication title: Counterpoints
Meetings/Conventions: Concert Series - annual

British Music Society
BMS

7 Tudor Gardens, Upminster, RM14 3DE, England, UK
Tel: 44 1708 224795
Website: http://www.musicweb.uk.net/BMS/index.htm
Founded: 1978
Members: 600
Contact: S.C. Trowell, Hon.Treas.
Fee: £22
Fee: £38
Description: Libraries, institutions, students, and other interested
individuals in 21 countries. Promotes the work of lesser-known British
composers, primarily from the years 1850-1975. Sponsors
competitions.
Publication: Book
Publication title: Arnold Cooke
Second publication: Book
Publication title: Aspects of British Song
Meetings/Conventions: - annual meeting London UK

British Mycological Society
BMS

Joseph Banks Bldg., Royal Botanic Gardens, Kew, Richmond, TW9
3AB, England, UK
Tel: 44 208 3325720
Email: info@britmycolsoc.org.uk
Website: http://www.britmycolsoc.org.uk
Founded: 1896
Members: 2000
Contact: Dr. George P. Sharples, Gen.Sec.
Fee: £60
Membership Type: regular member
Fee: £24

Membership Type: student
Description: Microbiologists, mycologists, and other scientists organized to promote mycology, the study of fungi.
Library Subject: mycology and plant pathology
Library Type: reference
Publication: Magazine
Publication title: Field Mycology
Second publication: Journal
Publication title: Mycological Research

British National Committee for Electroheat

30 Millbank, London, SW1P 4RD, England, UK
Tel: 44 207 3445917
Fax: 44 171 9635804
Founded: 1965
Contact: P.D. Bartlett, Exec.
Description: Electroheat equipment manufacturers, industrial users, consultants, research, academics, electricity supply industry, trade associations, Government and regulatory bodies. Aims to promote the safe, efficient and economic use of electroheat processes.

British Natural Hygiene Society
BNHS

Shalimar, 3 Harold Grove, Frinton-on-Sea, CO13 9BD, England, UK
Tel: 44 1255 672823
Website: http://members.rotfl.com/bnhs
Founded: 1959
Description: Promotes holistic and complementary health care as an alternative to conventional medical approaches to health disease.

British Naturalists' Association
BNA

PO Box 5682, Corby, NN17 2ZW, England, UK
Tel: 44 1536 262977
Fax: 44 1536 262977
Email: brit.naturalists@btinternet.com
Website: http://www.bna-naturalists.org
Founded: 1905
Staff: 1
Contact: Roger Tabor, Chm.
Fee: £15
Membership Type: EEC
Fee: £24
Membership Type: all others
Description: Professional and amateur naturalists. National body for both novice and experienced naturalists which offers its members field activities, lectures, branch programmes throughout the country, field trips in the UK and abroad, natural history publications at reduced prices. Also established Blake Shield BNA Trust Fund which organizes Blake Shield Competition for groups of young people.
Library Subject: natural history
Library Type: not open to the public
Publication: Magazine
Publication title: Country-Side. Advertisements.
Publication title: British Naturalist
Meetings/Conventions: - annual conference

British Naval Equipment Association
BNEA

c/o Society of Maritime Industries
30 Great Guildford St., 4th Fl., London, SE1 0HS, England, UK
Tel: 44 207 9289199
Fax: 44 207 9286599
Email: info@maritimeindustries.org
Website: http://www.maritimeindustries.org/about/bnea.jsp
Founded: 1973
Members: 67
Staff: 2
Contact: Christopher McHugh, Dir.
Description: Represents interests of builders of warships and suppliers of equipment and services for naval vessels.
Publication title: British Naval Equipment Association Directory and Product Guide

British Neuropathological Society
BNS

Beach Hill Rd., Sheffield, S10 2RX, England, UK
Tel: 44 114 2712949
Email: secretary@bns.org.uk
Website: http://www.bns.org.uk
Founded: 1950
Members: 250
Contact: Prof. Paul Glace, Hon.Sec.
Fee: £70
Membership Type: ordinary
Description: Promotes science and clinical practice related to neuropathology and diseases of the nervous system and skeletal muscle.

British Neuroscience Association
BNA

The Sherrington Buildings, Ashton St., Liverpool, L69 3GE, England, UK
Tel: 44 151 7945449
Fax: 44 151 7945516
Email: bna@liv.ac.uk
Website: http://www.bna.org.uk/
Contact: Dr. Yvonne Allen, Exec.Sec.
Fee: £45
Membership Type: full membership, direct debit
Fee: £50
Membership Type: full membership, check, debit and credit card
Description: Promotes study of the structure and functions of the nervous system.
Meetings/Conventions: - quarterly executive committee meeting

British Newsprint Manufacturers' Association

Papermakers House, Rivenhall Rd., Westlea, Swindon, SN5 7BD, England, UK
Tel: 44 1793 889616
Fax: 44 1793 878700
Email: rsexton@paper.org.uk
Members: 3
Contact: R.G. Sexton, Sec.
Description: Newsprint manufacturers.

British Non-Ferrous Metals Federation

10 Greenfield Crescent, Birmingham, B15 3AU, England, UK
Tel: 44 121 4563322
Fax: 44 121 4561394
Email: davidaparker@bnfmf.fsnet.co.uk
Founded: 1945
Members: 23
Contact: D.A. Parker, Tec.Sec.
Description: UK producers of copper and copper-based alloy semi-manufacture and ingots.

British Nuclear Energy Society

c/o Institution of Civil Engineers
1-7 Great George St., London, SW1P 3AA, England, UK
Fax: 44 207 7991325
Email: bnes@ice.org.uk
Website: http://www.bnes.com
Founded: 1962
Members: 1100
Staff: 1
Contact: Ian Andrews, Sec.
Fee: £25
Membership Type: open
Description: Research Institutes.
Library Type: not open to the public
Publication: Journal
Publication title: Nuclear Energy. Advertisements.
Meetings/Conventions: Nuclear Congress - annual conference - Exhibits.

British Nuclear Medicine Society
BNMS

291 Kirkdale, London, SE26 4QD, England, UK
Tel: 44 20 86767864
Fax: 44 20 86768417
Email: office@bnms.org.uk
Website: http://www.bnms.org.uk
Founded: 1969

British Nutrition Foundation

High Holborn House, 52-54 High Holborn, London, WC1V 6RQ, England, UK
Tel: 44 207 4046504
Fax: 44 207 4046747
Email: postbox@nutrition.org.uk
Website: http://www.nutrition.org.uk
Founded: 1967
Members: 41
Staff: 16
Contact: Mr. N.S. Porter, Sec.
Description: No individual members. Corporate membership open to any organisation, company or corporation (except trade associations) interested or concerned in achieving the objectives of the Foundation (which are listed in the Annual Report). Provides reliable information and scientifically based advice on nutrition and related health matters. Aims to help individuals understand how they may best match their diet with their lifestyle. Produces a wide range of publications on many aspects of diet and health.
Library Subject: nutrition as food science
Library Type: reference
Publication: Bulletin
Publication title: BNF Bulletin
Publication title: Food: A Fact of Life

British Occupational Hygiene Society
BOHS

Georgian House, Ste. 2, Great Northern Rd., Derby, DE1 1LT, England, UK
Tel: 44 1332 298101
Fax: 44 1332 298099
Email: admin@bohs.org
Website: http://www.bohs.org/
Founded: 1953
Members: 1000
Staff: 7
Contact: Mrs. P.M. Blythe, Secretariat Mgr.
Description: Individuals and companies. Promotes public and professional awareness of occupational and environmental hygiene practices and standards.
Publication: Journal
Publication title: Annals of Occupational Hygiene
Second publication: Directory
Publication title: Directory
Meetings/Conventions: - annual conference - Exhibits.

British Office Supplies and Services Federation

645 Ajax Ave., Slough, SL1 4BG, England, UK
Tel: 44 845 4501565
Fax: 44 845 6789
Email: info@bissfederation.co.uk
Website: http://www.bossfed.co.uk
Founded: 1905
Members: 950
Staff: 10
Contact: R. Wotherspoon, Chm.
Description: Retailers, manufacturers, associates and wholesalers of office and stationery equipment. Concerned with all aspects of stationery, office products, office furniture, and office machinery including computer hardware and software.
Formerly: British Office Systems and Stationery Federation
Publication: Newsletter
Publication title: Environmental Newsletter
Second publication: Directory
Publication title: Export Directory

British Oil Spill Control Association
BOSCA

c/o Society of Maritime Industries
30 Great Guildford St., 4th Fl., London, SE1 0HS, England, UK
Tel: 44 20 79289199
Fax: 44 20 79286599
Email: bosca@bmec.org.uk
Website: http://www.maritimeindustries.org/about/bosca.jsp
Founded: 1981
Members: 45
Staff: 2
Contact: Mr. Brian Webb, Dir.
Description: Represents the United Kingdom spill response industry. Membership includes equipment manufacturers, service contractors and consultants and covers every aspect of oil pollution prevention, control and clean-up at sea, along coastlines and inland. BOSCA has service contracts with both the Maritime and Coastguard Agency (MCA) and the environment regulators, under the terms of which it maintains the national equipment database for use in spill incidents, and through its members, the Association plays an active role in clean-up operations undertaken by these organizations. Members of

BOSCA also provide round-the-clock spill response services for commercial organizations and the general public.
Publication: Directory
Publication title: British Oil Spill Control Association Guide to Suppliers

British Oncological Association
BOA

c/o Institute of Cancer Research
15 Cotswold Rd., Sutton, Belmont, SM2 5NG, England, UK
Tel: 44 20 86438901
Fax: 44 20 86436940
Email: pamela@lcr.ac.uk
Founded: 1985

British Origami Society

2A The Chestnuts, Countesthorpe, Leicestershire, LE8 5TL, England, UK
Tel: 44 1494 675645
Fax: 44 1162 773870
Email: pauline@trewimage.co.uk
Website: http://www.britishorigami.org.uk
Founded: 1967
Members: 700
Contact: Mrs. Pauline Trew, Gen.Sec.
Fee: £23
Fee: £18
Membership Type: junior
Description: Seeks to encourage, inform, and educate on origami.
Library Subject: origami
Library Type: reference
Publication: Magazine
Publication title: British Origami
Meetings/Conventions: - semiannual convention York UK

British Ornithologists' Club
BOC

c/o British Ornithologists Association
Akeman St., Zoological Museum, Tring, HP23 6AP, England, UK
Tel: 44 1442 890080
Fax: 44 1442 890693
Founded: 1892

British Ornithologists' Union

The Natural History Museum, Tring, HP23 6AP, England, UK
Tel: 44 1442 890080
Fax: 44 20 79426150
Email: bou@bou.org.uk
Website: http://www.bou.org.uk
Founded: 1858
Members: 1800
Staff: 2
Contact: Mrs. G. Bonham
Fee: £26
Membership Type: ordinary
Fee: £660
Membership Type: life
Description: Professional and interested amateur ornithologists. To further the science of ornithology throughout the world.
Library Subject: ornithology
Library Type: not open to the public
Publication: Journal
Publication title: IBIS Journal. Advertisements.
Meetings/Conventions: - annual conference - Exhibits.

British Orthodontic Society

291 Gray's Inn Rd., London, WC1X 8QJ, England, UK
Tel: 44 207 8372193
Fax: 44 207 8372193
Website: http://www.bos.org.uk
Founded: 1994
Members: 1600
Staff: 1
Contact: C.J.R. Kettler, Sec.
Description: Persons interested in orthodontics eligible for membership. Members (normally resident in the UK), honorary members, life members, international members, associate members, retired members, laboratory and trades members. Concerned with the promotion of the study and practice of orthodontics. Orthodontics is a speciality of dentistry and involves the treatment of abnormalities of jaw size and dental arch relationship and irregularities of tooth position.
Publication: Newsletter
Publication title: BOS Newsletter
Second publication: Journal
Publication title: British Journal of Orthodontics

British Orthopaedic Association

c/o Royal College of Surgeons
35-43 Lincoln's Inn Fields, London, WC2A 3PN, England, UK
Tel: 44 207 4056507
Fax: 44 207 8312676
Email: secretary@boa.ac.uk
Website: http://www.boa.ac.uk
Founded: 1918
Members: 2700
Staff: 10
Contact: D.C. Adams, Chief Exec.
Description: Practising orthopaedic surgeons, orthopaedic surgeons in training, retired orthopaedic surgeons, orthopaedic surgeons resident abroad who have done all or part training in the United Kingdom. Concerned with the advancement of the science, art and practice of orthopaedic surgery with the aim of bringing relief to patients of all ages suffering from the effects of injury or disease to the musculo-skeletal system.
Publication title: British Orthopaedic News
Meetings/Conventions: - annual conference - Exhibits.

British Orthopaedic Foot Surgery Society
BOFSS

c/o British Orthopaedic Association
35-43 Lincoln's Inn Fields, London, WC2A 3PN, England, UK
Tel: 44 20 74056507
Founded: 1978

British Orthoptic Society

Tavistock House North, Tavistock Sq., London, WC1H 9HX, England, UK
Tel: 44 207 3877992
Fax: 44 207 3872584
Email: bos@orthoptics.org.uk
Website: http://www.orthoptics.org.uk
Founded: 1937
Members: 1200
Contact: Rosie Auld, Hon.Sec.
Description: Orthoptists, including students and retired orthoptists. Members work in both NHS and private practice.
Publication: Journal

Publication title: British Orthoptic Journal. Advertisements.
Meetings/Conventions: BOS Scientific Conference - annual - Exhibits.

British Osteopathic Association

Langham House West, Luton, LU1 2NA, England, UK
Tel: 44 158 2488455
Fax: 44 158 2481533
Email: enquiries@osteopathy.org
Website: http://www.osteopathy.org
Founded: 1911
Members: 1600
Staff: 4
Contact: Michael Murray, Ch.Exec.
Fee: £155
Membership Type: full
Description: Provides independent representation, care and support.
Publication: Directory
Meetings/Conventions: - annual convention - Exhibits.

British Overseas NGOs for Development
BOND

Regent's Wharf, 8 All Saints St., London, N1 9RL, England, UK
Tel: 44 207 8378344
Fax: 44 207 8374220
Email: bond@bond.org.uk
Website: http://www.bond.org.uk
Description: Aims to improve the United Kingdom's contributions to international development. Collaborates with nongovernmental organizations (NGOs) internationally.

British Parking Association

2 Clair Rd., West Sussex, Haywards Heath, RH16 3DP, England, UK
Tel: 44 1444 447300
Fax: 44 1444 454105
Email: info@bpauk.demon.co.uk
Website: http://www.britishparking.co.uk
Founded: 1967
Members: 550
Staff: 5
Contact: Andrew Sampson, Pres.
Description: Members represent central and local government, consultants, contractors, engineers, planners, architects, car park operators and equipment manufacturers. Holds seminars, exhibitions and meetings, publishes information on all aspects of parking and provides services to members. It is consulted by official bodies on matters affecting parking and is available for consultation by decision makers and thus serves as a channel through which those with parking interests can make their views known in the appropriate quarters. Operates technical information service; maintains speakers' bureau.
Library Subject: parking
Library Type: not open to the public
Publication: Journal
Publication title: Parking News. Advertisements.
Meetings/Conventions: Parkex - annual conference - Exhibits.

British Peanut Council

20 St. Dunstan's Hill, London, EC3R 8NQ, England, UK
Tel: 44 20 72832707
Email: info@peanuts.org.uk
Website: http://www.peanuts.org.uk
Founded: 1967

Members: 45
Staff: 2
Contact: Amanda Connor
Fee: £200
Membership Type: full
Description: Promotes and protects the interests of the British peanut industry.

British Performing Arts Medicine Trust

196 Shaftesbury Ave., London, WC2H 8JL, England, UK
Tel: 44 20 72403331
Fax: 44 20 72403335
Email: bpamt@dial.pipex.com
Website: http://www.bpamt.co.uk
Founded: 1987
Members: 700
Staff: 3
Contact: Eileen Quilter Williams, Gen.Admin.
Description: Provides helpline and free assessment and diagnosis for performers with performance-related injuries and illnesses.
Formerly: British Association for Performing Arts Medicine

British Pest Control Association
BPCA

Gleneagles House, Ground Fl., Vernongate, Derby, DE1 1UP, England, UK
Tel: 44 1332 294288
Fax: 44 1332 295904
Email: enquiry@bpca.org.uk
Website: http://www.bpca.org.uk
Founded: 1942
Members: 250
Staff: 12
Contact: Mr. R.J. Strand, Exec.Dir.
Description: Companies in Great Britain providing products and services to the pest control industry, including fumigation equipment, silo cleaning, and bird control.
Publication: Membership Directory
Publication title: Directory
Second publication: Magazine
Publication title: Professional Pest Controller
Meetings/Conventions: Pestex - semiannual show - Exhibits.

British Pharmacological Society

16, Angel Gate, City Road, London, EC1V 2SG, England, UK
Tel: 44 20 74170113
Fax: 44 20 74170114
Email: admin@bps.ac.uk
Website: http://www.bps.ac.uk/BPS.html
Founded: 1931
Members: 2500
Staff: 11
Contact: Sarah-Jane Stagg, Exec.Sec.
Fee: £70
Description: Pharmacologists and clinical pharmacologists in academia and industry in 20 countries. Conducts educational symposia and lectures; makes available travel bursaries.
Publication: Journal
Publication title: British Journal of Clinical Pharmacology. Advertisements.
Second publication: Journal
Publication title: British Journal of Pharmacology. Advertisements.
Meetings/Conventions: - quarterly meeting

British Phonographic Industry

Riverside Bldg., County Hall, Westminster Bridge Rd., London, SE1 7JA, England, UK
Tel: 44 20 78031300
Fax: 44 20 78031310
Email: general@bpi.co.uk
Website: http://www.bpi.co.uk
Founded: 1973
Members: 231
Staff: 23
Contact: Andrew Yeates, Dir.Gen.
Description: Trade Association for British record companies. Acts as a focal point both for its members and for individuals and organizations dealing with the record industry. It promotes the interests of the industry both in Westminster and Brussels.
Library Subject: music
Library Type: by appointment only
Publication: Handbook
Publication title: Statistical Handbook

British Photodermatology Group
BPG

St. Thomas Hospital, London, SE1 7EH, England, UK
Tel: 44 20 79289292

British Photographic Imaging Association
BPIA

c/o Photo Imaging Council
Orbital House, 85 Croydon Rd., Caterham, Surrey, CR3 6PD, England, UK
Tel: 44 1883 334497
Fax: 44 1883 334490
Email: pic@admin.co.uk
Website: http://www.bpia.co.uk
Founded: 1952
Members: 25
Contact: Pamela Hyde
Description: Importers of photographic imaging and related goods. Furthers the interests of members and promotes the photographic and digital industry in the UK so as to increase the photographic market through initiatives such as PR campaigns, generic research and the funding of prizes.
Formerly: British Photographic Importers' Association
Meetings/Conventions: - quarterly meeting

British Photovoltaic Association
PV-UK

c/o Delphine Gadenne, The National Energy Centre, Davy Ave., Knowlhill, Milton Keynes, MK5 8NG, England, UK
Tel: 44 1908 442291
Fax: 44 8700 529193
Email: enquiries@pv-uk.org.uk
Website: http://www.pv-uk.org.uk
Founded: 1991
Members: 47
Contact: Delphine Gadenne, Admin.
Description: Actively promotes the use of photovoltaic within the UK as well as in other regions. Members are drawn from industry; universities and consulting practices and many are world leaders in the field.
Publication: Newsletter
Publication title: Britsol

British Phycological Society
BPS

c/o Dr. Jackie Parry
Division of Biological Sciences, Lancaster University, Lancaster, LA1 4YQ, England, UK
Tel: 44 1524 593489
Fax: 44 1524 843854
Email: j.parry@lancaster.ac.uk
Website: http://www.brphycsoc.org
Founded: 1952
Members: 580
Contact: Dr. Jackie Parry, Hon.Sec.
Fee: £10
Membership Type: full
Fee: £35
Membership Type: full with journal
Description: Scientists, students, and other interested persons organized to further phycology, the study of algae. Conducts conservation activities and field excursions. Assists in mapping the geographical distributions of seaweeds of the British Isles. Maintains a scientific meeting fund to enable students to attend Society meetings.
Publication: Journal
Publication title: European Journal of Phycology
Second publication: Newsletter
Publication title: The Phycologist
Meetings/Conventions: - annual conference - Exhibits.

British Pig Association

Scotsbridge House, Scots Hill, Rickmansworth, WD3 3BB, England, UK
Tel: 44 1923 695295
Fax: 44 1923 695347
Email: bpa@britishpigs.org
Website: http://www.britishpigs.org
Founded: 1884
Members: 650
Staff: 4
Contact: Mr. Marcus Bates, Ch.Exec.
Description: Participants in the pig industry - principally pedigree pig farmers, representative body for the pedigree pig industry. BPA operates the UK's longest established, proven Herd Book recording service.
Library Subject: pig breeding
Library Type: reference
Meetings/Conventions: - semiannual conference

British Plant Gall Society
BPGS

c/o Dr. C.K. Leach, Hon.Sec.
Department of Biological Sciences, De Montfort University, The Gateway, Leicester, LE1 9BH, England, UK
Tel: 44 1162 577122
Fax: 44 1162 577286
Email: bioted@dmu.ac.uk
Website: http://www.btinternet.com/~bpgs/Society.html
Founded: 1985
Members: 300
Contact: Dr. C.K. Leach, Hon.Sec.
Fee: £10
Description: Promotes the study and recording of plant galls; coordinates activities of cecidologists from various backgrounds and interests, ranging from molecular biology to ecology with particular reference to the British Isles.

Publication: Journal
Publication title: Cecidology
Second publication: Newsletter
Meetings/Conventions: Field meetings & workshops meeting

British Plastics Federation

6 Bath Pl., Rivington St., London, EC2A 3JE, England, UK
Tel: 44 207 4575000
Fax: 44 207 4575045
Email: imcilwee@bpf.co.uk
Website: http://www.bpf.co.uk
Founded: 1933
Members: 400
Staff: 24
Contact: Iain McIlwee, Bus.Svc.Mgr.
Description: Open to all UK companies with an involvement in the plastics sector, whether polymer, machinery or additive producers or plastics processors. Exists to promote the growth and profitability of the UK Plastics Industry. It encourages co-operation between manufacturers to ensure a co-ordinated industry response to common opportunities and challenges. Represents its members' interests to UK government and EC institutions. Information service 9061 908070.
Publication title: Codes of Practice on Health & Safety
Second publication: Reports

British Plumbing Fittings Manufacturers Association

10 Greenfield Crescent, Birmingham, B15 3AU, England, UK
Tel: 44 121 4563322
Fax: 44 121 4561394
Email: copperuk@compuserve.com
Founded: 1988
Members: 5
Contact: David Parker, Sec.
Description: Represents UK manufacturers of tube fittings made of copper or copper alloy materials for connecting pipes to convey water or gas.
Formerly: Copper Tube Fittings Manufacturers Association

British Polarological Research Society

6 Beechvale, Hillview Rd., Woking, GU22 7NS, England, UK
Founded: 1970
Members: 45
Staff: 3
Contact: Prof. W.J. Parker, Pres.
Description: Individual post-doctoral polarological-research fellows, pure and applied operational-polarology research scientists; Corporate organisations supporting BPRS research projects. Society for promotion of operational research studies into polarological-phenomena in all disciplines, and the development of super-polarological operational-research theory and sciences for forecasting, optimisation, problem-solving and decision-making in non-orthodox scenarios; promotion of research into biopolarological communication-sensing, transmission, and control phenomena for blind-deaf-mute students; polarological operational-problem solving and decision making in OR, management, medical and environmental sciences, including cardiac-motivation polaro-analysis, cardiac-mobility polarotherapy, and polarochronophoton-psychotherapy; fog-polarodispersal research for hospital-helipads, hospital-ship helipads, hospital air-ambulance landing-strips, and approach-roads; polarological prevention of cot-deaths from cardiac QT syndrome and from CO poisoning and CO_2 asphyxiation by re-entrant infiltration from gas-heater exhaust wall-vents.
Publication: Papers
Meetings/Conventions: - periodic conference

British Ports Association

Africa House, 64-78 Kingsway, London, WC2B 6AH, England, UK
Tel: 44 207 2421200
Fax: 44 207 4051069
Email: info@britishports.org.uk
Website: http://www.britishports.org.uk
Founded: 1992
Members: 86
Staff: 4
Contact: David Whitehead, Dir.

British Pottery Managers' Association

c/o School of Art and Design
Staffordshire University, College Rd., Stoke-On-Trent, ST4 2XN, England, UK
Tel: 44 1782 294477
Fax: 44 1782 294873
Founded: 1903
Members: 400
Staff: 8
Contact: Miss Bernice Kontic, Sec.
Description: Ceramics/Pottery manufacturers. Examines and contributes to the members' advantage any considerations with regard to improvements or developments in practical, technical, social, commercial, educational or legislative measures and will offer assistance to any other body or organisation on matters concerning the ceramic industry to this end.
Publication: Newsletter

British Poultry Council
BPC

Europoint House, 5-11 Lavington St., London, SE1 0NZ, England, UK
Tel: 44 207 2024760
Fax: 44 207 9286366
Email: bpc@poultry.uk.com
Website: http://www.poultry.uk.com
Founded: 1973
Description: Associations of poultry breeders, producers, processors, and distributors. Conducts parliamentary and legislative lobbying on issues of research and development, farm animal welfare, trading standards, and import regulation. Analyzes poultry industry statistics covering the United Kingdom, European, and world markets. Monitors poultry diseases that could disrupt the industry; commissions clinical research.
Formerly: British Poultry Meat Federation

British Precast Concrete Federation
BPCF

60 Charles St., Leicester, LE1 1FB, England, UK
Tel: 44 116 2536161
Fax: 44 116 2514568
Email: info@britishprecast.org
Website: http://www.britishprecast.org.uk
Founded: 1964
Members: 114
Staff: 8
Contact: D.J. Zanker, Sec.
Description: Manufacturers of precast concrete products in factories in the United Kingdom. Represents members' interests before government bodies and regulatory agencies. Acts as forum for the exchange of technical information. Sponsors tours.
Formerly: Formed by Merger of, Bristish Cast Concrete Federation
Publication: Newsletter

Publication title: Newsletter
Second publication: Directory
Publication title: Products Directory
Meetings/Conventions: - annual luncheon - Exhibits. London UK

British Printing Industries Federation
BPIF

Farringdon Pt., 29-35 Farringdon Rd., London, EC1M 3JF, England, UK
Tel: 44 870 2404085
Fax: 44 207 4057784
Email: info@britishprint.com
Website: http://www.britishprint.com
Founded: 1903
Members: 3000
Staff: 120
Contact: Michael Johnson, Exec. Officer
Description: Promotes and represents the interests of the printing, packaging, and graphic communications industry in the United Kingdom. Offers technical and legal consulting services. Sponsors competitions. Compiles statistics. Conducts seminars.
Publication: Newsletter
Publication title: Action
Publication title: Directions
Meetings/Conventions: - annual congress

British Professional Toastmasters' Authority
BPTA

12 Little Bornes, Dulwich, London, SE21 8SE, England, UK
Tel: 44 181 6705585
Fax: 44 181 6790055
Email: ivor@ivorspencer.com
Founded: 1997
Contact: Ivor Spencer, Pres.
Description: Represents the interests of professional public speakers in the United Kingdom. Promotes the art of public speaking.

British Property Federation

1 Warwick Row, 7th Fl., London, SW1E 5ER, England, UK
Tel: 44 207 8280111
Fax: 44 207 8343442
Email: info@bpf.org.uk
Website: http://www.bpf.org.uk
Founded: 1974
Members: 500
Staff: 13
Contact: Andrea Sinclair
Description: The trade association of the property industry, membership includes property development companies, property investment companies, banks, insurance companies, pension funds, residential landlords, multiple retailers and professional firms.

British Psychoanalytical Society
BP-AS

Byron House, 112A Shirland Rd., London, W9 2EQ, England, UK
Tel: 44 20 7563 5000
Fax: 44 20 7563 5001
Email: editors@psychoanalysis.org.uk
Website: http://www.ijpa.org
Founded: 1919
Members: 500

Staff: 16
Contact: Mr. M. Mercer, Hon.Sec.
Fee: £380
Membership Type: full
Fee: £190
Membership Type: associate 3, associate 0-3, retired, guest
Description: Psychoanalysts in the United Kingdom. Offers instructional programs. Promotes members' interests.
Library Subject: Psychoanalysis.
Library Type: open to the public
Publication: Journal
Publication title: International Journal of Psychoanalysis. Advertisements.
Second publication: Newsletter
Meetings/Conventions: English-Speaking Weekend Conference - biennial London UK

British Psychoanalytical Society

112a-114 Shirland Rd., London, W9 2EQ, England, UK
Tel: 44 20 75635000
Fax: 44 20 75635001
Website: http://www.psychoanalysis.org.uk
Founded: 1924
Description: Provides training to become a qualified psychoanalyst; conducts research; provides treatment.

British Psychological Society
BPS

St. Andrews House, 48 Princess Rd. E, Leicester, LE1 7DR, England, UK
Tel: 44 116 2549568
Fax: 44 116 2470787
Email: enquiry@bps.org.uk
Website: http://www.bps.org.uk
Founded: 1901
Members: 34600
Staff: 104
Contact: Barry Brooking, Chief Exec.
Fee: £70
Membership Type: general
Description: Academic, research, and all branches of applied psychology. Promotes the advancement of psychological study and works to ensure high standards of professional education and conduct. Offers courses.
Library Subject: Psychology
Library Type: reference
Publication: Journal
Publication title: British Journal of Clinical Psychology
Second publication: Journal
Publication title: British Journal of Developmental Psychology

British Pteridological Society

42 Crown Woods Way, Eltham, London, SE9 2NN, England, UK
Email: secretary@ebps.org.uk
Website: http://www.ebps.org.uk
Founded: 1891
Members: 800
Contact: Jennifer M. Ide, Hon.Gen.Sec.
Fee: £15
Membership Type: full
Fee: £9
Membership Type: student

Description: Amateur and professional pteridologists interested in all aspects of the botany, natural history and cultivation of ferns and fern allies. Promotes the growing, study and conservation of fern and fern allies, and encourages interest in their taxonomy, distribution and ecology.
Publication: Bulletin
Publication title: BPS Bulletin
Publication title: The Cultivation and Propagation of British Ferns
Meetings/Conventions: Fern Flora Worldwide: Threats and Responses symposium

British Pump Manufacturers Association
BPMA

McLaren Bldg., 35 Dale Rd., Birmingham, B4 7LM, England, UK
Tel: 44 121 2001299
Fax: 44 121 2001306
Email: enquiry@bpma.org.uk
Website: http://www.bpma.org.uk
Founded: 1941
Members: 60
Staff: 3
Contact: Sharon Walters, Admin.
Description: Trade association for manufacturers and suppliers of pumps in Great Britain. Promotes pump manufacturing industry. Encourages exchange of information between members.
Publication: Directory
Publication title: Buyers Guide to Pumps
Meetings/Conventions: International Pump Technical Conference - biennial

British Puppet and Model Theatre Guild

Little Holme, Church Ln., Thames Ditton, KT7 0NL, England, UK
Tel: 44 20 89978336
Fax: 44 20 89978236
Email: michael.j.dixon@btinternet.com
Website: http://www.puppetguild.org.uk
Founded: 1925
Members: 250
Contact: Judith Shutt, Sec.
Fee: £14
Description: Promotes puppetry and toy theatre.
Library Subject: puppetry
Library Type: not open to the public
Publication: Magazine
Publication title: The Puppetmaster
Second publication: Newsletter
Meetings/Conventions: - monthly workshop

British Pyrotechnists Association

1 Waterloo Way, Leicester, LE1 6LP, England, UK
Tel: 44 116 2566000
Fax: 44 116 2566050
Members: 28
Staff: 1
Contact: M.A. Chamberlain
Description: The British Pyrotechnists' Association is an umbrella organisation incorporating the Firework Makers' Guild. Collects and passes on to all firework manufacturers information concerning Government and other regulations etc; acts as a source of information to the industry and promotes the safe handling of fireworks in the UK.
Publication: Video
Publication title: Celebrate Safely
Publication title: Firework Fact Sheet

British Rabbit Council

Purefoy House, 7 Kirkgate, Newark, NG24 1AD, England, UK
Tel: 44 1636 676042
Fax: 44 1636 611683
Email: info@thebrc.org
Website: http://www.thebrc.org
Founded: 1934
Members: 5042
Staff: 2
Contact: Mrs. Jo Jalland
Description: Protects, furthers and co-ordinates the interests of all British rabbit breeders; assists and extends the exhibition of rabbits. Influences, advises and co-operates with central and local authorities, departments of education and other committees and schools in promoting the extension of the breeding of rabbits and to promote and encourage education and research of a scientific and/or practical nature.
Publication title: Breeds Standard. Advertisements.
Publication title: Rules & Articles
Meetings/Conventions: - annual - Exhibits.

British Record Society

c/o College of Arms
Queen Victoria St., London, EC4V 4BT, England, UK
Tel: 44 171 2369612
Email: britishrecordsociety@hotmail.com
Website: http://www.britishrecordsociety.org.uk
Founded: 1889
Contact: P.L. Dickinson
Description: Concerned with the publishing of indexes to historical records

British Recording Media Association

Ambassador House, Brigstock Rd., Thornton Heath, CR7 7JG, England, UK
Tel: 44 20 86655395
Fax: 44 20 86656447
Email: brma@admin.co.uk
Founded: 1971
Contact: Elaine Cole, Sec.
Description: Manufacturers of blank audio, videotape & recording media.
Formerly: British Tape Industry Association

British Records Association
BRA

c/o London Metropolitan Archives
40 Northampton Rd., London, EC1R 0HB, England, UK
Tel: 44 207 8330428
Fax: 44 207 8330416
Email: britrecassoc@hotmail.com
Website: http://www.hmc.gov.uk/bra
Founded: 1932
Members: 1000
Staff: 2
Contact: Elizabeth Hughes, Hon.Sec.
Fee: £25
Membership Type: individual
Fee: £55
Membership Type: institutional
Description: Individuals and institutions involved in the use and preservation of historical documents. Aims to further the study of history through maintenance of public and private archives. Acts to

rescue and preserve documents that might otherwise be destroyed. Generates public interest in matters pertaining to archive preservation. Facilitates access to historical archives for interested students, authors, and other researchers.
Publication: Journal
Publication title: Archives. Advertisements.
Publication title: Archives and the User
Meetings/Conventions: - annual conference

British Reflexology Association

Monks Orchard, Whitbourne, Worcester, WR6 5RB, England, UK
Tel: 44 1886 821207
Fax: 44 1886 822017
Email: bra@britreflex.co.uk
Website: http://www.britreflex.co.uk
Founded: 1985
Members: 750
Contact: Nicola Hall, Chm.
Fee: £40
Membership Type: ordinary, fellow, associate, or student
Description: Reflexology practitioners and students training to become reflexology practitioners. Representative body for persons practising the method of reflexology as a profession and for students training in the method. The official teaching body of the BRA is the Bayly School of Reflexology.
Publication: Newsletter
Publication title: Footprints. Advertisements.
Publication title: Register of Members
Meetings/Conventions: lecture

British Refractories and Industrial Ceramics Association

Federation House, Station Rd., Stoke-On-Trent, ST4 2SA, England, UK
Tel: 44 1782 744631
Fax: 44 1782 744102
Email: ragb@ceramfed.co.uk
Founded: 1918
Members: 25
Contact: A. McRae, Sec.
Description: British corporations making use of refractories in metal processing; suppliers to the refractories industry. Represents members' interests before government agencies and international regulatory bodies; works to insure that members adhere to environmental protection standards; develops industry standards. Maintains Joint Technical Forum for discussion of proposed European standards for the steel industry. Compiles statistics.
Formerly: Refractories Association of Great Britian
Publication: Brochure
Publication title: Refractories Association of Great Britain
Second publication: Annual Report
Publication title: Refractories Association of Great Britain Annual Report

British Refrigeration Association

c/o Federation of Environmental Trade Association
Henley Rd., Medmenham, Marlow, SL7 2ER, England, UK
Tel: 44 1491578674
Fax: 44 1491575024
Email: info@feta.co.uk
Website: http://www.feta.co.uk
Founded: 1940
Members: 120

Staff: 6
Contact: Howard Roberts
Description: Manufacturers, distributors, contractors and training organisations working in the refrigeration industry. Trade association representing manufacturers, contractors, wholesalers and distributors of refrigeration plant, equipment and components.

British Resilient Flooring Manufacturers Association

4 Queen Sq., Brighton, BN1 3FD, England, UK
Tel: 44 1273 727906
Fax: 44 1273 206217
Contact: R.J.M. Crawt
Description: Concerned only with vinyl and linoleum floorcoverings.

British Resorts Association

Crown Buildings, Eastbank St., Southport, PR8 1DL, England, UK
Tel: 44 151 9342286
Fax: 44 151 9342287
Email: bresorts@sefton.u-net.com
Website: http://www.britishresorts.co.uk
Founded: 1921
Members: 86
Staff: 3
Contact: Mr. P. Hampson, Dir.
Description: Members are local authorities and tourist boards with an interest in promoting the cause of tourism in the United Kingdom. Represents the interests of all United Kingdom inland and seaside resorts and tourist regions by discussion, representations and co-ordination of views and initiatives, whether at local, national or international level and to provide advice and information both to members and other organisations.
Publication: Magazine
Publication title: British Resorts Factpack. Advertisements.
Meetings/Conventions: The Changing Face of Britain's Biggest Industry - annual conference - Exhibits. Llandudno UK

British Retail Consortium
BRC

21 Dartmouth St., 2nd Fl., London, SW1H 9BP, England, UK
Tel: 44 78548900
Fax: 44 78548901
Email: info@brc.org.uk
Website: http://www.brc.org.uk
Founded: 1992
Staff: 40
Contact: Ann Graun
Description: Trade association representing 90 percent of the retail industry in the U.K.
Library Type: reference
Formerly: Formed by Merger of, Retail Consortium
Publication: Annual Report
Second publication: Bulletin

British Retinitis Pigmentosa Society

PO Box 350, Buckingham, MK18 1GZ, England, UK
Tel: 44 1280 860363
Fax: 44 1280 815900
Email: info@brps.org.uk
Website: http://www.brps.org.uk
Founded: 1976
Members: 3000

Staff: 3
Contact: Mrs. Lynda M. Cantor, Trustee/Hon.Sec.
Fee: £10
Description: RP sufferers and their families and interested multidisciplinary members. Aims to help RP sufferers and their families cope with living with RP and to raise money for medical research.
Publication: Handbook
Second publication: Newsletter
Meetings/Conventions: - annual general assembly

British Rig Owners' Association

Carthusian Ct., 12 Carthusian St., London, EC3M 6EZ, England, UK
Tel: 44 20 74172827
Fax: 44 20 76001534
Email: edmund.brookes@broa.org
Website: http://www.broa.org
Founded: 1983
Members: 7
Contact: E.J.N. Brookes, Mgr.
Description: Owners/managers of mobile offshore units. Aims to promote and protect the interests of British rig owners/managers in respect of all aspects of design, construction, equipment and operation of mobile offshore units.

British Road Federation

Pillar House, 194-202 Old Kent Rd., London, SE1 5TG, England, UK
Tel: 44 207 7039769
Fax: 44 207 7010029
Email: brf@brf.uk.com
Founded: 1932
Members: 108
Staff: 9
Contact: Richard Diment, Dir. & Chief Exec.
Description: Road users in industry and commerce, private and public transport. Aims to promote intelligent, balanced and comprehensive transport planning throughout the country and presses for an adequate network of national and local roads.
Library Subject: transport planning
Library Type: by appointment only
Publication: Journal
Publication title: Basic Road Statistics
Publication title: Briefing
Meetings/Conventions: - annual conference - Exhibits. Warwick UK

British Rubber Manufacturers' Association
BRMA

6 Bath Pl., Rivongton St., London, EC2A 3JE, England, UK
Tel: 44 207 4575040
Fax: 44 207 9729008
Email: mail@brma.co.uk
Website: http://www.brma.co.uk
Founded: 1968
Contact: David E.P. Owen, Pres.
Description: British manufacturers of rubber and polyurethane. Serves as a forum for exchange of information among members and between members and the public. Gathers and disseminates information on the production and uses of rubber and polyurethane; lobbies for members' interests before government bodies and international trade organizations. Formulates and implements policies to ensure the safety of rubber and polyurethane workers.
Library Type: not open to the public
Publication: Directory

Publication title: Rubber and Polyurethane
Publication title: Toxicity and Safe Handling of Rubber Chemicals
Meetings/Conventions: - annual meeting

British Safety Council

70 Chancellors Rd., London, W6 9RS, England, UK
Tel: 44 20 87411231
Fax: 44 20 87414555
Email: mail@britsafe.org
Website: http://www.britishsafetycouncil.org
Founded: 1957
Members: 10000
Staff: 135
Contact: David Ballard, Dir.Gen.
Description: Aims to promote health, safety and environmental best practice for the benefit of society and the increase of productivity.
Publication: Booklets
Publication title: British Safety Council Guides
Second publication: Newsletter
Publication title: Health & Safety at Work Act Newsletter

British Sandwich Association

8 Home Farm, Ardington, Wantage, OX12 8PN, England, UK
Tel: 44 1235 821820
Fax: 44 1235 862200
Email: admin@sandwich.org.uk
Website: http://www.sandwich.org.uk
Founded: 1990
Members: 1280
Staff: 6
Contact: Les Jenkins
Description: Membership is made up of suppliers to the sandwich industry (meat/ cheese/ salad/ mayonnaise/ bread/ packaging/ refrig./ distrib. etc.), sandwich manufacturers, and sandwich bars/retail buyers. Represents all in the UK sandwich industry, promoting sandwich consumption as well as quality standards. Has developed its own Code of Practice for the industry which has the approval of the Institution of Environmental Health Officers and many retailers.
Publication: Magazine
Publication title: Sandwich and Snack News. Advertisements.
Meetings/Conventions: Food on the Move - periodic conference - Exhibits.

British Science Fiction Association

1 Long Row Close, Everdon, Daventry, NN11 3BE, England, UK
Tel: 44 1327 361661
Email: bsfa@enterprise.net
Website: http://www.bsfa.co.uk
Founded: 1958
Members: 700
Contact: Elizabeth Billinger, Ch.
Fee: £21
Membership Type: in United Kingdom
Fee: £26
Membership Type: world surface
Description: Promotes and encourages the reading, writing and publishing of science fiction, and provides a forum where SF fans, authors, publishers and critics can maintain contact and exchange ideas. Other services include writers' postal workshops and information service.
Publication: Magazine
Publication title: Focus. Advertisements.
Second publication: Newsletter
Publication title: Matrix

British Screen Advisory Council

13 Manette St., London, W1M 9AB, England, UK
Tel: 44 207 2891111
Fax: 44 207 2871123
Email: bsac@bsacouncil.co.uk
Founded: 1985
Members: 60
Staff: 4
Contact: Fiona Clarke-Hackston, Dir.
Description: Senior management of the audio visual industries invited on an individual basis for their expertise. Representing organisations and individuals within audio-visual industries in the UK. A unique forum advising national and European government and the industry itself on policy matters.
Publication: Reports
Second publication: Annual Report

British Secondary Metals Association

21 Sandford St., Lichfield, WS13 6QA, England, UK
Tel: 44 1543 255450
Fax: 44 1543 255325
Email: kaybsma@aol.com
Website: http://www.bsma.org.uk
Founded: 1941
Members: 300
Staff: 2
Contact: Mr. T.D. Wemyss, Exec.Dir.
Description: Trade association for non-ferrous metal merchants and traders.
Publication: Bulletin
Publication title: BSMA Bulletin

British Security Industry Association
BSIA

Security House, Barbourne Rd., Worcester, WR1 1RS, England, UK
Tel: 44 1905 21464
Fax: 44 1905 613625
Email: info@bsia.co.uk
Website: http://www.bsia.co.uk
Founded: 1967
Members: 400
Staff: 22
Contact: David Dickinson, Chief Exec.
Description: Trade association for manufacturers and suppliers of security products and services in Great Britain, including safes, alarms, guard and patrol services access control, closed circuit television, information destruction, and physical security.
Library Type: by appointment only
Publication: Membership Directory
Publication title: Security Direct. Advertisements.
Second publication: Newsletter
Publication title: Spectrum
Meetings/Conventions: - annual general assembly

British Sheep Dairying Association

c/o BSDA Secretary
The Sheep Centre, Malvern, WR13 6PH, England, UK
Tel: 44 168 4892661
Fax: 44 168 4892663
Email: bsda@btopenworld.com
Website: http://www.sheepdairying.com
Founded: 1983
Members: 150

Staff: 1
Contact: Sheila Spence, Chm.
Fee: £50
Membership Type: full, plus VAT
Fee: £20
Membership Type: associate, plus VAT
Description: Individuals and companies with an interest in sheep dairying. Promotes sheep dairying in the UK and worldwide.
Library Subject: dairy sheep, sheep milk products, and related subjects
Library Type: not open to the public
Publication: Journal
Publication title: Sheep Dairy News. Advertisements.
Meetings/Conventions: - annual conference - Exhibits.

British Shippers' Council

c/o Freight Transport Association
Hermes House, Saint John's Rd., Tunbridge Wells, TN4 9UZ, England, UK
Tel: 44 1892 552260
Fax: 44 1892 552328
Email: njohnson@fta.co.uk
Website: http://www.europeanshippers.com/public/councils/britain.htm
Contact: Dr. Andrew Trail
Description: UK import and export companies. Represents the interests of British importers and exporters in relation to the movement of their goods to and from overseas.
Publication: Newsletter
Publication title: Shippers Monthly Newsletter

British Shops and Stores Association

Middleton House, 2 Main Rd., Middleton Cheney, Banbury, OX17 2TN, England, UK
Tel: 44 1295 712277
Fax: 44 1295 711665
Email: info@bssa.co.uk
Website: http://www.british-shops.co.uk
Founded: 1990
Members: 3800
Staff: 32
Contact: John Dean, Chief Exec.
Description: Non-food retailers. Represents non-food retailers nationwide with specific sectors covering fashions and fabrics, men's and boys' wear, and furnishings. Services include clearing house, insurance, training, general advisory services and regular bulletins.
Publication title: Retail Review

British Sign and Graphics Association
BSGA

5 Orton Enterprise Centre, Bakewell Rd., Orton Southgate, Peterborough, PE2 6XU, England, UK
Tel: 44 1733 230033
Fax: 44 1733 230993
Email: bsa@sign.u-net.com
Website: http://www.bsga.co.uk
Founded: 1929
Members: 230
Staff: 3
Contact: Peter W. Tipton
Description: Any company or firm engaged in manufacturing illuminated or non-illuminated advertising signs, any company or firm who supplies raw materials, components, equipment or services to

the signmaking industry, or, any college or educational establishment. which provides training or qualification courses for the sign industry. To promote, develop, consolidate and protect the interests of sign manufacturers or suppliers to the industry. To promote a high standard of quality, design, workmanship and good commercial practice within the sign industry.
Formerly: British Sign Association
Publication: Magazine
Publication title: Sign Directions. Advertisements.
Meetings/Conventions: - periodic trade show - Exhibits.

British Small Animal Veterinary Association
BSAVA

Woodrow House, 1 Telford Way, Waterwells Business Pk., Quedgeley, Gloucester, GL2 4AB, England, UK
Tel: 44 1452 726700
Fax: 44 1452 726701
Email: adminoff@bsava.com
Website: http://www.bsava.com
Founded: 1957
Members: 5500
Staff: 16
Contact: Alison J. Phipps
Description: Veterinarians in 20 countries. Operates speakers' bureau; sponsors educational programs. Compiles statistics. Sponsors competitions; conducts charitable activities.
Library Type: reference
Publication: Handbook
Publication title: BSAVA Handbook
Second publication: Newsletter
Publication title: BSAVA News
Meetings/Conventions: - periodic regional meeting

British Society for Agricultural Labour Science
BSALS

Earley Gate, Reading, RG6 2AT, England, UK
Tel: 44 1734 85123
Founded: 1969

British Society for Allergy and Clinical Immunology
BSACI

66 Weston Park, Thames Ditton, K17 0HL, England, UK
Tel: 44 20 83989240
Fax: 44 20 83982766
Email: sduff@compuserve.com
Founded: 1948

British Society for Antimicrobial Chemotherapy
BSAC

11 The Wharf, 16 Bridge St., Birmingham, B1 2JS, England, UK
Tel: 44 121 6330410
Fax: 44 121 6439497
Email: enquiries@bsac.org.uk
Website: http://www.bsac.org.uk
Founded: 1971
Members: 770
Staff: 6
Contact: Tracey Guest, Exec. Officer
Description: Individuals in 33 countries working in the field of antimicrobial chemotherapy. Furthers research and understanding of chemotherapy.

Publication: Journal
Publication title: Journal of Antimicrobial Chemotherapy. Advertisements.
Meetings/Conventions: BSAC Scientific Meeting - annual meeting

British Society for Cell Biology
BSCB

c/o Dept. of Physiological Science
Medical School, University of Newcastle upon Tyne, Newcastle upon Tyne, NE2 4HH, England, UK
Tel: 44 191 2226953
Fax: 44 191 2226706
Email: physiology@ncl.ac.uk
Founded: 1959
Description: Promotes cell biology through scientific meetings and encourages understanding through public discussion of cell biology aims and achievements.

British Society for Clinical Cytology
BSCC

PO Box 352, Oxbridge, OB10 9TX, England, UK
Tel: 44 1895 274080
Founded: 1962

British Society for Clinical Neurophysiology

Dept. of Clinical Neurophysiology, Middlesex Hospital, Mortimer St., London, W1N 8AA, England, UK
Email: secretariat@bscn.org.uk
Website: http://www.bscn.org.uk
Founded: 1942
Members: 350
Contact: Dr. Alan Forster
Description: Medical practitioners, scientists and technologists. Medical and scientific study of electrical activity which can be recorded from the nervous system.
Formerly: EEG Society
Publication: Papers
Meetings/Conventions: - periodic conference

British Society for Dental and Maxillofacial Radiology

Department of Dental Radiology, University of British Dental School & Hospital, Lower Mardlen St., Bristol, BS1 2LY, England, UK
Tel: 44 113 2336209
Fax: 44 113 2336165
Email: jane.luker@nbht.swcst.nhi.uk
Website: http://www.bsdmfr.org.uk
Members: 150
Contact: Dr. Jane Luker, Hon.Sec.
Fee: £30
Description: Dental radiologists. Offers educational and public service programs. Conducts research.
Publication: Newsletter
Meetings/Conventions: - annual conference

British Society for Dental Research
BSDR

c/o Prof. Angus Walls, Sec.
The Dental School, Framington Pl., Newcastle Upon Tyne, NE2 4BW, England, UK
Tel: 44 191 2227823
Fax: 44 191 2228191
Email: a.w.g.walls@newcastle.ac.uk
Website: http://www.bsdr.org.uk
Contact: Prof. Colin Robinson, Pres.
Description: Individuals engaged in all aspects of dental research. Seeks to advance research and increase knowledge for the improvement of oral health worldwide. Provides support and assistance to the oral health research community; facilitates dissemination of new research findings. Conducts continuing professional development programs for members. Works closely with international public health and dental organizations.

British Society for Developmental Biology
BSDB

c/o Dr. Ivor J. Mason
MRC Brain Development Programme, Department of Developmental Neurobiology, Guy's Campus, King's College London, London, SE1 9RT, England, UK
Website: http://www.ana.ed.ac.uk/BSDB/
Contact: Dr. Ivor J. Mason, Sec.
Fee: £20
Membership Type: ordinary
Fee: £8
Membership Type: student
Description: Represents and promotes developmental biologists in the United Kingdom.
Publication: Newsletter
Meetings/Conventions: meeting

British Society for Developmental Disabilities

5 Handsworth Dr., Great Barr, Birmingham, B43 6ED, England, UK
Tel: 44 121 3602027
Fax: 44 121 3602027
Founded: 1954
Members: 24
Contact: J.G. Csucsmi, Hon. Admin.
Description: Multi-disciplinary professionals (4 trustees) concerned with the care and training of people with learning or developmental disabilities. Strives to provide relief to those with developmental disabilities, formally known as subnormal people. Works to advance public knowledge of developmental disabilities by means of publications, conferences and symposia.
Publication: Journal
Publication title: The British Journal of Developmental Disabilities. Advertisements.
Second publication: Monographs
Publication title: Despite Mental Handicap

British Society for Eighteenth Century Studies
BSECS

Burnaby Rd., Portsmouth, PO1 3AS, England, UK
Tel: 44 23 92876543
Fax: 44 23 92842174
Email: mark.Ledbury@port.ac.uk
Founded: 1971

British Society for Electronic Music
BSEM

49 Deodar Rd., London, SW15, England, UK
Tel: 44 20 88742363
Founded: 1969

British Society for Haematology

2 Carlton House Terr., London, SW1Y 5AF, England, UK
Tel: 44 208 6437305
Fax: 44 208 7700933
Email: janice@bshhya.demon.co.uk
Website: http://www.blackwell-science.com/uk/society/bsh/
Founded: 1960
Members: 1251
Staff: 1
Contact: Mrs. Janice O'Donnell, Admin.
Fee: £120
Membership Type: ordinary
Fee: £150
Membership Type: ordinary overseas
Description: Committed to advancing the practice and study of haematology; promotes good haematological practice and communication.
Publication: Journal
Publication title: British Journal of Haematology. Advertisements.
Second publication: Bulletins
Publication title: BSH Bulletins
Meetings/Conventions: - annual meeting - Exhibits.

British Society for Human Genetics
BSHG

Edgbaston, Birmingham, B15 2TG, England, UK
Tel: 44 121 6272634
Fax: 44 121 6272634
Email: bshg@bshg.org.uk
Website: http://www.bshg.org.uk
Founded: 1996
Description: Aims to advance the science of human genetics, to promote research and public awareness of human genetics related to health and disease, to guide professionals contributing to genetics in healthcare and to offer informed opinion on issues of public interest.

British Society for Immunology

Triangle House, Broomhill Rd., London, SW18 4HX, England, UK
Tel: 44 208 8752400
Fax: 44 181 8752424
Email: bsi@immunology.org
Website: http://immunology.org
Founded: 1956
Members: 4000
Staff: 16
Contact: Marcus Stephan, CEO
Fee: £50
Membership Type: ordinary
Fee: £15
Membership Type: concessionary
Description: Immunologists. To advance the science of immunology for the benefit of the public.
Publication: Journal
Publication title: Clinical & Experimental Immunology. Advertisements.
Second publication: Journal

Publication title: Immunology
Meetings/Conventions: Congress of Immunology - annual conference - Exhibits.

British Society for Medical Mycology
BSMM

Mycology Reference Centre, Department of Microbiology, Leeds General Infirmary, Leeds, LS1 3EX, England, UK
Tel: 44 113 3923390
Fax: 44 113 3435640
Email: h.r.ashbee@leeds.ac.uk
Website: http://www.bsmm.org
Founded: 1965
Members: 250
Contact: Dr. H.R. Ashbee, Hon.Sec.
Fee: £10
Publication: Newsletter

British Society for Middle Eastern Studies
BRISMES

Institute for Middle Eastern and Islamic Studies, University of Durham, Elvet Hill Rd., Durham, DH1 3TU, England, UK
Tel: 44 191 3345179
Fax: 44 191 3345661
Email: a.l.haysey@durham.ac.uk
Website: http://www.dur.ac.uk/brismes/
Founded: 1973
Contact: Dr. Noel Brehony, Pres.
Description: Teachers, researchers, students, diplomats, journalists, and other individuals with an interest in the Middle East. Promotes increased interest in Middle Eastern studies.
Publication: Newsletter
Publication title: BRISMES Newsletter
Second publication: Journal
Publication title: British Journal of Middle Eastern Studies
Meetings/Conventions: - periodic conference

British Society for Music Therapy

25 Rosslyn Ave., East Barnet, Barnet, EN4 8DH, England, UK
Tel: 44 208 3688879
Fax: 44 208 3688879
Email: denizeassistantbsmt.demon.co.uk
Website: http://www.bsmt.org
Founded: 1958
Members: 800
Staff: 1
Contact: Mrs. Denize Christophers
Fee: £40
Membership Type: individual
Fee: £25
Membership Type: student
Description: Open to all interested in music therapy. Promotes the use and development of music therapy in treatment, and rehabilitation of children and adults suffering from emotional, physical or mental handicap. Holds meetings and conferences.
Library Subject: music therapy
Library Type: not open to the public
Publication: Journal
Publication title: British Journal of Music Therapy. Advertisements.
Publication title: BSMT Bulletin
Meetings/Conventions: Children Need Music and Children with Special Needs conference - Exhibits.

British Society for Parasitology
BSP

c/o Dr. Geoff Hide
School of Environment and Life Sciences, Peel Bldg., University of Salford, Salford, M5 4WT, England, UK
Tel: 44 61 2953371
Fax: 44 61 2955210
Email: bsp@parasitology.org.uk
Website: http://www.parasitology.org.uk
Founded: 1962
Members: 1300
Contact: Dr. G. Hide, Hon.Comms.Sec.
Fee: £30
Description: Parasitologists employed in government agencies, pharmaceutical companies, research laboratories, and universities; students of parasitology. Promotes the study of parasitology and provides a forum for the exchange of ideas and experiences. Disseminates information on advances in the field.
Publication: Book
Publication title: Autumn Symposium
Second publication: Newsletter
Publication title: BSP Newsletter
Meetings/Conventions: Malaria Meeting - annual conference - Exhibits.

British Society for Plant Pathology
BSPP

Marlborough House, Basingstoke Rd., Spencers Wood, Reading, RG7 1AG, England, UK
Tel: 44 1707 284539
Fax: 44 1707 285258
Email: secretary@bspp.org.uk
Website: http://www.bspp.org.uk
Founded: 1981
Members: 800
Contact: Dr. Avice M. Hall, Sec.
Description: Individuals with an interest in any aspect of plant pathology. Promotes the study and advancement of plant pathology. Serves as a clearinghouse on plant pathology; encourages interaction and cooperation among members.
Publication: Newsletter
Publication title: BSPP Newsletter
Second publication: Journal
Publication title: Molecular Plant Pathology
Meetings/Conventions: BSPP Presidential Conference - annual conference

British Society for Restorative Dentistry
BSRD

Turner Dental School, University Dental Hospital Manchester, Manchester, M15 6FH, England, UK
Tel: 44 161 2756797
Fax: 44 161 2756797
Email: ann.shearer@man.ac.uk
Founded: 1968

British Society for Rheumatology

41 Eagle St., London, WC1R 4TL, England, UK
Tel: 44 207 2423313
Fax: 44 207 2423277
Email: bsr@rheumatology.org.uk
Website: http://www.rheumatology.org.uk

Founded: 1984
Members: 1500
Staff: 10
Contact: Ms. Samantha Peters, Chief Exec.
Fee: £150
Membership Type: ordinary
Fee: £60
Membership Type: retired
Description: Hospital doctors, non-clinical scientists, general practitioners, other professions allied to medicine. Promotes the treatment and prevention of rheumatic diseases, education and research.
Library Subject: rheumatology
Library Type: not open to the public
Publication: Journal
Publication title: Rheumatology. Advertisements.
Meetings/Conventions: - annual general assembly - Exhibits.

British Society for Strain Measurement

c/o Sally Cryer
16 Sweetlands Corner, Kents Hill, Milton Keynes, MK7 6DR, England, UK
Tel: 44 1908 559147
Fax: 44 1908 559147
Email: sallybssm@mac.com
Website: http://www.bssm.org
Founded: 1964
Members: 150
Staff: 2
Contact: Sally Cryer
Fee: £15
Membership Type: individual or corporate
Description: International organization that seeks to advance the knowledge of strain measurement, stress analysis and associated technologies. Provides a forum for the exchange of information between practising engineers and technicians. Promotes quality engineering design, and safety and reliability through properly conducted measurement, testing and analysis. Arranges conferences, national and regional meetings, and courses on all relevant topics. Validates engineers and technicians working in the stress and strain measurement fields.
Publication: Journal
Publication title: Strain. Advertisements.
Meetings/Conventions: - bimonthly conference

British Society for Surgery of the Hand

The Royal College of Surgeons of England, 34-43 Lincoln's Inn Fields, London, WC2A 3PE, England, UK
Tel: 44 20 78315162
Fax: 44 20 78314041
Email: secretariat@bssh.ac.uk
Website: http://www.bssh.ac.uk
Founded: 1970
Members: 653
Staff: 5
Contact: Mr. J.J. Dias, Hon.Sec.
Fee: £180
Membership Type: full
Fee: £110
Membership Type: overseas
Description: The membership is drawn from the two major parent specialties of orthopedic and plastic surgery; all members share an interest in the hand. To promote and direct the development of hand surgery and to foster and co-ordinate education, study and research in hand surgery including the dissemination and diffusion of knowledge of hand surgery among members of the Society and the medical profession.
Publication: Journal
Publication title: Journal of Hand Surgery
Meetings/Conventions: Scientific Meeting - annual conference - Exhibits. London UK

British Society for the History of Mathematics BSHM

20 Dunvegan Close, Exeter, EX4 4AF, England, UK
Email: mgc@dcs.warwick.ac.uk
Founded: 1971
Contact: Terry Darby, Adm.
Description: Researchers, educators, students, and other individuals with an interest in the history of mathematics. Promotes historical study of mathematics; seeks to further the use of history in the teaching of mathematics. Gathers and disseminates information on mathematics history, education, and research. Facilitates communication and cooperation among members. Conducts study tours of museum and library collections.
Publication: Newsletter
Meetings/Conventions: Christmas Meeting - annual seminar

British Society for the History of Medicine

Centre for the History of Medicine, University of Birmingham, Birmingham, B15 2TT, England, UK
Tel: 44 121 4146804
Fax: 44 121 4144036
Email: r.g.arnott@bham.ac.uk
Website: http://medweb.bham.ac.uk/histmed/bhsmindex.html
Founded: 1965
Contact: Mr. R. G. Arnott, Sec.
Description: Promotes meetings on the subject of the History of Medicine on a national scale and represents Britain in the affairs of the International Society for the History of Medicine.
Publication: Newsletter
Publication title: BHSM News. Advertisements.
Meetings/Conventions: - semiannual congress - Exhibits.

British Society for the History of Pharmacy BSHP

840 Melton Rd., Thurmaston, Leicester, LE4 88N, England, UK
Tel: 44 131 5564386
Fax: 44 131 5588850
Email: 101561.@compuserve.com
Website: http://www.bshp.org.uk
Founded: 1967

British Society for the History of Science

31 High St., Stanford in the Vale, Faringdon, Oxon, SN7 8LH, England, UK
Tel: 44 1367 718963
Fax: 44 1367 718963
Email: bshs@hidex.demon.co.uk
Website: http://www.bshs.org.uk
Founded: 1947
Members: 800
Contact: G. Bennett, Exec.Sec.
Fee: £33
Membership Type: UK and Europe
Fee: £41

Membership Type: rest of world
Description: Aims to promote and further the study of the history and philosophy of science.
Publication: Journal
Publication title: British Journal for the History of Science. Advertisements.
Second publication: Monograph
Publication title: Monograph Series

British Society of Audiology

80 Brighton Rd., Reading, RG6 1PS, England, UK
Tel: 44 118 9660622
Fax: 44 118 9351915
Email: ann@b-s-a.demon.co.uk
Website: http://www.b-s-a.demon.co.uk
Founded: 1968
Members: 1400
Staff: 3
Contact: Mrs. Ann Allen, Admin.Sec.
Fee: £43
Membership Type: full
Description: Anyone with an interest in audiology. To promote the science of audiology (i.e. the study of hearing and balance) and the diagnosis, alleviation and prevention of hearing and balance impairment. The advancement of education in audiology and the furtherance of research in audiology and the publication of the results of such research.
Publication: Magazine
Publication title: BSA News. Advertisements.
Second publication: Journal
Publication title: International Journal of Audiology
Meetings/Conventions: - annual conference

British Society of Baking

3 Upper Terr., Blockley, Moreton-in-Marsh, GL56 9BH, England, UK
Tel: 44 1386 700626
Fax: 44 1386 700626
Email: lsy@baketran.demon.co.uk
Website: http://www.bsb.org.uk
Founded: 1955
Members: 350
Contact: Linda Young, Sec.
Fee: £49
Description: Retail bakers, small craft bakers, independent group plant bakers, supermarket groups, research organizations, flour millers, ingredient and equipment suppliers. Provides a forum for learning more about the baking industry through conferences and associated events.
Library Type: not open to the public
Publication: Proceedings
Meetings/Conventions: - semiannual conference

British Society of Cinematographers

PO Box 2587, Gerrards Cross, SL9 7WZ, England, UK
Tel: 44 1753 888052
Fax: 44 1753 891486
Email: britcinematographers@compuserve.com
Website: http://www.bscine.com
Founded: 1949
Members: 290
Staff: 1
Contact: Mrs. Frances Russell
Description: Directors of photography working in motion pictures. Promotes and encourages the pursuit of the highest standards in the craft of motion picture photography. Aims to further the application by others of high standards and to encourage original and outstanding work. It also provides facilities for social intercourse between the members and arranges lectures, debates and meetings.
Publication: Directory
Publication title: BSC Directory

British Society of Criminology

The Law Department, Rm. A1024a, University of East London, Longbridge Rd., Dagenham, RM8 2AS, England, UK
Tel: 44 20 82232902
Fax: 44 1621 868219
Email: crimsoc@aol.com
Website: http://www.britsoccrim.org/
Contact: Paul Kiff
Description: Works to advance the interests and knowledge of persons engaged in teaching, research and public education about crime, criminal behavior, and the criminal justice system in the United Kingdom.

British Society of Dowsers

Hastingleigh, Ashford, TN25 5HW, England, UK
Tel: 44 1233 750253
Fax: 44 1233 750253
Email: secretary@britishdowsers.org
Website: http://www.britishdowsers.org/
Founded: 1933
Members: 1450
Staff: 2
Contact: Deidre Rust
Description: Anyone who is interested in dowsing. The scientific principles of dowsing including the knowledge of its application to the search for subterranean watercourses, cavities, tunnels, ores and other entities.
Library Subject: dowsing
Library Type: open to the public
Publication: Journal
Publication title: Dowsing Today. Advertisements.
Meetings/Conventions: - annual conference

British Society of Enamellers

Sainthill, Kingsland Rd., Shrewsbury, SY3 7AF, England, UK
Tel: 44 1743 235458
Email: maureen.carswell@which.net
Website: http://www.enamellers.org
Founded: 1984
Members: 80
Contact: Ian Robertson, Chmn.
Fee: £46
Membership Type: full
Fee: £25
Membership Type: associate
Description: Promotes the interests of professional enamellers.
Library Subject: enamel historical, members work
Library Type: reference
Publication: Newsletter

British Society of Experimental and Clinical Hypnosis

c/o Phyllis A. Alden, Hon.Sec.
Psychology Consultancy, District General Hospital, Scartho Rd., Grimsby, DN33 2BA, England, UK
Tel: 44 1472 873423
Fax: 44 1472 879238
Email: honsec@bsech.demon.co.uk
Website: http://www.alden-residence.demon.co.uk
Founded: 1977
Members: 300
Contact: Mrs. P. Alden, Hon.Sec.
Fee: £40
Membership Type: ordinary
Description: Medical doctors, dentists, psychologists, other health service personnel. A learned society for doctors, dentists, psychologists and other health care professionals interested in theory, research and therapeutic applications of hypnosis. It organizes meetings, training events and an annual conference.
Publication: Journal
Publication title: Contemporary Hypnosis
Meetings/Conventions: - annual conference

British Society of Flavourists
BSF

1 Brentwood Close, Brentwood, CM14 4PU, England, UK
Tel: 44 1440 704488
Website: http://www.bsf.org.uk
Founded: 1971

British Society of Gastroenterology

3 St Andrews Pl., London, NW1 4LB, England, UK
Tel: 44 20 73873534
Fax: 44 20 74873734
Email: bsg@mailbox.ulcc.ac.uk
Website: http://www.bsg.org.uk
Founded: 1937
Members: 2500
Staff: 3
Contact: Miss Di Tolfree
Fee: £100
Membership Type: full and international
Description: Physicians and surgeons with a special interest in gastroenterology. Associate nurse/clinical members. Concerned with the advancement of gastroenterology and the promotion of friendship amongst those who have a special interest in the subject.
Publication title: Gut
Meetings/Conventions: - annual meeting Glasgow UK

British Society of Gynaecological Endoscopy
BSGE

Duckworth Lane, Bradford, BD9 6RJ, England, UK
Tel: 44 1274 364618
Fax: 44 1274 366690
Founded: 1989

British Society of Hearing Aid Audiologists

9 Lukins Dr., Great Dunmow, Essex, CM6 1XQ, England, UK
Tel: 44 1371 876623
Fax: 44 1371 876623
Email: secretary@bshaa.com
Website: http://www.bshaa.com

Founded: 1957
Members: 700
Contact: Mrs. J. Humphreys
Fee: £95
Membership Type: qualified/fellow
Description: Educational and trade association for private hearing aid dispensers. Promotion of ethical standards through training, examination and codes of practice.
Formerly: BSHAA
Publication: Newsletter
Publication title: BSHAA News. Advertisements.
Meetings/Conventions: - annual conference

British Society of Hypnotherapists

37 Orbain Rd., London, SW6 7JZ, England, UK
Tel: 44 207 73851166
Fax: 44 207 73851166
Email: sy@bsh1950.fsnet.co.uk
Website: http://www.bsh1950.fsnet.co.uk
Founded: 1950
Members: 20
Staff: 1
Contact: S. Young, Hon.Sec.
Description: Specialising in the treatment of nervous disorders and addictions. Provides information service for public; conducts research on behalf of members and distributes information to them.

British Society of Master Glass Painters

c/o Ruth Cooke
PO Box 167, Ilkley, LS29 8WD, England, UK
Tel: 44 1943 602521
Fax: 44 1943 602521
Website: http://www.bsmgp.org.uk
Founded: 1921
Members: 500
Contact: Ruth Cooke, Hon. Sec.
Fee: £30
Membership Type: in the UK
Fee: £35
Membership Type: overseas
Description: Predominantly those active in the design, creation and conservation/restoration of stained glass and leaded lights. Those with a general interest in the history of stained glass and an appreciation of contemporary work are also welcomed. Represents the stained glass profession in Britain. It serves to promote professional standards and through its accreditation scheme, offers a validation of skills and expertise in conservation and restoration. Its journal is the only academic publication of its kind.
Library Subject: stained glass history and techniques
Library Type: open to the public
Publication: Journal
Publication title: The Journal of Stained Glass. Advertisements.
Second publication: Newsletter
Publication title: Stained Glass

British Society of Medical and Dental Hypnosis

The National Secretary, 28 Dale Park Gardens, Leeds, LS16 7PT, England, UK
Tel: 44 7000 560309
Fax: 44 7000 560309
Email: secretary@bsmdh.org
Website: http://www.bsmdh.com
Founded: 1952
Members: 369

Staff: 1
Contact: Angela Morris, Sec.
Fee: £65
Description: Qualified doctors, dentists and other registered health professionals Promotes the study and training in the principles and practice of hypnosis. It encourages research and publication of work relating to hypnosis.
Library Type: not open to the public
Formerly: British Society of Dental Hypnosis
Publication: Journal
Second publication: Newsletter
Meetings/Conventions: - annual conference

British Society of Painters in Oils, Pastels and Acrylics

41 Lister St., Riverside Gardens, Ilkley, LS29 9ET, England, UK
Tel: 44 1943 609075
Fax: 44 1943 603753
Founded: 1987
Members: 62
Contact: Margaret Simpson, Dir.
Description: Membership on merit-restricted by selection. Promotes all that is best in traditional values, allowing artists in any media to compete unrestricted in open exhibition - showing their works alongside those of the Fellows and Members - with the opportunity of being selected for Membership. Exhibitions biannually.
Publication: Catalog

British Society of Periodontology

44 Pool Rd., Hartley Wintney, Hook, RG27 8RD, England, UK
Tel: 44 1252 843598
Fax: 44 1252 844018
Email: bspadmin@btinternet.com
Website: http://www.bsperio.org
Founded: 1949
Members: 800
Contact: Mrs. A.S. Hallowes, Sec.
Description: Members are dental surgeons. To promote for the benefit of the public the art and science of dentistry and in particular the art and science of periodontology.
Publication: Journal
Publication title: Journal of Clinical Periodontology

British Society of Plant Breeders

Woolpack Chambers, 16 Market St., Ely, CB7 4ND, England, UK
Tel: 44 1353 653200
Fax: 44 1353 661156
Email: enquiries@bspb.co.uk
Website: http://www.bspb.co.uk
Members: 50
Staff: 15
Contact: Dr. P. Maplestone
Description: Represents members' interests; licenses and collects royalties on production of protected crop varieties.

British Society of Rehabilitation Medicine BSRM

11 St. Andrews Place, London, NW1 4LE, England, UK
Tel: 44 1992 638865
Fax: 44 1992 638905
Email: admin@bsrm.co.uk
Website: http://www.bsrm.co.uk
Founded: 1984

British Society of Scientific Glassblowers

8 Tanners Way, South Woodham Ferrers, Chelmsford, CM3 5PU, England, UK
Tel: 44 1954 785366
Email: paul@musgreaves.freeserve.co.uk
Website: http://www.bssg.co.uk
Founded: 1964
Members: 250
Contact: Chris Pittock, Sec.
Fee: £15
Description: Those engaged in scientific glassblowing and associated professions. Aims to uphold and further the status of scientific glassblowers; holds meetings, presents papers and encourages and promotes higher standards of skill and technical knowledge.
Library Type: not open to the public
Publication: Journal
Publication title: Journal of the British Society of Scientific Glassblowers. Advertisements.
Meetings/Conventions: - annual symposium - Exhibits.

British Society of Sports History

c/o University of Manchester
Institute of Science and Technology, Dinglebarn, Bradley, Frodsham, WA6 7EP, England, UK
Tel: 44 1928 733283
Email: r.cox@umist.ac.uk
Website: http://www.umist.ac.uk/sport/bssh.html
Founded: 1982
Members: 250
Contact: Dr. Richard William Cox
Fee: £15
Membership Type: institutional, full, unwaged
Description: Professional and amateur historians of sport. To promote, stimulate and encourage discussion, study, research and publications on the history of sport and physical education; to organize meetings and workshops and to publish materials that advance interest and scholarship in the area of study; to liaise with individuals and institutions having an interest in the aims of the Society.
Publication: Newsletter
Publication title: The BSSH Newsletter. Advertisements.
Publication title: Index to Sporting Manuscripts
Meetings/Conventions: British Society of Sports History - annual conference - Exhibits.

British Society of Toxicological Pathologists BSTP

PO Box 222, Horrogate, HG2 9XL, England, UK
Tel: 44 1423 870045
Fax: 44 1423 870045
Email: bstp@msn.com
Website: http://www.bstp.org.uk
Founded: 1985

British Sociological Association BSA

Unit 3F/G, Mountjoy Research Centre, Stockton Rd., Durham, DH1 3UR, England, UK
Tel: 44 191 3830839
Fax: 44 191 3830782
Email: enquiries@britsoc.org.uk
Website: http://www.britsoc.co.uk

Founded: 1950
Members: 2500
Staff: 5
Contact: Judith Mudd, Exec.Off.
Description: Individuals interested or employed in the fields of psychology, sociology, and other social sciences. Promotes the study of sociology and works to create a favorable climate for sociological research. Acts as a communication and information network.
Publication: Newsletter
Publication title: Network. Advertisements.
Second publication: Journal
Publication title: Sociology
Meetings/Conventions: - annual convention - Exhibits.

British Soft Drinks Association

20/22 Stukeley St., London, WC2B 5LR, England, UK
Tel: 44 20 74300356
Fax: 44 20 78316014
Email: bsda@britishsoftdrinks.com
Website: http://www.britishsoftdrinks.com
Founded: 1987
Members: 130
Staff: 11
Contact: Richard Laming, Public Relations Exec.
Description: Members are manufacturers, factors and franchisors of still and carbonated soft drinks, concentrates, freeze drinks, fruit juices and packaged waters. Provides an efficient, cost effective service to members which promotes, protects and represents their common industry interests.
Meetings/Conventions: - annual conference

British Stainless Steel Association

Broomgrove, 59 Clarkhouse Rd., Sheffield, S10 2LE, England, UK
Tel: 44 114 2671260
Fax: 44 114 2661252
Email: enquiry@bssa.org.uk
Website: http://www.bssa.org.uk
Members: 100
Staff: 3
Contact: Duncan Munro, Dir.
Description: Membership open to companies or individuals involved with stainless steel. To promote and develop the use of stainless steel to the benefit of all members.
Publication: Directory

British Stammering Association

15 Old Ford Rd., Bethnal Green, London, E2 9PJ, England, UK
Tel: 44 181 9831003
Fax: 44 181 9833591
Email: mail@stammering.org
Website: http://www.stammering.org
Founded: 1978
Members: 1600
Staff: 7
Contact: Norbert Liechfeldt, Ch.Exec.
Fee: £10
Membership Type: full or associate
Description: Self-help organization aimed at assisting individuals with stammering speech patterns. Conducts free information and advice service for all stammerers and parents/teachers with stammering children. Operates facilities and activities for members. Projects on early referral to speech therapy for dysfunctional children, and stammering pupils project.
Library Type: reference

Publication title: Annual Report
Publication title: Speaking Out
Meetings/Conventions: - annual conference

British Standards Institution
BSI

389 Chiswick High Rd., London, W4 4AL, England, UK
Tel: 44 208 9969000
Fax: 44 208 9967001
Email: cservicess@bsi-global.com
Website: http://www.bsi-global.com
Founded: 1901
Members: 28000
Staff: 4200
Description: Corporations, associations, individuals, and local governments. Produces national standards for British industry; conducts testing, certification, and quality assessment programs; provides information to exporters. Cooperates with the Joint European Standards Institution to develop uniform standards for the European union. Conducts research and educational programs. Maintains 3000 committees.
Library Type: reference
Publication title: Bibliotech
Second publication: Newsletter
Publication title: BSI News

British Stickmakers Guild

31 Springfield Close, Andover, SP10 2QR, England, UK
Tel: 44 1264 396757
Email: maclynn@ntworld.com
Website: http://www.thebsg.org.uk
Founded: 1984
Members: 1700
Contact: L. W. McIver, Sec.
Fee: £8
Membership Type: open
Fee: £14
Membership Type: overseas
Description: Open to all persons having an interest in making sticks, canes, and crooks for interest and pleasure and the promotion of this art. Promotes the art of stickmaking and joins together all those persons with an interest in the subject. Demonstrates throughout the country this craft and encourages all persons with an interest to join and promote the craft.
Publication: Newsletter
Publication title: The Stickmaker. Advertisements.
Meetings/Conventions: - annual meeting

British Sugar Beet Seed Producers Association
BSPSPA

c/o Dr. Penny Maplestone
Woolpack Chamber, Market St., Ely, CB7 4ND, England, UK
Tel: 44 1353 653200
Fax: 44 1353 661156
Email: penny@bspb.co.ukwww.bspb.co.uk
Members: 8
Contact: Penny Maplestone
Description: Sugar beet seed producers.

British Sugarcraft Guild

Wellington House, Messeter Pl., London, SE9 5DP, England, UK
Tel: 44 208 8596943
Fax: 44 208 8596117
Email: nationaloffice@bsguk.org
Website: http://www.bsguk.org
Founded: 1981
Members: 6500
Staff: 2
Contact: Lillian Davidson, Admin.
Fee: £23
Membership Type: international (overseas)
Fee: £18
Membership Type: in Great Britain
Description: Branch, individual and overseas membership open to anyone interested in the art of sugarcraft. Aims to promote and stimulate interest in sugarcraft as an art form, share knowledge, develop talent and improve standards.
Publication title: British Sugarcraft News. Advertisements.

British Sundial Society

4 New Wokingham Rd., Crowthorne, RG45 7NR, England, UK
Tel: 44 1344 772303
Email: douglas.bateman@btinternet.com
Website: http://www.sundialsoc.org.uk
Founded: 1989
Members: 640
Contact: D.A. Bateman, Hon.Sec.
Fee: £38
Membership Type: member
Fee: £44
Membership Type: family
Description: Promotes the science and knowledge of all types of sundials.
Library Subject: sundials
Library Type: by appointment only
Publication: Bulletin. Advertisements.
Meetings/Conventions: - annual conference Stone UK

British Support Group - Inter-African Committee Against Harmful Traditional Practices

Russell Lodge, Parkend, Lydney, GL15 4HS, England, UK
Tel: 44 1594 562617
Email: johnholman@namloh.fsnet.co.uk
Founded: 1990
Contact: Joan Higman Davies
Description: Expresses solidarity with African women who struggle against traditional health practices which are harmful to their lives, health, and personal dignity. Raises funds and conducts research. Arouses public awareness through the media. Offers educational programs related to the population in Africa and African immigrants in Britain.
Library Subject: Africa, family health, traditional practices, and religion
Library Type: reference
Publication: Newsletter
Meetings/Conventions: - periodic workshop - Exhibits.

British Suzuki Institute
BSI

39 High St., Wheathampstead, AL4 8BB, England, UK
Tel: 44 1582 832424
Fax: 44 1582 834488

Email: bsi@suzukimusic.force9.co.uk
Website: http://www.britishsuzuki.com
Founded: 1979
Members: 1850
Staff: 3
Contact: Suzanne Porter, Admin.
Fee: £13.5
Description: Music teachers, specialized educators, parents, and interested individuals in England. Promotes musical education among children using the educational philosophy and ideas of Shinichi Suzuki, a Japanese musician. (The Suzuki method teaches music as a language.) Sponsors and runs training programs using the Suzuki method for teachers of cello, flute, piano, and violin. Makes available children's services; participates in charitable programs.
Library Type: reference
Publication: Journal
Publication title: Ability Development. Advertisements.
Meetings/Conventions: conference

British Textile Machinery Association

Mount Pleasant, Glazebrook Ln., Glazebrook, Warrington, WA3 5BN, England, UK
Tel: 44 161 7755740
Fax: 44 161 7755485
Email: btma@btma.org.uk
Website: http://www.btma.org.uk
Founded: 1940
Members: 110
Staff: 5
Contact: R.E. France, Dir.
Description: The Association. aims to promote the interests, both at home and abroad, of the British textile machinery industry.
Publication: Directory
Meetings/Conventions: - annual meeting

British Tinnitus Association

Acorn Business Pk., Ground Fl., Unit 5, Woodseats Close, Sheffield, S8 0%B, England, UK
Tel: 44 114 2509922
Fax: 44 114 2557059
Email: info@tinnitus.org.uk
Website: http://www.tinnitus.org.uk
Founded: 1979
Members: 9000
Staff: 6
Contact: Mrs. V. Rose, Operations Mgr.
Fee: £10
Membership Type: in UK
Fee: £15
Membership Type: outside UK
Description: Individual Members or via a network of 80 local self-help groups and contacts. Offers information about tinnitus and helps to found and implement self-help groups to provide mutual support and varying degrees of counselling. BTA campaigns for better services for people with tinnitus and for more tinnitus clinics. A national conference is held annually.
Publication: Journal
Publication title: BTA Information Pack. Advertisements.
Publication title: QUIET

British Toxicology Society
BTS

PO Box 249, Macclesfield, SK11 6FT, England, UK
Tel: 44 1625 267881
Fax: 44 1625 267879
Email: secretariat@thebts.org
Website: http://www.thebts.org
Founded: 1979
Description: Promotes the science of toxicology through epidemiological evaluation of the prevalence of the chemical toxicity, bioanalysis of exposure to potentially harmful chemicals, and prediction of the toxicity of chemicals.

British Toy and Hobby Association
BTHA

c/o David L. Hawtin
80 Camberwell Rd., London, SE5 OEG, England, UK
Tel: 44 207 7017271
Fax: 44 207 7082437
Email: admin@btha.co.uk
Website: http://www.btha.co.uk
Founded: 1944
Members: 180
Staff: 9
Contact: David L. Hawtin, Gen.Sec.
Description: Manufacturers of toys and hobby-related items in the U.K. Promotes the toy and hobby industry; represents members' interests.

British Toy Importers Association
BTIA

Somers Mounts Hill, Benenden, Cranbrook, TN17 4ET, England, UK
Tel: 44 1580 240819
Fax: 44 1580 241109
Email: btia@chartsec.co.uk
Website: http://www.toycred.co.uk
Founded: 1930
Members: 100
Contact: Alan Milne, Sec.
Fee: £425
Description: Members import and distribute the majority of quality toys and components on sale in the UK and Republic of Ireland. Safeguards and promotes the interests of members by keeping them fully informed of matters affecting their trade. Advises on safety matters and quality assurance and the Safety Adviser ensures that the Association is given the opportunity to comment on new developments in safety legislation. Owner of Toycred Accreditation scheme.
Formerly: British Toy Importers and Distributors Association
Publication title: Advice on Toys Safety & Importing Quality Procedures
Second publication: Newsletter
Meetings/Conventions: Harrogate International Toy Fair - annual

British Toymakers Guild

124 Walcot St., Bath, BA1 5BG, England, UK
Tel: 44 1225 442440
Email: info@toymakersguild.co.uk
Website: http://www.toymakersguild.co.uk
Founded: 1955
Members: 220

Staff: 1
Contact: Robert Nathan
Description: Members are craftsmen toymakers, shops, galleries and collectors. Promotes and encourages excellence in toy making and the making of miniatures.
Publication title: The Toymaker
Second publication: Directory

British Transplantation Society
BTS

Broomhill Rd., Triangle House, London, SW18 4HX, England, UK
Tel: 44 20 88752430
Fax: 44 20 88742421
Email: secretariat@bts.org.uk
Founded: 1971

British Trombone Society

91 High St., Edgware, HA8 7DB, England, UK
Tel: 44 181 340 4109
Fax: 44 181 340 4109
Email: editbts@aol.com
Website: http://www.trombone-society.org.uk
Founded: 1986
Members: 1000
Contact: Chris Houlding, Pres.
Fee: £20
Membership Type: retired
Fee: £15
Membership Type: discounted
Description: Maintains and develops contact amongst trombonists.
Publication: Magazine
Publication title: The Trombonist. Advertisements.
Meetings/Conventions: - annual festival

British Trout Association
BTA

8/9 Lambton Pl., London, W11 2SH, England, UK
Tel: 44 207 2216065
Fax: 44 207 2216049
Email: mail@britishtrout.co.uk
Website: http://www.britishtrout.co.uk
Contact: Robin Scott, Chm.
Description: Trout producers in Britain. Conducts research and educational programs; represents members' interests.

British Trust for Ornithology

The Nunnery, Thetford, IP24 2PU, England, UK
Tel: 44 1842 750050
Fax: 44 1842 750030
Email: info@bto.org
Website: http://www.bto.org
Founded: 1933
Members: 12000
Staff: 80
Contact: Andy Elvin, Dir. of Services
Fee: £20
Membership Type: ordinary
Description: Birdwatchers and Bird Ringers. Promotes and encourages the wider understanding, appreciation and conservation of birds through scientific studies using the combined skills and enthusiasm of its members, other bird watchers and staff.
Library Subject: ornithology, ecology, and statistics

Library Type: not open to the public
Publication: Journal
Publication title: Bird Study. Advertisements.
Second publication: Magazine
Publication title: BTO News. Advertisements.
Meetings/Conventions: Annual Birdwatchers' Conference - annual conference - Exhibits.

British Tugowners' Association
Carthusian Ct., 12 Carthusian St., London, EC1M 6EZ, England, UK
Tel: 44 20 74172875
Fax: 44 20 76001534
Email: bta@british-shipping.org
Founded: 1935
Members: 20
Staff: 1
Contact: David Asprey, Sec.
Description: Coastal and harbour towage companies based in the majority of UK ports.

British Tunnelling Society
c/o Institution of Civil Engineers
1 Great George St., Westminster, Westminster, London, SW1P 3AA, England, UK
Tel: 44 207 6652233
Fax: 44 207 2227500
Email: bts@ice.org.org
Website: http://www.britishtunnelling.org
Founded: 1971
Members: 750
Staff: 1
Contact: Gavin Bowyer, Sec.
Fee: £550
Membership Type: corporate
Fee: £23
Membership Type: retired
Description: Individuals, corporate, students and companies in tunnelling/tunnelling equipment. To advance the education of the public in and to promote the art and science of tunnelling, including the creation and use of underground space by fostering, understanding experience, interest and research therein.
Publication: Magazine
Publication title: Tunnels & Tunnelling. Advertisements.
Meetings/Conventions: - monthly London

British Turf and Landscape Irrigation Association
PO Box 709, Garstang, Preston, PR3 1GT, England, UK
Tel: 44 7041 363130
Fax: 44 7041 363130
Email: info@btlia.org.uk
Website: http://www.btlia.org.uk
Founded: 1978
Members: 40
Contact: David G. Halford
Description: For those concerned with manufacture, installation or maintenance of turf and landscape irrigation equipment or design of irrigation systems.
Publication: Newsletter

British Turned-Parts Manufacturers Association
Pear Tree Cottage, Snitterfield Ln., Norton Lindsey, Warwick, CV35 8JQ, England, UK
Tel: 44 1789 730877
Fax: 44 1789 730899
Email: iangold@btmaonline.org.uk
Website: http://www.btma.org
Description: Represents turned-parts manufacturers.
Publication title: Buyers Guide

British UFO Research Association
BUFORA
BM Bufora, London, WC1N 3XX, England, UK
Tel: 44 1227 722916
Fax: 44 1227 722916
Email: enquiries@bufora.org.uk
Website: http://www.bufora.org.uk
Founded: 1964
Members: 500
Staff: 1
Contact: Peter Doye, Chm.
Fee: £20
Membership Type: full
Description: Organizations and individuals interested in investigating UFO reports. Promotes and conducts research on unidentified flying object phenomena in the United Kingdom. Compiles and disseminates UFO reports and related data; fosters cooperation and exchange in the field. Organizes research training courses.
Library Subject: UFOs
Library Type: not open to the public
Publication: Magazine
Publication title: Bufora Bulleting. Advertisements.
Second publication: Newsletter
Publication title: UFO Newsfile
Meetings/Conventions: - monthly lecture

British Union for the Abolition of Vivisection
16a Crane Grove, London, N7 8NN, England, UK
Tel: 44 20 77004888
Fax: 44 20 77000252
Email: info@buav.org
Website: http://www.buav.org
Founded: 1898
Staff: 25
Contact: Michelle Thew, Chf.Exec.
Description: Campaigns to end animal experiments.
Library Type: by appointment only
Publication: Magazine
Publication title: Campaign Report. Advertisements.

British Universities Film and Video Council
BUFVC
77 Wells St., London, W1T 3QJ, England, UK
Tel: 44 207 3931500
Fax: 44 207 3931555
Email: ask@bufvc.ac.uk
Website: http://www.bufvc.ac.uk
Founded: 1948
Members: 244
Staff: 18
Contact: Murray Weston, Dir.
Fee: £340

Membership Type: institutional
Description: Experts working with audiovisual media, materials, and techniques for teaching and research in institutions of higher and further education. Operates information service which includes an appraisals file on audiovisual materials currently available in the United Kingdom. Maintains specialist databases describing film and television archives in UK, British Newsreels (1910-1979) and an Index of British television broadcasts from May 1995 onwards.
Library Subject: film, television, and related media
Library Type: reference
Formerly: British Universities Film Council
Publication: Directories
Publication title: Audio-Visual Materials for Higher Education
Publication title: Researchers Guide to British Film and Television Collections
Meetings/Conventions: - periodic conference

British Universities Industrial Relations Association
BUIRA

Keele University, Keele, ST5 5BG, England, UK
Tel: 44 1782 583396
Fax: 44 1782 584271
Email: v.r.rowley@hrm.keele.ac.uk
Website: http://www.warwick.ac.uk
Founded: 1950

British Urban and Regional Information Systems Associations

c/o Alan Lodwick, Sec. Dorset County Council
County Hall, Dorchester, DT1 1XJ, England, UK
Tel: 44 1305 224984
Email: a.j.lodwick@dorset-cc.gov.uk
Founded: 1971
Members: 450
Contact: Alan Lodwick, Sec.
Fee: £20
Description: Practitioners whose common interest is in the use and management of information, and the development of information systems, for services to the public. Aims to promote better communications between people concerned with information and information systems in local and central government, the health services, utilities and the academic world through its regular newsletter, an annual conference and periodic workshops. Areas of interest include physical planning and development, social services, health, education, housing, economic development, transportation utilities and library services.
Publication: Newsletter
Publication title: BURISA Newsletter. Advertisements.
Meetings/Conventions: - annual conference - Exhibits.

British Vacuum Council

76 Portland Pl., London, W1B 1NT, England, UK
Tel: 44 20 74704800
Fax: 44 20 74704848
Email: peter.main@iop.org
Website: http://www.british-vacuum-council.org
Founded: 1969
Members: 18
Staff: 1
Contact: Peter Main
Fee: £500
Membership Type: organization

Description: Two representatives from each of the 2 bodies affiliated to the Council which are: The Institute of Physics and the Faraday Division of The Royal Society of Chemistry. To promote and advance the understanding and teaching of vacuum science, technology and its applications by coordinating and promoting conferences, seminars and courses and publications in these fields; encouraging excellence amongst postgraduate students and other young research workers in these fields.
Meetings/Conventions: - semiannual conference

British Valve and Actuator Manufacturers Association

The McLaren Bldg., 35 Dale End, Birmingham, B4 7LN, England, UK
Tel: 44 121 2001297
Fax: 44 121 2001306
Email: enquiry@bvama.org.uk
Website: http://www.bvama.org.uk
Founded: 1939
Members: 67
Staff: 3
Contact: David T. Pangbourne, Dir.
Description: Covers industrial valves and actuators for the control of fluids and gases.
Formerly: British Valve and Actuator Association
Publication title: Buyers Guide

British Vehicle Rental and Leasing Association

River Lodge, Badminton Ct., Amersham, HP7 0DD, England, UK
Tel: 44 1494 434747
Fax: 44 1494 434499
Email: info@bvrla.co.uk
Website: http://www.bvrla.co.uk
Founded: 1967
Members: 1000
Staff: 14
Contact: John Lewis, Dir.Gen.
Description: Trade association for the vehicle (cars/vans/commercial vehicles) rental and leasing/contract hire and vehicle management industries and other associated businesses. Promotes/supports the corporate objectives of its members by interfacing with Government/ Civil Service on strategic, economic and legislative issues relating to the industry. Offers support and advisory services, seminars and training; enforces Codes of Conduct and Quality Assurance Schemes.
Library Type: not open to the public
Publication: Magazine
Publication title: BVRLA News
Publication title: Residual Value Survey

British Venture Capital Association
BVCA, 3 Clements Inn, London, WC2A 2AZ, England, UK

Tel: 44 20 70252950
Fax: 44 20 70252951
Email: bvca@bvca.co.uk
Website: http://www.bvca.co.uk
Founded: 1983
Members: 300
Staff: 11
Contact: John Mackie, Chief Exec.
Description: Venture capital, private equity, and professional firms connected with the venture capital industry. Represents virtually every major source of venture capital in the UK. It provides information about members to entrepreneurs and investors; represents members'

views in discussions with Government and other bodies; provides a forum for the exchange of views among members; develops and maintains the highest standards of professional practice and provides training for members employees.
Library Type: not open to the public
Publication: Directory
Publication title: BVCA Directory of Members
Second publication: Report
Publication title: BVCA Report on Investment Activity

British Veterinary Association
BVA

7 Mansfield St., London, W1G 9NQ, England, UK
Tel: 44 207 6366541
Fax: 44 207 4362970
Email: bvahq@bva.co.uk
Website: http://www.bva.co.uk
Founded: 1882
Members: 10000
Staff: 40
Contact:
Fee: £200
Membership Type: full (veterinary surgeons and students)
Description: Veterinarians and veterinary students. Promotes interests of members and the animals in their care. Monitors activities of, provides advice to, and develops and maintains contact with organizations interested in animal health including government agencies, local authorities, professional societies, animal rights groups, and universities. Disseminates information to the public and the media. Conducts charitable programs. Sponsors seminars and symposia. Maintains 20 specialist divisions.
Library Type: reference
Formerly: National Veterinary Medical Association
Publication title: Annual Report
Publication title: In Practice
Meetings/Conventions: - annual congress Edinburgh UK

British Veterinary Nursing Association

Terminus House, Level 15, Terminus St., Harlow, CM20 1XA, England, UK
Tel: 44 1279 450567
Fax: 44 1279 420886
Email: bvna@bvna.co.uk
Website: http://www.bvna.org.uk
Founded: 1965
Members: 4500
Staff: 7
Contact: June Peachey, Exec.Dir.
Fee: £21
Membership Type: students
Fee: £35
Membership Type: qualified vn's
Description: Full membership qualified veterinary nurses; students; associate; supporter. To foster and promote the status of the veterinary nurse; representation on associated professional committees, and government committees. Gives advice on a career as a veterinary nurse. Membership benefits include an employment register, annual congress, reduced entry into BVNA regional and national meetings and BVNA Educational Courses.
Publication: Journal
Publication title: Veterinary Nurse Journal, bimonthly, through membership or subscription
Meetings/Conventions: - annual congress - Exhibits.

British Video Association

167 Great Portland St., London, W1W 5PE, England, UK
Tel: 44 20 74360041
Fax: 44 20 74360043
Email: general@bva.org.uk
Website: http://www.bva.org.uk
Founded: 1980
Members: 30
Staff: 3
Contact: Lavinia Carey, Dir. Gen.
Description: Full members are copyright owners of product for the pre-recorded video market. Associate members have affiliated operations, such as box manufacturers, wholesalers, printers, duplicators, etc. Represents, promotes and protects the collective interests of copyright owning companies who produce and/or distribute videos in the UK.
Publication: Brochure
Publication title: A Parent's Guide to Video
Second publication: Yearbook
Publication title: British Video Association Yearbook

British Watch and Clock Makers' Guild

PO Box 2368, Romford, RM1 2EH, England, UK
Tel: 44 170 8750616
Fax: 44 170 8750616
Founded: 1907
Members: 950
Staff: 2
Description: Watch, clock and allied professions. Aims to safeguard and promote the interest of watch and clock making and other allied trades.
Publication: Newsletter

British Water

1 Queen Anne's Gate, London, SW1 H9BT, England, UK
Tel: 44 207 9574554
Fax: 44 207 9574565
Email: info@britishwater.co.uk
Website: http://www.britishwater.co.uk
Founded: 1993
Members: 200
Staff: 9
Contact: David Neil-Gallacher, Chief Exec.
Description: UK water and waste water industries, designers, contractors, manufacturers, and suppliers of water purification plant equipment and chemicals, financial institutions, law firms, and training and research organizations, media, and travel service providers. Promotes involvement of members in water-related projects of British companies and organizations worldwide. Works with government bodies to establish water quality standards and methods of treatment; provides technical support to water quality programs of other organizations.
Formerly: Formed by Merger of, British Effluent Water Association and British Water Industries Group

British Watercolour Society

Briargate, 2 The Brambles, Ilkley, LS29 9DH, England, UK
Fax: 44 1943 603753
Founded: 1911
Members: 105
Contact: Margaret Simpson, Dir.
Description: Members and associate members show their works alongside amateur watercolourists - membership restricted by selection. Promotes the traditional values of watercolours, allowing

watercolourists to compete in unrestricted open exhibition, showing their works alongside those of the Members and Associate Members. Several thousands of pounds in prizes annually - two exhibitions per year.
Publication: Catalog

British Web Design and Marketing Association
BWDMA

c/o Patrick J. White
PO Box 3227, London, NW9 9LX, England, UK
Tel: 44 20 82042474
Fax: 44 20 89050364
Email: info@bwdma.com
Website: http://www.bwdma.co.uk
Members: 2000
Staff: 5
Contact: Patrick J. White, Founder
Fee: £120
Membership Type: certified corporate
Fee: £79
Membership Type: corporate
Description: Dedicated to the improvement of businesses and individuals in the new media sector, such as web design and marketing; aims to develop working relationships between suppliers and the industry.
Publication: Newsletter

British Wind Energy Association

c/o Renable Energy House
1 Aztec Row, Berners Rd., London, N1 0PW, England, UK
Tel: 44 207 6891960
Fax: 44 207 6891969
Email: info@bwea.com
Website: http://www.bwea.com
Founded: 1978
Members: 320
Staff: 7
Contact: Nick Goodall, Chief Exec.
Description: Trade and professional body for the UK wind energy industry. Members range from professional companies, organizations, engineers, scientists and others involved in the field of wind energy. Promotes the appropriate utilisation of the technology, through policy, development, and implementation. Acts as a central point of information for government, public, and the media. *VNU
Publication title: Best Practice Guide Lines
Publication title: Health and Safety in Wind Energy Industry
Meetings/Conventions: - annual conference - Exhibits. Glasgow UK

British Women Pilots' Association

Brooklands Museum, Brooklands Rd., Weybridge, KT13 0QN, England, UK
Email: enquires@bwpa.demon.co.uk
Website: http://www.bwpa.demon.co.uk
Founded: 1955
Members: 400
Contact: Mrs. Tricia Nelmes, Chmn.
Fee: £50
Membership Type: family, full, associate, under 18 years
Description: Assists women to gain pilots' licenses of all types. Advise women on training required and openings available to them. Promotes training and employment of women in aviation.
Library Subject: aviation
Library Type: by appointment only

British Wood Preserving and Damp-Proofing Association

1 Ground Fl., Gleneagles House, Vernon Gate, Derby, DE1 1UP, England, UK
Tel: 44 1332 225100
Fax: 44 1332 225101
Email: info@bwpda.co.uk
Website: http://www.bwpda.co.uk
Founded: 1930
Members: 510
Staff: 13
Contact: Jayne Hall
Description: Manufacturers and distributors of preservatives, fire retardants and treatment plants, producers and users of treated timber; specialists in remedial timber treatment and damp proofing; universities, colleges, learned societies and research. organisations in the UK and worldwide independent consultants and private members. Specialises in the technology of timber preservation, damp control and building repair. Provides impartial advice about wood preservation and building repair techniques, and plays a central role in setting standards and establishing operation codes of practice. Actively committed to raising standards of knowledge, quality and safety throughout the industry and to the promotion of technological innovation.
Library Subject: wood preservation, fire protection, and damp proofing
Library Type: open to the public
Publication: Magazine
Publication title: Preserve!. Advertisements.
Second publication: Journal
Publication title: Wood Protection
Meetings/Conventions: - biennial convention - Exhibits.

British Wood Pulp Association

Flat 5, Carlton House, 10 Carlton Rd., Tunbridge Wells, TN1 2JS, England, UK
Tel: 44 1892 616494
Email: bwpa@tinyworld.co.uk
Website: http://www.woodpulp.org.uk/
Founded: 1896
Members: 180
Staff: 1
Contact: L.M. DeVos

British Wood Turners Association
BWTA

Treetops, 78 St. Marks Ave., Salisbury, SP1 3DW, England, UK
Tel: 44 1722 328032
Fax: 44 1722 333558
Email: bwta@chalke.co.uk
Founded: 1946
Members: 36
Staff: 1
Contact: P.F. Chalke, Hon. Sec.
Description: Companies or individuals in Great Britain manufacturing items from wood using a lathe. Promotes the wood turning industry. Provides a forum for the exchange of information between members.
Publication: Directory. Advertisements.

British Woodworking Federation
BWF

56-64 Leonard St., London, EC2A 4JX, England, UK
Tel: 44 171 6085050
Fax: 44 171 6085051
Email: bwf@bwf.org.uk
Website: http://www.bwf.org.uk
Founded: 1976
Members: 450
Staff: 8
Contact: Richard Lambert, Dir.
Description: Manufacturers of building woodwork. Represents the collective interests of members engaged in the manufacture of builders woodwork.
Publication: Newsletter

British Wool Marketing Board

Wool House, Roydsdale Way, Euroway Trading Estate, Bradford, BD4 6SE, England, UK
Tel: 44 1274 688666
Fax: 44 1274 652233
Email: mail@britishwool.org.uk
Website: http://www.britishwool.org.uk
Contact: Frank Langrish, Chm.

British-Chilean Chamber of Commerce

12 Devonshire St., London, W1G 7DS, England, UK
Tel: 44 207 3233053
Fax: 44 207 5805901
Email: merilyn.potter@bccc.org.uk
Website: http://www.bccc.org.uk
Contact: Sondra Carey, Gen.Mgr.
Description: Promotes business and commerce.

British-Israel Chamber of Commerce

PO Box 4268, London, W1A 7WH, England, UK
Tel: 44 207 2243212
Fax: 44 207 4867877
Email: mail@b-icc.org.uk
Founded: 1950
Members: 500
Staff: 3
Contact: Hayley Davis, Bus.Mgr.
Fee: £250
Membership Type: ordinary
Description: Promotes business and commerce.
Publication: Magazine
Publication title: Trading Up

Broadcasting Entertainment Cinematograph and Theatre Union
BECTU

373-377 Clapham Rd., London, SW9 9BT, England, UK
Tel: 44 207 3460900
Fax: 44 207 3460901
Email: info@bectu.org.uk
Website: http://www.bectu.org.uk
Founded: 1991
Members: 26000
Staff: 50
Contact: Roger Bolton, Gen.Sec.

Description: Trade union for workers in the film, broadcasting, and theatre industries.
Formerly: Formed by Merger of, Association of Cinematograph, Television and Allied Technicians
Publication: Magazine
Publication title: Stage Screen & Radio. Advertisements.
Meetings/Conventions: - annual conference - Exhibits.

Bronte Society
IBS

Bronte Parsonage Museum, Haworth, Keighley, BD22 8DR, England, UK
Tel: 44 1535 642323
Fax: 44 1535 647131
Email: info@bronte.org.uk
Website: http://www.bronte.org.uk
Founded: 1893
Members: 2500
Staff: 26
Contact: Lyn Glading, Sec.
Fee: £20
Membership Type: Individual - U.K. and Europe
Fee: £475
Membership Type: Life - U.K. and Europe
Description: Preserves the literary works, manuscripts, and other objects of the Bronte sisters (Charlotte, 1816-55, Emily, 1818-48, and Anne, 1820-49). Maintains the Bronte Parsonage Museum. Provides research facilities by appointment.
Library Subject: lives and works of the Bronte family
Library Type: by appointment only
Publication: Newsletter
Publication title: Gazette. Advertisements.
Second publication: Journal
Publication title: Transactions
Meetings/Conventions: - biennial conference

Brooks Advisory Centres

421 Highgate Studios, 53-79 Highate Rd., London, WCIX 8UD, England, UK
Tel: 44 20 72846040
Fax: 44 20 72846050
Email: administration@brookcentres.org.uk
Founded: 1964
Contact: Paul Currie, Information/Advice Worker
Description: Seeks to decrease the incidence of unwanted pregnancy among young women. Conducts educational programs in matters of sex, contraception, and reproductive and social responsibility.

BTCV

Conservation Centre, 163 Balby Rd., Doncaster, DN4 0RH, England, UK
Tel: 44 1491 821600
Fax: 44 1491 839646
Email: international@btcv.org.uk
Website: http://www.btcv.org
Founded: 1959
Members: 8300
Staff: 339
Contact: Nikki Cripps, International Off.
Fee: £12
Membership Type: individual
Fee: £20

Membership Type: local group
Description: Charity protecting the environment through practical action. A network of over 150 field offices allows volunteers of all ages and from all sections of the community to train and take part in a wide range of environmental projects, including planting trees and hedges, repairing footpaths and drystone walls, improving access to the countryside and creating urban wildlife sanctuaries. Organizes conservation working holidays both in the UK and worldwide.
Formerly: British Trust for Conservation Volunteers
Publication title: The Conserver
Second publication: Handbooks

Builders Merchants Federation
BMF

15 Soho Sq., London, W1D 3HL, England, UK
Tel: 44 870 9013380
Fax: 44 207 7342766
Email: info@bmf.org.uk
Website: http://www.bmf.org.uk
Contact: Melanie Wiggins, Pr and Mktg. Officer
Description: Merchants specializing in the distribution of building materials in the United Kingdom. Promotes members' interests.
Publication title: Year Book and Buyers Guide

Building Cost Information Service of the Royal Institution of Chartered Surveyors

3 Cadogen Gate, London, SW1X OAS, England, UK
Tel: 44 20 76951500
Fax: 44 20 76951501
Email: bcis@bcis.co.uk
Website: http://www.bcis.co.uk
Founded: 1962
Contact: Joe Martin, Exec.Dir.
Description: Aims to provide a center of expertise and information exchange on building costs.

Building Research Establishment

Garston, Watford, WD25 9XX, England, UK
Tel: 44 1923 664000
Fax: 44 1923 664010
Email: enquiries@bre.co.uk
Website: http://www.bre.co.uk
Founded: 1921
Staff: 650
Contact: Martin Wyatt, Chief Exec.
Description: Centre of expertise for construction, fire, the built environment and risk sciences that provides research, consultancy, training, and information services to clients worldwide.
Publication: Newsletter
Publication title: Constructing the Future
Meetings/Conventions: Cabin Air Quality in Passenger Aircraft conference

Building Services Research and Information Association
BSRIA

Old Bracknell Ln. W, Bracknell, RG12 7AH, England, UK
Tel: 44 1344 426511
Fax: 44 1344 487575
Email: bsria@bsria.co.uk
Website: http://www.bsria.co.uk
Founded: 1955

Members: 750
Staff: 100
Contact: Andrew Eastwell, Ch.Exec.
Fee: £395
Membership Type: corporate
Description: Engineers, contracting firms, manufacturers, educational establishments, and commercial and public organizations. Is concerned with mechanical and electrical services associated with buildings, including heating and cooling, noise and vibration, fire protection, and plumbing and sanitation. Operates the BSRIA Information Centre for the collection and dissemination of technical information for staff and member organizations.
Library Subject: building services
Library Type: reference
Publication title: Application Guide
Second publication: Bulletin
Publication title: BSRIA Statistics Bulletin

Building Societies Association - England
BSA

3 Savile Row, London, W1S 3PB, England, UK
Tel: 44 207 4370655
Fax: 44 207 7346416
Website: http://www.bsa.org.uk
Members: 65
Staff: 20
Contact: Simon Rex, Info.Svcs.Mgr.
Description: Association of building societies in the United Kingdom. Promotes and protects members' interests.
Library Subject: savings, mortgages, housing
Library Type: by appointment only
Publication: Annual Report

Bulb Distributors Association

Springfields Gardens, Camelgate, Spalding, PE12 6ET, England, UK
Tel: 44 1775 724843
Fax: 44 1775 711209
Email: bda@mistral.co.uk
Website: http://www.bda.mistral.co.uk
Founded: 1945
Members: 30
Contact: David Norton, Sec.
Description: Bulb importers and wholesalers. Looks after the interest of the distributors and customers of the bulb (horticultural) industry within the UK and Europe.

Bureau of Freelance Photographers

Focus House, 497 Green Lanes, London, N13 4BP, England, UK
Tel: 44 20 88823315
Fax: 44 20 88865174
Email: info@thebfp.com
Website: http://www.thebfp.com
Founded: 1965
Members: 6500
Staff: 3
Contact: John Tracy
Fee: £60
Membership Type: outside UK
Fee: £45
Membership Type: U.K.
Description: Freelance photographers supplying editorial/publishing markets. Assists and advises members.
Publication: Handbook

Publication title: Freelance Photographer's Market Handbook
Second publication: Newsletter
Publication title: Market Newsletter

Business and Professional Women - UK

PO Box 214, 24 Knifesmithgate, Chesterfield, S4O 1XW, England, UK
Tel: 44 1246 211988
Fax: 44 1246 211983
Email: hq@bpwuk.org.uk
Website: http://www.bpwuk.org.uk
Founded: 1938
Members: 2000
Staff: 2
Contact: Sue Tonge, Off.Mgr.
Fee: £60
Membership Type: individual
Description: A networking and lobbying organization. Aims to enable business and professional women to achieve in their careers. Encourages women to take an active part in public life and decision making at all levels. Evaluates changing work patterns and press for development in education and training to meet them. Strives to ensure that the same opportunities and facilities are available to both men and women. Undertakes studies of problems common to business and professional women in Europe and worldwide.
Formerly: Formed by Merger of, Business and Professional Women of the United Kindom
Publication: Newsletter
Publication title: BPW News
Meetings/Conventions: - annual convention - Exhibits.

Business Application Software Developers Association

Templestowe, Longbottn Ln., Seer Green, Beaconsfield, HP9 2UL, England, UK
Tel: 44 1494 677699
Fax: 44 1494 681894
Email: info@basda.org
Website: http://www.basda.org/
Founded: 1993
Members: 280
Staff: 2
Contact: Dennis Keeling, Chief Exec.
Fee: £300
Membership Type: full and associate
Description: Open to developers of recognized accountancy or business application software products - as full members. It is also available to other organizations which have an interest in the development of the industry -as associate members. Aims to bring together organizations with an interest in the development, accreditation and marketing of business and accounting software products and to provide a forum for its members to influence the direction of the industry.
Formerly: Business and Accounting Software Developers Association
Publication: Handbook
Publication title: Changeover to the Euro
Second publication: Handbook
Publication title: EMU Specification for Application Software

Business Archives Council

c/o Fiona Maccoll
Rio Tinto plc, 6 St. James Sq., London, SW1Y 4LD, England, UK
Tel: 44 20 77532338
Fax: 44 20 77532211
Email: fiona.maccoll@riotinfo.com

Website: http://www.archives.gla.ac.uk/bac/default.html
Founded: 1934
Members: 300
Contact: Fiona Maccoll, Mgr.
Fee: £145
Membership Type: corporate/institutional
Fee: £55
Membership Type: institutional
Description: Records managers, archivists and anyone connected with the records of business. To encourage the preservation of archives of the business community and to promote the study of business history.
Publication: Newsletter
Publication title: BAC Newsletter
Second publication: Proceedings
Publication title: Conference Journal
Meetings/Conventions: - annual conference - Exhibits.

Butchers' Company

Butchers' Hall, 87 Bartholomew Close, London, EC1A 7EB, England, UK
Tel: 44 20 76064106
Fax: 44 20 76064108
Email: clerk@butchershall.com
Website: http://www.butchershall.com
Founded: 975
Members: 1600
Staff: 8
Contact: Mr. Graham J. Sharp, CEO
Fee: £60
Membership Type: professional, plus VAT
Description: Seeks to maintain and apply professional code of conduct in meat trading; promote education and training throughout the meat/food industry; promote excellence via technical presentations.
Library Subject: meat industry
Library Type: not open to the public
Publication: Newsletter. Advertisements.
Second publication: Bulletin. Advertisements.

Butterfly Conservation

Manor Yard, E Lulworth, Wareham, BH20 5QP, England, UK
Tel: 44 1929 400209
Fax: 44 1929 400210
Email: info@butterfly-conservation.org
Website: http://www.butterfly-conservation.org
Founded: 1968
Members: 11500
Staff: 35
Contact: Martin Warren, Chief Exec.
Fee: £24
Membership Type: standard
Fee: £14
Membership Type: individuals aged 18 or less
Description: Dedicated to saving butterflies, moths and their habitats. By making people aware of their declining numbers, funding research and by setting up reserves for the rarer species, the aim is to preserve these insects for future generations to enjoy.
Publication: Magazine
Publication title: Butterfly Conservation News. Advertisements.
Second publication: Reports
Publication title: Scientific Papers
Meetings/Conventions: Butterfly Conservation International Symposium - triennial symposium

CABI Bioscience

Bakeham Ln., Egham, TW20 9TY, England, UK
Tel: 44 1491 829000
Fax: 44 1491 829100
Email: bioscience.egham@cabi.org
Website: http://www.cabi-bioscience.org
Contact: David Dent, Dir.
Description: Entomologists, agricultural scientists, and other organizations and individuals with an interest in pest control. Promotes development and implementation of biological pest control strategies and techniques. Conducts research; gathers and disseminates information; provides technical support and assistance to local pest control organizations and projects worldwide.
Formerly: Absorbed, International Institute of Biological Control

Cable Communications Association

Artillery House, Artillery Row, 5th Fl., London, SW1P 1RT, England, UK
Tel: 44 20 72222900
Fax: 44 20 77991471
Founded: 1934
Members: 60
Staff: 20
Contact: Roy Payne, Dir. of Communications
Description: UK broadband cable operators. Represents the commercial, business and political interests on a national level, of the UK cable industry.
Publication title: Cable Companion
Publication title: Cablegram

Cafe Society

8 Home Farm, Ardington, OX12 8PN, England, UK
Tel: 44 1235 821820
Fax: 44 1235 862200
Email: enq@cafesociety.org.uk
Contact: Jim Winship
Description: Coffee bars and modern cafes. Promotes interest of industry; develops standards for operators. Provides training programs.

CALIBRE - Cassette Library for the Blind and Print Handicapped

New Rd., Weston Turville, Aylesbury, HP22 5XQ, England, UK
Tel: 44 1296 432339
Fax: 44 1296 392599
Email: enquiries@calibre.org.uk
Website: http://www.calibre.org.uk
Founded: 1974
Members: 15000
Staff: 37
Contact: J.R. Palmer, Dir.
Description: Provides a free postal library service of unabriged books on cassette for the blind and print disabled.
Library Subject: fiction
Library Type: not open to the public

Call Centre Management Association

International House, 174 Three Bridges Rd., Crawley, RH10 1LE, England, UK
Tel: 44 1293 538400
Fax: 44 1293 521313
Email: admin@ccma.org.uk
Website: http://www.ccma.org.uk

Founded: 1995
Members: 300
Contact: Roy Bailey, Sec.
Description: Individuals responsible for the management or supervision of a call centre. Promotes the profession and recognition of call centre management; acts as the professional body for call centre managers and supervisors, offers education and training, leading to professional qualifications.
Meetings/Conventions: meeting

Calligraphy and Lettering Arts Society
CLAS

54 Boileau Rd., London, SW13 9BL, England, UK
Tel: 44 20 87417886
Fax: 44 20 87417886
Email: suecavendish@compuserve.com
Website: http://www.clas.co.uk
Founded: 1994
Members: 1500
Contact: Sue Cavendish, Gen.Sec.
Fee: £25
Membership Type: individual
Fee: £32
Membership Type: outside UK
Description: Promotes the practice and teaching of calligraphy and lettering.
Library Subject: calligraphy, lettering and related subjects
Library Type: not open to the public
Publication: Magazine
Publication title: The Edge. Advertisements.
Meetings/Conventions: - annual festival

Cambridge and District Chamber of Commerce and Industry

Endeavor House, The Vision Park, Cambridge, CB4 9ZR, England, UK
Tel: 44 1223 237414
Fax: 44 1223 237405
Email: enquiries@cambscci.co.uk
Website: http://www.cambridgechamber.co.uk
Founded: 1917
Members: 1105
Staff: 15
Contact: Mr. Kim Norman, CEO
Description: Promotes business and commerce.

Cambridge Refrigeration Technology
CRT

140 Newmarket Rd., Cambridge, CB5 8HE, England, UK
Tel: 44 1223 365101
Fax: 44 1223 461522
Email: crt@crtech.demon.co.uk
Website: http://www.crtech.co.uk
Founded: 1945
Members: 60
Staff: 12
Contact: John Frith
Description: Shipowners carrying refrigerated cargoes (full). Any interested party (associate) including consultants, leasing companies, insurance companies and P & I Clubs. Covers research, development, testing, consultancy and information services related to

all forms of refrigerated transport; also cargo care & insurance & claims issues. Includes full size vehicle thermal test chambers.
Library Subject: transport, shipping, storage, commodities, perishables, equipment, legislation, standards, and patents
Library Type: not open to the public
Formerly: Shipowners Refrigerated Cargo Research Association
Publication: Newsletter
Publication title: CRT
Second publication: Newsletter
Publication title: RTIS CD-Rom
Meetings/Conventions: - periodic

Campaign Against Arms Trade
CAAT

11 Goodwin St., Finsbury Park, London, N4 3HQ, England, UK
Tel: 44 207 2810297
Fax: 44 207 2814369
Email: enquiries@caat.demon.co.uk
Website: http://www.caat.org.uk/
Founded: 1974
Members: 4000
Staff: 7
Description: Coalition of organizations and individuals united to end the international arms trade and Britain's role in it. Works in coordination with other peace organizations to promote awareness of the dangers of arms exports. Exchanges information with European anti-arms organizations. Seeks to convert the military industry to socially-useful production.
Library Type: reference
Publication: Newsletter
Publication title: Newsletter
Meetings/Conventions: - periodic convention

Campaign for Nuclear Disarmament
CND

162 Holloway Rd., London, N7 8DQ, England, UK
Tel: 44 171 7002393
Fax: 44 171 7002357
Email: enquiries@cnduk.org
Website: http://www.cnduk.org/
Founded: 1958
Members: 45000
Staff: 9
Description: Coordinates nuclear disarmament efforts in the United Kingdom through local groups. Activities include street campaigning, lobbying and elections work, public information and press campaigns, public relations, and information dissemination. Maintains speakers' bureau.
Library Type: reference
Publication: Magazine
Publication title: Campaign
Second publication: Magazine
Publication title: CND Today

Campaign for Press and Broadcasting Freedom

2nd Fl., Vi and Garner Smith House, 23 Orford Rd., Walthamstow, London, E17 9JU, England, UK
Tel: 44 20 85215932
Email: freepress@cpbf.org.uk
Website: http://www.cpbf.org.uk
Founded: 1979
Members: 700

Staff: 2
Contact: Barry White, Nat'l.Organizer
Fee: £15
Membership Type: individual
Fee: £25
Membership Type: organization
Description: Promotes media democracy.
Publication: Newsletter
Publication title: Free Press. Advertisements.
Meetings/Conventions: Media Democracy - annual conference - Exhibits.

Campaign for the Accountability of American Bases
CAAB

8 Park Row, Otley, LS21 1HQ, England, UK
Tel: 44 1943 466405
Fax: 44 1482 702033
Email: anniandlindis@caab.org.uk
Website: http://cndyorks.gn.apc.org/caab/caabinf.htm
Description: Committed to the opposition of weapons of mass destruction in general and nuclear weapons in particular, specifically the proposed American National Missile Defense/Theater Missile Defense systems, focusing on American military bases in the U.K. and abroad. Promotes public awareness, scrutiny and accountability of U.S. bases in the U.K.

Campden and Chorleywood Food Research Association, Chipping Campden, GL55 6LD, England, UK

Tel: 44 1386 842000
Fax: 44 1386 842100
Email: information@campden.co.uk
Website: http://www.campden.co.uk
Founded: 1919
Members: 1700
Staff: 300
Contact: B. Emond, Membership Mgr.
Description: Members are companies involved in agri-food, drink and allied industries including packaging and process innovation. Covers research, consultancy, and training into all areas of food and drink production, processing and preservation, including microbial and chemical contamination, quality management systems, sensory analysis and food hygiene requirements.
Library Type: not open to the public
Publication: Newsletter

Can Makers

1 Chelsea Manor Gardens, London, SW3 5PN, England, UK
Tel: 44 207 724083
Fax: 44 207 724020
Email: canmakers@gciuk.com
Website: http://www.canmakers.co.uk
Founded: 1981
Members: 17
Staff: 3
Contact: David Knowles, Dir.
Description: Drinks can manufacturers, raw material suppliers (steel, aluminium and coatings), detinning interests and secondary (multipack) suppliers. Represents the interests of the manufacturers of drinks cans and their raw material suppliers to promote the benefits of drinks cans and their environmental advantages.
Publication: Report

Publication title: Market Review
Second publication: Newsletter
Publication title: Thirst Choice

Canada-UK Chamber of Commerce

38 Grosvenor St., London, W1K 4DP, England, UK
Tel: 44 20 72586576
Fax: 44 20 72586594
Email: info@canada-uk.org
Website: http://www.canada-uk.org
Founded: 1921
Members: 330
Staff: 2
Contact: Karin Stephens, Exec.Dir.
Description: Promotes business and commerce.

Canon Collins Educational Trust for Southern Africa

22 The Ivories, 6 Northampton St., London, N1 2HY, England, UK
Tel: 44 20 73541462
Fax: 44 20 73594875
Email: ccetsa@gn.apc.org
Website: http://www.canoncollins.org.uk
Founded: 1981
Staff: 7
Contact: Ethel de Keyser, Dir.
Description: Promotes improved educational opportunities for people living in southern Africa, particularly people of color and women. Works with South African organizations to develop educational institutions and programs; assists students wishing to undertake postgraduate studies programs in the United Kingdom that are not available in southern Africa and in South Africa.
Meetings/Conventions: - annual conference

Captain Cook Society
CCS

13 Cowdry Close, Dewsbury, Thornhill, WF12 0LW, England, UK
Email: secretary@captaincooksociety.com
Website: http://www.captaincooksociety.com
Founded: 1975
Members: 400
Contact: Alwyn Peel, Sec.
Fee: £10
Fee: £19
Description: Individuals from 20 countries interested in the collection and study of material portraying the life and times of Captain James Cook (1728-79), English mariner and explorer. Conducts research on maritime history; disseminates information; announces related exhibitions; collects historical information on Cook and his sea voyages; reviews related maritime books.
Publication: Journal
Publication title: Cook's Log. Advertisements.
Meetings/Conventions: - annual meeting

Care for the Wild International
CFTWI

Tickfold Farm, Kingsfold, Horsham, RH12 3SE, England, UK
Tel: 44 1306 627900
Fax: 44 1306 627901
Email: info@careforthewild.org.uk
Website: http://www.careforthewild.com
Founded: 1984

Members: 30000
Staff: 10
Contact: Dr. Barbara Maas, Ch.Exec.
Description: Promotes the conservation and welfare of wildlife in Britain and abroad, particularly Africa and Asia. Provides fast, direct practical aid to animals in need by assisting to make areas safe from poachers, rehabilitation of sick or injured animals, and providing sanctuary for those unable to return to the wild. Work in the U.K. includes badgers, foxes, hedgehogs, seals and wild birds; abroad work focuses on the protection of tigers, elephants, rhinos, chimps, gibbons, orangutans, langurs, bears and wildcats.
Publication: Newsletter
Publication title: Newsletter. Advertisements.

CARE International UK

10-13 Rushworth St., London, SE1 0RB, England, UK
Tel: 44 207 9349334
Fax: 44 207 9349335
Email: info@ciuk.org
Website: http://www.careinternational.org.uk
Founded: 1938
Staff: 40
Contact: Will Day, Natl.Dir.
Description: National branch of the international organization. Individuals and organizations working to assist and provide relief to the underpriveleged, victims of natural disasters, and others in need. Assists communities in achieving long-term economic and social development while conserving natural resources through cooperation with community members and local organizations. Operates programs in health education, water sanitation, small business development, and education.
Formerly: CARE Britain

Careers Research and Advisory Centre

Sheraton House, Castle Park, Cambridge, CB3 0AX, England, UK
Tel: 44 1223 460277
Fax: 44 1223 311708
Email: web.enquiries@crac.org.uk
Website: http://www.crac.org.uk
Founded: 1964
Members: 155
Staff: 30
Contact: David Thomas, Dir.
Description: Aim is to support lifelong learning and career development through building strong links between education, training, and employment.
Publication: Newsletter
Publication title: Connections. Advertisements.
Meetings/Conventions: - periodic conference

Carers UK

Ruth Pitter House, 20-25 Glass House Yard, London, EC1A 4JS, England, UK
Tel: 44 207 4908818
Fax: 44 207 4908824
Email: info@ukcarers.org
Website: http://www.carersonline.org.uk
Founded: 1988
Members: 12000
Staff: 54
Contact: Diana Whitworth, Dir.
Fee: £8
Description: Provides information and support to carers, persons who provide assistance and support to ill, disabled, or elderly

individuals. Encourages carers to recognize and work towards meeting their own needs as caregivers through actively participating in social issues and legislative development that affects care givers and recipients. Offers training programs for professionals.
Library Type: not open to the public
Formerly: Carers National Association
Publication: Newsletter
Publication title: The Carer. Advertisements.
Second publication: Brochures
Meetings/Conventions: - annual meeting

Caribbean Banana Exporters Association
CBEA

c/o Gordon Myers, Exec.Sec.
Flagship Consulting - 67 Pall Mall, London, SW1Y 5ES, England, UK
Tel: 44 208 4286773
Fax: 44 208 4280014
Email: gem.cbea@btinternet.co
Website: http://www.cbea.org
Founded: 1958
Members: 4
Staff: 45
Contact: Malcolm Borthwick
Description: Banana associations of the Windward Islands, Belize, and Jamaica. To improve and develop the banana industry. Studies agronomic, economic, and statistical aspects of the banana industry; conducts research on plant pathology and fruit quality.
Formerly: Commonwealth Banana Exporters Association

Caribbean Council for Europe

Ste. 18, Westminster Palace Gardens, 1-7 Artillery Row, London, SW1P 1PR, England, UK
Tel: 44 207 7991521
Email: caribbean@compuserve.com
Founded: 1992
Members: 200
Staff: 7
Contact: David A. Jessop
Fee: £2000
Membership Type: premier
Fee: £500
Membership Type: standard
Description: Corporations and individuals. Provides advocacy and information to Caribbean private sector interests. Promotes understanding, cooperation, and trade between Europe and the Caribbean. Conducts educational and charitable programs.
Publication: Newsletter
Publication title: Europe/Caribbean Confidential
Meetings/Conventions: Europe Caribbean Conference - annual conference

Carlisle and West Cumbria Chamber of Commerce

Unit 3, Lakeland Business Park, Lamplugh Rd., Cockermouth, CA13 0QT, England, UK
Tel: 44 1900 824113
Fax: 44 1900 824951
Contact: Paul Fearn
Description: Promotes business and commerce.

Carpenters' Company

c/o Carpenters' Hall
Throgmorton Ave., London, EC2N 2JJ, England, UK
Tel: 44 20 75887001
Fax: 44 20 73821683
Email: info@carpentersco.com
Website: http://www.thecarpenterscompany.co.uk
Founded: 1333
Members: 250
Contact: Maj.Gen. P.T. Stevenson, Clerk
Description: A medieval craft guild which promotes the craft of carpentry and runs a building crafts college where courses are run in fine woodwork, shopfitting and stonemasonry. Also runs a convalescent home and alms houses.
Library Subject: historic carpentry
Library Type: not open to the public

Cast Metals Federation

The National Metalforming Centre, 47 Birmingham Rd., West Bromwich, B70 6PY, England, UK
Tel: 44 121 6016390
Fax: 44 121 6016391
Email: admin@cmfed.co.uk
Website: http://www.castmetalsfederation.com
Founded: 2001
Members: 225
Staff: 5
Contact: John Parker, Chief Exec.
Description: UK Foundries. Assists and encourages industry profitability; promotes image of the British Foundry Industry; extends membership with the Metal Casting Industry.
Formerly: Absorbed, British Investment Casting Trade Association
Publication title: Castings Buyers' Guide

Castings Technology International

7 E. Bank Rd., Sheffield, S2 3PT, England, UK
Tel: 44 114 2728647
Fax: 44 114 2730852
Email: info@castingstechnology.com
Website: http://www.castingstechnology.com
Founded: 1996
Members: 300
Staff: 110
Contact: Dr. M.C. Ashton, Ch.Exec.
Fee: £2500
Description: Carries out research and provides impartial expertise on all aspects of the design, materials, manufacture, use, quality, and performance of castings. Has extensive state-of-the-art facilities for design through to prototype manufacture and testing.
Library Subject: casting
Library Type: reference
Formerly: Formed by Merger of, Steel Castings Association
Publication: Book
Publication title: Specifications for Steel Castings
Second publication: Directory
Publication title: Where to Buy Iron Castings

Castor Manufacturers of United Kingdom Association

1 Perch Close, Marlow, SL7 2BQ, England, UK
Tel: 44 1628 475648
Fax: 44 1628 475648
Founded: 1965

Members: 7
Contact: A. Thorniley
Description: UK manufacturers of castors and wheels for domestic furniture, office equipment, hospital institutional and light/medium and heavy industrial applications. Promotes, develops and protects the UK castor and wheel industry for the benefit of both manufacturers and users, and is actively involved in the preparation of international and European dimensional and performance castor and wheel standards in conjunction with other national bodies and the specification for equipment using castors and wheels.
Publication: Brochure

Catering Equipment Distributors Association of Great Britain
CEDA

PO Box 194, Bingley, BD16 2XW, England, UK
Tel: 44 1274 826056
Fax: 44 1274 777260
Email: info@ceda.co.uk
Website: http://www.ceda.co.uk
Founded: 1972
Members: 88
Staff: 1
Contact: Bruce Furness, Chm.
Description: Companies primarily engaged in the distribution of commercial catering equipment. To promote and advance the interests and status of members; to foster the highest standards of efficiency; encourage, support and promote technical education for the benefit of members. To provide communication between members and foster discussion on matters of common interest.
Publication: Newsletter
Publication title: CEDA News
Second publication: Newsletter
Meetings/Conventions: - annual conference

Catering Equipment Suppliers Association

Carlyle House, 235-237 Vauxhall Bridge Rd., London, SW1V 1EJ, England, UK
Tel: 44 207 2337724
Fax: 44 207 8280667
Email: info@cesa.org.uk
Website: http://www.cesa.org.uk
Founded: 1938
Members: 86
Staff: 3
Contact: Becky Chick, Sec.
Description: Manufacturers of commercial catering equipment and/or suppliers of goods and services to the industry. Promotes co-operation and co-ordination between those engaged in the catering equipment manufacturing industry; makes representations to government departments and authorities, whether international, national or local on matters affecting members.

Catering Managers Association of Great Britain and the Channel Islands

c/o Mount Pleasant
Egton, Whitby, Y021 1UE, England, UK
Tel: 44 1947 895514
Fax: 44 1947 895514
Email: ptr.god@aol.com
Founded: 1947
Members: 100
Contact: P. Godbold

Fee: £25
Membership Type: full
Fee: £100
Membership Type: affiliate
Description: Professionals who work throughout different branches of the public and civil services, the armed forces, the prison service, hospitals, across the academic field, private and nationalised companies whether industrial, retail or service, airlines and. airports, hotels and restaurant chains and in smaller establishments. Aims to fight for greater recognition for professional managers in every sector of the industry; to improve, set and maintain standards in the catering industry; to give help to managers, potential managers and to develop their knowledge and expertise within our industry and to act as a stepping stone for student members.
Publication: Magazine
Publication title: The Catering Manager. Advertisements.
Meetings/Conventions: - quarterly meeting

Cathedral Architects Association

46 St. Mary's St., Ely, CB7 4EY, England, UK
Tel: 44 1353 660660
Fax: 44 1353 660661
Email: janekennedy@pmt.co.uk
Founded: 1948
Members: 80
Contact: Jane Kennedy
Fee: £35
Membership Type: full
Description: Architects looking after cathedrals. Mutual help of members of the association in dealing with the problems encountered with working on cathedrals.
Publication: Proceedings
Meetings/Conventions: - annual meeting

Catholic Institute for International Relations
CIIR

Unit 3 Canonbury Yard, 190A New North Rd., London, N1 7BJ, England, UK
Tel: 44 207 3540883
Fax: 44 207 3590017
Email: ciir@ciir.org
Website: http://www.ciir.org
Founded: 1940
Members: 3000
Staff: 39
Contact: Christine Allen, Exec.Dir.
Fee: £15
Membership Type: Individual
Fee: £20
Membership Type: outside UK
Description: Works to combine a heritage of radical Catholicism and secular thought. The values and goals include the eradication of poverty and exclusion through challenging unjust political, social and economic structures locally and globally; the full and active participation of the poorest groups in decision-making working to reduce vulnerability stemming from conflict, war and environmental degradation; and an equitable distribution of resources and power between men and women and communities and nations. Guatemala, Nicaragua, Yemen, Zimbabwe, Namibia, and Peru, providing skilled workers in agriculture, health, formal and non-formal education, and environment projects. Arranges forums providing resource material for members of British and European parliaments, policy-makers, and the media.
Library Subject: agriculture, drug trade, development, gender, global economics
Library Type: not open to the public

Publication title: Briefing Papers, Comment Series
Second publication: Newsletter
Publication title: CIIR Newsletter
Meetings/Conventions: - annual meeting

Cats Protection

17 Kings Rd., Horsham, RH13 5PN, England, UK
Tel: 44 1403 221900
Fax: 44 1403 218414
Email: cpl@cats.org.uk
Website: http://www.cats.org.uk
Founded: 1927
Members: 46000
Staff: 230
Contact: Derek Conway, Chief Exec.
Fee: £12
Membership Type: UK - individual
Fee: £18
Membership Type: Europe - individual
Description: Cat lovers, for the most part subscribers to the Charity's publications and passive supporters of the Charity's aims. A small percentage (around 5%) actively involved in cat rescue work on an unpaid voluntary basis. Aims to rescue stray and unwanted cats and kittens, rehabilitating and rehoming them where possible; to encourage the neutering of cats not required for breeding; to inform the public on the care of cats and kittens.
Publication: Magazine
Publication title: The Cat
Publication title: Junior News

Cement Admixtures Association
CAA

38A Tilehouse Screen Lane, Knowle, Solihull, B93 9EY, England, UK
Tel: 44 1564 776362
Fax: 44 1564 776362
Website: http://www.admixtures.org.uk
Founded: 1963
Staff: 1
Contact: John Dransfield, Sec.
Fee: £512
Membership Type: associate
Fee: £3650
Membership Type: full
Description: Cement admixtures production and marketing companies in the United Kingdom are full members; suppliers of materials and testing services to the cement admixtures industries are associate members. Encourages the safe and effective use of admixtures in concrete, cement, and sand mixes. Cooperates with government departments in the creation and monitoring of industry standards.
Publication title: Admixture Data Sheet
Second publication: Book
Publication title: Code of Practice for the Application of ISO 9000 to the Admixture Industry
Meetings/Conventions: - quarterly meeting

Central and West Lancashire Chamber of Commerce and Industry

9/10 Eastway Business Village, Olivers Pl., Fulwood, Preston, PR2 9WT, England, UK
Tel: 44 1772 653000
Fax: 44 1772 655544
Email: info@lancasterchamber.co.uk

Website: http://www.lancschamber.co.uk
Founded: 1916
Members: 1398
Staff: 20
Contact: Peter Milehan, Pres.
Description: Represents, promotes and supports business community of central and west Lancashire.
Publication: Journal
Publication title: Network

Central Association of Agricultural Valuers

Market Chambers, 35 Market Place, Coleford, GL16 8AA, England, UK
Tel: 44 1594 832979
Fax: 44 1594 810701
Email: enquire@caav.org.uk
Website: http://www.caav.org.uk
Founded: 1910
Members: 2100
Contact: Jeremy Moody, Sec. & Advisor
Fee: £150
Membership Type: full, probationer, or retired
Description: Members are land agents, agricultural valuers and auctioneers represented by the CAAV which awards the qualification FAAV on examination. Publisher technical guidance and briefings. Engager with government and others in professional matters.
Publication: Newsletter
Meetings/Conventions: - annual convention Bath UK

Central Association of Bee-Keepers

6 Oxford Rd., Teddington, TW11 OPZ, England, UK
Tel: 44 20 89775867
Founded: 1945
Members: 200
Contact: Mrs. M.R. English
Fee: £10
Membership Type: single
Fee: £12
Membership Type: dual
Description: Arranges lectures on scientific topics related to bees and beekeeping by acknowledged experts in their fields and publishes many of these lectures in booklet form. A weekend conference is held each October in Leamington Spa.
Publication: Book
Publication title: Honeybee Biology 1982
Second publication: Book
Publication title: Keeping Bees 1993
Meetings/Conventions: - semiannual conference

Centre for Agricultural Strategy
CAS

c/o The University of Reading
PO Box 237, Earley Gate, Whiteknights Rd., Reading, RG6 6AR, England, UK
Tel: 44 118 3788150
Fax: 44 118 9353423
Email: casagri@reading.ac.uk
Website: http://www.rdg.ac.uk/AgriStrat/
Founded: 1975
Staff: 9
Contact: Prof. Alan Swinbank, Dir.
Description: Provides independent and continuing assessments of agricultural and food industries across the countryside. Facilitates

strategic planning for the agricultural, food, and ancillary industries, together with relevant government departments and agencies.
Publication: Papers
Meetings/Conventions: - periodic conference

Centre for Business Transformation
Ashcroft International Business School, Anglia Polytecnic University, Danbury Park, CM3 4AT, England, UK
Tel: 44 1245 225511
Fax: 44 1245 224331
Email: j.sanger@apu.ac.uk
Website: http://www.cor.anglia.ac.uk
Founded: 1979
Contact: Prof. Jack Sanger
Description: Public and private sector organizations. Seeks to enhance the capabilities of managers through high quality research, consulting and training. Provides stat e of the art applications of research methodologies.
Formerly: Centre for Organisational Research
Publication: Monographs
Second publication: Papers

Centre for Deaf Studies
8 Woodland Rd., Bristol, BS8 1TN, England, UK
Tel: 44 117 9546900
Fax: 44 117 9546921
Email: coursesecretary-cds@bris.ac.uk
Website: http://www.bris.ac.uk/deaf/
Founded: 1978

Centre for Design and Technology Education
c/o University of Wolverhampton
Castle View, Dudley, DY1 3HR, England, UK
Tel: 44 1902 321050
Fax: 44 1902 323177
Email: sed-enquiries@wlv.ac.uk
Founded: 1987
Members: 200
Staff: 12
Contact: R.J. Booth
Description: Provides industry and teacher training in design and technology at the undergraduate and postgraduate levels.
Library Subject: humanities, technology, design
Library Type: open to the public
Publication: Newsletter
Publication title: CFACTS. Advertisements.
Meetings/Conventions: Design and Technolgy Inservice - annual seminar - Exhibits.

Centre for Ecology and Hydrology
Polaris House, Northstar Ave., Swindon, SN2 1EU, England, UK
Tel: 44 1491 838800
Fax: 44 1491 692424
Email: nrr@ceh.ac.uk
Website: http://www.ceh.ac.uk
Founded: 1965
Staff: 170
Contact: N. Runnalls
Description: Conducts fundamental and applied research concerning many aspects of the water cycle.
Library Subject: hydrology, water quality
Library Type: open to the public
Formerly: Institute of Hydrology

Publication: Newsletter
Publication title: Hydrological Summary
Second publication: Journal
Publication title: IH Report Series

Centre for Economic Policy Research
90-98 Goswell Rd., London, EC1V 7RR, England, UK
Tel: 44 20 78782900
Fax: 44 20 78782999
Email: cepr@cepr.org
Website: http://www.cepr.org
Founded: 1983
Members: 500
Staff: 23
Contact: Hilary Beech, CEO
Description: Research fellows throughout Europe. Enables members to collaborate in economic research; disseminates results to the public. Areas of interest include open economy macroeconomics, trade policy, and European economic integration.
Publication: Bulletin
Publication title: CEPR Bulletin
Second publication: Newsletter
Publication title: European Economic Perspectives

Centre for Interfirm Comparison
32 St. Thomas St., Winchester, SO23 9HJ, England, UK
Tel: 44 1962 844144
Fax: 44 1962 843180
Email: enquiries@cifc.co.uk
Website: http://www.cifc.co.uk
Founded: 1959
Staff: 12
Contact: Mr. H.W. Palmer, Dir.
Description: Provides expertise in performance measurement and financial control of companies and other organizations. Services include interfirm comparison; benchmarking; development of performance indicators; surveys, statistics and business information; and training in these topics. The Centre has worked in over 150 industries and the public and voluntary sectors in the UK and overseas.
Publication: Brochure

Centre for Photographic Conservation
233 Stanstead Rd., Forest Hill, London, SE12 1HU, England, UK
Tel: 44 181 6903678
Fax: 44 181 3141940
Email: xfa59@dial.pipex.com
Website: http://www.cpc.moor.dial.pipex.com
Description: Works to develop preservation and conservation techniques for photographic materials. Conducts research in historic process and material photographic technologies.

Centre for Policy on Ageing
CPA
19-23 Ironmonger Row, London, EC1V 3QP, England, UK
Tel: 44 207 5536500
Fax: 44 207 5536501
Email: cpa@cpa.org.uk
Website: http://www.cpa.org.uk
Founded: 1947
Members: 90
Staff: 16
Contact: Trish Harwood, Admin.

Description: Health care professionals; social workers; academics. Promotes policies in England which will result in higher standards of care and a better lifestyle for the elderly. Encourages informed debate about issues affecting older people and stimulates public awarenesss of their needs. Conducts studies and makes recommendations to policy makers. Maintains CPA Information Service which keeps readers abreast of trends in policy, practice, and research development. Areas of interest include residential care policy, educational and recreational activities for the elderly, and elderly people in ethnic minorities. Strives to address the needs of housebound and vulnerable elderly people and integrate all older people into the community. Currently investigating possible methods of providing for homeless elderly people.
Library Subject: social behavior health aspects of aging
Library Type: reference
Publication title: Age Info CD-ROM
Publication title: Aging and Society

Cereal Ingredients Manufacturers Association

6 Catherine St., London, WC2B 5JJ, England, UK
Tel: 44 207 8362460
Fax: 44 207 8360580
Email: charlottepatrick@fdf.org.uk
Founded: 1993
Members: 6
Contact: Charlotte Patrick
Description: Manufacturers of cereal ingredients, including rusk, batters and crumb coatings. Aims to promote and protect the interests of its members in all matters pertaining to the cereal ingredient trade.

Challenger Society for Marine Science
CSMS

c/o Southampton Oceanography Centre
Waterfront Campus, Ste. 251-20, Empress Dock, Southampton, SO14 3ZH, England, UK
Tel: 44 23 80596097
Fax: 44 23 80596149
Email: jxj@soc.soton.ac.uk
Website: http://www.soc.soton.ac.uk/OTHERS/CSMS/
Founded: 1903
Members: 550
Contact: Jennifer Jones, Exec.Sec.
Fee: £12
Membership Type: student
Fee: £25
Membership Type: full
Description: Scientists. Works to advance the study and application of marine science through research and education. Maintains specialist groups in different disciplines to provide a forum for technical discussion. Provides marine science information to the public in order to encourage study of the seas. Offers financial assistance to marine science students. Sponsors competitions.
Formerly: Challenger Society
Publication: Newsletter
Publication title: Ocean Challenge
Meetings/Conventions: - periodic conference - Exhibits.

Chamber of Commerce, Herefordshire and Worcestershire

Castle St., Enterprise House, Worcester, WR1 3EN, England, UK
Tel: 44 800 104010
Fax: 44 1905 616463
Email: information@hwcamber.co.uk

Website: http://www.hwccte.co.uk
Members: 2780
Staff: 185
Contact: Alan Curless, Chf.Exec.
Description: Promotes business and commerce and represents its members' interests.
Publication: Magazines
Publication title: Direction. Advertisements.

Chamber of Shipping
CoS

Cartusian Ct., 12 Carthusian St., London, EC1M 6EZ, England, UK
Tel: 44 207 4172800
Fax: 44 207 7262080
Website: http://www.british-shipping.org/index.htm
Founded: 1878
Members: 140
Staff: 35
Contact: Jeremy Harison, Hd.Pub.Rel.
Description: UK-based ship owners and managers, and associates from across the maritime sector. Promotes and protects members' interests. Represents the shipping industry before government agencies, international regulatory bodies.
Formerly: General Council of British Shipping
Publication: Journal
Publication title: Annual Review
Second publication: Bulletin
Publication title: Circular to Members

CHANGE - International Reports: Women and Society

PO Box 18333, London, EC1N 7XG, England, UK
Tel: 44 20 72428972
Fax: 44 20 74300254
Email: ncsm.change@sister.com
Founded: 1979
Staff: 4
Contact: Dr. Purna Sen, Dir.
Fee: £50
Membership Type: Supporter
Description: Researches and publishes reports concerning the status of women worldwide. Affirms that: the suppression of women in society has been a disadvantage to economic and political processes; the central purpose of a nongovernmental organization should be to represent the need for change; reports should be written by women natives of the relevant country; and although there exist real economic inequalities, developed and underdeveloped countries should not be separated, in order to prevent patronizing attitudes. Works to: educate the public about the inequalities women struggle against in society through: dissemination of information; encouraging an international exchange of information; promotion of recognition of women's human rights; the publication of such abuse by governments, businesses, or individuals. Contributes to campaigns, networks, and conferences worldwide. Offers gender training, and lobby and advocacy training.
Library Subject: human rights, women's rights, women and development
Library Type: reference
Publication title: Contradictions and Ironies: Women of Lesotho
Second publication: Book
Publication title: Economic Development and Women's Place: Women in Singapore
Meetings/Conventions: - periodic meeting

Charity Law Association
c/o Rollits
Rowntree Wharf, Navigation Rd., York, Y01 9WE, England, UK
Tel: 44 1904 625790
Fax: 44 1904 625807
Email: charitylaw@aol.com
Website: http://www.charitylawassociation.org.uk
Founded: 1992
Members: 615
Staff: 1
Contact: Ros Harwood, Sec.
Fee: £40
Description: Solicitors and barristers practising in the field of charity law, other professionals such as accountants having an interest in the development of charity law, charities and charity trustees. Aims to advance the education of the public in charity law and matters relating thereto and to improve the administration of charities.

Charles Lamb Society
BM Elia, London, WC1N 3XX, England, UK
Founded: 1935
Members: 350
Contact: Prof. John Beer, Pres.
Fee: £12
Membership Type: personal/single
Fee: £18
Membership Type: personal/double
Description: Seeks to advance knowledge and publish studies of the life, works, and times of the writer Charles Lamb (1775-1834) and his circle.
Library Subject: Charles Lamb and his circle
Library Type: by appointment only
Publication: Journal
Publication title: The Charles Lamb Bulletin

Charles Williams Society
CWS
c/o Richard Sturch
35 Broomfield, Stacey Bushes, Milton Keynes, MK12 6HA, England, UK
Tel: 44 1908 316779
Email: charles_wms_soc@yahoo.co.uk
Website: http://www.geocities.com/charles_wms_soc
Founded: 1975
Members: 117
Contact: Richard Sturch, Hon.Sec.
Fee: £10
Membership Type: ordinary
Description: Individuals interested in literary activities and in promoting interest in the life and works of Charles Walter Stansby Williams (1886-1945), writer and lay theologian.
Library Subject: the life and work of Charles Walter Stansby Williams (1886-1945)
Library Type: reference
Publication: Newsletter
Publication title: Charles Williams Society Newsletter
Meetings/Conventions: lecture

Chartered Institute of Arbitrators
International Arbitration Centre, 12 Bloomsbury Sq., London, WC1A 2LP, England, UK
Tel: 44 20 74217444
Fax: 44 20 74044023
Email: info@arbitrators.org
Website: http://www.arbitrators.org
Founded: 1915
Members: 10000
Staff: 33
Contact: Mr. Dair Farrar-Hockley, Dir.Gen.
Fee: £235
Membership Type: fellow
Fee: £160
Membership Type: associate
Description: Promotes and facilitates the determination of civil and commercial disputes by arbitration and alternative means of dispute resolution, including mediation and adjudication.
Library Subject: arbitrations and dispute resolution
Library Type: not open to the public
Publication: Journal
Publication title: Arbitration
Second publication: Newsletter
Publication title: Newsletter
Meetings/Conventions: - annual international conference

Chartered Institute of Building
Englemere, Kings Ride, Ascot, SL5 7TB, England, UK
Tel: 44 1344 630700
Fax: 44 1344 630777
Email: reception@ciob.org.uk
Website: http://www.ciob.org.uk
Founded: 1834
Members: 39000
Staff: 80
Contact: Shirley June Hartland, International Coor.
Description: Skilled managers and professionals with a common commitment to achieving and maintaining the highest possible standards. Concerned with the promotion, for the public benefit, of the science and practice of building; the advancement of education in the science and practice of building including all necessary research and the publication of the results of all such research; the establishment and maintenance of appropriate standards of competence and conduct of those engaged, or about to engage, in the science and practice of building.
Library Subject: construction management
Library Type: not open to the public
Publication: Magazine
Publication title: Construction Information Quarterly
Second publication: Magazine
Publication title: Construction Manager. Advertisements.

Chartered Institute of Environmental Health
Chadwick Court, 15 Hatfields, London, SE1 8DJ, England, UK
Tel: 44 207 9286006
Fax: 44 207 8275866
Email: information@cieh.org
Website: http://www.cieh.org
Founded: 1883
Members: 9800
Staff: 110
Contact: Graham Jukes, Ch.Exec.
Fee: £126
Description: The majority of its members are employed by local government to enforce a wide range of legislation on issues such as food safety, pollution, housing standards, safety at work and to educate the public on matters of hygiene and safety. An increasing number of its members are working in the commercial sector either for individual companies or as private environmental health consultants.

Responsible for the training and professional development of over 8000 environmental health officers. Its primary objective is the promotion of environmental health and the dissemination of knowledge about environmental health issues. The CIEH represents the views of its members on environmental and public health issues and is independent of central and local government.
Library Subject: environmental health
Library Type: by appointment only
Formerly: Institution of Environmental Health Offices
Publication: Journal
Publication title: Environmental Health. Advertisements.
Publication title: Environmental Health News
Meetings/Conventions: Annual Environmental Health Congress - Exhibits.

Chartered Institute of Housing

c/o Octavia House
Westwood Business Park, Westwood Way, Coventry, CV4 8JP, England, UK
Tel: 44 2476 851700
Fax: 44 2476 695110
Email: customer.services@cih.org
Website: http://www.cih.org
Founded: 1916
Members: 17000
Staff: 120
Contact: David Butler, CEO
Fee: £103
Membership Type: affiliate
Description: Aims to promote the highest standards of service in housing through education and training as the professional body for people working in all sectors of housing.
Library Subject: Social housing, social policy, home ownership
Library Type: not open to the public
Publication: Journal
Publication title: Housing. Advertisements.
Second publication: Journal
Publication title: Inside Housing. Advertisements.
Meetings/Conventions: - annual conference Harrogate UK

Chartered Institute of Journalists

2 Dock Offices, Surrey Quays Rd., London, SE16 2XU, England, UK
Tel: 44 207 2521187
Fax: 44 207 2322302
Email: memberservices@ioj.co.uk
Website: http://www.ioj.co.uk
Founded: 1884
Members: 1250
Staff: 3
Contact: C.J. Underwood, Gen.Sec.
Fee: £190
Membership Type: ordinary
Description: Print journalists, broadcasters, Internet communications, photographers, and public relations practitioners. Upholds and seeks to improve standards in journalism and also acts as an independent trade union.
Publication: Journal
Publication title: The Journal. Advertisements.
Publication title: What a Journalist Does
Meetings/Conventions: - annual conference Rochester, Kent UK

Chartered Institute of Logistics Transport
CIT

11/12 Buckingham Gate, London, SW1 6LB, England, UK
Tel: 44 20 75923110
Fax: 44 20 75923111
Email: gen@citrans.org.uk
Website: http://www.citrans.org.uk
Founded: 1919
Members: 32500
Contact: Prof. Cyril Bleasdale, Dir.Gen.
Description: Managers and others in 60 countries engaged in transport or logistics. Contributes to professional education in the field through the development of qualifications for those involved in the movement of people and goods. Promotes and coordinates the study and advancement of the science of transportation. Stimulates debate on transport issues and logistics with governments and the public. Sponsors studies undertaken by individuals. Administers exams and grants diplomas. Conducts student essay competitions.
Library Subject: transport, logistics
Library Type: reference
Publication: Journal
Publication title: CILT World. Advertisements.
Second publication: Reports
Meetings/Conventions: conference

Chartered Institute of Loss Adjusters

Peninsular House, 36 Monument St., London, EC3R 8LJ, England, UK
Tel: 44 207 3379960
Fax: 44 207 9293082
Email: info@cila.co.uk
Website: http://www.cila.co.uk
Founded: 1941
Members: 2300
Staff: 6
Contact: Graham L. Cave, Exec.Dir.
Description: Member institute for chartered loss adjusters.

Chartered Institute of Management Accountants - England
CIMA

26 Chapter St., London, SW1P 4NP, England, UK
Tel: 44 20 76635441
Fax: 44 20 76635442
Email: research@cimaglobal.com
Website: http://www.cimaglobal.com
Founded: 1919
Members: 50000
Staff: 220
Contact:
Fee: £60
Membership Type: professional institute
Description: Professional body devoted to the science and skill of management accountancy. Chartered Management Accountants work in industry, commerce and the public sector. Comprises commercially focused financial managers responsible for managing the resources of business enterprises. Offers professional qualification evaluation services.
Formerly: Institute of Cost and Management Accountants
Publication: Magazine
Publication title: Management Accounting. Advertisements.

Chartered Institute of Marketing
CIM

Moor Hall, Cookham, Maidenhead, SL6 9QH, England, UK
Tel: 44 1628 427500
Fax: 44 1628 427499
Email: membership@cim.co.uk
Website: http://www.cim.co.uk
Founded: 1911
Members: 60000
Staff: 150
Contact: Diane Thompson, Chief Exec.
Description: Seeks to increase knowledge of the principles and practices of marketing through the delivery of world class professional support to marketing professionals. Organizes residential training courses on all aspects of marketing; offers certificates and post-graduate diploma in Marketing.
Library Subject: marketing and business
Library Type: reference
Publication: Magazine
Publication title: Marketing Business. Advertisements.
Second publication: Report
Publication title: Marketing Success. Advertisements.

Chartered Institute of Patent Agents

95 Chancery Ln., London, WC2A 1DT, England, UK
Tel: 44 20 74059450
Fax: 44 20 74300471
Email: mail@cipa.org.uk
Website: http://www.cipa.org.uk
Founded: 1882
Members: 3000
Staff: 11
Contact: M.C. Ralph, Sec.
Description: Fellows are registered UK patent agents; Associates are part-qualified trainees, or members of associated professions; British Overseas or Foreign Members are patent attorneys qualified abroad. The professional body for patent agents and others in the intellectual property field.
Formerly: Formed by Merger of, CIPA
Publication: Journal
Publication title: CIPA. Advertisements.
Publication title: Membership List

Chartered Institute of Personnel and Development

Camp Rd., CIPD House, Wimbledon, London, SW19 4UX, England, UK
Tel: 44 208 9719000
Fax: 44 208 2633333
Email: cipd@cipd.co.uk
Website: http://www.cipd.co.uk
Founded: 1994
Members: 105000
Staff: 200
Contact: Barbara Salmon, Library Manager
Fee: £80
Membership Type: qualification/experience based
Description: Those involved in the management and development of people in the UK and the Republic of Ireland. Aims to position the CIPD as the leading organization in the United Kingdom and the Republic of Ireland responsible for the management and development of people and the dissemination of information on this.
Library Subject: personnel management, training and development, industrial relations, employment law, pay and benefits, human

resource planning, occupational psychology, and general management
Library Type: not open to the public
Formerly: Formed by Merger of, Institute of Personnel Management
Publication title: People Management. Advertisements.
Meetings/Conventions: Computers in Personnel - annual London UK

Chartered Institute of Public Finance and Accountancy

7th Fl., NLA Tower, 12-16 Addiscombe Rd., Croydon, CR0 0XT, England, UK
Tel: 44 207 5435600
Fax: 44 207 5435700
Website: http://www.cipfa.org.uk
Founded: 1885
Members: 13300
Staff: 200
Contact: Steve Freer, Chief Exec.
Fee: £234
Membership Type: ordinary
Description: Members manage finances across all sectors of the public services, in the Health Service, local and national government; National Audit; gas, electricity and water companies, education, and housing associations. Also in accountancy firms, in public audit sections. Provides education and training in accountancy and financial management, and sets and monitors professional standards. Professional qualification is high quality, relevant and practical, and is supported by a range of other products and services.
Publication: Magazine
Publication title: Public Finance

Chartered Institute of Purchasing and Supply

Easton House, Easton-on-the-Hill, Stamford, PE9 3NZ, England, UK
Tel: 44 1780 756777
Fax: 44 1780 751610
Email: info@cips.org
Website: http://www.cips.org
Founded: 1932
Members: 31000
Staff: 70
Contact: Carolyn Munton, Head of Mktg. & Commun.
Description: Those involved in the purchasing and supply management professions. The professional body for purchasing, supply and materials management staff in the public and private sectors of industry, local and central government.
Publication: Magazine
Publication title: Supply Management

Chartered Institute of Taxation
CIOT

12 Upper Belgrave St., London, SW1X 8BB, England, UK
Tel: 44 207 2359381
Fax: 44 207 2352562
Email: post@tax.org.uk
Website: http://www.tax.org.uk
Founded: 1930
Members: 10800
Staff: 40
Contact: R.A. Dommett, Sec.Gen.
Fee: £165
Membership Type: fellow
Fee: £150

Membership Type: associate
Description: Membership consists of tax advisers, most of whom are in practice, providing the widest range of taxation services to the public. Also includes accountants and solicitors who work in commerce and industry or are self employed. Members are known by the title chartered tax advisor. Promotes the study of the administration and practice of taxation. Makes recommendations to improve or simplify tax law and practice. Holds examinations throughout the UK twice a year and runs residential conferences, one-day courses and, through its branches, technical meetings and social activities.
Publication title: Essential Law for the Tax Practitioner
Publication title: Taxation Practitioner

Chartered Institution of Building Services Engineers - England
CIBSE

222 Balham High Rd., London, SW12 9BS, England, UK
Tel: 44 208 6755211
Fax: 44 208 6755449
Email: enquiries@cibse.org
Website: http://www.cibse.org/
Founded: 1897
Members: 15500
Staff: 32
Contact: Julian Amey, Chief Exec./Sec.
Description: Professional engineers and other interested individuals. Purpose is to promote the art, science, and practice of building services engineering and the advancement of education and research. Organizes educational and training courses. Sponsors charitable programs.
Formerly: Absorbed, Illuminating Engineering Society
Publication: Journal
Publication title: Building Services. Advertisements.
Publication title: Building Services Engineering Research and Technology
Meetings/Conventions: Lighting Conference - biennial conference - Exhibits.

Chartered Institution of Wastes Management

9 Saxon Court, St. Peters Gardens, Northampton, NN1 1SX, England, UK
Tel: 44 1604 620426
Fax: 44 1604 621339
Email: membership@ciwm.co.uk
Website: http://www.iwm.co.uk
Founded: 1898
Members: 4000
Staff: 29
Contact: Paul Frith, Info.Ofcr.
Fee: £93
Membership Type: corporate
Description: Qualified professional and technical persons experienced in all aspects of the management of wastes.
Library Subject: waste management
Library Type: by appointment only
Publication: Proceedings
Publication title: Scientific & Technical Review
Publication title: Waste Management. Advertisements.
Meetings/Conventions: - annual conference - Exhibits.

Chartered Institution of Water and Environmental Management
CIWEM

15 John St., London, WC1N 2EB, England, UK
Tel: 44 207 8313110
Fax: 44 207 4054967
Email: admin@ciwem.org.uk
Website: http://www.ciwem.org.uk
Founded: 1987
Members: 12000
Staff: 15
Contact: Nick Reeves, Exec.Dir.
Fee: £80
Membership Type: fellow
Fee: £80
Membership Type: member, graduate, associate, affiliate
Description: Engineers, chemists, biologists, geologists, hydrologists, and individuals engaged in water and environmental management issues in 100 countries. Advances the science and practice of water and environmental management, including the treatment and the distribution of drinking water and the treatment and disposal of domestic and industrial waste waters. Conducts symposia; sponsors study tours and competitions for young members.
Library Subject: Water supply, treatment of waste and wastewater, solid waste, sewage, and treatment plants.
Library Type: reference
Publication: Directory
Publication title: International Directory
Second publication: Magazine
Publication title: Water and Environment Manager. Advertisements.
Meetings/Conventions: - annual conference - Exhibits.

Chartered Insurance Institute

20 Aldermanbury, London, EC2Y 7HY, England, UK
Tel: 44 20 89898464
Fax: 44 20 85303052
Email: customer.serv@cii.co.uk
Website: http://www.cii.co.uk
Founded: 1912
Members: 65000
Staff: 150
Contact: Steve Radford, Mktg.Mgr.
Fee: £39
Membership Type: ordinary
Description: Persons employed or engaged in insurance or financial services. Plays a vital role in insurance and financial services promoting the highest standards of professionalism through education and training.
Publication: Journal
Publication title: CII Journal. Advertisements.
Second publication: Journal
Publication title: Society of Fellows Journal
Meetings/Conventions: - annual conference

Chartered Society of Designers
CSD

Freepost Lon5009, London, SE1 3YY, England, UK
Tel: 44 207 3578088
Fax: 44 207 4079878
Email: csd@csd.org.uk
Website: http://www.csd.org.uk/
Founded: 1930
Members: 7000

Staff: 10
Contact: Brian Lymbery, Dir.
Description: Represents interests of designers in U.K. Promotes high standards of design, fosters professionalism, and emphasises designers responsibilities to society.
Library Subject: design disciplines
Library Type: reference
Formerly: Society of Industrial Artists and Designers
Publication: Newsletter
Publication title: Business and Design
Second publication: Newsletter
Publication title: Chartered Designers' Newsletter
Meetings/Conventions: - periodic seminar

Chartered Society of Physiotherapy
CSP

14 Bedford Row, London, WC1R 4ED, England, UK
Tel: 44 207 3066666
Fax: 44 207 3066611
Email: csp@csp.org.uk
Website: http://www.csp.org.uk
Founded: 1894
Members: 40000
Staff: 130
Contact: Phillip Gray, Ch.Exec.
Fee: £149
Description: The professional association, educational body and trade union of the United Kingdom's 39,000 chartered psychotherapists, physical students and assistants. Aims to protect member's interests and help them to achieve the best possible patient care.
Library Subject: physiotherapy, health management
Library Type: not open to the public
Publication title: Frontline. Advertisements.
Second publication: Journal
Publication title: Physiotherapy Journal
Meetings/Conventions: - annual congress - Exhibits.

Cheirological Society

29 London Rd., Dereham, NR19 1AS, England, UK
Tel: 44 1362 693962
Fax: 44 1362 693962
Email: cheirology@x-stream.co.uk
Founded: 1889
Members: 250
Staff: 2
Contact:
Fee: £25
Description: Individuals with an academic interest in palm reading and study of the hand as a serious and systematic study bereft of supersitition and fakery. Promotes scientific inquiry into the analysis of hands from a psychological and medical perspective. Functions as a professional organization for hand analysts. Conducts courses; bestows diplomas. Makes available tutorial services.
Library Subject: cheirology, medicine, history, psychology, religion, Buddhism
Library Type: not open to the public
Publication: Journal
Publication title: Journal of the Cheirological Society
Second publication: Newsletter
Meetings/Conventions: - annual conference

Chemical and Industrial Consultants Association

53 Grovelands Ave., Herts, Hitchin, SG4 OQU, England, UK
Tel: 44 1462 458481
Fax: 44 1462 458481
Email: jim.b@jbsafety.co.uk
Website: http://www.chemical-consultants.co.uk
Founded: 1988
Members: 40
Contact:
Fee: £40
Description: Net work of consultants based in the UK, but it's members are prepared to undertake projects anywhere in the world solving problems, providing advice and carrying out tasks for companies and individuals in the chemical and related industries.

Chemical Hazards Communication Society

PO Box 222, Lymington, SO42 7GY, England, UK
Tel: 44 7000 790 337
Fax: 44 7000 790 338
Email: chcs@chcs.org.uk
Website: http://www.chcs.org.uk
Founded: 1994
Members: 400
Contact: Mr. D.C. Waight, Chm.
Fee: £65
Membership Type: member
Description: Aims to provide information and training guidance to as many individuals as possible, regardless of whether they work in small or large companies, for associations or for government involved with the ever increasing complexity of chemical hazards regulations and international codes.
Library Subject: hazard communication
Library Type: not open to the public

Chemical Industries Association
CIA

King's Bldgs., Smith Sq., London, SW1P 3JJ, England, UK
Tel: 44 20 78343399
Fax: 44 20 78344469
Email: enquiries@cia.org.uk
Website: http://www.cia.org.uk
Founded: 1965
Members: 170
Staff: 65
Contact: J.E. Hackitt, Dir.Gen.
Description: Assists members to secure sustainable profitability and improved recognition of contributions to society; works to influence relevant people and policies by stimulating and helping towards appropriate internal action.
Formerly: Formed by Merger of, Association of British Chemical Manufacturers
Publication: Report
Publication title: Basic International Chemical Industry Statistics
Second publication: Directory
Publication title: Directory of Products and Buyers' Guide
Meetings/Conventions: Business Outlook Conference - annual conference

Chester, Ellesmere Port and North Wales Chamber of Commerce and Indusry

Hilliards Ct., Chester Business Park, Wrexham, Chester, CH4 9QP, England, UK
Contact: Stepehn Welch, Chief Exec.
Description: Promotes business and commerce.

Chief Cultural and Leisure Officers Association

c/o Peter Cooke, Sec.
i-Space, Bridge End, Hexham, NE46 4DQ, England, UK
Tel: 44 1434 610424
Email: peter@cloa.org.uk
Website: http://www.cloa.org.uk
Founded: 1975
Members: 300
Contact: Peter Cooke, Sec.
Fee: £65
Membership Type: full
Description: Directors and Chief Officers in Local Government
Authorities (England and Wales) responsible for range of services
including arts, sports, amenities, libraries, museums, countryside,
economic development etc. Represents the views and interests of its
members in discussion with those who determine national policies in
the leisure arena and who influence the resourcing of those policies.
Provides a forum and a network for the exchange of knowledge and
the practical application of that knowledge.
Publication: Newsletter
Publication title: CLOA News. Advertisements.
Second publication: Paper
Meetings/Conventions: - quarterly workshop

Child Rights Information Network
CRIN

c/o Save the Children UK
17 Grove Ln., London, SE5 8RD, England, UK
Tel: 44 20 77162240
Fax: 44 2077937628
Email: info@crin.org
Website: http://www.crin.org
Founded: 1995
Members: 1300
Staff: 3
Contact: Veronica Yates, Commun.Asst.
Description: Global network of organizations sharing their
information on children's rights. Supports and promotes the
implementation of the United Nations Convention on the Rights of the
Child.
Publication: Newsletter

Children's Books History Society

c/o Pat Garrett, Sec.
25 Field Way, Hoddesdon, EN11 QQN, England, UK
Tel: 44 1992 464885
Fax: 44 1992 464885
Email: cbhs@abcgarrett.demon.co.uk
Founded: 1969
Members: 300
Contact: Pat Garrett, Sec.
Fee: £10
Membership Type: in England and Europe
Fee: £15
Membership Type: overseas
Description: Promotes appreciation of children's books in their
literary, historical, and biographical aspects. Fosters distribution and
exchange of information on children's literature.
Publication: Newsletter
Meetings/Conventions: meeting

Children's Legal Centre
CLC

University of Essex, Wivenhoe Park, Colchester, C04 3SQ, England,
UK
Tel: 44 1206 873820
Fax: 44 1206 874026
Email: clc@essex.ac.uk
Website: http://www2.essex.ac.uk/clc
Founded: 1980
Members: 12
Staff: 7
Contact: Carolyn Hamilton, Dir.
Description: Promotes children's rights in the United Kingdom.
Monitors policy and legislation affecting children. Asserts the rights of
children to exert influence on the policies and laws that affect them.
Offers confidential legal advice and information services; as well as an
education advocacy unit. Works to: make policy-makers accountable
to young people; make young people more independent; improve
health services; provide young people with freedom of information
and privacy; make available to children adequate opportunities for
education and employment.
Publication: Bulletin
Publication title: Childright
Second publication: Handbooks

Chilled Food Association

PO Box 6434, Kettering, NN15 5XT, England, UK
Tel: 44 1536 514365
Fax: 44 1536 515395
Email: cfa@chilledfood.org
Website: http://www.chilledfood.org
Founded: 1989
Members: 29
Contact: Kaarin Goodburn, Sec.Gen.
Fee: £600
Membership Type: corporate
Description: Participants in the chill chain: food manufacturers,
distributors, retailers. Promotes food safety and hygiene standards in
the chill chain.
Library Type: not open to the public
Publication: Manual
Publication title: CFA Hygiene Guidelines
Second publication: Newsletter
Publication title: Fire Risk Minimisation Guidance Published by the
Food Industry Panels Group

China Clay Association

John Keay House, St. Austell, PL25 4DJ, England, UK
Tel: 44 1726 74482
Fax: 44 1726 623019
Members: 3
Contact: Mrs. P.R. Jones, Sec.
Description: Members comprise the 3 china clay producing
companies, all based in S W England.
Meetings/Conventions: meeting

China, Glass and Giftware Retailers' Association

PO Box 26657, London, N14 4HZ, England, UK
Tel: 44 208 8868280
Fax: 44 208 4479600
Founded: 1921
Members: 120

Staff: 1
Contact: Josephine Hawkins
Fee: £62
Membership Type: personal
Description: Retailers of china, glassware, and giftware, or stores having a separate department for those products, in the UK and the rest of the world. Assists retailers to run their businesses more profitably and professionally, and aims to help them give a better service to the public.
Formerly: China and Glass Retailers' Association
Publication title: Conference Programme and Newsletter. Advertisements.
Second publication: Newsletter
Meetings/Conventions: - annual conference

China-Britain Business Council
CBBC
Abford House, 15 Wilton Rd., London, SW1V 1LT, England, UK
Tel: 44 20 78285176
Fax: 44 20 7630 5780
Email: enquiries@cbbc.org
Website: http://www.cbbc.org
Founded: 1991
Members: 350
Staff: 50
Contact: Leo Liu, Info.Off.
Fee: £1490
Membership Type: corporate and association, plus VAT
Description: British companies doing business in China. Promotes British trade in China. Acts as a liaison between the British and Chinese governments and member companies.
Library Subject: China economy, United Kingdom-China business
Library Type: open to the public
Publication: Magazine
Publication title: China-Britain Trade Review. Advertisements.

Choice in Personal Safety
Mount House, Urra, Chop Gate, Middlesborough, TS9 7H2, England, UK
Tel: 44 1489 896824
Website: http://users.aol.com/forgood/seatbelt/
Founded: 1982
Contact: Gordon Read, Chm.
Fee: £7.5
Membership Type: full
Description: Evaluates road safety measures. Promotes responsible personal behavior, and use of personal safety devices.

Choir Schools Association
c/o The Administrator
Minster School, Deangate, York, YO1 2JA, England, UK
Tel: 44 1904 624900
Fax: 44 1904 632418
Website: http://www.choirschools.org.uk
Founded: 1919
Members: 47
Contact: Wendy Jackson, Admin.
Description: Head teachers of schools regularly singing public services attached to cathedrals, colleges and churches. Exists to promote the interests of schools where choristers who sing regular public services in cathedrals, churches and college chapels, are educated. Also runs a bursay trust to help families with insufficient funds.
Publication title: Choir Schools Today

Christian Aid
35 Lower Marsh, Waterloo, London, SE1 7RL, England, UK
Tel: 44 20 76204444
Fax: 44 20 76200719
Email: info@Christian-aid.org
Website: http://www.christian-aid.org.uk
Founded: 1945
Staff: 279
Contact: Judith Knight, Admin.
Description: Aid and development arm of the Council of Churches for Britain and Ireland. Supports community development programs designed to help some of the world's poorest people. Works in partnership with other organizations in 70 countries throughout the world. Seeks to combat the causes of poverty through advocacy, campaigns, and public education.
Library Subject: Third World, theology, liberation, and development
Library Type: by appointment only
Publication: Magazine
Publication title: Christian Aid News
Second publication: Reports

Christian Booksellers' Association - England
Grampian House, 144 Deansgate, Manchester, M3 3ED, England, UK
Tel: 44 161 8333003
Fax: 44 161 8353000
Founded: 1984
Members: 600
Staff: 4
Contact: Barry Holmes, Gen.Mgr.
Description: Staff of religious bookshops. To promote training for religious bookshop staff. Membership services include advice on copyright, location of.
Publication title: The Christian News World Review
Second publication: Books
Publication title: European Christian Bookstore Journal

Christian Engineers in Development
22 Sherlock Close, Cambridge, CB3 0HW, England, UK
Tel: 44 1768 210589
Fax: 44 1768 210746
Email: admin@ced.org.uk
Website: http://www.ced.org.uk
Founded: 1985
Members: 70
Staff: 6
Contact: Gareth R. Cozens, Dir. & Sec.
Fee: £45
Membership Type: full
Fee: £45
Membership Type: over age 30
Description: Christian engineers and other professionals interested in equitable and sustainable development of economically underdeveloped areas worldwide. Seeks to apply engineering principles to the design and implementation of economic development programs; makes available technical assistance to local programs sharing similar goals. Promotes environmental protection and the development of indigenous leadership to guide local development.
Publication: Newsletter
Publication title: CED Newsletter
Meetings/Conventions: - annual meeting - Exhibits.

Christian Road Safety Association
The Flat Park Lane, Park Lane, Wembley, HA9 7SG, England, UK
Fax: 44 1342 554598

Email: crsa1937@msn.com
Website: http://www.crsa.org.uk
Founded: 1937
Members: 2000
Contact: Eric Thorn
Description: Christians from all churches concerned with safety for all road users throughout the world. To promote care and consideration for all road users.
Publication: Journal
Publication title: Christian Road Safety Journal. Advertisements.
Publication title: CRSA Member's Handbook

Chromatographic Society

c/o Clarendon Chambers
32 Clarendon St., Ste. 6, Nottingham, NG1 5JD, England, UK
Tel: 44 115 9500596
Fax: 44 115 9500614
Email: gill.caminow@chromsoc.com
Website: http://www.chromsoc.com
Founded: 1956
Members: 1000
Contact: G. Caminow, Exec.Sec.
Description: Workers in the field of Separation Science. Promotes all aspects of chromatography and separation techniques.
Publication title: Chromatography Abstracts

Church Monuments Society
CMS

Burlington House, Piccadilly, London, W1J 0BE, England, UK
Tel: 44 1837 851483
Fax: 44 1837 851483
Email: churchmonuments@aol.com
Website: http://www.churchmonumentssociety.org
Founded: 1979
Members: 500
Contact: John K. Bromilow, Hon. Publicity Off.
Fee: £16
Membership Type: ordinary
Fee: £18
Membership Type: family
Description: Art historians and historians of dress and armour, religion, and society; archaeologists, genealogists, geologists, heralds, masons, sculptors, and stone conservators in 7 countries. Promotes the study, care, and conservation of funerary monuments and related art of all periods and countries, including sculpture with its architectural framework, flat memorials, stained glass, and wall painting associated with burials. Visits sites; advises on all aspects of care and conservation of church monuments, including fundraising. A project is being conducted under the society's auspices for the listing of all medieval effigies in England.
Publication: Journal
Publication title: Journal of Church Monuments Society
Second publication: Newsletter
Publication title: Newsletter
Meetings/Conventions: - semiannual lecture

Churches Conservation Trust

1 W Smithfield, London, EC1A 9EE, England, UK
Tel: 44 207 2130660
Fax: 44 207 2130678
Email: central@tcct.org.uk
Website: http://www.visitchurches.org.uk/
Founded: 1969

Members: 7
Staff: 20
Contact: Catharine Gunningham, Head of Public Affairs
Description: Seeks to preserve redundant churches of historical, archaeological, or architectural interest. (Trust churches remain consecrated within the Church of England but are no longer used for regular worship. Currently, the Trust maintains more than 300 churches.) Encourages the holding of occasional services, concerts, art and history exhibitions, flower festivals, and other suitable events.
Formerly: Redundant Churches Fund
Publication title: Annual Report and Accounts
Publication title: Guides to Individual Churches

Churchill Society London

Ivy House, 18 Grove Lane, Ipswich, IP4 1NR, England, UK
Tel: 44 1473 413533
Fax: 44 1473 413533
Email: secretary@churchill-society-london.org.uk
Website: http://www.churchill-society-london.org.uk/Webmap.html
Founded: 1990
Members: 2800
Staff: 6
Contact:
Fee: £12
Description: Educational society for schools and young people; promotes the life and accomplishments of Churchill.
Publication: Newsletter
Meetings/Conventions: - annual meeting

CILT - The National Centre for Languages

20 Bedfordbury, London, WC2N 4LB, England, UK
Tel: 44 207 3795101
Fax: 44 207 3795082
Email: library@cilt.org.uk
Website: http://www.cilt.org.uk
Founded: 1966
Staff: 45
Contact: John Hawkins, Librarian
Description: Aims to promote greater national capability in languages. Supports the work of modern languages teaching professionals. Central to this work is the development of language teaching in schools. In addition, operates across all sectors and stages of education.
Library Subject: language, learning and teaching
Library Type: reference
Formerly: Centre for Information on Language Teaching and Research

CIMTECH

University of Hertfordshire, 45 Grosvenor Rd., St. Albans, AL1 3AW, England, UK
Tel: 44 1727 813651
Fax: 44 1727 813649
Email: c.cimtech@herts.ac.uk
Website: http://www.cimtech.co.uk
Founded: 1967
Members: 950
Staff: 10
Contact: Tony Hendley, Mng.Dir.
Fee: £200
Description: Publishers and consultants; private and public companies; educational institutions; records management and management service departments. Provides information about media and methods for originating, distributing, storing, and retrieving

information. Covers such topics as: computer assisted retrieval; document imaging; records management; optical character recognition; information processing. Conducts sponsored research projects. Offers educational courses. Provides consulting services in electronic content, document and records management.
Formerly: National Reprographic Centre for Documentation
Publication: Directory
Publication title: Document, Content & Records Management Guide 2003. Advertisements.
Second publication: Journal
Publication title: Information Management & Technology. Advertisements.
Meetings/Conventions: - periodic seminar

Cinema Advertising Association
CAA

12 Golden Sq., London, W1R 3AF, England, UK
Tel: 44 20 75346363
Fax: 44 20 75346464
Website: http://www.adassoc.org.uk/members/caa.html
Founded: 1953
Staff: 12
Contact: Terry Lince
Description: Screen contractors for cinema advertising. Enforces regulatory codes of advertising practice; monitors alcohol advertising. Gathers information on audience demographics. Convention/Meeting: none.
Formerly: Screen Advertising Association
Publication title: CAA Cinema Advertising Fact Sheet
Publication title: CAA Coverage and Frequency Guide

Cinema Exhibitors' Association

22 Golden Sq., London, W1R 3PA, England, UK
Tel: 44 207 7349551
Fax: 44 207 7346147
Email: cea@cinemaukoftech.co.uk
Founded: 1912
Members: 312
Staff: 3
Contact: John Wilkinson
Description: UK cinema operators. Safeguarding the commercial interests of UK cinema operators, including multi national operators, UK public companies, privately owned companies, independent operators, local authority cinemas and BFI regional film theatres.
Publication: Newsletter
Publication title: CEA Newsletter

Cinema Theatre Association

44 Harrowdene Gardens, Teddington, TW11 0DJ, England, UK
Tel: 44 181 9772608
Website: http://www.cinema-theatre.org.uk
Founded: 1967
Members: 1500
Contact: Adam Unger, Sec.
Fee: £12
Membership Type: full
Description: Those interested in the history, architectural, historical or technical of cinema buildings. Campaigns for the preservation and continued use of cinemas and theatres for their original purpose, organises visits to cinemas and theatre of interest; lectures and film shows are held from time to time, archive holding of related material.
Library Subject: cinema buildings, cinema architecture
Library Type: by appointment only

Publication: Newsletter
Publication title: CTA Bulletin. Advertisements.
Second publication: Magazines
Publication title: Picture House
Meetings/Conventions: Cinema Visits - monthly meeting

Circle of State Librarians
CSL

Hon Secretary, Home Office Rm. 1004, Queen Anne's Gate, London, SW1H 9AT, England, UK
Tel: 44 20 72734463
Fax: 44 20 72733957
Email: lynda.cooper@homeoffice.gsi.gov.uk
Website: http://www.circleofstatelibrarians.co.uk
Members: 500
Description: Aims to stimulate interest in the cost effective management of information. Promotes cooperation among staff in government and allied library and information services. Organizes training courses and visits to libraries and other places of interest, holds annual conference.
Publication: Journal
Publication title: State Librarian

Circle of Wine Writers

393 Ham Green, Holt, Trowbridge, BA14 6PX, England, UK
Tel: 44 1225 783007
Fax: 44 1225 783152
Email: secretary@winewriters.org
Website: http://www.circleofwinewriters.org
Founded: 1960
Members: 212
Staff: 1
Contact: Nicholas Faith, Hon. Treas.
Publication: Newsletter
Publication title: Up-Date

CIRIA

6 Storey's Gate, Westminster, London, SW1P 3AU, England, UK
Tel: 44 20 72228891
Fax: 44 20 72221708
Email: enquiries@ciria.org.uk
Website: http://www.ciria.org.uk
Founded: 1967
Description: Seeks to improve the performance of all involved with construction and the environment.
Formerly: Construction Industry Research and Information Association

CIRIA: Construction Industry Research and Information Association

6 Storey's Gate, London, SW1P 3AU, England, UK
Tel: 44 20 72228891
Fax: 44 20 72221708
Email: enquiries@ciria.org.uk
Website: http://www.ciria.org.uk
Founded: 1960
Members: 650
Staff: 55
Contact: Dr. T.W. Broyd, Ch.Exec.
Description: CIRIA identifies the research needs of the construction industry. Formulates research projects; arranges funding; assigns research contracts; assists in technology transfer; disseminates information. Research interests include structural design, civil

engineering, earthworks and foundations, management, building design and construction, water engineering, environmental management, and quality management.
Publication: Newsletter
Publication title: CIRIA News
Meetings/Conventions: conference

CISV International
MEA House, Ellison Pl., Newcastle upon Tyne, NE1 8XS, England, UK
Tel: 44 191 2324998
Fax: 44 191 2614710
Email: international@cisv.org
Website: http://www.cisv.org
Founded: 1950
Members: 48000
Staff: 5
Contact: Gabrielle Mandell, Sec.Gen.
Fee: £9
Fee: £75
Membership Type: lifetime
Description: Individuals and associations. Unites children from all over the world through summer camps in order to: further the education of children in international understanding without distinction of race, religion, or politics; fosters among youth a knowledge and understanding of the various customs of different countries; encourage friendships in the hope of achieving peaceful solutions to worldwide problems. The camps, called CISV Villages, are held in about 60 locations throughout the world; each village unites 48 11-year-olds from 12 countries for the 4-week experience. Participants are chosen on the basis of their learning aptitude, leadership skills, ability to make friends, and communication skills. Two boy and 2 girl participants form a delegation with 1 adult leader who leads camp activities; delegations are limited to 4 children to enhance international exchange. Other programs include: Interchange, through which 12- to 16-year-olds visit a family in another country for 1 month followed by a reciprocal visit; summer camps, which involves CISV youth ages 12-15 and adult leaders from each country who participate in a 3 week theme camp; Seminar Camps, in which 17- and 18-year-olds (a maximum of 4 per nation) discuss over a 3-week period such topics as world poverty, war, peace, race relations, and the arts. Encourages youth to continue their educational experiences through international and regional week long youth camps during major school holidays, and through year-round participation in community based CISV Local Work Program.
Library Type: not open to the public
Formerly: International Association of Children's International Simmer Villages
Publication: Magazine
Publication title: CISV Annual Report. Advertisements.
Second publication: Journal
Publication title: CISV News
Meetings/Conventions: - annual board meeting

City Women's Network
CWN
PO Box 353, Uxbridge, UB10 0UN, England, UK
Tel: 44 1895 272178
Fax: 44 1895 272178
Email: enquiries@citywomen.org
Founded: 1978
Members: 250
Contact: Anne De Suiza, Chm.
Fee: £95

Description: Senior executive and professional business women. Provides a forum for members to share common professional and social interests and experiences.
Publication: Newsletter
Publication title: Connections. Advertisements.
Second publication: Directory
Meetings/Conventions: - weekly meeting

Civic Trust
17 Carlton House Terrace, London, SW1Y 5AW, England, UK
Tel: 44 20 79300914
Fax: 44 20 73210180
Email: pride@civictrust.org.uk
Website: http://www.civictrust.org.uk
Founded: 1957
Staff: 35
Contact: Martin Bacon, Chief Exec.
Description: 800 component societies each of approximately 300 members. Civic Societies seek through voluntary effort to improve the quality of there environment. The Civic Trust takes up problems common to many societies and tries to achieve a national solution.
Library Subject: environment
Library Type: open to the public
Publication: Newsletter
Publication title: Civic Focus. Advertisements.

Civil Engineering Contractors Association
CECA
Construction House, 56-64 Leonard St., London, EC2A 4JX, England, UK
Tel: 44 20 76085060
Fax: 44 20 76085061
Email: enquirires@ceca.co.uk
Website: http://www.ceca.co.uk/
Members: 200
Contact: Rosemary Beales, Dir.
Description: Represents British civil engineering contractors as an integral part of the economy.
Publication: Newsletter
Publication title: CECA Communicates
Second publication: Survey
Publication title: Workload Trends Survey
Meetings/Conventions: CECA Contracts and Legal Committee meeting

Clarinet and Saxophone Society of Great Britain
Chase End, Abington Pigotts, Royston, SG8 0SD, England, UK
Tel: 44 1763 852504
Website: http://www.cassgb.co.uk
Founded: 1976
Members: 1225
Contact: Philip Tattersall, Sec.
Description: Promotes the playing of the instruments, clarinets and saxophones.
Publication title: Clarinet & Saxophone. Advertisements.

Classical Association - Cambridge
CA
c/o Dr. M. Schofield
St. John's College, Cambridge, CB2 1TP, England, UK
Tel: 44 1223 338644
Founded: 1904
Members: 3600
Contact: Dr. M. Schofield, Sec.
Fee: £5

Description: Supports academic endeavors in classical studies. Encourages improvement in the teaching of classical studies through discussion of scope and methods. Works to facilitate contact between individuals interested in classical studies; supports the work of similar organizations abroad.
Publication: Newsletter
Publication title: CA News
Publication title: Classical Quarterly
Meetings/Conventions: - annual convention

Clay Pipe Development Association

Copsham House, 53 Broad St., Chesham, HP5 3EA, England, UK
Tel: 44 1494 791456
Fax: 44 1494 792378
Email: cpda@aol.com
Website: http://www.cpda.co.uk
Founded: 1965
Members: 10
Contact: Les Richardson, Consultant
Description: All UK companies producing vitrified clay drainage and sewerage pipes and clay flue liners together with some overseas associate member companies in the same field. The trade association for manufacturers of vitrified clay drain and sewer pipes, fittings and flue liners, representing the industry on British and European standards work and to government. Organising research work, writing technical literature, giving advice on design and construction, giving lectures and troubleshooting.
Publication: Booklet
Publication title: Bedding Construction and Flow Capacity of Vitrified Clay Pipelines
Second publication: Booklet
Publication title: It Pays to Lay Clay

Clay Roof Tile Council

c/o British Ceramic Confederation
Federation House, Station Rd., Stoke-On-Trent, ST4 2SA, England, UK
Tel: 44 1782 744631
Fax: 44 1782 744102
Email: andrewm@ceramfed.co.uk
Website: http://www.clayroof.co.uk
Founded: 1981
Members: 6
Staff: 2
Contact: Andrew McRae, Con.
Description: Promotes the use of Clay Roof Tiles in the interest of members. Promotes, supports and improves technical education, knowledge and research in the field of Clay Roof Tiles.

Cleaning and Hygiene Suppliers' Association

PO Box 770, Marlow, SL7 2SH, England, UK
Tel: 44 1628 478273
Fax: 44 1628 478286
Email: secretary@chsa.co.uk
Website: http://www.chsa.co.uk
Founded: 1969
Members: 200
Staff: 1
Contact: Graham G. Fletcher, Gen.Sec.
Description: Suppliers and distributors of cleaning and hygiene materials and equipment. Concerned with raising industry standards, information and guidance to members on regulatory issues, warehousing and transport safety and environmental protection.

Cleaning and Support Services Association
CSSA

New Loom House, Ste. 3-01, 101 Black Church Lane, London, E1 1LN, England, UK
Tel: 44 207 4810881
Fax: 44 207 4810882
Email: enquiries@cleaningindustry.org
Website: http://www.cleaningassoc.org
Founded: 1967
Members: 180
Staff: 2
Contact: Mr. M. Vesey
Description: Cleaning and support industries in the Europe. Promotes cleaning and maintenance industry. Conducts research programs; compiles statistics.
Library Type: reference
Publication: Report
Publication title: Labor Market Survey
Second publication: Membership Directory
Publication title: Management Year Book. Advertisements.

Cleft Lip and Palate Association
CLPA

235-237 Finchley Rd., London, NW3 6LS, England, UK
Tel: 44 20 74310033
Fax: 44 20 74318881
Email: info@clapa.fsnet.co.uk
Website: http://www.clapa.com/
Founded: 1979
Contact: Goeth Davies, Chief Exec.
Description: Local groups comprising parents of children with cleft lips or palates and health care professionals. Seeks to improve treatment of cleft lips and palates; promotes an improved quality of life for children with cleft lips and palates. Provides support to children with cleft lips and palates and their parents; supports research into the causes and treatment of cleft lips and palates; conducts educational programs; undertakes fundraising campaigns. Maintains specialist service for parents having difficulty feeding children with cleft lips or palates.
Publication: Pamphlets

Clinical Dental Technicians Association

7 The Studios, The Row, New Ash Green, Longfield, DA3 8JL, England, UK
Tel: 44 1474 879430
Fax: 44 1474 872086
Email: cdta@btinternet.com
Website: http://www.cdta.org.uk
Founded: 1950
Members: 115
Staff: 2
Contact: Mr. C.J. Allen
Fee: £1000
Description: Dental technicians seeking legal status in the United Kingdom to train and qualify to make and fit dentures directly with the public under Act of Parliament.
Library Subject: dental technology
Library Type: open to the public
Formerly: Association for Denture Prosthesis
Publication: Newsletter
Publication title: The Denturist
Meetings/Conventions: - annual conference - Exhibits.

Clinical Genetics Society
CGS

c/o British Society for Human Genetics
Birmingham Women's Hospital, Edgabston, Birmingham, B15 2TF, England, UK
Email: bshg@bshg.org.uk
Website: http://www.bshg.org.uk
Founded: 1970

Clinical Pathology Accreditation

45 Rutland Park, Botanical Gardens, Sheffield, S10 2PB, England, UK
Tel: 44 114 2515800
Fax: 44 114 2515801
Email: office@cpa-uk.co.uk
Website: http://www.cpa-uk.co
Founded: 1992
Description: Provides a means to accredit clinical pathology services, including external audits and peer review.

Club for Acts and Actors

20 Bedford St., Strand, London, WC2E 9HP, England, UK
Tel: 44 207 8363172
Fax: 44 207 8363172
Founded: 1897
Members: 906
Staff: 4
Contact: Barbara Daniels, Sec.
Fee: £30
Description: Professional actors, actresses and entertainers and people connected with the stage or social members in allied professions. Run by artistes and actors for the benefit of fellow artistes and actors.
Formerly: Absorbed, Concert Artistes' Association
Publication title: But - What Do You Do in the Winter
Meetings/Conventions: - annual general assembly

Coal Merchants' Federation - England

7 Swanwick Court, Alfreton, DE55 7AS, England, UK
Tel: 44 1773 835400
Fax: 44 1773 834351
Email: cmf@solidfuel.co.uk
Website: http://www.coalmerchants.co.uk
Founded: 1918
Members: 1150
Staff: 5
Contact: Mrs. Jane Heginbotham, Sec.
Description: Coal merchants who fulfil prescribed standards for quality of products and services. Concerned with retail distribution of solid fuel.
Publication title: Coal Trader

Cobalt Development Institute
CDI

167 High St., Guildford, GU1 3AJ, England, UK
Tel: 44 1483 578877
Fax: 44 1483 573873
Email: 101637.2106@compuserve.com
Website: http://www.thecdi.com
Founded: 1982
Members: 45
Staff: 3
Contact: Dr. M. Hawkins, Gen.Mgr.
Fee: £11600
Membership Type: full and associate producer
Fee: £2600
Membership Type: industrial/associate
Description: Cobalt manufacturers and users in 14 countries; research organizations. Objectives are: to develop and promote uses for cobalt in industry, medicine, and science; to consult with governments, research organizations, and ecological groups on environmental and other questions connected with the utilization of cobalt and its compounds; to provide members with information regarding legislation and regulations affecting the cobalt industry; to arrange for the exchange of information relevant to the cobalt industry; to encourage cooperation between members and other international organizations. Compiles statistics.
Library Subject: Cobalt and its applications
Library Type: reference
Publication title: Cobalt Facts
Publication title: Cobalt News
Meetings/Conventions: Cobalt - annual conference - Exhibits. Hong Kong People's Republic of China

Coeliac Society of the United Kingdom
CSUK

Box 220, High Wycombe, HP11 2HY, England, UK
Tel: 44 1494 437278
Fax: 44 1494 474349
Email: admin@coeliac.co.uk
Website: http://www.coeliac.co.uk
Founded: 1968
Members: 55000
Contact: Andrew Ladds, Ch.Exec.
Description: National support organisation for people with intolerance to Gluten.
Publication: Directory
Publication title: Gluten Free Food & Drink Directory

Coffee Trade Federation

63a Union St., London, SE1 1SG, England, UK
Tel: 44 20 74033088
Fax: 44 20 74037730
Email: secretariat@coffeetradefederation.org.uk
Website: http://www.coffeetradefederation.org.uk
Description: Protects the interests of the UK coffee trade.

Coir Association

62 Wilson St., London, EC2A 2BU, England, UK
Tel: 44 20 77820007
Fax: 44 20 77820939
Email: coir@crouchchapman.co.uk
Founded: 1956
Members: 13
Contact: D.G. Sunderland, Sec.
Fee: £185
Membership Type: u.k. and overseas
Description: Represents UK and overseas importers and exporters of coir products.
Meetings/Conventions: - annual meeting

Coke Oven Managers' Association

c/o Universal Contractors
4 Sycamore Centre, Eastwood Trading Estate, Rotherham, S65 1EN, England, UK
Tel: 44 1709 360850

Email: stratag@aol.com
Website: http://www.coke-oven-managers.org
Founded: 1918
Members: 650
Staff: 1
Contact: R.G. Sargent, Hon.Gen.Sec.
Description: People involved in coking and associated industries. Furthers the cause of coking and allied industries.
Publication: Papers
Publication title: OCT Technical Papers
Second publication: Yearbook

Cold Rolled Sections Association

c/o National Metalforming Centre
47 Birmingham Rd., West Bromwich, West Midlands, B70 6PY, England, UK
Tel: 44 121 6016350
Fax: 44 121 6016373
Email: crsa@crsauk.com
Website: http://www.crsauk.com
Members: 16
Contact: Mrs. Sylvia Battersby
Description: Manufacturers of cold roll formed sections.

Cold Storage and Distribution Federation CSDF

Downmill Rd., Bracknell, RG12 1GH, England, UK
Tel: 44 1344 869533
Fax: 44 1344 869527
Email: dg@csdf.org.uk
Website: http://www.csdf.org.uk
Founded: 1911
Members: 150
Staff: 3
Contact: W.J. Bittles, Sec. Gen.
Description: Frozen food warehousers and distributors. Provides services for the advancement of the frozen food industry.
Publication: Directory
Publication title: CSDF Directory. Advertisements.

College of Optometrists

42 Craven St., London, WC2N 5NG, England, UK
Tel: 44 207 8396000
Fax: 44 207 8396800
Email: optometry@college-optometrists.org
Website: http://www.college-optometrists.org
Founded: 1980
Members: 10560
Staff: 21
Contact: Peter D. Leigh, Sec.
Description: Consists of Fellows and Members, both home and overseas, Associate Members who do not hold full qualifications, non-practising Fellows, Honorary and Life Fellows. Concerned with the improvement and conservation of human vision, advancement for the public benefit of the study of and research into optometry and publication of the results, promotion of the science and practice of optometry and encouragement of the highest possible standards of professional competence and conduct for the public benefit.
Library Subject: optometry and vision
Library Type: reference
Formerly: British College of Optometrists
Publication title: Ophthalmic and Physiological Optics

College of Phytotherapy

Bucksteep Manor, Bodle St. Green, Hailsham, BN27 4RJ, England, UK
Tel: 44 1323 834800
Fax: 44 1323 834801
Email: medherb@pavilion.co.uk.school
Founded: 1982
Members: 500
Staff: 6
Contact:
Fee: £150
Membership Type: College of Practitioners of Phytotherapy
Description: Runs a training school for practitioners of phytotherapy (herbal medicine) incorporating a 4 year Bachelor of Science degree course, a 5-year BSC Degree Distance Learning Course, specially structured course for practising general practitioners, plus a one-year basic home study course.
Library Subject: anatomy, physiology, pathology, pharmacology, sociology, nutrition, biology, chemistry, medicine, natural health, and psychology
Library Type: open to the public
Publication: Journal
Publication title: British Journal of Phytotherapy
Publication title: Training for a Career in Herbal Medicine

College of Teachers

33 John St., London, WC1N 2AT, England, UK
Tel: 44 20 74042008
Email: rpage@cot.ac.uk
Website: http://www.collegeofteachers.ac.uk
Founded: 1846
Members: 2000
Staff: 4
Contact: Prof. Ray Page, CEO
Fee: £90
Membership Type: fellow
Fee: £77
Membership Type: ordinary
Description: Teachers united to promote sound learning and advance the interests of education. Makes available programs and facilities enabling teachers to expand their knowledge and professional capabilities. Establishes in-service qualifications for teachers; conducts lectures and seminars.
Library Type: not open to the public
Publication: Journal
Publication title: Education Today
Second publication: Brochure
Meetings/Conventions: - quarterly board meeting

Combined Edible Nut Trade Association CENTA

62 Wilson St., London, EC2A 2BU, England, UK
Tel: 44 207 7820007
Fax: 44 207 7820939
Email: treenuts@compuserve.com
Website: http://www.centa.uk.com
Founded: 1970
Members: 50
Contact: D.G. Sunderland, Sec.
Fee: £395
Membership Type: UK and outside of UK
Fee: £405
Membership Type: overseas

Description: Aims to circulate members on topical issues relating to the nut trade; to discuss, debate all matters appertaining to the trade; to maintain arbitration rules and up to date trading terms on which contracts may be based; to have representation in Europe through membership of FRUCOM.
Publication: Brochure
Publication title: Terms and Conditions of Trading and Rules
Second publication: Newsletter
Meetings/Conventions: - annual meeting London UK

Combined Heat and Power Association
c/o Grosvenor Gardens House
35-37 Grosvenor Gardens, London, SW1W 0BS, England, UK
Tel: 44 207 8284077
Fax: 44 207 8280310
Email: info@chpa.co.uk
Website: http://www.chpa.co.uk
Founded: 1967
Members: 106
Staff: 8
Contact: Jane Andrews, Admin.
Description: Major energy suppliers; local authorities; CHP user; equipment suppliers etc. Promotes the wider use of CHP and community heating.
Library Subject: community heating and power
Library Type: by appointment only
Publication: Magazine
Publication title: Co-Gen. Advertisements.
Meetings/Conventions: - periodic

Commercial Boat Operators Association
CBOA
PO Box 7065, Milton Keynes, MK13 8YQ, England, UK
Tel: 44 1908 236261
Fax: 44 1908 236261
Email: secretary@cboa.org.uk
Website: http://www.cboa.org.uk
Contact: Tony Boston, Gen.Sec.
Description: Operators of boats or freight facilities are traders; other individuals who support the aims of the association are associates. Promotes increased use of British canals and other inland waterways for transportation of freight and as vacation destinations. Conducts promotional activities to increase public awareness of vacation opportunities associated with Britain's inland waterways and the environmental friendliness and economic efficiency of transporting freight by canal barge.

Commercial Horticultural Association, Stoneleigh Park, Kenilworth, CV8 2LG, England, UK
Tel: 44 2476 690330
Fax: 44 2476 690334
Email: info@cha-hort.com
Website: http://www.cha-hort.com
Founded: 1979
Members: 110
Staff: 4
Contact: Dr. Chris Wood, Sec.
Fee: £250
Membership Type: member
Description: Manufacturers and suppliers of equipment, products and services for the commercial horticultural industry worldwide. Trade association looking after interests of members; is particularly active in the area of exhibitions and regional shows covering commercial and amenity horticulture in UK and overseas.
Publication: Booklet
Publication title: Buyers Guide. Advertisements.
Second publication: Newsletter
Publication title: CHA Newsletter

Commerical Radio Companies Association
The Radiocentre, 77 Shaftesbury Ave., London, W1D 5DU, England, UK
Tel: 44 207 3062603
Fax: 44 207 4700062
Email: info@crca.co.uk
Website: http://www.crca.co.uk
Founded: 1973
Members: 250
Staff: 8
Contact: Paul Brown, Chief Exec.
Description: Trade body for the UK commercial radio. Represents commercial radio to Government, the Radio Authority, Copyright Societies and other organizations concerned with radio.

Commission for Local Administration in England
21 Queen Anne's Gate, London, SW1H 9BU, England, UK
Tel: 44 20 79153210
Fax: 44 20 72330396
Website: http://www.lgo.org.uk
Founded: 1974
Members: 4
Staff: 210
Contact: N.J. Karney, Sec.
Description: Provides independent, impartial and prompt investigation and resolution of complaints of injustice caused through maladministration by local authorities and certain other bodies and offers guidance intended to promote fair and effective administration in local government.
Publication: Booklets
Publication title: Complaint About the Council? How to complain to the Local Government Ombudsman
Second publication: Booklets
Publication title: Digest of Cases

Commission for Racial Equality
CRE
St. Dunston's House, 201-211 Borough High St., London, SE1 1G2, England, UK
Tel: 44 20 79390000
Fax: 44 20 79390001
Email: info@cre.gov.uk
Website: http://www.cre.gov.uk
Founded: 1975
Staff: 200
Description: Works to eliminate discrimination based on race. Promotes equal opportunity among persons of different races.
Library Subject: race relations
Library Type: open to the public
Publication: Magazine
Publication title: Connections. Advertisements.

Commission Internationale de Microflore du Paleozoique
CIMP

British Geological Survey, Keyworth, Nottingham, NG12 5GG, England, UK
Tel: 44 1142 223692
Fax: 44 1142 223696
Email: MHSTE@wpo.nerc.ac.uk
Website: http://www.shef.ac.uk/~cidmdp/index.html
Founded: 1958
Description: Supports collaboration in the field of Palaeozoic Palynology.

Committee of Advertising Practice

2 Torrington Pl., London, WC1E 7HW, England, UK
Tel: 44 207 5804100
Fax: 44 207 5804072
Email: enquiries@cap.org.uk
Website: http://www.cap.org.uk
Founded: 1961
Contact: Guy Parker
Description: Executive and policy-making body responsible for the advertising industry's system of self-regulation. The Codes its devises extend to all non-broadcast media and are independently supervised by the Advertising Standards Authority.

Committee of the Forest Nurseries in the European Union
CFNEU

25 Kenton Dr., Shrewsbury, SY2 6TH, England, UK
Tel: 44 1743 357252
Fax: 44 1743 365809
Email: a.gordon@dial.pipex.com
Founded: 1966
Members: 14
Contact: Dr. Andrew Gordon
Description: National organizations representing forest nurseries in the European Union. Promotes growth and development of the European forest industries; seeks to eliminate what the group feels is unfair competition between state and private sectors. Lobbies European Union agencies for policies favorable to forest nurseries and more effective legislation governing the development of and trade in forest reproductive material.
Library Subject: European Union legislation, European Union funding of forest nurseries
Library Type: reference

Commons, Open Spaces and Footpaths Preservation Society

25a Bell St., Henley-On-Thames, RG9 2BA, England, UK
Tel: 44 1491 573535
Website: http://www.oss.org.uk
Founded: 1865

Commonwealth Association for Mental Handicap and Developmental Disabilities
CAMHDD

36A Osberton Pl., Sheffield, S11 8XL, England, UK
Tel: 44 114 2682695
Fax: 44 114 2678883
Founded: 1980

Members: 200
Staff: 1
Contact: Dr. V.R. Pandurangi, Sec.Gen.
Description: Interested individuals and professionals in 30 countries employed in fields dealing with mental handicaps and developmental disability working to prevent mental retardation, especially in the developing countries. Promotes better health for the handicapped. Works to prevent mental handicaps through early detection of disabilities and to establish intervention programs in developing countries. Holds workshops and symposia; plans to organize a training course in developmental pediatrics. Sponsors children's services and charitable program; maintains speakers' bureau; compiles statistics.
Publication: Directory
Publication title: CAMHDD Directory
Second publication: Book
Publication title: Manual on Prevention of Handicap
Meetings/Conventions: - annual conference

Commonwealth Association of Architects
CAA

66 Portland Pl., London, W1N 4AD, England, UK
Tel: 44 20 74903024
Fax: 44 20 72533319
Email: admin@comarchitect.org
Website: http://comarchitect.org
Founded: 1965
Members: 39
Staff: 2
Contact: Tony Godwin, Exec.Dir.
Fee: £2
Membership Type: individual
Description: National architectural institutes and associations in 39 Commonwealth countries. Objectives are to: act as a clearinghouse for architects and architectural institutes, teachers, research workers, and students; promote the field of architecture and encourage professionalism; foster social, intellectual, artistic, scientific, and professional exchange; represent architectural interests before governmental bodies; evaluate the quality & standards of courses in architecture against set criteria and maintains a list of recognized courses in architecture.
Library Type: reference
Formerly: Absorbed, Commonwealth Board of Architectural Education
Second publication: Journal
Publication title: CAA Newsnet
Meetings/Conventions: - triennial assembly

Commonwealth Association of Public Sector Lawyers

The Coach House, Station Road, Godalming, GU7 1EX, England, UK
Tel: 44 1483 428400
Fax: 44 1483 419905
Email: cjdr@cjdr.screaming.net
Website: http://www.capsl.org
Founded: 1996
Contact: C.J.D. Robinson, Hon.Sec.
Description: Any person who is qualified to be a member of the Commonwealth Lawyers Association, any national, state, or regional professional body (or appropriate committee or group thereof) that represents such persons. Promotes interests within the Commonwealth in all aspects of public sector law; provides a focus and forum for the exchange of information and ideas; and supports public sector lawyers in carrying out their professional duties. Provides

opportunities for members visiting the UK to meet with professional colleagues working or visiting the UK; supports the Secretariats of the Commonwealth Law Conferences by organizing conference sessions of particular interest to public sector lawyers; encourages and supports exchange and secondary arrangements for public sector lawyers; maintains links with other bodies that have common interests; and seeks to develop training and consulting services for lawyers in need.
Publication: Newsletter
Meetings/Conventions: - biennial meeting Melbourne Australia

Commonwealth Association of Science, Technology and Mathematics Educators

c/o Education Department, Social Transformation Programming Division
Commonwealth Secretariat, Marlborough House, Pall Mall, London, SW1Y 5HX, England, UK
Tel: 44 20 77476282
Fax: 44 20 77476287
Email: v.goel@commonwealth.intwww.castme.org
Founded: 1973
Members: 290
Staff: 1
Contact: Dr. Ved Goel, Hon.Sec.
Fee: £11
Membership Type: individual
Fee: £36
Membership Type: institutional in the United Kingdom
Description: Teachers of science, technology, and mathematics. Provides social, cultural, human & economic context in the teaching of science technology and mathematics. Provides assistance to national and local teachers' organizations pursuing similar goals; conducts research and educational programs.
Publication: Journal
Publication title: CASTME Journal
Meetings/Conventions: Science Technology and Mathematics Education for Human Development - triennial conference - Exhibits.

Commonwealth Association of Surveying and Land Economy
CASLE

Faculty of the Built Environment, West of England University, Bristol, BS16 1QY, England, UK
Tel: 44 117 3443036
Fax: 44 117 3443002
Email: sspedding@rics.org.uk
Website: http://www.casle.org
Founded: 1969
Members: 50
Staff: 3
Contact: Prof. Alan Spedding, Pres.
Description: National professional societies concerned with land economy, land surveying, and quantity surveying. Objectives are: to provide Commonwealth countries with high quality surveying services; to encourage the establishment of research and technical information services; to strengthen relations among Commonwealth countries; and to encourage the interchange of relevant information among societies. Maintains Education Advisory Service that assists the evaluation of existing courses in surveying and land economy and in establishing new courses in the field. Appoints correspondents in countries having no surveying organization.
Formerly: Absorbed, Commonwealth Board of Surveying Education
Publication: Journal
Publication title: Survey Review. Advertisements.
Meetings/Conventions: - quinquennial general assembly

Commonwealth Association of Tax Administrators
CATA

Commonwealth Secretariat, Marlborough House, Pall Mall, London, SW1Y 5HX, England, UK
Tel: 44 20 77476473
Fax: 44 20 77476225
Email: cata@commonwealth.int
Website: http://www.cata-tax.org
Founded: 1978
Members: 47
Staff: 8
Contact: Mr. Zahir Kaleem, Exec.Dir.
Description: Government departments concerned with direct and indirect taxes and represented by senior tax officials. Works to improve all aspects of tax administration in 47 countries. Organizes annual management and technical training programs and assistance programs.
Library Subject: taxation, fiscal policy
Library Type: reference
Publication title: CATA Newsletter
Publication title: Survey Reports
Meetings/Conventions: Technical Conference - annual conference

Commonwealth Broadcasting Association
CBA

c/o Elizabeth Smith, Sec.Gen.
17 Fleet St., London, EC4 Y1AA, England, UK
Tel: 44 207 5835550
Fax: 44 207 5835549
Email: cba@cba.org.uk
Website: http://www.cba.org.uk
Founded: 1945
Members: 96
Staff: 4
Contact: Elizabeth Smith, Sec.Gen.
Description: Broadcasting organizations and groups of such organizations. Objectives are to: improve all aspects of broadcasting through group study and mutual assistance; advocate the role of public service broadcasting as a vital instrument in promoting social, cultural, and economic aspirations; operate an information clearinghouse; represent and promote members' interests worldwide.
Library Subject: broadcasting
Library Type: open to the public
Publication: Magazine
Publication title: Commonwealth Broadcaster. Advertisements.
Second publication: Booklet
Publication title: Commonwealth Broadcasters Directory
Meetings/Conventions: - biennial conference - Exhibits. Nadi Fiji

Commonwealth Countries' League
CCL

7 The Park, London, NW11 7SS, England, UK
Tel: 44 208 4553471
Email: info@ccl-int.org.uk
Website: http://www.ccl-int.org.uk
Founded: 1925
Contact: Mrs. R.E. Whitehouse, Hon.Sec.
Fee: £15
Membership Type: individual
Description: Societies of men and women interested in the British Commonwealth; spouses of High Commissioners in London, England; women members of Parliament. Strives to secure equality of liberties,

status, and opportunities for women and men in the Commonwealth. Promotes and funds secondary education for girls based on ability and financial need. Sponsors annual fundraising Commonwealth Fair.
Library Subject: Sadd-Brown library maintains collection of materials by and about women in the Commonwealth
Library Type: reference
Publication: Newsletter
Publication title: CCL News Update
Meetings/Conventions: - annual conference

Commonwealth Dental Association
CDA

13 Rodney House, 12/13 Pembridge Cres., London, W11 3DY, England, UK
Tel: 44 20 72293931
Fax: 44 20 76812758
Email: juliacampion@cdauk.com
Website: http://www.cdauk.com
Founded: 1991
Members: 44
Staff: 1
Contact: Julia Campion, Admin.
Description: Local dental associations. Serves as a forum for discussion of matters of interest to members; works to coordinate members' activities. Promotes dental hygiene and oral health. Develops primary preventive dental strategies; conducts training programs for dental health workers; provides technical support to members in implementing programs. Holds educational courses.
Publication: Newsletter
Publication title: CDA Bulletin. Advertisements.
Meetings/Conventions: - annual conference

Commonwealth Engineers Council
CEC

1-7 Great George St., London, SW1P 3AA, England, UK
Tel: 44 20 72227722
Fax: 44 20 72227500
Email: international@ice.org.uk
Founded: 1946
Members: 42
Contact: Mr. Tom Foulkes, Sec.Gen.
Description: Professional engineering societies in Commonwealth countries. Aims are: to advance the science, art, and practice of engineering for the benefit of mankind; to foster cooperation and the exchange of information among members and other related organizations; support the development of national engineering institutions in all countries of the Commonwealth; enhance the education, training, and development of engineers at all levels of professional and technical competence; to encourage and facilitate the exchange of technology among countries; to promote meetings on engineering and related subjects.
Publication title: Admission and Registration Qualifications
Meetings/Conventions: Commonwealth Young Professionals Millennium Conference - biennial conference

Commonwealth Forestry Association
CFA

c/o Oxford Forestry Institute
6-8 South Parks Rd., Oxford, OX1 3UB, England, UK
Tel: 44 1865 271037
Fax: 44 1865 275074
Email: cfa_oxford@hotmail.com

Founded: 1921
Members: 1100
Staff: 3
Contact: Michelle Brooks, Sec.
Fee: £45
Membership Type: individual
Fee: £150
Membership Type: corporate
Description: Organizations and individuals in 108 countries including foresters, forest and wood scientists, timber merchants, ecologists and resource managers, and conservationists interested in worldwide forestry; libraries. Seeks to unite all those concerned with forest conservation, development, and management.
Library Type: reference
Formerly: Empire Forestry Association
Publication: Handbook
Publication title: Commonwealth Forestry Handbook. Advertisements.
Second publication: Journal
Publication title: International Forestry Review
Meetings/Conventions: - semiannual conference

Commonwealth Foundation
CF

Marlborough House, Pall Mall, London, SW1Y 5HY, England, UK
Tel: 44 20 79303783
Fax: 44 20 78398157
Email: geninfo@commonwealth.int
Website: http://www.commonwealthfoundation.com
Founded: 1966
Members: 46
Staff: 12
Contact: Colin Ball, Dir.
Description: An intergovernmental organisation with a mandate to support the work of the non-governmental sector in the Commonwealth. Funding is provided by Commonwealth governments. Through the provision of travel grants and specific awards, supports professional development, training opportunities and the sharing of skills, experience and information among the people of the 54 Commonwealth member countries. Foundation programmes and grants benefit non-governmental organisations (NGOs), professional associations and cultural bodies. Encourages activities which facilitate co-operation between developing countries in priority areas including the eradication of poverty, rural development, health, non-formal education, community enterprise, gender and development, disability and the arts and culture.
Publication: Newsletter
Publication title: Commonwealth People
Publication title: Non-Governmental Organizations: Guidelines for Good Policy and Practice

Commonwealth Fund for Technical Co-Operation
CFTC

Commonwealth Secretariat, Marlborough House, Pall Mall, London, SW1Y 5HX, England, UK
Tel: 44 171 8393411
Fax: 44 171 9300827
Email: cftc@commonwealth.int
Website: http://www.thecommonwealth.org
Founded: 1971
Members: 54
Staff: 200
Contact: W. Cox, Dep.Sec.Gen.

Description: A fund of the Commonwealth Secretariat. Provides technical assistance by offering experts, training, in-house consultancy services and best practice guides to developing Commonwealth countries in areas of comparative advantage such as debt management, trade capacity building, export development, small and medium enterprise development, public sector reform, governance and democracy, sustainable development of natural resource sector: petroleum, gas and minerals, and capacity and institutional development in areas of priority for member countries.
Publication: Book
Publication title: Skills for Development

Commonwealth Geological Surveys Consultative Group

c/o Commonwealth Science Council
CSC Earth Sciences Programme, Marlborough House, Pall Mall, London, SW1Y 5HX, England, UK
Tel: 44 171 8393411
Fax: 44 171 9300827
Contact: Siyan Malomo
Description: Geologists and other earth scientists. Promotes cooperation and exchange of information among earth scientists in the British Commonwealth. Conducts surveys; disseminates information; compiles statistics.

Commonwealth Hansard Editors Association
CHEA

c/o Department of Official Report
House of Commons, Westminster, London, SW1 0AA, England, UK
Tel: 44 207 2193388
Fax: 44 207 2196323
Email: garlandb@parliament.uk
Website: http://www.hansard-westminster.co.uk/chea
Founded: 1984
Members: 60
Contact: Ian Church, Sec.
Description: Editors of Hansard (the body of reports containing verbatim parliamentary proceedings). Works to enhance the service provided by editors to their parliaments through the sharing of information.
Publication title: Report of Meetings
Meetings/Conventions: - triennial meeting - Exhibits.

Commonwealth Human Ecology Council
CHEC

Church House, Newton Rd., Bayswater, London, W2 5LS, England, UK
Tel: 44 20 77925934
Fax: 44 20 77925948
Email: chec@dialin.net
Website: http://chec.org.uk
Founded: 1969
Members: 500
Staff: 3
Contact: Mrs. Zena Daysh, Exec.V.Chm.
Fee: £12
Membership Type: personal
Fee: £25
Membership Type: corporate
Description: Governmental departments, academicians and universities, ecological associations, and interested individuals in 41 countries. Seeks to make the human ecology field a major component in national planning and policy and to increase awareness and improve programs concerned with the interrelationship of humans in the total environment; works for creation of human ecology institutions in Commonwealth countries. Conducts courses, seminars, and workshops.
Library Type: lending
Publication: Journal
Publication title: CHEC Journal. Advertisements.
Publication title: CHEC Points
Meetings/Conventions: - periodic international conference

Commonwealth Journalists Association
CJA

c/o Edna Tweedie
17 Nottingham St., London, W1M 3RD, England, UK
Tel: 44 171 4863844
Fax: 44 171 4863822
Email: ian.cjalon@virgin.net
Website: http://www.ozemail.com.au
Founded: 1977
Members: 750
Staff: 2
Contact: Mr. Ian Gillham, Exec.Dir.
Fee: £20
Description: Print, radio, and television journalists, government information officers, lecturers in journalism, press officers, and others in related professions in 25 countries. Promotes training and exchange opportunities enabling journalists from developing countries to learn their trade and gain a broader understanding of other countries and their problems. Works with other Commonwealth organizations to defend the independence of journalists. Addresses matters of professional concern including ethics, standards, recognition, and information access.
Publication: Newsletter
Publication title: CJA Newsletter. Advertisements.
Meetings/Conventions: - triennial meeting

Commonwealth Journalists Association - United Kingdom

17 Nottingham St., London, WLU 5EW, England, UK
Tel: 44 207 4863844
Fax: 44 207 4863822
Email: ian.cjalon@virgin.net
Contact: Patrick Keatley
Description: Journalists and broadcasters. Seeks to advance the practice of journalism, and to further the professional development of members. Facilitates exchange of information among members. Provides travel and legal assistance to journalists. Conducts educational programs.

Commonwealth Lawyers' Association
CLA

c/o Law Society
114 Chancery Ln., London, WC2A 1PL, England, UK
Tel: 44 20 73205911
Fax: 44 207 8310057
Email: cla@lawsociety.org.uk
Website: http://www.commonwealthlawyers.com
Founded: 1986
Members: 880
Staff: 1
Contact: Christine Amoh, Exec.Sec.
Fee: £75
Membership Type: lawyer

Description: Lawyers, bar associations, and law societies in Commonwealth countries. Works to raise and maintain the standard of legal services in the Commonwealth. Protects members' interests; conducts workshops and professional development programs. Seeks to stimulate a reappraisal of values, institutions, and methodologies among members of the legal profession. Facilitates the exchange of information among members concerning developments relevant to the organization and useful to legal professionals.
Publication: Newsletter
Publication title: Clarion
Second publication: Journal
Publication title: The Commonwealth Lawyer. Advertisements.
Meetings/Conventions: Commonwealth Law Conference - triennial conference - Exhibits. Melbourne Australia

Commonwealth Legal Advisory Service

c/o British Institute of International and Comparative Law
Charles Clore House, 17 Russell Sq., London, WC1B 5DR, England, UK
Email: t.aust@biicl.org
Website: http://www.biicl.org/research/clas.htm
Founded: 1959
Members: 60
Staff: 3
Contact: Michael Anderson
Description: Attorneys. Provides legal assistance and research support to government agencies and nongovernmental organizations working in the British Commonwealth.
Library Subject: international law, comparative law
Library Type: open to the public
Publication: Journal
Publication title: ICLQ. Advertisements.

Commonwealth Library Association
COMLA

Marlborough House, Pall Mall, London, SW1Y 5HX, England, UK
Tel: 44 207 7476385
Fax: 44 171 7476168
Email: info@commonwealth.int
Founded: 1972
Members: 50
Staff: 2
Contact: Norma Y. Amenu-Kpodo, Exec.Sec.
Description: National library associations or main library organizations of Commonwealth countries; members represent 40 countries. Works to improve the quality of library service in Commonwealth countries. Objectives are to: support member associations in their efforts to create and consolidate professional ties among librarians; enhance the professional status of and employment opportunities for librarians by demanding reciprocal recognition of library degrees among Commonwealth countries; stimulate research into library automation and other technological innovations. Organizes practical projects on electronic information systems, research methodologies, and other topics of interest to the profession. Nominates candidates for the Annual Commonwealth Foundation Fellowship Awards. Cooperates with other regional library groups.
Formerly: Formed by Merger of, COMLA
Publication: Newsletter
Publication title: COMLA Newsletter. Advertisements.

Commonwealth Magistrates and Judges' Association
CMJA

c/o Uganda House
58-59 Trafalgar Sq., London, WC2N 5DX, England, UK
Tel: 44 20 79761007
Fax: 44 20 79762395
Email: info@cmja.org
Website: http://cmja.org
Founded: 1970
Members: 1000
Staff: 2
Contact: Dr. Karen Brewer, Sec.Gen.
Fee: £1200
Membership Type: associations
Fee: £20
Membership Type: associates
Description: Associations of magistrates, judges, and legal officers in Commonwealth countries. Advances the administration of the law by the promotion of judiciary independence. Fosters education in the law, administration of justice, treatment for offenders, and prevention of crime within the Commonwealth. Disseminates information concerning the legal process within Commonwealth countries. Compiles statistics. Conducts seminars, study groups, and workshops. Sponsors charitable programs.
Library Type: reference
Publication: Journal
Publication title: Commonwealth Judicial Journal
Second publication: Proceedings
Publication title: Conference and Seminar Reports

Commonwealth Medical Association
CMA

BMA House, Tavistock Sq., London, WC1H 9JP, England, UK
Email: office@commat.org
Website: http://www.commedas.org
Founded: 1962
Members: 37
Staff: 3
Contact: Dr. Jane Richards, Sec.
Description: National medical associations in Commonwealth countries. Provides technical assistance and cooperation to the national medical associations of Commonwealth developing countries. Conducts projects in areas such as reproductive health, women's health, youth health, medical ethics and human rights. Acts as a clearinghouse for news and information.
Publication title: Manual on Ethics and Human Rights Standards for Health Professionals
Meetings/Conventions: Council Meeting - triennial meeting

Commonwealth Network for Science and Technology

Marlborough House, Pall Mall, London, SW1Y 5HX, England, UK
Tel: 44 171 7476220
Fax: 44 171 8396174
Email: science@commonwealth.int
Website: http://www.comsci.org
Members: 36
Description: Fosters the use of modern science and technology for sustainable economic, environmental, social and cultural development.

Commonwealth Nurses Federation
CNF

c/o International Office
Royal College of Nursing, 20 Cavendish Sq., London, W1G 0RN,
England, UK
Tel: 44 20 76473593
Fax: 44 20 76473413
Email: cnf@rcn.org.uk
Website: http://www.commonwealthnurses.org
Founded: 1973
Members: 54
Staff: 1
Contact: Michael Stubbings, Exec.Sec.
Description: Organization of national nurses associations in
Commonwealth countries. Strives to further the development of
nursing and midwifery for the benefit of the community in
Commonwealth nations. Promotes cooperation and coordinated
activities among member associations. Liaises with governmental and
health agencies to facilitate the delivery of appropriate health
services. Disseminates professional information, advice, and
assistance. Supports regional and pan-Commonwealth educational
nursing projects.
Publication: Newsletter
Publication title: CNF Newsletter. Advertisements.
Second publication: Directory
Publication title: Directory of Nursing Associations and Chief Nursing
Officers in Countries of the Commonwealth
Meetings/Conventions: - biennial conference London UK

Commonwealth Parliamentary Association
CPA

Westminster House, Ste. 700, 7 Millbank, London, SW1P 3JA,
England, UK
Tel: 44 20 77991460
Fax: 44 20 72226073
Email: pirc@cpahq.org
Website: http://www.cpahq.org
Founded: 1911
Members: 15000
Staff: 14
Contact: Hon. Denis Marshall, Sec.Gen.
Description: Members in more than 170 national, state, provincial,
and territorial Commonwealth Parliaments. Objectives are to: provide
for understanding, cooperation, and regular consultation among
Commonwealth parliamentarians; promote study of the theory and
practice of parliamentary democracy; act as clearinghouse on
parliamentary subjects and political events. Sponsors topical study
groups with senior parliamentarians; conducts exchange visits for
delegations, parliament officials, and parliamentary librarians; holds
seminars on parliamentary practice and procedure.
Library Subject: Parliamentary Information and Reference Center on
parliamentary procedures
Library Type: reference
Publication: Newsletter
Publication title: CPA News
Second publication: Journal
Publication title: The Parliamentarian. Advertisements.
Meetings/Conventions: Commonwealth Parliamentary Conference -
annual conference

Commonwealth Partnership for Technology Management
CPTM

CPTM Smart Partners Hub, 14 Queen Anne's Gate, London, SW1H
9AA, England, UK
Tel: 44 20 72223773
Fax: 44 20 79301543
Email: smart.partnership@cptm.orgwww.cptm.org
Founded: 1995
Members: 400
Staff: 8
Contact: Dr. Mihaela Y. Smith, CEO
Description: Public and private sector organizations. Seeks to
enhance national capabilities for the creation and participation in
wealth through sound management of technology, using public/private
sector partnerships. Operates: Country Task Programme, which
develops and implements a portfolio of projects to be implemented in
Commonwealth countries; and the National, Regional, and
International Smart Partnership Dialogue Programme, which brings
public, private, and labor organizations together to facilitate a
cooperative approach to the management of macroeconomic
development.
Formerly: Commonwealth Consultative Group on Technology
Management
Publication: Report
Meetings/Conventions: Interactive Dialogue - periodic seminar

Commonwealth Pharmaceutical Association
CPA

1 Lambeth High St., London, SE1 7JN, England, UK
Tel: 44 207 7522364
Fax: 44 207 7522508
Email: bfalconbridge@rpsgb.org.uk
Founded: 1970
Members: 550
Contact: Betty Falconbridge
Fee: £10
Description: Pharmaceutical organizations in 39 Commonwealth
countries; pharmacists. Objectives are to: maintain the honor and
traditions of the profession and promote high standards of conduct,
practice, and education at all levels; encourage close links among
members in the profession and facilitate personal contacts between
pharmacists and students; disseminate information about the
professional practice of pharmacy and the pharmaceutical sciences.
Publication: Newsletter
Publication title: Newsletter
Meetings/Conventions: - quadrennial conference - Exhibits.

Commonwealth Press Union - United Kingdom
CPU

17 Fleet St., London, EC4Y 1AA, England, UK
Tel: 44 207 5837733
Fax: 44 207 5836868
Email: lindsay@cpu.org.uk
Website: http://www.compressu.co.uk
Founded: 1909
Members: 800
Contact: Lindsay Ross, Dir.
Description: Newspapers or periodicals published in Commonwealth
countries and news agencies operating in the Commonwealth. Aims
to: uphold the ideals and values of the Commonwealth; promote
understanding and goodwill within the Commonwealth through the

press; advance the welfare of the Commonwealth's press and its employees; defend freedom of the press; provide training for all branches of the print media.
Meetings/Conventions: Commonwealth Press Union - biennial conference - Exhibits.

Commonwealth Science Council
CSC

Commonwealth Secretariat, Marlborough House, Pall Mall, London, SW1Y 5HX, England, UK
Tel: 44 207 7476220
Fax: 44 207 8396174
Email: science@commonwealth.int
Website: http://www.comsci.org
Founded: 1946
Members: 36
Staff: 11
Contact: Dr. K. Lum, Sec.
Description: An intergovernmental body established to enhance, through international cooperation, individual nations' capabilities in developing and using science and technology for economic, social, and environmental progress. Provides a forum for collaborative scientific and technological development efforts among governments and academic and professional institutions; facilitates the exchange of information, training, and techno-cultural traditions. Acts as a catalyst for research and development programs by defining projects, identifying members to conduct them, coordinating funds, and supporting networks of researchers working on collaborative projects. Conducts surveys and studies. Conducts surveys and studies.
Formerly: Absorbed, Commonwealth Committee on Mineral Resources and Geology
Publication: Magazine
Publication title: Commonwealth Scientist
Second publication: Proceedings
Meetings/Conventions: - triennial - Exhibits.

Commonwealth Secretariat
COMSEC

Marlborough House, Pall Mall, London, SW1Y 5HX, England, UK
Tel: 44 207 7476500
Fax: 44 207 9300827
Email: info@commonwealth.int
Website: http://www.thecommonwealth.org
Founded: 1965
Members: 54
Staff: 266
Contact: Ms. Ajoa Yeboah-Afari, Public Affairs Ofcr.
Description: Central body of 54 independent sovereign states organized to coordinate consultations and programs for the Commonwealth. Conducts cooperative technical projects, programs, services committees, and international conferences. Focuses on training, technical assistance, economics, industry, agriculture, food production, education, law, science, youth, health, human rights, and women and development. Areas of interest include: post-apartheid South Africa; recognition of democratically elected leaders; environmental protection and sustainable development; measures to counter international drug trafficking; alleviation of poverty; combating AIDS; international economic issues. Administers the Commonwealth Fund for Technical Co-Operation, the Commonwealth Science Council, and the Commonwealth Youth Programme.
Library Subject: developmental issues
Library Type: reference
Publication: Magazine

Publication title: Commonwealth Currents
Second publication: Bulletin
Publication title: Commonwealth Law Bulletin

Commonwealth Society for Deaf Charity
CSD

Sound Seekers, 34 Buckingham Palace Rd., London, SW1W 0RE, England, UK
Tel: 44 20 72335700
Fax: 44 20 72335800
Email: sound.seekers@btinternet.com
Website: http://www.sound-seekers.org.uk
Founded: 1959
Members: 102
Staff: 3
Contact: Graham Archer, Chair
Fee: £12
Membership Type: ordinary
Description: Works for the deaf, especially children, in developing Commonwealth countries. In conjunction with governmental and voluntary organizations, deploys working parties of ENT Surgeons/ Audiologists who are volunteers; trains technicians to support audiologists, and to maintain and repair electronic equipment; provides equipment for use by schools for the deaf. Conducts research into the prevention of deafness and compiles statistics on such research; has studied the incidence and causes of deafness in Gambia, Nigeria, and Botswana. Maintains contact with and disseminates information about schools, societies, and government councils for the deaf throughout the Commonwealth.
Publication: Newsletter
Publication title: Newsletter. Advertisements.
Second publication: Brochure
Publication title: Sound Seekers Zutomation Leaflet
Meetings/Conventions: - annual general assembly

Commonwealth Telecommunications Organization
CTO

c/o Clareville House, 26-27 Oxendon St., London, SW1Y 4EL, England, UK
Tel: 44 207 9762359
Fax: 44 207 9304248
Email: info@cto.int
Website: http://www.cto.int
Founded: 1948
Members: 34
Staff: 13
Contact: Dr. David Souter, Exec.Dir.
Description: Governments of Commonwealth countries. Promotes development of Commonwealth telecommunications through cooperative arrangements between countries. Aids in the dissemination of information and participates in consultations among member countries. Maintains Commonwealth Tele-communications Council and Commonwealth Tele-communications Headquarters.
Library Subject: telecommunications
Library Type: not open to the public
Formerly: Commonwealth Telecommunications Board
Publication: Journal
Publication title: CTO Briefing. Advertisements.
Meetings/Conventions: - annual meeting

Commonwealth Trade Union Council
CTUC

Congress House, 23-28 Great Russell St., London, WC1B 3LS, England, UK
Tel: 44 20 74671301
Fax: 44 20 74360301
Email: director@commonwealthtuc.org
Website: http://www.commonwealthtuc.org
Founded: 1979
Staff: 5
Contact: Annie Watson, Dir.
Description: Trade union organizations in British Commonwealth countries. Represents trade union views to Commonwealth governments and institutions; stimulates consultations, information sharing, and consensus. Promotes a better understanding of global interdependence; encourages efforts to improve the North-South dialogue and to create a fair international economic order. (The North-South dialogue represents efforts to create economic equality between the poverty-stricken countries of the South and the developed countries of the North.) Provides practical assistance to trade unions in developing countries through worker education and training programs. Compiles a register of members' needs and seeks aid-giving organizations for sponsorship of specific projects. Maintains liaison with the Commonwealth Secretary-General and the Commonwealth Secretariat.
Publication: Annual Report
Meetings/Conventions: - annual meeting Geneva Switzerland

Commonwealth Youth Exchange Council

7 Lion Yard, Tremadoc Rd., London, SW4 7NQ, England, UK
Tel: 44 20 74986151
Fax: 44 20 76224365
Email: mail@cyec.demon.co.ukwww.cyec.org.uk
Founded: 1970
Staff: 4
Contact: V.S.G. Craggs
Description: International youth exchange organizations; individuals and institutions with an interest in international exchange. Promotes international and intercultural understanding through supporting UK groups undertaking youth exchange with the Commonwealth. Facilitates international educational visits; gathers and disseminates information.

Communication Managers Association
CMA

CMA House, Ruscombe Business Park, Twyford, Reading, RG10 9JD, England, UK
Tel: 44 118 9342300
Fax: 44 118 9342087
Email: reception@cma.org.uk
Website: http://www.amicus-cma.org.uk
Members: 15000
Contact: Peter Skyte, Natl.Sec.
Description: Trade union for post office managers.
Publication: Journal
Publication title: CMA News. Advertisements.
Meetings/Conventions: - annual conference

Communication Workers Union - England

150 The Broadway, Wimbledon, London, SW19 1RX, England, UK
Tel: 44 20 89717200
Fax: 44 20 89717300
Email: info@cwu.org

Website: http://www.cwu.org
Founded: 1995
Members: 278522
Staff: 150
Contact: W. Hayes, Gen.Sec.
Description: British Telecom, the Post Office, Alliance Leicester related technologies and industries. Represents members employed in postal, telecommunications, information technology and related industries, and is committed to improving general working conditions, protecting individual employees, and increasing the influence of the union with employers and other bodies.
Library Subject: trade union, employment, health and safety, politics, postal services, telecommunications
Library Type: by appointment only
Publication: Journal
Publication title: CWU Voice. Advertisements.
Meetings/Conventions: - annual conference - Exhibits.

Communication, Advertising, and Marketing Education Foundation

Moor Hall, Cookham, Maidenhead, SI6 9QH, England, UK
Tel: 44 1628 427180
Fax: 44 1628 427159
Email: info@camfoundation.com
Website: http://www.camfoundation.com
Founded: 1970
Contact: Ann Rayner, Registar
Description: An examinations board serving the communications industry.
Publication title: Prospectus

Communications Management Association

c/o Ranmore House
The Crescent, Leatherhead, KT22 8DY, England, UK
Tel: 44 137 2361234
Fax: 44 137 2810810
Email: ckimber@thecma.com
Website: http://www.thecma.com
Contact: David Harrington, Dir.Gen.

Communications Network

PP 2D05, The Angel Centre, 403 St. John St., London, EC1V 4PL, England, UK
Tel: 44 20 8437622
Fax: 44 171 3567942
Email: information@ibte.org
Website: http://www.ibte.org
Founded: 1906
Members: 18000
Staff: 5
Contact: Miss. J. Gilbert, Mktg.Mgr.
Description: Employees from the BT Group of companies (worldwide). Works to increase understainding of the telecommunications industry through publications, lectures and other services. Conducts lectures programme on business and technical topics, visits, quizzes, competitions, family and celebrity events.
Library Subject: telecommunications, computing
Library Type: not open to the public
Formerly: Institution of British Telecommunications Engineers
Publication: Journal
Publication title: The Journal of the Institution of Telecommunication Engineers. Advertisements.

Community Foundation Network

Swallow House, 11 Northdown St., London, N1 9BN, England, UK
Tel: 44 207 7132326
Fax: 44 207 7139327
Email: network@communityfoundations.org.uk
Website: http://www.communityfoundations.org.uk
Founded: 1991
Members: 66
Staff: 7
Contact: Gaynor Humphreys, Dir.
Fee: £100
Membership Type: ordinary
Description: Support oganization for community foundations. Seeks to advance the community foundation movement in the United Kingdom. Provides educational support and technical assistance to community trusts and foundations; organizes staff exchanges between members and their counterparts abroad.
Formerly: Association of Community Trusts and Foundations
Publication: Newsletter. Advertisements.
Meetings/Conventions: - biennial conference

Community Hospitals Association

Meadow Brow, Broadway Road, Ilminster, TA19 9RG, England, UK
Tel: 44 1460 55951
Fax: 44 1460 3207
Email: irh@rural-health.ac.uk
Website: http://www.rural-health.ac.uk/ruralhealthworld/cha.php
Founded: 1969
Members: 409
Contact: Barbara Moore
Fee: £75
Membership Type: community hospital
Fee: £25
Membership Type: individual
Description: Community hospitals within and outside the NHS. Works towards developing the range and continuing improvement of services provided by community hospitals. Gathers and disseminates information on all aspects of work carried out in community hospitals; gives help and advice to members in furthering the interests of community hospitals.
Publication title: Community Hospital Association Newletter
Meetings/Conventions: - annual symposium - Exhibits.

Community Matters: The National Federation of Community Organisations

12-20 Baron St., London, N1 9LL, England, UK
Tel: 44 20 78377887
Fax: 44 20 72789253
Email: communitymatters@communitymatters.org.uk
Website: http://www.communitymatters.org.uk
Founded: 1945
Members: 920
Staff: 13
Contact: David Tyler, Natl.Dir.
Description: National federation of local community organizations in the United Kingdom. Promotes and supports action by local communities, community development. Supports member organizations in response to leisure, recreational educational and social needs in their communities. Designs, develops, and delivers training in the development and management of community buildings and management committees. Represents members' interests to central government and other agencies.
Library Subject: community development, employment, legal, government

Library Type: not open to the public
Formerly: National Federation of Community Organizations
Publication: Magazine
Publication title: Community. Advertisements.
Meetings/Conventions: - annual conference - Exhibits.

Community Transport Association

Highbank, Halton St., Chesire, Hyde, SK14 2NY, England, UK
Tel: 44 161 3666685
Fax: 44 161 3517221
Email: ctauk@communitytransport.com
Website: http://www.communitytransport.com
Founded: 1982
Members: 1500
Staff: 35
Contact: Jenny Meadows
Description: Operators of voluntary sector, non-profit and accessible transport services, and their supporters. A national, non-profit distributing organisation which exists to promote good practice in the community transport sector, and to provide services to operators, including advice; publications; training; representation; annual conference and trade exhibition.
Publication: Magazine
Publication title: Community Transport Magazine
Meetings/Conventions: - annual conference - Exhibits.

Compassion in World Farming
CIWF

Charles House, 5A Charles St., Petersfield, GU32 3EH, England, UK
Tel: 44 1730 264208
Fax: 44 1730 260791
Email: compassion@ciwf.co.uk
Website: http://www.ciwf.co.uk/intlinks/ciwfInternational.htm
Founded: 1967
Description: Campaigns against factory farming through peaceful protests and lobbying. Seeks to raise awareness of animal welfare.

Composers' Guild of Great Britain
CGGB

34 Hanway St., London, W1P 9DE, England, UK
Tel: 44 171 4360007
Fax: 44 171 4361913
Founded: 1944
Members: 530
Staff: 2
Contact: Naomi Moskovic, Gen.Sec.
Fee: £45
Membership Type: full
Fee: £35
Membership Type: associate
Description: Works to further the artistic and professional interests of classical composers in England. Promotes the performance and appreciation of classical music.
Library Subject: Composers and compositions.
Library Type: open to the public
Publication: Journal
Publication title: Composer News
Publication title: First Performances
Meetings/Conventions: - annual meeting

Computer Conservation Society

63 Collingwood Ave., Tolworth, Surbiton, KT5 9PU, England, UK
Tel: 44 208 3373176
Email: hamishc@globalnet.co.uk
Website: http://www.cs.man.ac.uk
Founded: 1989
Members: 750
Contact: Hamish Carmichael, Hon.Sec.
Fee: £1000
Membership Type: corporate
Fee: £50
Membership Type: library
Description: Seeks to preserve and restore computer hardware. Builds and maintains working original and replica examples. Preserves historic software, including operating systems, and emulates them on current machines. Maintains register of private and public collections. Seeks to find suitable homes for historic equipment becoming available for conservation, preferably in a major collection.
Library Subject: computer hardware and software
Library Type: reference
Publication: Journal
Publication title: Computer Resurrection
Meetings/Conventions: - bimonthly lecture

Computer Users Forum
CUF

1 Stuart Rd., Thornton Heath, CR7 8RA, England, UK
Tel: 44 181 7831 196693
Founded: 1984
Members: 9000
Staff: 20
Contact: Parveez Syed
Fee: £20000
Membership Type: corporate
Description: Offers legal and technical advice; discount on hard/software/maintenance.
Library Subject: computers, law
Library Type: not open to the public
Publication: Newsletter

Computing Suppliers Federation

26/27 Brookside Business Park, Cold Meece, Stone, ST15 0RZ, England, UK
Tel: 44 1785 769090
Fax: 44 1785 769082
Email: info@csf.org.uk
Website: http://www.csf.org.uk
Founded: 1985
Members: 200
Staff: 5
Contact: Valerie M. Cumming, Mng.Dir.
Fee: £1360
Membership Type: company
Description: Information management, digital AV, video communications, computer graphics, CADCAM, PDMEDM. Aims to ensure professional, educational and functional collaboration as well as orderly and ethical trading. Members are able to participate in a forum which reflects their industry and their interests.
Formerly: Computer Graphics Suppliers Association
Publication: Newsletter
Publication title: Reality. Advertisements.

Concert Promoters Association

6 St Mark's Rd., Henley-On-Thames, RG9 1LJ, England, UK
Tel: 44 1491 575060
Fax: 44 1491 414082
Email: carolesmith.cpa@virgin.net
Founded: 1986
Members: 29
Staff: 1
Contact: Carole Smith, Sec.
Description: Concert promoters in the UK. To represent the interests of concert promoters throughout the UK.

Conchological Society of Great Britain and Ireland

c/o R.E. Hill
447 B Wokingham Rd., Earley, Reading, RG6 7EL, England, UK
Tel: 44 1635 42190
Fax: 44 1635 820904
Email: mike_weideli@compuserve.com
Website: http://www.conchsoc.org/
Founded: 1876
Description: Promotes the study of the molluscs.

Concord Video and Film Council
CVFC

22 Hines Rd., Ipswich, IP3 9BG, England, UK
Tel: 44 1473 726012
Fax: 44 1473 274531
Email: concordvideo@btinternet.com
Website: http://www.btinternet.com/~concordvideo
Founded: 1962
Members: 5
Staff: 5
Contact: Lydia Vulliamy, Council Member
Description: Provides educational videocassettes and 16mm films on social issues including illiteracy, mental health, race relations, medical topics, unemployment, and world poverty, as well as other topics such as the arts, education, theatre, and youth.
Publication title: Catalogue and Supplements
Publication title: Concord Video and Film Catalogue

Concordia - Youth Service Volunteers
CYSV

20-22 Boundary Rd., 2nd Fl., 8 Brunswick Pl., Hove, BN3 1ET, England, UK
Tel: 44 1273 422293
Fax: 44 1273 422443
Founded: 1943
Contact: C. Lumb, Exec.Dir.
Description: Operates a youth agricultural work program that unites young people worldwide in an effort to help them gain insight into their own and other cultures. Places youth volunteers with fruit and other crop growers in Britain for a short period during harvest time. Also organizes short international voluntary work camps in the U.K. in summer, particularly in the field of nature conservation.

Concrete Block Association

60 Charles St., Leicester, LE1 1FB, England, UK
Tel: 44 116 2536161
Fax: 44 116 2514568
Email: info@britishprecast.org
Website: http://www.cba-blocks.org.uk
Founded: 1991

Members: 64
Contact: Ron Willers
Description: Block manufacturers and suppliers to the industry. Aims to promote the interests of the precast concrete block industry in expanding its markets; to act as the recognised trade association for the aggregate block industry; to undertake all necessary action with regulatory and similar bodies and especially in regard to European harmonisation, to ensure that the interests of the industry are protected.
Publication title: CBA Update

Concrete Repair Association
CRA

99 West St., Farnham, GU9 7EN, England, UK
Tel: 44 1252 739145
Fax: 44 1252 739140
Email: info@associationhouse.org.uk
Website: http://www.concreterepair.org.uk
Founded: 1989
Members: 40
Staff: 2
Contact: J. Farley, Sec.
Description: Contractors utilising concrete repair methods, manufacturers of materials and plant. Promotes and develops the practice of concrete repair; aims to advance education and technical training in concrete repair and to improve liaison with professional bodies, authorities and specifiers.
Publication: Directory
Publication title: Directory of Members
Publication title: Method of Measurement for Concrete Repair

Concrete Society

Century House, Telford Ave., Crowthorne, RG45 6YS, England, UK
Tel: 44 1344 466007
Fax: 44 1344 466008
Email: enquiries@concrete.org.uk
Website: http://www.concrete.org.uk
Founded: 1966
Members: 7000
Staff: 21
Contact: D.M. Powell, Chief Exec.
Description: All the disciplines within the construction industry, including contractors, engineers and architects. Brings together all those with an interest in concrete and provides information and advice on its uses.
Publication: Journal
Publication title: Concrete. Advertisements.
Second publication: Report
Publication title: Concrete Society Technical Report
Meetings/Conventions: - quarterly conference

CONFED

Humanities Bldg., University of Manchester, Oxford Rd., Manchester, M13 9PL, England, UK
Tel: 44 161 2758810
Fax: 44 161 2758811
Email: confedoffice@confed.org.uk
Website: http://www.confed.org.uk
Founded: 1971
Members: 900
Staff: 4
Contact: Chris Waterman, Exec.Dir.

Description: Education officers who work in the management of local education authorities in England, Wales and Northern Ireland. The professional association representing education officers who work in the management of local education authorities in England, Wales and Northern Ireland. It is not a trade union, but does maintain links with the Education Section of the Federated Union of Managerial and Professional Officers. Close links are also maintained with the Association of Directors of Education in Scotland (ADES).
Formerly: Society of Education Officers
Meetings/Conventions: Summer Conference - annual conference

Confederation of Aerial Industries

Fulton House Business Centre, Fulton Rd., Wembley Park, Middlesex, HA9 0TF, England, UK
Tel: 44 20 8902 8998
Fax: 44 20 8903 8719
Email: office@cai.org.uk
Website: http://www.cai.org.uk
Founded: 1978
Members: 750
Staff: 6
Contact: Mrs. B.K. Allgood, Sec.
Description: Members are contractors, manufacturers, retailers or wholesalers of domestic TV, FM and satellite including entryphones, warden call or other communication systems. Aims to raise standards within the industry; to represent its members to government, local authorities, nationalised bodies, etc to unite the industry on its common aims; to keep abreast of technological change.
Publication: Journal
Publication title: Codes of Practice. Advertisements.
Second publication: Newsletter
Publication title: Feedback
Meetings/Conventions: CAI Trade Fair - annual trade show - Exhibits.

Confederation of British Associations

840 Melton Rd., Thurmaston, Leicester, LE4 8BN, England, UK
Tel: 44 116 2640083
Fax: 44 116 2640141
Email: ae@associationhq.org.uk
Founded: 1990
Members: 45
Staff: 1
Contact: Colin Grimes, Chief Exec.
Fee: £250
Membership Type: corporate
Description: Associations, institutes, professional bodies, unions, federation, clubs, society and all kindred representative and membership organisations. A forum for the exchange of information. Concerned with all aspects of trade and professional association management and practice including the setting up and development of associations of all types and training of staff employed in them.

Confederation of British Industry
CBI

c/o Digby Jones, Contact
Centre Point, 103 New Oxford St., London, WC1A 1DU, England, UK
Tel: 44 207 3958247
Fax: 44 207 2401578
Website: http://www.cbi.org.uk
Founded: 1965
Members: 15000

Staff: 220
Contact: Digby Jones, Dir.Gen.
Description: Works to ensure that the government understands the intentions, needs, and problems of British business.
Publication: Newsletter
Publication title: CBI News
Second publication: Report
Publication title: Economic Situation Report

Confederation of British Metalforming

47 Birmingham Rd., West Midlands, West Bromwich, B70 6PY, England, UK
Tel: 44 121 6016350
Fax: 44 121 6016373
Email: info@britishmetalforming.com
Website: http://www.britishmetalforming.com
Contact: D. Powis
Description: Companies involved in the forging industry in Great Britain. Represents members' interests.
Formerly: Formed by Merger of, British Forging Industry Association and British Industrial Fasteners Federation
Publication title: Membership List: Buyers Guide

Confederation of British Wool Textiles

c/o Merrydale House
Roydsdale Way, Bradford, BD4 6SB, England, UK
Tel: 44 1274 652207
Fax: 44 1274 682293
Email: info@cbwt.co.uk
Website: http://www.cbwt.co.uk
Founded: 1979
Members: 220
Staff: 12
Contact: John Lambert
Description: Manufacturers of wool yarns and fabrics, textile dyers and finishers, dealers in, and processors of, raw wool and textile waste. To promote and protect the interests of the British wool textile industry, and to provide to member firms a wide range of services in the fields of employment law, health and safety, environmental issues and training.

Confederation of Construction Specialists

75-79 High St., Aldershot, GU11 1BY, England, UK
Tel: 44 1252 312122
Fax: 44 1252 343081
Email: confedcs@aol.com
Founded: 1983
Members: 500
Staff: 3
Contact: John Huxtable, Chief Exec.
Description: Specialist construction companies. Central representative body for specialist building and civil engineering companies. Provides wide range of management training and other services to members and campaigns against contractual abuse.
Library Subject: construction contracts and law
Library Type: not open to the public
Publication: Report
Publication title: Reports
Second publication: Newsletter
Meetings/Conventions: Contractual Training Course - periodic

Confederation of Dental Employers
CODE

c/o CODE Office
5a Stanhope Sq., Holsworthy, EX22 6AP, England, UK
Tel: 44 1409 254354
Fax: 44 1409 254364
Email: info@codeuk.com
Website: http://www.codeuk.com
Founded: 1978
Members: 450
Staff: 3
Contact: Tanya Gilmore, GM
Description: Owners of dental practices. Promotes success of dental businesses; seeks to advance the profession of dentistry. Develops codes of business ethics and standards of professional practice for members; conducts research and advises members on business issues including taxation, business management, and the law. Implements discount care schemes for promotional use by members.
Publication: Magazine
Publication title: Dentistry Opportunities. Advertisements.
Meetings/Conventions: - annual conference London UK

Confederation of European Computer User Associations
CECUA

100 Parkside, Wollaton, Nottingham, NG8 2NN, England, UK
Tel: 44 115 8773144
Fax: 44 1159 9280823
Email: stuart.gould@cecua.org
Website: http://www.cecua.org
Founded: 1978

Confederation of European Computer Users Associations
CECUA

100 Parkside, Wollaton, Nottingham, NG8 2NN, England, UK
Tel: 44 1159 9282091
Email: sgoold@cecua.org
Description: No further information was available for this edition.

Confederation of European National Societies of Anaesthesiology
CENSA

9 Bedford Sq., London, WC1B 3RA, England, UK
Tel: 44 20 76311650
Email: davidwilkinson1@compuserve.com

Confederation of Learned/Engineering Societies in the Mineral Industry

c/o Institution of Mining and Metallurgy
77 Hallam St., London, W1N 6BR, England, UK
Tel: 44 171 5803802
Fax: 44 171 4365388
Email: instmm@cix.compulink.co.uk
Founded: 1892
Members: 8000
Staff: 12
Contact: Dr. G.J.M. Woodrow, Sec.

Description: Those involved in the metallurgy and mining industry. Purpose to advance the science of economic and engineering geology and mining.
Library Subject: International minerals industry
Library Type: lending

Confederation of Passenger Transport - UK
CPT
Imperial House, 15/19 Kingsway, London, WC2B 6UN, England, UK
Tel: 44 207 2403131
Fax: 44 207 2406565
Email: cpt@cpt-uk.org
Website: http://www.cpt-uk.org/cpt
Founded: 1974
Members: 1140
Staff: 22
Contact: Stephen Head
Description: Corporate members are operators of the UK's buses, coaches and fixed track systems. Associate members are those companies who supply services to the industry ranging from chassis manufacturers and bodybuilders to tourist attractions and hotels. Acts as a forum for the industry representing the interests of its members to local, national and international government, and other external bodies related to the industry. Members of CPT can help to shape the direction and future of the industry.
Publication: Newsletter
Publication title: Newsline
Second publication: Annual Reports

Confederation of Roofing Contractors
CRC
72 Church Rd., Brightlingsea, Colchester, CO7 0JF, England, UK
Tel: 44 1206 306600
Fax: 44 1206 306200
Email: enquiries@corc.co.uk
Website: http://www.corc.co.uk/
Founded: 1985
Members: 600
Contact: Allan Buchan
Fee: £276
Membership Type: full and associate
Description: Committed to protecting the general public against unscrupulous roofing contractors; provides roofing services to all market sectors.
Publication: Magazine
Publication title: Roofing Today. Advertisements.

Conference of Drama Schools
PO Box 34252, London, NW5 1XJ, England, UK
Email: enquiries@cds.drama.ac.uk
Website: http://www.drama.ac.uk
Founded: 1970
Members: 19
Staff: 1
Contact: Flicky Ridel, Sec.
Fee: £1468
Description: Representatives from 19 schools which are concerned with the training of actors stagemanagers and theatre related professionals. Strengthens the voice of member schools in order to develop and encourage the highest standards in training for both actors and stage managers.
Publication: Directory
Publication title: Official Guide to U.K. Drama Training. Advertisements.

Conference of European Rabbis
CER
87 Hodford Rd., London, NW11 8NH, England, UK
Tel: 44 208 4559960
Fax: 44 208 4554968
Email: cllr.a.dunner@barnet.gov.uk
Founded: 1957
Members: 750
Staff: 2
Contact: Aba M. Dunner
Description: European rabbis. Promotes reconstruction and organization of Jewish communal life in Europe. Serves as a forum for the exchange of information among members; sponsors educational, social, and religious services.
Publication: Journal
Publication title: Sridim. Advertisements.
Meetings/Conventions: Medical Ethics - Jerusalem - biennial convention Strasbourg Germany

Conflict Research Society
CRS
c/o David Maxwell, Sec.
68 Chancer Rd., 6th Fl., Bedford, Mk40 2AP, England, UK
Tel: 44 1524 594266
Fax: 44 1524 594238
Email: dcmaxwell@talk21.com
Founded: 1963

Congleton Chamber of Commerce and Enterprise
Market Sq., Congleton, CW12 1EX, England, UK
Tel: 44 1260 285274
Fax: 44 1260 285251
Email: info@sece.co.uk
Website: http://www.congletonchamber.co.uk
Members: 240
Staff: 7
Contact: Jackie Kay
Description: Promotes business and commerce.
Library Subject: business
Library Type: reference
Publication: Directory
Publication title: South East Cheshire Enterprise Business Directory. Advertisements.
Second publication: Magazine
Publication title: South East Cheshire Enterprise Magazine. Advertisements.

CONNECT: The Union for Professionals in Communications
30 St. Georges Rd., London, SW19 4BD, England, UK
Tel: 44 20 89716000
Fax: 44 20 89716002
Email: union@connectuk.org
Website: http://www.connectuk.org
Members: 18000
Staff: 45
Contact: Leslie Manasseh, Dir. of Organisation
Description: Managers and professionals in communications industry. Represents the interests of members and works to negotiate their terms and conditions and provides a range of individual benefits.
Formerly: Society of Telecom Executives

Publication: Magazine
Publication title: The Review
Meetings/Conventions: - annual conference

Conservation Foundation

1 Kensington Gore, London, SW7 2AR, England, UK
Tel: 44 207 5913111
Fax: 44 207 5913110
Email: info@conservationfoundation.co.uk
Website: http://www.conservationfoundation.co.uk
Founded: 1982
Staff: 4
Contact: David Shreeve, Exec.Dir.
Description: Creates and manages environmental programmes many of which are sponsored by commercial organizations. Covers all environmental interests in the United Kingdom, Europe, and internationally. Operates as a registered charity housed at the headquarters of the Royal Geographical Society. Produces monthly Information Diary for the United Kingdom's environmental journalists and programme makers.
Publication: Magazine
Publication title: Network 21. Advertisements.

Conservative Future

32 Smith Sq., London, SW1P 3HH, England, UK
Tel: 44 20 72229000
Fax: 44 20 72221135
Email: cf@conservatives.com
Website: http://www.conservativefuture.com
Founded: 1998
Members: 10000
Staff: 1
Contact: David Pugh
Fee: £15
Membership Type: youth
Description: Official youth wing of the Conservative and Unionist Party of the United Kingdom.
Meetings/Conventions: Conservative Future National Weekend - annual conference - Exhibits.

Conservative Party Central Office

32 Smith Sq., London, SW1P 3HH, England, UK
Tel: 44 207 2229000
Fax: 44 171 2221135
Email: chairman@conservative-party.org.uk
Website: http://www.conservatives.com
Contact: Rt. Hon. David Davis, MP Chm.
Description: Conservative political party in England. Supports strengthened defense, free enterprise, decentralization, and aid to those in need.
Formerly: Formed by Merger of, Conservative Party
Meetings/Conventions: Party Conference - annual

Conservatory Association

44-48 Borough High St., London, SE1 1XB, England, UK
Tel: 44 20 72075873
Fax: 44 20 73577458
Founded: 1977
Contact: Nigel Rees, Chief Exec.
Description: Manufacturers and retailers of conservatories. The Conservatory Association is a specialist division of the Glass and Glazing Federation (GGF).

Consortium of European Building Control

53 Goodwood Close, Ipswich, IP1 6SY, England, UK
Tel: 44 1473 748182
Fax: 44 1473 741881
Email: d.m.smith@btinternet.com
Website: http://www.demon.com/instobc/consort
Founded: 1987
Members: 50
Contact: David Smith, Chm.
Fee: £500
Membership Type: building control-construction profession
Description: Representatives of building control organizations and health and safety organizations. Provides a forum for discussing technical and legal building issues. Conducts research.
Publication: Newsletter
Publication title: CEBC News. Advertisements.
Meetings/Conventions: meeting

Consortium of European Research Libraries
CERL

40 Bowling Green Ln., Clerkenwell, London, EC1R 0NE, England, UK
Tel: 44 20 79705642
Fax: 44 20 79705643
Email: secretariat@cerl.org
Website: http://www.cerl.org
Founded: 1992
Contact: Dr. Marian Lefferts, Mgr.
Description: Works to share resources and expertise between research libraries in Europe.

Construction Confederation
CC

Construction House, 56-64 Leonard St., London, EC2A 4JX, England, UK
Tel: 44 207 6085000
Fax: 44 207 6085001
Email: enquiries@thecc.org.uk
Website: http://www.thecc.org.uk
Founded: 1997
Members: 5500
Contact: Kurt Calder, External Rel.Mgr.
Description: Building and civil engineering contractors. Seeks to advance the building industries. Represents members' common interests before national and European government agencies. Negotiates agreements on members' behalf with pan-industry bodies; provides information and advice to members; conducts promotional campaigns.

Construction Economics European Committee
CEEC

12 Great George St., Parliament Sq., London, SW1P 3AD, England, UK
Tel: 44 207 3343877
Fax: 44 207 3343844
Email: john.frewen-lord@pgen.net
Website: http://www.ceec.org
Founded: 1979
Members: 34
Staff: 1
Contact: Ms. Laurence Marcouly, Sec.
Description: National bodies representing the construction economics profession. Provides for the exchange of information.

Works to establish professional guidelines; initiates studies leading to uniformity of training and qualifications. Represents the profession before the European Communities and other European institutions. **Meetings/Conventions:** - semiannual meeting

Construction Equipment Association
CEA

Orbital House, 85 Croydon Rd., Caterham, CR3 6PD, England, UK
Tel: 44 1883 334499
Fax: 44 1883 334490
Email: cea@admin.co.uk
Website: http://www.coneq.org.uk
Founded: 1942
Members: 100
Description: Represents construction equipment manufacturers, their component and accessory suppliers and service providers.
Formerly: Federation of Manufacturers of Construction Equipment and Cranes
Publication: Directory
Publication title: Business Tracker

Construction Fixings Association

c/o Institute of Spring Technology
Henry St., Sheffield, S3 7EQ, England, UK
Tel: 44 114 2789143
Fax: 44 114 2726344
Email: info@britishtools.com
Website: http://www.britishtools.com
Contact: Mr. J.R. Markham
Description: A trade association of manufacturers of construction fixings.

Construction History Society

c/o Library & Information Services Manager
The Chartered Institute of Bldg., Englemere, Kings Ride, Ascot, SL5 7TB, England, UK
Tel: 44 1344 630741
Fax: 44 1344 630764
Email: michael.tutton@virgin.net
Website: http://www.constructionhistory.co.uk
Founded: 1982
Members: 300
Contact: Michael Tutton, Sec.
Fee: £18
Description: Disseminates research and information about historical buildings and construction techniques; encourages today's industry to pay greater care to the safe keeping of its records' demonstrates the fascination of construction history studies through an active programme of visits and lectures.
Library Subject: construction history, construction techniques and materials, company histories
Library Type: by appointment only
Publication: Journal
Publication title: Construction History

Construction Industry Computing Association
CICA

1 Trust Ct., Histon, Cambridge, CB4 9PW, England, UK
Tel: 44 1223 236336
Fax: 44 1223 236337
Email: postmaster@cica.org.uk
Website: http://www.cica.org.uk

Founded: 1973
Members: 250
Staff: 7
Contact: Mr. I. Hamilton, GM
Description: Architects, civil engineers, contractors, and quantity surveyors; individuals affiliated with the software manufacturing industry and related university and government departments. Promotes the appropriate use of computers in the construction industry. Sponsors tutorials. Compiles statistics.
Formerly: Design Office Consortium
Publication: Directory
Publication title: Software Directory

Construction Plant Hire Association

27-28 Newbury St., Barbican, London, EC1A 7HU, England, UK
Tel: 44 20 77963366
Fax: 44 20 77963399
Email: enquiries@cpa.uk.net
Website: http://www.cpa.uk.net
Founded: 1941
Members: 1400
Staff: 7
Contact: Colin Wood
Description: Represents the interests of plant hirers.
Publication: Newsletter
Publication title: Bulletin. Advertisements.

Construction Plant-hire Association

52 Rochester Row, London, SW1P 1JU, England, UK
Tel: 44 207 6306868
Fax: 44 207 6306765
Email: enquiries@c-p-a.co.uk
Website: http://www.c-p-a.co.uk
Founded: 1941
Members: 1100
Staff: 7
Contact: Miss L.M. Abrahams
Description: Construction plant hire companies.

Construction Products Association
CPA

26 Store St., London, WC1E 7BT, England, UK
Tel: 44 207 3233770
Fax: 44 207 3230307
Email: enquiries@constprod.org.uk
Website: http://www.constprod.org.uk
Founded: 2000
Members: 66
Staff: 10
Contact: Michael Ankers, Ch.Exec.
Description: Acts as a single voice for the producers and suppliers of construction projects in the UK. Seeks to build a growing, profitable, and sustainable future for the construction products industry by focusing its activities in four specific areas: increasing investment in the built environment; developing a positive regulatory and fiscal framework; improving industry performance; and responding to the environmental challenge.
Library Subject: statistics, forecasts, and sector information available by telephone only
Library Type: reference
Formerly: National Council of Building Material Producers
Publication title: Construction Forecast
Publication title: Construction Market Trends

Consumer Credit Trade Association

The Wool Exchange, Ste. 8, 10 Hustlergate, Bradford, BD1 1RE, England, UK
Tel: 44 1274 390380
Fax: 44 1274 729002
Email: info@ccta.co.uk
Website: http://www.ccta.co.uk
Founded: 1891
Members: 500
Staff: 6
Contact: R. Keith Mather
Description: Credit grantors of many types who offer credit to consumers. Includes finance companies, retailers, some building societies, other lenders and suppliers of ancillary services. Represents to government, the media and EC authorities the interests of companies providing and operating credit, leasing and rental facilities. Offers a range of services to members including advice, courses and seminars, standard agreement forms, Short Guides on legislation, magazine and discussion groups and forums.
Publication: Journal
Publication title: Consumer Credit. Advertisements.

Consumers International - England

24 Highbury Crescent, London, N5 1RX, England, UK
Tel: 44 207 2266663
Fax: 44 207 3540607
Email: consint@consint.org
Website: http://www.consumersinternational.org
Founded: 1960
Members: 260
Staff: 70
Contact: Julian Edwards, Dir.Gen.
Description: Global association for consumers organizations from more than 100 countries. Objectives are to support the formation and development of strong and effective consumer organizations; foster international cooperation amongst consumer organizations and other supporting bodies; pursue an agenda for international action to protect consumers, especially the poor, the marginalised and the disadvantaged; and establish an authoritative and influential presence in global and regional policy making bodies. Works on such issues as sustainable consumption, food and technical standards, health concerns and international trade. Works closely with the United Nations agencies and other international decision-making bodies. Helped found and works closely with Health Action International, Pesticides Action Network, and International Baby Food Action Network.
Library Type: not open to the public
Formerly: International Organisation of Consumers Unions
Publication: Newsletter
Publication title: Consumer Currents
Second publication: Newsletter
Publication title: Regional
Meetings/Conventions: conference

Contemporary Art Society
CAS

Bloomsbury House, 74-77 Great Russell St., London, WC1B 3DA, England, UK
Tel: 44 207 6120730
Fax: 44 207 6314230
Email: cas@contempart.org.uk
Website: http://www.contempart.org.uk
Founded: 1910
Members: 1700

Staff: 6
Contact: Gill Hedley, Dir.
Fee: £40
Membership Type: individual
Fee: £500
Membership Type: corporate
Description: Purchases works of art by living artists and gives them to UK museums and galleries. Funding is obtained from arts council and other grants, membership dues and profits from the Contemporary Art Society Projects.
Library Subject: British contemporary art
Library Type: reference
Publication title: Annual Report
Second publication: Newsletter
Meetings/Conventions: - monthly tour - Exhibits.

Contemporary Glass Society

POB 1320, Stoke-On-Trent, ST4 2YS, England, UK
Email: admin@cgs.org.uk
Website: http://www.cgs.org.uk
Founded: 1997
Description: Facilitates and encourages communication between all those involved with glass in the artistic, technological, manufacturing and support capacity.
Publication: Newsletter
Publication title: Glass Network

Continuing Care at Home Association

Churchview, Sunningwell Willage, Abingdon, OX13 6RD, England, UK
Tel: 44 1865 326595
Fax: 44 1865 326595
Email: avis@concah.demon.co.uk
Website: http://www.concah.demon.co.uk/
Founded: 1992
Contact: Heather Hutchinson, Memb.Sec.
Description: Health and social service professionals. To improve the relief at home of those people suffering from chronic illness and disability, and to advance the learning and understanding of those caring for such persons

Contract Flooring Association

4c St. Mary's Pl., The Lace Market, Nottingham, NG1 1PH, England, UK
Tel: 44 115 9411126
Fax: 44 115 9412238
Email: info@cfa.org.uk
Website: http://www.cfa.org.uk
Founded: 1973
Members: 460
Staff: 4
Contact: Richard Wollerton, Exec.Dir.
Description: Manufacturers, contractors, distributors and consultants of carpets, vinyls, timber, rubber, cork linoleum etc. To promote standards within the flooring industry and provide advice and guidance to members.
Publication: Journal
Publication title: Contracts Flooring Journal
Publication title: Guide to Contract Flooring

Contractors Mechanical Plant Engineers

The White House, Whitby Rd., Easington, Saltburn by the Sea, TS13 4NW, England, UK
Tel: 44 1704 889129
Fax: 44 1704 880902

Email: cmpe.uk@virgin.net
Website: http://www.cmpe.org
Founded: 1957
Members: 1000
Contact: Stephen Mangham, Natl.Sec.
Description: Executives employed in connection with contractors mechanical plant used in the construction industry. Aims to broaden the scope of knowledge of such plant and its applications and other related activities.
Publication: Newsletter
Meetings/Conventions: - monthly meeting

Cooperative Women's Guild

446 Hertford Rd., Enfield, EN3 5QH, England, UK
Tel: 44 208 8045905
Fax: 44 208 8045905
Founded: 1883
Members: 2500
Staff: 2
Contact: Susan Bell, Sec.
Fee: £4.2
Description: Promotes equal opportunities for complete and free development. Educates women on principles and practices of cooperation so that they may participate in the women's movement. Works towards improving the status of women and encouraging their participation in community, national, and international affairs. Promotes world peace. Provides social, cultural, and recreational activities.
Publication: Newsletter
Meetings/Conventions: - annual congress

Copper Development Association

5 Grovelands Business Centre, Boundary Way, Hemel Hampstead, HP2 7TE, England, UK
Tel: 44 1442 275700
Fax: 44 1442 275716
Email: copperdev@compuserve.com
Website: http://www.cda.org.uk
Founded: 1933
Members: 9
Staff: 9
Contact: Angela Vessey, Dir.
Description: International copper producers and national copper fabricators. Encourages use of copper and copper alloys and promotes correct and efficient application.

Copyright Licensing Agency

90 Tottenham Court Rd., London, W1T 4LP, England, UK
Tel: 44 207 6315555
Fax: 44 207 6315500
Email: cla@cla.co.uk
Website: http://www.cla.co.uk
Founded: 1982
Members: 2
Staff: 54
Contact: Jonathon Leigh-Hunt
Description: Authors' Licensing & Collecting Society and the Publishers Licensing Society on whose behalf CLA acts as agent. Administers collectively photocopying and other copying rights that it is uneconomic for writers and publishers to administer for themselves. Issues collective and transactional licences, and the fees it collects, after the deduction of costs, are distributed at regular intervals to authors and publishers via their respective societies.
Publication: Newsletter
Publication title: CLArion Newsletter

Cork Industry Federation

13 Felton Lea, Sidcup, DA14 6BA, England, UK
Tel: 44 208 3024801
Fax: 44 208 3024801
Website: http://www.cork-products.co.uk
Founded: 1968
Members: 15
Staff: 1
Contact: Mrs. Joy Bell, Hon.Sec.
Description: The majority of firms involved in the import, manufacture and distribution of cork in the UK and export markets. Exists to monitor and uphold quality standards within the industry and to promote the use of cork in a host of different applications, closures (bottle stoppers), floor and wall tiles, industrial uses.
Publication: Membership Directory
Meetings/Conventions: conference

Cornwall Archaeological Society
CAS

Staff Flat, Truro College Tregeye, Truro, TR4 8QQ, England, UK
Tel: 44 1872 560351
Founded: 1961

Corona Worldwide

South Bank House, Black Prince Rd., London, SE1 7SJ, England, UK
Tel: 44 207 7934020
Fax: 44 207 7934042
Email: hq@coronaww.prestel.co.uk
Founded: 1950
Members: 4000
Staff: 1
Contact: Patrick Shine, Admin.Sec.
Fee: £15
Membership Type: full
Fee: £12
Membership Type: concession
Description: Assists women and families who have emmigrated from their native country. Strives to spread friendship and understanding between people. Works to make living in different cultures a stimulating and an enjoyable experience for the whole family. Disseminates practical information on resettlement. Conducts educational and research programs.

Coronary Artery Disease Research Association
CORDA

121 Sydney St., London, SW3 6NR, England, UK
Tel: 44 20 73498686
Fax: 44 20 73499414
Email: corda@rbh.nthames.nhs.uk
Website: http://www.corda.org.uk
Founded: 1975

Corporation of Insurance, Financial and Mortgage Advisers

174 High St., Guildford, GU1 3HW, England, UK
Tel: 44 1483 539121
Fax: 44 1483 301847
Founded: 1968
Members: 1000
Staff: 2
Contact: Mrs. Irene Bowman
Fee: £90

Membership Type: individual
Fee: £100
Membership Type: corporate
Description: Members are independent financial advisers and also appointed representatives, general insurance intermediaries and some registered brokers. Tries to raise ethics and professionalism within the financial services and insurance marketplace; to help members with any problems they may encounter in their business; to lobby on any legislative matter i.e. FSA which is important to members; to liaise with other Government and trade bodies on all matters that might affect membership.
Formerly: Corporation of Insurance and Financial Advisors
Publication: Newsletter. Advertisements.
Meetings/Conventions: - annual luncheon London UK

Corps of Drums Society
62 Gally Hill Rd., Church Crookham, Fleet, GU52 6RU, England, UK
Tel: 44 1252 614852
Email: reg@corpsofdrums.softnet.co.uk
Founded: 1977
Members: 469
Contact: Reg Davis, Hon. Sec.
Fee: £7
Membership Type: single
Description: Persons making or supporting drum and flute music based on the traditions of the British Army. Concerned with the presentation and promotion of the concept and traditions of the drum and flute Corps of Drums based on British Army practice.
Publication: Journal
Publication title: The Drummer's Call. Advertisements.
Meetings/Conventions: Music Meeting London UK

Corrugated Case Materials Association
c/o Papermakers House
Rivenhall Rd., Westlea, Swindon, SN5 7BD, England, UK
Tel: 44 1793 889600
Fax: 44 1793 886182
Email: djgillett@paper.org.uk
Contact: D.J. Gillett, Sec.
Description: Promotes the UK corrugated case materials industry.

Corrugated Packaging Association
2 Saxon Court, Freeschool St., Northampton, NN1 1ST, England, UK
Tel: 44 1604 621002
Fax: 44 1604 620636
Email: postbox@corrugated.org.uk
Website: http://www.corrugated.org.uk
Founded: 1919
Members: 40
Staff: 5
Contact: Dr. M. Oldman, Dir.
Description: Trade association.
Formerly: British Fibreboard Packaging Association

Cosmetic, Toiletry, and Perfumery Association - England
c/o Josaron House
5-7 John Princes St., London, W1G 0JN, England, UK
Tel: 44 207 4918891
Fax: 44 207 4938061
Email: info@ctpa.org.uk

Website: http://www.ctpa.org.uk
Founded: 1945
Members: 130
Staff: 9
Description: Manufacturers, raw material suppliers and contract services to the cosmetic toiletry and perfumery industry in the UK. Covers manufacturers and suppliers. Aims to provide a legislative and technical information service to members. Represents members' interests to UK Government, EC Commission and other opinion forums.

Council for Aluminium in Building
River View House, Bonds Mill, Stonehouse, GL10 3RF, England, UK
Tel: 44 1453 828851
Fax: 44 1453 828861
Email: enquiries@c-a-b.org.uk
Website: http://www.c-a-b.org.uk
Founded: 1994
Members: 74
Staff: 3
Contact: G. Reynolds, Dir.
Fee: £3000
Description: Members are drawn from all aspects of the architectural aluminium industry and allied suppliers. Aims to support the interests of the architectural aluminium industry by encouraging the increasing use of aluminium products in architecture and the construction industry as a whole; to provide technical information to specifiers and architects.
Publication: Newsletter
Publication title: Aluminium Angles

Council for British Archaeology
c/o Bowes Morrell House
111 Walmgate, York, YO1 9WA, England, UK
Tel: 44 1904 671417
Fax: 44 1904 671384
Email: info@britarch.ac.uk
Website: http://www.britarch.ac.uk
Founded: 1944
Members: 5500
Staff: 19
Contact: Mike Heyworth
Fee: £16
Membership Type: student
Fee: £27
Membership Type: individual or institution
Description: Societies, museums, universities, national and local government services, archaeological units and trusts, and other conservation bodies with mutual interests, as well as a large number of individuals, both professional and amateur. To promote the study and safeguarding of Britain's historic environment, to provide a forum for archaeological opinion, and to improve public knowledge of Britain's past.
Library Subject: British archaeology
Library Type: open to the public
Publication: Bibliography
Publication title: British and Irish Archaeological Bibliography
Publication title: British Archaeology

Council for British Archaeology
BAA

Bowes Morrell House, 111 Walmgate, York, YO1 9WA, England, UK
Tel: 44 1904 671417
Fax: 44 1904 671384
Email: info@britarch.ac.uk
Website: http://www.britarch.ac.uk
Founded: 1843

Council for Dance Education and Training - UK

Toynbee Hall, Commercial St., London, E1 6LS, England, UK
Tel: 44 20 72474030
Fax: 44 20 72473404
Email: info@cdet.org.uk
Website: http://www.cdet.org.uk
Founded: 1978
Members: 41
Staff: 4
Contact: Julie Crofts, Ch.Off.
Description: Dance teaching associations, dance training institutions and related dance professional bodies. Aims to maintain and improve standards of dance education and training at all levels throughout the country; advises, cooperates with and makes representation to government departments, local authorities and other interested bodies.
Publication title: Code of Conduct and Standards of Good Practice
Second publication: Directory
Publication title: UK Directory of Registered Dance Teachers
Meetings/Conventions: - annual general assembly London UK

Council for Education in the Commonwealth
CEC

c/o College of Preceptors
Commonwealth House, 7 Lion Yard, Tremadoc Rd., London, SW4 7NQ, England, UK
Tel: 44 207 4981202
Fax: 44 207 4981202
Email: secretariat@cecomm.org.uk
Website: http://www.personal.rdg.ac.uk/~esshonor/cec/
Founded: 1959
Members: 300
Contact: Malcolm Dalziel, Membership Sec.
Description: An organization based in the British parliament with academic institutions, corporations, nongovernmental organizations and interested individuals as supporters in 60 countries. Encourages discussion on problems in education and training in the Commonwealth, particularly in developing countries, and the role that Great Britain should play in the solution of these problems. Promotes educational cooperation; works to influence public opinion. Makes recommendations to the Commonwealth Secretariat, the Commission of the European Communities, the European Parliament, and other bodies. Initiates studies.
Publication: Newsletter
Publication title: CEC Newsletter
Meetings/Conventions: - bimonthly meeting

Council for Education in World Citizenship
CEWC

32 Carisbrooke Rd., London, E17 7EF, England, UK
Tel: 44 2852 16974
Email: info@cewc.org.uk
Founded: 1939

Contact: Titos Alexander
Description: Scholars and other individuals interested in international understanding and the concept of world citizenship. Seeks to help young people understand and confront global issues and challenges. Conducts civics and peace education courses; supports programs operated by other organizations pursuing similar goals; maintains speakers' bureau and resource center.

Council for Environmental Education
CEE

94 London St., Reading, RG1 4SJ, England, UK
Tel: 44 118 9502550
Fax: 44 118 9591955
Email: enquiries@cee.org.uk
Website: http://www.cee.org.uk
Founded: 1968
Members: 80
Staff: 11
Contact: Oby Onyekpe, Info.Off.
Description: Umbrella body for environmental and sustainable development education in England.
Library Subject: environmental education, education for sustainable development
Library Type: reference
Publication: Newsletter
Publication title: CEEview
Meetings/Conventions: - annual conference - Exhibits.

Council for Hospitality Management Education

c/o School of Tourism and Hospitality Management
Leeds Metropolitan University, Calverley St., Leeds, LS1 3HE, England, UK
Tel: 44 113 2835937
Fax: 44 141 2833111
Email: y.guerrier@sbu.ac.uk
Website: http://www.chme.co.uk
Founded: 1979
Members: 50
Contact: Yvonne Guerrier, Chair
Fee: £275
Description: Universities and colleges which offer degree and/or HND courses in hospitality management. Represents member institutions' interests in the field of hospitality management education at HE level, EC, government, industry and professional levels. It also promotes hospitality management education in general, as well as specialist levels, eg. industrial placement, research, access to courses etc.
Publication: Newsletter

Council for Independent Archaeology
CIA

c/o Kevan Fadden
7 Lea Rd., Ampthill, Bedford, MK45 2PR, England, UK
Tel: 44 1525 402273
Email: cia@archaeology.co.uk
Website: http://www.independents.org.uk
Founded: 1989
Members: 460
Contact: Andrew Selkirk, Chm.
Fee: £6
Membership Type: ordinary
Description: Amateur archeologists and other individuals with an interest in archeology. Promotes participation in archeological

activities by independent individuals. Serves as a forum for the exchange of information among members. Provides support to independent archeology projects; initiated development of resistivity meter.
Publication: Newsletter
Meetings/Conventions: - biennial conference Sheffield UK

Council for Music in Hospitals

74 Queens Rd., Hersham, Walton-On-Thames, KT12 5LW, England, UK
Tel: 44 1932 252809
Fax: 44 1932 252966
Email: info@music-in-hospitals.org.uk
Website: http://www.music-in-hospitals.org.uk
Contact: Diana Greenman, Ch.Exec.
Description: Provides live, professional concerts in hospitals, homes, hospices and day centres.

Council for National Parks

246 Lavender Hill, London, SW11 1LJ, England, UK
Tel: 44 207 9244077
Fax: 44 207 9245761
Email: info@cnp.org.uk
Website: http://www.cnp.org.uk
Founded: 1936
Members: 2500
Staff: 7
Contact: Vicki Elcoate, Dir.
Description: Campaigns to protect the National Parks of England and Wales and promotes their quiet enjoyment by everyone. Friends of National Parks support the work of the Council for National Parks. They receive a newsletter 3 times a year and take part in special events in the Parks.
Publication: Newsletter
Publication title: Viewpoint

Council for Registered Gas Installers
CORGI

Chineham Business Park, 1 Elmwood, Crockford Ln., Basingstoke, RG24 8WG, England, UK
Tel: 44 1256 37200
Email: enquiries@corgi-gas.co.uk
Website: http://www.corgi-gas.com/
Contact: Nicole Perry, Mng.Ed.
Description: Works as National Watchdog for Gas Safety in the United Kingdom; promotes and enhances gas safety, standards and quality.

Council for the Advancement of Arab-British Understanding

1 Gough Sq., London, EC4A 3DE, England, UK
Tel: 44 20 78321310
Fax: 44 20 78321329
Email: doylec@caabu.org
Website: http://www.caabu.org
Founded: 1967
Members: 900
Staff: 4
Contact: Chris Doyle, Dir.
Fee: £20
Membership Type: subscription
Description: Individuals united to promote mutual cultural appreciation between the peoples of Britain and the Arab World.

Advocates social policies tending to increase beneficial interaction between British and Arab peoples.
Library Subject: Middle East, Islam, politics
Library Type: not open to the public
Publication: Newsletter
Publication title: CAABU Briefings
Second publication: Newsletter
Publication title: Campaign Bulletin
Meetings/Conventions: - monthly meeting

Council for the Advancement of Communication with Deaf People

Durham University Science Park, Block 4, Stockton Rd., Durham, DH1 3UZ, England, UK
Tel: 44 191 3831155
Fax: 44 191 3837914
Email: durham@cacdp.org.uk
Website: http://www.cacdp.org.uk
Founded: 1982
Members: 1000
Staff: 23
Contact: M. Pickersgill
Description: Aims to improve communication between deaf and hearing people by the development of curricula and examinations in communication skills. Offers certification in British Sign Language, Lipspeaking. Communicating with Deafblind people and Deaf Awareness, and carries out the selection, training, monitering and registration of examiners.
Publication: Book
Publication title: CACDP Directory
Second publication: Newsletter
Publication title: CACDP Standard Newsletter

Council for the Protection of Rural England
CPRE

128 Southwark St., London, SE1 0SW, England, UK
Tel: 44 207 9812800
Fax: 44 207 9812899
Email: info@cpre.org.uk
Website: http://www.cpre.org.uk
Founded: 1926
Members: 60000
Staff: 40
Contact: Ms. Nicola Frank, Hd./Press & Pubs.
Fee: £20
Membership Type: individual
Fee: £27
Membership Type: joint
Description: Promotes the beauty, tranquility and diversity of rural England; encourages the sustainable use of land and other natural resources in town and country.
Library Subject: environment, planning, government policy on environment, transport
Library Type: not open to the public
Formerly: Council for Preservation of Rural England
Publication title: Annual Report
Second publication: Magazine
Publication title: Countryside Voice. Advertisements.
Meetings/Conventions: - semiannual convention - Exhibts. London UK

Council for the Registration of Schools Teaching Dyslexic Pupils
CRESTED

Greygarth, Littleworth, Winchcombe, Cheltenham, GL54 5BT, England, UK
Tel: 44 1242 604852
Fax: 44 1242 604852
Email: crested@crested.org.uk
Website: http://www.crested.org.uk
Founded: 1989
Contact: Dr. M.C.V. Cane, Chm.
Description: Offers guidance to parents seeking a school for their dyslexic child, providing a list of schools approved for their dyslexia provision.
Publication: Directory

Council of Academic and Professional Publishers

c/o Publishers Association
29 B Montague St., London, WC1B 5BH, England, UK
Tel: 44 20 76919191
Fax: 44 207 6919199
Email: gtaylor@publsihers.org.uk
Website: http://www.publishers.org.uk
Founded: 1977
Members: 90
Staff: 2
Contact: Graham Taylor, Dir.
Description: Academic/professional publishing companies specialising in books and journals. A subscription organization covering the following areas of activity on behalf of academic/professional publishers: representation to Government; collective marketing/promotion; specialist publishing services; copyright/licensing; information/ statistical services.
Formerly: University College Professional Publishers Council
Publication: Newsletter
Publication title: CAPP Bnef
Meetings/Conventions: - annual seminar

Council of European National Top-Level Domain Registries
CENTR

Sandford Gate, Sandy Ln. West, Oxford, OX4 6LB, England, UK
Tel: 44 1865 332400
Fax: 44 1865 332401
Email: secretariat@centr.org
Website: http://www.centr.org
Founded: 1998
Description: Maintains registry of top-level domain (TLD) names of Internet addresses. Acts as a channel of communication for Internet governing bodies.

Council of Forest Industries - UK

PO Box 1, Farnborough, GU14 6WE, England, UK
Tel: 44 1252 522545
Fax: 44 1252 522546
Email: cofiuk@aol.com
Website: http://www.cofi.org
Contact: John Park
Description: Representing, in the UK, Timber and plywood producers of British Columbia and Alberta, producing a wide range of timber and plywood products which are marketed throughout Europe, North America and the Pacific Rim. Provision of technical support for products of member companies. Head Office, Vancouver, BC.

Council of Mining and Metallurgical Institutions
CMMI

Danum House, 6A South Parade, Doncaster, DN1 2DY, England, UK
Tel: 44 1302 320486
Fax: 44 1302 380900
Email: hq@imm.org.uk
Founded: 1924
Members: 11
Contact: Dr. Graham Jm Woodrow, Sec.
Description: National mining and metallurgical institutes from Australia, Canada, Chile, India, Japan, South Africa, the United States and the United Kingdom. Promotes development of the world's mineral resources. Fosters a high level of technical efficiency and serves as an organ for communication and cooperation among members.
Publication: Proceedings
Publication title: Proceedings of the CMMI Congress
Meetings/Conventions: - quadrennial congress

Council of Mortgage Lenders

3 Savile Row, London, W1S 3PB, England, UK
Tel: 44 20 74370075
Fax: 44 20 74343791
Email: info@cml.org.uk
Website: http://www.cml.org.uk
Founded: 1989
Members: 138
Staff: 50
Contact: Michael J. Coogan, Sec.
Description: Mortgage lending institutions, including building societies, clearing banks, insurance companies and their subsidiaries, finance houses and centralised lenders. Has five main functions; to be a central representative body; to be a research and statistical centre; to be a technical centre; to be a forum for the exchange of information; and to be a focus of media relations, in relation to residential mortgage lending in the UK.
Publication title: Housing Finance
Second publication: Book
Publication title: Housing Finance Factbook

Council of National Beekeeping Associations in the United Kingdom
CONBA-UK

c/o Michael J. Badger Kara
14 Thorn Ln., Roundhay, Leeds, LS8 1NN, England, UK
Tel: 44 113 2945879
Fax: 44 113 2666303
Email: buzz.buzz@btinternet.com
Website: http://www.bbka.org.uk/conba-uk.htm
Founded: 1978
Contact: John A. Hall, Chm.
Description: Promotes the aims and objectives of the national beekeeping associations of England, Scotland, Ulster and Wales.
Meetings/Conventions: - semiannual meeting

Council of Occupational Therapists for the European Countries
COTEC

106-114 Borough High St., London, SE1 1LB, England, UK
Tel: 44 171 3576480
Fax: 44 171 4502349
Email: beryl.steeden@cot.co.uk

Website: http://www.cotec-europe.org
Founded: 1986
Members: 20
Contact: Maeve Groom, Pres.
Description: Works to enable national associations in European countries to develop, harmonize, and improve standards of professional practice and education, as well as to advance the theory of occupational therapy throughout Europe.
Meetings/Conventions: - quadrennial congress - Exhibits. Athens Greece

Council of Photographic News Agencies

Boswage Cottage, Boswague, Tregony, Truro, TR2 5ST, England, UK
Tel: 44 1872 501393
Founded: 1951
Members: 6
Staff: 110
Contact: George Freston
Description: Members are photographic news picture companies supplying the media with news, sport and stock pictures. Aims to supply all the media with photographic coverage of news and feature events. Also large archives of photographs going back to the early 1900s on news, sport, royalty etc.

Council of Subject Teaching Associations

The Niven Suite, The Mansion, Ottershaw Route, Chertsey, KT16 0TG, England, UK
Tel: 44 1757 706161
Fax: 44 1757 213699
Contact: Graeme Leen Smith
Description: To provide a forum for subject teaching associations to discuss issues of common concern and importance.

Country House Apartments

Aynhoe Park, Ste. 10, Aynho, Banbury, OX17 3BQ, England, UK
Tel: 44 1869 812800
Fax: 44 1869 812819
Email: hq@cha.org.uk
Website: http://www.cha.org.uk
Founded: 1955
Members: 2000
Staff: 200
Contact: S. Piltz, Chief Exec.
Fee: £15
Description: The main objective is saving, for the benefit of the public, buildings of historic and architectural interest of importance together with their gardens and grounds.
Publication: Annual Report
Second publication: Brochure
Meetings/Conventions: - annual meeting

Country Land and Business Association

16 Belgrave Sq., London, SW1X 8PQ, England, UK
Tel: 44 207 2350511
Fax: 44 207 2350528
Email: mail@cla.org.uk
Website: http://www.cla.org.uk
Founded: 1907
Members: 49400
Staff: 77
Contact: Mark Pendlington, Chief.Exec.
Description: Members are owners of rural land. To promote and safeguard the legitimate interests of owners of rural land; to safeguard and develop the capital invested in the ownership of agricultural and other rural land and to secure an appropriate return from these assets.
Formerly: Country Landowners Association
Publication title: CLA in Wales
Publication title: Country Landowner. Advertisements.
Meetings/Conventions: CLA Game Fair - annual - Exhibits.x

Countryside Alliance
CA

The Old Town Hall, 367 Kennington Rd., London, SE11 4PT, England, UK
Tel: 44 207 8409200
Fax: 44 207 7938484
Email: info@countryside-alliance.org
Website: http://www.countryside-alliance.org/
Founded: 1997
Members: 10000
Description: Individuals interested in the countryside and the preservation of rural areas of the United Kingdom. Seeks to preserve the freedoms of country people and their way of life and champion the countryside, country sports and the rural way of life. Conducts lobbying and advocacy campaigns to raise the awareness of rural issues among legislators at all levels of government; works on behalf of animal welfare and conservation programs; develops educational programs to improve public understanding of rural lifestyles and issues; sponsors research to develop solutions to problems facing rural areas.
Publication: Reports
Publication title: Real Countryside
Meetings/Conventions: - annual conference

Coventry and Warwickshire Chamber of Commerce

Oak Tree Court, Binley Business Park, Harry Weston Rd., Coventry, CV3 2UN, England, UK
Tel: 44 2476 654321
Fax: 44 2476 450242
Email: info@cw-chamber.co.uk
Website: http://www.cw-chamber.co.uk
Members: 1728
Staff: 194
Contact: Malcolm Gillespie, Chief Exec.
Description: Promotes business and commerce.

Craft Brewing Association
CBA

82 Elmfield Rd., London, SW17 8AN, England, UK
Founded: 1995
Members: 300
Contact: Bill Cooper, Membership Sec.
Description: Craft brewers. (A craft brewer is defined by the group as a home brewer who practices the true craft of brewing to the best of his or her ability.) Seeks to advance the art of home brewing. Serves as a support group for members; facilitates the establishment of local craft brewing clubs. Acts as a clearinghouse on home brewing techniques, beer making ingredients, and brewing equipment. Makes available beer tasting and evaluation services; sponsors educational and training programs; conducts social activities.
Publication: Journal
Publication title: Brewer's Contract

Craft Guild of Chefs

1 Victoria Parade, By 331 Sandycombe Rd., Richmond, TW9 3NB, England, UK
Tel: 44 208 9483870
Fax: 44 208 9483944
Email: john.retallick@craft-guild.org
Website: http://www.craft-guild.org
Founded: 1885
Members: 3000
Staff: 3
Contact: Mr. John Retallick, Mgr.
Description: Working cooks and chefs, catering teachers and trainees; members of the food and beverage industries, waiters, hotel managers. Aims to promote and develop the art and technology of cookery and supervisory and management skills related to cookery and associated professions, to foster and provide training and education especially for the young.
Formerly: Cookery and Food Association
Publication title: The Stockpot

Craft Potters Association of Great Britain

c/o William Blake House
7 Marshall St., London, W1V 1FD, England, UK
Tel: 44 207 4376781
Fax: 44 207 2879954
Email: contemporary.ceramics@virgin.net
Founded: 1957
Members: 900
Staff: 4
Contact: Tony Ainsworth, Admin.
Description: Aims to give support and encouragement to its members. It has three companies Ceramic Review, Craft Potters Trading Company Limited (which sells work of its members) and the Craft Potters Association.
Publication title: Ceramic Review

Crafts Council

c/o Reference Section
44a Pentonville Rd., Islington, London, N1 9BY, England, UK
Tel: 44 20 72787700
Fax: 44 20 78376891
Email: reference@craftscouncil.org.uk
Website: http://www.craftscouncil.org.uk
Founded: 1971
Staff: 60
Description: The national organization for contemporary crafts in Great Britain offering exhibition and educational programmes. Maintains picture and book libraries, a collection of contemporary craft, and runs a gallery shop and an outlet at the V&A Museum. Start-up grants are offered to makers.
Library Subject: contemporary crafts
Library Type: open to the public
Publication: Magazine
Publication title: Crafts. Advertisements.
Second publication: Catalogs

Craniosacral Therapy Association of the UK

Monomark House, 27 Old Gloucester St., London, WC1N 3XX, England, UK
Email: info@craniosacral.co.uk
Website: http://www.craniosacral.co.uk
Description: Craniosacral therapy practitioners in the United Kingdom.
Publication: Journal
Publication title: The Fulcrum

Credit Protection Association
CPA

CPA House, 350 King St., London, W6 0RX, England, UK
Tel: 44 208 8460000
Fax: 44 208 7417459
Email: cpaonline@cpa.co.uk
Website: http://www.cpa.co.uk
Founded: 1914
Description: Businesses and other organizations that offer their customers credit. Promotes prompt and effective action in cases of late or overdue payments. Provides support and advice to members attempting to collect on past due accounts; maintains nationwide network to screen potential credit recipients. Group claims to resolve 84 of overdue account situations within days by using interactive technologies that can track missing persons or corporations, and access legal and financial advice and business status reports.

Cremation Society of Great Britain
CSGB

Brecon House, 2nd Fl., 16/16A Albion Pl., Maidstone, ME14 5DZ, England, UK
Tel: 44 1622 688292
Fax: 44 1622 686698
Email: cremsoc@aol.com
Website: http://www.srgw.demon.co.uk/CremSoc
Founded: 1874
Staff: 5
Contact: Mr. R.N. Arber, Sec.
Description: Promotes the practice of cremation in the U.K. Compiles statistics and provides information on all aspects of cremation.
Publication: Directory
Publication title: Directory of Crematoria
Second publication: Journal
Publication title: Pharos International. Advertisements.
Meetings/Conventions: Annual Cremation Conference - annual conference - Exhibits. Harrogate UK

Crime Writers' Association
CWA

PO Box 6939, Birmingham, B14 7LT, England, UK
Tel: 44 121 4442536
Fax: 44 121 4442536
Email: info@thecwa.co.uk
Website: http://www.thecwa.co.uk
Founded: 1953
Members: 460
Contact: Lindsey Davis, Chair
Fee: £45
Membership Type: in U.K.
Fee: £75
Membership Type: in U.S.
Description: Writers, publishers, agents, and reviewers of crime fiction in 18 countries. Maintains speakers' bureau. Sponsors Awards.
Publication: Bulletin
Publication title: Red Herrings. Advertisements.
Meetings/Conventions: - annual conference

Cromwell Association
CA

49 St. Louis Rd., W. Norwood, London, SE27 9QJ, England, UK
Tel: 44 207 347341
Fax: 44 207 314095
Email: abbeygates@cs.com
Website: http://www.cromwell.argonet.co.uk
Founded: 1935
Members: 528
Contact: Joanne Smith
Fee: £15
Fee: £200
Membership Type: life
Description: Students and admirers of Oliver Cromwell (1599-1658), English statesman who directed English government from 1653 to 1658; individuals interested in the history of the period. Works to preserve the memory of Oliver Cromwell and to encourage study of the history of the Civil War, Commonwealth, and Protectorate. Maintains speakers' bureau; organizes competitions, organized conferences and day schools. Supports the Cromwell Museum.
Library Subject: Cromwell and related topics
Library Type: reference
Publication: Journal
Publication title: Cromwelliana. Advertisements.
Second publication: Newsletter
Publication title: Newsletter
Meetings/Conventions: Cromwell Day - annual

Crop Protection Association
CPA

4 Lincoln Ct., Lincoln Rd., Peterborough, PE1 2RP, England, UK
Tel: 44 1733 349225
Fax: 44 1733 562523
Email: info@cropprotection.org.uk
Website: http://www.cropprotection.org.uk
Founded: 1926
Members: 56
Staff: 14
Contact: Dr. A.H. Buckenham, Dir.Gen.
Description: Companies with manufacturing or technical control of the manufacture of pesticides in UK or which are substantial distributors of pesticides marketed under their own name. Supports and promotes the interests of major distributors and manufacturers of crop protection, amenity and garden products in the United Kingdom. As the trade association for the industry it represents the views of its members in any forum.
Formerly: British Agrochemicals Association
Publication: Handbook
Publication title: Annual Review and Handbook

Croydon Chamber of Commerce and Industry

Commerce House, 1 Wandle Rd., Croydon, CR9 1HY, England, UK
Tel: 44 208 6802165
Fax: 44 208 6884587
Email: enquiries@croydonchamber.org.uk
Website: http://www.croydonchamber.org.uk
Members: 1020
Staff: 16
Contact: Mike Wareham, Chief Exec.
Description: Promotes business and commerce.

CRUSE Bereavement Care Scotland
CRUSEBCS

126 Sheen Rd., Richmond, TW9 1UR, England, UK
Tel: 44 131 7705100
Fax: 44 131 5515234
Email: cruselochaber@freeuk.com
Founded: 1959
Contact: Ruth Hampton
Description: Individuals and organizations. Seeks to improve the quality of life of people who have lost a loved one. Provides support and services to bereaved individuals; conducts research and educational programs; makes available children's services; participates in charitable initiatives; compiles statistics.
Library Subject: bereavement
Library Type: by appointment only
Publication: Newsletter
Meetings/Conventions: - periodic board meeting

Cutlery and Allied Trades Research Association
CATRA

Henry St., Sheffield, S3 7EQ, England, UK
Tel: 44 114 2769736
Fax: 44 114 2722151
Email: info@catra.org
Website: http://www.catra.org
Founded: 1952
Staff: 20
Contact: R.C. Hamby
Description: Promotes and carries out research, development, testing, and consultancy into the cutlery and allied trades association, including knives, tools, cookware, surgical blades, razor blades, and machine and industrial blades.

Cyclamen Society

c/o Dr. David Bent
Little Pilgrims Way E, Otford, Sevenoaks, TN14 5QN, England, UK
Email: info@cyclamen.org
Website: http://www.cyclamen.org
Founded: 1977
Members: 1600
Contact: Dr. David Bent
Description: Encourages cultivation and conservation of the genus Cyclamen and its species, forms, and cultivars. The genus Cyclamen contains 20 species of plants, which are part of the Primrose family.
Publication: Journal

Cystic Fibrosis Trust

11 London Rd., Bromley, BR1 1BY, England, UK
Tel: 44 208 4647211
Fax: 44 208 3130472
Email: enquires@cftrust.org.uk
Website: http://www.cftrust.org.uk
Founded: 1964
Members: 62500
Staff: 64
Contact: Rosemary Barnes, Chief Exec.
Description: Individuals affected by Cystic Fibrosis.
Publication: Newsletter
Publication title: CF News
Meetings/Conventions: - biennial conference - Exhibits.

Dairy Council - United Kingdom
5-7 John Princes St., London, W1G 0JN, England, UK
Tel: 44 207 4997822
Fax: 44 207 4081353
Email: info@dairycouncil.org.uk
Website: http://www.milk.co.uk
Founded: 1920
Staff: 18
Contact: Michelle Stephens
Description: Co-ordinates the dairy industry's generic information and promotion activities. Funded by, and works on behalf of dairy farmers, dairy processors and manufacturers. Its prime role is to strengthen public perception of the quality and nutritional value of milk and dairy products.
Publication: Catalog
Second publication: Catalog

Dairy Industry Association
DIF
19 Cornwall Ter., London, NW1 4QP, England, UK
Tel: 44 207 4867244
Fax: 44 207 4874734
Email: info@dia-ltd.org.uk
Website: http://www.dia-ltd.org.uk
Founded: 1973
Members: 60
Staff: 17
Contact: Mr. Simon Bates, Company Sec.
Description: Trade association representing processors, manufacturers, wholesalers and retailers of milk and milk products.
Publication title: Dairy Affairs
Publication title: Management Matters

Daiwa Anglo-Japanese Foundation
Daiwa Foundation Japan House, 13/14 Cornwall Terr., London, NW1 4QP, England, UK
Tel: 44 207 4864348
Fax: 44 207 4862914
Email: office@dajf.org.uk
Website: http://www.daiwa-foundation.org.uk
Description: Fosters mutual understanding between the United Kingdom and Japan. Fosters research and education.

Danish-UK Chamber of Commerce
55 Sloane St., London, SW1X 9SR, England, UK
Tel: 44 20 72596795
Fax: 44 20 78231200
Email: info@ducc.co.uk
Website: http://www.ducc.co.uk
Founded: 1989
Members: 140
Staff: 3
Contact: Abigail Kirby-Harris, Dir.
Description: Promotes Anglo-Danish business and networking.

Dartmoor Sheep Breeders Association
The Old Rectory, Clannaborough, Crediton, EX17 6DA, England, UK
Tel: 44 1363 84256
Email: wilson.mitchell@care4free.net
Website: http://www.greyface-dartmoor.org.uk
Founded: 1909
Members: 200
Contact:

Fee: £18
Description: Promotes the Greyface Dartmoor Sheep.
Publication: Book
Publication title: Flock Book

Daycare Trust
NCCCDCT
21 St. George's Rd., London, SE1 6ES, England, UK
Tel: 44 207 84033500
Fax: 44 207 8403355
Email: info@daycaretrust.org.uk
Website: http://www.daycaretrust.org.uk
Founded: 1986
Staff: 25
Contact: Stephen Burke, Dir.
Fee: £25
Membership Type: individual
Fee: £15
Membership Type: unwaged individual
Description: Promotes the development of quality, affordable, accessible, and equitable child care. Works to improve child care nationwide through: dissemination of information; negotiations with politicians, administrators, and trade unions; and cooperation with other voluntary organizations having similar goals. Provides free childcare information to parents.
Library Subject: childcare, working women, equal opportunities
Library Type: reference
Formerly: National Childcare Campaign/Daycare Trust
Publication: Magazine
Publication title: Childcare Now
Second publication: Pamphlet
Publication title: Childwise
Meetings/Conventions: - periodic meeting

Deaf Broadcasting Council
50 Clevedon Rd., London, SE20 7QQ, England, UK
Fax: 44 7970 150006
Email: pennybes@aol.com
Website: http://deafbroadcastingcouncil.org.uk
Founded: 1980
Members: 315
Contact: Penny Beschizza
Fee: £3
Description: Concerned with the need for television and audiovisual communications to be accessible to deaf, deafened and hard of hearing people and such access to be of equal quality as hearing people.
Publication: Magazine
Publication title: Mailshot
Meetings/Conventions: - annual meeting - Exhibits.

Deaf Education Through Listening and Talking
DELTA
PO Box 20, Haverhill, CB9 7BD, England, UK
Tel: 44 1440 783689
Fax: 44 1440 783689
Email: enquiries@deafeducation.org.uk
Website: http://www.deafeducation.org.uk
Founded: 1980
Members: 800
Staff: 5
Contact: Wendy Barnes, Dir.

Fee: £12
Membership Type: ordinary
Description: Parents and teachers of children with hearing impairment; adults with hearing impairment. Promotes development of natural and effective spoken language among children with profound hearing impairment. Advocates use of the natural aural approach in teaching children with profound hearing impairment to use spoken language. Conducts workshops for teachers and families of children with profound hearing impairment; makes available teaching resources; sponsors research; provides children's services.
Formerly: National Aural Group
Publication: Newsletter
Publication title: Chat
Second publication: Newsletter
Publication title: Chatting
Meetings/Conventions: - periodic conference

Deafblind International
Dbl

c/o SENSE International
11-13 Clifton Terr., London, N4 3SR, England, UK
Tel: 44 20 72727774
Fax: 44 20 72726012
Email: dbi@sense.org.uk
Website: http://www.deafblindinternational.org
Founded: 1976
Members: 1000
Staff: 1
Contact: Emanuela Brahamsha
Fee: £30
Membership Type: individual
Fee: £300
Membership Type: corporate
Description: Serves as a network for deaf-blind people, their families, and professionals with an interest in their well-being. Seeks to develop public awareness of the needs and potential of deaf-blind people. Conducts charitable and educational programs.
Formerly: International Association for the Education of Deafblind People
Publication: Journal
Publication title: DBI Review. Advertisements.
Meetings/Conventions: European Conference - quadrennial

Deafblind UK

100 Bridge St., Peterborough, PE1 1DY, England, UK
Tel: 44 1733 358100
Fax: 44 1733 358356
Email: info@deafblinduk.org.uk
Website: http://www.deafblinduk.org.uk
Founded: 1928
Members: 2030
Staff: 150
Contact: Jackie Hicks, Chief Exec.
Description: Deafblind persons. Helps alleviate the isolation felt by those with dual sensory loss. Negotiates with government to secure better services and facilities for individuals with visual and hearing impairments. Conducts public service programs. Offers advice and financial consultation and some housing assistance. Organizes conferences, seminars, and communication courses.
Publication title: The Rainbow. Advertisements.
Second publication: Newspaper
Publication title: Snippets
Meetings/Conventions: - biennial meeting

DEBRA European

c/o Debra House
13 Wellington Business Park, Duke's Ride, Crowthorne, RG45 6LS, England, UK
Tel: 44 1344 771961
Fax: 44 1344 762661
Email: john.dart@btinternet.com
Website: http://www.debra-international.org
Founded: 1992
Members: 20
Staff: 1
Contact: John Dart, Dir.
Description: Umbrella organization of patient support groups for people whose lives have been affected by Epidemidysis Bullosa (EB). Activities include peer support, workshops, and dissemination of research findings.
Formerly: EUR Network of EB Support Groups

DEBRA International

13 Wellington Business Pk., Duke's Ride, Crowthorne, RG45 6LS, England, UK
Tel: 44 1344 771961
Fax: 44 1344 762661
Email: john.dart@btinternet.com
Website: http://www.debra-international.org
Founded: 1997
Members: 29
Staff: 1
Contact: John Dart, Dir.
Description: Seeks to promote the well being of people with EB and to promote research in the area.

Defense Manufacturers Association of Great Britain
DMA

Marlborough House, Headley Rd., Grayshott, Hindhead, GU26 6LG, England, UK
Tel: 44 1428 607788
Fax: 44 1428 604567
Email: enquiries@the-dma.org.uk
Website: http://www.the-dma.org.uk
Founded: 1976
Members: 500
Staff: 28
Contact: Brinley Salzmann, Exports Dir.
Description: UK companies, large or small, concerned with selling products or services to Government defence agencies and main defence contractors in the UK or overseas. Represents the views and needs of its members to Government and the MOD.
Library Subject: public security, police
Library Type: not open to the public
Publication: Report
Publication title: DMA Market Report
Publication title: Register of Members
Meetings/Conventions: - semimonthly seminar

Delius Society
DS

c/o Mr. S. Winstanley
Windmill Ridge, 82 Highgate Rd., Walsall, WS1 3JA, England, UK
Tel: 44 171 4364816
Fax: 44 1716374307
Email: deliussociety@tesco.net
Website: http://www.delius.org.uk/g_society.htm

Founded: 1962
Members: 529
Contact: Mr. Stewart Winstanley, Treas.
Fee: £20
Membership Type: U.K./Europe
Fee: £38
Membership Type: U.S./Canada
Description: Works for wider knowledge and appreciation of Frederick Delius (1862-1934), English composer. Objectives are: to share interest in Delius with others to promote performance, broadcasting, recording, and publishing of his works; to sustain isolated devotees. Sponsors lectures, discussions, and concert and opera visits.
Publication: Newsletter
Publication title: Journal
Meetings/Conventions: - periodic meeting

Dental Laboratories Association
DLA

44-46 Wollaton Rd., Nottingham, NG9 2NR, England, UK
Tel: 44 115 9254888
Fax: 44 115 9254800
Email: info@dla.org.uk
Website: http://www.dla.org.uk
Founded: 1961
Members: 1000
Staff: 8
Contact: Bill Courtney, C.E.
Description: Seeks to advance the study, teaching, and practice of dental technology and the dental sciences. Represents members' commercial and professional interests; facilitates communication and cooperation among members; sponsors research and educational programs.
Publication: Magazine
Publication title: Dental Laboratory. Advertisements.
Meetings/Conventions: Dental Technology Show - biennial conference - Exhibits.

Department for International Development
DFID

1 Palace St., London, SW1E 5HE, England, UK
Tel: 44 135 5843132
Fax: 44 135 843632
Email: enquiry@dfid.gov.uk
Website: http://www.dfid.gov.uk
Founded: 1964
Staff: 1449
Contact: Clare Short, Sec. of State for International Dev.
Description: Government department responsible for all aspects of international development policy. Administers the UK development programme, promotes more coherent UK and international policies in support of sustainable development.
Library Subject: international development
Library Type: not open to the public
Formerly: Overseas Development Administration
Publication: Magazine. Advertisements.

Depression Alliance

35 Westminster Bridge Rd., London, SE1 7JB, England, UK
Tel: 44 20 76330557
Fax: 44 20 76330559
Email: information@depressionalliance.org
Website: http://www.depressionalliance.org

Founded: 1979
Members: 3000
Staff: 9
Contact: Amelia Mustapha, Coord.
Fee: £10
Membership Type: waged
Fee: £5
Membership Type: unwaged
Description: Provides information and support to anyone affected by depression. Services include self-help groups, correspondence schemes and a unique range of literature.
Library Subject: depression
Library Type: reference
Publication: Newsletter
Publication title: A Single Step

Design and Technology Association

16 Wellesbourne House, Walton Rd., Wellesbourne, Warwick, CV35 9JB, England, UK
Tel: 44 1789 470007
Fax: 44 1789 841955
Email: data@data.org.uk
Website: http://www.data.org.uk
Founded: 1989
Members: 8000
Staff: 13
Contact: A.M. Breckon, Ch.Exec.
Fee: £36
Membership Type: individual or institution
Description: For those involved in delivering design and technology in the National Curriculum. Aims to: uphold high standards of teaching and learning, promote and disseminate good practice and act as catalyst for well planned change and development.
Library Subject: design and technology
Library Type: not open to the public
Publication: Newsletter
Publication title: DATANEWS. Advertisements.
Publication title: The Journal of Design and Technology Education
Meetings/Conventions: - annual conference - Exhibits.

Design Council

34 Bow St., London, WC2E 7DL, England, UK
Tel: 44 207 4205200
Fax: 44 207 4205300
Email: info@designcouncil.org.uk
Website: http://www.design-council.org.uk
Founded: 1944
Staff: 40
Contact: Andrew Sumner, Chief Exec.
Description: Organized to improve the design of British products by researching and communicating the benefits of design to government departments, agencies, companies, financial and educational institutions, medical practices, consultant groups, and industrial designers. Promotes improvements in design education. Organized to advise the government on national design policy, with particular reference to education curriculum developments.
Publication: Journal
Publication title: Design

Design History Society
DHS

Nottingham Trent University, Burton St., Nottingham, NG1 4BU, England, UK
Email: nichola.hebditch@ntu.ac.uk
Website: http://www.brighton.ac.uk/dhs/
Founded: 1977
Description: Promotes the study of and research into design history.

Despatch Association

The Lines, Stow Rd., Magdelen, King's Lynn, PE34 3BT, England, UK
Tel: 44 1553 813479
Email: phil@despatch.co.uk
Website: http://www.despatch.co.uk
Founded: 1985
Members: 250
Staff: 1
Contact: Phillip Stone, CEO
Fee: £200
Membership Type: full
Fee: £50
Membership Type: joining fee
Description: Express delivery services in UK. Represents the despatch industry, protects the interests of members, sets and maintains standards within the industry, improves the public image of the industry and improves safety standards within the industry.
Publication: Magazine
Publication title: Despatches Magazine. Advertisements.

Development Education Association

33 Corsham St., London, N1 6DR, England, UK
Tel: 44 207 4908108
Fax: 44 207 4908123
Email: dea@dea.org.uk
Website: http://www.dea.org.uk
Founded: 1993
Members: 330
Staff: 11
Contact: Doug Bourn, Dir.
Description: National umbrella body which aims to support and promote organizations and individuals working to raise awareness and understanding of global and development issues in the United Kingdom.
Library Subject: development education, development, environment, sustainable development, citizenship, and human rights
Library Type: not open to the public
Formerly: Absorbed, NADEC and Inter-Agencies Group
Publication: Journal
Publication title: DEA Journal. Advertisements.
Meetings/Conventions: - annual conference - Exhibits.

Development Planning Unit
DPU

9 Endsleigh Gardens, University College London, London, WC1H 0ED, England, UK
Tel: 44 20 76791111
Fax: 44 20 76791112
Email: dpu@ucl.ac.uk
Website: http://www.ucl.ac.uk/dpu/
Description: The Development Planning Unit is an international centre specialising in academic teaching, practical training, research and consultancy in the field of urban and regional development, planning and management. It is concerned with understanding the process of rapid urbanisation and the policy, planning and management responses to the economic and social development of both urban and rural areas. The full-time academic staff of the DPU is a multidisciplinary group of 17 professionals and academics (embracing 11 different nationalities), all with extensive and ongoing research and professional experience in various fields of urban and institutional development throughout the world. Annually, some 100 participants from more than 30 countries undertake courses or research degrees at the DPU.

Development Studies Association
DSA, University of Manchester, Crawford House, Oxford Rd., Manchester, M13 9GH, England, UK

Tel: 44 161 2752800
Fax: 44 161 27538829
Email: dsa@man.ac.uk
Website: http://www.devstud.org.uk/
Founded: 1977
Members: 560
Staff: 1
Contact: Linda Curry, Admin.
Fee: £20
Membership Type: individual
Fee: £10
Membership Type: concessionary
Description: Scholars with an interest in international economic development. Promotes the advancement of knowledge on international development. Serves as a clearinghouse on international development and international development studies; encourages research; facilitates interdisciplinary exchange and cooperation in the field of development studies.
Publication: Newsletter
Publication title: Forum. Advertisements.
Meetings/Conventions: - annual conference

Dickens Fellowship

The Dickens House, 48 Doughty St., London, WC1N 2LF, England, UK
Tel: 44 207 4052127
Fax: 44 207 8315175
Email: dickens.fellowship@btinternet.com
Website: http://www.dickens.fellowship.btinternet.co.uk
Founded: 1902
Members: 6500
Contact: Dr. Tony Williams, Gen.Sec.
Fee: £8.5
Description: Charles Dickens enthusiasts, scholars, professors, and literary and Victorian specialists in 23 countries. Seeks to: create a common bond of friendship between admirers of English novelist Charles Dickens (1812-70) and to preserve properties associated with Charles Dickens and his works. Maintains Dickens House as a museum.
Library Subject: Dickens' life and work; literary criticism
Library Type: reference
Publication: Journal
Publication title: The Dickensian. Advertisements.
Second publication: Newsletter
Publication title: Mr. Dick's Kite
Meetings/Conventions: - annual conference - Exhibits.

Diecasting Society

Broadway House, Calthorpe Rd., Five Ways, Birmingham, B15 1TN, England, UK
Tel: 44 121 4566103
Fax: 44 870 1389714
Members: 266
Staff: 2
Contact: Dr. David Harris

Digestive Disorders Foundation

3 St. Andrews' Place, London, NW1 4LB, England, UK
Tel: 44 207 4860341
Fax: 44 20 72242012
Email: ddf@digestivedisorders.org.uk
Website: http://www.digestivedisorders.org.uk
Founded: 1971
Staff: 5
Contact: Mark Lister, Ch.Exec.
Description: Aims to raise money for research into digestive disorders and diseases. Patient information leaflets are available on receipt of a stamped self-addressed envelope. These cover the most common digestive disorders.
Publication title: Annual Review

Dinosaur Society

PO Box 20, Heathfield, TN21 8GY, England, UK
Tel: 44 1435 860881
Email: enquiries@dinosaursociety.com
Website: http://www.dinosaursociety.com
Contact: Heidie Dwyer, Admin.
Description: Dedicated to supporting the work of individuals engaged in advancing the science of palaeontology, dinosaurs, and earth science in general.
Publication title: DinoMite
Second publication: Journal
Publication title: Quarterly Journal

Direct Marketing Association - United Kingdom
DMA

70 Market St., London, W1W 8SS, England, UK
Tel: 44 20 72913300
Fax: 44 20 73234165
Email: dma@dma.org.uk
Website: http://www.dma.org.uk
Founded: 1992
Members: 830
Staff: 51
Contact: Jo Scobie, Mgr.
Description: Direct marketing agencies, advertisers, and service suppliers in the United Kingdom. Represents members' interests and promotes self regulations and public awareness. Compiles statistics. Conducts seminars and training programs.
Library Subject: direct marketing media
Library Type: open to the public
Publication: Newsletter
Publication title: Weekly Fax
Second publication: Membership Directory
Publication title: Who's Who in Direct Marketing. Advertisements.
Meetings/Conventions: - semimonthly conference

Direct Selling Association - United Kingdom
DSA

29 Floral St., London, WC2E 9DP, England, UK
Tel: 44 207 4971234
Fax: 44 207 4973144
Email: ukdsa@globalnet.co.uk
Website: http://www.dsa.org.uk
Founded: 1965
Members: 66
Staff: 2
Contact: Richard Berry, Dir.
Description: Maintains high standards in the direct selling of consumer goods and services in the U.K. Represents members' interests before government agencies and consumer bodies; lobbies for favorable legislation. Disseminates market data and information concerning direct selling.
Library Subject: direct selling
Library Type: by appointment only
Publication: Book
Publication title: Direct Selling - From Door To Door to Network Marketing
Second publication: Newsletter
Publication title: The Direct Selling of Consumer Goods in the UK - DSA Annual Survey
Meetings/Conventions: - annual conference - Exhibits.

Directors Guild of Great Britain
DGGB

Acorn House, 314-320 Gray's Inn Rd., London, WC1X 8DP, England, UK
Tel: 44 207 2784343
Fax: 44 207 2784742
Email: guild@dggb.co.uk
Website: http://www.dggb.co.uk
Founded: 1982
Members: 1000
Staff: 3
Contact: Pat Trueman, Ch.Exec.
Description: Represents directors across media. Develops policy to influence the future of the industry, advice for members in dispute and contractual issues.
Publication: Magazine
Publication title: Direct. Advertisements.

Directory and Database Publishers Association
DPA

PO Box 23034, London, W6 0RJ, England, UK
Tel: 44 20 88469707
Fax: 44 870 1680552
Email: rosemarypettit@onetel.net.uk
Website: http://www.directory-publisher.co.uk
Founded: 1970
Members: 97
Staff: 1
Contact: Rosemary Pettit, Sec.
Fee: £120
Membership Type: full and associate
Description: Directory and database publishers in Britain and overseas. Seeks to: maintain a professional practice code; raise professional standards; promote business directories as an ideal advertising medium; promote and protect the trade's legal interests;

foster common interests and provide for exchange of technical, commercial, and managerial information.
Formerly: Association of British Directory Publishers
Publication: Newsletter
Publication title: DPA News
Second publication: Booklet
Publication title: Membership Book. Advertisements.
Meetings/Conventions: - annual conference - Exhibits.

Disability Alliance

Universal House, 89-94 Wentworth St., London, E1 7SA, England, UK
Tel: 44 20 72478776
Fax: 44 20 72478765
Email: office.da@dial.pipex.com
Website: http://www.disabilityalliance.org
Founded: 1974
Members: 380
Staff: 13
Contact: Michele Holland, Admin.Asst.
Description: Committed to breaking the link between poverty and disability by providing information to disabled people about entitlements; campaigns for improvements to social security system and for increases in disability benefits so persons can better reflect the real costs of disability.
Library Subject: disability benefits
Library Type: not open to the public
Formerly: Disability Alliance Education and Research Association
Publication: Handbook
Publication title: AA Guide and Checklist
Second publication: Handbook
Publication title: Disability Rights Handbook. Advertisements.

Disabled Drivers' Association - England
DDA

Ashwellthorpe, Norwich, NR16 1EX, England, UK
Tel: 44 870 7703333
Fax: 44 1508 488173
Email: ddahq@aol.com
Website: http://www.dda.org.uk
Founded: 1948
Members: 26500
Staff: 6
Contact: Douglas Campbell, Exec.Dir.
Fee: £10
Membership Type: full (disabled)
Fee: £14
Membership Type: joint (2 people at the same address)
Description: Available to all disabilities and also able bodied members. Offers advice and information, benefits and concessions with most ferry companies. Local and national campaigns.
Meetings/Conventions: - annual meeting

Disabled Living Foundation

380-384 Harrow Rd., London, W9 2HU, England, UK
Tel: 44 207 2896111
Fax: 44 207 2662922
Email: advice@dlf.org.uk
Website: http://www.dlf.org.uk
Founded: 1970
Staff: 35
Description: Provides impartial information on disability equipment for daily living.
Library Subject: disability equipment
Library Type: reference

Disabled Motorists Federation

Chester-le-Street & District, CVS Volunteer Centre, Clarence Terrace, Chester-Le-Street, DH3 3DQ, England, UK
Tel: 44 191 4163172
Fax: 44 191 4163172
Email: jkillick2214@compuserve.com
Members: 2500
Contact: J.E. Killick, Hon.Sec.
Fee: £25
Membership Type: affiliated clubs
Fee: £10
Membership Type: affiliated members
Description: Represents the interests of affiliated motor clubs and affiliated members.
Publication: Magazine
Publication title: The Way Ahead. Advertisements.
Meetings/Conventions: meeting

Disabled Photographers' Society

PO Box 130, Richmond, TW10 6XQ, England, UK
Tel: 44 1256 351990
Fax: 44 870 0542813
Website: http://www.dps-uk.org.uk/
Founded: 1968
Members: 300
Contact: Mark Roew, Hon. Sec.
Description: Disabled and handicapped persons involved in photography. Provides photographic equipment for disabled use, together with ancillary equipment, such as wheelchair supports etc. Holds annual exhibition.
Publication: Newsletter

Disinfected Mail Study Circle
DMSC

25 Sinclair Grove, London, NW11 9JH, England, UK
Tel: 44 208 4559190
Email: vdvpratique@aol.com
Founded: 1974
Members: 140
Contact: V. Denis Vandervelde, Chm.
Fee: £36
Description: Postal historians, doctors, researchers, libraries, and research foundations in 25 countries. Studies the historic treatment of mail so as to prevent the spread of contagious diseases. The study circle is continuing the research work of the late Dr. K. F. Meyer and his associates, many of whom are members. The study has been extended to include health certificates and passports, quarantine ephemera, anti-vaccination postal propaganda, and related subjects. Maintains speakers' bureau; conducts research programs.
Publication: Journal
Publication title: Cumulative Indexes. Advertisements.
Second publication: Magazine
Publication title: Pratique. Advertisements.
Meetings/Conventions: - annual conference - Exhibits.

District Surveyors Association

Avalon House, Chesil St., Winchester, SO23 0HU, England, UK
Tel: 44 1962 848151
Email: buildcon@winchester.gov.uk
Founded: 1991
Members: 400
Staff: 2
Contact: P.E. Chilvers, Sec.

Fee: £185
Membership Type: full, retiree, or honorary
Description: Head of the Building Control Service in each local authority in England and Wales. To improve the management of local authority building control; influence the training of building control surveyors; develop the science of building control; secure the legal position of the Association and its members; gives guidance to members, government, industry and local authorities.
Publication: Newsletter
Publication title: Insite. Advertisements.
Meetings/Conventions: - annual convention

Ditchley Foundation

Ditchley Park, Enstone, Chipping Norton, OX7 4ER, England, UK
Tel: 44 1608 677346
Fax: 44 1608 677399
Email: info@ditchley.co.uk
Website: http://www.ditchley.co.uk
Founded: 1958
Staff: 9
Contact: Sir Nigel Broomfield, Dir.
Description: Interested individuals united to promote, carry out, or advance any charitable activities, particularly in the sphere of education, likely to be of benefit to British or American citizens. Through weekend conferences, provides forum for individuals from the United States, the European Union, Japan, Canada, and elsewhere to meet and discuss issues facing their countries. Provides facilities for appropriate conferences sponsored by other groups.
Library Type: reference
Publication: Proceedings
Publication title: Ditchley Conference Reports
Second publication: Newsletter
Publication title: Newsletter
Meetings/Conventions: - periodic conference

DMA-ACHG

c/o Direct Marketing Associaton - UK Ltd.
70 Margaret St., London, W1W 8SS, England, UK
Tel: 44 207 2913300
Fax: 44 207 3234165
Email: dma@dma.org.uk
Founded: 1986
Members: 22
Staff: 15
Contact: James Kelly, Mng.Dir.
Description: Membership is open to service providers, information providers and consultants operating in the value-added sector of the UK audiotex/premium rate telephone and automated answering industry. The official voice of service and information providers who wish to encourage high standards in telephone publishing/automated answering industry. It provides a range of trade association services for members and represents the views and opinions of industry on commercial and policy matters to the media, general public, regulatory bodies, network providers, government bodies and opinion-leaders. Regular members meetings are held.
Formerly: Formed by Merger of, DMA

Domestic Appliance Service Association

69 The Maltings, Stanstead Abbotts, Ware, SG12 8HG, England, UK
Tel: 44 1920 872464
Fax: 44 1920 872498
Email: mail@dasa.org.uk
Website: http://www.dasa.org.uk
Founded: 1978

Members: 180
Staff: 1
Contact: Chris Hayter, Dir.
Fee: £290
Membership Type: ordinary
Description: Independent electrical and electronics service organisations. Aims to promote good service, efficiency and courtesy to all members of the public. Encourages communication between independent repairers, consults them on national issues and represents their interests within the trade. Sets national standards of competence and service quality.
Publication: Newsletter
Publication title: ORBIT Newsletter. Advertisements.
Meetings/Conventions: - annual general assembly

Doncaster Chamber

Enterprise House, White Rose Way, Doncaster, DN4 5ND, England, UK
Tel: 44 1302 341000
Fax: 44 1302 328382
Email: chamber@doncaster-chamber.co.uk
Website: http://www.doncaster-chamber.co.uk
Members: 1050
Staff: 43
Contact: Neville Dearden, Chief Exec.
Description: Promotes business and commerce.

Donizetti Society
DonSoc

146 Bordesley Rd., Morden, SM4 5LT, England, UK
Founded: 1973
Members: 200
Contact: J.P. Clayton
Description: Persons interested in promoting the works of Italian operatic composer Gaetano Donizetti (1797-1848), as well as the music of his period. Offers informational services to all opera companies performing Donizetti's operas. Offers sales services to members on books, scores, records, librettos, and other items pertaining to Donizetti and his musical period.
Publication: Journal
Second publication: Newsletter
Meetings/Conventions: - annual meeting - Exhibits. London UK

Donkey Sanctuary

Slade House Farm, Sidmouth, EX10 0NU, England, UK
Tel: 44 1395 578222
Fax: 44 1395 579266
Email: enquiries@thedonkeysactuary.com
Website: http://www.thedonkeysanctuary.org.uk
Founded: 1969
Staff: 280
Contact: Dr. Elisabeth D. Svendsen, CEO
Description: Seeks to prevent the suffering of donkeys worldwide through the provision of high quality, professional advice, training and support on donkey welfare. In the UK and Ireland permanent sanctuary is provided to any donkey in need of refuge.
Library Subject: donkey care and related veterinary matters
Library Type: reference
Publication: Newsletter
Publication title: Newsletter
Second publication: Handbook
Publication title: Professional Handbook of the Donkey
Meetings/Conventions: - periodic seminar

Door and Shutter Manufacturers Association
42 Heath St., Tamworth, B79 7JH, England, UK
Tel: 44 1827 52337
Fax: 44 1827 310827
Email: info@dsma.org.uk
Website: http://www.dsma.org.uk
Founded: 1940
Members: 90
Staff: 7
Contact: M.P. Skelding, Sec.
Description: Manufacturers of industrial and commercial metal doors, garage doors and shutters. Encourages the continual advancement of design, operational techniques, efficiency and safety standards throughout the metal door industry; participates in the preparation and finalisation of technical, trading and contractual standards involving metal door products, both on a national and international basis. It also provides a forum for discussion on matters of common interest.
Publication title: Open Door

Dorothy L. Sayers Society
DLS
Rose Cottage, Malthouse Ln., Hurstpierpoint, Hassocks, BN6 9JY, England, UK
Tel: 44 1273 833444
Fax: 44 1273 835988
Email: jasmine@sayers.org.uk
Website: http://www.sayers.org.uk/
Founded: 1976
Members: 500
Contact: Christopher J. Dean, Chm.
Fee: £14
Membership Type: U.K. - Regular
Fee: £7
Membership Type: U.K. - Student
Description: English teachers, detective fiction enthusiasts, and students of religious philosophy; those interested in medieval French and Italian literature. Promotes the study of the life and works of Dorothy Leigh Sayers (1893-1957), British dramatist, poet, novelist, essayist, and scholar of medieval French and Italian literature. Encourages the performance of Sayers' plays and the publication of books by and about her; seeks to preserve original materials. Encourages study and research into Sayers' life and works. Acts as forum and information center on the author; operates speakers' bureau. Sponsors competitions.
Library Type: reference
Publication title: Poetry of Dorothy L. Sayers
Meetings/Conventions: - annual convention Surrey UK

Dorset Chamber of Commerce and Industry
4 Newfields Business Park, Stinsford Rd., Poole, BH17 0BL, England, UK
Tel: 44 1202 448800
Fax: 44 1202 448838
Email: contact@dcci.co.uk
Website: http://www.dcci.co.uk
Members: 1100
Staff: 10
Contact: Beryl Kite, Chief Exec.
Description: Promotes business and commerce.

Down's Syndrome Association
DSA
155 Mitcham Rd., London, SW17 9PG, England, UK
Tel: 44 208 6824001
Fax: 44 208 6824012
Email: info@downs-syndrome.org.uk
Website: http://www.dsa-uk.com
Founded: 1970
Members: 12000
Staff: 35
Contact: Carol Boys, Chief Exec.
Fee: £4
Description: Provides information, advice, and support in England, Wales, and Northern Ireland on Down's Syndrome. Does this through its information service and helpline, regional offices, and parent-led local branches. Works toward creating the conditions whereby individuals with Down's Syndrome can receive necessary medical, educational, social, and financial support to develop to their full potential.
Library Subject: downs syndrome
Library Type: open to the public
Publication: Newsletter. Advertisements.
Meetings/Conventions: - annual conference

Drake Exploration Society
7 Rosewood Ave., Burnham-on-Sea, TA8 1HD, England, UK
Tel: 44 1278 783919
Email: sfdsociety@aol.com
Website: http://www.chantec.co.uk/drake-society/
Founded: 1996
Members: 40
Contact: Michael Turner, Found. Ed.
Fee: £25
Membership Type: ordinary overseas
Fee: £25
Membership Type: honorary & full
Description: Perpetuates the memory of Sir Francis Drake through research, fieldwork, lectures and publications.
Library Subject: historical with a geographical reference
Library Type: reference
Publication title: Drake Broadside

Draught Proofing Advisory Association
PO Box 12, Haslemere, GU27 3AH, England, UK
Tel: 44 1428 654011
Fax: 44 1428 651401
Email: dpaaassociation@cs.com
Website: http://dubois.vital.co.uk/database/creed/wall.html
Founded: 1980
Members: 60
Staff: 10
Contact: Gillian Allder, Dir.
Fee: £250
Membership Type: manufacturers/installers
Description: Manufacturers, contractors. Aims to promote the advantages of fitting high quality draught excluders, together with their good installation, and as original equipment by window and door manufacturers. The Association has adopted a Code of Professional Practice, by which all members agree to abide. It is aimed to further good technical and ethical practice, particularly in relation to the selling and installing of draught proofing products.
Publication: Pamphlet

Drilling and Sawing Association

PO Box 16, Belper, DE56 4WF, England, UK
Tel: 44 1773 820000
Fax: 44 1773 821284
Email: dsa@drillandsaw.org.uk
Website: http://www.drillandsaw.org.uk
Founded: 1984
Members: 105
Contact: Hugh Wylde
Description: Specialist contractors for the drilling, sawing and cutting of concrete and other construction materials using diamond cutting equipment. Also suppliers and distributors of the specialised machines and accessories. Aims to provide skilled experienced operatives on a contract basis. Also to raise standards of work through training and safety awareness, together with the provision of the appropriate specialist equipment.
Publication: Journal
Publication title: Concrete Cutter

Driving Instructors Association

Safety House, Beddington Farm Rd., Croydon, CR0 4XZ, England, UK
Tel: 44 208 6655151
Fax: 44 208 6655565
Email: driving@atlas.co.uk
Website: http://www.driving.org
Founded: 1978
Members: 10118
Staff: 11
Contact: Graham Fryer
Fee: £48
Membership Type: full
Description: Most of Britain's professional driving instructors are in membership. Aims to raise the standard of road user education, to create an increased awareness of road safety matters and to encourage and promote the interests and welfare of those engaged in professional driver training.
Publication: Newspaper
Publication title: Driving Instructor. Advertisements.
Second publication: Magazine
Publication title: Driving Magazine
Meetings/Conventions: SAFEX - biennial convention - Exhibits. Pula Croatia

DrugScope

32-36 Loman St., London, SE1 0EE, England, UK
Tel: 44 20 79281211
Fax: 44 20 79281771
Email: info@drugscope.org.uk
Website: http://www.drugscope.org.uk
Founded: 2000
Members: 1100
Staff: 50
Contact: Melissa Lawes, Info.Off.
Fee: £120
Fee: £90
Membership Type: voluntary groups
Description: One of UK's leading centres of expertise on the misuse of drugs. Aims to inform policy development and reduce drug-related risk. Offers self-help information through website.
Library Subject: drug use, drug misuse, and related issues
Library Type: by appointment only
Formerly: Formed by Merger of, Institute for the Study of Drug Dependence
Publication: Directories

Dry Stone Walling Association of Great Britain

PO Box 8615, Sutton Coldfield, B75 7HQ, England, UK
Tel: 44 121 3780493
Fax: 44 121 3780493
Email: j.simkins@dswa.org.uk
Website: http://www.dswa.org.uk
Founded: 1968
Members: 1200
Staff: 1
Contact: Jacqui Simkins, Sec.
Fee: £13
Membership Type: open
Fee: £25
Membership Type: professional wallers
Description: Professional wallers, part-time wallers, amateur wallers and many others who wish to support our work. Seeks to ensure the best craftsmanship of the past is preserved and the craft has a thriving future. DSWA is a registered charity.
Library Subject: dry stone walling
Library Type: by appointment only
Publication: Book
Publication title: Better Dry Stone Walling
Second publication: Book
Publication title: Building and Repairing Dry Stone Walls

Duke of Edinburgh's Award International Association

Award House, 7-11 St. Matthew St., London, SW1P 2JT, England, UK
Tel: 44 207 2224242
Fax: 44 207 2224141
Email: sect@intaward.org
Website: http://www.intaward.org
Founded: 1988
Members: 450000
Staff: 17
Contact: Paul Arengo-Jones, Sec.Gen.
Description: Self-development program, encourages personal development, perseverance, and community service among young people ages 14 to 25.
Publication: Magazine
Publication title: Award World
Meetings/Conventions: - triennial conference

Dyslexia Institute

Park House, Wick Rd., Egham, TW20 0HH, England, UK
Tel: 44 1784 222300
Fax: 44 1784 222333
Email: info@dyslexia-inst.org.uk
Website: http://www.dyslexia-inst.org.uk
Founded: 1972
Staff: 300
Contact: Shirley Cromer, Chief Exec.
Fee: £35
Description: Specializes in the development of individuals involved in the field of dyslexia; increases networking opportunities; broadens the sphere of influence, develops and maintains links with other bodies at all levels.
Publication: Newsletter
Publication title: As We See It
Second publication: Journal
Publication title: Dyslexia Review
Meetings/Conventions: Guild Symposium - annual symposium - Exhibits.

Dystrophic Epidermolysis Bullosa Research Association-Europe
DEBRA-Europe

Duke's Ride, 13 Wellington Business Park, Crowthorne, RG11 6LS, England, UK
Website: http://www.debra.org.uk

e.centre

10 Maltravers St., London, WC2R 3BX, England, UK
Tel: 44 207 6559000
Fax: 44 207 6812290
Email: info@e-centre.org.uk
Website: http://www.e-centre.org.uk
Founded: 1976
Members: 15000
Staff: 40
Contact: Kirstie Morris, Mktg.Exec.
Description: Business association that works to improve supply chain efficiency through the widespread adoption of e-business.
Library Type: not open to the public
Formerly: Formed by Merger of, Electronic Commerce Association
Publication: Journal
Publication title: ECQ
Publication title: EDI Manuals
Meetings/Conventions: - periodic conference

E.F. Benson Society
EFBS

c/o Allan Downend
The Old Coach House, High St., Rye, TN31 7JF, England, UK
Tel: 44 1797 223114
Website: http://www.efbenson.co.uk
Founded: 1984
Members: 200
Contact: Allan Downend, Sec.
Fee: £7.5
Membership Type: U.K. and Europe
Fee: £12.5
Membership Type: overseas
Description: Individuals with an interest in the English novelist Edward Frederic Benson (1867-1940). Aims to further knowledge and appreciation of Benson and the Benson Family. Visits places of Benson interest and holds Benson exhibitions and talks.
Publication: Booklet
Publication title: Bensoniana. Advertisements.
Second publication: Book
Publication title: The Bensons
Meetings/Conventions: - periodic lecture

Early English Text Society
EETS

Christ Church, Oxford, OX1 1DP, England, UK
Email: richard.hamer@chch.ox.ac.uk
Website: http://www.eets.org.uk
Founded: 1864
Members: 1250
Contact: R.F.S. Hamer, Exec.Sec.
Fee: £15
Membership Type: individual and institutional
Fee: £30
Membership Type: individual and institutional

Description: University teachers and other scholars; university and public libraries in 28 countries. Publishes pre-1558 texts not otherwise available in good editions; 1 or 2 such volumes are issued annually to subscriber-members. Texts already published include many well-known works from the Old and Middle English period and the Renaissance, such as Beowulf, works of King Alfred, Piers Plowman, several cycles of medieval drama, Sir Gawain and the Green Knight, and several biographies of Sir Thomas More. Editions available to nonmembers through booksellers.

Earth Science Teachers Association

Thomas Rotherham College, Mooregate Rd., Rotherham, S6Q 2RE, England, UK
Tel: 44 1709 300600
Fax: 44 1709 838193
Email: dawn.windles@thomroth.ac.uk
Website: http://www.esta-uk.org
Founded: 1967
Members: 800
Contact: Dr. Dawn Windley, Sec.
Fee: £22
Description: Teachers of earth sciences at all levels. Encourages and supports the teaching of earth sciences whether as a single subject such as geology, or as part of science or geography courses.
Publication title: Science of the Earth
Second publication: Journal
Publication title: Teaching Earth Sciences. Advertisements.
Meetings/Conventions: - annual conference - Exhibits.

East Lancashire Chamber of Commerce

Red Rose Ct., Clayton-le-Moors, Accrington, Lancashire, BB5 5JR, England, UK
Tel: 44 1254 356400
Fax: 44 1254 388900
Email: v.miles@chamber-elancs.co.uk
Website: http://www.chamber-elancs.co.uk
Members: 1002
Staff: 23
Contact: Michael Damms, Chief Exec.
Description: Promotes business and commerce.

East Mercia Chamber of Commerce and Industry

Chamber of Commerce House, Ward St., Walsall, WS1 2AG, England, UK
Tel: 44 1922 721777
Fax: 44 1922 647359
Email: membership@em-chamber.co.uk
Members: 1801
Staff: 125
Contact: John Tamberlin, Pres.
Description: Promotes business and commerce.

Eastern Africa Association
EAA

2 Vincent St., London, SW1P 4LD, England, UK
Tel: 44 207 8285511
Fax: 44 207 8285251
Email: jcsmall@eaa.co.uk
Website: http://www.eaa-lon.co.uk
Founded: 1964
Members: 189
Staff: 4
Contact: J.C. Small, Chief Exec.

Description: Companies from Belgium, Denmark, France, Germany, Monaco, Netherlands, South Africa, Switzerland, Sweden, Hong Kong, the United Kingdom, and the United States with business interests in Eritrea, Ethiopia, Kenya, Madagascar, Mauritius, Seychelles, Tanzania and Uganda. Interests include mining, manufacturing, agriculture, shipping, transportation, engineering, petroleum, publishing, insurance, and banking. Encourages foreign participation in the economic development of Eastern Africa. Works for the mutual benefit of Eastern African countries and foreign investors. Represents members interests before governments; maintains a network of contacts; disseminates information. information. information. information.
Library Type: not open to the public
Formerly: The East African Association
Publication: Newsletter
Publication title: Eastern Africa Association Newsletter
Meetings/Conventions: - periodic meeting

Eating Disorders Association
EDA

Wensum House, 1st Fl., 103 Prince of Wales Rd., Norwich, NR1 1DW, England, UK
Tel: 44 870 7703221
Fax: 44 1603 664915
Email: media@edauk.com
Website: http://www.edauk.com
Founded: 1989
Members: 3500
Staff: 32
Contact: Susan Ringwood, Ch.Exec.
Fee: £25
Membership Type: first year
Fee: £15
Description: Individuals affected by anorexia, bulimia nervosa, and related eating disorders, their families, and friends. Offers information, help, and support. Seeks to enhance awareness and understanding of these illnesses. Communicates with related organizations and individuals in the medical and counseling professions. Disseminates information. Organizes regional support days. Offers training for professionals.
Formerly: Formed by Merger of, Anorexic Aid
Publication: Journal
Publication title: European Eating Disorders Review. Advertisements.
Second publication: Magazine
Publication title: Signpost
Meetings/Conventions: - annual conference

Economic and Social Research Council
ESRC

Polaris House, North Star Ave., Swindon, SN2 1UJ, England, UK
Tel: 44 1793 413000
Fax: 44 1793 413001
Email: exrel@esrc.ac.uk
Website: http://www.esrc.ac.uk/home.html
Founded: 1967
Contact: Freda Lang, Mgr.
Description: Social science researchers. Conducts economic, social, demographic, and environmental studies. Focuses on current social and demographic trends in England and Scotland. Provides advisory services on data use. Offers courses and visiting fellowship program for researchers.
Publication: Bulletin

Publication title: Data Archive Bulletin
Second publication: Newsletter
Publication title: General Household Survey Newsletter
Meetings/Conventions: - periodic seminar

Economic Research Council
ERC

7 St. James Sq., London, SW1Y 4JU, England, UK
Tel: 44 207 4390271
Founded: 1942
Members: 300
Staff: 1
Contact: Peter Davidson
Fee: £25
Description: Economists, business executives, interested individuals. Promotes understanding of economics, particularly monetary practice. Encourages research and discussion among members; stimulates public interest in economic affairs; publicizes pertinent research findings. Maintains speakers' bureau.
Publication: Journal
Publication title: Britain Overseas
Second publication: Newsletter
Publication title: Newsletter
Meetings/Conventions: - annual convention

Economics and Business Education Association

1A Keymer Rd., Hassocks, BN6 8AD, England, UK
Tel: 44 1273 846033
Fax: 44 1273 844646
Email: ebeah@pavilion.co.uk
Website: http://www.ebea.org.uk
Founded: 1939
Members: 2500
Staff: 2
Contact: Carole Dyer
Fee: £42
Description: Teachers of economics, business studies and related subjects in schools and colleges. Represents teachers of economics, business studies and related subjects in schools and colleges throughout the UK and provides its members with the professional support they need in the classroom. It aims to encourage and promote the teaching and study of economics and related subjects within a broadly based curriculum.
Publication: Journal
Publication title: Teaching Business & Economics. Advertisements.

Edexcel International Foundation

Stewart House, 32 Russell Square, London, WC1B 5DN, England, UK
Tel: 44 20 77585656
Fax: 44 20 77585959
Email: international@edexcel.org.uk
Website: http://www.edexcel.org.uk/international
Founded: 1983
Members: 800
Staff: 600
Contact: Ian Reed, Gen.Mgr.
Description: Approves academic and work-related programmes of study including GNVQs, NVQs and GCSEs, A levels and A/S levels throughout England, Wales and Northern Ireland, and overseas and awards qualifications to students who successfully complete these and HND programmes.
Formerly: Formed by Merger of, University of London Examinations and Assessment Council, 1838
Publication: Report

Education in Human Rights Network

School of Education, University of Birmingham, Birmingham, B15 2TT, England, UK
Tel: 44 121 4143344
Fax: 44 121 4144865
Email: aosler@birmingham.ac.uk
Website: http://human-rights.net/ehrn
Founded: 1987
Contact: Dr. Audrey Osler, Sec.
Fee: £20
Membership Type: institutions
Description: Individuals interested in the global protection of basic human rights. Gathers and disseminates information to heighten public awareness of human rights issues; conducts educational programs.
Publication: Newsletter
Publication title: Human Rights Education Newsletter

Educational Centres Association

c/o Fareham Adult Education Centre
Wickham Rd., Fareham, PO16 7DA, England, UK
Tel: 44 1329 315753
Fax: 44 1329 826915
Founded: 1920
Members: 144
Contact: Mrs. Susan S. Dickinson
Description: Students, tutors and providers in furthering the development of adult education, locally, nationally and internationally. Concerned with adult education as a participatory process in which students engage with organizers in the management of institutions.
Library Subject: adult education materials
Library Type: by appointment only
Publication: Journal
Publication title: Centre Line
Second publication: Newsletter
Meetings/Conventions: - semiannual conference - Exhibits.

Educational Development Association

93 Lundhill Rd., Wombwell, Barnsley, S73 0RL, England, UK
Tel: 44 1226 210353
Fax: 44 1226 234711
Email: dave@e-d-a.co.uk
Founded: 1888
Contact: Dave Shevill, Gen.Sec.
Description: Teachers who are members of various regional Branches of the EDA. Teachers' association for in-service training and provider of summer schools for teachers.
Publication: Brochure
Publication title: Brochure for Summer Schools

Educational Publishers Council

The Publishers Association, 29B Montague St., London, WC1B 5BH, England, UK
Tel: 44 207 6919191
Fax: 44 207 6919199
Email: mail@publishers.org.uk
Website: http://www.publishers.org.uk
Founded: 1969
Members: 95
Staff: 2
Contact: Graham Taylor, Dir.
Description: Members publish school books. Covers the following areas of activity on behalf of educational publishers: representation to Government; supply and market services; exhibitions and promotion; subject panels; copyright/licensing; information/statistical services.
Publication: Newsletter
Publication title: EPC Brief
Meetings/Conventions: - annual meeting

EEMA - The European Forum for Electronic Business

Alexander House, High St., Inkberrow, Worcester, WR7 4DT, England, UK
Tel: 44 1386 793028
Fax: 44 1386 793268
Email: info@eema.org
Website: http://www.eema.org
Founded: 1987
Members: 250
Staff: 12
Contact: Jim Dickson, Membership Dir.
Description: Promotes electronic business across Europe.
Library Subject: electronic business
Library Type: not open to the public
Formerly: European Forum for Advanced Business Communication
Publication: Magazine
Publication title: EEMA Briefing. Advertisements.
Second publication: Newsletter
Publication title: EEMA Online
Meetings/Conventions: - annual conference

EFNARC

2 Beechwood Ct., Syderstone, PE31 8TR, England, UK
Tel: 44 1485 578796
Fax: 44 1485 578193
Email: poulson@btinternet.com
Website: http://www.efnarc.org
Founded: 1989
Members: 35
Staff: 6
Contact: John Fairley, Sec.Gen.
Description: European specialist contractors and materials suppliers, dealing with the repair and strengthening of all types of buildings and civil engineering structures. Acts as the technical, scientific and practical link between specialist contractors and material suppliers and the European construction repair and maintenance industry.
Formerly: European Federation of National Associations of Specialist Repair Contractors

Egypt Exploration Society
EES

3 Doughty Mews, London, WC1N 2PG, England, UK
Tel: 44 207 2421880
Fax: 44 207 4046118
Email: eeslondon@talk21.com
Website: http://www.ees.ac.uk
Founded: 1882
Members: 3000
Staff: 3
Contact: Dr. Patricia Spencer, Sec.
Description: Egyptologists and interested others organized to survey, explorate, and excavate at archaeological sites in Egypt. Promotes the study of the history, religion, and culture of ancient Egypt. Makes records of the monuments of Egypt and the Sudan. Graeco-Roman Branch publishes Greek and Latin papyri of the Ptolemaic and Roman periods.

Library Subject: egyptology
Library Type: reference
Formerly: Egypt Exploration Fund
Publication: Magazine
Publication title: Egyptian Archaeology. Advertisements.
Publication title: Graeco-Roman Memoirs
Meetings/Conventions: - annual meeting London UK

Eighteen Nineties Society

PO Box 97, Buckso, High Wycombe, HP14 4GH, England, UK
Tel: 44 1869 248340
Email: steve@ft-1890s-society.demon.co.uk
Website: http://www.1890s.org
Founded: 1972
Members: 200
Contact: Steven Halliwell, Hon.Sec.
Fee: £35
Description: Originally formed to unite admirers of the work of
Francis Thompson (1859-1907), English poet. The society has since
widened its scope to embrace the study of the entire artistic and
literary period of the 1890s, including theatre and book production.
Aids in members' research on the art and literature of this period;
arranges poetry readings. Hopes to acquire a house having
associations with Thompson or any 1890s figure for use as a research
center, museum and library.
Formerly: Supersedes, Francis Thompson Society
Publication: Journal
Publication title: Journal of the Eighteen Nineties Society
Second publication: Newsletter
Publication title: Keynotes
Meetings/Conventions: lecture

Electoral Reform Society

6 Chancel St., London, SE1 0UU, England, UK
Tel: 44 20 79281622
Fax: 44 20 74017789
Email: ers@reform.demon.co.uk
Website: http://www.electoral-reform.org.uk
Founded: 1884
Members: 2200
Staff: 6
Contact: Dr. Ken Ritchie, CEO
Fee: £25
Membership Type: full, life, student
Description: Campaigns for the strengthening of democracy among
members through changes to the voting system and electoral
arrangements.
Library Subject: political and electoral science, history of democracy
Library Type: open to the public
Publication title: ERS News
Meetings/Conventions: - annual meeting

Electric Railway Society
ERS

17 Catherine Dr., Sutton Coldfield, B73 6AX, England, UK
Tel: 44 121 3548332
Email: iain@ifrew.fsnet.co.uk
Founded: 1946
Members: 380
Contact: Dr. Iain D.O. Frew, Hon.Sec.
Fee: £13
Description: Professionals in rail industry and enthusiasts in 14
countries interested in researching electric railways, traction motor

design, and related equipment such as ticket machinery. Members
visit electric railway installations.
Publication: Journal
Publication title: The Electric Railway. Advertisements.
Meetings/Conventions: - monthly meeting

Electrical Contractors Association - England

c/o ESCA House
34 Palace Court, London, W2 4HY, England, UK
Tel: 44 207 3134800
Fax: 44 207 2217344
Email: electricalcontractors@eca.co.uk
Website: http://www.eca.co.uk
Founded: 1901
Members: 2000
Staff: 100
Contact: Ian Crosby, Pres.
Description: Trade association representing electrical engineering
and building services installation companies.
Publication title: Electrical Contractor

Electrical Installation Equipment Manufacturers' Association
EIEMA

Westminster Tower, 3 Albert Embankment, London, SE1 7SL,
England, UK
Tel: 44 207 7933013
Fax: 44 207 7933003
Email: cac@eiema.org.uk
Website: http://www.eiema.org.uk
Founded: 1972
Members: 60
Staff: 6
Contact: D.P. Dossett, Dir.
Description: Trade association for manufacturers of electrical wiring
accessories (e.g., fuses, plugs, sockets, LV circuit breakers,
switchboards, and power cable joints).

Electrical Insulation Association
EIA

PO Box 20630, London, NO6 6ZG, England, UK
Tel: 44 20 89606807
Fax: 44 20 89642009
Email: info@electrical-insulation.org.uk
Website: http://www.electrical-insulation.org.uk
Contact: Gordon Marshall, Chair
Description: Promotes the electrical insulation industry.

Electricity Association

30 Millbank, London, SW1P 4RD, England, UK
Tel: 44 20 79635700
Fax: 44 20 79635959
Email: enquiries@electricity.org.uk
Website: http://www.electricity.org.uk
Founded: 1990
Members: 25
Staff: 160
Contact: Jenny Kirkpatrick, Chief Exec.
Description: Any holder of a licence under the Electricity Act 1989.
Subject to the agreement of the Board, other companies involved in
the electricity business both in the UK and elsewhere who are not
eligible for full membership may become associate members.

Provides a forum where members can discuss matters of common interest; a collective voice for the electricity industry where members consider such a voice is needed; and professional services.

Electroheat Manufacturers Association of BEAMA EMAB

c/o BEAMAnergy Ltd.
Westminster Tower, 3 Albert Embankment, London, SE1 7SL, England, UK
Tel: 44 20 77933000
Fax: 44 20 77933003
Email: info@beama.org.uk
Website: http://www.beama.org.uk/emab_page.htm
Contact: Dr. H.W. Porter
Description: Manufacturers and suppliers of electroheat equipment including, industrial heading elements and induction and infrared and electric surface heating.

Electrophysiological Technologists' Association EPTA

c/o Atkinson Morley's Hospital
31 Loppe Hill, Wimbledon, London, SW20 0N6, England, UK
Fax: 44 20 87254637
Email: patricia.moore@lineone.net
Founded: 1950
Members: 600
Contact: Patricia Moore, Hon.Sec.
Description: Neurophysiology technicians; medical staff working in neurophysiology; individuals from commercial firms dealing with neurophysiology equipment. Promotes understanding of neurophysiology through preparation and presentation of scientific papers; oversees training of electrophysiology technology students.
Publication: Journal
Publication title: Journal of Electrophysiological Technology
Second publication: Newsletter
Publication title: Newsletter
Meetings/Conventions: - annual meeting

Embroiderers' Guild

Hampton Court Palace, Apt. 41, East Molesey, KT8 9AU, England, UK
Tel: 44 208 9431229
Fax: 44 208 9779882
Email: administrator@embroiderersguild.com
Website: http://www.embroiderersguild.com
Founded: 1906
Members: 14000
Staff: 18
Contact: Michael Spender, Dir.
Fee: £9
Membership Type: outside UK
Description: Open to anyone interested in embroidery, from beginner to professional. Full member through Hampton Court or through any of its 230 branches in the UK. Aims to promote the art and craft of embroidery to its highest standard, through workshops, lectures, conferences and exhibitions. Maintains Embroiderers' Development Scheme to help those with a high level of commitment to develop their skills at a professional and nationally recognized level. Has registered museum status for its textile collection.
Library Subject: embroidery and related subjects
Library Type: by appointment only
Publication: Newsletter
Publication title: Contact

Second publication: Magazine
Publication title: Embroidery
Meetings/Conventions: - periodic tour

Emergency Planning Society

Northumberland House, 11, The Pavement, Popes Lane, London, W5 4NG, England, UK
Tel: 44 208 5797971
Fax: 44 208 5797972
Email: headquarters@emergplansoc.org.uk
Website: http://www.emergplansoc.org.uk
Founded: 1993
Members: 1435
Contact: Shruti Patel, Admin.
Fee: £20
Membership Type: associate, fellow, member, affiliate, retired, honorary
Description: Any person who is involved in a professional, managerial or operational capacity in emergency planning or management. Aims to promote effective emergency planning and management in the UK and to promote the professional interests of its members. Provides a forum for the study of the most effective means of planning and managing local emergency preparation and response, and disseminating good practice.
Publication: Newsletter
Meetings/Conventions: - annual conference - Exhibits.

EMILY'S List

Garden Cottage, The Street, Oaksey, Malmesbury, SN16 9TG, England, UK
Tel: 44 1666 577955
Email: emily@oaksey.com
Founded: 1993
Members: 600
Contact: Mrs. Valerie Price
Description: Women members of the Labour Party. Conducts research and fundraising activities. Disseminates information.
Publication: Newsletter

Employers Forum on Age

2nd Fl., The Tower Bldg., 11 York Rd., London, SE1 7NX, England, UK
Tel: 44 20 79810341
Fax: 44 20 79810342
Email: efa@ace.org.uk
Founded: 1996
Members: 150
Staff: 4
Contact: Samantha Mercer, Campaign Dir.
Fee: £1800
Membership Type: large orgs
Fee: £900
Membership Type: medium orgs
Description: Supports member organizations in managing the skills and age mix of their workforces to obtain maximum business; removes barriers to achieving an age-balanced workforce by influencing key decision-makers, notably in government, education, training, recruitment, and the trade union movements; and informs all employers of the benefits of a mixed-age workforce.
Library Subject: age at work
Library Type: not open to the public

Enabling Education Network
EENET

c/o Susie Miles
University of Manchester, Oxford Rd., Manchester, M13 9PL,
England, UK
Tel: 44 161 2753711
Fax: 44 161 2753548
Email: eenet@man.ac.uk
Website: http://www.eenet.org.uk
Contact: Susie Miles
Description: Works to strengthen national, local, and regional
resource and information services for educators.
Publication: Newsletter

ENCAMS

The Pier, Elizabeth House, Wigan, WN3 4EX, England, UK
Tel: 44 1942 612621
Fax: 44 1942 824778
Email: info@encams.org
Website: http://www.encams.org
Founded: 1954
Members: 2000
Staff: 109
Contact: Alan Woods, Ch.Exec.
Description: Individuals and organizations interested in creating a
litter-free Britain. Seeks to restore pride and respect for the
environment in members and the public. Devises anti-litter programs
that enable local governments, industries, voluntary organizations,
school systems, and individuals to take coordinated action to clean up
their environs. Sponsors educational programs to increase awareness
of environmental damage done by litter and encourage individuals to
be more responsible about the way they dispose of their refuse;
makes available anti-litter curricula. Conducts research on type,
distribution, and impact of marine litter in the British Isles. Participates
in research programs and charitable activities. Maintains speakers'
bureau; compiles statistics.
Library Type: reference
Publication title: Annual Report
Second publication: Book
Publication title: Britain in Bloom
Meetings/Conventions: - annual convention - Exhibits.

End Child Prostitution, Pornography and Trafficking
ECPAT 'UK'

Thomas Clarkson House, Stableyard, Bromgrove Rd., London, SW9
9TL, England, UK
Tel: 44 207 5018927
Fax: 44 207 7384110
Email: ecpatuk@antislavery.org
Website: http://www.ecpat.org.uk
Founded: 1994
Members: 400
Staff: 2
Contact: Helen Veitch, Campaign Coord.
Fee: £5
Description: Individuals and organizations. Seeks to eradicate the
commercial sexual exploitation of children worldwide, and to end child
sex tourism. Coordinates activities of British organizations working to
end child prostitution; conducts educational programs to raise public
awareness of sexual tourism; lobbies government agencies to insure
British compliance with Article 34 of the United Nations Convention on
the Rights of the Child. Works with governments worldwide to improve

enforcement of laws banning the sexual exploitation of children.
Campaigns on the issue of child trafficking for sexual purposes.
Library Subject: child prostitution, child sex tourism, trafficking of
children for sex purposes
Library Type: reference
Publication: Brochure
Publication title: Campaigner
Second publication: Newsletter
Publication title: ECPAT News

Energy Systems Trade Association

PO Box 77, Benfleet, SS7 5EX, England, UK
Tel: 44 7041 492049
Fax: 44 7041 492050
Email: info@esta.org.uk
Website: http://www.esta.org.uk
Founded: 1982
Members: 70
Staff: 4
Contact: Alan Aldridge, Exec.Dir.
Fee: £950
Description: Companies offering energy efficiency goods and
services for industrial and commercial application. Aims to encourage
good practice by the suppliers of energy efficiency goods and services
to the industrial, commercial and public sectors. We promote
awareness of the financial and environmental benefits of good energy
management practice, and organise up to 20 national and regional
conferences for energy users -many of them free.
Publication: Yearbook
Publication title: Energy Efficiency Yearbook
Meetings/Conventions: Meeting the Energy Challenge - annual
seminar - Exhibits.

EnergyWatch

Artillary House, 4th Fl., Artillery Row, London, SW1P 1RT, England,
UK
Tel: 44 84 59060708
Fax: 44 207 77998341
Email: enquiries@energywatch.org.uk
Website: http://www.energywatch.org.uk
Founded: 1986
Staff: 81
Contact: Ann Robinson, Chair
Description: Works for interests of all 19 million gas users in the UK.
Offers free independent advisory and mediation service to all gas
consumers.
Formerly: Gas Consumers Council
Publication: Annual Report
Publication title: Consumers Council Annual Report

Enforcement Services Association

Ridgefield House, 14 John Dalton St., Manchester, M2 6JR, England,
UK
Tel: 44 161 8397225
Fax: 44 161 8342433
Email: enquiries@bailiffs.org.uk
Website: http://www.bailiffs.org.uk
Founded: 1906
Members: 106
Staff: 1
Contact: Vernon Phillips, Exec.Dir.
Description: Certificated bailiffs and civilian enforcement officers in
England and Wales. Promotes increased professionalism among

bailiffs; represents members' interests. Encourages development of civil law enforcement; conducts certification examinations.
Formerly: Certificated Bailiffs' Association
Publication: Newsletter
Publication title: Info. Advertisements.
Second publication: Membership Directory
Publication title: Yearbook. Advertisements.

Engineering and Physical Sciences Research Council

c/o Polaris House
North Star Ave., Swindon, SN2 1ET, England, UK
Tel: 44 1793 444000
Fax: 44 1793 444010
Email: infoline@epsrc.ac.uk
Website: http://www.epsrc.ac.uk
Founded: 1994
Staff: 300
Contact: Mrs. Glenys France, Zone Mgr.
Description: Government organisation funding research in the U.K.
Publication: Journal
Publication title: Newsline

Engineering Construction Industry Association

Broadway House, 5th Fl., Tothill St., London, SW1H 9NS, England, UK
Tel: 44 207 7992000
Fax: 44 207 2331930
Email: brenigwillliams@ecia.co.uk
Website: http://www.ecia.co.uk
Founded: 1994
Members: 300
Staff: 15
Contact: Brenig Williams, CEO
Description: Engineering construction firms. Represents the interests of its member firms, with government departments, the NJC, the Training Board and other outside bodies. It provides services to members of advice, information and direct assistance on industrial relations, health and safety, training and commercial and economic matters.
Publication: Papers
Publication title: Business Brief
Meetings/Conventions: - annual conference

Engineering Council (UK)

10 Maltravers St., London, WC2R 3ER, England, UK
Tel: 44 207 2407891
Fax: 44 207 3795586
Email: staff@engc.org.uk
Website: http://www.engc.org.uk
Founded: 1981
Members: 265000
Staff: 25
Contact: A.V. Ramsay, Exec.Dir.
Description: Engineers and engineering firms and institutions. Seeks to advance and promote the education, science, and profession of engineering. Conducts programs promoting the engineering profession; represents the interests of members before government agencies, academia, and industrial organizations. Maintains national register of engineers and technicians.
Publication: Newsletter
Publication title: Engineering First

Engineering Employers' Federation

c/o Broadway House
Tothill St., London, SW1H 9NQ, England, UK
Tel: 44 171 2227777
Fax: 44 171 2222782
Email: mtemple@eef-fed.org.uk
Website: http://www.eef.org.uk
Founded: 1896
Members: 5703
Staff: 55
Contact: Martin Temple, Dir.Gen.
Description: Members include small, medium and large engineering companies throughout the UK. Membership is on an individual site basis through our regional associations. Provides support and advisory services to member companies. On behalf of these members it lobbies government and politicians of all parties, the European Commission and civil servants in the UK and in mainland Europe.
Publication title: EEF Annual Review
Publication title: Engineering Outlook
Meetings/Conventions: - annual conference

Engineering Equipment and Materials Users Association

20 Long Ln., 3rd Fl., London, EC1A 9HL, England, UK
Tel: 44 20 77961293
Fax: 44 20 79961294
Email: info@eemua.co.uk
Website: http://www.eemua.co.uk
Founded: 1983
Members: 26
Staff: 6
Contact: Michael J. Darragh, Dir. & Sec.
Description: Large companies who are users of engineering equipment. To assist members to formulate and promote a common policy for their standardisation with the object of increasing industrial efficiency, and to present, through the British Standards Institution or otherwise, the user requirements in the preparation and adoption of specifications for such equipment or materials.
Publication: Catalog

Engineering Industries Association - England EIA

Broadway House, Tothill St., Westminster, London, SW1H 9NS, England, UK
Tel: 44 207 2222367
Fax: 44 207 7992206
Email: enquiries@eia.co.uk
Website: http://www.eia.co.uk
Founded: 1941
Members: 1700
Staff: 20
Contact: Sir. Ronald Halstead, Pres.
Description: Mechanical and electrical engineering firms. Promotes trade through overseas exhibitions and provides trade opportunities, advice, and representation to member firms. Conducts educational programs in quality assurance and advanced manufacturing technology. Sponsors competitions; bestows awards. Operates speakers' bureau.
Publication: Directory
Publication title: Engineering Buyers Guide and Directory
Publication title: Engineering Gazette

Engineering Integrity Society
EIS

5 Wentworth Ave., Sheffield, S11 9QX, England, UK
Tel: 44 114 2621155
Fax: 44 114 2621120
Email: cpinder@e-i-s.org.uk
Website: http://www.e-i-s.org.uk
Founded: 1985
Staff: 1
Contact: Catherine Pinder
Fee: £20
Membership Type: personal
Fee: £25
Membership Type: overseas
Description: Industrial engineers. Seeks to advance the study, teaching, and practice of industrial engineering. Serves as a forum for the exchange of information among members; organizes and conducts educational programs.
Publication: Journal
Publication title: Engineering Integrity. Advertisements.
Meetings/Conventions: Fatigue - periodic conference - Exhibits. Cambridge UK

Engineers' Hand Tools Association

c/o Institute of Spring Technology
Henry St., Sheffield, S3 7EQ, England, UK
Tel: 44 114 2789143
Fax: 44 114 2726344
Email: jrm@britishtools.com
Contact: J.R. Markham, Sec.
Description: Promotes the engineer hand tool industry.
Publication: Directory
Publication title: British Tools Directory

English Amateur Dancesport Association
EADA

515 Abbeydale Rd., Sheffield, S7 1FU, England, UK
Tel: 44 114 2555236
Fax: 44 114 2555236
Email: webmaster@eada.org
Website: http://www.englishdancesport.org.uk
Founded: 1983
Members: 3500
Contact: Rita Thomas, Chm.
Fee: £13
Membership Type: adult
Description: Amateur Dancesport governing body covering all Amateur competitors in England. Provides training for top Squads, selects couples and teams for international events.

English Association
EA

University of Leicester, University Rd., Leicester, LE1 7RH, England, UK
Tel: 44 116 2523982
Fax: 44 116 2522301
Email: engassoc@le.ac.uk
Website: http://www.le.ac.uk/engassoc/
Founded: 1906
Members: 2000
Staff: 3
Contact: Helen Lucas, Chief Exec.

Description: University and public libraries, schools, and individuals in 75 countries. Promotes appreciation and knowledge of English language and literature.
Publication: Journal
Publication title: English Four to Eleven
Second publication: Journal
Publication title: Use of English. Advertisements.
Meetings/Conventions: Shakespeare Conference - annual conference

English Folk Dance and Song Society
EFDSS

2 Regents Park Rd., Cecil Sharp House, London, NW1 7AY, England, UK
Tel: 44 207 4852206
Fax: 44 207 2840534
Email: efdss@efdss.org
Website: http://www.efdss.org
Founded: 1932
Members: 5500
Staff: 16
Contact: Hazel Miller, Ch.Off.
Description: Individual members, corporate members and affiliated groups, clubs and local societies who share the aims of the society. Aims to preserve and make known English folk dances, songs and music and to encourage their practice by means of classes, demonstrations and festivals; to promote and encourage collection and research into the development and traditional practice of English folk dances, songs and music.
Library Subject: traditional culture, music, dance, drama
Library Type: open to the public
Publication: Magazine
Publication title: EDS. Advertisements.
Second publication: Journal
Publication title: Folk Music Journal

English National Board for Nursing, Midwifery and Health Visiting

c/o Victory House
170 Tottenham Court Rd., London, W1P 0HA, England, UK
Tel: 44 20 73883131
Fax: 44 20 73834031
Email: link@enb.org.uk
Founded: 1983
Staff: 100
Contact: A.P. Smith, Chief Exec.
Description: The Board consists of 10 members who were appointed by the Secretary of State for Health - 7 non-executive members consisting of a nurse, midwife, and health visitor, and someone currently in education, and 3 executive members. Main purpose is to ensure that the institutions it approves conduct education programmes which equip nurses, midwives and health visitors to meet existing and changing health care needs.
Library Subject: nursing, education, health care, and midwifery
Library Type: reference
Meetings/Conventions: - bimonthly board meeting

English Nature

Northminster House, Peterborough, PE1 1UA, England, UK
Tel: 44 1733 455000
Fax: 44 1733568834
Email: enquiries@english-nature.org.uk
Website: http://www.english-nature.org.uk

Founded: 1991
Staff: 850
Description: Promotes wildlife conservation and wise land use in England. Selects, establishes, and manages wildlife and marine reserves; designates sites of special scientific interest; supports and conducts conservation research. Seeks to increase public awareness of the dangers posed to wildlife by loss of habitat.
Library Subject: Conservation, biodiversity
Library Type: by appointment only
Publication: Magazine
Publication title: English Nature

English Place-Name Society

c/o School of English Studies
University of Nottingham, University Park, Nottingham, NG7 2RD, England, UK
Tel: 44 115 9515919
Fax: 44 115 9515924
Email: janet.rudkin@nottingham.ac.uk
Website: http://www.nottingham.ac.uk/english/
Founded: 1923
Members: 650
Contact: Paul Cavill
Fee: £25
Description: Carries out the Survey of English Place-Names and publishes the results of the Survey, county by county.
Library Subject: onomastics and philology
Library Type: not open to the public
Publication: Journal
Publication title: EPNS Journal
Publication title: Field Names
Meetings/Conventions: - annual meeting

English Poetry and Song Society

76 Lower Oldfield Park, Bath, BA2 3HP, England, UK
Tel: 44 1225 313531
Fax: 44 1225 464333
Email: epss@members.v21.co.uk
Founded: 1983
Members: 50
Contact: Mr. Carder, Chm.
Fee: £12
Description: Composers, singers, pianists and anyone interested. Concerned with the promotion of English art songs, through recordings and publication; concerts and competitions for composers.
Library Subject: songs
Library Type: not open to the public
Publication: Newsletter
Meetings/Conventions: - quarterly

English Westerners Society

130 The Keep, Kingston Upon Thames, KT2 5UE, England, UK
Email: kgalvin.bas@gtnet.gov.uk
Website: http://www.english-westerners-society.org.uk/
Founded: 1954
Members: 175
Contact: Richard Platt, Chm.
Fee: £12
Membership Type: member (uk only)
Fee: £20
Membership Type: associate member (other countries)
Description: Publishes research materials on the American West on behalf of the members of the English Westerners' society.
Publication: Book

Publication title: Brand Book
Second publication: Newsletter
Publication title: Tally Sheet. Advertisements.
Meetings/Conventions: - annual general assembly

Entertainment and Leisure Software Publishers Association

c/o Roger Bennett
Ste. 1, Haddonsacre, Station Rd., Evesham, WR11 8JJ, England, UK
Tel: 44 1386 830642
Fax: 44 1386 833871
Email: info@elspa.com
Website: http://www.elspa.com
Founded: 1989
Members: 120
Staff: 16
Contact: Roger Bennett, Dir.Gen.
Fee: £2000
Membership Type: associate
Description: Aims to protect, promote, and provide for members' interests in the interactive leisure software industry. Collects and disseminates retail sales statistics; provides age rating of games; operates anti-piracy crime unit; conducts legislative lobbying with UK and EU governments.

Entomological Livestock Group
ELG

c/o John Green
11 Rock Gardens, Aldershot, GU11 3AD, England, UK
Email: pwbelg@clara.co.uk
Website: http://www.pwbelg.clara.net/
Founded: 1978
Members: 600
Contact: John Green, Sec.
Description: Promotes butterfly and insect breeders; works as entomological livestock exchange.
Publication: Newsletter

Envelope Makers' and Manufacturing Stationers' Association

Church View, 7A Church Ln., Arrington, Royston, SG8 0BD, England, UK
Tel: 44 1223 208665
Fax: 44 1223 208665
Email: emmsauk@aol.comwww.envelope.org
Founded: 1940
Members: 50
Staff: 1
Contact: Michael J. Dellar, Sec.
Description: Envelope makers and stationery manufacturers.

Environment and Development Group

41 Walton Crescent, Oxford, OX1 2JQ, England, UK
Tel: 44 1865 318180
Fax: 44 1865 318188
Email: admin@edg.org.uk
Website: http://www.edg.org.uk
Founded: 1990
Staff: 20
Contact: Sandra Mallinson, Admin.
Description: Promotes environmental protection and wise use of natural resources worldwide. Works with global corporation, governments and NGOs throughout the developing world, creating

practical solutions that meet the social, environmental and economic aspirations of clients.
Library Subject: conservation, environmental protection, wildlife, protected area management, natural resources
Library Type: reference

Environment Council

212 High Holborn, London, WC1V 7BF, England, UK
Tel: 44 207 8362626
Fax: 44 207 2421180
Email: info@envcouncil.org.uk
Website: http://www.the-environment-council.org.uk
Founded: 1969
Members: 2000
Staff: 30
Contact: Mhairi Dunlop, Communications Mgr.
Description: An independent charity dedicated to building awareness, dialogue and effective solutions to enhance and protect Britian's environment. Administers: Business Programmes to help businesses become more environmentally aware; Environmental Resolve, an environmental mediation and training service.
Library Type: not open to the public
Formerly: Absorbed, Conservation Trust
Publication title: Business and Environment Programme Handbook
Second publication: Newsletter
Publication title: Conservers at Work
Meetings/Conventions: - periodic seminar

Environmental Communicators' Organisation

8 Hooks Cross, Watton-at-Stone, Hertford, SG14 3RY, England, UK
Tel: 44 1920 830527
Fax: 44 1920 830538
Email: alanmassam@compuserve.com
Founded: 1972
Members: 246
Staff: 1
Contact: Alan Massam
Fee: £10
Membership Type: full
Description: Professional journalists and broadcasters.
Publication: Newsletter

Environmental Services Association

154 Buckingham Palace Rd., London, SW1W 9TR, England, UK
Tel: 44 207 8248882
Fax: 44 207 8248753
Email: info@esauk.org
Website: http://www.esauk.org
Founded: 1969
Members: 290
Staff: 17
Contact: Dirk Hazell, Chief Exec.
Description: ESA is the trade association for companies providing waste management and related environmental services. The members span the full spectrum of operations (including collection, treatment, disposal, re-use, recycling and recovery of waste), specialist equipment manufactures and environmental consultancies.
Publication: Newsletter
Publication title: ESA Briefing
Second publication: Membership Directory
Publication title: ESA Directory. Advertisements.
Meetings/Conventions: Charity Ball - annual

Environmental Transport Association

68 High St., Weybridge, KT13 8RS, England, UK
Tel: 44 1932 828882
Fax: 44 1932 829015
Email: eta@eta.co.uk
Website: http://www.eta.co.uk
Founded: 1990
Members: 20000
Staff: 15
Contact: Tracy Philpot
Fee: £20
Description: Environmentally aware motorists. Campaigns for environmentally sound transport, in particular, protection of the natural environment and national heritage from the damaging effects of transport. Provides a road rescue breakdown service for individuals and companies. Discount rates available for professional associations.
Publication: Magazine
Publication title: Going Green. Advertisements.
Second publication: Pamphlets

Equity

Guild House, Upper St. Martins Lane, London, WC2H 9EG, England, UK
Tel: 44 207 3796000
Fax: 44 207 3797001
Email: mbrown@equity.org.uk
Website: http://www.equity.org.uk
Founded: 1930
Members: 37000
Staff: 50
Contact: Ian McGarry, Gen. Sec.
Description: UK trade union representing actors, club and circus performers, stage managers, theatre designers, directors, choreographers, dancers, stunt performers, and singers. Works to secure the best possible terms and conditions for its members through collective bargaining. Makes representations to government and authorities on matters of policy relating to the performing arts. Negotiates terms of employment in all sections of entertainment including theatre, television, film, radio, and recording. Makes casting agreements with employers to encourage artists who are not already members to join the union. Offers legal counsel to members involved in disputes. Operates advisory service on insurance, pension, and investment matters.
Formerly: British Actors' Equity Association
Publication: Annual Report
Publication title: Equity Annual Report
Second publication: Journal
Publication title: Equity Journal. Advertisements.
Meetings/Conventions: Annual Representative Conference - annual convention

Ergonomics Society - England

c/o Devonshire House
Devonshire Sq., Loughborough, LE11 3DW, England, UK
Tel: 44 1509 234904
Fax: 44 1509 235666
Email: ergsoc@ergonomics.org.uk
Website: http://www.ergonomics.org.uk
Founded: 1949
Members: 1363
Staff: 5
Description: Academic and practitioners in ergonomics and allied fields. Furthering the discipline of ergonomics through publications, conferences, professional standards and educational material.

Publication: Journal
Publication title: Applied Ergonomics
Publication title: Ergonomics
Meetings/Conventions: Ergonomics Society Annual Conference - annual conference - Exhibits. Swansea UK

Esperanto Teachers Association

c/o Wedgwood Memorial College
Barlaston, Stoke-On-Trent, ST12 9DG, England, UK
Tel: 44 1782 372141
Email: eab@esperanto-gb.org
Founded: 1960
Members: 120
Contact: Mrs. Angela Tellier
Fee: £10
Description: Mainly members of the teaching profession but including non-teachers interested in the furtherance of Esperanto in schools. Aims to promote the teaching of the international language Esperanto in schools and other educational establishments in the UK and to support teachers of Esperanto through termly publication and through the organization of occasional seminars.
Publication title: La Brita Esperantisto

Essex Chamber of Commerce

Alexandra House, 36 A Church St., Great Baddow, Chelmsford, CM2 7HY, England, UK
Tel: 44 1245 241431
Fax: 44 1245 241500
Email: davidcrozier@essexchambers.co.uk
Website: http://www.essexchambers.co.uk
Members: 1800
Staff: 28
Contact: David Crozier, Chief Exec.
Description: Promotes business and commerce.

Estuarine and Coastal Sciences Association ECSA

c/o Dr. Michael Elliot
Dept. of Biological Sciences, Univerity of Hull, Hull, HU6 7RX, England, UK
Tel: 44 1482 465503
Fax: 44 1482 465458
Email: m.elliot@biosci.hull.ac.uk
Website: http://www.ecsa.ac.uk
Founded: 1971
Members: 700
Contact: Dr. Michael Elliot, Sec.
Fee: £10
Description: Professional scientists, estuarine and coastal managers, students, and interested individuals and organizations in 24 countries. Promotes: the production and dissemination of scientific knowledge and understanding of estuaries and other brackish and coastal waters; the prevention of environmental deterioration; management of natural resources for the public benefit. Fosters cooperation, coordination, and communication between producers and users of scientific information and among specialists from different disciplines. Sponsors professional training courses in estuarine methodology; holds symposia and workshops on such topics as numerical analyses, physical methods, and taxonomy of invertebrate groups.
Formerly: Estuarine and Brackish-Water Biological Association
Publication: Bulletin
Publication title: ECSA Bulletin. Advertisements.
Second publication: Journal

Publication title: Estuarine and Coastal Shelf Science
Meetings/Conventions: Scientific Meeting - semiannual conference - Exhibits.

EURISOL, The UK Mineral Wool Association

CIGA House, 3 Vimy Ct., Vimy Rd., Redbourn, Leighton Buzzard, LU7 1FG, England, UK
Tel: 44 1525 385886
Fax: 44 1525 385904
Email: info@eurisol.com
Website: http://www.eurisol.com
Founded: 1962
Members: 4
Staff: 3
Contact: Mr. I.S. Knight
Description: Large manufacturers of insulation materials. Aims to further the cause of energy conservation in the UK by promoting the benefits of mineral wool products in achieving effective solutions to better standards of thermal and acoustic insulation and fire protection in building, industry and commerce.

Eurocentres Business Institute

56 Eccleston Sq., London, SW1V 1PQ, England, UK
Tel: 44 20 78344155
Fax: 44 20 78341866
Email: vic-info@eurocenters.com
Website: http://www.eurocentres.com
Founded: 1990
Members: 2
Staff: 2
Contact: Mrs. Gillian Da Silva Rodrigues
Description: Members teach English to managers from abroad. Provides language training (English and foreign languages) for executives, managers and professional people. It also provides language training services (courses, materials, language audits) for corporate clients as well as specialized courses such as legal English.
Library Subject: business management
Library Type: by appointment only

Eurolink Age - England

1268 London Rd., London, SW16 4ER, England, UK
Tel: 44 208 7657717
Fax: 44 208 6796727
Email: eurolink@ace.org.uk
Founded: 1981
Members: 100
Staff: 1
Contact: Lesley Loughran, Policy Support and Info.Ofcr.
Description: Works to improve the quality of life of the elderly. Gathers and disseminates information on issues including social benefits, pensions, and employment.
Library Subject: gerontology
Library Type: by appointment only
Formerly: Eurolink Age - England

European Academy of Aesthetic Dentistry

47a Wimpole St., London, W1M 7DF, England, UK
Tel: 44 20 72241488
Fax: 44 20 71712241299

European Academy of Design

c/o Art & Design Research Centre
Sheffield Hallam University, Psalter Lane Campus, Sheffield, S11
8UZ, England, UK
Tel: 44 114 2252669
Fax: 44 114 2252603
Email: s.r.owen@shu.ac.uk
Website: http://www.artdes.salford.ac.uk/ead
Description: Promotes the publication and dissemination of research
in design.
Publication: Newsletter
Second publication: Journal
Meetings/Conventions: conference

European Academy of Facial Plastic Surgery
EAFPS

c/o British Association of Otothinolaryngologists - Head and Neck
Surgeons
35-43 Lincoln's Inn Fields, London, WC2A 3PN, England, UK
Tel: 44 20 74048373
Fax: 44 20 74044200
Email: eafps@bao-hns.demon.co.uk
Website: http://www.eafps.com
Founded: 1977
Members: 500
Staff: 1
Contact: Barbara Komoniewska
Description: Practicing and student facial and neck surgeons. Aims
to further plastic and reconstructive surgery by stimulating research in
neurosurgery, ophthalmology, otorhinolaryngology, and maxillofacial
surgery; encourages cooperation among members, particularly
between surgeons working in different specialties. Offers program on
techniques in reconstructive surgery.
Library Type: reference
Formerly: Joseph Society
Publication: Monograph
Publication title: Facial Plastic Surgery
Publication title: Membership List
Meetings/Conventions: - semiannual meeting

European Actuarial Consultative Group

Napier House, 4 Worcester St., Oxford, OX1 2AW, England, UK
Tel: 44 1865 268218
Fax: 44 1865 268233
Email: mlucas@gcactuaries.org
Website: http://www.gcactuaries.org
Founded: 1978
Members: 31
Staff: 2
Contact: Michael Lucas, Exec.Sec.
Description: Actuarial associations in Europe. Responds to requests
for opinions on matters of interest to the actuarial profession by
institutions of the EEC. Maintains contact with the International
Actuarial Association. Acts as a forum for all actuarial associations in
Europe.
Meetings/Conventions: - annual meeting

European Air Law Association
EALA

66 Chartfield Ave., London, SW15 6HQ, England, UK
Tel: 44 20 87883513
Fax: 44 20 87892467
Founded: 1988

European Alliance of Neuromuscular Disorders Associations
EANDA

7-11 Prescott Pl., London, SW4 6BS, England, UK
Tel: 44 207 7208055
Fax: 44 207 7498963
Email: mail@eamda.sonnet.co.uk
Founded: 1971
Members: 33
Staff: 1
Description: Organizations representing people with neurmuscular
disorders and health care professionals with an interest in
neurological maladies. Seeks to improve the quality of life of people
with neuromuscular disorders; promotes advances in the prevention,
diagnosis, and treatment of neurological diseases. Facilitates
exchange of information among members; serves as a clearinghouse
on neuromuscular disorders; sponsors research and educational
programs.

European Arboricultural Council
EAC

c/o Alice Holt Lodge, Wrecclesham, Farnham, GU10 4LH, England,
UK
Tel: 44 1794 522599
Fax: 44 1794 521640
Email: secretary@EAC-arboriculture.com
Website: http://www.eac-arboriculture.com/do/en/homepage.asp
Contact: Alice Holt Lodge, Sec.
Description: Works to improve the health and care for trees of
environmental importance. Fosters continued education among tree
care professionals.

European Aspirin Foundation
EAF

PO Box 7, Ripley, Woking, GU23 6YU, England, UK
Tel: 44 1483 225230
Fax: 44 1483 211043
Email: nickhen@pncl.co.uk
Website: http://www.aspirin-foundation.com
Contact: G.N. Henderson, Exec.Dir.
Description: Provides information to consumers, health
professionals, and journalists on scientific and general aspects of
aspirin usage. Supports medical and scientific studies.
Meetings/Conventions: - periodic symposium

European Association for Cancer Research
EACR

c/o Paul Saunders
University of Nottingham, The Pharmacy School, Nottingham, NG7
2RD, England, UK
Tel: 44 115 9515114
Fax: 44 115 9515115
Email: paul.saunders@nottingham.ac.uk
Website: http://www.eacr.org/
Founded: 1968
Members: 5000
Staff: 2
Contact: Paul Saunders, Admin.
Fee: £30
Membership Type: ordinary, student, Emeritus, honorary, sustaining

Description: Persons who have worked actively in cancer research for at least 2 years and who have an academic degree or the equivalent; membership in 40 countries. Seeks to advance cancer research by facilitating communication among research workers, particularly by organizing meetings. Sponsors: EACR Travel Fellowship Program, awarding travel expenses for member researchers to and from host institutions.
Publication: Directory
Publication title: Directory of the EACR
Second publication: Newsletter
Publication title: EACR Newsletter
Meetings/Conventions: - biennial conference - Exhibits. Copenhagen Denmark

European Association for Cardio-Thoracic Surgery
EACTS

The Cottage, 16 High St., Windsor, SL4 1LD, England, UK
Tel: 44 1753 832166
Fax: 44 1753 620407
Email: info@eacts.co.uk
Website: http://www.eacts.org
Founded: 1986
Description: Aims to advance education in the field of cardio-thoracic surgery. Promotes research into thoracic physiology, pathology and therapy.

European Association for Computer Assisted Language Learning
EUROCALL

Language Institute, University of Hull, Hull, HU6 7RX, England, UK
Tel: 44 1482 465872
Fax: 44 1482 466180
Email: eurocall@hull.ac.uk
Website: http://www.hull.ac.uk/cti/eurocall/
Founded: 1993
Members: 400
Staff: 2
Contact: June Thompson, Sec.
Fee: £35
Membership Type: individual
Description: Language teaching professionals. Promotes the use of foreign languages in Europe. Disseminates information and offers advice on all aspects of the use of technology for language learning, for those involved in education and training.
Publication: Journal
Publication title: ReCALL Journal. Advertisements.
Meetings/Conventions: Networked Language Learning - annual conference

European Association for Cranio-Maxillo-Facial Surgery
EACMFS

Thomond House, North St., Midhurst, GU29 9DJ, England, UK
Tel: 44 1730 810951
Fax: 44 1730 812042
Email: ea.cms@virgin.net
Website: http://www.eacmfs.org
Founded: 1970
Members: 800
Contact: Mr. J. Lowry, Sec.Gen.
Fee: £50
Membership Type: trainee

Fee: £150
Membership Type: active
Description: Surgeons involved in oral and cranio-maxillofacial surgery. Encourages discussion and conducts medical courses on subjects such as orthognathic and temporomandibular joint surgery and plastic and aesthetic surgery. Maintains speakers' bureau.
Publication: Journal
Publication title: Journal of Cranio-maxillo-facial Surgery. Advertisements.
Meetings/Conventions: - biennial congress - Exhibits.

European Association for Integrative Psychotherapy
EAIP

Ealing, London, W5 2QB, England, UK
Tel: 44 20 85792505
Founded: 1993
Description: Promotes and extends the practice of integrative psychotherapy in Europe.

European Association for Jewish Studies
EAJS

c/o European Centre for the University Teaching of Jewish Civilization Yarnton Manor, Yarnton, Oxford, OX5 1PY, England, UK
Tel: 44 1865 377946
Fax: 44 1865 375079
Email: eajs@herald.ox.ac.uk
Website: http://nonuniv.ox.ac.uk/~eajs
Founded: 1981
Members: 450
Staff: 2
Contact: Dr. Karina Stern
Fee: £15
Fee: £20
Membership Type: institutional
Description: Provides encouragement and support of the teaching of Jewish studies at university level in Europe; seeks to further an understanding of the importance of Jewish culture and civilization and the impact it has had on European cultures over many centuries.
Publication: Directory
Publication title: Directory of Jewish Studies in Europe
Meetings/Conventions: - biennial congress

European Association for Lexicography
EURALEX

c/o Paula Thomson, Membership Sec.
Oxford University Press, Journals Subscription Department, Great Clarendon St., Oxford, OX2 6DP, England, UK
Tel: 44 1865 556767
Email: thomsonp@oup.co.uk
Website: http://www.ims.uni-stuttgart.de/euralex/
Founded: 1983
Contact: Paula Thomson
Description: Works to advance all aspects in the field of lexicography.

European Association for Osseointegration
EAO

c/o Annie Nagem
1 Wimpoe St., London, W1M 8AE, England, UK
Tel: 44 207 2903948
Fax: 44 207 2902989
Email: eao-office@roysocmed.ac.uk
Website: http://www.eao.org
Contact: Annie Nagem
Description: Promotes the advancement of methods of treatment in reconstructive surgery and prosthetic rehabilitation based on the principles of osseointegration and related disciplines. Fosters research; disseminates information.

European Association for Passive Fire Protection
PFPF

Association House, 99 West St., Farnham, GU9 7EN, England, UK
Tel: 44 1252 739152
Fax: 44 1252 739140
Email: info@associationhouse.org.uk
Website: http://www.associationhouse.org.uk/eapfp/eapfp.html
Members: 9
Staff: 6
Contact: John Fairley, Sec.
Description: European manufacturers and contractors involved in passive fire protection, including steelwork, timber and other specialist applications. Promotes high industry standards.

European Association for Personnel Management
EAPM

CIPD House, Camp Rd., London, SW19 40X, England, UK
Tel: 44 208 2633273
Email: f.wilson@cipd.co.uk
Website: http://www.eapm.org
Founded: 1962
Members: 22
Contact: Frances Wilson, Gen.Sec.
Description: National personnel management associations. Purposes are to maintain professional standards of personnel management and to act as representative for personnel management associations in Europe. Disseminates information.
Meetings/Conventions: - biennial congress - Exhibits. Rome Italy

European Association for Planned Giving
EAPG

c/o Brakeley Ltd.
Paramount House, 162-170 Wardour St., London, W1V 4AB, England, UK
Tel: 44 20 77340777
Fax: 44 16 22850771
Email: info@plannedgiving.org.uk
Website: http://www.plannedgiving.co.uk
Description: Professional advisors involved in charitable giving. Seeks to advance the development of planned giving in Europe. Addresses cross-border and tax issues that arise in fundraising.
Publication: Bulletin
Publication title: EAPG Bulletin
Second publication: Newsletter
Publication title: Give a Thought

European Association for Special Education
EASE

Edgbaston, University of Birgmingham, Birmingham, B15 2TT, England, UK
Tel: 49 121 4144865
Email: H.R.J.Daniels@bham.ac.uk
Founded: 1970

European Association for the Treatment of Addiction - U.K.
EATA

Waterbridge House, 32-36 Loman St., London, SE1 0EE, England, UK
Tel: 44 20 79228753
Fax: 44 20 79284644
Email: secretariat@eata.org.uk
Website: http://www.box-1.freeserve.co.uk
Founded: 1992
Members: 80
Staff: 2
Contact: Mala Seecoomar
Fee: £29
Membership Type: full
Fee: £126
Membership Type: associate
Description: Substance abuse treatment centers; health care and other professionals with an interest in the treatment of people who abuse substances. Seeks to advance the treatment of people with substance abuse problems; promotes increased understanding of the scientific, psychological, and medical aspects of substance abuse. Facilitates communication and cooperation among members; facilitates research and educational programs.

European Association for Veterinary Pharmacology and Toxicology
EAVPT

North Mymms, Hatfield, AL9 7TA, England, UK
Tel: 44 1707 666294
Fax: 44 1707 666371
Email: plees@rvc.ac.uk
Founded: 1978
Description: Stimulates research and education in veterinary pharmacology and toxicology.

European Association of Acarologists
EURAAC

c/o Mr. D. Macfarlane
70 Hunters Way, Gillingham, ME7 3BT, England, UK
Tel: 44 1634 853107
Fax: 44 1634 302136
Email: donmacf@clara.co.uk
Website: http://www.fu-berlin.de/euraac/socinf.html
Founded: 1987
Contact: Donald Macfarlane, Treas.
Fee: £9
Fee: £5
Membership Type: student/retired
Description: Promotes the study of acarology.
Publication: Newsletter
Meetings/Conventions: meeting

European Association of Cognitive Ergonomics
EACE

c/o Sowerby
British Aerospace Place, FPC 267, PO Box 5, Bristol, BS12 7QW, England, UK
Tel: 44 117 9366988
Fax: 44 117 9363733
Email: civie.warren@src.bae.co.uk
Founded: 1987
Members: 150
Contact: Clive Warren, Chm.
Description: University instructors and researchers dealing with the human aspects of mental work, especially the integration of human activities with computers. Promotes cognitive sciences through the development of information systems designed to enhance effective interaction with users. Serves as a forum to enhance cooperation between researchers throughout Europe. Maintains contacts with other national and international scientific organizations. Edits reviews and books.
Publication: Newsletter
Publication title: EACE Newsletter
Meetings/Conventions: European Conference on Cognitive Ergonomics - biennial conference

European Association of Fibre Drum Manufacturers
SEFFI

St. Johns House, 4 London Rd., Crowborough, , England, UK
Tel: 44 1892 654414
Fax: 44 1892 654981
Email: seffi@kellys.uk.cowww.SEFFI.org
Founded: 1991
Members: 20
Contact: C.G. Stebbing, Sec.
Description: Works to develop useful product standards and to conduct activities to broaden the Industry's markets and create wider appreciation and acceptance of its products and services.

European Association of Fish Pathologists

c/o Dr. David Alderman
CEFAS Weymouth Laboratory, Barrack Rd., The Nothe, Weymouth, DT4 8UB, England, UK
Tel: 44 1305 206600
Fax: 44 1305 206601
Email: d.j.alderman@cefas.co.uk
Website: http://www.eafp.org
Founded: 1979
Contact: Dr. David Alderman, Pres.
Description: Promotes exchange of knowledge and coordinates research related to fish and shellfish pathology.
Publication: Bulletin
Meetings/Conventions: - biennial conference

European Association of Neurosurgical Societies
EANS

60 Cobden Ave., Southampton, SO18 1FT, England, UK
Tel: 44 23 80585115
Fax: 44 23 80585115
Email: stephanie.garfield@virgin.net
Website: http://www.eans.org
Founded: 1971
Contact: Prof. J. Lobo Antunes, Pres.

Description: National European neurosurgical societies in 32 countries. Sponsors two training courses per year and various other activities and research projects.
Publication: Journal
Publication title: Acta Neurochirurgica
Second publication: Bulletin
Publication title: EANS Newsletter
Meetings/Conventions: European Neurosurgical Congress - quadrennial conference - Exhibits. Lisbon Portugal

European Association of Science Editors
EASE

c/o Mrs. Jennifer Gretton
PO Box 426, Guildford, GU4 7ZH, England, UK
Tel: 44 1483 211056
Fax: 44 1483 211056
Email: secretary@ease.org.uk
Website: http://www.ease.org.uk/
Founded: 1982
Members: 960
Contact: Jennifer Gretton, Sec.-Treas.
Fee: £56
Membership Type: Individual
Fee: £28
Membership Type: Retired
Description: Editors of serial and other scientific publications in 49 countries; others responsible for editing or managing such a publication; individuals representing scientific publications or publishing bodies. Aims are to: promote improved communication in science by encouraging cooperation among editors in all disciplines of science; assist in the efficient operation of publications in the field. Encourages discussion on topics including: finding and keeping authors, editors, readers, publishers, and printers; producing publications quickly and economically; keeping up with modern technology in editing and printing; intellectual and practical problems in the transfer of scientific information.
Formerly: Formed by Merger of, European Association of Earth Science Editors
Publication: Journal
Publication title: European Science Editing. Advertisements.
Publication title: Science Editors' Handbook
Meetings/Conventions: Editing and Scientific Truth - periodic conference - Exhibits. Bath UK

European Association of Securities Dealers
EASD

112 Middlesex St., London, E1 7HY, England, UK
Tel: 44 207 2477080
Fax: 44 207 3770939
Email: info@apcims.co.uk
Description: Works to develop an efficient pan-European equity market that facilitates entrepreneurs' access to public funding. Sets pan-European market standards with an initial focus on high-growth companies.

European Association of Teachers - United Kingdom

c/o Brian Sandford, Sec.
20 Brookfield, Highgate Westhill, London, N6 6AS, England, UK
Tel: 44 1702 58662
Fax: 44 1702 586622
Email: eat@bsandford.freeserve.co.uk

Website: http://www.aede.org/uk
Founded: 1962
Members: 400
Staff: 1
Contact: Mary E. Duce
Description: Open to individual teachers. Schools or colleges may enrol. Aims to promote education about Europe with links between different sections in various projects. EAT/UK runs courses/ conferences for teachers, organises European Knowledge tests (approved by Schools Curriculum Assessment Authority), for pupils, and produces helpful publications.
Publication: Books
Second publication: Journal

European Beer Consumers' Union
EBCU

230 Hatfield Rd., St. Albans, AL1 4LW, England, UK
Tel: 44 1727 867201
Fax: 44 1727 867670
Email: camra@camra.org.uk
Website: http://www.camra.org.uk
Founded: 1990
Members: 85000
Contact: Terry Lock, Chm.
Description: National beer consumers' unions. Seeks to protect the economic and aesthetic rights of beer buyers. Represents members' before brewery operators and consumer protection agencies; facilitates communication and good fellowship among beer consumers.

European Biomedical Research Association
EBRA

58 Great Marlborough St., London, W1V 1DD, England, UK
Tel: 44 20 72872818
Fax: 44 20 72872627
Email: secretariat@ebra.org
Website: http://www.ebra.org/
Founded: 1994
Description: Promotes the best practice in animal research and high standards of laboratory animal welfare.

European Board for the Specialty of Cardiology
EBSC

Papworth Everard, Cambridge, CB3 8RE, England, UK
Tel: 44 1480 830541
Fax: 44 1480 831315
Founded: 1992
Description: Enhances the education and training of cardiologists in Europe.

European Business Travel Association
IBTA

34 Chester Rd., Macclesfield, Rickmansworth, SK11 8DG, England, UK
Tel: 44 1625 4410710
Fax: 44 1625 439183
Email: secretariat@itm.org.uk
Website: http://www.ibta.com
Contact: Ms. Caroline Prescot

Description: Aims to promote and facilitate the exchange of information between buyers and suppliers of corporate travel services throughout the world.

European Catering Association International
ECA

c/o Secretariat
Halm, Burgoine House, Burgoine Quay, 8 Lower Teddington Rd., Hampton Wick, Kingston Upon Thames, KT1 4ER, England, UK
Tel: 44 208 9774419
Fax: 44 208 9775519
Email: eca@halm.co.uk
Website: http://www.ecaint.org
Founded: 1964
Members: 712
Contact: Caroline Franklin, Sec.
Fee: £3000
Membership Type: affiliate
Fee: £6000
Membership Type: National section
Description: Industrial catering companies, self-employed caterers, catering managers' unions, and educational and research institutions. Promotes and represents the interests of the European catering industry. Fosters the exchange of experience and knowledge among members.
Library Type: open to the public
Publication title: Annual Report
Second publication: Newsletter
Publication title: ECA International News
Meetings/Conventions: Student of the Year Competition and Conference - annual meeting

European Cell Biology Organization
ECBO

c/o Dept. of Zoology
Downing St., Cambridge, CB2 3EJ, England, UK
Tel: 44 1223 336602
Fax: 44 1223 336676
Email: d.bray@zoo.cam.ac.uk
Founded: 1977
Members: 6600
Contact: Dr. Dennis Bray, Sec.Gen.
Description: European national cell biology societies in 18 countries. Promotes the study of cell biology and its applications. Encourages cooperation among individual cell biologists and their respective national societies.
Meetings/Conventions: - biennial congress - Exhibits.

European Centre for Medium-Range Weather Forecasts

Shinfield Park, Reading, RG2 9AX, England, UK
Tel: 44 118 9499101
Fax: 44 118 9869450
Email: dra@ecmwf.int
Website: http://www.ecmwf.int
Founded: 1973
Members: 18
Staff: 162
Contact: Dr. D. Burridge, Dir.
Description: National weather services and organizations. Promotes the development of numerical methods for medium-range weather forecasting. Prepares medium-range weather forecasts for distribution to members; conducts scientific and technical research to improve

weather forecasting; gathers and disseminates meteorological data. Assists in the implementation of the programs of the World Meteorological Organisation; provides advanced training to the scientific staff of national weather services; assists members conducting meteorological research. Produces and distributes weather forecasting products. Compiles data reception statistics.
Library Subject: meteorology
Library Type: reference

European Chilled Food Federation
CFA

PO Box 14811, London, NW10 9ZR, England, UK
Tel: 44 20 84510503
Fax: 44 20 84598061
Email: ecff@chilledfood.org
Website: http://www.ecff.net
Description: Promotes the chilled food industry in Europe.

European Chiropractors' Union
ECU

c/o Mrs. A. Kemp
9 Cross Deep Gardens, Twickenham, TW1 4QZ, England, UK
Tel: 44 181 8912546
Fax: 44 181 7442902
Founded: 1932
Members: 2300
Staff: 1
Contact: Mrs. A. Kemp, Exec.Sec.
Description: National associations (16) representing 2200 chiropractors; interested others (25). Promotes the development of chiropractic medicine and colleges through legal, educational, and research activities; maintains standards for chiropractic education in Europe. Works to foster unity among European chiropractors' associations. Provides research funds.
Library Type: reference
Publication: Directory
Publication title: European Chiropractors' Union Directory. Advertisements.
Second publication: Journal
Publication title: European Journal of Chiropractic
Meetings/Conventions: Rehabilitation Neurology & Sports - annual convention - Exhibits.

European Coalition to End Animal Experiments

16A Crane Grove, London, N7 8LB, England, UK
Tel: 44 171 7004888
Fax: 44 171 7000252
Email: eceae@buav.org
Website: http://www.tierrechte.de/european-coalition/
Founded: 1990
Description: Animal protection groups in the European Union. Works to eliminate animal experiments.

European Coastal Association for Science and Technology
EUROCOAST

c/o Jane Taussik
Centre for Coastal Zone Management, University of Portsmouth, Portland Bldg., Portland St., Portsmouth, PO1 3AH, England, UK
Tel: 44 23 92842934
Fax: 44 23 92842913

Email: jane.taussik@port.ac.uk
Website: http://www.eurocoast.org
Founded: 1989
Contact: Jane Taussik
Description: Scientists, engineers, and decision makers in the European Community. Promotes protection, development, management of he coastal zone. Fosters research; disseminates information.
Library Subject: coastal zones
Library Type: reference

European College of Hypnotherapy

5 Schroder Ct., Egham, TW20 0EH, England, UK
Tel: 44 1784 479930
Email: principal@european-college.co.uk
Website: http://www.european-college.co.uk/
Contact: Dr. Keith Hearne, Prin.
Description: Promotes the development of new techniques in hypnotherapy, including the conversion of nightmares into pleasant dreams, externalizing hypnotic imagery, new pain-control procedures, and the concept of the virtual self.
Publication: Articles

European Commission for Industrial Marketing
CEMI

18 St. Peters Steps, Brixham, , England, UK
Founded: 1969
Members: 39
Staff: 4
Contact: Dr. A.J. Williamson, Pres.
Description: Associations of industrial marketing executives in 16 countries. Represents members before the European and international industrial products market; facilitates the exchange of information among members. Develops training programs in industrial marketing and research through the European College of Marketing and Marketing Research in conjunction with the European Marketing Association. Compiles statistics.
Library Subject: marketing, selling, and market research
Library Type: not open to the public
Publication: Newsletter
Publication title: European Marketing Newsletter
Second publication: Journal
Publication title: Journal of International Marketing and Marketing Research
Meetings/Conventions: - quarterly symposium

European Committee for Agricultural and Horticultural Tools and Implements
CEOAH

Light Trades House, Melbourne Ave. 3, Sheffield, S10 2QJ, England, UK
Tel: 44 114 2663084
Fax: 44 114 2670910
Email: info@lighttradeshouse.co.uk
Founded: 1947
Members: 35
Staff: 2
Contact: M. Ponikowski, Sec.Gen.
Description: National associations of manufacturers of farm and garden tools in 12 European countries; manufacturing firms. Provides technical and statistical information.

Publication: Directory
Publication title: Directory
Meetings/Conventions: - biennial meeting

European Committee of Manufacturers of Compressors, Vacuum Pumps, and Pneumatic Tools
PNEUROP

33/34 Devonshire St., London, W1N 1RF, England, UK
Tel: 44 171 9352464
Fax: 44 171 9353077
Email: compressd.air@virgin.net
Website: http://www.pneurop.com
Members: 11
Staff: 3
Contact: R.D. Wall, Dir.
Description: Manufacturers of compressed air equipment in 11 countries. Examines technical and legislative issues.
Meetings/Conventions: - quarterly conference

European Committee on Radiopharmaceuticals

City Hospital NHS Trust, Birmingham, B18 7QH, England, UK
Fax: 44 121 5075223

European Communities Chemistry Council
ECCC

c/o Royal Soc. of Chemistry
Burlington House, Piccadilly, London, W1J 0BA, England, UK
Tel: 44 207 4403303
Fax: 44 207 4378883
Email: mcewane@rsc.org
Website: http://www.chemsoc.org/fecs
Founded: 1973
Members: 25
Contact: Evelyn K. McEwan, Sec.
Description: Western European national organizations whose interests include the theoretical and practical aspects of chemistry. Collaborates with the Commission of the European Communities to advise and consult in matters involving the science and practice of chemistry in member nations of the European Union and EEA. Awarding body for the designation of European Chemist.
Meetings/Conventions: - semiannual meeting

European Communities Clinical Chemistry Committee

Piccadilly, London, W1 0BN, England, UK
Tel: 44 20 74378656
Fax: 44 20 74378883
Founded: 1973

European Computer Leasing and Trading Association

Hall Green, 1285 Stratford Rd., Birmingham, B28 9AJ, England, UK
Tel: 44 121 7785327
Fax: 44 121 7785924
Email: jgsewel@ibm.net
Website: http://www.atchou.com/eclat.html
Founded: 1979
Members: 50
Staff: 3
Contact: Geoff Sewell, Dir.Gen.

Fee: £1000
Membership Type: ordinary
Description: Represents the interests of members before the European Commission, administrative authorities, economic groups, and other legal entities. Promotes adherence to high standards of ethics and practice by members. Provides a forum for members to establish and develop new international business relationships. Supplies members with information through a data network; enforces high standards of business ethics among members; serves as a clearinghouse on members.
Meetings/Conventions: - semiannual conference

European Consortium for Political Research
ECPR

University of Essex, Colchester, CO4 3SQ, England, UK
Tel: 44 1206 872501
Fax: 44 1206 872500
Email: ecpr@essex.ac.uk
Website: http://www.essex.ac.uk/ecpr
Founded: 1970
Members: 262
Staff: 5
Contact: Joe Foweraker, Exec.Dir.
Description: European universities and institutes in 28 countries engaged in teaching and research in political science. Aids scholars in their research and promotes the development of political science in Europe. Fosters collaboration and increases the levels of training. Enhances the dissemination of research information by facilitating exchanges and visits of European political science scholars and teachers. Holds 2 summer schools on quantitative research methods, taught in English and French, with workshops and research sessions. Research projects include the Political Economy of Interest Group Power and the Future of Party Government.
Publication title: Directory of European Political Scientists
Second publication: Newsletter
Publication title: ECPR News

European Construction Institute

Sir Frank Gibb Annex, West Park, Loughborough University, Loughborough, LE11 3TU, England, UK
Tel: 44 1509 223526
Fax: 44 1509 260118
Email: eci@lboro.ac.uk
Website: http://www.eci-online.org
Founded: 1990
Members: 126
Staff: 10
Contact: Gareth Thomas, Dir. of Oper.
Fee: £10000
Membership Type: corporate
Description: Construction client, contractor, and project support Organizations in Europe. Aligns the major contributors in the business to collectively devise techniques and practices to improve performance and share experiences on implementation.
Library Subject: best practices in engineering construction
Library Type: not open to the public
Publication: Newsletter
Publication title: ECI Newsletter
Second publication: Newsletter
Publication title: E-Newsletter
Meetings/Conventions: - annual conference

European Contact Lens Society of Ophthalmologists
ECLSO

143 Harley St., London, W1N 1DJ, England, UK
Tel: 44 20 79350886
Email: rene.mely@t-online.de
Website: http://www.ophtalmo.net/eclso/
Founded: 1969
Contact: Dr. Rene Mely, Gen.Sec.
Fee: £30
Fee: £30
Description: Ophthalmologists with an interest in eye disease; promotes the understanding and study of contact lenses.
Meetings/Conventions: - annual congress Venice Italy

European Control Manufacturers Association

c/o Honeywell Ltd.
Honeywell House, Bracknell, RG12 1EB, England, UK
Tel: 44 1344 656597
Founded: 1963
Members: 18
Contact: Mr. R. Glaser, Pres.
Description: Manufacturer of oil and gas controls. Works to establish uniform technical standards and certification procedures.
Meetings/Conventions: - semiannual meeting

European Cooperation in Legal Metrology
WELMEC

National Weights and Measures Laboratory, Stanton Ave., Teddington, TW11 0JZ, England, UK
Tel: 44 208 9437200
Fax: 44 181 9437270
Email: peter.badger@nwml.gov.uk
Website: http://www.welmec.org
Founded: 1990
Members: 28
Contact: Peter Badger
Description: National legal metrology organizations in the European Union and European Free Trade Association. Seeks to harmonize legal metrology (legal metrology refers the application of laws and regulations to the science of metrology, the study of weights and measurements) in Europe. Facilitates communication and cooperation among members.
Library Subject: guidance documents
Library Type: open to the public
Meetings/Conventions: - annual meeting

European Council for Blood Pressure and Cardiovascular Research
ECCR

127 High St., Teddington, TW11 8HH, England, UK
Tel: 44 20 89770011
Fax: 44 20 89770055
Email: eccr@hamptonmedical.com
Website: http://www.eccr.org
Founded: 1997
Members: 160
Contact: Gerry McCarthy, Sec.
Description: Promotes clinical and experimental research in hypertension and cardiovascular disease in Europe.
Meetings/Conventions: - annual conference Seeheim Germany

European Council for Classical Homeopathy
ECCH

Market Place, Kenninghall, NR16 2AH, England, UK
Tel: 44 1953 888163
Fax: 44 888163
Email: ecch@homeopathy-ecch.org
Website: http://www.homeopathy-ecch.org/
Founded: 1990
Members: 8000
Staff: 2
Contact: Stephen Gordon, Gen.Sec.
Description: Promotes and develops highest standards of homeopathic practice among the homeopathic profession.
Meetings/Conventions: Crossing Bridges - annual conference

European Council for Industrial Marketing

18 Saint Peters Steps, Brixham, TU5 9TE, England, UK
Tel: 44 1803 859575
Founded: 1968

European Council for the Village and Small Town

c/o CCRU
Cheltenham and Gloucester College, Swindon Rd., Cheltenham, GL50 4AZ, England, UK
Tel: 44 1242 544031
Fax: 44 1242 543273
Email: mdower@chelt.ac.uk
Website: http://www.ecovast.org
Founded: 1965
Members: 7000
Staff: 10
Contact: Michel Fontaine, Pres.
Description: Specialized in the study and conservation of vernacular architecture. Works for appropriate restoration of old rural houses, farm buildings and their vicinity, and generally by survival of this heritage.
Library Subject: protection of vernacular architecture
Library Type: open to the public

European Council of Civil Engineers
ECCE

3 Springfields, Amersham, Hp6 5JU, England, UK
Tel: 44 1494 723369
Email: eccescretariat@hotmail.com
Website: http://www.eccenet.org
Founded: 1985
Members: 19
Staff: 2
Contact: Diana Maxwell, Sec.Gen.
Fee: £48000
Membership Type: ordinary
Description: European national organizations representing civil engineers. Seeks to advance the study and practice of civil engineering. Serves as a forum for the exchange of information among members; conducts continuing professional development programs for civil engineers.
Publication title: Engineers in Europe

European Council of International Schools
ECIS

21 Lavant St., Petersfield, GU32 3EL, England, UK
Tel: 44 1730 268244
Fax: 44 1730 267914
Email: ecis@ecis.org
Website: http://www.ecis.org
Founded: 1965
Members: 1800
Staff: 25
Contact: T. Michael Maybury, Exec.Sec.
Description: Members include international schools, colleges, and institutions involved in the field of education worldwide; manufacturers of educational equipment and publishers; individuals interested in international education. Represents members' interests and serves as a liaison between member-schools and institutions of higher learning throughout the world. Evaluates and accredits schools according to standards set by international educational agencies. Provides guidance to schools regarding educational programs, teaching methods, and organizational questions. Assists schools in the recruitment of directors and teaching staff. Conducts research and gathers information of interest to members. Holds training courses on education in an international setting. Compiles statistics; operates placement service.
Publication: Directory
Publication title: ECIS International Schools Directory. Advertisements.
Publication title: Higher Education Directory
Meetings/Conventions: - annual conference - Exhibits.

European Council of Optics and Optometry
ECOO

61 Southwark St., London, SE1 6LN, England, UK
Tel: 44 207 9289269
Fax: 44 207 6201140
Website: http://www.europtom.com
Founded: 1960

European Council of Town Planners
ECTP

c/o Royal Town Planning Institute
41 Botolph Ln., London, EC3R 8DL, England, UK
Tel: 44 207 9299494
Fax: 44 207 9298199
Email: secretariat@ceu-ectp.org
Website: http://www.ceu-ectp.org
Founded: 1985
Members: 21
Contact: Robert Upton, Sec.Gen.
Description: National associations representing town planners and town planning institutes. Seeks to advance the study and practice of urban planning. Represents members' professional interests at the local, regional, national, and European levels; sponsors research and educational programs.

European Council on Eating Disorders
ECED

Department of Psychiatry, St. George's Hospital Medical School, London, SW17 0RE, England, UK
Tel: 44 208 7253489
Fax: 44 208 7253350
Email: eced@sghms.ac.uk

Founded: 1989
Members: 500
Contact: Mrs. Kathy Lawday, Admin.
Description: European medical clinicians and researchers with an interest in eating disorders. Seeks to advance the diagnosis and medical treatment of eating disorders. Facilitates exchange of information and clinical skills among members.
Publication: Newsletter
Meetings/Conventions: - biennial conference

European Council on Refugees and Exiles
ECRE

Clifton Centre, Unit 22, 110 Clifton St., London, EC2A 4HT, England, UK
Tel: 44 20 77295152
Fax: 44 20 77295141
Email: ecre@ecre.org
Website: http://www.ecre.org
Founded: 1974
Members: 72
Staff: 15
Contact: Peer Baneke, Gen.Sec.
Description: Organizations working to protect the human rights of refugees and other displaced people seeking refuge in Europe. Facilitates exchange of information regarding asylum policies of European countries; maintains the European Legal Network on Asylum to assist to individuals seeking political asylum; serves as a forum for discussion of legal issues among attorneys and other professionals. Conducts research and educational programs on refugees and international law. Works to enhance the capacities of nongovernmental organizations working with displaced people in central and eastern Europe.
Formerly: European Consultation on Refugees and Exiles
Meetings/Conventions: - periodic seminar

European Cutting Tools Association
ECTA

Light Trades House, 3 Melbourne Ave., Sheffield, S10 2QJ, England, UK
Tel: 44 114 2663084
Fax: 44 114 2670910
Email: info@lighttradeshouse.co.uk
Website: http://www.britishtools.com
Members: 9
Contact: Mike Ponikowski
Description: Cutting tools associations in Czech Republic, France, Germany, Italy, the Netherlands, Spain, Sweden, Switzerland, and United Kingdom. Seeks to ensure international representation of members' views on technical and economic issues.
Meetings/Conventions: - periodic conference

European Economic Association
EEA

Department of Economics, University of Warwick, Coventry, CV4 7AL, England, UK
Tel: 44 247 6523046
Fax: 44 247 6523032
Email: secretariat@eeassoc.org
Website: http://www.eeassoc.org
Founded: 1985
Members: 2000

Staff: 3
Description: Aims are: to contribute to the development and application of economics as a science in Europe; to improve communication and exchange between teachers, researchers and students in economics in the different European countries; to develop and sponsor co-operation between teaching institutions of university level and research institutions in Europe.
Publication: Journal
Publication title: Journal of the European Economic Association. Advertisements.
Meetings/Conventions: - annual congress

European Elasmobranch Association
EEA

Hambridge Rd., 36 Kingfisher Court, Newbury, RG14 5SJ, England, UK
Tel: 44 1635 550380
Fax: 44 1635 550230
Email: sharks@naturebureau.co.uk
Founded: 1997
Description: Coordinates activities of European organizations dedicated to study or conservation of sharks and rays.

European Federation for Pscyhoanalytic Psychotherapy

5 Windsor Rd., Finchley, London, , England, UK
Tel: 44 20 84399873
Fax: 44 20 83433197
Email: joycepiper@compuserve.com
Contact: Joyce Piper, Admin.Sec.
Description: Umbrella organization that links together national networks of adult, child, and adolescent and group psychoanalytic psychotherapists, and psychoanalysts involved in public sector services.

European Federation of Associations and Centres of Irish Studies
EFACIS

Castle View, Dudley, DY1 3HR, England, UK
Fax: 44 1902 323379
Email: c.norton@wlv.ac.uk
Website: http://www.geocities.com/efacis/links_organisations.html
Description: Promotes interest in and supports expansion of Irish studies in Europe.

European Federation of Associations of Market Research Organisations
EFAMRO

26 Chester Close N, Regent's Park, London, NW1 4JE, England, UK
Tel: 44 20 72243873
Fax: 44 20 72243873
Website: http://www.efamro.org/
Founded: 1992
Description: Works to bring together national associations of major countries in Western Europe representing research agencies responsible for 60-70 percent of total turnover in market research. Member countries include Belgium, Denmark, France, Czech Republic, Germany, Italy, The Netherlands, Portugal, Spain, Sweden and United Kingdom.

European Federation of Endocrine Societies

c/o Prof. JMC Connell
British Endocrine Societies, 17/18 The Courtyard, Woodlands, Bradley Stoke, Bristol, BS32 4NQ, England, UK
Tel: 44 1454 642200
Fax: 44 1454 642222
Email: julie.cragg@endocrinology.org
Website: http://www.euro-endo.org
Founded: 1984
Contact: John Wass, Pres.
Description: Promotes endocrinology in Europe. Seeks to advance research and education in endocrinology. Organizes postgraduate courses.
Meetings/Conventions: - biennial conference

European Federation of Foundation Contractors

c/o Forum Court
83 Copers Cope Rd., Beckenham, BR3 1NR, England, UK
Tel: 44 20 86630948
Fax: 44 20 630949
Email: effc@effc.org
Website: http://www.effc.org
Founded: 1989
Members: 366
Staff: 2
Contact: D. Jennings, Sec.
Description: Federations of specialist foundation contractors from all European and East European countries engaged in the construction of specialist foundations and ground improvement techniques.
Publication: Magazine
Publication title: European Foundations. Advertisements.
Meetings/Conventions: - periodic meeting

European Federation of Internal Medicine
EFIM

Eastern Rd., Brighton, BN2 5BE, England, UK
Tel: 44 1273 696955
Fax: 44 1273 684554
Email: info@efim.org
Website: http://www.efim.org/
Founded: 1969
Description: Promotes internal medicine at the scientific and professional level in the European Union.

European Federation of National Associations of Orthopaedics and Traumatology
EFORT

c/o Prof. George Bentley
Royal National Orthopedic Hospital, Stanmore, HA7 4LP, England, UK
Tel: 44 208 9095532
Fax: 44 208 9543036
Email: office@efort.org
Website: http://www.efort.org/
Founded: 1992
Description: Promotes the exchange of knowledge and ideas in the field of prevention, the conservative and surgical treatment of diseases and injuries to the musculoskeletal symptom.

European Federation of Societies for Ultrasound in Medicine and Biology
EFSUMB

Carpenters Court, 4a Lewes Rd., Bromley, BR1 2RN, England, UK
Tel: 44 20 84028973
Fax: 44 20 84029344
Email: efsumb@efsumb.org
Website: http://www.efsumb.org/
Founded: 1972
Members: 13500
Staff: 1
Contact: Mrs. Gianna Stanford, Gen.Sec.
Description: Interdisciplinary national organizations and subgroups of bodies representing 26 countries. Members promote the application of ultrasound in biology and medicine or engage in research and development in the field. Proposes standards for ultrasound use and interpretation; arranges congresses and study and development meetings; promotes the exchange of information on ultrasound as applied to biology and medicine. Represents the European national societies in the World Federation of Societies for Ultrasound in Medicine and Biology.
Publication: Journal
Publication title: European Journal of Ultrasound. Advertisements.
Meetings/Conventions: - periodic competition

European Federation of Wine and Spirit Importers

5 Kings House, 1 Queen St. Pl., London, EC4R 1XX, England, UK
Tel: 44 20 72485371
Fax: 44 20 74890322
Email: efwsid@wsa.org.uk
Founded: 1976
Members: 12
Staff: 7
Contact: Quentin Rappoport, Dir.
Description: Companies headquartered in the United Kingdom. Promotes and protects members' interests. Facilitates matching of members with foreign companies wishing to export wines and distilled beverages to Europe.

European Fishing Tackle Trade Association
EFTTA

73 St. John St., London, EC1M 4NJ, England, UK
Tel: 44 207 2530777
Fax: 44 207 2537779
Email: info@eftta.com
Website: http://www.eftta.com
Founded: 1982
Members: 250
Staff: 5
Contact: Janet Doyle
Fee: £550
Description: Promotes and protects the interests of European manufacturers, wholesalers, and distributors of fishing tackle and accessories in over 30 countries. Encourages the exchange of views on matters of concern, such as the environment, within the European industry. Develops and monitors specifications and standards for fishing tackle. Sponsors market research.
Publication: Newsletter
Publication title: EFTTA Newsline
Publication title: European Fishing Dictionary
Meetings/Conventions: European Fishing Tackle Trade Exhibition - annual trade show - Exhibits.

European Flexographic Technical Association - (UK)

4-5 Bridge Barns, Langport Rd., Sutton, TA10 9PZ, England, UK
Tel: 44 1458 241455
Fax: 44 1458 241684
Email: admin@efta.co.uk
Website: http://www.efta.co.uk
Founded: 1972
Members: 420
Staff: 4
Contact: Lesley Hide, Dir.
Description: Companies concerned with flexographic printing process. All technical and training aspects of the flexographic printing process.
Publication: Papers

European Foodservice Equipment Distributors Association
EFEDA

7 Hamilton Way, Wallington, SM6 9NJ, England, UK
Tel: 44 208 6698121
Fax: 44 208 6471128
Email: secretary@efeda.org
Website: http://www.efeda.org
Founded: 1990
Members: 110
Staff: 2
Contact: John Barton, Sec.
Description: Distributors of foodservice equipment in Europe. Acts as a voice for the industry. Close liaison with other trade associations and Government bodies: deals with technical standards and approvals in Europe. Provides trade information. Members must adhere to the constitution and rules of the association.
Formerly: Catering Equipment Importers Association
Publication: Membership Directory
Publication title: EFEDA Member Directory
Meetings/Conventions: EFEDA International - annual conference - Exhibits.

European General Galvanizers Association
EGGA

Maybrook House, Godstone Rd., Caterham, CR3 6RE, England, UK
Tel: 44 188 3331277
Fax: 44 188 3331287
Email: mail@egga.com
Website: http://www.egga.com
Founded: 1956
Members: 13
Staff: 2
Contact: Dr. M.G. Burcher, Dir.
Description: European galvanizing associations. Promotes the practice and technical development of hot-dip galvanizing of fabricated steel products. Arranges conferences, meetings, and study tours for members.
Publication title: Proceedings Volumes of International Conferences
Meetings/Conventions: International Galvanizing Conference - triennial conference - Exhibits. Amsterdam Netherlands

European Glass Container Manufacturers Committee
EGM

Northumberland Rd., Sheffield, S10 2UA, England, UK
Tel: 44 114 2686201
Fax: 44 114 2681073
Founded: 1951
Members: 24
Contact: Mr. D. Workman, Sec.
Description: National organizations in 15 countries that manufacture glass containers. To promote communication among members.
Meetings/Conventions: - annual conference

European Glaucoma Society

City Rd., London, EC1V 2PD, England, UK
Email: secretary@eugs.org
Website: http://www.eugs.org/
Founded: 1979

European Group for Organization Studies
EGOS

Drake Circus, Plymouth, PL4 8AA, England, UK
Tel: 44 1752 21312

European Herbal Practitioners Association
EHPA

45A Corsica St., London, N5 1JT, England, UK
Tel: 44 20 73455067
Fax: 44 20 73543605
Email: info@euroherb.com
Website: http://www.users.globalnet.co.uk/~ehpa/
Founded: 1993
Description: Herbal practitioners in Europe. Works to raise the standards of training and practice within the profession. Seeks to establish minimum standards of training and competence for herbal practitioners of all herbal traditions.

European Herpetological Society

c/o Environmental Initiatives
12 Cheyne Row, London, SW3 5HL, England, UK
Tel: 44 207 3526483
Fax: 44 207 3526483
Email: lambertmrk@aol.com
Website: http://www.gli.cas.cz/seh/
Founded: 1979
Members: 500
Contact: Dr. Michael R.K. Lambert, Gen.Sec.
Description: Specialist society with members from most countries in Europe and around the world. Promotes conservation of herpetofauna in all parts of Europe and adjacent regions, and maps species distributions in the western palaearctic biogeographical zone. Provides information, news, and conference announcements.
Publication: Journal
Publication title: Amphibia-Reptilia
Second publication: Book
Publication title: Atlas of Amphibians and Reptiles in Europe
Meetings/Conventions: - biennial conference - Exhibits. St. Petersburg Russia

European Historical Economics Society
EHES

St. Anothony's College, Oxford, OX2 6JF, England, UK
Email: enquiries@latin-american-centre.oxford.ac.uk
Website: http://www.eh.net/EHES/
Founded: 1995
Description: Organizes conferences and summer schools.

European Information Association

c/o Central Library
St. Peter's Sq., Manchester, M2 5PD, England, UK
Tel: 44 161 2283691
Fax: 44 161 2366547
Email: eia@libraries.manchester.gov.uk
Website: http://www.eia.org.uk
Founded: 1991
Members: 500
Staff: 2
Contact: Catherine Webb, Mgr.
Fee: £35
Membership Type: individual
Fee: £75
Membership Type: special
Description: Information intermediaries and others who provide European information services. Concerned with the development, coordination and improvement of the provision of information on the European Union and related matters. Regular EIA events and training courses allow members to develop skills, exchange experience and make new contacts. Also plays a major role in improving EU information through lobbying and its own publications.
Publication: Newsletter
Publication title: EIA Update. Advertisements.
Second publication: Journal
Publication title: European Information. Advertisements.

European Institute of Golf Course Architects

Chiddingfold Golf Club, Petworth Rd., Chiddinggfold, GU8 4SL, England, UK
Tel: 44 1428 681528
Fax: 44 1428 681528
Email: info@eigca.org
Website: http://www.eigca.org
Founded: 1970
Members: 108
Staff: 2
Description: Aims to ensure the future of golf for all by designing much needed courses which will enhance its natural environment. To this end the institute set up a training programme for students to teach them all aspects of golf course architecture. This course has been so successful that the institute has taken this another stage further by setting up a post graduate course in golf course architecture with a university.
Publication title: The Positive Face of Golf Development

European Intelligent Building Group

21 Seer Mead, Beaconsfield, HP9 2QL, England, UK
Tel: 44 149 4677924
Fax: 44 149 4670196
Email: 101676.3462@compuserve.com
Members: 65
Contact: Andy Ross
Description: Various organizations drawn from the architecture, building, planning, trade, management, supply and user groups.

Collection and dissemination of information relating to intelligent buildings.
Publication title: IB Focus

European Liquid Roofing Association

c/o Fields House
Gower Rd., Haywards Heath, RH16 4PL, England, UK
Tel: 44 1444 417458
Fax: 44 1444 415616
Email: info@elra.org.uk
Website: http://www.elra.org.uk
Founded: 1979
Members: 18
Contact: Bill Jenkins
Description: Manufacturers of liquid roofing systems (Full Members) and suppliers (Associate Members) of raw materials and services to the Full Members. To raise the level of awareness of the technical and financial benefits of specifying liquid roofing systems and to establish product and installation standards to ensure that optimum performance is achieved.
Publication title: Code of Practice
Publication title: Product Standards

European Lupus Erythematosus Federation
ELEF

27-43 Eastern Rd., St. James House, Romford, RM1 3NH, England, UK
Tel: 44 1708 731251
Fax: 44 1708 731252
Website: http://www.elef.rheumanet.org/
Founded: 1989
Description: promotes research and improves the knowledge of Systematic Lupus Erythematosus.

European Malt Extract Manufacturers Association

c/o Edme
1 Surrey Rd., Felixstone, 1P11 7SB, England, UK
Tel: 44 1394 271713
Fax: 44 1394 271713
Contact: R.E.A. Holt
Description: Malt extract manufacturers in Europe.

European Marketing Association
EMA

18 St. Peters Hill, Brixham, , England, UK
Founded: 1969
Staff: 10
Contact: Philip Allen, Gen.Sec.
Fee: £100
Membership Type: individual
Fee: £800
Membership Type: companies
Description: Marketing executives and researchers; manufacturing companies. Promotes the marketing profession in Europe. Facilitates the exchange of information and experience among members; informs members of current developments in marketing techniques. Offers training course in marketing and industrial marketing research through the European College of Marketing and Marketing Research.
Library Subject: marketing and marketing research
Library Type: not open to the public
Formerly: European Association for Industrial Marketing and Marketing Management

Publication: Directory
Publication title: European Industrial Marketing Research Personal Contact Directory. Advertisements.
Second publication: Journal
Publication title: Journal of International Marketing and Marketing Research
Meetings/Conventions: - semiannual meeting

European Mechanics Council
Euromech

University of Cambridge, Cambridge, CB3 9EW, England, UK
Fax: 44 1223 312984
Founded: 1964

European Movement

85 Frampton St., London, NW8 8NQ, England, UK
Tel: 44 207 7254300
Fax: 44 207 7254301
Email: info@euromove.org.uk
Website: http://www.euromove.org.uk
Founded: 1949
Members: 5000
Staff: 15
Contact: Ian Taylor, Chair
Fee: £20
Membership Type: individual
Fee: £25
Membership Type: couple
Description: Pro-Europe pressure group.

European Neutron Scattering Association
ENSA

University College London, Gower St., London, WC1E 6BT, England, UK
Tel: 44 207 6794392
Fax: 44 207 6791360
Email: k.mcewen@ucl.ac.uk
Website: http://www.psi.ch/ensa/
Founded: 1994
Description: Provides a focus for action in neutron scattering and related topics in Europe.

European Opthalmological Society
EOS

Moorfields Eye Hospital, City Rd., London, EC1V 2PD, England, UK
Tel: 44 171 2533411
Fax: 44 171 5662048
Founded: 1956
Contact: Mr. Z.J. Gregor, Sec.Gen.
Description: National associations of ophthalmologists. Seeks to advance ophthalmological research, study, teaching, and practice. Promotes continuing professional development among ophthalmologists. Facilitates exchange of information among members; conducts research and educational programs.
Meetings/Conventions: - biennial congress

European Orthodontic Society
EOS

49 Hallam St., Flat 20, London, W1W 6JN, England, UK
Tel: 44 20 79352795
Fax: 44 20 73230410

Email: eoslondon@compuserve.comwww.eoseurope.org
Founded: 1907
Members: 2700
Staff: 2
Contact: Prof. L. Dermaut
Fee: £48
Description: Orthodontists in 78 countries promoting the science of orthodontics.
Formerly: European Orthodontia Society
Publication: Journal
Publication title: European Journal of Orthodontics. Advertisements.
Meetings/Conventions: Congress of European Orthodontic Society - annual congress - Exhibits. Prague Czech Republic

European Phenolic Foam Association
99 West St., Association House, Farnham, GU9 7EN, England, UK
Tel: 44 1252 739148
Fax: 44 1252 739140
Email: info@epfa.org.uk
Website: http://www.epfa.org.uk
Members: 6
Staff: 2
Contact: John G. Fairley
Description: Members are either producers of phenolic foam insulation or are closely linked with the industry through the provision of raw materials. Exists to promote an awareness of the benefits of phenolic foam in insulation applications and consequently to increase its use.

European Plasticised PVC Film Manufacturers' Association
The Fountain Precinct, 1 Balm Green, Sheffield, S1 3AF, England, UK
Tel: 44 114 2766789
Fax: 44 114 2092421
Founded: 1978
Members: 5
Contact: P. Bradburn
Description: Furthers the common interests of the industry with especial reference to EC legislation.

European Policy Forum
EPF
125 Pall Mall, London, SW1Y 5EA, England, UK
Tel: 44 207 8397565
Fax: 44 207 8397339
Email: sarah.summers@epfltd.org
Website: http://www.epfltd.org
Founded: 1992
Staff: 5
Contact: Graham Mather, Pres.
Description: Promotes improved understanding of economic, regulatory, and constitutional issues facing the European Union. Serves as a clearinghouse on European public policies; sponsors educational programs; conducts policy studies.

European Prosthodontic Association
EPA
Eastman Dental Hospital, 256 Grays Inn Rd., London, WC1X 8LD, England, UK
Tel: 44 20 79151073
Fax: 44 20 79151246
Email: r.welfare@eastman.ucl.ac.uk

Website: http://www.eastman.ucl.ac.uk/~epa
Founded: 1978
Members: 528
Contact: Mr. R.D. Welfare, Hon.Sec.
Fee: £21
Membership Type: ordinary
Description: Prosthodontists. Seeks to advance the profession of dentistry; promotes continuing professional development of members. Serves as a forum for the exchange of information among European prosthodontists; sponsors research and educational programs.
Library Subject: Prosthodontics
Library Type: not open to the public

European Psycho-Analytical Federation
EPF
37 Wooddsome Rd., London, NW5 1SA, England, UK
Tel: 44 207 4857269
Fax: 44 207 2099963
Email: d.tuckett@ucl.ac.uk
Website: http://www.epf-eu.org
Founded: 1969
Contact: Prof. David Tuckett, Pres.
Description: Psychoanalysts from 19 countries belonging to European psychoanalytical societies. Seeks to further psychoanalysis as a comprehensive theory of personality and therapeutic method based on the teachings of Sigmund Freud (1856-1939), Austrian neurologist and founder of psychoanalysis. Works to maintain and improve standards of education and scientific inquiry and to foster theoretical research. Disseminates information on theoretical and practical aspects of psychoanalysis. Stimulates communication among psychoanalysts; provides a forum for discussion of psychoanalytic and related topics. Encourages the integration of psychoanalysis and other disciplines. Organizes seminars and symposia.
Publication title: Bulletin
Publication title: Psychoanalytic Training in Europe: 10 Years of Discussion
Meetings/Conventions: - biennial conference

European Public Relations Confederation
c/o Colin Farrington, Sec.
The Old Trading House, Northburgh St., London, EC1V 0PR, England, UK
Tel: 44 207 2535151
Fax: 44 207 4900588
Email: colinf@ipr.org.uk
Website: http://www.cerp.org
Founded: 1959
Contact: Patrick Alvarez, Sec.Gen.
Description: Promotes the public relations industry in the European Community. Represents members' interests. Compiles statistics.

European Ready-Mixed Concrete Organization
ERMCO
PO Box 19, Egham, TW20 8UT, England, UK
Tel: 44 1784 434990
Fax: 44 1784 435240
Founded: 1967
Members: 24
Contact: Francesco Biasioli, Sec.Gen
Description: Representatives from national ready mixed concrete associations. Establishes standards for the industry. Represents members' interests. Conducts seminars.

Publication: Annual Report
Publication title: Annual Report of Member Activities
Meetings/Conventions: - triennial congress - Exhibits. Helsinki Finland

European Regions Airline Association
ERA

Baker Ste., Fairoaks Airport, Chobham, Woking, GU24 8HX, England, UK
Tel: 44 1276 856495
Fax: 44 1276 857038
Email: info@eraa.org
Website: http://www.eraa.org
Founded: 1980
Members: 252
Staff: 18
Contact: Mike A. Ambrose, Dir.Gen.
Description: Seeks to be the principal body representing the interests of organizations involved in air transport in Europe's regions.
Formerly: European Regional Airlines Organisation
Publication: Journal
Publication title: ERA Yearbook. Advertisements.
Second publication: Journal
Publication title: International Report
Meetings/Conventions: - annual conference - Exhibits.

European Research Group on Experimental Contact Dermatitis
ERGECD

Alderley Park, Macclesfield, SK10 4TJ, England, UK
Tel: 44 1625 590249

European Resin Manufacturers' Association

8 Waldegrave Rd., Teddington, TW11 8LD, England, UK
Tel: 44 20 89778290
Fax: 44 20 89434705
Email: info@erma.org.uk
Website: http://www.erma.org.uk
Members: 36
Staff: 2
Contact: John Marshall, Sec.
Description: Resin Manufacturers.

European Sales and Marketing Association
ESMA

Victoria House, Desborough St., High Wycombe, HP11 2NF, England, UK
Tel: 44 1494 601105
Fax: 44 1494 451891
Email: info@esma.org
Website: http://www.esma.org
Founded: 1977
Members: 60
Staff: 1
Contact: Richard Onion
Description: Bona fide food brokerage companies in 25 European countries. Applicants for membership must be in business for at least three years before they can make application for membership. Holds an annual conference in different countries for its members. Conferences held in country of current ESMA president, who serves

for one year from June to July annually. Conference usually held in June.
Library Type: not open to the public
Publication: Membership Directory
Publication title: ESMA Directory of Members
Second publication: Newsletter
Publication title: News & Views
Meetings/Conventions: - annual convention - Exhibits.

European Shark Research Bureau

46 Lincoln Close, Welwyn Garden City, AL7 2NN, England, UK
Fax: 44 707 335259

European Snacks Association
ESA

37-41 Bedford Row, London, WC1R 4JH, England, UK
Tel: 44 20 76114660
Fax: 44 20 76114661
Email: esa@esa.org.uk
Website: http://www.esa.org.uk
Founded: 1961
Members: 200
Staff: 4
Contact: Steve Chandler, Sec.Gen.
Description: Promotes the production of potato chips, edible nuts, and snack food products in Europe. Promotes high quality standards for the industry. Represents members' interests; sponsors technical research. Promotes cooperation and the exchange of information among members.
Library Subject: food industry
Library Type: reference
Formerly: European Chips and Snacks Association
Publication: Magazine
Publication title: The Snacks Magazine. Advertisements.
Meetings/Conventions: Snackex - biennial trade show - Exhibits. Barcelona Spain

European Society for Animal Cell Technology
ESACT

PO Box 1723, Porton, Salisbury, SP4 0PL, England, UK
Tel: 44 1980 610405
Fax: 44 1980 610405
Email: jbgriffiths@compuserve.com
Website: http://www.esact.org
Founded: 1976
Members: 350
Staff: 9
Contact: Dr. J. B. Griffiths
Fee: £1
Membership Type: full and associate outside of Europe
Description: European and non-European scientists in 27 countries with a common interest in the application of animal cells for the generation of useful products and all areas of activity impinging on that operation. Aims to promote the communication of experiences among European investigators in basic and applied research and production whose work has a bearing on the large-scale production of animal cells. Areas of investigation include: development of new cell substrates; technology of large-scale animal cell culture; production, processing, characterization, and quantification of materials produced by using animal cells as substrates or as agents of conversion, tissue engineering and cell/gene therapy.
Publication title: Animal Cell Technology: From Target to Market
Second publication: Proceedings

Publication title: Animal Cell Technology: Products from Cells, Cells as Products
Meetings/Conventions: Animal Cell Technology Meets Genomics - biennial conference - Exhibits. Granada Spain

European Society for Cognitive Psychology
ESCP

c/o John Towse
Dept. of Psychology, Lancaster University, Bailrigg, Lancaster, LA1 4YF, England, UK
Email: andre.vandierendonck@rug.ac.be
Website: http://www.escop.org
Founded: 1985
Members: 512
Contact: Cesare Cornoldi, Pres.
Fee: £300
Membership Type: full, associate
Description: Stimulates research within the field of Cognitive Psychology and related subjects, particularly with respect to collaboration and exchange of information between researchers in different European countries.
Publication: Journal
Publication title: European Journal of Cognitive Psychology. Advertisements.
Meetings/Conventions: - biennial conference

European Society for Communicative Psychotherapy

c/o The School of Psychotherapy and Counselling
Regent's College, Inner Cir., Regent's Park, London, NW1 4NS, England, UK
Tel: 44 20 78477584
Fax: 44 20 78477446
Email: info@escp.org
Website: http://www.escp.org
Description: Psychiatrists and psychotherapists in Europe.

European Society for Developmental Psychology
ESDP

Loughborough University, Brighton, LE11 3TU, England, UK
Tel: 44 1509 223037
Fax: 44 1509 223940
Email: m.c.hewitt1@lboro.ac.uk
Website: http://devpsy.lboro.ac.uk/eurodev/
Founded: 1994
Description: Advances education in developmental psychology for the public benefit; supports or conducts relevant research in the European context.

European Society for Laser Aesthetic Surgery
ESLAS

23 Banbury Rd., Oxford, OX2 6NX, England, UK
Tel: 44 1865 244421
Fax: 44 1865 244421
Email: secretary@eslas.com
Website: http://www.eslas.com/
Description: Promotes instruction, research and exchange of information related to the use of light and lasers for application in plastic and aesthetic surgery.

European Society for Movement Analysis in Adults and Children
ESMAC

Nuffield Orthopaedic Centre, Windmill Rd., Headington, OX3 7LD, England, UK
Tel: 44 1865 227609
Fax: 44 1865 227943
Email: tim.theologis@noc.anglox.nhs.uk
Website: http://www.esmac.org
Founded: 1992
Members: 97
Contact: Tim Theologis, Sec.-Treas.
Fee: £60
Membership Type: ordinary
Fee: £25
Description: Orthopedists and other health care professionals, researchers, and scientists with an interest in human gait and posture and their impact on overall health. Works to advance scientific knowledge in the field of movement analysis; promotes continuing professional development of members. Facilitates communication and cooperation among members; conducts educational programs and courses.
Meetings/Conventions: - annual meeting Marseille France

European Society for Paediatric Endocrinology
ESPE

St. Bartholomew's Hospital, London, EC1A 7BE, England, UK
Tel: 44 20 76018468
Fax: 44 20 77262743
Email: research@eurospe.org
Website: http://www.eurospe.org
Founded: 1962
Description: Promotes research on paediatric endocrinology including metabolism, haematology, immunology, molecular biology, growth and development, nephrology, electrolytes and water metabolism.

European Society for Paediatric Infectious Diseases
ESPID

c/o Caroline Solway
Institute of Child Health, Education Centre, Royal Hospital for Children, Upper Maudlin St., Bristol, BS2 8BJ, England, UK
Email: espid-email@bristol.ac.uk
Website: http://www.e-luminaries.co.uk/espid/
Contact: Caroline Solway
Description: Promotes the exchange of information among individuals with special experience in the field of paediatric infectious diseases, as well as research and training in PID.
Publication: Proceedings
Meetings/Conventions: - annual meeting

European Society for Pediatric Endocrinology
ESPE

c/o Dr. Martin Savage
Division of Paediatric Endocrinology, St. Bartholomew's Hospital, London, EC1A 7BE, England, UK
Tel: 44 207 6018468
Email: secretariat@europe.org
Website: http://www.eurospe.org
Founded: 1961

Members: 450
Contact: Dr. Lorraine Greenwood, Sec.
Description: Pediatricians, medical practitioners, and scientific staff in 28 countries involved in research and clinical practice of pediatric endocrinology. Promotes discussion and collaboration in the field. Operates summer school for pediatric endocrinologists in training.
Publication title: Hormone Research
Publication title: Membership Directory
Meetings/Conventions: - annual conference - Exhibits.

European Society for Pigment Cell Research
ESPCR

St. George's Hospital Medical School, Cranmer Terrace, SW17 OR5, England, UK
Tel: 44 20 87255202
Fax: 44 20 87253326
Email: dbennett@sghms.ac.uk
Website: http://www.ulb.ac.be/medecine/loce/espcr.htm
Founded: 1985
Description: Promotes interdisciplinary research on the pigmentary system, including normal and pathological conditions.

European Society for Precision Engineering and Nanotechnology

Bldg 70, Cranfield University, Bedford, MK43 0AL, England, UK
Tel: 44 1234 754024
Email: info@euspen.org
Website: http://www.euspen.com/
Founded: 1998

European Society for Psychosocial Oncology
ESPO

Stanley House, Wilmslow Rd., Withington, M20 4BX, England, UK
Tel: 44 161 4463679
Fax: 44 161 4481655

European Society for Rural Sociology

c/o Centre for Rural Economy
University of Newscastle-upon-Tyne, Newcastle upon Tyne, NE1 7RU, England, UK
Tel: 44 191 2226460
Fax: 44 191 2226720
Email: christopher.ray@newcastle.ac.uk
Website: http://www.esrs.hu
Founded: 1957
Members: 300
Contact: Christopher Ray, Sec.
Description: Sociologists and other Individual interested in rural sociological issues. Promotes study of rural societies and development of strategies for insuring their continued viability. Facilitates communication among members; works to improve methods of rural sociological training and study; serves as a forum for discussion of issues affecting rural societies and their development.
Publication: Newsletter
Publication title: Rural Sociology News
Second publication: Journal
Publication title: Sociologia Ruralis
Meetings/Conventions: - annual board meeting

European Society for the History of Photography
ESHPH

Acorn House, 74-94 Cherry Orchard Rd., Croydon, CRO 6BA, England, UK
Tel: 44 208 6818339
Fax: 44 208 6811880
Founded: 1978
Members: 300
Staff: 1
Contact: Roy Green, Admin.
Description: Institutes, museums, and firms related to photography and its history. Examines the technical, scientific, social, and cultural aspects of photography; encourages the exchange of information and discussion of problems among members.
Library Type: reference
Publication: Magazine
Publication title: Photohistorica
Second publication: Magazine
Publication title: PhotoResearcher
Meetings/Conventions: - annual meeting

European Society for Toxicology In Vitro
ESTIV

Univ. of Surrey, Guildford, GU2 5XH, England, UK
Tel: 44 1483 259204
Fax: 44 1483 300374
Email: d.benford@surrey.ac.uk
Description: Promotes in vitro toxicology, scientifically and educationally.

European Society for Translation Studies
EST

c/o School of Languages and European Studies
Aston University, Birmingham, B4 7ET, England, UK
Tel: 44 121 3593611
Fax: 44 121 3596153
Email: c.schaeffner@aston.ac.uk
Website: http://est.utu.fi
Founded: 1992
Members: 250
Contact: Christina Schaeffner, Sec.Gen.
Fee: £25
Membership Type: ordinary
Fee: £25
Membership Type: ordinary
Description: Serves as a network for stimulating and coordinating research in translation and interpreting. Provides a forum for the exchange and dissemination of new ideas and insights in Translation Studies. Provides a center for information and know-how on issues of quality assessment and training in translation and interpreting. Provides a platform for the promotion of Translation Studies as an academic discipline.
Publication: Newsletter
Publication title: EST Newsletter
Meetings/Conventions: - triennial conference Lisbon Portugal

European Society for Vascular Surgery
ESVS

University of Bath, Rm. L2.27, Clavertown Down, Bath, BA2 7AY, England, UK
Tel: 44 1225 323770
Fax: 44 1225 323669
Email: s.needham@bath.ac.uk
Website: http://www.esvs.org
Founded: 1987
Contact: Michael Horrocks, Sec.Gen.
Fee: £75
Membership Type: ordinary
Description: Vascular surgeons and national vascular societies. Seeks to advance vascular surgical techniques; promotes continuing professional development among vascular surgeons. Serves as a clearinghouse on vascular surgery; facilitates exchange of information among members; sponsors research and educational programs.
Publication title: European Journal of Vascular and Endovascular Surgery
Meetings/Conventions: - annual meeting

European Society of Agricultural Engineers
EurAgEng

West End Rd., Silsoe, Bedford, MK45 4DU, England, UK
Tel: 44 1525 861096
Fax: 44 1525 861660
Email: secgen@eurageng.net
Website: http://www.eurageng.net
Founded: 1992
Members: 2200
Staff: 1
Contact: Michael Hurst, Sec.Gen.
Description: Agricultural engineers and agricultural engineering societies in Europe. Seeks to advance the study, teaching, and practice of agricultural engineering. Serves as a clearinghouse on agricultural engineering; conducts continuing professional development courses for members; represents the commercial and professional interests of agricultural engineers before European Union agencies.
Publication: Journal
Publication title: Biosystems Engineering. Advertisements.
Second publication: Newsletter
Meetings/Conventions: - biennial conference Leuven Belgium

European Society of Domestic Animal Reproduction
ESDAR

Univ. of Liverpool, Leahurst, L64 7TE, England, UK
Tel: 44 151 7946080
Fax: 44 151 7946082
Email: h.dobson@liv.ac.uk
Website: http://www.tzv.fal.de/esdar/
Description: Promotes education and research in domestic animal reproduction, especially for clinical aspects, biotechnology and physiology of reproduction.

European Society of Extracorporal Technology
EuroSECT

27 Tooley St, London, SE1 2PR, England, UK

European Society of Feline Medicine
ESFM

Taeselbury High St., Tisbury, Salisbury, SP3 6LD, England, UK
Tel: 44 870 7422278
Email: esfm@fabcats.org
Website: http://www.fabcats.org/esfm.html
Contact:
Fee: £70
Membership Type: individual in the United Kingdom (includes membership in the Feline Advisory Bureau)
Fee: £80
Membership Type: individual outside the United Kingdom (includes membership in the Feline Advisory Bureau)
Description: Veterinarians with an interest in feline medicine. Seeks to advance the medical treatment of cats; promotes continuing professional development of members. Facilitates exchange of information among veterinarians and researchers working in the field of feline medicine; sponsors educational courses.
Publication title: Journal of Feline Medicine and Surgery
Meetings/Conventions: - semiannual conference

European Society of Human Genetics

c/o Clinical Genetics Unit
Birmingham Women's Hospital, Birmingham, B15 2TG, England, UK
Tel: 44 121 6236830
Fax: 44 121 6236830
Email: eshg@eshg.org
Website: http://www.eshg.org
Founded: 1967
Contact: Ruth Cole, Admin.
Description: Clinicians, researchers, laboratory scientists, psychologists, bioethicists, nonmedical genetic counselors, and others involved in all disciplines of human genetics. Promotes research in basic and applied human and medical genetics
Publication: Journal
Publication title: European Journal of Human Genetics
Meetings/Conventions: European Human Genetics Conference - annual conference Birmingham UK

European Society of Regulatory Affairs
ESRA

7 Heron Quays, Marsh Wall, London, E14 4JB, England, UK
Tel: 44 207 5157673
Fax: 44 207 5157836
Email: esra@esra.org
Website: http://www.esra.org
Founded: 1985
Members: 2200
Staff: 7
Contact: Lynda Wight, Gen.Mgr.
Description: Professionals active in the field of regulatory affairs. Seeks to increase understanding of the affects of national and international manufacturing and trade regulations on business, with particular emphasis on the development and production of pharmaceutical products. Promotes professional advancement of members. Serves as a forum for the sharing of experience and knowledge among members; sponsors educational and training programs.

Publication: Journal
Publication title: ESRA Rapporteur. Advertisements.
Meetings/Conventions: - annual meeting Brussels Belgium

European Society of Thoracic Surgeons
ESTS

c/o ESTS Secretariat
PO Box 159, Stuttgart, Exeter, EX2 5SH, England, UK
Tel: 44 1392 662727
Fax: 44 1392 662900
Email: sue@ests.org.uk
Contact: Sue Hesford, Admin.Sec.
Description: Thoracic surgeons in Europe. Seeks to improve the study and practice of thoracic surgery.
Meetings/Conventions: - annual conference

European Society of Urogenital Radiology
ESUR

c/o Sameh K. Morcos, MD, Sec.-Treas.
Department of Diagnostic Radiology, Northern General Hospital, Herries Rd., Sheffield, S5 7AU, England, UK
Tel: 44 114 2434343
Fax: 44 114 2560472
Email: sameh.morcos@northngh-tr.trent.nhs.uk
Website: http://www.esur.org/
Contact: Nicolas Grenier, Pres.
Description: Promotes advancement of uro-genital imaging and intervention; stimulates the study of normal and abnormal kidney, urinary tract and genital organs with emphasis on integration of roentgenology, ultrasonography, computed tomography, magnetic resonance, nuclear medicine, and new imaging techniques as well as research on contrast media.

European Society of Veterinary Clinical Ethology
ESVCE

11 Cotebrook Dr., Upton, CH2 1RA, England, UK
Tel: 44 1244 377365
Fax: 44 1244 399228
Email: heath@vetethol.demon.co.uk
Website: http://www.esvce.org/
Founded: 1994
Contact: Sarah Heath, Pres.
Description: Promotes scientific progress in veterinary and comparative clinical ethology; furthers education in veterinary clinical ethology and behavior medicine, facilitates exchange of information.

European Sponsorship Consultants Association

Marash House, 2-5 Brook St., Tring, HP23 5ED, England, UK
Tel: 44 1442 826826
Fax: 44 1442 826826
Email: secretariat@sponsorship.org
Website: http://www.sponsorship.org
Founded: 1990
Members: 45
Staff: 1
Contact: Tony Rudge, Sec.Gen.
Fee: £500
Membership Type: full
Fee: £1200
Membership Type: role practitioner
Description: Consultancy companies who specialize in sponsorship consultancy and event management, audits and PR/promotions in

connection with sponsored events/activities/persons. An independent neutral and authoritative body comprising professional sponsorship consultants. Its aim is to set and maintain standards within the sponsorship industry and both to lobby on legislative and other matters relating to sponsorship as well as to act as a valuable independent reference point for current and first-time sponsors. Organizes a major international congress annually for the professionals in the sponsorship industry; conferences, seminars, educational meetings, and socials for its members; and educational/ training courses for students of universities/colleges and those from the commercial sector.
Publication: Directory
Publication title: Consultants Register
Publication title: Consumers' Guide
Meetings/Conventions: - annual conference

European Strategic Planning Federation
ESPLAF

c/o The Strategic Planning Society
17 Portland Pl., London, W1N 3AF, England, UK
Tel: 44 207 6367737
Fax: 44 171 3231692
Founded: 1976
Members: 9
Contact: Andre D'Olne, Chmn.
Description: European national planning societies. Furthers the principles and methods of strategic and corporate planning; encourages communication among national societies and the exchange of views and ideas.
Publication: Magazine
Publication title: Long Range Planning
Meetings/Conventions: - biennial meeting

European Study Group on Lysosomal Diseases
ESGLD

c/o Professor B. Winchester
Institute of Child Health, University of London, Biochemistry, Endocrinology and Metabolism Unit, 30 Guilford St., London, WC1N 1EH, England, UK
Tel: 44 20 79052114
Fax: 44 20 74046191
Email: b.winchester@ich.ucl.ac.uk
Website: http://www.technothesp.co.uk/esgld
Founded: 1978
Members: 90
Contact: Professor B. Winchester, Chairman
Fee: £30
Membership Type: laboratory
Description: Laboratories in 22 countries conducting research on lysosomal storage diseases. (Lysosomal storage diseases are hereditary disorders, resulting from defects in lysosomal enzymes or membrane components, characterized by accumulation of partially digested metabolites in tissues and excretion in urine.) Promotes research; encourages exchange of ideas and personnel among member laboratories.
Publication title: Register of Laboratories
Meetings/Conventions: - biennial workshop Prague Czech Republic

European Suzuki Association
ESA

Stour House, The Street, East Bergholt, Colchester, CO7 6TF, England, UK
Tel: 44 1206 299448
Fax: 44 1206 298490
Email: esc@stone-force9.co.uk
Founded: 1980
Members: 5800
Staff: 8
Contact: Dr. Birte Kelly
Description: Music teachers, specialized educators, parents, and interested individuals. Promotes musical education among children using the educational philosophy and ideas of Shinichi Suzuki, a Japanese musician. Methods include the mother tongue method which involves children learning music in the same way they learned their own native language. Conducts certification examinations for instructors.
Publication: Journal
Publication title: Journal. Advertisements.

European Templar Heritage Research Network
ETHRN

11 Dukes Rd., Totnes, TQ9 5YA, England, UK
Tel: 44 1803 868314
Fax: 44 1803 868377
Email: templartim@aol.com
Website: http://www.geocities.com/NapaValley/3511/kthome7.html
Description: Supports research into the authentic history of the Knights Templar era.

European Tourism Trade Fairs Association
ETTFA

PO Box 585, Richmond, TW9 1YQ, England, UK
Tel: 44 20 9399000
Email: secretariat@ettfa.org
Website: http://www.ettfa.org
Founded: 1992
Contact: Tom Nutley, Chairman
Description: Travel trade fairs. Seeks to enhance the quality and effectiveness of participation in travel trade fairs. Represents members before industrial organizations and the public; serves as a forum for the exchange of information among members.

European Tugowners Association
ETA

Docklands Business Centre, 10-16 Tiller Rd., London, E14 8PX, England, UK
Tel: 44 207 3455122
Fax: 44 207 3455722
Email: assocationservices1@compuserve.com
Members: 137
Contact: Mr. D.C. Randall
Description: Operators of towing vessels. Defends the rights of members; disseminates information.

European Union of Agrement
EUA

PO Box 195, Bucknalls Lane, Watford, WD25 9BA, England, UK
Tel: 44 1923 665300
Fax: 44 1923 665031

Email: mail@ueatc.com
Website: http://www.ueatc.com
Founded: 1960
Members: 18
Staff: 1
Contact: Joe Blaisdale, Gen.Sec.
Description: National organizations certifying procedure and product innovations in the construction field. Issues agrement certification which verifies the durability of materials and building techiques, purpose of construction, and safety. Promotes mutual recognition of agrement certification among member states.
Publication: Magazine
Publication title: UEATC Information

European Union of Dentists

62B Northgate, Regent's Park, London, NW8 7EH, England, UK
Tel: 44 207 5864056
Fax: 44 207 5864096
Founded: 1973
Members: 1000
Contact: Dr. Klaus Eicher
Description: Works to provide dental services to the socially and economically disadvantaged. Promotes solidarity and friendship among dentists of the EC.

European Union of Wholesale with Eggs, Egg-Products, Poultry and Game

89 Charterhouse St., 2nd Fl., London, EC1M 6HR, England, UK
Tel: 44 20 76083760
Fax: 44 20 76083860
Founded: 1959
Members: 10
Staff: 1
Contact: Mr. Jean-Yves Justeau, Pres.
Description: Those involved in the poultry and game business. Protects and defends the rights, functions, and professional interests of its members.

European Union of Women - British Section

Kersoe House, Kersoe, Worcester, WR10 3JD, England, UK
Tel: 44 1386 710 175
Fax: 44 1386 710176
Founded: 1953
Members: 4000
Contact: Frances Tubb, Sec.
Fee: £10
Description: Women affiliated with moderate and right wing political parties in Europe. Liaises with similar women's organizations to improve the status of women in politics. Provides a forum for exchange of ideas among members. Encourages women to involve themselves in national and local politics. Supports peace efforts worldwide. National Sections now exist in 21 European countries.
Publication title: Annual Commission Report. Advertisements.
Publication title: Gazette
Meetings/Conventions: Safeguarding Future Generations in Europe - annual general assembly

European Union Youth Orchestra
EUYO

65 Sloane St., London, SW1X 9SH, England, UK
Tel: 44 207 2357671
Fax: 44 207 2357370
Email: info@euyo.org.uk

Founded: 1976
Members: 140
Staff: 4
Contact: Joy Bryer, Sec.Gen.
Description: Musicians between the ages of 14 and 23 representing Belgium, Denmark, France, Germany, Greece, Italy, Luxembourg, Netherlands, Portugal, Republic of Ireland, Spain, Austria, Sweden, Finland, and the United Kingdom. Purpose is to promote orchestral music among young musicians and to help them launch their professional careers.
Formerly: European Community Youth Orchestra
Publication: Brochure
Publication title: Tour Brochure. Advertisements.
Meetings/Conventions: - annual meeting

European Venous Forum
EVF

St. Mary's Hospital, 10th Fl, QEQM Wing, London, W2 1NY, England, UK
Tel: 44 20 78861012
Fax: 44 20 78861022
Email: a.taft@ic.ac.uk
Founded: 2000
Description: Developes scientific knowledge, research, clinical expertise, training and education and aims to establish standards in the fields of venous disease; promotes collaboration between phlebological and vascular societies, health agencies and authorities at national and European levels.

European Veterinary Dental Society
EVDS

309 The Ridge, Hastings, TN34 2RA, England, UK
Tel: 44 1424 751595
Fax: 44 1424 756378
Email: pcooper@vetdent.softnet.co.uk
Website: http://www.vetdent.org
Founded: 1985
Description: Supports education in and promotion of clinical excellence in veterinary dentistry.

European Wound Management Association
EWMA

PO Box 864, London, SE1 8TT, England, UK
Tel: 44 207 8483496
Email: ewma@kcl.ac.uk
Website: http://www.ewma.org
Founded: 1991
Contact: Brian Gilchrist, Sec.
Fee: £15
Membership Type: individual
Description: Health care professionals, scientists, and pharmaceutical manufacturers with an interest in wound healing. Seeks to address clinical and scientific issues associated with wound healing, in areas including the native epidemiology, pathology, diagnosis, prevention, and management of wounds. Serves as a clearinghouse on wound healing; facilitates exchange of information among members; sponsors research and educational programs.
Publication: Journal
Publication title: EWMA Journal. Advertisements.
Meetings/Conventions: - annual conference Pisa Italy

Event Services Association

Centre Ct., 1301 Stratford Rd., Hall Green, Birmingham, B28 9HH, England, UK
Tel: 44 121 6937000
Fax: 44 121 6937100
Email: enq@tesa.org.uk
Website: http://www.tesa.org.uk
Founded: 1991
Members: 292
Staff: 6
Contact: Jim Winship
Description: Membership comprises both suppliers to the event industry and event organisers. Aims to work with other associations within the event industry to try and raise standards and increase safety measures. In particular, drawing up Codes of Practice to cover the different sectors of the industry e.g. safety, catering, marquees, seating, and staging. Where possible collaborates with other industry bodies and supports their guidelines/Codes where appropriate.
Publication: Magazine
Publication title: Event Organiser. Advertisements.
Meetings/Conventions: conference

Executives Association of Great Britain
EAGB

c/o David Britton
EAGB House, 5 Factory Yard, Wycombe End, Beaconsfield, HP9 1NA, England, UK
Tel: 44 1494 675940
Fax: 44 1494 677846
Email: info@eagb.co.uk
Website: http://www.eagb.co.uk
Contact: David Britton, Dir.Oper.
Description: Executives of businesses in the United Kingdom. Provides a forum for the exchange of information between members.
Publication title: Membership List. Advertisements.

Exeter Industrial Archaeology Group

Dept. of Economic History, Exeter University, Exeter, EX4 4RJ, England, UK
Tel: 44 1392 77911
Founded: 1969

Exmoor Horn Sheep Breeders Society

c/o Mrs. Yvonne Webber, Sec.
Holtom and Thomas, The Elms Office, Bishops Tawton, Barnstaple, EX32 OEJ, England, UK
Tel: 44 1271 326900
Fax: 44 1271 326692
Email: holtom.thomas@btinternet.com
Website: http://www.exmoor.org.uk/exmoorhorn.htm
Founded: 1957
Members: 180
Staff: 1
Contact: Ms. Yvonne Webber
Description: Seeks to promote improvement of sheep breeding.

Experimental Psychology Society
EPS

Earley Gate, Whiteknights, Reading, RG6 6AL, England, UK
Tel: 44 118 9875123
Fax: 44 118 9314404
Email: e.a.gaffan@reading.ac.uk

Website: http://www.eps.ac.uk
Founded: 1946
Description: Furthers scientific enquiry within the field of psychology and cognate subjects; disseminates information and educational material made available as a consequence of psychological research.

Exploring Parenthood
EP

4 Ivory Pl., 20a Treadgold St., London, W11 4BP, England, UK
Tel: 44 171 2216681
Fax: 44 171 2215501
Email: parenthd@itl.net
Founded: 1982
Contact: Julie Shorrock, Chief Exec.
Fee: £18
Description: Provides professional support and advice to parents through a free telephone advice line, publications, and special projects exploring parenthood. Offers training programs for professionals working with parents and families.
Publication title: Exploring Parenthood Factsheets
Second publication: Reports

Export Group for the Constructional Industries

c/o Construction House
56-64 Leonard St., London, EC2A 4JX, England, UK
Tel: 44 207 6085145
Fax: 44 207 6085146
Email: harpej@construct-confed.co.uk
Founded: 1940
Members: 18
Staff: 2
Contact: Alick Goldsmith, Dir.
Description: British construction and contracting companies working internationally. Promotes the execution by members of building, engineering or civil engineering projects outside the United Kingdom. The group is regarded by Government, and by similar associations overseas, as the representative organisation of British project contractors operating in international markets.

Factors and Discounters Association

2nd Floor, Boston House, The Little Green, Richmond, TW9 1QE, England, UK
Tel: 44 208 3329955
Fax: 44 208 3322585
Email: robin.clarke@factors.org.uk
Website: http://www.factors.org.uk
Founded: 1976
Members: 40
Staff: 5
Contact: Robin Clarke, CEO
Description: Brokers, business agents, and factors in the United Kingdom. Promotes and protects members' interests in the fields of factoring and invoice discounting. Conducts educational and research programs. Maintains a code of conduct; fosters the advancement of knowledge and experience; awards diplomas to students. Disseminates information; compiles statistics.
Formerly: Association of British Factors and Discounters

Faculty of Church Music

27 Sutton Park, Blunsdon, Swindon, SN26 7BB, England, UK
Tel: 44 181 6750180
Fax: 44 181 6750180
Founded: 1956

Members: 100
Contact: Rev. G. Gleed
Description: Those involved with music and worship and students of theology. Graded examinations in church music to postgraduate level and diploma in Bible reading. Some tuition available. Courses are aimed at mature students and are arranged individually within a broad syllabus. Awards are made by Central School of Religion.

Faculty of Dental Surgery
FDS

c/o The Royal College of Surgeons of England
35-43 Lincoln's Inn Fields, London, WC2A 3PE, England, UK
Tel: 44 20 78696810
Fax: 44 20 78696816
Email: fds@rcseng.ac.uk
Website: http://www.rcseng.ac.uk/dental/fds
Founded: 1947
Members: 2500
Staff: 20
Contact: Mrs. Mumtaz Rehman, Courses Admin.
Meetings/Conventions: conference

Faculty of Homeopathy

c/o British Homeopathic Association
15 Clerkenwell Close, London, EC1R 0AA, England, UK
Tel: 44 20 75667800
Fax: 44 20 75667815
Email: info@trusthomeopathy.org
Website: http://www.trusthomeopathy.org
Founded: 1950
Members: 1200
Staff: 12
Contact: Mrs. Sally Penrose, Hd. of Marketing
Fee: £80
Membership Type: full, licensed
Description: Professional body responsible for regulating the education, training and practice of homeopathy by medically qualified doctors, veterinary surgeons, dentists, pharmacists and other statutorily registered health care professionals. Accredited post-graduate training courses lead to the LFHom qualification and, for doctors and vets, medical/veterinary membership of the faculty.
Library Subject: homeopathic references
Library Type: reference
Publication: Journal
Publication title: Homeopathy. Advertisements.
Meetings/Conventions: British Homeopathic Congress - biennial congress

Faculty of Occupational Medicine

c/o Royal College of Physicians
6 St. Andrews Pl., Regent's Park, London, NW1 4LB, England, UK
Tel: 44 207 3175890
Fax: 44 207 3175899
Website: http://www.facoccmed.ac.uk/
Contact: Dr. W.J. Gunnyeon, Pres.

Faculty of Public Health Medicine

4 St Andrew's Pl., London, NW1 4LB, England, UK
Tel: 44 20 79350243
Fax: 44 20 72246973
Email: enquiries@fphm.org.uk
Website: http://www.fphm.org.uk
Founded: 1972

Members: 3000
Staff: 20
Contact: Paul Scourfield, Ch.Exec.
Description: Principally trainees and consultants in public health medicine. To promote, for the public benefit, the advancement of education in the field of public health medicine; and to develop public health medicine with a view to maintaining the highest possible standards of professional competence and practice, and act as an authoritative body for the purpose of consultation in matters of education or public interest concerning public health medicine.
Publication: Journal
Publication title: Journal of Public Health Medicine
Publication title: ph.com
Meetings/Conventions: Public Health - annual conference

Faculty of Secretaries and Administrators
15 Church St., Godalming, GU7 1EL, England, UK
Tel: 44 1483 425144
Fax: 44 1483 454213
Founded: 1930
Members: 500
Contact: W. Whitehouse
Description: Company secretaries and administrators.
Publication: Newsletter

Fair Organ Preservation Society
FOPS
43 Woolmans, Fullers Slade, Milton Keynes, MK11 2BA, England, UK
Tel: 44 1908 263717
Fax: 44 1908 263717
Email: memsec@fops.org
Website: http://www.fops.org
Founded: 1958
Members: 900
Contact: John Page, Membership Sec.
Fee: £14
Membership Type: outside UK
Fee: £10
Description: The promotion and encouragement of all forms of interest in and the preservation of fairground organs and mechanical musical instruments. Persons in 15 countries interested in fair organs, street organs, band organs, and dance organs united to promote interest in mechanical musical instruments. Makes available technical assistance to members.
Library Type: reference
Publication: Journal
Publication title: The Key Frame. Advertisements.
Publication title: Pocket Book of Coming Events
Meetings/Conventions: - annual meeting - Exhibits.

Fair Play for Children Association
35 Lyon St., Bognor Regis, PO21 1BW, England, UK
Tel: 44 124 3869922
Fax: 44 1243 869922
Email: fairplay@arunet.co.uk
Website: http://www.arunet.co.uk/fairplay/
Founded: 1972
Members: 450
Staff: 5
Contact: Jan Cosgrove, Natl. Organizer
Fee: £16
Membership Type: uk full
Fee: £30

Membership Type: international individual
Description: Campaigns for the child's right to play.
Library Subject: play rights, child development, childcare
Library Type: open to the public
Publication: Magazine
Publication title: Play Action. Advertisements.

Family Education Trust
The Mezzanine, Elizabeth House, 39 York Rd., London, SE1 7NQ, England, UK
Tel: 44 20 74015480
Fax: 44 20 74015471
Email: robert@ukfamily.org.uk
Website: http://www.famyouth.org.uk
Founded: 1971
Staff: 3
Contact: Robert Whelan, Dir.
Fee: £10
Description: Psychologists, psychiatrists, and other mental health professionals with an interest in dysfunctional families. Promotes improved understanding of family social and sexual dynamics. Conducts research into the social, psychological, and cultural consequences of sexual behavior and family breakdown.
Publication: Newsletter
Publication title: Family Bulletin
Second publication: Booklets
Meetings/Conventions: - annual conference

Family Farmers' Association
c/o Mrs. Pippa Woods, Chm.
Osborne Newton, Aveton Gifford, Kingsbridge, TQ7 4PE, England, UK
Tel: 44 1548 852794
Fax: 44 1548 852794
Founded: 1979
Members: 200
Contact: Mrs. Pippa Woods, Chm.
Fee: £37
Membership Type: standard
Description: Lobbies for survival of family farms.
Publication: Newsletter

Family Planning Association
FPA
2-12 Pentonville Rd., London, N1 9FP, England, UK
Tel: 44 20 78375432
Fax: 44 20 78373042
Email: melissad@fpa.org.uk
Website: http://www.fpa.org.uk
Founded: 1930
Description: Improves the sexual health and reproductive rights of all people throughout the UK.

Family Service Units
FSU
207 Old Marylebone Rd., London, NW1 5QP, England, UK
Tel: 44 207 4025175
Fax: 44 207 7241829
Email: centraloffice@fsu.org.uk
Website: http://www.fsu.org.uk
Founded: 1948

Staff: 300
Contact: Phillippa Gitlin, Chief Exec.
Description: Promotes the welfare of families and communities in some of the UK's most disadvantaged areas. Offers a 'one stop' model, providing family support services such as parenting skills, counselling, family case work, children's groups, etc. Also seeks to address the wider problems of poverty, injustice, and discrimination by delivering services such as advice and advocacy on welfare benefits, housing, and immigration. Actively encourages the development of self-help and local action groups which further enable people to take control for themselves. Studies the forces that lead to the disintegration of family and community life and disseminates information to improve social policy and practices. Frequently participates in conferences, seminars, and workshops on social policy and family issues.
Library Type: reference
Publication title: Annual Review
Meetings/Conventions: - annual meeting

Family Welfare Association
FWA

501-505 Kingsland Rd., Dalston, London, E8 4AU, England, UK
Tel: 44 207 2546251
Fax: 44 207 2495443
Contact: Lynne Berry, Dir.
Description: Organizations in the United Kingdom including national charities, adoption societies, almshouses, citizens' advice bureaus, councils for voluntary service, community councils, federations of community associations and foundations, legal advice centers, local associations for the hearing impaired and physically disabled, voluntary organizations for the blind, and volunteer bureaus. Coordinates members' effoerts to improve available social services in the United Kingdom.
Publication: Directory
Publication title: Charities Digest. Advertisements.

Fan Circle International
FCI

Cronk-y-Voddy, 21 Rectory Rd., Coltishall, Norwich, NR12 7HF, England, UK
Tel: 44 1603 737270
Email: jdm@coltishall.freeserve.co.uk
Website: http://www.fancircleinternational.org
Founded: 1975
Members: 400
Contact: Helen Marr, Treas.
Fee: £44
Description: Museums, art galleries, auction houses, and private collectors in 20 countries with an artistic, historical, or general interest in fans. Promotes interest in and knowledge of the fan in all aspects. Sponsors competitions and bestows awards. Organizes exhibitions; offers advice on preservation and repairs; arranges contacts among members for those traveling and wishing to view collections. Compiles statistics.
Library Subject: fans, related events
Library Type: reference
Publication: Bulletin
Publication title: Fans. Advertisements.
Meetings/Conventions: - periodic lecture - Exhibits.

Farm Retail Association

The Greenhouse, PO Box 575, Southampton, SO15 7BZ, England, UK
Tel: 44 23 80362150
Email: fra@farmshopping.com
Website: http://www.farmshopping.com
Founded: 1979
Members: 400
Staff: 2
Contact: Rita Exner, Exec.Sec.
Description: Represents farmers and growers who sell direct to the public through Pick-Your-Own, farmers' markets, farm shops, box-schemes, home delivery, mail order, Internet sales, and farmhouse catering. Promotes the experience of buying from the farm, or the farmer, including related festivals and entertainments (e.g., maize mazes). Develops quality and consistency of service and produce of members through best practice and accreditation. Also provides business development support and training for members. Aims to raise awareness of local foods, farm fresh produce, and added-value products.
Publication title: Harvet Times
Meetings/Conventions: - annual conference

Farmers' World Network
FWN

Arthur Rank Centre, National Agricultural Centre, Stoneleigh, CV8 2LZ, England, UK
Tel: 44 2476 696969
Fax: 44 2476 414808
Email: fwn@fwn.org.uk
Website: http://www.fwn.org.uk
Founded: 1984
Members: 1200
Staff: 5
Contact: Adrian Friggens, Exec.Dir.
Fee: £20
Description: Aims to widen the debate on the future of world food production and the associated questions of poverty and hunger.
Library Type: open to the public
Publication: Bulletin
Publication title: Landmark, Agri-Repere. Advertisements.

Farriers' Company

19 Queen St., Chipperfield, Kings Langley, WD4 9BT, England, UK
Tel: 44 1923 260747
Fax: 44 1923 261677
Email: theclerk@wcf.org.uk
Website: http://www.wcf.org.uk
Founded: 1356
Members: 375
Contact: Mrs. C.C. Clifford, Clerk
Description: Farriers.

Fauna and Flora International
FFI

Great Eastern House, Tenison Rd., Cambridge, CB1 2TT, England, UK
Tel: 44 1223 571000
Fax: 44 1223 461481
Email: info@fauna-flora.org
Website: http://www.fauna-flora.org
Founded: 1903
Members: 4000

Staff: 20
Contact: Mark Rose, Dir.
Description: Individuals, libraries, universities, natural history societies, other wildlife conservation organizations, and governmental departments responsible for wildlife, national parks, and tourism in 80 countries. Purpose is to prevent the extinction of species of wild animals and plants by promoting the conservation of wildlife, the establishment of new national parks, the enactment and enforcement of laws to protect wildlife, and the education of governments and individuals in the value of world wildlife as a non-renewable natural resource. Conducts research relating to endangered species.
Library Subject: conservation
Library Type: not open to the public
Formerly: Fauna and Flora Preservation Society
Publication: Newsletter
Publication title: Fauna and Flora News
Publication title: Good Bulb Guide
Meetings/Conventions: - annual conference - Exhibits. London UK

Fawcett Society

1-3 Berry St., London, EC1V 0AA, England, UK
Tel: 44 207 2532598
Fax: 44 207 2532599
Email: info@fawcettsociety.org.uk
Website: http://www.fawcettsociety.org.uk
Founded: 1866
Members: 3000
Staff: 6
Contact: Becky Gill, Officer
Fee: £15
Membership Type: standard
Fee: £8
Membership Type: concessionary
Description: Campaigns for equality between men and women; seeks to abolish all sex discrimination. Strives for new attitudes towards gender relationships in society. Conducts lobbying activities including equal value, equal pay, and equal partners campaign.
Library Type: open to the public
Formerly: London SOC of Obtaining Political Rights for Women
Publication: Newsletter
Publication title: Towards Equality
Meetings/Conventions: - annual meeting London UK

Federated Union of Managerial and Professional Officers

c/o Terminus House
The High, Harlow, CM20 1TZ, England, UK
Tel: 44 1279 434444
Fax: 44 1279 451176
Founded: 1986
Members: 14000
Staff: 40
Contact: Rob Newland, Act.Gen.Mgr.
Description: Senior officers and allied professionals from local government and public health services. Gives support to members with employment-related problems.
Publication title: Professional Officer
Meetings/Conventions: - semiannual conference

Federation of American Women's Clubs Overseas
FAWCO

22 Ember Lane, Esher, Surrey, KT10 8EP, England, UK
Tel: 44 208 2240901
Fax: 44 208 8731402
Email: president@fawco.org
Website: http://www.fawco.org
Founded: 1931
Members: 78
Contact: Pamela E. Dahlgren, Pres.
Description: American women's clubs or associations based in Europe, the Near East, the Far East, U.S.A. and Africa; represents over 17,000 individuals. Serves as a link among American women abroad and promotes better understanding between the U.S.A. and other nations. Is an NGO with consultative status with the ECOSOC. Studies cultural heritage, multi- and bilingualism, citizenship status including legislation pertaining to Americans married to nationals of other countries, and methods of improving voter registration for Americans abroad. Conducts research and educational programs on culture shock and women's legal status abroad; compiles statistics. Maintains a relief fund, fosters association with FAWCO Foundation, which bestows scholarship-merit awards and development grants.
Formerly: Federation of American Women's Clubs in Europe
Publication title: Conference Reports
Publication title: Handbook for the American Family Abroad
Meetings/Conventions: - periodic regional meeting

Federation of Bakers

6 Catharine St., London, WC2B 5JW, England, UK
Tel: 44 207 4207190
Fax: 44 207 3970542
Email: info@bakersfederation.org.uk
Website: http://www.bakersfederation.org.uk
Founded: 1942
Members: 70
Staff: 5
Contact: John White, Dir.
Description: Large scale plant bakers - predominantly wholesale. To promote and maintain the economic stability of the bread industry; to represent members' interests within the United Kingdom and Europe in areas of legislation, media and in co-operation with other organisations and associations; to provide a forum for members to pursue common interests and resolve problems; to provide statistics as required by members.
Publication: Annual Report
Publication title: Annual Report
Second publication: Booklet
Publication title: Bread is Good for You
Meetings/Conventions: - annual meeting

Federation of British Artists
FBA

17 Carlton House Terr., London, SW1Y 5BD, England, UK
Tel: 44 207 9306844
Fax: 44 207 8397830
Email: info@mallgalleries.com
Website: http://www.mallgalleries.org.uk
Founded: 1960
Members: 600
Staff: 8
Contact: John Sayers
Description: Artists, societies, and patrons of the arts. Promotes educational activities that increase public awareness of art. Assists

individual artists and art societies with showings and sale of art works. Operates the Mall Galleries in London, England, where each member society holds its annual exhibition. Also runs a commissioning service.
Publication: Catalog. Advertisements.
Meetings/Conventions: - periodic lecture

Federation of British Conservatoires

c/o Royal College of Music
Birmingham Conservatoire, Paradise Circus, Birmingham, B3 3HG, England, UK
Tel: 44 207 5914363
Fax: 44 207 5897740
Contact: Dr. Janet Kitterman, Chm.
Description: Principals of British conservatories.
Formerly: Committee of Principals of Conservatoires

Federation of British Engineers' Tool Manufacturers

c/o Institute of Spring Technology
Henry St., Sheffield, S3 7EQ, England, UK
Tel: 44 114 2789143
Fax: 44 114 2726344
Email: light.trades@virgin.net
Website: http://www.britishtools.com
Founded: 1943
Members: 78
Staff: 9
Contact: J.R. Markham, Sec.Gen.
Description: Servicing trade associations in the UK and EC.
Publication: Directory
Publication title: British Tools Directory

Federation of British Hand Tool Manufacturers FBHTM

Light Trades House, 3 Melbourne Ave., Sheffield, S10 2QJ, England, UK
Tel: 44 114 2663084
Fax: 44 114 2670910
Email: jrm@lighttradeshouse.co.uk
Website: http://www.britishtools.com
Members: 48
Staff: 9
Contact: Mike Ponikowski, Sec.Gen.
Description: British manufacturers of hand and engineering tools. Promotes the tool industry.
Publication: Directory
Publication title: British Tools

Federation of British Port Wholesale Fish Merchants Association

Wharncliffe Rd., Fish Docks, Grimsby, DN31 3QJ, England, UK
Tel: 44 1472 350022
Fax: 44 1472 240838
Email: ceqgrimsbey@fishmerchants.co.uk
Founded: 1928
Members: 300
Contact: Stephen J. Norton, Chm.
Description: Fish merchants/processors. A federation of trade associations within the fish industry which looks after matters of legal importance to the membership, particularly Department for Environment, Food & Rural Affairs.

Federation of Building Specialist Contractors

Construction House, 56/64 Leonard St., London, EC2A 4JX, England, UK
Tel: 44 207 6085080
Fax: 44 207 6085081
Email: enquiries@fbsc.org.uk
Founded: 1970
Members: 200
Staff: 3
Contact: Stephen Kennefick, Company Sec.
Description: Represents building specialists in the United Kingdom construction industry.

Federation of Children's Book Groups

2 Bridge Wood View, Horsforth, Leeds, LS18 5PE, England, UK
Tel: 44 113 2588910
Fax: 44 113 2588920
Email: info@fcbg.org.uk
Website: http://www.fcbg.org.uk
Founded: 1968
Members: 500
Contact: Sinead Kromer
Description: Parents, teachers, librarians, publishers and schools. Fosters the education of children by the provision of books, National Share-a-Story Month, and local group events.
Publication: Newsletter
Meetings/Conventions: - annual conference - Exhibits.

Federation of City Farms and Community Gardens

c/o The Green House
Hereford St., Bedminster, Bristol, BS3 4NA, England, UK
Tel: 44 117 9231800
Fax: 44 117 9231900
Email: admin@farmgarden.org.uk
Website: http://www.farmgarden.org.uk
Founded: 1980
Members: 210
Staff: 12
Contact: Jeremy Iles, Dir.
Description: Network organization coordinating community farm and garden groups in city environments throughout the UK. Promotes and supports sustainable regeneration through community managed farming and gardening.
Library Subject: City farming, environmental issues, and gardening
Library Type: reference
Formerly: National Federation of City Farms
Publication title: City Farms List
Second publication: Newsletter
Publication title: Growing Places
Meetings/Conventions: - annual conference - Exhibits.

Federation of Clothing Designers and Executives

56 Eden Park Ave., Beckenham, BR3 3HW, England, UK
Tel: 44 208 6505429
Fax: 44 208 6630073
Founded: 1935
Members: 287
Contact: M.J. Watts, Hon. Gen. Sec.
Description: Members are clothing designers, fashion designers, stylists, pattern technologists, clothing company executives, senior production controllers, technicians, senior quality controllers. Affiliate members are senior clothing college lecturers,. clothing technicians in allied trades, after two years total involvement they can apply for membership. The four Associations are based in London, Manchester

and Midlands. From September to June, Associations hold monthly meetings connected to clothing manufacture and open to guests of members. The Annual Convention includes a practical Conference for members and non members. There are other social functions during the year.
Publication: Newsletter
Second publication: Yearbook
Meetings/Conventions: - annual seminar

Federation of Cocoa Commerce
Cannon Bridge House, 1 Cousin Lane, London, EC4R 3XX, England, UK
Tel: 44 207 3792884
Fax: 44 207 3792389
Email: fcc@liffc.com
Website: http://www.cocoafederation.com
Founded: 1929
Members: 102
Staff: 2
Contact: Philip M. Sigley, Chief Exec.
Description: Aims to protect and promote interests of those engaged in physical cocoa trade.
Publication title: Cocoa News

Federation of Commodity Associations
FCA
c/o Robert Stein
Gafta House, 6 Chapel Pl., Rivington St., London, EC2A 3SH, England, UK
Tel: 44 207 8149666
Fax: 44 207 8148383
Email: fca@gafta.demon.co.uk
Founded: 1943
Members: 58
Staff: 16
Contact: Pamela Kirby Johnson, Sec.
Fee: £600
Membership Type: commodity associations
Description: Commodity trade associations; companies, firms, or individual traders in commodities. Promotes and protects the commercial interests of members. Seeks to establish an effective liaison between members and the European Commission through the exchange of information and the coordination of problem-solving procedures. Offers information service on current and projected legislation. Maintains close links with educational establishments.
Library Type: reference
Publication: Book
Publication title: Book of Rules

Federation of Communication Services
FCS
Burnhill Business Centre, Provident House, Burrell Row, High St., Beckenham, BR3 1AT, England, UK
Tel: 44 20 2496363
Fax: 44 87 1205927
Email: fcs@fcs.org.uk
Website: http://www.fcs.org.uk
Founded: 1981
Members: 150
Staff: 5
Contact: Jacqui Brookes, CEO
Description: Representative body for the mobile and telecommunication services industry including network operators,

service providers, equipment manufacturers and suppliers, dealers in GSM, PMR, Public Access Mobile Radio-Tetra, paging, fixed telephony, and all supporting businesses.
Library Type: not open to the public
Publication: Bulletin
Publication title: FCS Bulletin. Advertisements.
Meetings/Conventions: PMR in the Future - annual conference - Exhibits.

Federation of Drum Reconditioners
Deans Rough Farm, Lower Withington, Macclesfield, SK11 9DF, England, UK
Founded: 1951
Members: 26
Staff: 1
Contact: B.E. Chesworth
Description: Companies operating a full reconditioning process according to Code of Practice, and a registered to BS5750.

Federation of Engine Re-Manufacturers
FER
59 Mewstone Ave., Wembury, Plymouth, PL9 0JT, England, UK
Tel: 44 1752 863681
Fax: 44 1752 863682
Email: ferm@btintenet.com
Website: http://www.fer.co.uk/home.htm
Founded: 1937
Members: 200
Staff: 1
Contact: Brian Ludford, Sec.
Fee: £280
Description: Promotes the reconstruction of gasoline and diesel engines and the sale and exchange of such engines. Sponsors technical lectures and work visits.
Publication: Journal
Publication title: Fer News. Advertisements.
Meetings/Conventions: - annual conference - Exhibits.

Federation of Engineering Design Companies
13 High Rd., Rayleigh, SS6 7SA, England, UK
Tel: 44 1268 772996
Fax: 44 1268 772996
Email: gthomas@fedc.org.uk
Website: http://www.fedc.org.uk
Founded: 1955
Members: 66
Staff: 1
Contact: W.H. Mitchell, Gen.Mgr.
Fee: £650
Membership Type: full
Description: Subcontract design and technical publications offices. Represents the interests of companies involved in engineering design, technical publications, information services and technical recruitment in the UK.
Publication: Brochure
Publication title: Federation of Engineering Design Companies Ltd.
Second publication: Membership Directory

Federation of Entertainment Unions
c/o Steve Harris
1 Highfield, Twyford, Winchester, SO21 1QR, England, UK
Tel: 44 1962 713134
Fax: 44 1962 713134

Email: harris@interalpha.co.uk
Founded: 1990
Staff: 1
Contact: Steve Harris, Sec.
Description: Entertainers, broadcasters, musicians, writers, members of the media. Collective body of six affiliated trade unions, representing the interests of its members in the broadcasting and entertainment industries.

Federation of Environmental Trade Associations

Henley Rd., Medmenham, Marlow, SL7 2ER, England, UK
Tel: 44 1491 578674
Fax: 44 1491 575024
Email: info@feta.co.uk
Website: http://www.feta.co.uk
Founded: 1977
Members: 250
Staff: 6
Contact: C. Sloan
Description: Members are manufacturers, distributors and contractors serving the heating, ventilating, air conditioning, refrigeration, chimney and flues industries. Serves the interests of the heating, ventilating, air conditioning and refrigeration industries and the users of HVACR equipment

Federation of European Chemical Societies - England
FECS

c/o Royal Society of Chemistry
Burlington House, Piccadilly, London, W1J 0BA, England, UK
Tel: 44 20 74403303
Fax: 44 20 74378883
Email: mcewane@rsc.org
Website: http://www.chemsoc.org/fecs
Founded: 1970
Members: 40
Contact: Evelyn K. McEwan, Sec.Gen.
Description: National societies throughout Europe representing 200,000 chemists. Fosters cooperation among member societies. Encourages discussion in all fields of chemistry.
Meetings/Conventions: - annual general assembly

Federation of European Employers

Adam House, 7-10 Adam St., The Strand, London, WC2N 6AA, England, UK
Tel: 44 207 5209264
Fax: 44 1359 269900
Email: robin.charter@fedee.com
Website: http://www.fedee.com/index.shtml
Founded: 1989
Contact: Robin Chafer, Sec.Gen.
Description: Represents the interests of employers in Europe.

Federation of European Pedestrian Associations
FEPA

31-33 Bondway, London, SW18 1SJ, England, UK
Tel: 44 20 78208208
Email: w.de.jong@3vo.nl
Founded: 1992
Members: 10
Staff: 3
Contact: Mr. B. Plowden, Pres.

Description: Promotes the rights of pedestrians. Works to insure that pedestrians and motorized traffic share roadways in a safe and equitable manner.
Library Subject: traffic safety, pedestrians, city buildings
Library Type: not open to the public
Meetings/Conventions: - annual general assembly

Federation of European Societies of Plant Physiology
FESPP

School of Biological Sciences, University of Bristol, Woodland Rd., Bristol, BS8 1UG, England, UK
Tel: 44 117 9289757
Fax: 44 117 3316771
Email: mike.jackson@bristol.ac.uk
Website: http://www.fespp.org/
Founded: 1978
Description: Advances science of plant physiology in Europe; establishes cooperation among member societies and individuals.

Federation of Image Consultants

Mallory House, 27 Verulam Rd., St. Albans, AL3 4DG, England, UK
Tel: 44 7010 701018
Fax: 44 7010 701018
Email: info@tfic.org.uk
Website: http://www.tfic.org.uk/index.html
Founded: 1988
Members: 200
Contact: Polly Holman, Pres.
Fee: £75
Membership Type: fellow
Fee: £75
Membership Type: member
Description: Represents professionals working or specialising in the field of personal image development. Sets and maintains standards for the profession. Supports and promotes consultants. Acts as a media source for the press and an information source for the general public.
Library Subject: image consultancy
Library Type: by appointment only

Federation of Managerial Professional and General Associations

c/o Tavistock House
Tavistock Sq., London, WC1H 9JP, England, UK
Tel: 44 171 3836094
Members: 7
Contact: Chris Minta, Gen.Sec.
Description: Trades unions. Promotes the interests of members in the field of trade unions in UK and Europe.

Federation of Manufacturing Opticians

37-41 Bedford Row, London, WC1R 4JH, England, UK
Tel: 44 207 4058101
Fax: 44 207 8312797
Email: ofice@fmo.co.uk
Website: http://www.fmo.co.uk
Founded: 1917
Members: 164
Staff: 4
Contact: R. Wilshin

Description: Manufacturers, wholesalers and distributors of ophthalmic optical products. Aims to further the interests of its members.
Publication: Newsletter
Publication title: In Focus

Federation of Master Builders

c/o Gordon Fisher House
14-15 Great James St., London, WC1N 3DP, England, UK
Tel: 44 207 2427583
Fax: 44 207 4040296
Email: central@fmb.org.uk
Website: http://www.fmb.org.uk
Founded: 1941
Members: 15000
Staff: 58
Contact: Mr. I.P. Davis, Dir.Gen.
Description: Members may be self-employed, in partnership or limited companies. Principal responsibility is to organise, represent and promote the interests of employers in the building industry on a national basis. Its warranty scheme provides insurance-backed cover for the customer for a period of 2 years or 5 years on major structural alterations.
Library Subject: buildings & employment law
Library Type: open to the public
Publication title: BATJIC Working Rule Agreement
Second publication: Journal
Publication title: Masterbuilder

Federation of National Associations of Shipbrokers and Agents
FONASBA

3 St. Helen's Pl., London, EC3A 6EJ, England, UK
Tel: 44 20 76285559
Fax: 44 20 75887836
Email: fonasba@ics.org.uk
Website: http://www.fonasba.com
Founded: 1969
Members: 43
Staff: 2
Contact: J.C. Williams, General Mgr.
Description: National associations of shipbrokers and ship's agents united in promotion of fair and equitable practices within the profession. Seeks recognition and acceptance of the traditional role of shipbrokers and agents as intermediaries and advisers to ship owners and merchants. Coordinates efforts to improve, modernize, simplify, and standardize shipping contracts and documents. Cooperates with and represents members' interests before other national and international bodies, authorities, and organizations. Conducts lectures and conferences.
Meetings/Conventions: - annual meeting

Federation of Oils, Seeds, and Fats Associations

20 St. Dunstan's Hill, London, EC3R 8NQ, England, UK
Tel: 44 207 2835511
Fax: 44 207 6231310
Email: contact@fosfa.org
Website: http://www.fosfa.org
Founded: 1971
Members: 720
Staff: 10
Contact: S.R. Logan, Chief Exec.

Description: Trade association primarily involved with contacts for the international trade in oils and fats, oilseeds, and selected groundnuts.
Library Subject: trade
Library Type: not open to the public
Publication: Newsletter. Advertisements.
Meetings/Conventions: - annual dinner

Federation of Overseas Property Developers Agents and Consultants

St. Clare Business Park, Lacey House, Holly Rd., Hampton Hill, TW12 1QQ, England, UK
Tel: 44 20 89415588
Fax: 44 20 89410202
Email: info@fopdac.com
Website: http://www.fopdac.com
Founded: 1973
Members: 87
Staff: 12
Contact: Linda Travella, Chp.
Fee: £200
Membership Type: full, probationary, associate
Description: Overseas property agents, developers and consultants.

Federation of Petroleum Suppliers

3 Slaters Ct., Princess St., Knutsford, WA16 6BW, England, UK
Tel: 44 1565 631313
Fax: 44 1565 631314
Email: office@fpsonline.co.uk
Website: http://www.fpsonline.co.uk
Founded: 1979
Members: 280
Staff: 5
Contact: S. Hancock, Ch.Exec.
Fee: £415
Membership Type: company
Description: Distributors of petroleum products.
Publication: Journal
Publication title: Downstream. Advertisements.
Meetings/Conventions: - annual conference - Exhibits. Dublin Ireland

Federation of Piling Specialists

c/o Forum Court
83 Copers Cope Rd., Beckenham, BR3 1NR, England, UK
Tel: 44 20 86630947
Fax: 44 20 86630949
Email: fps@fps.org.uk
Website: http://www.fps.org.uk
Founded: 1964
Members: 18
Staff: 2
Contact: D. Jennings, Sec.
Description: Specialist contractors offering all types of foundation, earth retaining and soil improving techniques.

Federation of Plastering and Drywall Contractors

c/o Construction House
56/64 Leonard St., London, EC2A 4JX, England, UK
Tel: 44 207 6085092
Fax: 44 207 6085081
Email: admin@fpdc.org
Website: http://www.fpdc.org

Founded: 1942
Members: 250
Staff: 2
Contact: Emma Ayad, Dir.
Description: Plastering and drywall contractors.
Publication: Directory
Publication title: Spec Finish. Advertisements.

Federation of Private Residents' Associations

Enterprise House, 113-115 George Ln., South Woodford, London, E18 1AB, England, UK
Tel: 44 208 5308464
Fax: 44 208 9893153
Email: info@fpra.org.uk
Website: http://www.fpra.org.uk
Founded: 1972
Members: 3000
Staff: 2
Contact: Cheryl Francis, Adm.
Description: Residents' associations in England and UK. For those holding long leases on their properties or who have purchased the freehold. Offers assistance in setting up residents' associations; advice given on legal matters in connection with landlords, agents, purchase of freehold, maintenance of blocks of flats.
Library Type: not open to the public
Publication: Newsletter
Publication title: FPRA Newsletter
Meetings/Conventions: - annual general assembly

Federation of Professional Association

c/o Hayes Court
West Common Rd., Bromley, BR2 7AU, England, UK
Tel: 44 181 4627755
Fax: 44 181 3158234
Founded: 1971
Members: 45000
Staff: 17
Contact: Michael Murdoch, National Sec.
Description: Trade Union representing supervisory, administrative, managerial and professional staffs in the industries covered by the component associations.
Publication: Journal
Publication title: Union News. Advertisements.
Meetings/Conventions: - biennial conference

Federation of Recorded Music Societies
FRMS

2 Fulmar Pl., Meir Park, Stoke-On-Trent, ST3 7QF, England, UK
Tel: 44 1782 399291
Email: frms.sec@virgin.net
Website: http://www.musicweb.force9.co.uk/music/frms/index.htm
Founded: 1937
Members: 235
Contact: F.A. Baines, Hon.Sec.
Description: Musical organizations. Promotes the appreciation of all types of music; sponsors lectures and recitals.
Publication: Bulletin
Publication title: Bulletin. Advertisements.
Meetings/Conventions: Music Weekend - annual meeting

Federation of Small Businesses

Blackpool Business Park, Blackpool, FY4 2FEF, England, UK
Tel: 44 1253 336000
Fax: 44 1253 348046
Email: membership@fsb.org.uk
Website: http://www.fsb.org.uk
Founded: 1974
Members: 168000
Contact: John Emmins, Natl.Chm.
Description: Lobby organization representing the interests of small business and the self-employed. Provides benefits to members, does not provide grants.
Publication: Magazine
Publication title: First Voice. Advertisements.
Meetings/Conventions: - annual conference Brighton UK

Federation of Tour Operators

170 High St., Lewes, BN7 1YE, England, UK
Tel: 44 1273 477722
Fax: 44 1273 483746
Email: fto@ifto.demon.co.uk
Website: http://www.fto.co.uk
Founded: 1967
Members: 18
Staff: 3
Contact: Alan Flook, Sec.Gen.
Description: Major tour operators. Aims to improve conditions for tourists from the UK, both on their journey and in resort.

Federation of Wholesale Distributors

1st Fl, Berkeley House, 26 Gildredge Rd., Eastbourne, BN21 4SA, England, UK
Tel: 44 1323 724952
Fax: 44 1323 732820
Contact: Alan Toft, Dir. Gen.
Description: UK food and drink, grocery, tobacco and allied product cash and carry and delivered wholesalers. To defend and promote the interests of cash and carry and delivered wholesalers in the grocery, alcohol and related markets.
Publication title: Pro Wholesaler

Federation of Worker Writers and Community Publishers
FWWCP

Burslem School of Art, Queen St., Stoke-On-Trent, ST6 3EJ, England, UK
Email: thefwwcp@tiscali.co.uk
Website: http://www.fwwcp.mcmail.com
Founded: 1976
Members: 70
Contact: Timothy Diggles
Description: Independent writers' groups, community publishers, and adult literacy and literature development organizations. Creates and supports a national community of writers and publishers; offers people greater access to developing skills in participatory writing and publishing activities; encourages people to write and read creatively, especially those who may be socially excluded. Hosts creative writing events and performances; provides training in organizational and management skills; offers advice and information.
Meetings/Conventions: Festival of Writing - annual workshop

Federation of Zoological Gardens of Great Britain and Ireland

Regent's Park, London, NW1 4RY, England, UK
Tel: 44 20 75860230
Fax: 44 20 77224427
Email: admin.fedzoo@zsl.org
Website: http://www.zoofederation.org.uk
Founded: 1966
Members: 63
Staff: 3
Contact: Gwen Manning, Sec.
Description: Professional body representing the zoo community in Britain and Ireland. A conservation, education and scientific wildlife charity dedicated to the maintenance of the world's biodiversity, the welfare of animals in zoos and the advancement of scientific knowledge. Achieves these objectives through conservation breeding programmes and support for projects in the wild; inspiring an understanding of the natural world through environmental education; and non-invasive scientific studies which contribute to greater knowledge and understanding of animals.
Publication title: Guidelines for the Management of Cheetah
Publication title: Guidelines for the Management of Giraffes
Meetings/Conventions: - annual convention

Feline Advisory Bureau
FABCFFS

Taeselbury,, High Street, Tisbury, SP3 6LD, England, UK
Tel: 44 870 7422278
Fax: 44 1747 871873
Email: information@fabcats.org
Website: http://www.fabcats.org
Founded: 1958
Members: 3000
Staff: 5
Contact: Claire Bessant, Chief Exec.
Fee: £20
Membership Type: within UK
Fee: £55
Membership Type: European Society of Feline Medicine member
Description: Veterinary surgeons, cat breeders, and pet owners. Promotes humane behavior toward cats and provides information on feline health and care. Raises funds for feline clinical research. Provides cat boarding information service.
Library Type: not open to the public
Publication: Journal
Publication title: Fab Journal. Advertisements.
Second publication: Journal
Publication title: Journal of Feline Medicine and Surgery
Meetings/Conventions: - annual conference - Exhibits.

Fellowship at St. Nicholas
FSN

66 London Rd., East Sussex, St. Leonards-on-Sea, TN37 6AS, England, UK
Tel: 44 1424 423683
Fax: 44 1424 460446
Email: fsn@stleonards3.fsnet.co.uk
Website: http://www.fellowshipofstnicholas.org.uk
Founded: 1939
Staff: 10
Contact: A.M. Cox, Dir.

Description: Provides mobile projects; operates after-school care and day care for preschool children. Works to protect children from exploitation.

Fellowship of Makers and Researchers of Historical Instruments
FoMRHI

c/o Lewis Jones, Hon.Sec.
London Metropolitan University, 4171 Commercial Rd., London, E1 1LA, England, UK
Fax: 44 20 73201830
Email: ljones@londonmet.ac.uk
Website: http://www.nrinstruments.demon.co.uk/fomrhi.html
Founded: 1975
Members: 500
Contact: Lewis Jones, Hon.Sec.
Fee: £10.5
Description: Makers and researchers of historical musical instruments and interested others in 33 countries. Promotes the preservation, reconstruction, and use of historical musical instruments; upholds standards of authenticity.
Publication: Journal
Publication title: FoMRHI Quarterly
Publication title: Index of Articles
Meetings/Conventions: - periodic meeting

Fellowship of Sports Masseurs and Therapists

BM Soigneur, London, WC1N 3XX, England, UK
Tel: 44 1992 537778
Email: admin@fsmt-uk.org
Founded: 1975
Members: 500
Contact: Frank J. Westell, Chief Exec.
Fee: £25
Description: Sports masseurs and therapists having produced evidence of skills and knowledge in dealing with sports persons in competition, industry, rehabilitation. Sets and maintains standards in sports massage and therapy; advises on courses, helps to set up specific courses for national sports governing bodies, educational establishments sports centres and local authorities.
Publication: Newsletter

Felt Roofing Contractors Employers Association

c/o Fields House
Gower Rd., Haywards Heath, RH16 4PL, England, UK
Tel: 44 1444 440027
Fax: 44 1444 415616
Founded: 1975
Members: 80
Staff: 2
Contact: Mr. W.A. Jenkins
Description: Administered by Flat Roofing Contractors Advisory Board.

Feminist Library and Information Centre
FLRC

5-5a Westminster Bridge Rd., London, SE1 7XW, England, UK
Tel: 44 207 9287789
Founded: 1975
Members: 1500
Staff: 10
Contact: Feride Cork

Fee: £5
Membership Type: student
Fee: £20.5
Description: Women interested in feminist issues.
Library Subject: Women's studies and feminism
Library Type: reference
Formerly: Feminist Library
Publication: Newsletter
Publication title: Feminist Library Newsletter
Meetings/Conventions: - annual meeting

FERFA Resin Flooring Association
FeRFA

99 West St., Farnham, GU9 7EN, England, UK
Tel: 44 1252 739149
Fax: 44 1252 739140
Email: info@associationhouse.org.uk
Website: http://www.ferfa.org.uk
Founded: 1969
Members: 35
Staff: 5
Contact: Brian Poulson, Technical Off.
Description: Major product manufacturers, raw material suppliers and specialist contractors of resin, polymer and cementitious based materials and systems for the repair and protection of structures. Sets and maintains high standards of product quality; health and safety, technical competence and application capability. Promotes and develops understanding and knowledge of the benefits of cement, polymer and resin based products, their uses and applications.
Formerly: Federation for the Repair and Protection of Structures
Publication title: The Resin Flooring Handbook

Fertiliser Manufacturers' Association

Great North Rd., Peterborough, PE8 6HJ, England, UK
Tel: 44 1780 781360
Fax: 44 1780 781369
Email: enquire@fma.org.uk
Founded: 1875
Members: 33
Staff: 4
Contact: D.J. Heather
Description: Represents the views and interests of UK fertiliser manufacturers to government and appropriate organisations.
Publication: Report
Publication title: Fertiliser Review

Fibre Bonded Carpet Manufacturers' Association

c/o A.E.G. Gardiner
3 Manchester Rd., Bury, BL9 0DR, England, UK
Tel: 44 161 7645401
Fax: 44 161 7641114
Founded: 1968
Members: 13
Staff: 1
Contact: A.E.G. Gardiner, Sec.
Fee: £700
Membership Type: full
Fee: £350
Membership Type: associate
Description: Aims to advance generally the interests of the manufacturers to fibre bonded carpet. Aims for quality production to be worthy of the industry. Fosters co-operation with all other sections of the floor-covering trade. Provides a means of collaboration with allied and connected industries.

Fibreoptic Industry Association
FIA

The Manor House, Buntingford, SG9 9AB, England, UK
Tel: 44 1763 273039
Fax: 44 1763 273255
Email: jane@fiasec.demon.co.uk
Website: http://www.fibreoptic.org.uk
Founded: 1990
Members: 220
Staff: 1
Contact: Jane Morrison
Description: Installers, manufacturers, distributors, consultants and educational establishments associated with fibre optic communications. Aims to improve professional standards of manufacture, installation and training throughout the fibre optics industry.
Library Subject: communications
Library Type: not open to the public
Publication title: Cable Selection Guide
Second publication: Newsletter
Publication title: FIA Newsletter
Meetings/Conventions: Breakfast Seminars - quarterly seminar

Field Studies Council

Preston Montford, Montford Bridge, Shrewsbury, SY4 1HW, England, UK
Tel: 44 1743 852100
Fax: 44 1743 852101
Email: enquiries@field-studies-council.org
Website: http://www.field-studies-council.org
Founded: 1943
Members: 3800
Contact: Mr. Tony Thomas, Chief Exec.
Fee: £10
Membership Type: individual
Description: Registered charity with 12 residential field study centres throughout England and Wales. Offers a wide range of enviornmental education and special interest courses for adults and school groups.
Publication: Journal
Publication title: Field Studies

File Association

c/o Institute of Spring Technology
Henry St., Sheffield, S3 7EQ, England, UK
Tel: 44 114 2789143
Fax: 44 114 2726344
Email: jrm@britishtools.com
Contact: J.R. Markham, Sec.
Publication: Directory
Publication title: British Tools Directory

Film Artistes Association
FAA

373-377 Clapham Rd., London, SW9 9BT, England, UK
Tel: 44 20 73460900
Fax: 44 20 73460901
Email: smacdonald@bectu.org.uk
Website: http://www.bectu.org.uk
Founded: 1940
Members: 1400
Contact: Spencer MacDonald
Fee: £60

Description: Supporting artistes, stand-ins and doubles employed in the film and television industry.
Formerly: Absorbed, Film Artistes Association
Publication: Journal
Publication title: Stage Screen and Radio

Film Distributors' Association

22 Golden Sq., London, W1F 9JW, England, UK
Tel: 44 20 74374383
Fax: 44 20 77340912
Email: info@fda.uk.net
Website: http://www.launchingfilms.com
Founded: 1915
Members: 14
Contact: Mark Batey, CEO
Description: Includes all major distribution companies and several independent companies. Promotes and protects its members' interests and co-operates with all other film organizations and government agencies where distribution interests are involved.
Formerly: Society of Film Distribution

Filtration Society
FS

5 Henry Dane Way, Newbold, Coleorton, LE67 8PP, England, UK
Tel: 44 1530 223124
Fax: 44 1530 223124
Email: r.j.wakeman@lboro.ac.uk
Website: http://www.filtsoc.com
Founded: 1964
Members: 800
Contact: Prof. Richard Wakeman, Sec.
Description: Users of filtration and separation technology and equipment; research scientists and engineers in government establishments, universities, and technical colleges; manufacturers and designers of equipment. Promotes knowledge of filtration and separation in all industries. Has established award fund to stimulate research and innovation in the field. Organizes and sponsors conferences, symposia, and laboratory and industrial visits.
Publication: Journal
Publication title: Journal of the Filtration Society. Advertisements.
Second publication: Journal
Publication title: Transactions of the Filtration Society
Meetings/Conventions: - periodic meeting

Finance and Leasing Association
FLA

Imperial House, 2nd Fl., 15-19 Kingsway, London, WC2B 6UN, England, UK
Tel: 44 20 78366511
Fax: 44 20 74209600
Email: info@fla.org.uk
Website: http://www.fla.org.uk
Founded: 1992
Members: 180
Staff: 22
Contact: Martin Hall, Dir.Gen.
Description: Trade association representing the UK asset, consumer, and motor finance sectors. Provides high level representation and lobbying at both national and EU levels, supported by first class technical information and industry statistics. Members must comply with the relevant FLA code of conduct, which is supported by FLA's conciliation and arbitration schemes. Provides a focus and forum for the industry, and has a high level of member involvement in its many

working groups. Organizes conferences, workshops, and training courses.
Formerly: Formed by Merger of, Finance Houses Association
Publication title: Annual Report
Publication title: Annual Survey of Business Finance
Meetings/Conventions: Asset Management Convention - annual convention

Financial Services Authority

25 The North Colonnade, Canary Wharf, London, E14 5HS, England, UK
Tel: 44 207 6761000
Fax: 44 207 6761099
Website: http://www.fsa.gov.uk
Founded: 1986
Staff: 200
Description: Concerned with the regulation of investments and investor protection.
Formerly: Securities and Investments Board

Find Your Feet
FYF

Bon Marche Centre, Unit 316, 241-251 Ferndale Rd., London, SW9 8BJ, England, UK
Tel: 44 20 73264464
Fax: 44 20 77338848
Email: fyf@fyf.org.uk
Website: http://www.fyf.org.uk
Founded: 1960
Staff: 5
Contact: Sue Stoessl, Chair
Description: Works in partnership with NGOs in Southern Africa and South Asia in longterm development programes promoting sustainable livelihoods. Helping to break the cycle of poverty by providing investment to enable people to increase their income and achieve longterm food security.
Publication: Newsletter

Fine Art Trade Guild

16-18 Empress Pl., London, SW6 1TT, England, UK
Tel: 44 20 73816616
Fax: 44 20 73812596
Email: info@fineart.co.uk
Website: http://www.fineart.co.uk
Founded: 1910
Members: 1800
Staff: 10
Contact: Christrose Sumner, Mng.Dir.
Description: Art dealers; fine art printers and publishers; framing materials suppliers; art galleries; picture framers; artists; agents. Association for all those involved in the picture industry. Aims to help members develop their businesses via consumer marketing, retail and craft training and testing, setting of industry standards, financial savings and information services.
Publication: Magazine
Publication title: Art Business Today. Advertisements.
Publication title: The Directory

Fingerprint Society
FS

Fingerprint Bureau, City of London Police, 37 Wood St., London, EC2P 2NQ, England, UK
Tel: 44 171 6012333
Founded: 1974
Members: 1000
Contact: Mr. Stephen E. Haylock, Chm.
Description: Fingerprint and scene of the crime officers employed by police, civilian, or military organizations in 74 countries. Purpose is to further the study of fingerprints. Facilitates communication and cooperation among members and others interested in the field of personal identification.
Publication: Handbook
Publication title: The Fingerprint Society Handbook
Second publication: Magazine
Publication title: Fingerprint Whorld
Meetings/Conventions: - annual conference - Exhibits.

Fire and Risk Sciences

c/o Building Research Establishment
Bucknalls Ln., Garston, Watford, WD25 9XX, England, UK
Tel: 44 1923 664700
Fax: 44 1923 664910
Email: frsenquiries@bre.co.uk
Website: http://www.bre.co.uk/frs
Founded: 1947
Staff: 110
Contact: Mr. Gary Neal, Business Development Mgr.
Description: Environmental scientists, physicists, engineers, risk scientists, professional researchers, chemists. Aims to reduce loss of life and property due to fire.
Library Type: by appointment only
Formerly: Fire Research Station

Fire Brigades Union
FBU

68 Coombe Rd., Kingston Upon Thames, KT2 7AE, England, UK
Tel: 44 20 85411765
Fax: 44 20 85465187
Email: office@fbu.org.uk
Website: http://www.fbu.org.uk
Founded: 1918
Members: 50000
Staff: 25
Contact: Andy Gilcrest, Gen.Sec.
Description: Uniformed members of local authority fire brigades in the United Kingdom. Serves its members by winning for them the best possible conditions, and to serve the community by encouraging its members to be skilled at their craft.
Publication: Journal
Publication title: Firefighter

Fire Extinguishing Trades Association

Neville House, 55 Eden St., Kingston-upon-Thames, Kingston Upon Thames, KT1 1BW, England, UK
Tel: 44 208 5498839
Fax: 44 208 5471564
Email: feta@abft.org.uk
Website: http://www.feta.org.uk
Founded: 1916
Members: 80

Staff: 12
Contact: B. Gately, Gen.Mgr.
Description: Committed to upholding and where appropriate, to raising the standards of performance and reliability of portable firefighting equipment and fiting and fire hoses manufactured and/or maintained by its members.
Publication title: Guide to Servicing Portable Fire Extinguishers and Hose Reels
Publication title: Review
Meetings/Conventions: - annual conference

Fire Fighting Vehicles Manufacturers' Association
FFVMA

c/o Forbes House
Halkin St., London, SW1X 7DS, England, UK
Tel: 44 207 2357000
Fax: 44 207 2357112
Email: ffvma@smmt.co.uk
Founded: 1970
Members: 11
Staff: 2
Contact: C.J. Ford, Dir.
Fee: £1200
Description: Companies manufacturing fire appliance chassis and bodywork and other equipment. Sole UK trade association representing the interests of companies building fire appliances. Regular liaison with Home Office, Fire Service and other legislative and standards making bodies.

Fire Industry Confederation

c/o Neville House
55 Eden St., Kingston Upon Thames, KT1 1BW, England, UK
Tel: 44 20 85498839
Fax: 44 20 85471564
Email: fic@abft.org.uk
Website: http://www.the-fic.org.uk
Founded: 1988
Staff: 5
Contact: Wilf Butcher, Pres.
Description: To provide a forum for the fire protection industry for subjects beyond any individual trade association's scope of interest.
Publication title: Competitiveness of the UK Fire Industry

Fire Protection Association - England
FPA

Bastille Ct., 2 Paris Garden, London, SE1 8ND, England, UK
Tel: 44 20 7902 5300
Fax: 44 20 7902 5301
Email: fpa@thefpa.co.uk
Website: http://www.thefpa.co.uk
Founded: 1946
Members: 5850
Staff: 25
Contact: J.O. Neill, Managing Dir.
Fee: £110
Membership Type: within U.K.
Fee: £125
Membership Type: outside UK
Description: Insurers, brokers, loss adjusters, industrial, commercial and private sector companies/organizations, fire brigades, fire liaison panels, Industrial Fire Protection Association and local FPAs, engineers, architects and fire safety specialists/. consultants. Identifying and drawing attention to fire dangers, and the means by

which their potential for loss can be minimized, FPA services are designed to assist fire, security and safety managers - and their professional advisors, achieve and maintain the highest standards of fire safety within the premises for which they are responsible.
Library Subject: fire safety, loss prevention, related subjects
Library Type: not open to the public
Formerly: See parent group for further info, Loss Prevention Council
Publication: Video
Publication title: Extinguishing Fires in the Workplace
Second publication: Magazine
Publication title: Fire Prevention. Advertisements.

First Steps to Freedom
7 Avon Ct., School Lane, Kenilworth, CV8 2GX, England, UK
Tel: 44 1926 864473
Fax: 44 1926 864473
Email: fstf1234@aol.com
Website: http://www.first-steps.org
Founded: 1991
Members: 1500
Staff: 60
Contact: Sheila Harris, Sec.
Fee: £12
Membership Type: regular
Fee: £6
Membership Type: senior citizens
Description: People who suffer from phobias, panic attacks, general anxiety, obsessive compulsive disorders, and tranquilizer withdrawal. Makes available telephone help line, support groups, relaxation audio tapes. Conducts educational programs.
Publication title: NWL

Fitness Industry Association
115 Eastbourne Mews, London, W2 6LQ, England, UK
Tel: 44 207 2986730
Fax: 44 207 2986731
Email: info@fia.org.uk
Website: http://www.fia.org.uk
Founded: 1989
Members: 1400
Staff: 7
Contact: Nigel Wallace, Exec.Dir.
Description: Operators, suppliers, educational establishments, and professionals in the fitness industry. Aims to raise standards across the industry via the publicising of the Code of Practice.
Library Subject: fitness club retention and attention, health and safety, business excellence
Library Type: reference
Publication: Magazine
Publication title: Club Business International. Advertisements.
Publication title: Health Club Management
Meetings/Conventions: Bodylife - annual convention

Fitness League
52 London St., Chertsey, KT16 8AJ, England, UK
Tel: 44 1932 564567
Fax: 44 1932 567566
Email: tfl@thefitnessleague.com
Website: http://www.thefitnessleague.com
Founded: 1930
Members: 18000
Staff: 4
Contact: Mrs. V.A. Augustine, Admin. Officer
Fee: £6

Description: Charity organization. Promotes education for women in physical training, health, and fitness. Offers training courses and exercise classes.
Formerly: Women's League of Health and Beauty
Publication: Booklet
Publication title: History of the League
Second publication: Annual Report

Flag Institute
44 Middleton Rd., Acomb, York, YO24 3AS, England, UK
Tel: 44 1904 339985
Email: info@flaginstitute.org
Website: http://www.flaginstitute.org
Founded: 1971
Members: 504
Staff: 1
Contact: Graham Bartram, Sec.
Description: Individual, trade, group, junior. A documentation and resource centre to which trade members, national libraries, government departments and museums subscribe, together with a body of individual members. It offers advice, information, guidelines and publications on all aspects of flags.
Publication: Journal
Publication title: Flagmaster

Flat Glass Council
44-48 Borough High St., London, SE1 1XB, England, UK
Tel: 44 20 74037177
Fax: 44 20 73577458
Contact: Mr. N. Rees
Description: Promotes the flat glass industry.

Flat Roofing Alliance
c/o Fields House
Gower Rd., Haywards Heath, RH16 4PL, England, UK
Tel: 44 1444 440027
Fax: 44 1444 415616
Email: info@fra.org.uk
Website: http://www.fra.org.uk
Founded: 1938
Members: 80
Staff: 3
Contact: Bill Jenkins
Description: Major contractors and small specialists involved with flat roofing and, through its affiliate members, most of the manufacturers supplying materials to the industry. Covering built-up flat roofing and ancillary materials. Promotes the interests of flat roofing contractors by providing up to date technical information. Representing them in discussions at all levels, ensuring availability of suitable training and promoting the correct use of materials and specification of systems.
Formerly: Flat Roofing Contractors Advisory Board
Publication: Handbook
Publication title: FRA Roofing Handbook

Flora Europaea Residuary Body
FERB
c/o Dr. Stephen L. Jury
Plant Science Laboratories, University of Reading, Whiteknights, Reading, RG6 6AS, England, UK
Tel: 44 118 9318169
Fax: 44 118 9753676
Email: s.l.jury@reading.ac.uk
Members: 5

Contact: Dr. Stephen L. Jury
Description: Botanists and other natural scientists with an interest in the plants of Europe. Continues to see to the interests of Flora Europaea.

Flour Advisory Bureau

21 Arlington St., London, SW1A 1RN, England, UK
Tel: 44 207 4932521
Fax: 44 207 4936785
Email: fab@nabim.org.uk
Website: http://www.fabflour.co.uk/
Founded: 1956
Members: 68
Staff: 2
Contact: Tamnia Grassi
Description: Acts as the promotional arm of the National Association of British and Irish Millers which provides information on wheat, flour and bread.

Flowers and Plants Association

266 Flower Market, New Covent Garden Market, London, SW8 5NB, England, UK
Tel: 44 20 77388044
Fax: 44 20 77388083
Email: info@flowers.org.uk
Website: http://www.flowers.org.uk
Founded: 1984
Members: 200
Staff: 3
Contact: Veronica Richardson, Chief Exec.
Fee: £125
Membership Type: full
Fee: £1000
Membership Type: research
Description: Growers, wholesalers, importers, retailers, colleges and associated companies. Encourages the sales of cut flowers and indoor plants and educates consumers about these products through promotional campaigns, advertising, information service, and press office offering statistics, facts, advice, and spokespersons.
Library Subject: flowers, plants
Library Type: not open to the public
Publication: Newsletter

FOCAL International

Pentax House, South Hill Ave., South Harrow, HA2 0DU, England, UK
Tel: 44 20 84235853
Fax: 44 20 89334826
Email: info@focalint.org
Website: http://www.focalint.org
Founded: 1985
Members: 360
Staff: 2
Contact: Anne Johnson, Commercial Mgr.
Fee: £90
Membership Type: individual
Fee: £550
Membership Type: company
Description: Footage, stills and sound libraries; film and stills researchers; production companies and producers; research companies; facility companies. Promotes the use of library footage, stills and sound in programming, advertising, multimedia, corporate videos etc. Holds seminars and meetings, publishes a journal quarterly and a Directory of Members.

Formerly: Federation of Commercial Audio Visual Libraries International
Publication: Journal
Publication title: Archive Zones. Advertisements.
Publication title: Members Guide
Meetings/Conventions: - monthly meeting - Exhibits.

Folklore Society

c/o The Warburg Institute
Woburn Sq., London, WC1H 0AB, England, UK
Tel: 44 20 78628564
Email: folklore.society@talk21.com
Website: http://www.folklore-society.com
Founded: 1876
Members: 950
Staff: 2
Contact: Susan Vass, Admin.
Fee: £30
Fee: £90
Membership Type: institutions
Description: Includes the collection and study of popular custom and belief; traditional narrative, drama, music, song and dance; foodways; language; arts and crafts; and children's folklore. Interests also extend to the related areas of oral history and popular culture.
Library Subject: folklore
Library Type: reference
Publication title: FLS Library Publications
Publication title: FLS News

Food Additives and Ingredients Association

10 Whitchurch Close, Maidstone, MEI6 8UR, England, UK
Tel: 44 1622 68219
Fax: 44 1622 682119
Email: rbr1@tconnect.com
Website: http://www.faia.org.uk
Founded: 1977
Members: 26
Contact: Richard Ratcliffe, Exec.Sec.
Description: Company membership comprising manufacturers, blenders and distributors of food additives and ingredients. Represents the interests of the UK food additives and ingredients industry by promoting a better understanding of the importance of food additives and ingredients among food manufacturers, legislators and consumers, providing a centre of expertise on food additives and ingredients technology and safe use and making representation to relevant authorities on all aspects of food additives and ingredients legislation.
Formerly: Food Additives Industry Association
Publication: Booklet
Publication title: The Chemistry On Your Table
Publication title: Food Issues

Food Aid Committee
FAC

c/o International Grains Council
1 Canada Sq., Canary Wharf, London, E14 5AE, England, UK
Tel: 44 207 5131122
Fax: 44 207 5130630
Email: igc-fac@igc.org.uk
Website: http://www.igc.org.uk
Founded: 1967
Members: 23

Staff: 18
Contact: Mr. G.A. Denis, Exec.Dir.
Description: Implements the Food Aid Convention 1999 (FAC), which is part of the International Grains Agreement, 1995.
Publication: Report
Publication title: Food Aid Shipments
Meetings/Conventions: - semiannual meeting

Food and Drink Federation - England
FDF

6 Catherine St., London, WC2B 5JJ, England, UK
Tel: 44 207 8362460
Fax: 44 207 8360580
Email: generalenquiries@fdf.org.uk
Website: http://www.fdf.org.uk
Description: Represents the interests of the U.K. food and drink manufacturers.
Library Type: not open to the public

Food for the Hungry - UK

44 Copperfield Rd., Bassett, Southampton, SO16 3NX, England, UK
Tel: 44 23 80902327
Fax: 44 23 80902327
Email: uk@fhi.net
Website: http://www.uk.fhi.net
Founded: 1971
Staff: 1
Contact: Doug Wakeling, Exec.Ofcr.
Description: Christian relief and development organisation, seeking to feed both spiritual and physical hunger. Primary emphasis is on long-term development among the extremely poor, recognising their dignity, creativity and ability to solve their own problems. Programmes are designed to strengthen and empower the local churches, leaders and families, to move their communities toward their God-given potential. Part of the International FHI Partnership, with operations in 25 nations in Africa, Central and South America, and eastern Europe. Key activities include food production, land reclamation and agroforestry, primary health care, education, water development for drinking and irrigation, emergency relief and rehabilitation and micro-enterprise development.

Forecourt Equipment Federation

PO Box 35084, London, NW1 4XE, England, UK
Tel: 44 20 79358532
Fax: 44 20 79358532
Email: fef@gpda.com
Website: http://www.fef.org.uk
Founded: 1958
Members: 9
Contact: C. Dunn-Meynell
Description: Forecourt equipment manufacturing companies in the UK. Represents the interest of forecourt equipment in the UK.
Formerly: Petrol Pump Manufacturers Association

Foreign Press Association in London

11 Carlton House Terrace, London, SW1Y 5AJ, England, UK
Tel: 44 20 79300445
Fax: 44 20 79250469
Email: secretariat@foreign-press.org.uk
Website: http://www.foreign-press.org.uk
Founded: 1888
Members: 700

Staff: 4
Contact: Ms. Tine Van Houts, Pres.
Description: Mainly foreign journalists representing overseas media covering UK news. Membership also open to freelance/British press and Embassy press attaches, and PR executives. Facilitates the work of UK based foreign correspondents covering British news.
Publication: Membership Directory

Forensic Science Society
FSSOC

Clarke House, 18 A Mount Parade, Harrogate, HG1 1BX, England, UK
Tel: 44 1423 506068
Fax: 44 1423 566391
Email: michele@forensic-science-society.org.uk
Website: http://www.forensic-science-society.org.uk
Founded: 1959
Members: 2200
Staff: 5
Contact: Dr. Angela Gallop, Pres.
Description: Forensic scientists, lawyers, pathologists, police officers, odontologists and police surgeons in 80 countries. Promotes the study and application of forensic science.
Publication: Journal
Publication title: Journal of the Forensic Science Society. Advertisements.
Second publication: Directory
Publication title: World List of Forensic Science Laboratories and Practices
Meetings/Conventions: - annual general assembly

Forest Peoples Programme

Fosseway Business Center, Ste. 1C, Stratford Rd., Moreton-in-Marsh, GL56 9NQ, England, UK
Tel: 44 1608 652893
Fax: 44 1608 652878
Email: info@fppwrm.gn.apc.org
Website: http://forestpeoples.gn.apc.org
Founded: 1990
Staff: 13
Contact: Marcus Colchester, Dir.
Description: Citizen's groups. Promotes protection of rainforests and the people and wildlife that inhabit them worldwide. Campaigns for the defense of the civil and human rights of people indigenous to the rainforest; provides support and assistance to environmental protection organizations operating in rainforests.
Formerly: World Rainforest Movement

Forest School Camps
FSC

Rhianon Gale, 363A Holloway Rd., London, N7 0RN, England, UK
Tel: 44 20 88833057
Email: gensec@fsc.org.uk
Website: http://www.fsc.org.uk
Founded: 1947
Members: 2000
Staff: 600
Contact: Lottie Davies, Gen.Sec.
Description: Educational youth camps and youth leaders. Promotes the healthy physical and spiritual development of youth through woodcraft and increased understanding of nature. Maintains forest camps providing young people with the opportunity to develop improved self-esteem while learning woodcraft skills. Conducts

woodcraft and environmental education programs; sponsors recreational activities; makes available children's services.
Publication: Catalog
Publication title: Forest School Camps
Second publication: Newsletter
Meetings/Conventions: - monthly board meeting London UK

Fork Lift Truck Association

c/o Riverview House
London Rd., Old Basing, Basingstoke, RG24 7JL, England, UK
Tel: 44 1256 381441
Fax: 44 1256 381735
Website: http://www.fork-truck.org.uk
Founded: 1972
Members: 158
Staff: 2
Contact: Barry Lea
Fee: £950
Membership Type: full
Description: Manufacturers, dealers and associated members offering the hire and supply of fork truck services and services to other members in the UK and Europe. To ensure the highest standards of quality and service and ensure the safe, reliable hiring of fork trucks for both casual and contract hire and to promote the virtues of hire as a means of funding the acquisition of capital plant.
Publication title: Good Hire Guide
Second publication: Manual
Publication title: Health & Safety Manual
Meetings/Conventions: meeting - Exhibits. Coventry UK

Fortress Study Group
FSG

c/o Bernard Lowry
The Severals, Bentleys Rd., Market Drayton, TF9 1LL, England, UK
Tel: 44 1630 653433
Email: bclowryfsg@aol.com
Website: http://www.fortress-study-group.com/
Founded: 1975
Members: 700
Contact: Bernard C. Lowry, Sec.
Fee: £25
Membership Type: U.K and Europe
Fee: £35
Membership Type: All others
Description: Societies, libraries, and individuals in 34 countries. Studies fortification as developed since the introduction of gunpowder and artillery. Organizes annual trips to places of interest.
Publication: Newsletter
Publication title: Casemate
Second publication: Journal
Publication title: Fort
Meetings/Conventions: - annual conference

FOSFA International

20 St. Dunstan's Hill, London, EC3R 8NQ, England, UK
Tel: 44 20 72835511
Fax: 44 20 76231310
Email: contact@fosfa.org
Website: http://www.fosfa.org
Founded: 1971
Members: 700

Description: Supports the world trade of oilseeds, fats and edible nuts. Aims to provide standard forms of contract and a well-established system for resolving disputes.

Fostering Network

87 Blackfriars Rd., London, SE1 8HA, England, UK
Tel: 44 20 76206400
Fax: 44 20 76206401
Email: info@fostering.net
Website: http://www.fostering.net
Founded: 1974
Members: 19000
Staff: 39
Contact:
Fee: £34
Membership Type: individuals
Description: Foster care workers, social workers, and advisors. Promotes good foster care practice and supports carers in their work. Offers training for foster care service; conducts educational and research programs; disseminates Information on changes in child care policy.
Library Subject: foster care, adoption, childcare and development, child abuse, childrens rights
Library Type: open to the public
Formerly: National Foster Care Association
Publication: Newsletter
Publication title: Foster Care Finance
Second publication: Magazine
Publication title: Foster Care Magazine
Meetings/Conventions: - biennial conference

Foundation for International Environmental Law and Development
FIELD

52-53 Russell Sq., London, WC1B 4HP, England, UK
Tel: 44 207 6377950
Fax: 44 207 6377951
Email: field.org@field.org.uk
Website: http://www.field.org.uk
Founded: 1989
Members: 12
Staff: 16
Contact: Megan Addis, Admin.
Description: Attorneys, jurists, and other individuals with an interest in environmental law. Promotes environmental protection through legal action and reform. Provides consulting services to legal and governmental agencies with an interest in environmental protection.
Publication: Journal
Publication title: Review of European Community International Environmental Law (RECIEL). Advertisements.
Meetings/Conventions: conference

Foundation for the Study of Infant Deaths
FSID

11-19 Artillery Row, London, SW1P 1RT, England, UK
Tel: 44 870 7870885
Fax: 44 870 7870725
Email: fsid@sids.org.uk
Website: http://www.sids.org.uk/fsid/
Founded: 1971
Staff: 34
Contact: Joyce Epstein, Sec.

Description: Works to prevent sudden infant death syndrome (SIDS) and to promote infant health. Offers emotional support services to families who have suffered the loss of a child to SIDS. Provides networking and a forum for discussion and support among bereaved parents. Disseminates information about infant death and infant care to families, health professionals, the media, and government agenices.
Library Subject: cot death, sudden infant death syndrome, infant health and care
Library Type: not open to the public
Publication: Annual Report
Second publication: Brochures
Meetings/Conventions: - annual convention

Foundation for Women's Health Research and Development
FORWARD

40 Eastbourne Terrace, London, W2 3QR, England, UK
Tel: 44 171 7252606
Fax: 44 171 7252796
Email: forward@forwarduk.co.uk
Website: http://www.forwarduk.org.uk
Founded: 1983
Members: 951
Staff: 4
Contact: Adwoa Kwateug-Kluritse, Actg.Dir.
Fee: £16
Membership Type: individual sponsorship
Fee: £8
Membership Type: claimant, student, and OAP sponsorship
Description: Promotes the studies of women's health research and development throughout Europe and other western countries and Africa. Supports the rights of women and children. Promotes the prevention of early childhood marriage that contributes to VVF and RVF. Protects women and children from becoming victims of abuse. Opposes and fights for the elimination of the practice of genital mutilation of young girls. Disseminates information. Conducts training programs.
Library Type: open to the public
Publication: Video
Publication title: Another Form of Physical Abuse: Prevention of Female Genital Mutilation in the United Kingdom
Second publication: Book
Publication title: Child Protection and Female Genital Mutilation: Advice for Health, Education, and Social Work Professionals

Foundry Equipment and Supplies Association

c/o Queensway House
2 Queensway, Queensway House, Redhill, RH1 1QS, England, UK
Tel: 44 1737 768611
Fax: 44 1737 855469·
Email: marywhite@uk.dmgworldmedia.comwww.fesa.org.uk
Founded: 1925
Members: 41
Staff: 2
Contact: Mary White, Sec.
Description: Promotes the industry of foundry equipment and supplies.

Fountain Society

Weather Tower Hill, Dorking, RH4 2AP, England, UK
Tel: 44 207 5849004
Fax: 44 207 5842917

Email: peterkmowlson@hotmail.com
Website: http://www.fountainsoc.org.uk
Founded: 1986
Contact: Peter Knowlson, Chm.
Fee: £20
Membership Type: ordinary, UK and Channel Islands
Fee: £30
Membership Type: ordinary, overseas
Description: Concerned with the conservation and restoration of fountains, cascades, and waterfalls of aesthetic merit for public and domestic enjoyment; also to promote the provision and restoration of cascades, waterfalls and other water features for public enjoyment. Offers advice on the design, construction, sighting and maintenance of fountains.
Publication: Reports
Second publication: Paper
Meetings/Conventions: - periodic conference

Fourth World Educational and Research Association Trust
FWERAT

c/o John Papworth
The Close, 26 High St., Purton, Swindon, SN5 9AE, England, UK
Tel: 44 179 3772214
Email: john.papworth@bt.com
Founded: 1981
Members: 2000
Staff: 4
Contact: John Papworth
Description: Individuals who support the establishment of the Fourth World, distinct from the Old, New, and Third worlds, in which power would belong not to the centralized government or mass society, but to the village and small urban neighborhood. Promotes a world ordered on the human scale, in opposition to what it considers to be to the giantism of modern social institutions; believes that the solution to the global crisis of power and to the current deterioration of mankind through war, population excess, environmental pollution, and mass alienation of many kinds, will come only through the creation of an organically structured and decentralized form of participatory democracy. Acts as a think-tank to study existing expressions of Fourth World thought such as communes and alternative schooling and to consider problems such as global communications, bioregionalism, ethnic identity, decolonization, urban life, and war and nonviolence in a Fourth World context. Links similar groups from 32 countries in the Fourth World Network.
Publication: Booklet
Publication title: Crisis Wisdom
Second publication: Magazine
Publication title: Fourth World Review. Advertisements.
Meetings/Conventions: Radical Consultation (RADCON) - annual general assembly - Exhibits.

FPA - England

2-12 Pentonville Rd., London, N1 9FP, England, UK
Tel: 44 20 78375432
Fax: 44 171 8373042
Website: http://www.fpa.org.uk
Founded: 1936
Members: 2000
Staff: 36
Contact: Anne Weyman, CEO
Fee: £30
Membership Type: individual
Fee: £90

Membership Type: corporate
Description: Promotes family planning and sexual health in England. Conducts public education programs; conducts research. Provides helpline and reference library.
Library Subject: family planning, contraception, sexual and reproductive health
Library Type: by appointment only
Formerly: Family Planning Association
Publication: Newsletter
Publication title: Contraceptive Education Bulletin

Fragile X Society

c/o Mrs. Lesley Walker
53 Winchelsea Lane, Hastings, TN35 4LG, England, UK
Tel: 44 142 4813147
Email: lesleywalker@fragile.k-web.co.uk
Website: http://www.fragilex.org.uk
Founded: 1990
Members: 1400
Contact: Mrs. Lesley Walker
Fee: £30
Membership Type: families overseas
Fee: £12
Membership Type: professor UK
Description: Aims to provide support and comprehensive information to families whose children and adult relatives have fragile X syndrome, to raise awareness of fragile X and to encourage research.
Library Subject: learning disabilities, children and adults, genetics, fragile X syndrome
Library Type: reference
Publication: Newsletter
Meetings/Conventions: - biennial conference Birmingham UK

Francis Brett Young Society

c/o Mrs. J. Hadley
92 Gower Rd., Halesowen, B62 9BT, England, UK
Tel: 44 1214228969
Website: http://www.fbysociety.co.uk
Founded: 1979
Members: 202
Contact: Mr. M. Hall, Chm.
Fee: £7
Membership Type: individual
Fee: £10
Membership Type: husband & wife
Description: Aims to provide opportunities for those interested in the life and writings of Francis Brett Young to meet, to correspond and to share their enjoyment of the author's work.

Freedom Organisation for the Right to Enjoy Smoking Tobacco
FOREST

Audley House, 13 Palace St., London, SW1E 5HX, England, UK
Tel: 44 20 72336155
Fax: 44 20 76306226
Email: forest@forest-on-smoking.org.uk
Website: http://www.forest-on-smoking.org.uk
Founded: 1979
Members: 5000
Staff: 3
Contact: Simon Clark, Dir.
Fee: £20
Membership Type: full

Fee: £80
Membership Type: corporate
Description: Defends the freedom of choice of adults to smoke. Works to counter campaigns launched by smoking and tobacco prohibitionists. Maintains that it is not the role of the state to restrict smoking rights. Sponsors representatives attending debates and discussions on the topic and appearing on television and radio shows to advocate smoking rights.
Publication: Newsletter
Publication title: Burning Issues
Second publication: Papers
Meetings/Conventions: - periodic meeting

Freight Transport Association

Hermes House, St. Johns Rd., Tunbridge Wells, TN4 9UZ, England, UK
Tel: 44 1892 526171
Fax: 44 1892 534989
Email: enquiries@fta.co.uk
Website: http://www.fta.co.uk
Founded: 1890
Members: 11000
Staff: 350
Contact: Richard Turner, Chief Exec.
Description: Companies with a transport interest whether by road, rail, sea or air. Represents the transport interests of British industry.
Library Subject: transport
Library Type: not open to the public
Publication: Magazine
Publication title: Freight Magazine
Second publication: Yearbook
Meetings/Conventions: Freight Summit - annual conference

French Chamber of Commerce in Great Britain

21 Dartmouth St., Westminster, London, SW1H 9BP, England, UK
Tel: 44 207 3044040
Email: mail@ccfgb.co.uk
Website: http://www.ccfgb.co.uk
Founded: 1883
Members: 600
Staff: 25
Contact: Alain Soulas, Mng.Dir.
Fee: £485
Membership Type: corporate, plus VAT
Fee: £1400
Membership Type: corporate, plus VAT
Description: Promotes business and commerce between Great Britain and France.
Library Subject: Franco-British trade
Library Type: reference
Publication: Directory
Publication title: Cross Channel Freight Transport Directory. Advertisements.
Second publication: Directory
Publication title: Franco British Trade Directory
Meetings/Conventions: - biennial

Fresh Produce Consortium - UK

Minerva House, Minerva Business Park, Lynch Wood, Peterborough, PE2 6FT, England, UK
Tel: 44 1733 237117
Fax: 44 1733 237118
Email: info@freshproduce.org.uk
Website: http://www.freshproduce.org.uk

Founded: 1992
Members: 1200
Staff: 3
Contact: D.W. Henderson, Ch.Exec.
Description: Growers, producers, importers, retailers (independent and multiple), marketing organizations, wholesalers, pre-packers of fresh produce and flowers/plants. Represents the industry in negotiations, consultations and with DEFRA, EU Commission, NFU and National Association of British Market Authorities, and CIMO.
Publication title: Code of Practice for Pesticide Controls
Second publication: Handbook
Publication title: Fresh Produce Consortium Handbook. Advertisements.
Meetings/Conventions: - periodic convention UK

Freshwater Biological Association
FBA

The Ferry House, Ambleside, Cumbria, LA22 0LP, England, UK
Tel: 44 15394 42468
Fax: 44 15394 46914
Email: info@fba.org.uk
Website: http://www.fba.org.uk
Founded: 1929
Members: 1750
Staff: 4
Contact: Dr. R.A. Sweeting, Chief Exec.
Fee: £20
Membership Type: ordinary
Fee: £10
Membership Type: student
Description: Promotes freshwater science through an innovative research programme, an active membership organisation, and by providing sound, independent scientific opinion.
Library Subject: freshwater biology
Library Type: reference
Publication: Newsletter
Publication title: FBA Newsletter. Advertisements.
Second publication: Journal
Publication title: Freshwater Forum
Meetings/Conventions: Scientific Meeting - annual conference - Exhibits.

Friends Historical Society

c/o Patricia Sparks
173-177 Euston Rd., The Library, London, NW1 2BJ, England, UK
Founded: 1803
Members: 400
Contact:
Fee: £8
Membership Type: personal
Fee: £8
Membership Type: Quaker institutions
Description: Promotes the study of Quaker History.

Friends of the Earth - England, Wales, and Northern Ireland
FOE

26-28 Underwood St., London, N1 7JQ, England, UK
Tel: 44 207 4901555
Fax: 44 207 4900881
Email: info@foe.co.uk
Website: http://www.foe.co.uk

Founded: 1971
Members: 90000
Staff: 120
Contact:
Fee: £21
Membership Type: individual
Fee: £29
Membership Type: family
Description: Operates as an environmental pressure group, campaigning on a wide range of issues including pollution, transport, energy, waste, habitats, forests, and sustainable development. Exists to protect and improve the environment, now and for the future, through changing political policies and business practices, empowering individuals and communities to take personal and political action, and stimulating wide and intelligent public debate on sustainability issues.
Publication: Magazine
Publication title: Earth Matters. Advertisements.
Publication title: Publications List

Friends of the National Libraries

c/o Department of Manuscripts
The British Library, 96 Euston Rd., London, NW1 2DB, England, UK
Tel: 44 20 74127559
Fax: 44 20 74127787
Founded: 1931
Members: 750
Contact: Michael Borrie, Hon. Sec.
Fee: £30
Membership Type: personal
Fee: £60
Membership Type: corporation
Description: Assists British libraries and record offices in acquiring printed books, manuscripts, and archives by eliciting donations and sponsorship.
Publication: Annual Report
Publication title: Friends of the Libraries Annual Report
Meetings/Conventions: - annual general assembly

Friends of the Royal Watercolour Society and Royal Society of Painter-Printmakers

c/o Bankside Gallery
48 Hopton St., Blackfriars, London, SE1 9JH, England, UK
Tel: 44 20 9287521
Fax: 44 20 9282820
Email: bankside@freeuk.com
Founded: 1986
Contact: Victoria Weir, Deputy Dir.
Fee: £22
Membership Type: ordinary
Description: Patrons of the Royal Watercolour Society and the Royal Society of Painter-Printmakers. Supports the activities of the RWS and RE. Receives free admission and invitations to art events.
Formerly: Formed by Merger of, Friends of the Royal Society of Painters in Water-Colours
Publication: Bulletin
Publication title: Bankside Bulletin

Frontier (Society for Environmental Exploration - United Kingdom)

50-52 Rivington St., London, EC2A 3QP, England, UK
Tel: 44 207 6132422
Fax: 44 207 6132922
Email: info@frontier.ac.uk

Website: http://www.frontier.ac.uk
Founded: 1989
Staff: 42
Description: Promotes conservation and environmental protection. Conducts operations in areas including forest, protected areas, and coastal zone management, wildlife conservation, and artisanal fisheries research.
Library Subject: tropical biodiversity, rainforests, savannah habitats, coastal and marine environments
Library Type: reference
Publication: Reports

Full Employment League
FEL

6 Southgate Green, Bury St. Edmunds, IP33 2BL, England, UK
Tel: 44 1284 754123
Founded: 1993
Staff: 3
Contact: Robert Corfe
Fee: £5
Membership Type: individual
Description: Members of the public with an active interest in job creation, from all walks of life and social strata, who feel that a body which transcends vested party interests is necessary to achieve this purpose. Acts as a non-party socio-economic movement to work for full employment policies through increasing the UK's manufacturing base and promoting the primary industries. It works particularly for legislation in changing patterns of investment into high- earning job-creating home-based activities to raise sufficient taxable income for pension and other social needs.
Library Subject: social science
Library Type: not open to the public
Publication: Booklets
Publication title: The Crisis of Anglo-Saxon Capitalism

Funeral Furnishing Manufacturers Association

12 Amherst Rd., Kenilworth, CV8 1AH, England, UK
Tel: 44 1926 855225
Email: kenmidgley@hotmail.com
Founded: 1939
Members: 40
Staff: 1
Contact: K.J. Midgley, Gen.Sec.
Fee: £130
Description: Manufacturing and supply companies to the funeral industry.
Meetings/Conventions: - semiannual conference

Furniture History Society
FHS

c/o Dr. Brian Austen
1 Mercedes Cottages, St. John's Rd., Haywards Heath, RH16 4EH, England, UK
Tel: 44 1444 413845
Fax: 44 1444 413845
Email: furniturehistorysociety@hotmail.com
Founded: 1964
Members: 1700
Contact: Dr. Brian Austen, Membership Sec.
Fee: £30
Membership Type: UK
Fee: £35
Membership Type: Europe

Description: Libraries and museums, antique dealers, furniture historians, and others in 28 countries interested in the study of furniture. Sponsors visits to important furniture collections; organizes seminars, lectures, and international tours.
Publication: Journal
Publication title: Furniture History
Second publication: Newsletter
Meetings/Conventions: - annual symposium

Furniture Industry Research Association
FIRA

Maxwell Rd., Stevenage, SG1 2EW, England, UK
Tel: 44 1438 777700
Fax: 44 1438 777800
Email: info@fira.co.uk
Website: http://www.fira.co.uk
Founded: 1961
Staff: 75

Futures and Options Association

150 Minories, 4th Fl., London, EC3N 1LS, England, UK
Tel: 44 207 4267250
Fax: 44 207 4267251
Email: info@foa.co.uk
Website: http://www.foa.co.uk
Founded: 1993
Members: 200
Staff: 9
Contact: Anthony Belchamers, Chief Exec.
Description: Banks and other financial institutions, commodity trade houses, brokerage houses, fund managers, corporate users of the markets, exchanges, clearing houses and specialist firms of lawyers and accountants. Monitors and responds to regulatory and tax developments likely to affect the carrying on of members' business; provides training programmes; heightens product and market awareness and promotes the business of members.
Publication title: Members Briefing
Second publication: Booklets
Publication title: Training and careers
Meetings/Conventions: workshop

Galpin Society
GS

c/o Pauline Holden
32 Eastergate Green, Nustington, Littlehampton, BN16 3EN, England, UK
Tel: 44 1903 776675
Fax: 44 1903 776675
Website: http://dionysos.music.ed.ac.uk/euchmi/galpin/
Founded: 1946
Members: 950
Contact: Pauline Holden, Sec.
Fee: £18
Membership Type: UK
Fee: £28
Membership Type: outside Europe
Description: Individuals, libraries, and institutions in 33 countries. Formed for the publication of original research into the history, construction, development, and use of musical instruments. Society commemorates the late Canon F.W. Galpin, a pioneer in this field. Conducts symposia, holds exhibitions and organises visits to major collections worldwide.
Publication: Journal. Advertisements.
Second publication: Newsletter
Meetings/Conventions: - monthly meeting

Galvanizers Association
GA

Wrens Ct., 56 Victoria Rd., Sutton Coldfield, B72 1SY, England, UK
Tel: 44 121 3558838
Fax: 44 121 3558727
Email: ga@hdg.org.uk
Website: http://www.hdg.org.uk
Founded: 1947
Members: 50
Staff: 8
Contact: David Baron, Mktg.Mgr.
Description: Firms engaged in hot dip galvanizing in the United Kingdom and the Republic of Ireland. Prmotoes the use of hot dip goelvanijed steel and provides authoritative information and advice to users and potential users.
Publication: Directory
Publication title: Directory of General Galvanizers
Second publication: Journal
Publication title: Hot Dip Galvanizing

GAMBICA, Association for Instrumentation, Control, Automation and Laboratory Technology

St. George's House, 155-203 Waterloo Rd., London, SE1 8WB, England, UK
Tel: 44 20 76428080
Fax: 44 20 76428096
Email: assoc@gambica.org.uk
Website: http://www.gambica.org.uk
Founded: 1971
Members: 300
Staff: 14
Contact: Geoff Young, Ch.Exec.
Description: Associates in instrumentation, control, laboratory technology, and automation industry in the UK. Represents the interests of members.
Formerly: Gambica Association for the Instrumentation, Control and Automation Industry in the United Kingdom
Publication title: Product Guides
Second publication: Annual Report

Game Conservancy Trust

Fordingbridge, Hampshire, SP6 1EF, England, UK
Tel: 44 1425 652381
Fax: 44 1425 651026
Email: info@gct.org.uk
Website: http://www.gct.org.uk
Founded: 1968
Members: 26000
Staff: 100
Contact: Stephen Tapper, Dir. of Policy & Public Affairs
Fee: £50
Description: Research is undertaken on all aspects of game and the environment with a view to the development of practical management plans for landowners and farmers.
Library Subject: conservation, wildlife, farming, botany, biodiversity, fisheries, ornithology
Library Type: by appointment only
Publication title: Game Conservancy Review. Advertisements.
Second publication: Magazine
Publication title: Gamewise

Game Farmers Association

Church End House, Church End, Great Rollright, Chipping Norton, OX7 5RX, England, UK
Description: Game Farmers.

Garage Equipment Association
GEA

2-3 Church Walk, Daventry, NN11 4BL, England, UK
Tel: 44 1327 312616
Fax: 44 1327 312606
Email: john@gea.co.uk
Website: http://www.gea.co.uk
Founded: 1946
Members: 112
Staff: 2
Contact: John Nelson, Chief Exec.
Description: Manufacturers, distributors, importers, service and installation technicians, and other interested individuals of the garage equipment industry. Strives to produce and maintain quality garage equipment. Promotes high standards in the technical and economic aspects of garage equipment.
Library Subject: Automotive
Library Type: reference
Publication: Book
Publication title: Auto-Solve Diagnostic Assistance
Second publication: Book
Publication title: Code of Practice
Meetings/Conventions: - bimonthly

Garden Centre Association

19 High St., Theale, Reading, RG7 5AH, England, UK
Tel: 44 118 9323360
Fax: 44 118 9308915
Email: info@gca.org.uk
Website: http://www.gca.org.uk
Founded: 1966
Members: 350
Staff: 3
Contact: Gillie Westwood, Admin.
Fee: £500
Membership Type: full
Fee: £320
Membership Type: associate
Description: Leading garden centres throughout the UK. Represents the interests of Britain's leading garden centres. Maintains standards by annual inspection.
Publication: Yearbook
Meetings/Conventions: - annual conference - Exhibits.

Garden History Society

70 Cowcross St., London, EC1M 6EJ, England, UK
Tel: 44 207 6082409
Fax: 44 207 4902974
Email: enquiries@gardenhistorysociety.org
Website: http://www.gardenhistorysociety.org
Founded: 1965
Members: 2400
Staff: 4
Contact: Andrew Plumridge, Dir.
Fee: £30
Membership Type: ordinary single
Fee: £35
Membership Type: outside UK, ordinary single

Description: Persons interested in garden history. Campaigns to protect and conserve garden heritage and to ensure its appreciation.
Publication: Journal
Publication title: Garden History. Advertisements.
Publication title: News
Meetings/Conventions: conference

Garden Industry Manufacturers Association

225 Bristol Rd., Edgbaston, Birmingham, B5 7UB, England, UK
Tel: 44 121 446 6688
Fax: 44 121 446 5215
Email: info@gima.org.uk
Website: http://www.gima.org.uk
Founded: 1982
Members: 135
Staff: 2
Contact: Peter Marsh, Dir.
Description: Suppliers of garden products for use by consumers. Provides an opportunity to exchange views and for co-operation between members on matters of importance to garden industry: Represents their opinions and views to other bodies, associations, the media, government and trade generally. Organises a calender of events that are of business value to member companies.
Library Type: open to the public
Meetings/Conventions: - annual dinner

GARDENEX: Federation of Garden and Leisure Manufacturers

The White House, High St., Brasted, TN16 1JE, England, UK
Tel: 44 1959 565995
Fax: 44 1959 565885
Email: info@gardenex.com/index.html
Website: http://www.gardenex.com
Founded: 1961
Members: 185
Staff: 9
Contact: Amanda Sizer, Dir.Gen.
Description: Gardenex promotes and expands the exports of British garden and leisure products. Its membership is comprised of British garden and leisure product manufacturers who export their products; associate member category open to companies who supply services to exporters. Services to members include: regular export leads; joint ventures to overseas exhibitions; a product sourcing service for the use of overseas buyers; discounts on a wide range of business services; organizing inward and outward trade missions; publicising members' garden products worldwide.
Library Subject: gardening market information world-wide; export procedure information
Library Type: by appointment only
Publication: Directory
Publication title: British Garden Products and Services Guide for International Buyers. Advertisements.
Second publication: Magazine
Publication title: Gardenex News. Advertisements.
Meetings/Conventions: Growing Worldwide - annual conference - Exhibits.

Gasket Cutters Association
GCA

105 St. Peter's St., St. Albans, AL1 3EJ, England, UK
Tel: 44 1727 896084
Fax: 44 1727 896026
Email: info@gcassociation.co.uk

Website: http://www.gcassociation.co.uk
Contact: Paul Neale, Sec.Gen.
Fee: £250
Membership Type: member
Fee: £200
Membership Type: associate
Description: Companies engaged in the conversion of materials into gaskets for all types of industrial use. Furthers and protects the commercial interests of members.

Gauchers Association
GA

25 W. Cottages, London, NW6 1RJ, England, UK
Tel: 44 207 4331121
Email: office@gauchersassociation.org.uk
Website: http://www.gaucher.org.uk
Founded: 1991
Description: Individuals with Gaucher's disease. (Gaucher's disease is a genetic disorder resulting in enzyme deficiency, producing symptoms including anemia, fatigue, bone pain and degeneration, easy bruising, and a tendency to bleed. The rare Type 2 and Type 3 forms of Gaucher's disease can also cause various neurological problems.) Seeks to improve the quality of life of people with Gaucher's disease; encourages medical research on the diagnosis, prevention, and treatment of the disease. Serves as a support group for people with Gaucher's disease; works to increase the availability of enzyme treatments; facilitates contact among the families of people with Gaucher's disease in the UK.

Gauge and Tool Makers' Association

3 Forge House, Summerleys Rd., Princes Risborough, HP27 9DT, England, UK
Tel: 44 1844 274222
Fax: 44 1844 274227
Email: gtma@gtma.co.uk
Website: http://www.gtma.co.uk
Founded: 1942
Members: 310
Staff: 7
Contact: J.L. Moore, Exec.Mgr.
Description: Gauge and tool making companies. Concerned with jigs, fixtures, press tools, moulds and dies, measuring equipment, special tooling and precision machining.
Publication: Directory
Publication title: Buyer's Guide

Gemini News Service

9 White Lion St., London, N1 9PD, England, UK
Tel: 44 207 2781111
Fax: 44 207 2780345
Email: alexw@panoslondon.org.uk
Founded: 1963
Members: 80
Staff: 7
Contact: Dipankar De Sarkar, Editor-in-Chief
Description: Economically developing countries are subscribers. Nonprofit news service focusing on issues in international development. Seeks to produce a greater public understanding of economic development issues, and to inform governments of trends in development program design and implementation.
Publication title: Gemini News Service

GEMMA

BM Box 5700, London, WC1N 3XX, England, UK
Founded: 1976
Members: 150
Contact: Elsa Beckett, Coord.
Fee: £8
Description: Lesbian and bisexual women with and without disabilities. Works towards diminishing the isolation of lesbian and bisexual women with disabilities through a pen-, tape-, phone-, and braille-friend network. Provides information on other lesbian groups and helplines.
Library Subject: Silver Leaves anthology, members fiction and non-fiction
Library Type: open to the public
Publication: Magazine
Publication title: Facets/Silver Leaves
Second publication: Newsletter
Meetings/Conventions: - monthly meeting London UK

Gemmological Association and Gem Testing Laboratory of Great Britain

GAGTL

27 Greville St., London, EC1N 8TN, England, UK
Tel: 44 207 4043334
Fax: 44 207 4048843
Email: gagtl@btinternet.com
Website: http://www.gem-a.info
Founded: 1931
Members: 3500
Staff: 19
Contact: Mary Burland
Fee: £75
Membership Type: outside UK
Fee: £250
Membership Type: laboratory membership
Description: Ordinary - those members not having achieved exam passes; laboratory - mainly trade for use of testing and identifying stones; Fellow - those members having passed exams. Lectures for members/non-members throughout year. Education activities - taking exams and issuing results. Selling of Gemological instruments. Testing of gemstones for members and trade. Attending various jewelery trade shows throughout the year.
Publication: Newsletter
Publication title: Gem and Jewellery News
Second publication: Journal
Publication title: The Journal of Gemology. Advertisements.
Meetings/Conventions: - annual conference London UK

General Aviation Manufacturers and Traders Association

ATOA

19 Church St., Brill, Aylesbury, HP18 9RT, England, UK
Tel: 44 1844 238020
Fax: 44 1844 238087
Email: ga@gamta.org
Website: http://www.gamta.org
Founded: 1975
Members: 130
Contact: G.S. Forbes, Exec. Officer
Description: Aircraft operators; individuals and companies concerned with air taxi, charter, and commuter flight transportation. Promotes and represents members' interests before regulatory bodies. Maintains liaisons with other organizations in the air transport industry.

General Aviation Safety Council

Rochester Airport, Chatham, ME5 9SD, England, UK
Tel: 44 1634 200203
Fax: 44 1634 200203
Email: info@gen-av-safety.demon.co.uk
Founded: 1964
Members: 60
Staff: 2
Contact: Mr. J. Campbell, Chief Exec.
Fee: £12
Description: Private and business aviation, flying and gliding clubs, commercial operation. Fosters the development of general aviation in the UK along safe lines by encouraging competence among general aviation pilots and operators.
Library Type: not open to the public
Publication: Magazine
Publication title: Flight Safety. Advertisements.
Meetings/Conventions: - quarterly meeting

General Chiropractic Council

GCC

344-354 Gray's Inn Rd., London, WC1X 8BP, England, UK
Tel: 44 20 77135155
Fax: 44 20 77135844
Email: enquiries@gcc-uk.org
Website: http://www.gcc-uk.org/
Founded: 1999
Contact: Margaret Coats, Ch.Exec./Reg.
Description: Aims to protect the public by regulating Chiropractors; set standards of chiropractic education, practice and conduct.

General Council and Register of Naturopaths

Goswell House, 2 Goswel Rd., Somerset, BA16 0JG, England, UK
Tel: 44 870 7456984
Fax: 44 870 7456985
Email: admin@naturopathy.org.uk
Website: http://www.naturopathy.org.uk
Founded: 1964
Members: 325
Staff: 3
Contact: M.W.F. Szewiel, Sec.
Fee: £110
Membership Type: professional
Description: Fully qualified naturopathic practitioners. Maintains educational, professional and ethical standards and the safe practice of naturopathy for the benefit and protection of the public.
Publication: Membership Directory

General Council of the Bar

3 Bedford Row, London, WC1R 4DB, England, UK
Tel: 44 207 2420082
Fax: 44 207 8319217
Email: generaloffice@barcouncil.org.uk
Website: http://www.barcouncil.org.uk
Founded: 1894
Members: 16000
Contact: David Bean, Chm.
Description: The professional and governing body for barristers.

General Dental Council
GDC

c/o Antony Townsend, Chief Exec./Registrar
37 Wimpole St., London, W1G 8DQ, England, UK
Tel: 44 207 8873800
Fax: 44 207 2243294
Email: information@gdc-uk.org
Website: http://www.gdc-uk.org
Founded: 1956
Members: 29
Staff: 60
Contact: Antony Townsend, Ch.Exec./Registrar
Fee: £300
Membership Type: dentist
Fee: £250
Membership Type: orthodontic
Description: Regulatory body of the dental profession; registers all qualified dentists, dental hygienists and dental therapists.
Publication title: Dentists Register
Second publication: Proceedings
Publication title: Minutes of Meeting of the Council and Professional Conduct Committee
Meetings/Conventions: meeting London UK

General Federation of Trade Unions

c/o Central House
Upper Woburn Pl., London, WC1H 0HY, England, UK
Tel: 44 171 3872578
Fax: 44 171 3830820
Email: gftuhq@gftu.org.uk
Website: http://www.gftu.org.uk
Founded: 1899
Members: 35
Contact: Mike Bradley, Gen.Sec.
Description: Specialist trades unions. Provides members with education courses, research facilities, training, technology and information.
Publication title: Federation News

General Hypnotherapy Register

Hazelwood Broadmead, Sway Lymington, Lymington, S041 6DH, England, UK
Tel: 44 1590 683770
Fax: 44 1590 683770
Email: admin@general-hypnotherapy-register.com
Website: http://www.general-hypnotherapy-register.com
Founded: 2000
Members: 750
Staff: 2
Contact: William Broom
Fee: £60
Membership Type: registered
Description: Counselors and therapists, mainly offering short-term treatment in private practice. Most members offer hypnotherapy as their main method of treatment. To represent and protect the interests of independent therapists and hypnotherapists. To provide referrals lists of practitioners in which the public may have full confidence by maintaining high standards of practice and conduct among members. Provides register of practitioners.
Formerly: National Council of Psychotherapists and Hypnotherapy Register
Publication: Bulletin. Advertisements.
Meetings/Conventions: - periodic workshop

General Medical Council

178 Great Portland St., London, W1N 5JE, England, UK
Tel: 44 207 5807642
Fax: 44 207 9153641
Email: gmc@gmc.uk.org
Founded: 1858
Members: 102
Staff: 180
Contact: Finlay Scott, Chief Exec. & Registrar
Description: Doctors elected by UK doctors or appointed by UK universities with medical schools and by Royal Colleges. Lay members nominated by Privy Council. Protects the public by overseeing medical education, keeping a register of qualified doctors and taking action where a doctor's fitness to pratise is in doubt.
Publication title: Duties of a Doctor - Guidance on Professional Ethics
Second publication: Newsletter
Publication title: GMC News Review
Meetings/Conventions: - semiannual meeting

General Optical Council

41 Harley St., London, W1G 8DJ, England, UK
Tel: 44 20 75803898
Fax: 44 20 74363525
Email: goc@optical.org
Website: http://www.optical.org
Founded: 1958
Members: 16000
Staff: 14
Contact: Peter C. Coe, Registrar/Chief Exec.
Fee: £85
Membership Type: ordinary
Description: Registered opticians and enrolled bodies (corporate) carrying out work as opticians. The 1958 Opticians Act established the General Optical Council. The Council registers opticians in the UK and deals with matters relating to the Opticians professional education and Professional discipline.
Publication title: Annual Register
Second publication: Annual Report

General Osteopathic Council
GOsC

Osteopathy House, 176 Tower Bridge Rd., London, SE1 3LU, England, UK
Tel: 44 171 3576655
Email: concerns@osteopathy.org.uk
Website: http://www.osteopathy.org.uk/index.htm
Contact: Nigel Clark, Chm.
Description: Promotes the profession of Osteopathy in the United Kingdom; provides a Code of Practice which sets out standards of conduct and practice for all osteopaths.
Publication: Journal
Publication title: The Osteopath. Advertisements.

Geographical Association of England
GA

160 Solly St., Sheffield, S1 4BF, England, UK
Tel: 44 114 2960088
Fax: 44 114 2967176
Email: ga@geography.org.uk
Website: http://www.geography.org.uk
Founded: 1893
Members: 10000

Staff: 17
Contact: Ian Gregg, Coord.
Description: Corporations and individuals. Works to promote the study of geography at all educational levels. Represents its members in national and international matters. Conducts educational programs. Maintains working groups and speakers' bureau.
Publication: Journal
Publication title: Geography. Advertisements.
Publication title: Primary Geographer. Advertisements.
Meetings/Conventions: - annual conference - Exhibits.

Geological Society
GSL

Burlington House, Piccadilly, London, W1J 0BG, England, UK
Tel: 44 207 4349944
Fax: 44 207 4398975
Email: enquiries@geolsoc.org.uk
Website: http://www.geolsoc.org.uk
Founded: 1807
Members: 9000
Staff: 32
Contact: E. Nickless, Exec.Sec.
Fee: £88
Description: Geologists, geophysicists, geotechnical engineers, students, and interested individuals. Promotes the study and practice of geology and allied disciplines. Holds scientific and technical meetings at its Piccadilly headquarters and its regional branches. Bestows the title of Chartered Geologist to candidates with the appropriate academic qualifications, practical training, and professional responsibility.
Formerly: Absorbed, Institution of Geologists
Publication: Journal
Publication title: Engineering Geology
Second publication: Directory
Publication title: Geologists Directory
Meetings/Conventions: - annual convention

Geologists Association

Burlington House, Piccadilly, London, W1V 9AG, England, UK
Tel: 44 207 4349298
Fax: 44 207 2870280
Email: geol.assoc@btinternet.com
Website: http://www.geologist.demon.co.uk
Founded: 1858
Members: 2500
Staff: 1
Contact: John Crocker, Gen.Sec.
Description: Amateur and professional geologists. Serving the interests of the amateur geologist.
Publication: Proceedings
Publication title: Proceedings of the Geologists' Association

George MacDonald Society
GMS

38 S Vale, Upper Norwood, London, SE19 3BA, England, UK
Tel: 44 1342 823859
Fax: 44 1342 823859
Email: webmaster@george-macdonald.com
Website: http://www.gmsociety.org.uk
Founded: 1980
Members: 170
Contact: Richard Lines, Chm.

Fee: £10
Membership Type: individual and institutional
Fee: £20
Membership Type: outside UK
Description: Individuals devoted to the study of the life and works of George MacDonald (1824-1905), Scottish novelist and lecturer remembered primarily for his fairy tales and adult fantasies. Aim is to expose modern generations to the writings and religious views of MacDonald. Aims to establish biographical archives. Sponsors discussions.
Library Type: reference
Publication: Journal
Publication title: North Wind. Advertisements.
Second publication: Newsletter
Publication title: ORTS Newsletter
Meetings/Conventions: - periodic conference - Exhibits.

German History Society

c/o Dr. Mark Hewitson
Dept. of German, University College of London, Grower St., London, BS8 1TE, England, UK
Tel: 44 20 76793038
Fax: 44 20 78130168
Email: m.hewitson@ucl.ac.uk
Website: http://members.tripod.co.uk/GHS
Members: 300
Contact: Dr. Jill Stephenson, Chm.
Fee: £20
Membership Type: full
Fee: £10
Membership Type: postgraduate
Description: Professional association for historians of the German Speaking world.
Publication: Journal
Publication title: German History
Meetings/Conventions: conference

German-British Chamber of Industry and Commerce

Mecklenburg House, 16 Buckingham Gate, London, SW1E 6LB, England, UK
Tel: 44 20 79764100
Fax: 44 20 79764101
Email: mail@ahk-london.co.uk
Website: http://www.ahk-london.co.uk
Founded: 1971
Members: 910
Staff: 31
Contact: Ulrich Hoppe, Mng.Dir.
Fee: £127
Description: Businesses and individuals. Promotes trade and investment between Germany and the U.K. Disseminates information on import and export requirements, and wholesale, distribution, and retail companies. Offers advice on legal matters, management and marketing problems, tax and VAT matters, debt collection, and purchasing. Organizes seminars, lectures, and market research and analysis programs.
Library Type: not open to the public
Publication: Magazine
Publication title: Initiative
Second publication: Membership Directory
Publication title: Members

Ghost Club

PO Box 160, St. Leonards-On-Sea, TN38 8WA, England, UK
Email: r.m.snow@ghostclub.org.uk
Website: http://www.ghostclub.org.uk
Founded: 1851
Contact: Alan Murdie, Chm.
Description: Membership by invitation only. Investigates and researches all subjects not yet fully understood or accepted by science. Focuses on both spontaneous and induced psychic phenomena. Compiles statistics.
Library Subject: paranormal research, ghosts, hauntings
Library Type: reference
Publication: Book
Publication title: Peter Underwood's Guide to Ghosts & Haunted Places
Second publication: Journal
Publication title: Society News
Meetings/Conventions: meeting

Giftware Association

Federation House, 10 Vyse St., Birmingham, B18 6LT, England, UK
Tel: 44 121 2362657
Fax: 44 121 2371106
Email: enquiries@ga-uk.org
Website: http://www.ga-uk.org
Founded: 1947
Members: 1500
Staff: 5
Contact: Isabel Martinson, Chief Exec.
Description: Manufacturers, importers, distributors, wholesalers and retailers of giftware. Services offered by the Association include Code of Practice, discounts-trade fairs, healthcare, hotels, export assistance, free legal advice, copyright assistance, training, seminars, credit management services, newsletters.
Publication: Newsletter
Publication title: Newsline. Advertisements.

Gilbert and Sullivan Society

7/20 Hampden Gurney St., London, W1H 5AX, England, UK
Founded: 1924
Members: 450
Contact: Valerie Colin-Russ, Hon.Sec.
Fee: £10
Membership Type: within the United Kingdom
Fee: £12
Membership Type: outside UK
Description: Encourages interest in the Gilbert and Sullivan operas and enables members to develop their knowledge of all aspects appertaining to the operas and their authors.
Library Subject: Gilbert and/or Sullivan, D'oyly Carte opera
Library Type: open to the public
Publication: Magazine
Publication title: Gilbert & Sullivan News. Advertisements.
Meetings/Conventions: - triennial convention London UK

Gilt Edged Market Makers Association

c/o Barclays Capital
5 The North Colonnade, Canary Wharf, London, E14 4BB, England, UK
Tel: 44 207 7762323
Fax: 44 171 7734868
Founded: 1986
Members: 17
Contact: Ecian Haricness, Chmn.

Description: Firms which are registered with the Bank of England and London Stock Exchange as market makers in gilt-edged securities. Adjudicates on changes thought necessary by GEMMS in the interests of the market and communicates matters arising to the Bank of England.

Gin and Vodka Association of Great Britain

Cross Keys House, Queen St., Salisbury, SP1 1EY, England, UK
Tel: 44 1722 415892
Fax: 44 1722 415840
Email: ginvodka@lineone.net
Website: http://www.ginvodka.org
Founded: 1991
Members: 25
Staff: 3
Contact: Edwin Atkinson
Description: Producers, brand owners and importers of gin and/or vodka. Protects and promotes the interests of the UK gin and vodka trades at home and abroad and aims to prevent malpractice or abuses within the trade. Puts the trade's views to UK Government and to EC bodies and informs members of relevant developments and of business opportunities.
Formerly: Formed by Merger of, Gin Rectifiers and Distillers Association
Publication: Newsletter
Publication title: Newsletter
Second publication: Annual Report

Gingerbread

7 Sovereign Close, Sovereign Court, London, E1W 3HW, England, UK
Tel: 44 207 4889300
Fax: 44 207 4889333
Email: office@gingerbread.org.uk
Website: http://www.gingerbread.org.uk
Founded: 1970
Members: 3600
Staff: 36
Contact: Amanda Ball, Chief Exec.
Publication: Newsletter
Publication title: Ginger Junior
Second publication: Newsletter
Publication title: Ginger Update

Girl Guiding UK

17-19 Buckingham Palace Rd., London, SW1W 0PT, England, UK
Tel: 44 20 78346242
Fax: 44 20 76306199
Email: website@girlguiding.org.uk
Website: http://www.guides.org.uk
Members: 700000
Description: Committed to enabling girls and young women to fulfill potential and to take an active and responsible role in society through distinctive, stimulating and enjoyable program of activities delivered by trained volunteer leaders.

Girls Friendly Society - United Kingdom - GFS Platform
GFS

Townsend House, 126 Queens Gate, London, SW7 5LQ, England, UK
Tel: 44 207 5899628
Fax: 44 207 2251458

Email: admin@gfsplatform.org.uk
Website: http://www.gfsplatform.org.uk
Founded: 1875
Members: 2000
Staff: 70
Contact: Sarah Coulam, Admin.Asst.
Fee: £5
Description: Girls and women over the ages of 6. Conducts creative and challenging recreational and training activities for young women. Offers low-cost, secure housing for women. Provides guidance and support to troubled young women.
Library Type: reference
Publication: Newsletter
Publication title: Platform News
Meetings/Conventions: World Council - triennial - Exhibits.

Girls' Schools Association

130 Regent Rd., Leicester, LE1 7PG, England, UK
Tel: 44 116 2541619
Fax: 44 116 2553792
Email: info@girls-schools.org.uk
Website: http://www.girls-schools.org.uk
Contact: Ms. S. Cooper, Gen.Sec.
Description: Girls schools.

Glass and Glazing Federation

44-48 Borough High St., London, SE1 1XB, England, UK
Tel: 44 20 74037177
Fax: 44 20 73577458
Email: info@ggf.org.uk
Website: http://www.ggf.org.uk
Founded: 1977
Members: 550
Staff: 23
Contact: Nigel Rees, Chief Exec./Sec.
Description: Members are manufacturers, processors and installers of architectural glass and frames. Writes and maintains technical standards within the industry and all GGF members abide by a Code of Good Practice. GGF is the voice of the window and cladding industry. Developed government-approved self-assessment scheme for the industry (FENSA), to allow companies in England and Wales comply with changes to building regulations relating to energy efficiency.
Publication: Newsletter
Publication title: Glass Eye. Advertisements.
Second publication: Book
Publication title: The Glazing Manual
Meetings/Conventions: - annual convention - Exhibits.

Global Ideas Bank
GIB

c/o Institute for Social Inventions
6 Blackstock Mews, Blackstock Rd., London, N4 2BT, England, UK
Tel: 44 20 82082853
Fax: 44 20 84526434
Email: rhino@dial.pipex.com
Website: http://www.globalideasbank.org
Founded: 1985
Staff: 3
Contact: Nick Temple
Fee: £15
Membership Type: annual subscription

Description: Seeks to gather and disseminate ideas for improving the quality of life worldwide. Maintains registry of socially innovative ideas and projects contributed by interested individuals worldwide.
Library Subject: social innovation
Library Type: by appointment only
Publication: Journal
Publication title: Encyclopedia of Best Ideas

Glosa Education Organisation
GEO

c/o Glosa International Language Network
PO Box 18, Richmond, TW9 2GE, England, UK
Website: http://www.glosa.org
Founded: 1987
Members: 600
Staff: 2
Contact: Wendy Ashby
Description: Promotes the teaching and use of Glosa (a language having no grammar and a vocabulary based on Latin and Greek root words) in 20 countries for international communications, particularly between Third World workers and representatives of industrialized nations. Encourages the publication of scientific and technical papers in Glosa; provides consultative services and educational programs; sponsors courses; discussions; speakers; sample talks.
Formerly: Formed by Merger of, Glosa International Language Network
Publication title: Dictionaries & Teaching Materials
Second publication: Newsletter
Publication title: Plu Glosa Nota
Meetings/Conventions: Local Conferences - periodic

Glued Laminated Timber Association

c/o Chiltern House
Stocking Lane, Hughenden Valley, High Wycombe, HP14 4ND, England, UK
Tel: 44 1494 565180
Fax: 44 1494 565487
Website: http://www.glulam.co.uk
Founded: 1988
Members: 4
Description: Manufacturers and suppliers of glued laminated timber. Concerned with the promotion and awareness of glued laminated timber.
Publication: Brochures

GMB

22-24 Worple Rd., London, SW19 4DD, England, UK
Tel: 44 20 89473131
Fax: 44 20 89446552
Email: john.edmonds@gmb.org.uk
Website: http://www.gmb.org.uk
Founded: 1889
Members: 690000
Staff: 704
Contact: John Edmonds, Gen.Sec.
Fee: £8
Description: Advances the economic and social interests of working people. Regulates relations between members and their employers. Promotes favorable legislation. Provides employment assistance and legal aid; offers educational programs covering shop standards, staff representatives, pensions, negotiations, and health and safety; conducts research into work injuries and health and safety.
Library Type: not open to the public

Formerly: Formed by Merger of, Association of Professional, Executive, Clerical, and Computer Staff and GMB
Meetings/Conventions: - biennial - Exhibits. Blackpool UK

Goat Veterinary Society

c/o John Matthews
The Limes, Chalk St., Rettendon Common, Chelmsford, CM3 5DA, England, UK
Tel: 44 1245 353741
Fax: 44 1245 348564
Email: goatvetsoc@vetweb.co.uk
Website: http://www.vetweb.co.uk/sites/goatsoc1.htm
Founded: 1979
Contact: John Matthews, Sr. VP
Description: Works to improve knowledge about goats in the veterinary profession.
Publication: Journal
Publication title: The Goat Veterinary Society Journal
Meetings/Conventions: - semiannual meeting

Gold Foundation

c/o Teresa Needs, Sec.
Foundation House, Hanbury Manor, Ware, SG12 OUH, England, UK
Tel: 44 1920 484044
Fax: 44 1920 484055
Founded: 1952
Staff: 16
Contact: Alan Bough, Admin. and Finance Mgr.

Goldsmiths' Company

Goldsmiths' Hall, Foster Ln., London, EC2V 6BN, England, UK
Tel: 44 20 76067010
Fax: 44 20 76061511
Email: the.clerk@thegoldsmiths.co.uk
Website: http://www.thegoldsmiths.co.uk
Founded: 1327
Members: 1900
Staff: 100
Contact: R.D. Buchanan-Dunlop
Description: Mainly serving and retired members of the silversmithing, jewellery and allied trades, but includes members from many other professions. A livery company of the City of London, the Goldsmiths' Company operates the London Assay Office and promotes excellence in design and craftsmanship for modern silverware and jewellery.
Library Subject: hallmarks, silver and jewellery
Library Type: by appointment only
Publication: Magazine
Publication title: Goldsmiths Review

Grace and Compassion Benedictines

St. Benedict's Generalate, 1 Manor Rd., Kemp Town, Brighton, BN2 5EA, England, UK
Tel: 44 1273 680720
Fax: 44 1273 680527
Email: generalate@graceandcompassion.co.uk
Website: http://www.dabnet.org/gcb.htm
Founded: 1954
Members: 201
Staff: 20
Contact: Mother Mary Garson
Description: Individuals, Benedictine congregations, and long-term care facilities for the elderly. Seeks to improve the quality of life of

elderly people requiring residential care and other living assistance. Maintains network of nursing homes, group residences, and shelters for the elderly. Provides charitable assistance to the elderly, frail and sick.
Library Subject: religion, fiction and non-fiction
Library Type: reference
Publication: Newsletter
Publication title: Our Lady's Newsletter
Meetings/Conventions: - semiannual board meeting

Grain and Feed Trade Association
GAFTA

GAFTA House, 6 Chapel Place, Rivington St., London, EC2A 3SH, England, UK
Tel: 44 207 8149666
Fax: 44 207 8148383
Email: post@gafta.com
Website: http://www.gafta.com
Founded: 1971
Members: 850
Staff: 16
Contact: Pamela Kirby Johnson, Dir.Gen.
Description: Promotes international trade in grain, animal feedingstuffs, pulses and rice and to protect the interests of members worldwide, providing support and international contacts,
Publication: Newsletter
Publication title: GAFTA Newsletter. Advertisements.
Second publication: Handbook
Publication title: Member's Yearbook

Grantham Chamber of Commerce

Springfield House conference, Springfield Business Park Centre, Springfield Rd., Grantham, NG31 7BJ, England, UK
Contact: J S P Smith
Description: Promotes business and commerce.

Graphical, Paper and Media Union
GPMU

c/o Keys House
63/67 Bromham Rd., Bedford, MK40 2AG, England, UK
Tel: 44 1234 351521
Fax: 44 1234 270580
Email: general@gpmu.org.uk
Website: http://www.gpmu.org.uk
Founded: 1991
Members: 269881
Contact: Tony Dubbins, Gen.Sec.
Description: Those concerned with paper and board making, ink making, graphic design, reproduction, printing, bookbinding and print finishing. Clerical workers in all areas of printing, publishing and allied trades.
Publication: Journal
Publication title: GPMU Journal

Great Britain Postcard Club

c/o Mrs. Drene Brennan
34 Harper House, St. John Crescent, London, SW9 7LW, England, UK
Tel: 44 207 7719404
Founded: 1961
Members: 400

Staff: 1
Contact:
Fee: £10
Description: Promotes world friendship.
Library Subject: postcards
Library Type: not open to the public
Publication: Magazine
Publication title: Postcard World. Advertisements.

Greater London Industrial Archaeology Society

31 The High St., Farnborough Village, Orpington, BR6 7BQ, England, UK
Tel: 44 1689852186
Email: chairman@glias.org.uk
Website: http://www.glias.org.uk
Founded: 1968
Members: 600
Contact: Dr. Denis Smith, Chm.
Fee: £8
Membership Type: individual
Fee: £7
Membership Type: student & retired
Description: Concerned with recording and, where applicable, conserving London's Industrial past and bringing this to the notice of general public.
Library Subject: industrial history and archaeology
Library Type: not open to the public

Greater Peterborough Chamber of Commerce, Training and Enterprise

5 The Forum, Minerva Business Park, Peterborough, PE2 6FT, England, UK
Tel: 44 1733 393333
Fax: 44 1733 393330
Email: gpcci@gpcci.co.uk
Members: 1100
Staff: 125
Contact: Barry Mason, Chief Exec.
Description: Promotes business and commerce.

Green Organisation

The Mill House, Mill Ln., Earls Barton, Northampton, NN6 0NR, England, UK
Tel: 44 1604 810507
Fax: 44 1604 810507
Website: http://www.thegreenorganisation.info
Founded: 1992
Members: 150
Staff: 2
Contact: Roger Wolens, Nat'l.Organizer
Fee: £250
Description: Individuals interested in environmental protection and the conservation of natural resources. Assists companies wishing to become environmentally responsible, and to be recognized as such by the public.
Library Subject: environment
Library Type: not open to the public
Publication title: Environmental Best Practice Work of Reference. Advertisements.
Meetings/Conventions: Environmental Best Practice - annual seminar London UK

GreenNet

74-77 White Lion St., 33 Islington High St., London, N1 9LH, England, UK
Tel: 44 845 554011
Fax: 44 207 8375551
Email: info@gn.apc.org
Website: http://www.gn.apc.org
Founded: 1986
Members: 1500
Staff: 7
Contact: Karen Banks
Fee: £13.5
Membership Type: standard
Description: Computer network seeking to bring together individuals interested in issues of global concern, particularly environmental protection. Gathers and disseminates information; conducts charitable and educational programs.
Publication: Newsletter
Publication title: GreenNet News
Second publication: Bulletin

Greenpeace UK

Canonbury Villas, London, N1 2PN, England, UK
Tel: 44 20 78658100
Fax: 44 20 78658200
Email: info@uk.greenpeace.org
Website: http://www.greenpeace.org.uk
Founded: 1971
Members: 20
Contact: Dan Mills
Description: Individuals interested in environmental protection and human and animal rights. Conducts campaigns to end exploitation of people, animals, and the environment.
Library Type: by appointment only
Meetings/Conventions: - periodic board meeting London UK

Greeting Card Association

United House, North Rd., London, N7 9DP, England, UK
Tel: 44 207 6190396
Fax: 44 207 6076411
Email: gca@max-publishing.co.ukgreetingcardassociation.org.uk
Founded: 1994
Members: 170
Staff: 1
Contact: Sharon Little
Description: Publishers of greeting cards and related products. Represents, promotes and protects the greeting card industry in the United Kingdom.
Publication: Magazine
Publication title: Progressive Greetings. Advertisements.

Grieg Society of Great Britain

c/o Beryl Foster
25 Belgrave Sq., London, SW1X 8QD, England, UK
Founded: 1992
Members: 100
Contact: Beryl Foster, Chm.
Fee: £12
Membership Type: single
Fee: £18
Membership Type: joint
Description: Promotes British interest in Grieg and other Norwegian composers and to pursue the cultural links between Britain and Norway.
Library Subject: Grieg and Norwegian Music
Library Type: not open to the public

Group-Analytic Society

258 Belize Rd., London, NW6 4BT, England, UK
Tel: 44 207 3161824
Fax: 44 207 3161880
Email: groupanalytic.society@virgin.net
Website: http://www.groupanalyticsociety.org/
Founded: 1952
Members: 600
Staff: 3
Contact: Mrs. Brenda Ling
Description: Group-analysts, doctors, psychiatrists, professors, educationalists, caring professions. Receives and administers funds to be used for the promotion and development of group analysis as a treatment, prophylaxis and science; its advancement through study, research and teaching, and the provision of advisory services, lectures and publications.
Publication: Journal
Publication title: Journal - Group Analysis

Guide Association UK

Atlantic St., Broadheath, Altrincham, WA14 5EQ, England, UK
Tel: 44 161 9412237
Fax: 44 161 9416326
Email: jonT@girlguiding.org.uk
Website: http://www.guides.org.uk
Founded: 1910
Members: 650000
Staff: 170
Contact: Ms. Denise King, Chief Exec.
Description: Assists the emotional, spiritual, mental, and physical development of girls and young women in the United Kingdom. Promotes the development of self-awareness, self-respect, and self-confidence; teaches teamwork and leadership skills. Promotes the protection of the environment. Fosters the ideals of multicultural youth work.
Formerly: Girl Guides Association
Publication: Magazine
Publication title: Brownie. Advertisements.
Publication title: Guiding

Guide Dogs for the Blind Association

Hillfields, Burghfield Common, Reading, RG7 3YG, England, UK
Tel: 44 118 9835555
Fax: 44 118 9835433
Email: guidedogs@gdba.org.uk
Website: http://www.guidedogs.org.uk
Founded: 1934
Members: 5000
Contact: Geraldine Peacock, Chief Exec.
Description: Provides guide dogs, mobility and other rehabilitation services that meet the needs of blind and partially sighted people.
Publication: Magazine
Publication title: FORWARD

Guild of Agricultural Journalists

47 Court Meadow, Rotherfield, Crowborough, TN6 3LQ, England, UK
Tel: 44 189 2853187
Fax: 44 189 2853551
Email: don.gomery@farmline.com
Website: http://www.gaj.org.uk
Founded: 1943
Members: 580
Contact: D. Gomery
Fee: £40
Description: Agricultural and horticultural journalists (full members); and those in the agricultural/horticultural industry with media connections (PRs, etc) (associate members). Aims to promote a high professional standard among journalists who specialize in agriculture, horticulture and allied subjects; to represent members' interests; to provide a forum, through business meetings and social activities, to maintain contact with associations of agricultural journalists overseas and to promote schemes for the education of members of the Guild.
Publication: Bulletin
Publication title: Bulletin
Second publication: Yearbook
Publication title: GAJ Yearbook

Guild of Air Pilots and Air Navigators

9 Warwick Ct., Gray's Inn, London, WC1R 5DJ, England, UK
Tel: 44 207 4044032
Fax: 44 207 4044035
Email: gapan@gapan.org
Website: http://www.gapan.org
Founded: 1929
Members: 1650
Staff: 5
Contact: Duncan M.S. Simpson, Master
Fee: £130
Membership Type: freeman, upper freeman, liveryman
Description: Professional, civil and military, and private pilots and navigators covering lighter than air, fixed and rotary wing aircraft. Aims to maintain the highest standards of air safety; to enhance the knowledge and status of air pilots and air navigators; to advise, consult and facilitate the exchange of information; to assist air pilots and air navigators and their dependants in need through a Benevolent Fund.
Library Subject: aviation
Library Type: by appointment only
Publication title: Guild News
Meetings/Conventions: Sir Alan Cobham Presentation - annual general assembly London UK

Guild of Air Traffic Control Officers

24 The Greenwood, Guildford, GU1 2ND, England, UK
Tel: 44 1483 578347
Fax: 44 1483 578347
Email: caf@gatco.org
Website: http://www.gatco.org
Founded: 1954
Members: 2100
Staff: 1
Contact: Mr. Richard Dawson, Pres.
Fee: £78
Membership Type: full
Fee: £300
Membership Type: corporate
Description: Promotes members' interests.
Library Subject: aviation
Library Type: not open to the public
Publication: Journal
Publication title: Transmit. Advertisements.
Meetings/Conventions: Balpa/Gatco Forum - annual workshop

Guild of Antique Dealers and Restorers
GADAR

c/o Maureen Edmondson
111 Belle Vue Rd., Shrewsbury, Shropshire, SY3 7NJ, England, UK
Tel: 44 1743 271852
Website: http://www.gadar.co.uk
Founded: 1989
Members: 300
Staff: 3
Contact: Maureen Edmondson, Admin.
Fee: £40
Membership Type: member
Description: Promotes the image and standards of the Guild, thus creating public awareness of the trade of GADAR. Represents its members' views wherever their interests are involved. Assists members with information to benefit them in their day-to-day trading.
Library Subject: antiques, architecture, restoration
Library Type: not open to the public
Publication: Newsletter

Guild of Architectural Ironmongers

8 Stepney Green, London, E1 3JU, England, UK
Tel: 44 207 7903431
Fax: 44 207 7908517
Email: info@gai.org.uk
Website: http://www.gai.org.uk
Founded: 1961
Members: 525
Staff: 3
Contact: Peter Spill, Dir.
Description: Architectural ironmongers and manufacturers of architectural ironmongery products are corporate members; individual members are those who have passed the guilds examination. Serves to further all aspects of architectural ironmongery, promote the interchange of information to encourage better product design and high professional standards of ironmongery scheduling and specification. Operates a four year programme leading to the GAI Diploma, an industry recognised qualification.
Publication: Journal
Publication title: Architectural Ironmongery Journal. Advertisements.
Second publication: Membership Directory

Guild of Aviation Artists

71 Bondway, London, SW8 1SQ, England, UK
Tel: 44 207 7350634
Fax: 44 207 7350634
Email: admin@gava.org.uk
Website: http://www.gava.org.uk
Founded: 1970
Members: 450
Contact: Ian Burnstork
Description: Professional artists, part time amateur artists and non painting supporters. Encouragement of aviation art in all its forms.
Publication: Newsletter

Guild of British Camera Technicians

c/o Panavision
Britol Rd., Greenford, UB6 8UQ, England, UK
Tel: 44 208 8131999
Fax: 44 208 8132111
Email: admin@gbct.org
Website: http://www.gbct.org
Founded: 1978
Members: 541
Staff: 4
Contact: Christine Henwood, Off.Mgr.
Fee: £120
Membership Type: freelance camera persons
Description: All qualified freelance camera technicians.
Publication: Newsletter
Publication title: GBCT. Advertisements.
Meetings/Conventions: - annual meeting

Guild of British Film Editors

72 Pembroke Rd., London, W8 6NV, England, UK
Tel: 44 20 76028319
Email: secretarygbfe@btopenworld.com
Founded: 1966
Members: 100
Contact: Sally Fisher, Sec.
Description: Senior film and sound editors, by invitation only. To ensure that the true art of film and sound editing is recognised throughout the industry.
Publication: Newsletter

Guild of Drama Adjudicators

14 Elmwood, Welwyn Garden City, AL8 6LE, England, UK
Tel: 44 1707 326488
Fax: 44 1707 326488
Website: http://www.amdram.co.uk/goda
Founded: 1947
Members: 135
Contact: Judith Claxton
Description: Persons with knowledge of the stage and drama especially those who have had some experience of adjudication at drama festivals, verse-speaking and can lecture on drama and theatrical art. Aims to improve the standards of adjudication of amateur drama by establishing recognised principles of practice to which members must adhere.
Publication title: Directory of Adjudicators. Advertisements.
Publication title: News and Views
Meetings/Conventions: - quarterly meeting

Guild of Experienced Motorists

Station Rd., Forest Row, RH18 5EN, England, UK
Tel: 44 1342 825676
Fax: 44 1342 824847
Email: gem@roadsafety.org.uk
Website: http://www.roadsafety.org.uk
Founded: 1932
Members: 60000
Staff: 16
Contact: David Williams, Ch.Exec.
Fee: £14.5
Description: Membership is available to all motorists who have been disqualified from driving during the previous five years; members are encouraged to drive showing Care Courtesy and Concentration at all times.
Formerly: The Company of Veteran Motorists
Publication: Magazine
Publication title: Good Motoring Magazine. Advertisements.

Guild of Fine Food Retailers

PO Box 1525, Gillingham, SP8 4WA, England, UK
Tel: 44 1747 822290
Fax: 44 1747 822289

Email: bob.farrand@finefoodworld.co.uk
Website: http://www.finefoodworld.co.uk/
Founded: 1994
Members: 500
Staff: 5
Contact: Bob Farrand
Fee: £75
Membership Type: retail
Fee: £150
Membership Type: corporate
Description: Fine food retailers.
Publication: Magazine
Publication title: Fine Food Digest. Advertisements.
Meetings/Conventions: Specialty and Fine Food Fair - annual trade show Leeds UK

Guild of Food Writers

48 Crabtree Lane, London, SW6 6LW, England, UK
Tel: 44 207 6101180
Fax: 44 207 6100299
Email: gfw@gfw.co.uk
Website: http://www.gfw.co.uk
Founded: 1984
Members: 350
Staff: 1
Contact: Ms. C. Thomas, Admin.
Fee: £70
Description: Brings together professional food writers including journalists, broadcasters and authors. Prints and issues an annual list of members; extends the range of members' knowledge and experience; contributes to the growth of the public's interest in, and knowledge of, the subject of food.
Publication: Membership Directory
Publication title: Guild of Food Writers Directory

Guild of Glass Engravers

87 Nether St., Finchley, London, N1Z 7NP, England, UK
Fax: 44 20 87319352
Email: enquiries@gge.org.uk
Website: http://www.gge.org.uk
Founded: 1975
Members: 500
Staff: 1
Contact: Christine Weatherhead, Admin.
Fee: £25
Membership Type: lay member
Description: Membership of the Guild is worldwide and is open to anyone who is interested in glass engraving. Lay members may or may not be practising engravers. Craft members, associate fellowship, and fellowship are levels of competence in design and technique. which may be attained through assessment within the Guild. To promote the highest quality of creative design and craftsmanship among glass engravers and to encourage a better understanding of the engravers' skill for those visiting exhibitions or commissioning engraved glass and to advance the education of the public in the art of glass engraving.
Publication: Newsletter
Publication title: Guild of Glass Engravers. Advertisements.
Meetings/Conventions: - annual conference

Guild of Incorporated Surveyors
GS

1 Alexandra St., Queens Rd., Oldham, OL8 2AU, England, UK
Tel: 44 161 6272389
Fax: 44 161 6273336
Website: http://www.aecportico.co.uk/directory/GIS.shtm
Founded: 1950
Members: 1025
Staff: 3
Contact: D.B. Birchenall
Description: Approved surveyors in 6 countries organized to safeguard and further the interests of the surveying profession. Provides professional education; acts as a clearinghouse of legal and technical data and other information. Maintains advisory service; offers technical and social activities and lectures.
Library Type: reference
Formerly: Guild of Surveyors
Publication title: Seminar Technical Papers
Publication title: Survey
Meetings/Conventions: - semiannual seminar

Guild of International Butler Administrators and Personal Assistants
GIBAPA

c/o Ivor Spencer
12 Little Bornes, Dulwich, London, SE21 8SE, England, UK
Tel: 44 20 87605585
Fax: 44 20 86700055
Email: ivor@ivorspencer.com
Website: http://www.ivorspencer.com
Founded: 1982
Members: 75
Staff: 3
Contact: Ivor Spencer, Pres.
Description: Butlers trained in the Ivor Spencer International School for Butler Administrators and Personal Assistants; speakers and masters of ceremonies. Provides a forum for discussion of professional problems and concerns. Encourages the highest standards among British-trained butlers throughout the world. Seeks to keep members informed of current methods of operating a household. Provides consultancy services to film and television companies regarding British-trained butlers. Maintains speakers' bureau and placement service.
Formerly: Guild of British Butlers
Publication: Newsletter
Meetings/Conventions: - periodic competition

Guild of International Professional Toastmasters

12 Little Bornes, London, SE21 8SE, England, UK
Tel: 44 181 6705585
Fax: 44 181 6700055
Email: ivor@ivorspencer.com
Website: http://www.ivorspencer.com
Founded: 1990
Members: 20
Staff: 2
Contact: Ivor Spencer, Pres.
Description: A toastmaster is accepted into the Guild when he has had 5 years experience in the UKs top hotels and livery companies or to have received a Diploma from the Ivor Spencer School for Professional Toastmasters. Aims to meet and to discuss ways of keeping professional standards as high as possible. Also acts as advisers to firms of repute and to promote for them special traditional banquets with authentic ceremonies world wide. Only the finest toastmasters are accepted into the Guild.

Guild of International Songwriters and Composers

Sovereign House, 12 Trewartha Rd., Praa Sands, Penzance, TR20 9ST, England, UK
Tel: 44 1736 762826
Fax: 44 1736 763328
Email: songmag@aol.com
Website: http://www.songwriters-guild.co.uk
Founded: 1936
Members: 8000
Staff: 9
Contact: Carole A. Jones, Gen.Sec.
Fee: £50
Description: Songwriters, composers, publishers, record companies, management companies, recording studios, musicians, singers, lyricists, producers. Advises and assists with the needs of its members in the many aspects of the music industry. Members vary from amateur to professional songwriters, composers, lyricists, poets, musicians, music publishers, record companies, managers, etc. Membership is open to all persons throughout the world. Free songwriters' news magazine available on request with S.A.E./ International Reply Coupons.
Publication title: Songsearch
Second publication: Magazine
Publication title: Songwriting and Composing

Guild of Master Craftsmen

166 High St., Lewes, BN7 1XU, England, UK
Tel: 44 1273 478449
Fax: 44 1273 478606
Email: theguild@themcgroup.com
Website: http://www.guildmc.com
Founded: 1976
Members: 15000
Staff: 58
Description: Trade association for skilled craftspeople. Aims to protect the public by instilling among members a greater sense of responsibility and by encouraging members always to strive for excellence. The Guild runs a help line and can provide selective lists of skilled craftsmen and women, across the country.
Publication: Magazine
Publication title: Business Matters. Advertisements.
Second publication: Magazine
Publication title: Dolls House

Guild of Motoring Writers

30 The Cravens, Smallfield, Horley, RH6 9QS, England, UK
Tel: 44 1342 843294
Fax: 44 1342 844093
Email: sharon@scott-fairweather.freeserve.co.uk
Website: http://www.newspress.co.uk/guild
Founded: 1944
Members: 420
Contact: Sharon Scott-Fairweather
Fee: £60
Description: Members may be of any nationality whose occupation has been for at least two years, that of a journalist, author, artist, photographer, broadcaster or film maker whose work is either wholly concerned with motoring or concerned to a. significant degree with motoring topics. Activities include training days for new journalists and several social functions for members.
Publication: Yearbook
Publication title: Who's Who in the Motor Industry/The Guild of Motoring Writers Yearbook

Guild of Professional After Dinner Speakers

c/o Ivor Spencer
12 Little Bornes, Dulwich, London, SE21 8SE, England, UK
Tel: 44 20 86705585
Fax: 44 20 86700055
Description: Promotes after dinner speakers in England.

Guild of Psychotherapists

47 Nelson Sq., London, SE1 02A, England, UK
Tel: 44 20 74013260
Email: guild@psycho.org.uk
Website: http://www.psycho.org.uk
Founded: 1974
Members: 190
Staff: 2
Contact: Peter Berry, Chm.
Fee: £274
Description: Qualified and registered psychoanalytic psychotherapists practising in London and all parts of the country. Aims to train psychoanalytic psychotherapists and to offer a clinical referral service with qualified psychotherapists in all areas of the country. Reduced fees available.
Meetings/Conventions: Study Days - annual meeting London UK

Guild of Railway Artists

45 Dickins Rd., Warwick, CV34 5NS, England, UK
Tel: 44 1926 499246
Email: frankhodges@railart.co.uk
Website: http://www.railart.co.uk
Founded: 1979
Members: 190
Contact: F.P. Hodges, HonGRA
Description: Artists who depict railway as one of their subject matters. Provides a tangible link between artists depicting the heritage and the modern practices of the railway scene.
Publication: Book
Publication title: A Century of Railways
Second publication: Book
Publication title: The Great Western Collection

Guild of Stunt and Action Coordinators

c/o Sally Fisher
72 Pembroke Rd., London, W8 6NX, England, UK
Tel: 44 20 76028319
Fax: 44 20 76028319
Email: stunts.uk@btinternet.com
Founded: 1986
Members: 20
Staff: 1
Contact: Sally Fisher, Sec.
Description: Promotes the interests of stunt and action coordinators.

Guild of Television Cameramen

April Cottage, The Chalks, Chew Magna, Bristol, BS40 8SN, England, UK
Tel: 44 1822 614405
Fax: 44 1822 614405
Email: membership@gtc.org.uk
Website: http://www.gtc.org.uk
Founded: 1972
Members: 1100
Contact: Sheila Lewis, Admin. Officer
Fee: £20

Description: Television cameramen united to ensure the professional status of the art. Activities include meetings, discussions, demonstrations of new equipment, and cooperation with similar groups in other countries.
Meetings/Conventions: - annual meeting - Exhibits.

Guild of Vision Mixers

147 Ship Lane, Farnborough, GU14 8BJ, England, UK
Tel: 44 1252 514953
Fax: 44 1252 656756
Email: gg@visionmixers.tv
Website: http://www.visionmixers.tv
Founded: 1980
Members: 100
Contact: Peter Turl, Chm.
Fee: £12
Description: Vision mixers employed in the TV industry; associate membership available to other TV professionals. Maintains and improves standards in vision-mixing and television production in the UK.

Guild of Wedding Photographers
GWP

5 Fore St., Trowbridge, BA14 8ET, England, UK
Tel: 44 1225 760088
Fax: 44 1225 759159
Email: info@gwp-uk.co.uk
Website: http://www.gwp-uk.co.uk/
Description: Professional wedding photographers whose work has been deemed of acceptable quality by the guild. Seeks to: put potential clients in touch with qualified wedding photographers; improve the standard of wedding photography. Assesses the quality of wedding photographs and certifies qualifying photographers and studios; maintains registry of accredited photographers; matches photographers with potential clients.

Gun Trade Association

PO Box 43, Tewkesbury, GL20 5ZE, England, UK
Tel: 44 1684 291868
Fax: 44 1684 291864
Email: enquiries@guntradeassociation.com
Website: http://www.guntradeassociation.com
Founded: 1912
Members: 475
Staff: 3
Contact: John Batley, Dir. & Sec.
Description: Manufacturers (gunmakers etc), distributors and retailers of firearms, ammunition and related components and accessories, and those who offer a service related to the production, maintenance and legitimate use of such items. Represents the interests of those involved in all aspects of the legitimate trade in firearms, ammunition and related items in the United Kingdom and offers associate membership to those based outside the United Kingdom.
Publication: Newsletter
Publication title: GTA Newsletter. Advertisements.

Gunmakers' Company

c/o Proof House
48-50 Commercial Rd., London, E1 1LP, England, UK
Tel: 44 171 4812695
Fax: 44 171 4805102
Contact: J.M. Riches, Clerk
Description: Gunmakers.

Gypsum Products Development Association

PO Box 350 84, London, NW1 4XE, England, UK
Tel: 44 20 79358532
Fax: 44 20 79358532
Email: admin@gpda.com
Website: http://www.gpda.com
Founded: 1956
Members: 4
Contact: C. Dunn-Meynell
Description: Gypsum product manufacturers in the U.K. and Ireland. Promotes, encourages and develops the use of gypsum products.

H.G. Wells Society
HGWS

c/o J.R. Hammond
49 Beckingthorpe Dr., Bottesford, Nottingham, NG13 0DN, England, UK
Website: http://hgwellsusa.50megs.com
Founded: 1960
Members: 200
Contact: J.R. Hammond, Sec.
Fee: £16
Membership Type: UK and EC
Fee: £19
Membership Type: outside EC
Description: Individual members are students, scholars, other and interested persons; corporate members are universities, libraries, and institutes. Purpose is to encourage and promote an active interest in and an appreciation of the life, work, and thought of H.G. Wells (1866-1946), British novelist, sociological writer, and historian. Provides book service, information service, and speakers' panel.
Library Subject: H.G. Wells
Library Type: reference
Publication: Bibliography
Publication title: H.G. Wells Bibliography
Second publication: Book
Publication title: Human Rights and World Order
Meetings/Conventions: - annual conference

Haberdashers' Company

39/40 Bartholomew Close, Haberdasher's Hall, London, EC1A 7JN, England, UK
Tel: 44 20 76060967
Fax: 44 20 76065738
Email: enquiries@haberdashers.co.uk
Website: http://www.haberdashers.co.uk
Contact: Nicholas Lundesq, Master
Description: Haberdashers.

Hairdressing Council

c/o 12 David House
45 High St., South Norwood, London, SE25 6HJ, England, UK
Tel: 44 20 87716205
Fax: 44 181 7713392
Email: registrar@haircouncil.org.uk
Website: http://www.haircouncil.org.uk
Founded: 1964
Members: 18000
Staff: 5
Contact: John Byrne, Registrar
Fee: £28
Membership Type: state registered hairdresser

Description: Hairdressers trained and qualified to a prescribed standard may apply to become State Registered Hairdressers. The statutory authority for hairdressing. Provides the administration for the Hairdressing Industry Coordinating Committee, the industry umbrella body, and is the contact point for the government, European Commission and other areas of officialdom.
Publication: Magazine
Publication title: State Registered Hairdresser. Advertisements.

Hairdressing Employers' Association
6 Coldbath Sq., London, EC1R 5NA, England, UK
Tel: 44 207 8330633
Fax: 44 207 8332192
Website: http://www.norfolk-careers.co.uk/links/trainingsupps/hair-dressing.html
Founded: 1981
Members: 100
Staff: 12
Contact: B.E. Howe, Chief Exec.
Description: The major hair and beauty salon chains in the UK, together with the major product manufacturing houses. Represents the major hairdressing salon groups in the UK to government, EC bodies and trade organisations. It has direct representation on key industry bodies, and a direct line to relevant government departments such as the Department of Trade and the Department of Employment and Education and their agencies.
Publication: Newsletter
Publication title: Newsline
Meetings/Conventions: - semiannual conference

Hairdressing Manufacturers' and Wholesalers' Association
25 West St., Haslemere, GU27 2AP, England, UK
Tel: 44 1428 654336
Fax: 44 1428 658233
Founded: 1927
Members: 80
Contact: Richard Coleman, Sec.
Description: Manufacturers and suppliers of products and services for hairdressers and beautician.
Publication title: A Guide to the Health and Safety of Salon Hair Products

Hakluyt Society - England
HS
c/o Map Library, British Library
96 Euston Rd., London, NW1 2DB, England, UK
Tel: 44 1428 641850
Fax: 44 1428 641933
Email: office@hakluyt.com
Website: http://www.hakluyt.com
Founded: 1846
Members: 2300
Staff: 1
Contact: Richard Bateman
Fee: £35
Membership Type: UK
Fee: £70
Membership Type: US
Description: Individuals in 64 countries interested in the literature of geographical discovery and travel. Publishes original and rare narratives of notable voyages and naval expeditions (in addition to other geographical materials) in order to educate and enlighten the public; such published volumes currently number more than 300. Society is named after Richard Hakluyt.
Publication: Directory
Publication title: List of Members
Second publication: Directory
Publication title: List of Publications in Print
Meetings/Conventions: meeting

Halton Chamber of Commerce and Industry
Halton Business Forum, Victoria Square, Widnes, WA8 7QZ, England, UK
Tel: 44 151 4209400
Fax: 44 151 4209424
Email: dianek@shalton-businesslink.co.uk
Founded: 1995
Members: 300
Staff: 3
Contact: Bill Badrock, Chief Exec.
Description: Promotes business and commerce.
Library Subject: management, international exports
Library Type: not open to the public
Publication title: Alliance. Advertisements.
Meetings/Conventions: - monthly meeting

Handbell Ringers of Great Britain
87 The Woodfields, Sanderstead, South Croydon, CR2 OHJ, England, UK
Tel: 44 208 6512663
Fax: 44 20 86512663
Email: info@hrgb.org.uk
Website: http://www.hrgb.org.uk
Founded: 1967
Members: 3000
Contact: Mrs. Sandra Winter, Hon.Sec.
Description: Handbell tune ringing teams throughout the UK. Caters for active ringers, ringers of handchimes and belleplates and also those with merely an interest in ringing. To promote the art of handbell tune ringing, through rallies, workshops, concerts etc. Many of these are arranged by the eight regional branches. Advice and information available to all. Occasional publications of music etc. Registered Charity no. 298945.
Publication: Magazine
Publication title: Reverberations. Advertisements.
Meetings/Conventions: National Rally and Conference - annual - Exhibits.

Handsaw Association
c/o Institute of Spring Technology
Henry St., Sheffield, S3 7EQ, England, UK
Tel: 44 114 2789143
Fax: 44 114 2726344
Email: jrm@britishtools.com
Contact: J.R. Markham, Sec.
Description: Promotes the handsaw industry.
Publication: Directory
Publication title: British Tools Directory

Hansard Society
9 Kingsway, London, WC2B 6FX, England, UK
Tel: 44 207 9557459
Fax: 44 207 9557492
Email: hansard@hansard.lse.ac.uk
Website: http://www.hansardsociety.org.uk

Founded: 1944
Members: 400
Staff: 7
Contact: Shelagh Diplock, Dir.
Fee: £15
Membership Type: ordinary
Fee: £60
Membership Type: outside the United Kingdom
Description: Promotes knowledge of and interest in parliamentary governments and procedures. Conducts research, educational programs, and training courses for companies and teachers; sponsors international student exchange programs. Organizes academic competitions and lobbying seminars.
Publication: Book
Publication title: Agenda for Change
Second publication: Book
Publication title: Making the Law: The Legislative Process
Meetings/Conventions: - periodic conference

Harris Tweed Authority

6 Garden Rd., Stornoway, HS1 2QJ, England, UK
Tel: 44 1851 702269
Fax: 44 1851 702600
Email: enquiries@harristweed.org
Website: http://www.harristweed.org
Founded: 1909
Members: 10
Staff: 5
Contact: Ian A. Mackenzie, Chief Exec.
Description: Concerned with the promotion, protection, certification and authentication of Harris Tweed.

Harveian Society of London

11 Chandos St., London, W1M 0EB, England, UK
Tel: 44 20 75801043
Founded: 1831
Members: 350
Staff: 2
Contact: Col. Richard Kinsella-Bevan, Exec.Sec.
Fee: £25
Membership Type: individual
Description: Promotes discussion of the medical, surgical, and philosophical subjects connected with medical subjects.
Library Type: by appointment only

Harvest Help
HH

3-4 Old Bakery Row, Wellington, Telford, TF1 1PS, England, UK
Tel: 44 1952 260699
Fax: 44 1952 247158
Email: info@harvesthelp.org
Website: http://www.harvesthelp.org
Founded: 1985
Members: 1500
Staff: 5
Contact: Andrew Jowett, Dir.
Description: A charity in the United Kingdom which works in poor rural villages in Africa. Aims to raise the standards of farming, nutrition, and primary education in less-developed countries.
Publication: Newsletter
Publication title: Harvest Helper
Meetings/Conventions: Supporters Open Day - annual meeting - Exhibits.

Havergal Brian Society

5 Eastbury Rd., Watford, WD19 4PT, England, UK
Tel: 44 1923 224607
Fax: 44 1923 250506
Email: hbs@havergal.demon.co.uk
Website: http://www.musicweb.uk.net/brian
Founded: 1974
Members: 230
Contact: Alan Marshall, Sec.
Fee: £12
Membership Type: in U.K.
Fee: £16
Membership Type: in Europe
Description: Individuals in 15 countries interested in the work of English composer Havergal Brian (1876-1972). Provides information about Brian and his music; gathers information on the location of Brian's missing scores. Advises and assists prospective performers of Brian's music; arranges and sponsors recitals, recordings, and concerts.
Publication: Book
Publication title: Brian's Complete Music for Solo Piano
Second publication: Book
Publication title: Havergal Brian's Gothic Symphony: Two Studies
Meetings/Conventions: - annual meeting

Hawk and Owl Trust

Regents Park, London, NW1 4RY, England, UK
Tel: 44 20 84500662
Founded: 1969

Headmasters' and Headmistresses' Conference

130 Regent Rd., Leicester, LE1 7PG, England, UK
Tel: 44 116 2551567
Fax: 44 116 2556972
Email: hmc@hmc.org.uk
Website: http://www.hmc.org.uk
Founded: 1869
Members: 243
Staff: 4
Contact: Geoff Lucas
Description: Heads of major independent boys and co-educational schools. Responds to any major government initiatives, like those on the curriculum, examinations, teacher training and children's welfare. Provides professional training, inspection of schools and general advice on educational matters.
Library Subject: past papers of conference
Library Type: not open to the public
Formerly: Formed by Merger of, Headmasters' Conference
Publication title: Conference and Common Room. Advertisements.
Second publication: Newsletter
Publication title: NCCA Newsletter. Advertisements.
Meetings/Conventions: - annual meeting - Exhibits.

Health Care Supplies Association

32 Etron Close, Chester House, Datchet, Slough, SL3 9BE, England, UK
Tel: 44 1753 580176
Fax: 44 1753 580176
Founded: 1960
Members: 490
Contact: Mrs. C.B. Jones, Exec.Dir.
Fee: £15
Description: To promote maintain and seek continuously to improve professional standards and training relating to supplies and

associated services within the healthcare sector. To establish and maintain a professional link with appropriate statutory bodies. To liaise with professional and other organizations. Activities include two annual training schools for junior grades in the supplies discipline and an annual conference.
Publication: Book
Publication title: Official Procurement Guide. Advertisements.
Meetings/Conventions: - annual conference

Health Food Manufacturers' Association
63 Hampton Court Way, Thames Ditton, KT7 0LT, England, UK
Tel: 44 208 3984066
Fax: 44 208 3985402
Email: hfma@hfma.co.uk
Website: http://www.hfma.co.uk
Founded: 1965
Members: 160
Staff: 6
Contact: Penny Viner, Dir.
Description: Trade association covering manufacturers, distributors and suppliers of specialist health products including foods, supplements, natural medicines and cosmetics. Covers legislation, training and education, standards and ethics and the dissemination of information. It is also involved in the more commercial aspects of export and trade exhibitions but primarily it is concerned with providing a safe and expanding marketing arena within which its members can increase their sales and influence.
Publication title: Nutrition Research
Meetings/Conventions: - monthly

Health in Prisons Project
ICPMS
Wicken House, Weston Rd., Aston Clinton, Buckinghamshire, HP22 5EP, England, UK
Tel: 44 1296 630448
Fax: 44 1296 632448
Email: england&wales@hipp-europe.org
Founded: 1976
Members: 200
Contact: Chunilal Roy, Sec.Gen.
Description: Medical and health care professionals; associate members are administrators of prison health care agencies. Promotes discussion among prison health professionals. Strives to improve health care worldwide; encourages postgraduate training for doctors working in prison settings.
Publication: Proceedings
Meetings/Conventions: - annual symposium

Healthcare Financial Management Association
Ste. 32 Albert House, 111 Victoria St., Bristol, BS1 6AX, England, UK
Tel: 44 117 9294789
Fax: 44 117 9294844
Email: info@hfma.org.uk
Website: http://www.hfma.org.uk
Founded: 1950
Members: 2000
Staff: 12
Contact: Mark Knight, Chief Exec.
Description: Any qualified accountant and/or financial employee working in the NHS - with a retired membership also. Promotes professional standards of financial practice in the management and audit of the NHS.
Publication: Newsletter

Publication title: HFMA. Advertisements.
Publication title: NHS Health Authorities
Meetings/Conventions: - annual conference - Exhibits.

Healthlink Worldwide
Cityside, 40 Adler St., London, E1 1EE, England, UK
Tel: 44 20 75391570
Fax: 44 20 75391580
Email: info@healthlink.org.uk
Website: http://www.healthlink.org.uk
Founded: 1977
Members: 70
Staff: 24
Contact: Dr. Roger Drew, Exec.Dir.
Description: Works in partnership with organisations in developing countries seeking to improve the health and well-being of poor and vulnerable communities by strengthening the provision, use, and impact of information. Offers expertise in various aspects of health and disability-related communications, including development of print and electronic materials, resource centre, and database development.
Library Subject: primary health care in developing countries
Library Type: reference
Formerly: Appropriate Health Resources and Technologies Action Group
Publication: Newsletter
Publication title: AIDS Action
Publication title: Annual Report
Meetings/Conventions: - periodic seminar

Hearing Concern
7/11 Armstrong Rd., London, W3 7JL, England, UK
Tel: 44 181 7429151
Fax: 44 181 7429043
Email: info@hearingconcern.org.uk
Website: http://www.hearingconcern.org.uk
Founded: 1947
Members: 3000
Staff: 8
Contact: Fiona Robertson, Ch.Exec.
Fee: £7
Description: Dedicated to improving the quality of life for those who are hard of hearing. Provides advice, information and support, as well as communication access and raises public and professional awareness of the issues associated with hearing loss.
Formerly: Hearing Concern, British Association of the Hard of Hearing
Publication: Magazine
Publication title: Hearing Concern. Advertisements.
Meetings/Conventions: - annual conference - Exhibits.

Heating and Ventilating Contractors' Association
c/o ESCA House
34 Palace Court, London, W2 4JG, England, UK
Tel: 44 207 3134900
Fax: 44 207 7279268
Email: contact@hvca.org.uk
Website: http://www.hvca.org.uk
Founded: 1904
Members: 1167
Staff: 42
Contact: Robert Stirland, Pres.
Description: Contractors involved in heating, ventilating, air conditioning, refrigeration, duct work, and related work. Aims to provide a range of services to the membership and to represent,

promote and protect their interests in the broadest possible sense and at the highest possible levels.
Publication: Magazine
Publication title: The Specifier. Advertisements.
Publication title: Specifier's Guide
Meetings/Conventions: Summit - annual conference Birmingham Oklahoma

Heating, Ventilating and Air Conditioning Manufacturers' Association

Henley Rd., Medmenham, Marlow, SL7 2ER, England, UK
Tel: 44 1491 578674
Fax: 44 1491 575024
Email: info@feta.co.uk
Website: http://www.feta.co.uk
Founded: 1961
Members: 130
Staff: 6
Contact: Terry Seward
Description: Manufacturers and distributors of heating, ventilating and air conditioning equipment. Serves the interests of manufacturers and users of heating, ventilating and air conditioning equipment.

Heavy Transport Association

Worley Bank House, Bolesworth Road, Tattenhall, Chester, CH3 9HL, England, UK
Tel: 44 1829 773104
Fax: 44 1829 773109
Email: jbd@wdl.co.uk
Website: http://www.wdl.co.uk/htaindex.htm
Founded: 1983
Members: 100
Contact: John Dyne, Sec.
Fee: £225
Membership Type: honorary, ordinary, associate, affiliate, advisory
Description: Professional operators of special type vehicles and equipment pertaining to the heavy haulage industry. Aims to represent and promote the profession and trade interests of its members and improve the standard of the heavy haulage industry.
Library Subject: heavy haulage transport issues
Library Type: not open to the public
Publication: Newsletter
Publication title: Heavy Talk. Advertisements.
Meetings/Conventions: - quarterly

Hebe Society

c/o Geoffrey Scoble
Rosemercy, Hain Walk, St. Ives, TR26 2AF, England, UK
Tel: 44 1736795225
Founded: 1985
Members: 300
Contact: Geoffrey Scoble, Hon.Sec.
Fee: £12
Membership Type: individual
Fee: £14
Membership Type: joint
Description: Aims to encourage, improve, conserve and extend the cultivation of Hebe, parahebe and all New Zealand native plants.
Library Subject: hebes and other New Zealand native plants
Library Type: lending
Publication: Magazine
Publication title: Hebe News. Advertisements.
Meetings/Conventions: - annual conference - Exhibits.

Helpage International

PO Box 32832, London, N1 9UZ, England, UK
Tel: 44 207 2787778
Fax: 44 207 7137993
Email: hai@helpage.org
Website: http://www.helpage.org/
Founded: 1983
Members: 65
Staff: 178
Contact: Austin Hall, Info.Ofcr.
Description: Works with and for disadvantaged older people worldwide, to achieve lasting improvement in the quality of their lives. Supports the development of grass roots activity and the growth of local organisations working with older people. Projects focus on health, social services, residential, community and home care, income generation, advocacy, training and organisational development.
Library Subject: aging, health, refugees, disaster relief
Library Type: not open to the public
Publication: Handbook
Publication title: Adding Health to Years
Second publication: Newsletter
Publication title: Helpage International News

Henry Doubleday Research Association
HDRA

Ryton Organic Gardens, Coventry, CV8 3LG, England, UK
Tel: 44 2476 303517
Fax: 44 2476 639229
Email: enquiry@hdra.org.uk
Website: http://www.hdra.org.uk
Founded: 1958
Members: 30000
Staff: 100
Contact: Jackie Gear, Exec.Dir.
Fee: £23
Membership Type: standard
Fee: £27
Membership Type: family
Description: Provides research and advice on all aspects of organic horticulture, primarily on a small or garden scale. Examines the problem of peasant agriculture in developing countries.
Library Subject: Organic horticulture and agriculture.
Library Type: reference
Publication: Catalog
Publication title: Organic Gardening Catalogue
Second publication: Magazine
Publication title: The Organic Way
Meetings/Conventions: - annual meeting - Exhibits.

Henry Williamson Society

c/o Mrs. Margaret Murphy
16 Doran Dr., Redhill, RH1 6AX, England, UK
Tel: 44 1737 763228
Email: mm@misterman.freeserve.co.uk
Website: http://www.henrywilliamson.org
Founded: 1980
Members: 540
Description: Aims to encourage interest in and a deeper understanding of the life and work of the writer Henry Williamson.
Publication: Journal
Publication title: Henry Wiliamson Society

Henty Society
c/o Bruce Lees
Hayfield, Bourne Fields, Twyford, Winchester, S0Z1 1NY, England, UK
Tel: 44 1962 713164
Website: http://www.gahenty.co.uk
Founded: 1977
Members: 180
Contact: Bruce Lees, Hon.Sec.
Fee: £13
Fee: £38
Description: Researches into life and works of George Alfred Henty.
Publication: Journal
Publication title: Bulletin

Herb Society
c/o Nicky Westwood
Sulgrave Manor, Sulgrave, Banbury, OX17 2SD, England, UK
Tel: 44 1295 768899
Fax: 44 1295 768069
Email: nickey@herbsociety.co.uk
Website: http://www.herbsociety.co.uk
Founded: 1927
Members: 2000
Staff: 1
Contact: Nicky Westwood
Fee: £20
Membership Type: normal
Fee: £17
Description: Aims to disseminate information on all aspects of herbs.
Library Subject: herbs
Library Type: reference
Publication: Magazine
Publication title: Herbs. Advertisements.

Heritage Protection Society
c/o Dr. F.R. Hampson
128 Lowndes Lane, Stockport, SK2 6DH, England, UK
Tel: 44 161 4873230
Founded: 1982
Members: 1934
Contact: Dr. F.R. Hampson
Description: Promotes the preservation of our heritage and environment.
Library Subject: architectural and environmental preservation
Library Type: not open to the public

Heritage Railway Association
c/o John Crane
7 Robert Close, Potters Bar, EN6 2DH, England, UK
Tel: 44 1654 710344
Fax: 44 1654 710344
Website: http://ukhrail.uel.ac.uk/
Founded: 1959
Members: 250
Contact: David Woodhouse, Mng.Dir.
Description: Open to Railway Preservation Organizations World Wide and individuals. Co-ordinates the activities of railway preservation societies and groups, and represents the membership in matters of relevant legislation, and regulations eg. The Health and Safety Executive. It also publishes lists and details of preserved railway activities in UK and Eire. The Association is managed by an elected Council. Its officers function in a voluntary capacity as staff.
Publication: Journal

Publication title: Heritage Railways Journal
Publication title: Railways Restored
Meetings/Conventions: general assembly

Herpes Viruses Association
41 North Rd., London, N7 9DP, England, UK
Tel: 44 207 6099061
Email: info@herpes.org.uk
Website: http://www.herpes.org.uk
Founded: 1985
Members: 1300
Staff: 3
Contact: Marlan Nicholson, Dir.
Fee: £40
Membership Type: personal
Fee: £40
Membership Type: professional
Description: Provides accurate information on herpes simplex virus (to counteract the herpes hype), to the media, health professionals and the public.
Library Subject: herpes viruses
Library Type: reference
Publication: Journal
Publication title: Sphere. Advertisements.

Hertfordshire Chamber of Commerce and Industry
45 Grosvenor Rd., St. Albans, AL1 3AW, England, UK
Tel: 44 1727 813680
Fax: 44 1727 813694
Email: enquiries@hertschamber.com
Website: http://www.hertschamber.com
Members: 1450
Staff: 9
Contact: Tim Hutchings, Chief Exec.
Description: Promotes business and commerce.
Publication: Newsletter
Publication title: Chamber News

Higher Education Funding Council for England HEFCE
Northavon House, Coldharbour Ln., Bristol, BS16 1QD, England, UK
Tel: 44 117 9317317
Fax: 44 117 9317203
Email: hefce@hefce.ac.uk
Website: http://www.hefce.ac.uk/
Description: Non-departmental public body set up under the Further and Higher Education Act of 1992. Distributes public funding for teaching and research and related activities in universities and colleges, within the context of the government's policy for higher education. Advises the Secretary of State for Education and Skills on the funding needs of the higher education sector. Also promotes and supports the development of high-quality socially inclusive teaching and learning within universities and colleges, which are well governed and managed and deliver value for money to students, business, sponsors, and other stakeholders.

Highland Railway Society
c/o J. Roake
Ringmarsh Cottage, Horsington Marsh, Templecombe, BA8 0EL, England, UK
Tel: 44 1889 207010
Email: johnroake@brink.net.com
Website: http://www.hrsoc.org.uk

Founded: 1989
Members: 300
Contact: John Roake, Hon.Treas.
Fee: £11
Membership Type: full
Fee: £9.5
Membership Type: senior citizen
Description: Studies the Highland railway, its constituents, and successors.
Library Subject: Highland railway
Library Type: not open to the public
Publication: Journal
Publication title: Highland Railway Journal
Meetings/Conventions: - annual convention

Hire Association Europe

2 Holland Rd. W, Waterlinks, Birmingham, B6 4DW, England, UK
Tel: 44 121 3804600
Fax: 44 121 3334109
Email: memserve@hae.org.uk
Website: http://www.hae.org.uk
Founded: 1973
Members: 1100
Staff: 16
Contact: John Coyne, Mng.Dir.
Fee: £350
Membership Type: full and supplier
Description: Companies which hire out equipment and vehicles including tools, audio-visual equipment catering and leisure equipment, portable toilets and access equipment, boats, trailers, and recreational vehicles. Aims to represent, promote and enhance the hire industry for the benefit of its members and their customers.
Publication title: Focus
Second publication: Newsletter
Publication title: Hire Standard. Advertisements.
Meetings/Conventions: - annual conference - Exhibits.

Historic Commercial Vehicle Society

c/o Michael J. Banfield
Iden Grange, Cranbrook Rd., Staplehurst, Tonbridge, TN12 0ET, England, UK
Tel: 44 1580 892929
Fax: 44 1580 893227
Email: hcvs@btinternet.com
Website: http://www.hcvs.co.uk
Members: 4000
Staff: 2
Contact: Michael J. Bainfield, Exec.Ofr.
Fee: £80
Membership Type: full member
Description: Promotes events to display commercial vehicles 20 years old or older.
Library Subject: historic commercial vehicles
Library Type: reference
Publication: Magazine
Publication title: Historic Commercial News. Advertisements.

Historic Houses Association

2 Chester St., London, SW1X 7BB, England, UK
Tel: 44 207 2595688
Fax: 44 207 2595590
Email: info@hha.org.uk
Website: http://www.hha.org.uk
Founded: 1973

Members: 1600
Staff: 4
Contact: Edward Leicester, Pres.
Fee: £28
Membership Type: single
Fee: £40
Membership Type: double
Description: Owners of privately owned historic houses and gardens around 300 of which are open regularly, to the public. Represents the owners of historic houses, parks and gardens in private ownership in Britain. It provides practical advice and services to owners and seeks to establish a fiscal, political and economic climate in which owners can maintain Britain's historic houses for the benefit of the nation. Operates a friends scheme for people who support the aims and enjoy visiting houses which are open to the public. Friends have free access to around 280 HHA members' properties.
Publication: Journal
Publication title: Historic House. Advertisements.
Second publication: Manuals

Historical Association
HA

59 A Kennington Park Rd., London, SE11 4JH, England, UK
Tel: 44 207 7353901
Fax: 44 207 5824989
Email: enquiry@history.org.uk
Website: http://www.history.org.uk
Founded: 1906
Members: 7500
Staff: 7
Contact: Linda Davidson, Membership Off.
Fee: £20
Description: Individuals in 10 countries dedicated to the promotion of the study and teaching of history at all educational levels. Organizes lectures, study tours, and vacation history courses.
Publication: Magazine
Publication title: Historian. Advertisements.
Second publication: Journal
Publication title: History
Meetings/Conventions: - annual conference

Historical Diving Society
HDS

Little Gatton Lodge, 25 Gatton Rd., Reigate, RH2 0HD, England, UK
Tel: 44 1737 249961
Fax: 44 1384 896079
Email: info@thehds.com
Website: http://www.thehds.com
Founded: 1990
Contact: Dr. John Bevan, Chair
Description: Individuals with an interest in diving and the history of underwater exploration. Seeks to identify, protect, and preserve artefacts and archival materials pertaining to the history of diving. Serves as a forum for the exchange of information among members; encourages public awareness of diving and its history; provides support and assistance in the maintenance of working diving equipment. Maintains membership, profile, and historical equipment registries.
Library Subject: diving, diving history
Library Type: reference
Publication: Newsletter
Meetings/Conventions: - annual conference

Historical Manuscripts Commission
HMC
Quality House, Quality Court, Chancery Lane, London, WC2A 1HP, England, UK
Tel: 44 20 72421198
Fax: 44 20 78313550
Email: nra@hmc.gov.uk
Website: http://www.hmc.gov.uk
Founded: 1869
Staff: 24
Contact: Dr. C. J. Kitching, Sec.
Description: Functions as the U.K.'s central coordinating and advisory body on all matters relating to manuscript sources for British history. Maintains the National Register of Archives and the Manorial Documents Register.
Library Subject: contains published and unpublished lists and catalogs of major manuscript collections
Library Type: open to the public

History of Education Society
20 Bedford Way, London, WC1H 0AL, England, UK
Founded: 1967

Hockey Writers' Club
37 Orchard Rd., Old Windsor, Windsor, SL4 2RZ, England, UK
Tel: 44 1753 861750
Fax: 44 1753 861750
Email: mike@haymonds.freeserve.co.uk
Founded: 1972
Members: 150
Staff: 3
Contact: Mike Haymonds, Hon. Sec.
Fee: £5
Membership Type: UK member
Fee: £5
Membership Type: non-UK members
Description: All regular contributors on field hockey to press, television, or radio, whether as writers, broadcasters, or photographers within the United Kingdom as full members and as Associate members if non resident in the UK. To promote increased publicity for field hockey and to advance the interests of writers, broadcasters and photographers in the execution of their duties relating to the game. To seek the provision of satisfactory facilities for press, radio and television when covering the game.
Publication: Newsletter
Publication title: The Hockey Writer

Holiday Centres Association
Pilars, Eastacombe Lane, Heanton Punchardon, North Devon, WD1 35Y, England, UK
Tel: 44 1271 816696
Fax: 44 1271 817411
Email: holidaycentres@aol.comwww.holidaycentres.co.uk
Founded: 1936
Members: 50
Contact: David Howell, CEO
Description: Majority of holiday centre operators in UK. Trade Organisation representing majority of holdiay centre operators in the UK. Holiday centres meeting the standards of the NAHC include such as Butlins, Pontins and Warners.
Formerly: National Association of Holiday CentreS
Meetings/Conventions: meeting

Home Beer and Wine Manufacturers Association
304 Northridge Way, Hemel Hempstead, HP1 2AB, England, UK
Tel: 44 1442 267228
Fax: 44 1442 267228
Founded: 1986
Members: 18
Staff: 1
Contact: Evelyn Barrett, Sec.
Description: Full membership is open only to those companies who are producers of substantial brands used for homebrewing and winemaking and/or manufacturers of raw materials for the industry. Allied members includes companies who make a substantial contribution. to the industry but do not fulfil the criteria for full membership. Aims to facilitate discussions with and explanations by and to national and local government authorities in relation to technical, administrative and procedural matters of interest to all or the majority of Members of the Association; and in relation to such matters, to promote the interest of Members.
Meetings/Conventions: Home Brew-X - annual conference - Exhibits.

Home Brewing and Winemaking Trade Association
c/o Valley House
68 Frome Rd., Southwick, Trowbridge, BA14 9QD, England, UK
Founded: 1986
Members: 110
Contact: Dr. D. Harrild
Description: Retail stockists of home brew items. Represents retail members in all matters concerning the homebrew trade. Organizes an annual exhibition.
Publication: Newsletter

Home Decoration Retailer's Association
Box 44, Walsall, WS2 8GH, England, UK
Tel: 44 1922 631134
Founded: 1955
Members: 700
Staff: 2
Contact: Diana Truman, Admin.
Description: Promotes the well being of the home decor market in the United Kingdom. Assists retailers of home decorating products.
Formerly: Wallcovering, Fabric, and Decor Retailers Association
Publication: Membership Directory
Publication title: Gold Decor Directory. Advertisements.
Second publication: Magazine
Publication title: Home Decor & Furnishings. Advertisements.

Home Laundering Consultative Council
5 Portland Pl., London, W1N 3AA, England, UK
Tel: 44 207 6367788
Fax: 44 207 6367515
Email: enquiries@care-labeling.com
Website: http://www.care-labelling.com
Members: 40
Contact: Adam Mansell
Description: Represents members' interests.

Homoeopathic Medical Association
HMA
6 Livingstone Rd., Gravesend, DA12 5DZ, England, UK
Tel: 44 1474 560336
Fax: 44 1474 327431
Email: info@the-hma.org

Website: http://www.the-hma.org
Founded: 1985
Members: 300
Description: Develops, supports and encourages the practice of homeopathic medicine in the UK and in other countries; increase public awareness and acceptance of homeopathy.
Publication: Journal
Publication title: Homeopathy International
Publication title: Register of Qualified Homeopathic Practitioners
Meetings/Conventions: - annual congress

Hong Kong Tourist Association - London
HKTA

6 Grafton St., London, W1S 4EQ, England, UK
Tel: 44 207 5337100
Fax: 44 207 5337111
Email: info@discoverhongkong.com
Website: http://www.hkta.org
Description: Transportation and hospitality industries in Hong Kong. Promotes Hong Kong as a tourism destination. Represents members' commercial and regulatory interests; conducts promotional activities.

Honourable Company of Master Mariners

c/o HQS Wellington
Temple Stairs, Victoria Embankment, London, WC2R 2PN, England, UK
Tel: 44 207 8368179
Fax: 44 207 2403082
Email: info@hcmm.org.uk
Website: http://www.hcmm.org.uk
Contact: J.A.V. Maddock, Clerk

Horticultural and Contractors' Tools Association

c/o Institute of Spring Technology
Henry St., Sheffield, S3 7EQ, England, UK
Tel: 44 114 2789143
Fax: 44 114 2726344
Email: jrm@britishtools.com
Contact: J.R. Markham, Sec.
Description: Promotes the horticultural and contractor tool industry.
Publication: Directory
Publication title: British Tools Directory

Horticultural Trades Association

c/o Horticulture House
19 High St., Theale, Reading, RG7 5AH, England, UK
Tel: 44 118 9303132
Fax: 44 118 9323453
Email: info@the-hta.org.uk
Website: http://www.the-hta.org.uk
Founded: 1899
Members: 3000
Staff: 30
Contact: David Gwyther, Dir.
Description: Trade association; supports needs of United Kingdom horticulture, including garden centers, retail/wholesale nurseries, landscapers, manufacturers and suppliers, and service-providing associate members.
Library Subject: horticulture, general management, landscape, environment-agriculture reference
Library Type: not open to the public
Publication: Magazine
Publication title: HTA News
Meetings/Conventions: - annual conference Manchester UK

Horticulture Research International Association

Wellesbourne, Warwick, CV35 9EF, England, UK
Tel: 44 1789 470382
Fax: 44 1789 470552
Email: hri.association@hri.ac.uk
Website: http://www.hri.ac.uk/hria
Founded: 1994
Members: 450
Description: Growers, agrochemical suppliers, seed trade, supermarkets, consultants, education/research, and other horticultural occupations. Provides members' days, subject days, and Grower Workshops at which information is supplied on horticultural research or overviews of the growing of the different horticultural crops grown principally in the UK.
Formerly: Horticultural Research Association
Meetings/Conventions: - periodic workshop

Hospital Consultants and Specialists Association
HCSA

1 Kingsclere Rd., Overton, Basingstoke, RG25 3JA, England, UK
Tel: 44 1256 771777
Fax: 44 1256 770999
Email: enquiries@hcsa.com
Website: http://www.hcsa.com
Founded: 1948
Contact: Graham Poynton, Admin.Dir.
Description: Membership is open to hospital consultants, associate specialists, senior registrars, and staff grade doctors working in the National Health Service. Concerned with the interests of senior hospital doctors and their patients. Aims to improve the conditions of service of members, informing them on matters affecting their practice and endeavouring to ensure that key health decisions are taken with due regard to their views.
Publication title: The Consultant
Second publication: Newsletter
Publication title: Consultant Newsletter
Meetings/Conventions: - 3/year meeting

Hospital Doctors' Association

Old Court House, London Rd., Ascot, SL5 7EN, England, UK
Tel: 44 1344 26613
Founded: 1966
Members: 600
Staff: 1
Contact: Pam Morrisroe, Chief Exec.
Description: All hospital doctors below consultant level. The organisation exclusively representing junior doctors interests. It is concerned with their pay and terms and condition of service. At present it is concerned with the changes in specialist training and the reduction in hours of work
Publication: Directory
Publication title: Official Reference Directory

Hospital Infection Society
HIS

University of Leeds, Leeds, LS2 9JT, England, UK
Email: markwi@pathology.leeds.ac.uk
Website: http://www.his.org.uk/
Description: Furthers medical knowledge and disseminates information on the subject of Hospital associated infection.

Hot Extruded Sealants Association

18 Furness Ave., Simonstone, Burnley, BB12 7SU, England, UK
Tel: 44 1282 771260
Fax: 44 1282 771260
Email: pliles@hts.u-net.com
Founded: 1979
Members: 10
Contact: P.A. Liles, Sec.-Treas.
Fee: £400
Membership Type: full
Fee: £100
Membership Type: joining subscription
Description: Promotes the hot extruded sealant industry.
Meetings/Conventions: - semiannual meeting

Hotel and Catering International Management Association
HCIMA

Trinity Ct., 34 West St., Sutton, SM1 1SH, England, UK
Tel: 44 20 86614900
Fax: 44 20 86614901
Email: recep@hcima.co.uk
Website: http://www.hcima.org.uk/
Founded: 1971
Members: 23000
Staff: 34
Contact: Sarah Hathaway, CEO
Description: Managers and potential managers in the hospitality/foodservice industry. Concerns itself with the setting of standards by the development and provision of hotel and catering management education and the collation and dissemination of industry and technical information. It works with government, industry and education and is a focal point for debate. It plans seminars and conferences.
Library Subject: hospitality industry
Library Type: open to the public
Publication: Bulletin
Publication title: Current Awareness Bulletin
Second publication: Journal
Publication title: Hospitality Management Magazine
Meetings/Conventions: Fellows Diner - annual

House Builders Federation
HBF

56-64 Leonard St., London, EC2A 4JX, England, UK
Tel: 44 20 76085100
Fax: 44 20 76085101
Email: hbf@hbf.co.uk
Website: http://www.hbf.co.uk
Founded: 1946
Members: 350
Staff: 35
Contact: Robert Ashmead, Chief Exec.
Description: Represents and promotes the political, land use planning and economic interests of residential house builders in the United Kingdom. Conducts lobbying and advocacy campaigns. Gathers and disseminates industry information.
Publication: Magazine
Publication title: House Builder. Advertisements.
Meetings/Conventions: - triennial conference

Housman Society
HS

80 New Rd., Bromsgrove, B60 2LA, England, UK
Tel: 44 1527 874136
Email: info@housman-society.co.uk
Website: http://www.housman-society.co.uk
Founded: 1973
Members: 300
Contact: J.C. Page, Chm.
Fee: £12
Fee: £10
Description: Purpose is to bring together all those interested in the lives and works of members of the Housman family, particularly the poet Alfred Edward (1859-1936), his brother Laurence (1865-1959), and his sister Clemence (1861-1955). Collects and preserves letters, manuscripts, personal belongings, and published works of the Housmans; supports, develops, and collates research; preserves Housman family graves and monuments.
Library Type: reference
Publication title: A.E. Housman Poet and Scholar
Second publication: Book
Publication title: A Westerly Wanderer-A Life of A.E. Housman

Howard League for Penal Reform
HLPL

1 Ardleigh Rd., London, N1 4HS, England, UK
Tel: 44 20 72497373
Fax: 44 20 72497788
Email: howard.league@ukonline.co.uk
Website: http://web.ukonline.co.uk/howard.league/
Founded: 1866
Members: 1700
Staff: 8
Contact: Frances Crook, Dir.
Description: Lawyers, judges, and other practitioners in the criminal justice system; academics; prisoners and their families; interested individuals. Aim is to increase professional and public awareness of issues relating to criminal justice. Encourages discussion and analysis, and makes recommendations for change. Believes that prison is the severest penalty on the statute book, and to use it more than can be shown to be the minimum necessary to protect the public is wrong in principle, besides being ineffective and costly. Undertakes research; offers training programs; holds seminars; operates speakers' bureau.
Library Type: reference
Publication: Newsletter
Publication title: Criminal Justice
Second publication: Journal
Publication title: Howard Journal
Meetings/Conventions: - annual conference

Hull and Humber Chamber of Commerce, Industry and Shipping

34/38 Beverley Rd., Hull, HU3 1YE, England, UK
Tel: 44 1482 324976
Fax: 44 1482 213962
Email: info@hull-humber-chamber.co.uk
Website: http://www.hull-humber-chamber.co.uk
Founded: 1837
Members: 1500
Staff: 35
Contact: Ian Kelly, Chief Exec.
Description: Promotes business and commerce.

Human Genome Organization
HUGO

144 Harley St., London, W1G 7LD, England, UK
Tel: 44 20 79358085
Fax: 44 20 79358341
Email: hugo@hugo-International.org
Website: http://www.gene.ucl.ac.uk/hugo

Human Rights Society

c/o Mariners Hard
Cley, Holt, NR25 7RX, England, UK
Tel: 44 1263740990
Fax: 44 1263740990
Email: human-rights-society@ukgateway.net
Founded: 1969
Staff: 1
Contact: Mrs. J.J. Murray
Fee: £10
Membership Type: annual
Fee: £5
Membership Type: student
Description: Opposes the legislation of euthanasia, because there is no way in which any law could provide the necessary safeguards. Provides information about hospice care and the relief of pain in terminal illness and educational material for students projects.
Library Subject: euthanasia, hospice care, pain relief
Library Type: reference
Publication: Newsletter
Meetings/Conventions: - annual conference

Humane Slaughter Association and Council of Justice to Animals
HSA&CJA

The Old School, Brenhouse Hill, Wheathampstead, AL4 8AN, England, UK
Tel: 44 1582 831919
Fax: 44 1582 831414
Email: info@hsa.org.uk
Website: http://www.hsa.org.uk
Founded: 1911
Members: 650
Staff: 5
Contact: Dr. James K. Kirkwood
Fee: £15
Membership Type: corporate or individual
Fee: £5
Membership Type: student
Description: Promotes humane methods of slaughter and the introduction of reforms in livestock markets, including transport facilities.
Library Subject: animal welfare
Library Type: by appointment only
Publication: Newsletter
Publication title: Annual Report
Second publication: Papers
Publication title: Guidance Notes on Killing Poultry

Hunter Archaeological Society

34 Elwood Rd., Sheffield, S17 4RH, England, UK
Tel: 44 114 2361850

Founded: 1912
Description: Promotes history and archaeology of Southern Yorkshire and Northern Derbyshire.

Huntington's Disease Association
HDA

108 Battersea High St., London, SW11 3HP, England, UK
Tel: 44 207 2237000
Fax: 44 207 2239489
Email: info@hda.org.uk
Website: http://www.hda.org.uk
Founded: 1971
Members: 5700
Staff: 17
Description: Individuals united to provide assistance, treatment, and information on the effects of Huntington's Disease, a hereditary nervous disorder causing terminal physical and mental disability. Services include: counseling program designed for families and involved professionals; network of regional advisers and local groups throughout the country; confidential telephone and correspondence service; financial assistance; aid to patients undergoing presymptomatic tests or brain tissue donations. Encourages research on the medical and social effects of Huntington's Disease; raises funds.
Publication: Newsletter. Advertisements.
Second publication: Pamphlets

Hydrographic Society
THS

PO Box 103, Plymouth, PL4 7YP, England, UK
Tel: 44 1752 223512
Email: helen@hydrographicsociety.org
Website: http://www.hydrographicsociety.org
Founded: 1972
Members: 1500
Staff: 2
Contact: Helen Atkinson, Mgr.
Fee: £48
Membership Type: Individual
Fee: £24
Membership Type: Student/Retired
Description: Hydrographers and persons in 68 countries working in associated academic, business, commercial, engineering, and professional disciplines. Promotes the science of surveying at sea and related sciences and encourages the exchange of information between technologists and others engaged in hydrography and related disciplines. Conducts workshops. Maintains a travel fund and an educational fund for those starting a career in hydrography and allied sciences.
Library Type: not open to the public
Publication: Journal
Publication title: Hydrographic Journal. Advertisements.
Publication title: Hydrographic Society Diary
Meetings/Conventions: - biennial symposium - Exhibits.

Hymn Society of Great Britain and Ireland

c/o Rev. Geoffrey Wrayford
7 Paganel Rd., Minehead, TA24 5ET, England, UK
Tel: 44 1643 703530
Fax: 44 1643 703530
Email: g.wrayford@breathemail.net
Website: http://www.dsg.freeispshares.co.uk/Hsoc/
Founded: 1936

Members: 500
Description: Promotes the study and research in the field of hymnody. Promotes good standards of hymn signing. Encourages the discerning use of hymns and songs in worship. Sponsors relevant publications.

Hypnotherapy Association
14 Crown St., Chorley, Lancashire, PR7 1DX, England, UK
Tel: 44 1257 262124
Fax: 44 1257 262124
Email: bha@lineone.net
Website: http://www.zednet.co.uk/bhahypnotherapy/
Founded: 1958
Members: 483
Staff: 2
Contact: Alison Wookey, Sec.
Description: Practitioners with at least 4 years post graduate of training in psychotherapy and hypnotherapy who comply with the Association's code of competence and ethics. Concerned with professional standards in the treatment of nervous disorders by trained psychotherapists who use hypnosis when appropriate to facilitate recall by the patient, as well as using other methods proven by research into long-term results. Referrals, research, lectures, broadcasts, talks, papers, articles, books and seminars arranged.
Library Subject: relationship problems, psychodynamics, therapy
Library Type: not open to the public

I CAN
4 Dyer's Buildings, Holborn, London, EC1N 2QP, England, UK
Tel: 44 870 104066
Fax: 44 870 104067
Email: info@ican.org.uk
Website: http://www.ican.org.uk
Founded: 1888
Staff: 250
Contact: Natasha Rees, Mktg.Off.
Description: Works as charity helping children with speech and language difficulties. Services include three residential schools, an early years program, mainstream support language resources in secondary schools, and a national training program for professionals.
Publication title: Annual Report
Meetings/Conventions: I Can National Forum - annual conference - Exhibits.

ICC Commercial Crime Services
Maritime House, 1 Linton Rd., Barking, IG11 8HG, England, UK
Tel: 44 208 5913000
Fax: 44 208 5942833
Email: ccs@icc-ccs.org.uk
Website: http://www.iccwbo.org/index_ccs.asp
Founded: 1981
Contact: P. Mukundan, Dir.
Description: Works to combat commercial fraud. Maintains ICC Counterfeiting Intelligence Bureau, ICC International Maritime Bureau, and CC Commercial Crime Bureau.
Library Subject: commercial fraud, maritime crime
Library Type: reference
Publication: Brochure
Second publication: Bulletin
Meetings/Conventions: International Trading Problems - Pitfalls and Remedies - annual workshop

ICC Counterfeiting Intelligence Bureau
CIB
c/o ICC Commercial Crime Services
Maritime House, 1 Linton Rd., Barking, London, 1G11 8HG, England, UK
Tel: 44 208 5913000
Fax: 44 208 5942833
Email: cib@icc-cib.org.uk
Website: http://www.iccwbo.org/ccs/menu_cib_bureau.asp
Founded: 1985
Contact: Peter Lowe, Asst.Dir.
Fee: £1420
Description: Specialized division of the International Chamber of Commerce. Manufacturers and trade associations in 23 countries; staff members include former officers of commercial police fraud squads with international investigative experience, experts in the detection and analysis of forged documents, and consultants from industries affected by counterfeiting. Serves as a focal point for industries to combat economic crime by investigating and seeking to prevent counterfeiting of trademarked goods and trade dress, patents, copyrights, and industrial designs and models. Gathers information on activities of product counterfeiters and disseminates findings to members. Conducts international inquiries on the sources and distribution of counterfeit products, thereby enabling law enforcement agencies worldwide to make arrests and seize counterfeit goods. Provides investigative services to members; conducts seminars.
Publication: Bulletin
Publication title: Bulletin
Second publication: Pamphlets
Meetings/Conventions: Product Counterfeiting Protection - biennial conference - Exhibits.

ICC International Maritime Bureau
Maritime House, 1 Linton Rd., Barking, Essex, IG11 8HG, England, UK
Tel: 44 20 85913000
Fax: 44 20 85942833
Email: imb@icc-ccs.org.uk
Website: http://www.iccwbo.org/ccs/menu_imb_bureau.asp
Founded: 1981
Contact: P. Mukundan, Dir.
Fee: £1250
Fee: £2850
Description: Works to prevent and investigate combat maritime and trading crime.
Library Subject: Maritime crime
Library Type: not open to the public
Meetings/Conventions: Pitfalls and Remedies in International Trading - annual workshop

Ice Cream Alliance
5 Pelham Court, Pelham Rd., Nottingham, NG5 1AP, England, UK
Tel: 44 115 9858505
Fax: 44 115 9857985
Email: info@ice-cream.org
Website: http://www.ice-cream.org
Founded: 1920
Members: 800
Staff: 4
Contact: Tricia Mobbs, Membership Administrator
Fee: £100
Membership Type: domestic
Fee: £100
Membership Type: outside UK

Description: Companies and individuals connected with the ice cream industry in the UK. Aims to promote the UK ice-cream industry, protect individuals who work within it and encourage good practice within the industry. All efforts are combined at the annual conference and exhibition. Also an information point via the Ice Cream Information Service.
Publication: Magazine
Publication title: Ice Cream. Advertisements.
Meetings/Conventions: Ice Cream Alliance Annual Exhibition - annual trade show - Exhibits.

Immigration Advisory Service
IAS

County House, 3rd Fl., 190 Great Dover St., London, SE1 4YB, England, UK
Tel: 44 20 73577511
Fax: 44 20 74035875
Email: info@iasuk.org
Website: http://www.iasuk.org
Founded: 1993
Staff: 80
Contact: Keith Best, CEO
Description: Provides independent and confidential advice, assistance, and representation to persons subject to immigration control.
Library Subject: Law reports and immigration law; country bundles for asylum claims
Library Type: not open to the public
Formerly: UK Immigrants' Advisory Service
Publication title: Annual Report
Second publication: Book
Publication title: Digest of Immigration Law
Meetings/Conventions: - annual conference - Exhibits.

Imperial Society of Teachers of Dancing

Imperial House, 22-26 Paul St., London, EC2A 4QE, England, UK
Tel: 44 207 3715777
Fax: 44 207 72478979
Email: marketing@istd.org
Website: http://www.istd.org
Founded: 1904
Members: 10000
Staff: 27
Contact: Jon Singleton, Hd.
Description: Teachers of dancing by examination at three levels. A qualifying body for many forms of dance providing grade examinations and medal tests for children and adults. Courses, congresses and competitions are provided for professional teachers and the public.
Library Subject: dance
Library Type: open to the public
Publication: Magazine
Publication title: Dance. Advertisements.

Imported Tyre Manufacturers' Association

c/o Peter Taylor
5A Pindock Mews, London, W9 2PY, England, UK
Tel: 44 20 72891043
Fax: 44 20 72899859
Email: prt@itma1.freeserve.co.uk
Website: http://www.itma-europe.com
Founded: 1980
Members: 16

Description: Tire manufacturers and importers. Provides information, help, and a promotion forum for overseas tire manufacturers and their brands in the UK and the European Union.
Library Subject: tire manufacturing, tire recycling, statistics
Library Type: not open to the public

Impotence Association

c/o Ann Tailor
PO Box 10296, London, SW17 9WH, England, UK
Tel: 44 20 87677791
Fax: 44 20 85167725
Email: info@impotence.org.uk
Website: http://www.impotence.org.uk
Founded: 1995
Members: 1300
Staff: 6
Contact: John Pryor, Chm.
Fee: £15
Membership Type: patient, patient partner
Fee: £20
Membership Type: health professional
Description: Raises awareness among the public and health professionals on impotence. Offers free advice and information via a telephone hotline. Maintains up to date information on the causes and treatments available for impotence.

Inclusion International
II

Administrative Office, 115 Golden Ln., London, EC1Y 0TJ, England, UK
Tel: 44 20 76966904
Fax: 44 20 76965589
Email: info@inclusion-international.org
Website: http://www.inclusion-international.org
Founded: 1960
Members: 200
Staff: 5
Contact: Ute Michel, Dir.
Description: Grassroots human rights organization of families, self-advocates and committed citizens. Dedicated to protecting and promoting the rights of persons with intellectual disabilities and to help them live in the mainstream of society. improved public attitudes towards persons with mental disabilities.
Formerly: International League of Societies for Persons with Mental Handicap
Publication: Newsletter
Publication title: Inclusion News
Meetings/Conventions: Inclusion International World Congress - quadrennial congress

Incorporated Association of Organists

17 Woodland Rd. Birmingham, Northfield, Birmingham, B31 2HU, England, UK
Tel: 44 121 4754408
Fax: 44 121 4754408
Email: w.j.stormout@btinternet.com
Website: http://www.iao.org.uk
Founded: 1927
Members: 6000
Contact: John Stormont, Gen.Sec.
Description: Lovers of (classical) organ music, players and listeners alike. Many are church organists and choirmasters. Most are members of local organists' associations affiliated to the IAO. An

educational charity. It arranges an annual week-long Organ Festival that includes concerts, recitals, lectures, tuition and master-classes with international artists. It also promotes and sponsors educational events in London and the provinces.
Publication title: Organists' Review. Advertisements.
Meetings/Conventions: Organ Festival - annual

Incorporated Association of Preparatory Schools

11 Waterloo Pl., Leamington Spa, CV32 5LA, England, UK
Tel: 44 1926 887833
Fax: 44 1926 888014
Email: hq@iaps.org.uk
Website: http://www.iaps.org.uk
Founded: 1892
Members: 600
Staff: 13
Contact: John Morris, Gen.Sec.
Description: Heads of independent preparatory schools. Fosters the interchange of experience and ideas on education between Heads of preparatory schools, promoting collective views and providing a channel of communication with senior independent schools and other bodies concerned with education. A wide variety of services and a broad range of training courses are offered to members and their staff.
Publication: Magazine
Publication title: Prep School. Advertisements.

Incorporated Phonographic Society

c/o Bishopsgate Institute
230 Bishopsgate, London, EC2M 4QH, England, UK
Tel: 44 171 2476198
Fax: 44 171 2476318
Founded: 1872
Members: 250
Contact: Mary Sorene
Description: Users of Shorthand - i.e. verbatim reporters, secretaries, journalists, teachers of shorthand and typewriting. Aims to encourage users and learners of shorthand (any recognised system) to achieve the highest standard possible, by providing weekly meetings, advice, examinations in shorthand and typewriting.
Publication: Journal
Publication title: IPS Journal

Incorporated Society for Psychic Research

49 Marloes Rd., Kensington, London, W8 6LA, England, UK
Tel: 44 207 9378984
Fax: 44 207 9378984
Founded: 1882
Members: 1000
Staff: 1
Contact: Peter Johnson, Sec.
Description: To advance the understanding of events and abilities commonly described as psychic or paranormal, without prejudice and in a scientific manner. Holds no collective opinions.
Library Type: by appointment only
Publication: Journal
Publication title: Journal of the Society for Psychical Research
Second publication: Newsletter
Publication title: Paranormal Review
Meetings/Conventions: - annual conference

Incorporated Society of British Advertisers

44 Hertford St., London, W1J 7AE, England, UK
Tel: 44 20 74997502
Fax: 44 20 76295355
Email: info@isba.org.uk
Website: http://www.isba.org.uk
Founded: 1900
Members: 300
Staff: 15
Contact: Malcom Earnshaw, Dir.Gen.
Description: Major UK advertiser companies. Represents the interests of the majority of British advertisers on everything connected with advertising and communication.

Incorporated Society of Musicians

10 Stratford Pl., London, W1C 1AA, England, UK
Tel: 44 20 76294413
Fax: 44 20 74081538
Email: membership@ism.org
Website: http://www.ism.org
Founded: 1882
Members: 5000
Staff: 10
Contact: Neil Hoyle, Ch.Exec.
Fee: £103
Membership Type: full (professionals)
Fee: £47
Membership Type: associate (amateurs)
Description: All professional musicians - performers, composers, conductors, lecturers, schoolteachers and private teachers. Protects the interests of everyone who works with music; promotes higher standards through codes of conduct and by professional development and training schemes; offers members comprehensive legal, financial and technical services, as well as careers advice, publications, discounts and insurances.
Publication: Booklet
Publication title: Careers with Music. Advertisements.
Second publication: Journal
Publication title: Music Journal. Advertisements.
Meetings/Conventions: - annual meeting - Exhibits.

Incorporated Society of Organ Builders - England ISOB

c/o Smithy Steads
Freepost, Cragg Vale, Hebben Bridge, West Yorkshire, HX7 5SQ, England, UK
Tel: 44 870 1393645
Fax: 44 870 1393645
Email: admin@isob.co.uk
Website: http://www.musiclink.co.uk/isob
Founded: 1947
Members: 200
Contact: Anthony K. Bishop, Pres.
Description: Students, ordinary members, associates, fellows and counsellors. Advances the science and practice of organ building, by discussion, inquiry, research, experiment, and other means and aims to diffuse knowledge regarding organ building by means of lectures, publications and exchange of information.
Publication: Journal

Incorporated Society of Valuers and Auctioneers ISVA

3 Cadogan Gate, London, SW1X OAS, England, UK
Tel: 44 207 2352282
Fax: 44 207 2354390
Email: hq@isva.co.uk
Founded: 1924
Members: 7000
Staff: 26
Contact: C. Evans, Chief Exec.
Description: Auctioneers, valuers, surveyors, estate agents, and students in the U.K and overseas. Promotes cooperation between members in all aspects of valuation, use, acquisition, and disposal of property. Offers training programs; conducts examinations.
Formerly: Formed by Merger of, Incorporated Society of Auctioneers and Landed Property
Publication: Book
Publication title: Assets Valuation
Second publication: Book
Publication title: Buying and Selling Chattels at Auctions
Meetings/Conventions: - periodic convention

Independent Battery Distributors Association

c/o J. Godfrey Ferris
3 Blakeley Dene, Raby Mere, Wirral, CH63 0QE, England, UK
Tel: 44 151 3342040
Fax: 44 151 3342040
Email: godfreyferris@lineone.net
Founded: 1991
Members: 30
Staff: 1
Contact: J.Godfrey Ferris, Gen.Sec.
Fee: £450
Membership Type: full
Fee: £400
Membership Type: associate/supplier
Description: Represents the interest of the independent battery distributor and provides services to it's members. Helps to promote the interests of all sectors of the battery industry in the UK.
Publication: Newsletter
Publication title: IBDA NEWS. Advertisements.
Meetings/Conventions: National Battery Conference - quadrennial conference

Independent Footwear Retailers' Association

PO Box 123, Banbury, OX15 6WB, England, UK
Tel: 44 1295 738726
Fax: 44 1295 738275
Email: ifra@netcomuk.co.uk
Website: http://www.shoeshop.org.uk
Founded: 1944
Members: 306
Staff: 2
Contact: Arthur F. Spencer-Bolland
Description: Independent footwear retailers.
Publication: Magazine
Publication title: Footprint. Advertisements.
Meetings/Conventions: - annual conference Oxford UK

Independent Healthcare Association

Westminster Tower, 3 Albert Embankment, London, SE1 7SP, England, UK
Tel: 44 20 77934620
Fax: 44 20 78203738
Email: info@iha.org.uk
Website: http://www.iha.org.uk
Founded: 1987
Members: 1000
Staff: 11
Contact: Barry Hassell, Chief Exec.
Description: Independent hospitals and homes registered under the 1984 Registered Homes Act. The representative body for independently-owned healthcare providers, whether voluntary or private, funded largely by member subscriptions based on a fee per bed. Its charitable status derives from its objectives to promote high standards of care in the independent sector.
Publication title: Focus
Second publication: Bulletin

Independent Living Centre

St. Loyes Foundation, Topsham Rd., Exeter, EX2 6EP, England, UK
Tel: 44 1392 286239
Fax: 44 1392 286239
Founded: 1986
Staff: 1
Contact: Mrs. Sue Morris
Description: Provides a permanent exhibition and demonstration centre of equipment for people of all ages with a variety of needs and disabilities providing information to their families, carers, health professionals, students and the general public.
Publication: Brochure

Independent Midwives Association

1 The Great Quarry, Guildford, Surrey, GU1 3XN, England, UK
Tel: 44 1483 821104
Email: info@independentmidwives.org.uk
Website: http://www.independentmidwives.org.uk
Founded: 1982
Members: 60
Contact: Andrea Dombrowe, Sec.
Description: Midwives practicing in England. Promotes the involvement of midwives in childbirth, doing mainly house births. Promotes education in midwifery. Represents members' interests.

Independent Publishers Guild

PO Box 93, Royston, SG8 5GH, England, UK
Tel: 44 1763 247014
Fax: 44 1763 246293
Email: info@ipg.uk.com
Website: http://www.ipg.uk.com
Founded: 1962
Members: 430
Staff: 2
Contact: Sheila Bounford
Description: Independent publishing companies of all sizes, book packagers and publishing suppliers. Offers a forum for the exchange of ideas and information in the changing world of publishing. Activities include open meetings, training seminars, an annual conference, and corporate stands at major book fairs.
Publication: Bulletin
Publication title: IPG

Independent Schools Council

Grosvenor Gardens House, 35-37 Grosvenor Gardens, London,
SW1W OBS, England, UK
Tel: 44 20 77981500
Fax: 44 20 77981591
Email: isc@iscis.uk.net
Website: http://www.iscis.uk.net
Founded: 1974
Members: 1300
Staff: 24
Contact: Dr. Alistar Cooke, Gen.Sec.
Description: Independent schools.
Publication: Handbook
Publication title: ISC Guide. Advertisements.

Independent Schools Council Information Service
ISCIS

35-37 Grosvenor Gardens, London, SW1W 0BS, England, UK
Tel: 44 20 77981500
Fax: 44 20 77981501
Email: info@iscis.uk.net
Website: http://www.iscis.uk.net
Founded: 1972
Members: 1300
Staff: 13
Contact: David Woodhead
Description: Information and PR and Press services for independent
schools.
Publication title: Choosing Your Independent School.
Advertisements.
Second publication: Magazine
Publication title: ISIS Magazine

Independent Theatre Council

12 The Leathermarket, Weston St., London, SE1 3ER, England, UK
Tel: 44 207 4031727
Fax: 44 207 4031745
Email: admin@itc-arts.org
Website: http://www.itc-arts.org
Founded: 1974
Members: 450
Staff: 5
Contact: Charlotte Jones, Dir.
Description: Small to middlescale touring theatre and performing arts
companies or venues.
Publication: Booklets
Publication title: Equal Opportunities Booklets: Race, Gender,
Disability and Sexuality

Independent Waste Paper Processors Association

19 High St., Daventry, NN11 4BG, England, UK
Tel: 44 1327 703223
Fax: 44 1327 300612
Email: admin@iwppa.co.uk
Website: http://www.iwppa.co.uk
Founded: 1974
Members: 95
Staff: 4
Contact: M.J. Nicholls, Pres.
Description: Independent waste paper merchants. Formed to
develop the interests of independent waste paper merchants, the
IWPPA works to ensure its members views are represented to the
relevant organisations.

Indian Military Historical Society

33 High St., Tilbrooj, Huntingdon, PE28 0JP, England, UK
Tel: 44 20 85744425
Email: imhs@zetnet.co.uk
Founded: 1983
Members: 230
Staff: 3
Contact: A.N. McClenaghan, Sec.
Fee: £8
Membership Type: UK
Fee: £8
Membership Type: overseas (surface)
Description: Conducts research into the military history of the Indian
sub-continent.
Publication: Journal
Publication title: Durbar. Advertisements.

Indian Volunteers for Community Service
IVCS

12 Eastleigh Ave., South Harrow, Harrow, HA2 0UF, England, UK
Tel: 44 208 8644740
Fax: 44 208 9308338
Email: endah@btinternet.com
Website: http://www.ivcs.org.uk
Founded: 1981
Members: 200
Staff: 2
Contact: Nayan Shukla, Chm.
Fee: £15
Membership Type: ordinary
Description: Programme intended for people over the age of 18 who
wish to learn about India. Places selected individuals in a rural
development project in North India for a three week trial period as
paying guests. Participants may then move on for up to six months as
community service volunteers.
Publication: Journal
Publication title: International Journal of Rural Studies.
Advertisements.

Indonesia Human Rights Campaign
TAPOL

111 Northwood Rd., Thornton Heath, CR7 8HW, England, UK
Tel: 44 208 7712904
Fax: 44 208 6530322
Email: tapol@gn.apc.org
Website: http://tapol.gn.apc.org
Founded: 1973
Members: 750
Staff: 5
Contact: Carmel Budiardjo, Dir.
Description: Objectives are to: inform individuals worldwide about
human rights violations in Indonesia, East Timor, and West Papua;
obtain the assistance of British and other governments to pressure the
Indonesian military government to change; stop all British arms sales
to Indonesia; cooperate with British and other peace organizations in
order to further human rights concerns. Indonesia has been under
military rule since 1965, when the state military, supplied with British
and U.S. weapons, took control. Since then millions of Indonesians
have been denied jobs, been forced to resettle, been executed or
imprisoned, and suffered other human rights abuses for holding
beliefs differing from those of the military government. The
government, still in possession of weapons supplied by the United
Kingdom and the United States, invaded East Timor and retains

control of West Papua. Both these island nations now suffer human rights abuses similar to those suffered by Indonesians, in addition to being denied the right to self-determination.
Library Subject: human rights
Library Type: by appointment only
Publication: Bulletin
Publication title: Tapol Bulletin

Industrial Cleaning Machine Manufacturers' Association
ICMMA

Westminster Tower, 3 Albert Embankment, London, SE1 7SL, England, UK
Tel: 44 20 77933039
Fax: 44 20 77933003
Email: icmma@beama.org.uk
Website: http://www.icmma.org.uk
Founded: 1961
Members: 15
Contact: A A Bullen
Description: Represents manufacturers of cleaning machinery, in the entire spectrum of industrial cleaning technology from floor and carpet maintenance through to fixed installation cleaning systems and mechanised sweeping. Liaison is effected with departments of government. It is actively involved in the drafting of national and international standards for the industry.
Publication title: Product Guide to Member Companies

Industry Council for Electronic Equipment Recycling

6 Bath Pl., Rivington St., London, EC2A 3JE, England, UK
Tel: 44 20 77294766
Fax: 44 20 77299121
Email: ws@icer.org.uk
Website: http://www.icer.org.uk
Founded: 1992
Members: 60
Contact: Claire Snow, Dir.
Fee: £1500
Membership Type: associate
Description: Members are drawn from all who have a stake in the electronic and electrical product chain. Includes raw material suppliers, manufacturers, distributors, retailers, waste management companies, local authorities, and recyclers. Aims to develop industry-led solutions to management of end-of-life products - solutions which are both environmentally sound and commercially realistic. Working with government - UK and EC to put those solutions into practice.
Publication title: ICER Design
Second publication: Newsletter
Publication title: ICER Update
Meetings/Conventions: - semiannual conference

Industry Council for Packaging and the Environment
INCPEN

Sussex House, Ste. 108, 6 The Forbury, Reading, RG1 3EJ, England, UK
Tel: 44 118 9253486
Fax: 44 118 9253467
Email: info@incpen.org
Website: http://www.incpen.org
Founded: 1974

Members: 60
Staff: 6
Contact: Jane Bickerstaff, Dir.
Fee: £12000
Membership Type: full council
Description: Members are major British and international corporations involved in the manufacture of packaging and its use for packaged goods. They have an active interest in minimising the impact of packaging on the environment. Brings together all sectors of industry involved in the manufacture of packaging and the manufacture and retailing of packaged goods; leads in the rational debate on packaging and the environment, promotes the positive social and environmental benefits of packaging. Encourages environmentally responsible industrial practices for packaging and tries to ensure that balanced environmentally effective legislation on packaging is effected.
Publication: Journal
Publication title: The Pen
Second publication: Newsletter
Meetings/Conventions: seminar

Information for School and College Governors
ISCG

c/o Avondale Park School
Sirdar Rd., London, W11 4EE, England, UK
Tel: 44 207 2290200
Fax: 44 207 2290651
Email: iscg@governors.fsnet.co.uk
Website: http://www.governors.fsnet.co.uk/
Founded: 1990
Staff: 6
Contact: Mrs. F. Hollis, Co.Sec.
Description: The ISCG provides a unique independent research and information service for governors and LEAs.
Library Subject: education
Library Type: not open to the public
Formerly: Institution for School and College Governors
Meetings/Conventions: - periodic conference

Inn Sign Society

c/o Alan Rose
9 Denmead Dr., Wednesfield, Wolverhampton, WV11 2QS, England, UK
Tel: 44 1902 721808
Email: alanarose@btinternet.com
Website: http://www.bjcurtis.force9.co.uk/
Founded: 1988
Members: 400
Contact: Mr. Alan Rose
Fee: £30
Membership Type: full
Fee: £15
Membership Type: full
Description: Dedicated to investigating information about inns, their names and their signs.
Library Subject: inn and public house signs/pub histories
Library Type: not open to the public
Publication: Journal
Publication title: At The Sign Of

Insol International
II

2/3 Philpot Ln., London, EC3M 8AQ, England, UK
Tel: 44 207 9296679
Fax: 44 207 9296678
Email: claireb@insol.ision.co.uk
Website: http://www.insol.org
Founded: 1982
Members: 31
Staff: 3
Contact: Claire Broughton, Exec.Dir.
Fee: £50
Membership Type: by association
Fee: £100
Membership Type: individual
Description: Organizations representing 7,300 insolvency practitioners from 62 countries worldwide. Seeks international professional recognition of insolvency practitioners. Works to improve communication and cooperation among members; facilitates the exchange of information; establishes working committees to examine international issues of insolvency practice. Is developing a bibliographic database of insolvency publications.
Publication: Membership Directory
Publication title: INSOL International Membership
Second publication: Newsletter
Publication title: INSOL World
Meetings/Conventions: - quadrennial congress - Exhibits. Sydney NSW Australia

Insolvency Aid Society

68 Barcombe Rd., Brighton, BN1 9JR, England, UK
Tel: 44 1273 606067
Fax: 44 1273 606067
Email: ukphotoahp@aol.com
Website: http://users.aol.com/ukphotoahp/ias.htm
Founded: 1985
Members: 1273049
Staff: 224
Contact:
Fee: £10
Membership Type: full, complementary, temporary
Description: Open to debtors and creditors in Britain. Aims to reduce costs and losses to debtors and creditors; improve efficiency of debt payment and collection; to educate debtors and creditors.

Insolvency Practitioners Association
IPA

52-54 Gracechurch, London, EC3V 0EH, England, UK
Tel: 44 207 6235108
Fax: 44 207 6235127
Email: secretariat@ipa.co.uk
Website: http://www.ipa.uk.com
Founded: 1961
Members: 800
Staff: 3
Contact: C.M.T. Haig, Pres.
Description: Individuals licensed to act as insolvency practitioners in England, Wales, Scotland and Northern Ireland. Represents members' interests and indirectly the public.
Publication: Magazine
Publication title: Index of Members

Institute for African Alternatives - England

Lyndhurst Hall, Warden Rd., Room A, London, NW5 4RE, England, UK
Tel: 44 207 4824660
Fax: 44 207 4824662
Email: ifaanet@gn.apc.org
Founded: 1986
Members: 550
Staff: 6
Contact: Mohammed Suliman, Dir.
Fee: £30
Membership Type: associate
Description: Promotes innovative solutions to problems facing Africa. Maintains centers in Nigeria, Senegal, South Africa, Tanzania, and Zimbabwe to gather information on economic and social development in Africa; conducts research to determine the efficacy of various development programs. Sponsors educational and training courses to develop indigenous African expertise in development issues. Maintains liaison with government agencies throughout Africa. Advocates on behalf of development strategies designed to enhance social justice and ensure equality for women and minorities.
Library Subject: African culture
Library Type: open to the public
Publication: Papers
Second publication: Proceedings
Meetings/Conventions: - periodic conference

Institute for Animal Health

Compton, Newbury, RG20 7NN, England, UK
Tel: 44 1635 578411
Fax: 44 1635 577237
Email: animal.health@bbsrc.ac.uk
Website: http://www.iah.bbsrc.ac.uk
Founded: 1985
Staff: 480
Contact: Professor Paul-Pierre Pastoret, Dir.
Description: Aims to understand the pathogenesis of infectious diseases from which knowledge disease control methods will emerge.
Publication: Annual Report

Institute for Complementary Medicine
ICM

PO Box 194, London, SE16 7QZ, England, UK
Tel: 44 207 2375165
Fax: 44 207 2375175
Email: info@icmedicine.co.uk
Website: http://www.icmedicine.co.uk
Founded: 1982
Members: 6000
Staff: 8
Contact: Clive Teal, Gen.Mgr.
Fee: £100
Description: Registered charity of individuals united to promote the practice of alternative medicine. Seeks to establish educational standards for practitioners and to establish ties between therapy groups, organizations, teachers, and practitioners. Cooperates with the British government to develop natural therapy curricula. Maintains British Register of Complementary Practitions. Conducts research; disseminates information. Advises groups establishing healing practices on legal, organizational, and practical matters.
Library Type: reference
Formerly: Absorbed, Healing Research Trust
Publication: Journal
Publication title: Journal for Complementary Medicine

Second publication: Newsletter
Publication title: Newsletter
Meetings/Conventions: - annual conference - Exhibits. London UK

Institute for Development Policy and Management
IDPM

University of Manchester, The Harold Hankins Bldg , Precinct Ctr., Booth St. W, Manchester, M13 9QH, England, UK
Tel: 44 161 2752800
Fax: 44 161 2738829
Email: idpm@man.ac.uk
Website: http://www.man.ac.uk/idpm/
Staff: 40
Contact: Jayne Hindle, Admin.
Description: Development professionals. Promotes appropriate and sustainable economic and community development worldwide. Provides technical support and consulting services to development organizations and government agencies regulating development; sponsors research and educational programs.

Institute for European Environmental Policy
IEEP

Dean Bradley House, 5th Fl., 52 Horseferry Rd., London, SW1P 2AG, England, UK
Tel: 44 207 7992244
Fax: 44 207 7992600
Email: central@ieeplondon.org.uk
Website: http://www.ieep.org.uk
Founded: 1980
Staff: 17
Contact: Dr. David Baldock, Dir.
Description: Leading independent body for the analysis and advancement of environmental policies in Europe. Undertakes research, analysis, and consultancy on the European dimension of environmental protection with a main focus placed on the development, implementation, and evaluation of EU environmental policy. Encompasses several other EU policies of environmental significance, including agriculture, transport, regional development, and fisheries. Seeks both to increase awareness of the European dimension of environmental protection and to advance European policy-making in this field.
Library Type: reference
Publication title: Annual Report
Second publication: Newsletter
Publication title: Rural Areas Newslink
Meetings/Conventions: - quarterly conference

Institute for Fiscal Studies
IFS

7 Ridgmount St., 3rd Fl., London, WC1E 7AE, England, UK
Tel: 44 207 2914800
Fax: 44 207 3234780
Email: mailbox@ifs.org.uk
Website: http://www.ifs.org.uk
Founded: 1969
Members: 1300
Staff: 35
Contact: Emma Hyman, Marketing and Publicity Officer
Fee: £35
Membership Type: individual
Fee: £125
Membership Type: institution

Description: Academics, civil servants, financiers, industrialists, accountants, solicitors, industry, professions, trade unions, universities, civil service. Looks at public policy with particular reference to taxation.
Library Type: not open to the public
Publication: Journal
Publication title: Fiscal Studies. Advertisements.
Second publication: Reports
Meetings/Conventions: conference

Institute for Jewish Policy Research
JPR

79 Wimpole St., London, W1G 9RY, England, UK
Tel: 44 20 79358266
Fax: 44 20 79353252
Email: jpr@jpr.org.uk
Website: http://www.jpr.org.uk
Founded: 1941

Institute for Manufacturing
IMANF

Mill Lane, Cambridge, CB2 1RX, England, UK
Tel: 44 1223 766141
Fax: 44 1223 464217
Email: ifm-enquiries@eng.cam.ac.uk
Website: http://www.ifm.eng.cam.ac.uk/
Founded: 1978
Members: 400
Staff: 4
Contact: Prof. H.J. Manners, Pres. and Founder
Fee: £40
Description: Individuals involved in manufacturing in 40 countries. Provides information to members on new developments, techniques, processes, and methods in the field of manufacturing. Conducts seminars and programs in management training and education.
Publication: Journal
Publication title: Manufacturing Management and Manufacturers. Advertisements.
Meetings/Conventions: - periodic conference

Institute for Outdoor Learning

Plumpton Old Hall, Plumpton, Penrith, CA11 9NP, England, UK
Tel: 44 1768 885800
Fax: 44 1768 885801
Email: institute@adventure-ed.ca.uk
Website: http://www.outdoor-learning.org
Founded: 2001
Members: 800
Staff: 3
Contact: Melanie Bardgett, Hon.Sec.
Fee: £30
Membership Type: individual in the United Kingdom
Fee: £75
Membership Type: group/organization
Description: Supports, develops and promotes learning through outdoor experiences.
Library Subject: outdoor education
Library Type: by appointment only
Formerly: National Association for Outdoor Education
Publication: Magazine
Publication title: Horizons. Advertisements.
Second publication: Newsletter
Publication title: IOL Newsletter
Meetings/Conventions: - annual conference - Exhibits.

Institute for Scientific Information - Europe, Middle East, and Africa

14 Great Queen St., London, WC2B 5DF, England, UK
Tel: 44 20 73442800
Fax: 44 20 73442830
Email: uksales@isinet.co.uk
Website: http://www.isinet.com
Description: Provision of databases and other information services covering published research in all areas of science, technology, social sciences and humanities.
Publication: Newsletter
Publication title: Current Contents

Institute for Social Inventions
ISI

6 Blackstock Mews, Blackstock Rd., London, N4 2BT, England, UK
Tel: 44 20 73598391
Fax: 44 20 73543831
Email: rhino@dial.pipex.com
Website: http://www.globalideasbank.org/ISI.html
Founded: 1985
Members: 400
Staff: 3
Contact: Nick Temple
Fee: £15
Membership Type: subscription
Description: Promotes non-technological social innovations for improving the quality of life. Also runs the Global Ideas Bank on the Internet.
Library Subject: social innovations collected by the Institute
Library Type: not open to the public
Publication: Book
Publication title: Book of Inspirations
Second publication: Journal
Publication title: Social Inventions
Meetings/Conventions: Ideas Walks in Countryside - weekly

Institute for the Management of Information Systems
IMIS

5 Kingfisher House, New Mill Rd., Orpington, BR5 3QG, England, UK
Tel: 44 70 00023456
Fax: 44 70 00023023
Email: central@imis.org.uk
Website: http://www.imis.org.uk
Founded: 1978
Members: 11000
Staff: 14
Contact: Ian M. Rickwood, Chief Exec.
Description: Professional and student information systems practitioners in 56 countries. Seeks to advance the interests of the information systems profession, set professional standards, and recognize practitioners meeting these standards. Serves as an examining body for IMIS students.
Formerly: Formed by Merger of, Data Processing Management Association
Publication: Journal
Publication title: IMIS Journal. Advertisements.
Meetings/Conventions: - annual conference - Exhibits.

Institute of Acoustics

77A St. Peter's St., St. Albans, AL1 3BN, England, UK
Tel: 44 1727 848195
Fax: 44 1727 850553
Email: ioa@ioa.org.uk
Website: http://www.ioa.org.uk
Founded: 1974
Members: 2450
Staff: 5
Contact: Roy D. Bratby, Chief Exec.
Description: Membership covers all aspects of acoustics.
Publication: Magazine
Publication title: Acoustics Bulletin. Advertisements.

Institute of Actuaries - United Kingdom

Staple Inn Hall, High Holborn, London, WC1V 7QJ, England, UK
Tel: 44 207 6322100
Fax: 44 207 6322111
Email: institute@actuaries.org.uk
Website: http://www.actuaries.org.uk
Founded: 1848
Members: 11069
Staff: 81
Contact: Caroline Instance, Ch.Exec.
Description: Actuaries - student and qualified. Professional and examining body for the actuarial profession. Promotes actuarial science and sets standards for the actuarial profession. Holds meetings and conferences and publishes on actuarial and related topics. A recognized professional body under the terms of the United Kingdom Financial Services Act 1986.
Library Subject: actuarial sciences, life assurance, general insurance, pensions, employee benefits, friendly societies, social security, investment, demography, mortality, probability, risk theory, and histories of insurance companies
Library Type: by appointment only
Publication: Journal
Publication title: British Actuarial Journal

Institute of Administrative Management
IAM

16 Park Cres., London, W1B 1BA, England, UK
Tel: 44 207 6127099
Fax: 44 207 6127094
Email: membership@instam.org
Website: http://www.instam.org
Founded: 1915
Members: 10000
Staff: 20
Contact: David Woodgate, Ch.Exec.
Fee: £90
Membership Type: fellow
Fee: £85
Membership Type: regular
Description: To promote and develop, for the public benefit, the science of administrative management in all branches; encourage the attainment of professional academic qualifications. Provides the latest techniques and developments in the field of administrative management via conferences, seminars, meetings and publications.
Library Subject: Management
Library Type: reference
Publication: Journal
Publication title: British Manager, Journal of Administrative

Management. Advertisements.
Second publication: Manuals
Meetings/Conventions: - annual convention

Institute of Advanced Motorists

c/o IAM House
510 Chiswick High Rd., London, W4 4HS, England, UK
Tel: 44 208 9969600
Fax: 44 208 9949249
Website: http://www.iam.org.uk
Founded: 1956
Members: 108000
Staff: 37
Contact: Christopher T. Bullock, Chief Exec.
Fee: £15
Description: These who have passed the Advanced Driving Test or who have recognised standards for exemption. Aims to enhance road safety through improved driving standards; conducts advanced driving tests (for cars, motorcycles, minibuses and commercial vehicles); provides commercial fleet driver training through IAM Fleet Training Limited.
Publication: Magazine
Publication title: Advanced Driving. Advertisements.
Publication title: Pass Your Advanced Driving Test

Institute of Agricultural Management
IAM

c/o Farm Management Unit
University of Reading, Reading, RG6 6AT, England, UK
Tel: 44 1189 316578
Fax: 44 1189 756467
Email: d.j.ansell@rdg.ac.uk
Website: http://www.rdg.ac.uk/iagrm
Founded: 1966
Members: 1200
Staff: 1
Contact: D. Ansell
Fee: £32
Membership Type: associate
Fee: £60
Membership Type: member
Description: Promotes high standards in the practice and business of management in agriculture. Promotes training and to encourage the provision and attainment of professional qualifications in the principles and practice of management in agriculture.
Formerly: Centre of Management in Agriculture
Publication: Journal
Publication title: Farm Management
Meetings/Conventions: Farm Management Conference - annual conference

Institute of Agricultural Secretaries and Administrators
IAgSA

c/o National Agricultural Centre
Stoneleigh, Kenilworth, CV8 2LZ, England, UK
Tel: 44 2476 696592
Fax: 44 2476 417937
Email: iagsa@iagsa.co.uk
Website: http://www.iagsa.co.uk
Founded: 1967
Members: 900

Contact: Charlotte O'Kane
Fee: £50
Description: Secretaries and managers employed within the agricultural industry. The professional body for those engaged in agricultural secretaryship and rural business administration. It offers support to all practising agricultural secretaries and administrators, advises student members on education and training, helps the new entrant to the profession and maintains close links with all relevant education bodies.
Publication: Bulletin. Advertisements.
Second publication: Journal
Meetings/Conventions: - annual conference - Exhibits.

Institute of Animal Technology

5 South Parade, Summertown, Oxford, OX2 7JL, England, UK
Website: http://www.iat.org.uk
Founded: 1950
Description: Promotes high ethical standards in technology and the practice of laboratory animal care and welfare.
Publication: Bulletin
Second publication: Journal
Publication title: Animal Technology
Meetings/Conventions: - annual congress

Institute of Archaeo-Metallurgical Studies
IAMS

31-34 Gordon Sq., London, WC1H 0PY, England, UK
Tel: 44 207 6794918
Email: b.rothenberg@ucl.ac.uk
Website: http://www.ucl.ac.uk/iams/
Founded: 1973
Description: Fosters research into the origins of metallurgy.

Institute of Association Management

21 Bloomsbury Way, London, WC1A 2TH, England, UK
Tel: 44 207 8311979
Fax: 44 207 8311842
Email: sae@martex.co.uk
Founded: 1933
Members: 400
Contact: Peter Wigginton, CEO
Description: Executives of associations and association suppliers in the United Kingdom. Provides a forum for the exchange of information between members.
Formerly: Society of Association Executives
Publication: Newsletter
Publication title: Association
Publication title: Handbook. Advertisements.
Meetings/Conventions: - annual conference - Exhibits.

Institute of Automotive Engineer Assessors
IAEA

Stowe House, Netherstowe, Lichfield, WS13 6TJ, England, UK
Tel: 44 1543 251346
Fax: 44 1543 415804
Website: http://guideto.iaea.org.uk/
Contact: J.R. Morris, Sec.
Description: Automotive engineer assessors in England. Promotes and protects members' interests.
Publication: Directory
Publication title: Register of Members Arrangement

Institute of Biology

20-22 Queensberry Pl., London, SW7 2DZ, England, UK
Tel: 44 20 75818333
Fax: 44 20 78239409
Email: info@iob.org
Website: http://www.iob.org
Founded: 1950
Members: 14000
Staff: 20
Contact:
Fee: £80
Membership Type: full
Fee: £116
Membership Type: fellow
Description: Provides a forum for the advancement of education and research in biology. Conducts educational programs.
Formerly: Absorbed, Biological Council
Publication: Magazine
Publication title: Biologist. Advertisements.
Second publication: Journal
Publication title: Journal of Biological Education. Advertisements.
Meetings/Conventions: - annual meeting

Institute of Biomedical Science

12 Coldbath Sq., London, EC1R 5HL, England, UK
Tel: 44 207 7130214
Fax: 44 207 4364946
Email: mail@ibms.org
Website: http://www.ibms.org
Founded: 1912
Members: 15000
Staff: 28
Contact: Inga Smith
Fee: £94
Membership Type: associate
Fee: £76
Membership Type: student
Description: Biomedical scientists (medical laboratory scientists) and related staff in the National Health Service, private sector, commercial sector, and overseas. To promote the study and development of biomedical science and maintain high standards of professional education and practice.
Library Subject: biomedical science
Library Type: not open to the public
Publication title: Biomedical Scientist. Advertisements.
Second publication: Journal
Publication title: British Journal of Biomedical Science
Meetings/Conventions: - biennial congress - Exhibits.

Institute of Building Control

92-104 East St., Epsom, KT17 1EB, England, UK
Tel: 44 1372 745577
Fax: 44 1372 748282
Email: admin@building-control.org
Founded: 1971
Members: 3600
Staff: 8
Description: Building Control practitioners in the private and public sectors. Concerns itself exclusively with building control. Its sole object has been to advance public education in matters relating to the law and science of building control.
Publication title: Building Control
Publication title: IBC News

Institute of Burial and Cremation Administration

Kelham Hall, Kelham, Newark, 5QX, England, UK
Tel: 44 1753 771518
Fax: 44 1753 770984
Email: tmlgo3882@bluegondar.co.uk
Founded: 1913
Members: 650
Contact: Tim Morris, Natl.Sec.
Fee: £75
Membership Type: plus $50 registration fee
Description: Managers and staff of burial and cremation authorities. Promotes and advances the burial and cremation service within the United Kingdom. Disseminates information; Administers a course of study leading to the award of a diploma. Training schemes for cemetery operatives and crematorium technicians.
Publication: Journal
Publication title: The Journal
Meetings/Conventions: Joint Conference of Burial and Cremation Authorities - annual conference

Institute of Business Administration and Management

16 Park Crescent, London, W1B 1AH, England, UK
Tel: 44 20 75804741
Fax: 44 20 76127027
Email: info@ibam.org
Website: http://www.ibam.org
Founded: 1992
Members: 1850
Staff: 4
Contact: J. Smith, Exec.Dir.
Description: Administrators of small and medium sized enterprises. To promote professional standards of administration in small and medium sized organizations by providing a professional qualification enabling individuals to apply for membership of IBA.
Formerly: Institute of Business Administration
Publication: Journal
Publication title: IBA News. Advertisements.

Institute of Business Advisers

Response House, Queen St. N., Chesterfield, EC1N 8LD, England, UK
Tel: 44 1246 453322
Fax: 44 1246 453300
Email: info@iba.org.uk
Website: http://www.iba.org.uk
Founded: 1989
Members: 2100
Staff: 8
Contact: Maggie Hall, Chief Exec.
Description: Professional, independent business advisers, business counsellors, business menters, trainers and support staff in a wide range of business support organizations. The professional body responsible for the accreditation of independent business advisers. Their services are available to small and medium size businesses through Business Links, local Enterprise Agencies and Training and Enterprise Councils (TECs) or Local Enterprise Companies (LECs). Some members are available for private business advisory services.
Formerly: Institute of Business Counsellors
Publication: Magazine
Publication title: The Business Adviser
Meetings/Conventions: - annual conference - Exhibits.

Institute of Career Guidance

27a Lower High St., Stourbridge, DY8 1TA, England, UK
Tel: 44 1384 376464
Fax: 44 1384 440830
Email: hq@icg-uk.org
Website: http://www.icg-uk.org
Founded: 1961
Members: 3000
Staff: 15
Contact: Bryony Pawinska, Chief Exec.
Description: Careers guidance practitioners, including those employed by careers services. Professional body for those engaged in careers advisory work.
Library Subject: practice and policy in career guidance
Library Type: not open to the public
Publication: Newsletter
Publication title: A Career in Careers Guidance
Second publication: Journal
Publication title: Careers Guidance Today
Meetings/Conventions: - annual conference

Institute of Cast Metals Engineers

c/o National Metalforming Centre
47 Birmingham Rd., West Bromwich, B70 6PY, England, UK
Tel: 44 121 6016979
Fax: 44 121 6016981
Email: info@icme.org.uk
Website: http://www.icme.org.uk
Founded: 1904
Members: 2200
Staff: 9
Contact: Mr. Andrew Turner
Description: Workers in the cast metals industry. Offers educational, research, and public service programs. Offers placement service.
Library Subject: cast metals, pattern making
Library Type: reference
Formerly: Institute of British Foundrymen
Publication: Journal
Publication title: Foundryman. Advertisements.
Second publication: Proceedings
Meetings/Conventions: Castcon - annual conference

Institute of Chartered Accountants in England and Wales
ICAEW

Chartered Accountants Hall, PO Box 433, London, EC2P 2BJ, England, UK
Tel: 44 207 9208100
Fax: 44 207 9208547
Website: http://www.icaew.co.uk
Contact: Andrew Colquhoun, Sec.
Description: Accounting firms and individual accountants in the United Kingdom. Promotes the interests of members. Provides career adviser contact information; promotes job placement of individuals interested in accounting in England.
Publication: Membership Directory
Publication title: Complete List of Members
Publication title: Training Vacancies

Institute of Chartered Secretaries and Administrators

16 Park Crescent, London, W1B 1AH, England, UK
Tel: 44 207 5804741
Fax: 44 207 3231132
Email: info@icsa.org.uk
Website: http://www.icsa.org.uk
Members: 73000
Description: Chartered secretaries and administrators in England.

Institute of Chartered Shipbrokers - England

3 St. Helens Place, London, EC3A 6EJ, England, UK
Tel: 44 207 6285559
Fax: 44 207 6285445
Email: info@ics.org.uk
Website: http://www.ics.org.uk
Founded: 1920
Members: 3300
Staff: 10
Contact: D.A. Phillips, Dir.Gen.
Description: Professional, qualified Chartered Shipbrokers. Education and examination - qualification for shipping personnel. Guidance and promotion of company members' interests.
Library Subject: maritime economics
Library Type: reference
Publication: Journal
Publication title: Shipbroker. Advertisements.

Institute of Chiropodists and Podiatrists

27 Wright St., Southport, PR9 0TL, England, UK
Tel: 44 1704 546141
Fax: 44 1704 500477
Email: editor@inst-chiropodist.org.uk
Website: http://www.inst-chiropodist.org.uk
Founded: 1938
Members: 2500
Staff: 4
Contact: Mrs. S.M. Kirkham
Fee: £110
Description: State registered and non-state registered chiropodists. Members governed by strict code of ethics. Third party surgery risks insurance provided for members.
Formerly: Institute of Chiropodists
Publication: Journal
Publication title: Chiropody Review. Advertisements.
Meetings/Conventions: - annual conference - Exhibits.

Institute of Clay Technology

101 Ball Lane, Norton Green, Stoke-On-Trent, ST6 8SW, England, UK
Tel: 44 1782 503341
Fax: 44 1782 503341
Website: http://www.aecportico.co.uk/Directory/ICIT.shtm
Founded: 1927
Members: 1154
Contact: W.M. Churchill
Description: Employees of heavy clay industry. To promote and provide facilities for the discussion of practical, technical, geological, chemical and other matters which affect the working of clay and other ceramic raw materials for use in the production of clay bricks, clay tiles, clay pipes, refractories and other similar goods, and which relate to the control of clayworks and the education of clayworkers. To

encourage closer personal associations and fellowship among its members.
Publication title: Clay Technology. Advertisements.
Meetings/Conventions: - annual conference

Institute of Clerks of Works of Great Britain
41 The Mall, Ealing, London, W5 3TJ, England, UK
Tel: 44 20 85792917
Fax: 44 20 85790554
Email: gensec@icwgb.sagehost.co.uk
Founded: 1882
Members: 4200
Staff: 6
Contact: A.P. Macnamara
Description: Qualified clerks of works working to ensure the client obtains value for money in all areas of the construction industry - civil engineering, building, M and E and landscape. Recognised as the authoritive organization for Clerks of Works, ICW has 24 UK meeting centres and a Hong Kong branch. It arranges an annual residential seminar, regional CPD events, offers guidance on employment matters, publishes a number of guides and leaflets and provides annual examinations worldwide to corporate membership.
Publication title: The Clerk of Works
Second publication: Directory
Publication title: Directory of Self-Employed, Private Practice and Freelance Clerks of Works

Institute of Clinical Research
PO Box 1208, Maidenhead, SL6 3GD, England, UK
Tel: 44 1628 829900
Fax: 44 1628 829922
Email: info@instituteofclinicalresearch.org
Website: http://www.instituteofclinicalresearch.org
Founded: 1978
Members: 4200
Staff: 8
Contact: John Kolthammer, Bus.Mgr.
Fee: £30
Membership Type: within the U.K.
Fee: £45
Membership Type: outside UK
Description: Any person who is engaged in the design, organization or conduct of clinical trials for the pharmaceutical industry. Aims to establish and maintain the professional identity of members; to facilitate communications between members of clinical research departments in the industry, to provide a forum for discussion and to foster good relations with other professional groups. Maintains resource center.
Formerly: Association of Clinical Research for the Pharmaceutical Industry
Publication title: Clinical Research Focus. Advertisements.
Second publication: Handbook
Publication title: Handbook of Clinical Research
Meetings/Conventions: Introductory Course - 3/year

Institute of Commerce
50 BurnHill Rd., Beckenham, BR3 3LA, England, UK
Tel: 44 208 663577
Fax: 44 208 6633212
Members: 500
Contact: Mr. P. Van Berckel
Description: To promote and develop business education.

Institute of Commercial Management
The Fusee, 20A Bargates, Christchurch, BH23 1QL, England, UK
Tel: 44 1202 490555
Fax: 44 1202 490666
Email: info@icm.ac.uk
Website: http://www.icm.ac.uk
Founded: 1979
Members: 158000
Staff: 18
Contact: A.F. Somerville Ford, CEO
Fee: £30
Membership Type: associate
Fee: £45
Membership Type: ordinary
Description: Managers/supervisors in industry and commerce. An examining body for business and management students providing a range of recognised qualifications. Seeks to provide a range of high quality global education, training, and consulting services which raise performance standards for business and enhance the professional status of individuals. Offers certification programs.
Publication title: ICM Review
Publication title: The Manager

Institute of Commonwealth Studies
University of London, 28 Russell Sq., London, WC1B 5DS, England, UK
Tel: 44 207 8628844
Fax: 44 207 8628820
Email: ics@sas.ac.uk
Website: http://www.sas.ac.uk/commonwealthstudies/
Founded: 1949
Members: 2000
Staff: 20
Contact: Timothy M. Shaw, Dir.
Description: Academics, educators, students, and other individuals with an interest in the history of the British Commonwealth and its component countries. Promotes interest in and study of the economic, social, and cultural aspects of the Commonwealth. Conducts research and educational programs.
Library Subject: commonwealth-related history, politics, economics, social sciences, human rights
Library Type: reference

Institute of Community Studies
18 Victoria Park Sq., Bethnal Green, London, E2 9PF, England, UK
Tel: 44 208 9806263
Fax: 44 208 9816719
Email: info@icstudies.org.uk
Founded: 1953
Staff: 10
Contact: John Stevens

Institute of Company Accountants
IComA
40 Tyndalls Park Rd., Bristol, BS8 1PL, England, UK
Tel: 44 117 9738261
Fax: 44 117 9238292
Founded: 1974
Members: 6000
Staff: 8
Contact: B.T. Banks, Dir.Gen.
Description: Accountants, secretaries, and financial directors in 25 countries. Works to advance the interests of accountants employed by

companies, corporations, public bodies, and those in public practice. Seeks to elevate the status of the profession. Sponsors lectures.
Library Subject: Accountancy, computers, law, and management
Library Type: reference
Formerly: Formed by Merger of, British Association of Accountants and Auditors
Publication: Newsletter
Publication title: Student Digest
Meetings/Conventions: - annual dinner

Institute of Concrete Technology
ICT

PO Box 7827, Crowthorne, RG45 6FR, England, UK
Tel: 44 1344 752096
Fax: 44 1344 752096
Email: ict@ictech.org
Website: http://www.ictech.org
Founded: 1972
Members: 700
Staff: 1
Contact: Graham Taylor, Exec. Ofc.
Fee: £12
Membership Type: graduate/student
Fee: £63
Membership Type: member
Description: Professionally qualified concrete technologists (UK and overseas). Promotes concrete technology through technical meetings; representation on national technical committees; newsletter and technical information to members.
Publication: Yearbook
Publication title: ICT Yearbook. Advertisements.
Second publication: Papers
Meetings/Conventions: - annual convention - Exhibits.

Institute of Consumer Affairs

21 Wood St., Woburn Sands, MK17 8PH, England, UK
Founded: 1974
Members: 100
Contact: Kathryn Walker
Description: People who are employed as consumer advisers within Consumer Advice Centres, those who manage a Consumer Advice Centre at any level or people who are involved in consumer education or information at any level. Aims to protect the status of consumer advisers and encourage, maintain and improve standards of consumer service.
Publication: Newsletter

Institute of Contemporary Arts
ICA

The Mall, London, SW1Y 5AH, England, UK
Tel: 44 207 9303647
Fax: 44 207 8730051
Email: info@ica.org.uk
Website: http://www.ica.org.uk
Founded: 1947
Members: 7000
Staff: 50
Contact: Philip Dodd, Dir.
Fee: £30
Description: Available to all people with an interest in live and contemporary art, including artists, young people and students (concessions available). Aims to encourage debate around central

issues of contemporary art. Provides a forum for young people to display their work.
Publication: Videos

Institute of Corrosion

Corrosion House, Vimy Ct., Leighton Buzzard, LU7 1FG, England, UK
Tel: 44 1525 851771
Fax: 44 1525 376690
Email: admin@icorr.demon.co.uk
Website: http://www.icorr.demon.co.uk
Founded: 1975
Members: 1550
Staff: 2
Contact: Dr. J. Burnell-Gray, Hon.Sec.
Description: Corrosion engineers, technologists and scientists interested in corrosion prevention and control. To advance the understanding of the science of corrosion and the technology of corrosion prevention and control, and to encourage the exchange of information and ideas of these subjects for the public benefit.
Publication: Magazine
Publication title: Corrosion Management. Advertisements.
Second publication: Report
Meetings/Conventions: - annual conference

Institute of Cost and Executive Accountants
ICEA

Tower House, 139 Fonthill Rd., 3rd Fl., London, N4 3HF, England, UK
Tel: 44 171 2723925
Fax: 44 171 2815723
Email: icea@enta.net
Website: http://www.icea.enta.net
Founded: 1958
Members: 3600
Staff: 4
Contact: Sushil K. Das Gupta, Sec.Gen.
Fee: £57
Membership Type: associate
Fee: £67
Membership Type: fellow
Description: Professional society of accountants, financial directors, financial controllers, and commercial consultants in over 30 countries. Seeks to advance the status and interests of the profession, and upgrade knowledge and efficiency in accounting. Provides examinations and certificates of proficiency. Facilitates the exchange of information and ideas; offers employment services; provides assistance to students. Compiles statistics.
Library Subject: Accounting, finance, taxation, and management.
Library Type: reference
Publication: Journal
Publication title: Executive Accountant. Advertisements.
Second publication: Newsletter
Publication title: Newsletter
Meetings/Conventions: - annual meeting

Institute of Credit Management

Station Rd., The Water Mill, South Luffenham, LE15 8NB, England, UK
Tel: 44 1780 722900
Fax: 44 1780 721333
Email: info@icm.org.uk
Website: http://www.icm.org.uk
Founded: 1939
Members: 9000

Staff: 24
Contact: Peter A. Rowe, Dir. General
Fee: £70
Membership Type: individual
Description: Those working in credit management and its ancillary services. The central reference point in the UK on all matters relating to credit management. The Institute raises professional standards through the provision of examinations, seminars, conferences and publications. Courses are offered at local colleges, by the Rapid Results Correspondence College and by distance learning.
Library Subject: credit management
Library Type: not open to the public
Publication: Journal
Publication title: Credit Management. Advertisements.
Meetings/Conventions: - annual conference - Exhibits.

Institute of Credit Management

Station Rd., The Water Mill, South Luffenham, LE15 8NB, England, UK
Tel: 44 1780 722900
Fax: 44 1780 721333
Email: info@icm.org.uk
Website: http://www.icm.org.uk
Founded: 1939
Members: 9000
Staff: 24
Contact: Peter A. Rowe, Dir. General
Fee: £70
Membership Type: individual
Description: Those working in credit management and its ancillary services. The central reference point in the UK on all matters relating to credit management. The Institute raises professional standards through the provision of examinations, seminars, conferences and publications. Courses are offered at local colleges, by the Rapid Results Correspondence College and by distance learning.
Library Subject: credit management
Library Type: not open to the public
Publication: Journal
Publication title: Credit Management. Advertisements.
Meetings/Conventions: - annual conference - Exhibits.

Institute of Development Studies
IDS

c/o Communications Officer
University of Sussex, Brighton, BN1 9RE, England, UK
Tel: 44 1273 606261
Fax: 44 1273 621202
Email: ids@ids.ac.uk
Website: http://www.ids.ac.uk
Founded: 1966
Staff: 180
Contact: Zoe Mars, Sec.
Description: Research and teaching institute seeking to reduce poverty and create economies capable of providing secure livelihoods to individuals worldwide. Aims to influence development policies; through research, training, and post-graduate teaching.
Publication: Journal
Publication title: IDS Bulletin. Advertisements.
Second publication: Reports
Meetings/Conventions: - periodic conference

Institute of Directors - England

116 Pall Mall, London, SW1Y 5ED, England, UK
Tel: 44 20 78391233
Fax: 44 20 79301949
Email: enquiries@iod.com
Website: http://www.iod.co.uk
Founded: 1903
Members: 53000
Staff: 225
Contact: Alan Morkel, Sec.
Description: Membership is available to company directors or those holding a similar position in industry, commerce, the professions or government organizations. A business organisation aimed at advancing company directors' interests, and fostering free enterprise. Services to members include a Branch network, professional development activities and conferences, information and advisory services. The IoD also provides meeting rooms and restaurant facilities to its members.
Library Type: reference
Publication title: also publishes Guidelines for Directors
Publication title: Director
Meetings/Conventions: - annual conference London UK

Institute of Ecology and Environmental Management

45 Southgate St., Winchester, Farnborough, SO23 9EH, England, UK
Tel: 44 1962 868626
Fax: 44 1962 868625
Email: enquiries@ieem.demon.co.uk
Website: http://www.ieem.org.uk
Founded: 1991
Members: 1400
Contact: Dr. Jim Thompson, Exec.Dir.
Fee: £100
Membership Type: full
Fee: £70
Membership Type: associate
Description: Individuals working in local authorities, government departments and agencies, environmental consultants; ecologists and environmental managers in industry, conservation bodies (voluntary and public), academic and research institutes. Concerned to raise the profile of the profession of ecology and environmental management, to establish, maintain and enhance professional standards and to promote an ethic of environmental care within the profession and to clients and employers of the members.
Library Type: not open to the public
Publication: Magazine
Publication title: In Practice. Advertisements.
Meetings/Conventions: Upland Ecology - semiannual conference London UK

Institute of Economic Affairs
IEA

2 Lord North St, London, SW1P 3LB, England, UK
Tel: 44 20 77998909
Fax: 44 20 77992137
Email: jblundell@iea.org.uk
Website: http://www.iea.org.uk
Founded: 1955

Institute of Ecotechnics

24 Old Gloucester St., London, WC1N 3AL, England, UK
Tel: 44 207 4051824
Fax: 44 207 4051851
Email: marknelson1@cs.com
Website: http://www.ecotechnics.edu
Founded: 1972
Members: 12
Contact: Mark Nelson, Chm.
Description: Council members only. Concerned with the development of a conceptual model for ecosystem management which includes human cultures, technics and decision-making populations. These dynamic factors together with studies of soil, plant and animal interactions, energy flows and material cycles, facilitate a total systems approach to complex environmental issues.

Institute of Employment Rights

177 Abbeville Rd., London, SW4 9RL, England, UK
Tel: 44 207 4986919
Fax: 44 207 4989080
Email: ier@gn.apc.org
Website: http://www.ier.org.uk
Founded: 1989
Members: 800
Staff: 3
Contact: Carolyn Jones, Dir.
Fee: £40
Membership Type: individual
Fee: £45
Membership Type: trade union
Description: Trade union general secretaries, academics and legal practitioners. To analyze, discuss and promote issues relating to employment law. Wide network of experts - legal practitioners, academics and trade unionists - to develop an alternative legal agenda for the future through publications and seminars.
Publication: Books. Advertisements.
Meetings/Conventions: - periodic conference

Institute of Energy
InstE

18 Devonshire St., London, W1G 7AU, England, UK
Tel: 44 20 75807124
Fax: 44 20 78504420
Email: secretariat@instenergy.org.uk
Website: http://www.instenergy.org.uk
Founded: 1927
Members: 4500
Staff: 11
Contact: Ms. L. Kingham, Sec./CEO
Description: Individuals interested in energy issues. Maintains charitable program; bestows awards.
Publication: Magazine
Publication title: Energy World. Advertisements.
Publication title: Energy World Yearbook
Meetings/Conventions: - periodic conference

Institute of Entertainment and Arts Management

c/o S. Carpenter
17 Drake Close, Horsham, RH12 5UB, England, UK
Tel: 44 870 2417248
Fax: 44 870 2417248
Email: admin@ieam.co.uk
Website: http://www.ieam.co.uk

Founded: 1982
Members: 300
Staff: 2
Contact: Shirley Carpenter, Admin.
Fee: £50
Membership Type: individual
Fee: £100
Membership Type: corporate
Description: Management in the local government grant-aided and commercial sectors in the entertainment and arts industry. Conducts training seminars at the national and regional levels; sponsors venue visits and social and professional networking.
Publication: Yearbook. Advertisements.
Meetings/Conventions: - annual general assembly

Institute of Estuarine and Coastal Studies
IECS

Wolfson Bldg., University of Hull, Hull, HU6 7RX, England, UK
Tel: 44 1482 465667
Fax: 44 1482 465001
Email: iecs@hull.ac.uk
Website: http://www.hull.ac.uk/iecs
Founded: 1982
Staff: 14
Contact: Dr. M. Elliott, Dir.
Description: Covers the entire range of coastal studies, from fundamental scientific research to the preparation of management plans and environmental impact assessment. A major part of work involves field measurement and monitoring both of physical and biological systems and using a variety of surveying and instrumental techniques.
Library Subject: estuarine and coastal science and management
Library Type: not open to the public
Publication: Reports
Meetings/Conventions: International Symposium on Estuarine and Lagoon Fish and Fisheries - periodic symposium

Institute of Explosives Engineers

Centenary Business Centre, Hammond Close, Attleborough Fields, Nuneaton, CV11 6RY, England, UK
Tel: 44 2476 350846
Fax: 44 2476 350831
Email: info@iexpe.org
Website: http://www.iexpe.org
Founded: 1974
Members: 1000
Staff: 2
Contact: G.C. Bonar, Sec.
Description: Civil and Military engineers, academics and scientists engaged in the development and/or manufacture of explosives/munitions. Aims to promote the profession of explosive engineering and to achieve professional standing so that the Institute takes its place alongside other specialised Engineering bodies and provides technical consultative facilities for government departments and other external agencies within its field.
Publication: Journal
Publication title: Explosives Engineering. Advertisements.
Second publication: Directory

Institute of Export

c/o Export House
Minerva Business Park, Lynch Wood, Peterborough, PE2 6FT,
England, UK
Tel: 44 1733 404400
Fax: 44 1733 404444
Email: institute@export.org.uk
Website: http://www.export.org.uk
Founded: 1935
Members: 6700
Staff: 17
Contact: Hugh Allen, Chief Exec.
Description: Professionally Qualified Exporters. Enhances and
promotes the UK's international trade and the support of the
professional exporter in both the corporate and personal context. Sets
and maintains the standards for professional education and training in
international trade.
Publication: Yearbook

Institute of Field Archaeologists

c/o University of Reading
2 Earley Gate, PO Box 239, Reading, RG6 6AU, England, UK
Tel: 44 118 3786446
Fax: 44 118 3786448
Email: admin@archaeologists.net
Website: http://www.archaeologists.net
Founded: 1982
Members: 1700
Staff: 6
Contact: Mr. P. Hinton, Dir.
Description: Provides an active professional organization, involving
and offering appropriate services to its membership; develops proper
professional guidelines and standards for the execution of
archaeological work and establishes these guidelines and standards
by promoting membership of the institute to all those practicing field
archaeology.
Publication: Magazine
Publication title: The Archaeologist. Advertisements.
Second publication: Directory
Publication title: Yearbook and Directory
Meetings/Conventions: - annual conference - Exhibits. Bangor
Wales

Institute of Financial Accountants
IFA

Buford House, 44 London Rd., Sevenoaks, TN13 1AS, England, UK
Tel: 44 1732 458080
Fax: 44 1732 455848
Email: mail@ifa.org.uk
Website: http://www.ifa.org.uk
Founded: 1916
Members: 8000
Staff: 15
Contact: J. Malcolm Dean, Chief Exec.
Fee: £84
Membership Type: associate
Fee: £90
Membership Type: fellow
Description: Financial accountants and controllers, finance directors,
lecturers, secretaries, and teachers in 80 countries engaged in
commerce, industry, and public service. Purpose is to promote and
protect the status and high standards of members. Administers
examinations. Bestows awards; sponsors charitable program.
Operates speakers' bureau. Compiles statistics. Conducts seminars.

Publication: Journal
Publication title: Financial Accountant
Meetings/Conventions: - annual conference

Institute of Financial Planning

Lewins Mead, Whitefriars Centre, Bristol, BS1 2NT, England, UK
Tel: 44 117 9452470
Fax: 44 117 9292214
Email: enquiries@finanicalplanning.org.uk
Website: http://www.financialplanning.org.uk
Founded: 1987
Members: 1000
Staff: 6
Contact: Nick Cann, Chief Exec.
Description: Members provide holistic financial planning objectively
to members of the public and to companies. Membership includes
IFAs, accountants, solicitors, bankers and tax-consultants. Intends to
continue to promote the profession and practice of financial planning,
to increase public awareness of the need for financial planning and to
ensure high professional and ethical standards amongst its members.
Sharing knowledge and skills with other professionals for the benefit
of mutual clients is of paramount importance. Confers certified
financial planner license to qualified individuals. Affiliated to Certified
Financial Planner Board of Standards.
Formerly: Absorbed, Financial Planning Association
Publication: Journal
Publication title: Financial Planning. Advertisements.
Meetings/Conventions: - annual conference - Exhibits.

Institute of Financial Services - England

90 Bishopsgate, London, EC2N 4DQ, England, UK
Tel: 44 20 74447111
Fax: 44 20 74447115
Email: customerservices@ifslearning.com
Website: http://www.ifslearning.com
Founded: 1879
Members: 50000
Staff: 150
Contact: Gavin Shreeve, Chief Exec.
Fee: £51
Membership Type: Individual
Description: Develops and delivers life long career support services
and a range of appropriate qualifications to the wider financial
services community, for which the CIB acts as an examining and
awarding body. A faculties based structure allows for the provision of
targeted services an specialist educational programmes to particular
sectors, including the areas of Banking and Finance, E-commerce
and Technology, and Regulatory and Retail.
Library Subject: financial services
Library Type: reference
Formerly: Chartered Institute of Bankers - England
Publication: Magazine
Publication title: CIB News. Advertisements.
Second publication: Magazine
Publication title: Financial World
Meetings/Conventions: - annual conference - Exhibits. London UK

Institute of Fisheries Management
IFM

39 Chelveston Rd., Raunds, NN9 6DA, England, UK
Tel: 44 115 9822317
Fax: 44 115 9826150
Email: admin@ifm.org.uk

Website: http://www.ifm.org.uk
Founded: 1970
Members: 1400
Contact: John Gregory, Chair
Fee: £30
Membership Type: registered member
Description: Mainly professional people who are interested in fisheries management. Aims to promote the advancement of fisheries management in all or any of its branches, to improve and elevate the technical and general knowledge and efficiency of persons engaged in, or about to engage in, fisheries management so as to advance the standing of the profession.
Publication: Magazine
Publication title: Fish. Advertisements.
Meetings/Conventions: - annual conference - Exhibits.

Institute of Food Science and Technology - UK

5 Cambridge Court, 210 Shepherds Bush Rd., London, W6 7NJ, England, UK
Tel: 44 207 6036316
Fax: 44 207 6029936
Email: info@ifst.org
Website: http://www.ifst.org
Founded: 1964
Members: 3100
Staff: 5
Contact: Helen G. Wild, Chief Exec.
Description: Food scientists and technologists. Professional qualifying body for food scientists and technologists. Educational charity.
Publication: Journal
Publication title: Food Science & Technology Today. Advertisements.
Meetings/Conventions: - annual conference - Exhibits.

Institute of Funraisers

Market Towers, 1 Nine Elms Lane, London, SW8 5NQ, England, UK
Tel: 44 20 76273436
Fax: 44 20 76273508
Email: enquiries@icfm.co.uk
Website: http://www.icfm.org.uk
Founded: 1983
Members: 2700
Staff: 7
Contact: Stephen Lee, Dir.
Description: Those working as fundraisers, or in support of fundraising activities. Exists to promote the highest standards of fundraising. Through its associated charitable trust, ICFM provides training and education in all aspects of fundraising. Regional groups organize networking and training meetings at a local level.
Formerly: Institute of Charity Fundraising Managers
Publication title: Who's Who in Fundraising
Meetings/Conventions: National Fundraisers Convention - annual

Institute of Grocery Distribution
IGD

Grange Ln., Letchmore Heath, Watford, WD25 8GD, England, UK
Tel: 44 1923 857141
Fax: 44 1923 852531
Email: igd@igd.com
Website: http://www.igd.com
Members: 460

Staff: 70
Contact: Louise Spillard
Description: Provides information, research and education for the food and grocery industry.
Meetings/Conventions: - bimonthly - Exhibits.

Institute of Groundsmanship

19-23 Church St., Wolverton, Milton Keynes, MK12 5LG, England, UK
Tel: 44 1908 312511
Fax: 44 1908 311140
Email: iog@iog.org
Website: http://www.iog.org
Founded: 1934
Members: 4200
Staff: 4
Contact: P.H.B. Gosset, Chief Exec.
Description: From all sectors of the sports and leisure management and maintenance industry. Disseminates information and enhances the training of groundsmen. Organizes training in UK and Europe on Sportsturf management. Runs the trade exhibition (SALTEX) annually for the Sport and Leisure maintenance industry. Organizes a conference each year and runs a consultancy service on all aspects of turf management.
Library Subject: grounds management
Library Type: not open to the public
Publication: Magazine. Advertisements.
Second publication: Manual
Meetings/Conventions: - annual meeting - Exhibits.

Institute of Group Analysis

1 Daleham Gardens, London, NW3 5BY, England, UK
Tel: 44 20 74312693
Fax: 44 20 74317246
Email: iga@igalondon.org.uk
Website: http://www.igalondon.org.uk
Founded: 1971
Members: 300
Staff: 8
Contact: Mrs. Sue Stevenson, Mgr.
Fee: £300
Membership Type: IGA-qualified group analysts
Description: Counsellors, social workers, psychologists, psychiatrists, caring professionals, probation officers. Responsible for the establishment of a widely recognised professional qualification in group-analytic psychotherapy. The principal aim is to promote and forward the selection, education and training of persons in order to qualify them for the conduct and study of group analysis and related forms of psychotherapy.
Library Subject: group analysis, psychotherapy, and psychiatry
Library Type: not open to the public
Publication: Newsletter
Publication title: Dialogue

Institute of Health Promotion and Education

University Dental Hospital, Dept. of Oral Health and Development, Higher Cambridge St., Manchester, M15 6FH, England, UK
Tel: 44 161 2756610
Fax: 44 161 2756299
Email: anthony.blinkhorn@man.ac.uk
Website: http://www.ihpe.org.uk
Founded: 1962
Members: 1000
Contact: Prof. A.S. Blinkhorn, Gen.Sec.
Fee: £24

Membership Type: member
Fee: £21
Membership Type: associate
Description: Members are individuals concerned with the promotion of health and the prevention of illness in all sections of the community at home, school, work and leisure.
Publication: Journal
Publication title: International Journal of Health Promotion and Education. Advertisements.

Institute of Healthcare Engineering and Estate Management
IHEEM

2 Abingdon House, Cumberland Business Centre, Portsmouth, PO5 1DS, England, UK
Tel: 44 23 92823186
Fax: 44 23 92815927
Email: office@iheem.org.uk
Website: http://www.iheem.org.uk
Founded: 1943
Members: 2500
Staff: 4
Contact: William Pym, Ch.Exec.
Description: Individuals involved in hospital engineering in 24 countries; hospital engineering and estate management students. Works to enhance the education and training of hospital engineers and other professionals working in estate management. Sponsors qualified members for registration as chartered engineer, incorporated engineer, and engineering technician.
Library Type: reference
Formerly: Institute of Hospital Engineering
Publication title: Guidance to Engineering Commissioning
Publication title: Health Estate Journal. Advertisements.
Meetings/Conventions: Building a Healthier Future Together - annual conference - Exhibits.

Institute of Healthcare Management

46 Grosvenor Gardens, London, SW1, England, UK
Tel: 44 207 8819235
Fax: 44 207 8819236
Email: enquiries@ihm.org.uk
Website: http://www.ihm.org.uk
Founded: 1902
Members: 8000
Staff: 22
Contact: Stuart Marples, Dir.
Fee: £119.5
Membership Type: full
Description: Those involved in the management and administration of health care. To promote excellence in health services management and the development of good managers, to affect health services policy and its implementation and to create and sustain a professional community of health services managers. It is a forum, network and management development association for individuals both inside and outside the NHS.
Formerly: Institute of Health Services Management
Publication: Magazine
Publication title: Health Management. Advertisements.
Second publication: Book
Publication title: The IHSM Health and Social Services Yearbook
Meetings/Conventions: - annual conference - Exhibits.

Institute of Highway Incorporated Engineers
IHIE

20 Queensberry Place, London, SW7 2DR, England, UK
Tel: 44 207 8239093
Fax: 44 207 5818087
Email: information@ihie.org.uk
Website: http://www.ihie.org.uk
Founded: 1965
Members: 3000
Staff: 4
Contact: Ms. J.M. Walker, Sec.
Fee: £84
Membership Type: fellow
Description: Engineers and technicians in highway and traffic engineering and transportation; students. Promotes professionalism among members. Conducts educational and training programs; offers certification testing. Determines qualifications for incorporated engineers and engineering technicians.
Formerly: Highway and Traffic Technicians Association
Publication title: Home Zone Design Guidelines
Second publication: Journal
Publication title: Transportation Professional. Advertisements.
Meetings/Conventions: - quarterly meeting - Exhibits.

Institute of Holistic Therapies

PO Box 37, Scarborough, YO11 1AR, England, UK
Tel: 44 1723 378573
Fax: 44 1723 378573
Email: lnroche@talk21.com
Founded: 1989
Members: 1200
Staff: 4
Contact: K. Jones, Chief Registrar
Fee: £49
Membership Type: full
Description: Qualified holistic practitioners only. Provides indemnity and malpractice insurance cover and a register of all qualified professional holistic therapists who have satisfactorily completed a recognised study course worldwide.
Library Subject: hypnotherapy, remedial massage, noesitherapy, reflexology
Library Type: not open to the public
Meetings/Conventions: - annual workshop

Institute of Horticulture

14-15 Belgrave Sq., London, SW1X 8PS, England, UK
Tel: 44 207 2456943
Fax: 44 207 2456943
Email: ioh@horticulture.org.uk
Website: http://www.horticulture.org.uk
Founded: 1984
Members: 2010
Staff: 3
Contact: Angela Clarke, Gen.Sec.
Description: Professional horticulturists. Aims to promote and encourage good horticultural practice by the dissemination of information, consultation with governments and other bodies, promoting educational and training opportunities, and conferring status upon professionally qualified horticulturists. There are various categories of membership, each requiring specific entry qualifications.
Publication: Journal
Publication title: The Horticulturist. Advertisements.
Meetings/Conventions: - annual conference

Institute of Indirect Taxation Practitioners

116-118 Chancery Lane, London, WC2A 1PP, England, UK
Tel: 44 171 6370333
Fax: 44 171 6371893
Founded: 1991
Members: 400
Staff: 1
Contact: Nicola Cohen, Admin.
Description: Those involved In the law and practice of indirect taxation. Trains, regulates and represents practitioners in VAT and Customs and Excise Duties (also Stamp Duty).
Publication: Handbook

Institute of Insurance Brokers

Higham Business Centre, Midland Rd., Higham Ferrers, Northamptonshire, NN10 8DW, England, UK
Tel: 44 1933 410003
Fax: 44 1933 410020
Email: inst.ins.brokers@iib-uk.com
Website: http://www.iib-uk.com
Founded: 1987
Members: 1100
Staff: 12
Contact: Andrew N. Paddick, Dir.Gen.
Description: Promotes and represents brokers in the insurance industry.
Library Subject: insurance, finance, law
Library Type: not open to the public
Publication: Magazine
Publication title: ARS

Institute of Internal Auditors - UK and Ireland IIA

13 Abbeville Mews, 88 Clapham Park Rd., London, SW4 7BX, England, UK
Tel: 44 207 4980101
Fax: 44 207 9782492
Email: info@iia.org.uk
Website: http://www.iia.org.uk
Founded: 1947
Members: 6000
Staff: 24
Contact: G. Easterbrook, CEO
Fee: £102
Membership Type: voting
Fee: £102
Membership Type: affiliate
Description: Internal auditors in the United Kingdom. Examines and certifies auditors. Promotes members' interests. Provides training and information.
Library Subject: Auditing and computers.
Library Type: by appointment only
Publication: Magazine
Publication title: Internal Auditing & Business Risk. Advertisements.
Meetings/Conventions: - annual convention - Exhibits. London UK

Institute of International Licensing Practitioners IILP

87 Regent St., Ste. 73, London, W1R 7HF, England, UK
Tel: 44 207 2870200
Fax: 44 207 2870400
Email: iilp.web@virgin.net

Website: http://freespace.virgin.net/iilp.web/
Founded: 1969
Members: 30
Staff: 6
Contact: Guy Reeves, Exec.Sec.
Fee: £85
Membership Type: fellow, associate, affiliate
Description: Independent licensing consultants and agents. Administers a professional code of practice; disseminates information and enquiries for professional services to fellow members; educates on licensing matters; maintains register of members.
Publication: Directory
Publication title: Directory of Fellows and Associates
Publication title: Information Brochure
Meetings/Conventions: - periodic seminar

Institute of Inventors

19-21-23 Fosse Way, Ealing, London, W13 0BZ, England, UK
Tel: 44 208 9983540
Email: mikinvent@aol.com
Website: http://www.newgadgets.freeserve.co.uk
Founded: 1964
Members: 1350
Staff: 3
Contact: Michael V. Rodrigues, Pres.
Fee: £120
Membership Type: first year
Fee: £40
Description: Private inventors, professional inventors, business members. Voluntary inventor's club, to help inventors at all stages of invention -appraisal, patent searches, patent drafting, licensing agreements, business consultations/funding advice.
Library Subject: science, technology, innovation
Library Type: not open to the public

Institute of Irrigation and Development Studies

c/o Dept. of Civil and Environmental Engineering
University of Southampton, Southampton, SO17 1BJ, England, UK
Tel: 44 23 80593728
Fax: 44 23 80677519
Email: jt8@soton.ac.uk
Founded: 1964
Staff: 7
Contact: Ben Fawcett
Description: Concerned with education, training, research and consultancy in rural development, specializing in irrigation, water supply and sanitation, planning and management for development.
Library Subject: irrigation management, water supply, sanitation
Library Type: not open to the public
Formerly: Institute of Irrigation Studies
Meetings/Conventions: - annual

Institute of Leadership and Management

c/o Stowe House
Netherstowe, Lichfield, WS13 6TJ, England, UK
Tel: 44 1543 251346
Fax: 44 1543 26681
Email: mes@i-l-m.com
Website: http://www.i-l-m.com
Founded: 1947
Members: 24000
Staff: 40
Contact: V. Nurcombe, Info.Svcs.Mgr.

Description: Fellows, Members and Associates - Corporate grades; Affiliates and Students - Non-corporate grades. To encourage and develop the science and practice of management and gain recognition of management as a profession.
Library Subject: management, training
Library Type: reference
Formerly: Institute of Supervisory Management
Publication: Journal. Advertisements.

Institute of Legal Cashiers and Administrators
146-148 Eltham Hill, Eltham, London, SE9 5DX, England, UK
Tel: 44 208 2942887
Fax: 44 208 8591682
Email: info@ilca.org.uk
Founded: 1978
Members: 2500
Staff: 4
Contact: Maria Maloney/Editor
Fee: £59
Membership Type: ordinary, associate, diploma, or fellow
Description: Legal-cashiers, administrators, partnership secretaries, financial controllers, office managers, some legal executives and solicitors. Dedicated to the education, support and promotion of specialist financial and administrative personnel working within the legal community.
Formerly: Absorbed, Institute of Legal Cashiers
Publication title: ILCA Listed Legal Software Suppliers Pocket Guide
Second publication: Journal
Publication title: Legal Abacus. Advertisements.
Meetings/Conventions: - annual conference - Exhibits.

Institute of Legal Executives
Kempston Manor, Kempston, Bedfordshire, MK42 7AB, England, UK
Tel: 44 1234 841000
Fax: 44 1234 840373
Email: info@ilex.org.uk
Website: http://www.ilex.org.uk
Founded: 1963
Members: 22000
Staff: 50
Contact: Mrs. Diane Burleigh, Sec.Gen.
Description: Members are staff working in solicitors' offices or legal departments, or who are studying for a career in the law. They have a wide range of educational and career backgrounds. The professional and examining body representing Legal Executives in England and Wales. A Legal Executive is a trained, qualified and experienced lawyer working in a law firm, private company or government department.
Publication: Journal
Publication title: Legal Executive Journal. Advertisements.
Meetings/Conventions: - annual conference - Exhibits. Stratford-upon-Avon UK

Institute of Leisure and Amenity Management
ILAM
ILAM House, Lower Basildon, Reading, RG8 9NE, England, UK
Tel: 44 1491 874800
Fax: 44 1491 874801
Email: info@ilam.co.uk
Website: http://www.ilam.co.uk
Founded: 1983
Members: 6500

Staff: 50
Contact: Andy Worthington, Ch.Exec.
Description: Managers working in art and entertainment complexes, health and fitness clubs, museums, parks and playgrounds, and sports centers in the United Kingdom and the Republic of Ireland. Aims to: promote high standards in the field of leisure management; encourage cooperation and information exchange; represent the interests of members in legislative matters; promote professional development and improved management methods and skills; encourage research in the field of leisure management. Provides career and course advisory service and contract arbitration service. Offers training courses and seminars; grants certificates and diplomas.
Library Subject: leisure, sports, arts, tourism, parks and open spaces, play
Library Type: by appointment only
Publication: Magazine
Publication title: Leisure Manager. Advertisements.
Meetings/Conventions: - annual conference - Exhibits.

Institute of Linguists
Saxon House, 48 Southwalk St., London, SE1 1UN, England, UK
Tel: 44 207 9403100
Fax: 44 207 9403101
Email: info@iol.org.uk
Website: http://www.iol.org.uk
Founded: 1910
Members: 6700
Contact: Jana Teteris, Membership Sec.
Description: Professional membership organization and examinations body working to promote and maintain standards of the professional linguist and to enhance the status of the profession.

Institute of Logistics and Transport
ILT
Logistics and Transport Centre, PO Box 5787, Corby, NN17 4XQ, England, UK
Tel: 44 1536 740100
Fax: 44 1536 740101
Email: enquiry@iolt.org.uk
Website: http://www.iolt.org.uk
Founded: 1999
Members: 22500
Staff: 50
Contact: Richard Ebbage, Operations
Fee: £102
Membership Type: statutory fellow
Fee: £72
Membership Type: statutory member or individual (nonstatutory) friend of the institute
Description: Professional body for individuals and organisations involved in all aspects of logistics, transport, and supply-chain management. Members have privileged access to a unique range of benefits and services, which are designed to support them, personally and professionally, throughout their careers.
Publication: Journal
Publication title: Logistics Focus. Advertisements.
Second publication: Yearbook
Publication title: Members Directory. Advertisements.

Institute of Machine Woodworking Technology

St. Keynes, Bowl Rd., Charing, Kent, TN27 0HB, England, UK
Tel: 44 1233 713768
Fax: 44 1233 713768
Email: imwoodt@aol.com
Founded: 1952
Members: 390
Contact: John E. Fryer, Hon.Sec.
Description: Those involved in machine loading, studying, training, operating, managing, research on selling. Covering the field of machine woodworking from the conversion of log and round timber, sawmilling, building, joinery etc to the numerous branches concerned with woodwork manufacturing and various forms of composition timber and plastics.

Institute of Management

c/o Chartered Management Institute
2 Savoy Ct., Strand, London, WC2R OEZ, England, UK
Tel: 44 171 4970580
Fax: 44 207 4970463
Founded: 1992
Members: 80000
Staff: 150
Contact: Mary Chapman, Dir.Gen.
Description: Membership grades are affiliate, student, associate, member, fellow and companion. These grades are available to managers from all sectors, levels and disciplines. To promote the development, exercise and recognition of professional management. Provides services in the areas of management development, management advice, management information and management networks. Leading provider of management qualifications and development programmes in the UK.
Library Subject: management
Library Type: open to the public

Institute of Management Consultancy

17-18 Hayward's Pl., 3rd Fl., London, EC1R 0EQ, England, UK
Tel: 44 20 75665220
Fax: 44 20 75665230
Email: consult@imc.co.uk
Website: http://www.imc.co.uk
Founded: 1962
Members: 3800
Staff: 8
Contact: Ian Barratt, CEO
Description: Individual professional management consultants in the UK, from practices of all sizes and covering all functional and business specialisms. Seeks to advance the profession of management consultancy through the establishment and maintenance of the highest standards of performance and conduct by its members. Conducts qualification, certification, and regulatory programs in the field of management consultancy; makes available support and services to members.
Publication: Newsletter
Publication title: Update
Second publication: Annual Report
Meetings/Conventions: Special Interest Group Meeting - weekly - Exhibits.

Institute of Management Services

Stowe House, Netherstowe, Lichfield, WS13 6TJ, England, UK
Tel: 44 1543 251346
Fax: 44 1543 266833
Email: admin@ims-stowe.fsnet.co.uk

Website: http://www.ims-productivity.com/
Founded: 1941
Members: 5000
Staff: 5
Contact: Harry Downes, Chm.
Fee: £98
Membership Type: 3 corporate grades
Description: From industry, commerce and the public sector including armed services and police. A professional, qualifying body whose main activities are to provide qualifications and education and to disseminate knowledge in the field of management services. Members investigate, advise and carry out solutions to management and organizational problems.
Publication: Journal
Publication title: Management Services. Advertisements.

Institute of Management Specialists
IMS

Warwick Corner, 42 Warwick Rd., Kenilworth, CV8 1HE, England, UK
Tel: 44 1926 855498
Fax: 44 1926 513100
Founded: 1971
Members: 1200
Staff: 4
Contact: Prof. H.J. Manners, Pres. and Founder
Fee: £40
Membership Type: student, companion, associate, full member, fellow
Description: Management personnel and specialists in commercial business, industry, and professional and technical fields from 40 countries. Provides services to management specialists and works to improve the status of management disciplines. Keeps members informed of new developments, controls, methods, and techniques. Offers advanced training and development to members through private study courses leading to the Management Specialist Certificate/Diploma of Merit.
Publication: Journal
Publication title: The Management Specialist. Advertisements.

Institute of Marine Engineers, Science and Technology
ImarEST

80 Coleman St., London, EC2R 5BJ, England, UK
Tel: 44 207 3822600
Fax: 44 207 3822670
Email: info@imarest.org
Website: http://www.imare.org.uk
Founded: 1889
Members: 17000
Staff: 50
Contact: Mr. K. Read, Dir.Gen.
Description: Professionals in 43 countries involved in marine engineering, naval architecture, and offshore and subsea engineering. Promotes the development of all branches of marine engineering and advances the professional status of the engineer; facilitates advancement in the field. Sponsors seminars, symposia, and technical meetings. Serves as a forum for the exchange of information among members; disseminates information.
Library Subject: Marine engineering and related topics.
Library Type: reference
Publication: Journal
Publication title: Journal of Offshore Technology. Advertisements.
Publication title: Marine Engineers Review. Advertisements.
Meetings/Conventions: - biennial conference - Exhibits.

Institute of Masters of Wine

Five Kings House, 1 Queen St. Pl., London, EC4R 1QS, England, UK
Tel: 44 207 2364427
Fax: 44 207 2130499
Email: jcarr@imow.demon.co.uk
Website: http://www.masters-of-wine.org
Founded: 1955
Members: 240
Staff: 5
Contact: Jane Carr, Exec.Dir.
Description: Members of the wine industry who have passed the Master of Wine Examination.
Publication: Journal
Publication title: Journal of Wine Research

Institute of Materials
IOM

1 Carlton House Terr., London, SW1Y 5DB, England, UK
Tel: 44 207 4517300
Fax: 44 207 8391702
Email: webmaster@materials.org.uk
Website: http://www.materials.org.uk
Founded: 1869
Members: 18000
Staff: 45
Contact: Dr. B.A. Rickinson, Sec.
Description: Industrial and commercial firms, governmental institutions, research institutes, universities, and individuals in 80 countries who promote the science, manufacture, conversion, working, properties, and use of metals, polymers, ceramics, and composite materials. Provides international forum for discussion among those interested in engineering materials, and the environment in which such materials are used.
Library Subject: materials science
Library Type: reference
Formerly: Absorbed, Plastics and Rubber Institute
Publication: Journal
Publication title: British Corrosion Journal
Second publication: Magazine
Publication title: Historical Metallurgy
Meetings/Conventions: - biennial congress - Exhibits.

Institute of Mathematics and its Applications

c/o Catherine Richards House
16 Nelson St., Southend-on-Sea, Essex, SS1 1EF, England, UK
Tel: 44 1702 354020
Fax: 44 1702 354111
Email: post@ima.org.uk
Website: http://www.ima.org.uk
Founded: 1964
Members: 5000
Staff: 12
Contact: Prof. J.G. McWhirter, Pres.
Description: Promotes and supports the understanding, teaching, research, and application of mathematics.
Publication: Bulletin
Publication title: Mathematics Today. Advertisements.
Second publication: Journals

Institute of Measurement and Control
INSTMC

87 Gower St., London, WC1E 6AA, England, UK
Tel: 44 207 3874949
Fax: 44 207 3888431
Email: m.yates@instmc.org.uk
Website: http://www.instmc.org.uk
Founded: 1944
Members: 4750
Staff: 9
Contact: Michael Yates, Sec.
Description: Measurement and control technology practitioners in manufacturing and user companies and in research and academic establishments. Advances the science and practice of measurement and control technology. Maintains seven technical committees.
Publication: Journal
Publication title: Measurement and Control
Publication title: Transactions of the Institute
Meetings/Conventions: - periodic conference

Institute of Metal Finishing

c/o Exeter House
Holloway Head, Birmingham, B1 1NQ, England, UK
Tel: 44 121 6227387
Fax: 44 121 6666316
Email: info@uk-finishing.org.uk
Website: http://www.uk-finishing.org.uk
Founded: 1925
Members: 1100
Staff: 3
Contact: Mrs. J. Sturch
Fee: £42
Description: Professional people working in surface engineering industry. Metal finishing processs include electro-plating, organic (paint) finishing, anodising, printed circuitry and ancillary methods of surface treatment.
Publication title: Newsletters. Advertisements.
Second publication: Journal
Publication title: Transitions of the Institute of Metal Finishing. Advertisements.
Meetings/Conventions: - annual conference - Exhibits.

Institute of Musical Instrument Technology
IMIT

11 Kendal Ave. S, Sanderstead, London, CR2 0QR, England, UK
Website: http://www.imit.org.uk
Founded: 1938
Members: 500
Contact: Malcolm Dalton, Hon.Sec.
Fee: £20
Membership Type: fellow
Fee: £15
Description: Concerned with the advance of musical instrument technology through the exchange of information and ideas; the promotion of professional status of members engaged in musical instrument design manufacture or repair.
Library Subject: musical instrument manufacture and repair
Library Type: not open to the public
Publication title: Soundings
Second publication: Journal

Institute of Operations Management
c/o University of Warwick Science Park
Sir William Lyons Rd., Coventry, CV4 7EZ, England, UK
Tel: 44 2476 692266
Fax: 44 2476 692305
Email: info@iomnet.org.uk
Website: http://www.iomnet.org.uk
Founded: 1969
Members: 5055
Staff: 9
Contact: R.G. Turner
Fee: £60
Membership Type: fellow
Fee: £55
Membership Type: associate
Description: Directors, senior, middle and junior management of manufacturing and service companies who are actively engaged in the fields of production and inventory management, materials and operations management, logistics and related activities. Aims to assist British industry to compete more effectively in the world market by improving the knowledge and skill base of production and inventory management professionals through the provision of conferences, courses, seminars, meetings, journals and qualifications appropriate to their needs.
Library Subject: operations management
Library Type: open to the public
Formerly: British Production & Inventory Control Society
Publication: Magazine
Publication title: Control. Advertisements.
Meetings/Conventions: - periodic conference

Institute of Ophthalmology
Bath St., London, EC1V 9EL, England, UK
Tel: 44 207 6086800
Fax: 44 207 6086852
Email: k.bonstein@ucl.ac.uk
Website: http://www.ucl.ac.uk/ioo
Founded: 1948
Staff: 230
Contact: Prof. A.M. Sillito, Dir.
Description: Promotes research into eye diseases and other causes of blindness.

Institute of Packaging
Sysonby Lodge, Nottingham Rd., Melton Mowbray, LE13 0NU, England, UK
Tel: 44 1664 500055
Fax: 44 1664 564164
Email: info@iop.co.uk
Website: http://iop.co.uk
Founded: 1947
Members: 3000
Staff: 15
Contact: Paul Burns, Mktg.Mgr.
Fee: £75
Membership Type: member/associate
Fee: £30
Membership Type: student
Description: The only UK professional and qualifying body for individuals working in or with the packaging industry.
Library Subject: packaging
Library Type: by appointment only
Publication: Book
Publication title: Institute of Packaging Directory and Review.
Advertisements.
Second publication: Magazine
Publication title: The Packaging Professional

Institute of Paper
Hamilton Court, Gogmore Lane, Chertsey, KT16 9AP, England, UK
Tel: 44 8707 500332
Fax: 44 1932 569749
Email: admin@instituteofpaper.com
Website: http://www.instpaper.org.uk
Founded: 1992
Staff: 6
Contact: Veronica Bowen, Information Officer
Description: Those employed in, or associated with, the paper industry.

Institute of Paper Conservation
IPC
Bridge House, Waterside, Upton Upon Severn, Worcestershire, WR8 0HG, England, UK
Tel: 44 1684 591150
Fax: 44 1684 592380
Email: information@ipc.org.uk
Website: http://www.ipc.org.uk
Founded: 1976
Members: 1600
Staff: 2
Contact: Clare Hampson, Exec.Sec.
Fee: £50
Membership Type: U.K. individual
Fee: £70
Membership Type: outside UK individual
Description: Conservators and custodians of artifacts such as prints, drawings, watercolors, books, manuscripts, and documents; others interested in the conservation of paper artifacts. Encourages the exchange of information on the conservation of prints, drawings, archives, and books; provides a focus for professional awareness to aid conservation craftsmen, scientists, museum curators, private collectors, and commercial organizations interested in paper conservation. Maintains research programs.
Library Subject: book and paper conservation
Library Type: reference
Publication: Pamphlet
Publication title: Guidelines to Conservation Framing of Works of Art on Paper
Second publication: Directory
Publication title: Membership Directory. Advertisements.

Institute of Paralegal Training
c/o The Mill
Clymping St., Clymping, Littlehampton, BN17 5RN, England, UK
Tel: 44 1903 714276
Fax: 44 1903 713710
Founded: 1976
Staff: 6
Contact: Mrs. A. Ibberson, Sec.Gen.
Description: Provides an organization for men and women of education and ability and experience who desire to qualify as legal secretaries/administrators and to secure professional status. Sets, moderates and controls qualifying examinations which will reflect the high standard required of all legal personnel.
Publication: Booklet

Institute of Patentees and Inventors

Triumph House, Ste. 505A, 189 Regent St., London, W1B 4JY,
England, UK
Tel: 44 207 4341818
Fax: 44 207 4341727
Email: enquiries@invent.org.uk
Website: http://www.invent.org.uk
Founded: 1919
Members: 1000
Staff: 1
Contact: R. Magnus, Sec.
Fee: £43
Membership Type: individual
Fee: £85
Membership Type: corporate
Description: Inventors who have applied for or received a patent,
aspiring inventors who have product ideas but are unaware of the
patent application process, and companies wishing to stimulate
innovation are members; elected members who submit an accepted
thesis are fellows. Seeks to further the interests of individual and
employee patentees and inventors; serves as a clearinghouse for
members in all areas pertaining to the inventive process. Makes
recommendations to government agencies regarding changes to
patent laws.
Publication: Journal
Publication title: Future and the Inventor. Advertisements.
Meetings/Conventions: - bimonthly board meeting

Institute of Payroll and Pensions Management

Shelly House, Monkspath, Solihull, B90 4EH, England, UK
Tel: 44 121 7121080
Fax: 44 121 7121001
Email: info@ippm.org
Website: http://www.ippm.org
Founded: 1980
Members: 5000
Staff: 50
Contact: Trevor Lakin, Mng.Dir.
Fee: £85
Membership Type: associate and full
Description: Payroll and pensions administrators in the public and
private sector. Concerned with the promotion of a higher professional
standard; the provision of a nationally recognised body; awareness of
developments in payroll and pensions; identification and satisfaction
of training needs; national and regional exchange of information; the
provision of an advisory service.
Formerly: Association of Payroll and Superannuation Administrators
Publication: Magazine
Publication title: PAYadvice. Advertisements.
Meetings/Conventions: Payroll Conference - annual conference
Cheltenham UK

Institute of Petroleum
IP

61 New Cavendish St., London, W1G 7AR, England, UK
Tel: 44 207 4677100
Fax: 44 207 2551472
Email: ip@petroleum.co.uk
Website: http://www.petroleum.co.uk
Founded: 1913
Members: 8400
Staff: 45
Contact: Louise Kingham, Dir.Gen.
Fee: £70

Membership Type: individual and corporate
Description: Individuals (8000) and corporations (400). Promotes
advancement of knowledge in the science, technology, and
economics of the oil and gas industry. Compiles statistics; maintains
library and information service.
Library Subject: Petroleum industry
Library Type: reference
Publication: Books
Publication title: Codes of Safe Practice
Second publication: Journal
Publication title: Petroleum Review. Advertisements.
Meetings/Conventions: - annual conference

Institute of Pharmacy Management International

The Seasons, Parkwood, Doddinghurst, Brentwood, CM15 0SN,
England, UK
Tel: 44 1277 823889
Email: enelwood@compusreve.com
Website: http://www.pharmweb.net/pwmirror/pw9/ipmi
Founded: 1964
Members: 500
Contact: Nicholas Wood, Gen.Sec.
Fee: £50
Membership Type: member, associate, fellow, student, corporate
Description: Members are pharmaceutical chemists, and managers
in the hospitals and pharmaceutical industry. Provides research and
study of management within the pharmaceutical industry and
profession of pharmacy in hospital and community practice with
particular reference to the National Health Service pharmaceutical
service; sales and marketing activities in connection with OTC
medicines and allied healthcare products. Hosts twice in a year
conferences on management subjects.
Publication: Journal
Publication title: IPMI Institute News. Advertisements.
Meetings/Conventions: - biennial conference - Exhibits. Harogate
UK

Institute of Physics
IOP

76 Portland Pl., London, W1B 1NT, England, UK
Tel: 44 207 4704800
Fax: 44 207 4704848
Email: physics@iop.org
Website: http://www.iop.org
Founded: 1874
Members: 23000
Staff: 220
Contact: Dr. A. Jones, Chief Exec.
Description: International learned society and professional body for
physicists. Chartered by a royal charter to promote the advancement
and dissemination of knowledge and education in the science of pure
and applied physics. Represents the physics community to
government and other legislative or policy-making bodies. Sets and
supports professional standards and qualifications.
Formerly: Formed by Merger of, Institute of Physics
Publication: Journal
Publication title: Classical and Quantum Gravity
Second publication: Journal
Publication title: Clinical Physics and Physiological Measurement

Institute of Physics and Engineering in Medicine

Fairmount House, 230 Tadcaster Rd., York, YO24 1ES, England, UK
Tel: 44 1904 610821
Fax: 44 1904 612279
Email: office@ipem.org.uk
Website: http://www.ipem.org.uk
Founded: 1943
Members: 2700
Staff: 8
Contact: Robert W. Neilson, Gen.Sec.
Description: Scientists, engineers and technologists working in the field of medical physics and bioengineering. Promotes for public benefit the advancement of physics and engineering applied to medicine and biology and to advance public education in this field. Represents the needs and interests of engineering and physical sciences in the provision and advancement of health care.
Library Subject: medical physics and engineering, physiological measurement
Library Type: not open to the public
Formerly: Institution of Physics and Engineering in Medicine and Biology
Publication: Journal
Publication title: Medical Engineering and Physics. Advertisements.
Second publication: Journal
Publication title: Physics in Medicine and Biology. Advertisements.
Meetings/Conventions: - annual conference - Exhibits.

Institute of Plumbing
IOP

c/o Kevin Wellman
64 Station Ln., Hornchurch, RM12 6NB, England, UK
Tel: 44 1708 472791
Fax: 44 1708 448987
Email: info@plumbers.org.uk
Website: http://www.plumbers.org.uk
Founded: 1906
Members: 11500
Staff: 15
Contact: Kevin Wellman
Description: Promotes professionalism in the plumbing industry.
Formerly: Absorbed, Registered Plumbers Association
Publication: Directory
Publication title: Directory. Advertisements.
Second publication: Newsletter
Publication title: Plumbing
Meetings/Conventions: - annual conference - Exhibits.

Institute of Practitioners in Advertising
IPA

44 Belgrave Sq., London, SW1X 8QS, England, UK
Tel: 44 207 2357020
Fax: 44 207 2459904
Email: info@ipa.co.uk
Website: http://www.ipa.co.uk
Founded: 1917
Members: 1786
Contact: Hamish Pringle, Dir.Gen.
Description: Advertising agencies (225) and individuals (1500) in Britain. Provides programs in: training, leadership, legal advising, marketing, and public relations. Represents members' interests to government agencies, media, and advertising related organizations. Conducts research and educational programs.
Formerly: Association of British Advertising Agents

Publication: Magazine
Publication title: Annual Report
Second publication: Directory
Publication title: IPA Member Companies List
Meetings/Conventions: - periodic conference

Institute of Printing

The Mews, Hill House, Clanricarde Rd., Tunbridge Wells, TN1 1NU, England, UK
Tel: 44 1892 538118
Fax: 44 1892 518028
Email: admin@instituteofprinting.org
Website: http://www.instituteofprinting.org
Founded: 1893
Members: 2000
Staff: 4
Contact: Davik Freeland, Sec. Gen.
Description: Two corporate grades, five categories of individual membership for people with greatly differing qualifications, experience and occupations. Concerned with the advancement of the science and art of printing and its associated occupations.
Publication: Journal
Publication title: Professional Printer. Advertisements.
Second publication: Membership Directory
Meetings/Conventions: - annual conference UK

Institute of Professional Investigators
IPI

Burnhill Business Centre, Provident House, Burrell Row, High St., Beckham, BR3 1AT, England, UK
Tel: 44 20 82496605
Fax: 44 20 82496606
Email: admin@ipi.org.uk
Website: http://www.ipi.org.uk
Founded: 1976
Members: 450
Staff: 2
Contact: James D. Cole, Sec.Gen.
Fee: £150
Description: Criminal, police, civil investigators, handwriting experts, pathologists, and others in 32 countries working in the investigative field. Provides for the regulation of principles and codes of ethics in the field. Encourages investigators to achieve internationally recognized professional and academic standards and distinctions and to improve their technical expertise through correspondence courses. Seeks to establish and operate an examination structure allowing members to improve their academic and business knowledge in investigation.
Publication: Directory
Publication title: Institute of Professional Investigators Register of Members
Second publication: Newsletter
Publication title: The Professional Investigator. Advertisements.
Meetings/Conventions: conference - Exhibits.

Institute of Psychiatry

c/o Kings College London
De Crespigny Park, Denmark Hill, London, SE5 8AF, England, UK
Tel: 44 20 78365454
Email: enquiries@iop.kcl.ac.uk
Website: http://www.iop.kcl.ac.uk/iop/home.shtml
Founded: 1948

Staff: 525
Contact: L. Carlisle, Sec.
Description: To promote excellence in the research, development and teaching of psychiatry and its allied subjects and to apply and disseminate this knowledge through the development of treatment for the relief of suffering.
Library Type: not open to the public
Publication: Annual Report
Second publication: Papers

Institute of Psychosexual Medicine
12 Chandos St., Cavendish Sq., London, W1G 9DR, England, UK
Tel: 44 207 5800631
Fax: 44 207 5800631
Email: ipm@ipm.org.uk
Website: http://www.ipm.org.uk
Founded: 1974
Members: 450
Staff: 2
Contact: Susan Beck, Admin.
Description: Medical practitioners only. Seeks to promote the study and practice of psychosexual medicine through seminar training and research.
Publication: Journal
Publication title: Journal of the Institute of Psychosocial Medicine
Meetings/Conventions: conference

Institute of Public Loss Assessors
14 Red Lion St., Chesham, HP5 1HB, England, UK
Tel: 44 1494 782342
Fax: 44 1494 774928
Founded: 1966
Members: 100
Contact: J.D. Turberville
Description: Those actively engaged in Loss Assessing.

Institute of Public Relations
IPR
Old Trading House, 15 Northburgh St., London, EC1V 0PR, England, UK
Tel: 44 207 2535151
Fax: 44 207 4900588
Email: info@ipr.org.uk
Website: http://www.ipr.org.uk
Founded: 1948
Members: 6600
Staff: 17
Contact: Colin Farrington, Dir.Gen.
Fee: £155
Membership Type: Full
Fee: £130
Membership Type: Associate
Description: Employees of local and central governments, consulting and industrial firms, and voluntary organizations in 40 countries. Promotes the development, recognition, and understanding of the public relations field. Encourages members to attain professional academic qualifications and to comply with standards of professional conduct. Maintains vocational committees and special interest groups. Provides placement services. Sponsors competitions; bestows awards. Compiles statistics.
Library Subject: public relations
Library Type: reference
Publication: Magazine

Publication title: Profile. Advertisements.
Second publication: Directory
Publication title: Register of Members
Meetings/Conventions: - annual meeting - Exhibits.

Institute of Qualified Private Secretaries
IQPS
6 Bridge Ave., 1st Fl., Maidenhead, SL6 1RR, England, UK
Tel: 44 1628 625007
Fax: 44 1628 624990
Email: office@iqps.org
Website: http://www.iqps.org
Founded: 1957
Members: 2000
Staff: 2
Contact: Julia Philipson, Gen.Mgr.
Fee: £52
Description: Secretaries, lecturers and managers with secretarial qualifications to our defined standard. Seeks to be recognised as the leading UK professional organisation for career minded secretaries, personal assistants, administrators, and lecturers in business studies. Aims to facilitate and encourage the training and continuing professional development of Secretaries and to enable them to make a maximum contribution in their field of activity. Conferences, meetings, seminars and discussions are held.
Library Subject: training and development
Library Type: not open to the public
Publication: Magazine
Publication title: Career Secretary. Advertisements.
Meetings/Conventions: - semiannual convention - Exhibits.

Institute of Quality Assurance
12 Grosvenor Crescent, London, SW1X 7EE, England, UK
Tel: 44 20 72456722
Fax: 44 20 72456788
Email: iqa@iqa.org
Website: http://www.iqa.org
Founded: 1919
Members: 13409
Staff: 50
Contact: Frank Steer, Dir.Gen
Description: Those involved with the attainment and improvement of quality in any product or service. Concerned with the promotion and advancement of quality management and practices, together with the promotion of education, training and professional development of those involved in quality assurance and quality management.
Library Type: by appointment only
Publication: Magazine
Publication title: Quality World. Advertisements.
Meetings/Conventions: conference

Institute of Quarrying - England
7 Regent St., Nottingham, NG1 5BS, England, UK
Tel: 44 115 9453880
Fax: 44 115 9484035
Email: mail@quarrying.org
Founded: 1917
Members: 6000
Staff: 4
Contact: Jack Berridge, Exec.Dir.
Description: Individuals in 70 countries employed in the quarrying and related industries. Promotes education and training in order to improve all aspects of quarry operation and business management.

Works to enhance recognition of professional managers in the quarrying industry. Organizes courses and field trips to factories, plants, and quarries and occasional international study tours. Conducts examinations.
Publication: Newsletter
Publication title: Quarry Management. Advertisements.
Meetings/Conventions: - annual conference - Exhibits.

Institute of Race Relations
IRR

2-6 Leeke St., King's Cross Rd., London, WC1X 9HS, England, UK
Tel: 44 207 8370041
Fax: 44 207 2780623
Email: info@irr.org.uk
Website: http://www.irr.org.uk
Founded: 1956
Members: 200
Staff: 5
Contact: A. Sivanandan, Dir.
Description: Promotes good race relations. Encourages research and educational work. Supports solidarity committees; services organizations opposing racism.
Library Subject: imperialism, race and minority relations
Library Type: reference
Publication title: How Racism Came to Britain
Second publication: Journal
Publication title: Race and Class. Advertisements.

Institute of Refrigeration

c/o Kelvin House
76 Mill Lane, Carshalton, SM5 2JR, England, UK
Tel: 44 20 86477033
Fax: 44 20 87730165
Email: ior@ior.org.uk
Website: http://www.ior.org.uk
Founded: 1899
Members: 2600
Staff: 1
Description: Those engaged in the science and practice of refrigeration.
Publication: Papers

Institute of Revenues, Rating and Valuation

41 Doughty St., London, WC1N 2LF, England, UK
Tel: 44 207 8313505
Fax: 44 207 8312048
Email: enquiries@irrr.org.uk
Website: http://www.irrv.org.uk
Founded: 1882
Members: 5000
Staff: 25
Contact: David Magor, Dir.
Description: Local government revenues, rating, benefit and valuation officers in local government, valuation office officials and private practice valuers. To develop the knowledge of professionals involved in the levying, collection and administration of local revenues, the valuation of property etc. The Institute also organizes national and international conferences and advises its members on technical matters as well as responding to government (and other bodies') proposals in its sphere of interest.
Publication: Books
Second publication: Journal

Institute of Risk Management
IRM

Lloyds Ave. House, 6 Lloyds Ave., London, EC3N 3AX, England, UK
Tel: 44 207 7099808
Fax: 44 207 7090716
Email: enquiries@theirm.org
Website: http://www.theirm.org
Founded: 1986
Members: 1600
Staff: 4
Contact: Steve Fowler, Exec.Dir.
Fee: £135
Membership Type: individual
Description: Professionals in 45 countries in the area of risk management. (Risk management is a multidisciplinary field which requires familiarity with the concepts of such specialized areas as fire engineering, security, occupational safety, insurance, and legal liability.) Promotes and protects professional standing of members; conducts continuing professional education seminars for members; holds certification examinations.
Library Subject: Business organization and finance, risk analysis, risk control, corporate risk management, risk financing, occupational health and safety, insurance liability exposures, health sector risk management, and local authority risk management
Library Type: reference
Publication title: Careers Leaflet
Second publication: Journal
Publication title: Inform. Advertisements.
Meetings/Conventions: - annual conference

Institute of Road Safety Officers

Pin Point, 1-2 Rosslyn Crescent, Harrow, HA1 2SB, England, UK
Tel: 44 870 0104442
Fax: 44 870 3337772
Email: irso@dbda.co.uk
Founded: 1971
Members: 570
Contact:
Fee: £50
Membership Type: individual
Description: Provides recognition of the professional standing of road safety officers by accrediting qualification courses and being involved in vocational training. The institute is made up of local groups to provide an open forum for all members to discuss road safety matters.
Publication: Journal
Publication title: Inroads. Advertisements.
Meetings/Conventions: Getting It Right - annual conference

Institute of Roofing

24 Weymouth St., London, W1N 3FA, England, UK
Tel: 44 207 4360103
Fax: 44 207 6361287
Email: info@instituteofroofing.org.uk
Website: http://www.instituteofroofing.org.uk
Founded: 1980
Members: 1350
Staff: 2
Contact: Brian Clarke
Fee: £65
Membership Type: examination
Description: Professional qualifications for all sectors of the roofing industry namely contracting, manufacturing, and stocking, by examination or assessed vocational experience. Promotes and stimulates the improvement of the technical and general knowledge of

individuals engaged in management in the roofing industry; confers a recognised status on individuals in the industry and conducts training by the management of courses, seminars, lectures work visits, study tours.
Publication: Newsletter
Meetings/Conventions: - periodic seminar

Institute of Sales and Marketing Management

c/o Romeland House
Romeland Hill, St. Albans, St. Albans, AL3 4ET, England, UK
Tel: 44 1727 812500
Fax: 44 1727 812525
Email: sales@ismm.co.uk
Website: http://www.ismm.co.uk
Founded: 1966
Members: 12000
Staff: 12
Contact: Jennie Harnaman
Fee: £75
Description: Open to all sales and marketing professionals, from students to main board directors. Actively promotes the prestige and integrity of the sales and marketing professions. It makes legal, recruitment and consultancy services available to its members and, through publications, supplies market intelligence and sales information.
Publication: Magazine
Publication title: Sales & Marketing Professional. Advertisements.
Meetings/Conventions: Successful Selling - annual convention - Exhibits.

Institute of Science Technology
IST

Stowe House, Netherstowe, Lichfield, WS13 6TJ, England, UK
Tel: 44 1543 251346
Fax: 44 1543 266811
Email: ist@ismstowe.demon.co.uk
Website: http://www.ISTonline.org.uk
Founded: 1948
Members: 1500
Contact: John Robinson
Fee: £29
Description: Fellows, Members (Corporate Grades) Associates, affiliates. Grades awarded by examination standard and experience and thesis. Most members work in education or research e.g. universities, colleges of further education, schools, hospitals, agricultural establishments with a few in industry. Provides own qualifications in analytical chemistry techniques, biochemical techniques, microbiological techniques, animal sciences techniques HPLC and gas chromatography. Makes available training support packages for science technicians.
Publication: Journal. Advertisements.
Meetings/Conventions: - annual seminar

Institute of Scientific and Technical Communicators
ISTC

PO Box 522, Peterborough, PE2 5WX, England, UK
Tel: 44 1733 390141
Fax: 44 1733 390126
Email: istc@istc.org.uk
Website: http://www.istc.org.uk
Founded: 1972
Members: 1500

Staff: 1
Contact: Carol Hewitt, Exec.Off.
Fee: £64
Membership Type: fellow
Fee: £43
Membership Type: associate
Description: Technical authors, technical editors, illustrators, publication managers, freelance and contract technical writers. Maintains professional codes of practice for members, who are employed in all branches of scientific and technical communication throughout industry, commerce, IT, finance, education, and the public sector. It provides a forum for exchange of views and disseminates information through local meetings, publications, an annual conference, and lectures.
Publication: Magazine
Publication title: Communicator. Advertisements.
Second publication: Newsletter. Advertisements.
Meetings/Conventions: - annual conference - Exhibits.

Institute of Sheet Metal Engineering
ISME

47 Birmingham Rd., West Bromwich, B70 6PY, England, UK
Tel: 44 121 6016350
Fax: 44 121 6016373
Founded: 1946

Institute of Social Psychiatry

c/o Sutton Manor Clinic
London Rd., Stapleford Tawney, Romford, RM4 1SR, England, UK
Tel: 44 1992 814661
Fax: 44 1708 688583
Founded: 1947
Contact: Mrs. N. Weeks
Description: Aims to further and finance, if feasible, research into psychiatry. Runs a nursing home for elderly mentally handicapped. The Institute of Social Psychiatry is a Registered Charity.

Institute of Sport and Recreation Management

Sir John Beckwith Centre for Sport, Loughborough University, Loughborough, LE11 3TU, England, UK
Tel: 44 1509 226474
Fax: 44 1509 226475
Email: info@isrm.co.uk
Website: http://www.isrm.co.uk
Founded: 1921
Members: 4900
Staff: 15
Contact: Ralph Riley, Chief Exec.
Description: Full membership for those who have passed the Sport & Recreation Management Certificate. Diploma Membership for those members that pass the Diploma Examination. Provides approved industry led education and training programmes leading to recognised qualifications in the management and operation of sports and recreation facilities. Associated activities include annual conference and exhibition, advisory and consultancy services and ISRM publications.

Institute of Spring Technology
IST

Henry St., Sheffield, S3 7EQ, England, UK
Tel: 44 114 2760771
Fax: 44 114 2726344
Email: ist@ist.org.uk

Website: http://www.ist.org.uk
Founded: 1946
Members: 280
Staff: 21
Contact: Arthur Hooper, CEO
Description: Manufacturers of testing and special purpose equipment to the spring industry. Promotes the industry and its products through information and technical support. Maintains accredited testing laboratory.
Library Subject: Spring and materials technology.
Library Type: reference
Formerly: Spring Research Association

Institute of Sterile Services Management

c/o Frank Waller
2 Grange Close, Winchester, SO23 9RS, England, UK
Tel: 44 1962 843988
Email: frank_waller@yahoo.co.uk
Website: http://www.issm.org.uk
Contact: Frank Waller, Dir.Info.
Description: Different grades of membership - Fellow, Member, Student member, Associate, Corporate, Honorary, Associate Technician. Aims to organise and initiate training programmes for members/students, with the object of achieving high professional standards; provides a forum for members through regional branches to consider and discuss matters relating to sterilization and disinfection and promotes and encourages research and development in the world of sterile service.
Publication: Journal
Publication title: The ISSM Journal. Advertisements.
Publication title: Official Reference Book
Meetings/Conventions: - annual conference - Exhibits.

Institute of Stock Auditors and Valuers

Monomark House, 27 Old Gloucester St., London, WC1N 3XX, England, UK
Tel: 44 207 2422474
Fax: 44 1625 610161
Email: admin@tvi.org.uk
Website: http://www.tvi.org.uk
Founded: 1972
Members: 103
Contact: N.A. Addy, Hon.Sec.
Fee: £35
Membership Type: student
Fee: £55
Membership Type: ordinary
Description: Proprietors and staff of firms who provide stocktaking, stock auditing, and other related professional services for trade and industry. Represents the interests of professional stocktakers/valuers; protects the interests of both members and their clients by exercising control/supervision through rules and code of conduct; enhances the professional expertise of members; publicises the professional skills of the membership.
Library Subject: trade valuation training and standards of practice
Library Type: not open to the public
Formerly: Trade Valuers Institute
Publication: Journal
Publication title: Count Me In. Advertisements.
Meetings/Conventions: - annual general assembly - Exhibits.

Institute of Surface Science and Technology

c/o Loughborough University
Ashby Rd., Loughborough, LE11 3TU, England, UK
Tel: 44 1509 223314
Fax: 44 1509 219702
Email: isst@lboro.ac.uk
Contact: D.D. Hall, Dir.

Institute of Swimming Pool Engineers

PO Box 3089, Halstead, CO9 4SB, England, UK
Tel: 44 1440 785999
Founded: 1979
Members: 700
Staff: 2
Contact: Mr. R. Alcock
Description: UK and overseas personnel from all areas of the swimming pool industry. Concerned with training and education across all sectors of the swimming pool industry. Arranges seminars, workshops, home study courses and technical papers.
Library Subject: swimming pool engineering
Library Type: not open to the public
Publication: Handbook
Publication title: Design Planning of Swimming Pools
Second publication: Magazine
Publication title: ISPG Magazine. Advertisements.
Meetings/Conventions: - quarterly seminar - Exhibits. UK

Institute of Terrestrial Ecology

Monks Wood, Huntingdon, PE17 2LS, England, UK
Tel: 44 1487 773381
Fax: 44 1487 773590
Contact: Suzanne Stefanelli
Description: Ecologists and other natural and social scientists. Promotes high-quality, interdisciplinary research in areas including environmental impact assessment, habitat restoration, and conservation. Conducts research; gathers and disseminates information.

Institute of the Motor Industry

Fanshaws, Brickendon, Hertford, SG13 8PQ, England, UK
Tel: 44 1992 511521
Fax: 44 1992 511548
Email: imi@motor.org.uk
Website: http://www.motor.org.uk
Founded: 1920
Members: 25000
Staff: 38
Contact: Nigel Beaven, Dir. of Mktg.
Description: Professional body for individuals employed in the motor industry and associated sectors. Performs the role of promoting and recognizing professionalism in the motor industry. Also acts as an awarding body for a wide variety of qualifications including National Vocational qualifications (NVQ), learning programmes, and sales and management qualifications.
Publication: Magazine
Publication title: Motor Industry Management. Advertisements.

Institute of Trade Mark Attorneys

c/o Canterbury House
2-6 Sydenham Rd., Croydon, CR0 9XE, England, UK
Tel: 44 208 6862052
Fax: 44 208 6805723
Email: tm@itma.org.uk
Website: http://www.itma.org.uk

Founded: 1934
Members: 1700
Staff: 5
Contact: Mrs. M.J. Tyler
Description: Exists to protect the interests of its members, and, by extension those of trade mark proprietors; it acts as an information exchange, and arranges meetings and conferences on subjects of interest to all those concerned with trade marks. Also lobbies for changes in trade mark law.
Publication: Newsletter
Meetings/Conventions: - annual international conference - Exhibits.

Institute of Transactional Analysis

3 Kents Ln., Soham, Ely, CB7 5DX, England, UK
Tel: 44 1353 724982
Fax: 44 1353 724982
Email: admin@ita.org.uk
Website: http://www.ita.org.uk
Founded: 1973
Members: 1100
Staff: 1
Contact: Charlie King, Admin.
Fee: £45
Membership Type: regular
Description: Professional members, qualified to teach and supervise the practice of TA. Certified TA analysts and trainee TA analysts. Also those interested in TA. Promotes and maintains the practice of TA, sets and maintains standards of professional practice and training.
Publication: Newsletter
Publication title: ITA News
Second publication: Journal
Publication title: Transactions
Meetings/Conventions: - annual conference Swansea UK

Institute of Translation and Interpreting

Fortuna House, S 5th St., Milton Keynes, MK9 2EU, England, UK
Tel: 44 1908 325250
Fax: 44 1908 325259
Email: info@iti.org.uk
Website: http://www.iti.org.uk
Founded: 1986
Members: 2800
Staff: 6
Contact: Alan Wheatley, Gen.Sec.
Fee: £162
Membership Type: student, associate, member or fellow
Description: Professional translators and interpreters; translation companies; universities; commercial firms (translation and interpreting services buyers); students; lecturers. Promotes professional standards, offers guidance and training to those wishing to enter the profession, and advice to users of translation and interpreting services. Primary aim is to promote the profession and thereby ensure improved conditions of work.
Library Subject: languages
Library Type: not open to the public
Publication: Proceedings
Publication title: Conference Proceedings
Second publication: Membership Directory
Publication title: Directory of Translators & Interpreters
Meetings/Conventions: Fair Course and Open Forum - annual conference - Exhibits.

Institute of Transport Administration
IoTA

Mill House, 11 Nightingale Rd., Horsham, RH12 2NW, England, UK
Tel: 44 1403 242412
Fax: 44 1403 242413
Website: http://www.iota.org.uk
Founded: 1944
Members: 3000
Staff: 4
Contact: Kerr Millar, Dir.
Description: Persons engaged in transportation management and administration of transportation via air, land, rail, or sea in 25 countries. Works to formulate standards of training, education, and experience required for proper administration and registration within the transportation industry. Encourages exchange of information among members. Offers educational programs; grants diplomas by examination. Compiles statistics.
Library Subject: General transportation.
Library Type: reference
Publication title: Rule Book
Publication title: Transport Management. Advertisements.
Meetings/Conventions: - annual conference - Exhibits.

Institute of Travel and Tourism

113 Victoria St., Crane Mead, Ware, SG12 9PY, England, UK
Tel: 44 870 7707960
Fax: 44 870 7707961
Email: admin@itt.co.uk
Website: http://www.itt.co.uk
Founded: 1956
Members: 3125
Staff: 7
Contact: Pat Dinner, Office Mgr.
Description: The majority of the members are owner/managerial/director level and represent a wide cross section of the senior personnel in the travel industry. The professional body for the travel and tourism industry offering membership to appropriately qualified individuals.
Publication: Journal. Advertisements.
Meetings/Conventions: Overseas Conference - annual

Institute of Trichologists
IT

20/22 Queensberry Place, London, SW7 2D2, England, UK
Tel: 44 870 6070602
Fax: 44 115 9384303
Email: trichologists@ambernet.co.uk
Website: http://www.ambernet.co.uk/trichologists/
Founded: 1902
Members: 240
Staff: 2
Contact: Alan Samuel, Sec.
Fee: £9
Membership Type: Retired
Fee: £80
Membership Type: Individual
Description: Promotes study, research, and application in the treatment and care of human scalp and hair. Provides scientific training of individuals qualified to advise and offer treatment of hair and scalp disorders and serves as an examining body for students of trichology. Provides centers for clinical study. Maintains Scalp and Hair Hospital where students conduct clinical observations and gain

practical experience. Bestows awards; sponsors charitable program; maintains speakers' bureau.
Publication: Membership Directory
Publication title: Membership Directory
Publication title: Monograph
Meetings/Conventions: - annual conference

Institute of Vehicle Engineers

31 Redstone Farm Rd., Hall Green, Birmingham, B28 9NU, England, UK
Tel: 44 121 7784354
Fax: 44 121 7022615
Email: info@ivehe.org
Website: http://www.ivehe.org
Founded: 1881
Members: 3000
Staff: 3
Contact: James Walker
Description: Middle management and upwards in all sections of the automotive industry - major motor manufacturers, component and materials suppliers, together with design houses, systems suppliers, etc. Aims to maintain improvement in design, engineering and manufacturing processes of land transport, utilising conferences, lectures, publications, and skill competitions, thus keeping abreast of new developments in materials and their uses, safety, performance, economy and ecology, which influence the production of vehicles of ever higher safety and quality.
Formerly: Institute of British Carriage and Automobile Manifacturers
Publication: Magazine
Publication title: Vehicle Technology. Advertisements.

Institute of Vehicle Recovery

201 Great Portland St., London, W1N 6AB, England, UK
Tel: 44 1788 540494
Fax: 44 1788 547565
Founded: 1983
Members: 431
Contact: Simon McCormack
Description: Persons normally active in vehicle recovery work. To promote training and professionalism in the vehicle recovery industry.

Institute of Vitreous Enamellers

Wych House, 37 Avenue Rd., Astwood Bank, Redditch, B96 6AQ, England, UK
Tel: 44 152 7893031
Fax: 44 152 7460868
Email: info@ive.org.uk
Website: http://www.ive.org.uk
Founded: 1936
Members: 105
Staff: 1
Contact: M.A. Collins, Hon.Sec.
Fee: £53
Membership Type: personal
Fee: £440
Membership Type: corporate, UK & EU
Description: Promotes vitreous enameller industry; provides technical support, education and training.
Library Subject: vitreous enamel
Library Type: reference
Publication: Journal
Publication title: The Vitreous Enameller. Advertisements.
Meetings/Conventions: - annual congress Bilboa Spain

Institute of Welfare Officers

Newland House, 3rd Fl., 137-139 Hagley Rd., Edgbaston, Birmingham, B16 8UA, England, UK
Tel: 44 121 4548883
Fax: 44 121 4547873
Email: i.w.o@virgin.net
Founded: 1945
Members: 3000
Staff: 5
Contact: Tom Dean, CEO
Fee: £50
Membership Type: corporate
Description: Registered Professional Welfare Officers and others engaged in the provision of Welfare Services. Students studying the Certificate and Diploma in Welfare Studies UK wide. Aims to promote education and training for persons desirous of attaining a career in welfare and its related issues. The establishment, maintenance and promotion of professional standards amongst practitioners and students. The only body authorised to register professional Welfare Officers.
Publication: Journal
Publication title: Welfare World. Advertisements.
Meetings/Conventions: - annual conference - Exhibits.

Institute of Wood Science

Stocking Lane, Hughenden Valley, High Wycombe, HP14 4NU, England, UK
Tel: 44 1494 565374
Fax: 44 1494 565395
Email: info@iwsc.org.uk
Website: http://www.iwsc.org.uk
Founded: 1954
Members: 1735
Staff: 1
Contact: M.W. Holloway
Description: Fellows, Associates, Members, Certificated Members, Student Members. To advance and encourage the scientific, technical, practical and general knowledge of timber and wood-based materials.
Library Subject: timber technology
Library Type: not open to the public
Publication: Journal
Meetings/Conventions: - annual conference - Exhibits.

Institution of Agricultural Engineers
IAgrE

West End Rd., Silsoe, Bedford, MK45 4DU, England, UK
Tel: 44 1525 861096
Fax: 44 1525 861660
Email: secretary@iagre.org
Website: http://www.iagre.org
Founded: 1938
Members: 1700
Staff: 5
Contact: Christopher Whetnall, Ch.Exec.Sec.
Fee: £75
Description: Agricultural engineers and students in many countries. Promotes and defends the interests of members; disseminates information on technical subjects.
Publication: Journal
Publication title: Landwards. Advertisements.
Meetings/Conventions: - annual convention - Exhibits.

Institution of Analysts and Programmers

c/o Charles House
36 Culmington Rd., London, W13 9NH, England, UK
Tel: 44 20 85672118
Fax: 44 20 85674379
Email: admin@iap.org.uk
Website: http://www.iap.org.uk
Founded: 1972
Members: 3000
Contact: Michael Ryan, Dir.Gen.
Description: Members consist of those professionally engaged in computer programming or systems analysis for commerce, industry or the public service. Aims to assist members to advance in their profession, and to secure public recognition of their professional status. There are four grades of membership, and members are entitled to use designatory letters as a public assurance of their experience and professional status.
Publication: Directory
Second publication: Newsletter

Institution of Chemical Engineers
IChemE

Davis Bldg., 165-189 Railway Terr., Rugby, CV21 3HQ, England, UK
Tel: 44 1788 578214
Fax: 44 1788 560833
Email: bgarratt@icheme.org.uk
Website: http://www.icheme.org
Founded: 1922
Members: 25000
Staff: 85
Contact: Dr. T.J. Evans, Ch.Exec.
Description: Chemical engineers united to promote and develop the science of chemical engineering and to further scientific and economic development and application of manufacturing processes in which chemical and physical changes of materials are involved. Promotes research into chemical engineering and communicates with governments on behalf of industry; compiles statistics. Holds symposia; offers continuing education courses.
Library Subject: chemical engineering and related topics
Library Type: reference
Publication: Journal
Publication title: The Chemical Engineer. Advertisements.
Second publication: Journal
Publication title: Chemical Engineering Research and Design
Meetings/Conventions: - annual meeting

Institution of Civil Engineering Surveyors

Dominion House, Sibson Rd., Sale, M33 7PP, England, UK
Tel: 44 161 9723100
Fax: 44 161 9723118
Email: training.membership@ices.org.uk
Website: http://www.ices.org.uk
Founded: 1970
Members: 3200
Staff: 5
Contact: CK Blackwell, Exec.Dir.
Fee: £115
Membership Type: professional qualification
Description: Land/engineering and quantity surveyors within the civil engineering industry. Entry is subject to qualifications, approved training and examination. The continuing development and promotion of the Institution as a centre of excellence in the art and science of civil engineering surveying to serve the public benefit and satisfy the needs of industry.

Publication: Survey
Publication title: Civil Engineering Surveyor
Publication title: Surveyors Guide to Civil Engineering Plans
Meetings/Conventions: - annual convention - Exhibits.

Institution of Civil Engineers
ICE

One Great George St., Westminster, London, SW1P 3AA, England, UK
Tel: 44 20 72227722
Fax: 44 20 72227500
Email: membership@ice.org.uk
Website: http://www.ice.org.uk
Founded: 1818
Members: 78000
Staff: 380
Contact: Adrian Long, Pres.
Description: Professional organization of chartered civil engineers in England. Sponsors competitions.
Library Subject: civil engineering, related sciences
Library Type: reference
Formerly: Absorbed, Society of Civil Engineering Technicians
Publication: Magazine
Publication title: NCE International. Advertisements.
Publication title: New Civil Engineer. Advertisements.

Institution of Diesel and Gas Turbine Engineers

P O Box 43, Bedford, MK40 4JB, England, UK
Tel: 44 1234 214340
Fax: 44 1234 355493
Email: secretary@idgte.org
Founded: 1913
Members: 700
Staff: 3
Contact: K.S. Edmanson
Fee: £68
Membership Type: corporate
Fee: £62
Membership Type: associate
Description: Diesel and gas turbine engineers, manufacturers, consultants and operators. Provides a forum for exchanging information on gas turbines, diesel, gas, and dual-fuel reciprocating engines CHP technologies and practices. Regular discussion meetings are arranged, and the paper's subsequent oral and written contributions are published in the transactions of the Institution. Seminars, conferences and exhibitions are arranged.
Library Type: open to the public
Formerly: Diesel Engineers and Users Association
Publication: Journal
Publication title: The Power Engineer. Advertisements.
Meetings/Conventions: - bimonthly meeting - Exhibits.

Institution of Economic Development
IED

PO Box 396, High Wycombe, HP15 6EL, England, UK
Tel: 44 1494 714201
Fax: 44 1494 718556
Email: admin@ied.co.uk
Website: http://www.ied.co.uk
Founded: 1983
Members: 1000
Contact: Stephanie Wakefield

Description: Economic development practitioners in both public and private sector organisations. Committed to demonstrating the value of economic development work for local and regional communities and to the pursuit of best practice in economic development and to the attainment of the highest standards of professional training and competence.
Publication: Journal

Institution of Electrical Engineers - England
IEE

Savoy Pl., London, WC2R 0BL, England, UK
Tel: 44 20 72401871
Fax: 44 20 72407735
Email: postmaster@iee.org.uk
Website: http://www.iee.org
Founded: 1871
Members: 130000
Staff: 450
Contact: Dr. A. Roberts, CEO
Description: Individuals in 121 countries united to promote the advancement of electrical and electronic science and engineering. Represents the profession of electrical and electronic engineering and related sciences; sets qualification standards for electrical, electronics, and software engineers; accredits industrial training schemes and courses at universities, polytechnics, and colleges; assists in the formulation of safety standards for the installation of electrical and electronic equipment. Operates schools liaison service, providing information and advice to young people; provides career information and advice to members. Conducts lectures, meetings, conferences, and residential vacation schools; sponsors competitions and bestows scholarships, grants, and prizes.
Library Subject: Technical and commercial aspects of electrotechnology, computer science, and control.
Library Type: reference
Formerly: Formed by Merger of, Institution of Electronic and Radio Engineers
Publication: Journal
Publication title: Computing and Control Engineering Journal. Advertisements.
Second publication: Journal
Publication title: Electronics and Communication Engineering Journal. Advertisements.

Institution of Engineering Designers

Courtleigh, Westbury Leigh, Westbury, BA13 3TA, England, UK
Tel: 44 1373 822801
Fax: 44 1373 858085
Email: ied@ied.org.uk
Website: http://www.ied.org.uk/
Founded: 1945
Members: 5500
Staff: 7
Contact: Mrs. E.K. Brodhurst, Sec./Chief Exec.
Fee: £68
Membership Type: mied
Description: Persons working in the field of engineering design as designers, managers or educators. Fellows (FIED), Members (MIED), are corporate members, Associates (AIED) and Competent Design Associates (CDAIED) are non-corporate, while Students and Diplomates may join as affiliate members. A professional body for designers who operate in widely diverse fields of engineering practice, including product, domestic appliance, jog and tool, special purpose machine, electro-mechanical, piping, design etc., in industry, in consultative practice and in education.

Library Subject: engineering design, engineering
Library Type: not open to the public
Publication: Journal
Publication title: Engineering Designer. Advertisements.

Institution of Environmental Sciences
IES

PO Box 16, Bourne, PE10 9FB, England, UK
Tel: 44 1778 394846
Fax: 44 1778 394846
Email: ies-uk@breathemail.net
Website: http://ies-uk.org.uk
Founded: 1971
Members: 800
Contact: Dr. R.A. Fuller, Hon.Sec.
Description: Professional and educational institutions, industrial companies, environmental consultants and agencies and college and graduate students (overseas members from many countries). Seeks to increase public interest, awareness, and involvement in the problems of world environment and environmental sciences. Promotes interdisciplinary studies of the environment and educational research in related sciences. Provides advisory services to schools, agencies, libraries, and the public on environmental matters. Conducts seminars.
Library Type: reference
Publication: Handbook
Publication title: Environmental Careers Handbook. Advertisements.
Second publication: Magazine
Publication title: The Environmental Scientist. Advertisements.
Meetings/Conventions: Burntwood Memorial Lecture - annual lecture - Exhibits.

Institution of Fire Engineers - England
IFE

148 Upper New Walk, Leicester, LE1 7QB, England, UK
Tel: 44 116 2553654
Fax: 44 116 2471231
Email: info@ife.org.uk
Website: http://www.ife.org.uk
Founded: 1918
Members: 11000
Staff: 8
Contact: David Evans, Gen.Sec.
Description: Members are involved in all areas of the fire world operating in both the public and private sectors. A professional organisation to promote and improve the science and practice of fire extinction, fire prevention and fire engineering.
Publication: Journal

Institution of Gas Engineers & Managers

12 York Gate, London, NW1 4QG, England, UK
Tel: 44 207 4870650
Fax: 44 207 2244762
Email: general@igaseng.demon.co.uk
Website: http://www.igem.org.uk
Founded: 1863
Members: 5000
Staff: 12
Contact: Gordon Davis, CEO
Description: Gas engineers.
Library Subject: gas engineering and technology from the 19th century onward

Library Type: open to the public
Publication: Journal
Publication title: International Car Engineering and Management. Advertisements.
Meetings/Conventions: - annual conference

Institution of Highways and Transportation
6 Endsleigh St., London, WC1H 0DZ, England, UK
Tel: 44 207 3872525
Fax: 44 207 3872808
Email: info@iht.org
Website: http://www.iht.org
Founded: 1930
Members: 10000
Staff: 14
Contact: Mary Lewis, Chief Exec. and Sec.
Description: Professionals working in the highways and transportation sector. Aims to provide a forum for the exchange of technical information; give specialist advice to government and other bodies; encourage education and training; and to make roads safer.
Library Subject: road infrastructure
Library Type: open to the public
Publication: Journal
Publication title: HET. Advertisements.

Institution of Incorporated Engineers
c/o Savoy Hill House
Savoy Hill, London, WC2R 0BS, England, UK
Tel: 44 20 7836 3357
Fax: 44 20 7497 9006
Email: info@iie.org.uk
Website: http://www.iie.org.uk
Founded: 1884
Members: 40000
Staff: 40
Contact:
Fee: £53
Description: Incorporated engineers and engineering technicians in the electronic, electrical, mechanical, and allied engineering fields worldwide. Dedicated to serving the professional interests of Incorporated Engineers and Engineering Technicians in electronic, electrical, mechanical, and allied engineering fields. It is committed to offering full support to members' professional career needs and continuing professional development.
Library Type: not open to the public
Formerly: Formed by Merger of, Institution of Electronics and Electrical Incorporated Engineers
Publication: Journal
Publication title: Engineering Technology. Advertisements.
Meetings/Conventions: - periodic seminar

Institution of Incorporated Executive Engineers
Wix Hill House, West Horsley, Leatherhead, KT24 6DZ, England, UK
Tel: 44 1483 222383
Fax: 44 1483 211109
Email: exec@iiexe.demon.co.uk
Founded: 1914
Members: 3400
Staff: 5
Contact: D.J. Dacam, Sec.
Fee: £88
Description: Practising professional managers in engineering. Learned society and professional Institution for practising engineers of all disciplines, engaged in (or retired from) engineering management.

Library Subject: engineering and engineering management
Library Type: open to the public
Publication: Journal
Publication title: Executive Engineer. Advertisements.
Second publication: Handbook
Publication title: Management Handbooks
Meetings/Conventions: - annual meeting - Exhibits.

Institution of Lighting Engineers
ILE
Lennox House, 9 Lawford Rd., Rugby, CV21 2DZ, England, UK
Tel: 44 1788 576492
Fax: 44 1788 540145
Email: ile@ile.org.uk
Website: http://www.ile.org.uk
Founded: 1924
Members: 2200
Staff: 5
Contact: Mr. R.G. Frost
Fee: £70
Membership Type: individual
Description: Promotes advancements in the science and art of efficient lighting. Facilitates the exchange of information and ideas.
Library Subject: all forms of lighting
Library Type: reference
Publication: Journal
Publication title: Lighting Journal. Advertisements.
Meetings/Conventions: - annual convention - Exhibits.

Institution of Mechanical Engineers
Birdcage Walk, Westminster, London, SW1H 9JJ, England, UK
Tel: 44 207 2407891
Fax: 44 207 3795586
Email: ils@imeche.org.uk
Website: http://www.imeche.org.uk/
Founded: 1847
Members: 80000
Staff: 180
Contact: Sir Michael Moore, Ch.Exec.
Fee: £104
Membership Type: corporate
Description: Mechanical and mechanical related engineers working in industry, academia, government departments, research associations and representative of all levels of responsibility from chief executive to student. Involved in the education, training and professional development of engineers, acting as an international centre for technology transfer in mechanical engineering. It is active in professional ethics and representation, collaborative activities with government and industry, provision of services to its members and provision for the future of the profession.
Library Subject: mechanical engineering, automotive, rail, power, manufacturing, mathematics, bioengineering, tribology, and aerospace
Library Type: open to the public
Publication: Journal
Publication title: Automotive Engineer
Second publication: Journal
Publication title: Environmental Engineering
Meetings/Conventions: - periodic meeting

Institution of Mining and Metallurgy
IMMM

Danum House, South Parade, Doncaster, DN1 2DY, England, UK
Tel: 44 1302 320486
Fax: 44 1302 380900
Email: hq@imm.org.uk
Website: http://www.imm.org.uk
Founded: 1892
Members: 6500
Staff: 16
Contact: Graham Woodrow
Description: Metallurgists, geologists, mining engineers, and petroleum engineers. Promotes advancement in the scientific and practical aspects of the mineral industry. Serves as a qualifying body for engineers in the field.
Library Subject: minerals industry
Library Type: reference
Formerly: Absorbed, Institution of Mining and Metallurgy
Publication title: IMM Abstracts. Advertisements.
Publication title: International Mining & Minerals
Meetings/Conventions: - annual conference - Exhibits.

Institution of Nuclear Engineers

Allan House, 1 Penerley Rd., London, SE6 2LQ, England, UK
Tel: 44 208 6981500
Email: inucewh@aol.com
Website: http://www.inuce.org.uk
Founded: 1959
Members: 1425
Staff: 4
Contact: Prof. K.L. Barratt, Pres.
Fee: £88
Membership Type: member
Fee: £106.5
Membership Type: fellow
Description: Professional engineers. Encourages the promotion and advancement of nuclear engineering and allied branches of science and engineering. In addition it endeavors to promote contact between nuclear engineers throughout the world, particularly by encouraging the establishment of branches both in the UK and overseas. It also promotes educational qualifications to engineers.
Publication: Journal
Publication title: Nuclear Engineer. Advertisements.

Institution of Occupational Safety and Health

The Grange, Highfield Dr., Wigston, LE18 1NN, England, UK
Tel: 44 116 2573100
Fax: 44 116 2573101
Email: enquiries@iosh.co.uk
Website: http://www.iosh.co.uk
Founded: 1945
Members: 26500
Staff: 70
Contact: Irene Plackett
Description: Represents individuals safety and health professionals. Promotes and sustains safety and health at work through training, and professional development courses.
Library Subject: safety, health, welfare, and the environment
Library Type: reference
Publication: Journal
Publication title: Journal of the Institution of Occupational Safety and Health

Second publication: Book
Publication title: Principles of Health and Safety at Work
Meetings/Conventions: - annual conference - Exhibits.

Institution of Physics and Engineering in Medicine
IPEMB

Fairmount House, 230 Tadcaster Rd., York, YO24 1ES, England, UK
Tel: 44 1904 610821
Fax: 44 1904 612279
Email: office@ipem.org.uk
Website: http://www.ipem.org.uk
Founded: 1960
Members: 2200
Staff: 5
Contact: Mr. R. Neilson, Hon.Sec.
Description: To promote to the public benefit the advancement of physics and engineering applied to medicine and biology and to advance public education in the field.
Formerly: Biological Engineering Society
Publication: Journal
Publication title: Journal of Biomedical Engineering
Second publication: Journal
Publication title: Medical Engineering and Physics
Meetings/Conventions: - annual convention

Institution of Population Registration

c/o The Register Office
Wycombe Area Office, Easton St., High Wycombe, HP11 1NH, England, UK
Tel: 44 1270 505106
Fax: 44 1270 505107
Founded: 1962
Members: 350
Contact: Mrs. A. Birrs, Sec.
Description: Those involved in registration of births deaths and marriages and associated professions - statistical surveying, genealogy etc. Aims to promote and facilitate training and examinal qualifications for registration officers within the UK. Stimulates interest and encourages debate on all matters relating to, or affecting, vital registration.
Publication: Journal
Second publication: Newsletter

Institution of Railway Signal Engineers

Savoy Hill House, 3rd Fl., Savoy Hill, London, WC2R 0BS, England, UK
Tel: 44 207 2403290
Fax: 44 207 2403281
Email: david@dwcrab.freeserve.co.uk
Website: http://www.irse.org
Founded: 1912
Members: 3000
Staff: 6
Contact: David Crabtree
Description: Membership from railways and manufacturers of railway signaling and telecommunications apparatus worldwide. Encourages the advancement of the science and practice of railway signaling and telecommunications by means of discussion enquiry research and experiments. The diffusion of knowledge, regarding railway signaling by means of lectures, publications and otherwise.
Library Subject: railway signal engineering and control systems
Library Type: not open to the public
Publication: Reports

Publication title: Technical Reports
Second publication: Books
Publication title: Textbooks
Meetings/Conventions: - annual convention

Institution of Structural Engineers
IStructE

11 Upper Belgrave St., London, SW1X 8BH, England, UK
Tel: 44 207 2354535
Fax: 44 207 2354294
Email: mail@istructe.org.uk
Website: http://www.istructe.org.uk
Founded: 1908
Members: 21000
Staff: 46
Contact: Dr. Keith Eaton
Description: Structural engineers in 105 countries. Promotes the advancement of structural engineering through continuing professional and technical development programs. Bestows awards; holds charitable programs; sponsors competitions. Maintains committees and task groups.
Library Subject: Structural engineering.
Library Type: lending
Formerly: Concrete Institute
Publication: Yearbook
Publication title: Directory of Members
Publication title: Structural Engineer. Advertisements.
Meetings/Conventions: - periodic conference

Institution of Water Officers
IWO

4 Carlton Ct., Team Valley, Gateshead, NE11 0AZ, England, UK
Tel: 44 191 4220088
Fax: 44 191 4220087
Email: lynn@iwo.org.uk
Website: http://www.iwo.org.uk
Founded: 1945
Members: 2000
Staff: 4
Contact: Lynn Cooper, Gen.Sec.
Description: Membership is open to all employees of the UK water industry, whatever their discipline. Offers members the opportunity to attend seminars, conferences, study tours, technical visits and weekend schools. Also provides registration as Chartered Engineer, Incorporate Engineer, and Engineering Technician.
Publication: Journal
Publication title: IWO Journal
Meetings/Conventions: - annual conference Cardiff UK

Instock Footwear Suppliers Association

c/o Marlow House
Churchill Way, Fleckney, Leicester, LE8 8UD, England, UK
Tel: 44 116 2403232
Fax: 44 116 2402762
Founded: 1947
Members: 10
Contact: Mrs. B. Beattie
Description: Wholesale footwear suppliers. An association for exchange of information, represents footwear distributing trade to Government and acts as a regulating body for relations with customers, suppliers and service industries. Also acts as a general

safety valve and suitable body for promoting the activities of members.
Meetings/Conventions: executive committee meeting

Insulated Render and Cladding Association
INCA

PO Box 12, Haslemere, GU27 3AH, England, UK
Tel: 44 1428 654011
Fax: 44 1428 651401
Email: incaassociation@aol.com
Website: http://www.inca-ltd.org.uk
Founded: 1981
Members: 62
Staff: 10
Contact: Ms. L. Onslow-Dewey
Fee: £720
Description: System designers, component manufacturers, contractors and others with an interest in external wall insulation. Aims to establish good technical, ethical and legal standards for the industry; to give impartial advice and to promote the concept and advantages of external wall insulation, as designed and applied by recognized member companies; and to represent the industry when liaising with government, local authorities and other bodies.
Formerly: External Wall Insulation Association
Publication: Brochure

Insurance Institute of London

20 Aldermanbury, London, EC2V 7HY, England, UK
Tel: 44 207 6001343
Fax: 44 207 6006857
Email: iil.london@cii.co.uk
Website: http://www.iilondon.co.uk
Founded: 1907
Members: 13000
Staff: 6
Contact: Laon Hulme
Fee: £39
Membership Type: ordinary
Fee: £66
Membership Type: associate
Description: Professional men and women in the insurance industry in London. Aims to raise the levels of professional knowledge of those working in insurance in London and to assist members in their career development and to support and reinforce the role and work of the Chartered Insurance Institute.
Publication: Journal
Publication title: Journal of the Insurance Institute of London
Second publication: Report
Meetings/Conventions: IIL Lecture Programme luncheon

Intellect

Russell Sq. House, 10-12 Russell Sq., London, WC1B 5EE, England, UK
Tel: 44 207 3312000
Fax: 44 207 3312040
Email: info@intellectuk.org
Website: http://www.intellectuk.org
Founded: 1945
Members: 16
Staff: 11
Contact: Abigail Grossman
Description: Covers manufacturers of radio and television receivers, video recorders, and all consumer electronic products. Aims to

promote, encourage, foster, develop and protect the radio and electronic equipment manufacturing industry and all ancillary and allied trades in the United Kingdom.
Formerly: Formed by Merger of, British Radio and Electronic Equipment Manufacturers' Association, Federation of the Electronics Industry and Computing Services and Software Association
Publication title: Statistical Press Notices
Second publication: Annual Report

Intensive Care Society
ICS

29 B Montague St., 3rd Fl., London, WC1B 5BH, England, UK
Tel: 44 20 72910690
Fax: 44 20 75800689
Email: marie@ics.ac.uk
Website: http://www.ics.ac.uk
Founded: 1970
Members: 2000
Staff: 3
Contact: Pauline Kemp, Admin.Mgr.
Fee: £130
Membership Type: consultant
Fee: £60
Membership Type: trainee
Description: Medical and scientific specialists in the field of intensive care. Seeks to provide the scientific and professional basis necessary for the research activities related to intensive care issues, and to make advice and information available to interested parties. Promotes communication among related organizations.
Publication: Book
Publication title: Fire Safety in the Intensive Care Unit
Second publication: Newsletter
Publication title: ICS Newsletter
Meetings/Conventions: - semiannual conference - Exhibits.

Interights, the International Centre for the Legal Protection of Human Rights

33 Islington High St., Lancaster House, London, N1 9LH, England, UK
Tel: 44 20 72783230
Fax: 44 20 72784334
Email: ir@interights.org
Website: http://www.interights.org
Founded: 1982
Staff: 13
Contact: Jerry McBride, Acting Dir.
Description: Attorneys and other individuals with an interest in human rights. Seeks to protect and expand the rights of the individual by strengthening their statutory underpinning worldwide. Drafts model human rights legislation and statutes; provides legal representation for individuals and groups appearing before international human rights tribunals; sponsors public education programs.
Library Subject: human rights
Library Type: open to the public
Publication: Journal
Publication title: Interights Bulletin

Interim Management Association

36-38 Mortimer St., London, W1N 7RB, England, UK
Tel: 44 207 4623296
Website: http://www.interimmanagement.uk.com
Founded: 1989
Members: 24

Contact: Eileen Simpson
Description: Recruitment consultancies specializing in interim managers for industry and commerce at senior level.
Formerly: Association of Temporary and Interim Executive Secretaries
Publication title: Annual Guide

Interior Decorators and Designers Association
IDDA

1/4 Chelsea Harbour Design Centre, Chelsea Harbour, Lots Rd., London, SW10 0XE, England, UK
Tel: 44 20 73490800
Fax: 44 20 73490500
Email: enquiries@idda.co.uk
Founded: 1966
Members: 450
Staff: 3
Contact: Joy Whittaker
Fee: £270
Membership Type: full
Description: Interior decorators and designers worldwide. Promotes the interior decorating and design industry.
Library Type: open to the public
Publication title: Directory of Members
Second publication: Newsletter
Publication title: Update
Meetings/Conventions: - monthly seminar - Exhibits.

Intermediate Technology Development Group
ITDG

The Schumacher Centre for Technology and Development, Bourton Hall, Bourton-on-Dunsmore, Rugby, CV23 9QZ, England, UK
Tel: 44 1926 634400
Fax: 44 1926 634401
Email: itdg@itdg.org.uk
Website: http://www.itdg.org
Founded: 1965
Members: 7078000
Staff: 450
Contact: Cowan Coventry
Description: Organizations and interested individuals. Enables poor people in developing areas to acquire and use skills and technologies which give them more control over their lives and which contribute to the sustainable development of their communities.
Library Subject: development issues
Library Type: reference
Formerly: Intermediate Technology Development Group - England
Publication title: Intermediate Technology Report
Publication title: Publications Catalogue

International Academy of Periodontology

5 Battery Green Rd., Lowestoft, NR32 1DE, England, UK
Tel: 44 1502 511522
Fax: 44 1502 583152
Email: perioiap@btclick.com
Website: http://www.perioiap.org

International Accounting Standards Board
IASB

30 Cannon St., London, EC4M 6XH, England, UK
Tel: 44 20 72466410
Fax: 44 20 72466411
Email: iasb@iasb.org.uk
Website: http://www.iasc.org.uk
Founded: 1973
Members: 143
Staff: 21
Contact: Sir David Tweedie, Chair
Description: Professional accountancy bodies representing more than 2,000,000 accountants in 104 countries. Aim is to formulate and publish, in the public interest, International Accounting Standards to be observed in the presentation of audited financial statements and to promote their worldwide acceptance and observance. (International Accounting Standards are statements regulating the representation and disclosure of figures within financial statements; such standards do not nullify local laws and may not be in accordance with local legislature.) Works for the improvement and harmonization of regulations, accounting standards, and procedures relating to the presentation of financial statements. Provides standards developed in response to the needs and problems of both developed and developing nations. Provides liaison between members and stock exchanges, representative bodies of accountants, industry groups, and other international organizations. Operates several technical committees to research current programs; maintains consultative group of representatives from banks, business, labor, law, securities commissions, stock exchanges, and international governmental organizations who offer advice on the process of setting International Accounting Standards.
Library Type: reference
Publication: Journal
Publication title: IASC Insight
Second publication: Newsletter
Publication title: IASC Update
Meetings/Conventions: board meeting

International Advertising Festival

27 Mortimer Street, London, W1T 3JF, England, UK
Tel: 44 20 72918444
Fax: 44 20 72918401
Website: http://www.canneslions.com
Founded: 1954
Members: 44
Staff: 10
Contact: Romain Hatchuel, Mng.Dir.
Description: Film, television, and print advertisers. Sponsors International Advertising Festival in Cannes, France. Encourages exchange among members. Sponsors competition; bestows awards.
Publication title: EuroBest
Meetings/Conventions: - annual meeting - Exhibits. Cannes France

International African Institute
IAI

SOAS, Thornhaugh St., Russell Sq., London, WC1H 0XG, England, UK
Tel: 44 20 78984420
Fax: 44 20 78984435
Email: iai@soas.ac.uk
Website: http://www.iaionthe.net
Founded: 1926
Members: 22
Staff: 4
Contact: Prof. Paul Spencer, Hon.Dir.
Description: Engages in encouraging the study of African society and disseminating the results of research. Prime objective is to facilitate communications between scholars within the continent and Africans throughout the world on issues that are of direct relevance to the peoples of this region. Achieves this through its publication programme which embraces the journal Africa, monographs, ethnographic and linguistic surveys, directories, bibliographies, and other reference works; seminars which bring together African and non-African scholars; and projects which are concerned with the infrastructure for learning and research in Africa.
Formerly: International Institute of African Languages and Cultures
Publication: Journal
Publication title: Africa
Second publication: Bibliography
Publication title: Africa Bibliography

International Agricultural Exchange Association - United Kingdom
IAEA

The Y.F.C. Centre, National Agricultural Centre, Kenilworth, CV8 2LG, England, UK
Tel: 44 1203 696578
Fax: 44 1203 696684
Email: post@agriventure.com
Founded: 1963
Members: 8000
Contact: R.F. Gregor, Sec.Gen.
Fee: £18
Description: Provides rural youth in 23 countries with the opportunity to study agricultural practices in other countries through placements with host families on approved training farms. Seeks to develop an understanding of the cultural patterns and way of life in host countries. Works to strengthen and improve mutual understanding among countries through contacts between trainees and hosts; increases trainees' knowledge of foreign languages. Maintains placement service of agricultural trainees in foreign countries. Sponsors exchange programs in which students spend 6 to 8 months in one host country or in which students travel to 2 host countries for 6 months for training in each country.
Publication title: World Agri-News
Meetings/Conventions: - annual international conference

International Alliance of Orchestra Associations
IAOA

c/o Association of British Orchestras
Enterprise House, Upper Ground, London, SE1 9PCE, England, UK
Tel: 44 20 72611555
Fax: 44 20 72611555
Email: russell@abo.org.uk
Founded: 1992
Members: 22
Contact: Russell Jones, Dir.
Description: Seeks to encourage by international means the development of orchestras in all respects; to initiate, develop, and participate in international activities concerned with orchestras; and to exchange information among the member orchestras.
Library Subject: copyright, labour law and professional music, dance and theatre
Library Type: not open to the public

International Aluminium Institute
IAI

New Zealand House, 8th Fl., Haymarket, London, SW1Y 4TE, England, UK
Tel: 44 207 9300528
Fax: 44 207 3210183
Email: iai@world-aluminium.org
Website: http://www.world-aluminium.org
Founded: 1972
Members: 35
Staff: 8
Contact: Robert Chase, Sec.Gen.
Description: Producers of primary aluminum from 23 countries. Seeks to increase world understanding of the aluminum industry and to develop additional uses of primary aluminum. Provides a forum for the exchange of information and the discussion of developments affecting the industry; conducts studies on problem areas affecting the industry including energy, the environment, and health and safety; collects and disseminates information.
Formerly: International Primary Aluminum Institute
Publication: Report
Publication title: Aluminium Recovered from Purchased or Tolled Scrap
Second publication: Report
Publication title: Electrical Power Utilization

International Apparel Federation

5 Portland Pl., London, W1N 3AA, England, UK
Tel: 44 171 6367788
Fax: 44 171 6367515
Email: iaf@dial.pipex.com
Website: http://www.iafnet.org
Founded: 1985
Members: 50
Contact:
Fee: £600
Membership Type: full
Fee: £500
Membership Type: associate
Description: Apparel manufacturers. Promotes international fair trade.
Meetings/Conventions: - annual conference - Exhibits.

International Artificial Intelligence in Education Society

University of Sussex, Falmer, BNI 9QH, England, UK
Tel: 44 113 2334626
Fax: 44 1273 671320
Email: aiedsoc@cogs.susx.ac.uk
Website: http://cbl.leeds.ac.uk/ijaied/aiedsoc.html
Founded: 1997
Description: Promotes research and development in the field of artificial intelligence in education.

International Artist Managers' Association
IAMA

23 Garrick St., Covent Garden, London, WC2E 9BN, England, UK
Tel: 44 20 73797336
Fax: 44 20 73797338
Email: info@iamaworld.com
Website: http://www.iamaworld.com
Founded: 1954

Members: 145
Staff: 3
Contact: Atholl Swainston-Harrison, Exec.Dir.
Description: Trade association for classical music artist managers and concert agents with affiliate membership available to other professionals in related areas of the classical music business.
Formerly: British Association of Concert Agents
Publication: Directory
Publication title: Directory of Artists. Advertisements.
Publication title: International (Technical) Guide
Meetings/Conventions: - annual international conference

International Association Against Painful Experiments on Animals
IAAPEA

PO Box 14, Hayling Island, PO11 9BF, England, UK
Tel: 44 2392 463738
Fax: 44 2392 462744
Email: iaapea@hotmail.com
Website: http://www.iaapea.com
Founded: 1969
Members: 60
Contact: Brian Gunn, Gen.Sec.
Description: Animal welfare organizations in 30 countries united to abolish painful experiments on animals. Supports the campaign against the exploitation of animals and encourages the development of research techniques that would replace experiments on animals. Established World Day for Laboratory Animals (April 24) to draw attention to the plight of animals in laboratories throughout the world. Provides assistance to societies and individuals working to eliminate laboratory experiments on animals. Operates an international photo agency to provide the media with photographs of animal experiments; produces documentary films; organizes seminars.
Publication: Bulletin
Publication title: Information Bulletin
Publication title: International Animal Action
Meetings/Conventions: - biennial general assembly

International Association for Citizenship Social and Economics Education

c/o John Price Consultants
22 Willows Dr., Meir Heath, Stoke-On-Trent, ST3 7LZ, England, UK
Tel: 44 1782 394898
Fax: 44 1782 394898
Email: iacsee@aol.com
Website: http://www.iacsee.org
Founded: 1994
Members: 130
Contact: Dr. Marie Wilson, Chm.
Fee: £44
Membership Type: individual
Fee: £62
Membership Type: school
Description: Teachers at all levels, researchers, and individuals working in support services or networks. Promotes the advancement of theoretical and practical knowledge about children in the areas of social studies and economics education and understanding.
Publication: Journal
Publication title: Children's Social and Economics Education

International Association for Educational and Vocational Guidance
IAEVG

c/o Linda Taylor, Chief Exec.
Essex Careers and Business Partnership, Westergaard House, The Matchyns, London Rd., Rivenhall, CM8 3HA, England, UK
Tel: 44 1376 391304
Fax: 44 1376 391498
Email: linda.taylor@careersessex.co.uk
Website: http://www.iaevg.org
Founded: 1951
Members: 300
Staff: 1
Contact: Linda Taylor, Sec.Gen.
Description: Individuals, institutions, and national associations in 54 countries concerned with educational and vocational guidance. Collects and distributes information pertaining to educational and vocational guidance; promotes professional training and encourages research by granting scholarships for study and travel. Collaborates with international organizations, governmental and nongovernmental, and individuals involved in educational and vocational guidance and related matters; participates in activities relating to educational and vocational guidance in research as well as in practical application. Organizes seminars, colloquia, conferences, workshops, and study tours in conjunction with related organizations. Advises government and national and international organizations on the development of guidance systems.
Library Subject: vocational guidance
Library Type: reference
Publication: Bulletin
Publication title: Educational and Vocational Guidance Bulletin
Second publication: Book
Publication title: Glossary of Educational and Vocational Guidance Terms in English, French, German, and Spanish
Meetings/Conventions: - annual congress - Exhibits.

International Association for Forensic Psychotherapy
IAFP

Cranmer Terrace, London, SW17 0RE, England, UK
Tel: 44 20 87255568
Fax: 44 20 87252475
Email: gmcgaule@sghms.ac.uk
Founded: 1991
Description: Promotes scientific research into causes and prevention of crime; establishes observation centres and clinics for diagnosis and treatment of delinquency and crime; secures cooperation between all bodies engaged in similar work.

International Association for Insurance Law - United Kingdom
IAIL

c/o Mr. Peter Tyldesley
London Guildhall University, Department of Management and Professional Development, 84 Mooregate, London, EC2M 65Q, England, UK
Tel: 44 20 73201596
Fax: 44 20 73201585
Email: bila@lqu.ac.uk
Website: http://www.aida.org.uk
Founded: 1960
Members: 56

Contact: Michael Mendelowitz, Asst.Sec.Gen.
Description: Associations whose membership comprises university professors, those working in the field of law, and others interested in international and comparative aspects of insurance law representing 56 countries.
Publication: Newsletter
Publication title: AIDA Mail
Publication title: Boletin Informativo
Meetings/Conventions: - quadrennial congress

International Association for Malacology

Crowell Rd., London, SW7 5BD, England, UK
Tel: 44 20 79425210
Fax: 44 20 79425054
Email: pbm@nhm.ac.uk
Website: http://www.ucmp.berkeley.edu/mologis/mollia.html

International Association for Marine Electronics Companies

Southbank House, Black Prince Rd., London, SE1 7SJ, England, UK
Tel: 44 207 5871245
Fax: 44 207 5871436
Email: secgen@cirm.org
Website: http://www.cirm.org
Founded: 1928
Members: 75
Staff: 3
Contact: Capt. Chris Cobley, Sec.-Gen.
Description: Represents marine electronics and radio communications companies from 23 nations. Promotes the application of electronic technology to the safety of life and efficient conduct of vessels at sea, and represents the industry at IMO, ITU and IEC, providing technical advice in the development of international standards. Sponsors technical committee and working groups.
Publication title: Technical Papers
Second publication: Brochure
Meetings/Conventions: - semiannual meeting

International Association for Mass Communication Research
IAMCR

University of Leicester, Leicester, LE1 7LT, England, UK
Founded: 1957

International Association for Pattern Recognition
IAPR

66 Weston Park, Thames Ditton, KT7 0HL, England, UK
Tel: 44 208 3982766
Fax: 44 208 3982766
Email: susanmduff@cs.com
Website: http://www.iapr.org
Founded: 1976
Members: 38
Staff: 1
Contact: Dr. R. Kasturi, Pres.
Description: National societies in the field of pattern recognition (38). Sponsors international conferences in the field. Maintain 18 technical committees. Fosters educational and research programs.
Publication: Brochure
Publication title: IAPR
Second publication: Newsletter
Publication title: IAPR Newsletter

International Association for Religious Freedom
IARF

2 Market St., Oxford, OX1 3EF, England, UK
Tel: 44 1865 202744
Fax: 44 1865 202746
Email: hq@iarf.net
Website: http://www.iarf-religiousfreedom.net
Founded: 1900
Members: 3000
Staff: 10
Contact: Andrew C. Clark, Gen.Sec.
Fee: £10
Membership Type: national chapter or member organization
Fee: £5
Membership Type: national chapter or member organization
Description: Religious groups in 30 countries subscribing to the principles of openness. Collaborates in worldwide efforts to liberate religion from exclusionary tendencies. Conducts interreligious dialogues and intercultural encounters. Offers computerized services. Maintains consultative status at the United Nations.
Library Type: reference
Publication title: Congress Proceedings
Publication title: IARF World
Meetings/Conventions: - annual conference

International Association for the History of Glass

16 Lady Bay Rd., West Bridgeford, Nottingham, NG2 5BJ, England, UK
Tel: 44 115 9819065
Email: hilary.cool@btinternet.com
Website: http://www.aihv.org
Founded: 1958
Members: 420
Contact: H. Cool
Fee: £50
Membership Type: institutional
Fee: £32
Membership Type: individual
Description: Promotes the historic, archaeological, and artistic study of glass in 30 countries. Facilitates international scientific collaboration among members and specialists in examining the cultural aspects of glass heritage within a larger historical context. Examines problems of conservation and technology, excluding those regarding the industrial production of contemporary glass; studies all periods in the history of glass.
Publication: Proceedings
Publication title: Annales de l'AIHV
Second publication: Monographs
Meetings/Conventions: - triennial congress - Exhibits. London UK

International Association for the Psychology of Food and Nutrition
IAPFoN

Edgbaston, Birmingham, B15 2TT, England, UK
Tel: 44 121 4144932
Fax: 44 121 4144897
Email: d.a.booth@bham.ac.uk
Website: http://www.westenhoefer.de/iapfon/welcome.html
Founded: 1992
Description: Brings together basic and applied psychologists in research and practice on food and nutrition.

International Association for the Study of Maritime Mission
IASMM

School of Technology, The College of Ripon and York St. John, Lord Mayor's Walk, York, YO31 7EX, England, UK
Tel: 44 1904 716861
Fax: 44 1904 612512
Email: s.friend@ucrysj.ac.uk
Website: http://www.ucc.uconn.edu/~shpark/english.html
Founded: 1990
Members: 200
Contact: Stephen Friend, Sec.
Fee: £20
Membership Type: individual
Fee: £25
Membership Type: organization
Description: Individuals and organizations involved in chaplaincy work in ports worldwide, and education, social, pastoral, and medical work among seafarers. Promotes the preservation, cataloguing, and publicising of sources for research in maritime mission and encourages maritime mission studies in places of learning.
Library Subject: seafarers missions
Library Type: reference
Publication: Journal
Publication title: Maritime Mission Studies
Meetings/Conventions: - biennial international conference

International Association for the Study of Obesity
IASO

231 North Gower St., London, NW1 2NS, England, UK
Tel: 44 207 3876033
Fax: 44 207 6911914
Email: kate.baillie@iaso.org
Website: http://www.iaso.org
Founded: 1986
Description: Improves prevention, management and treatment of obesity worldwide by promoting medical research, extending and disseminating knowledge, facilitating contact between investigators and promoting public education.

International Association for the Study of Popular Music

c/o Keith Kahn Harris, Mem.Sec.
57 Goring Rd., London, N11 2BT, England, UK
Tel: 44 795 7695823
Fax: 44 870 1307784
Email: kharrus@sociocult.u-net.com
Website: http://www.iaspm.net/iaspm/
Founded: 1980
Members: 700
Staff: 5
Contact: Claire Levy, Gen.Sec.
Fee: £16
Membership Type: waged
Fee: £8
Membership Type: unwaged
Description: Scholars and other individuals and institutions committed to furthering and promoting knowledge of this vital area of contemporary cultural activity.
Publication: Proceedings
Publication title: Conference Proceedings
Second publication: Newsletter
Publication title: RPM
Meetings/Conventions: - biennial conference

International Association of Agricultural Information Specialists
IAALD

c/o Ms. Margot Bellamy
14 Queen St., Dorchester-on-Thames, Wallingford, OX10 7HR,
England, UK
Tel: 44 1865 340054
Email: margot.bellamy@fritillary.demon.co.uk
Website: http://www.iaaid.org
Founded: 1955
Members: 500
Contact: Ms. Margot Bellamy, Sec.Treas.
Fee: £45
Membership Type: individual
Fee: £15
Membership Type: developing country
Description: Agriculturists, librarians, documentalists, extensionists, and related associations and information institutions in over 80 countries. Promotes library science and documentation, information and knowledge management, and the professional interests of agricultural librarians and documentalists, including forestry, agricultural engineering, veterinary science, fisheries, food and nutrition, and agricultural and food industries.
Formerly: International Committee Agricultural Librarians
Publication title: Quarterly Bulletin of the IAALD
Publication title: World Directory of Agricultural Information Resource Centers 2000, 3rd Ed.

International Association of ALS/MND Associations

PO Box 246, Northampton, NN1 2PR, England, UK
Tel: 44 1604 611821
Fax: 44 1604 611852
Email: alliance@alsmndalliance.org
Founded: 1992
Contact: Diane Heron, Chair
Description: Umbrella organization for Amyotrophic Lateral Sclerosis (ALS) and Motor Neruone Disease (MND) associations. ALS and MND are muscle-wasting conditions. Provides a forum for support and exchange of information for ALS and MND associations worldwide.
Publication: Directory

International Association of Book-Keepers
IAB

Burford House, 44 London Rd., Sevenoaks, TN13 1AS, England, UK
Tel: 44 1732 458080
Fax: 44 1732 455848
Email: vburrows@iab.org.uk
Website: http://www.iab.org.uk
Founded: 1973
Members: 1275
Staff: 15
Contact: J. Malcolm Dean, Chief Exec.
Fee: £42
Membership Type: associates and fellows
Description: Associated with the Institute of Financial Accountants. Professionals in the field of bookkeeping in 55 countries. Purpose is to bring together members of the profession and administer professional examinations.
Publication: Journal
Publication title: Professional Book Keeper. Advertisements.
Meetings/Conventions: - annual conference

International Association of Broadcasting Manufacturers
IABM

PO Box 2264, Reading, RG31 6WA, England, UK
Tel: 44 118 9418620
Fax: 44 118 9418630
Email: info@theiabm.org
Website: http://www.theiabm.org
Founded: 1976
Members: 160
Staff: 4
Contact: Mr. Martin Salter, Chm.
Fee: £300
Membership Type: corporate
Fee: £100
Membership Type: associate
Description: Companies in 10 countries engaged in the manufacture of broadcasting equipment and associated products. Works to coordinate the common interests of manufacturers of sound and television broadcasting equipment and associated products. Areas of interest include: equipment and specification standards; tendering procedures; participation in international broadcasting conventions and equipment exhibitions.
Publication: Newsletter
Publication title: ScanLine

International Association of Business Computing

31 High St., Wooten Basset, Swindon, SN4 7AF, England, UK
Tel: 44 1793 772254
Fax: 44 1793 772254
Email: admin@iabc.demon.co.uk
Founded: 1995
Staff: 2
Contact: Pippa Lewis, Admin. Officer
Description: Non-profit examining body providing vocational qualifications in business computing and information systems at three levels: certificate, diploma, and advanced diploma.
Formerly: Association of Business and Administrative Computing
Publication: Journal
Publication title: Networking International

International Association of Classification Societies
IACS

5 Old Queen St., London, SW1H 9JA, England, UK
Tel: 44 207 9760660
Fax: 44 207 9760440
Email: permsec@iacs.org.uk
Website: http://www.iacs.org.uk
Founded: 1968
Members: 12
Staff: 8
Contact: Robin Bradley, Sec.
Description: Classification societies worldwide whose goals are: to work toward the improvement of standards of safety at sea and for the prevention of pollution of the marine environment; to provide consultation and cooperation with relevant international and national maritime organizations; to cooperate closely with marine industries worldwide. Has worked in a variety of areas relative to ship safety and reliability. Maintains liaison with International Maritime Organization and International Organization for Standardization.

International Association of Craniofacial Identification

Oxford Rd., Manchester, M13 9PT, England, UK
Email: rneave@fs2.scg.man.ac.uk

International Association of Dry Cargo Shipowners
INTERCARGO

4 London Wall Bldgs, 2nd Fl., Blomfield St., London, EC2M 5NT, England, UK
Tel: 44 207 6383989
Fax: 44 207 6383943
Email: info@intercargo.org
Website: http://www.intercargo.org
Founded: 1980
Members: 180
Staff: 6
Contact: Roger Holt, Sec.Gen.
Description: Promotes and protects the interests of its members, exchange views, frames policies, especially in the areas of safety and freedom of navigation, and cooperates with other bodies avoiding duplication where possible. Is a consultative member of I.M.O.
Library Type: open to the public
Publication: Journal
Publication title: Intercargo Annual Review
Second publication: Bulletin
Publication title: Intercargo Bulletin
Meetings/Conventions: - annual general assembly

International Association of Engineering Insurers
IMIA

PO Box 296, Macclesfield, SK11 9FR, England, UK
Tel: 44 1625 861637
Fax: 44 1625 890092
Email: archie.watt@imiasec.demon.co.uk
Website: http://www.imia.com
Founded: 1968
Members: 40
Contact: A. Watt, Sec.
Description: Leading international machinery insurers in 18 countries. Provides a forum for the international exchange of information, knowledge, and experience in the engineering insurance field. Promotes practical cooperation in meeting complex technological developments and changing risks in engineering insurance.
Formerly: International Machinery Insurers Association
Meetings/Conventions: - annual meeting Stockholm Sweden

International Association of Environmental Coordinators
IAEC

Corylus Burton Way, Chalfont St. Giles, , England, UK
Founded: 1976

International Association of Forensic Phonetics
IAFP

86 The Mount, York, Y024 1AR, England, UK
Tel: 44 1904 634821
Fax: 44 1904 634626
Email: enquiries@jpfrench.com
Website: http://www.iafp.net/
Founded: 1988

Description: Promotes basic research in forensic phonetics; provides a forum for the interchange of ideas and information of its practice, development and research.

International Association of Language Centres
IALC

PO Box 798, Canterbury, CT1 2WX, England, UK
Tel: 44 1227 769007
Fax: 44 1227 769014
Email: info@ialc.org
Website: http://www.ialc.org
Founded: 1983
Members: 45
Staff: 2
Contact: Sonia D. Centa, Pres.
Description: Promotes learning the language where it is spoken through study in private, independent language schools of high quality.

International Association of Maritime Institutions
IAMI

Faculty of Nautical Sciences, South Tyneside College, St. George's Ave., South Shields, NE34 6ET, England, UK
Tel: 44 191 4273696
Fax: 44 191 4273653
Email: nautical@stc.ac.uk
Founded: 1950
Members: 40
Contact: Dr. C.E.C. May, Hon.Sec.
Fee: £360
Membership Type: full
Fee: £120
Membership Type: associate
Description: Maritime institutions. Works to further marine education and training.
Meetings/Conventions: - annual conference

International Association of Oral Pathologists
IAOP

Eastman Dental Institute for Oral Health Care Sciences, University College London, 256 Gray's Inn Rd., London, WC1X 8LD, England, UK
Tel: 44 20 79151000
Fax: 44 20 79151039
Email: academic@eastman.ucl.ac.uk
Website: http://www.eastman.ucl.ac.uk
Founded: 1976
Members: 380
Contact: Prof. Paul M. Speight
Fee: £20
Description: Dentists who have had postgraduate instruction in pathology. Seeks to advance the science of oral pathology; works to foster international cooperation in the field.
Publication: Journal
Publication title: Journal of Oral Pathology and Medicine
Publication title: Membership List

International Association of Packaging Research Institutes

Randalls Rd. 1, Leatherhead, KT22 7RU, England, UK
Tel: 44 137 2802000
Fax: 44 137 2802238
Email: benparsons@tinyonline.co.uk
Founded: 1971
Members: 42
Staff: 9
Contact: Ben Parsons, Sec.Gen.
Fee: £300
Membership Type: member
Description: Individuals and groups involved in the packaging industry.

International Association of Paediatric Dentistry
IAPD

123 Gray's Inn Rd., London, WC1X 8WD, England, UK
Tel: 44 20 79051251
Fax: 44 20 79051285
Email: iapd@eastman.ucl.ac.uk
Website: http://www.iapd.org.uk
Founded: 1969
Members: 700
Contact: Dr. M.P. Hector, Hon.Sec./Treas.
Fee: £33
Membership Type: individual
Description: Dentists, dental and medical libraries, bookshops, and research institutions in 36 countries. Encourages research and foster progress in the field of children's dental health. Provides a forum for the exchange of information concerning children's dentistry worldwide.
Publication: Journal
Publication title: International Journal of Paediatric Dentistry.
Second publication: Newsletter
Publication title: Newsletter
Meetings/Conventions: - biennial congress - Exhibits.

International Association of Practising Accountants

Stafford House, 2nd Fl., 33-39 Station Rd., Aldershot, GU11 1BA, England, UK
Tel: 44 1252 325981
Fax: 44 1252 350733
Email: admin@iapa-accountants.com
Website: http://www.iapa-accountants.com
Founded: 1987
Members: 16
Contact: Mark Hayward, Ch.Exec.
Description: Medium sized firms of chartered accountants. An informal association of medium sized firms of chartered accountants to promote and advance the interests of medium sized firms of chartered accountants by means of discussion, publicity, cooperation and exchange of information.
Publication: Booklet
Publication title: Becoming A Chartered Accountant - Training With A Medium Sized Firm
Second publication: Booklet
Publication title: Medium Sized Firms of Chartered Accountants - The Vital Link Between Growing Businesses and The City

International Association of Professional Congress Organizers
IAPCO

42 Canham Rd., London, W3 7RS, England, UK
Tel: 44 20 87496171
Fax: 44 20 87400241
Email: iapco@xs4all.be
Website: http://www.iapco.org
Founded: 1968
Members: 70
Staff: 1
Contact: Sarah Storie-Pugh, PVGM Admin.
Description: Professional congress organizers including freelance organizers and organizing companies in 26 countries. Promotes high professional standards in the organization and administration of international congresses, conferences, and meetings. Encourages the study of theoretical and practical aspects of international congresses. Seeks to further the recognition of the profession of congress organizer. Conducts research and educational programs.
Publication: Pamphlet
Publication title: Guidelines for International Scientific Programme Committee
Meetings/Conventions: - annual general assembly

International Association of Schools of Social Work
IASSW

c/o Prof. Lena Dominelli
Dept. of Social Work Studies, Southampton Univ., Highfield, Southampton, SO17 1BJ, England, UK
Tel: 44 23 80593054
Fax: 44 23 80594800
Email: ld@socsci.soton.ac.uk
Website: http://www.iassw.soton.ac.uk
Founded: 1928
Members: 600
Contact: Lena Dominelli, Pres.
Description: Schools of social work in 80 countries; national and regional associations of schools of social work. Provides international leadership and encourages high standards in social work education; represents the interests of social work education in connection with activities of other public and private international bodies. Sponsors study groups on social work education; offers consultative to educational institutions; undertakes projects of concern to social work educators; maintains an updated information system on social work education worldwide; and organizes conferences and seminars.
Publication: Journal
Publication title: International Social Work
Meetings/Conventions: Congress on Social Work Education - biennial congress - Exhibits. Adelaide Australia

International Association of Structural Tectonic Geologists
IASTG

University of Manchester, Manchester, M13 9PL, England, UK
Fax: 44 161 2753947
Email: iastg@man.ac.uk
Founded: 1990
Description: Promotes communication among structural/tectonic geologists.

International Association of Teachers of English as a Foreign Language
IATEFL

3 Kingsdown Chambers, Whitstable, CT5 2FL, England, UK
Tel: 44 1227 276528
Fax: 44 1227 274415
Email: generalenquiries@iatefl.org
Website: http://www.iatefl.org
Founded: 1967
Members: 4000
Staff: 7
Contact: Mrs. G. Smart, Exec. Officer
Fee: £37
Membership Type: teachers
Description: Teachers of English as a foreign or second language; educational institutions. Aim is to exchange experience, views, and information among members in 112 countries so that the teaching of English might be improved at all age levels and in all countries.
Publication: Newsletter
Publication title: IATEFL Issues. Advertisements.
Meetings/Conventions: - semiannual symposium

International Association of Technological University Libraries
IATUL

c/o Dr. Judith Palmer
Radcliffe Science Library, University of Oxford, Parks Rd., Oxford, OX1 3QP, England, UK
Tel: 44 1865 27282
Fax: 44 1865 27283
Email: judith.palmer@bodley.ox.ac.uk
Website: http://www.iatul.org
Founded: 1955
Members: 234
Contact: Judith Palmer, Sec.
Description: Libraries of academic institutions in 41 countries that offer courses in engineering or technology at the doctoral level; nonvoting associate members are libraries of academic institutions that offer such courses to the Master's or equivalent level; observer members are libraries housed in national patent offices and science museums with technological collections that meet research standards. Works to facilitate international cooperation among member libraries to stimulate and develop library projects of international and regional importance.
Publication: Journal
Publication title: IATUL Conference Proceedings
Meetings/Conventions: - annual conference - Exhibits. Ankara Turkey

International Association of Tour Managers

397 Walworth Rd., London, SE17 2AW, England, UK
Tel: 44 20 77039154
Fax: 44 20 77030358
Email: iatm@iatm.co.uk
Website: http://www.iatm.co.uk
Founded: 1962
Members: 1500
Staff: 3
Contact: Ron Julian, Gen.Mgr.
Description: Active members are professional tour managers. Allied and Associate members are companies involved with group tourism. Promotes the highest standards of professional competence and improves the status and welfare of tour managers. Represents the interests of tour managers within the industry and to all governmental and non-governmental organisations concerned with group tourism.
Publication: Newsletter
Meetings/Conventions: - annual general assembly - Exhibits.

International Association of University Professors of English
IAUPE

Penwithian Higher Fore St., Marazion, TR17 0BQ, England, UK
Founded: 1951

International Association of Wool Textile Laboratories

Merrydale House, Roydsdale Way, Bradford, BD4 6SB, England, UK
Tel: 44 1274 470040
Fax: 44 1274 652133
Email: info@interwoollabs.com
Website: http://www.interwoollabs.com
Founded: 1969
Members: 125
Staff: 2
Contact: Dimitri Orekhoff, Sec.Gen.
Description: Wool textile laboratories in 35 countries. Seeks to ensure correct and uniform application of measuring and sampling methods among member laboratories in order to obtain consistent test results. Aids member laboratories in settling disputes resulting from measurement discrepancies. Conducts research.
Meetings/Conventions: - annual conference

International Association on Water Quality

Duchess House, 20 Masons Yard, Duke St., St. James, London, SW1Y 6BU, England, UK
Tel: 44 20 78398299
Contact: A. Milburn, Exec.Dir.
Description: Individuals, organizations, and agencies. Promotes preservation and sustainable use of global water resources. Seeks to limit water pollution. Serves as a clearinghouse on water resources and pollution; provides assistance to corporations and agencies wishing to adopt pollution control programs; sponsors research and educational programs.

International Autistic Research Organization
IARO

49 Orchard Ave., Croydon, CR0 7NE, England, UK
Tel: 44 20 87770095
Fax: 44 20 87762362
Email: iaro@autismresearchww.freeservice.co.uk
Website: http://www.charitynet.org/~iaro
Founded: 1981
Members: 300
Staff: 3
Contact: Gerda I.M. McCarthy, Dir.-Sec./Founder
Description: Provides information about scientific research into autism.
Publication: Magazine
Meetings/Conventions: conference

International Balint Federation
IBF

c/o Dr. David Watt
Tollgate Health Ctr., 220, Tollgate Rd., London, E64 JS, England, UK
Tel: 44 20 89042844
Email: jvsalinsky@aol.com
Website: http://www.balint.co.uk/international.html
Founded: 1975
Contact: Dr. John Salinsky, Sec.
Description: Groups and corresponding members in 34 countries. Promotes group training and practice according to the principles of Michael Balint (1896-1970), psychiatrist and author. Studies the patient-physician relationship on a psychosocial level and encourages improved psychological training and research in practice.
Publication: Journal
Publication title: Balint. Advertisements.
Meetings/Conventions: - biennial Berlin Germany

International Bar Association
IBA

271 Regent St., London, W1B 2AQ, England, UK
Tel: 44 207 6291206
Fax: 44 207 4090456
Email: member@int-bar.org
Website: http://www.ibanet.org
Founded: 1947
Members: 18000
Staff: 50
Contact: Mark Ellis, Exec.Dir.
Fee: £40
Membership Type: individual
Description: National bar associations and individual members of the legal profession working in the field of international law in 183 countries. Works to advance the science of jurisprudence; promotes uniformity in related legal fields and administration of justice under law. Seeks to establish and maintain friendly relations among members of the legal profession worldwide. Supports the legal principles and aims of the United Nations.
Library Type: not open to the public
Publication title: Business Law Int'l
Publication title: Directory of Members. Advertisements.
Meetings/Conventions: - annual conference - Exhibits.

International Biodeterioration and Biodegradation Society

c/o John Gillatt
Thor Specialties Ltd., Wincham Ave., Wincham, Northwich, CW9 6GB, England, UK
Tel: 44 1606 818869
Fax: 44 1606 818801
Email: info@biodeterioration.org
Website: http://www.biodeterioration.org
Founded: 1968
Members: 250
Contact: John Gillatt, Hon.Sec.
Fee: £43
Description: Academics, representatives of the biocide industry, and research scientists from industry and government organizations. Promotes the sciences of biodeterioration and biodegradation. Sponsors symposia; conducts the Bunker Memorial Lecture.
Publication: Journal
Publication title: International Biodeterioration and Biodegradation
Second publication: Newsletter

Publication title: Newsletter
Meetings/Conventions: International Biodeterioration and Biodegradation Symposium convention - Exhibits.

International BIPAVER

Elsinore House, Buckingham St., Aylesbury, HP20 2NQ, England, UK
Tel: 44 1296 399837
Fax: 44 870 9000610
Email: bipaver@ntda.co.uk
Founded: 1954
Contact: Richard Edy, Sec.Gen.
Description: Tire retailers and retreaders in European. Develops standards for tire retreading and repair. Seeks to develop a tire disposal policy that meets legislative requirements and the practical and commercial needs of the industry. Provides a forum for communication between members and other European tire manufacturing associations. Encourages training to ensure the technical skills of people working tire retreading and retailing. Lobbies European institutions. Compiles statistics; disseminates information.

International Boundaries Research Unit
IBRU

Dept. of Geography, University of Durham, South Rd., Durham, DH1 3LE, England, UK
Tel: 44 191 3747701
Fax: 44 191 3747702
Email: ibru@dur.ac.uk
Website: http://www-ibru.dur.ac.uk/index.html
Founded: 1989
Staff: 4
Contact: Martin Pratt, Dir. of Res.
Description: Seeks to enhance the resources available for the peaceful resolution of problems associated with international boundaries on land and at sea around the world. Conducts research.
Library Subject: cartography, border disputes
Library Type: open to the public
Publication: Report
Publication title: Boundary and Territory Briefing
Second publication: Report
Publication title: Maritime Briefing
Meetings/Conventions: - periodic conference

International Brewers Guild
IBG

8 Ely Pl., London, EC1N 6SD, England, UK
Tel: 44 171 4054565
Fax: 44 171 8314995
Founded: 1906
Members: 2000
Staff: 7
Contact: W.D.J. Carling, Gen.Sec.
Fee: £69
Membership Type: general
Description: Brewing professionals and students in 12 countries. Seeks to raise the status and advance the interests of the brewing profession and act as the representative of brewers.
Library Type: not open to the public
Formerly: Incorporated Brewers' Guild
Publication: Journal
Publication title: The Brewer. Advertisements.
Second publication: Directory
Publication title: International Brewery Guild Directory

International Bunker Industry Association
IBIA

The Baltic Exchange, 38 St. Mary Ave., London, EC3A 8BH, England, UK
Tel: 44 20 79291616
Fax: 44 20 79291717
Email: ian.adams@ibia.net
Website: http://www.ibia.net
Founded: 1993
Contact: Ian Adams, Sec.Gen.
Fee: £500
Membership Type: corporate
Fee: £100
Membership Type: individual
Description: Anyone who has an interest in bunkering. Including ship owners, charterers, managers, bunker suppliers, traders, brokers, barging companies, storage companies, surveyors, port authorities, credit reporting companies, lawyers, equipment manufacturers, shipping journalists and marine consultants. Aims to provide an international forum to address the concerns of all sectors of the bunker industry.

International Cabin Crew Association
ICCA

Head Office, Rm. 14, Runnymede Malthouse, Runnymede Rd., Egham, Surrey, TW20 9BD, England, UK
Tel: 44 1784 497060
Fax: 44 1784 497061
Email: 10650.3130@compuserve.com
Website: http://ourworld.compuserve.com/homepages/ICCA_EG-HAM/
Founded: 1976
Members: 40000
Staff: 1
Contact: P. R. Miller, U.S. Rep.
Description: Flight attendants and flight attendant associations and unions. Strengthens bonds of solidarity among flight attendants through consultation and industry-related projects. Conducts investigations and research projects on cabin safety, health, and training. Undertakes studies on psychological after-effects of crashes, evacuations, and in-flight incidents producing stress. Plans to present Antonio de Souza Award. Sponsors seminars.
Formerly: International Flight Attendants Association
Publication: Newsletter
Publication title: ICCA Newsletter

International Cable Protection Committee
ICPC

PO Box 150, Lymington, SO41 6WA, England, UK
Tel: 44 1590 681673
Fax: 44 870 526049
Email: secretary@iscpc.org
Website: http://www.iscpc.org
Founded: 1958
Members: 80
Staff: 1
Contact: Graham Marle, Sec.
Fee: £1000
Description: Governmental administrations and commercial companies in 39 countries that own or operate submarine telecommunications cables as well as commercial companies that own or operate submarine power cables. Promotes the safeguarding of submarine telecommunications cables against man-made and natural hazards. Serves as a forum for the exchange of technical and legal information pertaining to submarine cable protection methods and programmes.
Publication: Video
Publication title: Share the Seabed
Second publication: Brochures
Meetings/Conventions: ICPC Plenary Meeting - periodic meeting - Exhibits.

International Cargo Handling Coordination Association
ICHCA

85 Western Rd., Ste. 2, Romford, RM1 3LS, England, UK
Tel: 44 1708 734787
Fax: 44 1708 734877
Email: info@ichca.org.uk
Founded: 1952
Members: 2000
Staff: 8
Contact: Gerry Askham, CEO
Fee: £500
Description: Individuals and organizations in 84 countries with interests in international handling and transport of goods. Works to increase efficiency and economy in the handling and movement of goods from origin to destination by all modes and at all phases of transportation. Maintains information service and expert committees; sponsors research programs, and intergovernmental representation (NGO).
Library Subject: cargo handling and international transportation
Library Type: reference
Publication: Magazine
Publication title: Cargo Today. Advertisements.
Publication title: ICHCA Buyer's Guide to Manufacturers
Meetings/Conventions: - biennial conference - Exhibits.

International Centre for Child Studies
ICCS

86 Cumberland Rd., Hotwells, Bristol, BS1 6UG, England, UK
Tel: 44 117 9250835
Fax: 44 117 9093739
Email: nrbutler@aol.com
Website: http://www.charitiesdirect.com

International Centre for Conservation Education

Brockelbank, Butts Lane, Woodmancote, Cheltenham, GL52 9QH, England, UK
Tel: 44 1242 674839
Fax: 44 1242 674839
Email: info@icce.org.uk
Website: http://www.icce.org.uk
Founded: 1984
Staff: 1
Contact: Mark Boulton
Description: Works to promote greater understanding of global environmental issues and sustainable development.
Library Subject: environmental education
Library Type: not open to the public
Publication: Catalog

International Cerebral Palsy Society
ICPS

19 St. Mary's Grove, London, W4 3LL, England, UK
Tel: 44 208 9946386
Fax: 44 208 7478528
Email: a.loring@easynet.co.uk
Website: http://www.icps.org.uk
Founded: 1969
Members: 317
Staff: 1
Contact: Anita Loring, Sec.Gen.
Description: Professionals, parents, handicapped persons, and organizations in 60 countries. Seeks to stimulate research in cerebral palsy and promote related improvements and developments in early diagnosis, methods of treatment, and appropriate teaching and rehabilitation programs. Acts as the international coordinating organization for collection, distribution, and exchange of specialized information on cerebral palsy. Disseminates information about: architectural design for the handicapped; operation and equipment of a mobile visiting aid unit; aids and appliances; how to obtain entry visas for handicapped children emigrating with their families; medical matters; sex education; research on integration; publications for parents; alternative forms of physiotherapy; employment opportunities. Offers consulting services and referrals.
Formerly: Supersedes, World Commission of Cerebral Palsy of the International Society for Rehabilitation of the Disabled
Publication: Bulletin
Publication title: Bulletin
Meetings/Conventions: - semiannual meeting

International Chamber of Commerce - UK

14-15 Belgrave Sq., London, SW1X 8PS, England, UK
Tel: 44 207 823 2811
Fax: 44 207 2355447
Email: katharinehedger@iccorg.co.uk
Website: http://www.iccwbo.org
Founded: 1919
Members: 350
Staff: 4
Contact: Caroline McGrath, Policy Exec.
Description: Small, medium and large companies; multinationals; trade associations; chambers of commerce; academic institutions; law firms; banks. Promotes trade and investment and the free market system. Practical services to business include the ICC International Court of Arbitration; the ICC Institute of International Buisiness Law. ICC conferences and its triennial congress are held in cities throughout the world.

International Chamber of Shipping
ICS

12 Carthusian St., London, EC1M 6EZ, England, UK
Tel: 44 20 74178844
Fax: 44 20 74178877
Email: ics@marisec.org
Website: http://www.marisec.org
Founded: 1921
Members: 45
Contact: Mr. Chris Horrocks, Sec.Gen.
Description: International trade association for national associations of ship owners. Promotes interests of members worldwide in shipping matters such as documentation, insurance, marine safety, maritime law, navigation, and pollution control. Facilitates exchange of information and ideas. Represents members' concerns before governments and intergovernmental organizations throughout the world in an effort to formulate policies for national and international application. Produces a number of operational guides on safety and pollution prevention for the shipping industry. Maintains consultative status with the International Maritime Organization and other agencies of the United Nations; participates in the work of international organizations with common interests.
Formerly: International Shipping Conference

International Clematis Society

c/o Fiona Woolfenden, Sec.
3 Cuthberts Close, Waltham Cross, EN7 5RB, England, UK
Tel: 44 1992 636524
Email: clematis@dial.pipex.com
Website: http://www.clematisinternational.com
Founded: 1984
Members: 275
Contact: Klaus Korber, Pres.
Fee: £30
Membership Type: member
Description: Individuals worldwide who cultivate, research, or share an interest in the Clematis flower. Seeks to improve and extend the cultivation of Clematis; disseminate knowledge; stimulate scientific research and international cooperation and exchange. Provides a seed exchange program.
Publication: Journal
Publication title: Clematis International. Advertisements.
Meetings/Conventions: - annual tour

International Cocoa Organization
ICCO

22 Berners St., London, W1P 3DB, England, UK
Tel: 44 207 6373211
Fax: 44 207 6310114
Email: info@icco.org
Website: http://www.icco.org
Founded: 1973
Members: 42
Staff: 16
Contact: Dr. Jan Vingerhoets
Description: International organization of cocoa-exporting and importing countries established to implement the International Cocoa Agreement. (The ICCA was first negotiated in 1972 to bring stability to the world cocoa market by preventing excessive fluctuation in the price of cocoa, which adversely affects the long-term interests of producers and consumers.) Acts as a center for the collection and distribution of information on all aspects of the world cocoa economy. Compiles statistics. Is governed by the International Cocoa Council.
Library Subject: cocoa-related material
Library Type: by appointment only
Publication: Newsletter
Publication title: Cocoa Newsletter. Advertisements.
Publication title: ICCO Annual Report
Meetings/Conventions: - quarterly meeting

International Coffee Organization
ICO

22 Berners St., London, W1T 3DD, England, UK
Tel: 44 207 5808591
Fax: 44 207 5806129
Email: info@ico.org
Website: http://www.ico.org
Founded: 1962

Members: 61
Staff: 38
Contact: Mr. Celsius A. Lodder, Exec.Dir.
Description: Countries that export and import coffee. Seeks to further international cooperation among coffee-exporting and coffee-importing countries and to achieve fair prices for consumers and producers. Goals are: to promote economic development of coffee-producing countries; to bring supply and demand into reasonable balance; to avoid excessive fluctuation in coffee prices; to promote and increase the consumption of coffee.
Library Type: by appointment only
Publication: Newsletter
Publication title: Coffee Newsletter
Second publication: Report
Publication title: Country Coffee Profiles
Meetings/Conventions: - periodic meeting

International College of Psychosomatic Medicine
ICPM

Roehampton, London, SW15 5JJ, England, UK
Tel: 44 20 83924227
Fax: 44 20 83922632
Founded: 1970
Description: Advances principles of psychosomatic medicine worldwide, achieves highest standards of research.

International Color Vision Society

c/o Prof. J.D. Mollon
Dept. of Experimental Psychology, University of Cambridge, Downing St., Stafford, CB2 3EB, England, UK
Tel: 44 1782 583060
Fax: 44 7071 295038
Email: anne.kurtenbach@uni-tuebingen.de
Website: http://orlab.optom.unsw.edu.au/icvs
Founded: 1971
Members: 200
Contact: Andre Roth, Pres.
Description: Ophthalmologists, optometrists, physicists, physiologists, psychologists, and zoologists. Seeks to collaborate on the study of congenital and acquired color vision deficiencies.
Formerly: International Research Group on Coloru Vision Deficiencies
Publication: Newsletter
Publication title: Daltoniana
Publication title: Proceedings of the IRGCVD Symposia
Meetings/Conventions: - biennial - Exhibits.

International Commission for the History of Representative and Parliamentary Institutions
ICHRPI

c/o John Rogister
Dept. of History, 43-46 N. Bailey, Durham, DH1 3EX, England, UK
Tel: 44 191 3864299
Fax: 44 191 3744754
Founded: 1936
Members: 250
Contact: John Rogister, Pres.
Fee: £60
Description: Historians and political scientists interested in the research and study of the origin and development of worldwide parliamentary and representative institutions. Is concerned with the political theory and institutional practice of parliaments and estate

assemblies as well as the internal organization and the social and political backgrounds of these institutions.
Publication: Journal
Publication title: Parliaments, Estates & Representation. Advertisements.
Second publication: Monograph
Publication title: Studies presented to ICHRPI
Meetings/Conventions: - annual congress

International Commission on General Relativity and Gravitation
ICGRG

Queen Mary, University of London, Mile End Rd., London, E1 4NS, England, UK
Tel: 44 20 78825555
Fax: 44 20 89819587
Email: m.a.h.maccallum@qmul.ac.uk
Website: http://www.maths.qmul.ac.uk/grgsoc/
Founded: 1957
Description: Fosters the study of general relativity and gravitation (GRG).
Publication: Journal
Publication title: General Relativity & Gravitation

International Commission on Irrigation and Drainage - England

c/o Institution of Civil Engineers
1 Great George St., Westminster, London, SW1P 3AA, England, UK
Tel: 44 207 6652234
Fax: 44 207 9971325
Email: icid@ice.org.uk
Website: http://www.icid.org.uk
Founded: 1950
Members: 288
Contact: Tim Fuller, Sec.
Fee: £35
Membership Type: individual
Fee: £250
Membership Type: corporate
Description: Organizes a regular programme of meetings and events; periodic meetings for the presentation and discussion of technical papers; an annual weekend symposium; field events; an annual memorial lecture.
Publication: Newsletter
Publication title: News and Views

International Commission on Zoological Nomenclature
ICZN

Natural History Museum, Cromwell Rd., London, SW7 5BD, England, UK
Tel: 44 20 79425653
Email: iczn@nhm.ac.uk
Website: http://www.iczn.org
Founded: 1895
Members: 28
Staff: 3
Contact: Dr. A. Wakeham-Dawson, Exec.Sec.
Description: Zoologists, paleozoologists, scientists, and others interested in zoological nomenclature in 19 countries. Serves as a bureau to assist zoologists worldwide with problems in zoological nomenclature.

Publication: Journal
Publication title: Bulletin of Zoological Nomenclature
Second publication: Book
Publication title: International Code of Zoological Nomenclature
Meetings/Conventions: - triennial congress

International Committee for the Science of Photography
ICSP

Headstone Dr, Harrow, HA1 4TY, England, UK
Tel: 44 20 84274380
Founded: 1976
Description: Advances discussions on science and applications of photography, information recording, and related fields.

International Committee on Bionomenclature

Hendon, London, NW4 1DG, England, UK
Tel: 44 20 82034282
Fax: 44 20 82034282
Email: myconova@btinternet.com
Founded: 1995

International Committee on Seafarer's Welfare Office
ICSW

Cassiobury House, 11-19 Station Rd., Watford, WD17 1EZ, England, UK
Tel: 44 1923 222653
Fax: 44 1923 222663
Email: icsw@icsw.org.uk
Website: http://www.seafarerswelfare.org
Founded: 1980
Members: 24
Staff: 2
Contact: Andrew Elliott, Sec.
Fee: £500
Membership Type: subscription
Description: National agencies and international organizations in 14 countries concerned with maritime welfare. Promotes and fosters the provision of welfare services at sea and ashore for seafarers of all nationalities, races, colours, and creeds in line with the International Labour Organisation (ILO) instruments concerning seafarers' welfare. Identifies the need for facilities and services such as clubs, advisory centres, welfare officers, sporting events, and sports facilities as well as entertainment and cultural provisions for seafarers visiting ports. Provides advice and assistance to international, national, municipal and port authorities and agencies, shipowners, seafarers, welfare organisations, and other interested bodies. Maintains close working relationships with the ILO and acts as an advisory body to the ILO regarding the objectives of the ILO instruments concerning seafarers' welfare.
Publication: Brochure
Publication title: Port of the Seven Seas Directory 2000/2001
Second publication: Newsletter
Publication title: Seven Seas. Advertisements.
Meetings/Conventions: - annual seminar

International Communications Consultancy Organization
ICCO

3A Holnest Park House, Holnest, DT9 6HA, England, UK
Tel: 44 777 9807223
Email: chris@iccopr.com
Website: http://www.iccopr.com
Founded: 1986
Members: 25
Staff: 3
Contact: Chris McDowall, Sec.Gen.
Description: Corporate public relations bodies.
Formerly: International Committee of Public Relations Consultancies Associations
Publication: Directory. Advertisements.
Meetings/Conventions: Berlin Summit - biennial conference Berlin Germany

International Confederation of Art Dealers

20 Rutland Gate, London, SW7 1BD, England, UK
Tel: 44 20 75894128
Fax: 44 20 75819083
Email: secretary@cinoa.org
Website: http://www.cinoa.org
Founded: 1935
Members: 29
Staff: 1
Contact: Rudolf Otto, Pres.
Description: National trade associations and federations in 24 countries representing 5,000 individuals. Coordinates the art works of chambers, unions, associations, and federations of dealers. Contributes, by legal means, to artistic and economic expansion. Organizes exhibitions. Maintains inquiry and research bureau.
Publication title: List of Members
Second publication: Directory
Meetings/Conventions: Antiques Fair - annual trade show

International Conference on Social Science and Medicine

Falmer, Brighton, BN1 9RF, England, UK
Tel: 44 1273 66755
Founded: 1968

International Congress of African Studies

Thornbaugh St., School of Oriental and Asian Studies, Russell Sq., London, WC1H 0XG, England, UK
Tel: 44 207 3236035
Fax: 44 207 3236118
Email: iai@soas.ac.uk
Description: Institutions with African studies programs; educators and students in the field. Promotes advancement in the teaching of African studies. Facilitates communication and cooperation among members.

International Congress of Americanists
ICA

22 Bollin Hill, Wilmslow, SK9 4AW, England, UK
Tel: 44 1625 528000
Fax: 44 1625 539924
Email: david.fox@man.ac.uk
Founded: 1875
Members: 2000

Contact: David J. Fox, Sec.Gen.
Description: Archaeologists, anthropologists, historians, linguists, sociologists, political scientists, geographers, and other scholars interested in the study of man in the Americas. Conducts congresses, general sessions, specialized symposia, and formal and informal discussions of recent and continuing research. Honors distinguished scholars.
Publication: Proceedings
Publication title: Conference Proceedings
Second publication: Book
Publication title: Past and Present in the Americas
Meetings/Conventions: International Congress of Americanists - triennial conference - Exhibits. Santiago Chile

International Continence Society
ICS

c/o Victoria Rees, Admin.
Southmead Hospital, Bristol, BS10 5NB, England, UK
Tel: 44 117 9503510
Fax: 44 117 9503469
Email: vicky@icsoffice.org
Website: http://www.icsoffice.org
Founded: 1971
Members: 1500
Staff: 1
Contact: Vicky Rees, Sec.
Fee: £50
Membership Type: full
Description: Physicians, surgeons, nurses, physicists, physiotherapists, bio-engineers, and scientists. Promotes the study of the storage and voiding function of the lower urinary tract, its diagnosis, and the management of lower urinary tract dysfunction. Encourages research into pathophysiology, diagnostic techniques, and treatment.
Library Subject: incontinence
Library Type: not open to the public
Publication: Journal
Publication title: Neurourology and Urodynamics
Meetings/Conventions: - annual conference Florence Italy

International Cooperative and Mutual Insurance Federation
ICMIF

PO Box 21, Altrincham, WA14 4PD, England, UK
Tel: 44 161 9295090
Fax: 44 161 9295163
Email: icmif@icmif.org
Website: http://www.icmif.org
Founded: 1922
Members: 150
Staff: 21
Contact: Hans Dahlberg, CEO
Description: Promotes co-operation and collaboration between members; provides technical and financial assistance for the information and development of insurance organizations; conducts collaborative research projects; offers training in reinsurance; organizes technical seminars, workshops and study visits; publishes research reports, training manuals and regular newsletters; facilitates personnel exchanges; fosters alliances with related external organizations.
Publication: Directory
Publication title: Member Directory

Second publication: Newsletter
Publication title: Network
Meetings/Conventions: - biennial conference - Exhibits.

International Council of Jewish Women
ICJW

24-32 Stephenson Way, London, NW1 2JW, England, UK
Tel: 44 171 3888311
Fax: 44 171 3872110
Email: hq@icjw.demon.co.uk
Founded: 1912
Members: 1750000
Staff: 1
Contact: June Jacobs, Pres.
Description: National organizations linking nearly 1,500,000 Jewish women. Objectives are to: promote friendly relations, understanding, and mutual support among Jewish women; uphold and strengthen the bonds of Judaism; show solidarity with Israel and support the efforts of Israel to secure a just and lasting peace; economic security and social, educational, and cultural development in Israel; further the highest interests of humanity in the fields of international relations, government, social welfare and education; cooperate with national and international organizations working for goodwill among all peoples and for equal rights for humanity; supports the Universal Declaration of Human Rights of the United Nations, and encourages work for the improvement of the social, economic, and leagal status of all women under Jewish and civil law; encourage and assist in the education, training and use of volunteers.
Publication title: Cooking Time Around the World
Second publication: Directory
Publication title: Directory of ICJW Affiliates
Meetings/Conventions: - triennial convention

International Council of Marine Industry Associations
ICOMIA

Marine House, Thorpe Lea Rd., Egham, TW20 8BF, England, UK
Tel: 44 1784 223700
Fax: 44 1784 223705
Email: info@icomia.com
Website: http://www.icomia.com
Founded: 1966
Members: 35
Staff: 5
Contact: T.P.T. Donkin, Sec.Gen.
Description: Marine industry associations united to remove trade barriers and promote boating as an international recreational activity by establishing a medium for the exchange of information on common matters such as safety, service, quality, and marinas, in order to stimulate the sale and usage of boats and their equipment. Compiles statistics.
Library Subject: Environmental issues connected to the use of marine engines
Library Type: reference
Publication title: Boating Industry Statistics
Second publication: Yearbook. Advertisements.
Meetings/Conventions: - annual congress

International Council of Tanners
ICT

Leather Trade House, Kings Park Rd., Moulton Park, Northampton, NN3 6JD, England, UK
Tel: 44 1604 679917
Fax: 44 1604 679998
Email: sec@tannerscouncilict.org
Website: http://www.tannerscouncilict.org
Founded: 1926
Members: 33
Staff: 2
Contact: Mr. R. Paul Pearson, Sec.
Description: Leather trade associations united to promote the leather industry throughout the world. Fosters research and development in the industry.
Publication: Newsletter
Publication title: ICT Update
Second publication: Booklet
Publication title: International Glossary of Leather Terms
Meetings/Conventions: - annual meeting Hong Kong People's Republic of China

International Council on Mining and Metals
ICMM

19 Stratford Pl., 3rd Fl., London, W1C 1BQ, England, UK
Tel: 44 207 2904920
Email: info@icmm.com
Website: http://www.icmm.com
Founded: 1991
Members: 27
Staff: 11
Contact: Gary Nash, Sec.Gen.
Description: Producers of nonferrous and precious metals. Promotes environmentally responsible production and disposal of metals and increased use of recycling in the metal-producing industries. Disseminates information on environmentally sustainable mining and metal production.
Formerly: International Council on Metals and the Environment
Publication: Newsletter
Publication title: ICME Newsletter
Meetings/Conventions: - semiannual meeting

International Council on Monuments and Sites

10 Barley Mow Passage, London, W4 4PH, England, UK
Tel: 44 208 9946477
Fax: 44 208 7478464
Email: icomos-uk@icomos.org
Website: http://www.icomos.org/uk/
Founded: 1964
Members: 274
Staff: 2
Contact: Susan Denyer
Fee: £40
Membership Type: individual
Fee: £200
Membership Type: institutions
Description: Professionals interested in all aspects of architectural conservation. Works for higher standards in conservation. It also works for international education, and has special responsibilities for World Heritage Sites. Members enjoy a wide range of benefits throughout the world.
Library Type: by appointment only

International Cranial Association

478 Baker St., Enfield, EN1 3QS, England, UK
Tel: 44 20 83675561
Fax: 44 20 82026686
Founded: 1965
Members: 84
Staff: 8
Contact: W. Wright
Fee: £50
Membership Type: full
Description: Osteopaths, chiropractors, manipulative therapists. Holds a register of members for enquiries from the public; provides a training course each year; holds an annual conference for members and the public; provides a code of ethics.
Library Subject: cranial osteopathy and related subjects
Library Type: not open to the public
Formerly: Cranial Osteopathic Association
Publication: Newsletter. Advertisements.
Meetings/Conventions: - annual conference - Exhibits.

International Credit Insurance and Surety Association
ICISA

1-2 Castle Ln. , 2nd Fl., London, SW1E 6DR, England, UK
Tel: 44 20 72338880
Fax: 44 20 72338544
Email: secretariat@icisa.org
Website: http://www.icisa.org
Founded: 1928
Members: 50
Description: Insurance companies specializing in credit and guarantee insurance. Analyzes questions pertaining to credit and guarantee insurance and acts as a forum for international cooperation.
Formerly: International Credit Insurance Association
Meetings/Conventions: - annual meeting

International Cremation Federation
ICF

Brecon House, 2nd Fl., 16/16a Albion Pl., Maidstone, ME14 5DZ, England, UK
Tel: 44 1622 688293
Fax: 44 1622 686698
Email: rogrna@aol.com
Website: http://www.cremator.org
Founded: 1937
Members: 53
Staff: 1
Contact: Mr. R.N. Arber, Sec.Gen.
Fee: £720
Membership Type: general
Description: Cremation societies and organizations in 22 countries. Promotes the practice of cremation and disseminates information on its qualities from a hygienic, ethical, economic, and aesthetic viewpoint. Maintains information and documentation center.
Publication: Journal
Publication title: Pharos International. Advertisements.
Meetings/Conventions: - triennial congress - Exhibits.

International Dance Teachers' Association

International House, 76 Bennett Rd., Brighton, BN2 5JL, England, UK
Tel: 44 1273 685652
Fax: 44 1273 674388
Email: info@idta.co.uk
Website: http://www.idta.co.uk
Founded: 1967
Members: 6000
Staff: 32
Contact: Liz Murphy
Fee: £50
Membership Type: dance teachers
Description: Dance schools and commercial dance instructors who pass a qualifying examination in the United Kingdom. Strives to uphold the highest ideals of the dance profession. Organizes and grants the right to organize certified theatre dance championship competitions. Formulates and administers amateur grade and medal tests to measure students' progress. Offers low-cost equipment and services to support members' educational activities; sponsors competitions. Produces media advertisements promoting participation in dance programs.
Library Subject: dance
Library Type: not open to the public
Formerly: IDMA
Publication: Magazine
Publication title: Dance Teacher. Advertisements.
Publication title: The Year Book
Meetings/Conventions: Ballroom and Theatre Seminar - annual congress

International Democrat Union
IDU

2 Queen Anne's Gate, London, SW1H 9AA, England, UK
Tel: 44 20 72220847
Fax: 44 20 72225999
Email: rnormington@idu.org
Website: http://www.idu.org
Founded: 1983
Members: 41
Staff: 2
Contact: Richard Normington, Exec.Sec.
Description: Conservative and similar central right political parties in over 40 countries. Seeks to foster among member parties the common philosophy of a free, open, and democratic society emphasizing the rule of law, social justice, the role of the family, and a free competitive market economy. Encourages closer cooperation among member parties and its regional groups, the European Democrat Union, the Asia-Pacific Democrat Union the Americas Democrat Union, and the African Democratic Union/Dialogue Group. Provides a forum for the exchange of ideas and information.
Meetings/Conventions: Party Leaders Meeting - triennial meeting

International Dendrology Society
IDS

Hergest Estate Office, Kington, HR5 3EG, England, UK
Tel: 44 1544 232045
Fax: 44 1544 230160
Email: ids@hergest.kc3ltd.co.uk
Founded: 1952
Description: Promotes the enjoyment and study of trees, woody plants and shrubs.

International Dental Federation
IDF

7 Carlisle St., London, W1V 5RG, England, UK
Founded: 1900

International Egg Commission
IEC

89 Charterhouse St., 2nd Fl., London, EC1M 6HR, England, UK
Tel: 44 20 74903493
Fax: 44 20 74903495
Email: ieclondon@aol.com
Website: http://www.internationalegg.com
Founded: 1962
Contact: Neil Mackenzie, Sec.Gen.
Description: National organizations of commercial egg producers in 37 countries. Works to: improve egg statistics; estimate import-export trends; maintain cooperation with authorities in importing-exporting countries; examine means of increasing consumption; improve marketing techniques; standardize egg products; dispose of surpluses. Provides an international statistical service.
Meetings/Conventions: Production and Marketing Conference - annual conference

International Enamellers Institute
IEI

Wych House, 37 Avenue Rd., Astwood Bank, Redditch, B96 6AQ, England, UK
Tel: 44 1527 893031
Fax: 44 1527 460868
Email: info@iei-world.org
Website: http://www.iei-world.org
Founded: 1957
Members: 15
Contact: M.A. Collins, Sec.Gen.
Fee: £120
Membership Type: national institute
Description: Technical organizations representing the vitreous enamelling industry. Promotes the exchange of technical information and sponsors investigations into the testing, nomenclature, and developments in the enamelling industry. Offers advice on holding international conferences.
Meetings/Conventions: congress - Exhibits. Istanbul Turkey

International Farm Management Association
IFMA

Farm Management Unit, Univ. of Reading, PO Box 217, Reading, RG6 6AH, England, UK
Tel: 44 118 9351458
Fax: 44 118 9756467
Email: pjjames@waitrose.com
Founded: 1974
Members: 1000
Staff: 1
Contact: P.J. James, Hon.Sec./Treas.
Fee: £30
Description: Farmers, extension workers, academics, resource use planners, and managers in 68 countries concerned with the planning, production, and marketing in agriculture. Furthers the knowledge and understanding of farm business management and fosters the exchange of ideas and information about farm management theory and practice worldwide.
Publication: Proceedings

Publication title: Congress Proceedings
Second publication: Journal
Publication title: Journal of International Farm Management
Meetings/Conventions: - biennial congress Perth Australia

International Federation for Heat Treatment and Surface Engineering
IFHTSE

1 Carlton House Terrace, London, SW1Y 5DB, England, UK
Fax: 44 1483 222185
Email: ifhtwood@aol.com
Website: http://www.ifhtse.org
Founded: 1971
Members: 25
Staff: 2
Contact: Robert B. Wood, Sec.Gen.
Fee: £2000
Membership Type: association
Description: Federation of scientific and technological societies and associations worldwide. Promotes the study and development of the science, practice, and application of heat treating and surface engineering.
Publication: Newsletter
Publication title: IFHTSE Bulletin
Meetings/Conventions: - biennial congress

International Federation for Modern Languages and Literatures

c/o Prof. David A. Wells
Birkbeck Coll., Malet St., London, WC1E 7HX, England, UK
Tel: 44 20 76316103
Fax: 44 20 73833729
Email: d.wells@bbk.ac.uk
Website: http://vicu.utoronto.ca/staff/kushner/fillm.htm
Founded: 1928
Members: 18
Contact: Prof. David A. Wells, Sec.Gen.
Description: Federation of modern language and literature societies. Objectives are to establish permanent contact between literary scholars, to develop facilities for there work, and encourage their academic disciplines under the aegis of United Nations Educational, Scientific and Cultural Organization. Promotes the study of the history of medieval and modern languages and literatures.
Publication title: Acta
Meetings/Conventions: - triennial congress

International Federation for Theatre Research
IFTR

Department of European Languages and Cultures, University of Lancaster, Lancaster, LA1 4YN, England, UK
Tel: 44 1524 592664
Fax: 44 1524 593942
Email: d.whitton@lancaster.ac.uk
Website: http://www.firt-iftr.org
Founded: 1957
Members: 400
Contact: David Whitton, Sec.Gen.
Fee: £240
Membership Type: institutional
Fee: £90
Membership Type: individual

Description: Public and private organizations in over 40 countries devoting all or part of their activity to theatre research; individual researchers and other interested persons. Promotes and coordinates the study of theatre history; disseminates scholarly, technical, and other important works on theatre research; assists in the preservation of historic theatre buildings and theatre material. Aids theatrical researchers in obtaining facilities in libraries and museums; helps members obtain research grants. Promotes relations with other historical and artistic studies departments.
Publication: Bulletin
Publication title: News Bulletin
Second publication: Journal
Publication title: Theatre Research International. Advertisements.
Meetings/Conventions: - annual conference Jaipur India

International Federation for Tropical Medicine

Keppel St., London, WC1E 7HT, England, UK
Tel: 44 20 76368739
Email: g.targett@lshtm.ac.uk
Website: http://www.iftm.org

International Federation of Actors
FIA

Guild House, Upper Saint-Martin's Ln., London, WC2H 9EG, England, UK
Tel: 44 20 73790900
Fax: 44 20 73798260
Email: info@fia-actors.com
Website: http://www.fia-actors.com
Founded: 1952
Members: 100
Staff: 2
Contact: Dominick Luquer, Gen.Sec.
Fee: £1.79
Membership Type: in developed countries.88
Membership Type: in developing countries
Description: 100 trade unions of professional performers in 70 countries. Defends the artistic, economic, legal, and social interests of performers. Represents performers at intergovernmental and international meetings that national trade unions are not permitted to attend. Coordinates activities of affiliated cinema, radio, television, and theatre performers' unions to resist social slumping and ensure that the employment of actors respects the minimum conditions set by trade unions, national legislation and international treaties. Attempts to control commercial and other repeated uses of recordings made for specific media. Advocates: payment of residuals to individuals performing in multilateral television relays; protection against the broadcast or recording of performances without consent of the performer. Maintains Solidarity and Aid Fund for emergency assistance to performers' unions in dispute. Has organized symposia and seminars to examine the concerns of professional dancers, variety and circus artists, and performers working in commercials. Maintains consultative status with International Labor Organization, United Nations Educational, Scientific and Cultural Organization; and World Intellectual Property Organization.
Publication: Newsletter
Publication title: FIA Focus
Publication title: FIA - The First 30 Years
Meetings/Conventions: - quadrennial congress

International Federation of Air Line Pilots Associations
IFALPA

Interpilot House, Gogmore Ln., Chertsey, KT16 9AP, England, UK
Tel: 44 1932 571711
Fax: 44 1932 570920
Email: globalpilot@ifalpa.org
Website: http://www.ifalpa.org
Founded: 1948
Members: 94
Staff: 19
Contact: Cathy Bill, Exec.Dir.
Fee: £15.33
Membership Type: per capita
Description: National pilot associations representing more than 100,000 pilots. Promotes the development of a safe and orderly system of air transportation and the protection of the interests of airline pilots. Activities include: the regular exchange of information and ideas; examination of common problems; coordination of policies. Maintains team of accident investigation experts to assist pilots involved in accidents. Works to standardize legislation concerning hijacking. Conducts surveys. Maintains liaison with the International Civil Aviation Organization and the International Air Transport Association.
Publication: Magazine
Publication title: IFALPA Quarterly Review. Advertisements.
Second publication: Booklet
Publication title: Introducing IFALPA
Meetings/Conventions: - annual conference - Exhibits.

International Federation of Air Traffic Safety Electronics Association
IFATSEA

75-79 York Rd., London, SE1 7AQ, England, UK
Tel: 44 207 9026618
Fax: 44 207 9026667
Email: ifatsea@prospect.org.uk
Website: http://www.ifatsea.org
Founded: 1972
Members: 44
Contact: Iain Findlay, Exec.Sec.
Description: National electronic engineering associations representing electronic engineers in civil aviation who install, modify, and repair all ground safety equipment. Promotes safety, efficiency, and regularity in international air navigation. Furthers the development of electronics systems and seeks to maintain the safe and orderly flow of air traffic. Collects and disseminates information. Sponsors and supports legislation and regulations that increase and protect the safety of air navigation through the improvement of working conditions of air traffic safety electronics personnel.
Publication: Journal
Publication title: Navaire. Advertisements.
Meetings/Conventions: - annual assembly - Exhibits.

International Federation of Airworthiness
IFA

UK Secretariat, 14 Railway Approach, East Grinstead, RH19 1BP, England, UK
Tel: 44 1342 301788
Fax: 44 1342 317808
Email: sec@ifairworthy.org
Website: http://www.ifairworthy.org
Founded: 1975
Members: 122
Staff: 6
Contact: J.W. Saull, Exec.Dir.
Fee: £800
Membership Type: corporate
Description: Aerospace manufacturers, airlines, aircraft engineering and service facilities, international flight safety associations, professional aeronautical societies, and airworthiness authorities in 47 countries. Provides a forum for the exchange of experience and ideas on all areas of airworthiness including maintenance, design, and operations. Encourages a mutual understanding between airlines and airworthiness authorities. Organizes working parties to investigate specific problems in the aerospace industry.
Formerly: International Federation of Airworthiness Technology and Engineering
Publication title: Annual Report of Accounts
Publication title: Conference Proceedings
Meetings/Conventions: - annual conference - Exhibits.

International Federation of Anti-Leprosy Associations
ILEP

234 Blythe Rd., London, W14 0HJ, England, UK
Tel: 44 20 76026925
Fax: 44 20 73711621
Email: ilep@ilep.org.uk
Website: http://www.ilep.org.uk
Founded: 1966
Members: 16
Staff: 7
Contact: Dominique Martineau-Needham, Gen.Sec.
Description: International federation of autonomous non-governmental anti-leprosy organizations, most of which generate their income by raising funds from private donors to support more than a thousand projects in more than 90 countries. Members support medical, scientific, social, and humanitarian activities throughout the world to cure and rehabilitate people affected by leprosy and to prevent and eventually eradicate the disease.
Publication: Newsletter
Publication title: ILEP Connect
Meetings/Conventions: - annual general assembly

International Federation of Automotive Engineering Societies

1 Birdcage Walk, London, SW1H 9JJ, England, UK
Tel: 44 207 9731275
Fax: 44 207 9731285
Email: info@fisita.com
Website: http://www.fisita.com
Founded: 1948
Members: 169000
Contact: Mr. Ian Dickie, Ch.Exec.
Description: Mission is to help create efficient, affordable, safe and sustainable automotive transportation. By providing a global forum involving engineers together with representatives from industry, government, academia and standardization bodies, FISITA makes sure that everyone concerned with automotive transportation is working together towards the development of cleaner, safer, more sustainable vehicles.
Library Type: open to the public
Publication: Magazine

Publication title: Auto Technology. Advertisements.
Meetings/Conventions: World Automotive Congress - biennial congress Yokohama Japan

International Federation of Boat Show Organisers
IFBSO

c/o Val Thornborough
22 St. Johns Rd., Woking, GU21 7SA, England, UK
Tel: 44 1483 751506
Fax: 44 1483 751021
Email: info@ifbso.com
Website: http://www.ifbso.com
Founded: 1964
Members: 39
Contact: Val Thornborough, Sec.Gen.
Description: Promotes the interests of organizers of international boat shows.
Publication: Handbook
Meetings/Conventions: - annual congress

International Federation of Business and Professional Women
IFBPW

PO Box 568, Horsham, RH13 9ZP, England, UK
Tel: 44 1403 739343
Fax: 44 1403 734432
Email: members@bpwintl.com
Website: http://www.bpwintl.com
Founded: 1930
Members: 100000
Staff: 3
Contact: Antoinette Ruegg, Pres.
Fee: £3.5
Description: Promotes the status of women worldwide. Seeks higher business and professional standards.
Library Subject: Organization history, statistics on business and professional women, health, housing, crime, and development projects
Library Type: not open to the public
Publication: Book
Publication title: A Measure Filled
Second publication: Bulletin
Publication title: UN Bulletin
Meetings/Conventions: - triennial congress - Exhibits. Lucerne Switzerland

International Federation of Clinical Neurophysiology

c/o IFCN Secretariat
42 Canham Rd., London, W3 7SR, England, UK
Tel: 44 208 7433106
Fax: 44 208 7431010
Email: ifcn@ifcn.info
Website: http://www.ifcn.info
Contact: Wendy Holloway, contact
Description: Neurologists, physiologists, and other medical professionals; scientists and researchers. Seeks to advance knowledge in clinical neurophysiology and related fields; promotes development of more effective neurological diagnostic and surgical procedures. Serves as a clearinghouse on neurophysiology; conducts educational, training, and continuing professional development courses.

International Federation of Essential Oils and Aroma Trades
IFEAT

6 Catherine St., London, WC2B 5JJ, England, UK
Tel: 44 20 78362460
Fax: 44 20 78360580
Email: ifeatadministrator@fdf.org.uk
Website: http://www.ifeat.org
Founded: 1978
Members: 220
Staff: 2
Contact: Mrs. Julie Young
Fee: £350
Membership Type: company
Description: Producers, compounders, and traders of fragrance and flavor materials. Purpose is to promote and advance commercial interests of members of the aroma chemicals and essential oils industry throughout the world. Awards diplomas in perfumery to students completing one year correspondence course offered by Plymouth University (UK).
Publication: Newsletter
Publication title: IFEAT Newsletter
Meetings/Conventions: International Conference on Aromas & Essential Oils - annual international conference - Exhibits.

International Federation of Ex-Libris Societies

c/o Prof. W.E. Butler
Stratton Audley Park, Bicester, OX27 9AB, England, UK
Fax: 44 1869 277820
Email: webakademik@aol.com
Founded: 1966
Members: 42
Staff: 1
Contact: Prof. W.E. Butler, Exec.Sec.
Description: Promotes research on bookplates and encourages quality bookplate design.
Meetings/Conventions: - biennial congress Wels Australia

International Federation of Free Journalists
IFFJ

4 Overton Rd., London, N14 4SY, England, UK
Tel: 44 181 3602991
Founded: 1942
Members: 94
Contact: Krystyna Asipowicz, Gen.Sec.
Description: Journalists of Central and Eastern European origin in 7 countries. Promotes and defends the principles of a free and honest press; works in the defense of freedom of information and of human and national rights. Strives to raise standards and ethics of journalism and to foster cooperation among journalistic organizations. Provides articles to the British and East European press; sponsors periodic seminars on political, social, cultural, and economic problems in Eastern and Central Europe.
Meetings/Conventions: - biennial conference

International Federation of Gynecology and Obstetrics
FIGO

70 Wimpole St., London, W1G 8AX, England, UK
Tel: 44 207 2243270
Fax: 44 207 9350736
Email: figo@figo.org

Website: http://www.figo.org
Founded: 1954
Members: 102
Staff: 4
Contact: Prof. Giuseppe Benagiano, Sec.Gen.
Description: Objectives are to: promote and assist in the development of scientific and research work relating to all facets of gynecology and obstetrics; improve the physical and mental health of women, mothers, and their children; provide an exchange of information and ideas; improve teaching standards; promote international cooperation among medical bodies. Acts as liaison with World Health Organization and other international organizations.
Publication: Annual Report
Publication title: Figo Annual Report on the Results of Treatment of Gynecologic Cancer
Second publication: Newsletter
Publication title: Figo Newsletter
Meetings/Conventions: - triennial congress - Exhibits. Santiago Chile

International Federation of Hardware and Housewares Associations

225 Bristol Rd., Birmingham, B5 7UB, England, UK
Tel: 44 121 4466688
Fax: 44 121 4465215
Email: iha@ihaworldwide.org
Website: http://www.ihaworldwide.org
Founded: 1909
Members: 22
Staff: 1
Contact: Jonathan Swift, Gen.Sec.
Fee: £350
Membership Type: full
Description: National associations in 21 countries representing 75,000 firms dealing with wholesale and retail trade of hardware and household goods. Objectives are to: promote exchange of information among members; establish special committees on technical questions; coordinate advertising and sales promotions; further professional training and development. Performs market and motivation research and supports an international student exchange. Compiles statistics; operates placement service.
Library Type: reference
Publication: Newsletter
Publication title: IHA Bulletin
Meetings/Conventions: - biennial congress - Exhibits. Dublin Ireland

International Federation of Health Plans
IFHP

46 Grosvenor Gardens, London, SW1W 0EB, England, UK
Tel: 44 20 78819281
Fax: 44 20 77309234
Email: maria@ifhp.com
Website: http://www.ifhp.com
Founded: 1968
Members: 100
Staff: 3
Contact: Tom Sackville, Ch.Exec.
Fee: £310
Membership Type: associate
Description: Nongovernmental organizations involved in the execution of independent health care finance (100); associations of health funds (11) and individuals (26) in 20 countries. Promotes the study and development of independent health care services. Encourages research and the exchange of information. Operates conferences and meetings; information and research; sharing of information in cohesive network of member health funds. Offers study tours and educational programmes.
Formerly: International Federation of Voluntary Health Service Funds
Publication title: Conference Proceedings
Second publication: Directory
Publication title: Membership Directory
Meetings/Conventions: Amsterdam Biennial Conference - biennial conference - Exhibits. San Diego California United States

International Federation of Park and Recreation Administration
IFPRA

Globe House, Crispin Close, Caversham, Reading, RG4 7JS, England, UK
Tel: 44 118 9461680
Fax: 44 118 9461680
Email: ifpraworld@aol.com
Website: http://www.ifpra.org
Founded: 1957
Members: 456
Contact: Alan Smith, Gen.Sec.
Fee: £18
Membership Type: retired
Fee: £40
Membership Type: professional or supporting
Description: Individuals from the fields of parks, recreation, amenity, leisure, and related services; government departments, municipal and public authorities, universities, and scientific and educational institutions; national allied professional associations are affiliates. Objectives are to: establish a world coordinating center; collect and disseminate general and statistical information to members; promote the establishment of national associations for affiliation with the federation. Attempts to facilitate the exchange of students and professionals between countries and to adopt internationally acceptable training and qualification standards. Establishes special committees to study matters of professional interest; promotes research. study matters of professional interest; promotes research.
Publication: Bulletin
Publication title: IFPRA Bulletin. Advertisements.
Second publication: Proceedings
Meetings/Conventions: - annual congress

International Federation of Practitioners of Natural Therapeutics
IFPNT

21 Bingham Pl., London, W1M 3FH, England, UK
Tel: 44 20 79356933
Founded: 1963

International Federation of Professional Aromatherapists

82 Ashby Rd., Hinckley, LE10 1SN, England, UK
Tel: 44 1455 637987
Fax: 44 1455 890956
Email: admin@ifparoma.org
Website: http://www.ifparoma.org
Founded: 1990
Members: 2300
Staff: 3
Contact: Lisa Brown, Admin.

Description: Various categories of membership, the main group of which has trained with or meet the high standards required by ISPA accredited schools. Only full membership, members are entitled to use the letter MISPA. To develop and stimulate high professional standards, through qualification and practice. Accredited schools across the country. Local practitioner lists and public hot-line service.
Formerly: Formed by Merger of, International Society of Professional Aromatherapists, International Federation of Aromotherapists and Register of Qualified Aromatherpists
Publication: Journal
Publication title: Aromatherapy World. Advertisements.
Meetings/Conventions: - annual conference - Exhibits.

International Federation of Reflexologists

Surrey, Croydon, CRO 1EF, England, UK
Tel: 44 181 6679458
Fax: 44 181 6499291
Email: ifr44@aol.com
Website: http://www.reflexology-ifr.com
Description: Promotes reflexology therapist profession enforcing a code of ethics and practice.

International Federation of Settlements and Neighborhood Centers - USA
IFS

Winchester House, Crammer Rd., London, SW9 6EJ, England, UK
Contact: Carol R. Lubih
Description: Community centers, neighborhood houses and settlements, and interested individuals. Promotes forging of links between communities worldwide. Encourages cooperation among similar organizations across cultural, national, and economic boundaries.
Publication: Newsletter
Publication title: IFS Newsletter
Meetings/Conventions: conference

International Federation of Shipmasters' Associations
IFSMA

202 Lambeth Rd., London, SE1 7JY, England, UK
Tel: 44 207 2610450
Fax: 44 207 9289030
Email: hq@ifsma.org
Website: http://www.ifsma.org
Founded: 1974
Members: 8500
Staff: 3
Contact: Capt. R. MacDonald, Sec.Gen.
Fee: £10
Membership Type: association
Fee: £40
Membership Type: individual
Description: National associations of qualified seagoing master mariners and shipmasters in 44 countries. Promotes safety at sea and serves as professional representative at meetings of the International Maritime Organization.
Library Subject: safety at sea, protection of marine environment
Library Type: by appointment only
Publication: Papers
Publication title: Conference Papers
Second publication: Newsletter

Publication title: IFSMA Newsletter - The International Shipmasters Link
Meetings/Conventions: - annual general assembly - Exhibits.

International Federation of Societies of Cosmetic Chemists
IFSCC

G.T. House, 24/26 Rothesay Rd., Luton, LU1 1QX, England, UK
Tel: 44 1582 726661
Fax: 44 1582 405217
Email: ifscc.scs@btconnect.com
Website: http://www.ifscc.org
Founded: 1959
Members: 42
Staff: 2
Contact: Mrs. L.K. Weston, Gen.Sec.
Description: National societies representing over 14,000 cosmetic chemists or cosmetic scientists throughout the world. Fosters advancement in cosmetic science by encouraging fundamental research in industry and academia; provides information and documentation. Works to develop standardized procedures for analyses of raw materials and finished products and for estimating efficiency of products.
Publication: Magazine
Publication title: IFSCC Magazine. Advertisements.
Meetings/Conventions: - semiannual conference - Exhibits.

International Federation of Teratology Societies
IFTS

Dept. of Anatomy & Developmental Biology, St. George's Hospital Medical School, University of London, Cramner Terrace, London, SW17 0RE, England, UK
Tel: 44 208 7252830
Fax: 44 208 6727098
Email: ifts@sghms.ac.uk
Founded: 1983
Members: 2600
Contact: Dr. W.S. Webster, Sec.
Description: Individuals from the European Teratology Society, Teratology Society, Japanese Teratology Society, and Australian Teratology Society. Fosters international cooperation, increased understanding, and a greater interest in the global aspects of teratology. (Teratology is the study of congenital malformations and serious deviations from normal characteristics.) Encourages information exchange and collaboration with health and charitable agencies. Provides education to organizations and individuals interested in prevention and treatment of birth defects. Supports research in the area of teratology.
Meetings/Conventions: - triennial conference

International Federation of the Periodical Press
FIPP

Queens House, 55/56 Lincoln's Inn Fields, London, WC2A 3LJ, England, UK
Tel: 44 207 4044169
Fax: 44 207 4044170
Email: info@fipp.com
Website: http://www.fipp.com
Founded: 1925
Members: 120
Staff: 3
Contact: Don Kummerfeld, Pres.

Description: National associations of periodical publishers (37) and individual periodical publishing companies (93) in 31 countries. Organized to: support press freedom; protect and represent the interests of its members before international bodies; compile and distribute information internationally; promote the image of the periodical press as an advertising medium; encourage the adoption of uniform standards. Maintains liaison with United Nations Educational, Scientific and Cultural Organization, International Chamber of Commerce, and Universal Postal Union.
Library Subject: all aspects of periodical publishing
Library Type: open to the public
Publication: Paper
Publication title: FIPP/FAEP Environment Position Paper
Publication title: FIPP Membership Directory
Meetings/Conventions: - biennial congress - Exhibits.

International Federation of the Phonographic Industry - England
IFPI

IFPI Secretariat, 54 Regent St., London, W1B 5RE, England, UK
Tel: 44 207 8787900
Fax: 44 207 8787950
Email: info@ifpi.org
Website: http://www.ifpi.org
Founded: 1933
Members: 1319
Contact: Jay Berman, Chm./Chief Exec.
Description: Producers and distributors of phonograms and videograms in 72 countries. Promotes the interests of members through the use of statutes, case law, contracts, and agreements. Represents members on national and international copyright issues; coordinates anti-piracy actions. Compiles statistical information on the international recording industry. Provides industry contacts and advisory services.
Library Subject: Copyright and other intellectual property matters.
Library Type: reference
Publication title: Annual Review
Second publication: Newsletter
Publication title: Newsletter
Meetings/Conventions: - annual meeting

International Federation of Tour Operators
IFTO

170 High St., Lewes, BN7 1YE, England, UK
Tel: 44 1273 477722
Fax: 44 1273 483746
Founded: 1970
Members: 18
Contact: Alan Flook, Sec.
Description: National associations of tour operators. Offers member associations the opportunity for joint action in matters of mutual interest. Acts as liaison among national and international organizations in areas such as air licensing, airport and route charges, tourist and hotel legislation, and facilities.
Meetings/Conventions: - quarterly meeting

International Federation on Aging - European Office
IFA

1268 London Rd., London, SW16 4EJ, England, UK
Tel: 44 20 86798000
Fax: 44 20 86796069
Founded: 1973

International Feed Industry Federation
IFIF

214 Prestbury Rd., Cheltenham, GL52 3ER, England, UK
Tel: 44 1242 267702
Fax: 44 1242 267701
Email: roger.gilbert@ifif.org
Founded: 1987
Contact: Roger Gilbert, Sec.Gen.
Description: Feed companies, industry associations and federations, financial institutions, and suppliers to the feed industry. Promotes growth and development of the global feed industry. Gathers and disseminates information on the feed industries; represents members' interests before government agencies and industrial and international trade organizations. Compiles statistics.
Publication: Newsletter
Publication title: IFIF News
Meetings/Conventions: - periodic conference

International Fertiliser Society - England

PO Box 4, York, Y032 5YS, England, UK
Tel: 44 1904 492700
Fax: 44 1904 492700
Email: secretary@fertiliser-society.org
Website: http://www.fertiliser-society.org
Founded: 1947
Members: 450
Contact: C.J. Dawson, Sec.
Fee: £65
Membership Type: ordinary
Description: Agronomists, environmentalists, chemists, engineers, journalists, equipment manufacturers, contractors, marketing and purchasing managers. Provides a medium for the discussion of scientific, technical, economic and environmental aspects of production, use and application of fertilisers.
Formerly: Fertiliser Society - England
Publication: Proceedings
Publication title: Proceedings of the International Fertiliser Society
Meetings/Conventions: - annual conference

International Fish Meal and Fish Oil Organization

2 College Yard, Lower Dagnall St., St. Albans, AL3 4PA, England, UK
Tel: 44 1727 842844
Fax: 44 1727 842866
Email: secretariat@iffo.org.uk
Website: http://www.iffo.org.uk
Founded: 1960
Members: 19
Staff: 9
Contact: Dr. Stuart M. Barlow, Dir.Gen.
Description: National fish meal and oil producing organizations and companies in 18 countries. Organizes and finances the interchange of production and trade statistics. Conducts research and promotes development. Acts as a network for technical and scientific information. Represents the industry before international organizations and users of fish meal and oil.
Library Subject: Fish meal, fish oil research
Library Type: not open to the public
Formerly: International Fish Meal and Oil Manufacturer Association
Publication: Booklet
Publication title: Digest of Selected Statistics
Second publication: Proceedings
Publication title: Record of Proceedings of Annual Conference
Meetings/Conventions: - annual conference

International Flight Catering Association

Surrey Place, Mill Lane, Godalming, GU7 1EY, England, UK
Tel: 44 1483 419449
Fax: 44 1483 419780
Email: ifca@associationservices.co.uk
Website: http://www.ifcanet.com
Contact: A. Todd, Sec.Gen.

International Food Information Service Publishing
IFISP

Lane End House, Shinfield Rd., Shinfield, Reading, RG2 9BB, England, UK
Tel: 44 1189 883895
Fax: 44 1189 885065
Email: ifis@ifis.org
Website: http://www.ifis.org
Founded: 1968
Staff: 30
Contact: Dr. John Metcalf, Mng.Dir.
Description: Gathers and disseminates information on food science and technology.
Publication: Journal
Publication title: Food Science and Technology Abstracts

International Fur Trade Federation
IFTF

PO Box 495, Weybridge, KT13 8WD, England, UK
Tel: 44 1932 232866
Fax: 44 1932 232656
Email: pressoffice@iftf.com
Website: http://www.iftf.com/
Founded: 1949
Members: 33
Contact: Mrs. J. Bailey, Exec.Dir.
Description: Associations that trade, manufacture, or process fur skins. Seeks to: promote and organize joint action; collect statistics and other information; promote conservation of species scientifically proven to be threatened; develop and protect the fur trade. Seeks to establish commercial trade uniformity. Appoints or acts as arbitrator in disputes.
Publication: Newsletter
Publication title: Newsletter

International General Produce Association

Gafta House, 6 Chapel Pl., Rivington St., London, EC2A 3SH, England, UK
Tel: 44 20 78149666
Fax: 44 20 78148383
Email: igpa@gafta.com
Website: http://www.igpa.com
Founded: 1876
Members: 100
Staff: 16
Contact: Pamela Kirby Johnson, Sec.
Description: Traders in general produce.
Meetings/Conventions: - annual meeting

International Glaciological Society
IGS

Lensfield Rd., Cambridge, CB2 1ER, England, UK
Tel: 44 1223 355974
Fax: 44 1223 336543
Email: int_glaciol_soc@compuserve.com
Website: http://www.igsoc.org/
Founded: 1936
Members: 850
Staff: 3
Contact: Simon Ommanney, Sec.Gen.
Fee: £60
Membership Type: full
Fee: £30
Membership Type: junior
Description: Persons with a scientific, practical, or general interest in any aspect of ice and snow study; membership comprises scientists and others from 33 countries in such fields as physics, meteorology, oceanography, geology, geography, engineering, and chemistry. The society also has 500 libraries as subscribers. Aim is to stimulate research and interest in the practical and scientific problems of snow and ice. Conducts symposia, discussions, and meetings.
Library Subject: Glaciology.
Library Type: not open to the public
Formerly: British Glaciological Society
Publication: Journal
Publication title: Annals of Glaciology
Second publication: Newsletter
Publication title: Ice
Meetings/Conventions: Fast Glacier Flow - semiannual symposium

International Glaucoma Association
IGA

108C Warner Rd., Camberwell Hill, London, SE5 9HQ, England, UK
Tel: 44 20 77373265
Fax: 44 20 73465929
Email: info@iga.org.uk
Website: http://www.iga.org.uk
Founded: 1974
Members: 14500
Staff: 9
Contact: David Wright, Chief Exec.
Fee: £12.5
Membership Type: standard
Fee: £35
Membership Type: professional
Description: Glaucoma patients. Seeks to educate the public about glaucoma, its causes, detection, and treatment. Provides patients, doctors, opticians, optometrists, and others a forum for the exchange of ideas on glaucoma. Supports research; bestows grants. Conducts surveys; disseminates information.
Formerly: Glaucoma Association
Publication: Booklet
Publication title: Glaucoma 98 - A Guide for Patients
Second publication: Newsletter
Meetings/Conventions: meeting

International Grains Council
IGC

1 Canada Sq., Canary Wharf, London, E14 5AE, England, UK
Tel: 44 207 5131122
Fax: 44 207 5130630
Email: igc-fac@igc.org.uk
Website: http://www.igc.org.uk
Founded: 1949
Members: 29
Staff: 18
Contact: Mr. G.A. Denis, Exec.Dir.

Description: Administers the Grains Trade Convention (1995), which is part of the International Grains Agreement (1995), an intergovernmental agreement whose main objectives are international cooperation in all aspects of grains, the expansion of grains trade and its freest possible flow, stability of international grains markets and enhanced food security. Provides a forum for the exchange of information and discussion of members' concerns regarding grains.
Library Type: not open to the public
Formerly: International Wheat Council
Publication title: Grain Market Report
Publication title: Report of the Council
Meetings/Conventions: IGC Grains Conference - annual conference

International Guild of Artists
IGA

Briargate, 2 The Brambles, Ilkley, LS29 9DH, England, UK
Tel: 44 1943 609075
Fax: 44 1943 603753
Website: http://www.britpaint.co.uk
Founded: 1981
Members: 150
Contact: Margaret Simpson, Dir.
Fee: £100
Membership Type: selected artists
Description: Professional artists. Provides assistance and support to members. Operates a telephone helpline to answer members' art questions. Fosters communication among members.
Publication: Catalog
Publication title: Exhibition Catalogue. Advertisements.
Meetings/Conventions: - quarterly show - Exhibits. Ilkley UK

International Harbour Masters' Association
IHMA

c/o Mr. Mike Hadley
Maritime Centre, Northney Marina, Hayling Island, PO11 ONH, England, UK
Tel: 44 1329 832771
Fax: 44 1329 834975
Email: secretary.ihma@harbourmaster.org
Website: http://www.harbourmaster.org
Founded: 1996
Members: 300
Staff: 3
Contact: Mr. Mike Hadley, Sec.
Fee: £102
Membership Type: full member
Fee: £54
Membership Type: associate
Description: Harbour masters from ports large and small, publicly and privately owned. Provides up-to-date, hands-on expertise in a range of maritime operations, including: safety of navigation, vessel traffic control, shipping movements, port management, protection of the marine environment, the ship/port interface, cargo handling, safety management and training, and the good practice of seamanship in port and harbor environs.
Library Subject: port and harbour management, safety of navigation
Library Type: open to the public
Publication: Newsletter
Publication title: Harbour Master. Advertisements.
Meetings/Conventions: - biennial congress - Exhibits. Bremen Germany

International Headache Society
IHS

Oakwood, 9 Willowmead Dr., London, SKIO 4BU, England, UK
Tel: 44 1625 828663
Fax: 44 1625 828494
Email: rosemary@ihs.u-net.com
Website: http://www.i-h-s.org
Founded: 1982
Description: Conducts research into the causes, mechanisms, treatment and other aspects of headache.

International Headquarters of the Salvation Army
IHSA

c/o Gen. John Larsson
101 Queen Victoria St., London, EC4P 4EP, England, UK
Tel: 44 20 73320101
Fax: 44 20 72364981
Email: the_general@salvationarmy.org
Website: http://www.salvationarmy.org
Founded: 1865
Members: 1500000
Staff: 125000
Contact: Gen. John Larsson
Description: Ordained ministers, volunteers, and others donating time to religious and social welfare activities in 109 countries and colonies. Christian church and charity; embraces Christian ideals and high moral standards; seeks to minister to the physical, spiritual, and emotional needs of mankind. Serves to propagate Christianity, provide education, relieve poverty, and establish charitable projects. Works for the betterment of the poor through evangelistic and social enterprises including alcohol and drug rehabilitation programs, hostels for the homeless, children's homes, schools, hospitals, clinics, and institutes for the blind and handicapped. Preaches the Gospel and publishes in over 175 languages. Cooperates with international relief agencies and governments.
Library Type: reference
Publication: Newsletter
Publication title: All the World
Publication title: Salvation Army YearBook
Meetings/Conventions: - periodic international conference - Exhibits.

International Health Exchange
IHE

1st Floor, 134 Lower Marsh, London, SE1 7AE, England, UK
Tel: 44 207 6203333
Fax: 44 207 6202277
Email: info@ihe.org.uk
Founded: 1980
Members: 1200
Staff: 8
Contact: Ivan Scott, Dir.
Fee: £20
Membership Type: student
Fee: £27
Membership Type: ordinary
Description: Health care professionals and others working health in humanitarian relief and development programs worldwide. Recruits health workers for relief and development programs. Offers career advice and training program.
Publication: Magazine
Publication title: Health Exchange Magazine. Advertisements.
Second publication: Annual Report
Meetings/Conventions: - periodic board meeting UK

International Humanist and Ethical Union
IHEU

47 Theobald's Rd., London, WC1X 8SP, England, UK
Tel: 44 207 8314817
Fax: 44 207 4048641
Email: humanism@iheu.org
Website: http://www.iheu.org/
Founded: 1952
Members: 4000000
Staff: 3
Contact: Mr. Gogineni, Exec.Dir.
Description: Members of humanist and ethical organizations in 37 countries, which work against authoritarian traditions and encourage activities in the interest of a more humane world. Working parties coordinate activities in the field of moral education and human rights. Maintains an active part in issues of education, racism, pollution, mental health, and human rights through its relations with the Council of Europe, the United Nations Educational, Scientific and Cultural Organization, UNICEF, and the United Nations. Engages in development work in various parts of the world including Africa, Asia, the European Union, and Latin America through the Humanistic Institute for Cooperation with Developing Countries. Africa, Asia, the European Union, and Latin America through the Humanistic Institute for Cooperation with Developing Countries.
Publication: Newsletter
Publication title: International Humanist News
Meetings/Conventions: - periodic conference

International Institute for Conservation of Historic and Artistic Works
IIC

6 Buckingham St., London, WC2N 6BA, England, UK
Tel: 44 207 8395975
Fax: 44 207 9761564
Email: iicon@compuserve.com
Website: http://www.iiconservation.org
Founded: 1950
Members: 4000
Staff: 2
Contact: David Bomford, Sec.Gen.
Fee: £30
Membership Type: Individual
Fee: £60
Membership Type: Institution
Description: Restorers and conservators in private or museum practice, scientists, educators, and collection managers; supporting institutions include museums, galleries, libraries, universities, and research establishments. Provides a permanent organization for coordinating and improving the knowledge, methods, and working standards needed to protect and preserve historic and artistic works.
Publication: Newsletter
Publication title: Bulletin
Second publication: Proceedings
Publication title: Conference Proceedings
Meetings/Conventions: - biennial conference Bilbao Spain

International Institute for Environment and Development

3 Endsleigh St., London, WC1H 0DD, England, UK
Tel: 44 207 3882117
Fax: 44 207 3882826
Email: info@iied.org
Website: http://www.iied.org

Founded: 1971
Staff: 55
Contact: Nigel Cross, Exec.Dir.
Description: Aims to provide expertise and leadership in researching and achieving sustainable development at local, national, regional, and global levels. In alliance with others, seeks to help shape a future that ends global poverty and delivers and sustains efficient and equitable management of the world's natural resources.
Library Subject: national environmental planning
Library Type: open to the public
Formerly: International Institute for Environmental Affairs
Publication: Journal
Publication title: Environment and Urbanisation
Second publication: Newsletter
Publication title: Haramata
Meetings/Conventions: Equity for a Small Planet? Making Globalization Work - annual conference

International Institute for Strategic Studies
IISS

Arundel House, 13-15 Arundel St., Temple Place, London, WC2R 3DX, England, UK
Tel: 44 20 73797676
Fax: 44 20 78363108
Email: iiss@iiss.org
Website: http://www.iiss.org
Founded: 1958
Members: 2140
Staff: 50
Contact: Dr. John Chipman, Dir.
Fee: £175
Description: Journalists, politicians, businesspersons, academic personnel, retired service officers, economists, and interested others in 80 countries; associate members are active service officers and government officials; corporate members are newspapers, universities, television stations, embassies and government ministries, service colleges, and other corporate entities. Prepares studies on topical strategic subjects.
Library Subject: International security
Library Type: reference
Publication: Papers
Publication title: Adelphi Papers
Publication title: Military Balance

International Institute of Communications
IIC

3rd Fl., Westcott House, 35 Portland Pl., London, W1B 1AE, England, UK
Tel: 44 207 3239622
Fax: 44 207 3239623
Email: enquiries@iicom.org
Website: http://www.iicom.org
Founded: 1968
Members: 1500
Staff: 8
Contact: Gerry Jayasuriya, Sec.
Description: Broadcasters, academics, professionals, technologists, journalists and others; broadcasting organizations, telecommunications, computer and electronic firms, news agencies, corporations, foundations, and universities. Objectives are the provision of an independent forum for those concerned with present use and future development of communication and the promotion and dissemination of research and policy studies concerned with the

impact of electronic media on society and with the economic, social, legal, and political implications of contemporary communication technology. Examines issues such as ownership, control of the media, cultural ecology, international telecommunications structures, communications, and development.
Library Subject: Communications
Library Type: reference
Publication title: InterMedia
Publication title: Reports of Seminars
Meetings/Conventions: - annual conference

International Institute of Reflexology
IIR

255 Turleigh, Bradford-on-Avon, BA15 2HG, England, UK
Tel: 44 1225 865899
Fax: 44 1225 865899
Email: reflexology_uk@hotmail.com
Website: http://www.reflexology-uk.co.uk
Contact: Hildegard Fdwards, VP
Description: Dedicated to professional standards in reflexology based on the Ingham Method of Foot Reflexology.
Meetings/Conventions: seminar

International Institute of Risk and Safety Management
IIRSM

70 Chancellors Rd., London, W6 9RS, England, UK
Tel: 44 20 86005538
Fax: 44 20 87411349
Email: enquiries@iirsm.org
Website: http://www.iirsm.org
Founded: 1975
Members: 6600
Contact: Julie Silvester
Fee: £40
Membership Type: individuals
Description: Membership in various grades, is open to all individuals who have an interest in occupational health, safety and risk management. Benefits include Newletters, Magazines, Designatory letters (where qualified). health and safety information service; seminars and events.
Publication: Newsletter
Publication title: Health & Safety Managers Newsletter

International Institute of Security

The Business Centre, 57 Torquay Rd., Ste. 8, Paignton, TQ3 3DT, England, UK
Tel: 44 1803 663275
Fax: 44 1803 663251
Email: iisec@btconnect.com
Website: http://www.iisec.co.uk
Founded: 1968
Members: 750
Staff: 2
Contact: P.J. Stanbridge, Company Sec.
Description: Membership is obtainable by examination. Examinations are jointly accredited, Certificate in Security Management 7251 and 7252, with the City & Guilds of London Institute. The professional body specialising in the provision of security measures against loss through theft, fire, fraud, other damage and waste.
Publication: Pamphlet

International Institute of Social Economics
IISE

Enholmes Hall, Patrington, Hull, HU12 0PR, England, UK
Tel: 44 1964 630033
Fax: 44 1964 631716
Email: n24@dial.pipe.com
Founded: 1972
Members: 550
Staff: 2
Contact: Prof. Barrie O. Pettman, Dir.
Description: Persons experienced in, studying, or interested in social economics. Aims are to: assist in the development of social economics as a recognized discipline with a scientific foundation and accepted standards of qualifications and ethics; enhance communication and the exchange of ideas; help social economists to understand and apply newly developed ideas and techniques and translate them into practical terms; aid and motivate colleges and universities to develop and maintain sound and adequate social economics teaching. Seeks to broaden the discipline of social economics through research, publication, and meetings. Conducts comparative studies concerning: the definition of social economics; economic systems; population growth and its ramific ations; changes in the workforce; income distribution and policy. Develops relationships with international bodies associated with specific facets of social economics; makes presentations to government departments and related institutions to improve the quality and extent of statistical sources.
Library Type: reference
Publication: Journal
Publication title: International Journal of Social Economics
Meetings/Conventions: - annual conference

International Institute of Tropical Agriculture
IITA

26 Dingwall Road, Croydon, CR9 3EE, England, UK
Tel: 44 20 86869031
Fax: 44 20 86818583
Email: iita@cgiar.org
Website: http://www.iita.org/
Founded: 1967

International Jewish Vegetarian Society
IVJS

Bet Teva, 855 Finchley Rd., Golders Green, London, NW11 8LX, England, UK
Tel: 44 20 84550692
Fax: 44 20 84551465
Email: ijvs@yahoo.com
Founded: 1966
Members: 5000
Contact: Shirley Labelda, Exec. Officer
Fee: £12
Description: Jewish vegetarians in 65 countries; nonvegetarians sympathetic to the ideas of the society and concerned with the promotion of natural health and vegetarianism through social activities. Objectives are to: promote action to advance ethical vegetarianism as related to Jewish religious teachings; advocate living on pure and wholesome natural foods; foster the concept of respect for all life. Organizes cultural and social activities. Provides information on health, travel, and facilities offering vegetarian cuisine. Advocates vegetarianism as a solution to world hunger; conducts classes on topics such as cruelty to animals, cookery, religious precepts, health, diet, travel and nutrition.

Library Type: reference
Publication: Newsletter
Publication title: Jewish Vegetarian. Advertisements.
Second publication: Book
Publication title: Jewish Vegetarian Cooking
Meetings/Conventions: - semiannual conference

International Language Union
Victoria Rd., Harrogate, HG2 O1J, England, UK
Founded: 1908

International Law Association
ILA
Charles Clore House, 17 Russell Sq., London, WC1B 5DR, England, UK
Tel: 44 20 73232978
Fax: 44 20 73233580
Email: info@ila-hq.org
Website: http://www.ila-hq.org
Founded: 1873
Members: 3500
Staff: 1
Contact: Juliet Fussell
Description: Lawyers and representatives in 85 countries active in the shipping, commercial, and banking industries. Fosters interest in the study, advancement and unification of international public and private law and comparative law, and in resolving legal conflicts. Conducts seminars.
Publication: Proceedings
Publication title: Conference Reports
Second publication: Book
Publication title: The Effect of Independence on Treaties
Meetings/Conventions: - biennial conference

International Lead and Zinc Study Group
ILZSG
2 King St., London, SW1Y 6QP, England, UK
Tel: 44 20 78398550
Fax: 44 20 79304635
Email: root@ilzsg.org
Website: http://www.ilzsg.org
Founded: 1959
Members: 28
Staff: 7
Contact: Donald Smale, Sec.Gen.
Description: Representatives of governments and ministerial and industry advisers in 28 countries. Provides for intergovernmental consultation on international trade in lead and zinc and for studies of the world situation in lead and zinc, particularly the supply and demand position and its probable development. Compiles statistics.
Library Subject: lead and zinc
Library Type: reference
Publication: Directory
Publication title: World Directory: Lead and Zinc Mines
Second publication: Directory
Publication title: World Directory: Primary and Secondary Lead Plants
Meetings/Conventions: - annual conference

International League for the Protection of Horses
ILPH
Anne Colvin House, Snetterton, NR16 2LP, England, UK
Tel: 44 870 8701927
Fax: 44 870 9041927
Email: hq@ilph.org
Website: http://www.ilph.org/
Founded: 1927
Contact: John Smales, Ch.Exec.
Description: Works to prevent ill treatment of horses exported to Europe for slaughter.

International Lifeboat Federation
ILF
Royal National Lifeboat Institution, W Quay Rd., Poole, BH15 1HZ, England, UK
Tel: 44 1202 663152
Fax: 44 1202 663306
Email: iventham@rnli.org.uk
Website: http://www.lifeboats.org
Founded: 1924
Members: 85
Staff: 3
Contact: Ian Ventham, Sec.
Description: Government-organized and voluntary lifeboat services. Activities include the design and operation of lifeboats, search and rescue at sea, communications, and medical, financial, and training programs. Demonstrates boats and equipment. Exchanges information regarding new methods of rescue.
Library Type: reference
Publication: Proceedings
Publication title: Conference Report
Second publication: Magazine
Publication title: Lifeboat International
Meetings/Conventions: - quadrennial conference Cape Town Republic of South Africa

International Marine Contractors Association
Carlyle House, 235 Vauxhall Bridge Rd., London, SW1 1EJ, England, UK
Tel: 44 20 79318171
Fax: 44 20 79318935
Email: imca@imca-int.com
Website: http://www.imca-int.com
Founded: 1995
Members: 195
Staff: 6
Contact: Hugh Williams, Chief Exec.
Description: Companies active in the offshore marine contracting industry, including vessel owners/operators, and marine and underwater contractors. Represents members on an international basis with particular reference to improvements in safety standards.
Formerly: Absorbed, The AODC
Publication: Newsletter

International Maritime Industries Forum
IMIF
c/o The Baltic Exchange
38 St. Mary, London, EC3A 8BH, England, UK
Tel: 44 20 79296429
Fax: 44 20 79296430
Email: imif@btconnect.com

Website: http://web.ukonline.co.uk/imif/main.htm
Founded: 1975
Members: 130
Contact: J.G. Davis, Chm.
Fee: £950
Membership Type: boardroom level
Fee: £475
Membership Type: observer status
Description: Shipowners and builders, shipbreakers, oil companies, insurance companies, classification societies, and bankers in 25 countries. Seeks to: maintain a healthy commercial and financial climate for all sectors of shipping, including ownership, operation, construction, and international trade; encourage discussions of mutual interest; foster change and stimulate action to benefit the maritime industry. Strives to upgrade the standards of ships, port state control and to establish shipbreaking plants in the Third World to promote its large market for rerolled and recycled ship scrap.
Publication: Booklet
Publication title: All About IMIF
Second publication: Newsletter
Publication title: Newsletter
Meetings/Conventions: - annual conference

International Maritime Organization
IMO

4 Albert Embankment, London, SE1 7SR, England, UK
Tel: 44 207 7357611
Fax: 44 207 5873210
Email: info@imo.org
Website: http://www.imo.org
Founded: 1948
Members: 162
Staff: 300
Contact: W.A. O'Neil, Sec.Gen.
Description: Governments involved in promoting the safety of international merchant shipping and preventing pollution at sea caused by ships.
Library Subject: Maritime and organizations of the United Nations (see separate entry). 17,000 holdings
Library Type: reference
Publication: Magazine
Publication title: IMO News. Advertisements.
Second publication: Catalog
Publication title: IMO Publications Catalog
Meetings/Conventions: - periodic meeting

International Maritime Pilots Association
IMPA

HQS Wellington , Temple Stairs, Victoria Embankment, London, WC2R 2PN, England, UK
Tel: 44 207 2403973
Fax: 44 207 2403518
Email: secgen@impahq.org
Website: http://www.impahq.org
Founded: 1970
Members: 8000
Staff: 2
Contact: Nick Cutmore, Sec.Gen.
Description: Associations of maritime pilots in 40 countries. Disseminates information on matters of mutual interest to members.
Publication: Newsletter
Publication title: International Pilot. Advertisements.
Publication title: Required Boarding Arrangements for Pilots
Meetings/Conventions: - biennial congress

International Marketing Commission
CIM

18 St. Peters Steps, Brixham, , England, UK
Tel: 44 1803 859575
Founded: 1964
Members: 56
Staff: 5
Contact: Dr. T.A. Voss, Sec.
Description: National and regional professional marketing or market research associations. Furthers cooperation and communication between member organizations.
Publication title: International Marketing Directory. Advertisements.
Publication title: Journal of International Marketing and Marketing Research
Meetings/Conventions: - periodic meeting

International Marketing Federation
IMF

c/o J.A. Curtis
Institute of Industrial Selling, 18 St. Peters Steps, Brixham, TQS 9TE, England, UK
Founded: 1959
Contact: Dr. J.A. Curtis, Dir.
Description: Associations and educational institutions cencerned with marketing. Promotes communication and cooperation between member bodies. Places an emphasis on global marketing.

International Mohair Association
IMA

10/12 The Grove, Ilkley, LS29 9EG, England, UK
Tel: 44 1943 817149
Fax: 44 1943 817150
Email: info@int-mohair.com
Website: http://www.int-mohair.com
Founded: 1974
Members: 60
Staff: 3
Contact: Mrs. Carole Shaw, Mgr.
Fee: £1150
Description: Promotes, advances, and protects the interests of members and their manufactured Mohair products. Ensures the maintenance of the highest quality standards associated with this luxurious natural fibre through the works of the Association's council. The main producing countries are South Africa, USA, Turkey, Lesotho, Argentina, Australia, and New Zealand.
Publication: Book
Publication title: Mohair: A Review of its Properties, Processing and Applications
Meetings/Conventions: - annual conference

International Molinological Society
TIMS

c/o Michael Harverson
125 Parkside Dr., Watford, WD17 3BA, England, UK
Tel: 44 1923 219672
Email: harversontims@aol.com
Website: http://www.timsmills.info
Founded: 1973
Members: 605
Contact: Michael Harverson, Pres.
Fee: £28

Description: Individuals and institutions united for the appreciation and preservation of mills, specifically those powered by water, wind, or animal power. Conducts and encourages studies of the history and technology of mills and milling.
Publication: Journal
Publication title: International Molinology
Publication title: Symposium Transactions
Meetings/Conventions: conference

International Monarchist League
ML

PO Box 5307, Bishop's Stortford, Hertfordshire, CM23 3DZ, England, UK
Tel: 44 1279 465551
Fax: 44 1279 466111
Email: league@monarchy.net
Website: http://www.monarchy.net/leaguei.htm
Founded: 1943
Members: 4000
Staff: 1
Contact: Count Nikolai Tolstoy, Chancellor
Fee: £400
Membership Type: Life
Fee: £20
Membership Type: ordinary
Description: Works to promote, support, and defend the monarchical system of government in the U.K. and abroad.
Library Subject: Monarchy
Library Type: reference
Publication: Journal
Publication title: Monarchy. Advertisements.
Meetings/Conventions: - periodic meeting

International Network for Home-Based Workers

HomeNet, 24 Harlech Terrace, 30-38 Dock St., Leeds, LS11 7DX, England, UK
Fax: 44 113 773269
Email: homenet@gn.apc.org
Website: http://www.homenetww.org.uk
Founded: 1994
Members: 40
Staff: 3
Contact: Jane Tate, International Coor.
Fee: £50
Membership Type: homeworker organization, homeworker support organization
Fee: £50
Membership Type: supporter
Description: Promotes grass-roots organizing and national and international lobbying and advocacy in the interest of home-based workers.
Library Subject: home-based work, informal employment
Library Type: reference
Publication: Newsletter
Publication title: Homenet

International Network Towards Smoke-free Hospitals

c/o John Bickerstaff, Gen.Sec.
45 Brookscroft, Linton Glade, Croydon, CR0 9NA, England, UK
Tel: 44 20 86515436
Fax: 44 20 86513428
Email: jbickerstaff@cix.co.uk

Founded: 1991
Contact: Mr. John Bickerstaff, Gen.Sec.
Fee: £20
Membership Type: ordinary
Description: Physicians, nurses, hospital administrators, healthcare workers, and other interested parties. Seeks to protect, preserve, and improve the health of patients, visitors, and person working in hospitals or in connection with health services, in the U.K. and overseas, by promoting smoke-free environments in hospitals and other healthcare facilities. Provides advice and briefings to hospitals wishing to become smoke-free.
Publication title: Making Hospitals Smoke Free. Advertisements.
Publication title: Smoke-Free Hospitals International

International NGO Training and Research Centre

PO Box 563, Oxford, OX2 6RZ, England, UK
Tel: 44 1865 201851
Fax: 44 1865 201852
Email: info@intrac.org
Website: http://www.intrac.org
Founded: 1991
Staff: 22
Contact: Natasha Thurlow, Admin.Asst.
Description: Provides specialist training, consultancy, and research services to international relief and development organizations. Focuses on key areas such as North/South NGO relations, strategic policy issues, performance assessment, small enterprise development, and strengthening Southern NGOs and training centres. Works to improve the effectiveness and performance of Northern and Southern NGOs.
Library Type: reference
Publication: Book
Publication title: Governance, Democracy and Conditionality: What Role for NGOs?
Second publication: Book
Publication title: Institutional Development and NGOs in Africa: Policy Perspectives for European Development Agencies
Meetings/Conventions: - periodic workshop

International Oil Pollution Compensation Funds
IOPC Funds

Portland House, Stag Place, London, SW1E 5PN, England, UK
Tel: 44 207 5927100
Fax: 44 207 5927111
Email: info@iopcfund.org
Website: http://www.iopcfund.org
Founded: 1978
Members: 83
Staff: 29
Contact: Mans Jacobsson, Dir.
Description: Provides compensation for oil pollution damage resulting from spills of persistent oil from tankers.
Publication: Manual
Publication title: Claims Manual
Publication title: Explanatory Note Prepared by the Secretriat mage
Meetings/Conventions: - annual general assembly

International Opticians Association

Godmersham Park Mansion, Canterbury, Kent, CT4 7DT, England, UK
Tel: 44 207 7060289
Fax: 44 207 7241175
Email: general@abdo.org.uk

Founded: 1985
Members: 7
Staff: 2
Contact: Sir Anthony Garrett, CBE
Fee: £100
Description: Companies engaged in the business of retail opticians which are optical employers. Represents the interests of optical employers, in legislation, relating with the Department of Health, with the General Optical Council and other optical bodies. Issues advice and guidance to members and is involved in European matters through the Joint Optical Committee on the EC.
Formerly: Federation of Ophthalmic and Dispensing Opticians

International Orthoptic Association
IOA

c/o Mrs. Bronia Unwin
Moorfields Eye Hospital, Orthoptic Department, City Rd., London, EC1B 2PD, England, UK
Tel: 44 171 5662163
Fax: 44 171 3885066
Website: http://home.vicnet.net.au/~ioaorth/
Founded: 1967
Members: 4000
Contact: Bronia Unwin, Sec.-Treas.
Description: Orthoptists in 22 countries certified to treat defects in binocular vision, faulty visual habits, and low visual acuity. Organizes and conducts an international congress of orthoptists; shares information through newsletters.
Publication: Journal
Publication title: Abstracts of Congress. Advertisements.
Second publication: Newsletter
Publication title: Newsletter
Meetings/Conventions: International Orthoptic Congress - quadrennial congress - Exhibits. Melbourne Australia

International Ostomy Association
IOA

15 Station Rd., Reading, RG1 1LG, England, UK
Tel: 44 1189 391537
Fax: 44 1189 569095
Email: sue@bcass.org.uk
Website: http://www.ostomyinternational.org
Founded: 1975

International P.E.N. - England

9/10 Charterhouse Bldgs., Goswell Rd., London, EC1M 7AT, England, UK
Tel: 44 20 72534308
Fax: 44 20 72535711
Email: intpen@dircon.co.uk
Website: http://www.internatpen.org
Founded: 1921
Members: 14000
Staff: 5
Contact: Terry Carlbom, Sec.
Description: Poets, playwrights, essayists, novelists, editors, translators, radio and television scriptwriters, historians, and other types of writers from 96 countries. (P.E.N. stands for poets, playwrights, essayists, editors, and novelists.) Objectives are to: act as a forum to promote intellectual exchange, friendship, and goodwill among writers internationally; support freedom of expression and promote freedom for the exchange of literature among all countries regardless of political situations; and inform publishers, editors,

librarians, and university departments about literature in languages of lesser currency. Encourages translation of contemporary literature in minority languages. Works to defend writers suffering from governmental harassment, imprisonment, or other forms of oppression. Holds special subject conferences and literary sessions.
Formerly: Federation Internationale des P.E.N. Clubs
Publication: Magazine
Publication title: Pen International
Second publication: Pamphlets
Meetings/Conventions: - annual congress Mexico City Mexico

International P.E.N. Writers Association

9/10 Charterhouse Bldgs., Goswell Rd., London, EC1M 7AT, England, UK
Tel: 44 20 72534308
Fax: 44 20 72535711
Email: intpen@dircon.co.uk
Website: http://www.internatpen.org
Founded: 1921
Members: 14000
Staff: 7
Contact: Jane Spender, Admin.Dir.
Description: Works for international cooperation and the maintenance of the free exchange of ideas between writers of all nations; operates for freedom of expression.
Publication: Magazine
Publication title: PEN International
Meetings/Conventions: - annual congress Mexico City Mexico

International Pancreas and Islet Transplant Association
IPITA

John Radcliffe Hosp Headington, Oxford, 0X3 9DU, England, UK
Tel: 44 1865 225092
Fax: 44 1865 225616
Email: derek.gray@nds.ox.ac.uk
Website: http://www.ipita.org/
Founded: 1993
Description: Encourages research and training relevant to transplantation of insulin producing tissue in the treatment of diabetes mellitus; promotes and encourages contacts between clinical and experimental researchers from different institutions.

International Petroleum Exchange of London

c/o International House
1 St. Katharine's Way, London, E1W 1UY, England, UK
Tel: 44 207 4810643
Fax: 44 207 4818485
Email: info@ipe.uk.com
Website: http://www.ipe.uk.com
Founded: 1981
Members: 45
Staff: 110
Contact: Dr. Richard Ward, CEO
Fee: £10000
Publication: Magazine
Publication title: Pipeline

International Petroleum Industry Environmental Conservation Association
IPIECA

5th Fl., 209-215 Blackfriars Rd., London, SE1 8NL, England, UK
Tel: 44 20 76332388
Fax: 44 20 76332389
Email: info@ipieca.org
Website: http://www.ipieca.org/
Founded: 1974
Members: 35
Staff: 6
Contact: Mr. Chris Morris, Gen.Sec.
Description: Petroleum enterprises; petroleum industry associations concerned with the environmental aspects of petroleum operations. Purpose is to represent members' views in consultations and collaborations with agencies of the United Nations and other organizations active in areas of environmental protection. Acts as clearinghouse and promotes cooperation and mutual assistance among other oil industry associations. Deals with subjects such as oil spill contingency planning.
Meetings/Conventions: - annual meeting

International Petroleum Marketing Association

4 Belgrave Close, Walton-On-Thames, KT12 5PH, England, UK
Founded: 1995
Contact: Edward Bradfield, Sec.
Description: Marketers of motor fuels and alternative fuels. Fosters information exchange on issues of interest to members, such as payment systems information technology. Conducts training programs.

International Planned Parenthood Federation - United Kingdom
IPPF

Regent's College, Inner Circle, Regent's Park, London, NW1 4NS, England, UK
Tel: 44 20 74877900
Fax: 44 20 74877950
Email: info@ippf.org
Website: http://www.ippf.org
Founded: 1952
Members: 147
Staff: 248
Contact: Dr. Steven Sinding, Dir.Gen.
Description: Initiates and supports worldwide sexual and reproductive health searvices, including family planning, HIV prevention and care and support programs.
Library Subject: sexual and reproductive health and rights, family planning, HIV/AIDS, sex education, gender issues, demography, country studies
Library Type: reference
Publication: Handbook
Publication title: Family Planning Handbook for Health Professionals
Second publication: Annual Report
Publication title: IPPF Annual Report

International Planning History Society

Gipsy Ln., Headington, OX3 0BP, England, UK
Tel: 44 1865 483450
Fax: 44 1865 483559

International Police Association
IPA

International Administration Centre, Arthur Troop House, 1 Fox Rd., West Bridgford, Nottingham, NG2 6AJ, England, UK
Tel: 44 115 9455985
Fax: 44 115 9822578
Email: isg@ipa-iac.org
Website: http://www.ipa-iac.org
Founded: 1950
Members: 310000
Staff: 2
Contact: Alan F. Carter, Int'l.Sec.Gen.
Description: Police officers, either on active service or retired. Seeks to unite all active and retired members of the police service to establish ties of friendship and mutual aid among them. Organizes exchange holidays, pen-friendships, and group visits; encourages and stimulates public service to promote respect for law and the maintenance of order among members of the police service in all countries. Engages in social and cultural activities; Works to establish a correspondence service. NGO (consultative status) with UN and council of Europe.
Publication: Journal
Publication title: Information Guide - World Edition. Advertisements.
Publication title: International Executive Council Proceedings
Meetings/Conventions: - annual conference

International Powered Access Federation
IPAF

PO Box 16, Carnforth, LA6 1LB, England, UK
Tel: 44 1524 781393
Fax: 44 1524 781301
Email: mewp@ipaf.org
Founded: 1983
Members: 200
Staff: 9
Contact: Paul A. Adorian, Mng.Dir.
Description: Manufacturers and distributors of all types of elevating work platforms worldwide. Seeks to promote and extend the use of members' products; take action on matters of interest to powered access equipment industry; encourage high standards of safety and good trading by members; promote safety for operators; represent the industry in discussions at government level in user countries; liaise with other trade associations' encourage technical efficiency by cooperation in the establishment of standards and the discussion of common problems.
Formerly: Formed by Merger of, International Work Platform Association and International Federation of Hydraulic Platform Manufacturers
Publication: Magazine
Publication title: Access International. Advertisements.
Publication title: Mobile Elevating Work Platforms Operators' Safety Guide
Meetings/Conventions: - annual meeting

International Primary Market Association
IPMA

c/o Mr. C.R. Dammers
36-38 Cornhill, London, EC3V 3NG, England, UK
Tel: 44 207 6239353
Fax: 44 207 6239356
Email: cdammers@ipma.org.uk
Website: http://www.ipma.org.uk
Founded: 1984

Members: 65
Staff: 5
Contact: Mr. C.R. Dammers, Sec.Gen.
Description: Represents the interests of managers in 17 countries with debt and equity concerns.
Publication: Booklet
Publication title: Code of Conduct
Second publication: Booklet
Publication title: Standard Documentation

International Professional Security Association - England
IPSA

Northumberland House, Business Ctr. 11, The Pavement, Popes Ln., Ealing, London, W5 4NG, England, UK
Tel: 44 20 88327417
Fax: 44 20 88327418
Email: post@ipsamail.org.uk
Website: http://www.ipsa.org.uk
Founded: 1958
Members: 1000
Staff: 6
Contact: Patrick J. Lemerville, Sec.
Fee: £52
Membership Type: member
Description: Employers and employees in the field of industrial and commercial security. Works to improve the status of the industry by organizing educational activities for security staff, including lectures, seminars, and training courses.
Library Subject: security
Library Type: reference
Publication: Book
Publication title: 1001 Things To Know About Security
Second publication: Directory
Publication title: The Red Book/Directory of Members
Meetings/Conventions: - annual conference

International Psychoanalytical Association
IPA

Broomhills, Woodside Ln., London, N12 8UD, England, UK
Tel: 44 208 4468324
Fax: 44 208 4454729
Email: ipa@ipa.org.uk
Website: http://www.ipa.org.uk
Founded: 1910
Members: 10700
Staff: 8
Contact: Daniel Wildlocher, Pres.
Fee: £250
Membership Type: full
Description: Organizations in 30 countries involved in psychoanalysis. Encourages communication among members and promotes high educational standards. Organizes training programs, conferences, and gives research grants.
Publication: Bulletin
Publication title: Bulletin
Second publication: Booklet
Publication title: Information Booklet
Meetings/Conventions: Psychoanalysis: Working at the Frontiers - biennial congress - Exhibits. Toronto Ontario Canada

International Psychoanalytical Association Trust

Broomhills, Woodside Ln., London, N12 8UD, England, UK
Tel: 44 20 84468324
Fax: 44 20 84454724
Email: ipa@ipa.org.uk
Website: http://www.ipa.org.uk/
Founded: 1910
Members: 10800
Staff: 8
Description: Promotes communication among psychoanalysts and psychoanalytic component organizations; supports development of psychoanalytical organizations.
Meetings/Conventions: Working at the Frontiers - semiannual conference Toronto Ontario Canada

International Public Relations Association
IPRA

c/o James Holt
Cheltonian House, Portsmouth Rd., Esher, KT10 9AA, England, UK
Tel: 44 1372 461188
Fax: 44 1372 461188
Website: http://www.ipra.org
Founded: 1955
Members: 800
Staff: 3
Contact: Carolyn R. Fazio, Pres.
Fee: £225
Membership Type: individual
Description: Senior public relations practitioners from 84 countries. Provides for exchange and dissemination of professional information, standards, and education. Supports the International Foundation for Public Relations Research and Education. Compiles statistics.
Publication: Journal
Publication title: Frontline 21. Advertisements.
Publication title: IPRA Gold Papers
Meetings/Conventions: - annual conference

International Records Management Trust

12 John St., London, WC1N 2EB, England, UK
Tel: 44 20 78314101
Fax: 44 20 78317404
Email: info@irmt.org
Website: http://www.irmt.org
Founded: 1989
Staff: 9
Contact: Neil McCallum
Description: Committed to providing records and archive management services and support to developing countries to preserve official records. Provides technical consultancy, educational projects and research projects.

International Research Group on Law and Urban Space
IRGLUS

Hereford Rd., London, W2 5BA, England, UK
Fax: 44 171 7271271
Email: edesiofernandes@compuserve.com

International Rubber Research and Development Board - United Kingdom
IRRDB

Brickendonbury, Hertford, SG13 8NP, England, UK
Tel: 44 1992 584966
Fax: 44 1992 504267
Email: irrdb@aol.com
Founded: 1960
Description: Promotes cooperation between member institutes and provides a forum for concerted action on matters of common interest.

International Rubber Study Group
IRSG

Heron House, 109/115 Wembley Hill Rd., Wembley, HA9 8DA, England, UK
Tel: 44 208 9005400
Fax: 44 208 9032848
Email: irsg@rubberstudy.com
Website: http://www.rubberstudy.com
Founded: 1944
Members: 17
Staff: 9
Contact: Dr. A. F. S. Budiman, Sec.Gen.
Description: Members are 17 governments of countries producing and consuming natural and synthetic rubber and rubber products. Provides a forum to discuss the problems affecting the rubber industry worldwide including natural and synthetic raw materials and manufacturing. Conducts economic studies; makes available statistics on the rubber industry.
Library Subject: history, economics, statistics of rubber industry
Library Type: reference
Publication: Journal
Publication title: Rubber Industry Report
Second publication: Bulletin
Publication title: Rubber Statistical Bulletin

International Securities Market Association - London

7 Limeharbour, London, E14 9NQ, England, UK
Tel: 44 207 5385656
Fax: 44 207 5384902
Email: info@isma.co.uk
Website: http://www.isma.org
Founded: 1969
Members: 630
Staff: 130
Contact: Rijnhard W.F. Van Tets, Chr.
Fee: £10000
Membership Type: trade association and self-regulatory organisation
Description: All major European banks, investment houses and financial institutions active in the international securities markets as well as a number of firms in North America, the Middle East and Australasia. Seeks to establish uniform market practices governing transactions in international securities. Provides market information and statistical services; conducts educational seminars.
Meetings/Conventions: - annual general assembly

International Seismological Centre
ISC

Pipers Ln., Thatcham, Newbury, RG19 4NS, England, UK
Tel: 44 1635 861022
Fax: 44 1635 872351
Email: admin@isc.qc.uk
Website: http://www.isc.ac.uk/
Founded: 1964
Members: 64
Staff: 10
Contact: Dr. R.J. Willemann, Dir.
Description: National seismological academies of science, research institutes, and government departments (45); reinsurance companies, engineering consultancies, and oil and instrument companies requiring earthquake information are associate members (19). Objectives are to: collect, analyze, and disseminate information on earthquakes worldwide; continually refine information on earthquake times and positions; act as an international source for information on earthquake locations and statistics; search for undetected earthquakes. Collects earthquake readings from 2000 seismograph stations. Conducts consulting services; maintains collection of computer programs and files.
Library Type: reference
Publication: Bulletin
Publication title: ISC Bulletin
Second publication: Book
Publication title: ISC Regional Catalogue of Earthquakes
Meetings/Conventions: - biennial meeting

International SGML/XML Users' Group

Copse House, 15 Upton Close, Swindon, SN25 4UL, England, UK
Fax: 44 1793 721106
Email: admin@isgmlug.org
Website: http://www.isgmlug.org
Members: 1100
Contact: Francis J. Cave, Chm.
Fee: £40
Membership Type: individual
Fee: £80
Membership Type: company
Description: Users of SGML/XML computer software worldwide. Promotes efficient use of this program and full exploitation of its capabilities. Serves as a forum for discussion of matters of common interest to members.
Publication: Newsletter
Publication title: InterChance. Advertisements.

International Ship Electrical and Engineering Service Association
ISES

27 Britton St., 2nd Fl., London, EC1M 5UD, England, UK
Tel: 44 207 4903840
Fax: 44 207 4903843
Email: secretariat@isesassociation.com
Website: http://www.isesassociation.com
Founded: 1962
Members: 70
Staff: 3
Contact: Thomas S. Cash, Sec.Gen.
Description: Repair and service companies. Provides quality electrical, electronic, and specialised marine services, either in port or during a voyage.
Formerly: International Ship Electric Service Association
Publication title: ISES Marine Service Guide
Second publication: Journal
Publication title: ISESnews
Meetings/Conventions: - annual general assembly

International Ship Suppliers Association
ISSA

The Baltic Exchange, St. Mary Ave., London, EC3A 8BH, England, UK
Tel: 44 207 6266236
Fax: 44 207 6266234
Email: issa@dial.pipex.com
Website: http://www.shipsupply.org
Founded: 1955
Members: 1620
Staff: 3
Contact: S. Eade, Sec.
Description: Companies in 82 countries engaged in the supplying of merchant shipping with ship stores; associated groups. Aims to unite the industry for the improvement, efficiency, and modernization of the system and method of supplying merchant vessels.
Library Type: reference
Publication title: International Ship Suppliers Register
Publication title: Ship Stores Catalogue
Meetings/Conventions: - annual convention - Exhibits.

International Shipping Federation
ISF

c/o Carthusian St.
12 Carthusian St., London, EC1M 6EZ, England, UK
Tel: 44 20 74178844
Fax: 44 20 74178877
Email: isf@marisec.org
Website: http://www.marisec.org
Founded: 1909
Members: 32
Staff: 4
Contact: Mr. Chris Horrocks, Sec.Gen
Description: National shipowners' associations and maritime employers' federations in 30 countries. Monitors and disseminates information on all aspects of maritime employment and social affairs; proposes and coordinates international shipowners' positions concerning employment and other public issues; represents members before governments and unions, particularly before the international bodies concerned with these issues. Promotes the exchange of views and policies among members on questions pertaining to the employment of seamen, such as pay conditions and benefits of officers and ratings at the national level, relations with unions, developments in manning organization on board, the role of management in ship operations, safe working practices, and maritime training.
Publication: Directory
Publication title: ISF Guide to International Ship Registers
Second publication: Directory
Publication title: ISF Maritime Labour Supply Guide
Meetings/Conventions: - annual meeting

International Social Service - United Kingdom
ISSUK

Cranmer House, 39 Brixton Rd., London, SW9 6DD, England, UK
Tel: 44 20 77358941
Email: issuk@charity.vfree.com
Founded: 1955
Members: 500
Staff: 16
Contact: Peter Fry

Description: National independent organizations that form part of the existing social service structure. Seeks to assist individuals who, as a consequence of voluntary or forced migration or other social problems of an international character, have to overcome personal or family difficulties requiring coordinated efforts in several countries for their solution. Studies the conditions and consequences of migration in relation to individual and family life. Collaborates with international organizations pursuing similar goals.

International Society for Anthrozoology
ISAZ

c/o Dr. Garry Marvin
School of Sociology and Social Policy, University of Surrey
Roehampton, 80 Roehampton Ln., London, SW15 5SL, England, UK
Email: D.Wells@qub.ac.uk
Website: http://www.vetmed.ucdavis.edu/ccab/isaz.htm
Founded: 1991
Contact: Dr. D. Wells, Sec.
Fee: £12
Membership Type: full
Fee: £240
Membership Type: life
Description: Aims to promote the study of all aspects of human-animal relationships. Activities include publishing research, holding public meetings, and dissemination information to support objectives.

International Society for Boundary Elements
ISBE

Wessex Institute of Technology, WIT Press, Ashurst Lodge, Ashurst, Southampton, SO40 7AA, England, UK
Tel: 44 238 0293223
Fax: 44 238 0292853
Email: isbe@wessex.ac.uk
Founded: 1989
Members: 300
Contact: C.A. Brebbia, Dir.
Fee: £110
Membership Type: individual
Fee: £296
Membership Type: corporate or institutional
Description: Facilitates exchange of ideas and knowledge of computational methods in engineering in 30 countries. Promotes application of applied mechanics and mathematical modeling to traditional fields of engineering. Conducts training courses.
Publication: Newsletter
Publication title: Boundary Element Communications
Publication title: Conference Proceedings
Meetings/Conventions: Boundary Element Methods Conference - annual conference

International Society for Child and Adolescent Injury Prevention
ISCAIP

c/o Child Accident Prevention Trust
18-20 Farringdon Ln., London, EC1R 3AU, England, UK
Email: iscaip@capt.demon.co.uk
Website: http://www.iscaip.org/
Founded: 1993
Contact:
Fee: £35
Membership Type: individuals, U.S.
Fee: £75

Membership Type: non-profit or charity institutions (includes all employees and one journal subscription)
Description: Persons with interest or involvement in prevention of childhood and adolescent injuries. Promotes reduction and severity of injury to children and adolescents; provides multi-disciplinary forum; provides advocacy at national and international levels; fosters national injury prevention initiatives; disseminates research findings and funding opportunities; proposes policy on international basis.
Publication: Journal
Publication title: Injury Prevention
Second publication: Newsletter
Meetings/Conventions: conference - Exhibits.S

International Society for Chronobiology
ISC

Research Institute of Sport and Exercise Science, Liverpool, L3 3AF, England, UK
Founded: 1937

International Society for Clinical Electrophysiology of Vision

c/o Prof. Colin Barber
Medical Physics Dept., Queens Medical Ctr., Nottingham, NG7 2UH, England, UK
Tel: 44 115 9709131
Fax: 44 115 9422745
Email: colin.barber@nottingham.ac.uk
Website: http://www.iscev.org
Founded: 1962
Members: 700
Staff: 25
Contact: Prof. Colin Barber, Sec.Gen.
Fee: £100
Description: Ophthalmologists and other individuals with an interest in the electrophysiology of vision. Seeks to advance understanding of the mechanics of vision; promotes development of new ophthalmologic techniques and technologies. Functions as a clearinghouse on the electrophysiology of vision; facilitates cooperation and communication among workers in the field of the clinical and basic electrophysiology of vision; formulates standards of terminology, research, and practice in the field.
Library Type: reference
Publication: Newsletter
Publication title: Documents of Ophthalmology
Meetings/Conventions: - annual meeting

International Society for Clinical Haemorheology
ISCH

Bldg. South Kensington, London, SW7 2AZ, England, UK
Tel: 44 20 75943187
Fax: 44 20 75943100
Email: m.rampling@ic.ac.uk
Founded: 1993
Description: Advances study of clinical haemorheology.

International Society for General Relativity and Gravitation

School of Mathematical Sciences, Queen Mary and Westfield College, Mile End Rd., London, E1 4NS, England, UK
Tel: 44 20 78825445
Fax: 44 20 89819387
Email: m.a.h.maccallum@qmul.ac.uk
Website: http://www.maths.qmw.ac.uk/grgsoc/
Founded: 1957
Members: 400
Staff: 2
Contact: M.A.H. MacCallum, Sec.
Fee: £30
Description: Scientists from 38 countries active in the field of general relativity and gravitation. Offers information services.
Publication: Journal
Publication title: General Relativity and Gravitation
Second publication: Directory
Meetings/Conventions: International Conference on General Relativity and Gravitation - triennial conference - Exhibits. Dublin Ireland

International Society for Human and Animal Mycology

c/o Prof. E.G.V. Evans, Sec.
Dept. of Microbiology, University of Leeds, Leeds, LS2 9JT, England, UK
Tel: 44 113 2335590
Fax: 44 113 2335640
Email: e.g.v.evans@leeds.ac.uk
Website: http://www.ishamsociety.org
Founded: 1954
Members: 1000
Contact: Dr. D.H. Ellis, Gen.Sec.
Fee: £40
Description: Mycologists and other interested individuals. Seeks to advance scholarship and practice in the field of mycology, the study and classification of fungi. Conducts research on the health effects of fungi on humans and animals. Serves as a clearinghouse on mycology.
Publication: Journal
Publication title: Medical Mycology. Advertisements.
Second publication: Newsletter
Publication title: Mycoses Newsletter. Advertisements.
Meetings/Conventions: - triennial congress - Exhibits. San Antonio Texas United States

International Society for Microelectronics

Tapestries Coach House, Harbertonford, , England, UK

International Society for Mushroom Research
ISMS

c/o Kerry Burton
196 Rugby Road, Leamington Spa, CV32 6DU, England, UK
Email: kerry.burton@hri.ac.uk
Website: http://www.hri.ac.uk/isms
Founded: 1980
Members: 135
Staff: 3
Contact: Kerry Burton, Exec.Sec.
Fee: £55
Membership Type: individual
Fee: £12
Membership Type: corporate/1,000 tons of mushrooms produced
Description: Aims to further the cultivation of edible macrofungi. Activities include dissemination of information on new developments and the science of mushrooms and to stimulate exchange of new ideas between growers and scientists around the world.

421

International Society for Mushroom Science
ISMS

196 Rigby Rd., Leamingtonspa, CV32 6DU, England, UK
Email: kerry.burton@hri.ac.uk
Website: http://www.hri.ac.uk/isms
Founded: 1968
Contact: Kerry Burton, Exec.Sec.
Fee: £30
Membership Type: individual
Description: National mushroom research institutes, national organizations of mushroom growers and individuals in over 30 countries. Aims to further the cultivation of mushrooms by improving international cooperation in the study of scientific and technical problems. Conducts symposia.
Publication: Newsletter
Publication title: Newsletter
Second publication: Proceedings
Meetings/Conventions: - quadrennial congress - Exhibits.

International Society for Mushroom Sciences
ISMS

196 Rugby Rd., Leamington Spa, CV32 6DU, England, UK
Tel: 44 1926 882150
Fax: 44 1926 882150
Email: kerry.burton@hri.ac.uk
Website: http://www.hri.ac.uk/isms/
Founded: 1968
Description: Furthers the cultivation of mushrooms by international cooperation relating scientific and technical problems.

International Society for Oral Literature in Africa
ISOLA

Charterhouse, Godalming, GU7 2ED, England, UK
Email: jeffopland@compuserve.com
Website: http://www.sas.upenn.edu/African_Studies/Org_Institutes/isola.html
Founded: 1998
Description: Celebrates, studies and promotes the oral arts of Africa.

International Society for Photogrammetry and Remote Sensing
ISPRS

c/o Ian Dowman
Department of Geomatic Engineering, University College London, Gower St., London, WC1E 6BT, England, UK
Tel: 44 20 76797226
Fax: 44 20 73800453
Email: idowman@ge.ucl.ac.uk
Website: http://www.isprs.org
Founded: 1910
Members: 165
Contact: Ian Dowman, Sec.Gen.
Description: National societies and committees of photogrammetry and remote sensing; national mapping agencies; only one organization per country may acquire Ordinary Membership but Associate Members from these countries are also entitled to join without voting rights. Regional members are multi-national associations working in photogrammetry and/or remote sensing. Photogrammetry and remote sensing are used to make maps from aerial and space photographs to determine descriptions of terrain cover types and to measure objects from images at close range.

Works to advance photogrammetric and remote sensing science, research, technology, and applications. Sponsors competitions; compiles statistics and conducts research programs.
Publication: Proceedings
Publication title: International Archives of the Photogrammetry, Remote Sensing, & Spatial Information Sciences
Second publication: Newsletter
Publication title: ISPRS Highlights
Meetings/Conventions: ISPRS Congress of Photogrammetry and Remote Sensing - quadrennial congress - Exhibits. Istanbul Turkey

International Society for Reef Studies
ISRS

c/o Peter Mumby, Sec.
Centre for Tropical Coastal Management, Ridley Bldg., University of Newcastle, Newcastle Upon Tyne, NE1 7RU, England, UK
Email: p.j.mumby@exeter.ac.uk
Website: http://www.uncwil.edu/isrs
Founded: 1980
Contact: Dr. Terry Done, Pres.
Description: Promotes production and dissemination of scientific knowledge and understanding of coral reefs, both living and fossil.

International Society for Soil Mechanics and Geotechnical Engineering

City University, Northampton Sq., London, EC1V 0HB, England, UK
Tel: 44 20 70408154
Fax: 44 20 70408832
Email: secretariat@issmge.org
Website: http://www.issmge.org/
Founded: 1936
Members: 73
Staff: 2
Contact: Prof. R. N. Taylor, Sec.Gen.
Description: National societies of engineers in soil mechanics and related areas representing 17,000 individuals. Fosters international fellowship and cooperation among engineers and scientists for the advancement of knowledge in the field of geotechnics and its engineering applications. Facilitates exchange of information among member societies. Maintains 29 technical committees.
Publication title: Conference Proceedings
Second publication: Newsletter
Publication title: ISSMGE News
Meetings/Conventions: - triennial conference - Exhibits.

International Society for Strategic Studies - Africa
ISSSA

9 Cave St., Oxford, OX4 1BA, England, UK
Tel: 44 1865 727777
Fax: 44 1865 295063
Email: cres@technocom.com
Founded: 1980
Description: Analyses conflict and conflict resolution in Africa; works together with African governmental authorities to promote a wider distribution of information and views on conflict in the regions; provides training in International Dispute Resolution.

International Society for the Philosophy of Chemistry
ISPC

Great Horton Rd., Bradford, BD7 1AY, England, UK
Email: m.akeroyd@bilk.ac.uk
Website: http://www.georgetown.edu/earleyj/ISPC.html

International Society for the Prevention of Water Pollution
ISPWP

Little Orchard, Bentworth, Alton, GU34 5RB, England, UK
Tel: 44 1420 562225
Founded: 1980
Members: 750
Staff: 6
Contact: Earl Maitland, Chm.
Fee: £10
Membership Type: environmentalist
Description: Experts in water problems from 14 countries united to prevent the pollution or contamination of water throughout the world. Raises and provides funds for research into the causes and effects of, and solutions to, water pollution problems. Seeks to attract the attention of governments, states, and municipalities affected by water pollution; recommends improvements. Offers children's services. Conducts research and charitable programs. Maintains speakers' bureau.
Library Subject: water pollution
Library Type: reference
Publication: Newsletter
Publication title: ISFTPOWP Newsletter
Meetings/Conventions: - quarterly meeting

International Society for the Study of Hypertension in Pregnancy

Royal Victoria Infirmary, Newcastle upon Tyne, NE1 4LP, England, UK
Founded: 1978
Description: Conducts research in the field of hypertension in pregnancy; advances education in the field.

International Society for the Study of Tension in Performance

c/o 28 Emperor's Gate
Kingston University, School of Music, London, SW7 4HS, England, UK
Tel: 44 207 3737307
Fax: 44 207 3735440
Email: carogrindea@yahoo.com
Founded: 1981
Members: 360
Staff: 3
Contact: Carola Grindea, Chm.
Fee: £5
Membership Type: student
Fee: £16
Membership Type: individual
Description: Musicians, actors, dancers, medical practitioners, consultants, psychologists, physiotherapists, Alexander Technique, yoga, Feldenkrais disciplines teachers and practitioners and others interested in the subject and in the problems created by muscular and nervous tensions, physical injuries, among instrumentalists. Aims to collect and disseminate information regarding the debilitating effects of excess anxiety and tensions experienced by musicians, actors, dancers, public speakers, sportsmen, etc; to foster research and related activities; to provide advisory service for members and to assist performers with their physical or psychological problems offering free consultations.
Library Type: not open to the public
Publication: Journal. Advertisements.
Meetings/Conventions: Performing Arts Clinic - annual conference - Exhibits.

International Society for the Understanding, Prevention and Treatment of Mental Illness Relating to Child Bearing

Goldhawk Rd., London, W6 0XG, England, UK
Tel: 44 20 87417407
Fax: 44 20 87411948
Email: marcesoc@rpms.ac.uk
Description: Organizes research conferences.

International Society for Trenchless Technology
ISTT

14/15 Belgrave Sq., London, SW1X 8PS, England, UK
Tel: 44 20 72596755
Fax: 44 20 72356976
Email: info@istt.co.uk
Website: http://www.istt.com
Founded: 1986
Members: 3500
Staff: 2
Contact: John Castle
Fee: £250
Membership Type: corporate
Fee: £25
Membership Type: individual
Description: Promotes the use of trenchless methods of installing, renovating, and replacing underground utilities.
Publication: Proceedings
Publication title: International No-Dig Congress
Second publication: Directory
Publication title: ISTT Yearbook and Trenchless Technology Directory. Advertisements.
Meetings/Conventions: International No-Dig - semiannual conference - Exhibits. Las Vegas Nevada United States

International Society for Utilitarian Studies
ISUS

University College London, Bentham Project, Gower St., London, WC1E 6BT, England, UK
Tel: 44 20 76793610
Fax: 44 171 9168510
Email: p.schofield@ucl.ac.uk
Website: http://www.ucl.ac.uk/Bentham-Project
Founded: 1986
Members: 150
Contact: Prof. Philip Schofield, Hon.Sec.
Fee: £38
Membership Type: Individual
Description: Historians, lawyers, political scientists, and philosophers interested in the teachings of Jeremy Bentham (1748-1832), English author, philosopher, and developer of Utilitarianism (a doctrine maintaining that the propriety of an action depends on its tendency to promote the greatest happiness of the greatest number). Encourages

study of Utilitarian ideas and serves as a liaison for scholars working in the field. Organizes activities to raise funds for publication of a new scholarly edition of Bentham's books and literary treatises; conducts seminars.
Formerly: International Bentham Society
Publication: Journal
Publication title: Utilitas. Advertisements.
Meetings/Conventions: conference Lisbon Portugal

International Society of Biomechanics in Sports
ISBS

c/o Technical Mgr., International Tennis Federation
Bank Ln., Roehampton, SW15 5XZ, England, UK
Tel: 44 20 83924676
Fax: 44 20 83924773
Email: stuart.miller@iftennis.com
Website: http://www.uni-stuttgart.de/External/isbs/
Founded: 1983

International Society of Chemotherapy
ISC

c/o Dr. Faridah Moosdeen
31 St. Olav's Ct., City Business Centre, 25 Lower Rd., London, SE16 2XB, England, UK
Tel: 44 20 72312944
Fax: 44 20 72312124
Email: moosdeen@ischemo.demon.co.uk
Website: http://www.ischemo.org
Founded: 1961
Members: 16000
Staff: 1
Contact: Dr. Faridah Moosdeen, Adm.Sec.
Description: Societies or specialized groups within societies that are concerned with chemotherapy; scientists and clinicians working in chemotherapy. (Chemotherapy is the use of chemical agents in the treatment or control of infectious and neoplastic diseases and immunological disorder.) Promotes the development of chemotherapy through scientific and educational means. Encourages cooperation between members and scientists in related fields. Urges formation of new societies in countries where such groups do not exist. Promotes and/or sponsors formation of international working groups and training projects in the field of antimicrobial, antiparasitic, and antineoplastic chemotherapy; coordinates their activities. Appoints commissions for special activities.
Library Subject: antimicrobial therapy
Library Type: open to the public
Publication: Newsletter
Publication title: Antibiotics Chemotherapy. Advertisements.
Publication title: Congress Proceedings
Meetings/Conventions: - periodic symposium

International Society of Endocrinology
ISE

c/o Prof. Lesley H. Rees
51-53 St. Bartholomew's Hospital, Bartholomew Close, London, EC1A 7BE, England, UK
Tel: 44 207 6064012
Fax: 44 207 7964676
Email: l.h.rees@mds.gmw.ac.uk
Website: http://www.jingo.com/ise/
Founded: 1966
Members: 53

Contact: Prof. Lesley H. Rees, Sec.Gen.
Fee: £2.5
Description: Federation of national endocrinology societies with 15,000 individual members. Disseminates information on endocrinology and facilitates collaboration between national endocrinological societies and persons interested in the field.
Publication: Newsletter
Publication title: Abstracts of Congresses
Publication title: Symposia Abstracts
Meetings/Conventions: - quadrennial conference - Exhibits.

International Society of Magnetic Resonance in Medicine - British Chapter
ISMRM

c/o Prof. Peter Morris, Treas.
Magnetic Resonance Centre, University of Nottingham, University Park, Nottingham, NG7 2RD, England, UK
Email: martin@icr.ac.uk
Website: http://www-ipg.umds.ac.uk/ismrm-bc/bylaws.html
Contact: Prof. Martin Leach, Sec.
Fee: £20
Membership Type: full
Fee: £5
Membership Type: student
Description: Promotes communication, research, development, applications and availability of information on magnetic resonance in medicine and biology and other related topics.

International Society of Nurses in Cancer Care
ISNCC

PO Box 297, Macclesfield, SK11 7FZ, England, UK
Tel: 44 1625 669588
Fax: 44 1625 428128
Email: secretariat@isncc.org
Website: http://www.isncc.org
Founded: 1984
Members: 60
Contact: Christine Armstrong, Sec.
Description: Provides communication network for cancer nursing societies and professionals; works as resource for nurses working in clinical practice, education, research and management for cancer nursing and the nurse's role in cancer care.
Publication: Directory
Publication title: International Cancer Nursing News
Publication title: Palliative Care Curriculum
Meetings/Conventions: International Conference on Cancer Nursing - biennial conference - Exhibits. Sydney Australia

International Society of Typographic Designers
ISTD

Chapelfield Cottage, Randwick, Stroud, GL6 6HS, England, UK
Tel: 44 1453 759311
Fax: 44 1453 767466
Email: info@istd.org.uk
Website: http://www.istd.org.uk
Founded: 1928
Members: 630
Staff: 1
Contact: Helen Cornish
Fee: £100
Description: Promotes professionalism among typographic designers. Offers annual student assessment; conducts lectures.

Publication: Journal
Publication title: Typographic
Meetings/Conventions: Council Meeting - monthly - Exhibits.

International Society of Ultrasound in Obstetrics and Gynecology

Unit 4, Blythe Mews, Blythe Rd., London, W14 OHW, England, UK
Tel: 44 20 74719955
Fax: 44 20 74719959
Email: info@isuog.org
Website: http://obg.med.wayne.edu/ISUOG/home.htm
Founded: 1991
Members: 2000
Staff: 2
Contact: Sarah Johnson, Exec.Dir.
Fee: £180
Description: Healthcare practitioners in the field of ultrasound in obstetrics and gynecology. Fosters scientific and educational advancements in ultrasound technology in obstetrics and gynecology. Conducts training programs.
Publication: Journal
Publication title: Ultrasound in Obstetrics and Gynecology
Second publication: Newsletter
Meetings/Conventions: - annual congress

International Songwriters Association - England

37 New Cavendish St., London, W1M 8JR, England, UK
Tel: 44 20 74865353
Fax: 44 20 74862094
Email: jliddane@songwriter.iol.ie
Website: http://www.songwriter.co.uk/
Founded: 1967
Contact: Anna M. Sinden
Description: Songwriters, professional, semi-professional and amateur. A protective and advisory organization for songwriters, with members in more than 50 countries.

International Spinal Cord Society

c/o National Spinal Injuries Centre
Stoke Mandeville Hospital, Aylesbury, HP21 8AL, England, UK
Tel: 44 1296 315866
Fax: 44 1296 315870
Email: admin@iscos.org.uk
Website: http://www.iscos.org.uk
Founded: 1961
Members: 1200
Staff: 2
Contact: Prof. T. Ikata, Pres.
Fee: £50
Membership Type: full
Fee: £10
Membership Type: associate
Description: Qualified medical practitioners with an interest and activity in research or treatment and rehabilitation of spinal cord afflictions. To study all problems concerning traumatic and non-traumatic problems of the spinal cord. To advance research, treatment and prevention; social integration of paraplegics - encourage medical services throughout the world especially in developing countries. To sponsor young specialists to attend annual scientific meetings and undertake research work.
Formerly: International Medical Society of Paraplegia
Publication: Journal

Publication title: Spinal Cord
Meetings/Conventions: - annual meeting Beijing People's Republic of China

International Spinal Research Trust
ISRT

River Front, Enfield, EN1 3TR, England, UK
Tel: 44 20 83673555
Fax: 44 20 83667999
Email: isrt@isrthq.demon.co.uk
Founded: 1980

International Sports Engineering Association
ISEA

Mappin St., Sheffield, S1 3JD, England, UK
Tel: 44 114 2227891
Fax: 44 114 2227855
Email: s.j.haake@sheffield.ac.uk
Website: http://www.sports-engineering.org
Founded: 1998
Members: 98
Contact: Ms. Amanda Staley
Fee: £85
Description: Promotes sports engineering.

International Steel Trade Association

Broadway House, Tothill St., London, SW1H 9NQ, England, UK
Tel: 44 207 7992662
Fax: 44 207 7992468
Email: hbailey@steeltrade.co.uk
Website: http://www.steeltrade.co.uk
Contact: H. W. Bailey
Description: International steel traders. Assists members in manner determined by executive committee.

International Study Association for Teachers and Teaching
ISATT

c/o Maureen Pope
University of Reading, Faculty of Education & Communication Studies, Bulmershe Ct., Earley, Reading, RG6 1HY, England, UK
Tel: 44 173 4318811
Fax: 44 173 4352080
Email: m.l.pope@reading.ac.uk
Website: http://www.ipn.uni-kiel.de/projekte/isatt
Founded: 1983
Contact: Maureen Pope, Treas.
Fee: £60
Membership Type: member
Fee: £40
Membership Type: student
Description: Tearcher-researchers worldwide at every academic level from a range of disciplines. Promotes, presents, discusses, and disseminates research on teachers and teaching, with a focus on the way teachers understand teaching and their roles in it.
Publication: Journal
Publication title: Teachers and Teaching - Theory and Practice
Meetings/Conventions: - biennial international conference

International Study Group for Mathematics Learning
ISGML

Acton, London, W3 9DN, England, UK
Tel: 44 20 89926944
Founded: 1961

International Sugar Organization
ISO

1 Canada Sq., Canary Wharf, Docklands, London, E14 5AA, England, UK
Tel: 44 207 5131144
Fax: 44 207 5131146
Email: economics@isosugar.org
Website: http://www.isosugar.org
Founded: 1969
Members: 63
Staff: 10
Contact: Dr. P. Baron, Exec.Dir.
Description: Governments of sugar exporting and importing countries. Is currently administering the 1992 International Sugar Agreement. Promotes the sugar industry.
Library Subject: Sugar production, agriculture, economics, and international trade
Library Type: reference
Publication: Bulletin
Publication title: Statistical Bulletin

International Tanker Owners Pollution Federation
ITOPF

Staple Hall, Stone House Ct., 87-90 Houndsditch, London, EC3A 7AX, England, UK
Tel: 44 207 6211255
Fax: 44 207 6211783
Email: deborahansell@itopf.com
Website: http://www.itopf.com
Founded: 1968
Members: 4000
Staff: 22
Contact: Dr. Ian C. White, Mng.Dir.
Description: Tanker owners, bareboat charterers, and other ship owners. Responds to spills from all types of vessels; offers advice on clean-up, investigates the impact of spills, and assesses the technical merits of subsequent claims for compensation for clean-up costs and damage. Undertakes contingency planning and training assignments and maintains various databases, including are an oil spills from tankers.
Library Subject: oil pollution, clean-up techniques, environmental effects, case histories
Library Type: reference
Publication: Newsletter
Publication title: Ocean Orbit
Second publication: Book
Publication title: Response to Marine Oil Spills
Meetings/Conventions: - annual board meeting

International Task Force for the Rural Poor
INTAF

12 Eastleigh Ave., South Harrow, HA2 0UF, England, UK
Tel: 91 5921 270567
Fax: 91 5921 270567

Email: apk_gram@yahoo.co.uk
Website: http://www.aede.org/intaf5.html
Founded: 1989
Members: 210
Staff: 20
Contact: Mrs. Jyoti Singh
Fee: £30
Membership Type: life
Fee: £5
Membership Type: Individual
Description: Seeks to raise the consciousness of the world community regarding the plight of the rural poor. Aims to ease the economic and social problems of the underpriveliged internationally.
Library Subject: Poverty, Nutrition, Economic Development
Library Type: open to the public
Publication: Journal
Publication title: International Journal of Rural Studies
Second publication: Journal
Publication title: Vikas Seva
Meetings/Conventions: - triennial general assembly - Exhibits. Harrow UK

International Tea Committee
ITC

Sir John Lyon House, 5 High Timber St., London, EC4V 3NH, England, UK
Tel: 44 207 2484672
Fax: 44 207 3296955
Email: inteacom@globalnet.co.uk
Website: http://www.intteacomm.co.uk
Founded: 1933
Members: 18
Staff: 3
Contact: Manuja Peiris, Statistician
Description: Tea-producing and consuming governments and associations. Collects and disseminates information and statistics on tea.
Publication: Bulletin
Publication title: Annual Bulletin of Statistics. Advertisements.
Publication title: Monthly Statistical Summary

International Theatre Institute - British Centre

Goldsmith College, Univ. of London, Lewisham Way, Newcross, London, SE14 6NW, England, UK
Tel: 44 207 9197276
Fax: 44 207 9197277
Email: iti@gold.ac.uk
Website: http://iti.gold.ac.uk
Founded: 1948
Members: 400
Staff: 1
Contact: Neville Shulman, Dir.
Fee: £10
Membership Type: student
Fee: £85
Membership Type: organizations
Description: Arts professionals, academics and anyone with an interest in international performing arts. To promote cultural exchange between nations and thereby deepen mutual understanding and participate in the strengthening of peace. Provides information and contacts worldwide.
Library Type: open to the public

Publication: Bulletin
Second publication: Newsletters
Meetings/Conventions: conference

International Toy Libraries Association

68 Churchway, London, NW1 1LT, England, UK
Tel: 44 171 3879592
Fax: 44 171 3832714
Founded: 1972
Members: 1000
Staff: 10
Contact: Glenis Carter, Dir.
Fee: £70
Membership Type: national
Fee: £30
Membership Type: individual
Description: National associations, informal groups or individuals. Representatives from each country receives and shares information on toys and leisure library information.
Publication: Newsletter
Publication title: Broadsheet
Second publication: Directory
Publication title: Good Toy Guide 600 Toys Assessed. Advertisements.
Meetings/Conventions: conference - Exhibits.

International Transport Workers' Federation
ITF

49-60 Borough Rd., London, SE1 1DR, England, UK
Tel: 44 20 74032733
Fax: 44 20 73577871
Email: mail@itf.org.uk
Website: http://www.itf.org.uk
Founded: 1896
Members: 604
Staff: 90
Contact: David Cockroft, Gen.Sec.
Description: Trade unions representing 5 million workers in railways, road transport, inland navigation, ports and docks, shipping, fisheries, civil aviation, tourism services, and a special seafarers' department for the promotion of fair practices in the maritime industry. Promotes and defends the economic and social interests of transport workers internationally.
Library Subject: transport, labour information
Library Type: reference
Publication title: Congress Proceedings
Publication title: Transport International
Meetings/Conventions: - quadrennial congress

International Tree Foundation

Sandy Ln., Crawley, RH10 4HS, England, UK
Tel: 44 1342 712536
Fax: 44 1342 718282
Email: hq.itf@tree-foundation.org.uk
Website: http://www.internationaltreefoundation.org/
Founded: 1922
Members: 3000
Staff: 4
Contact: Mrs. Kay Sexton, Ch.Exec.
Fee: £12.5
Membership Type: individual

Description: Dedicated to the planting and protecting of trees at home and abroad. Offers advice on all aspects of tree care. Provides support to well-researched planting projects in the Third World.
Formerly: Men of the Trees
Publication: Journal
Publication title: Trees
Second publication: Newsletter
Publication title: Trees are News
Meetings/Conventions: - annual meeting

International Tube Association
ITA

46 Holly Walk, Leamington Spa, CV32 4HY, England, UK
Tel: 44 1926 334137
Fax: 44 1926 314755
Email: ita@intras.co.uk
Website: http://www.itatube.org
Founded: 1979
Members: 1300
Staff: 12
Contact: Phillip Knight, Exec.Sec.
Description: Professional association of tube and pipe engineers in 71 countries. Promotes and organizes exhibitions, conferences and seminars covering all aspects of tube production and processing. Industry partner to Tube Dusseldorf.
Publication: Journal
Publication title: Tube and Pipe Technology. Advertisements.
Second publication: Papers
Meetings/Conventions: - annual conference - Exhibits.

International Tungsten Industry Association
ITIA

2 Baron's Gate, 33 Rothschild Rd., London, W4 5HT, England, UK
Tel: 44 208 7422274
Fax: 44 208 7427345
Email: info@itia.info
Website: http://www.itia.info
Founded: 1988
Members: 55
Staff: 2
Contact: Michael Maby, Sec.Gen.
Description: Organizations and companies engaged in the production, processing, and consumption of tungsten; trading companies; assayers. Promotes cooperation among members in research, production, processing, and use of tungsten. Protects the common interests of members in technical, environmental, and health matters. Collects and disseminates information; compiles statistics.
Formerly: Supersedes, Primary Tungsten Association
Publication: Newsletter
Publication title: Newsletter
Second publication: Brochure
Publication title: Tungsten
Meetings/Conventions: - annual meeting

International Tyre, Rubber, and Plastic Federation
ITRPF

28 Stone Cross Lane, Lowton, Warrington, WA3 2SE, England, UK
Tel: 44 1942 728335
Fax: 44 1942 728335
Email: tony@cowell.fsbusiness.co.uk
Founded: 1958
Members: 70

Staff: 1
Contact: A.W. Cowell
Description: Tire dealers and plastics and rubber manufacturers. Promotes trade between members; offers advice on pertinent legislation. Works to solve the problem of disposal and recycling of tires.
Meetings/Conventions: - annual congress

International Underwriting Association of London
IUA

London Underwriting Centre, 3 Minster Ct., Mincing Ln., London, EC3R 7DD, England, UK
Tel: 44 207 6174444
Fax: 44 207 6174440
Email: info@iua.co.uk
Website: http://www.iua.co.uk
Founded: 1998
Members: 180
Staff: 30
Contact: Miss M.L. Rossi, Chief Exec.
Description: Insurance and reinsurance companies across all classes, central accounting and policy checking firms. Provides central accounting and processing services for ordinary members; representational activities and information and research services for all members.
Formerly: Institute of London Underwriters
Meetings/Conventions: - biennial seminar - Exhibits.

International Union Against Sexually Transmitted Infections - United Kingdom
IUSTI

c/o Dr. Raj Patel
Royal South Hants Hospital, Brintons Terrace, South Hampton, SE1 7EH, England, UK
Tel: 44 207 9289292
Fax: 44 207 4036459
Email: raj.patel@iusti.org
Website: http://www.iusti.org
Founded: 1923
Contact: Dr. James Bingham, Pres.
Description: Promotes international cooperation in the control of sexually transmitted diseases, including HIV infection, with an emphasis on the medical, social, and epidemiological aspects.

International Union Against The Venereal Diseases and The Treponematoses
IUVDT

Saint Mary's Hospital, London, W2 1NY, England, UK
Tel: 44 20 72621123
Founded: 1923

International Union for Land Value Taxation and Free Trade
IULVTFT

c/o London Fruit and Wool Exchange
Brushfield St., Ste. 427, London, E1 6EL, England, UK
Tel: 44 20 73778885
Fax: 44 20 73778686
Email: iu@interunion.org.uk
Website: http://www.interunion.org.uk
Founded: 1926

Members: 300
Staff: 3
Contact: B.P. Sobrielo, Sec.
Fee: £15
Membership Type: ordinary, corporate
Description: Concerned persons in 32 countries. Works to gain worldwide support for permanent peace and prosperity for all peoples, which the union believes is achievable through the progressive removal of the basic economic causes of poverty and war as demonstrated in the writings of Henry George (1839-97), American economist. (George developed the single tax theory, according to which only the rental value of land should be taxed.) Encourages the raising of public revenues by land value taxation (apart from improvements) in order to secure economic rent for the community and promotes abolition of taxes, tariffs, or imposts that interfere with free production and exchange of wealth.
Library Subject: land economics, social justice
Library Type: not open to the public
Publication title: Conference Proceedings
Second publication: Journal
Publication title: Georgist Journal
Meetings/Conventions: conference

International Union of Air Pollution Prevention and Environmental Protection Associations
IUAPPA

44 Grand Parade, Brighton, BN2 2QA, England, UK
Tel: 44 1273 878770
Fax: 44 1273 606626
Email: iuappa@nsca.org.uk
Founded: 1965
Members: 34
Staff: 3
Contact: R. Mills, Dir.Gen.
Description: National air pollution prevention and environmental protection associations in 36 countries. Promotes global public education relating to the importance of clean air and methods and results of pollution control. Facilitates the exchange of information and publications; encourages the use of uniform scientific and technical terminology; promotes uniform methods of measurement and monitoring. Acts as liaison with other international and national scientific and technical organizations. Maintains information service.
Library Type: reference
Formerly: International Union of Air Pollution Prevention Associations
Publication: Book
Publication title: Clean Air Around the World
Publication title: IUAPPA Members Handbook
Meetings/Conventions: World Clean Air Congress and Exhibition - triennial - Exhibits. Israel

International Union of Aviation Insurers
IUAI

6 Lovat Ln., London, EC3R 8DT, England, UK
Tel: 44 207 6265314
Fax: 44 207 9293534
Email: dg.iuai@virgin.net
Website: http://www.iuai.org
Founded: 1934
Members: 43
Staff: 2
Contact: D.R. Gasson, Sec.Gen.
Description: Associations, groups, underwriting pools, and organizations in 35 countries engaged in aviation insurance. To

constitute a body which shall be able to form a focal point for international aviation insurance interests, to provide a forum for members to liaise and discuss aviation and space risks insurance matters, to provide a central office for the circulation of information between members, to assist in and provide for the better understanding and conduct of international aviation and space insurance; to do all such things as many be beneficial for the development and conduct of these branches of insurance.
Publication: Handbook
Publication title: Aviation Legal Liability Handbook
Second publication: Handbook
Publication title: Aviation Statistical Handbook
Meetings/Conventions: - annual meeting

International Union of Credit and Investment Insurers/ The Berne Union

1-2 Castle Ln., London, SW1E 6DR, England, UK
Tel: 44 20 72338228
Fax: 44 20 72338208
Email: bu-sec@berneunion.org.uk
Website: http://www.berneunion.org.uk
Founded: 1934
Members: 51
Staff: 6
Contact: Kimberly Wiehl, Sec.Gen.
Fee: £10000
Membership Type: corporate
Description: Organizations insuring or guaranteeing export credit insurance transactions and/or foreign investments; organizations whose activities are related to export credit insurance. Seeks to: promote international cooperation in fostering a favorable investment climate; develop and maintain sound principles of export credit insurance; establish and sustain discipline in the terms of credit for international trade. Facilitates exchange of information, continuing consultation, and close cooperation among members. Acts as liaison between members and other international institutions. Maintains technical and ad hoc sub-committees, groups, and working parties to study specific problems and issues.
Publication: Magazine
Publication title: Yearbook. Advertisements.
Meetings/Conventions: - biennial meeting

International Union of Crystallography
IUCr

2 Abbey Sq., Chester, CH1 2HU, England, UK
Tel: 44 1244 345431
Fax: 44 1244 344843
Email: execsec@iucr.org
Website: http://www.iucr.org
Founded: 1948
Members: 40
Staff: 21
Contact: Mr. M.H. Dacombe, Exec.Sec.
Description: National academies, national research councils, scientific societies, and similar bodies in 40 countries. Objectives are to: promote international cooperation in crystallography (the study of crystal form, structure, and modes of aggregation); contribute to all aspects of its advancement including related topics concerning the non-crystalline states; facilitate international standardization of methods used such as units, nomenclature, and symbols; form a focus for the relations of crystallography to other sciences. Organizes training schools on various aspects of crystallography. Maintains 18 commissions.
Publication: Journal

Publication title: Acta Crystallographica Section A. Advertisements.
Publication title: Acta Crystallographica Section C
Meetings/Conventions: - triennial congress - Exhibits.

International Union of Physiological Sciences
IUPS

University Laboratory of Physiology, Oxford Univ., Parks Rd., Oxford, OX1 3PT, England, UK
Tel: 44 1865 272478
Fax: 44 1865 272469
Email: frances.ashcroft@physiol.ox.ac.uk
Website: http://iups.mcw.edu/
Founded: 1953
Members: 52
Staff: 1
Contact: Frances Ashcroft, Council
Description: Physiological societies united to exchange scientific information. Coordinates research and educational programs.
Publication: Journal
Publication title: News in Physiological Sciences
Second publication: Directory
Publication title: World Directory of Physiologists
Meetings/Conventions: International Congress of Physiological Sciences - quadrennial congress - Exhibits. Washington District of Columbia United States

International Union of Soil Sciences
IUSS

Department of Soil Science, University of Reading, Reading, RG6 6DW, England, UK
Tel: 44 118 3786559
Fax: 44 118 3786666
Email: iuss@rdg.ac.uk
Website: http://www.iuss.org
Founded: 1924
Members: 45000
Staff: 1
Contact: Stephen Nortcliff, Sec.Gen.
Description: Non-profit, non-governmental, scientific society with individuals from 143 countries engaged in the study and application of soil science. Promotes contacts among scientists; stimulates scientific research to further the application of soil research.
Library Type: reference
Formerly: International Society of Soil Science
Publication: Bulletin
Publication title: Bulletin of the IUSS. Advertisements.
Publication title: Membership List
Meetings/Conventions: World Congress of Soil Science - periodic meeting - Exhibits. Philadelphia Pennsylvania United States

International Vegetarian Union
IVU

Parkdale, Dunham Rd., Altringham, Cheshire, WA14 4QG, England, UK
Email: chair@ivu.org
Website: http://www.ivu.org
Founded: 1908
Members: 300
Staff: 1
Contact: Saurabu Oalar, Sec.
Fee: £20
Membership Type: group, individual, corporate

Description: Union of societies from 40 countries whose members live on a diet of cereals, vegetables, fruit, pulses, nuts, and herbs, with or without the addition of eggs and dairy products, but excluding animal flesh whether meat, fish, fowl or their derivatives. Seeks to coordinate the work of all affiliated and associated member societies. Sponsors information service on vegetarian/vegan accommodation, restaurants, and health food stores in the world. Conducts and continuously reviews world census of vegetarian/vegan organizations. Promotes the publication of leaflets on horticulture, balanced vegetarian recipes, lectures, and articles. Compiles statistics.
Library Type: reference
Publication: Magazine
Publication title: IVU Magazine. Advertisements.
Meetings/Conventions: - biennial conference - Exhibits.

International Visual Communication Association

19 Pepper St., Glengall Bridge, London, E14 9RP, England, UK
Tel: 44 20 75120571
Fax: 44 20 75120591
Email: info@ivca.org
Website: http://www.ivca.org
Founded: 1988
Members: 920
Staff: 6
Contact: Wayne Drew, Ch.Exec.
Fee: £750
Description: Patrons, corporate commissioner/user, corporate supplier, institutional/non profit making, individual, student/trainee. A professional association which represents the users and suppliers of visual communication. The association strives to advance the standing and recognition of the industry and its practitioners, and provides a comprehensive range of membership services. The IVCA has a proactive role in marketing visual communications to potential users.
Publication: Newsletter
Publication title: IVCA Update
Meetings/Conventions: - annual conference

International Water Association

Alliance House, 12 Caxton St., London, SW1H 0QS, England, UK
Tel: 44 20 76545500
Fax: 44 20 76545555
Email: water@iwahq.org.uk
Website: http://www.iawq.org.uk
Founded: 1965
Members: 6850
Staff: 14
Contact: Paul Reiter, Exec.Dir.
Fee: £50
Membership Type: ordinary
Fee: £570
Membership Type: corporate
Description: Individuals, national organizations, municipal authorities, pollution control agencies, government departments, research institutes, and commercial concerns in 120 countries. Objectives are to: contribute to the advancement of research, development, and applications in drinking water treatment and supply, wastewater treatment, water pollution control and water quality management; encourage communication and a better understanding among those engaged in the solution of water quality problems and water quality management. Promotes the exchange of information on drinking water treatment and supply, wastewater treatment, water pollution control, water quality management, and its practical application.
Formerly: International Association on Water Pollution Research and Control

Publication: Yearbook
Publication title: IAWQ Yearbook. Advertisements.
Second publication: Magazine
Publication title: Water Quality International
Meetings/Conventions: - biennial conference - Exhibits.

International Whaling Commission
IWC

The Red House, 135 Station Rd., Impington, Cambridge, CB4 9NP, England, UK
Tel: 44 1223 233971
Fax: 44 1223 232876
Email: secretariat@iwcoffice.org
Website: http://www.iwcoffice.org
Founded: 1946
Members: 49
Staff: 16
Contact: Dr. N. Grandy, Sec.
Description: Commissioners representing member countries. Works for the conservation of whale studies in order to develop the whaling industry. Encourages and helps organize studies on whales and whaling; compiles statistics on current condition of whale stocks; disseminates information on methods of estimating the size of whale stocks. Collects and publishes whaling statistics previously compiled by Norway's Bureau of International Whaling Statistics.
Library Subject: whales, whaling, law, history
Library Type: open to the public
Publication: Journal
Publication title: Journal of Cetacean Research and Management
Second publication: Reprints
Publication title: Scientific Papers
Meetings/Conventions: - annual meeting Berlin Germany

International Wildlife Coalition - England
IWC

141A High St., Edenbridge, TN8 5AX, England, UK
Tel: 44 1732 866955
Fax: 44 1732 866995
Email: iwcuk@iwcmail.demon.co.uk
Founded: 1989
Members: 15000
Staff: 3
Contact: Mr. Charles Wartenberg
Description: Works to preserve wildlife habitats worldwide. Publicizes issues affecting wildlife; conducts research and educational programs.

International Wire and Machinery Association
IWMA

46 Holly Walk, Leamington Spa, CV32 4HY, England, UK
Tel: 44 1926 334137
Fax: 44 1926 314755
Email: iwma@intras.co.uk
Website: http://www.iwma.org
Founded: 1970
Members: 330
Staff: 2
Contact: Phillip Knight, Exec.Sec.
Description: A trade association for manufacturers of wire, cable, and fibre optic machinery and products and suppliers of related production and process machinery in 52 countries. Promotes the exchange of technology and standards and seeks to advance quality control among industries internationally.

Library Subject: Technical information.
Library Type: reference
Publication: Newsletter
Publication title: WCN-Wire Cable Newsletter
Meetings/Conventions: - periodic conference

International Wrought Copper Council
IWCC

6 Bathurst St., Sussex Sq., London, W2 2SD, England, UK
Tel: 44 207 7237465
Fax: 44 207 7240308
Email: iwcc@coppercouncil.org
Website: http://www.coppercouncil.org
Founded: 1953
Members: 19
Contact: Simon Payton, Sec.Gen.
Description: National trade associations of the copper and copper alloy fabricating industries. Promotes information exchange and cooperation within the industry; conducts promotional activities.
Publication: Report
Publication title: Survey of Capacities of Copper Mines, Smelters, Refineries and Copper Wire Rod Plants
Second publication: Directory
Meetings/Conventions: - annual meeting

International Young Democrat Union
IYDU

32 Smith Sq., Westminster, London, SW1P 3HH, England, UK
Tel: 44 207 2220847
Fax: 44 207 2221459
Email: iydu@andrew1.tory.org.uk
Founded: 1991
Members: 60
Contact: Andrew Rosindell, Chair
Description: Organizations comprising students and young people with center-right political viewpoints. Promotes freedom and democracy worldwide. Conducts research and educational programs in areas including government policies and human rights.

International Youth Hostel Federation
IYHF

1st Fl., Fountain House Pkwy., Welwyn Garden City, AL8 6JH, England, UK
Tel: 44 1707 324170
Fax: 44 1707 323980
Email: iyhf@iyhf.org
Website: http://www.iyhf.org
Founded: 1932
Members: 60
Staff: 28
Contact: Rawdon Lau, Sec.Gen.
Description: National youth hostel associations in 60 countries representing 4 million members. Encourages cooperation among national youth hostel associations and seeks to educate young people of all nations by promoting youth tourism and an appreciation of travel. Provides low-cost accommodation and programs on outdoor education, recreation, and touring; holds periodic travel seminars; sponsors annual international youth travel forum and manager training program. Carries out development projects in Asia and Latin America. Conducts research and compiles statistics. Maintains numerous committees.
Publication title: Annual Report

Second publication: Book
Publication title: Guide to Budget Accommodation
Meetings/Conventions: Conference of the International Youth Hostel Federation - biennial conference - Exhibits.

Intervega - Movement for Compassionate Living the Vegan Way
MCL

31 Walton Close, Coventry, CV3 2LJ, England, UK
Tel: 44 2476 441446
Fax: 44 2476 441446
Email: oldkaie@beeb.net
Founded: 1985
Members: 800
Staff: 2
Contact: Peter Kempadoo, Coord./Sec.
Fee: £5
Description: Individuals in 32 countries. Vegans eat no animal products and promote a way of life that the movement believes will enable all people to live within the resources of the planet. Opposes exploitation of any living being.
Library Type: open to the public
Publication: Booklet
Publication title: Abundant Living in the Coming of Age of the Tree
Second publication: Journal
Publication title: New Leaves. Advertisements.
Meetings/Conventions: Fellowship and Policy Meeting - quarterly meeting

Intumescent Fire Seals Association

20 Park St., Princes Risborough, HP27 9AH, England, UK
Tel: 44 1844 275500
Fax: 44 1844 274002
Email: ifc@intfire.com
Founded: 1982
Members: 19
Contact: Graham Wiles
Description: Manufactures of intumescent fire seals. Aims to promote the life safety benefits associated with the use of intumescent and smoke seals; to promote research and development into extending the areas where these benefits can be utilised. To participate in the development of test procedures for fire protection products. Offers technical advice on fire doors, fire resistant glazing and penetration sealing systems.
Library Type: open to the public
Meetings/Conventions: - periodic workshop

Invertebrate Link
JCCBI

c/o Royal Entomological Society of London
41 Queen's Gate, London, SW7 5HU, England, UK
Tel: 44 1491 829071
Email: o.cheeseman@cabi.org
Founded: 1968
Members: 31
Contact: Stephen J. Brooks
Description: Representatives from national entomological societies plus some other invertebrate societies, observers from UK statutory conservation bodies, National Trust, etc. Advises on the conservation of UK invertebrates and their habitats, policy for legislation etc. Organizes surveys for selected species and monitors rare species conservation. The Committee has recently expanded to all terrestrial

and freshwater invertebrates - previously covered insects only, hence still entomological bias.

Formerly: Joint Committee for the Conservation of British Invertebrates

Meetings/Conventions: Maintaining the Biodiversity of British Invertebrates - periodic conference - Exhibits.

Investment Management Association
IMA

65 Kingsway, London, WC2B 6TD, England, UK
Tel: 44 20 8310898
Fax: 44 20 8319975
Email: ima@investmentuk.org
Website: http://www.investmentfunds.org.uk
Founded: 1959
Members: 235
Staff: 26
Contact: Philip Warland, Dir.Gen.
Description: The trade association for unit trust and investment fund management companies. Aims to improve the regulatory, fiscal and legal environment for unit trusts and investment funds; to increase public awareness of collective investments; to provide information, guidance, assistance and other services to its members.
Formerly: Association of Unit Trusts and Investment Funds
Meetings/Conventions: - annual conference

Investor Relations Society

3 Bedford St., Bedford House, London, WC2E 9HD, England, UK
Tel: 44 207 3791763
Fax: 44 207 2401320
Email: enquiries@irs.org.uk
Website: http://www.ir-soc.org.uk
Founded: 1980
Members: 630
Staff: 5
Contact: Andrew Hawkins, Dir.Gen.
Fee: £350
Membership Type: full
Fee: £250
Membership Type: associate
Description: UK's professional body for investor relations practitioners. Seeks to promote excellence in investor relations and enhance corporate value through effective communication. Has contributed to proposals for regulatory change and legislation, represented its members on relevant working parties and committees, and promoted education and training at all levels of investor relations. Is also a founder member of the International Investor Relations Federation and maintains contact with fellow organizations in Europe, the Americas, and the Far East.
Publication: Bulletin. Advertisements.
Second publication: Journal. Advertisements.
Meetings/Conventions: - annual conference - Exhibits.

Involvement and Participation Association

42 Colebrooke Row, London, N1 8AF, England, UK
Tel: 44 207 3548040
Fax: 44 207 3548041
Email: involve@ipa-involve.com
Website: http://www.ipa-involve.com
Founded: 1884
Members: 210
Staff: 8
Contact: William Cowpar

Description: All organizations, private and public, who want to release the full potential of their employees. Promotes employee involvement and participation at work.
Library Subject: employee involvement, management
Library Type: reference
Publication: Magazine
Publication title: IPA Magazine
Second publication: Papers
Meetings/Conventions: Company Visit tour

Irish Heritage

32 The Grove, London, N3 1QJ, England, UK
Tel: 44 20 83462726
Founded: 1973
Description: Promotes the best of Irish and Anglo-Irish music and literature.

Irish Texts Society
ITS

Royal Bank of Scotland, Drummonds Branch, 49 Charing Cross, London, SW1A 2DX, England, UK
Founded: 1898
Members: 500
Contact: Mr. Sean Hutton, Hon.Sec.
Fee: £25
Membership Type: subscription
Description: Individuals in 13 countries. Strives to advance public education by promoting the study of Irish literature.
Library Subject: Irish literature, history, and folklore, hagiography, mythology, poetry, tales, and romance
Library Type: reference
Publication title: Irish-English Dictionary
Second publication: Books
Publication title: Main Series
Meetings/Conventions: - periodic seminar

Ironmongers' Company

c/o Ironmongers' Hall
Barbican, London, EC2Y 8AA, England, UK
Tel: 44 171 7762304
Fax: 44 171 6003519
Founded: 1463
Members: 220
Contact: James A. Oliver, Clerk
Description: City of London Livery Company administering charitable trusts for the care of the elderly, education and the relief of needy people. No longer involved in the trade of its name but makes grants towards iron-related projects. Tudor-style Hall is available for public use.

ISCO Careerscope

12A Princess Way, Camberley, GU15 3SP, England, UK
Tel: 44 1276 21188
Fax: 44 1276 691833
Email: admin@isco.org.uk
Website: http://www.isco.org.uk
Founded: 1942
Members: 191000
Staff: 60
Contact: K.L.F. Beale, Admin.Dir.
Fee: £830
Description: Individual - children enrolled in our Student Scheme. Corporate Independent Schools in subscription paying membership

from where the individual membership arises. Aims to advise and assist careers and other staff in its member schools, to advise individual students and their parents on all careers and higher education matters and to advise and assist employers in contacts with independent schools and vice versa.
Publication: Directory
Publication title: Awards - Directory of Bursaries and Scholarships
Second publication: Magazine
Publication title: CareerScope. Advertisements.

Islamic Text Society
ITS

22A Brooklands Ave., Cambridge, CB2 2DQ, England, UK
Tel: 44 1223 314387
Fax: 44 1223 324342
Email: mail@its.org.uk
Website: http://www.its.org.uk
Founded: 1981
Staff: 3
Contact: Ms. Fatima Azzam, Dir.
Description: Educational charity registered in the UK and specializing in the publication of works of traditional importance to the Islamic faith and culture including translations of heritage titles.

Isle of Wight Natural History and Archaeological Society

Rylstone Gardens, Shanklin, PO37 6RG, England, UK
Tel: 44 1983 867016
Founded: 1919

Isle of Wright Chamber of Commerce

Mill Court, Furrlongs, Newport, PO30 2AA, England, UK
Tel: 44 198 3520777
Fax: 44 198 3554555
Email: chamber@wpartnership.com
Website: http://www.iwchamber.co.uk
Members: 418
Staff: 3
Contact: Barry Groves, Chief Exec.
Description: Promotes business and commerce.

ISSUE, the National Fertility Association

114 Lichfield St., West Midlands, Walsall, WS1 1SZ, England, UK
Tel: 44 1922 722888
Fax: 44 1922 640070
Email: info@issue.co.uk
Website: http://www.issue.co.uk
Founded: 1976
Members: 6000
Staff: 5
Contact: Glenis Ratcliffe, Gen.Mgr.
Fee: £20
Membership Type: First year
Fee: £20
Membership Type: Renewal
Description: Infertile women and men. Disseminates information and provides support and offers telephone counseling to infertile individuals on all aspects of infertility.
Publication: Magazine
Publication title: ISSUE
Meetings/Conventions: - annual conference - Exhibits.

Italian Chamber of Commerce in Britian

1 Princess St., London, W1R 8AY, England, UK
Contact: Barry Walker
Description: Promotes business and commerce.

Jacob Sheep Society

Foxholes Farm, Hanbury, Burton on Trent, DE13 8QT, England, UK
Tel: 44 1283 820487
Fax: 44 1283 820487
Email: secretary@jacobsheep.org.uk
Website: http://www.jacobsheep.org.uk
Founded: 1979
Members: 800
Staff: 1
Contact: Mrs. Val Hunt, Sec.
Fee: £20
Membership Type: full
Description: Small flock owners and large breeders of Jacob sheep. Saves and promotes the Jacob sheep breed and encourages and supports Society members. Registers pedigree sheep in flock book.
Publication: Journal
Publication title: Jacob Journal

Jane Austen Society - England
JAS

c/o Mrs. Maggie Lane
1 Brookleaze, Bristol, BS9 2ET, England, UK
Tel: 44 1420 562469
Website: http://www.janeaustensociety.org.uk
Founded: 1940
Members: 2050
Contact: Maggie Lane, Hon.Sec.
Fee: £15
Membership Type: regular individual
Fee: £18
Membership Type: outside UK individual
Description: Individuals worldwide interested in the life and works of Jane Austen (1775-1817), English novelist. Acts as a clearinghouse for information on Jane Austen.
Library Subject: Austen's works and related books.
Library Type: reference
Publication title: Collected Reports. Advertisements.
Second publication: Book
Publication title: Jane Austen in Bath
Meetings/Conventions: - annual general assembly - Exhibits. Chawton UK

Japanese Chamber of Commerce and Industry in the UK

Rooms 493-495, 2nd Fl. Salisbury House, 29 Finsbury Circus, London, EC2M 5QQ, England, UK
Tel: 44 207 6280069
Fax: 44 207 6280248
Email: chamber@jsecci.org.uk
Contact: Mr. Masaki Takahashi
Description: Promotes business and commerce.

Jennifer Trust for Spinal Muscular Atrophy
JTSMA

Elta House, Birmingham Rd., Stratford-Upon-Avon, CV37 0AQ, England, UK
Tel: 44 1789 267520
Fax: 44 1789 268371
Email: jennifer@jtsma.org.uk
Website: http://www.jtsma.org.uk
Founded: 1985
Members: 1500
Staff: 7
Contact: Ms. Anita Macaulay, Ch.Exec.
Description: Offers support information and advice to all those whose lives have been affected by spinal muscular atrophy (SMA).
Library Type: lending
Publication: Newsletter
Publication title: Holding Hands
Meetings/Conventions: - annual conference Stratford-upon-Avon UK

Jerome K. Jerome Society

35 Park St., Walsall, WS1 1LY, England, UK
Tel: 44 1922 629000
Fax: 44 1922 721065
Email: tonygray@fraserwood.demon.co.uk
Website: http://www.jeromekjerome.com
Founded: 1984
Members: 200
Contact: Tony Gray, Hon. Sec.
Fee: £9
Membership Type: single member
Fee: £3
Membership Type: student, OAP
Description: Promotes the life and works of Jerome K. Jerome and funds the birthplace museum in Bradford Street, Walsall. Hosts an annual dinner in May, a Christmas Concert, and a trip to the Black Forest to celebrate the 100th anniversary of the publication Three Men on the Bummel.
Library Type: not open to the public

Jewellery Distributors' Association of the United Kingdom

Federation House, 10 Vyse St., Birmingham, B18 4BR, England, UK
Tel: 44 121 2362657
Fax: 44 121 2363921
Email: secretariat@jda.org.uk
Website: http://www.jda.org.uk
Founded: 1943
Members: 80
Staff: 1
Contact: Lynn B. Snead, Mgr.
Description: Wholesalers, distributors and importers in the gold and silver jewellery, fashion jewellery and allied trades. Offers trade protection, export services, debt collection. Discounts are available at certain trade fairs and source information is available to promote business opportunities to members; represents the industry to government and other bodies, to provide a forum for discussion on topics of concern to the industry.
Publication: Newsletter
Publication title: The Distributer. Advertisements.
Meetings/Conventions: - annual general assembly

Jewish Historical Society of England
JHSE

33 Seymour Pl., London, W1H 5AP, England, UK
Tel: 44 20 77235852
Fax: 44 20 77235852
Email: jhse@dircon.co.uk
Website: http://www.users.dircon.co.uk/~jhse/
Founded: 1893
Members: 700
Staff: 1
Contact: Anita Black, Admin.
Fee: £30
Description: Libraries and other institutions; academics, amateur historians, students and other interested persons. Works to research and promote Jewish and Anglo-Jewish history and literature. Encourages research; sponsors lecture program.
Publication: Annual Report
Publication title: Bulletin of the Jewish Historical Society of England
Publication title: Jewish Historical Studies
Meetings/Conventions: - monthly lecture

Jewish Refugees Committee
JRC

The Forum, 74/80 Camden St., London, NW1 OEG, England, UK
Tel: 44 207 6911782
Fax: 44 207 6911780
Email: wjri@wjr.org.uk
Founded: 1933
Staff: 5
Description: Individuals united to assist Jewish refugees fleeing persecution. Works to provide sanctuary and ongoing support for them in the United Kingdom.
Publication title: Annual Report
Meetings/Conventions: - annual convention

Johann Strauss Society of Great Britain

12 Bishams Court, Church Hill, Caterham, CR3 6SE, England, UK
Tel: 44 1883 349681
Fax: 44 1883 349681
Email: jss@johann-strauss.org.uk
Website: http://www.johann-strauss.org.uk
Founded: 1964
Members: 500
Contact: Mrs. Viola Coates, Hon.Sec.
Description: Promotes the performance and recording, and furthers the study and deeper appreciation of the music of the Strauss family and their Viennese contemporaries.
Publication: Journal
Publication title: Vienna Music
Second publication: Newsletter

John Clare Society

59 Bryony Rd., Selly Oak, Birmingham, B29 4BY, England, UK
Tel: 44 121 4751805
Email: l.j.curry@bham.ac.uk
Website: http://vzone.virgin.net/linda.curry/jclaresociety.htm
Founded: 1981
Members: 600
Contact: Linda Curry, Hon.Treas.
Description: Promotes the work of John Clare, the 19th Century Northhamptonshire peasant poet.
Library Type: by appointment only

Publication: Journal
Publication title: John Clare Society Journal. Advertisements.
Meetings/Conventions: John Clare Festival in Helpston - annual festival Helpston UK

John Hampden Society
31 Craigwell Ave., Bucks, Avlesbury, HP21 7AF, England, UK
Tel: 44 1488 648441
Fax: 44 8700 522514
Email: enquiries@johnhampden.org
Website: http://www.johnhampden.org
Founded: 1992
Members: 150
Contact: Lord Hollenden, Chm.
Fee: £7
Membership Type: UK adult
Fee: £12
Membership Type: UK joint
Description: Works to make the character and achievements of John Hampden better known, to stimulate research into his life and times, and encourage and assist the preservation and/or renovation of the monument and artifacts associated with him. Provides access to compiled information.
Library Subject: 17th century, John Hampden, Civil War
Library Type: reference

John Innes Manufacturers Association
c/o Brian L. Dunsby, Sec.&PRO
(M14GI) PO Box 8, Harrogate, HG2 8XB, England, UK
Tel: 44 1423 879208
Fax: 44 1423 870025
Email: bdunsby@ntlworld.com
Founded: 1975
Members: 6
Contact: Brian L. Dunsby, Sec. & PRO
Fee: £500
Membership Type: corporate
Description: Manufacturers of John Innes loam-based potting mixes for both amateur gardeners and professional growers. Represents the leading UK manufacturers of traditional loam-based John Innes potting mixes, who all use the JIMA seal of approval on the packaging. The JIMA seal of approval is a registered trademark which can only be used by approved JIMA members who produce to JIMA quality standards.
Publication title: Brochure and Technical Data Sheets

John Judkyn Memorial
JJM
Claverton Manor, Bath, BA2 7BD, England, UK
Tel: 44 1225 444278
Fax: 44 1225 444279
Email: exhibits@jjm.org.uk
Website: http://www.jjm.org.uk
Founded: 1963
Staff: 3
Contact: James E. Ayres, Dir.
Description: Circulates American exhibits to British schools and provides exhibitions on American themes for museums, art galleries, embassies, and other educational bodies. Maintains a separate identity under the Trustees of the American Museum in Britain. Judkyn (1913-63), a British-born American citizen, was director of the English-Speaking Union of the United States, active in the American

Friends Service Committee, and cofounder with Dr. Dallas Pratt (1914-94) of the American Museum in Britain.
Library Subject: American history and decorative arts
Library Type: reference
Publication: Catalogs

Johnson Society - Lichfield
JS
Johnson Birthplace Museum, Breadmarket St., Lichfield, WS13 6LG, England, UK
Tel: 44 1543 2264972
Email: j.dudley@btinternet.com
Website: http://www.nbbl.demon.co.uk
Founded: 1910
Members: 800
Contact: Mr. J. Dudley, Lit.Sec.
Fee: £5
Description: Individuals in 6 countries interested in the life and works of Dr. Samuel Johnson (1709-84), English author and lexicographer. Fosters interest in Johnson and preserves the writer's birthplace as well as objects associated with him. Organizes tours and social events.
Publication title: Transactions. Advertisements.
Meetings/Conventions: - periodic lecture

Johnson Society of London
JSL
c/o Mrs. Z. O'Donnell
255 Baring Rd., Grove Park, London, SE12 OBQ, England, UK
Tel: 44 181 8510173
Email: jsl@nbbl.demon.co.uk
Website: http://www.nbbl.demon.co.uk
Founded: 1928
Members: 200
Contact: Mrs. Z. O'Donnell, Hon.Sec.
Fee: £13
Membership Type: single
Fee: £15
Membership Type: joint
Description: Individuals in 8 countries interested in the study of the 18th century and Dr. Samuel Johnson (1709-84), English author and lexicographer.
Publication: Journal
Publication title: The New Rambler. Advertisements.
Meetings/Conventions: - monthly meeting London UK

Joint Association of Classical Teachers
Senate House, Malet St., London, WC1E 7HU, England, UK
Tel: 44 20 78628706
Fax: 44 20 78628729
Email: croberts@sas.ac.uk
Website: http://www.jact.org
Founded: 1962
Members: 1500
Staff: 1
Contact: Clare Roberts, Sec.
Fee: £39
Membership Type: full
Description: Teachers of classics in schools and universities.
Publication: Newsletter
Publication title: JACT Bulletin. Advertisements.

Second publication: Journal
Publication title: JACT Review. Advertisements.
Meetings/Conventions: - annual meeting

Joint Committee of National Amenity Societies

c/o Ancient Monuments Society
St. Ann's Vestry Hall, 2 Church Entry, London, EC4V 5HB, England, UK
Tel: 44 20 72363934
Fax: 44 20 7329 3677
Email: office@ancientmonumentssociety.org.uk
Founded: 1972
Staff: 1
Contact: Matthew Saunders
Description: Coordinates strategic activities of the 8 National Amenity Societies recognized as statutory consultees on applications affecting listed buildings.

Joint Commonwealth Societies Council

c/o The Royal Commonwealth Society
18 Northumberland Ave., London, WC2N 5BJ, England, UK
Tel: 44 20 79309705
Fax: 44 20 77669200
Email: jcsc@rcsint.org
Members: 20
Staff: 2
Contact: Nicholas Hercules, Hon.Sec.
Description: Links official and unofficial British Commonwealth organizations. Shares information regarding the modern commonwealth through educational programs and events. Organizes the annual multi-faith Commonwealth Day Observance at Westminster Abbey.

Joint Council for the Welfare of Immigrants

115 Old St., London, EC1V 9RT, England, UK
Tel: 44 20 72518708
Fax: 44 20 72518707
Email: info@jcwi.org.uk
Website: http://www.jcwi.org.uk
Founded: 1967
Members: 1000
Staff: 14
Contact: Habib Rahman
Fee: £20
Membership Type: individual, unwaged
Fee: £70
Membership Type: corporate
Description: Independent national organization which exists to campaign for justice in immigration, nationality and refugee law and policy. Undertakes strategic casework and acts as an expert training resource for others who work in this field. Mission is to eliminate discrimination in this sphere.
Library Type: not open to the public
Publication: Handbook
Publication title: Immigration, Nationality & Refugee Law Handbook
Second publication: Bulletin
Publication title: JCWI Bulletin

Joint Group of Experts on the Scientific Aspects of Marine Environmental Protection
GESAMP

c/o International Maritime Organization
4 Albert Embankment, London, SE1 7SR, England, UK
Tel: 44 171 7357611
Fax: 44 171 5873210
Founded: 1969
Members: 25
Contact: Oleg Khalimonov, Adm.Sec.
Description: Individuals nominated by: Food and Agricultural Organization of the United Nations; International Atomic Energy Agency; International Maritime Organization; United Nations Educational, Scientific and Cultural Organization; United Nations Environment Programme; World Health Organization; World Meteorological Organization. Provides: assessment of the potential effects of marine pollutants; scientific bases for research and monitoring programs; international exchange of scientific information relevant to the assessment and control of marine pollution; scientific principles for the control and management of marine pollution sources; and scientific bases and criteria relating to legal instruments and other measures for the prevention, control, or abatement of marine pollution. or abatement of marine pollution.
Publication: Reports
Publication title: GESAMP Reports and Studies
Meetings/Conventions: - annual meeting

Joint Nature Conservation Committee

Monkstone House, City Rd., Peterborough, PE1 1JY, England, UK
Tel: 44 1733 562626
Fax: 44 1733 555948
Email: feedback@jncc.gov.uk
Website: http://www.jncc.gov.uk
Description: Serves as a forum through which the three country nature conservation agencies, the Countryside Council for Wales, English Nature, and Scottish Natural Heritage, deliver their statutory responsibilities as a whole and internationally. Contributes to sustaining and enriching biological diversity, enhancing geological features and sustaining natural systems. Advises ministers on the development of policies. Establishes common standards throughout Great Britain for the monitoring of nature conservation and for research. Commissions or supports research which the Committee deems relevant.

Joint Radio Co.
JRC

30 Millbank, London, SW1P 4RD, England, UK
Tel: 44 20 79635885
Fax: 44 20 79635995
Email: info@jrc.co.uk
Website: http://www.jrc.co.uk
Founded: 1934
Members: 24
Staff: 5
Contact: Mr. Adrian Grilli, Managing Dir.
Description: Manages the block allocation of spectrum for the gas and electricity industries in order that this scarce natural resource is used efficiently and in a way amenable to use by the utilities.
Formerly: Joint Radio Committee for the Nationalised Fuel and Power Industries
Meetings/Conventions: - annual meeting

Joint University Council

c/o Faculty of Economics and Social Sciences
Nottingham Trent University, Burton St., Nottingham, NG1 4BU,
England, UK
Tel: 44 115 8485537
Fax: 44 115 8486808
Email: sandra.odell@ntu.ac.uk
Website: http://www.york.ac.uk/depts/poli/juc/jucwelc.htm
Founded: 1918
Members: 100
Staff: 1
Contact: Prof. David Stanley, Ch.
Description: Academic institutions with up to 3 academic
representatives in each institution representing the Council's Public
Administration, Social Policy and Social Work Education Committees.
Co-ordinates and develops the work of universities, university colleges
and other relevant centers teaching the applied social sciences to
degree level.
Publication: Journal
Publication title: Public Policy and Administration. Advertisements.
Meetings/Conventions: - annual conference

Josephine Butler Society
JBS

60 Rotherwick Rd., London, NW11 7DB, England, UK
Tel: 44 208 4551664
Founded: 1869
Members: 100
Staff: 1
Contact: Ruth M. Cass, Hon.Corr.Sec.
Fee: £12
Membership Type: waged
Fee: £8
Membership Type: unwaged
Description: Individuals and organizations in the United Kingdom.
Espouses the principle of social justice and equality for all people and
the need for a high and equal standard of morality and sexual
responsibility. Promotes the principles of the International Abolitionist
Federation in an effort to abolish state regulation of prostitution,
combat traffic in persons, and prevent exploitation of prostitution by
third parties. Addresses legislation concerning prostitution; opposes
the lowering of the age of consent and the licensing of brothels.
Operates the Josephine Butler Educational Trust. The society is
named for Josephine Butler (1828-1906), a British social reformer.
Library Subject: campaign for repeal of Contagious Diseases Act
Library Type: reference
Formerly: Victorian Association for Moral and Social Hygiene
Publication: Newsletter
Publication title: News and Views
Meetings/Conventions: - annual meeting - Exhibits. London UK

Jubilee Research

New Economics Foundation, Cinnamon House, 6-8 Cole St., London,
SE1 AYH, England, UK
Tel: 44 207 0892853
Fax: 44 207 4076473
Website: http://www.jubilee2000uk.org
Contact: Ann Pettifor, Coordinator
Description: Individuals and organizations concerned about
international debt among developing countries. Seeks to secure
forgiveness of the international debts of developing nations by the
year 2000. Serves as a clearinghouse on international debt; conducts
lobbying and advocacy campaigns.
Formerly: Jubilee 2000

Justices' Clerks' Society

2nd Fl., Port of Liverpool Bldg., Pier Head, Liverpool, L3 1BY,
England, UK
Tel: 44 151 2550790
Fax: 44 151 2364458
Email: secretariat@jc-society.co.uk
Website: http://www.jc-society.co.uk
Founded: 1839
Members: 367
Staff: 5
Contact: Sid Brighton, Chief Exec.
Description: Clerks and chief executives of justices. Promotes
communication and cooperation among members.
Meetings/Conventions: - annual conference

Kaolin and Ball Clay Association

Park House, Courtenay Park, Newton Abbot, TQ12 4PS, England, UK
Tel: 44 1626 332345
Fax: 44 1626 322387
Founded: 1948
Members: 2
Contact: W.J.C. Watts
Description: UK producers of ball clay. Trade association for
employers.
Formerly: British Ball Clay Producers' Association

Karg-Elert Archive

38 Lyndhurst Ave., Twickenham, TW2 6BX, England, UK
Tel: 44 20 88946859
Fax: 44 20 88946859
Email: anthony@caldicott247.fs.life.co.uk
Website: http://www.karg-elert-archive.org.uk
Founded: 1987
Members: 55
Staff: 4
Contact: Anthony Caldicott, Chmn.
Fee: £10
Membership Type: ordinary
Description: Encourages and implements the recording performance,
publications and study of the music and writings of Sigfrid Karg-Elert.
Library Subject: recordings, performances, reviews, research
material relevant to archives objectives
Library Type: reference
Publication title: Review
Second publication: Newsletter. Advertisements.

Karuna Trust
KT

72 Holloway Rd., London, N7 8JG, England, UK
Tel: 44 207 7003434
Fax: 44 207 7003535
Email: info@karuna.org
Website: http://www.karuna.org
Founded: 1987
Staff: 8
Contact: Peter Joseph, Dir.
Fee: £16
Description: Buddhist charity. Coordinates and supports health,
education, and employment projects that promote self-reliance for
individuals in India.
Library Subject: Buddhism and charity.
Library Type: not open to the public
Publication title: A Peaceful Revolution
Publication title: Ambedkar and Buddhism

Kendal and South Lakeland Chamber of Commerce
Unit 1, Lake District Business Park, Mint Bridge Rd., Kendal, LA9 6NF, England, UK
Contact: Graham Haworth
Description: Promotes business and commerce.

Keygraphica
PO Box 1381, Rugby, CV21 2ZF, England, UK
Tel: 44 1788 536389
Fax: 44 1788 550152
Email: keygraphica@assocbureau.demon.co.uk
Website: http://www.keygraphica.com
Founded: 1934
Members: 37
Staff: 1
Contact: Ms. Yasmin Chopin
Description: Companies manufacturing nameplates and other graphics made of metal or plastic. Some also make membrane switches, dashboard graphics and their components.
Formerly: Formed by Merger of, Association of Industrial Graphics and Nameplate Manufacturers and Industrial Graphics Association
Meetings/Conventions: - semiannual conference

Kids' Clubs Network
Bellerive House, 3 Muirfield Crescent, London, E14 9SZ, England, UK
Tel: 44 207 5122112
Fax: 44 207 5122010
Email: information.office@kidsclub.org.uk
Website: http://www.kidsclubs.org.uk
Founded: 1981
Members: 4000
Staff: 50
Contact:
Fee: £10
Membership Type: individual
Fee: £25
Membership Type: club
Description: Aims to provide support for those setting up out of school care by providing information, publications, training and advice.

Kilvert Society
The Old Forge, Kinnersley, HR3 6QB, England, UK
Tel: 44 1544 327426
Website: http://communigate.co.uk/here/kilvertsociety
Founded: 1948
Members: 667
Staff: 7
Contact: Michael Sharp, Hon.Sec.
Fee: £6
Membership Type: annual
Description: Aims to foster an interest in the Rev. Francis Kilvert, his work, his diary and the countryside.
Library Subject: Francis Kilvert
Library Type: reference
Publication: Journal
Publication title: Journal of the Kilvert Society
Meetings/Conventions: - annual meeting

Kipling Society
6 Clifton Rd., London, W9 1SS, England, UK
Tel: 44 20 72860194
Fax: 44 20 72860194
Email: jane@keskar.fsworld.co.uk

Website: http://www.kipling.org.uk
Founded: 1927
Members: 850
Contact: Mrs. Jane Keskar, Hon.Sec.
Fee: £22
Membership Type: individual or corporate
Description: Individuals, universities and libraries from 25 countries interested in the life and works of English poet and prose writer Rudyard Kipling (1865-1936). Promotes exchange and discussion among members. Maintains speakers' bureau and makes occasional visits to the house Kipling lived in from 1902 until his death. Maintains a library and archive at City University London, and a Kipling exhibition in Rottingdean, Brighton, Sussex, England.
Library Subject: Kipling's life and work.
Library Type: reference
Publication: Journal
Publication title: Kipling Journal. Advertisements.
Meetings/Conventions: - quarterly lecture London UK

Kitchen, Bathroom, Bedroom Specialists Association
12 Top Barn Business Centre, Holt Heath, Worcester, WR6 6NH, England, UK
Tel: 44 1905 621787
Fax: 44 1905 621887
Email: info@kbsa.co.uk
Website: http://www.kbsa.co.uk
Founded: 1977
Members: 400
Staff: 3
Contact: Graham Hayden, Chief Exec.
Fee: £895
Membership Type: full retail
Description: Members design, supply or install fitted kitchens, bedrooms, bathrooms. Recognized body for the professional kitchen, bedroom and bathroom supplier who can prove to the consumer the design, supply and installation services they provide. Consumercare scheme protects consumer deposits and marketing message enforces and reinforces that security to the general public Helpline 01905 726066.
Formerly: Kitchen Specialists Association
Publication: Magazine
Publication title: The Kitchen Specialist. Advertisements.
Meetings/Conventions: - annual meeting

Knitting Industries' Federation
53 Oxford St., Leicester, LE1 5XY, England, UK
Tel: 44 116 2541608
Fax: 44 116 2542273
Email: directorate@knitfed.co.uk
Website: http://www.emnet.co.uk/kif/
Founded: 1970
Members: 250
Staff: 3
Contact: Anne Carvell
Description: Knitting manufacturers in UK, including dyers and finishers. Provides a service of representation, advice and information to members both as knitting manufacturers and employers, nationally and internationally.
Publication: Bulletins

Kvakera Esperanto-Servo
Webbs Cottage Pottery and Press, Woolpits Rd., Great Saling, Braintree, CM7 5DZ, England, UK
Tel: 44 1371 850423
Fax: 44 1371 850423
Founded: 1921
Contact: Martin Howard, Sec.
Description: Fosters the use of Esperanto among Quakers and interests Esperantists in Quakerism. Translations of Quaker literature into Esperanto.
Formerly: Kuakera Esperantista Societo
Publication: Journal
Publication title: Kvakera Esperantisto. Advertisements.
Second publication: Booklet

Laban Guild
LG
c/o Ann Ward
7 Coates Close, Heybridge, Maldon, CM9 4PB, England, UK
Tel: 44 1621 850441
Email: awardglenkeen@bigfoot.com
Website: http://www.labanguild.f9.co.uk/
Founded: 1946
Members: 450
Contact: Ann Ward, Membership Sec.
Fee: £20
Membership Type: in UK
Fee: £25
Membership Type: outside UK
Description: Individuals who work in the fields of movement analysis and professional and recreational dance in education, industry, and therapy. Founded by Rudolf von Laban and his pupils in order to ensure the development of his studies. (Laban, 1879-1958, was a German innovator in the fields of modern dance and the analysis of human movement.) The influence of Laban's work has been felt in theatrical dance and drama, in educational dance and kinetography (movement notation), and in industry and therapy. Offers tutorial service; provides training scheme for leaders of community dance groups.
Publication: Magazine
Publication title: Movement and Dance. Advertisements.
Second publication: Report
Meetings/Conventions: - annual conference - Exhibits.

Laboratory Animal Science Association
LASA
PO Box 3993, Tamworth, B78 3QU, England, UK
Tel: 44 1827 259130
Fax: 44 1827 259188
Email: lasa@globalnet.co.uk
Founded: 1976

Labour Party - Britain
16 Old Queen St., London, SW1H 9HP, England, UK
Tel: 44 8705 900200
Fax: 44 207 8021234
Email: info@new.labour.org.uk
Website: http://www.labour.org.uk
Members: 375000
Contact: Dsvid Triesman, Gen.Sec.
Description: British centre/left political party.
Meetings/Conventions: - annual conference - Exhibits.

Labour Party Women's Organisation - NEC Women's Committee
Millbank Tower, Millbank, London, SW1P 4AT, England, UK
Tel: 44 171 8021210
Email: rachel-cashman@new.labour.org.uk
Contact: Rachel Cashman, National Women's Officer
Description: Women members of the British Labour party representing the labor constituency. Represents women's views within the labor party. Campaigns for the election of labor party members to office.
Publication: Newsletter
Publication title: Women's News
Meetings/Conventions: - annual conference - Exhibits.

Labour Women's Network
Garden Cottage, The Street, Oaksey, Malmesbury, SN16 9TG, England, UK
Tel: 44 1666 577955
Fax: 44 1666 575009
Email: lwn@oaksey.com
Founded: 1988
Members: 500
Contact: Valerie Price, Admin.
Description: Supports and advises women in the Labour Party who are seeking selection for public office.
Publication: Newsletter
Second publication: Booklets

Lace Guild
The Hollies, 53 Audnam, Stourbridge, DY8 4AE, England, UK
Tel: 44 1384 390739
Fax: 44 1384 444415
Email: hollies@laceguild.org
Website: http://www.laceguild.demon.co.uk
Founded: 1976
Members: 5000
Staff: 3
Contact: Isobel Aizlewood, Hon.Sec.
Fee: £21
Membership Type: UK
Fee: £25
Membership Type: Europe
Description: Worldwide, adult and junior, amateur and professional, all abilities. Promotes the craft of lace making, its history and use, and with these objects in mind, organizes courses and workshops, lace study days, exhibitions and events.
Library Subject: lace and related topics
Library Type: not open to the public
Publication: Magazine
Publication title: Lace. Advertisements.
Second publication: Newsletter
Meetings/Conventions: - annual convention - Exhibits.

Lancaster District Chamber of Commerce, Trade and Industry
Commerce House, Fenton St., Lancaster, LA1 1AB, England, UK
Tel: 44 1524 381331
Fax: 44 1524 389505
Email: info@lancaster-chamber.org.uk
Website: http://www.lancaster-chamber.org.uk
Members: 353
Staff: 28
Contact: R B Scoffin, Chief Exec.
Description: Promotes business and commerce.

Land Institute

16 Hippodrome Mews, Holland Park, London, W11 4NN, England, UK
Tel: 44 171 2292830
Fax: 44 171 2432128
Founded: 1966
Members: 403
Staff: 1
Contact: Clifford Tippett, Sec.
Fee: £40
Membership Type: professional
Description: Solicitors, surveyors, valuers, property managers and others having an interest in the valuation, management and use of land in all its forms. The advancement of education for the public benefit of all persons in the law, economics, public and local administration, town and county planning and other relevant fields associated with the land, through conferences and seminars.
Meetings/Conventions: - quarterly seminar

Landscape Institute

LI

6/8 Barnard Mews, London, SW11 1QU, England, UK
Tel: 44 20 73505200
Fax: 44 20 73505201
Email: mail@l-i.org.uk
Website: http://www.l-i.org.uk
Founded: 1929
Members: 4500
Staff: 13
Contact: M. Wetherall, Dir.Gen.
Description: Professional body for chartered landscape architects in the United Kingdom. Aims to protect, conserve and enhance the natural and built environment for the benefit of the public.
Library Type: reference
Publication: Directory
Publication title: Directory of Registered Landscape Practices
Second publication: Journal
Publication title: Landscape Design

Landscape Research Group

LRG

Department of Social Sciences & Law, Oxford Brookes University, Gipsy Ln., Headington, Oxford, OX3 0BP, England, UK
Tel: 44 1865 483950
Fax: 44 1865 483937
Email: pgraham@brookes.ac.uk
Website: http://www.landscaperesearch.org.uk
Founded: 1967
Members: 650
Staff: 1
Contact: Pauline Graham, Sec.
Fee: £35
Membership Type: individual
Description: Individuals and corporations in 30 countries with a professional, academic, or practical interest in the landscape. Promotes education and research; encourages exchange of information for public benefit in the field of landscaping and related subjects. Conducts symposia and seminars on landscape research.
Publication: Journal
Publication title: Landscape Research. Advertisements.
Second publication: Bulletin
Publication title: Landscape Research Extra
Meetings/Conventions: conference

Latin America Bureau

LAB

1 Amwell St., London, EC1R 1UL, England, UK
Tel: 44 207 2782829
Fax: 44 207 2780165
Email: info@lab.org.uk
Website: http://www.lab.org.uk
Founded: 1977
Staff: 4
Contact: Marcela Lopez Levy
Fee: £15
Membership Type: Supporter
Description: Research and publishing organization seeking to increase British and European public awareness of problems facing Latin America and the Caribbean. Provides economic, political, social, and human rights information to educators, the media, and the public.
Publication: Newsletter
Publication title: Lab News
Second publication: Books

Law Centres Federation

Duchess House, London, W1T 5LR, England, UK
Tel: 44 3207 3878570
Fax: 44 3207 3878368
Email: info@lawcentres.org.uk
Website: http://www.lawcentres.org.uk
Founded: 1968
Members: 52
Staff: 4
Contact: Lynn Evans
Description: Law Centres give free legal advice to their local communities. The national voice of Law Centres. It acts as a co-ordinator, promoter and facilitator of Law Centre activities. Where appropriate, it comments on the provision of legal services.
Publication: Annual Report
Publication title: Legal & Advice Services: A Pathway of Exclusion
Meetings/Conventions: - annual conference - Exhibits.

Law Services Association

84 Temple Ave., London, EC4Y 0HP, England, UK
Tel: 44 2073539471
Fax: 44 2075831531
Email: j.cowdry@londonlaw.co.uk
Founded: 1919
Members: 40
Contact: Jeremy A. Cowdy
Description: Promotes the interests of law agents publishers and law printers.

Law Society

113 Chancery Ln., London, WC2A 1PL, England, UK
Tel: 44 20 72421222
Fax: 44 20 78310344
Email: info.services@lawsociety.org.uk
Website: http://www.lawsociety.org.uk
Description: Solicitors in England and Wales. Provides services and support for members; sets standards for the legal profession. Works to improve access to the law by the general public.

Law Society of England

113 Chancery Lane, London, WC2A 1PL, England, UK
Tel: 44 207 2421222
Fax: 44 207 8310344

Email: info.services@lawsociety.org.uk
Website: http://www.lawsoc.org.uk
Founded: 1831
Members: 58431
Staff: 571
Description: Members of the Law Society are solicitors in England and Wales. Membership is voluntary but practising certificates are required in order to practise - 98% of all practising solicitors are members. Since 1990, membership has been free to all holders. of practising certificates. Makes rules for the profession, guiding the regulation of conduct, education & training, remuneration, financial services, professional indemnity, keep records of solicitors and complaints against solicitors. Also aims to serve law & justice; to increase public confidence in the profession, to promote a free and independent profession. Encourages solicitors' good practice and is working to develop the legal profession in Europe.

Law Society of England and Wales
113 Chancery Ln., London, WC2A 1PL, England, UK
Tel: 44 20 72421222
Fax: 44 20 78310344
Founded: 1825

Lead Contractors Association
LCA
Centurion House, 38 London Rd., East Grinstead, RH19 1AB, England, UK
Tel: 44 1342 317888
Fax: 44 1342 303200
Email: rwr@lca.gb.com
Website: http://www.lca.gb.com
Founded: 1984
Members: 120
Staff: 2
Contact: R.W. Robertson, Sec.
Description: Contracting firms which provide leadworking services to the construction industry in the United Kingdom. Promotes the use of lead in construction. Protects members' interests. Sponsors competitions.
Publication: Membership Directory
Publication title: Directory of Specialist Leadworking Contractors. Advertisements.
Second publication: Newsletter
Meetings/Conventions: - annual seminar

Lead Development Association International
LDA
42 Weymouth St., London, W1G 6NP, England, UK
Tel: 44 20 74998422
Fax: 44 20 74931555
Email: enq@ldaint.org
Website: http://www.ldaint.org
Founded: 1956
Members: 20
Staff: 6
Contact: Dr. D.N. Wilson, Dir.
Description: Mining companies, metal producers, semi-fabricators, associations, and user groups in 10 countries. Promotes use of lead in all forms; represents the lead industry at national and international levels. Provides promotional and technical information concerning lead to developing countries. Organizes seminars on technical and environmental aspects of the production and use of lead. Conducts market surveys.

Library Type: reference
Publication title: Proceedings
Meetings/Conventions: European Lead Battery Conference - biennial - Exhibits. Berlin Germany

Lead Sheet Association
Hawkwell Business Centre, Maidstone Rd., Pembury, Tunbridge Wells, TN2 4AH, England, UK
Tel: 44 1892 822773
Fax: 44 1892 823003
Email: leadsa@globalnet.co.uk
Website: http://www.leadsheetassociation.org.uk
Founded: 1926
Members: 4
Staff: 6
Contact: B. Hawkes, Sec.
Description: Trade association representing manufacturers of lead sheet. Promotes and encourages the use of rolled lead sheet in building applications throughout the UK. Also provides a technical advisory service and operates a national network of educational centers and a mobile training unit.
Publication: Manual
Publication title: Technical Manual

Lead Smelters and Refiners Association
42 Weymouth St., London, W1G 6NP, England, UK
Tel: 44 20 74998422
Fax: 44 20 74931555
Email: enq@ldaint.org
Founded: 1967
Members: 7
Staff: 5
Contact: Dr. David Wilson, Sec.
Description: Lead smelters and refiners.

League for the Exchange of Commonwealth Teachers
LECT
7 Lion Yard, Tremadoc Rd., Clapham, London, SW4 7NQ, England, UK
Tel: 44 870 7702636
Fax: 44 870 7702637
Email: info@lect.org.uk
Website: http://www.lect.org.uk
Founded: 1901
Members: 3000
Staff: 10
Contact: Ms. Anna Tomlinson, Dir.
Fee: £10
Description: Participating schools in Australia, Bahamas, Bangladesh, Barbados, Bermuda, Canada, India, Jamaica, Kenya, New Zealand, Sierra Leone, Singapore, South Africa, Trinidad and Tobago, and other countries. Conducts 12-month teacher exchanges among Commonwealth countries to enhance professional growth while providing exposure to diverse cultures and educational systems. Seeks to foster professional adaptability through participation in teacher exchanges at all academic levels; encourages long-term realtionships among participating schools. Exchanges are arranged on a one-to-one basis; applicants correspond with and arrange accommodation for their exchange partners. Collects information through study projects. Provides grants for air fare, conferences, dependent children, and personal allowance; offers in-service training.
Publication: Magazine

Publication title: Annual Report. Advertisements.
Publication title: The Story of the League 1901-1991
Meetings/Conventions: - quarterly conference

League of Jewish Women

6 Bloomsbury Sq., London, WC1A 2LP, England, UK
Tel: 44 20 72428300
Fax: 44 20 72428313
Email: office@leagueofjewishwomen.org.uk
Website: http://www.leagueofjewishwomen.org.uk
Founded: 1943
Members: 5000
Contact: Sandra Harris
Description: Promotes friendly relations, understanding, and mutual support among Jewish women. Seeks to: improve the status of women in the Jewish and general communities; intensify in each Jewish woman her sense of Jewish consciousness; and encourage solidarity among members.
Publication: Newsletter
Publication title: Around the League

Learning Agency

9 Tavistock Pl., London, WC1H 9SN, England, UK
Tel: 44 171 2882041
Fax: 44 171 3873614
Founded: 1965
Members: 50
Staff: 11
Contact: Peter Riches
Description: Local authority social services, education welfare and housing developments, voluntary organizations and health trusts. To provide high quality training and consultancy to the core sector at all different levels and to many different disciplines and agencies.

Learning Information Network Association
LINA

c/o Vocational Technologies Ltd.
PO Box 186, Alton, GU34 3WZ, England, UK
Tel: 44 1937 843867
Fax: 44 1937 843867
Email: ronan@openline.go-learning.net
Website: http://www.lina.demon.co.uk
Contact: Robin Twining, Sec.
Fee: £100
Membership Type: organizational, associate
Description: To provide support for anyone involved in running or funding a lifelong learning database or information service.

Leatherhead Food International

Randalls Rd., Leatherhead, KT22 7RY, England, UK
Tel: 44 1372 376761
Fax: 44 1372 386228
Email: help@leatherheadfood.com
Website: http://www.leatherheadfood.com
Founded: 1919
Members: 950
Staff: 200
Contact: Mr. John Bevington, CEO
Description: Manufacturers and suppliers of food products. Seeks to advance members' commercial interests. Provides national and international support and services to food products manufacturers and suppliers.
Library Subject: food science technology and market information

Library Type: not open to the public
Publication: Manual
Publication title: European Legislation Manual
Second publication: Report
Publication title: Market Report
Meetings/Conventions: - weekly conference - Exhibits.

Leeds Chamber of Commerce

102 Wellington St., Leeds, LS1 4LT, England, UK
Tel: 44 113 2470000
Fax: 44 113 2471111
Email: info@leedschamber.co.uk
Website: http://www.leedschamber.co.uk
Members: 1456
Staff: 60
Contact: Richard Mansell, Chief Exec.
Description: Promotes business and commerce.

Legal Technology Insider

Ferndale House, Harling Rd., North Lopham, Stratford-Upon-Avon, IP22 2NQ, England, UK
Tel: 44 1379 687518
Fax: 44 1379 687704
Email: news@legaltechnology.com
Website: http://www.lssa.co.uk
Founded: 1995
Contact: Roger Hancock, Sec.
Description: Provides a regulatory body to legal software suppliers in England.

Leicester Chamber of Trade

279 London Rd., Leicester, LE2 3BE, England, UK
Description: Promotes business and commerce.

Leicestershire Chamber of Commerce and Industry

Charnwood Ct., New Walk, Leicester, LE1 6TE, England, UK
Tel: 44 116 2471800
Fax: 44 116 2470430
Email: leics@chamberofcommerce.co.uk
Website: http://www.chamberofcommerce.co.uk
Members: 1930
Staff: 40
Contact: Martin Traynor, Chief Exec.
Description: Promotes business and commerce.

Leisure and Outdoor Furniture Association

113 Worcester Rd., Chichester, PO19 4EE, England, UK
Tel: 44 1243 839593
Fax: 44 1243 839467
Email: info@lofa.com
Website: http://www.lofa.com
Founded: 1967
Members: 65
Contact: Richard Ploldman
Description: Manufacturers and distributors of garden furniture and barbecues. Works to represent and promote members' interests and products.

Leisure Studies Association
LSA

c/o M. McFee
The Chelsea School, University of Brighton, Gaudick Rd., Eastbourne, BN20 7SP, England, UK
Tel: 44 1323 640357
Fax: 44 1323 644641
Email: mcfee@solutions-inc.co.uk
Website: http://www.leisure-studies-association.info/LSAWEB/index.html
Founded: 1975
Members: 200
Contact: Mrs. Myrene L. McFee, Admin.Asst.
Fee: £70
Membership Type: corporate in United Kingdom
Fee: £40
Membership Type: individual in United Kingdom
Description: Researchers, planners, policy-makers, administrators and practitioners involved in leisure studies/research. Covers sociology, geography, psychology, management, planning, government, tourism, media, environment, education, economics, leisure industries. Themes - culture, politics, sport, social history, unemployment, consumerism, aging, gender, arts, etc.
Publication: Newsletter
Meetings/Conventions: Journeys in Leisure: Current and Future Alliances - annual conference

Leonard Cheshire International

30 Millbank, London, SW1P 4QD, England, UK
Tel: 44 171 8028200
Fax: 44 171 8028275
Email: international@london.leonard-chesire.org.uk
Website: http://www.lcint.org.uk
Founded: 1948
Staff: 10
Contact: Rupert Ridge, Dir.
Description: Locally operated programs for people with disabilities and their families in 54 countries. Seeks to improve the quality of life of people with disabilities. Maintains rehabilitation centers, skills training centers, support for employment and education programs, independent living programs, community-based support and residential services.
Publication: Magazine
Publication title: COMPASS
Second publication: Directory
Publication title: The Leonard Cheshire International

Leopold Stokowski Society
LSS

12 Market St., Deal, CT14 6HS, England, UK
Email: stowkoski@mcmail.com
Founded: 1977
Members: 1250
Staff: 5
Contact: Dr. Christine Ducrotoy, Sec.
Fee: £17
Membership Type: UK
Fee: £33
Membership Type: United States
Description: Individuals dedicated to celebrating the life and works of Leopold Stokowski (1882-1977), American conductor, composer, and founder of the American Symphony Orchestra. Strives to ensure that his works remain available for pleasure and study; advocates the release on digital disc of important Stokowski recordings; transfers old recordings onto records. Assists members in the acquisition of recordings. Sponsors lectures, discussions, and concert and opera outings. Operates speakers' bureau.
Publication: Magazine
Publication title: List of Available Recordings. Advertisements.
Second publication: Journal
Publication title: Tocatta
Meetings/Conventions: - quarterly meeting - Exhibits.

LEPRA - England

Fairfax House, Causton Rd., Colchester, CO1 1PU, England, UK
Tel: 44 1206 562286
Fax: 44 1206 762151
Email: lepra@lepra.org.uk
Website: http://www.lepra.org.uk
Founded: 1924
Members: 50
Staff: 50
Contact: Mr. Terry Vasey, Ch.Exec.
Fee: £1
Membership Type: Executive - one-time payment
Description: Objective is to eradicate leprosy throughout the world. Operates training programs for medical personnel. Supports research for the development of leprosy drugs and vaccines, and research projects of the World Health Organization. Concentrates efforts in Africa, Asia, and Brazil. Maintains special children's, eye, and hand remobilization funds. Investigates potential for treatment of leprosy in conjunction with that of other diseases. Sponsors competitions; bestows awards.
Library Subject: leprosy, TB, and HIV
Library Type: reference
Publication: Journal
Publication title: Leprosy Review. Advertisements.
Meetings/Conventions: - annual convention - Exhibits.

Leprosy Relief Association
LEPRA

c/o Terry Vasey, Esq.
Fairfax House, Causton Rd., Colchester, CO1 1PU, England, UK
Tel: 44 1206 562286
Fax: 44 1206 762151
Email: terry_vasey@lepra.org.uk
Website: http://www.leprosy.org.uk
Contact: Terry Vasey, Ch.Exec.
Description: Works as medical development charity restoring health, hope and dignity to people affected by leprosy and other diseases of poverty.

Lesbian and Gay Beereavement Project
LGBP

LGBP Vaughn Williams Centre, Colindale Hospital, London, NW9 5HG, England, UK
Tel: 44 20 84558894
Email: lgbp@aol.com
Founded: 1980
Members: 60
Staff: 2
Contact: Tristan Alexander Yates, Dir.
Description: Provides support and assistance to gay and lesbian individuals who have suffered the loss of a gay or lesbian loved one. Makes available counseling services. Conducts educational programs for heterosexual members of the caring professions regarding the

particular problems faced by gay and lesbian individuals suffering the loss of a same-gender loved one.
Library Subject: bereavement
Library Type: reference
Meetings/Conventions: - periodic seminar

Letter File Manufacturers Association

6 Wimpole St., London, W1M 8AS, England, UK
Tel: 44 207 6377692
Fax: 44 207 4363137
Email: info@bossfed.co.uk
Contact: J.S. Roscoe
Description: Promotes the interests of manufacturers of filing products in the UK.

Lewis Carroll Society

69 Cromwell Rd., Hertford, SG13 7DP, England, UK
Email: alanwhite@tesco.net
Website: http://www.aznet.co.uk/lcs/
Founded: 1969
Members: 400
Contact: Alan White, Sec.
Fee: £13
Membership Type: UK
Fee: £15
Membership Type: Europe
Description: Admirers of British author Lewis Carroll (1832-98), whose works include Alice's Adventures in Wonderland and Through the Looking Glass. Promotes appreciation of Carroll's works.
Library Subject: Lewis Carroll, Victorian life and literature
Library Type: reference
Publication: Journal
Publication title: The Carrollian
Meetings/Conventions: Summer Outing - annual

Liberal Democrat Youth and Students - UK
LDYS

4 Cowley St., London, SW1P 3NB, England, UK
Tel: 44 20 72271387
Fax: 44 20 77992170
Email: ldys@cix.co.uk
Website: http://www.ldys.org.uk
Founded: 1993
Members: 3000
Staff: 4
Contact: Veena Hudson, Hd. of Off.
Fee: £3
Description: Youth and Student organization of the Liberal Democrats.
Publication: Magazine
Publication title: Free Radical. Advertisements.
Meetings/Conventions: - biennial conference - Exhibits.

Liberal International
LI

1 Whitehall Pl., London, SW1A 2HD, England, UK
Tel: 44 20 78395905
Fax: 44 20 79252685
Email: all@liberal-international.org
Website: http://www.liberal-international.org
Founded: 1947
Members: 80

Staff: 4
Contact: Federica Sabbati, Sec.Gen.
Description: National liberal political parties and groups. Promotes: the welfare and protection of economic, racial, political, and ethnic minorities; the respect of human rights; decentralization of political and economic power; individual liberty and tolerance; conflict resolution by peaceful means. Monitors national elections. Coordinates international activities of liberal parties; conducts study visits. Cooperates with liberal forces in the developing world and cultural and research institutions.
Publication: Magazine
Publication title: Liberal Aerogramme. Advertisements.
Meetings/Conventions: congress - Exhibits. Istanbul Turkey

Liberal International

1 Whitehall Pl., London, SW1A 2HD, England, UK
Tel: 44 207 8395905
Fax: 44 207 9252685
Email: all@liberal-international.org
Website: http://www.liberal-international.org
Founded: 1947
Members: 500
Staff: 1
Contact: Tom Dale, Org.Sec.
Fee: £17.15
Membership Type: individual
Fee: £5
Membership Type: youth
Description: Liberal Democrat political activists in the U.K. organized to promote cooperation with liberals worldwide. Raises money for the work of worldwide liberal organizations. Conducts study visits to other countries and hosts visiting liberal political personalities. Offers study programs on the liberal view of world problems and provides education for British political activists on liberal politics worldwide. Arranges British representation at international gatherings of liberals and liberal organizations. Maintains speakers' bureau; sponsors fundraising social events.
Publication title: Annual Report. Advertisements.
Meetings/Conventions: - annual conference

Libertarian Alliance
LA

25 Chapter Chambers, Esterbrooke St., London, SW1P 4NN, England, UK
Tel: 44 171 8215502
Fax: 44 207 8212031
Email: chris@libertarian.co.uk
Website: http://www.libertarian.co.uk/
Founded: 1965
Contact: Dr. Chris R. Tame, Dir.
Fee: £15
Fee: £30
Description: Members in 10 countries. Promotes libertarian ideas through activities including publishing, maintaining a speakers' bureau, and holding seminars.
Formerly: Radical Libertarian Alliance
Publication title: Foreign Policy Perspectives
Second publication: Magazine
Publication title: Free Life Magazine. Advertisements.
Meetings/Conventions: - annual conference

Liberty

21 Tabard St., London, SE1 4LA, England, UK
Tel: 44 20 74033888
Fax: 44 20 74075354
Email: info@liberty-human-rights.org.uk
Website: http://www.liberty-human-rights.org.uk
Founded: 1934
Members: 7000
Staff: 16
Contact: Nwsrat Chagtai
Fee: £24
Membership Type: Individual
Fee: £8
Membership Type: Student
Description: Individuals committed to the defense and extension of civil liberties in the United Kingdom. Campaigns for: a Bill of Rights, protection against inhumane or degrading punishment; equality before the law; freedom from discrimination on grounds of disability, political opinion, race, religion, sex, or sexual orientation; protection from arbitrary arrest and unnecessary detention and for fair hearings and associated legal rights; freedom of thought and belief, speech and publication, and peaceful assembly and association; free movement, privacy, and the right of access to official information. Lobbies Parliament; takes important test cases to court; advises people on legal rights. Commissions research.
Library Type: by appointment only
Publication title: Annual Report
Second publication: Magazine
Publication title: Liberty
Meetings/Conventions: - annual meeting

Librarians of Institutes and Schools of Education

c/o Anglia Polytechnic University Library
Sawyers Hall Lane, Brentwood, CM15 9BT, England, UK
Tel: 44 1277 264504
Fax: 44 1277 211363
Email: lbryab@vaxe.anglia.ac.uk
Website: http://www.educ.cam.ac.uk/lise
Founded: 1954
Members: 47
Contact: John Makin, Chair
Description: Universities with Schools, Faculties or Departments of Education providing initial teacher education or INSET for teachers. Concerned with the provision of materials and services in support of studies and research in education and serving information needs of students, teachers, and researchers engaged in education.
Publication: Journal
Publication title: Education Libraries Journal. Advertisements.

Library and Information Research Group
LIRG

Learning and Information Services, Learning Centre, Leeds Metropolitan University, Leslie Silver Bldg., Leeds, LS1 3HE, England, UK
Tel: 44 113 2835966
Fax: 44 113 2833123
Email: p.payne@lmn.ac.uk
Founded: 1977
Members: 200
Contact: Philip Payne, Chm.
Fee: £25
Membership Type: personal
Description: Promotes awareness of the need for library and information research. Is concerned with bridging the gap between library research and practice. Organizes conferences and seminars. Publishes newsletter.
Publication: Magazine
Publication title: Library and Information Research News. Advertisements.

Licensed Taxi Drivers Association

LTDA Taxi House, Woodfield Rd., London, W9 2BA, England, UK
Tel: 44 20 72861046
Fax: 44 20 72862494
Email: info@ltda.co.uk
Website: http://www.ltda.co.uk/
Founded: 1967
Members: 6500
Staff: 10
Contact: Robert Oddy, Gen.Sec.
Description: Licensed taxi drivers. Represents members in consultation with government, local and international authorities and organizations in matters affecting the taxi trade.
Publication: Newspaper
Publication title: Taxi. Advertisements.

Licensing Executives Society - Britain and Ireland

c/o Highbury Consultants Ltd.
1 Highbury Rd., Hitchen, SG4 9RW, England, UK
Tel: 44 1462 436894
Fax: 44 1462 442647
Email: christimitchell@compuserve.com
Website: http://www.les-europe.org
Members: 750
Contact: Renate Siebrasse
Description: Businessmen, financiers, academics, scientists, engineers, lawyers and other professionals, united by a common interest in the successful commercialisation of technology and intellectual property rights by licensing or assignment. Membership is open. to all who have an interest in technology transfer and are prepared to abide by proper professional standards.

LIFE

Life House, Newbold Terrace, Leamington Spa, CV32 4EA, England, UK
Tel: 44 1926 421587
Fax: 44 1926 336497
Email: info@lifeuk.org
Website: http://www.lifeuk.org
Founded: 1970
Members: 35000
Staff: 50
Contact: Nuala Scarisbrick, Hon.Admin./Trustee
Fee: £5
Membership Type: unwaged
Fee: £15
Membership Type: waged
Description: Individuals dedicated to the abolition of abortion in the United Kingdom. Seeks to increase knowledge of the potential health risks involved in abortion. Operates 120 pregnancy care centers offering free pregnancy counseling, abortion counseling and counseling after abortion, free testing, welfare advice, and provision of baby and maternity clothes and equipment. Maintains 40 Life houses providing shelter and aid to impoverished pregnant women. Offers speakers' bureau.
Library Type: open to the public

Publication: Newsletter
Publication title: Life News. Advertisements.
Meetings/Conventions: Life National Conference - annual conference - Exhibits.

Life Insurance Association
LIA

c/o LIA House
Chorleywood, Rickmansworth, WD3 5PF, England, UK
Tel: 44 845 6442288
Fax: 44 1923 285395
Email: info@lia.co.uk
Website: http://www.lia.co.uk
Founded: 1972
Members: 25000
Staff: 25
Contact: Lyn New, Dir.
Fee: £90
Fee: £9
Description: Financial advisers, both independent and tied, broker consultants and managers in financial services. Aims to unify the profession of financial advisers in one body, the hallmarks of which are integrity, competance and service to clients. Representation at government and regulatory organization level. Provision of education courses and designatory recognition of examination success.
Publication: Magazine
Publication title: Prospect. Advertisements.
Meetings/Conventions: - annual convention

Lift and Escalator Industry Association
LEIA

33/34 Devonshire St., London, W1G 6PY, England, UK
Tel: 44 20 79353013
Fax: 44 20 79353321
Email: enquiries@leia.co.uk
Website: http://www.leia.co.uk
Founded: 1996
Members: 122
Staff: 6
Contact: David M. Fazakerley
Description: Manufacturers. Covers the manufacture, installation, service and repair, also provision of components for lifts, escalators and passenger conveyors. In addition the LEIA Educational Trust, a registered charity for the furtherance of education and training in the lift industry.
Formerly: Formed by Merger of, National Association of Lift Makers

Lifting Equipment Engineers Association
LEEA

Waggoners Ct., 77 The Street, Manuden, Bishop's Stortford, CM23 1DW, England, UK
Tel: 44 1279 816504
Fax: 44 1279 816524
Email: mail@leea.leea.co.uk
Website: http://www.leea.co.uk
Founded: 1944
Members: 135
Staff: 6
Contact: D. Bailes, Ch.Exec.
Fee: £815
Membership Type: full & assoc.
Fee: £300

Membership Type: overseas assoc.
Description: Companies that supply, service, or use lifting equipment in the United Kingdom. Promotes the use of lifting equipment. Maintains standards for the industry. Conducts educational programs. Provides a forum for the exchange of information between members in order to increase product quality and efficiency.
Library Type: reference
Publication: Handbook
Publication title: Code of Practice for the Safe Use of Lifting Equipment
Second publication: Directory
Publication title: Membership List

Light Music Society

Lancaster Farm, Chipping Lane, Preston, , England, UK
Tel: 44 1772 783646
Fax: 44 1772 786026
Email: hilary.ashton@talk21.com
Founded: 1957
Members: 300
Staff: 1
Contact: Ernest Tomlinson, Chm.
Fee: £15
Membership Type: member
Fee: £36
Membership Type: member
Description: Acts as the backing organization for the Library of Light Orchestral Music, an archive of light-orchestral performance material from the 1850s to the present.
Library Subject: orchestral sets
Library Type: lending
Publication: Newsletter
Publication title: Light Music Society Newsletter. Advertisements.
Meetings/Conventions: General Meeting & Matinee Musicale - annual general assembly Lancashire UK

Light Rail Transit Association
LRTA

PO Box 302, Gloucester, GL4 4ZD, England, UK
Tel: 44 1452 419900
Fax: 44 1452 419900
Email: office@lrta.org
Website: http://www.lrta.org
Founded: 1937
Members: 4000
Contact: Mike Taplin, Chm.
Fee: £37.5
Fee: £70
Membership Type: outside Europe
Description: Professionals, firms, and libraries involved in public transport and light rail systems. (Light rail transit is a flexible form of electric railway which can, where appropriate, mix with motor traffic or pedestrians.) Encourages the development of light rail transit worldwide, particularly in the United Kingdom. Advocates the reduction of motor traffic, improvement of public transport, and energy conservation through the utilization of light rail systems. Promotes the exchange of information concerning light rail transit and its historical aspects. Organizes study tours; collects data on tramways and light rail systems.
Library Subject: trainways and light rail transit
Library Type: not open to the public
Publication: Magazine

Publication title: Tramway Review
Second publication: Magazine
Publication title: Tramways & Urban Transit. Advertisements.

Lighting Association

Stafford Park 7, Telford, TF3 3BQ, England, UK
Tel: 44 1952 290905
Fax: 44 1952 290906
Email: enquiries@lightingassociation.com
Website: http://www.lightingassociation.com
Founded: 1939
Members: 350
Staff: 16
Contact: Graham Samuel, Sec.
Description: Manufacturers, importers and wholesalers of lighting and lighting accessories, lighting retailers. Trade Association for lighting which has a code of practice scheme, provides technical advice and retailer training courses, and supplies product safety labels. The Association also organizes the annual Lightshow Exhibition at the national exhibition centre in Birmingham and holds a student design competition. Provides full test laboratory facilities for luminaires.
Publication: Catalog
Publication title: Buyers' Guide. Advertisements.
Second publication: Newsletter
Publication title: LA Update
Meetings/Conventions: Lighting Show - annual show - Exhibits.

Lighting Industry Federation

c/o Swan House
207 Balham High Rd., London, SW17 7BQ, England, UK
Tel: 44 20 86755432
Fax: 44 20 86735880
Email: info@lif.co.uk
Website: http://www.lif.co.uk
Founded: 1969
Members: 90
Staff: 7
Contact: Ernest Magog
Description: Manufacturers of lighting equipment. Promotes the United Kingdom's lighting industry.
Publication: Brochure

Lightweight Cycle Manufacturers' Association

c/o Witcomb Cycles
21-25 Tanners Hill, London, SE8 4PJ, England, UK
Tel: 44 181 6921734
Contact: E.W. Witcomb
Description: Persons who are able to build from the bare materials into a complete frameset and/or cycle wheel building, etc. Concerned with hand built cycles and cycle framesets. All types of cycle repairs ie. brazing etc by craftsmen.

Limbless Association

Rehabilitation Centre, Roehampton Ln., London, SW15 5PR, England, UK
Tel: 44 20 87881777
Fax: 44 20 87883444
Email: membership@limbless.association.org
Website: http://www.limbless-association.org
Founded: 1983
Members: 5000
Staff: 7
Contact: Zafer Khan, Ch.

Fee: £15
Membership Type: full (limbless individual)
Fee: £75
Membership Type: life (limbless individual)
Description: Provides information and advice to people who have had amputations or who have been born without upper or lower limbs. Through a nationwide network of volunteer representatives who are all amputees themselves, offers support and encouragement to prospective amputees, careers, and those already trying to come to terms with limb loss or deficiency.
Publication: Magazine
Publication title: Step Forward. Advertisements.

LIMRA Europe

31-35 Clarendon Rd., Watford, WD17 1JA, England, UK
Tel: 44 1923 650500
Fax: 44 1923 241889
Email: info@limra.com
Website: http://www.limra.com
Founded: 1974
Members: 145
Staff: 18
Contact: George Strang, Exec.Dir. of Research
Description: Financial Services companies with an interest in long term business. Aims to enhance the marketing function of member companies through industry supported research, products and services.
Library Subject: life insurance, pensions, health insurance
Library Type: not open to the public
Formerly: Life Insurance Marketing and Research Association
Publication: Magazine
Publication title: LIMRA's Market Facts. Advertisements.
Second publication: Catalog
Meetings/Conventions: - annual meeting - Exhibits.

Lincolnshire Chamber of Commerce and Industry

Commerce House, Outer Circle Rd., Lincoln, LN2 4HY, England, UK
Tel: 44 152 2523333
Fax: 44 152 2546667
Email: enquiries@lincs-chamber.co.uk
Website: http://www.lincs-chamber.co.uk/frames.htm
Members: 1190
Staff: 17
Contact: David Wilson, Gen. Mgr.
Description: Promotes business and commerce.

Linguistics Association of Great Britain
LAGB

University of Lancaster, Lancaster, LA1 4YW, England, UK
Tel: 44 1524 594473
Fax: 44 1524 843085
Email: a.siewirska@lancaster.ac.uk
Founded: 1959

Linnean Society of London
LSL

Burlington House, Piccadilly, London, W1J 0BF, England, UK
Tel: 44 20 74344479
Fax: 44 20 72879364
Email: john@linnean.org
Website: http://www.linnean.org
Founded: 1788

Members: 2100
Staff: 7
Contact: Dr. John C. Marsden, Exec.Sec.
Fee: £50
Description: Professional scientists and others interested in natural sciences. Promotes study in all disciplines of pure biology such as agriculture, anatomy, biochemistry, genetics, medicine, and paleobiology while focusing on evolution, ecology, and systematics. Bestows awards. Organization is named for Swedish naturalist Carl Linnaeus (1707-78), who is credited with classifying and naming over 9000 plants, 828 shells, 2100 insects, and 477 fish using a method of binomial nomenclature for species and plants (fundamentals of which are still used today).
Library Subject: Topics in biology.
Library Type: by appointment only
Publication title: Biological Journal
Publication title: Botanical Journal
Meetings/Conventions: - periodic conference - Exhibits.

Liquid Food Carton Manufacturers Association

3-5 Latimer Rd., Teddington, TW11 8QA, England, UK
Tel: 44 208 9776116
Fax: 44 208 9776909
Email: jenny.francis@lfcma.org.uk
Website: http://www.drinkscartons.com
Founded: 1989
Members: 3
Staff: 1
Contact: Ms. Jenny Francis, Dir.
Description: Major manufacturers of liquid food cartons in the UK. Lobbies both UK and European governments on issues relevant to the beverage carton industry to avoid legislative discrimination. Promotes the environmental and other benefits of the beverage carton and acts as an information service.
Publication: Newsletter
Publication title: Alliance Information
Second publication: Newsletter
Publication title: Beverage Carton News

Little Theatre Guild of Great Britain

181 Brampton Rd., Carlisle, CA3 9AX, England, UK
Tel: 44 1228 522649
Fax: 44 1228 522649
Email: barbaraw@carlisle-city.gov.uk
Website: http://www.uktw.co.uk/clubs/ltg.htm
Founded: 1946
Members: 92
Contact: Mrs. B.C. Watson, Sec.
Fee: £45
Description: Independent and self-governing theatre companies, non-commercial in character and controlling and established theatre. To extend close co-operation between members in all areas of theatre; to organize national and regional conferences and seminars; to act as a co-ordinating body for the development of little theatres, and to lobby on their behalf on matters of national interest, such as taxation, charitable status, licensing, sponsorship, insurance and royalties.
Publication: Newsletter. Advertisements.
Meetings/Conventions: - annual conference

Live and Let Live Animals and Connected Human Rights

88 Cobden St., Luton, LU2 0NG, England, UK
Email: kittyplant@netscapeonline.co.uk

Founded: 1990
Contact: Debby Wakeham, Founder
Fee: £10
Membership Type: group
Fee: £5
Membership Type: individual
Description: Supports the connected right to life of people of all ages and of animals. Opposes war, abortion, euthanasia, capital punishment, economic injustice, cruelty to animals, and eugenic killing. Works to make abortion unnecessary through education and improvement in the social and economic status of women; facilitates access to family planning programs; advocates comprehensive sex education as part of public school curricula. Hopes to eradicate vivisection, blood sports, and the meat trade.
Publication title: Euthanasia Briefing Pack
Second publication: Reports

Liverpool Chamber of Commerce and Industry

1 Old Hall St., Liverpool, L3 9HG, England, UK
Tel: 44 151 2271234
Fax: 44 151 2360121
Email: chamber@liverpoolchamber.org.uk
Website: http://www.liverpoolchamber.org.uk
Members: 1200
Staff: 67
Contact: Peter Ralphs, CEO
Description: Promotes business and commerce.

Livestock Auctioneers' Association

Audley House, 5 Woolley St., Bradford-on-Avon, BA15 1AD, England, UK
Tel: 44 1225 862666
Fax: 44 1225 860907
Email: db@laa.co.uk
Website: http://www.laa.co.uk
Founded: 1954
Members: 213
Staff: 2
Contact: D.A. Brown
Description: Open to firms operating livestock auction markets in England and Wales. Membership dependent on recommendation from local Livestock Auctioneers Association. All matters affecting the marketing of cattle, sheep and pigs.
Publication: Booklet
Publication title: Future Trends in Livestock Market
Second publication: Pamphlet
Publication title: Livestock Markets - Open to All
Meetings/Conventions: - annual general assembly

Living Streets, 31-33 Bondway, London, SW8 1SJ, England, UK

Tel: 44 207 8201010
Fax: 44 207 8208208
Email: info@livingstreets.org.uk
Website: http://www.livingstreets.org.uk
Founded: 1929
Members: 1200
Staff: 7
Contact: Terence Bendixson, Pres.
Fee: £15
Membership Type: individual
Description: Seeks to make roads safer for all users, particularly pedestrians. Works to insure that public walkways are both safe and scenic; promotes establishment of pedestrians only areas cities;

lobbies for strict observance and enforcement of speed limits, and for the rights of pedestrians at crosswalks and intersections. Maintains Walkways advice service to assist local communities with traffic problems; makes available Walk Talk environmental education program.
Library Subject: roads, transportation, road safety
Library Type: by appointment only
Formerly: Pedestrians' Association
Publication: Journal
Publication title: WALK. Advertisements.
Meetings/Conventions: - quarterly board meeting - Exhibits.

Lloyd's Aviation Underwriters' Association
Lloyd's Building, Lime St., London, EC3M 7DQ, England, UK
Tel: 44 171 3274045
Fax: 44 171 3274711
Email: laua@laua.e-market.net.uk
Founded: 1935
Members: 22
Staff: 3
Contact: Ian S. MacFarlane, Sec.
Description: Lloyd's Underwriters of Aviation business. Presents members' views to, and their negotiation with, other bodies regulatory authorities. The provision of information to members from such bodies.

Lloyd's Motor Underwriters' Association
c/o Irongate House
Dukes Pl., London, EC3A 7LQ, England, UK
Tel: 44 207 6267006
Fax: 44 207 9291224
Email: lmua@lloyds.com
Founded: 1931
Members: 15
Staff: 4
Contact: R.M. Jones
Description: All syndicates at Lloyd's which transact motor insurance in the UK.

Local Authorities Coordinators of Regulatory Services
10 Albert Embankment, London, SEI 7SP, England, UK
Tel: 44 20 78407200
Fax: 44 20 77359977
Email: faisal.hossain@lacots.gov.uk
Website: http://www.lacots.com
Founded: 1978
Members: 500
Staff: 22
Contact: Maragaret Humphreys
Description: Local authorities in England, Wales, Scotland and Northern Ireland. Aims to provide a uniform interpretation of legislation and be a centre for conciliation and exchange of information. Promotes good enforcement practice, maintains a register of overloading convictions and liaises with trade and consumer organisations; advises government and European institutions. Develops contacts with enforcement practitioners overseas.
Library Subject: enforcement and regulations
Library Type: not open to the public
Publication: Report

Local Authorities Research and Intelligence Association
c/o Graham Smith
9 Cortland Rd., Nunthorpe, Middlebrough, TS7 0JX, England, UK
Tel: 44 1642 316576
Fax: 44 1642 314892
Email: larioffice@aol.com
Website: http://www.laria.gov.uk
Founded: 1974
Members: 1100
Staff: 1
Contact: Graham Smith, Admin.
Fee: £5
Description: Mainly research officers in local government, health service, academia and central government. To promote the further development of research practices and to encourage communication between those engaged in research and intelligence in local government by providing a national forum for the sharing of technical knowledge and research methods.
Publication: Newsletter
Publication title: Laria News. Advertisements.
Meetings/Conventions: - annual conference - Exhibits.

Local Authority Caterers Association
Bourne House, Horsell Park, Woking, GU21 4LY, England, UK
Tel: 44 1483 766777
Fax: 44 1483 751991
Email: admin@laca.co.uk
Website: http://www.laca.co.uk
Founded: 1990
Members: 1052
Staff: 2
Contact: Vivianne Buller, Chair
Fee: £60
Membership Type: full
Fee: £60
Membership Type: associate
Description: Qualified catering managers in local authority departments. Promotes the professionalism of local authority caterers by running annual national conferences and exhibitions for national members. Regional seminars and training programmers. Also lobbies MPs on concerns of members.
Formerly: National Association of Senior Meals Organizers
Publication: Annual Report. Advertisements.
Second publication: Handbook
Meetings/Conventions: - annual conference - Exhibits. Birmingham UK

Local Authority Road Safety Officers' Association
5 Farriers Ct., Scopwick, Lincoln, LN4 3PL, England, UK
Tel: 44 1526 322199
Fax: 44 1526 322391
Email: bhogarth@bun.com
Website: http://www.larsoa.org
Founded: 1974
Members: 200
Contact: Wendy Broome, Chm.
Fee: £100
Description: Senior road safety education personnel operating in all the local authorities throughout the UK, except London. Advises local authorities on policy matters relating to the safety of road users and represents local authorities in national matters related to road safety education, training and publicity.
Meetings/Conventions: - semiannual

Locomotive and Carriage Institution

20 Savill Gardens, Raynes Park, London, SW20 0UJ, England, UK
Tel: 44 20 83953713
Email: alan.spencer@lococarriage.org.uk
Website: http://www.lococarriage.org.uk
Founded: 1911
Members: 295
Contact: Mr. A.J. Spencer
Fee: £13
Membership Type: railway staff and managers
Description: Employees of rail transport administrations or associated industries. Aims to promote knowledge concerning all aspects of the railway industry. Enables members to meet to facilitate the exchange of ideas and information and to discuss technical developments. Also arranges speakers from the industry to address meetings. Visits to railway installations and those of the associated industries as well as visits abroad are arranged.
Formerly: Loco & Carr Inst
Publication title: Prospectus
Publication title: Syllabus of Winter Meetings
Meetings/Conventions: - monthly general assembly

London and Middlesex Archaeological Society LAMAS

c/o The Museum of London
150 London Wall, London, EC2Y 5HN, England, UK
Email: postmaster@london-arch-soc.demon.co.uk
Website: http://www.lamas.org.uk
Founded: 1855
Members: 654
Contact:
Fee: £15
Membership Type: individual
Fee: £17
Membership Type: joint
Description: Encourages the study of and interest in the archaeology local history and historic buildings of the London area.
Publication: Journal
Publication title: Transactions
Second publication: Newsletter

London Association of Primal Psychotherapists

West Hill House, 6 Swains Ln., London, N6 6QS, England, UK
Tel: 44 207 2679616
Fax: 44 207 4820858
Email: info@lapp.org
Website: http://www.lapp.org
Founded: 1986
Members: 55
Staff: 5
Contact: Susan Cowan-Jenssen
Description: Student membership open to trainees; associate membership open to people with an interest in the field of psychotherapy; full membership open to those qualified to work as primal psychotherapists. Aims to refine and develop primal psychotherapy. To this end a four year training programme is run that is recognized by the United Kingdom Council for Psychotherapy. Also has a trust fund devoted to working with people facing life threatening illness.

London Boroughs Grants

59 Southwark St., London, SE1 0EL, England, UK
Tel: 44 207 9349999

Email: info@lbgrants.org.uk
Founded: 1985
Members: 33
Staff: 35
Contact: Ian Brown
Description: One councillor from each of the 33 London councils is elected to represent its borough on the committee. Strategic funding body for the voluntary sector. It funds about 500 voluntary organizations from an annual budget. Part of the Association of London Government.
Publication: Newsletter
Publication title: London Grants News

London Chamber of Commerce and Industry

33 Queen St., London, EC4R 1AP, England, UK
Tel: 44 207 2484444
Fax: 44 207 4890391
Email: lc@londonchamber.co.uk
Website: http://www.londonchamber.co.uk
Members: 3100
Staff: 100
Contact: Peter Bishop, CEO
Description: Promotes business and commerce.

London International Financial Futures and Options Exchange

Cannon Bridge House, 1 Cousin Ln., London, EC4R 3XX, England, UK
Tel: 44 20 76230444
Fax: 44 20 75883624
Website: http://www.liffe.com
Founded: 1982
Members: 200
Staff: 500
Contact: Hugh Freedberg, Chief Exec.
Description: Members represent a variety of sectors and geographical areas of the international financial community.
Library Type: by appointment only

London Investment Banking Association LIBA

6 Frederick's Pl., London, EC2R 8BT, England, UK
Tel: 44 20 77963606
Fax: 44 20 77964345
Email: liba@liba.org.uk
Website: http://www.liba.org.uk
Founded: 1988
Members: 45
Staff: 13
Contact: Peter E. Beales, Dir./Sec.
Description: Principal trade association in the UK for firms active in the investment banking and securities industry. Represents the interests of its members on all aspects of their business and promotes their views to the authorities in the UK, the European Union, and elsewhere.
Formerly: British Merchants Banking and Securities Houses Association
Publication title: Annual Report
Second publication: Membership Directory

London Mathematical Society
LMS

De Morgan House, 57-58 Russell Sq., London, WC1B 4HS, England, UK
Tel: 44 207 6373686
Fax: 44 207 3233655
Email: lms@lms.ac.uk
Website: http://www.lms.ac.uk
Founded: 1865
Members: 2400
Staff: 12
Contact: P.R. Cooper, Exec.Sec.
Fee: £27
Membership Type: individual
Fee: £54
Membership Type: individual
Description: Academic mathematicians. Concerned with the promotion and extension of mathematical knowledge. It is also actively interested in matters concerning mathematical education.
Publication: Journal
Publication title: Bulletin
Second publication: Journal
Publication title: Journal

London Money Market Association

c/o Investec Bank (UK)
2 Gersham St., London, EC2V 7QP, England, UK
Tel: 44 171 5974485
Fax: 44 171 5974491
Founded: 1998
Members: 18
Contact: R.J. Vardy, Sec.
Description: Represents members' interests.

London Natural History Society
LNHS

c/o Natural History Museum
Cromwell Rd., London, SW7 5BD, England, UK
Tel: 44 20 79389123
Website: http://www.lnhs.org.uk
Founded: 1858
Members: 1400
Contact: Prof. John Edgington, Sec.
Fee: £30
Fee: £20
Description: Promotes natural history within 20 miles of central London, through scientific investigations, nature conservation and publication.
Library Subject: natural history
Library Type: open to the public
Publication: Journal
Publication title: The London Naturalist
Second publication: Journal
Publication title: The London Bird Report

London Record Society

c/o Institute of Historical Research
Senate House, London, WC1E 7HU, England, UK
Tel: 44 2078628798
Fax: 44 2078628793
Email: heather.creaton@sas.ac.uk
Website: http://www.history.ac.uk/cmh/cmh.main.html
Founded: 1964
Members: 350
Contact: Heather Creaton, Hon.Sec.
Fee: £22
Membership Type: individual
Fee: £35
Membership Type: institutional
Description: Publishes transcripts, abstracts and lists of primary sources for the history of London, and generally to stimulate interest in archives relating to London.
Meetings/Conventions: - annual meeting

London Sisal Association

162 Stirling Cres., Hedge End, Southampton, S030 2AL, England, UK
Tel: 44 1489 788529
Email: barbara@bfrench40frnet.co.uk
Founded: 1953
Members: 25
Staff: 1
Contact: Mrs. B. French, Sec.

London Society
LS

Mortimer Wheeler House, 46 Eagle Wharf Rd., London, N1 7ED, England, UK
Tel: 44 207 2539400
Fax: 44 207 2539400
Email: londonsociety@hotmail.com
Website: http://www.londonsociety.org.uk
Founded: 1912
Contact: B. Jones, Hon.Sec.
Fee: £6
Membership Type: ordinary
Fee: £9
Membership Type: corporate
Description: Individuals and organizations with an interest in the growth and development of the city of London. Promotes economically and environmentally sustainable urban growth. Provides advice and assistance to city planning and development organizations and corporations; represents the environmental interests of local inhabitants when new developments are proposed. Conducts architectural tours
Library Subject: history, topography, urban environments
Library Type: reference
Publication: Journal
Publication title: Journal of the London Society
Second publication: Newsletter
Meetings/Conventions: Banister Fletcher Lecture - annual lecture

London Subterranean Survey Association
LSSA

98 Cambridge Gardens, London, W10 6HS, England, UK
Tel: 44 20 73612097
Fax: 44 20 73613463
Email: plnrm@rbkc.gov.uk
Founded: 1968
Contact: Dr. Roger J. Morgan
Description: Promotes study of man made and used underground space beneath London and its interaction with surface development.

London Swing Dance Society

31 Rashleigh House, Thanet St., London, WC1H 9ER, England, UK
Tel: 44 207 3871011
Email: swinguk@zetnet.co.uk
Website: http://www.swingdanceuk.com
Founded: 1986
Members: 2000
Staff: 2
Contact: Mr. Simon Selmon, Dir.
Fee: £1
Membership Type: full
Description: Supports and promotes swing dance events, classes and performances. Performs as Sugarfoot Stompers.

London Topographical Society

36 Old Deer Park Gardens, Richmond, TW9 2TL, England, UK
Tel: 44 20 89405419
Email: patfrazer@yahoo.co.uk
Website: http://www.topsoc.org
Founded: 1880
Members: 900
Contact: Patrick Frazer, Hon.Sec.
Fee: £20
Membership Type: member
Description: Individuals interested in maps and the history of London. Publishes reproductions of maps, prints, and views of London, and promotes original research into London's history and topography.

London Transport Users Committee

6 Middle St., London, EC1A 7JA, England, UK
Tel: 44 20 75059000
Fax: 44 20 75059003
Email: enquiries@ltuc.org.uk
Website: http://www.ltuc.org.uk
Founded: 1984
Members: 26
Staff: 23
Contact: Rufus Barnes, Dir.
Description: Members are appointed by the Greater London Assembly. Represents the interests of users of London Transport's bus network, the Underground, Heathrow Express, Eurostar, and the national railways in and around London.
Library Subject: London public transportation
Library Type: by appointment only
Formerly: London Regional Passengers Committee
Publication: Annual Report
Meetings/Conventions: - bimonthly executive committee meeting

London Welsh Association

LWA

157 Gray's Inn Rd., London, WC1X 8UE, England, UK
Tel: 44 20 78373722
Founded: 1920

Longhorn Cattle Society

Gidleys, 36 Ide Lane Alphington, Exeter, EX2 8UT, England, UK
Tel: 44 1392 270421
Fax: 44 1392 270421
Email: longhorncs@aol.com
Website: http://longhorncattlesociety.com
Founded: 1878
Members: 400

Staff: 1
Contact: Elizabeth Henson
Fee: £15
Membership Type: full
Fee: £7
Membership Type: associate
Description: Seeks to maintain, conserve and promote the British Longhorn breed of cattle.
Publication: Newsletter. Advertisements.
Second publication: Books
Meetings/Conventions: - annual meeting

Long-term Medical Conditions Alliance

LMCA

Unit 212, 16 Baldwins Gardens, London, EC1N 7RJ, England, UK
Tel: 44 2078133637
Fax: 44 2078133640
Email: info@lmca.org.uk
Website: http://www.lmca.demon.co.uk
Founded: 1989
Members: 115
Staff: 8
Contact:
Fee: £300
Membership Type: voluntary health organizations
Description: Umbrella body working with member organisations towards better lives for people with long-term health conditions. Aims to gain recognition of people's needs and ensure resources are available to meet them, to campaign to achieve change in areas of common concern, to develop effective partnerships between service providers and service users, and to promote participation by individuals in their own care and treatment.

Loriners' Company

8 Portland Square, London, E1W 9QR, England, UK
Tel: 44 171 709 0222
Founded: 1261
Contact: G.B. Forbes, Clerk
Description: Makers of bits, spurs, and stirrups. Represents members' interests.

Loss Prevention Council

Melrose Ave., Borehamwood, WD6 2BJ, England, UK
Tel: 44 181 2072345
Fax: 44 20 82369601
Email: info@lpc.co.uk
Founded: 1986
Staff: 170
Contact: Mr. G. Orme, Chief Exec.
Library Subject: loss prevention, fire safety, related subjects
Library Type: not open to the public

Low Power Radio Association

LPRA

c/o Walker Mitchell Ltd., Secretariat
Brearley Hall, Halifax, HX2 6HS, England, UK
Tel: 44 1422 886463
Fax: 44 1422 886950
Email: info@lpra.org
Website: http://www.lpra.org
Founded: 1990
Members: 160

Staff: 2
Contact: Stella E. Stiegeler
Fee: £417
Membership Type: ordinary
Description: Companies involved in telemetry, telecommand, RFID and alarms in the licence-exempt frequency bands. Membership includes manufacturers, suppliers, installers, designers, consultants and end users of low power radio. Aims to promote the responsible use of low power radio equipment and to act as a channel of communication between the European radio authorities and LPRA members.
Publication: Newsletter
Publication title: LPRA News. Advertisements.
Publication title: LPRA Yearbook and Buyers' Guide
Meetings/Conventions: Radio Solutions - annual conference - Exhibits. London UK

LP Gas Association
Pavilion 16, Headlands Business Pk., Salisbury Rd., Ringwood, BH24 3PB, England, UK
Tel: 44 1425 461612
Fax: 44 1425 471131
Email: mail@lpga.co.uk
Website: http://www.lpga.co.uk
Founded: 1970
Members: 197
Staff: 5
Contact: Tom Fidell, Dir.Gen.
Description: Full members are involved in the sale of LP Gas or the manufacture of gas appliances or equipment. Aims to promote the safe use and development of the LPG industry and represents the industry in consultation with government departments and the EU in respect of environmental, health and safety and fiscal duty issues affecting the UK. It also provides technical advice on safety in installation and use of LPG.
Formerly: Liquified Petroleum Gas Technical Association
Meetings/Conventions: - annual conference

Lute Society
LS
Southside Cottage, Brook Hill, Albury, Guildford, GU5 9DJ, England, UK
Tel: 44 1483 202159
Fax: 44 1483 203088
Email: lutesoc@aol.com
Website: http://www.lutesoc.co.uk/
Founded: 1956
Members: 700
Staff: 1
Contact: Christopher Goodwin, Sec.
Fee: £30
Description: Individuals and university libraries in 23 countries interested in the lute and associated instruments. Promotes appreciation of lute playing and knowledge of lute history, technique, and construction. Maintains picture collection.
Library Subject: lute music, musicology
Library Type: reference
Publication: Journal
Publication title: The Lute. Advertisements.
Second publication: Magazine
Publication title: Lute News
Meetings/Conventions: - quarterly meeting

Lymphoma Association
PO Box 386, Aylesbury, HP20 2GA, England, UK
Tel: 44 1296 619400
Fax: 44 1296 619414
Email: support@lymphoma.org.uk
Website: http://www.lymphoma.org.uk
Founded: 1986
Members: 2000
Staff: 15
Description: Provides information and emotional support for anyone affected by lymphoma. Provides a Help line; telephone links to helpers with similar experience of lymphoma; a network of regional support groups and a quarterly newsletter for members.
Library Subject: lymphomas, living with cancer, treatments
Library Type: lending
Publication title: Fundraising News
Second publication: Newsletter
Publication title: Lymphoma News
Meetings/Conventions: - annual conference

Macclesfield Chamber of Commerce and Enterprise
Churchill Chambers, Churchill Way, Macclesfield, SK11 6AS, England, UK
Tel: 44 1625 664400
Fax: 44 1625 664415
Email: macclesfieldchamber@sectec.co.uk
Website: http://www.maccdirectory.co.uk/chamber/chamber.asp
Members: 660
Staff: 14
Contact: John Lamond, Chief Exec.
Fee: £71
Description: Promotes business and commerce.
Library Type: open to the public

Macular Disease Society
Darwin House, 13a Bridge St., Andover, SP10 1BE, England, UK
Email: info@maculardisease.org
Website: http://www.maculardisease.org
Founded: 1986
Members: 12000
Staff: 2
Contact: Tom Bremridge, Exec.
Fee: £15
Membership Type: large print
Fee: £15
Membership Type: audio tape
Description: Aims to provide information, fellowship and support to those with macular disease.

Made-up Textiles Association
42 Heath St., Tamworth, B79 7JH, England, UK
Tel: 44 1827 52337
Fax: 44 1827 310827
Email: info@muta.org.uk
Website: http://www.muta.org.uk
Founded: 1919
Members: 283
Contact: M.P. Skelding, Sec.
Description: Companies engaged in the manufacture and processing of tarpaulins, marquees, tents, awnings, sails flags, inflatables, reusable healthcare textiles, and banners. Represents the interests of companies which manufacture and process heavy textiles. It represents its members in international, European and national standards organizations and by lobbying government departments in

London and Brussels. MUTA members use their collective expertise to develop codes of practice for the industry and to initiate research in relevant technologies.
Publication: Magazine
Publication title: Industrial Textiles. Advertisements.
Meetings/Conventions: MUTA Trade Fair - annual conference - Exhibits.

Magistrates' Association of England and Wales

28 Fitzroy Sq., London, W1T 6DD, England, UK
Tel: 44 20 73872353
Fax: 44 20 73834020
Email: secretariat@magistrates-association.org.uk
Website: http://www.magistrates-association.org.uk
Founded: 1920
Members: 29000
Staff: 12
Contact: Ms. S.J. Dickinson, Sec./CEO
Fee: £22
Description: Magistrates.
Library Subject: law
Library Type: not open to the public
Publication: Journal
Publication title: The Magistrate. Advertisements.

Mail Order Traders' Association

PO Box 1023, Liverpool, L69 2WS, England, UK
Tel: 44 151 2275456
Fax: 44 151 2275678
Email: ukmota@cs.com
Founded: 1948
Members: 7
Staff: 2
Contact: Mr. M. Hogarth, Chief Exec.
Description: The large general catalogue mail order companies and firms trading in the United Kingdom. Protects and enhances the interests of its membership, deals with queries and complaints made by members of the public including the supervision and enforcement of the Association's Code of Practice, to deal with enquiries from the media and consumer organizations. In addition, the Association responds to points raised by Central government, the European Commission, the Parliament of Westminster and the European Parliament.

Mail Users' Association

70 Main Rd.d, Hermitage, Emsworth, PO10 8AX, England, UK
Founded: 1976
Members: 100
Contact: Jeremy Partridge, Exec.Dir.
Description: Open to any business, large or small, wishing to support the aims of the MUA. Business sectors currently represented include financial services, publishing, communications, print distribution, direct marketing, banking and charities. Aims to strive for the improvement of postal services to/from all addresses in terms of reliability, security, choice and value. Its activities revolve around bringing pressure to bear upon the Post Office and government to achieve its goals. Funded by membership subscriptions.

Maine-Anjou Cattle Society of the UK

20 Mill St., Shipston-On-Stour, CV36 4AW, England, UK
Founded: 1972
Members: 10
Staff: 2
Contact: Mr. S. Bosley, Pres.

Fee: £12
Membership Type: full member
Description: Develops and promotes the Maine-Anjou cattle breed in Great Britain and abroad.
Library Type: reference

Making Music

7-15 Rosebery Ave., London, EC1R 4SP, England, UK
Tel: 44 870 9033780
Fax: 44 870 9033785
Email: info@makingmusic.org.uk
Website: http://www.makingmusic.org.uk
Founded: 1935
Members: 1922
Staff: 8
Contact: Rachel Tuxford, Asst.
Description: Members belong to amateur music clubs, choral and orchestral societies.
Formerly: National Federation of Music Societies
Publication: Newsletter
Publication title: NFMS News. Advertisements.
Second publication: Annual Report
Meetings/Conventions: - annual conference - Exhibits.

Malone Society
MS

c/o Anne Ashby
Oxford University Press, Arts and Reference Division, Walton St., Oxford, 0X2 6DP, England, UK
Tel: 44 1865 558229
Email: creaser@holl.u-net.com
Website: http://www.smuc.ac.uk/malone/
Founded: 1906
Members: 650
Contact: Prof. John Creaser, Exec.Sec.
Fee: £20
Membership Type: individual or institutional
Description: Individuals worldwide interested in English Renaissance drama; libraries. Prints 1 or 2 volumes each year of edited texts of early English dramatic works, particularly rare and inaccessible texts of Renaissance plays, and of documents relating to the drama.
Publication: Book
Publication title: Malone Society Reprints
Meetings/Conventions: - annual general assembly Oxford UK

Maltsters' Association of Great Britain

31b Castle Gate, Newark, NG24 1AZ, England, UK
Tel: 44 1636 700781
Fax: 44 1636 701836
Email: info@magb.org.uk
Website: http://www.ukmalt.com
Founded: 1827
Members: 14
Staff: 3
Contact: I.R. Murrell, Dir.Gen.
Description: Sales maltsters, selling malt on the open market, and brewer and distiller maltsters, who make malt for brewing and distilling in-house. Promotes the interests of the trade, and to keep a watch on all legislation, litigation, public proceedings etc which may affect the trade; secures the benefits of co-operation to members in aspects of training, health and safety etc.

Mammal Society
MS

15 Cloisters House, 8 Battersea Park Rd., London, SW8 4BG, England, UK
Tel: 44 20 74984358
Fax: 44 20 76228722
Email: enquiries@mammal.org.uk
Website: http://www.mammal.org.uk
Founded: 1954
Members: 2000
Staff: 3
Contact: Georgette Shearer
Fee: £20
Membership Type: full
Fee: £10
Membership Type: student
Description: Individuals interested in the study of mammals. Promotes the conservation and study of British mammals. Organizes conservation projects, surveys, and symposia.
Publication: Newsletter
Publication title: Mammal News and Mammalaction News. Advertisements.
Publication title: Mammal Review
Meetings/Conventions: Mammal Society Easter Conference and AGM - annual conference

Management Consultancies Association

49 Whitehall, London, SW1A 2BX, England, UK
Tel: 44 20 73213990
Fax: 44 20 73213991
Email: bruce.petter@mca.org.uk
Website: http://www.mca.org.uk
Founded: 1956
Members: 70
Staff: 8
Contact: Bruce Petter, Exec.Dir.
Fee: £7000
Description: Full and associate. Both memberships must fulfil the same criteria and principles but the qualifications required differ. Principal activities are the enhancement of the management consultancy profession and the furthering of the collective objectives and interests of its members. It is the focal point for those wishing to seek advice on management consultancy, and the forum for members of the Association to discuss matters of current interest and future policy.

Manchester Chamber of Commerce and Industry

56 Oxford St., Manchester, M6O 7HJ, England, UK
Tel: 44 161 2374029
Fax: 44 161 2364160
Email: sheenah.grant@mcci.org.uk
Website: http://www.mcci.co.uk
Founded: 1874
Members: 3000
Staff: 12
Contact: Angie Robinson, Chief Exec.
Description: Businesses, professionals, and interested individuals. Promotes the commercial and industrial interests of businesses throughout England. Facilitates the development of national and international trade by providing traders and investors with information and advice on new markets and products. Services offered include research and information gathering on trade opportunities, educational programs, and consumer and business assistance.

Manorial Society of Great Britain
MSGB

104 Kennington Rd., London, SE11 6RE, England, UK
Tel: 44 207 7356633
Fax: 44 207 5827022
Email: manorial@msgb.co.uk
Website: http://www.msgb.co.uk
Founded: 1906
Members: 1200
Staff: 5
Contact: Robert Alexander Smith, Chm.
Fee: £20
Membership Type: holder of a British title
Description: Aristocrats, gentry, landowners, lawyers, and real estate agents in Europe and the United States; others interested in British manors. Provides legal and estate advice; gathers historical information concerning manors in the United Kingdom. Sponsors research and educational programs. Organizes annual exhibitions, auctions, receptions, and dinners.
Library Subject: manorial and Aristocratic history
Library Type: reference
Publication: Bulletin
Publication title: Bulletin of the Manorial Society of Great Britain. Advertisements.
Publication title: House of Commons, 700 Years of British Tradition
Meetings/Conventions: - annual conference - Exhibits.

Manpower Society

34 Downview Rd., Felpham, Bognor Regis, PO22 8HH, England, UK
Tel: 44 1243 837355
Fax: 44 1243 837355
Email: heather@mansoc.org.uk
Website: http://www.mansoc.demon.co.uk
Founded: 1970
Members: 400
Contact: H.M. Gale, Admin.Mgr.
Fee: £324
Membership Type: corporate
Fee: £30
Membership Type: individual
Description: Corporate - companies and public authorities may hold corporate membership and nominate up to ten members of staff to represent them. Individual - open to interested persons who may come from a wide range of organizations. The society does not administer examinations or require formal qualifications for membership. Promotes the study of manpower policy, management and planning utilisation. Activities include information exchange, presidential forums, and special interest groups for the financial sector and health sector.
Publication: Newsletter. Advertisements.
Meetings/Conventions: - periodic seminar

Manufacturers' Agents' Association of Great Britain and Ireland

Unit 16, Thirales End, Harpenden, AL5 5UD, England, UK
Tel: 44 1582 767618
Fax: 44 1582 766092
Email: prw@themaa.co.uk
Website: http://www.themaa.co.uk
Founded: 1909
Members: 400
Contact: Paul Wakeling, Sec.
Fee: £60

Membership Type: sales agents
Description: Self-employed professional sales agents. To promote the interests of manufacturers' agents.
Publication: Magazine
Publication title: Agents News. Advertisements.
Meetings/Conventions: workshop

Manufacturers of Domestic Unvented Systems

17 Victoria Rd., Saltaire, Shipley, BD18 3LQ, England, UK
Tel: 44 1274 594593
Fax: 44 1274 594593
Email: admin@modusse.co.uk
Website: http://www.modusse.co.uk
Founded: 1976
Members: 15
Contact: David A. Walker
Fee: £1160
Description: Manufacturers of domestic unvented supply systems equipment and accessories. Offers advice and expertise on all aspects of high pressure unvented supply systems.
Meetings/Conventions: meeting

Manufacturing Science Finance
MSF

c/o The MSF Centre
33-37 Moreland St., London, EC1V 8HA, England, UK
Tel: 44 20 75053000
Fax: 44 20 75053030
Email: info@msf.org.uk
Website: http://www.msf.org.uk
Members: 482000
Contact: Roger Lyons, Gen.Sec.
Description: Engineers, craftspeople, scientists, technologists, professional and managerial staff in manufacturing industry eg aerospace and defence, engineering, automobiles, civil aviation, chemicals and pharmaceuticals, electronics and telecommunications,. shipbuilding, tobacco, food and drink, energy, textiles, ceramics and paper. Professional staff in universities, commercial sales, the voluntary sector, financial services and the National Health Service. Trade union offering support, advice and representation to people at work; collectively bargaining on pay and conditions; and campaigning for manufacturing, a strong service sector, the NHS and a better society.

Manufacturing Technologies Association

62 Bayswater Rd., London, W2 3PS, England, UK
Tel: 44 207 2986400
Fax: 44 207 2986430
Email: marketing@mta.org.uk
Website: http://www.mta.org.uk
Founded: 1919
Members: 250
Staff: 20
Contact: Clare Kelly, PR Mgr.
Description: Represents manufacturers and suppliers of machine tools and related equipment in the United Kingdom. Promotes the development of the machine tool industry. Represents members' interests before government agencies. Conducts research and compiles statistics. Sponsors competitions. Organizes exhibitions.
Library Type: not open to the public
Formerly: Machine Tool Technologies Association
Publication: Directory
Publication title: British Machine Tools & Equipment

Second publication: Newsletter
Publication title: Machine Tool Enterprise
Meetings/Conventions: MACH Exhibition - biennial trade show - Exhibits.

Margarine and Spreads Association
MSMA

6 Catherine St., London, WC2B 5JJ, England, UK
Tel: 44 207 4207122
Fax: 44 207 3795735
Email: jhowarth@fdf.org.uk
Website: http://www.margarine.org.uk
Contact: Mr. Tim Mustin
Description: Margarine and spreads Association in England. Represents members' interests; disseminates information.
Formerly: Margarine and Shortening Manufacturers Association
Publication: Brochure

Margery Allingham Society

2B Hiham Green, Winchelsea, TN36 4HB, England, UK
Tel: 44 1797222363
Fax: 44 1797222363
Email: bruxnerwinchelsea@talk21.com
Website: http://www.margeryallingham.fsnet.co.uk/home1.html
Founded: 1988
Members: 86
Contact: Mrs. Pamela Bruzner, Sec.
Fee: £10
Membership Type: ordinary
Fee: £15
Membership Type: ordinary
Description: Aims to celebrate the life and work of Margery Allingham.
Publication: Journal
Publication title: The Bottle Street Gazette
Meetings/Conventions: Margery Allingham Society Weekend - annual conference

Marie Curie Cancer Care
MCCC

89 Albert Embankment, London, SE1 7TP, England, UK
Tel: 44 207 5997777
Fax: 44 207 5997708
Email: info@mariecurie.org.uk
Website: http://www.mariecurie.org.uk
Founded: 1948
Description: Health care professionals working with people who have cancer. Seeks to improve the quality of life of people with cancer; promotes increased availability and effectiveness of cancer care. Operates nationwide network of Marie Curie Nurses in the community and operates ten hospices across England, Scotland, Wales, and Northern Ireland; provides specialist care for people with cancer; conducts cancer research. Conducts educational programs.
Publication: Newsletter
Publication title: Marie Curie News
Second publication: Pamphlets

Marie Stopes International - United Kingdom
MSI

153-157 Cleveland St., London, W1T 6QW, England, UK
Tel: 44 207 5747400
Fax: 44 207 5747417

Email: msi@stopes.org.uk
Website: http://www.mariestopes.org.uk
Founded: 1975
Contact: Dr. Timothy Black, CEO
Description: Provides a wide range of maternal health and family planning services. Programs conducted include: contraceptive social marketing; male oriented services. Specializes in working with indigenous personnel to develop clinical family planning services and social marketing programs.

Marine Conservation Society
MCS

9 Gloucester Rd., Ross-On-Wye, HR9 5BU, England, UK
Tel: 44 1989 566017
Fax: 44 1989 567815
Email: info@mcsuk.org
Website: http://www.mcsuk.org
Founded: 1977
Members: 5000
Staff: 16
Contact: Tony Martin, Ch.Exec.
Fee: £20
Membership Type: individual or family
Fee: £10
Membership Type: student
Description: Individuals and organizations concerned with and interested in marine conservation. Protects the marine environment for wildlife and future generations.
Library Type: not open to the public
Publication: Book
Publication title: Common Reef Fishes of Sri Lanka
Second publication: Book
Publication title: Mangrove - The Forgotten Habitat
Meetings/Conventions: - annual conference

Marine Society

202 Lambeth Rd., London, SE1 7JW, England, UK
Tel: 44 207 2619535
Fax: 44 207 4012537
Email: enq@marine-society.org
Website: http://www.marine-society.org
Founded: 1756
Members: 300
Staff: 30
Contact: Capt. J.J. Howard, Dir.
Description: Governors who subscribe annually or are life governors support the society and elect its council. The training, education and general welfare of professional seafarers (both RN and MN) and the support of those intending to make a career at sea, or who have been professional seafarers, and their dependants. Activities include Seafarers Library Service, College of the Sea, Training Ships and financial support for the education and training of seafarers.
Library Subject: maritime and marine
Library Type: not open to the public
Publication: Magazine
Publication title: Seafarer. Advertisements.

Maritime Information Association
MIA

c/o Michael Naxton
202 Lambeth Rd., London, SE1 7JW, England, UK
Tel: 44 118 9479535
Fax: 44 118 9476693
Founded: 1972
Members: 120
Contact: Michael Naxton, Chair
Fee: £10
Description: Librarians and information officers from 11 countries who are concerned with maritime and nautical subjects. Promotes contact and cooperation among marine librarians and information officers and the development of a body of professional expertise on relevant literature and information sources. Acts as a forum for exchange of problems and information.
Formerly: Marine Librarians Association
Publication: Proceedings
Publication title: Conference Proceedings
Second publication: Book
Publication title: Maritime Information: A Guide to Libraries and Sources of Information in the U.K.
Meetings/Conventions: - annual conference

Market Research Society
MRS

15 Northburgh St., London, EC1V 0JR, England, UK
Tel: 44 207 4904911
Fax: 44 207 4900608
Email: info@mrs.org.uk
Website: http://www.mrs.org.uk
Founded: 1946
Members: 8000
Staff: 40
Contact: Jackie Lomas, Info. & Website Coord.
Description: Represents professional researchers and others engaged or interested in market, social and opinion research. Offers training and professional development resources; acts as the official awarding body for vocational qualifications in market research in the U.K.
Library Subject: market research methodology
Library Type: not open to the public
Publication: Journal
Publication title: International Journal of Market Research
Second publication: Proceedings
Publication title: Market Research Society Conference
Meetings/Conventions: - annual conference - Exhibits. Birmingham UK

Marlowe Society

c/o Membership Secretary
9 Middlefield Gardens, Hurst Green Rd., Halesowen, B62 9QH, England, UK
Tel: 44 121 4211482
Fax: 44 1242 579472
Email: marsot@ntlworld.com
Website: http://www.marlowe-society.org
Founded: 1955
Members: 150
Staff: 12
Contact: Dr. Collin Niven, Pres.
Fee: £12
Membership Type: individual

Fee: £7
Membership Type: concessionary
Description: Presents Christopher Marlowe in his true light as a great poet and dramatist
Publication: Newsletter
Publication title: The Marlowe Story
Meetings/Conventions: - annual meeting

Marquee Contractors Association

South Eastern Area, 47 Osborne Rd., Thornton Heath, Surrey, CR7 8PD, England, UK
Tel: 44 208 6531988
Fax: 44 208 6532932
Email: barkers@mcmail.com
Founded: 1963
Members: 12
Contact: A.C. Barker
Description: Marquee and tent hirers and manufacturers. To promote co-operation among marquee contractors and facilitate the exchange of information on matters of mutual interest. To protect and further the business interests of members and to take action in any matter affecting the trade locally or nationally.

MARQUES - Association of European Trademark Owners

840 Melton Rd., Thurmaston, Leicester, LE4 8BN, England, UK
Tel: 44 116 2640080
Fax: 44 116 2640141
Email: info@marques.org
Website: http://www.marques.org
Founded: 1984
Members: 500
Staff: 6
Contact: Colin Grimes, Sec.Gen.
Description: Assists European-based brand owners in the selection, management, and protection of their trademarks. Protects members interests. Acts as an information exchange.
Publication: Newsletter
Meetings/Conventions: - annual conference Istanbul Turkey

Mars Society

4 Chievely Ct., Emerson Valley, Milton Keynes, MK4 2DD, England, UK
Email: bo@marssociety.org.uk
Website: http://www.marssociety.org.uk/
Founded: 1998
Members: 700
Contact: Philip Dembo
Description: Committed to a vision of pioneering the planet Mars. Special interests include space exploration, the exploration of Mars and the generation of an international space effort.
Meetings/Conventions: conference

Master Carvers Association

Workshop 20, 21 Wren St., London, WC1X 0HF, England, UK
Tel: 44 20 72788759
Fax: 44 20 72788759
Email: info@mastercarvers.co.uk
Website: http://www.mastercarvers.co.uk
Founded: 1897
Members: 40
Contact: Paul Ferguson

Description: Companies and employers of wood and/or stone carvers and self employed wood/stone carvers. Areas covered include: Architectural carving in wood and stone, architectural joinery, cabinet making and carving, carved picture frame making, ecclesiastical carving, figure carving in wood and stone, furniture restoration, ornamental carving and gilding, Heraldic carving and modelling, letter cutting in wood and stone, modelling for casting, mould making for casting and GRP casting.

Master Locksmiths Association

5D Great Central Way, Woodford Halse, Daventry, NN11 3PZ, England, UK
Tel: 44 1327 262255
Fax: 44 1327 262539
Email: admin@locksmiths.co.uk
Website: http://www.locksmiths.co.uk
Founded: 1958
Members: 1550
Staff: 4
Contact: Lorraine Stanley, CEO
Description: Membership is divided into four divisions: British Locksmiths Institute (professional body); MLA Trade Division (trade association); MLA Affiliate Division (manufacturers, wholesalers, etc); Guild of Keycutters. Concerned with promoting the interests of those in the locksmithing industry, advancing the education and training of persons preparing to enter or engaged in the trade, encouraging the issue of standards by members, and ensuring high standards are maintained for the protection of the public.
Publication: Magazine
Publication title: Keyways. Advertisements.
Meetings/Conventions: - biennial convention - Exhibits. Donington Park UK

Master Photographers Association

c/o Jubilee House
1 Chancery Ln., Darlington, DL1 5QP, England, UK
Tel: 44 1325 356555
Fax: 44 1325 357813
Email: mpa@mpauk.com
Website: http://www.mpauk.com
Founded: 1952
Members: 2000
Staff: 5
Contact: Colin Buck, Chief Exec.
Description: Photographers practising full time may be accepted into membership.
Publication: Magazine
Publication title: Master Photographers. Advertisements.

Mastic Asphalt Council

PO Box 77, Hastings, TN35 4WL, England, UK
Tel: 44 1424 814400
Fax: 44 1424 814446
Email: masphaltco@aol.com
Website: http://www.masticasphaltcouncil.co.uk
Founded: 1969
Members: 72
Staff: 2
Contact: J.K. Blowers
Description: Mastic asphalt contractors. Support for member contractors and a free technical advisory service for potential specifiers. Supplying handbooks and offering in house technical seminars/presentations (free).
Formerly: Mastic Asphalt Council and Employer's Federation

Publication: Handbooks
Publication title: MAC Technical Guide

Maternity Alliance
MA

2-6 Northburgh St., 3rd Fl. W, London, EC1V 0AY, England, UK
Tel: 44 20 74907639
Fax: 44 20 70141350
Email: info@maternityalliance.org.uk
Website: http://www.maternityalliance.org.uk
Founded: 1980
Members: 70
Staff: 17
Contact: Christine Gowdridge, Dir.
Fee: £25
Membership Type: Associate
Description: Individuals and organizations concerned with rights and services for parents and babies. Campaigns for improvements in rights and services for mothers, fathers, and babies. Concerns include: improvement in health care before conception and the first year of life; financial support for low income families; protection of working mothers' rights; and availability of transportation and housing. Conducts research programs.
Library Subject: maternity services, maternal and child health, employment, welfare benefits, gender discrimination, equal opportunity
Library Type: by appointment only
Publication: Bulletin
Publication title: Maternity Action
Publication title: Money for Mothers and Babies
Meetings/Conventions: - periodic conference

Mathematical Association

259 London Rd., Leicester, LE2 3BE, England, UK
Tel: 44 116 2210013
Fax: 44 116 2122835
Email: office@m-a.org.uk
Website: http://www.m-a.org.uk
Founded: 1871
Members: 4500
Staff: 6
Contact: Marcia Murray, Office Mgr.
Description: Students, teachers, lecturers, advisers/inspectors across all age ranges. Represented on all major national bodies concerned with mathematics education, it has wide influence through its members and activities. It is a lively organization which can help teachers through its publications, support networks and branches, national conferences, developing mathematical thinking and giving ideas for the classroom.
Library Subject: mathematics and mathematics education
Library Type: not open to the public
Publication: Journal
Publication title: Mathematical Gazette. Advertisements.
Second publication: Journal
Publication title: Mathematics in School. Advertisements.
Meetings/Conventions: - annual conference - Exhibits.

Max Steiner Film Music Society
MSFMS

1 Rotherwood Rd., Putney, London, 5W15 ILA, England, UK
Founded: 1965
Contact: Brian A. Reeve, Dir.

Description: Supplies schools, colleges, and libraries with information on Max Steiner (1888-1971), Academy Award-winning composer of film scores including Gone With the Wind, Casablanca, and Now, Voyager.
Formerly: Max Steiner Memorial Society
Publication title: Centennial Brochure
Second publication: Journal
Publication title: Max Steiner Journal 2000

McLibel Support Campaign - UK

5 Caledonian Rd., London, N1 9DX, England, UK
Tel: 44 171 7131269
Fax: 44 171 7131269
Founded: 1990
Description: Organized to generate solidarity and financial support for campaigners involved in GreenPeace (London) being sued for libel in the United Kingdom by the McDonald's restaurant chain. Conducts campaigns against McDonald's; advocates an end to the exploitation of people, animals, and the environment by multinational companies and others.
Library Type: by appointment only
Publication: Bulletin
Publication title: McLibel Trial Bulletin
Meetings/Conventions: - weekly board meeting London UK

Mechanical-Copyright Protection Society
MCPS

29-33 Berners St., London, W1T 3AB, England, UK
Tel: 44 20 75805544
Fax: 44 20 73064350
Email: classicalquery@mcps-prs-alliance.co.uk
Website: http://www.mcps.co.uk
Founded: 1924
Members: 17000
Staff: 320
Contact: John Hutchinson, Chief Exec.
Description: Music copyright owners/composers/music publishers. Collects and distributes the mechanical royalties on behalf of its members whenever their copyright musical works are recorded. Such royalties accrue from recording music on to CDs, cassettes, videos, audio-visual and broadcast material. MCPS maintains a comprehensive database of recordings known as the National Discography, this is available as an on-line service.
Publication: Newsletter
Publication title: For The Record

Medau Movement

East St., 86 Robson House, Epsom, KT17 1HH, England, UK
Tel: 44 1372 729056
Fax: 44 1372 729056
Email: medau@nascr.net
Website: http://www.medau.org.uk
Founded: 1952
Members: 2000
Staff: 2
Contact: Mrs. Barbara Norton, Chmn.
Description: Trains and supports movement teachers. Maintains a national register of media movement classes and runs recreational courses.

Media Society

56 Roseneath Rd., London, SW11 6AQ, England, UK
Tel: 44 171 2235631
Fax: 44 171 2235631
Founded: 1973
Members: 270
Contact: Peter Dannheisser, Sec.
Description: Editors, journalists, broadcasters, media executives, media lawyers, public relations executives, politicians, academics etc. Provides a forum for the exchange of knowledge and opinion between those in public and political life, the professions, industry and education, mostly in the form of evening lectures and luncheons and dinners in London.

mediawatch - UK

3 Willow House, Kennington Rd., Ashford, TN24 0NR, England, UK
Tel: 44 1233 633936
Fax: 44 1233 633836
Email: info@mediawatchuk.org
Website: http://www.mediawatchuk.org/
Founded: 1965
Members: 7000
Staff: 2
Contact: John C Beyer, Dir.
Fee: £10
Membership Type: individual
Description: Campaigns for better standards of taste and decency in broadcasting and media generally.
Library Subject: broadcasting, film, video, Internet, media
Library Type: reference
Formerly: National Viewers and Listeners Association
Publication: Newsletter
Publication title: Mediawatch-UK Newsbrief

Medical Defence Union
MDU

230 Blackfriars Rd., London, SE1 8PJ, England, UK
Tel: 44 20 72021500
Fax: 44 20 72021667
Email: mdu@the-mdu.com
Website: http://www.the-mdu.com
Founded: 1885

Medical Foundation for AIDS and Sexual Health

BMA House, Tavistock Sq., London, WC1H 9JP, England, UK
Tel: 44 20 73836345
Fax: 44 20 73882544
Email: enquiries.medfash@medfash.bma.org.uk
Website: http://www.medfash.org.uk
Description: Works with policy-makers and health professional to promote excellence in the prevention and management of HIV and other sexually transmitted infections. Develops materials to support health professionals.
Publication: Report
Publication title: Standards for NHS Hospital HIV services
Second publication: Pamphlet
Publication title: Take the HIV Test

Medical Officers of Schools Association

21 St. Botorpa's Rd., Sevenoaks, TN13 3AQ, England, UK
Tel: 44 1732 459255
Fax: 44 1732 750586
Website: http://www.mosa.org.uk

Founded: 1884
Members: 440
Staff: 2
Contact: Dr. Neil D. Arnott, Hon.Sec.
Fee: £34
Description: School doctors and doctors with an interest in the health of the school child. To represent school doctors and those doctors with an interest in the health of the school child; to provide an advisory service for members, and non-members, on any aspect of school medicine.
Publication: Handbook
Publication title: Handbook of School Health. Advertisements.
Second publication: Newsletter
Meetings/Conventions: - annual - Exhibits.

Medical Protection Society
MPS

33 Cavendish Sq., London, W1G 0PS, England, UK
Tel: 44 207 3991300
Fax: 44 207 3991301
Email: info@mps.org.uk
Website: http://www.mps.org.uk/
Description: Physicians, dentists, and other health care professionals. Seeks to assist members in protecting themselves from patient complaints and litigation. Provides technical and customer service assistance to members in matters involving disputes and litigation arising from patient care. Represents members before health boards, hospital inquiries, and other professional conduct or competence proceedings. Makes available legal and ethical advice to members.

Medical Research Society
MRS

c/o Dr. A. Chaudhry, Sec.
Renal Unit, L Block, Hammersmith Hospital, DuCane Rd., London, W12 0NN, England, UK
Tel: 44 1438 314333
Fax: 44 7092 388555
Email: mrs@dial.pipex.com
Website: http://www.medres.org
Members: 1300
Contact: Dr. Jonathen Rhodes, Hon.Sec.
Description: Individuals engaged in basic and clinical medical research. Facilitates interdisciplinary exchange of information and provides a forum for data presentations by biomedical researchers.
Publication title: Clinical Science
Publication title: Clinical Science Abstracts
Meetings/Conventions: - semiannual meeting

Medical Sciences Historical Society

117 Woodland Dr., Cassiobury, Watford, WD17 3DA, England, UK
Founded: 1981
Members: 60
Contact: H. Taylor
Fee: £10
Description: Holds four annual meetings. Publishes two newsletters and a journal.
Publication: Newsletter
Second publication: Journal

Medical Society for the Study of Venereal Diseases

1 Wimpole St., London, W1M 8AE, England, UK
Tel: 44 20 72902968
Fax: 44 20 72902989
Email: mssvd@rsm.ac.uk
Website: http://www.mssvd.org.uk
Founded: 1955

Medical Society of London

11 Chandos St., London, W1M 0EB, England, UK
Tel: 44 20 75801043
Fax: 44 20 75805793
Founded: 1773

Medical Women's Federation

Tavistock House N, Tavistock Sq., London, WC1H 9HX, England, UK
Tel: 44 20 73877765
Fax: 44 20 73889216
Email: admin@mwfonline.org.uk
Website: http://www.mwfonline.org.uk
Founded: 1917
Members: 1500
Staff: 3
Description: Women doctors and medical students. The professional association of women doctors in the UK.
Publication: Newsletter
Publication title: Medical Woman. Advertisements.

Medico-Legal Society

33 Henrietta St., London, WC2E 8NH, England, UK
Tel: 44 20 78360011
Fax: 44 20 78362783
Founded: 1901

Mediterranean Association to Save the Sea Turtles - United Kingdom
MEDASSET

c/o 24 Park Towers, 2 Brick St., London, W1J 7DD, England, UK
Tel: 44 20 76290654
Fax: 44 20 76290654
Email: medasset@medasset.org
Founded: 1988
Members: 100
Staff: 4
Contact: Lily Venizelos, Pres.
Description: Promotes the preservation and conservation of all species of sea turtle, their natural environment, and associated biotope in the Mediterranean, and other international waters. Promotes the formulation of protective legislation and it's enforcement. Supports scientific research and assessment projects and education, public awareness, publicity, and political liaison activities. Observer NGO at Bern Convention meetings and an NGO partner to the UNEP/MP (Barcelona Convention).
Library Subject: marine turtle biology and conservation, ecology, biodiversity
Library Type: reference
Formerly: Mediterranean Association to Save the Sea Turtles - United Kingdom
Publication: Newsletter
Publication title: MEDASSET Progress Reports
Second publication: Brochures
Publication title: Public Awareness

Medway Chamber of Commerce

Medway Business Point, Stirling House, Sunderland Quay, Medway City Estate, Rochester, ME2 4HN, England, UK
Tel: 44 1634 311411
Fax: 44 1634 311450
Email: chamber@medway.co.uk
Founded: 1891
Members: 420
Staff: 10
Contact: Tracey Manley
Description: Promotes business and commerce.

Mensa International
MIL

15 The Ivories, 6-8 Northampton St., London, N1 2HY, England, UK
Tel: 44 207 2266891
Fax: 44 207 2267059
Email: mensainternational@mensa.org
Website: http://www.mensa.org
Founded: 1946
Members: 100000
Staff: 3
Contact: Edward J. Vincent, Exec.Dir.
Fee: £12
Description: Individuals from 100 countries whose intelligence, as measured by standardized tests, is within the top 2 percent of the general population. Aims to promote: social contact among intelligent people; research in psychology and the social sciences; the identification and development of human intelligence. Mensa's policy is to include intelligent people of every opinion and background. Maintains no religious or political affiliations and is open to all who meet the intelligence criterion. Conducts research on public opinions and sociological potential of the highly intelligent. Provides volunteers for research workers requiring a high I.Q. group. Sponsors projects to foster intelligence and provides educational facilities. Sponsors periodic competitions; maintains speakers' bureau. Offers children's services and charitable program.
Publication: Journal
Publication title: International Journal
Publication title: Registers
Meetings/Conventions: - annual board meeting

Mental After Care Association
MACA

Lincoln House, 1st Fl., 296-302 High Holborn, London, WC1V 7JH, England, UK
Tel: 44 20 70613400
Fax: 44 20 70613401
Email: maca@maca.org.uk
Website: http://www.maca.org.uk
Founded: 1879
Members: 100
Staff: 800
Contact: Gil Hitchon, Ch.Exec.
Fee: £15
Description: MACA is a leading mental health charity providing high quality services in the community, hospitals and prisons. With more than 90 services throughout the country, we support more than 1,500 people with severe and enduring mental health needs and their carers. We work in partnership with health authorities, local authorities, housing associations and other voluntary agencies.
Publication title: Annual Report. Advertisements.
Second publication: Pamphlets
Meetings/Conventions: - annual meeting London UK

Mental Health Foundation

83 Victoria St., 7th Fl., London, SW1H 0HW, England, UK
Tel: 44 207 8020300
Fax: 44 207 8020301
Email: mhf@mhf.org.uk
Website: http://www.mentalhealth.org.uk
Founded: 1949
Contact: Andrew McCulloch, Ch.Exec.
Description: Plays a vital role in pioneering new approaches to prevention, treatment and care. Allocates grants for research and community projects, contributes to public debate and strives to reduce the stigma attached to mental illness and learning disabilities.

Mental Health Media

356 Holloway Rd., London, N7 6PA, England, UK
Tel: 44 20 77008171
Fax: 44 20 76860959
Email: info@mhmedia.com
Website: http://www.mhmedia.com
Founded: 1965
Staff: 10
Contact: Kelly Chester, Proj.Asst.
Description: Specializes in the use of the full range of communications media to promote understanding of mental health or learning difficulties issues from a user perspective in order to reduce discrimination and prejudice. Operates a media bureau, which supports mental health service users in working with journalists, writers, and broadcasters to improve their coverage of mental health issues. Also acts as a production house for a full range of information publications, including videos and CDs, about mental health and learning difficulties issues from the user perspective.
Formerly: Mental Health Film Council
Meetings/Conventions: - periodic workshop - Exhibits.

Mercers' Company

Mercer's Hall, Ironmonger Lane, London, EC2V 8HE, England, UK
Tel: 44 207 7264991
Fax: 44 207 6001158
Email: mail@mercers.co.uk
Website: http://www.mercers.co.uk
Contact: G.M.M. Wakeford, Clerk
Description: Mercers.

Merchant Taylors' Company

c/o Merchant Taylors' Hall
30 Threadneedle St., London, EC2R 8AY, England, UK
Tel: 44 207 4504440
Fax: 44 207 5582776
Contact: Capt. D.A. Wallis, Clerk
Description: Merchant tailors.

Metal Packaging Manufacturers Association

Siena Ct., The Broadway, Maidenhead, SL6 1NJ, England, UK
Tel: 44 1628 509029
Fax: 44 1628 509100
Email: mpma.enquiries@btinternet.com
Website: http://www.mpma.org.uk
Founded: 1977
Members: 46
Staff: 3
Contact: A.R. Woods, Dir.
Description: Trade association of companies involved in the manufacture of light metal containers, closures and components. Aims to promote common interests and protect members through representation and debate with government.

Metalforming Machinery Makers' Association

The Maclaren Building, 35 Dale End, Birmingham, B4 7LN, England, UK
Tel: 44 121 2002100
Fax: 44 121 2001306
Email: dbrotherton@mmma.org.uk
Website: http://www.mmma.org.uk
Founded: 1949
Members: 42
Staff: 2
Contact: D.C. Brotherton, Sec.
Fee: £325
Membership Type: corporate
Description: Metalforming machinery makers.
Publication: Handbook
Publication title: Member's Handbook

Metamorphic Association

PO Box 32368, London, SW17 8YB, England, UK
Tel: 44 870 7707984
Website: http://www.metamorphicassociation.org.uk
Founded: 1979
Members: 200
Contact: G. Saint-Pierre
Fee: £60
Membership Type: practitioners
Fee: £100
Membership Type: teachers
Description: Promotion of good health and well-being through awareness, understanding and use of Metamorphic Technique in the UK and internationally, and to uphold standards and procedures and teaching the technique.
Publication: Newsletter
Publication title: The Programme
Meetings/Conventions: - monthly workshop

Microwave Technologies Association

3 Popham Gardens, Richmond, TW9 4LJ, England, UK
Tel: 44 208 8765454
Fax: 44 208 8765454
Email: jennywebb@blueyonder.co.uk
Website: http://www.microwaveassociation.org.uk
Founded: 1978
Members: 38
Contact: Jenny Webb
Description: Companies, producers, colleges, universities and individuals who are involved in the microwave and attendant food industries and wish to exchange technical and general information as well as to ensure users are informed of the best way to prepare. food safely and well. Runs an annual conference and periodic seminars at educational establishments and a number of public exhibitions and demonstration are held in the year. The MA takes part in major food/equipment exhibitions. The MA worked closely with MAFF on the voluntary labelling scheme for microwaves and microwave foods and sits on the UK Microwave Working Group.
Formerly: Microwave Association
Publication: Handbook
Second publication: Newsletter

Mid Yorkshire Chamber of Commerce and Industry

Commerce House, Wakefield Rd., Aspley, Huddersfield, HD5 9AA, England, UK
Tel: 44 148 4438800
Fax: 44 148 4514199

Email: post@chambercom6.bdx.co.uk
Website: http://www.chambercom.co.uk
Members: 2000
Staff: 400
Contact: Roger Staples, Pres.
Description: Promotes business and commerce.

Middle East Association
MEA

Bury House, 33 Bury St., St. James, London, SW1Y 6AX, England, UK
Tel: 44 207 8392137
Fax: 44 207 8396121
Email: mail@the-mea.co.uk
Website: http://www.the-mea.co.uk
Founded: 1961
Members: 400
Staff: 12
Contact: Brian Constant, Dir.Gen.
Fee: £950
Description: Firms in the United Kingdom doing business with companies in the Middle East. Promotes trade and business between the United Kingdom and the Middle East. Provides information regarding all aspects of trade with the Middle East.
Library Subject: Middle East trade
Library Type: not open to the public
Publication title: Handbook and Classified List of Members
Publication title: Information Digest. Advertisements.
Meetings/Conventions: - periodic conference

Middle England Fine Foods

Three Kings Farm, Mareham Ln., ThreeKingham, Sleaford, NG34 0BQ, England, UK
Tel: 44 1529 241034
Fax: 44 1529 241093
Email: office@meff.co.uk
Founded: 1997
Members: 300
Contact: Diana Goodband
Description: Small food producers within UK. Aims to actively promote producers' interests and to raise the profile of British speciality food and drink.
Formerly: National Association of Speciality Food and Drink Producers
Publication: Directory
Second publication: Newsletter
Meetings/Conventions: - periodic meeting

Midland General Galvanizers Association

1A Buckingham Rd., Wolverhampton, WV3 5TL, England, UK
Tel: 44 1902 338617
Founded: 1934
Members: 20
Contact: C.J. Carder, Sec.
Fee: £100
Description: Galvanizers to the trade. Provides inter alia for discussion on matters of common interest; for the dissemination of technical information and the promotion of the use of hot dip galvanizing; organizes international work/study tours.
Meetings/Conventions: - semiannual general assembly

Midwives Information and Resource Service
MIDIRS

9 Elmdale Rd., Clifton, Bristol, BS8 1SL, England, UK
Tel: 44 117 9251791
Fax: 44 117 9251792
Email: sales@midirs.org
Website: http://www.midirs.org
Founded: 1983
Members: 14000
Staff: 16
Contact: Sue Penn
Description: Provides information for midwives and nurses who want to keep up-to-date with contemporary knowledge and thinking in the world of midwifery care, women's health, and care of new borns. Offers articles, books, and other information concerning midwifery. Conducts educational programs.
Library Subject: midwifery, maternity services
Library Type: not open to the public
Publication: Directory
Publication title: Directory of Maternity Organisations
Publication title: MIDIRS Midwifery Digest. Advertisements.
Meetings/Conventions: conference - Exhibits.

Migraine Action Association

Oakley Hay Lodge Business Park, Unit 6, Great Folds Rd., Great Oakley, NN18 9AS, England, UK
Tel: 44 1536 461333
Fax: 44 1536 461444
Email: info@migraine.org.uk
Website: http://www.migraine.org.uk
Founded: 1958
Members: 17000
Staff: 5
Contact: Jackie Bonella, Sec.
Fee: £9
Description: Migraine sufferers, their families and friends, or anyone else who is interested, including medical professionals. Support for research into aspects of migraine, grants, information, understanding and encouragement to migraine sufferers.
Formerly: British Migraine Association
Publication: Newsletter
Publication title: Migraine Action News
Second publication: Handbook
Publication title: The Migraine Handbook
Meetings/Conventions: - annual meeting

Military Heraldry Society

Windy Ridge, 27 Sandbrook, Ketley, Telford, TF1 5BB, England, UK
Tel: 44 1952 408830
Email: billbowbagins@hotmail.com
Founded: 1951
Members: 320
Staff: 8
Contact: Hubert H. Long, Pub.Off.
Fee: £10
Membership Type: all
Fee: £12
Description: For collectors and others interested in cloth military insignia worldwide.
Library Subject: militaria
Library Type: lending
Publication: Journal
Publication title: Formation Sign. Advertisements.

Military Historical Society - England

National Army Museum, Royal Hospital Rd., London, SW3 4HT, England, UK
Tel: 44 1380 723371
Founded: 1948
Members: 1150
Contact: Lt.Col. Robin Hodges, Sec.
Fee: £10
Membership Type: overseas
Fee: £15
Description: Covers research into the dress, arms, history and tradition of Britain's armed forces and those of the Commonwealth.
Publication: Journal
Publication title: Bulletin of the Military Historical Society. Advertisements.
Publication title: Map of the pre 1947 Indian Army
Meetings/Conventions: - monthly meeting - Exhibits.

Milling Cutter and Toolbit Association

c/o Institute of Spring Technology
Henry St., Sheffield, S3 7EQ, England, UK
Tel: 44 114 2789143
Fax: 44 114 2726344
Email: info@britishtools.com
Contact: Mr. J.R. Markham
Description: Manufacturers of milling cutters and toolbits.

Milton Keynes and North Buckinghamshire Chamber of Commerce

Tempus, 249 Midsummer, Milton Keynes, MK9 1EU, England, UK
Tel: 44 190 8259000
Fax: 44 190 8230130
Email: enquiry@mk-chamber.co.uk
Website: http://www.mk-chamber.co.uk
Members: 1375
Staff: 130
Contact: Sean Hickey, Managing Dir.
Description: Promotes business and commerce.

MIND - Mental Health Charity

Granta House, 15-19 Broadway, London, E15 4BQ, England, UK
Tel: 44 20 85192122
Fax: 44 20 85221725
Email: contact@mind.org.uk
Website: http://www.mind.org.uk
Founded: 1948
Members: 1700
Staff: 105
Contact: Richard Brook, Ch.Exec.
Fee: £15
Membership Type: ordinary
Description: Promotes mental health and encourages a better understanding of mental health problems. Seeks to eliminate the stigma associated with mental illness. Conducts research; disseminates information. Offers legal referral services. Sponsors charitable program. Maintains information service. Conducts training and educational courses and seminars.
Library Type: reference
Publication title: Annual Report
Second publication: Magazine
Publication title: OpenMIND. Advertisements.
Meetings/Conventions: - annual conference - Exhibits.

Mineral Industry Research Organisation

c/o Hazel Pexton, Admin.
1 City Sq., Leeds, LS1 2ES, England, UK
Tel: 44 113 3002040
Fax: 44 113 3002640
Email: mail@miro.co.uk
Founded: 1972
Members: 60
Staff: 9
Contact: Hazel Pexton, Admin.
Fee: £1500
Membership Type: corporate
Fee: £750
Membership Type: university
Description: Companies or organisations that are involved in the exploration, mining, extraction or processing of primary and secondary raw materials. Technology brokerage that identifies, promotes and manages new technology research projects for its members. It aims wherever possible to obtain co-funding from European, national or regional agencies. Studies are contracted to either universities or independent research laboratories.
Library Subject: technical, statistical, research output related to mineral industry
Library Type: not open to the public
Publication: Newsletter
Publication title: MIRONEWS. Advertisements.
Meetings/Conventions: - annual meeting - Exhibits.

Mineralogical Society of Great Britain and Ireland MSGBI

41 Queen's Gate, London, SW7 5HR, England, UK
Tel: 44 20 75847516
Fax: 44 20 78238021
Email: adrian@minersoc.org
Website: http://www.minersoc.org
Founded: 1876
Members: 1020
Staff: 6
Contact: Dr. Adrian Lloyd-Lawrence, Exec.Sec.
Description: Museum and research scientists, research organizations, students, and university staff involved in mineralogical studies in 57 countries. Aims to advance the knowledge of crystallography, geochemistry and petrology, and mineralogy through scientific gatherings and publications.
Publication: Journal
Publication title: Clay Minerals
Publication title: Mineralogical Abstracts
Meetings/Conventions: - periodic conference

Minerals Engineering Society

2 Ryton Close, Blyth, Worksop, S81 8DN, England, UK
Tel: 44 1909 591787
Fax: 44 1909 591940
Email: hon.sec.mes@lineone.net
Website: http://www.mineralsengineering.org
Founded: 1957
Members: 630
Contact: A.W. Howells, Hon.Sec.
Fee: £20
Membership Type: fellow
Fee: £16
Membership Type: member

Description: Learned society to promote minerals engineering
Publication: Journal
Publication title: Mine and Quarry Magazine
Meetings/Conventions: - annual convention - Exhibits.

Minewatch

218 Liverpool Rd., London, N1 1LE, England, UK
Tel: 44 171 6091852
Fax: 44 171 7006189
Contact: Christine Lancaster, Coordinator
Description: Individuals and organizations concerned about the human and environmental danger posed by land mines. Promotes efforts to remove land mines left behind following military conflicts; seeks to secure an international ban on future land mine use. Serves as a clearinghouse on land mines; sponsors advocacy activities.

Mining Association of the UK

Expert House, Sandford St., Lichfield, WS13 6QA, England, UK
Tel: 44 1543 262957
Fax: 44 1543 262183
Email: mauk@mauk.org.uk
Founded: 1946
Members: 25
Contact: R.A. Fenton, Sec.
Description: Services provided by member companies UK mineral producers (excluding coal and aggregates) and overseas mining groups. Covering the interests of the mining of metals and minerals in any part of the world.
Publication: Annual Report
Second publication: Newsletter

Minor Metals Trade Association

c/o Mr. N.B.Jaynes, Sec.
Tamesis House, 35 St. Phillip's Ave., Worcester Park, KT4 8JS, England, UK
Tel: 44 208 3307456
Fax: 44 208 3307447
Email: secretary@mmta.co.uk
Website: http://www.mmta.co.uk
Founded: 1973
Members: 75
Staff: 3
Contact: N.B. Jaynes, Sec.
Description: UK and overseas traders in minor metals. Also associate non-trading members. Encourages, participates in and fosters the activities of traders in minor metals in order to maintain good trade practices and healthy competition on the basis of sound commercial principles.
Formerly: Minor Metals Traders Association
Meetings/Conventions: - annual conference

Minority Rights Group International
MRGI

379 Brixton Rd., London, SW9 7DE, England, UK
Tel: 44 207 9789498
Fax: 44 207 7386265
Email: minority.rights@mrgmail.org
Website: http://www.minorityrights.org
Founded: 1969
Staff: 27
Contact: Mark Lattine, Dir.
Fee: £25
Membership Type: individual

Fee: £35
Membership Type: institution
Description: An information and research organization dedicated to obtaining justice for minority and indigenous groups. Aims to enhance awareness of groups suffering discrimination. Attends meetings of the United Nations. Maintains nongovernmental organization and consultative status with the Economic and Social Council.
Publication: Report
Publication title: MRG Reports
Second publication: Newsletter
Publication title: Outsider
Meetings/Conventions: - annual conference

MIRA

Watling St., Nuneaton, CV10 0TU, England, UK
Tel: 44 24 76355000
Fax: 44 24 76358000
Email: enquiries@mira.co.uk
Website: http://www.mira.co.uk
Founded: 1946
Members: 100
Staff: 540
Contact: Keith R. Read
Description: A contract research organization serving the automotive and wider transport industries. It has a substantial number of laboratories and test facilities at its 700-acre technology center and proving ground. MIRA operates on behalf of customers in virtually every aspect of design and development of vehicles and components, safety and legislation.
Library Subject: vehicle design, development engineering, and general motor industry
Library Type: reference
Formerly: Motor Industry Research Association
Publication: Newsletter
Publication title: Automotive Business News
Second publication: Report
Publication title: Car Manufacturers of the World

Miscarriage Association

c/o Clayton Hospital, Northgate, Wakefield, WF1 3JS, England, UK
Tel: 44 1924 200799
Fax: 44 1924 298834
Email: info@miscarriageassociation.org.uk
Website: http://www.miscarriageassociation.org.uk
Founded: 1982
Members: 1400
Staff: 5
Contact: Mrs. Ruth Bender Atik, Dir.
Fee: £20
Membership Type: overseas
Description: Provides support and information for all on the subject of pregnancy loss. Gathers information about causes and treatments and promote good practice in the way pregnancy loss is managed in hospitals and in the community.
Publication: Newsletter

Mission to Seafarers

St. Michael Paternoster Royal, College Hill, London, EC4R 2RL, England, UK
Tel: 44 207 2485202
Fax: 44 207 2484761
Email: pr@missiontoseafarers.org
Website: http://www.missiontoseafarers.org
Founded: 1856

Members: 3000
Staff: 125
Contact: Rev. Canon Bill Christiansen, Sec.Gen.
Description: Charity of the Anglican Church concerned with the well-being of merchant seamen of all races in ports throughout the world. Maintains fully staffed seafarers' clubs in over 100 ports and part-time chaplains in 200 others.
Formerly: Missions to Seamen
Publication: Newspaper
Publication title: Flying Angel News
Second publication: Directory
Publication title: The Mission to Seafarers Directory

Mobile and Outside Caterers Association (Great Britain)

c/o Centre Court
1301 Stratford Rd., Hall Green, Birmingham, B28 9HH, England, UK
Tel: 44 121 6937000
Fax: 44 121 6937100
Email: enq@moca.org.uk
Website: http://www.moca.org.uk
Founded: 1987
Members: 850
Staff: 2
Contact: R.W. Fox
Fee: £339
Membership Type: caterer or supplier
Description: Mobile and outside caterers and suppliers to the trade. Acts as a voice for the industry, discourages inexperienced and unscrupulous operators, maintains high quality standards and practices. Encourages all Members in professional activities only. Close liaison with other organizations and Government Departments. Hygiene training and due diligence systems adopted code of practice.
Publication: Book
Publication title: Getting Started. Advertisements.
Publication title: The MOCA Industry Reference Guide. Advertisements.
Meetings/Conventions: Food on the Move - annual trade show - Exhibits.

Modern Humanities Research Association
MHRA

c/o Dr. D.C. Gillespie
University of Bath, Bath, BA2 7AY, England, UK
Tel: 44 1225 826826
Email: d.c.gillespie@bath.ac.uk
Website: http://www.mhra.org.uk
Founded: 1918
Members: 600
Contact: Dr. David Gillespie, Hon.Sec.
Fee: £54
Membership Type: subscription
Description: Scholars working in the area of modern European languages and literatures; university graduates interested in the humanities. Encourages study and research in modern European languages and literatures; promotes academic diversity. Recognizes accomplishments in the humanities.
Publication: Bulletin
Publication title: Annual Bulletin of the Modern Humanities Research Association
Publication title: Modern Language Review

Money Advice Association

c/o Norman Laws
Kempten House, Kempten way, Dysart Rd., Grantham, NG31 7LE, England, UK
Tel: 44 1476 594970
Fax: 44 1476 591204
Email: office@m-a-a.org.uk
Website: http://www.m-a-a.org.uk
Founded: 1984
Members: 717
Staff: 2
Contact: Jane Guy
Fee: £41
Membership Type: individual/organization
Description: Those who give free and impartial money advice. Works to promote the development of money advice services, to offer training and support for money advisers and to provide policy feedback to government and other bodies on matters affecting the financial situation of people in debt.
Publication: Journal
Meetings/Conventions: - annual conference - Exhibits.

Monumental Brass Society
MBS

c/o H. Martin Stuchfield, Hon.Sec.
Lowe Hill House, Stratford, St. Marys, C07 6JX, England, UK
Tel: 44 208 5205249
Fax: 44 208 5218387
Email: martin.stuchfield@intercitygroup.co.uk
Website: http://www.mbs-brasses.co.uk/contacts.htm
Founded: 1887
Members: 500
Contact: H. Martin Stuchfield, Hon.Sec.
Fee: £18
Membership Type: individual
Fee: £25
Membership Type: family
Description: Libraries, schools, and interested individuals. Promotes the preservation and study of monumental brasses and incised slabs as well as the study of indents of lost brasses.
Publication: Bulletin
Publication title: MBS Bulletin
Publication title: Portfolio
Meetings/Conventions: - annual conference

Mothers for Peace - U.K.
MFP-UK

70 Station Rd., Burley-in-Wharfedale, Ilkley, LS29 7NG, England, UK
Tel: 44 1943 864577
Founded: 1981
Members: 200
Contact: Beryl Milner
Fee: £12
Membership Type: general
Description: Individuals, peace organizations, and Quaker societies. Fosters world peace movements and ideals; promotes cooperation among members.
Publication: Newsletter
Publication title: International Newsletter
Second publication: Book
Publication title: Mother for Peace: Lucy Behenna

Mothers' Union - England

24 Tufton St., London, SW1P 3RB, England, UK
Tel: 44 207 2225533
Fax: 44 207 2221591
Email: mu@themothersunion.org
Website: http://www.themothersunion.org
Founded: 1876
Members: 1000000
Staff: 45
Contact: Reg Bailey, Chf.Exec.
Description: An Anglican organization which promotes the well-being of families world-wide.
Publication: Magazine
Publication title: Home & Family. Advertisements.

Motor Neurone Disease Association

PO Box 246, Northampton, NN1 2PR, England, UK
Tel: 44 1604 250505
Fax: 44 1604 638289
Email: enquiries@mndassociation.org
Website: http://www.mndassociation.org
Founded: 1979
Members: 7000
Staff: 100
Contact: Gayle Sweet, Hd.
Fee: £12
Membership Type: single
Description: Aims to ensure that people affected by MND can secure the care and support needed; funds research into the disease. Services included a national telephone helpline, literature on all aspects of living with MND, free loan of specialist equipment, network of Regional Care Advisors, support groups and limited financial support to those with the disease.
Library Subject: motor neurone disease
Library Type: not open to the public
Publication: Booklets
Publication title: Annual Review
Second publication: Magazine
Publication title: Thumb Print. Advertisements.
Meetings/Conventions: - annual conference - Exhibits.

Motor Schools Association of Great Britain

101 Wellington Rd. N, Stockport, SK4 2LP, England, UK
Tel: 44 161 4299669
Fax: 44 161 4299779
Email: mail@msagb.co.uk
Website: http://www.msagb.co.uk
Founded: 1935
Members: 7500
Staff: 4
Contact: John Lepine
Description: Department of Transport approved driving instructors. Keeps members informed on any matters of practical interest to them and sets standards of professional and ethical behaviour for teachers of driving. Also prides itself on the information and representation available to its members. Most of the information passed on to members is contained in MSA's national and regional publications.

Motorcycle Industry Association
MCI

Starley House, Eaton Rd., Coventry, CV1 2FH, England, UK
Tel: 44 870 3307808
Fax: 44 870 0703291

Email: motorcycling@mcia.co.uk
Website: http://www.mcia.co.uk
Founded: 1910
Members: 146
Staff: 24
Contact: Jeanette Taverner, Proj.Coord.
Description: Works for the benefit of its members and motorcycling in general. Represents members' interests; organizes exhibitions.
Library Type: reference
Formerly: MCIA
Publication title: Statistics Booklet
Meetings/Conventions: International Motorcycle & Scooter Show - annual show

Moving Image Society

5 Walpole Ct., Ealing Studios, Ealing Green, London, W5 5EP, England, UK
Tel: 44 20 85845220
Fax: 44 20 85845220
Email: info@bksts.demon.co.uk
Website: http://www.bksts.com
Founded: 1931
Members: 1500
Staff: 6
Contact: John Graham, Dir.
Fee: £75
Membership Type: full and associate
Fee: £40
Membership Type: affiliate
Description: Technicians and management in the film, television and related industries. Assists in establishing technical standards, recommended practices and processes of production. It encourages study and research in all aspects of film and television production and distribution of allied arts and sciences. Holds meetings and conferences and organizes training courses and seminars.
Library Subject: film, television, and technical
Library Type: not open to the public
Formerly: British Kinematograph Sound and TV Society
Publication: Journal
Publication title: Cinema Technology. Advertisements.
Publication title: Image Technology
Meetings/Conventions: - biennial workshop - Exhibits.

Multiple Sclerosis International Federation

3rd. Fl., Skyline House, 200 Union St., London, SE1 0LY, England, UK
Tel: 44 207 6201911
Fax: 44 207 6201922
Email: info@msif.org
Website: http://www.msif.org
Founded: 1967
Members: 36
Staff: 6
Contact: Christine Purdy, Ch.Exec.
Description: Key aims are to stimulate scientific research at a global scale, disseminate information internationally, assist the development of national MS societies, and encourage full integration and participation of all people affected by MS.
Library Subject: multiple sclerosis
Library Type: reference
Formerly: International Federation of Multiple Sclerosis Societies
Publication: Magazine
Publication title: Annual Report
Publication title: Federation Updates
Meetings/Conventions: - biennial international conference - Exhibits.

Multiple Sclerosis Society of Great Britain and Northern Ireland

MS National Centre, 372 Edgware Rd., Staples Corner, London, NW2 6ND, England, UK
Tel: 44 208 4380700
Fax: 44 208 4380701
Email: info@mssociety.org.uk
Founded: 1953
Members: 60000
Staff: 95
Contact: Peter Cardy, Chief Exec.
Fee: £5
Membership Type: in U.K.
Fee: £20
Membership Type: outside UK
Description: Persons with an interest in multiple sclerosis. Promoting and funding research to find the cause and cure of multiple sclerosis and the provision of a welfare and support service for anyone affected by MS.
Library Subject: multiple sclerosis
Library Type: open to the public
Publication: Magazine
Publication title: MS Matters. Advertisements.
Meetings/Conventions: - annual conference

Museums Association - England

24 Calvin St., London, E1 6NW, England, UK
Tel: 44 20 74266970
Fax: 44 20 74266961
Email: katie@museumsassociation.org
Website: http://www.museumsassociation.org
Founded: 1889
Members: 4770
Staff: 27
Contact: Kate Dawson, Info.Ofcr.
Description: Museums and people who work in them. A non-governmental organization that represents the interests of museum employees, museums, and their collections.
Publication: Journal
Second publication: Yearbook
Meetings/Conventions: - annual conference - Exhibits.

Mushroom Growers Association
MGA

PO Box 192, Ketton, Stamford, PE9 3ZT, England, UK
Tel: 44 1780 722074
Fax: 44 1780 729006
Email: Mel@mushjournal.fsnet.co.uk
Website: http://www.mushgrowersassoc.fsnet.co.uk/
Founded: 1945
Members: 700
Staff: 5
Contact: Miss T.C.U. Johnston, Dir.
Description: Mushroom growers, trade members, scientists, and research institutes in 60 countries. Represents and acts as liaison to the mushroom growing industry at all levels, both nationally and internationally, particularly in the European Union. Disseminates information through publications, tours, farm walks, and visits. Arranges legal advice for members and supports planning applications. Actively supports mushroom research, acting as a link between growers and researchers.
Publication title: International Congress Proceedings

Second publication: Journal
Publication title: Mushroom Journal
Meetings/Conventions: - annual conference - Exhibits.

Music Education Council
MEC

54 Elm Rd., Hale, WA15 9AP, England, UK
Tel: 44 161 9283085
Fax: 44 161 9299648
Email: ahassan@easynet.co.uk
Website: http://www.mec.org.uk/
Founded: 1974
Members: 250
Staff: 1
Contact: Anna Hassan, Adm.
Fee: £21
Membership Type: subscribing member
Description: Organizations, institutions, and individuals involved in music education. Represents members' interest to central government. Offers advice concerning music education and training in Great Britain to domestic and international enquirers.
Publication: Newsletter
Meetings/Conventions: British Music Educators Conference - Exhibits.

Music Industries Association - England

Ivy Cottage Offices, Finch's Yard, Eastwick Rd., Gt. Bookham, Surrey, KT23 4BA, England, UK
Tel: 44 1372 750600
Fax: 44 1372 750515
Email: office@mia.org.uk
Website: http://www.mia.org.uk
Founded: 1919
Members: 230
Staff: 4
Contact: Bob Kelley, Sec.Gen.
Description: Manufacturers distributors and retailers of musical instruments and accessories. Gives active support to members in the marketing and promotion of musical instruments and accessories; promotes the making of music as an enjoyable and worthwhile activity in work, leisure and education.
Publication: Newsletter
Publication title: Business to Business
Meetings/Conventions: British Music Fair - annual - Exhibits.

Music Masters' and Mistresses' Association

Wayfaring, Smithers Ln., East Peckham, Tonbridge, TN12 5HT, England, UK
Tel: 44 1622 872758
Email: mma.admin@cwcom.net
Website: http://www.mma-online.org.uk
Founded: 1924
Members: 950
Contact: Kate Le Page, Admin.
Description: Music educators. Aims to further all aspects of music in schools. Annual conferences are held at a different school every year, courses and regional meetings are held throughout the year.
Publication: Journal
Publication title: Ensemble. Advertisements.

Music Producers Guild

PO Box 32, Harrow, HA2 7ZX, England, UK
Tel: 44 20 73718888
Fax: 44 20 73718887
Email: office@mpg.org.uk
Website: http://www.mpg.org.uk
Founded: 1985
Members: 220
Contact: Andrew East, Admin.
Fee: £150
Membership Type: full
Fee: £50
Membership Type: associate
Description: Record producers and engineers in the UK and overseas.
Formerly: Guild of Recording Producers, Directors and Engineers
Publication title: A & R Guides
Publication title: Legal Guides
Meetings/Conventions: V & A Show - annual show - Exhibits.

Music Publishers Association

18-20 York Buildings, 3rd Fl., Strandgate, London, WC2N 6JU, England, UK
Tel: 44 207 8397779
Fax: 44 207 8397776
Email: info@mpaonline.org.uk
Website: http://www.mpaonline.org.uk
Founded: 1881
Members: 200
Staff: 5
Contact: Sarah Faulder, Chief Exec.
Description: Represents and promotes the interests of its music publisher members to Government, within the music industry and generally.
Publication title: Catalogue of Printed Music
Publication title: List of Members

Musical Box Society of Great Britain

c/o Secretary
PO Box 299, Waterbeach, Cambridge, CB4 8PJ, England, UK
Email: mbsgb@kreedman.globalnet.co.uk
Website: http://www.mbsgb.org.uk
Founded: 1962
Members: 500
Contact:
Fee: £65
Membership Type: member
Description: Aims to further the interest in an appreciation of all forms of mechanical music.
Library Type: reference
Publication: Journal
Publication title: Music Box. Advertisements.

Musicians Union

MU

60/62 Clapham Rd., London, SW9 0JJ, England, UK
Tel: 44 20 75825566
Fax: 44 20 75829805
Email: webmaster@musiciansunion.org.uk
Website: http://www.musiciansunion.org.uk
Founded: 1894
Members: 31000

Staff: 48
Contact: Andy Knight, Dep.Gen.Sec.
Description: Performers engaged in the music profession including music writers and instrumental music teachers and instructors. To secure the organization of members for their mutual protection and advancement; to improve the status and remuneration of members and to provide assistance to them when needed.
Publication title: Musician. Advertisements.

Musicworld

23 Hitchin St., Biggleswade, SG18 8AX, England, UK
Tel: 44 1767 316521
Fax: 44 1767 317221
Email: musicworld@lindsaymusic.co.uk
Founded: 1988
Members: 1500
Staff: 2
Contact: Carole Lindsay-Douglas
Fee: £14.5
Membership Type: personal or school
Description: Individual teachers in primary schools with responsibility for teaching music. Provides a constant source of practical music-making material for the primary classroom for both specialist and generalist teachers.
Formerly: National Junior Music Club of Great Britain
Publication: Magazine
Publication title: NJM. Advertisements.
Meetings/Conventions: Teachers' One-Day Training Course - periodic

Muzzle Loaders Association of Great Britain

82A High St., Sawston, Cambridge, CB2 2HJ, England, UK
Tel: 44 1223 830665
Fax: 44 1223 839804
Email: membership@mlagb.com
Website: http://www.mlagb.com
Founded: 1952
Members: 2500
Staff: 2
Contact: David Cole
Fee: £30
Membership Type: full
Description: Collectors, students, shooters of antique muzzle loading firearms and replicas thereof. Concerned with the use and study of antique firearms, particularly the safe and effective use of muzzle loading rifles, pistols and shotguns together with safeguarding of the rights of members to own and use them.
Publication: Newsletter
Publication title: Black Powder Newsletter. Advertisements.

Myasthenia Gravis Association

Keynes House, Chester Pk., Alfreton Rd., Derby, DE21 4AS, England, UK
Tel: 44 1332 290219
Fax: 44 1332 293641
Email: mg@mgauk.org.uk
Website: http://www.mgauk.org
Founded: 1976
Members: 1125
Staff: 18
Contact: Joy Elliot
Description: Supports research into the management and cure of Myasthenia.
Publication: Newsletter
Publication title: MGA News

NACRO

169 Clapham Rd., London, SW9 0PU, England, UK
Tel: 44 207 5826500
Fax: 44 207 7351673
Email: helpline@nacro.org.uk
Website: http://www.nacro.org
Founded: 1966
Staff: 1100
Contact: Richard Garside
Description: Individuals and organisations in sympathy with NACRO's aims; organisations actively concerned with after-care or the prevention of crime. Helps people who have been in trouble with the law and those at risk of becoming so to deal with the problems they face and to be reaccepted into society without stigma. NACRO exists to promote a more humane and constructive criminal justice system and to prevent crime.
Formerly: National Association for the Care and Resettlement of Offenders
Publication: Catalog
Publication title: Publications Catalogue
Meetings/Conventions: - annual meeting London UK

NAPAEO

c/o H. W. Petch
67 The Meadows, Cherry Burton, Beverley, H417 7RL, England, UK
Tel: 44 1964 550736
Fax: 44 1964 550736
Email: howard@petchh.freeserve.co.uk
Founded: 1950
Members: 46
Staff: 1
Contact: Howard W. Petch, Exec.Dir.
Fee: £500
Description: Principals/Chief Executives of agricultural colleges in England, Scotland and Wales.
Formerly: National Association of Principal Agricultural Education Officers
Meetings/Conventions: - annual meeting

Napoleonic Association
NA

c/o Christine Binmore
26 Copse Dr., Wokingham, RG41 1LX, England, UK
Tel: 44 118 9783006
Email: john.binmore@ntlworld.com
Website: http://www.n-a.co.uk/index.htm
Founded: 1975
Members: 750
Staff: 6
Contact: Christine Binmore, Sec.
Fee: £18
Membership Type: individual
Fee: £20
Membership Type: family
Description: Members of the armed forces, civil servants, film and stage professionals, historians, academics, and others interested in the study of battles fought by European armies from 1796 to 1815 and known as the Napoleonic Wars. Studies and recreates, for public entertainment and instruction, the uniforms, equipment, and tactics of the European armies during the Napoleonic Wars and periods of the French Empire. Performs drills and battle maneuvers of the period including wargames and re-enactments. Provides drill groups and live firing for film and televison work; makes available to members collections of memoirs, orders of battles, and drill manuals. Compiles statistics.
Publication: Magazine
Publication title: The Adjutant
Meetings/Conventions: Historical Reenactment - Exhibits.

Narcolepsy Association United Kingdom
UKAN

Craven House, 1st Floor, 121 Kingsway, London, WC2B 6PA, England, UK
Tel: 44 20 77218904
Fax: 44 1322 863056
Email: info@narcolepsy.org.uk
Founded: 1981
Members: 700
Contact:
Fee: £10
Membership Type: UK and Europe
Fee: £15
Membership Type: outside of Europe
Description: Narcoleptics, their relatives, and others interested in improving the lives of those afflicted with narcolepsy. Promotes awareness of narcolepsy and provides authoritative information about it to narcoleptics, the medical profession, and to the public. Supports the establishment of local self-help groups; encourages research; co-operates with narcolepsy associations overseas.
Publication: Newsletter
Publication title: Catnap

National Abortion Campaign
NAC

The Print House, 18 Ashwin St., London, E8 3DL, England, UK
Tel: 44 207 9234976
Fax: 44 207 9234979
Email: nac@gn.apc.org
Website: http://nac.gn.apc.org
Founded: 1975
Members: 600
Staff: 2
Contact: Sarah Colbourne
Description: Campaigns for the right of all women to have equal access to safe and free abortions on requests.
Library Subject: abortion and contraception
Library Type: reference
Publication: Newsletter
Publication title: NAC Newsletter
Meetings/Conventions: - annual meeting

National Acrylic Painters' Association

134 Rake Ln., Wirral, Wallasey, CH45 1JW, England, UK
Tel: 44 151 6392980
Fax: 44 151 6392980
Email: alan.edwards420@ntlworld.com
Website: http://www.art-arena.com/napa
Founded: 1985
Members: 433
Contact: Alwyn Crawshaw, Pres.
Fee: £30
Membership Type: membership
Description: Promotes usage and understanding of the need for acrylic paints.
Library Subject: acrylics

Library Type: reference
Publication: Newspaper
Publication title: International NAPA Newspaper

National Adult School Organisation
NASO

Riverton, 370 Humberstone Rd., Leicester, LES OSA, England, UK
Tel: 44 116 2538333
Fax: 44 116 2513626
Email: gensec@naso.org.uk
Website: http://www.naso.org.uk
Founded: 1899
Members: 900
Staff: 1
Contact: Mrs. P.C. Dean, Gen.Sec.
Fee: £10
Membership Type: individual
Fee: £11
Membership Type: individual
Description: Members belong to groups situated throughout the country affiliated either directly to the national organisation or through local area organisation (County Unions). Provides a broad-based education through groups which seek to deepen understanding and enrich life through friendship, discussion and social service. Opportunities are available to join either local or national one-day or residential schools and international visits.
Library Type: reference
Publication: Handbook
Publication title: Homelands. Advertisements.
Second publication: Magazine
Publication title: One and All
Meetings/Conventions: National Council - annual general assembly - Exhibits. Liverpool UK

National AIDS Trust

New City Cloisters, 188/196 Old St., London, EC1V 9FR, England, UK
Tel: 44 207 8146767
Fax: 44 207 2160111
Email: info@nat.org.uk
Website: http://www.nat.org.uk
Founded: 1987
Staff: 19
Contact: Derek Bodell, Dir.
Description: Individuals and organizations in the United Kingdom interested in preventing the spread of HIV/AIDS. Conducts educational programs, fundraising, policy work, employers initiatives, research, lobbying, and parliamentary liaison.
Publication: Magazine
Publication title: Impact

National Ankylosing Spondylitis Society
NASS

PO Box 179, Mayfield, TN20 6ZL, England, UK
Tel: 44 1435 873527
Fax: 44 1435 873027
Email: nass@nass.co.uk
Website: http://www.nass.co.uk
Founded: 1976
Members: 8000
Staff: 3
Contact: Fergus J Rogers, Dir.
Fee: £12

Membership Type: UK
Fee: £15
Membership Type: overseas
Description: Promotes patient education in the medical and social aspects of the condition. Provides support through local UK groups for supervised physiotherapy one evening per week.
Library Type: not open to the public

National Anti-Vivisection Society

261 Goldhawk Rd., London, W12 9PE, England, UK
Tel: 44 20 88469777
Fax: 44 20 88469712
Email: info@navs.org.uk
Website: http://www.navs.org.uk
Founded: 1875
Members: 30000
Staff: 25
Contact: Jan Creamer, Dir.
Description: Campaigns to end all animal experiments. Aims to educate parliament and the public about the dangers of relying upon animal research.
Library Subject: animal welfare, vivisection
Library Type: by appointment only

National Artists Association

Studio 234, Cable Street Studios, 566 Cable St., London, E1 9HB, England, UK
Tel: 44 20 77906696
Fax: 44 20 77906630
Email: naa@gn.apc.org
Founded: 1985
Members: 600
Staff: 2
Contact: Sally Labern, Sr.Mgr.
Fee: £15
Membership Type: artist
Fee: £25
Membership Type: nonartist
Description: Practising artists around the UK (individual members); existing artists' groups (affiliate members); artists from outside the UK, organisations and non-artists (associate members). Exists to improve artists' working conditions and to advance their status and economic situation. The Association aims to raise awareness amongst artists of the value of sharing information and the power of collective action. One conference is held each year, a range of seminars; representing artists at all levels.
Library Type: open to the public
Publication: Booklet
Publication title: Code of Practice for the Visual Arts
Meetings/Conventions: - annual conference

National Assembly of Women
NAW

Belvedere, Savile Rd., Hebden Bridge, HX7 6ND, England, UK
Tel: 44 1422 846302
Fax: 44 181 7617532
Email: naw@belvedere.clara.net
Website: http://www.sisters.org.uk
Founded: 1952
Members: 1000
Contact: Margaret Boyle, Gen.Sec.
Fee: £8
Membership Type: individual

Fee: £25
Membership Type: affiliate
Description: Women of all classes, intellectual and physical description, color, race, sexual orientation and religion. Works to raise the economic, social, and legal status of women. Campaigns for international peace and understanding. Organizes educational and campaign meetings for both members and nonmembers.
Publication: Pamphlet
Publication title: A Short History of the National Assembly of Women
Second publication: Journal
Publication title: SISTERS (Sisterhood and International Solidarity to End Racism and Sexism). Advertisements.
Meetings/Conventions: - annual general assembly - Exhibits.

National Association Agricultural Contractors
NAAC

Samuelson House, Paxton Rd., Orton Centre, Peterborough, PE2 5LT, England, UK
Tel: 44 1733 362920
Fax: 44 1733 362921
Email: members@naac.co.uk
Website: http://www.naac.co.uk
Members: 300
Staff: 2
Contact: Jill Hewitt, Exec.Off.
Description: Agricultural contractors, farm workers, farmers, farm equipment manufacturers, and other providers of support and services to agricultural industries. Seeks to advance the interests of agribusinesses. Represents members' commercial and regulatory interests at the national level.
Publication: Newsletter
Publication title: Contractors Bulletin. Advertisements.

National Association for Colitis and Crohn's Disease
EFCCA

4 Beaumont House, Sutton Rd., St. Albans, AL1 5HH, England, UK
Tel: 44 1727 830038
Fax: 44 1727862550
Email: Rod.Mitchell@InfoDor.FsNet.Co.Uk
Website: http://www.nacc.org.uk/
Founded: 1990
Description: Encourages scientific research into inflammatory bowel disease causes, diagnosis and treatment.

National Association for Environmental Education

Walsall Campus, Gorway Rd., University of Wolverhampton, Walsall, WS1 3BD, England, UK
Tel: 44 1922 631200
Fax: 44 1922 631200
Email: info@naee.org.uk
Website: http://www.naee.org.uk
Founded: 1960
Members: 1000
Staff: 16
Contact: Gabrielle Back, Gen.Sec.
Fee: £30
Membership Type: individual, institutional
Fee: £45
Membership Type: Europe
Description: Teachers and lecturers. The association of teachers, lecturers and others concerned with education and the environment.

Its members work in all types of schools, colleges, polytechnics and universities. The Association produces a timely journal and a series of practical guides for promoting environmental education in schools.
Library Subject: environmental education
Library Type: by appointment only
Publication: Journal
Publication title: Environmental Education. Advertisements.

National Association for Gifted Children
NAGC

Challenge House, Ste. 14, Sherwood Dr., Bletchley, Milton Keynes, MK3 6DP, England, UK
Tel: 44 870 7703217
Fax: 44 870 7703219
Email: amazingchildren@nagcbritain.org.uk
Website: http://www.nagcbritain.org.uk
Founded: 1966
Members: 2000
Staff: 10
Contact: Ken Bore, Dir.
Fee: £30
Membership Type: Family
Fee: £20
Membership Type: Individual
Description: Institutions, families, and individuals. Seeks to enable gifted children to fulfill their potential and to render parents, health visitors, and persons who care for very young children more aware of the special needs of gifted children. Provides parents of gifted children with confidential counselling and support as well as opportunities for exchange of ideas and information. Works to improve the provision of the school system for gifted children.
Publication: Book
Publication title: A Bright Start
Second publication: Journal
Publication title: Gifted and Talented
Meetings/Conventions: - annual general assembly

National Association for Pastoral Care in Education

c/o Institute of Education
University of Warwick, Coventry, CV4 7AL, England, UK
Tel: 44 2476 523810
Fax: 44 2476 574137
Email: base@napce.org.uk
Website: http://www.napce.org.uk
Founded: 1982
Members: 1000
Staff: 2
Contact: Katie Hall
Fee: £58
Membership Type: group
Fee: £33
Membership Type: individual
Description: Secondary schools and teachers in the United Kingdom; also includes primary and further education, advisers, inspectors, lecturers, consultants etc. The Association includes a number of overseas members, drawn mainly, but not exclusively, from the. English-speaking world. To support all those who have a professional concern for pastoral care, to promote the theoretical study of pastoral care in education and to disseminate good practice in pastoral care in education. Also aims to promote the education, training and development of those engaged in pastoral care and to liaise with other organizations having similar objects.
Library Subject: pastoral care in education
Library Type: by appointment only

Publication: Journal
Publication title: Pastoral Care in Education. Advertisements.
Meetings/Conventions: Pastoral Curriculum - annual conference - Exhibits.

National Association for Premenstrual Syndrome

41 Old Rd., East Peckham, Kent, TN12 5AP, England, UK
Tel: 44 870 7772178
Fax: 44 870 7772177
Email: contact@pms.org.uk
Website: http://www.pms.org.uk
Founded: 1983
Members: 1000
Staff: 7
Contact: Mr. Christopher Ryan, CEO
Fee: £15
Membership Type: standard
Fee: £7
Membership Type: concessionary
Description: Provides help, information and support to PMS sufferers and their families; promotes a better understanding of PMS and its treatment by the medical profession.
Library Subject: bibliographical database on PMS maintained by volunteer research manager, understanding PMS, dietary guidelines for PMS
Library Type: reference
Publication: Newsletter
Publication title: NAPS News

National Association for Pre-Paid Funeral Plans

618 Warwick Rd., Solihull, B91 1AA, England, UK
Tel: 44 121 7111343
Fax: 44 121 7111351
Members: 7

National Association for Primary Education
NAPE

University of Leicester, Moulton College, Moulton, Northampton, NN3 7RR, England, UK
Tel: 44 1604 647646
Fax: 44 1604 647660
Email: nationaloffice@nape.org.uk
Website: http://www.nape.org.uk
Founded: 1980
Members: 1500
Staff: 1
Contact: John Coe, Info.Off.
Fee: £12
Membership Type: individual
Fee: £28
Membership Type: school
Description: Membership includes teachers, school communities, parents and all interested in the primary phase of schooling and child development. Concerned that all children should enjoy access to full educational opportunity, that the primary phase of education should receive equal resourcing per pupil to every other phase. Also that the education of children is a partnership between parents, schools and other concerned groups and that good practice is a matter of continual debate.
Library Subject: primary education
Library Type: not open to the public
Publication: Journal
Publication title: New Childhood. Advertisements.

Second publication: Newsletter
Publication title: Newsbrief. Advertisements.
Meetings/Conventions: - annual conference - Exhibits.

National Association for Small Schools

Cloudshill Cottage, High Street Shutford, Banbury, OX15 6PQ, England, UK
Tel: 44 1295 780308
Fax: 44 1295 780308
Email: mbenford@bigfoot.com
Website: http://www.smallschools.org.uk
Founded: 1978
Members: 300
Contact: Mervyn Benford, Natl.Coor.
Fee: £8
Membership Type: individual
Fee: £10
Membership Type: school
Description: Parish councils, rural community councils, governing bodies, schools, parents' and friends' groups, charities, Diocesean boards of education and individuals interested in supporting village schools. Aims to provide a voice and a link for those who believe that small schools, particularly in rural areas, have educational and social roles to perform, too precious to lose. Provides advice and assistance to schools facing closure proposals.
Library Subject: small school issues, small school advantages
Library Type: reference
Publication: Newsletter
Publication title: NASS News. Advertisements.
Second publication: Papers
Meetings/Conventions: - annual conference

National Association for Special Educational Needs
NASEN

Nasen House, 4/5 Amber Business Village, Amber Close, Amington, Tamworth, B77 4RP, England, UK
Tel: 44 1827 311500
Fax: 44 1827 313005
Email: welcome@nasen.org.uk
Website: http://www.nasen.org.uk
Founded: 1992
Members: 11300
Staff: 12
Contact: Miss Beverley Walters, Office Mgr.
Fee: £38
Membership Type: individual
Fee: £62
Membership Type: school
Description: Mainly teachers and other practitioners in special education, also lectures in further and higher education, LEA staff, HMI and those from the caring professions. Promotes the development of children and young people with special educational needs, wherever they are located, and supports those who work with them. Details of course, conferences, and publications may be obtained.
Publication: Journal
Publication title: British Journal of Special Education and Support for Learning. Advertisements.
Second publication: Magazine
Publication title: Special!
Meetings/Conventions: conference

National Association for Staff Development in the Post-16 Sector

36 Kimbolton Ave., Bedford, MK40 3AA, England, UK
Tel: 44 1234 309678
Email: jojohnbedford@aol.com
Website: http://www.nasd.org.uk
Founded: 1978
Members: 300
Contact: Jo Faccenda, Sec.
Fee: £50
Membership Type: corporate
Fee: £15
Membership Type: individual
Description: Corporate: Institutions of further, higher and adult education and sixth form colleges, national examining bodies in F Individual: Researchers and consultants. Established to encourage self-reliance within the profession amongst those keen to innovate, to explore issues, to share good practice and to keep abreast of developments related to human resource development in all Post-16 education.
Formerly: National Association for Staff Development in Post-16 Education
Publication: Journal
Publication title: National Association of Staff Development
Meetings/Conventions: conference - Exhibits.

National Association for Teaching English and other Community Languages to Adults

NATECLA

c/o NATECLA National Centre
South Birmingham College, 99-103 Clifton Rd., Birmingham, B12 85R, England, UK
Tel: 44 121 6888121
Fax: 44 121 4499070
Email: co-ordinator@natecia.fsnet.co.uk
Website: http://www.natecla.org.uk
Founded: 1978
Members: 600
Staff: 2
Contact: Jane Arstall, Asst.Natl.Coord.
Fee: £30
Membership Type: paid teacher/organizer over 18.5 hours per week
Fee: £15
Membership Type: paid teacher/organizer 4.5-18.5 hours per week
Description: Individual teachers, volunteers and community workers using English or community languages with multilingual groups; colleges and adult education institutions and organisations providing vocational training as associate members. A forum for ESOL and community language tutors, and others working with multilingual people settled in the UK. Its publications include practical ideas and reviews. Expertise is shared through conferences and training events; new initiatives in the field may be developed through working parties.
Formerly: NATESLA
Publication: Journal
Publication title: Language Issues. Advertisements.
Second publication: Newsletter
Publication title: NATECLA News. Advertisements.
Meetings/Conventions: Inspiration & Innovation - annual conference - Exhibits. Leeds UK

National Association for the Teaching of English

c/o Broadfield Business Centre
50 Broadfield Rd., Sheffield, S8 0XJ, England, UK
Tel: 44 114 2555419
Fax: 44 114 2555296
Email: natehq@btconnect.com
Website: http://www.nate.org.uk
Founded: 1963
Members: 5000
Staff: 8
Contact: Trevor Millum, Commun.Dir.
Description: Individuals, school departments, colleges, university libraries, advisers in English. Aims to support the teaching of English at all levels by publishing books for and by teachers, organising conferences and INSET courses and a network of local branches. Gives English teachers a forum for discussion and a national voice.
Publication: Magazine
Publication title: English in Education. Advertisements.
Second publication: Newsletter
Publication title: NATENews
Meetings/Conventions: - annual conference

National Association for Therapeutic Education

59 Birdham Rd., Chichester, PO19 2TB, England, UK
Tel: 44 1243 776042
Email: nathed@ukonline.co.uk
Website: http://www.n-a-t-e.co.uk
Founded: 1995
Members: 100
Contact: John Tierney, Dir.
Description: Promotes concept of therapeutic education. Promotes conditions in context of child education for formative emotional development.

National Association of Advisory Officers for Special Educational Needs

Princes Street, Tunbridge Wells, TN2 4SL, England, UK
Tel: 44 1892 534034
Fax: 44 1799 521257
Email: diana.robinson@btclick.com
Contact: Diana Robinson, Hon.Sec.
Description: Advisory officers for special education.
Formerly: National Association of Advisor Officers for Special Education

National Association of Alcohol and Drug Abuse Counsellors

122a Wilton Rd., London, SW1V 1JZ, England, UK
Tel: 44 870 7636139
Email: office@naadac.org.uk
Website: http://www.naadac.org.uk
Founded: 1984
Members: 160
Contact: Yasmin Chopin, Sec.
Fee: £50
Membership Type: full individual
Fee: £25
Membership Type: associate individual
Description: Individual counsellors dedicated to the development of the professional specialism of alcoholism and drug abuse counselling as a means of securing the provision of quality care to those who experience primary and secondary addiction problems, their families and. dependants and others significant to them. Promotes recognition of the qualified alcoholism and drug abuse counsellor as a health care

professional; fosters interaction and exchange of knowledge and experience between counsellor associations; advocates on a national level for alcoholism and drug abuse counsellors on issues affecting the profession; promotes a code of ethics.
Publication: Newsletter
Publication title: NAADAC News. Advertisements.
Meetings/Conventions: - quarterly general assembly

National Association of Bereavement Services

2 Plough Yard, London, EC2A, England, UK
Tel: 44 207 2470617
Fax: 44 207 2470617
Founded: 1988
Members: 400
Staff: 3
Contact: Carole Lambert
Fee: £20
Membership Type: individual in United Kingdom
Fee: £30
Membership Type: individual outside United Kingdom
Description: A coordinating body for those working in the field of bereavement and loss. Initiates and encourages Regional Support Groups for those involved in bereavement services, provides a forum for members and arranges training activities for volunteers, counsellors, co-ordinators and other professional workers. Acts as a referral service for bereaved people, referring them to the nearest, most appropriate local service.
Publication: Book
Publication title: Guidelines for Setting Up a Bereavement Counselling or Support Service
Second publication: Directory
Publication title: The National Directory of Bereavement and Loss Services

National Association of Brass Band Conductors

33 Deansway, Chippenham, SN15 1QZ, England, UK
Tel: 44 1249 655700
Website: http://www.nabbc.org.uk
Founded: 1946
Contact:
Fee: £27
Membership Type: full/associate
Fee: £50
Membership Type: students
Description: Aims to promote the interests of its members, and to provide an effective organization of such members.
Library Subject: full scores of brass band compositions and arrangements
Library Type: not open to the public

National Association of Breeders' Services

c/o Avoncroft Sires Ltd.
Delta House, 17a Harris Business Park, Stoke Prior, Bromsgrove, B60 4DJ, England, UK
Tel: 44 1527 831481
Fax: 44 1527 834091
Email: frank.degraaf@avoncroft.com
Founded: 1978
Members: 11
Contact: Frank de Graaf
Description: Cattle breeding companies. Offers sales advice and after-sales service connected with the insemination of cattle.

National Association of British and Irish Millers

21 Arlington St., London, SW1A 1RN, England, UK
Tel: 44 207 4932521
Fax: 44 207 4936785
Email: info@nabim.org.uk
Website: http://www.nabim.org.uk
Founded: 1878
Members: 32
Staff: 14
Contact: N.F. Bennett, Sec.
Description: Acts as a trade association for UK flour milling industry.

National Association of Careers and Guidance Teachers

9 Lawrence Leys, Bloxham, Banbury, OX15 4NU, England, UK
Tel: 44 1295 720809
Email: info@nacgt.org.uk
Website: http://www.nacgt.org.uk
Founded: 1969
Members: 2000
Contact: Alan Vincent, Gen.Sec.
Fee: £40
Description: Membership is not confined to teachers. It is open to anyone involved in careers and guidance work in education. Represents the views of members in regular meetings with various branches of Government and Government agencies and has continuing links with other professional careers associations in Europe. Services to members include 6 distributions per year and an annual study conference.
Publication: Journal
Publication title: Careers Education and Guidance
Meetings/Conventions: - annual conference Essex UK

National Association of Catering Butchers

217 Central Markets, Smithfield, London, EC1A 9LH, England, UK
Tel: 44 171 4890005
Fax: 44 171 2484733
Website: http://www.haighs.com/nacb.htm
Founded: 1983
Members: 90
Staff: 3
Contact: Chris J. Gasden, Sec.Gen.
Description: Catering butchers whose premises have been inspected and approved by the NACB Plant Evaluation Committee and who maintain the required standard. Seeks to raise the standards of catering butchery throughout the UK; to promote the NACB through the catering press so as to ensure a greater volume of business for NACB members and to protect the interests of its members through negotiations with the authorities in London and Brussels.

National Association of Chimney Sweeps

Unit 15, Emerald Way, Stone Business Park, Stone, ST15 0SR, England, UK
Tel: 44 1785 811732
Fax: 44 1785 811712
Email: nacs@chimneyworks.co.uk
Website: http://www.chimneyworks.co.uk
Founded: 1982
Members: 250
Staff: 1
Contact: Patricia A. Coulthard-Jones, Administrator
Description: Individual chimney sweeps and allied suppliers. Promotion of the Association to the public to encourage regular sweeping of flues for safety and environmental reasons. Also aims to

raise the standard of professional work through training, qualifications, etc.

Meetings/Conventions: Chimney Works - annual trade show - Exhibits.

National Association of Choirs

64 Church Ln., Dore, Sheffield, S17 3GS, England, UK
Tel: 44 114 2350431
Email: laurie@ukchoirsassoc.f9.co.uk
Website: http://www.ukchoirsassoc.co.uk
Founded: 1920
Members: 451
Contact: Peter Marshall, Gen.Sec.
Fee: £25
Description: To promote, develop, and maintain public education in, and appreciation of the art and science of choral music. The service to choirs is fully comprehensive, covering music loan/search, festivals information, insurance, organization of group choral activities and annual conference/concert.
Publication: Newsletter
Publication title: News and Views. Advertisements.
Second publication: Yearbook
Meetings/Conventions: - annual meeting

National Association of Cigarette Machine Operators

PO Box 132, Macclesfield, SK11 6FL, England, UK
Tel: 44 1948 664850
Fax: 44 1948 663671
Founded: 1968
Members: 200
Contact: Ken Simcox
Description: Cigarette vending machine operators. Protects the interest of membership in the UK and Northern Ireland.
Publication: Handbook. Advertisements.
Meetings/Conventions: NACMO Exhibition - annual trade show - Exhibits. UK

National Association of Citizens Advice Bureaux

115-123 Pentonville Rd., London, N1 9LZ, England, UK
Tel: 44 207 8332181
Fax: 44 207 8334371
Website: http://www.citizensadvice.org.uk
Founded: 1939
Staff: 300
Description: All Citizens Advice Bureaux are independent charities, each funded by its local authority. Together they form the largest advice service in the country. There are 691 main bureaux which are members of NACAB. Supports CABx with the national information system, updated monthly. Citizens Advice Bureaux provide free, confidential and impartial advice and information on every subject including debt and benefits, and answer around 6.1 million enquiries a year. Drawing on its experience of clients' problems, the CAB Service seeks to exercise a responsible influence on the development of social policies and services, both locally and nationally. nationally. nationally.
Meetings/Conventions: - annual conference

National Association of Clubs for Young People

369 Kennington Lane, London, SE11 5QY, England, UK
Tel: 44 20 77930787
Fax: 44 20 78209815
Email: office@nabc-cyp.org.uk

Website: http://www.nacyp.org.uk
Founded: 1925
Members: 301890
Staff: 24
Contact: Andrew Mabey
Fee: £18
Membership Type: full or associate
Description: Aims to enable young people to develop spiritually, morally, culturally, mentally and physically, thereby helping them to prepare for life and adult responsibility.
Formerly: NACYP - Clubs for Young People
Publication: Magazine
Publication title: Club Connection
Second publication: Manual
Publication title: Leader's Guide
Meetings/Conventions: National Staff Conference - annual conference - Exhibits. UK

National Association of Colitis and Crohn's Disease
NACC

4 Beaumont House, Sutton Rd., St. Albans, AL1 5HH, England, UK
Tel: 44 1727 830038
Fax: 44 1727 862550
Email: nacc@nacc.org.uk
Website: http://www.nacc.org.uk
Founded: 1979
Members: 30000
Staff: 12
Contact: Richard Driscoll, Dir.
Description: Patients, relatives, health professionals, and anyone interested in colitis and Crohn's disease. Provides support and information for patients and families living with these conditions.
Publication: Newsletter

National Association of Co-operative Officials
NACO

6a Claredon House, Hyde, Cheshire, SK14 2Q2, England, UK
Tel: 44 161 3517900
Fax: 44 161 3666800
Founded: 1917
Members: 2400
Contact: Lindsay Ewing
Description: Those employed within retail distribution, food manufacturing, insurance, dairy industry, funeral services, motor trades (retail), retail pharmacy, travel industry, agriculture.
Publication: Newsletter
Publication title: The Co-Operative Official

National Association of Counsellors, Hypnotherapists and Psychotherapists

PO Box 719, Cambridge, CB5 0NX, England, UK
Tel: 44 163 8741363
Fax: 44 163 8744190
Email: mail@nachp.org
Website: http://www.nachp.org
Contact: Brian Beber, Chm.
Description: Aims to maintain a register of qualified therapists which is available to members of the public seeking treatment.

National Association of Deafened People

PO Box 50, Amersham, HP6 6XB, England, UK
Tel: 44 1494 724830
Fax: 44 1494 431932
Email: enquiries@nadp.org.uk
Website: http://www.nadp.org.uk
Founded: 1984
Members: 500
Staff: 1
Contact: Jenny Dunning, Admin.Off.
Fee: £10
Description: People with acquired profound hearing loss and professionals associated with them. Aims to work for improvements in the quality of life of deafened people, by providing a support service of information and advice and promoting an improvement in education, training and rehabilitation opportunities available. It also aims to increase public awareness of the needs and problems of deafened people, and to support research.
Publication: Booklet
Publication title: An Introduction to Cochlear Implants
Publication title: Information Booklet

National Association of Decorative and Fine Arts Societies

NADFAS House, 8 Guilford St., London, WC1N 1DA, England, UK
Tel: 44 20 74300730
Fax: 44 20 72420686
Email: enquiries@nadfas.org.uknadfas.org.uk
Founded: 1968
Members: 88000
Staff: 14
Contact: Dr. Thomas Cocke, CEO
Description: Membership is through local societies. There are no qualifications for membership other than an interest in the decorative and fine arts. Concerned with the promotion and advancement of the aesthetic education of the public, the cultivation, appreciation and study of the decorative and fine arts and the giving of aid to the preservation of our national artistic heritage for the benefit of the public.
Publication: Magazine
Publication title: NADFAS News. Advertisements.

National Association of Estate Agents
NAEA

Arbon House, 21 Jury St., Warwick, CV34 4EH, England, UK
Tel: 44 1926 496800
Fax: 44 1926 400953
Email: info@naea.co.uk
Website: http://www.naea.co.uk
Founded: 1962
Members: 9500
Staff: 23
Description: Estate agents in the United Kingdom. Promotes the use of estate agents. Sets standards for members.
Publication: Journal
Publication title: The Estate Agent. Advertisements.
Second publication: Membership Directory

National Association of Farriers, Blacksmiths and Agricultural Engineers

10 National Agricultural Centre, Stoneleigh Park, Kenilworth, CV8 2LG, England, UK
Tel: 44 2476 696595
Fax: 44 2476 696708
Email: nafbae@compuserve.com
Website: http://www.nafbae.org
Founded: 1905
Members: 1000
Staff: 2
Contact: Jackie Webb
Fee: £102
Membership Type: trade
Description: Farriers, blacksmiths and trade suppliers. Association for the craft of farriers and blacksmiths.
Publication: Magazine
Publication title: Forge. Advertisements.

National Association of Flower Arrangement Societies

Osborne House, 12 Devonshire Sq., London, EC2M 4TE, England, UK
Tel: 44 20 72475567
Fax: 44 20 72477232
Email: flowers@nafas.org.uk
Website: http://www.nafas.org.uk
Founded: 1959
Members: 104000
Staff: 4
Contact:
Fee: £1.4
Membership Type: local club
Description: Dedicated amateur flower arrangers. Aims to advance public education in the art of flower arranging and related subjects; to encourage the love of flowers and to demonstrate their decorative value; to instruct, train and qualify judges, demonstrators, teachers and speakers in order to raise the standard of work throughout the Country.
Library Subject: all floral art/horticultural related handbooks
Library Type: not open to the public
Publication: Magazine
Publication title: The Flower Arranger. Advertisements.

National Association of Funeral Directors

618 Warwick Rd., Solihull, B91 1AA, England, UK
Tel: 44 121 7111343
Fax: 44 121 7111351
Email: info@nafd.org.uk
Website: http://www.nafd.org.uk
Founded: 1905
Members: 1010
Staff: 6
Contact: A.B. Slater
Description: Funeral director firms and suppliers within the UK and overseas. Represents funeral service interests to government departments, local authorities etc. Protects and assists the rights of members.
Library Type: reference
Publication: Magazine
Publication title: Funeral Director Monthly. Advertisements.
Meetings/Conventions: - annual conference UK

National Association of Governors and Managers

Western House, 4th Fl., Ste. 1, Smallbrook Queensway, Birmingham, B5 4HQ, England, UK
Tel: 44 121 6435787
Fax: 44 121 6435787
Email: governorhq@nagm.org.uk
Website: http://www.nagm.org.uk
Founded: 1970
Members: 37000
Staff: 4
Contact: G. Down, Sec.
Fee: £12
Membership Type: individual
Fee: £40
Membership Type: governing bodies
Description: Individual governors, LEA representatives and groups comprising governing bodies. Information, training and advice for school governors.
Publication: Journal
Publication title: Governors News. Advertisements.
Second publication: Papers
Meetings/Conventions: - annual conference

National Association of Head Teachers

1 Heath Sq., Boltro Rd., Haywards Heath, RH16 1BL, England, UK
Tel: 44 1444 472472
Fax: 44 1444 472473
Email: info@naht.org.uk
Website: http://www.naht.co.uk
Founded: 1897
Members: 38500
Staff: 33
Contact: David M. Hart, Gen.Sec.
Description: Heads/principals, deputy heads/vice-principals of schools and colleges. To provide a ready means of communication for all members to ascertain and give expression to their opinions and to take action, when necessary on their behalf; to render help to all members in cases of professional difficulty; to further the cause of education generally; to uphold a high standard of professional conduct among members and to regulate relations between members and their employers.
Publication: Magazine
Publication title: Head Teachers Review

National Association of Hospital and Community Friends

Fairfax House, 2nd Fl., Causton Rd., Colchester, CO1 1RJ, England, UK
Tel: 44 1206 761227
Fax: 44 1206 560244
Email: info@hc-friends.org.uk
Website: http://www.hc-friends.org.uk
Founded: 1949
Members: 800
Staff: 7
Contact: David Wood, Ch.Exec.
Description: Works to promote and strengthen the work of member leagues throughout the United Kingdom. Membership services and benefits include advice and information, insurance and other group schemes, training, publications, grants and conferences. Each league is in individual charity supporting anyone disadvantaged by illness, injury, age or disability in hospitals, communities, GP practices and nursing homes.
Formerly: National Association of Leagues of Hospital Friends

Publication: Magazine
Publication title: The Hospital and Community Friend
Meetings/Conventions: - periodic conference - Exhibits.

National Association of Hospital Fire Officers

c/o Ken Bullas
Bolton Hospitals NHS Trust, Bolton General Hospital, Minerva Rd., Farnworth, Bolton, BL4 0JR, England, UK
Tel: 44 1204 390948
Fax: 44 1204 390838
Email: kenbullas@boltonh-tr.nwest.nhs.uk
Website: http://www.nahfo-healthfire.org.uk
Founded: 1971
Members: 350
Contact: Ken Bullas, Gen.Sec.
Description: Hospital fire prevention officers throughout the UK. Promotes and encourages the furtherance of the highest standards of fire safety in health service premises.
Publication: Newsletter
Meetings/Conventions: - annual conference - Exhibits.

National Association of Language Advisers

c/o Redcar, Cleveland ICT Centre
Corporation Rd., Redcar, TS10 1HA, England, UK
Tel: 44 1642 286688
Email: j.mcelwee@btinternet.com
Website: http://www.nala.org.uk
Founded: 1969
Members: 210
Contact: Mr. J. McElwee, Hon.Sec.
Fee: £45
Membership Type: ordinary
Description: Advisers, inspectors and consultants in modern languages in education. To support modern language professionals in their work.
Meetings/Conventions: - annual conference - Exhibits.

National Association of Laryngectomy Clubs

6 Rickett St., Ground Fl., Fulham, London, SW6 1RU, England, UK
Tel: 44 207 3819993
Fax: 44 207 3810025
Founded: 1976
Members: 4000
Staff: 2
Contact: Ms. V. Reed, Gen.Sec.
Fee: £20
Membership Type: clubs
Description: Promotes the welfare of laryngectomees by providing literature to them, their friends and their families and also the relevant professionals. Membership is via a club only.
Publication: Annual Report
Second publication: Newsletter
Meetings/Conventions: - annual meeting - Exhibits.

National Association of Licensed House Managers NALHM

c/o Peter Love, National Officer
Transport House, Warrington, M5 2SG, England, UK
Tel: 44 161 8480909
Fax: 44 161 8726068
Website: http://www.nalhm.org/
Founded: 1969
Members: 8500

Staff: 21
Contact: P.B. Love, Gen.Sec.
Description: Licensed house managers. Negotiates terms and conditions of employment for members and provides representation for discipline and grievance cases.
Publication: Yearbook

National Association of Local Councils
109 Great Russell St., London, WC1B 3LD, England, UK
Tel: 44 207 6371865
Fax: 44 207 4367451
Email: nalc@nalc.gov.uk
Website: http://www.nalc.gov.uk
Founded: 1947
Members: 7500
Staff: 11
Contact: John Findlay, Chief Exec.
Description: Parish, town and community councils in England and Wales. Represents the national interests generally of member councils and gives advice and guidance to individual member councils normally supplied through the 48 County Associations (addresses available on request).
Publication: Magazine
Publication title: Local Council Review. Advertisements.
Meetings/Conventions: - semiannual conference

National Association of Master Bakers - England
21 Baldock St., Ware, SG12 9DH, England, UK
Tel: 44 1920 468061
Fax: 44 1920 461632
Email: namb@masterbakers.co.uk
Website: http://www.masterbakers.co.uk/
Founded: 1887
Members: 2050
Staff: 11
Contact: D.G. Smith, CEO
Description: Small and medium bakery and confectionery businesses in England and Wales. Protects and promotes the interests of master bakers throughout England and Wales.

National Association of Master Letter Carvers
Bucklers Cottage, 74 West St., Marlow, SL7 2BP, England, UK
Tel: 44 162 8485638
Founded: 1920
Members: 50
Contact: A G Dickens, Honorary Sec.-Treas.
Fee: £25
Membership Type: full
Description: Promotes and preserves the craft of hand carved lettering in stone, marble, granite, and slate. Sets prices for piecework.
Library Type: reference

National Association of Mathematics Advisers
c/o Mary May
Bede Cottage, Inglestone Cottage, Hawkesbury, South Gloucestershire, GL9 1BX, England, UK
Tel: 44 1507 527793
Fax: 44 1384 410436
Email: c-matthews@uneone.net
Website: http://www.nama.org.uk
Founded: 1973
Members: 365

Staff: 1
Contact: Mary May, Admin.
Fee: £40
Description: Members are mathematics inspectors, advisers and consultants. Aims to ensure that inspection, advice and support, individually and collectively, make an effective contribution to and provide information on mathematics education.
Publication: Newsletter. Advertisements.
Meetings/Conventions: - annual conference - Exhibits. Oxford UK

National Association of Memorial Masons
27A Albert St., Rugby, CV21 2SG, England, UK
Tel: 44 1788 542264
Fax: 44 1788 542276
Email: enquiries@namm.org.uk
Website: http://www.namm.org.uk
Founded: 1907
Members: 400
Staff: 4
Contact: Barri N. Stirrup, Nat'l.Exec.Ofcr.
Description: Retail and wholesale memorial masonry companies throughout the UK and suppliers of ancillary products (Associate Members). Also some overseas companies interested in the UK market. Employers organization for the memorial masonry trade. Concerned with liaison with burial authorities; drawing up Codes of Practice and technical information; running a Conciliation and Arbitration Service; training; disseminating memorialisation information; organizing trade and public exhibitions and negotiating wages for the industry.
Library Subject: memorial masonry and related topics
Library Type: not open to the public
Formerly: NAMM
Publication: Journal
Publication title: Review

National Association of Mining History Organisantions
c/o Peak District Mining Museum
The Pavilion, Matlock Bath, Matlock, DE4 3NR, England, UK
Tel: 44 1629 583834
Email: secretary@namho.org
Website: http://www.namho.org
Founded: 1979
Members: 80
Contact: W.J. Taylor, Editor
Fee: £15
Membership Type: full member
Description: Mining museums, mining history societies and other organizations interested in mining history. Representation of member organizations and furtherance of mining history. Contact point for enquiries about any aspect of mining history or exploration of disused mines.
Publication: Book
Publication title: Mining History Heritage Guide. Advertisements.
Meetings/Conventions: - biennial conference

National Association of Music Educators
Gordon Lodge, Snitterton Rd., Matlock, DE4 3LZ, England, UK
Tel: 44 1629 760791
Fax: 44 1629 760791
Email: musiceducation@name.org.uk
Website: http://www.name.org.uk
Founded: 1983
Members: 530

Staff: 1
Contact: Helen Fraser, Admin.
Fee: £56
Membership Type: individual
Fee: £82
Membership Type: individual corporate
Description: A broad cross-section of music educators. Presses for the continued supply of well qualified music educators in schools and colleges; promotes professional dialogue and research and acts as a forum for exchange of good practice.
Formerly: Absorbed, Association for the Advancement of Teacher Education in Music
Publication: Journal
Publication title: Name Magazine. Advertisements.
Second publication: Newsletter
Publication title: Postbag
Meetings/Conventions: - annual conference - Exhibits. Stone UK

National Association of Ovulation Method Instructors UK

Oakfield, Wineham Lane, Bolney, Haywards Heath, RH17 5SD, England, UK
Tel: 44 1444 881744
Fax: 44 1444 881744
Website: http://www.woomb.org
Founded: 1977
Contact: Dr. Helen Davies
Description: Provides information on the Billings Ovulation Method of natural family planning; provides training for instructors.
Library Type: reference
Publication title: Resource List
Meetings/Conventions: - annual workshop

National Association of Paper Merchants

Hamilton Court, Gogmore Lane, Chertsey, KT16 9AP, England, UK
Tel: 44 8707 500249
Fax: 44 1932 569749
Email: info@napm.org.uk
Website: http://www.napm.org.uk
Founded: 1920
Members: 40
Staff: 6
Contact: David J. Pryke, Dir.Gen.
Description: Trade association representing the interests of UK paper merchants.
Publication: Magazine
Publication title: Distribute

National Association of ParaLegals

401 Langham House, 29-30 Margaret St., London, W1W 8SA, England, UK
Tel: 44 20 76255211
Fax: 44 20 73285931
Email: napl@compuserve.com
Founded: 1987
Members: 4000
Staff: 7
Contact: John C. Stacey-Hibbert, Gen.Sec.
Fee: £30
Membership Type: student
Fee: £35
Membership Type: associate
Description: Seeks to re-enforce and constantly increase it's position as the professional organization catering solely for the needs of the

Para-Legal; to strive to ensure the proper recognition of it's members by the auditing of it's qualifications, professional development and standards of behavior laid down for it's members; to encourage and develop the role and practice of the Para-Legal and to represent the best interests' of it's members.
Library Subject: all legal areas
Library Type: reference

National Association of Pension Funds
NAPF

NIOC House, 4 Victoria St., London, SW1H 0NX, England, UK
Tel: 44 207 8081300
Fax: 44 207 2227585
Email: membership@napf.co.uk
Website: http://www.napf.co.uk
Founded: 1923
Members: 1450
Contact: Dr. Ann Robinson
Description: Firms in the United Kingdom offering pensions. Provides a forum for the exchange of information between members. Promotes the availability of pensions.
Publication title: Year Book. Advertisements.

National Association of Percussion Teachers

11 Mallard Close, Kempshott, Basingstoke, RG22 5JP, England, UK
Tel: 44 1256 329009
Email: wendy.harding@bigfoot.com
Website: http://www.percussion.co.uk
Founded: 1986
Members: 200
Contact: Wendy Harding, Sec.
Fee: £20
Description: Percussion teachers. Brings together percussion teachers to share views and improve the quality of percussion teaching. Organizes an annual October conference.
Publication: Newsletter. Advertisements.
Meetings/Conventions: meeting London UK

National Association of Poultry Suppliers

1 Belgrove, Tunbridge Wells, TN1 1YW, England, UK
Tel: 44 1892 541412
Fax: 44 1892 535462
Email: naps@nfmft.co.uk
Founded: 1939
Staff: 1
Contact: G.E. Bidston
Description: Wholesale poultry merchants and suppliers. Represents wholesale poultry merchants and distributors within the UK. Willing to offer spokesmen on the wholesale poultry trade, including supplies and prices.
Formerly: National Federation of Wholesale Poultry Merchants

National Association of Press Agencies

41 Lansdowne Crescent, Leamington Spa, CV32 4PR, England, UK
Tel: 44 1926 424181
Fax: 44 1926 424760
Email: secretariat@napa.org.uk
Website: http://www.napa.org.uk
Founded: 1983
Members: 50
Contact: Julie Tracey
Description: Members include some of Britain's major news and picture agencies, established correspondents for all leading

newspapers, magazines, TV and broadcasting outlets. Concerned with safeguarding and promoting members' interests, with agencies covering most of Britain.
Publication: Handbook

National Association of Primary Care

Lettsom House, 11 Chandos St., Cavendish Sq., London, W1G 9DP, England, UK
Tel: 44 207 6367228
Fax: 44 171 6361601
Email: napc@primarycare.co.uk
Website: http://www.primarycare.co.uk
Founded: 1991
Members: 1000
Staff: 2
Contact: Pete Smith
Description: GP fundholding practices in England, Scotland, Wales & N Ireland. Aims to: promote good communication amongst fundholding practices; develop and extend the scope of services to patients offered by fundholding practices; encourage education research for and within fundholding practices; maintain and promote the highest ethical standards on the part of practitioners in fundholding practices; encourage the creation of new fundholding practices.
Formerly: National Association of Fundholding Practices

National Association of Prison Visitors

32 Newnham Ave., Bedford, MK41 9PT, England, UK
Tel: 44 1234 359763
Fax: 44 1234 359763
Email: info@napv.org.uk
Website: http://www.napv.org.uk
Founded: 1924
Members: 1300
Staff: 1
Contact: Mrs. A.G. McKenna
Fee: £5
Description: To befriend prisoners whilst in prison.
Publication: Newsletter
Meetings/Conventions: - annual meeting

National Association of Private Ambulance Services

21 Bassenhally Rd., Whittlesey, Peterborough, PE7 1RN, England, UK
Tel: 44 1733 350916
Fax: 44 1733 350916
Email: napas@ambulanceservices.co.uk
Website: http://www.ambulanceservices.co.uk
Founded: 1992
Members: 47
Staff: 450
Contact: Peter A. Littledyke, Dir.
Description: Provides self-regulation for private and professional ambulance service throughout the U.K and Ireland.
Library Subject: ambulance service all sections
Library Type: reference

National Association of Probation Officers
NAPO

4 Chivalry Rd., London, SW11 1HT, England, UK
Tel: 44 20 72234887
Fax: 44 20 72233503

Email: info@napo.org.uk
Website: http://www.napo.org.uk
Founded: 1912
Members: 7000
Staff: 17
Contact: Judy McKnight, Gen.Sec.
Description: Probation officers and other grades of staff in the Probation Service in England, Wales and Northern Ireland. Salaries and conditions of service. Probation practice issues. Campaigning on wide range of legal, penal and social issues and the promotion of anti-discriminatory practice in probation and the criminal justice system.
Publication: Journal
Meetings/Conventions: - annual meeting

National Association of Radiator Specialists

9 North St., Rugby, CV21 2AB, England, UK
Tel: 44 1788 538321
Fax: 44 1788 547361
Email: name@rmif.co.uk
Founded: 1945
Members: 50
Staff: 2
Contact:
Fee: £306
Description: Manufacturers, re-manufacturers, repairers and allied suppliers to the automotive radiator/industrial industry. Aims to provide a central organization for automotive radiator and heat exchange specialists both in the UK and overseas so that they can advance their interests. Also to secure for them a recognised status in trade circles and take such measures as considered desirable to promote greater efficiency on their behalf.
Publication: Handbook

National Association of Schoolmasters and Union of Women Teachers
NASUWT

Hillscourt Educ. Centre, Rednal, Birmingham, B45 8RS, England, UK
Tel: 44 121 4536150
Fax: 44 121 4576209
Email: nasuwt@mail.nasuwt.org.uk
Website: http://www.teachersunion.org.uk
Founded: 1919
Members: 250000
Staff: 180
Contact: Barry Gandy, Asst.Sec.
Fee: £114
Description: Active, retired, and student teachers. Regulates relations between members and other employees in the education field. Works to ensure competitive salary scale. Advises government and local education authorities on educational matters. Offers members insurance coverage, legal assistance, and housing. Conducts research. Maintains speakers' bureau.
Library Type: reference
Formerly: Formed by Merger of, National Association of Schoolmasters
Publication: Journal
Publication title: Career Teacher. Advertisements.
Meetings/Conventions: - annual conference - Exhibits. Bournemouth UK

National Association of Seed Potato Merchants

Bldg. 5, Bentwaters Parks, Rendlesham, Woosbridge, IP12 2TW, England, UK
Tel: 44 1394 460075
Fax: 44 1394 461117
Email: dfradd@naspm.org.ukwww.naspm.org.uk
Founded: 1940
Members: 94
Staff: 1
Contact: C.D. Fradd, Sec.
Description: Association of seed potato merchants.
Publication: Newsletter
Publication title: NASPM News
Meetings/Conventions: - annual conference

National Association of Self Employed

91 Mansfield Rd., Nottingham, NG1 3FN, England, UK
Tel: 44 115 9475046
Fax: 44 115 9509139
Email: nas@n-a-s.org.uk
Website: http://www.n-a-s.org.uk
Founded: 1942
Members: 5000
Staff: 5
Contact: Mr. T Hiley
Description: Provides the best possible advice and support to the self-employed and furthers their interests.

National Association of Shopfitters

411 Limpsfield Rd., The Green, Warlingham, CR6 9HA, England, UK
Tel: 44 1883 624961
Fax: 44 1883 626841
Email: nas@clara.net
Website: http://www.shopfitters.org
Founded: 1919
Members: 175
Staff: 3
Contact: G.F. Elliott, Dir.
Description: Bespoke shopfitting and interior contractors. Represents the major shopfitting companies throughout Great Britain. Work carried out by member companies covers interiors of all kinds, including shops, bars, offices, banks, public buildings, hotels and restaurants.
Publication: Annual Report
Second publication: Directory

National Association of Social Workers in Education

6 Highgrove Ct., Poringland, Norwich, NR14 7RS, England, UK
Tel: 44 1603 223473
Founded: 1884
Contact: Grace Cheese, Gen.Sec.
Description: Social workers in education and education welfare officers employed by local authorities in the UK. Aims to promote the status of social work in the service, to encourage the development of training and professional practice, to protect the rights of children and young people.

National Association of Steel Stockholders
NASS

The McLaren Bldg., 6th Fl., Dale End, Birmingham, B4 7LN, England, UK
Tel: 44 121 2002288
Fax: 44 121 2367444
Email: info@nass.org.uk
Website: http://www.nass.org.uk
Founded: 1928
Members: 100
Staff: 4
Contact: G. Polson, Dir.Gen.
Fee: £405
Membership Type: full
Fee: £700
Membership Type: associate
Description: Steel stockholders, processors, and firms providing services to steel stockholders. Represents members' interests before governmental and European Community agencies; encourages exchange of ideas and information between members. Organizes training courses; compiles statistics.
Library Subject: U.K., European, and world steel industry, especially stockholding
Library Type: not open to the public
Publication: Video
Publication title: Beating the Odds - Safety in Steel Stockholding
Second publication: Membership Directory
Publication title: List of Members
Meetings/Conventions: - annual conference

National Association of Street Entertainers

27 Howard Rd., Brighton, BN2 2TP, England, UK
Tel: 44 1273 683339
Website: http://www.streetentertainers-association.org
Founded: 1994
Members: 130
Staff: 1
Contact: John Arno, Sec.
Fee: £20
Description: Street performers, festival and corporate acts.
Publication: Newsletter
Publication title: The Busker. Advertisements.

National Association of Theatre Nurses

Daisy Ayris House, 6 Grove Park Ct., Harrogate, HG1 4DP, England, UK
Tel: 44 1423 508079
Fax: 44 1423 531613
Email: hq@natn.org.uk
Website: http://www.natn.org.uk
Founded: 1964
Members: 8000
Staff: 13
Contact: John Beesley, Prof.Ofr.
Fee: £33
Membership Type: ordinary
Description: Operating theatre nurses. Workshops and study days are organized locally and nationally throughout the year.
Publication: Journal
Publication title: British Journal of Perioperitive Nurses. Advertisements.
Meetings/Conventions: - annual congress - Exhibits. Harrogate UK

National Association of Tool Dealers

225 Bristol Rd., Edgbaston, Birmingham, B5 7UB, England, UK
Tel: 44 121 4466688
Fax: 44 121 4465215
Email: natd@bhfgroup.demon.co.uk
Founded: 1899
Members: 3500
Staff: 52
Contact: Jonathan Swift, Dir.
Fee: £124
Membership Type: retail corporate
Description: Represents members' interests, including marketing and finance.
Library Subject: hardware house wares garden tools
Library Type: reference

National Association of Training Officers in Personal Social Services

c/o Selly Wick House
59/61 Selly Wick Rd., Selly Park, Birmingham, B29 7JE, England, UK
Tel: 44 121 4156805
Fax: 44 121 4156806
Email: office@natopss.info
Website: http://www.natopss.info/
Contact: David Leavy, Chair
Description: Training officers in personal social services.

National Association of Waste Disposal Officers
NAWDO

Nottinghamshire County Council, Environment Department, Fl. 1, Trent Bridge House, Fox Rd., W. Bridgford, Nottingham, NG2 6BJ, England, UK
Tel: 44 115 9774893
Fax: 44 115 9772148
Email: chris.drew@nottscc.gov.uk
Founded: 1992
Members: 90
Contact: Chris Drew
Fee: £25
Membership Type: U.K. waste disposal authorities
Description: Waste disposal client representatives from waste disposal authorities in the UK. Bulk of membership from England and Wales. Aims to provide a national forum for waste disposal client functions, including matters relating to legislation, contracts, contract administration and recycling. The Association will set up working parties to examine and report on a number of matters of national interest in terms of waste management. The Association will maintain a working liaison with the regulation authority.
Meetings/Conventions: - quarterly meeting

National Association of Women Pharmacists
NAWP

c/o Office Manager, Royal Pharmaceutical Society of Great Britain, 1 Lambeth High St., London, SE1 7JN, England, UK
Email: enquiries@nawp.org.uk
Website: http://www.nawp.org.uk
Founded: 1905
Members: 300
Contact: Brenda Ecclestone, Hon.Sec.
Fee: £15
Membership Type: Full-time pharmacists.
Fee: £20
Membership Type: Part-time pharmacists.

Description: Women pharmacists. Promotes the careers of women in pharmacy and the role of women pharmacists in public life. Encourages continuing education and career development for women pharmacists. Maintains communication with pharmacists who have left the Register of the Royal Pharmaceutical Society of Great Britain (RPSGB) during a career break. Works with other women's organizations. Conducts courses and lectures, provides mentoring for members.
Publication: Book
Publication title: Careers in Pharmacy
Second publication: Newsletter
Publication title: NAWP. Advertisements.
Meetings/Conventions: Kare of Kids Children's Health and Treatment - annual conference - Exhibits.

National Association of Writers in Education

PO Box 1 Sheriff Hutton, York, YO60 7YU, England, UK
Tel: 44 165 3618429
Email: paul@nawe.co.uk
Website: http://www.nawe.co.uk
Founded: 1987
Members: 500
Contact: Paul Munden, Dir.
Fee: £12
Membership Type: individual
Fee: £50
Membership Type: institutional
Description: Open to all, including writers, teachers, arts advisers, students and librarians. Supports writers and creative writing of all genres in all educational settings throughout the United Kingdom. Maintains an online directory of extensive details on over 1000 writers. Produces Writing in Education sent free to members three times per year.
Library Type: reference

National Association of Youth Theatres
NAYT

Arts Centre, Vane Terrace, Darlington, DL3 7AX, England, UK
Tel: 44 1325 363330
Fax: 44 1325 363313
Email: naytuk@aol.com
Website: http://www.nayt.org.uk/
Founded: 1982
Members: 250
Staff: 4
Contact: Stuart Hawkes, Dir.
Description: Youth theater groups linked to professional theater, amateur theater, local government youth projects, special needs groups, and the voluntary arts sector. Promotes increased participation by people between the ages of 16 and 24 in theater programs. Represents the interests of youth theater programs; advocates for increased public funding of youth theater. Conducts regional youth theater training and support projects. Makes available advice, resources, financial assistance, and other support services to youth theater projects. Advises national and county government agencies responsible for arts programs and funding.
Library Subject: youth theatre
Library Type: by appointment only
Publication title: Strategies for Success
Second publication: Bulletin. Advertisements.
Meetings/Conventions: B & G Youth Theatre Festival

National Auricula and Primula Society

67 Warnham Ct. Rd., Carshalton Beeches, SM5 3ND, England, UK
Founded: 1876
Members: 400
Contact: Lawrence E. Wigley, Hon.Sec.
Fee: £8
Membership Type: single
Fee: £8
Membership Type: family
Description: Promotes the interest of individuals who raise and show Auriculas, Gold Laced Polyanthus and other primulas, some rare and difficult to grow and others well known and easily recognizable as garden and wild plants.
Library Type: reference
Publication: Yearbook
Second publication: Newsletter
Meetings/Conventions: show

National Autistic Society
NAS

393 City Rd., London, EC1V 1NG, England, UK
Tel: 44 20 78332299
Fax: 44 20 78339666
Email: nas@nas.org.uk
Website: http://www.nas.org.uk
Founded: 1962
Members: 11500
Staff: 1400
Contact: Vernon Beauchamp, Chief Exec.
Fee: £16
Membership Type: individual overseas
Fee: £11
Membership Type: individual UK
Description: Parents of people with autism; professionals; caregivers. Exists to champion the rights and interests of all people with autism and to ensure that they and their families receive quality services appropriate to their needs. It has developed a range of educational and support services; runs schools and adult centres; offers families and carers information, advice and support; works to improve awareness of autism; offers a diagnostic and assessment service; and provides training and promotes research.
Library Subject: autism
Library Type: by appointment only
Publication: Journal
Publication title: Communication. Advertisements.
Meetings/Conventions: - annual conference

National Bed Federation

Victoria House, Victoria St., Tauton, Somerset, TA1 3FA, England, UK
Tel: 44 182 3368008
Fax: 44 182 3350526
Email: info@bedfed.org.uk
Website: http://www.bedfed.org.uk
Founded: 1912
Members: 135
Staff: 2
Contact: Mr. Patrick Quigley, Ch.Exec.
Description: Bed manufacturers and manufacturers engaged in trade allied to bed manufacture. Represents bed manufacturers and their suppliers.

National Begonia Society

33 Findern Ln., Willington, Derby, DE65 6DW, England, UK
Tel: 44 1283 702681
Email: natbegonia@aol.com
Website: http://www.begoniasouthcoast.co.uk/
Founded: 1948
Members: 800
Contact: Colin Nicklin, Sec.
Fee: £7
Membership Type: member
Fee: £8
Membership Type: affiliated
Description: Promotes the growing of begonias.
Library Subject: begonias
Library Type: not open to the public

National Canine Defence League
NCDL

17 Wakley St., London, EC1V 7RQ, England, UK
Tel: 44 207 8370006
Fax: 44 207 8332701
Email: info@ncdl.org.uk
Website: http://www.ncdl.org.uk
Founded: 1891
Members: 20000
Staff: 380
Contact: Clarissa Baldwin, CEO
Description: Largest dog welfare charity in the UK. Dedicated to the rescue and rehoming of stray and abandoned dogs. Working towards the day when all dogs can enjoy a happy life, free from the threat of unnecessary destruction.
Library Subject: dogs, animal welfare
Library Type: by appointment only
Publication: Newsletter
Publication title: Wag
Meetings/Conventions: International Companion Animal Welfare Conference conference

National Caravan Council

Catherine House, Victoria Rd., Aldershot, GU11 1SS, England, UK
Tel: 44 1252 318251
Fax: 44 1252 322596
Email: info@nationalcaravan.co.uk
Website: http://www.thecaravan.net
Founded: 1939
Members: 800
Staff: 20
Contact: Alan Bishop, Dir.
Description: Members include manufacturers, distributors, park operators and suppliers of components, accessories and services. Acts as the trade association for all aspects of the caravan industry in the UK. Includes touring caravans, motor caravans, caravan holiday homes and park residential (mobile) homes.
Publication: Magazine
Publication title: Caravan Business. Advertisements.
Second publication: Handbook
Publication title: NCC Handbook
Meetings/Conventions: - annual convention - Exhibits.

National Care Homes Association

45/49 Leather Ln., 4th Fl., London, EC1N 7TJ, England, UK
Tel: 44 20 78317090
Fax: 44 20 78317040

Email: ncha@btclick.com
Founded: 1981
Members: 3000
Staff: 5
Contact: Sheila Scott, Chief Exec.
Description: Independent sector care and nursing homes. Serves as a trade association representing members' interests.
Library Type: not open to the public
Publication: Newsletter
Publication title: Newsletter
Meetings/Conventions: - annual conference - Exhibits.

National Caving Association

c/o Guy Smith
108 Brookhouse Hill, Sheffield, S10 3TE, England, UK
Tel: 44 114 2303575
Email: admin@nca.org.uk
Website: http://www.nca.org.uk
Founded: 1969
Members: 9
Contact: Mick Day, Chm.
Fee: £460
Membership Type: constituent bodies
Description: Consists of 5 regional Caving Councils in the UK, plus 4 other, national caving bodies, which cover, education, research, cave rescue and mine exploration; 340 caving clubs. Covers, safety, conservation, equipment, training, access and liaison with many bodies such as the Sports Council, Central Council for Physical Recreation, English Nature, etc.
Library Subject: caving, training, conservation
Library Type: not open to the public
Publication: Handbook
Publication title: Cave Conservation Handbook
Publication title: Cave Conservation Policy
Meetings/Conventions: - annual meeting

National Childbirth Trust
NCT

Alexandra House, Oldham Terrace, Acton, London, W3 6NH, England, UK
Tel: 44 870 7703236
Fax: 44 870 7703237
Website: http://www.nctpregnancyandbabycare.com
Founded: 1956
Members: 56000
Staff: 30
Contact: Bernadette Matus, Ch.
Fee: £36
Membership Type: National
Fee: £26
Membership Type: renewal
Description: Provides information regarding pregnancy, childbirth, and parenting to interested individuals. Sponsors support groups for disabled parents and parents who have experienced miscarriage. Conducts educational programs in antenatal care and breastfeeding in schools and colleges. Disseminates information.
Library Subject: parenting, antenatal care, and breastfeeding
Library Type: by appointment only
Publication title: New Digest
Second publication: Magazine
Publication title: New Generation Magazine. Advertisements.
Meetings/Conventions: - annual meeting - Exhibits.

National Childminding Association
NCMA

8 Masons Hill, Bromley, BR2 9EY, England, UK
Tel: 44 208 4646164
Fax: 44 208 2906834
Email: info@ncma.org.uk
Website: http://www.ncma.org.uk
Founded: 1977
Members: 50000
Staff: 30
Contact: Lynn Daley, Chair
Description: Child care professionals, parents, and interested individuals. Promotes quality day care, recreation, and education for young children and seeks to advance the education of child care professionals. Offers seminars; conducts research.
Publication: Magazine
Publication title: Who Minds?
Second publication: Pamphlets
Meetings/Conventions: - annual conference - Exhibits.

National Children's Bureau

8 Wakley St., London, EC1V 7QE, England, UK
Tel: 44 20 78436000
Fax: 44 20 78436007
Email: library@ncb.org.uk
Website: http://www.ncb.org.uk
Founded: 1963
Members: 2800
Staff: 150
Contact: Nicola Hilliard, Head of Library and Info. Serv.
Description: Professionals and policy makers from health education and social services; parents and individuals from many different organizations. To identify and promote the interests of all children and young people and to improve their status in a diverse society.
Library Subject: children
Library Type: open to the public
Publication: Newsletter
Publication title: Children Now
Second publication: Journal
Publication title: Children & Society
Meetings/Conventions: - periodic conference

National Chrysanthemum Society

George Gray House, 8 Amber Business Village, Amber Close, Tamworth, B77 4RP, England, UK
Tel: 44 1827310331
Fax: 44 1827310331
Email: ncs1846@aol.com
Founded: 1846
Members: 5000
Staff: 3
Contact: Wallace Farr Frics, Gen.Mgr.
Fee: £13
Membership Type: fellow
Fee: £22
Membership Type: patron
Description: Promotes the growing of Chrysanthemums.
Library Subject: chrysanthemums
Library Type: reference

National Coalition of Anti-Deportation Campaigns
NCADC

110 Hamstead Rd., Birmingham, B20 2QS, England, UK
Tel: 44 121 5546947
Email: ncadc@ncadc.org.uk
Website: http://www.ncadc.org.uk
Founded: 1995
Staff: 3
Contact: John O.
Description: Families and individuals facing deportation (asylum seekers and economic migrants) and organizations which defend asylum seekers and economic migrants. Seeks to prevent the deportation of families and individuals seeking asylum and economic migrants in the United Kingdom. Publicizes the cases of anyone facing deportation; works to reform statutes governing immigration and asylum.

National College of Hypnosis and Psychotherapy

12 Cross St., Nelson, BB9 7EN, England, UK
Tel: 44 1282 699378
Fax: 44 1282 698633
Email: hypnosis_nchp@compuserve.com
Website: http://www.hypnotherapyuk.net
Founded: 1977
Members: 200
Staff: 11
Contact: P.J.D. Savage, Principal
Description: Mature students seeking a reputable, externally accredited (by the British Accreditation Council) training with a view to running their own practices, for interest or to augment their existing professional skills. Concerned with training in hypnotherapy/ psychotherapy/counselling on part-time basis to appropriate, suitably motivated, mature students in London, Liverpool, Glasgow, and Northern Ireland. Courses are held at regular intervals throughout the year. Member of United Kingdom Council for Psychotherapy and European Association for Hypnopsychotherapy. Higher Education. Courses are held at regular intervals throughout the year. Member of United Kingdom Council for Psychotherapy.

National Compost Development Association

c/o Dept of Civil Engineering
The University of Leeds, Leeds, LS2 9JT, England, UK
Tel: 44 113 2332298
Fax: 44 113 2332243
Email: 106234.1137@compuserve.com
Founded: 1995
Members: 70
Staff: 4
Contact: Stuart Brown
Fee: £500
Membership Type: corporate
Description: To promote composting and the use of compost.
Library Type: not open to the public
Meetings/Conventions: - bimonthly workshop

National Council for Drama Training

5 Tavistock Pl., Bloomsbury, London, WC1H 9SS, England, UK
Tel: 44 20 73873650
Fax: 44 20 76814733
Email: info@ncdt.co.uk
Website: http://www.ncdt.co.uk
Founded: 1976
Staff: 2
Contact: Adele Bailey, Exec.Sec.

Description: Promotes drama industry employers, Equity and vocational drama schools. Ensures the professional relevance of training and good practice. possible links between those engaged in training and those working in the profession.
Publication title: A Practical Guide to vocational training in dance and drama
Publication title: An Applicant's Guide to auditioning and interviewing at dance and drama schools

National Council for Hospice and Specialist Palliative Care Services

34-44 Britannia St., London, WC1X 9JG, England, UK
Tel: 44 207 5208299
Fax: 44 207 5208298
Email: enquiries@hospice-spc-council.org.uk
Website: http://www.hospice-spc-council.org.uk
Founded: 1991
Members: 35
Staff: 4
Contact: Mrs. Eve Richardson, Ch.Exec.
Description: Members are nominated by national charities and professional organisations or elected by regional hospice and palliative care units. To represent the views and interests of hospice and palliative care services to ministers, civil servants, MPs, the media and statutory and other agencies. To provide advice to hospice and specialist palliative care services in their relations with health authorities, local authorities and other agencies.
Publication: Newsletter
Publication title: Information Exchange
Second publication: Papers

National Council for the Conservation of Plants and Gardens

c/o The Stable Courtyard
Wisley Gardens, Wisley, Woking, GU23 6QP, England, UK
Tel: 44 1483 211465
Fax: 44 1483 212404
Email: info@nccpg.org.uk
Website: http://www.nccpg.com
Founded: 1978
Members: 5000
Staff: 5
Contact: Genevieve Melbourne Webb, Gen.Admin.
Fee: £15
Membership Type: national members
Fee: £10
Membership Type: overseas
Description: A mixture of amateur and professional horticulturists and botanists. Aims to conserve garden plants for future generations through a network of local groups of supporters and 650 'collection' holders.
Formerly: NCCPG
Publication: Directory
Publication title: Directory of The National Plant Collection. Advertisements.
Second publication: Journal
Publication title: Plant Heritage. Advertisements.
Meetings/Conventions: - annual conference

National Council for the Training of Journalists

Latton Bush Centre, Southern Way, Harlow, CM18 7BL, England, UK
Tel: 44 1279 430009
Fax: 44 1279 438008
Email: info@nctj.com

Website: http://www.nctj.com
Founded: 1951
Members: 6
Staff: 10
Contact: Rob Selwood, Chief Exec.
Description: Representatives of the newspaper employers, Editors Guild, national trade unions throughout UK. Aims to advance the education and training of trainee journalists including press photographers.
Publication: Newsletter
Publication title: NTCJ News. Advertisements.
Meetings/Conventions: seminar

National Council for Voluntary Organisations
NCVO

Regent's Wharf, 8 All Saints St., London, N1 9RL, England, UK
Tel: 44 207 7136161
Fax: 44 207 7136300
Email: ncvo@ncvo-vol.org.uk
Website: http://www.ncvo-vol.org.uk
Founded: 1919
Members: 1600
Staff: 80
Contact: Stuart Etherington, Ch.Exec.
Fee: £85
Description: Voluntary organizations, professional associations, and government bodies in Britain. Promotes and protects members' interests. Encourages the formation of voluntary and charitable organizations. Offers advisory services; acts as a liaison between members and government authorities; works with national and international government bodies.
Formerly: National Council of Social Service
Publication: Book
Publication title: Voluntary Agencies Directory. Advertisements.
Second publication: Magazine
Publication title: Voluntary Sector. Advertisements.
Meetings/Conventions: Building Communities - annual conference - Exhibits.

National Council of Voluntary Child Care Organisations

Unit 4, Pride Court, 80-82 White Lion St., London, N1 9PF, England, UK
Tel: 44 20 78333319
Fax: 44 20 78338637
Email: office@ncvcco.org
Website: http://www.ncvcco.org
Founded: 1942
Members: 108
Staff: 8
Contact: Erica DeAth, Chief Exec.
Description: Voluntary organisations providing child care or supporting child care work throughout England. Aims to be an independent, identifiable member-led organisation maintaining the distinctive voice of voluntary child care; promotes and sustains the voluntary sector's contribution to the provision of services for children and families.
Publication: Bulletin
Publication title: Magnet. Advertisements.
Second publication: Newsletter
Publication title: Outlook. Advertisements.

National Courier Association
NCA

7 Canons Rd., Old Wolerton, Milton Keynes, MK12 5TL, England, UK
Tel: 44 1908 315315
Fax: 44 1908 314000
Email: ncaadmin@london-link.co.uk
Website: http://www.nca.couk.com/
Founded: 1988
Members: 110
Contact: Ian Dafter, Pres.
Description: Same-day courier companies. Seeks to allow members to inter-trade and provide customers with same-day collection and delivery services. Screens courier companies and confers membership upon qualifying services; facilitates communication and cooperation among members. Represents members' interests before government agencies, labor and industrial organizations, and the public. Plans to establish courier services in the Republic of Ireland as associate members.
Formerly: National Network of Courier Companies

National Dairymen's Association

19 Cornwall Terrace, London, NW1 4QP, England, UK
Tel: 44 171 9354562
Fax: 44 171 4874734
Email: info@dairymen.org.uk
Founded: 1937
Members: 2500
Staff: 16
Contact: John A. Kerr, Dir.
Description: Individual dairymen and large dairy companies. Promotes and protects the interests of members who represent the liquid and fresh products sectors of the dairy industry in England and Wales. It negotiates with and makes dairymen's views known to the UK government, producer organizations, the European Union, local authorities, trade bodies and others on all subjects associated with members' businesses.
Publication: Journal
Publication title: Milk Industry International. Advertisements.
Meetings/Conventions: Dairy Industry Show - annual conference - Exhibits. Blackpool UK

National Day Nurseries Association

Brighouse, West Yorkshire, HD6 4AB, England, UK
Tel: 44 870 7744244
Fax: 44 870 7744243
Email: info@ndna.org.uk
Website: http://www.ndna.org.uk
Founded: 1991
Members: 1700
Staff: 40
Contact: Rosemary Murphy, CEO
Description: Aims to enhance the development and education of children in their early years, through the provision of support services to members.
Library Type: reference
Publication: Magazine
Publication title: Nursery News. Advertisements.

National Deaf Children's Society

15 Dufferin St., London, EC1Y 8UR, England, UK
Tel: 44 20 74908656
Fax: 44 20 72515020
Email: ndcs@ndcs.org.uk

Website: http://www.ndcs.org.uk
Founded: 1944
Members: 9000
Staff: 64
Contact: Molly Baack, Press Contact
Fee: £10
Membership Type: U.K.
Fee: £20
Membership Type: outside UK
Description: Supports families and young deaf people, chiefly through providing information and advice on education, state benefits, audiology and equipment.
Library Subject: small, specialized library
Library Type: not open to the public
Publication: Pamphlet
Publication title: Communication Tips and Terms
Second publication: Magazine
Publication title: TALK. Advertisements.
Meetings/Conventions: - semiannual meeting - Exhibits.

National Dog Wardens Association

Tewkesbury Borough Council Offices, Gloucester Rd., Tewkesbury, GL20 5TT, England, UK
Tel: 44 1452 840785
Fax: 44 1452 840832
Email: topdogk9@amserve.co
Founded: 1988
Members: 300
Contact: Mrs. Susan Bell, Pres.
Fee: £50
Membership Type: associate
Fee: £25
Membership Type: full member
Description: Promotes the compassionate enforcement of animal welfare, both statutory and voluntary at the local government level.
Library Subject: animal welfare with particular emphasis on canines
Library Type: reference
Meetings/Conventions: - periodic seminar

National Dried Fruit Trade Association

Castle House, 25 Castlereach St., Ste. 13, London, W1Y 5YR, England, UK
Tel: 44 171 7232083
Founded: 1956
Members: 48
Contact: W.J. Anzer, Sec.
Description: Dried fruit importers and packers. Protects the interests of the dried fruit trade.

National Eczema Society
NES

Hill House, Highgate Hill, London, N19 5NA, England, UK
Tel: 44 207 2813553
Fax: 44 207 2816395
Email: helpline@excema.org
Website: http://www.eczema.org/
Founded: 1975
Members: 12000
Staff: 15
Contact: Margaret Cox, Ch.Exec.
Fee: £20
Membership Type: standard, healthcare professionals
Fee: £40

Membership Type: practice
Description: People with eczema, dermatitis, and sensitive skin. Seeks to improve the quality of life of people with eczema; promotes advancement of the diagnosis and treatment of eczema and related disorders. Provides information and support to those affected by the condtion. Conducts information days to raise public awareness of eczema; raises funds to support dermatological research; represents the interests of people with eczema before pertinent government agencies and health care organizations.
Publication: Journal
Publication title: Exchange. Advertisements.

National Endometriosis Society

Ste. 50, Westminster Place Gardens, 1-7 Artillery Row, London, SW1P 1RL, England, UK
Tel: 44 207 222 2781
Fax: 44 207 222 2786
Email: nes@endo.org.uk
Website: http://www.endo.org.uk
Founded: 1982
Members: 3500
Staff: 4
Contact: Robert Music, Ch.Exec.
Fee: £18
Membership Type: UK resident
Fee: £25
Membership Type: overseas
Description: Women with personal experience of endometriosis and clinicians. Funds research into endometriosis and raises public awareness of it among medical professionals and the public.
Publication: Newsletter
Publication title: Endolink

National Entertainment Agents Council

PO Box 112, Seaford, BN25 2DQ, England, UK
Tel: 44 870 7557612
Fax: 44 870 7557613
Email: info@neac.org.uk
Website: http://www.neac.org.uk
Founded: 1977
Members: 100
Contact: C.N. Bray, Gen.Sec.
Fee: £160
Description: Members are entertainment agents. Provides a medium through which members can trade, communicate, be kept updated in current matters via newsletters and other circulations, complain, confer and lobby for the mutual benefit of members. The Council is self-policing, and its members all adhere to its published code of conduct.
Formerly: Central Entertainment Agents Council
Publication: Newsletter
Publication title: The Agent. Advertisements.

National Farmers' Union - England

164 Shaftesbury Ave., London, WC2H 8HL, England, UK
Tel: 44 207 3317200
Fax: 44 207 3317313
Email: nfu@nfu.org.uk
Website: http://www.nfuonline.com
Founded: 1908
Members: 100000
Staff: 650
Description: Membership is restricted to working farmers. Represents farmers and growers of England and Wales.

National Federation of 18 Plus Groups

8-10 Church St., Newent, GL18 1PP, England, UK
Tel: 44 1531 821210
Fax: 44 1531 821474
Email: office@18plus.org.uk
Website: http://www.eng.warwick.ac.uk/18plus
Founded: 1941
Members: 1000
Staff: 2
Contact: Christine George, Admin.Off.
Fee: £26
Membership Type: full
Description: Volunteers 18-35 years old engaged in social activities. Offers training.
Publication title: Plus News
Second publication: Directory
Meetings/Conventions: - periodic convention - Exhibits.

National Federation of Access Centres

SW Regional Access Centre, disability Assist Service, University of Plymouth, Drake Circus, Plymouth, PL4 8AA, England, UK
Tel: 44 1752 232696
Fax: 44 1752 232279
Email: m.m.kemp@plymouth.ac.uk
Website: http://www.nfac.org.uk
Contact: Judith Waterfield, Mgr.
Description: Provides clients with disabilities with an opportunity to evaluate a range of enabling technologies relevant to their learning, teaching, or other daily communication needs.

National Federation of Builders

c/o Construction House
56-64 Leonard St., London, EC2A 4JX, England, UK
Tel: 44 20 76085150
Fax: 44 20 76085151
Email: national@builders.org.uk
Website: http://www.builders.org.uk
Founded: 1984
Members: 2500
Staff: 35
Contact: Barry Stephens, Chief Exec.
Description: Acts as the principal focus for the views of small and medium sized general building contractors in England and Wales. Presents those views to government, clients etc and generally promotes the role of the general contractor. Also advises and assists individual member with legal, technical, tax and employment problems.
Formerly: Building Contractors Federation

National Federation of Bus Users

PO Box 320, Portsmouth, PO5 3SD, England, UK
Tel: 44 2392 814493
Fax: 44 2392 863080
Email: caroline@nfbu.fsnet.co.uk
Website: http://www.nfbu.org
Founded: 1985
Members: 750
Staff: 6
Contact: Dr. Caroline Cahm, Chm.
Fee: £7
Membership Type: individual
Fee: £12
Membership Type: group

Description: Individual bus passengers, passenger groups, and groups/organisations interested in public transport. Helps to set up local user groups and provides them with help and advice in dealing with local bus issues. Develops links between passengers and those responsible for provision of local bus services as well as bus manufacturers. Campaigns for government policies to encourage improvements in both the level and quality of bus transport.
Publication: Newsletter
Publication title: Bus User
Publication title: The Clean and Green Bus Guide
Meetings/Conventions: - annual general assembly

National Federation of Cemetery Friends

42 Chestnut Grove, South Croydon, CR2 7LH, England, UK
Email: gwyneth1@btinternet.com
Founded: 1986
Members: 40
Contact: Gwyneth Stokes, Hon.Sec.
Description: Acts as a link for voluntary groups who aim to conserve and preserve cemeteries and encourage public use for educational and recreational purpose.
Publication: Newsletter

National Federation of Demolition Contractors NFDC

Resurgam House, 1A New Rd., The Causeway, Staines, TW18 3DH, England, UK
Tel: 44 1784 456799
Fax: 44 1784 461118
Email: info@demolition-nfdc.com
Website: http://www.demolition-nfdc.com
Founded: 1941
Members: 201
Staff: 3
Contact: Christine MacFarlane, Ch.Exec.
Fee: £1351.23
Membership Type: Corporate
Fee: £1057.5
Membership Type: Associate
Description: Contractors that provide demolition services to the building and construction industry in the United Kingdom. Represents and protects members' interests.
Publication: Journal
Publication title: Demolition and Dismantling. Advertisements.
Publication title: List of Members
Meetings/Conventions: - annual convention - Exhibits. Prague Czech Republic

National Federation of Enterprise Agencies

Trinity Gardens, 9-11 Bromham Rd., Bedford, MK40 2UQ, England, UK
Tel: 44 1234 354055
Fax: 44 1234 543055
Email: enquiries@nfea.com
Website: http://www.nfea.com
Founded: 1992
Members: 133
Staff: 5
Contact: Alan Bretherton, Chief Executive
Fee: £350
Membership Type: annual subscription

Description: Aims to influence Government, the EU and other key decision makers in the development of effective strategies which will assist small businesses to sustain themselves and, ultimately, to prosper.

National Federation of Fish Friers
c/o New Federation House
4 Greenwood Mount, Leeds, LS6 4LQ, England, UK
Tel: 44 113 2307044
Fax: 44 113 2307010
Email: mail@federationoffishfriers.co.uk
Founded: 1913
Members: 2300
Staff: 3
Contact: Mrs. Ann M. Kirk, Gen.Sec.
Description: Representing bona fide fish and chip shop proprietors. Offers three day trade training courses from own training school monthly, specially designed for new and prospective entrants to the trade.

National Federation of Fishermen's Organisations NFFO
c/o NFFO Services Ltd., Marsden Rd., Grimsby, DN31 3SG, England, UK
Tel: 44 1472 349009
Fax: 44 1472 242486
Email: nffo@nffo.org.uk
Website: http://www.nffo.org.uk
Founded: 1977
Members: 2500
Staff: 7
Contact: R. Casson, Pres.
Description: Fishermen's associations in England and Wales. Represents and promotes the interests of commercial fishermen. Compiles statistics.
Publication title: Official Yearbook
Second publication: Newsletter
Meetings/Conventions: - monthly executive committee meeting

National Federation of Fishmongers
c/o Pisces
London Rd., Feering, Colchester, CO5 9ED, England, UK
Tel: 44 1376 571391
Fax: 44 1376 571391
Founded: 1932
Members: 1000
Contact: Mrs. H.E. Leftwich
Description: Retail fishmongers. Represents fishmongers to government departments and other statutory bodies and the press. Annual competition and conference organised.

National Federation of Glaziers
27 Old Gloucester St., London, WC1N 3XX, England, UK
Tel: 44 20 74043099
Founded: 1991
Members: 200
Staff: 2
Contact: Anthony C. Jones, Chm.
Fee: £85
Membership Type: full
Description: Promotes members' interests. Provides advice, a code of installation practice, insured guarantees, customer questionnaire and a arbitration service. Provides glazing information to consumers.

Publication: Booklet
Publication title: Commitment to Good Practice
Second publication: Newsletter

National Federation of Master Steeplejacks and Lightning Conductor Engineers
4d St. Mary's Pl., The Lace Market, Nottingham, NG1 1PH, England, UK
Tel: 44 115 9558818
Fax: 44 115 9412238
Email: info@nfmslce.co.uk
Website: http://www.nfmslce.co.uk
Founded: 1946
Members: 59
Contact: R. Wollerton, Sec.
Description: Members, affiliates, (with less than 2 years trading) and special members (suppliers to the industry).
Publication: Booklet

National Federation of Meat and Food Traders
1 Belgrove, Tunbridge Wells, TN1 1YW, England, UK
Tel: 44 1892 541412
Fax: 44 1892 535462
Email: info@nfmft.co.uk
Website: http://www.butchers-online.net
Founded: 1888
Members: 2000
Staff: 7
Contact: Graham Bidston, Ch.Exec.
Fee: £170
Membership Type: core (full)
Fee: £350
Membership Type: affiliate
Description: Members include independent retail butchers, slaughterhouse operators, bacon curers, meat manufacturers and wholesale distributors.
Publication: Journal
Publication title: Food Trader for Butchers. Advertisements.
Meetings/Conventions: - annual conference

National Federation of Retail Newsagents
c/o Yeoman House
Sekforde St., London, EC1R 0HF, England, UK
Tel: 44 207 2534225
Fax: 44 207 2500927
Email: r.clarke@nfrn.org.uk
Website: http://www.nfrn.org.uk
Founded: 1919
Members: 25000
Staff: 104
Contact: Roger Clarke, Chief.Exec.
Fee: £3.8
Membership Type: full and full partner
Description: Members are mainly independent retail newsagents with some managers of multiple newsagents. Improves the conditions and raises the status of the independent newsagent, trade and business, and protects their interests. Provides legal aid and constant advice, with a wide ranging benefits package for fee paying members. Maintains two limited companies which negotiate commercial deals on behalf of members and publish and distribute promotional materials.
Library Type: reference
Publication: Journal
Publication title: Retail Newsagent. Advertisements.
Meetings/Conventions: - annual conference - Exhibits.

National Federation of Roofing Contractors
NFRC

24 Weymouth St., London, W1G 7LX, England, UK
Tel: 44 207 4360387
Fax: 44 207 6375215
Email: info@nfrc.co.uk
Website: http://www.nfrc.co.uk
Founded: 1898
Members: 785
Contact: Rachel Chambers
Description: Roofing contractors and manufacturers of roofing products and equipment in the United Kingdom. Promotes the interests of members.
Publication: Directory
Publication title: Organization Directory
Second publication: Annual Report

National Federation of Sea Schools

24 Peterscroft Ave., Ashurst, Southampton, SO40 7AB, England, UK
Tel: 44 2380 293822
Fax: 44 2380 293822
Email: info@nfss.co.uk
Website: http://www.nfss.co.uk
Founded: 1947
Members: 83
Staff: 1
Contact: Brigid Howells, Gen.Sec.
Description: Open to RYA recognised teaching establishments that have been fully recognised for over one year. Representative body of sailing and motor cruising schools in the UK. It provides a representative voice for various committees, pursues a joint advertising and marketing policy, exhibits at major boat shows, and provides information and advice to the public.
Publication: Newsletter
Meetings/Conventions: - annual meeting

National Federation of Spiritual Healers

Old Manor Farm Studio, Church St., Sunbury-On-Thames, TW16 6RG, England, UK
Tel: 44 8451 232777
Fax: 44 1932 779648
Email: office@nfsh.org.uk
Website: http://www.nfsh.org.uk
Contact: K. Wyatt
Description: Spiritual Healers.
Publication: Magazine
Publication title: Healing Today. Advertisements.

National Federation of Terrazzo Marble and Mosaic Specialists

PO Box 2843, London, W1A 5PG, England, UK
Tel: 44 845 6090050
Fax: 44 845 6078610
Email: dslade@nftmms.demon.co.uk
Website: http://www.nftmms.co.uk
Founded: 1932
Members: 50
Staff: 1
Contact: Donald A. Slade, Sec.
Description: Firms engaged in supplying and fixing terrazzo, marble, mosaic and other stone products. Provides technical and other information to architects and other specifiers in the building industry, together with a service of inspection and report on works involving their materials, and is represented on British and European Standards Committees relevant to our trades.

National Federation of Young Farmers' Clubs
NFYFC

c/o YFC Centre, NAC
Stoneleigh Park, Kenilworth, CV8 2LG, England, UK
Tel: 44 2476 857200
Fax: 44 2476 857229
Email: post@nfyfc.org.uk
Website: http://www.nfyfc.org.uk
Founded: 1932
Members: 27000
Staff: 21
Contact: Laura Papadopoulos, Admin.
Description: Clubs representing 27,000 rural young people. Seeks to develop self-reliance and responsibility in members and to increase knowledge of agriculture, home crafts, and country life. Offers courses and competitions. Raise funds for UK charities. Participates in farming unions. Operates exchange service. Cooperates with branches of government promoting agricultural skills.
Publication title: International Competitions
Second publication: Magazine
Publication title: Ten 26. Advertisements.
Meetings/Conventions: - annual conference - Exhibits.

National Fillings Trades Association

263a Monton Rd., Monton, Eccles, Manchester, M30 9LF, England, UK
Tel: 44 161 7889018
Fax: 44 161 7877741
Founded: 1933
Members: 16
Contact: J.G. Mellor
Description: Manufacturers of synthetic and natural filling materials. Serves the interests of employer members within the industry of synthetic and natural upholstery and bedding fillings manufacture.

National Fireplace Association

McLaren Bldg., 6th Fl., 35 Dale End, Birmingham, B4 7LN, England, UK
Tel: 44 121 2001310
Fax: 44 121 2001306
Email: enquiries@nfa.org.uk
Website: http://www.nfa.org.uk
Members: 260
Staff: 2
Contact: David Brotherton, Dir.
Description: Retail showrooms, manufacturers of fireplaces, appliances, flues, chimneys and accessories, fuel suppliers and other fireplace industry trade associations or bodies. Aims to unite all who have an interest in fires, fireplaces, fuels, chimneys and associated products, and promote their businesses. It works closely with other organizations and trade associations, and with its diversity of membership, represents the whole fire and fireplace industry as well as specialist groups within it, caring for their interests at home and abroad.
Publication: Yearbook
Publication title: Fireplace Yearbook. Advertisements.

National Foundation for Educational Research
NFER
The Mere, Upton Park, Slough, SL1 2DQ, England, UK
Tel: 44 1753 574123
Fax: 44 1753 691632
Email: enquiries@nfer.ac.uk
Website: http://www.nfer.ac.uk
Founded: 1947

National Game Dealers Association
Aycliffe Industrial Park, 18 Leaside, Newton Aycliffe, DL5 6DE, England, UK
Tel: 44 1325 316320
Fax: 44 1325 320634
Email: sales@yorkshiregame.co.uk
Founded: 1979
Contact: Sandra Baxter, Chm.
Description: Mainly licensed wholesale game dealers. Represents major wholesale game dealers within UK. Willing to offer spokesmen on the game trade.

National Hairdressers' Federation
11 Goldington Rd., Bedford, MK40 3JY, England, UK
Tel: 44 1234 360332
Fax: 44 1234 269337
Founded: 1942
Members: 5000
Staff: 4
Contact: R.J. Seymour
Fee: £88
Membership Type: individual/salon
Description: Hairdressing and/or beauty salon owners. Offers support, advice, a comprehensive legal advisory service, industrial tribunal representation, a tax advisory and protection service, a commercial property emergency service, management and artistic seminars, and many other benefits to assist salon owners with the conduct of their business and to stimulate their artistic talents.
Publication: Newsletter
Publication title: Headline News

National Harmonica League
112 Hag Hill Rise, Taplow, Maidenhead, SL6 OLT, England, UK
Tel: 44 1628 604069
Email: nhl@harmonica.co.uk
Website: http://harmonica.co.uk
Founded: 1951
Contact: Dr. Roger Trobridge, Chm.
Fee: £20
Membership Type: inside the United Kingdom
Fee: £24
Membership Type: inside the United States
Description: Members range from beginners to virtuoso amateurs and professionals, and include non players with an interest, collectors, traders etc. Concerned with the presentation and advancement of the harmonica. Encourages amateur participation at national events, which also include inspiring virtuosos. Competitions inspire many to reach high standards of musical attainment. Social events provide for enthusiasts at all levels from raw beginners upwards. Teaching material is also available.
Publication: Journal
Publication title: Harmonica World. Advertisements.
Meetings/Conventions: Blue Saturday - quarterly workshop

National Hedgelaying Society
16 Narcot Ln., Chalfont St. Giles, CV8 2LG, England, UK
Tel: 44 1203 696544
Fax: 44 1203 696559
Email: juliehallam@beeb.net
Members: 250
Staff: 3
Contact: Julie Hallam, Sec.
Fee: £7.5
Fee: £5
Description: To encourage the craft of hedgelaying and to maintain local styles.
Publication: Booklet
Publication title: Hedgelaying Explained
Meetings/Conventions: National Hedgelating Championships - annual competition - Exhibits.

National Home Improvement Council
Carlyle House, 235 Vauxhall Bridge Rd., London, SW1V 1EJ, England, UK
Tel: 44 207 8288230
Fax: 44 207 8280667
Email: info@nhic.org.uk
Website: http://www.nhic.org.uk/
Founded: 1974
Members: 35
Staff: 2
Contact: Graham Ponting, Exec.Dir.
Description: Manufactuers, distributors, contractors and trade associations involved in all aspects of home improvement, repair and maintenance. Aims to increase awareness of the benefits of home improvement and proper presentation of existing homes; to ensure co-operation between private manufacturers, distributors etc and Housing Associations and Local Authorities to achieve the most effective level of improvement; to ensure Government and MPs are kept abreast of the industry's issues.
Publication title: Home Improvement Progress
Publication title: Spring and Autumn Press Packs on Home Improvement

National Hop Association of England
754 Fulham Rd., London, SW6 5SH, England, UK
Tel: 44 20 73841333
Fax: 44 20 73840335
Email: rupert@randr.co.uk
Website: http://www.hops.co.uk
Founded: 1987
Members: 130
Contact: Tony Redsell, Chmn.
Description: Aims to look after the interests of English hop growers after the disbanding of the obsolescent Hops Marketing Board and its replacement by the Hop Producer Groups.

National House-Building Council
c/o Buildmark House
Chiltern Ave., Amersham, HP6 5AP, England, UK
Tel: 44 1494 735363
Fax: 44 1494 735369
Email: cssuport@nhbc.co.uk
Website: http://www.nhbc.co.uk
Founded: 1936
Members: 181000
Staff: 1000
Contact: Andrew Howard, Hd. of Corp.Commun.

Description: Registers housebuilders and developers across the UK. Sets the standards for house-building, inspects homes built to those standards, and then provides its 'Buildmark' insurance cover on around 85% of all private sector new homes in the UK.
Publication title: NHBC Technical Standards
Publication title: Statistics

National Household Hazardous Waste Forum
NHHWF

74 Kirkgate, Leeds, LS2 7DJ, England, UK
Tel: 44 113 2467584
Fax: 44 113 2344222
Email: enquiry@nhhwf.org.uk
Website: http://www.nhhwf.org.uk
Founded: 1993
Members: 190
Staff: 3
Contact: Roland Arnison, Mgr.
Fee: £450
Membership Type: full
Description: Manufacturers, trade associations, packaging manufacturers, equipment suppliers, retailers, local authorities, local authority institutions, waste management companies, research institutes and voluntary organizations. Seeks practical solutions to the many problems associated with the collection, recycling and safe disposal of household hazardous waste and its packaging.
Publication: Report
Publication title: A Evaluation of Silver Oxide Bitten Cell Recycling
Publication title: Good Practice Guide
Meetings/Conventions: - 3/year meeting

National Illumination Committee of Great Britain

c/o Chartered Institution of Building Services Engineers
Delta House, 222 Balham High Rd., London, SW12 9BS, England, UK
Tel: 44 208 6755211
Fax: 44 208 6755449
Website: http://www.cie-uk.org.uk
Founded: 1913
Members: 52
Contact: I.F. Davies
Description: Organizations, companies, universities, government departments. Aims to provide an international forum for the discussion of all matters relating to the science, technology and art in the fields of light and lighting and for the interchange of information in these fields between countries.

National Inspection Council for Electrical Installation Contracting
NICEIC

Vintage House, 37 Albert Embankment, London, SE1 7UJ, England, UK
Tel: 44 20 75642323
Fax: 44 20 75642370
Email: enquiries@niceic.org.uk
Website: http://www.niceic.org.uk/
Founded: 1956
Staff: 46
Description: Devoted to the protection of consumers against the hazards of unsafe and unsound electrical installations.
Publication title: The Roll

National Institute for Biological Standards and Control
NIBSC

Blanche Lane, South Mimms, Potters Bar, EN6 3QG, England, UK
Tel: 44 1707 641000
Fax: 44 1707 646730
Email: enquiries@nibsc.ac.uk
Website: http://www.nibsc.ac.uk
Staff: 260
Contact: Dr. G. Schild, Exec. Officer
Description: Research institution and national control laboratory for biologicals used in medicine.
Library Subject: vaccines, blood products, AIDS, biochemistry, hematology, virology, microbiology, immunology, and endocrinology
Library Type: by appointment only
Publication: Catalog
Publication title: Catalogue of Biological Standards and Reference Materials
Publication title: Corporate Plan
Meetings/Conventions: Scientific Meeting - periodic

National Institute of Adult Continuing Education
NIACE

21 De Montfort St., Leicester, LE1 7GE, England, UK
Tel: 44 116 2044200
Fax: 44 116 2854514
Email: enquiries@niace.org.uk
Website: http://www.niace.org.uk
Founded: 1983
Members: 473
Staff: 100
Contact: Carolyn Winkless, Information Officer
Description: Government departments, local education authorities, voluntary sector agencies, educational institutions, broadcasts, universities, individuals. Promotes the study and general advancement of the education of adults. The Institute therefore offers a means of consultation and co-operation for all those interested in the education of adults.
Library Subject: adult education
Library Type: reference
Publication: Journal
Publication title: Adults learning, 10 issues per annum. Advertisements.
Second publication: Yearbook
Publication title: Adults Learning Yearbook

National Institute of Agricultural Botany

Huntingdon Rd., Cambridge, CB3 0LE, England, UK
Tel: 44 1223 276381
Fax: 44 1223 277602
Email: info@niab.com
Website: http://www.niab.com
Founded: 1919
Members: 4000
Staff: 252
Contact: Shelley Davison, Assn.Off.
Fee: £83
Membership Type: associate membership
Description: Farmers, seed trade, agrochemical, plant breeders, universities and colleges, consultants and advisers, individuals.

Promotes the improvement of existing varieties of seed, plants and crops and aids the introduction or distribution of new varieties.
Library Type: not open to the public
Publication: Handbook
Publication title: Cereal Variety

National Institute of Carpet and Floorlayers

4d St. Mary's Pl., The Lace Market, Nottingham, NG1 1PH, England, UK
Tel: 44 115 9583077
Fax: 44 115 9412238
Email: info@nicfltd.org.uk
Website: http://www.nicfltd.org.uk
Founded: 1979
Members: 415
Contact: Richard Wollerton, Sec.
Description: Mainly individual installers of carpets with some manufacturers corporate patron members. To promote standards within the carpet industry and provide advice and guidance to members.
Formerly: National Institute of Carpet Fitters
Publication: Newsletter
Publication title: NICF Bulletin

National Institute of Economic and Social Research NIESR

2 Dean Trench St., London, SW1P 3HE, England, UK
Tel: 44 20 72227665
Fax: 44 20 72221435
Email: gchisham@niesr.oc.uk
Website: http://www.niesr.ac.uk
Founded: 1938
Staff: 40
Contact: Gill Chisham, Sec.
Description: Promotes economic and social research.
Publication: Journal
Publication title: National Institute Economic Review. Advertisements.
Meetings/Conventions: meeting London UK

National Institute of Hardware

225 Bristol Rd., Edgbaston, Birmingham, B5 7UB, England, UK
Tel: 44 121 4466688
Fax: 44 121 4465215
Email: nih@bhfgroup.demon.co.uk
Website: http://www.bhfgroup.co.uk
Founded: 1947
Members: 3500
Staff: 12
Contact: Jonathan Swift, Mng.Dir.
Fee: £60
Membership Type: corporate
Description: Non-statutory training organization for the hardware/housewares retail trade, administered for the Council by the British Hardware Federation.
Library Subject: hardware, housewares
Library Type: open to the public
Publication: Magazine
Publication title: Hardware Today. Advertisements.
Meetings/Conventions: - annual convention - Exhibits.

National Institute of Medical Herbalists

56 Longbrook St., Exeter, EX4 6AH, England, UK
Tel: 44 1392 426022
Fax: 44 1392 498963
Email: nimh@ukexeter.freeserve.co.uk
Website: http://www.nimh.org.uk
Founded: 1864
Members: 625
Staff: 2
Description: Practitioners of herbal medicine.
Publication: Journal
Publication title: European Journal of Herbal Medicine. Advertisements.
Second publication: Directory
Publication title: Register of Members

National Insulation Association

PO Box 12, Haslemere, GU27 3AH, England, UK
Tel: 44 1428 654011
Fax: 44 1428 651401
Email: nciaassociation@cs.com
Website: http://www.ncia-ltd.org.uk
Founded: 1975
Members: 118
Staff: 10
Contact: Gillian Allder, Dir.
Fee: £250
Membership Type: manufacturers/installers
Description: Manufacturers and contractors. It aims to raise and maintain high standards of competence and conduct in the business of cavity wall insulation and to ensure a good service to the specifier, the public and to industry. The Association has its own Code of Practice and all companies applying for membership are closely vetted.
Formerly: National Cavity Insulation Association
Publication: Pamphlet

National Joint Council for the Motor Vehicle Retail and Repair Industry

201 Great Portland St., London, W1N 6AB, England, UK
Tel: 44 171 3073408
Fax: 44 171 3073404
Founded: 1945
Members: 200000
Contact: Cory Roberts, Sec.
Description: Trade associations and trade unions covering approx 200, 000 individuals. Covers the member companies of the two trade associations - the Retail Motor Industry Federation and the Scottish Motor Trades Association. It negotiates periodically new minimum terms and conditions of employment of the retail motor industry and operates a procedure for avoiding disputes.
Publication: Handbook
Publication title: NJC

National League of the Blind and Disabled NLBD

Swinton House, 324 Gray's Inn Rd., London, WCIX 8DD, England, UK
Tel: 44 207 8376103
Fax: 44 207 2780436
Founded: 1893
Members: 2371

Staff: 3
Contact: Joe Mann, Gen.Sec.
Description: Blind, partially sighted and seeing disabled people 16 years of age and over. Represents, negotiates, campaigns for provisions of equality of resources and services for people with disabilities in education, rehabilitation, training, employment and benefits by the State and local authorities.
Publication: Magazine
Publication title: Advocate

National Market Traders Federation

Hampton House, Hawshaw Ln., Hoyland, Barnsley, S74 0HA, England, UK
Tel: 44 1226 749021
Fax: 44 1226 740329
Email: enquiries@nmtf.co.uk
Website: http://www.nmtf.co.uk
Founded: 1899
Members: 26854
Staff: 13
Contact: D.E. Feeny
Description: Market Traders and licensed street traders. To promote and protect markets and market traders and to make representation to the EC and national and local government on behalf of members and their interests
Publication: Newsletter
Publication title: Conference Supplement
Publication title: Federation News. Advertisements.
Meetings/Conventions: - annual conference - Exhibits.

National Music Council of The United Kingdom

60/62 Clapham Rd., London, SW9 0JJ, England, UK
Tel: 44 20 78209992
Fax: 44 20 78209972
Email: nationalmusiccouncil@ukonline.co.uk
Founded: 1953
Members: 30
Staff: 1
Contact: Fiona Penny, Admin.
Fee: £120
Description: Musical societies and related organizations. Objective is to represent and promote the interests of the music industry in the United Kingdom.
Publication: Annual Report

National Music for the Blind

2 High Park Rd., Southport, PR9 7QL, England, UK
Tel: 44 1704 228010
Email: pir8ship@postmaster.co.uk
Website: http://Derek.wsmcafe.com
Founded: 1971
Members: 850
Staff: 9
Contact: Charlie Chester
Fee: £50
Membership Type: individual
Fee: £40
Membership Type: individual
Description: Provides a weekly tape to all partially sighted or blind members and also awards radio/cassette recorders to the needy blind.
Library Subject: music, all kinds of recordings material
Library Type: open to the public
Publication: Audiotape

Publication title: Guiding Star. Advertisements.
Second publication: Audiotape
Publication title: Merry-Go-Round. Advertisements.

National Operatic and Dramatic Association NODA

NODA House, 58-60 Lincoln Rd., Peterborough, PE1 2RZ, England, UK
Tel: 44 870 7702480
Fax: 44 870 7702490
Email: everyone@noda.org.uk
Website: http://www.noda.org.uk
Founded: 1899
Members: 5000
Staff: 7
Contact: Mark Pemberton, Chief Exec.
Fee: £20
Membership Type: individual
Description: Opera and drama societies (2500) and interested individuals (2500). Encourages information exchange and mutual assistance among members dedicated to amateur stage performances. Offers consulting services. Sponsors competitions. Operates a summer school for one week each year covering all aspects of theater.
Library Subject: Musicals, opera, play scripts, pantomime
Library Type: reference
Publication: Magazine
Publication title: NODA National News. Advertisements.
Second publication: Magazine. Advertisements.
Meetings/Conventions: - annual conference Peebles UK

National Osteoporosis Society

Camerton, Bath, BA2 0PJ, England, UK
Tel: 44 1761 471771
Fax: 44 1761 471104
Email: info@nos.org.uk
Website: http://www.nos.org.uk
Founded: 1986
Members: 27000
Staff: 50
Contact:
Fee: £15
Description: National charity dedicated to improving the diagnosis, prevention, and treatment of osteoporosis. Works with health care professionals to facilitate greater understanding of the needs of individuals with the disease. Offers support to people with osteoporosis and their families through a range of detailed information booklets, a national telephone helpline and a network of regional support groups throughout the UK. Raises funds for research to increase understanding of the disease and improve treatment options and patient care. Raises awareness of the disease and campaigns to promote bone health.
Meetings/Conventions: conference Bath UK

National Outdoor Events Association

7 Hamilton Way, Wallington, SM6 9NJ, England, UK
Tel: 44 208 6698121
Fax: 44 208 6471128
Email: secretary@noea.org.uk
Website: http://www.noea.org.uk
Founded: 1979
Members: 250

Staff: 2
Contact: John W. Barton
Description: Local authorities, show organisers, suppliers of equipment and services and general practitioners for the outdoor events industry. Forum between suppliers of equipment and the clientele - show organisers, local authorities etc. Initiates meetings between various organisations for the benefit of industry; promotes technical standards at outdoor events and various Codes of Practice. Members must adhere to Code of Professional Practice.
Publication: Magazine
Publication title: Access All Areas - The Events Industry Magazine
Publication title: Code of Practice for Outdoor Events
Meetings/Conventions: Regular Outdoor Event

National Pawnbrokers' Association

1 Bell Yard, London, WC2A 2JP, England, UK
Tel: 44 207 2421114
Fax: 44 207 4054266
Email: nfinch@parknelson.co.uk
Website: http://www.thenpa.com
Founded: 1892
Members: 250
Staff: 3
Contact: T.G. Ford, Sec.Gen.
Fee: £550
Membership Type: head office
Fee: £150
Membership Type: branch
Description: Pawnbrokers.
Publication title: NPA Times
Meetings/Conventions: - semiannual meeting

National Pharmaceutical Association

Mallinson House, 38-42 Saint Peter's St., St. Albans, AL1 3NP, England, UK
Tel: 44 1727 832161
Fax: 44 1727 840858
Email: npa@npa.co.uk
Website: http://www.npa.co.uk
Founded: 1921
Members: 7000
Staff: 122
Contact: Veronica Wray
Description: Represents 7000 pharmacy owners in UK, who collectively own 12,000 retail pharmacies. Provides members with legal and financial services; insurance; defence and indemnity; training; publications; public relations; business services and pharmacy planning.
Publication: Journal
Publication title: Professional Practice Notes
Second publication: Journal
Publication title: The Supplement

National Phobics Society

Zion Centre, 339 Stretford Rd., Hulme, Manchester, M15 4ZY, England, UK
Tel: 44 870 7700456
Fax: 44 161 2279862
Email: natphob.soc@good.co.uk
Website: http://www.phobics-society.org.uk
Founded: 1970
Members: 6000
Staff: 2
Contact: G. Kingsley-Nunes, Chief Exec.

Fee: £15
Membership Type: individual
Fee: £20
Membership Type: professional individual
Description: Provides information, support, and advice to anyone affected by anxiety disorders, including panic attacks, OCD, BDD, agoraphobia, social phobia, and PTSD.
Publication: Newsletter
Publication title: Don't Panic

National Pony Society

c/o Willingdon House
102 High St., Alton, GU34 1EN, England, UK
Tel: 44 1420 88333
Fax: 44 1420 80599
Website: http://www.nationalponysociety.org.uk
Founded: 1893
Members: 3000
Staff: 3
Contact: Mrs. L. Wilkins, Sec.
Description: Pony owners, breeders, exhibitors, competitors, equine students, people with general interest in pony matters. Encourages the breeding, registration and improvement of British riding ponies and mountain and moorland ponies and to foster the welfare of ponies in general.
Publication title: The National Pony Society Review
Second publication: Newsletter
Meetings/Conventions: meeting

National Portage Association

PO Box 3075, Yeovil, BA21 3FB, England, UK
Tel: 44 1935 471641
Fax: 44 1935 471641
Email: npa@portageuk.freeserve.co.uk
Website: http://www.portage.org.uk
Founded: 1979
Members: 550
Staff: 2
Contact: Brenda Paul, Admin.
Fee: £20
Membership Type: parent or professional
Description: Aims to campaign for Portage Services to be made more available to all families caring for a young child with special needs. Supports standards of service. Develops positive monitoring procedures, offers a code of practice and encourages new developments.

National Portraiture Association

59-60 Fitzjames Ave., London, W14 0RR, England, UK
Tel: 44 20 76020892
Fax: 44 20 76026705
Email: enquiries@natportrait.com
Website: http://www.natportrait.com
Founded: 1971
Members: 25
Staff: 12
Contact: William Henderson
Description: Non-profit on-line portrait galleries designed for client self-select from nationally recognised artists. Increases UK demand for high quality portraiture in all media.

National Prefabricated Building Association
NPBA

The Hardmoors, London Road, East Retford, Nottingham, DN22 7JJ, England, UK
Tel: 44 1777 869563
Fax: 44 1777 703448
Email: enquiries@npba.co.uk
Website: http://www.npba.co.uk
Founded: 1938
Members: 1
Staff: 2
Contact: Robert Ford, Sec.
Description: Large and small companies in the prefabricated building industry may qualify by experience and practice for full membership. Associate membership also available for companies and individuals with an interest in the industry. Promotion and marketing of prefabricated buildings. Members make, sell and hire buildings, many of which are relocatable and some portable. Government, commerce, leisure and domestic requirements are covered. Standards are set, codes of practice and model terms of business produced. Market surveys are conducted.
Publication: Newsletter
Publication title: NPBA News. Advertisements.
Second publication: Book
Meetings/Conventions: - annual conference - Exhibits.

National Register of Hypnotherapists and Psychotherapists

12 Cross St., Nelson, BB9 7EN, England, UK
Tel: 44 1282 716839
Fax: 44 1282 698633
Email: nrhp@btconnect.com
Website: http://www.nrhp.co.uk
Founded: 1985
Members: 390
Staff: 2
Contact: Julie Young
Fee: £100
Membership Type: professional
Description: Therapists who have graduated from the National College of Hypnosis and Psychotherapy or equivalent trainings. Promotes and protects the professional status, standards, ethics and interest of its members and also promotes the interests of those members of the public who seek professional help, and for whom it provides a nationwide referral service. Member of the United Kingdom Council for Psychotherapy.
Publication: Directory
Publication title: Directory of Practitioners
Publication title: Information Leaflet

National Register of Personal Trainers
NRPT

16 Borough High St., London, SE1 9QG, England, UK
Tel: 44 20 74079223
Fax: 44 20 74079225
Email: info@nrpt.co.uk
Website: http://www.nrpt.co.uk
Founded: 1992
Members: 1000
Staff: 5
Contact: Will Broome
Fee: £60

Description: Qualified fitness instructors available for one to one personal training throughout the UK. Representative and advisory body for personal fitness trainers in UK. Acts as a referral service for the general public when looking for a personal trainer; provides networking and secures the best possible services and products for personal trainers to enhance their professionalism.
Formerly: National Register of Personal Fitness Trainers
Publication: Newsletter
Publication title: One to One. Advertisements.

National Register of Warranted Builders

14-15 Great James St., London, WC1N 3DP, England, UK
Tel: 44 171 2427583
Fax: 44 171 4040296
Email: central@fmb.org.uk
Website: http://www.fmb.org.uk
Founded: 1980
Members: 3000
Staff: 5
Contact: J.H. Gentry, Registrar
Description: Small to medium size building companies and allied trades. Provision of insurance backed warranties on building work.
Publication: Journal
Publication title: MasterBuilder Journal

National School Band Association

72 Broomfield Rd., Churchdown, Gloucester, GL3 2PC, England, UK
Tel: 44 1664 434379
Fax: 44 1452 714976
Email: info@nsba.org.uk
Website: http://www.nsba.org.uk
Founded: 1952
Members: 300
Contact: Scott Stroman, Pres.
Description: Aims to foster an interest in music through the playing of brass and woodwind instruments and the formation of brass and wind bands in schools.
Publication title: The Trumpeter

National Secular Society

25 Red Leon Sq., London, WC1R 4RL, England, UK
Tel: 44 20 74043126
Fax: 44 20 74043126
Email: enquiries@secularism.org.uk
Website: http://www.secularism.org.uk
Founded: 1866
Contact: K. Porteous Wood, Exec.Dir.
Fee: £15
Membership Type: annual
Fee: £300
Membership Type: life
Description: Campaigns against religious privilege.

National Security Inspectorate

Queenstate House, 14 Cookham Rd., Maidenhead, SL6 8AJ, England, UK
Tel: 44 870 2050000
Fax: 44 1628 773367
Email: nacoss@nsi.org.uk
Website: http://www.nsi.org.uk/
Founded: 1990

Description: Works as the national approval service for companies in the electronic security sector, including intruder alarms, access control, and CCTV systems. Four groups of standards are applied: Technical Standards, Business Standards, Codes of Practise, and Quality Management.

National Sewerage Association
NSA

98 Alric Ave., New Malden, KT3 4JW, England, UK
Tel: 44 208 9429391
Fax: 44 208 9429391
Email: nsa@tinyonline.co.uk
Website: http://www.sewerage.org
Founded: 1980
Members: 26
Staff: 2
Contact: Mrs. Val Gibbens, Sec.
Fee: £660
Membership Type: company
Description: Companies engaged in the survey, operation, renovation, and maintenance of sewers, drains, and pipelines. Promotes adherence to high standards of ethics and practice by members. Works with external bodies to monitor and advance technical and technological capabilities in the sewerage and pipeline industries.
Formerly: Absorbed, Association of Flow Survey Contractors
Publication: Directory
Publication title: Directory of Members. Advertisements.
Meetings/Conventions: - quarterly general assembly Nuneaton UK

National Sheep Association

The Sheep Centre, Malvern, WR13 6PH, England, UK
Tel: 44 1684 892661
Fax: 44 1684 892663
Email: enquiries@nationalsheep.demon.co.uk
Website: http://www.nationalsheep.org.uk
Founded: 1892
Members: 24000
Staff: 6
Contact: Mr. J. Thorley, Ch.Exec.
Fee: £35
Membership Type: UK
Fee: £40
Membership Type: outside UK
Description: Almost entirely sheep farmers in UK and some 35 other countries. Represents the sheep industry in discussions with all bodies influencing the industry. Researches, compiles and publishes a diverse array of publications and holds technical conferences.
Library Subject: sheep
Library Type: not open to the public
Publication: Book
Publication title: British Sheep. Advertisements.
Second publication: Magazine
Publication title: The Sheep Farmer. Advertisements.

National Society for Clean Air and Environmental Protection
NSCA

44 Grand Parade, Brighton, BN2 9QA, England, UK
Tel: 44 1273 878770
Fax: 44 1273 606626
Email: admin@nsca.co.uk

Website: http://www.nsca.org.uk
Founded: 1899
Members: 800
Staff: 10
Contact: Richard Mills, Sec.
Description: Local authority, industry, academic, individual. To secure environmental improvement by promoting clean air through the reduction of air pollution, noise and other contaminants while having due regard for other aspects of the environment. NSCA brings together pollution expertise from industry; local and central government; technical, academic and institutional bodies.
Library Subject: environment
Library Type: by appointment only
Publication: Newsletter
Publication title: Briefing
Second publication: Journal
Publication title: Clean Air. Advertisements.
Meetings/Conventions: Environmental Protection - annual convention - Exhibits. Torquay UK

National Society for Education in Art and Design
NSEAD

The Gatehouse, Corsham Court, Corsham, SN13 0BZ, England, UK
Tel: 44 1249 714825
Fax: 44 1249 716138
Email: johnsteers@nsead.org
Website: http://www.nsead.org
Founded: 1888
Members: 2500
Staff: 6
Contact: Dr. John Steers, Gen.Sec.
Fee: £132
Membership Type: full
Fee: £72
Membership Type: associate
Description: Instructors, students, and individuals interested in art, craft, and design education. Aims to strengthen the role of the arts in general education and promote high professional standards in art education. Provides legal advice and insurance benefits to members.
Library Subject: art, design education
Library Type: not open to the public
Formerly: Formed by Merger of, National Society for Art Education
Publication: Journal
Publication title: Journal of Art and Design Education. Advertisements.
Publication title: NSEAD Newsletter
Meetings/Conventions: - annual conference - Exhibits.

National Society for Epilepsy

Chesham Ln., Chalfont St. Peter, Gerrards Cross, SL9 0RJ, England, UK
Tel: 44 1494 601300
Fax: 44 1494 871927
Website: http://www.epilepsynse.org.uk
Founded: 1892
Members: 2000
Staff: 450
Contact: Graham Faulkner, Chief Exec.
Fee: £15
Membership Type: associate membership
Description: Individuals with an interest in epilepsy who wish to support epilepsy education and research. Provides assessment, treatment, rehabilitation, long term and respite care for adults with

epilepsy. The education department provides support and information, produces educational resources and runs conferences and seminars. Coordinates a national network of trained volunteers offering information services.
Library Subject: epilepsy
Library Type: open to the public
Publication: Magazine
Publication title: Epilepsy Review
Meetings/Conventions: conference

National Society for Research into Allergy

PO Box 45, Hinckley, LE10 0SZ, England, UK
Tel: 44 1455 250715
Fax: 44 1455 851546
Email: nsra.allergy@virgin.net
Founded: 1980
Members: 1000
Contact: Eunice L. Rose
Fee: £15
Membership Type: in UK
Fee: £25
Membership Type: outside UK
Description: Main aim is to educate the populace on the devastating effects of allergy/intolerance and to see effective treatment in all teaching hospitals. Offers elimination diet and recipe books as well as councelling, advice, etc. on all types of allergy/intolerance/ hyperventilation and the tests and treatments for same.

National Society for the Prevention of Cruelty to Children

Weston House, 42 Curtain Rd., London, EC2A 3NH, England, UK
Tel: 44 207 8252500
Fax: 44 207 8252525
Email: marcomm@nspcc.org.uk
Website: http://www.nspcc.org.uk
Founded: 1884
Staff: 1400
Contact: Mr. J. Harding, Dir.
Description: Exists to prevent children suffering from significant harm as a result of ill treatment; help and protect children who are at risk from such harm; help abused children to overcome the effects of abuse and works to protect abused children from further harm. Convention/Meeting: none.
Library Subject: child protection, child development, family relations, social work charities, therapeutic issues
Library Type: not open to the public

National Society of Allied and Independent Funeral Directors

3 Bullfields, Sawbridgeworth, CM21 9DB, England, UK
Tel: 44 1279 726777
Fax: 44 1279 726300
Email: info@saif.org.uk
Website: http://www.saif.org.uk/
Founded: 1989
Description: Family-owned and operated funeral homes. Seeks to promote and protect the future of the independent funeral director. Serves as a trade association for independent funeral directors. Maintains code of practice to which members must adhere; monitors members' services and certifies qualifying homes.
Publication: Magazine
Publication title: Saiflink. Advertisements.

National Society of Master Thatchers

20 The Laurels, Tetsworth, Thame, OX9 7BH, England, UK
Tel: 44 1844 281568
Fax: 44 1844 281568
Email: info@nsmt.co.uk
Website: http://www.nsmt.co.uk
Founded: 1967
Members: 95
Staff: 1
Contact: Mrs. C.J. Miller, Sec.Treas.
Fee: £125
Membership Type: full
Description: Represents all member thatchers and negotiates on their behalf with official and other bodies. Aims to promote, encourage and uphold high standard of craftsmanship, and to regulate the needs of the craft.
Meetings/Conventions: - annual meeting

National Specialist Contractors Council
NSCC

Construction House, 56/64 Leonard St., London, EC2A 4JX, England, UK
Tel: 44 207 6085090
Fax: 44 207 6085081
Email: enquiries@nscc.org.uk
Website: http://www.nscc.org.uk
Members: 26
Staff: 3
Contact: Stephen Kennefick
Description: Represents the specialists in the United Kingdom construction industry.

National Taxicab Association

5 Clifton Hill, Brighton, BN1 3HL, England, UK
Tel: 44 1273 729403
Fax: 44 1273 728122
Email: enquiries@brighton-streamline.co.uk
Website: http://www.brighton-streamline.co.uk
Founded: 1961
Members: 100
Staff: 2
Description: Taxi associations in the United Kingdom, excluding Scotland. Aims to carry on important activities in the common interest of all its members, to cultivate acquaintance, fellowship, co-operation, goodwill and a professional spirit among them; to facilitate the exchange of ideas and methods; to recognize and honor their exceptional services and achievements.
Formerly: National Federation of Taxicab Associations

National Trust

London Central Office, 36 Queen Anne's Gate, London, SW1H 9AS, England, UK
Tel: 44 870 6095380
Fax: 44 20 72225097
Email: enquiries@thenationaltrust.org.uk
Website: http://www.nationaltrust.org.uk
Founded: 1895
Members: 2600000
Description: Seeks to preserve places of historic interest or natural beauty for the enjoyment of everyone in the nation. Protects and keeps open to the public over 200 historic houses and 49 monuments and mills. Seeks to protect farms, forests, woods, archaeological remains and natural reserves.

National Trust Volunteering and Community Involvement Office
NTVO

Rowan, Kembrey Park, Swindon, GL7 1RQ, England, UK
Tel: 44 870 6095383
Fax: 44 1793 496813
Email: volunteers@ntrust.org.uk
Website: http://www.nationaltrust.org.uk/volunteering
Founded: 1895
Members: 2900000
Staff: 3200
Contact: Jenny Baker, Head of Volunteers
Description: Volunteers in England, Wales, and Northern Ireland (38,000), working to restore and preserve the historical properties owned by the National Trust.
Publication: Brochure
Publication title: Working Holidays

National Tyre Distributors Association

Elsinore House, Buckingham St., Aylesbury, HP20 2NQ, England, UK
Tel: 44 870 9000600
Fax: 44 870 9000610
Email: info@ntda.co.uk
Website: http://www.ntda.co.uk
Founded: 1930
Members: 2000
Staff: 5
Contact: Richard Edy, Dir.
Description: Companies in tyre specialist and fast-fit trade. UK Trade Association for tyre specialist companies and fast fit business.
Publication: Bulletin
Publication title: NTDA Service
Second publication: Manual
Publication title: Technical

National Union of Domestic Appliances and General Operatives
NUDAGO

7-8 Imperial Buildings, 1st Fl., Corporation St., Rotherham, S60 1PB, England, UK
Tel: 44 1709 382820
Fax: 44 1709 362826
Website: http://www.gftu.org.uk/html/nudago_index.html
Founded: 1890
Members: 2402
Contact: Anthony McCarthy, Gen.Sec.
Description: Domestic appliance industries, engineering, foundries (grey iron), electronics and general workers.

National Union of Journalists - England
NUJ

Headland House, 308 Grays Inn Rd., London, WC1X 8DP, England, UK
Tel: 44 207 2787916
Fax: 44 207 8378143
Email: jeremyd@nuj.org.uk
Website: http://www.nuj.org.uk
Founded: 1907
Members: 30000
Staff: 40
Contact: Jeremy Dear

Description: Trade union of journalists in the United Kingdom and the Republic of Ireland. Defends members' interests.
Publication: Journal
Publication title: Journalist

National Union of Knitwear, Footwear and Apparel Trades
KFAT

55 New Walk, Leicester, LE1 7EB, England, UK
Tel: 44 116 2556703
Fax: 44 116 2544406
Email: head-office@kfat.org.uk
Website: http://www.kfat.org.uk
Founded: 1991
Members: 16000
Contact: Paul Gates, Gen.Sec.
Fee: £1.45
Description: Trade union for workers in knitwear, textiles, lace, dyeing and finishing, footwear, leather, gloving, made-up leathergoods. Regulates the relations between members and their employers; and seeks the social, educational, economic and political advancement of members. Provides members with advice and representation (including legal) in connection with issues arising out of their employment.
Library Subject: trade unions
Library Type: open to the public
Publication: Journal
Publication title: KFAT News. Advertisements.

National Union of Lock and Metal Workers
NULMW

Wilkes St., Bellamy House, Willenhall, WV13 2BS, England, UK
Tel: 44 1902 366651
Fax: 44 1902 368035
Founded: 1889
Members: 4100
Staff: 6
Contact: Ray Ward
Fee: £200
Description: Lock and manufacturing industries.

National Union of Marine, Aviation and Shipping Transport Officers
NUMAST

Oceanair House, 750/760 High Rd., Leytonstone, London, E11 3BB, England, UK
Tel: 44 20 89896677
Fax: 44 20 85301015
Email: enquiries@numast.org
Website: http://www.numast.org
Founded: 1863
Members: 19000
Staff: 37
Contact: Brian Orrell, Gen. Sec.
Fee: £136.8
Description: Merchant navy and all related areas. An independent, financially viable organization recruiting and retaining members from maritime, maritime related, and other sectors by providing a high quality, cost-effective service covering their professional, industrial, legal, financial welfare and trade union needs.
Publication: Newspaper
Publication title: Telegraph. Advertisements.

National Union of Rail, Maritime and Transport Workers
RMT

c/o Unity House
39 Chalton St., London, NW1 1JD, England, UK
Tel: 44 207 3874771
Fax: 44 207 3874123
Email: info@rmt.org.uk
Website: http://www.rmt.org.uk
Founded: 1990
Members: 60000
Staff: 60
Contact: Jimmy Knapp, Gec.Sec.
Description: Railways and shipping.
Publication: Magazine
Publication title: RMT News. Advertisements.

National Union of Students - United Kingdom
NUS

Nelson Mandela House, 461 Holloway Rd., London, N7 6LJ, England, UK
Tel: 44 20 72728900
Fax: 44 20 72635713
Email: nusuk@nus.org.uk
Website: http://www.nusonline.co.uk
Description: Students and student organizations. Seeks to advance the educational, social, and cultural interests of students. Represents members before educational institutions and government agencies; serves as a clearinghouse on higher education; sponsors educational and social programs.

National Vegetable Society

c/o NVS Webmaster
5 Whitelow Rd., Heaton Moor, Stockport, SK4 4BY, England, UK
Tel: 44 161 4227190
Fax: 44 161 4227190
Email: webmaster@nvsuk.org.uk
Website: http://www.nvsuk.org.uk
Founded: 1960
Members: 2500
Contact: Len Cox, Hon.Natl.Sec.
Fee: £10
Membership Type: ordinary
Fee: £50
Membership Type: married couple
Description: Promotes members' interests.
Library Subject: vegetable cultivation, association problems
Library Type: lending

Natural Slate Quarries Association

26 Store St., London, WC1E 7BT, England, UK
Tel: 44 171 3233770
Fax: 44 171 3230307
Founded: 1943
Members: 7
Staff: 1
Contact: Richard H. Toms
Description: Safeguards the interests of the slate quarry industry, represents collective interests and is the focal point for communication of interest, information and views to promote the use of slate.

Nautical Archaeology Society
NAS

Eastney, Portsmouth, PO4 9LD, England, UK
Tel: 44 23 92818419
Fax: 44 23 92818419
Email: nas@nasportsmouth.org.uk
Website: http://www.nasportsmouth.org.uk
Founded: 1981
Description: Promotes the preservation of nautical heritage in the area; provides training courses, awareness courses; publishes international journals and additional volumes.

Nautical Campus
NI

202 Lambeth Rd., London, SE1 7LQ, England, UK
Tel: 44 207 9281351
Fax: 44 207 4012817
Email: info@nauticalcampus.org
Founded: 1972
Members: 7000
Staff: 12
Contact: C.J. Parker, Sec.
Fee: £65
Description: Qualified mariners in navies and the merchant marine; membership represents 70 countries. Promotes high standards of knowledge and competence among those operating sea-going vessels. Conducts research and educational programs. Sponsors competitions.
Publication: Journal
Publication title: Seaways
Second publication: Proceedings
Meetings/Conventions: - periodic conference - Exhibits.

Needleloom Underlay Manufacturers' Association

3 Manchester Rd., Bury, BL9 0DR, England, UK
Tel: 44 161 7645401
Fax: 44 161 7641114
Founded: 1958
Members: 5
Contact: A.E.G. Gardiner, Sec.
Description: Manufacturers of needled underfelts. Representing members interests with the government etc. working through BSI in setting standards for the industry in the UK and Europe. Providing a forum for discussion of matters of common concern.

Neonatal Society

Queen's Medical Ctr., Nottingham, NG7 2UH, England, UK
Tel: 44 115 9709257
Fax: 44 115 9709382
Email: michael.symonds@nottingham.ac.uk
Founded: 1959

Netherlands British Chamber of Commerce

The Dutch House, 307 High Holborn, London, WC1V 7LS, England, UK
Tel: 44 207 2421064
Fax: 44 207 8314831
Email: nbcc@btinternet.com
Website: http://www.nbcc.co.uk
Contact: Enid Kemp
Description: Promotes business and commerce.

Netherlands Chamber of Commerce in Britain

The Dutch House, 307 High Holborn, London, WC1V 7LS, England, UK
Contact: Willem Offenberh
Description: Promotes business and commerce.

Network

National Office, Perran Cottage, New Rd., Swanmore, SO32 2PE, England, UK
Tel: 44 1489 893910
Website: http://www.topwomenuk.com
Founded: 1981
Members: 800
Contact: Sandra Cox
Description: Professional women in England. Seeks to enhance the status of women. Provides a forum for women to develop social and professional contacts.

Network of Alternative Technology and Technology Assessment
NATTA

c/o David Elliott
Energy and Environment Research Unit, Faculty of Technology, Walton Hall, Open Univ., Milton Keynes, MK7 6AA, England, UK
Tel: 44 1908 654638
Fax: 44 1908 858407
Email: s.j.dougan@open.ac.uk
Website: http://www.eeru.open.ac.uk/natta/rol.html
Founded: 1976
Members: 500
Staff: 2
Contact: David A. Elliott, Coord.
Fee: £18
Membership Type: individual
Fee: £50
Membership Type: institution
Description: Coalition of individuals active in renewable energy and related fields. Promotes the development of alternative technology for renewable energy sources, alternative food production, transport, building construction and design, and work organization. Engages in direct lobbying efforts and maintains liaison with environmental pressure groups. Conducts and supports research projects. Maintains speakers' bureau; offers technical and career advice. Supports national campaign for renewable energy.
Publication: Newsletter
Publication title: RENEW
Second publication: Report
Meetings/Conventions: - periodic conference - Exhibits.

Neurofibromatosis Association

82 London Rd., Kingston Upon Thames, KT2 6PX, England, UK
Tel: 44 208 5471636
Fax: 44 208 9745601
Email: nfa@zetnet.co.uk
Website: http://www.nfa.zetnet.co.uk
Founded: 1981
Members: 1870
Staff: 21
Contact: Roberta Tweedy, Chief Exec.
Fee: £20
Membership Type: overseas
Fee: £12
Membership Type: family
Description: Seeks to establish and maintain a network of family support workers who are able to support and offer practical help and advice to those affected by Neurofibromatosis and their families. Neurofibromatosis is a genetic disorder of the nerve tissue, the characteristics of which include six or more coffee colored marks on the skin in the first two years of life and nodules on or just below the surface of the skin, or tumors on both acoustical nerves. Fosters research; disseminates information.
Publication: Newsletter
Second publication: Annual Report

New English Art Club
NEAC

c/o Federation of British Artists
17 Cariton House Terrace, London, SW1Y 5BD, England, UK
Tel: 44 207 9306844
Fax: 44 207 8397830
Email: info@mallgalleries.com
Founded: 1886
Members: 45
Contact: Briony Chaplin
Description: Promotes excellence in drawing and painting. Organizes annual exhibits and sales.
Publication: Catalog
Publication title: Annual Exhibition Catalogue. Advertisements.

New Forest Pony Breeding and Cattle Society

The Corner House, Ringwood Rd., Bransgore, BH23 8AA, England, UK
Tel: 44 1425 672775
Fax: 44 1425 672775
Email: forestpony@enterprise.net
Website: http://www.newforestpony.com
Founded: 1938
Members: 1100
Staff: 1
Contact: Miss D Macnair, Hon.Sec.
Fee: £10
Membership Type: individual
Description: Owners and breeders of New Forest ponies. Strives for the conservation and preservation of New Forest ponies. Sponsors point to point races; encourages breed registration; compiles and distributes sales lists.
Publication: Book
Publication title: Forest Pony Stud Book
Second publication: Newsletter

New Producers Alliance

9 Bourlet Close, London, W1W 7BP, England, UK
Tel: 44 207 5802480
Fax: 44 207 5802484
Email: queries@npa.org.uk
Website: http://www.npa.org.uk
Founded: 1993
Members: 1200
Staff: 3
Contact: David Castro, CEO
Fee: £45
Membership Type: producer, writer, and director
Fee: £65
Membership Type: affiliate
Description: Membership organization for first and second time filmakers. Affiliate membership for entertainment lawyers,

accountants, etc. is also available. To educate and inform film producers in the UK; to promote the role of the film producer; to share information and experience; to seek creative partnerships with producers worldwide.
Library Subject: coproduction treaties, form contracts
Library Type: reference
Publication: Newsletter
Publication title: The New Producer. Advertisements.

Newcomen Society for the Study of the History of Engineering and Technology
NSSHET

The Science Museum, London, SW7 2DD, England, UK
Tel: 44 207 3714445
Fax: 44 207 3714445
Email: thomas@newcomen.com
Website: http://www.newcomen.com
Founded: 1920
Members: 1100
Staff: 1
Contact: Mr. R.M. Swann
Fee: £30
Membership Type: U.K. individual
Fee: £33
Membership Type: outside UK individual
Description: Institutions (120) and individuals (1000) in 28 countries. Promotes study of the history of engineering, industry, and technology. Disseminates information.
Library Subject: history of technology and engineering
Library Type: not open to the public
Publication title: Bulletin
Publication title: History of Thermionic Valves
Meetings/Conventions: - annual meeting

Newspaper Publishers Association

34 Southwark Bridge Rd., London, SE1 9EU, England, UK
Tel: 44 171 2072200
Fax: 44 171 9282067
Founded: 1906
Members: 8
Staff: 7
Contact: Steve Oram, Dir.
Description: The trade association for national daily and Sunday newspapers.

Newspaper Society

74-77 Great Russell St., Bloomsbury House, London, WC1B 3DA, England, UK
Tel: 44 207 6367014
Fax: 44 207 6315119
Email: ns@newspapersoc.org.uk
Website: http://www.newspapersoc.org.uk
Founded: 1836
Members: 142
Staff: 40
Contact: Gill Salim, Director's Sec.
Description: Represents regional and local press in the United Kingdom. Covers an immense range of activities, from individual advertisement control advice to lobbying in Brussels, Westminster and Whitehall on all political and legislative issues of concern to publishers. Also provides marketing services, promoting the regional press and national advertisers.
Formerly: Newspaper Society of England

Publication: Journal
Publication title: Headlines
Second publication: Journal
Publication title: Production Journal

NHS Consultants Association

Hill House, Banbury, Oxon, OX17 1QH, England, UK
Tel: 44 1295 750407
Fax: 44 1295 750407
Email: nhsca@pop3.poptel.org.uk
Website: http://www.nhsca.org.uk
Founded: 1976
Members: 600
Contact: Dr. P.W. Fisher, Pres.
Fee: £30
Membership Type: standard
Fee: £15
Membership Type: retired
Description: Senior doctors committed to the NHS and the basic principles on which it was founded. Acts as a pressure group lobbying politicians and others concerned with health.
Formerly: National Health Service Consultants Association
Publication: Reports

Nicaragua Solidarity Campaign
NSC

129 Seven Sisters Rd., London, N7 7QG, England, UK
Tel: 44 207 2729619
Fax: 44 207 2725476
Email: nsc@nicaraguasc.org.uk
Website: http://www.nicaraguasc.org.uk
Founded: 1978
Members: 1000
Staff: 4
Contact: Helen Yuill
Fee: £20
Fee: £7
Membership Type: unwaged
Description: Campaigning organization concerned with political solidarity work for Nicaragua. Promotes support in the United Kingdom for grass roots organizations. Aims to channel material and financial support to Nicaragua and to publicize political and social developments. Maintains speakers' bureau.
Library Subject: Nicaragua
Library Type: reference
Publication: Journal
Publication title: Central America Report
Meetings/Conventions: - annual meeting

Nickel Development Institute - England

c/o European Technical Information Centre
The Holloway, Alvechurch, Birmingham, B48 7QB, England, UK
Tel: 44 1527 584777
Fax: 44 1527 585562
Email: pcutler@nidi.org
Website: http://www.nidi.org
Founded: 1984
Members: 11
Staff: 3
Contact: Dr. Peter Cutler, Tech. Dir.
Description: Membership is open to primary nickel producers. Associate membership is available to other industries. Head office in Toronto can advise on this. The market development and applications

research organisation of the primary nickel industry. Its objective is sustained growth in the consumption of nickel. It carries out market development and technical research, and provides a technical service of information and advice to nickel and nickel alloy users worldwide.
Library Type: not open to the public
Publication: Magazine
Publication title: Nickel
Meetings/Conventions: - monthly congress

NOF
Derwent House, District 1, Tyne & Wear, Washington, NE38 7SY, England, UK
Tel: 44 191 4174254
Fax: 44 191 4174257
Email: team@nof.co.uk
Website: http://www.nof.co.uk
Founded: 1988
Members: 280
Staff: 9
Description: Assists member companies to become competitive in the national and international marketplace. Assists with the development of members' capabilities in response to changing demands of the industry. Provides consultancy, financial assistance, and support for innovation and training initiatives. Gathers and disseminates information.
Formerly: Northern Offshore Federation
Publication: Membership Directory

Non-Marine Association
c/o Lloyd's of London
1 Lime St., 1986 Bldg., Ste. 1085, London, EC3M 7DQ, England, UK
Tel: 44 20 73273333
Fax: 44 20 73274443
Email: nma@lloyds.com
Website: http://www.nma.org.uk
Founded: 1910
Members: 260
Staff: 12
Contact: Rob Gillies
Description: Underwriters at Lloyd's of syndicates writing principally Non-Marine business (Property, General Liability, Accident & Health, Term Assurance). To disseminate information to members on non-marine insurance worldwide; to represent members' interests within the Society so that non-marine business may be written as efficiently and as widely as possible.

Norfolk and Waveney Chamber of Commerce and Industry
St Andrews House, St Andrews St., Norwich, NR2 4TP, England, UK
Tel: 44 1603 729701
Fax: 44 1603 633032
Email: caroline.williams@norfolkchamber.co.uk
Members: 2000
Staff: 12
Contact: Caroline Williams, Chief Exec.
Description: Promotes and supports business and commerce.

North Cheshire, Wirral and North Wales Group
6 Wimmarleigh St., Warrington, WA1 1NB, England, UK
Members: 1889
Staff: 18
Contact: Colin Daniels, Chief Exec.
Description: Promotes business and commerce.

North Derbyshire Chamber of Commerce and Industry
Commerce Centre, Canal Wharf, Chesterfield, S41 7NA, England, UK
Tel: 44 1246 207207
Email: chamber@derbyshire.org
Founded: 1899
Members: 989
Staff: 63
Contact: Glenys Goucher, Chief Exec.
Description: Promotes business support and training.
Library Type: not open to the public
Publication: Journal
Publication title: Chamber Today. Advertisements.

North East Chamber of Commerce
Aykley Heads Business Centre, Aykley Heads, Durham, DH1 5TS, England, UK
Tel: 44 191 3861133
Fax: 44 191 3861144
Email: information@ne-cc.com
Website: http://www.ne-chamber.co.uk
Members: 4500
Staff: 252
Contact: Michael Bird, Chief Exec.
Description: Promotes business and commerce.
Publication: Magazine
Publication title: Contact. Advertisements.

North Hampshire Chamber of Commerce and Industry
Business Support Centre, Deanes Building, London Rd., Basingstoke, Hampshire, RG21 7YP, England, UK
Tel: 44 1256 352275
Fax: 44 1256 479391
Email: info@nhcci.co.uk
Website: http://www.nhcci.co.uk
Contact: Barbara Bryant
Description: Promotes business and commerce.

North of England Institute of Mining and Mechanical Engineers
Westgate Rd., Newcastle upon Tyne, NE1 1SE, England, UK
Tel: 44 191 2322201
Fax: 44 191 2322201
Email: info@infomine.com
Founded: 1852

North of England Zoological Society
NEZS
Upton, Chester, CH2 1LH, England, UK
Tel: 44 1244 380280
Fax: 44 1244 371273
Founded: 1934
Description: Saves animal species from extinction.

North Staffordshire Chamber of Commerce and Industry
Commerce House, Festival Park, Stoke-On-Trent, ST1 5BE, England, UK
Tel: 44 1782 202222
Fax: 44 1782 202448
Email: membership@northstaffs.chamber.co.uk

Website: http://www.nscci.co.uk
Founded: 1851
Members: 1150
Staff: 20
Contact: Bryan Carnes, Chief Exec.
Description: Promotes business and commerce.
Publication: Journal
Publication title: Focus
Second publication: Bulletin
Meetings/Conventions: - monthly meeting

Northamptonshire Chamber of Commerce

Royal Pavilion, Summerhouse Rd., Moulton Park, Northampton, NN3 6BJ, England, UK
Tel: 44 1604 671200
Fax: 44 1604 670362
Email: info@northants-chamber.co.uk
Website: http://www.northants-chamber.co.uk
Members: 1550
Staff: 132
Contact: Martyn Wylie, CEO
Description: Promotes business and commerce.
Formerly: Northhamptonshire Chamber of Commerce, Training and Enterprise

North-East Atlantic Fisheries Commission NEAFC

22 Berners St., London, W1T 3DY, England, UK
Tel: 44 207 6310016
Fax: 44 207 6369225
Email: info@neafc.org
Website: http://www.neafc.org
Founded: 1963
Members: 6
Staff: 3
Contact: Mr. Sigmond Engesaeter, Sec.
Description: Government representatives from Denmark (representing Greenland and the Faroe Islands), European Union, Iceland, Norway, Poland, and the Russian Federation contracting parties. Objective is to promote the conservation and optimun utilization of the fish resources of the North East Atlantic area. Encourage international cooperation and discussion on fish stock management. The Commission has no regulatory powers over waters within member states' jurisdiction, unless the relevant member states agree.
Meetings/Conventions: - annual meeting London UK

Northern Horticultural Society

Crag Ln., Harrogate, HG3 1QB, England, UK
Tel: 44 1423 565418
Fax: 44 1423 530663
Founded: 1946

Norwegian Chamber of Commerce in Britain

Norway House, 21-24 Cockspur St., London, SW1Y 5BN, England, UK
Contact: Robert Leggatt
Description: Promotes business and commerce.

Not Forgotten Association

4th Fl., 2 Grosvenor Gardens, London, SW1W 0DH, England, UK
Tel: 44 207 7302400
Fax: 44 207 7300020

Email: director@nfassociation.freeserve.co.uk
Website: http://www.nfassociation.freeserve.co.uk
Founded: 1920
Staff: 6
Description: Exists to help disabled ex-service men and women nation-wide. Aims to enhance the quality of their lives and give them something to which they can look forward; provides television sets, holiday outings and concerts.
Publication: Annual Report

Nottinghamshire Chamber of Commerce and Industry

309 Haydn Rd., Nottingham, NG5 1DG, England, UK
Tel: 44 115 9624624
Fax: 44 115 9856612
Email: marketing@nottschamber.co.uk
Website: http://www.nottschamber.co.uk
Founded: 1860
Members: 2500
Staff: 91
Contact: Geoffrey Hulse, Chief Exec.
Description: Promotes business and commerce.
Publication title: Network Nottinghamshire Magazine. Advertisements.

Nuclear Stock Association

PO Box 126, Terrington St. Clement, King's Lynn, PE34 4EP, England, UK
Tel: 44 1553 829076
Fax: 44 1553 829076
Email: nsagrant@aol.com
Founded: 1953
Members: 100
Contact: A.J. Grant, Sec.
Fee: £25
Membership Type: shareholder
Description: Members are plant propagators and fruit growers dedicated to ensuring the supply of healthy planting stock to the fruit growing industry. Aims to ensure the supply of healthy planting stock of commercially required varieties of soft fruit plants and fruit trees. This is achieved by funding, with others, disease indexing programmes and the propagation of indexed material under stringent conditions of isolation and hygiene demanded by plant health division of MAFF.

Nuffield Council on Bioethics

28 Bedford Sq., London, WC1B 3JS, England, UK
Tel: 44 20 76819619
Fax: 44 20 76371712
Email: bioethics@nuffieldfoundation.org
Website: http://nuffieldbioethics.org
Founded: 1991
Members: 18
Staff: 8
Contact: Dr. Sandra Thomas, Dir.
Description: Clinicians, educators, attorneys, nurses, philosophers, scientists, and theologians. Established by the Trustees of the Nuffield Foundation to identify, examine, and report on ethical questions raised by recent advances in biological and medical research. Seeks to play a role in policy-making and in stimulating debate in bioethics. Has published six major reports on the ethical issues associated with genetic screening, ownership of tissue, xenotransplantation, genetics and mental disorders, and genetically modified crops. Recent

discussion paper deals with new report on ethics of research related to healthcare in developing countries.
Library Subject: bioethics
Library Type: by appointment only
Publication: Report
Publication title: Animal-to-Human Transplantation: The Ethics of Xenotransplantation
Second publication: Report
Publication title: Genetic Screening: Ethical Issues
Meetings/Conventions: Ethical Issue of Clinical Research in Developing Countries - annual workshop

Nutrition Society
NS

10 Cambridge Ct., 210 Shepherds Bush Rd., London, W6 7NJ, England, UK
Tel: 44 20 76020228
Fax: 44 20 76021756
Email: office@nutsoc.org.uk
Website: http://www.nutsoc.org.uk
Founded: 1941
Members: 2200
Staff: 7
Contact: Prof. John Mathers, Pres.
Fee: £45
Membership Type: Professional
Fee: £10
Membership Type: Student
Description: Persons involved in nutrition research or in health maintenance organized to promote the scientific study of nutrition. Maintains special regional groups; disseminates information via journals.
Publication: Journal
Publication title: British Journal of Nutrition
Second publication: Magazine
Publication title: Gazette
Meetings/Conventions: - annual conference

Occupational and Environmental Diseases Association
OEDA

PO Box 26, Enfield, Middlesex, EN1 2NT, England, UK
Tel: 44 208 3608490
Website: http://www.oeda.demon.co.uk
Founded: 1995
Contact: Dr. Nancy Tait, Management Committee
Description: Asbestos is still responsible for much of our work.
Formerly: Society for the Prevention of Asbestosis and Industrial Diseases

Ockenden International - England
OI

Constitution Hill, Woking, GU22 7UU, England, UK
Tel: 44 1483 772012
Fax: 44 1483 750774
Email: oi@ockenden.org.uk
Website: http://www.ockenden.org.uk
Founded: 1951
Members: 40
Staff: 120
Contact: James Beale, Ch.Exec.

Description: Promotes self-reliance for displaced people in eight countries in Asia and Africa; establishes skills training courses and micro credit systems; establishes and maintains schools.

Office of Health Economics

12 Whitehall, London, SW1A 2DY, England, UK
Tel: 44 207 9309203
Fax: 44 207 7471419
Email: ohegeneral@ohe.org
Website: http://www.ohe.org
Founded: 1962
Staff: 7
Contact: Elizabeth Aulsford, Sec.
Description: Undertakes research on the economic aspects of medical care, with particular reference to the pharmaceutical industry.
Publication: Papers

Offshore Pollution Liability Association
OPOL

29 High St., Ewell, KT17 1SB, England, UK
Tel: 44 208 7863640
Fax: 44 208 7863641
Email: opol@compuserve.com
Website: http://www.opol.org.uk
Founded: 1974
Members: 76
Staff: 1
Contact: Roger Segal, Mng.Dir.
Description: European offshore oil company operators in European Union, Norway, Isle of Man, Faroe Islands. Aims to administer the OPOL Agreement which relates to the settlement of claims made against offshore oil companies as a result of oil spills.
Meetings/Conventions: - annual meeting

Oil and Colour Chemists' Association

Priory House, 967 Harrow Rd., Wembley, HA0 2SF, England, UK
Tel: 44 20 89081086
Fax: 44 20 89081219
Email: membership@occa.org.uk
Website: http://www.occa.org.uk
Founded: 1918
Members: 2573
Staff: 5
Contact: C. Pacey-Day, Gen.Sec.
Fee: £65
Membership Type: individual
Description: Technical, commercial staff in world wide surface coatings industry. Learned society/professional body for technical staff employed in surface coatings companies. Organizes exhibitions and technical meetings.
Publication: Journal
Publication title: Surface Coatings International. Advertisements.
Second publication: Bulletin
Publication title: Surface Coatings International Bulletin
Meetings/Conventions: SURFEX - semiannual - Exhibits. Manchester UK

Oil Companies International Marine Forum
OCIMF

27 Queen Anne's Gate, London, SW1H 9BU, England, UK
Tel: 44 207 6541200
Fax: 44 207 6541205

Email: enquiries@ocimf.com
Website: http://www.ocimf.com
Founded: 1970
Members: 40
Staff: 8
Contact: R.C. Oldham, Dir.
Description: Oil companies worldwide united to promote safety in the transportation and storage of crude oil and its products, including gas and petrochemicals, and to prevent pollution from tankers and at terminals. Works to establish guidelines for equipment at terminals and offshore moorings, and for tanker and gas carrier manifolds. Conducts studies and research projects on such projects as effects of wind and currents, safe terminal moorings of large ships, tanker salvage, and the handling of disabled ships. Is involved with other organizations in the consideration of governmental and industrial contingency plans to handle spills. Participates in work of the International Maritime Organization in areas of carriage of bulk chemicals and gases, equipment, fire protection, navigation safety, ship design, standards of training, and watchkeeping. Works with governments represented by IMO and provides information and assistance. Cooperates with other industry organizations, including the International Chamber of Shipping and the Society of International Gas Tanker and Terminal Operators, on the operation of tankers and gas carriers such as the ship to ship transfer for oil tankers and gas carriers, and planned passage in the Malacca/Singapore Straits.
Publication: Book
Publication title: Clean Seas Guide for Oil Tankers
Meetings/Conventions: - annual meeting

Oil Firing Technical Association for the Petroleum Industry

Foxwood House, Dobbs Ln., Kesgrave, Ipswich, IP5 2QQ, England, UK
Tel: 44 845 6585080
Fax: 44 845 6585181
Email: enquiries@oftec.org
Website: http://www.oftec.org.uk
Founded: 1991
Contact: J.M. Spenser, CEO
Description: Promotes members' interests.
Library Subject: oil central heating and oil distribution
Library Type: reference

Oil Industry International Exploration and Production Forum

25/28 Old Burlington St., London, W1X 1LB, England, UK
Tel: 44 171 4376291
Fax: 44 171 4343721
Founded: 1974
Members: 59
Staff: 9
Contact: Mike Cloughley, Exec.Sec.
Description: Private or government-owned oil companies engaged in exploration and drilling for crude oil and natural gas and its production, treatment, or transportation by pipeline; petroleum industry associations. Represents the industry with international regulatory bodies and produces guidelines for sound operating practices. Encourages communication among members; maintains contact with other professional and industrial organizations in order to ensure the resolution of problems and to avoid duplication of effort; generates and distributes information on developments in the field. Promotes protection of the environment, health and safety.

OISTAT Centre of Great Britain

c/o Association of British Theatre Technicians
47 Bermondsey St., London, SE13 3XT, England, UK
Tel: 44 171 4033778
Fax: 44 171 3786170
Email: office@abtt.org.uk
Website: http://www.abtt.org.uk
Contact: Jenny Straker
Description: National office of the Organisation Internationale des Scenographes, Techniciens, et Architectes de Theatre. Facilitates exchange of ideas and information among professional theatrical technicians. Gathers and disseminates information on subjects relating to technical installations with theatrical applications.

Older Lesbians Network

c/o VAC
295-299 Kentish Town Rd., London, WC1X 9BD, England, UK
Founded: 1988
Members: 180
Description: Lesbians over 40 years of age. Strives to create a network of contacts for lesbians.
Library Subject: lesbianism, feminism, fiction
Library Type: lending
Publication: Newsletter
Publication title: OLN Newsletter
Meetings/Conventions: - monthly meeting

Oldham Chamber of Commerce

Oldham Business Centre, Cromwell St., Oldham, OL1 1BB, England, UK
Tel: 44 161 6200006
Fax: 44 161 6200030
Email: enquiries@oldhamchamber.co.uk
Website: http://www.oldhamchamber.co.uk
Members: 750
Staff: 22
Contact: E. Stacey, Chief Exec.
Description: Promotes business and commerce.
Formerly: Oldham Chamber of Commerce, Training and Enterprise

Omnibus Society
OS

185 Southlands Rd., Bromley, Ashtead, BR2 2QZ, England, UK
Tel: 44 1372 272631
Website: http://www.omnibussoc.org/
Founded: 1929
Members: 950
Contact: Tony Francis, Sec.
Description: Individuals in 15 countries interested in preserving the history of bus, coach, trolleybus, and tramway vehicles and records. Provides for the exchange of information and the discussion of traffic and engineering matters. Organizes field trips and study tours. Maintains news and historical service, photographic register, route recording scheme, ticket and timetable collection.
Library Type: reference
Publication: Magazine
Publication title: Omnibus Magazine
Second publication: Monographs
Meetings/Conventions: Presidential Weekend - annual

One Village
OV

Charlbury, Chipping Norton, OX7 3SQ, England, UK
Tel: 44 1608 811811
Fax: 44 1608 811911
Email: progress@onevillage.org
Website: http://www.onevillage.org
Founded: 1979
Contact: R. Scott
Description: Campaigns to enhance public understanding of global interdependence and encourages community action to increase the well-being of communities and the worldwide community. Operates with workers' cooperatives and community associations involved in craft production in Africa, Asia, and Central and South America.

One World Action

Bradley's Close, White Lion St., London, N1 9PF, England, UK
Tel: 44 207 8334075
Fax: 44 207 8334102
Email: owa@onewordaction.org
Website: http://www.oneworldaction.org
Founded: 1989
Staff: 12
Contact: Graham Bennett, Dir.
Description: OWA works in Europe and with partner organizations in poor countries to defeat poverty and to promote democracy and respect for human rights. Through such partners for change we are working for a just and equal world.
Publication title: A Family of the Musseque: Survival and Development in Postwar Angola
Second publication: Newsletter
Publication title: A Partnership for Change
Meetings/Conventions: Local Democracy and Local Governance conference

Open and Distance Learning Quality Council

16 Park Crescent, London, W1B 1AH, England, UK
Tel: 44 20 76127090
Fax: 44 20 76127092
Email: info@odlqc.org.uk
Website: http://www.odlqc.org.uk
Founded: 1969
Members: 49
Staff: 4
Contact: David Morley
Description: Organisations awarded accreditation. Aims to raise standards in distance education and training, protect the interests of learners and increase awareness of the work of ODLQC and its accredited organisations.
Formerly: Council for the Accreditation of Correspondence Colleges
Publication: Brochure
Publication title: Buyers Guide to Distance Learning
Second publication: Brochure
Publication title: Courses Offered by Accredited Providers

Open Spaces Society

25a Bell St., Henley-On-Thames, RG9 2BA, England, UK
Tel: 44 1491 573535
Email: hq@aol.com
Website: http://www.oss.org.uk
Founded: 1865
Members: 2300

Staff: 5
Contact: Kate Ashbrook, Gen.Sec.
Fee: £27
Membership Type: new
Fee: £21
Membership Type: renewal
Description: Individuals groups, parish councils, national organizations, local authorities. Campaigns to create and conserve common land, village greens, open spaces and rubric paths and country in England and Wales.
Library Type: not open to the public
Publication: Book
Publication title: Getting Greens Registered-A Guide to Law and Procedure for Town and Village Greens
Second publication: Book
Publication title: Making Space-Protecting and Creating Open Space for Local Communities

Operational Research Society - United Kingdom

Seymour House, 12 Edward St., Birmingham, B1 2RX, England, UK
Tel: 44 121 2339300
Fax: 44 121 2330321
Email: email@orsoc.org.uk
Website: http://www.orsoc.org.uk
Founded: 1948
Members: 3080
Staff: 7
Contact: Bob Miles, Sec.
Fee: £45
Membership Type: individual
Fee: £15
Membership Type: student
Description: Practitioners and academics in operational research, decision support systems, business research, management science, decision science. Aims to further knowledge and good practice in the use of scientific, analytic, systematic, and structured, approaches to assist in planning and decision-making in industry, commerce, government at all levels and in public and private services.
Library Subject: operational research
Library Type: open to the public
Publication: Journal
Publication title: European Journal of Information Systems
Second publication: Journal
Publication title: European Journal of Information Systems
Meetings/Conventions: - annual conference - Exhibits.

Optical Frame Importers' and Manufacturers Association

37-41 Bedford Row, London, WC1R 4JH, England, UK
Tel: 44 171 4058101
Fax: 44 171 8312797
Founded: 1980
Members: 53
Staff: 4
Contact: R.H.J. Forsyth
Description: Importers and manufacturers of optical frames. Aims to further the interests of its members.
Formerly: Formed by Merger of, OFSA
Publication title: In Focus

Optra Exhibits UK

37-41 Bedford Row, London, WC1R 4JH, England, UK
Tel: 44 171 4058101
Fax: 44 171 8312797

Founded: 1968
Members: 44
Staff: 4
Contact: R. Wilshin
Description: Members of the Federation of Manufacturing Opticians who exhibit at Optrafair (biennial ophthalmic trade fair). Aims to further the interests of its members.
Formerly: Opthalmic Exhibitors' Association
Publication title: In Focus (Federation of Manufacturing Opticians)

Oral History Society
OHS

c/o Department of History
Essex University, Colchester, CO4 3SQ, England, UK
Tel: 44 207 4127405
Email: rob.perks@bl.uk
Website: http://www.ohs.org.uk
Founded: 1969
Members: 1000
Contact: Dr. Robert Perks, Sec.
Description: Historians and other individuals with an interest in oral history. Promotes recording and preservation of oral histories as a method of historical research. Provides practical support to individuals wishing to record oral histories; serves as a clearinghouse on oral history; conducts research and educational programs.
Publication: Journal
Publication title: Oral History Journal. Advertisements.
Second publication: Book
Publication title: Talking in Class
Meetings/Conventions: - periodic conference

Orders and Medals Research Society
OMRS

PO Box 248, Snettisham, King's Lynn, PE31 7TA, England, UK
Tel: 44 1295 690009
Email: gensec@omrs.org.uk
Founded: 1942
Members: 2750
Contact: P.M.R. Helmore, Gen.Sec.
Fee: £12
Membership Type: UK
Fee: £20
Membership Type: outside the U.K.
Description: Individuals (2700); firms and military museums (50). Objectives are: to promote and foster interest in the study of orders, decorations, and medals, and all related material; to assist collectors and students in their research; to advance the interests of members as collectors. Organizes lectures.
Publication title: The Miscellany of Honours
Second publication: Journal
Publication title: Orders and Medals. Advertisements.
Meetings/Conventions: - annual convention - Exhibits.

Organic Food Federation

c/o The Tithe House
Peaseland Green, Elsing, East Dereham, Dereham, NR20 3DY, England, UK
Tel: 44 1362 637314
Fax: 44 1362 637398
Founded: 1986
Members: 350
Staff: 5
Contact: J.C.G. Wade

Description: Manufacturers, processors, importers and producers of organic foods or ingredients. Provides organic certification. Represents manufacturers' and importers' interests on governmental and other bodies. Disseminates information on organic food and ingredients and relevant matters to members. It is the focal point for organic manufacturers, distributors, and importers to establish contact and meet regularly.
Publication: Bulletin
Meetings/Conventions: Certification and Management Committee meeting

Organic Living Association

St. Mary's Villa, Hanley Swan, Worcester, WR8 0EA, England, UK
Fax: 44 1684 310703
Founded: 1971
Members: 200
Staff: 1
Contact: Dennis C. Nightingale-Smith, Dir. Sec.
Fee: £10
Membership Type: subscription
Description: Aims to integrate the production and consumption of vegetables, fruit, cereals and dairy produce grown on healthy, naturally fertilized soil. Promotes human health by whatever humane means may be necessary; promotes establishment of ecological, self-reliant, self-sufficient villages. Disseminates knowledge of alternatives to allopathic medicine.
Library Type: by appointment only
Publication: Newsletter

Organisation of European Aluminum Refiners and Remelters
OEA

OEA Technical Office, Broadway House, Calthorpe Rd., Birmingham, B15 1TN, England, UK
Tel: 44 121 4561103
Fax: 44 870 1329790
Email: oeato@alfed.org.uk
Founded: 1960
Members: 50
Staff: 1
Contact: Mark Askew
Description: Companies in the secondary aluminum industry producing foundry ingot, deoxidant for the steel industry, master alloys, rolling slab and extrusion billet predominantly from recycled aluminum. Represents the common interests of smelters in Europe. It helps members to operate in an environmentally acceptable way and assists in the search for new markets. Represents members interests to the public, to legislative organisations and provides a forum for members co-operation on technical and economic areas.
Formerly: Organisation of European Aluminium Smelters
Publication: Journal
Publication title: Comparison of National Standards for Aluminium Casting Alloys
Second publication: Annual Report
Publication title: OEA
Meetings/Conventions: - annual meeting

Organisation of Professional Users of Statistics

c/o Lancaster House
More Lane, Esher, KT10 8AP, England, UK
Tel: 44 1372 463121
Fax: 44 1372 469847

Email: bts@dial.pipex.com
Contact: Ian Maclean
Description: Professional users of statistics.

Oriental Ceramic Society
OCS

30B Torrington Sq., London, WC1E 7JL, England, UK
Tel: 44 20 76367985
Fax: 44 20 75806749
Email: ocs-london@beeb.net
Website: http://www.ocs-london.com
Founded: 1921
Members: 1100
Staff: 1
Contact: Jean Martin, Sec.
Fee: £45
Membership Type: inside UK
Fee: £65
Membership Type: outside UK
Description: Individuals, museums, and libraries. Increases knowledge of Eastern ceramics and other arts. Organizes loan exhibitions of objects from members' private collections and museums.
Publication title: Transactions of the Oriental Ceramic Society
Second publication: Journal
Publication title: Transactions of the Oriental Ceramic Society (TOCS). Advertisements.
Meetings/Conventions: Exhibition on Blue and White Ceramics - annual meeting London UK

Ornithological Society of the Middle East
OSME

c/o The Lodge, Sandy, Bedfordshire, SG19 2DL, England, UK
Fax: 44 1442 822623
Email: ag@osme.org
Website: http://www.osme.org
Founded: 1978
Members: 1000
Contact: O. Roberts, Hon.Sec.
Fee: £20
Membership Type: family, non-UK address
Fee: £15
Membership Type: individual, non-UK address
Description: Individuals and organizations in 50 countries interested in birds of the Middle East. Encourages knowledge and conservation of Middle Eastern birds. Collects and collates ornithological data. Seeks to develop working relationships with environmental, conservation, and natural history societies concerned with the Middle East.
Library Subject: ornithology in the Middle East
Library Type: reference
Publication: Journal
Publication title: Sandgrouse. Advertisements.
Meetings/Conventions: - annual meeting

Orthoptic and Binocular Vision Association
OBVA

48 Church St., Tamworth, B79 7DE, England, UK
Tel: 44 1827 61600
Email: d.b.stidwill@aston.ac.uk
Founded: 1958
Members: 150

Staff: 4
Contact: David B. Stidwill, Hon.Sec.
Fee: £2
Membership Type: associate
Fee: £5
Membership Type: full
Description: Optometrists are full members; optometry students and other health care professionals are associate members. Promotes orthoptic and vision training among health care professionals. Conducts educational programs in orthoptics and binocular vision.
Library Subject: orthoptics, binocular vision, pediatric optometry
Library Type: lending
Publication: Newsletter
Publication title: OBVA Newsletter. Advertisements.
Meetings/Conventions: Clinical Meeting - annual meeting

Oscar Wilde Society
OWS

100 Peacock Str., Gravesend, DA12 1EQU, England, UK
Tel: 44 1474 535978
Email: vanessa@salome.co.uk
Founded: 1990

OSPAR Commission

New Ct., 48 Carey St., London, WC2A 2JQ, England, UK
Tel: 44 207 4305200
Fax: 44 207 4305225
Email: secretariat@ospar.org
Website: http://www.ospar.org
Founded: 1992
Members: 16
Staff: 12
Contact: Alan Simcock, Exec.Sec.
Description: Governments of Belgium, Denmark, Germany, Finland, France, Iceland, Luxembourg, Netherlands, Norway, Portugal, Republic of Ireland, Spain, Sweden, Switzerland, the United Kingdom, and the Commission of European Communities.
Library Type: reference
Publication: Annual Report
Meetings/Conventions: - annual meeting

Outdoor Advertising Association of Great Britain

Summit House, 27 Sale Place, London, W2 1YR, England, UK
Tel: 44 207 9730315
Fax: 44 207 9730318
Email: enquiries@oaa.org.uk
Website: http://www.oaa.org.uk
Staff: 2
Contact: Alan James, Chief Exec.
Description: Members are poster advertising contractors.

Outdoor Industries Association

Morritt House, 58 Station Approach, South Ruislip, Ruislip, HA4 6SA, England, UK
Tel: 44 20 88421111
Fax: 44 20 88420090
Email: info@go-outdoors.org.uk
Website: http://www.go-outdoors.org.uk
Founded: 1961
Members: 300
Staff: 5
Contact: Ms. P.M. Edwards
Fee: £100

Description: Trade association representing manufacturers, retailers, wholesalers, importers and distributors of outdoor leisure equipment and accessories. Provides an organization for the promotion and development of the outdoor leisure and camping trades.
Formerly: Camping and Outdoor Leisure Association
Publication: Newsletter
Publication title: Go Outdoors Bulletin
Meetings/Conventions: Go Outdoors - annual trade show - Exhibits. Harrogate UK

Outdoor Writer's Guild
259 Preston Rd., Coppull Moor, Chorley, PR7 5DS, England, UK
Tel: 44 1772 696732
Fax: 44 1772 696732
Email: info@owg.org.uk
Website: http://www.owg.org.uk
Founded: 1980
Members: 180
Contact: Dennis Kelsall, Membership Sec.
Fee: £35
Description: Professional writers and journalists who write, film, photograph, broadcast, etc., about walking, climbing, mountaineering and similar outdoor activities, along with general travel. Aims to promote professional standards among writers specialising in outdoor writing; to represent members' interests; to provide a forum through meetings and social activities for members to meet colleagues and others in the outdoor leisure industry.
Publication: Newsletter
Publication title: Bootprint. Advertisements.
Second publication: Handbook
Publication title: OWG Handbook and Directory

Overseas Development Institute
ODI
111 Westminister Bridge Rd., Stag Place, London, SE1 7JD, England, UK
Tel: 44 20 79220300
Fax: 44 20 79220399
Email: d.evans@odi.org.uk
Website: http://www.odi.org.uk
Founded: 1960
Staff: 80
Contact: Simon Maxwell, Dir.
Description: An independent non-governmental centre for development research and a forum for discussion of the problems facing developing countries. Research programme has four main components: Natural Resources, Forestry, Human Security and Development, and International Economic Development. Also has networks linking research to practitioners in Agricultural Research and Extension, rural Development Forestry and Relief and Rehabilitation.
Library Type: reference
Publication: Annual Report

Overseas Development Institute
111 Westminster Bridge Rd., London, SE1 7JD, England, UK
Tel: 44 20 79220300
Fax: 44 20 79220399
Email: d.evans@odi.org.uk
Website: http://www.odi.org.uk
Members: 2200
Contact: Simon Maxwell, Dir.
Description: Gathers and disseminates information on research in social- and agroforestry.

Library Subject: Project and implementation case studies. Material highlights gaps in current knowledge.
Library Type: reference
Publication title: Network Papers & Newsletters

Overseas Press and Media Association
OPMA
c/o Smyth International Media
Archgate Business Center, 825 High Rd., London, N12 8UB, England, UK
Tel: 44 208 4466400
Fax: 44 208 84466402
Email: alastair@smyth-international.com
Website: http://www.opma.co.uk
Founded: 1965
Members: 150
Contact: John Howard, Hon.Sec.
Fee: £95
Membership Type: full
Description: Represents overseas media to markets in the United Kingdom.
Publication: Book
Publication title: OPMA Guide

OXFAM - U.K.
274 Banbury Rd., Oxford, OX2 7DZ, England, UK
Tel: 44 1865 312610
Fax: 44 1865 312600
Email: oxfam@oxfam.org.uk
Website: http://www.oxfam.org.uk
Founded: 1942
Staff: 1343
Contact: Barbara Stocking, Dir.
Description: Supported by 180,000 financial donors and assisted by 30,000 volunteers. Provides food and shelter to people in emergency situations. Assists people in their efforts to gain economic self-sufficiency. Feels that all people have a right to good living conditions; believes in the fundamental dignity of people and their inherent ability to overcome obstacles imposed by geopolitical and socioeconomic hardships. Contends that the world's material resources can, if equitably distributed, satisfy the basic needs of all people. Administers charitable program; maintains 50 field offices and operates over 2900 relief and development projects in more than 70 countries. Conducts educational programs and campaigns in the United Kingdom and the Republic of Ireland.
Library Subject: development, health, gender
Library Type: by appointment only
Publication: Journal
Publication title: Development in Practice
Second publication: Journal
Publication title: Gender and Development
Meetings/Conventions: - periodic meeting

Packaging and Industrial Films Association
2 Mayfair Ct., North Gate, New Basford, Nottingham, NG7 7GR, England, UK
Tel: 44 1159 422445
Fax: 44 1159 422650
Email: pifa@pifa.co.uk
Website: http://www.pifa.co.uk
Founded: 1957
Members: 150

Staff: 6
Contact: J.R. Pugh, Chief Exec.
Description: Open to companies in the UK engaged in the manufacture, conversion and supply of plastic film. Associate Membership is open to those companies whose activities are closely related to the film industry. Acts as forum for developing industry consensus, a channel for information, advice and education, a regime for policing performance and quality standards, a centre for trade statistics and a focus for representation.
Publication: Brochures
Second publication: Reports
Meetings/Conventions: - annual luncheon

Pain Society

21 Portland Pl., London, W1B 1PY, England, UK
Tel: 44 20 76318870
Fax: 44 20 73232015
Email: info@painsociety.org
Website: http://www.painsociety.org
Founded: 1967
Members: 1400
Staff: 3
Contact: Dr. Doug Justins, Pres.
Description: Professional body representing healthcare professionals working in chronic and acute pain. Aims to relieve the suffering of pain by the promotion of education, training and research. Supplies general information and a list of pain clinics by county.
Publication: Newsletter
Publication title: Pain Society Newsletter. Advertisements.
Meetings/Conventions: - annual meeting - Exhibits. Glasgow UK

Paint Research Association

8 Waldegrave Rd., Teddington, TW11 8LD, England, UK
Tel: 44 208 6144800
Fax: 44 208 9434705
Email: information@pra.org.uk
Website: http://www.pra.org.uk
Founded: 1926
Members: 200
Staff: 55
Contact: John Marshall, Mng.Dir.
Description: Raw materials suppliers, all coating manufacturers including paints, inks and adhesives and users. Acts as an international centre for coatings technology, catering for manufacturers of coatings, its raw materials suppliers & users. Major activities are research, information, provision, testing, analysis, environmental and consultancy services and training.
Library Subject: paint and related technologies
Library Type: not open to the public
Publication: Journal
Publication title: Coatings Comet
Second publication: Journal
Publication title: World Surface Coatings Abstracts
Meetings/Conventions: Addcoat - semiannual conference - Exhibits.

Painter-Stainers' Company

c/o Painters' Hall
9 Little Trinity Lane, London, EC4V 2AD, England, UK
Tel: 44 207 2366258
Fax: 44 207 2360500
Email: beadle@painters-hall.co.uk
Website: http://www.painters-hall.co.uk
Founded: 1502
Members: 550

Staff: 5
Contact: Col. W.J. Chesshyre, Clerk
Description: Livery company.

Painting and Decorating Association of Great Britain

32 Coton Rd., Nuneaton, CV11 5TW, England, UK
Tel: 44 2476 353776
Fax: 44 2476 354513
Email: info@paintingdecoratingassociation.co.uk
Website: http://www.british-decorators.co.uk
Founded: 1894
Members: 2400
Staff: 4
Contact: D. Powis, Chief Exec.
Description: Painters, decorators and decorating contractors. Aims to promote the continuous and progressive improvement of the painting and decorating industry, to advance the well-being and status of all connected with it. Also aims to federate the various regional and local associations, persons and companies engaged in the trade of painting and decorating and to act jointly by amalgamation, and to co-operate with any other associations, in promoting the objects of the Association.
Formerly: Formed by Merger of, British Decorators Association and Painting and Decorating Federation
Publication title: The Decorator
Second publication: Handbook
Publication title: Members Reference Handbook

Palaeontographical Society

c/o P.C. Ensom
Department of Palaeontology, Natural History Museum, Cromwell Rd., London, SW7 5BD, England, UK
Tel: 44 207 9425195
Fax: 44 207 9425546
Email: p.ensom@nhm.ac.uk
Website: http://www.nhm.ac.uk/hosted_sites/palsoc/
Founded: 1847
Members: 260
Contact: Paul C. Ensom
Fee: £17
Membership Type: student
Fee: £33
Membership Type: ordinary
Description: Professional and amateur paleontologists and libraries world-wide. For figuring and describing British fossils.
Publication: Monographs
Publication title: Monographs of the Palaeontographical Society

Panos Institute - London

9 White Lion St., London, N1 9PD, England, UK
Tel: 44 20 72781111
Fax: 44 20 72780345
Email: panos@panoslondon.org.uk
Website: http://www.panos.org.uk
Founded: 1986
Staff: 30
Contact: James Dean, Exec.Dir.
Description: Promotes greater awareness of sustainable development; facilitates development journalism. Gathers and disseminates information on sustainable development; works with local organizations to conduct public education programs.
Publication title: Panos Features
Second publication: Report
Publication title: Panos Reports

Paper Agents' Association

Bucklands, Chapmans Hill, Meopham, DA13 0QP, England, UK
Tel: 44 1474 812527
Fax: 44 1474 812940
Email: radam@paa.org.uk
Website: http://www.paa.org.uk
Founded: 1924
Members: 50
Contact: John DeLittle, Pres.
Description: Paper agents. Representing overseas paper and board manufacturers.
Meetings/Conventions: - quarterly

Paper Federation of Great Britain

Papermakers House, Rivenhall Rd., Westlea, Swindon, SN5 7BD, England, UK
Tel: 44 1793 889600
Fax: 44 1793 886182
Email: fedn@paper.org.uk
Website: http://www.paper.org.uk
Founded: 1872
Members: 63
Staff: 36
Contact: D. Fogerty, Sec.
Description: Manufacturers of paper and board. Presents to Government, the European Commission and others the considered views of the paper and allied industries.
Publication: Report
Publication title: Annual Review & Members List

Paper Industry Technical Association
PITA

5 Frecheville Ct., Bury, BL9 0UF, England, UK
Tel: 44 161 7645858
Fax: 44 161 7645353
Email: info@pita.co.uk
Website: http://www.pita.co.uk
Founded: 1920
Members: 1975
Staff: 4
Contact: John Clewley, Exec.Dir.
Fee: £99
Membership Type: Full
Fee: £29
Membership Type: Junior
Description: An independent body. Stimulates discussion of technical matters to promote the cost effective application of new ideas and procedures. Promotes scientific and technical education. Cooperates with other scientific organizations. Maintains committees that organize paper presentations, annual meetings and programs, and field visits.
Library Subject: paper maker and associations
Library Type: open to the public
Publication title: Essential Guide to Aqueous Coating
Publication title: Membership Yearbook
Meetings/Conventions: - biennial conference - Exhibits. Edinburgh UK

Paper Makers' Allied Trades Association

24 Beatrice Rd., Worsley, Manchester, M28 2TN, England, UK
Tel: 44 161 7945734
Fax: 44 161 7930827
Founded: 1931
Contact: D.G. McNay, Hon.Sec.

Description: Membership covers suppliers of plant and raw materials to paper mills. Fosters good relations between the paper industry and its suppliers.

Parenteral Society

99 Ermin St., Stratton St. Margaret, Swindon, SN3 4NL, England, UK
Tel: 44 1793 824254
Fax: 44 1793 832551
Email: secretary@parenteral.demon.org.uk
Website: http://www.parenteral.org.uk
Founded: 1981
Members: 1250
Staff: 2
Contact: Phil Precious, Chm.
Fee: £50
Membership Type: individual
Fee: £293
Membership Type: corporate
Description: Fosters the advancement in the interests of public health, the practice and science of parenteral therapy and to preserve and improve the integrity and standards of the parenteral industry.

Parentline Plus

c/o Dr. Dorit Braun
520 Highgate Studios, 53-79 Highgate Rd., London, NW5 1TL, England, UK
Tel: 44 207 2845500
Fax: 44 207 2845501
Email: centraloffice@parentlineplus.org.uk
Website: http://www.parentlineplus.org.uk
Founded: 1983
Members: 600
Staff: 8
Contact: Dr. Dorit Braun
Fee: £20
Membership Type: family
Fee: £50
Membership Type: associate
Description: Provides information and advice and support services to parents. Supports research. Trains professionals.
Library Type: not open to the public
Formerly: Absorbed, National Stepfamily Association
Publication: Magazine
Publication title: Changing Families
Second publication: Newsletter
Publication title: Stepladder
Meetings/Conventions: - annual conference London UK

Parents at Work
PAW

1-3 Berry St., London, EC1V 0AA, England, UK
Tel: 44 20 72537243
Fax: 44 20 72536253
Email: info@parentsatwork.org.uk
Website: http://www.parentsatwork.org.uk
Founded: 1985
Members: 1500
Staff: 7
Contact: Sarah Jackson, Chief Exec.
Fee: £18
Membership Type: individual
Description: Campaign to improve quality of life for all working parents and their children. Lobbies employers and policy makers for

improvement of childcare facilities. Provides working parents with childcare information.
Library Subject: Child care and family policies.
Library Type: not open to the public
Formerly: Working Mothers Association
Publication: Newsletter
Publication title: Balanced Lives
Second publication: Newsletter
Publication title: Waving Not Drowning
Meetings/Conventions: - annual conference

Parkinson's Disease Society of the United Kingdom

215 Vauxhall Bridge Rd., London, SV1W 1EJ, England, UK
Tel: 44 20 79318080
Fax: 44 20 72339908
Email: enquiries@parkinsons.org.uk
Website: http://www.parkinsons.org.uk
Founded: 1969
Members: 27000
Staff: 160
Contact: Linda Kelly, Ch.Exec.
Fee: £4
Membership Type: member
Description: Promotes awareness of Parkinson's disease.
Library Subject: Parkinson's disease.
Library Type: open to the public

Parrot Society - U.K.
PS

108 B Fenlake Rd., Bedford, MK42 0EU, England, UK
Tel: 44 1234 358922
Fax: 44 1234 358922
Website: http://www.theparrotsocietyuk.org
Founded: 1964
Members: 5000
Staff: 3
Contact: L. Rance, Sec.
Fee: £12
Description: Zoos, bird gardens, traders, and individuals in the United Kingdom interested in the breeding and study of parrots. Disseminates information on parrots; advises pet owners. Conducts seminars; operates charitable program; compiles statistics.
Library Type: reference
Publication: Directory
Publication title: Breeding Register
Second publication: Magazine
Publication title: Magazine of the Parrot Society
Meetings/Conventions: - annual convention

Partially Sighted Society
PSS

9 Plato Pl., 72-74 St. Dionis Rd., London, SW6 4TU, England, UK
Tel: 44 1302 323132
Fax: 44 171 3170289
Founded: 1973
Members: 2000
Staff: 21
Description: Strives to improve social, medical, and domestic services available to the visually impaired in the United Kingdom and to increase educational and employment opportunities. Offers information and advice; provides visual aids and special printing and enlargement services. Operates 3 sight centers that offer vision

assessment and training services. Arranges conferences, exhibitions, and displays.
Publication: Newsletter
Publication title: Oculus
Second publication: Brochures
Meetings/Conventions: - annual conference - Exhibits.

PARTIZANS

41A Thornhill Square, London, N1 1BE, England, UK
Tel: 44 207 7006189
Fax: 44 207 7006189
Email: info@minesandcommunities.org
Website: http://www.minesandcommunities.org
Founded: 1978
Members: 400
Staff: 3
Contact: Digby Knight, Coor.
Fee: £20
Membership Type: individual
Description: Supports indigenous peoples and their organizations, particularly in anti-nuclear and land rights campaigns. Focuses on RTZ, the world's largest mining company.
Library Subject: Aborigines and other indigenous peoples
Library Type: reference
Formerly: Colonialism and Indigenous Minorities Research/Action
Publication: Newsletter
Publication title: Parting Company. Advertisements.
Second publication: Book
Publication title: Plunder!
Meetings/Conventions: - annual conference

Passenger Shipping Association

4th Fl. Walmar House, 288-242 Regent St., London, W1R 5HE, England, UK
Tel: 44 207 4362449
Fax: 44 207 6369206
Email: hayleypsara@aol.com
Website: http://www.cruiseinformationservice.co.uk
Founded: 1957
Members: 50
Staff: 5
Contact: Bill Gibbons, Dir.
Description: Passenger shipping companies (cruising and ferry). Owners trade association for cruise lines and ferry operators. Provides market information to members as well as acting as contact body for wide ranging membership in consultation and liaison with UK government and industry bodies.

Pastel Society

17 Carlton House Terrace, London, SW1Y 5BD, England, UK
Tel: 44 207 9306844
Fax: 44 207 8397830
Email: info@mallgalleries.com
Website: http://www.mallgalleries.org.uk
Founded: 1898
Members: 56
Contact: Briony Chaplin
Description: Professional artists specialising in dry medium. Organises pastel exhibitions, helps to educate public in pastel medium through exhibitions and demonstrations.

Pathological Society of Great Britain and Ireland

2 Carlton House Terrace, London, SW1Y 5AF, England, UK
Tel: 44 20 79761260
Fax: 44 20 79761267
Email: administrator@pathsoc.org.uk
Website: http://www.pathsoc.org.uk
Founded: 1906
Members: 1100
Staff: 2
Contact: Roselyn Pitts, Admin.
Description: Those engaged in research or teaching in connection with pathology or allied science. Holds one scientific meetings each year.
Publication: Journal
Publication title: Journal of Pathology
Meetings/Conventions: - annual meeting Bristol UK

Pattern, Model, and Mould Manufacturers Association

National Metalforming Centre, 47 Birmingham Rd., West Bromwich, B70 6PY, England, UK
Tel: 44 121 6016976
Fax: 44 121 6016981
Email: info@pmmma.co.uk
Website: http://www.pmmma.co.uk
Members: 52
Staff: 2
Contact: Mr. A. Turner, Sec.
Fee: £300
Description: Pattern, model and mould manufacturers.
Library Type: reference
Publication: Journal
Publication title: Patternmaking. Advertisements.
Meetings/Conventions: congress Warwick UK

Pax Christi - Great Britain

Christian Peace Education Centre, St. Joseph's, Watford Way, Hendon, London, NW4 4TY, England, UK
Tel: 44 20 82034884
Fax: 44 20 82035234
Email: paxchristi@gn.apc.org
Website: http://www.paxchristi.org.uk
Founded: 1965
Members: 1600
Staff: 2
Contact: Patricia Gaffney, Gen.Sec.
Description: Purposes are to: work for peace while bearing witness to the peace of Christ; contribute to the construction of a more genuinely humane world, with respect for the life of each human being; collaborate with other Christian groups and peace movements; struggle against sources of injustice such as violence, war, hatred, and economic inequality. Condemns the arms race; urges arms control and disarmament. Stresses the importance of detente between the East and West, human rights, the Catholic church's duty to emphasize peace, and the problems of the Third World.
Library Subject: peace
Library Type: by appointment only
Publication: Newsletter
Publication title: Justpeace
Meetings/Conventions: - periodic meeting

Peace Pledge Union
PPU

41B Brecknock Rd., London, N7 0BT, England, UK
Tel: 44 20 74249444
Fax: 44 20 74826390
Email: enquiry@ppu.org.uk
Website: http://www.ppu.org.uk
Founded: 1934
Members: 2000
Staff: 5
Contact: Jan Melichar, Coor.
Description: Individuals who pledge to renounce war or aggressive action in order to achieve a world in which justice and freedom are personal experiences and not abstract definitions. Furthers discussion of nonviolent approaches to problem solving and strives to develop conflict resolutions that satisfy pacifist aims. Focuses attention on societal influences on young people that encourage aggressive behavior. Campaigns for a voluntary ban on the sale of war toys and promotes development of cooperative play. Distributes educational materials on the causes of war and on alternative solutions. Sponsors speakers bureau; compiles statistics on wars and war deaths.
Library Type: reference
Formerly: Sheppard Peace Movement
Publication: Magazine
Publication title: Peace Matters
Second publication: Pamphlets
Meetings/Conventions: - annual general assembly

Peat Producers Association
PPA

PO Box 15, Stowmarket, IP14 3RD, England, UK
Tel: 44 7071 780273
Fax: 44 1449 614614
Email: peatprods@aol.com
Website: http://www.peatproducers.co.uk
Members: 24
Contact: Robert Stockdale, Dir.
Description: Commercial peat companies in England. Establishes standards for commercial peat cutting operations. Represents members' interests before governmental organizations. Disseminates information.
Publication title: Code of Practice
Publication title: Growing Media and the British Economy

Penal Reform International
PRI

Unit 450, The Bon Marche Centre, 241-251 Ferndale Rd., Brixton, London, SW9 8BJ, England, UK
Tel: 44 207 9249575
Fax: 44 207 9249697
Email: headofsecretariat@pri.org.uk
Website: http://www.penalreform.org
Contact: Vivien Stern
Description: Promotes humane operation of criminal justice systems worldwide. Meets with national criminal justice officials to discuss issues and propose solutions to problems; advocates alternative sentencing and treatment of offenders.
Meetings/Conventions: - periodic seminar

Pensioners for Peace International
PPI

16 Sandy Ln., Richmond, TW10 7EL, England, UK
Tel: 44 181 9402611
Fax: 44 1273 492855
Founded: 1981
Contact: Kenneth Glynn
Fee: £3
Membership Type: pensioners
Description: International organization of senior citizens working for peace and disarmament. Promotes the formation of local groups; organizes Peace and Friendship Tours.
Publication: Newsletter
Publication title: Newsletter
Meetings/Conventions: - annual meeting

Pensions Management Institute
PMI

4-10 Artillery Ln., London, E1 7LS, England, UK
Tel: 44 207 2471452
Fax: 44 207 3750603
Email: enquires@pensions-pmi.org.uk
Website: http://www.pensions-pmi.org.uk
Founded: 1976
Members: 4500
Staff: 20
Contact: Mrs. S.M. Howlett, Sec.Gen.
Description: Promotes professional standards for employees working in pensions/employee benefits.
Publication: Directory
Publication title: Yearbook
Meetings/Conventions: - semiannual conference London

People's Trust for Endangered Species
PTES

15 Cloisters House, 8 Battersea Park Rd., London, SW8 4BG, England, UK
Tel: 44 20 74984533
Fax: 44 20 74984459
Email: enquiries@ptes.org
Website: http://www.ptes.org
Founded: 1977
Staff: 10
Contact: Dr. Valerie Keeble
Description: Aims to help to ensure a future for many species of endangered creatures worldwide. Committed to working in an effort to preserve them in their natural habitat for future generations to enjoy by funding scientific research whose results lead to the drawing up of effective conservation strategies.
Library Subject: natural history, conservation, environmental issues
Library Type: not open to the public
Publication: Newsletter
Publication title: Appeal Letters
Second publication: Report
Publication title: Changes in the British Badger Population, 1988-1997
Meetings/Conventions: - annual conference - Exhibits.

Percussive Arts Society UK

c/o Matt King
27 Catalina Dr., Baiter Park, Poole, BH15 1UZ, England, UK
Tel: 44 1202 466700
Fax: 44 181 4615910
Founded: 1994
Members: 50
Contact: Christine Skinner, Memb.Sec.
Description: Professional percussion players and teachers. Brings together like minded percussion teachers and professional percussion players with the aim of sharing information on skills and techniques.

Percy Grainger Society

6 Fairfax Crescent, Aylesbury, HP20 2ES, England, UK
Tel: 44 1296 428609
Fax: 44 1296 428609
Email: info@percygrainger.org.uk
Website: http://www.percygrainger.org.uk
Founded: 1976
Members: 500
Staff: 1
Contact: Barry Peter Ould, Pres.
Fee: £18
Membership Type: normal
Fee: £160
Membership Type: life
Description: Promotes knowledge and understanding in the life and works of the Australian/British/American composer/pianist Percy Aldridge Grainger.
Library Subject: music
Library Type: reference
Publication: Journal
Publication title: Grainger Society Journal

Performing Right Society
PRS

29-33 Berners St., London, W1T 3AB, England, UK
Tel: 44 207 5805544
Fax: 44 207 3064350
Email: info@prs.co.uk
Website: http://www.prs.co.uk
Founded: 1914
Members: 30000
Staff: 750
Contact: Terri Anderson, Dir./Planning & Corp.Comm.
Description: Composers, authors and/or music publishers. To license the public performance and broadcasting of copyright music on behalf of its composer author and music publisher members. When music is used in public, eg in a pub, shop etc., a PRS licence is required. The money collected is distributed, as fairly as possible, to composers, authors and publishers.
Publication title: PRS Handbook
Publication title: PRS News

Perfumers Guild

61 Abbots Rd., Abbots Langley, WD5 0BJ, England, UK
Tel: 44 1923 260502
Fax: 44 1923 268200
Email: perfumersguild@aol.com
Founded: 1981
Contact: John Bailey
Description: Perfumers.

Periodical Publishers Association
PPA

Queens House, 28 Kingsway, London, WC2B 6JR, England, UK
Tel: 44 207 4044166
Fax: 44 207 4044167
Email: info1@ppa.co.uk
Website: http://www.ppa.co.uk
Founded: 1913
Members: 180
Staff: 28
Contact: Ian Locks, Chief Exec.
Description: Compiles statistics. Promotes and protects the magazine industry.
Library Type: reference
Publication: Report
Publication title: Annual Review
Second publication: Directory
Publication title: Directory of WEB Offset Printers
Meetings/Conventions: - annual conference - Exhibits.

Permaculture Association

BCM Permaculture Association, London, WC1N 3XX, England, UK
Tel: 44 845 4581805
Fax: 44 845 4581805
Email: office@permaculture.org.uk
Website: http://www.permaculture.org.uk
Founded: 1983
Members: 1000
Staff: 4
Contact: Andy Goldring
Fee: £10
Membership Type: concession
Fee: £15
Membership Type: individual
Description: Advanced design principles for food production and sustainable lifestyles, especially perennial crops and mixed plantings, water and energy conservation and permaculture design courses.
Publication: Newsletter
Publication title: Permaculture Works. Advertisements.
Meetings/Conventions: AGM Convergence - annual - Exhibits.

Permanent Service for Mean Sea Level
PSMSL

Proudman Oceanographic Laboratory, Bidston Observatory, Birkenhead, CH43 7RA, England, UK
Tel: 44 151 6538633
Fax: 44 151 6536269
Email: psmsl@pol.ac.uk
Website: http://www.pol.ac.uk/psmsl
Founded: 1933
Staff: 4
Contact: Prof. P.L. Woodworth, Dir.
Description: Member of the Federation of Astronomical and Geophysical Data Analysis Services. Collects, analyzes, and publishes data regarding changes in global sea levels.

Permanent Way Institution
PWI

11 Caraway Pl., Stoke-on-Trent, ST3 7FE, England, UK
Tel: 44 1782 397880
Fax: 44 1782 397546
Email: pwi.bjn@virgin.net

Website: http://www.permanentwayinstitution.com
Founded: 1884
Members: 4500
Contact: Brian J. Newman, Sec.
Fee: £35
Membership Type: fellowship by award
Description: Railway civil engineers, technical staff, supervisors, and trackmen in 46 countries. Seeks to advance the knowledge of railway permanent way and its exchange between the railway systems of the world.
Library Subject: railway civil engineering
Library Type: not open to the public
Publication: Book
Publication title: British Railway Track, 7th Ed.. Advertisements.
Second publication: Book
Publication title: The Evolution of Permanent Way. Advertisements.
Meetings/Conventions: - annual convention

Personal Managers' Association

1 Summer Rd., East Molesey, KT8 9LX, England, UK
Tel: 44 208 3989796
Fax: 44 208 3929796
Email: info@thepma.com
Founded: 1950
Members: 122
Contact: Angela Adler, Sec.
Fee: £250
Membership Type: ordinary
Description: Theatrical agents. For artists, technicians and writers in the entertainment industry.

Personal Safety Manufacturers Association

c/o Mr. N.B. Jaynes, Sec.
Tamesis House, 35 St. Philip's Ave., Worcester Park, KT4 8JS, England, UK
Tel: 44 208 3306446
Fax: 44 208 3307447
Email: psma@tamgroup.co.uk
Founded: 1998
Members: 60
Staff: 3
Contact: N.B. Jaynes, Sec.
Description: Manufacturers and suppliers of personal protective equipment in the United Kingdom. Represents the interests of the protective equipment industry. Establishes and monitors industry standards. Represents members' interests.
Formerly: Safety Equipment Association
Publication: Membership Directory
Publication title: Reference Book of Protective Equipment

Pet Care Trust

Bedford Business Centre, 170 Mile Rd., Bedford, MK42 9TW, England, UK
Tel: 44 1234 273933
Fax: 44 1234 273550
Email: info@petcare.org.uk
Website: http://www.petcare.org.uk
Founded: 1986
Members: 1600
Staff: 4
Contact: Stephanie Freakley, Projects & Spec. Events Mgr.
Description: Professional dog groomers; retail pet stores; boarding kennels; manufacturers and distributors of livestock, pet foods, and accessories. Promotes the interests of the pet care industry.

Encourages responsible pet ownership through education and training. Offers certificates in pet store management and dog grooming. Joint organiser of Petindex, Europe's leading annual pet trade exhibition. Organiser for the industry's annual conference.
Publication: Directory
Publication title: Buyers' Guide. Advertisements.
Second publication: Yearbook
Publication title: Pet Trade Industry Yearbook

Pet Food Manufacturers' Association
20 Bedford St., London, WC2E 9HP, England, UK
Tel: 44 207 3799009
Fax: 44 207 3798008
Email: info@pfma.org.uk
Website: http://www.pfma.com
Founded: 1970
Members: 54
Staff: 4
Contact: Tamara Garmston, Association Sec.
Description: Trade association of manufacturers, packers, and importers for the prepared pet food industry. Promotes products which are safe, of sound nutrition, palatable, and offer value for money. Works to raise industry standards. Encourages responsible pet ownership.

Peter Warlock Society
PWS
c/o Malcolm Rudland
32 A Chipperfield House, Cale St., London, SW3 3SA, England, UK
Tel: 44 207 5899595
Fax: 44 207 5899595
Email: mrudland@talk21.com
Website: http://www.peterwarlock.org
Founded: 1963
Members: 300
Contact: Malcolm Rudland, Sec.
Fee: £15
Description: Individuals in 14 countries who have an interest in the music of British composer Peter Warlock (1894-1930); Peter Warlock is a pseudonym for Philip Heseltine. Aims to act as a center of information concerning Warlock's music, and to arouse greater interest in this field. Sponsors competitions, concerts, and jaunts.
Library Subject: Choral music
Library Type: reference
Publication: Newsletter
Meetings/Conventions: - annual meeting

Petroleum Exploration Society of Great Britain
2nd Fl. Kent House (Ste. 41-48), 87 Regent St., London, W1B 4EH, England, UK
Tel: 44 207 4941933
Fax: 44 207 4941944
Email: gail@pesgb.org.uk
Website: http://www.pesgb.org.uk
Founded: 1964
Members: 5200
Staff: 4
Contact: Gail Williamson, Exec.Dir.
Fee: £25
Membership Type: individual

Description: Promotes, for the public benefit, education in the scientific and technical aspects of petroleum exploration.
Publication title: Tales of Early U.K. Oil Exploration
Second publication: Directory
Meetings/Conventions: - periodic conference - Exhibits.

Philological Society
School of Oriental and African Studies, Thornhaugh St., Russell Sq., London, WC1H 0XG, England, UK
Tel: 44 207 3236318
Fax: 44 207 4363844
Email: ns5@soas.ac.uk
Founded: 1842
Members: 600
Contact: Dr. Andrew Simpson, Sec.
Fee: £10
Membership Type: individual
Description: Individuals united to promote the study of the structure and history of languages.
Publication: Journal
Publication title: Transactions of the Philological Society. Advertisements.
Meetings/Conventions: meeting

Photo Imaging Council
Ambassador House, Brigstock Rd., Thornton Heath, CR7 7JG, England, UK
Tel: 44 20 86656181
Fax: 44 20 86656447
Email: pic@admin.co.uk
Website: http://www.pic.uk.net
Founded: 1918
Contact: Rob Oliver, Chief Exec.
Description: Photographic manufacturers and photographic associations.

Photographic Waste Management Association
c/o Photo Imaging Council
Orbital House, 85 Croydon House, Caterham, Surrey, CR3 6PD, England, UK
Tel: 44 1883 334497
Fax: 44 1883 334490
Email: pic@admin.co.uk
Founded: 1993
Members: 12
Contact: A.C. Skipper, Sec.
Description: Encourages environmental responsibility of manufacturers, users and waste processors in the photographic and allied industries; quality of service and operational procedures by Trade member companies; corporate representation and dialogue between member companies on current and future concerns.

Photoluminescent Safety Products Association
42-44 Albert Rd., Braintree, Essex, RH20 3FR, England, UK
Tel: 44 1376 551955
Fax: 44 1376 550744
Email: phosphor20@aol.com
Website: http://www.pspa.org.uk
Founded: 1991
Members: 28
Staff: 1
Contact: Mr. Brian Milton, Sec.
Fee: £550
Membership Type: full

Description: Promotes the use and knowledge of photo luminescent products in the field of safety applications.

Physical Education Association of the United Kingdom

Ling House, Bldg. 25, London Rd., Reading, RG1 5AQ, England, UK
Tel: 44 118 9316240
Fax: 44 118 9316242
Email: enquiries@pea.uk.com
Website: http://www.pea.uk.com
Founded: 1899
Members: 4000
Contact: Sue Capel, Pres.
Description: Works to advance physical education in the United Kingdom; promotes the improvement of physical health of the community through physical education, health education and recreation.

Physiological Society - UK

PO Box 11319, London, WC1V 6YB, England, UK
Tel: 44 20 72695710
Fax: 44 20 72695720
Email: admin@physoc.org
Website: http://www.physoc.org
Founded: 1876
Members: 2500
Staff: 26
Contact: Esther Williams, Chief Exec.
Description: Physiologists at senior levels in universities, research institutions, hospitals and relevant industries and government departments, about a third of who are resident overseas. Affiliation is now available for younger physiologists such as. postgraduate students and postdoctoral workers. To promote the advancement of physiology. Covers all areas of physiology. Main activities are Scientific publishing; organising/funding scientific meetings, symposia, seminars, workshops, lectures for members, students, school-teachers, sixthformers; school and university liaison; 25 special interest groups, plus 13 subcommittees.
Publication title: Experimental Physiology
Second publication: Journal
Publication title: The Journal of Physiology

Phytochemical Society of Europe
PSE

The Gateway, Leicester, LE1 9BH, England, UK
Tel: 44 116 2506385
Fax: 44 116 2577287
Email: rrjarroo@dmu.ac.uk
Website: http://www.dmu.ac.uk/ln/pse
Founded: 1957

Piano Trade Suppliers Association

78-80 Borough High St., London, SE1 1XG, England, UK
Tel: 44 207 4032300
Fax: 44 207 4038140
Founded: 1904
Members: 11
Contact: D. Hart
Description: Suppliers of parts for the music industry especially pianoforte. A small trade association with limited activities.

Pianoforte Tuners' Association

10 Reculver Rd., Herne Bay, CT6 6LD, England, UK
Tel: 44 1227 368808
Fax: 44 1227 368808
Email: members@pianotuner.org.uk
Website: http://www.pianotuner.org.uk
Founded: 1913
Members: 280
Contact: Mrs. V.M. Addis
Fee: £75
Description: Piano tuners and technicians. Aims to bring together piano tuners and technicians for mutual protection and benefit; to educate the public on the need for regular and skilled tuning and servicing and to proclaim the importance of high professional standards; to provide the strength of association which is necessary to protect and represent the tuning profession.
Publication: Newsletter. Advertisements.
Second publication: Yearbook
Meetings/Conventions: - annual convention - Exhibits.

Picon

c/o St. Christopher's House
Holloway Hill, Godalming, GU7 1QZ, England, UK
Tel: 44 1483 412000
Fax: 44 1483 412001
Email: info@picon.co.uk
Website: http://www.picon.com
Founded: 1880
Members: 150
Staff: 7
Contact: John Brazier, Chief Exec.
Description: UK based companies manufacturing or supplying equipment and consumables for publishing, graphic arts, printing, paper-making and paper converting industries.
Formerly: British Federation of Printing Machinery and Supplies
Publication: Paper
Publication title: Paper and Converting Machinery News
Second publication: Magazine
Publication title: Picon News

Pigging Products and Services Association
PPSA

PO Box 2, Stroud, GL6 8YB, England, UK
Tel: 44 1285 760597
Fax: 44 1285 760470
Email: ppsa@gdhbiz.demon.com.uk
Website: http://www.piggingassnppsa.com
Founded: 1990
Members: 70
Contact: Gill Hornby, Exec.Sec.
Fee: £1420
Membership Type: full
Fee: £675
Membership Type: associate
Description: Provides information and services for pipeline operators. Promotes knowledge of pigging and its related services. Pipeline pigs are devices that is inserted into and travel throughout the length of a pipeline driven by product flow.
Publication: Book
Publication title: An Introduction to Pipeline Pigging
Publication title: The Buyers' Guide and Directory of Members
Meetings/Conventions: - annual seminar

Pipe Jacking Association

Hamilton House, 1 Temple Ave., London, EC4Y 0HA, England, UK
Tel: 44 20 74892072
Fax: 44 20 74892074
Email: secretary@pipejacking.org
Website: http://www.pipejacking.org
Founded: 1973
Members: 24
Contact: Andrew Marshall
Description: Companies, firms or individuals who specialise in
carrying out, or supplying equipment and materials for, the process of
pipe jacking and/or microtunnelling. The objects of the Association are
to promote the use of pipejacking and microtunnelling as
environmentally, socially and economically beneficial trenchless
construction techniques; to promote the common interests of PJA
members; to improve standards of workmanship; and to maintain high
levels of technical competence and innovation.
Publication: Handbook
Publication title: A Guide to Pipe Jacking and Microtunnelling Design
(Handbook)

Pipeline Industries Guild

14/15 Belgrave Sq., London, SW1X 8PS, England, UK
Tel: 44 207 2357938
Fax: 44 207 2350074
Email: hqsec@pipeguild.co.uk
Website: http://www.pipeguild.co.uk
Founded: 1957
Members: 1000
Staff: 4
Contact: A.A. Reed, Gen.Sec.
Fee: £60
Membership Type: individual
Fee: £750
Membership Type: corporate
Description: Engineers and representatives from pipeline owning
companies, engineering companies, consultants, contractors,
manufacturers and associated companies.
Publication: Directory
Publication title: Pipeline Industry Directory. Advertisements.
Second publication: Journal
Publication title: Pipeline World. Advertisements.
Meetings/Conventions: - biennial trade show - Exhibits.

PIRA International
PIRAI

Randalls Rd., Leatherhead, KT22 7RU, England, UK
Tel: 44 1372 802000
Fax: 44 1372 802238
Email: infocentre@pira.co.uk
Website: http://www.pira.co.uk
Founded: 1939
Members: 2500
Staff: 200
Contact: Diana Deavin, Bus.Mgr.
Description: Provides research services for the paper and board
making, printing, publishing, and packaging industries. Disseminates
information on management, marketing, publishing, legislation, and
technical and business developments. Services include manual
literature searching, consulting, research, and referrals.
Library Subject: paper, packaging, printing, publishing
Library Type: reference
Publication title: Digital Demand
Publication title: Management and Marketing Abstracts
Meetings/Conventions: - periodic conference

Plan - United Kingdom

5-6 Underhill St., London, NW1 7HS, England, UK
Tel: 44 207 4829777
Fax: 44 207 4829778
Email: mail@plan-international.org.uk
Website: http://www.plan-uk.org
Founded: 1937
Contact: John Greensmith, Dir.
Description: Seeks to address the needs of children and families
worldwide. Conducts services including: provision of health care, food,
and clothing; educational programs for children and adults; community
and individual skills development initiatives. Makes available
emergency relief services to victims of natural and man-made
disasters.

Plastics and Board Industries Federation
PBIF

Rock House, Maddacombe Rd., Kingskerswell, Newton Abbott,
Devon, TQ12 5LF, England, UK
Tel: 44 1803 403303
Fax: 44 1803 873167
Email: pbifoffice@aol.com
Website: http://www.pbif.co.uk/
Founded: 1987
Members: 220
Staff: 2
Contact: Alison Ainsworth, Chief.Exec.
Fee: £300
Membership Type: full
Fee: £175
Membership Type: small business
Description: Promotes the high frequency welding and allied
industries.
Library Subject: high frequency welding
Library Type: not open to the public
Formerly: Federation of High Frequency Welders

Plastics Historical Society
PHS

c/o Hon.Sec. RH Chambers
31A Maylands Dr., Sidcup, DA14 4SB, England, UK
Tel: 44 20 83020684
Website: http://www.plastiquarian.com
Founded: 1986
Members: 350
Contact: Richard H. Chambers, Sec.
Fee: £20
Membership Type: individual
Fee: £25
Membership Type: individual (overseas)
Description: Historians, collectors, and other individuals with an
interest in the history of plastics. Encourages the study and
preservation of all historical aspects of plastics and related materials.
Promotes the recording of current developments for future
generations; acts as an information center for collectors; maintains
close contact with museums and galleries interested in conservation.
Library Subject: all areas concerned with polymeric materials
Library Type: reference
Publication: Newsletter
Publication title: PHS Newsletter. Advertisements.
Second publication: Journal
Publication title: Plastiquarian

Plastics Land Drainage Manufacturers' Association
c/o Robson Rhodes
Centre City Tower, 7 Hill St., Birmingham, B5 4UU, England, UK
Tel: 44 121 6976000
Fax: 44 121 6976113
Members: 6
Contact: Sylvia Battersby
Description: Manufacturers of plastic pipes for land drainage.

Plastics Machinery Distributors Association
PMDA
PO Box 1414, Dorchester, PT2 84H, England, UK
Tel: 44 1305 250002
Fax: 44 1305 250996
Founded: 1966
Members: 90
Staff: 1
Contact: Vivienne Page, Comm. Sec.
Description: Suppliers and manufacturers of processing machinery for the plastics industry in the United Kingdom and overseas. Promotes the plastics industry in the United Kingdom. Sets standards for the industry.
Library Subject: buyers guide, history
Library Type: not open to the public
Publication: Membership Directory
Meetings/Conventions: - periodic seminar

Plastics Window Federation
c/o Federation House
85-87 Wellington St., Luton, LU1 5AF, England, UK
Tel: 44 1582 456147
Fax: 44 1582 412215
Email: ins@pwfed.co.uk
Website: http://www.pwfed.co.uk/
Founded: 1989
Members: 500
Staff: 20
Contact: Ken Wiltsher
Description: Companies engaged in the installation of PVC windows and doors. Provides survey, arbitration, commercial cover and sales staff licensing services. Offers purchasers of PVC-u products, via its member companies total protection.
Publication title: Federation News

Play Therapy International
PTI
Fern Hill Centre, Fern Hill, Fairwarp, Uckfield, TN22 3BU, England, UK
Tel: 44 1825 712360
Fax: 44 1825 713679
Email: ptiorg@aol.com
Website: http://www.playtherapy.org/
Founded: 1996
Members: 1200
Staff: 4
Contact: Joanne Ginter, Pres.
Fee: £30
Membership Type: student
Fee: £50
Membership Type: individual
Description: Professional child psychotherapists and play therapists, students, and other individuals with an interest in child psychology. Promotes advancement in the teaching, theory, and practice of play therapy and child psychotherapy. Conducts examinations and bestows certification to child psychotherapists and play therapists; makes available continuing professional advancement programs to members. Serves as a clearinghouse on play therapy; represents members within the psychological community and before public bodies. Sponsors research; provides children's services; maintains speakers' bureau.
Library Subject: child psychology, play therapy
Library Type: not open to the public
Publication: Newsletter
Publication title: Play News
Second publication: Journal
Publication title: World of Children
Meetings/Conventions: World Congress on Child & Play Therapy - annual convention

Player Piano Group
PPG
2 St. Giles Barton, Hillesley, Gloucestershire, GL12 8RG, England, UK
Tel: 44 1895 634288
Email: jrd@ngscd.demon.co.uk
Website: http://www.playerpianogroup.org.uk
Founded: 1959
Members: 300
Contact: Tony Austin, Hon.Sec.
Fee: £12
Membership Type: UK
Fee: £15
Membership Type: international
Description: Persons in 8 countries with an interest in the mechanical and musical aspects of player pianos. Fosters sharing of information and experience concerning player pianos; provides a forum for selling, purchasing, repairing, and restoring player pianos and music rolls among members; promotes public concerts.
Publication: Bulletin
Publication title: The Player Piano Group Bulletin
Meetings/Conventions: meeting

PLAYLINK
The Co-op Centre, Unit 5 Upper, 11 Mowll St., London, SW9 6BG, England, UK
Tel: 44 20 78203800
Fax: 44 20 75870790
Email: info@playlink.org.uk
Website: http://www.playlink.org.uk
Founded: 1962
Members: 30
Staff: 5
Contact: Sandra Melville, Dir.
Fee: £15
Description: Individuals, local voluntary organizations, local authorities, national and regional voluntary sector organizations with an interest in play services and playwork. Connects practical playwork experience to the broader policy issues affecting children's play and works with other organizations in support of children and their right to play. Services include advice, information, training design and build, safety inspections, and risk assessment. Registered charity no. 303322.
Publication: Booklet
Publication title: Play As Culture
Second publication: Booklet
Publication title: A Playworkers Taxonomy of Play Types
Meetings/Conventions: conference - Exhibits.

Plumbers' Company

49 Queen Victoria St., Rm. 28, London, EC4N 4SA, England, UK
Tel: 44 20 72367816
Founded: 1365
Members: 330
Staff: 3
Contact: Lt.Col. R.J.A. Paterson-Fox, Clerk
Description: Plumbers.
Meetings/Conventions: - annual lecture

Plunkett Foundation

23 Hanborough Business Park, Long Hanborough, Oxford, OX29 8SG, England, UK
Tel: 44 1993 883636
Fax: 44 1993 883576
Email: info@plunkett.co.uk
Website: http://www.plunkett.co.uk
Founded: 1919
Members: 120
Staff: 7
Contact: Quintin Fox, Devel.Exec.
Fee: £45
Membership Type: individual
Fee: £185
Membership Type: corporate
Description: Educational charity that supports the development of rural group enterprise world-wide. Draws on practical experience of working with partners from the public and private sectors to promote and implement economic self-help solutions to rural problems.
Library Subject: Co-operatives worldwide; rural development, diaries and correspondence of Sir Horace Plunkett
Library Type: by appointment only
Publication: Newsletter
Publication title: Rural Connections
Meetings/Conventions: Plunkett Milk Groups Conference - annual convention

Poetics and Linguistics Association
PALA

c/o Dr. Peter Stockwell
School of English Studies, Nottingham University, University Park, Nottingham, NG7 2RD, England, UK
Tel: 44 115 9515908
Email: peter.stockwell@nottngham.ac.uk
Website: http://www.pala.lancs.ac.uk
Contact: Dr. Peter Stockwell
Description: Academic association for individuals working in sylistics, poetics, and associated fields of language and linguistics.
Publication: Journal
Publication title: Language and Literature
Meetings/Conventions: - annual conference

Poetry Society

22 Betterton St., London, WC2H 9BX, England, UK
Tel: 44 2074209880
Fax: 44 207 2404818
Email: info@poetrysociety.org.uk
Website: http://www.poetrysociety.org.uk
Founded: 1909
Members: 3500
Staff: 9
Contact:
Fee: £50

Membership Type: outside England
Description: Readers and writers of poetry. Helps poets and poetry thrive in Britain; publishes poetry and acts as an advocate for contemporary poetry; provides information for schools.
Library Subject: Poetry review
Library Type: not open to the public
Publication: Newsletter
Publication title: Poetry News. Advertisements.
Second publication: Journal
Publication title: Poetry Review

Police Federation of England and Wales

15-17 Langley Rd., Surbiton, KT6 6LP, England, UK
Tel: 44 208 3351000
Fax: 44 208 3902249
Email: jweeks@jcc.polfed.org
Website: http://www.polfed.org
Founded: 1919
Members: 126000
Staff: 60
Contact: John Weeks
Description: Police officers from constable to chief inspector.
Publication: Magazine
Publication title: Police. Advertisements.
Meetings/Conventions: - annual conference

Police History Society

37 Greenhill Rd., Timperley, Altrincham, WA15 7BG, England, UK
Tel: 44 161 9802188
Email: alanhayhurst@greenhillroad.fsnet.co.uk
Website: http://www.policehistorysociety.co.uk
Founded: 1985
Members: 400
Contact: Alan Hayhurst, Hon.Sec.
Fee: £8
Membership Type: personal
Fee: £8
Membership Type: corporate
Description: Acts as a forum for those interested in the history of police and policing.
Publication: Journal. Advertisements.
Second publication: Newsletter
Meetings/Conventions: - annual conference Lincoln UK

Police Superintendents' Association of England and Wales

67A Reading Rd., Pangbourne, Reading, RG8 7JD, England, UK
Tel: 44 118 9844005
Fax: 44 118 9845642
Email: enquiries@policesupers.com
Website: http://www.policesupers.com
Founded: 1920
Members: 1300
Staff: 6
Contact: Supt. David Palmer, Natl.Sec.
Fee: £282
Description: Superintending ranks of the British Police Service in England and Wales. Represents the interests of all superintending ranks in Home Office maintained police forces in England or Wales.
Publication: Newsletter
Publication title: The Superintendent
Second publication: Annual Report
Meetings/Conventions: - annual conference - Exhibits.

Polish Underground Movement 1939-1945 Study Trust
PUMST

11 Leopold Rd., London, W5 3PB, England, UK
Tel: 44 208 9926057
Fax: 44 208 9926057
Email: spplondon@ukgateway.net
Founded: 1947
Staff: 23
Contact: Dr. K. Stolimski, Chm.
Description: Established to collect materials and conduct historical documentary research on the Polish Underground Movement, Polish Home Army, and Polish Secret State during World War II. Compiles statistics.
Library Subject: World War II (1939-45)
Library Type: reference
Formerly: Formed by Merger of, Polish Institute
Publication: Books
Publication title: Armia Krajowa w Dokumentach 1939-45
Meetings/Conventions: - annual meeting

Political Studies Association

Department of Politics, University of Newcastle, Newcastle upon Tyne, NE1 7RU, England, UK
Tel: 44 191 2228021
Fax: 44 191 2223499
Email: psa@ncl.ac.uk
Website: http://www.psa.ac.uk
Contact: Prof. Wyn Grant, Chair
Description: Political scientists and political science students and educators. Seeks to develop and promote the study of politics. Serves as a clearinghouse on politics and political science; facilitates communication and cooperation among members.
Publication: Journal
Publication title: Political Studies

Politics Association

Old Hall Lane, Manchester, M13 0XT, England, UK
Tel: 44 161 2563906
Fax: 44 161 2563906
Email: info@politics-association.org.uk
Website: http://www.politics-association.org.uk
Founded: 1970
Members: 1300
Staff: 2
Contact: Philip Norton, Pres.
Fee: £25
Membership Type: individual in the UK
Fee: £33
Membership Type: in Europe
Description: Individuals and organizations involved in teaching or understanding politics. Promotes the study of local, national, and international politics, both theory and practice.
Publication: Journal
Publication title: Talking Politics

Polymer Machinery Manufacturers and Distributors Association
PMMDA

c/o Sandy Weaver
PO Box 2539, Rugby, CV23 9YF, England, UK
Tel: 44 87 2411474
Fax: 44 87 2411475
Email: pmmda@pmmda.org.uk
Website: http://www.pmmda.org.uk
Founded: 1966
Members: 90
Staff: 1
Contact: Sandy Weaver, Sec.
Fee: £365
Description: Promotes polymer machinery manufacturing and distributing in the U.K.
Publication: Newsletter

Ponies Association - UK

Chesham House, 56 Green End Rd., Sawtry, Huntingdon, PE28 5UY, England, UK
Tel: 44 1487 832086
Email: info@poniesuk.co
Website: http://www.poniesuk.org
Founded: 1988
Members: 3000
Staff: 5
Contact:
Fee: £25
Membership Type: adult
Fee: £10
Membership Type: junior
Description: Promotes and improves standards of horse management and breeding.
Meetings/Conventions: - annual competition

Pony Club

NAC Stoneleigh Park, Kenilworth, CV8 2RW, England, UK
Tel: 44 2476 698300
Fax: 44 2476 696836
Email: becky@pcuk.org
Website: http://www.pcuk.org
Founded: 1929
Members: 40000
Staff: 7
Contact: Rebecca Elvin, Sec.
Fee: £32
Description: Young people with an interest in horses and riding. To encourage young people to ride and learn to enjoy all sport connected with horses and riding; to provide instruction in riding and horsemanship and instil in members the proper care of their animals; to promote the highest ideals of sportsmanship, citizenship and loyalty, thereby cultivating strength of character and self-discipline.
Publication: Book
Publication title: The Manual of Horsemanship
Second publication: Book
Publication title: Pony Club Year Book
Meetings/Conventions: The Pony Club Conference - annual conference - Exhibits.

Pool Promoters Association
100 Old Hall St., Liverpool, L3 9TD, England, UK
Tel: 44 151 2377777
Fax: 44 151 2377676
Contact: Roger Calvert, Sec.
Description: Trade association of football pool promoters.

Population Concern
Studio 325, Highgate Studios, 53-79 Highgate Rd., London, NW5 1TL, England, UK
Tel: 44 870 7702476
Fax: 44 207 2676788
Email: info@populationconcern.org.uk
Website: http://www.populationconcern.org.uk
Founded: 1974
Staff: 22
Contact: Ros Davies, Chief Exec.
Description: Works for the improvement of the quality of life worldwide by advancing the right of all people to exercise free and informed reproductive choice and to have access to confidential sexual and reproductive health services including family planning. Also works with partner organisations in over 20 countries to provide these services and have an education and advocacy programme in the UK.
Library Subject: population, environment, development, women, health, youth issues, reproductive and sexual health, family planning
Library Type: by appointment only
Formerly: Population Countdown
Publication: Magazine
Publication title: Annual Review
Second publication: Newsletter
Publication title: Update
Meetings/Conventions: Youth Conference - biennial - Exhibits.

Portable Electric Tool Manufacturers' Association
PO Box 35084, London, NW1 4XE, England, UK
Tel: 44 20 79358532
Fax: 44 20 79358532
Email: office@petma.org.uk
Founded: 1942
Members: 3
Contact: C. Dunn-Meynell
Description: Portable electric tool manufacturing companies in the UK. Represents the interests of portable electric tool manufacturers in the UK.

Portsmouth and South East Hampshire Chamber of Commerce and Industry
Regional Business Centre, Harts Farm Way, Havant, PO9 1HR, England, UK
Tel: 44 2392 449449
Fax: 44 2392 449444
Email: sehants@chamber.org.uk
Website: http://www.chamber.org.uk
Founded: 1879
Members: 900
Staff: 14
Contact: Max Breeze, Intl.Trade Mgr.
Description: Promotes business and commerce.
Library Subject: business, international business
Library Type: open to the public
Publication: Magazine
Publication title: Business News. Advertisements.

Portugese Chamber of Commerce in Britain
1st Fl, 22-25a Sackville St., London, W15 3DR, England, UK
Tel: 44 207 4941844
Fax: 44 207 4941822
Email: info@portugese-chamber.org.uk
Contact: Ronnie Price
Description: Promotes business and commerce.

Portuguese Chamber
22/25a Sackville St., 1st Fl., London, W1S 3DR, England, UK
Tel: 44 20 74941844
Fax: 44 20 74941822
Email: info@portuguese-chamber.org.uk
Website: http://www.portuguese-chamber.org.uk
Founded: 1980
Members: 320
Staff: 4
Contact: Ronnie Price, Dir.Gen.
Fee: £412
Membership Type: corporate status, sustaining class, standard overseas
Description: Provides business services for bilateral business between Portugal/United Kingdom-Ireland.
Publication: Directory
Publication title: Directory Yearbook
Second publication: Newsletter
Publication title: E Tradewindows.com
Meetings/Conventions: meeting

Positively Women
347-349 City Rd., London, EC1V 1LR, England, UK
Tel: 44 20 77130444
Fax: 44 20 77131020
Email: info@positivelywomen.org.uk
Website: http://www.positivelywomen.org.uk/
Founded: 1987
Staff: 20
Contact: Elisabeth Crafer, Dir.
Description: Offers peer support and self-help services to women with HIV and/or AIDs and their children. Provides information; maintains a resource facility.
Publication: Newsletter
Publication title: Positively Women Newsletter
Meetings/Conventions: - semiweekly support group meeting London UK

Post Tensioning Association
Cabco House, Elland Rd., Leeds, LS11 8BH, England, UK
Tel: 44 113 2701221
Fax: 44 113 2760138
Contact: Graham Bowring, Chair

Postal History Society
7 Manor Croft, Leeds, LJ15 9BW, England, UK
Tel: 44 113 2601978
Email: randys@ringworld.co.uk
Founded: 1936
Members: 450
Contact: Claire Angier
Fee: £24
Description: Exists to bring together the collectors, researchers, dealers and academic institutions around the world who study one or more of the varied aspects of postal history.

Library Type: not open to the public
Publication: Journal
Publication title: Postal History. Advertisements.
Meetings/Conventions: - quarterly convention Preston UK

Postwatch

28 Grosvenor Gardens, London, SW1W 0TT, England, UK
Tel: 44 8456 013265
Fax: 44 207 7303044
Email: info@postwatch.co.uk
Website: http://www.postwatch.co.uk
Founded: 2001
Contact: Peter Carr, Chm.
Description: Protects, promotes and develops the interests of all customers of postal services in the United Kingdom.

Powder Actuated Systems Association

c/o Institute of Spring Technology
Henry St., Sheffield, S3 7EQ, England, UK
Tel: 44 114 2789143
Fax: 44 114 2726344
Email: info@britishtools.com
Website: http://www.britishtools.com
Contact: Mr. J.R. Markham
Description: A trade association of manufacturers of fixing systems.

Power Fastenings Association

42 Heath St., Tamworth, B79 7JH, England, UK
Tel: 44 1827 52337
Fax: 44 1827 310827
Email: enquiries@powerfasteningts.org.uk
Website: http://www.powerfastenings.org.uk
Founded: 1978
Members: 6
Staff: 2
Contact: A.D. Skelding
Description: Manufacturers and suppliers of pneumatically operated nailing and stapling equipment. To promote the safe use of pneumatic nailing and stapling equipment.
Publication: Pamphlet
Publication title: Play It Safe

Power Generation Contractors Association
PGCA

c/o BEAMA
Westminster Tower, 3 Albert Embankment, London, SE1 7SL, England, UK
Tel: 44 20 77933040
Fax: 44 20 77933003
Email: angela.samuel@beama.org.uk
Website: http://www.beama.org.uk/pgca/pgca.htm
Founded: 1989
Members: 12
Staff: 2
Contact: Khanum Chaiwala, Sec.
Description: Power generation contractors.

Powys Society
PS

82 Linden Rd., Gloucester, GL1 5HD, England, UK
Tel: 44 1452 304539
Email: pjf@retepssof.freeserve.co.uk

Website: http://www.powys-society.org
Founded: 1967
Members: 350
Contact: Dr. Peter J. Foss, Hon.Sec.
Fee: £14
Membership Type: UK
Fee: £16
Membership Type: outside UK
Description: Individuals in 17 countries interested in the lives and works of John Cowper Powys (1872-1963), Theodore Francis Powys (1875-1953), and Llewelyn Powys (1884-1939), English brothers and authors of fiction, poetry, and criticism. Promotes the study and appreciation of the Powys family. Maintains speakers' bureau; provides information service.
Publication: Journal
Publication title: Powys Journal. Advertisements.
Second publication: Newsletter
Publication title: Powys Society Newsletter
Meetings/Conventions: - annual conference

Precast Concrete Paving and Kerb Association
INTERPAVE

60 Charles St., Leicester, LE1 1FB, England, UK
Tel: 44 116 2536161
Fax: 44 116 2514568
Email: info@paving.org.uk
Website: http://www.paving.org.uk
Members: 7
Staff: 2
Contact: C.J. Budge, Sec.
Description: Manufacturers of precast concrete block and flag paving and kerbs. Information is published for the benefit of users and seminars are held. Research is undertaken to develop improved product application.
Publication: Handbook
Publication title: The Design Handbook
Publication title: The Design of Heavy Duty Pavements for Ports and Other Industries

Precast Flooring Federation

60 Charles St., Leicester, LE1 1FB, England, UK
Tel: 44 116 2536161
Fax: 44 116 2514568
Email: info@pff.org.uk
Website: http://www.pff.org.uk
Members: 8
Staff: 2
Contact: Clive Budge, Sec.
Description: Manufacturers of precast concrete flooring. The national trade association for the precast flooring industry. It speaks with authority for the industry, and it publishes information for the benefit of users.
Publication: Book
Publication title: Code of Practice for Safe Erection of Precast Concrete Flooring

Prefabricated Aluminium Scaffold Manufacturers Association

PO Box 1828, West Mersea, Colchester, CO5 8HY, England, UK
Tel: 44 1206 382666
Fax: 44 1206 382666
Founded: 1978
Members: 30

Staff: 1
Contact: Eric Abbey
Description: Aluminium scaffold tower manufacturers. Advises members on matters related to manufacture, hire and sale of aluminium scaffold systems. Provides training for operators and promotes safety in the use of aluminium towers.
Publication: Booklet
Publication title: Operators Code of Practice
Second publication: Video
Publication title: Setting Standard For Safe Use of Scaffolding Towers

Prehistoric Society
PS

University College London, Institute of Archaeology, 31-34 Gordon Sq., London, WC1H 0PY, England, UK
Email: prehistoric@ucl.ac.uk
Website: http://www.ucl.ac.uk/prehistoric
Founded: 1908
Members: 2100
Contact: T. Machling, Admin.Asst.
Fee: £30
Membership Type: Individual
Fee: £45
Membership Type: Institutions
Description: Interested individuals in 30 countries concerned with the study of prehistory. Encourages prehistoric study and excavation. Conducts lectures and study tours.
Publication: Newsletter
Publication title: Past. Advertisements.
Second publication: Journal
Publication title: Proceedings
Meetings/Conventions: - annual conference - Exhibits.

Premenstrual Society

PO Box 429, Addlestone, KT15 1DZ, England, UK
Tel: 44 1932 872560
Founded: 1986
Members: 500
Staff: 4
Contact: Dr. M.G. Brush, Chm.
Fee: £10
Membership Type: ordinary
Fee: £5
Membership Type: student
Description: Seeks to provide advice and support for sufferers of premenstrual syndrome (PMS). Provides support for local groups and professionals in the field.
Library Subject: premenstrual syndrome, nutrition endocrinology
Library Type: not open to the public
Publication: Newsletter
Publication title: Premsol Newsletter

Pre-Raphaelite Society
PRS

c/o Michael Wollaston. Treas.
18, Floyd Grove, Balsall Common, Coventry, CV7 7RP, England, UK
Email: info@pre-raphaelitesociety.org
Website: http://www.pre-raphaelitesociety.org
Founded: 1988
Members: 325

Staff: 10
Contact: Michael Wollaston, Treas.
Fee: £35
Membership Type: individual
Fee: £35
Membership Type: corporate
Description: Promotes the art of the Pre-Raphaelite period.
Publication: Newsletter
Publication title: The Pre-Raphaelite Society Newsletter of the U.S.. Advertisements.
Second publication: Journal
Publication title: Review. Advertisements.

Pre-Retirement Association
PRA

9 Chesham Rd., Guildford, GU1 3LS, England, UK
Tel: 44 1483 301170
Fax: 44 1483 300981
Email: info@pra.uk.com
Website: http://www.pra.uk.com
Founded: 1964
Members: 404
Staff: 7
Contact: Dr. Mary Davies
Description: People with associated interests in a personal or professional capacity and companies willing to be associated with the development of retirement/redundancy advice/mid life planning. Promoting awareness of the needs of all those preparing for retirement. It provides education, planning and support services that relate to the successful management of transitional changes from an increasing diversity of employment patterns. Runs a course leading to a certificate in pre-retirement education with life planning.
Library Subject: mid and later life issues, adult continuing education
Library Type: not open to the public
Formerly: Pre-Retirement Association of Great Britain and Northern Ireland
Second publication: Newsletter
Publication title: PRA Resources Unit News
Meetings/Conventions: - annual conference

Pre-school Learning Alliance

69 Kings Cross Rd., London, WC1X 9LL, England, UK
Tel: 44 20 78330991
Fax: 44 20 78374942
Email: pla@pre-school.org.uk
Website: http://www.pre-school.org.uk
Founded: 1961
Members: 16000
Staff: 60
Contact: Margaret Lochrie, Chief Exec.
Fee: £29.5
Membership Type: family
Fee: £62.6
Membership Type: group
Description: Enhances the development and education of children under statutory school age by encouraging parents to understand and provide for the needs of their children through community pre-schools and nurseries.
Publication title: Under-Five Contact. Advertisements.
Second publication: Catalog
Meetings/Conventions: - annual conference - Exhibits.

Press Complaints Commission

1 Salisbury Sq., London, EC4Y 8JB, England, UK
Tel: 44 20 73531248
Fax: 44 20 73538355
Email: complaints@pcc.org.uk
Website: http://www.pcc.org.uk
Founded: 1991
Members: 16
Staff: 13
Contact: Tonia Milton, Info.Ofcr.
Description: Sixteen members drawn from the lay public and the press; includes seven editors of national, regional and local newspapers and magazines. Non-press members are in the majority. Upholds a Code of Practice covering issues such as accuracy, harassment and invasion of privacy; it deals with complaints about the editorial content of British newspapers and magazines and advises editors on journalistic ethics.
Publication title: Code of Practice
Publication title: How to Complain

Pressure Gauge and Dial Thermometer Association

136 Hagley Rd., Birmingham, B16 9PN, England, UK
Tel: 44 121 4544141
Fax: 44 121 4544949
Email: infohealth@btinternet.com
Website: http://pgdt.org
Founded: 1951
Members: 13
Description: Provides assistance for purchasers of pressure gauges and thermometers.

Pressure Sensitive Manufacturers Association

Sysonby Lodge, Nottingham Rd., Melton Mowbray, LE13 0NU, England, UK
Tel: 44 1664 500055
Fax: 44 1664 564164
Website: http://www.confedpaper.org.uk
Founded: 1974
Members: 8
Contact: T. Chasemore, Pres.
Description: Represents member companies and promotes their interests by representation on committees and liaison meetings with other trade associations.

Prestressed Concrete Association

60 Charles St., Leicester, LE1 1FB, England, UK
Tel: 44 116 2536161
Fax: 44 116 2514568
Email: pca@britishprecast.org
Website: http://www.britishprecast.org/pca
Members: 2
Staff: 2
Contact: C.J. Budge, Sec.
Description: Manufacturers of precast concrete bridge beams. Promotes growth and development of members' businesses. Represents members' interests before government agencies and labor and industrial organizations.
Publication: Book
Publication title: Integral Abutments for Prestressed Beam Bridges
Second publication: Book
Publication title: Prestressed Beam Integral Bridges

Primary Immunodeficiency Association

Alliance House, 12 Caxton St., London, SW1H 0QS, England, UK
Tel: 44 20 79767640
Fax: 44 20 79767641
Email: info@pia.org.uk
Website: http://www.pia.org.uk
Description: Immunologists, physicians, and others working to raise awareness of immunodeficiency. Conducts research; disseminates information.
Publication: Booklet
Publication title: Primary Immunodeficiency Disease
Meetings/Conventions: - annual workshop

Prince of Wales International Business Leaders Forum
PWBLF

15-16 Cornwall Terrace, Regent's Park, London, NW1 4QP, England, UK
Tel: 44 207 4673600
Fax: 44 207 4673610
Email: info@iblf.org
Website: http://www.iblf.org
Founded: 1990
Members: 41
Staff: 30
Contact: Robert Davies, Chief Exec.
Description: Business leaders in the United Kingdom. Promotes socially responsible business practices; seeks to achieve socially, economically, and environmentally responsible development worldwide.
Library Subject: business, development
Library Type: open to the public
Publication: Book
Publication title: Building Competitiveness and Community
Second publication: Book
Publication title: Building Competiveness and Communities

Principal's Professional Council

1 Heath Square, Boltro Road, Haywards Heath, RH16 1BL, England, UK
Tel: 44 1444 472499
Fax: 44 1444 472493
Email: ceoapc@naht.org.uk
Founded: 1920
Members: 800
Contact: Ken Clarke, Gen.Sec.
Description: Principals and Deputies of Colleges of Further Education, Adult Education, Colleges of Art, Colleges of Agriculture and Horticulture, Colleges of Building, Colleges of Commerce, Colleges of Music. Aims to discuss all matters relating to the work of the Colleges listed above and to represent the views of members to national, regional and local bodies through its national council and branches throughout the UK. To provide professional and legal support to members.
Formerly: Association of Principals of Colleges
Publication: Newsletter
Publication title: News Link

Printing Historical Society
PHS

St. Bride Institute, Bride Ln., Fleet St., London, EC4Y 8EE, England, UK
Founded: 1964
Members: 700
Contact: John Bowman, Hon.Sec.
Fee: £20
Fee: £35
Description: Printers, librarians, bibliographers, typographers, and graphic designers; libraries, printing firms, and learned societies. Aims: to foster interest in the history and traditions of printing and its methods, equipment, materials, and products; to preserve items of historical interest, including printing equipment and printed matter; to commemorate notable figures in the history of printing; to encourage study and discussion of such subjects in schools and among printers, designers, bibliophiles, and the public. Programs include: reading and discussion of papers on the history of printing and the allied trades; exhibitions and displays; visits to libraries, museums, and printing offices of historical interest.
Publication: Bulletin. Advertisements.
Second publication: Journal. Advertisements.
Meetings/Conventions: - annual meeting

Prisoners Abroad

89-93 Fonthill Rd., Finsbury Park, London, N4 3JH, England, UK
Tel: 44 20 75616820
Fax: 44 20 75616821
Email: info@prisonersabroad.org.uk
Website: http://www.prisonersabroad.org.uk
Founded: 1978
Members: 4000
Staff: 21
Contact: Carlo Laurenzi, Dir.
Description: Looks after the interests and welfare of British citizens lawfully or unlawfully detained overseas, and to their families and dependents. Facilitates the choosing of lawyers; advises on parole, prisoner transfer, and related matters; provides money for food and medical supplies where necessary. Helps with accomodation, employment, and financial assistance to released prisoners. Provides emotional and practical support to families and dependants. Liaises with the British Foreign Office; works to uphold and improve prisoner transfer treaties and other legislation affecting British prisoners overseas.
Publication: Newsletter
Second publication: Annual Report

Prisoners Wives and Families Society

254 Caledonian Rd., London, N1 0NG, England, UK
Tel: 44 20 72783981
Fax: 44 20 72783981
Email: pwfs@yahoo.co.uk
Founded: 1975
Members: 8
Staff: 10
Contact: Pauline Hoare, Organiser
Description: Supports, advises and gives information to the families of those in prison. Overnight accomodation for families visiting London prisons or courts.

Privacy International

Lancaster House, 33 Islington High St., 2nd Fl., London, N1 9LH, England, UK
Tel: 44 7947 778247
Email: privacyint@privacy.org
Website: http://www.privacyinternational.org
Founded: 1990
Contact: Simon Davies, Dir.Gen.
Description: Human rights advocates, journalists, information technology experts, academics, and data protection experts. Works to protect personal privacy and monitor surveillance activities by governments and other organizations worldwide. Establishes guidelines for police files in emerging democracies.

Private Libraries Association
PLA

Ravelston, South View Rd., Pinner, HA5 3YD, England, UK
Email: dchambrs@aol.com
Website: http://www.the-old-school.demon.co.uk/pla.htm
Founded: 1956
Members: 800
Contact: David Chambers, Hon.Chm.
Fee: £25
Fee: £40
Description: Individuals who collect or who are interested in books from an amateur or professional point of view, including collectors of rare books, fine books, single authors, reference books on special subjects, and individuals who collect books for the pleasure of reading and ownership. Encourages cooperation among book collectors. Sponsors Society of Private Printers, an informal group of owners of private presses who exchange ideas and printed specimens.
Publication title: Membership List
Second publication: Newsletter
Publication title: Newsletter and Exchange List
Meetings/Conventions: - annual meeting London UK

Probation Boards' Association
PBA

8/9 Grosvenor Pl., 4th Fl., London, SW1X 7SH, England, UK
Tel: 44 20 78087722
Fax: 44 207 8232553
Email: association@probationboards.co.uk
Website: http://www.probationboards.co.uk
Founded: 1982
Members: 435
Staff: 12
Contact: George Barrow, PR Officer and Head of Officer
Description: Chief, deputy chief, assistant chief probation officers and other top managers in the 58 probation services of England, Wales, Northern Ireland, Jersey and Isle of Man. Promotes and co-ordinates the work of the probation services of England and Wales.
Formerly: Association of Chief Officers of Probation

Processors' and Growers' Research Organisation

Great North Rd., Thornhaugh, Peterborough, PE8 6HJ, England, UK
Tel: 44 1780 782585
Fax: 44 1780 783993
Email: info@pgro.co.uk
Website: http://www.pgro.co.uk
Founded: 1944
Members: 4750
Staff: 16
Contact: G.P. Gent, Dir.
Description: Farmers, food processors, merchant seedsman, agrochemical companies, higher education institutes and research stations. Research, evaluation and advice on the growing, harvesting and usage of different types of peas and beans. This includes the

evaluation of new varieties, crop protection product and growing and harvesting techniques. Technical services are also provided, including seed and soil testing and instrument calibration.
Library Subject: agriculture
Library Type: not open to the public
Publication: Annual Report
Second publication: Journal

Producers Alliance for Cinema and Television
PACT

45 Mortimer St., London, W1W 8HJ, England, UK
Tel: 44 207 3316000
Fax: 44 207 3316700
Email: enquiries@pact.co.uk
Website: http://www.pact.co.uk
Founded: 1991
Members: 1000
Staff: 19
Contact: David Alan Mills, Info.Mgr.
Description: Represents the commercial interests of independent feature film, television, animation, and interactive media companies.
Publication: Magazine
Publication title: PACT. Advertisements.
Second publication: Directory
Publication title: PACT Directory of British Film & Television Producers

Production Engineering Association
PEA

c/o OTM Consulting Ltd.
44 Quarry St., Guildford, GU1 3XQ, England, UK
Tel: 44 1483 598000
Fax: 44 1483 598010
Email: shreekant.mehta@otmnet.com
Website: http://www.peajip.com
Founded: 1989
Members: 25
Contact: Shreekant Mehta, Sec.
Fee: £3200
Description: Companies concerned with all operations and equipment related to the production or injection of oil, water, gas from the reservoir to separation facilities. Identifies members' technology requirements and fosters a common view for the future of production technology. Promotes high industry standards.
Library Type: not open to the public

Production Engineering Research Association
PERA

PERA Innovation Park, Melton Mowbray, LE13 0PB, England, UK
Tel: 44 1664 501501
Fax: 44 1664 501554
Email: marketing@pera.com
Website: http://www.pera.com
Founded: 1946
Members: 1200
Staff: 300
Contact: Rachel Spencer
Description: Technical and management consultancy and training organisation.

Production Guild of Great Britain

c/o Pinewood Studios
Pinewood Rd., Iver Heath, SL0 0NH, England, UK
Tel: 44 1753 651767
Fax: 44 1753 652803
Email: lynne@productionguild.com
Website: http://www.productionguild.com
Founded: 1967
Members: 500
Staff: 2
Contact: Michael O'Sullivan, Pres.
Fee: £250
Membership Type: application
Description: Freelance film production accountants, freelance assistant production accountants, financial administrators in permanent employment and retired members. To promote, maintain and protect the highest standards of film production accounting, costing and financial administration and to safeguard the interests of the Guild and its members.
Formerly: Formed by Merger of, Guild of Film Production Executives
Publication: Membership Directory. Advertisements.
Meetings/Conventions: - annual convention

Production Managers Association

Ealing Studios, Ealing Green, London, W5 5EP, England, UK
Tel: 44 2087588699
Fax: 44 2087588647
Email: pma@pma.org.uk
Website: http://www.pma.org.uk
Founded: 1991
Members: 175
Staff: 2
Contact: Justin Johnson, Chair
Description: Professional organization representing over 175 production managers working in film, television and multimedia.
Publication: Magazine
Publication title: The Bottom Line. Advertisements.

Production Services Association

Centre Ct., 1301 Stratford Rd., Hall Green, Birmingham, B28 9HH, England, UK
Tel: 44 121 6937127
Fax: 44 121 6937100
Email: admin@psa.org.uk
Website: http://www.psa.org.uk
Founded: 1994
Members: 1100
Staff: 2
Contact: Bob Fox, Sec.
Description: Personnel and companies working in the production, design, touring, technical and support services in the live entertainment industry. Seeks to make representations to the government and EC Commission and other local national and overseas governmental bodies on legislation and other public matters and policies which affect the business or professional interests of its members.
Publication: Newsletter
Publication title: Backstage. Advertisements.
Meetings/Conventions: - annual trade show - Exhibits.

Professional Association of Alexander Teachers

2 Roshven Rd., Birmingham, B12 8DB, England, UK
Email: info@paat.org.uk
Website: http://www.paat.org.uk

Founded: 1987
Contact: J. Walker, Sec.
Description: Aims to promote the principles of the Alexander Technique as laid down in the books of F M Alexander, and to provide help and support for members. PAAT conducts a four-year training course in Birmingham for those wishing to become teachers of the Alexander Technique.
Publication: Pamphlets
Publication title: Pamphlets and brochures about the Alexander Technique

Professional Association of Nursery Nurses
PANN

c/o Professional Association Teachers
2 St. James' Ct., Friar Gate, Derby, DE1 1BT, England, UK
Tel: 44 1332 372337
Fax: 44 1332 290310
Email: pann@pat.org.uk
Website: http://www.pat.org.uk
Founded: 1982
Members: 5000
Staff: 6
Contact: Tricia Pritchard, Professional Officer
Description: Qualified and experienced child care practitioners within education, social services, the health service, the private sector (including nannies). Represents the interests of qualified and student nursery nurses, nannies, and other child care workers throughout the UK. Promotes professionalism at all times.
Publication title: All You Need to Know About Working as a Nanny
Second publication: Journal
Publication title: Professionalism in Practice. Advertisements.
Meetings/Conventions: - annual conference - Exhibits. Harrogate UK

Professional Association of Teachers - UK
PAT

2 St. James' Ct., Friar Gate, Derby, DE1 1BT, England, UK
Tel: 44 1332 372337
Fax: 44 1332 290310
Email: hq@pat.org.uk
Website: http://www.pat.org.uk
Founded: 1970
Members: 35000
Staff: 40
Contact: Mrs. Jean Gemmell, Gen.Sec.
Description: Teachers, lecturers and student teachers, nursery nurses and nannies and education support staff in all parts of the UK, from nursery to tertiary and in both maintained and independent sectors. To promote professional standards amongst teachers, support staff, and childcarers, emphasizing the need to give priority to the well-being of children and students; to further the advancement of education and childcare by initiating proposals for reform and by resisting any lowering of standards; to provide services to members and to negotiate salaries and conditions of service. No strike policy.
Publication: Journal
Publication title: Professionalism in Practice: the PAT Journal. Advertisements.
Meetings/Conventions: - annual conference - Exhibits. Harrogate UK

Professional Bodyguards Association

72 New Bond St., Mayfair, London, W1S 1RR, England, UK
Email: xsas@hotmail.com

Website: http://www.bodyguards-pba.com
Founded: 1985
Members: 1300
Contact: M.J. Tombs, Chmn.
Fee: £45
Membership Type: executive
Description: Represents bodyguards worldwide. All members must be trained up to PBA standards.
Library Subject: bodyguarding and surveillance
Library Type: reference

Professional Business and Technical Management

Warwick Corner, 42 Warwick Rd., Kenilworth, CV8 1HE, England, UK
Tel: 44 1926 855498
Fax: 44 1926 513100
Founded: 1983
Members: 500
Staff: 3
Contact: Prof. H.J. Manners, Pres.
Fee: £45
Membership Type: student, associate, fellow, companion
Description: Professional people in industry, commerce, computing, technology and associated management. Aims to equip members with knowledge, skill and experience in the combined disciplines of business and technical management through journals, courses, contact with other professional bodies and giving advice and information.

Professional Computing Association

PO Box 48, Royston, SG8 6JS, England, UK
Tel: 44 1763 262987
Fax: 44 1763 261907
Email: admin@pcauk.org
Founded: 1993
Members: 150
Staff: 2
Contact: Keith Warburton, Exec.Dir.
Fee: £250
Membership Type: corporate
Fee: £1250
Membership Type: individual
Description: Companies active in the UK personal computer business. To equally and fairly represent the interests of members and to promote the best practice within the computer industry via a code of practice, available free. Please send large SAE.
Formerly: Absorbed, Personal Computer Direct Marketers' Association
Publication: Newsletter
Publication title: Interface. Advertisements.
Meetings/Conventions: - semiannual conference - Exhibits.

Professional Lighting and Sound Association

38 St. Leonards Rd., Eastbourne, BN21 3UT, England, UK
Tel: 44 1323 410335
Fax: 44 1323 646905
Email: info@plasa.org
Website: http://www.plasa.org
Founded: 1977
Members: 460
Staff: 14
Contact: Anne Angel, Coord.
Fee: £450
Membership Type: international
Fee: £150

Membership Type: corparate
Description: Members are designers, manufacturers, suppliers and installers of sound, lighting and effects equipment for the entertainment and presentation industries. Aims to increase the professionalism of the entertainment technology industry world-wide.
Publication: Yearbook
Publication title: The Best of Entertainment Technology
Second publication: Magazine
Publication title: Lighting and Sound International. Advertisements.
Meetings/Conventions: PLASA Show Live at Earls Court - annual trade show - Exhibits. London UK

Professional Photographic Laboratories Association

29 Hempfield Rd., Littleport, Ely, CB6 1NW, England, UK
Tel: 44 1353 863255
Fax: 44 12353 863522
Email: pmauk@pmai.org
Website: http://pmai.org/sections/ppla.htm
Founded: 1984
Members: 190
Staff: 1
Contact: Malcolm Pyrah, Sec.
Fee: £25
Membership Type: ordinary, plus VAT starting membership
Description: Professional photographic imaging laboratories throughout the United Kingdom. Seeks to represent professional photographic processing laboratories exclusively. Committed to the highest standards of professionalism in laboratory work and therefore expects members to monitor carefully the standard of work carried out.
Library Subject: imaging issues
Library Type: reference
Publication: Newsletter
Publication title: PPLA Lablink. Advertisements.
Meetings/Conventions: - annual trade show - Exhibits.

Professional Plant Users Group

c/o Landscape Institute
6-8 Barnard Mews, London, SW11 1QU, England, UK
Tel: 44 20 73505200
Fax: 44 20 73505201
Founded: 1987
Members: 5
Contact: Tom La Dell, Chm.
Description: Landscape Institute; Institute of Leisure and Amenity Management; British Association of Landscape Industries; Institute of Horticulture; Arboricultural Association. Furthers the better use of plants in amenity landscapes, including plant selection, plant establishment and maintenance. Encourages research in all areas and informing members of constituent bodies through Plant User.
Publication title: Plant User

Progress Educational Trust

140 Gray's Inn Rd., London, WC1X 8AX, England, UK
Tel: 44 207 2787870
Fax: 44 207 2787862
Email: admin@progress.org.uk
Website: http://www.progress.org.uk
Founded: 1992
Members: 200
Staff: 1
Contact: Juliet Tizzard
Fee: £20

Membership Type: individual
Fee: £30
Membership Type: organization
Description: Promotes reproductive rights and supports pre-embryo research into human reproduction. Promotes the development of medical technology to eliminate infertility, miscarriage, and congenital handicap. Conducts educational activities.
Formerly: Progress Campaign for Research into Human Reproduction
Publication: Journal
Publication title: Progress in Reproduction
Meetings/Conventions: Progress Educational Trust Science Week Forum - annual conference - Exhibits.

Property Consultants Society

107a Tarrant St., Arundel, BN18 9DP, England, UK
Tel: 44 1903 883787
Fax: 44 1903 889590
Email: pes@propco.freeserve.co.uk
Website: http://www.propco.freeserve
Founded: 1954
Members: 650
Staff: 3
Contact: D.J. May, Sec.
Fee: £55
Membership Type: fellow
Fee: £45
Membership Type: associate
Description: Persons engaged in the property industry. Provides a central organization for persons engaged as consultants in the property business whether as principals or employees. Aims to advance members' interests and standing within the context of sound and professional advice.
Library Type: not open to the public
Publication: Newsletters. Advertisements.

Proprietary Association of Great Britain

Vernon House, Sicilian Ave., London, WC1A 2QH, England, UK
Tel: 44 207 2428331
Fax: 44 207 4057719
Email: pagb@pagb.org.uk
Website: http://www.pagb.org.uk/
Founded: 1919
Members: 70
Staff: 15
Contact: Sheila Kelly, Exec.Dir.
Description: Trade association representing manufacturers of over-the-counter (OTC) medicines, health care and food supplements. Promotes responsible consumers and aims to increase the size of the OTC market.
Library Type: not open to the public
Publication: Newsletter
Publication title: The Monitor
Second publication: Bulletin
Publication title: PAGB Bulletin
Meetings/Conventions: - monthly workshop

Proprietary Crematoria Association

3 Woodlands, Hove, BN3 6TJ, England, UK
Tel: 44 01273 562256
Founded: 1944
Members: 15
Contact: G.C. Scott

Description: Firms who are actively engaged in the operation of proprietary crematoria and cemetery undertakings. The administration of privately owned crematoria and cemeteries.

ProShare (United Kingdom)
Centurion House, 24 Monument St., London, EC3R 8AQ, England, UK
Tel: 44 207 2201730
Fax: 44 207 2201731
Email: diane.hay@proshare.org
Website: http://www.proshare.org
Founded: 1992
Staff: 15
Contact: Tony Hobman
Description: Promotes responsible share based investment, including employee share ownership, through education and research.
Publication: Magazine
Publication title: Dividend. Advertisements.

Prospect
75-79 York Rd., London, SE1 7AQ, England, UK
Tel: 44 20 79026600
Fax: 44 20 79026667
Email: enquiries@prospect.org.uk
Website: http://www.prospect.org.uk
Founded: 1919
Members: 105000
Staff: 151
Contact: Paul Noon, Gen.Sec.
Description: Professional, technical engineering and scientific grades in the Civil Service, other government bodies and private sector organisations - prospect members and branches are organised through professional sectors, such as agriculture, defence,. health and safety, environment and energy, with additional sector bases in Scotland, Liverpool, Bristol, and Birmingham. Concerned with the interests of members; to maintain and improve conditions of employment; to provide services for the benefit of members and personal assistance in time of need. Areas of representation include government departments and agencies, other public and private sector organizations such as CAA, British Energy, BNFL, AEA Technology, MLC, BAA, Unilever etc.
Formerly: Formed by Merger of, Engineers and Managers Association and Institution of Professionals, Managers and Specialists
Publication: Annual Report

Provincial Booksellers' Fairs Association
The Old Coach House, 16 Melbourn St., Royston, SG8 7BZ, England, UK
Tel: 44 1763 248400
Fax: 44 1763 248921
Email: info@pbfa.org
Website: http://www.pbfa.org
Founded: 1974
Members: 750
Staff: 3
Contact: Gina Dolan
Description: Antiquarian and second-hand booksellers. Organizes book fairs throughout the country, with the Hotel Russell Fair in London the focal point of the British book trade. Aims to promote interest in the collection of antiquarian and secondhand books.
Publication: Book

Publication title: Book Collecting: A Guide to Antiquarian and Secondhand Books
Publication title: Childhood Recollected: Early Children's Books from the Library of Marjorie Moon

Provision Trade Federation
17 Clerkenwell Green, London, EC1R 0DP, England, UK
Tel: 44 207 2532114
Fax: 44 207 6081645
Email: info@provtrade.co.uk
Website: http://www.provtrade.co.uk
Founded: 1887
Members: 154
Staff: 5
Contact: Mrs. C. Cheney, Dir.Gen.
Description: Manufacturers, traders, importers, exporters, distributors, and retailers involved in trading dairy products, chilled and processed meats, and canned foods in the UK. Represents, protects, and promotes the interests of members by negotiating with organizations and official bodies representing EU institutions, the UK government, trade associations, or local and regional authorities.
Formerly: UK Provision Trade Federation
Publication: Magazine
Publication title: Yearbook. Advertisements.

Psoriasis Association
7 Milton St., Northampton, NN2 7JG, England, UK
Tel: 44 1604 711129
Fax: 44 1604 792894
Website: http://wisdom.wellcome.ac.uk
Founded: 1968
Description: Provides up to date information and promotes self-help and support to people with psoriasis; works to raise standards of patient care and improves education about psoriasis with the public and healthcare professionals.

Psoriatric Arthropathy Alliance
PAA
PO Box 111, St. Albans, AL2 3JQ, England, UK
Tel: 44 870 703212
Fax: 44 870 703212
Email: jill.hewitt@naac.co.uk
Website: http://www.paalliance.org
Founded: 1993
Staff: 2
Contact: David Chandler, Dir.
Fee: £13
Membership Type: subscriber in the United Kingdom
Fee: £20
Membership Type: subscriber outside the United Kingdom
Description: Individuals with psoriatic arthritis and its associated skin disorder, psoriasis. Seeks to protect, serve, and respect the interests and rights of people who have or might become susceptible to psoriatic arthritis. Conducts educational programs to raise public awareness of psoriatic arthritis and related disorders; provides support and assistance to people with psoriatic arthritis and their families; sponsors advocacy programs benefiting members.
Publication title: Psoriatic Care Fact File
Publication title: Skin 'N' Bones Connection

PTO
1 Regent Pl., Rugby, CV21 2PJ, England, UK
Tel: 44 870 4435252
Fax: 44 870 4435160
Email: bacp@bacp.co.uk
Founded: 1970
Members: 820
Staff: 2
Contact: Gemma Peters, Div.Admin.
Fee: £35
Membership Type: individual
Fee: £35
Membership Type: organizational
Description: Counsellors in institutions of further and higher education. Aims to promote student counselling as an integral part of the educational process of institutions of Further and Higher Education.
Formerly: Association for University and College Counselling
Publication: Annual Report
Second publication: Newsletter. Advertisements.
Meetings/Conventions: Annual Training Conference - annual conference - Exhibits.

Public and Commercial Services Union
CPSA
160 Falcon Rd., London, SW11 2LN, England, UK
Tel: 44 20 79242727
Fax: 44 20 79241847
Email: pauld@pcs.org.uk
Website: http://www.pcs.org.uk
Members: 250000
Description: Clerical, secretarial, computer support, and communications grades in the civil service, certain fringe organizations and public sector areas. Protects and promotes the interests of its members, regulates their relations with the employing body, and improves their employment conditions.
Formerly: Civil and Public Services Association

Public Health Association
58 Langdale Rd., Manchester, M14 5PN, England, UK
Email: info@dukpha.org.uk
Founded: 1989
Members: 1000
Staff: 3
Contact: John Nicholson, Chm.
Description: Aims to promote public health, by bringing people together across UK, especially tackling inequalities.

Public Monuments and Sculpture Association
c/o Courtauld Institute of Art
Somerset House, Strand, London, WC2R 0RN, England, UK
Tel: 44 207 8482777
Fax: 44 207 8482410
Email: pmsa@pmsa.org.uk
Website: http://www.courtauld.ac.uk
Founded: 1991
Members: 275
Contact: Jo Darke, CEO
Fee: £20
Membership Type: ordinary
Fee: £25

Membership Type: family
Description: Aims to protect and promote the public monuments and sculpture dating from post-medieval to tomorrow.

Public Relations Consultants Association
PRCA
Willow House, Willow Pl., Victoria, London, SW1P 1JH, England, UK
Tel: 44 207 2336026
Fax: 44 207 8284797
Email: flora@prca.org.uk
Founded: 1969
Members: 180
Staff: 6
Contact: Flora Hamilton, Dir.Gen.
Description: Public relations consultants in England. Maintains professional standards in the field; promotes confidence in public relations consulting. Assists members with problems in financial management, industrial relations, and consulting practice, recruitment and training. Conducts research; compiles statistics. Bestows awards. Operates referral system.
Library Type: reference
Publication: Booklets
Second publication: Yearbook
Meetings/Conventions: - periodic conference

Publicity Club of London
112 St. Martins Ln., London, WC2N 4BD, England, UK
Tel: 44 20 2406005
Fax: 44 20 2408005
Email: sue@ashcommunications.com
Website: http://www.thepcl.co.uk
Founded: 1913
Members: 340
Contact: Sue Ash, Hon.Sec.
Fee: £54
Membership Type: standard
Description: Organizes three or four events a month that vary from attending operas to theatre events.

Publishers Association
29B Montague St., London, WC1B 5BH, England, UK
Tel: 44 20 76919191
Fax: 44 20 76919199
Email: mail@publishers.org.uk
Website: http://www.publishers.org.uk
Founded: 1896
Members: 200
Staff: 20
Description: Book, journal and electronic publishers. Promotes the publishing industry in the U.K. Provides industry information, market statistics, and notice of training opportunities.

Publishers Licensing Society
37-41 Gower St., London, WC1E 6HH, England, UK
Tel: 44 207 2997330
Fax: 44 207 2997780
Email: info@pls.org.uk
Website: http://www.pls.org.uk
Founded: 1981
Members: 1500

Staff: 4
Contact: Caroline Elmslie
Description: Book, magazine and journal publishers.
Publication title: PLS Plus
Second publication: Annual Report

Publishers Publicity Circle

65 Airedale Ave., London, W4 2NN, England, UK
Tel: 44 20 89941881
Email: ppc-@lineone.net
Website: http://www.publisherspublicitycircle.co.uk
Founded: 1956
Members: 300
Contact: Heather White
Fee: £70
Description: People involved in book publicity at all levels in both publishing houses and independent PR companies. Monthly meetings provide a forum for press journalists, television and radio researchers and producers to meet publicists. The Circle enables publicists to meet and share information.
Publication: Directory
Publication title: Directory of Members
Second publication: Newsletter

Pullet Hatcheries Association

Second Fl., 89 Charter House St., London, EC1M 6HR, England, UK
Tel: 44 2076083760
Fax: 44 2076083860
Email: british.edd.industry@farmline.com
Members: 8
Description: Promotes the more efficient production, distribution and sale of layer strain hatching eggs and chicks.

Pump Distributors Association
PDA

c/o Ian Castle, Dir.
PO Box 993, Pewsey, SN9 5ZA, England, UK
Tel: 44 1474 815750
Fax: 44 1474 815750
Email: iancastle@pda-uk.com
Website: http://www.pumpmasters.co.uk/pda
Founded: 1985
Members: 35
Staff: 1
Contact: Ian Castle, Dir.
Description: Pump distributors in the United Kingdom. Aims to be the representative body of the pump distributive industry of the UK and by the setting and maintaining of proper standards for the professional conduct of its members to thereby protect and further enhance their reputation and interests.
Publication: Handbook
Meetings/Conventions: - annual meeting

Puppet Centre Trust

The Puppet Centre, BAC, Lavender Hill, London, SW11 5TN, England, UK
Tel: 44 20 72285335
Email: pct@puppetcentre.demon.co.uk
Website: http://www.puppetcentre.com
Founded: 1974
Staff: 1
Description: Puppeteers, puppetry enthusiasts, teachers, students, bookers and funders of puppetry, arts boards and arts councils. Aims to further the arts of puppetry and animation, to service the needs of anyone involved in professional, amateur and educational puppetry. To evolve a more professional and scientific base for the development of the art form in partnership with funding bodies, community groups, local authorities, arts organizations and educational establishments.
Library Subject: Puppetry, animation
Library Type: open to the public
Publication title: Education Pack - Alive 'an Kickin'
Meetings/Conventions: workshop - Exhibits.

Quaker Peace and Social Witness
QPS

Friends House, 173-177 Euston Rd., London, NW1 2BJ, England, UK
Tel: 44 20 76631048
Fax: 44 20 76631049
Email: lizc@quaker.org.uk
Website: http://www.quaker.org.uk/peace/index.html
Founded: 1978
Staff: 30
Contact: Linda Fielding, Gen.Sec.
Description: The international department of the Religious Society of Friends of Britian. Primary aim is to build international peace and reduce violence. Also tries to advance social and economic change and reduce poverty and injustice in the world. Supports long term programmes with experienced representatives in working on the tools of reconciliation at all levels, including the victims of wars or violence. Helps reconciliation work in Africa, Asia, the Middle East and Europe. Gives training in peacemaking skills, places workers with local service agencies and supports work in Britian which addresses the causes of economic injustice and violence.
Formerly: Formed by Merger of, Friends Peace and International Relations Council
Publication: Report
Publication title: Journal Letters
Second publication: Newsletter
Publication title: Opportunities for Action
Meetings/Conventions: - annual conference

Qualifications and Curriculum Authority

83 Picadilly, London, W1J 8QA, England, UK
Tel: 44 207 5095555
Fax: 44 20 75096666
Email: info@qca.org.uk
Website: http://www.qca.org.uk
Founded: 1993
Members: 15
Staff: 200
Description: Teachers, educationalists and industrialists with expertise, experience and a direct interest in education. Keeps under review all aspects of the curriculum for maintained schools in England and all aspects of school examinations and assessment, and advises the Secretary of State on these curriculum examinations and assessment matters. Publishes and disseminates information relating to the curriculum, examinations and assessment. Responsible for making arrangements for school-based assessments.
Formerly: School Curriculum and Assesment Authority
Publication: Newsletter
Publication title: Inform

Quality Scheme for Ready Mixed Concrete
QSRMC

3 High St., Hampton, Twickenham, TW12 2SQ, England, UK
Tel: 44 208 9410273
Fax: 44 208 9794558
Email: qsrmc@qsrmc.co.uk
Founded: 1984
Staff: 19
Contact: C.A. Head, Sec.
Description: Works to: provide a nationally accredited product conformity certification scheme for supply and production of ready mixed concrete; establish and enforce prescribed standards for the industry; promote the development of new standards and specifications.
Publication title: QSRMC Directory of Registered Companies and Certificated Plants
Publication title: QSRMC Quality and Product Conformity Regulations

Quarry Products Association
QPA

156 Buckingham Palace Rd., London, SW1W 9TR, England, UK
Tel: 44 20 77308194
Fax: 44 20 77304355
Email: info@qpa.org
Website: http://www.qpa.org
Founded: 1997
Members: 130
Staff: 20
Contact: Simon van der Byl, Dir.Gen.
Description: Trade association for the aggregates, asphalt, surfacing, ready-mixed concrete, silica sand, and mortar industries. Represents 90% of crushed rock and sand and gravel production in the UK.
Formerly: British Ready Mixed Concrete Association

Quaternary Research Association
QRA

c/o Prof. David Keen
Department of Geography, Coventry University, Priory St., Coventry, CV1 5FB, England, UK
Email: gex028@coventry.ac.uk
Website: http://qra.org.uk
Founded: 1964
Contact: Prof. D.H. Keen, Pres.
Description: Archaeologists, botanists, civil engineers, geographers, geologists, soil scientists, zoologists and others interested in the problems of the Quaternary. Promotes the study of the Quaternary period of time.

Quekett Microscopical Club

c/o Natural History Museum
Cromwell Rd., London, SW7 5BD, England, UK
Email: tonysd@cix.co.uk
Website: http://www.nhm.ac.uk/hosted_sites/quekett
Founded: 1865
Members: 450
Contact: Mr. P.M. Greaves, Hon.Sec.
Fee: £28
Membership Type: ordinary
Fee: £11
Membership Type: junior

Description: Encourages the study of every branch of microscopical science.
Library Subject: microscopy
Library Type: reference

Quilters' Guild of the British Isles

Rm. 190, Dean Clough, Halifax, HX3 5AX, England, UK
Tel: 44 1422 347669
Fax: 44 1422 345017
Email: administrafor@qghalifax.org.uk
Website: http://www.quiltersguild.org.uk
Founded: 1979
Members: 7000
Staff: 8
Contact: Jane Fellows, Admin.
Fee: £26
Membership Type: in U.K.
Fee: £30
Membership Type: in Europe
Description: Quilters with varying experience and skills. Collectors, traders, teachers. Promotes the art, understanding, appreciation, technique and heritage of patchwork, quilting and applique.
Library Subject: patchwork, quilting, applique, embroidery
Library Type: open to the public
Publication title: Quilt Treasures
Second publication: Magazine
Publication title: The Quilter. Advertisements.
Meetings/Conventions: - annual general assembly - Exhibits.

Quit

Ground Fl., 211 Old St., London, EC1V 9NR, England, UK
Tel: 44 207 2511551
Fax: 44 207 2511661
Email: info@quit.org.uk
Website: http://www.quit.org.uk
Founded: 1926
Staff: 170
Contact: Steve Crone
Description: Offers information, advice and support to people who want to stop smoking.
Publication: Brochures

Radio, Electrical and Television Retailers' Association

RETRA House, St. John's Ter., 1 Ampthill St., Bedford, MK42 9EY, England, UK
Tel: 44 1234 269110
Fax: 44 1234 269609
Email: retra@retra.co.uk
Website: http://www.retra.co.uk
Founded: 1942
Members: 1500
Staff: 8
Contact: Mr. F.F. Round, Chief Exec.
Description: Independent and multiple electrical retailers, together with Associate members (47). In addition to representing the views of its members, RETRA provides a host of time and cost saving services including free legal and business advice, business and consumer credit stationery, point of sale material, extended warranty insurance and subsidies on security equipment, shop insurance, workwear and credit referencing, discounts with HSBC, Barclaycard; operates Code of Practice; conducts useful surveys.
Publication: Magazine
Publication title: Alert magazine, monthly, free to all members,

circulated also to Associate members, Trade Press, Broadcasters, European Counterpart organisations, I. Advertisements.
Second publication: Directory
Meetings/Conventions: - annual conference

Radioactive Waste Management Advisory Committee

Zone 4/F4, Ashdown House, 123 Victoria St., London, SWE1 6DE, England, UK
Tel: 44 20 79446267
Fax: 44 20 79446319
Email: robert.jackson@defra.gsi.gov.uk
Website: http://www.defra.gov.uk/rwmac
Founded: 1978
Members: 20
Staff: 4
Contact: Dr. Robert L. Jackson, Sec.
Fee: £162
Description: Members appointed by the Secretary of State for the Environment, Food and Rural Affairs. Advises the Ministers in the Department for Environment Food and Rural Affairs, the Scottish Executive and the National Assembly for Wales on technical and environmental implications of major issues concerning the development and implementation of an overall policy for all aspects of the management of civil radioactive waste, including research and development, and on any other matters.
Publication: Report
Publication title: Topic Report
Second publication: Annual Report
Meetings/Conventions: Plenary Committee Meeting meeting

Radionic Association
RA

Baerlein House, Goose Green, Deddington, Banbury, OX15 0SZ, England, UK
Tel: 44 1869 338852
Fax: 44 1869 338852
Email: secretary@radionic.co.uk
Website: http://www.radionic.co.uk
Founded: 1943
Members: 501
Staff: 2
Contact: Penelope Harris, Sec.
Fee: £20
Membership Type: voting associateship
Description: Individuals who have trained in radionics and are qualified to practice professionally and laymen who are interested in radionics and wish to support the association. (Radionics is described as a method of healing at a distance through the medium of a specially designed instrument using the faculty of extra-sensory perception.) Main objectives of the association are to promote knowledge and understanding of radionics and to maintain the highest standards of competence and conduct among its practicing members. Maintains School of Radionics which provides professional training.
Library Subject: medical
Library Type: reference
Publication: Journal
Publication title: Radionic Journal. Advertisements.
Second publication: Monograph
Meetings/Conventions: - annual meeting

Railway Canal Historical Society

3 West Court, West St., Oxford, OX2 0NP, England, UK
Email: ms@bodley.ox.ac.uk
Website: http://www.bodley.ox.ac.uk/external/rchs/
Founded: 1956
Members: 780
Contact: Matthew Searle, Hon. Sec.
Description: Unites those interested in the history of transport, with particular reference to British railways and waterways. Promotes historical research and raises the standards of published history.

Railway Correspondence and Travel Society
RCTS

365 Old Bath Rd., Cheltenham, GL53 9AH, England, UK
Tel: 44 1242 523917
Email: peter.littlecote@freeserve.co.uk
Website: http://www.rcts.org.uk
Founded: 1928
Members: 3500
Contact: Peter Davies, Asst.Treas.
Fee: £18
Library Subject: railways
Library Type: not open to the public
Publication: Journal
Publication title: Railway Observer. Advertisements.

Railway Development Society

207 The Colourworks, 2 Abbot St., London, E8 3DP, England, UK
Tel: 44 207 2495533
Fax: 44 207 2546777
Email: info@railfuture.org.uk
Website: http://www.railfuture.org.uk
Founded: 1978
Members: 3500
Staff: 5
Contact: Alix Stredwick
Fee: £15
Description: Individuals, rail users' groups, local authorities, companies interested in the objectives of the Society. Aims to encourage development of a modern rail system fit for the next century, as a more environmentally friendly means of transport. To maintain intact the existing system, fight closures, encourage re-openings/opening of new lines and stations where justified. Fifteen branches cover the UK.
Library Type: not open to the public
Publication title: A-Z of Rail Re-openings (4th edition)
Second publication: Magazine
Publication title: Railwatch. Advertisements.
Meetings/Conventions: - annual conference - Exhibits.

Railway Industry Association
RIA

22 Headfort Pl., London, SW1X 7RY, England, UK
Tel: 44 207 2010777
Fax: 44 207 2355777
Email: ria@riagb.org.uk
Website: http://www.riagb.org.uk
Founded: 1875
Members: 130
Staff: 10
Contact: Jeremy Candfield, Dir.Gen.

Description: Works to supply the world's railways with equipment, services and consultancy. Promotes use and development of railroads.
Publication: Directory
Publication title: Members & Products

RAPRA Technology
Shawbury, Shrewsbury, SY4 4NR, England, UK
Tel: 44 1939 250383
Fax: 44 1939 251118
Email: info@rapra.net
Website: http://www.rapra.net
Founded: 1919
Members: 190
Staff: 150
Contact: Andrew Ward, CEO
Description: Provides the rubber and plastics industry with technology, information, and consultancy on all aspects of rubber and plastics. Operates extensive processing, analytical, and testing laboratory facilities.
Library Subject: rubber, plastics, adhesives, polymer composites
Library Type: reference
Formerly: Research Association of British Rubber Manufacturers
Publication title: Adhesives Abstracts
Second publication: Journal
Publication title: Cellular Polymers

Rating Surveyors' Association
c/o Lambeth Smith Hampton
79 Mosley St., Manchester, M2 3LQ, England, UK
Tel: 44 161 2286411
Fax: 44 161 2287354
Email: gbuckley@lsh.co.uk
Website: http://www.rsarating.mixed.org
Founded: 1909
Members: 383
Contact: Gareth Buckley
Description: Persons practising or employed as rating surveyors. To uphold and improve the status of rating surveyors, to regulate the customs and usages of the profession; to encourage harmonious action between members; to discuss matters or questions in connection with rating.

Ray Society
RAYS
Natural History Museum, Cromwell Rd., London, SW7 5BD, England, UK
Tel: 44 20 79425532
Fax: 44 20 79425433
Email: nje@nhm.ac.uk
Founded: 1844
Members: 350
Contact: Dr. N.J. Evans, Hon.Sec.
Fee: £6
Membership Type: individual
Description: Individuals from 20 countries interested in natural history. Prints and promotes books and monographs on zoology and botany, with special but not exclusive relevance to British flora and fauna.
Publication: Pamphlet
Publication title: Annual Report of the Council of the Ray Society

Second publication: Books
Meetings/Conventions: - semiannual executive committee meeting London UK

Raynaud's and Scleroderma Association
RSAT
112 Crewe Rd., Alsager, Cheshire, ST7 2JA, England, UK
Tel: 44 1270 872776
Fax: 44 1270 883556
Email: info@raynauds.org.uk
Website: http://www.raynauds.demon.co.uk
Founded: 1982
Members: 8000
Staff: 4
Contact: Anne H. Mawdsley, Dir.
Fee: £6
Membership Type: in the United Kingdom
Fee: £15
Membership Type: outside the United Kingdom
Description: Individuals afflicted with Raynaud's Disease or scleroderma; concerned medical professionals. Raynaud's Disease is marked by interruption of blood flow to the extremities, primarily the toes and fingers but can include the ears and nose, due to spasmodic contraction of small blood vessels; in severe cases this phenomenon is often noted in individual suffering from scleroderma, which affects the blood vessels, immune system and connective tissue. Encourages better communication among doctors and patients and provides mutual support among those with the condition. Strives to heighten public awareness on Raynaud's Disease and scleroderma. Conducts fundraising activities to help finance research.
Formerly: Raynaud's Association Trust
Publication: Newsletter
Publication title: Raynaud's Association Newsletter. Advertisements.
Second publication: Books
Meetings/Conventions: - annual conference - Exhibits.

REACH: Association for Children with Hand or Arm Deficiency
PO Box 54, Helston, Cornwall, TR13 8WD, England, UK
Tel: 44 845 1306225
Fax: 44 872 262098
Email: reach@reach.org.uk
Website: http://www.reach.org.uk
Founded: 1978
Members: 1200
Staff: 1
Contact: Sue Stokes, Coor.
Fee: £20
Membership Type: full
Fee: £20
Membership Type: associate
Description: Aims to offer support to families of children with upper limb deficiency.

Records Management Society of Great Britain
Woodside, Coleheath Bottom, Speen, Princes Risborough, HP27 0SZ, England, UK
Tel: 44 1494 488599
Fax: 44 1494 488590
Email: info@rms-gb.org.uk
Website: http://www.rms-gb.org.uk
Founded: 1983
Members: 560

Staff: 1
Contact: Mrs. Jude Awdry, Admin.Sec.
Fee: £12
Membership Type: student
Fee: £56
Membership Type: individual
Publication: Journal
Publication title: Bulletin. Advertisements.
Publication title: Society Newsletter
Meetings/Conventions: - annual conference - Exhibits.

Recreation Managers Association of Great Britian

PO Box 166, Rawmarsh, Rotherham, S62 7QZ, England, UK
Tel: 44 1709 522463
Fax: 44 1709 523001
Email: mel@rmagb.freeserve.co.uk
Website: http://www.rma-of-gb.org
Founded: 1956
Members: 900
Staff: 1
Contact: M.F. Johnson, Exec.Ofc.
Fee: £95
Membership Type: corporate
Description: Recreation or club managers of large industrial sports clubs, leisure centre, health clubs. Covers the organization of a club and planning activities, office management, licensing and bar controls, catering, motivation and management style, financial systems and budgeting.
Publication: Brochure
Publication title: Conference
Second publication: Magazine
Publication title: Leisure Opportunities
Meetings/Conventions: - annual conference - Exhibits.

Recruitment and Employment Confederation

36-38 Mortimer St., London, W1W 7RG, England, UK
Tel: 44 20 74623260
Fax: 44 20 72552878
Email: info@rec.uk.com
Website: http://www.rec.uk.com
Founded: 1963
Members: 14000
Staff: 45
Contact: Tim Nicholson, Ch.Exec.
Description: Promotes the recruitment industry in Britain by supplying membership services, legal advice, education and training; represents members' interests before parliament and in Europe.
Formerly: Formed by Merger of, Institute of Employment Consultants and Federation of Recruitment and Employment Services
Publication: Journal
Publication title: Recruitment Matters. Advertisements.
Meetings/Conventions: - annual international conference

Red Poll Cattle Society

52 Border Cot Ln., Wickham Market, Woodbridge, IP13 0EZ, England, UK
Tel: 44 1728 747230
Fax: 44 1728 748226
Email: secretary@redpoll.co.uk
Website: http://www.redpoll.org
Founded: 1877
Members: 212
Staff: 1
Contact: Mrs. T.J. Booker, Sec.

Fee: £20
Membership Type: registering
Fee: £10
Membership Type: associate
Description: Promotes the Red Poll breed of cattle.
Library Subject: cattle
Library Type: reference
Publication: Book
Publication title: Herd Book

Refined Sugar Association

Forum House, 15-18 Lime St., London, EC3M 7AQ, England, UK
Tel: 44 207 6261745
Fax: 44 207 2833831
Email: moond@sugar-assoc.co.uk
Founded: 1891
Members: 115
Contact: D.G. Moon
Fee: £500
Description: Members are active traders in white sugar. Provides for the proper conduct of the international white sugar trade; provides contract rules and arbitration services and looks after the interests of members in the white sugar trade.
Library Subject: rules & regulations for the white sugar trade, price on application
Library Type: reference
Publication title: The Rules and Regulations
Second publication: Brochure

Refractory Users Federation

Docklands Business Centre, 10-16 Tiller Rd., London, E14 8PXT, England, UK
Tel: 44 207 3455122
Fax: 44 207 3455722
Founded: 1947
Members: 19
Contact: D. Randell
Description: Companies in the refractory construction and repair industry. Brings together members of the Refractory Users Federation and the British Industrial Furnace Constructions Association to enable them to negotiate wages and conditions of employment with the Trade Unions representing the industry.
Publication title: National Agreements

Regional Studies Association
RSA

PO Box 2058, Seaford, BN25 4QU, England, UK
Tel: 44 1323 899698
Fax: 44 1323 899798
Email: rsa@mailbox.ulcc.ac.uk
Website: http://www.regional-studies-assoc.ac.uk
Founded: 1965
Members: 800
Staff: 3
Contact: Sally Hardy, Ch.Exec.
Fee: £63
Membership Type: individual
Fee: £130
Membership Type: corporate
Description: Individuals (550) and corporate groups (250) such as government departments, ministries, county councils, local authorities, research bodies, educational institutions, consultants' offices, geographers, economists, town planners, architects, and engineers

interested in regional planning. Promotes education and research in the field of regional planning and development internationally; provides a forum for exchange of ideas and information; disseminates research results. Maintains European Regional Research Network which produces reports, directories, surveys, and lists of contact addresses in Europe; promotes regional studies and research at European rather than national levels; develops contact among teachers and researchers throughout Europe.
Publication title: Annual Report
Publication title: European Urban and Regional Research Directory
Meetings/Conventions: - annual conference - Exhibits.

Registered Nursing Home Association
15 Highfield Rd., Edgbastion, Birmingham, B15 3DU, England, UK
Tel: 44 121 4542511
Fax: 44 121 4540932
Email: rnhaho@aol.com
Website: http://www.rnha.co.uk
Founded: 1968
Members: 1600
Staff: 8
Contact: F.E. Ursell, CEO
Fee: £12
Membership Type: direct
Description: Nursing Home Owners.
Publication: Journal
Publication title: Nursing Home News. Advertisements.
Second publication: Book
Publication title: RNHA Reference Book. Advertisements.
Meetings/Conventions: - annual conference - Exhibits.

Relate
Herbert Gray College, Little Church St., Rugby, CV21 3AP, England, UK
Tel: 44 1788 573241
Fax: 44 1788 535007
Email: enquires@relate.org.uk
Website: http://www.relate.org.uk
Founded: 1938
Members: 5500
Staff: 200
Contact: Angela Sibson, Chief Executive
Description: Provides relationship counselling and sex therapy services to couples in England, Wales, and Northern Ireland.
Publication: Newsletter
Publication title: Relate News. Advertisements.
Meetings/Conventions: - annual meeting

Relatives and Residents Association
5 Tavistock Place, London, WC1H 9SN, England, UK
Tel: 44 20 76924302
Fax: 44 20 79166093
Email: relres@totalise.co.uk
Founded: 1992
Members: 2500
Staff: 12
Contact: Sue Adams, Ch.Exec.
Fee: £12
Membership Type: individual
Fee: £50
Membership Type: corporate
Description: Provides advice and support to relatives and friends of older people in residential care homes, nursing homes and long stay

hospitals. Also offers training to homes in order to promote good practice through involvement of relatives.
Publication: Newsletter
Publication title: The Relatives & Residents Association
Meetings/Conventions: - annual conference

Remote Sensing and Photogrammetry Society
c/o School of Geography, University of Nottingham, University Park, Nottingham, NG7 2RD, England, UK
Tel: 44 115 9515435
Fax: 44 115 9515249
Email: rspsoc@nottingham.ac.uk
Website: http://www.rspsoc.org
Founded: 2001
Members: 1200
Staff: 2
Contact: Dr. J. Finch, Hon.Gen.Sec.
Fee: £40
Membership Type: Ordinary
Description: Seeks to promote the knowledge and understanding of remote sensing and photogrammetry. workshops. workshops.
Library Subject: remote sensing, photogrammetry
Library Type: reference
Formerly: Remote Sensing Society
Publication: Journal
Publication title: International Journal of Remote Sensing. Advertisements.
Second publication: Journal
Publication title: The Photogrammetric Record
Meetings/Conventions: - annual conference - Exhibits. Nottingham UK

Renal Association
Triangle House, Unit 2, Broomhill Rd., London, SW18 4XH, England, UK
Tel: 44 208 8752413
Fax: 44 208 8752434
Email: renal@immunology.org
Website: http://www.renal.org/
Contact: Prof. Andy Rees, Pres.
Description: Works as the professional body for nephrologists in the United Kingdom; promotes development of renal services within the U.K, including prevention and treatment of renal disorders.
Meetings/Conventions: - annual meeting

Research and Development Society
20 Queensberry Pl., London, SW7 2DZ, England, UK
Tel: 44 207 5818333
Fax: 44 207 8239409
Email: rdsoc@iob.org
Website: http://www.rdsoc.org
Founded: 1962
Members: 450
Staff: 1
Contact: Amy Scales, Admin.Sec.
Fee: £60
Membership Type: individual
Fee: £300
Membership Type: corporate
Description: Senior R&D personnel in industry, public sector and academic, private R&D consultants. Aims to promote and advance the

better understanding of R&D and associated activities and to assist those concerned with its organization and management.
Publication: Newsletter
Publication title: The R & D Society Newsletter
Meetings/Conventions: - monthly lecture

Re-Solv, the Society for the Prevention of Solvent and Volatile Substance Abuse
RS

30A High St., Stone, ST15 8AW, England, UK
Tel: 44 1785 817885
Fax: 44 1785 813205
Email: information@re-solv.org
Website: http://www.re-solv.org
Founded: 1984
Members: 300
Staff: 10
Contact: Barrie Liss, Chm.
Fee: £150
Membership Type: Corporate
Fee: £75
Membership Type: Public
Description: Promotes increased awareness on the part of parents, local authorities, retailers, and law enforcement officials of the problem of the sniffing of solvents and volatile substances. Acts as an information clearinghouse on solvent abuse. Liaises with other agencies, the Home Office, and other government bodies in the dissemination of information. Supports legislation that seeks to control solvent abuse. Provides videos and other materials for use in primary and secondary schools and by parents, teachers, doctors, social workers, retailers, and law enforcement personnel. doctors, social workers, retailers, and law enforcement personnel. doctors, social workers, retailers, and law enforcement personnel.
Library Subject: solvent and volatile substance abuse
Library Type: reference
Publication: Video
Publication title: The Adolescent Epidemic
Second publication: Video
Publication title: Chicken!
Meetings/Conventions: - periodic lecture

Restaurant Association

Queen's House, 55-56 Lincoln's Inn Fields, London, WC2A 3BH, England, UK
Tel: 44 207 4047744
Fax: 44 207 4047799
Email: feedback@ragb.co.uk
Website: http://www.ragb.co.uk
Founded: 1967
Members: 2500
Staff: 6
Contact: Ian McKerracher, Chief Exec.
Fee: £195
Membership Type: Restaurant
Fee: £3000
Membership Type: Patron Supplier
Description: Trade Association for independently owned and operated restaurants throughout the UK. Protects the interests and advances the views and opinions of independent and group restaurateurs.
Formerly: Restaurateurs Association of Great Britain
Publication: Newsletter

Publication title: Digest
Second publication: Magazine
Publication title: Dine-Out. Advertisements.

Restricted Growth Association

PO Box 4744, Dorchester, DT2 9FA, England, UK
Tel: 44 1308 898445
Email: rga1@talk21.com
Website: http://www.rgaonline.org.uk
Founded: 1970
Members: 650
Staff: 2
Contact: Honor Rawlings
Fee: £13
Membership Type: full and associate in the United Kingdom
Fee: £16
Membership Type: family and joint in the United Kingdom
Description: Open to persons with restricted growth, families with a child with restricted growth, health professionals, and other interested persons. Aims to help reduce the distress and disadvantages of persons of restricted growth by trying to reduce social barriers, improve the quality of life and enhance their role in society. Offers counselling training, family support, medical information and other practical help. Regional co-ordinators.
Library Subject: Restricted growth
Library Type: not open to the public
Publication: Magazine
Publication title: RGA Information Magazine. Advertisements.
Second publication: Newsletter
Publication title: RGA News. Advertisements.
Meetings/Conventions: - annual convention - Exhibits.

Retail Confectioners and Tobacconists Association

Unit 4 Manor Place, Manor Way, Borehamwood, WD6 5WG, England, UK
Tel: 44 181 2076775
Fax: 44 181 2076484
Founded: 1976
Members: 1000
Staff: 8
Contact: Paul Rambridge, Chm.
Fee: £35
Description: Deals mainly in trade affairs matters within the tobacco and confectionery industries. Primary service is that of a retail buying group with central distribution facilities (within M25 area).
Publication title: Link Buyers Guide

Retail Motor Industry Federation
RMI

201 Great Portland St., London, W1W 5AB, England, UK
Tel: 44 207 5809122
Fax: 44 207 5806376
Email: suerobinson@rmif.co.uk
Founded: 1913
Members: 10000
Contact: Sue Robinson, Media Dir.
Description: Serves and represents businesses concerned with the provision of motor industry products and services and aims to assist, support and promote members in providing the highest standards of operation for the mutual benefit of themselves and their customers.
Publication: Magazine
Publication title: Forecourt
Second publication: Magazine
Publication title: RM Eye

Retail Trade Centre
NRTC

Adam House, Waterworks Rd., Worcester, WR1 1EZ, England, UK
Tel: 44 1905 612733
Fax: 44 1905 21501
Email: alliance@indretailer.co.uk
Website: http://www.indretailer.co.uk/Pages/rtc.html
Founded: 1983
Members: 92
Staff: 4
Contact: Beryl Davis, Chief Exec.
Fee: £2500
Membership Type: manufacturers & wholesalers
Description: Works in conjunction with Alliance of Independent Retailers. Seeks to: promote greater understanding and cooperation between independent retailers and their customers; review and introduce new services; improve communications among members; support the independent retailers.
Publication: Magazine
Publication title: Hotelier
Second publication: Magazine
Publication title: Independent Retailer. Advertisements.
Meetings/Conventions: - annual conference - Exhibits.

Rethink

30 Tabernacle St., London, EC2A 4DD, England, UK
Tel: 44 20 73309100
Fax: 44 20 73309102
Email: info@rethink.org
Website: http://www.rethink.org
Founded: 1972
Members: 7102
Staff: 1200
Contact: Cliff Prior, Chief Exec.
Fee: £12
Membership Type: in U.K.
Fee: £22
Membership Type: outside of U.K.
Description: Exists to improve the lives of everyone affected by schizophrenia and other severe mental illnesses by providing quality support, services, and information and by influencing local, regional, and national policies.
Formerly: National Schizophrenia Fellowship
Publication: Video
Publication title: A Meeting Of Minds - A Positive Response To Mental Disorder
Second publication: Report
Publication title: Cognitive Therapy
Meetings/Conventions: - annual meeting London UK

Retinoblastoma Society
RS

St. Bartholomew's Hospital, London, EC1A 7BE, England, UK
Tel: 44 207 6003309
Fax: 44 207 6008579
Email: rbinfo@rbsociety.org.uk
Website: http://www.rbsociety.org.uk
Founded: 1986
Members: 750
Staff: 2
Contact: Sonia Home, Natl.Coord.
Description: Children with retinoblastoma (eye cancer) and their families; other interested individuals. Seeks to improve the quality of life of people with eye cancer; promotes advancement in the prevention, diagnosis, and treatment of retinoblastoma. Provides support for people with retinoblastoma and their families; promotes awareness with health professionals; fundraising activities to support eye cancer research.
Publication: Newsletter
Publication title: ORBS. Advertisements.
Meetings/Conventions: - annual meeting

Retread Manufacturers' Association

2nd Fl., Federation House, Station Road, Stoke-On-Trent, ST4 2TJ, England, UK
Tel: 44 1782 417777
Fax: 44 1782 417766
Email: retreads@ukonline.co.uk
Website: http://www.greentyres.com
Founded: 1946
Members: 60
Staff: 3
Contact: S. Ikin
Fee: £2000
Membership Type: level 1
Fee: £1000
Membership Type: level 2
Description: Consists of UK tyre retreaders, suppliers to the industry ie machinery, equipment materials and casings. Processing members retread all categories of tyre from car to heavy commercial, earthmover, tractor etc. Represents the interests of the independent retreader and associated businesses and is the national body, recognised by government, the British Standards Institution, tyre manufacturers, press, and other trade associations.
Publication title: Directory of Membership

Returned Volunteer Action
RVA

1 Amwell St., London, EC1R 1TH, England, UK
Tel: 44 20 72780804
Fax: 44 20 72787019
Email: retvolact@lineone.net
Founded: 1966
Members: 300
Staff: 1
Contact: John Sayers
Fee: £7
Membership Type: ordinary
Description: Individuals who have completed a voluntary tour of services with an international development or relief organization. Promotes improved effectiveness among international development programs. Conducts research and educational programs to assist development programs in becoming more appropriate to local needs and more effective in their implementation. Sponsors training programs for prospective international development volunteers; serves as a clearinghouse on voluntary opportunities in international development; maintains speakers' bureau.
Library Subject: international development, voluntarism
Library Type: by appointment only
Publication: Newsletter
Publication title: Development Action. Advertisements.

Reunite - International Child Abduction Centre

PO Box 24875, London, E1 6FR, England, UK
Tel: 44 116 2555345
Email: reunite@dircon.co.uk

Website: http://www.reunite.org
Founded: 1986
Staff: 5
Contact: Denise Carter, Dir.
Description: Offers support and information on the issue of child abduction. Advises lawyers and other interested professionals working in the area of child abduction. Provides a telephone advice line. Liaises with government organizations and similar associations. Conducts research on the legal issues of child custody and abduction.
Publication title: Child Abduction Prevention Pack
Second publication: Newsletter
Meetings/Conventions: - annual conference

Reuter Foundation

85 Fleet St., London, EC4P 4AJ, England, UK
Tel: 44 20 7542705
Fax: 44 20 75428599
Email: foundation@reuters.com
Website: http://www.foundation.reuters.com
Founded: 1982
Staff: 13
Contact: Rosemary Martin, Dir.
Description: Promotes professional development of journalists worldwide. Conducts study and training programs for journalists from the developing world and from central and eastern Europe; sponsors research and educational programs and schools and universities; provides financial and technical support for charitable and cultural organizations. New service launched in 1997 AlertNet - online rapid news and communications service for international disaster relief organizations.
Publication: Newsletter
Publication title: ReutersLink

Rice Association

21 Arlington St., London, SW1A 1RN, England, UK
Tel: 44 207 4932521
Fax: 44 207 4936785
Email: damiantesta@nabim.org.uk
Website: http://www.riceassociation.org.uk/
Description: Promotes interests of members in all areas pertaining to the import, preparation, processing, packaging, marketing and use of rice. Promotes public awareness and consumption of all types of rice in the United Kingdom.

Richard Jefferies Society
RJS

Eidsvoll, Bedwells Heath, Boars Hill, Oxford, OX1 5JE, England, UK
Tel: 44 1865 735678
Website: http://www.bath.ac.uk/~lissmc/rjeffs.htm
Founded: 1950
Members: 350
Contact: Phyllis Treitel, Hon.Sec.
Fee: £7
Membership Type: single
Fee: £8
Membership Type: couples
Description: Conservationists, writers, academics, and other admirers of British writer, naturalist, and mystic Richard Jefferies (1848-87). Promotes knowledge of the life and works of Jefferies and maintains interest in places connected with him; is involved in the restoration of Jefferies' birthplace. Fosters fellowship among admirers of Jefferies. Circulates contemporary articles among readers, writers, lecturers, and students. Organizes trips to places related to Jefferies. Holds lectures, readings, and discussions. Maintains museum.

Library Type: reference
Publication: Bulletin
Publication title: Annual Report and Bulletin
Second publication: Newsletter
Publication title: Spring Newsletter
Meetings/Conventions: - annual meeting - Exhibits.

Richmond Fellowship International
RFI

16 Europoint, 5-11 Lavington St., London, SE1 0NZ, England, UK
Tel: 44 20 79456187
Fax: 44 20 79456190
Email: rfi.uk@virgin.net
Website: http://www.rfinternational.org
Founded: 1981
Members: 18
Staff: 7
Contact: Archie McCarron, CEO
Description: Promotes the establishment and operation of halfway houses and day centers for abused children, former psychiatric patients and recovering drug addicts. Organizes mental health training programs for social workers, psychologists, psychotherapists, and psychiatric nurses. Supports development of community based psychosocial rehabilitation services and service user advocacy.
Publication title: Annual Report
Second publication: Newsletter
Meetings/Conventions: - biennial conference

Rider Haggard Society

c/o Mr. Roger Allen
27 Deneholm, Monkseaton, Whitley Bay, NE25 9AU, England, UK
Tel: 44 191 2524516
Fax: 44 191 2524516
Email: RB27Allen@aol.com
Website: http://www.riderhaggardsociety.org.uk/enterdor.htm
Founded: 1984
Members: 100
Contact: Roger Allen, Hon. Sec., Ed.
Fee: £9
Membership Type: UK
Fee: £15
Membership Type: U.S.
Description: Works toward the dissemination of information on and enjoyment of the author. Publishes 4 journals per year. Sponsors a national meeting every 18 months.
Publication: Journal
Publication title: Rider Haggard Journal. Advertisements.
Meetings/Conventions: meeting Herefordshire UK

Rights of Women
ROW

52-54 Featherstone St., London, EC1Y 8RT, England, UK
Tel: 44 207 2516577
Fax: 44 207 4905377
Email: info@row.org.uk
Website: http://www.rightsofwomen.org.uk
Founded: 1975
Members: 200
Staff: 5
Contact: Ranjit Kaur
Fee: £20
Membership Type: women only

Fee: £10
Membership Type: low income individual
Description: Women's organizations, companies, and individuals. Informs women of their legal rights and promotes the interests of women through legal action. Provides legal advice for women regarding: relationship breakdown; sexual and domestic violence; lesbian parenting; housing; and immigration. Defends the rights of women. Operates an advice line offering legal advice and referrals to women solicitors. Organizes and sponsors talks, conferences, and training; undertakes research and policy work.
Publication: Bulletin
Publication title: Results of Women
Second publication: Newsletter
Publication title: Rights of Women Bulletin
Meetings/Conventions: Violence Against Women - annual conference - Exhibits. London UK

Road Emulsion Association

50 Beach Rd., Clacton-on-Sea, CO15 1UE, England, UK
Tel: 44 255 422202
Fax: 44 255 436195
Website: http://rea.org.uk
Founded: 1928
Members: 6
Staff: 2
Contact: Robert W N Welton, Sec.
Description: Represents companies who supply or produce road emulsion products used in constructing and maintaining roads and footways.
Library Type: not open to the public
Publication title: Technical Data Sheets
Meetings/Conventions: - quarterly meeting

Road Haulage Association
RHA

Roadway House, 35 Monument Hill, Weybridge, KT13 8RN, England, UK
Tel: 44 1932 841515
Fax: 44 1932 852516
Email: international@rha.net
Website: http://www.rha.net
Founded: 1946
Members: 10000
Staff: 91
Contact: J. Falkner, Sec.
Description: Training associations and licensing authorities in the British trucking industry. Promotes all aspects of the hire and reward transport in the U.K.; supports international operators.
Publication: Membership Directory
Publication title: National Directory of Haulers. Advertisements.
Meetings/Conventions: - annual conference

Road Operators' Safety Council

395 Cowley Rd., Oxford, OX4 2DJ, England, UK
Tel: 44 1865 775552
Fax: 44 1865 711745
Website: http://www.rosco.org.uk
Founded: 1955
Members: 90
Contact: A. Beetham, Sec.
Description: Bus and coach operators. Aims to promote among owners and operators of road transport vehicles, employees, measures to prevent accidents and encourage safety on the road.

Publication: Newsletter
Publication title: Safety First
Meetings/Conventions: Getting the Message Across - semiannual workshop

Road Surface Dressing Association

Westwood Park, London Rd., Colchester, Essex, C06 4BS, England, UK
Tel: 44 120 6274052
Fax: 44 120 6274053
Email: enquiries@rsda-gb.co.uk
Website: http://www.rsda-gb.co.uk
Founded: 1942
Members: 29
Staff: 1
Contact: John Baxter, Consultant Dir. & Sec.
Fee: £1000
Membership Type: full
Fee: £750
Membership Type: associate
Description: Contractors in the surface dressing industry. Represents contractors and suppliers of equipment and materials used in the surface dressing process. Concerned with the improvement in the quality of surface dressing carried out within the United Kingdom as well as the extended use of the process.
Publication: Book
Publication title: Advice Notes on Surface Dressing Binders, Racked-in Surface Dressing, Preparing Roads for Surface Dressing, Surface Dressing Aggregates, etc.
Publication title: Code of Practice

Rochdale Chamber of Commerce, Training and Enterprise

The Old Vicarage, Sparrow Hill, Rochdale, OL16 1QT, England, UK
Contact: MC Ellison
Description: Promotes business and commerce.

Romany Society

10 Haslam St., Bury, BL9 6EQ, England, UK
Tel: 44 161 7647078
Founded: 1996
Members: 300
Contact: Mrs. Romany Watt, Pres.
Fee: £5
Membership Type: individual
Fee: £9
Membership Type: family
Description: Promotes and encourages the study and appreciation of Romany, his life and works.

ROOM, the National Council for Housing and Planning

41 Botolph Ln., London, EC3R 8DL, England, UK
Tel: 44 20 79299477
Fax: 44 20 79298199
Email: mail@room.org.uk
Website: http://www.room.org.uk
Founded: 1900
Members: 573
Contact: Chris Griffin, Commun.Mgr.
Description: Local authorities, housing associations, developers, building societies, housing and planning consultants, companies with housing and planning interests, public utilities, and individuals. Works

to achieve better standards and conditions in housing, promote more effective town and country planning, and improve the built and natural environments. It aims to bring together people from a wide variety of backgrounds concerned with these issues.
Formerly: National Housing and Town Planning Council
Publication: Journal
Publication title: Axis, the Journal of Housing, Planning and Regeneration. Advertisements.
Meetings/Conventions: National Regeneration Convention - annual convention

Rotating Electrical Machines Association
Westminster Tower, 3 Albert Embankment, London, SE1 7SL, England, UK
Tel: 44 20 77933041
Fax: 44 20 75828020
Email: rema@beama.org.uk
Website: http://www.rema.uk.com
Founded: 1971
Members: 11
Staff: 2
Contact: Clive Betts, Dir.
Description: Manufacturers of rotating electrical machines. Represents members' interests.

Rotherham Chamber of Commerce, Training and Enterprise
15 High St., Rotherham, S60 1PT, England, UK
Tel: 44 1709 386200
Fax: 44 1709 836688
Email: j.lewis@rotherhamchamber.org.uk
Website: http://www.rotherhamchamber.org.uk
Members: 1210
Staff: 127
Contact: John Lewis, Chief Exec.
Description: Promotes business and commerce.

Rough Fell Sheep Breeders Association
Weasdale Farm, Newbiggin on Lune, Kirkby Stephen, CA17 4LY, England, UK
Website: http://www.roughfellsheep.co.uk
Founded: 1926
Members: 175
Description: Maintains records of Rough Fell Rams

Royal Academy of Arts
RA
Piccadilly, London, W1J 0BD, England, UK
Tel: 44 20 73008000
Fax: 44 20 73008001
Email: library@royalAcademy.org.uk
Website: http://www.royalAcademy.org.uk
Founded: 1768
Description: Encourages the creation, enjoyment and appreciation of the visual arts through exhibitions, education and debate; mounts a continuous programme of internationally renowned loan exhibitions complemented by education events.

Royal Academy of Dance
RAD
36 Battersea Sq., London, SW11 3RA, England, UK
Tel: 44 20 72368000
Fax: 44 20 79243129
Email: info@rad.org.uk
Website: http://www.rad.org.uk
Founded: 1920
Members: 20000
Staff: 57
Contact: Luke Rittner, Chief Exec.
Fee: £66
Membership Type: teaching
Fee: £53
Membership Type: full
Description: World's largest teaching and examining body for classical ballet, with ballet teachers in more than 75 countries. Strives to advance standards of classical ballet teaching and classical ballet performance throughout the world. Offers training programs for students, teachers, former professional dancers, notators leading to qualifications validated by the University of Durham. Provides students with a comprehensive range of courses and examinations. Sponsors special needs dance programs and competitions.
Library Subject: dance and related subjects
Library Type: reference
Formerly: Association of Operatic Dancing of Great Britain
Publication: Magazine
Publication title: Dance Gazette. Advertisements.
Second publication: Book
Publication title: Dictionary of Classical Terminology
Meetings/Conventions: - periodic convention

Royal Academy of Dramatic Art
RADA
18 Chenies St., London, WC1E 7EX, England, UK
Tel: 44 20 76367076
Fax: 44 20 73233865
Founded: 1904

Royal Academy of Engineering
29 Great Peter St., Westminster, London, SW1P 3LW, England, UK
Tel: 44 207 2222688
Fax: 44 207 2330054
Website: http://www.raeng.org.uk/
Founded: 1976
Members: 1196
Staff: 41
Contact: Jon Burch, Exec.Sec.
Fee: £160
Membership Type: fellow
Description: Chartered engineers, multi-disciplinary. The pursuit, encouragement and maintenance of excellence in the whole field of engineering in order to promote the advancement of the science, art and practice of engineering for the benefit of the public.
Library Subject: engineering
Library Type: reference
Publication: Newsletter
Publication title: Higher Education News
Second publication: Annual Report
Publication title: Royal Academy of Engineering Annual Review

Royal Aeronautical Society - United Kingdom
RAeS

4 Hamilton Pl., London, W1J 7BQ, England, UK
Tel: 44 207 6704300
Fax: 44 207 6704309
Email: antonia.price@raes.org.uk
Website: http://www.raes.org.uk
Founded: 1866
Members: 18000
Staff: 32
Contact: Keith Mann, Dir.
Description: All those professionally engaged in the aerospace indsutry. Founded in 1866 for the general advancement of aeronautical art, science and engineering. To stimulate research, debate and expert opinion. As a nominated body of the Engineering Council, the Society is the preferred route to registration for engineers working in the aerospace industry. Membership is open to all aerospace professionals; there are thirty-four branches in the United Kingdom and nine overseas in Cyprus, Dublin, Hong Kong, Malaysia, Munich, Northern Germany, Shannon, Toulouse and United Arab Emirates. Each branch has its own management committee and runs a programme of events independently of the main Society. There are also five overseas divisions, in Australia, New Zealand, Pakistan, Southern Africa and Zimbabwe. These are larger organisations with more authority than branches.
Library Subject: Aerospace science
Library Type: reference
Formerly: Absorbed, Institute of Aeronautical Engineers
Publication: Journal
Publication title: Aeronautical Journal. Advertisements.
Second publication: Magazine
Publication title: Aerospace International. Advertisements.
Meetings/Conventions: - periodic conference

Royal African Society
RAS

SOAS, Thornhaugh St., Russell Sq., London, WC1H OXG, England, UK
Tel: 44 207 8984390
Fax: 44 207 8984389
Email: ras@soas.ac.uk
Website: http://www.royalafricansociety.org
Founded: 1901
Members: 850
Staff: 4
Contact: Mrs. M.L. Allan, Sec.
Fee: £29
Membership Type: individual
Fee: £15
Membership Type: student
Description: Individuals in 45 countries united to increase knowledge of peoples and countries of Africa and of encouraging interest in the continent.
Publication: Journal
Publication title: African Affairs. Advertisements.
Meetings/Conventions: - periodic conference

Royal Agricultural Society of England

National Agricultural Centre, Stoneleigh Park, Warwickshire, CV8 2LZ, England, UK
Tel: 44 2476 696969
Fax: 44 2476 696900
Email: info@rase.org.uk

Website: http://www.rase.org.uk/
Contact: James Johnson, Sec.
Description: Individuals and organizations. Promotes the advancement of British agriculture through good science and the caring stewardship of land, animals, and people. Conducts educational programs; facilitates international agricultural programs and exchanges; maintains Arthur Rank Centre.
Library Subject: agriculture
Library Type: reference
Meetings/Conventions: - periodic conference

Royal Agricultural Society of the Commonwealth
RASC

2 Grosvenor Gardens, London, SW1W 0DH, England, UK
Tel: 44 207 2599678
Fax: 44 207 2599675
Email: rasc@commagshow.org
Website: http://www.commagshow.org
Founded: 1957
Members: 37
Staff: 3
Contact: C.D. Runge Frags, Hon.Sec.
Description: Agricultural member societies from 20 Commonwealth countries. Assists developing countries in their efforts to increase agricultural production; encourages major agricultural producers within the Commonwealth to provide advice and assistance to developing Commonwealth countries as a means of resolving the problem of hunger and poverty; stimulates and facilitates the exchange of knowledge and experience among members to improve methods of land cultivation and livestock breeding; works to increase the efficiency of agricultural equipment and machinery; maintains appeal fund to assist representatives of developing Commonwealth countries to attend RASC conferences.
Publication: Journal
Publication title: Conference Report
Second publication: Newsletter
Publication title: RASC News
Meetings/Conventions: Commonwealth Agricultural Conference - biennial conference

Royal Anthropological Institute of Great Britain and Ireland

50 Fitzroy St., London, W1T 5BT, England, UK
Tel: 44 207 3870455
Fax: 44 207 3834235
Email: admin@therai.org.uk
Website: http://www.therai.org.uk
Founded: 1843
Members: 2000
Staff: 10
Contact: Hilary Callan, Dir.
Fee: £70
Membership Type: U.K. Fellow
Fee: £61
Membership Type: fellow outside UK
Description: Acts as the learned society for anthropologists and interested laypeople worldwide. Fellows of the Institute have full access to the famous library at the Museum of Mankind. Films are available for hire in the UK internationally. The Institute's principal commitment is international journal publishing.
Publication title: Anthropological Index
Publication title: Anthropology Today

Royal Archaeological Institute

c/o Society of Antiquaries of London
Burlington House, Piccadilly, London, W1V 0HS, England, UK
Email: caroline@craison.freeservice.co.uk
Website: http://www.royalarchaeolinst.org
Founded: 1844
Members: 1550
Staff: 2
Contact: Brian Dix, Sec.
Fee: £25
Membership Type: ordinary
Fee: £8
Membership Type: associate
Description: Honorary, ordinary and associate. Takes a leading part in stimulating interest in archaeology, assists in the preservation of national antiquities and in the field of architectural conservation. It has high standards of research and preservation, publishes material on archaeology of all periods in the Archaeological Journal. It also offers research grants and is represented on many committees and is in touch with local societies.
Publication: Journal
Publication title: The Archaeological Journal
Publication title: Building on the Past
Meetings/Conventions: - monthly lecture

Royal Asiatic Society of Great Britain and Ireland

60 Queen's Gardens, London, W2 3AF, England, UK
Tel: 44 207 7244741
Fax: 44 207 7064008
Email: info@royalasiaticsociety.co.uk
Website: http://www.royalasiaticsociety.org
Founded: 1823
Members: 900
Staff: 6
Contact: Adrian Thomas, Sec.
Fee: £38
Description: Promotes the study of Asian science, literature, history, and arts. Provides a forum for communication and exchange among members.
Library Subject: Asian studies
Library Type: reference
Publication: Journal

Royal Association for Deaf People
RAD

Walsingham Rd., Colchester, CO2 7BP, England, UK
Tel: 44 1206 509509
Fax: 44 1206 769755
Email: tom.fenton@royaldeaf.org.uk
Website: http://www.royaldeaf.org.uk
Founded: 1841
Contact: Tom Fenton, Chief.Exec.
Description: Meets the needs of profoundly deaf people.
Formerly: Royal Association in Aid of Deaf People

Royal Association for Disability and Rehabilitation
RADAR

12 City Forum, 250 City Rd., London, EC1V 8AF, England, UK
Tel: 44 207 2503222
Fax: 44 207 2500212
Email: radar@radar.org.uk
Website: http://www.radar.org.uk
Founded: 1977
Members: 500
Staff: 40
Description: Represents the rights and interests of disabled individuals in the United Kingdom. Strives to improve educational, health, and social services for disabled people and stresses their full integration and participation in community life. Seeks to eliminate barriers that impose restrictions on disabled people. Provides advice. UK Secretariat of Rehabilitation International.
Formerly: Formed by Merger of, British Council for Rehabilitation of the Disabled
Publication title: Holiday Guides
Second publication: Bulletin
Meetings/Conventions: - periodic conference

Royal Association of British Dairy Farmers

Dairy House, 60 Kenilworth Rd., Leamington Spa, CV32 6JX, England, UK
Tel: 44 1926 887477
Fax: 44 1926 887585
Email: office@rabdf.co.uk
Website: http://www.rabdf.co.uk
Founded: 1876
Members: 3000
Staff: 3
Contact: N. Everington, Ch.Exec.
Description: Dairy farmers and those associated with the dairy farming industry. Represents the interests of practical dairy farmers in the UK by representations, and open days, conferences, published material and support of research. Organises the UKs major specialist technical event for dairy farming and dairy farmers. This, The Dairy Event is held at the National Agricultural Centre, Stoneleigh, Warwickshire each September.
Publication: Newsletter
Publication title: RABDF News

Royal Astronomical Society

Burlington House, Piccadilly, London, W1J 0BQ, England, UK
Tel: 44 20 77343307
Fax: 44 20 74940166
Email: info@ras.org.uk
Website: http://www.ras.org.uk
Founded: 1820
Members: 3000
Staff: 12
Contact: J.E.J. Lane, Exec.Sec.
Description: Elected by fellow members. Individuals cannot join freely. A learned society to encourage and promote astronomy and geophysics both with the European Communities and worldwide.
Publication title: BIAMU Post Graduate Opportunity Information
Second publication: Journal
Publication title: Geophysical Journal International

Royal British Legion Women's Section
RBLWS

48 Pall Mall, London, SW1Y 5JY, England, UK
Tel: 44 207 9737214
Fax: 44 207 8397917
Email: lbunting@britishlegion.org.uk
Website: http://www.britishlegion.org.uk
Founded: 1921
Members: 72000

Staff: 14
Contact: Mrs. Diane A. Myers, Natl.Sec.
Fee: £3
Membership Type: women
Description: Wives, widows, female dependents, and relatives of Service and ex-Service men and women. Promotes and defends the interests of those who have served or are serving in the military or Red Cross in Britain and their dependents. Raises funds.
Publication: Report
Publication title: Annual Report & Accounts Report
Second publication: Newsletter
Meetings/Conventions: - annual conference - Exhibits.

Royal Choral Society
RCS

Studu 9, 92 Lots Rd., London, SW10 0QD, England, UK
Tel: 44 207 3763718
Fax: 44 207 3763719
Email: helenbody@royalchoralsociety.co.uk
Website: http://www.royalchoralsociety.co.uk
Founded: 1871
Members: 200
Staff: 2
Contact: Helen Body, Admin.
Fee: £80
Description: Individuals interested in singing choral music. Promotes performance of choral repertoire.
Library Type: reference
Meetings/Conventions: - weekly

Royal College of Anaesthetists

48-49 Russell Sq., London, WC1B 4JY, England, UK
Tel: 44 20 78131900
Fax: 44 20 78131876
Email: info@rcoa.ac.uk
Website: http://www.rcoa.ac.uk
Founded: 1988

Royal College of General Practitioners

14 Princes Gate, Hyde Pk., London, SW7 1PU, England, UK
Tel: 44 207 5813232
Fax: 44 207 2253047
Email: info@rcgp.org.uk
Website: http://www.rcgp.org.uk
Founded: 1952
Members: 18400
Staff: 130
Contact: Prof. Dame Lesely Southgate, Pres.
Description: General practitioners. Responsible for the promotion of high quality general practice through education, research and standard setting.
Publication: Journal
Publication title: British Journal of General Practice. Advertisements.

Royal College of Midwives

15 Mansfield St., London, W1G 9NH, England, UK
Tel: 44 20 73123535
Fax: 44 20 73123536
Email: info@rcm.org.uk
Website: http://www.rcm.org.uk/
Founded: 1881
Members: 36000

Staff: 60
Contact: Karlene Davis, Gen.Sec.
Fee: £155
Description: Promotes the practice of midwifery, and works to maintain high standards in the field. Provides educational programs to midwives in the areas of maternity, child care, and personal development. Represents worker rights of midwives to national legal and political authorities. Encourages and supports research.
Library Subject: midwifery
Library Type: reference
Publication: Magazine
Publication title: Midwives
Second publication: Journal
Publication title: RCM Midwives Journal. Advertisements.
Meetings/Conventions: - annual general assembly - Exhibits.

Royal College of Nursing

20 Cavendish Sq., London, W1G 0RN, England, UK
Tel: 44 207 4093333
Fax: 44 207 6473425
Email: webteam@rcn.org.uk
Website: http://www.rcn.org.uk
Founded: 1916
Members: 310000
Staff: 480
Contact: Dr. Beverly Malone, Gen.Sec.
Fee: £114.5
Description: Nurses, midwives and health visitors. Represents nurses working at all levels of responsibility and in a wide variety of settings, from the NHS to the independent sector and from local government to private industry.
Library Subject: Nursing
Library Type: open to the public
Publication: Journal
Publication title: Nursing Standard. Advertisements.
Meetings/Conventions: - annual congress - Exhibits.

Royal College of Obstetricians and Gynaecologists

27 Sussex Pl., Regent's Park, London, NW1 4RG, England, UK
Fax: 44 207 7230575
Email: pbarnett@rcog.org.uk
Website: http://www.rcog.org.uk
Founded: 1929
Members: 10324
Staff: 95
Contact: Paul Barnett, College Sec.
Description: Obstetricians and gynecologists, having completed a period of training recognised by the College and passed all components of the MRCOG examination. The encouragement of the study and the improvement of the practice of obstetrics and gynaecology. This is achieved by running examinations, postgraduate meetings, publications, committees and working parties.
Library Type: reference
Publication: Journal
Publication title: British Journal of Obstetrics and Gynaecology. Advertisements.
Second publication: Journal
Publication title: Journal for Continuing Professional Development from the Royal College of Obstetricians and Gynaecologists

Royal College of Ophthalmologists

17 Cornwall Terr., London, NW1 4QW, England, UK
Tel: 44 207 9350702
Fax: 44 207 9359838

Email: margaret@rcophth.ac.uk
Website: http://www.rcophth.ac.uk
Founded: 1988
Members: 3027
Staff: 14
Contact: Miss M. Hallendorff
Fee: £190
Membership Type: within U.K.
Fee: £170
Membership Type: outside UK
Description: Medical Practitioners (ophthalmologists).
Publication: Journal
Publication title: EYE. Advertisements.
Meetings/Conventions: Scientific Congress - annual - Exhibits.

Royal College of Organists

7 St. Andrews St., London, EC4A 3LQ, England, UK
Tel: 44 20 79363606
Fax: 44 20 73538244
Email: admin@rco.org.uk
Website: http://www.rco.org.uk
Founded: 1864
Members: 3100
Staff: 7
Contact: Alan Dear, Ch.Exec.
Fee: £45
Membership Type: open
Description: Open to all who take an interest in the work and profession of the organist and in organ music as well as to those who wish to gain the College's Diplomas. To promote the art of organ playing and chroal directing, to hold examinations in these studies and related areas, to offer education at all levels in these studies, and to generate professional support to organists.
Library Subject: organ and choral music
Library Type: reference
Publication: Newsletter
Publication title: RCO News. Advertisements.
Second publication: Yearbook
Publication title: RCO Yearbook. Advertisements.

Royal College of Paediatrics and Child Health

50 Hallam St., London, W1W 6DE, England, UK
Tel: 44 207 3075600
Fax: 44 207 3075601
Email: enquiries@rcpch.ac.uk
Website: http://www.rcpch.ac.uk
Founded: 1928
Members: 6500
Staff: 50
Contact: Patricia Hamilton, Hon.Sec.
Description: Consultant paediatricians, community child health doctors, trainee paediatricians, research workers, general practitioners and other medical specialists who work with children. Aims to advance the understanding, treatment and prevention of disease in childhood, to further the study of child health and to promote excellence in paediatric practice.
Formerly: British Paediatric Association
Publication: Journal
Publication title: Archives of Disease in Children
Second publication: Newsletter
Publication title: College Newsletter
Meetings/Conventions: - annual meeting York UK

Royal College of Pathologists - United Kingdom

2 Carlton House Terrace, London, SW1Y 5AF, England, UK
Tel: 44 20 74516700
Fax: 44 20 74516701
Email: info@rcpath.org
Website: http://www.rcpath.org
Founded: 1962
Members: 7500
Staff: 25
Contact: Daniel Ross, CEO
Fee: £229
Membership Type: UK member
Fee: £294
Membership Type: UK fellow
Description: Postgraduate medical and scientific graduates who have successfully completed all or part of the college's examinations following a specified period of approved training, or elected under specified college ordinances. Advances the science and practice of pathology, furthers public education, promotes study and research work in pathology and related subjects and publishes the results of such study and research.
Library Subject: pathology disciplines
Library Type: not open to the public
Publication: Journal
Publication title: College Bulletin. Advertisements.
Publication title: Manpower and Management Policy Documents
Meetings/Conventions: Inhouse Scientific Update Meeting - monthly

Royal College of Physicians
RCP

11 St. Andrew's Pl., Regent's Park, London, NW1 4LE, England, UK
Tel: 44 20 79351174
Fax: 44 20 74867038
Email: linda.cuthbertson@rcplondon.ac.uk
Website: http://www.rcplondon.ac.uk
Founded: 1518
Members: 17500
Staff: 190
Contact: Mr. Philip Masterson-Smith, Chief Exec.
Description: Individuals in 64 countries. Responsible for the postgraduate education and training of physicians in England, Wales, and Northern Ireland. Committed to maintaining the highest standards of medical practice. Advises the government, public, and members of the profession on health and medical issues. Conducts educational and training programs; organizes examinations; operates clinical effectiveness unit.
Library Subject: medical history and biography
Library Type: open to the public
Publication title: Annual Report
Publication title: College List
Meetings/Conventions: - periodic conference

Royal College of Psychiatrists

17 Belgrave Sq., London, SW1X 8PG, England, UK
Tel: 44 20 72352351
Fax: 44 20 72451231
Email: rcpsych@rcpsych.ac.uk
Website: http://www.rcpsych.ac.uk
Founded: 1971
Members: 10000
Staff: 90
Contact: Deborah Hart
Description: Psychiatrists.

Publication: Journal
Publication title: British Journal of Psychiatry, Psychiatric Bulletin. Advertisements.
Meetings/Conventions: - annual conference

Royal College of Radiologists
RCR

38 Portland Pl., London, W1B 1JQ, England, UK
Tel: 44 207 6364432
Fax: 44 207 3233100
Email: enquiries@rcr.ac.uk
Website: http://www.rcr.ac.uk
Founded: 1939
Members: 5679
Staff: 20
Contact: Damion Clarke, PR
Description: Diagnostic and interventional radiologists, nuclear medicine specialists, oncologists, radiotherapists, and ultrasound specialists. Works to advance the science and practice of radiological technology. Offers courses to further the education of practitioners. Establishes qualifications and examinations for fellowships and diplomas.
Formerly: Formed by Merger of, British Association of Radiologists
Publication: Journal
Publication title: Clinical Oncology
Second publication: Journal
Publication title: Clinical Radiology
Meetings/Conventions: - periodic

Royal College of Speech and Language Therapists

2 White Hart Yard, London, SE1 1NX, England, UK
Tel: 44 207 3781200
Fax: 44 207 4037254
Email: postmaster@rcslt.org
Website: http://www.rcslt.org
Founded: 1945
Members: 8500
Staff: 21
Contact: Kamini Gadhok, Chief Exec.
Fee: £45
Membership Type: affiliate
Description: Speech and language therapists, including practising members, non-practising and retired members. All members have a certificate to practise (or its equivalent) issued by the college. Supports qualified speech and language therapists working for the relief of disorders of communication among both adults and children and the accreditation of courses leading to qualification as a speech and language therapist. Careers information available on request.
Formerly: College of Speech Therapists
Publication: Magazine
Publication title: Bulletin. Advertisements.
Publication title: Bulletin Supplement
Meetings/Conventions: - periodic conference - Exhibits.

Royal College of Surgeons of England
RCS Eng

35/43 Lincoln's Inn Fields, London, WC2A 3PE, England, UK
Tel: 44 20 74053474
Fax: 44 20 78319438
Email: external@rcseng.ac.uk
Website: http://www.rcseng.ac.uk
Founded: 1800

Members: 15000
Staff: 250
Contact: Mr. Craig Duncan, Sec.
Description: Surgeons and dental surgeons in the United Kingdom. Aims to promote and encourage the study and practice of surgery as an art and a science. Maintains professional standards through examinations; establishes criteria for the qualification of consultant and dental surgeons in the National Health Service; advises government and other professional bodies on surgical matters; conducts research. Offers postgraduate courses in surgery and related subjects; sponsors seminars and workshops. Operates the Hunterian Museum.
Library Subject: Surgical procedures and medical history
Library Type: reference
Formerly: Supersedes, Company of Surgeons of London
Publication: Report
Publication title: Annals of the Royal College of Surgeons of England
Meetings/Conventions: - annual conference - Exhibits.

Royal College of Veterinary Surgeons

Belgravia House, 62-64 Horseferry Rd., London, SW1P 2AF, England, UK
Tel: 44 207 2222001
Fax: 44 207 2222004
Email: admin@rcvs.org.uk
Website: http://www.rcvs.org.uk
Founded: 1844
Members: 21200
Staff: 50
Contact: Andrea Samuelson, Head of External Affairs
Fee: £217
Membership Type: home
Fee: £108
Membership Type: outside UK
Description: Graduates possessing a veterinary degree, registerable with the RCVS who intend to practice in the UK. Statutory body governing the veterinary profession in the UK. Responsible for quality of veterinary undergraduate education at the UK veterinary schools, provision of membership examination, and discipline of members. Establishment of certificate and diploma examinations.
Library Subject: veterinary science
Library Type: open to the public
Publication: Directory
Publication title: Directory of Veterinary Practices. Advertisements.
Publication title: Guide to Professional Conduct
Meetings/Conventions: - annual meeting

Royal Commonwealth Society

18 Northumberland Ave., London, WC2N 5BJ, England, UK
Tel: 44 207 9306733
Fax: 44 207 9309705
Email: info@rcsint.org
Website: http://www.rcsint.org
Founded: 1868
Members: 6000
Staff: 40
Contact: Stuart Mole, Dir.Gen.
Description: Individuals and organizations with an interest in the nations and cultures of the Commonwealth. To educate about the commonwealth. Serves as a forum for the exchange of information on the peoples, nations, and cultures of the Commonwealth.
Publication: Annual Report
Second publication: Newsletter
Meetings/Conventions: - biennial international conference

Royal Economic Society

c/o Dept. of Economics
London Business School, Sussex Pl., Regent's Park, London, NW1
4SA, England, UK
Tel: 44 207 7066783
Fax: 44 207 7241598
Email: eburke@london.edu
Website: http://www.res.org.uk
Founded: 1890
Members: 3300
Contact: Prof. Richard Portes, Sec-Gen.
Description: Members are mainly professional economists in business, government service or higher education. Concerned with the promotion and encouragement of the study of economic science.
Publication: Journal
Publication title: Economic. Advertisements.
Second publication: Newsletter
Publication title: RES
Meetings/Conventions: - annual conference

Royal Entomological Society

41 Queen's Gate, London, SW7 5HR, England, UK
Tel: 44 207 5848361
Fax: 44 207 5818505
Email: reg@royensoc.co.uk
Website: http://www.royensoc.co.uk
Founded: 1833
Members: 2000
Staff: 6
Contact: G.G. Bentley, Registrar
Description: An academic qualification is not required but must show genuine interest in entomology; Fellowships are open to those who have made a substantial contribution to entomology, through publications or other evidence of achievement. Concerned with the improvement and diffusion of entomological science. Holds meetings on all aspects of entomology, publishing the results of entomological research, supporting entomological expeditions. Generates discourse between entomologists.
Library Subject: entomology
Library Type: by appointment only

Royal Forestry Society of England, Wales and Northern Ireland

102 High St., Tring, HP23 4AF, England, UK
Tel: 44 1442 822028
Fax: 44 1442 890395
Email: rfshq@rfs.org.uk
Website: http://www.rfs.org.uk
Founded: 1882
Members: 4400
Staff: 4
Contact: Dr. J.E. Jackson, Dir.Mgr.
Fee: £24
Description: Open - cosmopolitan. To encourage the positive management of Britain's woodlands so that they may be conserved, improved and expanded. Multi-purpose forestry; woodland, tree management; education; conservation; arboriculture; study tours; field meetings.
Library Subject: forestry
Library Type: open to the public
Publication: Journal
Publication title: Quarterly Journal of Forestry. Advertisements.
Second publication: Proceedings
Meetings/Conventions: - annual symposium - Exhibits.

Royal Geographical Society with the Institute of British Geographers
RGS

1 Kensington Gore, London, SW7 2AR, England, UK
Tel: 44 207 5913000
Fax: 44 207 5913001
Email: info@rgs.org
Website: http://www.rgs.org
Founded: 1830
Members: 13500
Staff: 50
Contact: Dr. Rita Gardner, Dir.
Description: Businesses, schools, student exploration societies, university departments, and individuals in 45 countries interested in geography. Works to advance and improve geographical science by facilitating information exchange. Organizes overseas scientific projects; offers financial support for scientific expeditions; operates the Expedition Advisory Centre, offering advice and training to anyone planning an expedition. Conducts lectures, symposia, and exhibitions. Maintains museum. Active research groups in all aspects of geography in higher education. Advises on and responds to government and NGO's on geographical matters. Professional body and learned society for geography.
Library Subject: geography and related subjects
Library Type: reference
Formerly: Absorbed, African Association
Publication: Journal
Publication title: Area
Publication title: Geographical
Meetings/Conventions: Environmental Forum conference - Exhibits.

Royal Guild of Toastmasters

Petit Coin, 96 Millbank Ct., 24 John Islip St., Westminster, London, SW1P 4LQ, England, UK
Tel: 44 1534 865005
Fax: 44 1534 865005
Founded: 1996
Members: 10
Contact: Robert Luigi Michieli
Fee: £5000
Description: Toastmasters, masters of ceremonies, and other individuals who speak at public gatherings. Promotes professionalism among members; seeks to enhance public recognition of members' professional status. Conducts educational programs; participates in charitable activities; sponsors competitions; maintains hall of fame.
Publication: Directory
Publication title: Royal Guild of Toastmasters. Advertisements.
Second publication: Brochure
Meetings/Conventions: - annual convention

Royal Historical Society - United Kingdom

University London College, Gower St., London, WC1E 6BT, England, UK
Tel: 44 171 3877532
Fax: 44 171 3677532
Email: rhsinfo@rhs.ac.uk
Website: http://ihr.sas.ac.uk/rhs/
Founded: 1868
Members: 2600
Staff: 2
Contact: Joy McCarthy

Publication title: Camden
Second publication: Handbooks
Publication title: RHS

Royal Horticultural Society
80 Vincent Sq., London, SW1P 2PE, England, UK
Tel: 44 207 8213000
Email: info@rhs.org.uk
Website: http://www.rhs.org.uk
Founded: 1804
Members: 250000
Staff: 400
Contact:
Fee: £24
Description: Encourages horticulture in all its branches.
Library Subject: horticulture and botany
Library Type: open to the public
Publication: Journal
Publication title: The Garden (Journal of the Royal Horticultural Society)
Publication title: The New Plantsman

Royal Humane Society
Brettenham House, Lancaster Pl., London, WC2E 7EP, England, UK
Tel: 44 20 78368155
Fax: 44 20 78368155
Email: rhs@supanet.com
Website: http://www.royalhumane.org
Founded: 1774
Staff: 4
Contact: Maj.Gen. C. Tyler
Description: Makes awards to those who, at risk to their own lives, save or attempt to save a fellow citizen.
Library Type: not open to the public
Publication: Annual Report

Royal Institute of British Architects
c/o Jane Oldfield
66 Portland Pl., London, W1B 1AD, England, UK
Tel: 44 20 75805533
Fax: 44 20 72551541
Email: info@inst.riba.org
Website: http://www.architecture.com
Founded: 1834
Members: 32000
Staff: 150
Contact: Richard Hastilow, Chief Exec.
Description: Chartered architects; students in Schools of Architecture are also able to become student members. Concerned with the general advancement of civil architecture and the promotion and facilitating of the acquirement of the various arts and sciences connected therewith. It also aims to see that in meeting clients' requirements, architects have regard to the broader user and environmental implications of their work.
Library Type: open to the public

Royal Institute of British Architects - Women Architects' Group
66 Portland Pl., London, W1B 1AD, England, UK
Tel: 44 171 5805533
Fax: 44 171 2551541
Email: admin@inst.riba.org
Founded: 1985

Members: 15
Contact: Pamela Edwards
Description: Promotes the interests of women architects in England. Provides a forum for discussion and professional information exchange among women architects.

Royal Institute of International Affairs
Chatham House, 10 St. James Sq., London, SW1Y 4LE, England, UK
Tel: 44 207 9575700
Fax: 44 207 9575710
Email: contact@riia.org
Website: http://www.riia.org
Founded: 1920
Members: 3385
Staff: 73
Contact: Dr. Victor Bulmer-Thomas
Description: Members come from the fields of politics, academia, the media and business, and usually are active in, or have special knowledge of, international issues. Promotes the study and understanding of international affairs. Operates seven research programmes on: Europe; Russia & Eurasia; International Economics; International Security; Asia Pacific; Middle East; Energy and Environment.
Library Subject: economics, politics security, environment, energy
Library Type: reference
Publication title: The World Today
Meetings/Conventions: conference

Royal Institute of Navigation
IAIN
1 Kensington Gore, London, SW7 2AT, England, UK
Tel: 44 207 5913130
Fax: 44 207 5913131
Email: info@rin.org.com
Website: http://www.rin.org.uk
Founded: 1975
Members: 18
Staff: 6
Contact: David M. Page, Sec.Gen
Description: National navigation institutes. Facilitates relations and coordinates activities among members. Promotes meetings and projects related to navigation. Maintains liaison with relevant intergovernmental and other organizations and provides specialized advice where appropriate.
Publication: Newsletter
Publication title: IAIN Newsletter
Meetings/Conventions: - triennial general assembly - Exhibits. Berlin Germany

Royal Institute of Oil Painters
ROI
c/o Federation of British Artists
17 Carlton House Terrace, London, SW1Y 5BD, England, UK
Tel: 44 207 9306844
Fax: 44 207 8397830
Email: info@mallgalleries.com
Website: http://www.mallgalleries.org.uk
Founded: 1882
Members: 73
Contact: Briony Chaplin
Description: Professional painters in oils. The exhibition of oil paintings; sales and commissions of oil paintings; educating the public

in oil paintings through its exhibitions. Most work for sale at annual exhibition.
Publication: Catalog
Publication title: Annual Exhibition Catalogue. Advertisements.
Meetings/Conventions: - annual specialty show - Exhibits.

Royal Institute of Painters in Water Colours

17 Carlton House Terrace, London, SW1Y 5BD, England, UK
Tel: 44 171 9306844
Fax: 44 171 8397830
Email: info@mallgalleries.com
Founded: 1831
Members: 56
Contact: Briony Chaplin
Description: Professional water colour artists. Organises the exhibition of watercolour paintings, sales and commissions of watercolours, demonstrations of watercolour paintings. Educates the public about watercolour paintings through exhibitions and demonstrations.

Royal Institute of Philosophy

14 Gordon Sq., London, WC1H 0AG, England, UK
Tel: 44 207 3874130
Fax: 44 207 3834061
Email: j.garvey@royalinstitutephilosophy.org
Website: http://www.royalinstitutephilosophy.org
Founded: 1925
Members: 680
Contact: Ingrid Purkiss, Sec.
Description: All those interested in philosophy. To promote the study and discussion of philosophy and original work in it through its journal and by arranging and sponsoring programmes of lectures and conferences.
Publication title: Philosophy

Royal Institute of Public Health
RIPH

28 Portland Pl., London, W1B 1DE, England, UK
Tel: 44 20 75802731
Fax: 44 20 75806157
Email: marketing@riph.org.uk
Website: http://www.riph.org.uk
Founded: 1897
Members: 2500
Staff: 26
Contact: Sir. Nichola Wilkins, Chief Exec.
Fee: £28
Membership Type: Associate
Fee: £43
Membership Type: Member
Description: Caterers, doctors, environmental health officers, food technologists, laboratory and mortuary technicians, microbiologists, nurses, and teachers promoting the advancement of domestic, industrial, and personal health and hygiene. Encourages the study of hygiene, preventive medicine, and public health. Offers courses; holds seminars.
Formerly: Formed by Merger of, Institute of Hygiene' Royal Institute of Public Health
Publication title: Handbook of Mortuary Practice and Safety for Anatomical Pathology Technicians
Second publication: Journal
Publication title: Health & Hygiene
Meetings/Conventions: - periodic conference

Royal Institute of Public Health

28 Portland Place, London, W1B 1DE, England, UK
Tel: 44 207 5802731
Fax: 44 207 5806157
Email: marketing@riph.org.uk
Website: http://www.riph.org.uk
Founded: 1856
Members: 1700
Staff: 18
Contact: Nichola Wilkins, Ch.Exec.
Fee: £50
Membership Type: fellow, plus 30 reg.
Description: Medical practitioners, dental practitioners, and environmental health officers from 19 countries. Seeks to advance public health and integrated health services. Provides a forum for information exchange among specialists. Reviews existing methodologies and proposes new practices. Serves as an advisory body to governmental and other organizations. Assists in developing continuing professional training for specialists in public health and preventive medicine. Conducts research.
Formerly: Society of Public Health
Publication: Journal
Publication title: Health & Hygiene. Advertisements.
Second publication: Journal
Publication title: Public Health. Advertisements.
Meetings/Conventions: conference - Exhibits.

Royal Institution of Chartered Surveyors
RICS

Surveyor Ct., Westwood Way, Coventry, CV4 8JE, England, UK
Tel: 44 870 3331600
Email: contactrics@rics.org.uk
Website: http://www.rics.org
Members: 110000
Description: Committed to addressing all aspects of land, property, construction and associated environmental issues and uphold industry standards.

Royal Institution of Chartered Surveyors
AEBS

12 Great George St., Parliament Sq., London, SW1P 3AD, England, UK
Tel: 44 870 3331600
Fax: 44 20 72229430
Email: contactrics@rics.org.uk
Website: http://www.rics.org
Founded: 1868
Members: 110000
Staff: 433
Contact: Hilary Oakley
Description: Professional building surveyors. Seeks to ensure quality in the building and maintenance of structures; promotes development of international standards of building survey practice. Facilitates communication among members; develops building survey standards; sponsors research and continuing professional development programs.
Library Subject: commercial/residential property, surveying, construction, valuation, town and country planning
Library Type: open to the public
Formerly: Association of European Building Surveyors
Publication: Journal
Publication title: CSM

Royal Institution of Chartered Surveyors - England
RICS

12 Great George St., Parliament Sq., London, SW1P 3AD, England, UK
Tel: 44 207 2227000
Fax: 44 207 2229430
Email: contactrics@rics.org.uk
Website: http://www.rics.org
Founded: 1868
Members: 87655
Staff: 280
Contact: James Rebbeck, Chief Press Officer
Description: Surveyors. Seeks to improve the surveying profession. Represents members' interests; organizes educational courses; administers examinations; offers placement service.
Library Subject: Surveying and surveying history, valuation, construction economics, real estate, appraisal
Library Type: reference
Formerly: Absorbed, Institute of Quanitity Surveyors
Publication: Magazine
Publication title: Abstracts and Reviews
Second publication: Bulletin
Publication title: Chartered Surveyor Monthly

Royal Institution of Great Britain

21 Albemarle St., London, W1S 4BS, England, UK
Tel: 44 207 4092992
Fax: 44 207 6293569
Email: ri@ri.ac.uk
Website: http://www.rigb.org
Founded: 1799
Members: 3000
Staff: 30
Contact: Baroness Susan Greenfield, Dir.
Description: All who are interested in science - no special scientific qualification being required. Concerned with the pursuit of independent research, the popularisation of science and custodianship of its historic premises.
Library Subject: science
Library Type: by appointment only
Publication title: Essays on Science and Technology
Second publication: Proceedings
Publication title: Proceedings of the Royal Institution

Royal Institution of Naval Architects
RINA

10 Upper Belgrave St., London, SW1X 8BQ, England, UK
Tel: 44 20 72354622
Fax: 44 20 72595912
Email: hq@rina.org.uk
Website: http://www.rina.org.uk
Founded: 1860
Members: 6900
Staff: 25
Contact: Mr. Trevor Blakeley, Chief Exec.
Description: International professional institution whose members are involved in the design, construction, and repair of ships, boats, and maritime structures worldwide. Organises an extensive programme of international conferences covering all aspects of naval architecture and maritime technology.
Library Subject: collection known as the Denny Library
Library Type: reference
Publication: Journal

Publication title: Naval Architect
Second publication: Journal
Publication title: Ship and Boat International
Meetings/Conventions: - periodic meeting

Royal Isle of Wight Agricultural Society
48-49 High St., Newport, PO30 1SE, England, UK
Tel: 44 1983 826275
Fax: 44 1983 826275
Founded: 1882

Royal Meteorological Society
RMS

104 Oxford Rd., Reading, RG1 7LL, England, UK
Tel: 44 118 9568500
Fax: 44 118 9568571
Email: roysteven@royalmetsoc.org
Website: http://www.royal-met-soc.org.uk
Founded: 1850
Members: 3200
Staff: 9
Contact: Dr. D.M. Burridge, Pres.
Fee: £45
Description: Encourages research and information exchange on all aspects of meteorology and related sciences.
Publication: Journal
Publication title: International Journal of Climatology. Advertisements.
Second publication: Journal
Publication title: Journal of the Royal Meteorological Society. Advertisements.
Meetings/Conventions: - monthly

Royal Microscopical Society
RMS

37/38 St. Clements, Oxford, OX4 1AJ, England, UK
Tel: 44 1865 248768
Fax: 44 1865 791237
Email: info@rms.org.uk
Website: http://www.rms.org.uk
Founded: 1839
Members: 1500
Staff: 7
Contact: P.B. Hirst, Admin.
Fee: £43
Membership Type: individual
Description: Academic and industrial scientists; researchers and technicians using microscopes; university, industrial, and government research departments; microscope manufacturers. Promotes the advancement of microscopy. Fosters research into improved microscope construction and application. Offers training courses in basic and specialized microscopic techniques; conducts periodic scientific meetings and workshops. Has established undergraduate and postgraduate certificate programs in practical microscopy.
Formerly: Microscopical Society of London
Publication: Journal
Publication title: Journal of Microscopy
Publication title: Proceedings of the RMS
Meetings/Conventions: - biennial meeting London UK

Royal Musical Association
RMA

c/o Dr. Jeffrey Dean
4 Chandos Rd., Chorlton-cum-Hardy, Manchester, M21 OST,
England, UK
Tel: 44 161 8617542
Fax: 44 161 8617543
Email: jeffrey.dean@stingrayoffice.com
Website: http://www.rma.ac.uk/
Founded: 1874
Members: 900
Contact: Dr. Jeffrey Dean, Membership Sec.
Fee: £37
Fee: £18
Membership Type: students
Description: Musicologists and music students; plus interested
amateurs. Exists to promote research and exchange of ideas in
musicology. To this end it holds meetings and conferences at which
scholarly papers are read on aspects of musicology, music theory,
and music analysis.
Library Subject: musicology
Library Type: reference
Publication: Journal
Publication title: Journal of the Royal Musical Association.
Advertisements.
Second publication: Monographs
Publication title: Royal Musical Association
Meetings/Conventions: - annual conference - Exhibits. Cardiff UK

Royal National Institute for Deaf People

19-23 Featherstone St., London, EC1Y 8SL, England, UK
Tel: 44 20 72968000
Fax: 44 207 2968199
Email: informationline@rnid.org.uk
Website: http://www.rnid.org.uk
Founded: 1911
Members: 25455
Staff: 1500
Contact:
Fee: £16.5
Description: Individual registered members. Provides the following
quality services for the deaf, deaf blind and hard of hearing people:
information, residential care, training (deaf awareness), specialist
telephone services (Typetalk), assistive devices for sale from Sound
Advantage, and Communication Support Units. All services are
accessed through Regional offices, except Typetalk and Sound
Advantage.
Library Subject: deafness, speech problems
Library Type: open to the public
Publication: Magazine
Publication title: One In Seven. Advertisements.
Meetings/Conventions: - annual general assembly London

Royal National Institute of the Blind England
RNIB

105 Judd St., London, WC1H 9NE, England, UK
Tel: 44 207 3881266
Fax: 44 207 3882034
Email: helpline@rnib.org.uk
Website: http://www.rnib.org.uk
Founded: 1868
Staff: 2000
Contact: Ian Bruce, Dir.Gen.

Description: Wants a world in which blind and partially sighted
people enjoy the same rights, freedoms, and responsibilities and
quality of life as people who are fully sighted. Mission is to challenge
blindness. Challenges the disabling effects of blindness by providing
services to help people determine their own lives. Challenges
society's actions, attitudes, and assumptions. Works to dismantle
barriers that are put into the path of the blind and partially sighted
people. Works to prevent, cure, and alleviate blindness.
Library Type: open to the public
Publication title: Publications Catalogue

Royal Navy Bird Watching Society
RNBWS

16 Cutlers Ln., Stubbington, Fareham, P014 2JN, England, UK
Tel: 44 1329 665931
Email: fsward@lincone.net
Founded: 1946
Members: 299
Staff: 6
Contact: Comdr. F.S. Ward, Sec.
Fee: £8
Membership Type: member and associate
Fee: £8
Membership Type: library member
Description: Aims to provide a forum for the exchange of information
and observations of seabirds, and of landbirds at sea, by members for
whom birdwatching is first and foremost a hobby, and to provide
advice and support to make best use of such opportunities at sea.
Library Subject: ornithology
Library Type: reference
Publication: Newsletter
Publication title: Bulletin. Advertisements.
Second publication: Magazine
Publication title: Sea Swallow. Advertisements.
Meetings/Conventions: - annual meeting

Royal Over-Seas League
ROSL

Over-Seas House, Park Pl., St. James's St., London, SW1A 1LR,
England, UK
Tel: 44 207 4080214
Fax: 44 207 4996738
Email: info@rosl.org.uk
Website: http://www.rosl.org.uk
Founded: 1910
Members: 22000
Staff: 140
Contact: Mr. Robert F. Newell, Dir.Gen.
Description: Represents members' interests.
Publication: Journal
Publication title: Overseas Journal. Advertisements.
Meetings/Conventions: - periodic

Royal Pharmaceutical Society of Great Britain
RPSGB

1 Lambeth High St., London, SE1 7JN, England, UK
Tel: 44 207 7359141
Fax: 44 207 7357629
Email: enquiries@rpsgb.org.uk
Website: http://www.rpsgb.org.uk
Founded: 1841
Members: 40000

Staff: 170
Contact: Ann Lewis, Sec./Registrar
Fee: £186
Membership Type: statutory
Description: Pharmacists. Professional, statutory and regulatory body for practicing pharmacists in Great Britain.
Library Subject: pharmacy, pharmaceutical sciences, health care
Library Type: open to the public
Publication: Book
Publication title: The Extra Pharmacopeia
Second publication: Newsletter
Publication title: Martindale Online Newsletter
Meetings/Conventions: British Pharmaceutical Conference - annual conference - Exhibits.

Royal Philharmonic Society
RPS

10 Stratford Pl., London, W1C 1BA, England, UK
Tel: 44 207 4918110
Fax: 44 207 4937463
Email: admin@royalphilharmonicsociety.org.uk
Website: http://www.royalphilharmonicsociety.org.uk
Founded: 1813
Members: 350
Staff: 2
Contact: Rosemary Johnson, Gen.Admin.
Description: Professional musicians and music lovers. Supports creativity, excellence, and understanding in music. Provides support for composers, new music, and young musicians.
Library Subject: history of the Royal Philharmonic Society since 1813
Library Type: reference
Publication: Newsletter
Publication title: Fanfare. Advertisements.
Publication title: First Philharmonic
Meetings/Conventions: - periodic competition

Royal Photographic Society of Great Britain
RPS

The Octagon, Milsom St., Bath, BA1 1DN, England, UK
Tel: 44 1225 462841
Fax: 44 1225 448688
Email: rps@rps.org
Website: http://www.rps.org
Founded: 1853
Members: 9500
Staff: 20
Contact: John Page, Pres.
Fee: £77
Membership Type: in the United Kingdom
Fee: £67
Membership Type: outside the United Kingdom
Description: Individuals interested in the science and art of photography. Organizes international touring exhibitions. Conducts lectures, seminars, and conferences; offers children's services. Sponsors competitions; bestows awards. Maintains museum housing 19th and 20th century photography, photographic equipment, and journals.
Library Subject: photography
Library Type: reference
Publication title: Imaging Abstracts
Second publication: Journal
Publication title: Imaging Science Journal. Advertisements.
Meetings/Conventions: RPS Touring Exhibitions - periodic

Royal Sailors' Rests

Castaway House, 311 Twyford Ave., Portsmouth, PO2 8PE, England, UK
Tel: 44 23 92650505
Fax: 44 23 92652929
Email: info@rsr.org.uk
Website: http://www.rsr.org.uk
Founded: 1876
Members: 3000
Staff: 60
Contact: Brian Deverson, Exec.Dir.
Description: Society of counseling centers proclaiming the Christian faith and preaching temperance to the men and women of the Royal Navy. Operates children's services and charitable programs.
Publication: Newsletter
Publication title: Ashore and Afloat
Meetings/Conventions: - annual conference

Royal Society
RS

6-9 Carlton House Terr., London, SW1Y 5AG, England, UK
Tel: 44 207 4512500
Fax: 44 207 9302170
Email: info@royalsoc.ac.uk
Website: http://www.royalsoc.ac.uk
Founded: 1660
Members: 1200
Staff: 125
Contact: Mr. Stephen Cox, Exec.Sec.
Description: Recognizing excellence in science and its application, promoting authoritative advice, notably to Government, on science and engineering-related matters; offers research fellowships and grants to individual scientists; disseminates the results of research through meetings, lectures and exhibitions; fosters public understanding of science; promotes science education and awareness; supports international scientific exchange and international scientific relations; provides resources for research into the history of science and acts as a forum and focus for discussion of issues relating to the wider scientific community.
Library Subject: history of science, scientific biography, and science policy
Library Type: reference
Publication: Book
Publication title: Biographical Memoirs of Fellows of the Royal Society
Second publication: Newsletter
Publication title: Excellence in Science
Meetings/Conventions: meeting

Royal Society for Asian Affairs

2 Belgrave Sq., London, SW1X 8PJ, England, UK
Tel: 44 20 72355122
Fax: 44 20 72596771
Email: sec@rsaa.org.uk
Website: http://www.rsaa.org.uk
Founded: 1901
Members: 1200
Staff: 4
Contact: Mr. Norman Cameron, Sec.
Fee: £55
Membership Type: in London
Fee: £45
Membership Type: international

Description: Promotes greater knowledge and understanding of Asian countries. Conducts educational activities and tours. Maintains speakers' bureau.
Library Subject: Asian history, geography, politics, travel
Library Type: reference
Publication: Journal
Publication title: Asian Affairs. Advertisements.
Meetings/Conventions: - biennial dinner

Royal Society for Mentally Handicapped Children and Adults
MENCAP

123 Golden Ln., London, EC1Y 0RT, England, UK
Tel: 44 20 74540454
Fax: 44 20 76965540
Email: information@mencap.org.uk
Website: http://www.mencap.org.uk
Founded: 1947
Contact: Fred Heddell, Exec.Off.
Fee: £12
Membership Type: individual
Description: Works with children and adults with learning disabilities in England, Wales and Northern Ireland; campaigns to ensure that people with learning disabilities have the best opportunities to live as full citizens; aims to influence new legislation and raise the profile of learning disability issues; conducts research into issues affecting people with learning disabilities. Provides housing advice, residential services, employment assistance, leisure clubs, holiday advice.
Publication: Newspaper
Publication title: Viewpoint

Royal Society for the Encouragement of Arts, Manufactures, and Commerce
RSA

8 John Adam St., London, WC2N 6EZ, England, UK
Tel: 44 207 9305115
Fax: 44 207 8395805
Email: general@rsa.org.uk
Website: http://www.theRSA.org
Founded: 1754
Members: 23000
Staff: 120
Contact: Penny Egan, Dir.
Fee: £100
Membership Type: fellowship, by election
Description: Individuals in 70 countries. Works to embolden enterprise, enlarge science, refine art, improve our manufacturers and extend our commerce. Seeks to encourage sustainable economic development and release human creativity.
Library Subject: manufacturing and commerce, modern collection covering the Society's core interests, plus historic collection dating back to 1750s
Library Type: by appointment only
Publication: Journal
Publication title: RSA Journal. Advertisements.

Royal Society for the Prevention of Accidents
Edgbaston Park, 353 Bristol Rd., Birmingham, B5 7ST, England, UK
Tel: 44 121 2482314
Fax: 44 121 2482001
Email: rvincent@rospa.co.uk
Website: http://www.rospa.org.uk

Founded: 1917
Members: 6900
Staff: 120
Contact: Roger Vincent
Description: Companies, local authorities, road safety officers, schools, leisure centres. Aims to enhance quality of life by exercising a powerful influence for accident prevention.
Library Subject: safety
Library Type: not open to the public
Publication title: Care on the Road. Advertisements.
Second publication: Bulletin
Publication title: Occupational Safety and Health Bulletin
Meetings/Conventions: Home Safety Conference - annual

Royal Society for the Prevention of Cruelty to Animals
RSPCA

Wilberforce Way, Horsham, RH13 9RS, England, UK
Tel: 44 870 01001181
Fax: 44 870 7530048
Website: http://www.rspca.org.uk
Founded: 1824
Members: 53754
Staff: 1207
Contact: Chris Reed, Info.Off.
Fee: £15
Membership Type: adult
Description: Individuals and organizations concerned about the well-being of wild and domestic animals in the United Kingdom. Opposes: unnecessary animal experimentation; habitat destruction; factory farming; blood sports. Promotes: attitudes and behaviors supporting the rights and dignity of all animals; spaying and neutering of pets; proper treatment of pets. Makes available low cost veterinary care
Library Subject: animal welfare, animal care, ethics
Library Type: by appointment only
Publication: Journal
Publication title: Animal Action. Advertisements.
Second publication: Journal
Publication title: Animal Life. Advertisements.
Meetings/Conventions: - annual general assembly

Royal Society for the Promotion of Health
38A St. George's Dr., London, SW1V 4BH, England, UK
Tel: 44 207 6300121
Fax: 44 207 9766847
Email: rshealth@rshealth.org.uk
Website: http://www.rsph.org
Founded: 1876
Members: 6000
Staff: 23
Contact: Hugh Alowson, Ch.Exec.
Description: Members are drawn from a wide variety of professions and occupations with an interest in improving the health of the population. They range from architects and engineers, the health related profession, to food scientists and caterers. Aims to improve the quality and dignity of human life worldwide and to promote the continuous improvement of health and safety through education communication and the encouragement of scientific research.
Formerly: Royal Society of Health
Publication: Journal
Publication title: JRSH

Royal Society for the Protection of Birds
RSPB

The Lodge, Sandy, SG19 2DL, England, UK
Tel: 44 1767 680551
Fax: 44 1767 692365
Website: http://www.rspb.org.uk
Founded: 1889
Members: 1012000
Staff: 1000
Contact: Graham Wynne, CEO
Fee: £27
Membership Type: single
Fee: £36
Membership Type: joint
Description: Voluntary wildlife conservation organization. Encourages better conservation and protection of wild birds, especially rare species. Promotes public interest and appreciation. Assists efforts to protect nesting grounds; purchases land for bird sanctuaries and reserves. Conducts research and surveys; offers educational programs.
Library Subject: birds, nature conservation
Library Type: reference
Publication: Magazine
Publication title: Bird Life. Advertisements.
Second publication: Magazine
Publication title: Birds. Advertisements.
Meetings/Conventions: Members Weekend - annual convention - Exhibits.

Royal Society of British Artists

c/o Federation of British Artists
17 Carlton House Terrace, London, SW1Y 5BD, England, UK
Tel: 44 207 9306844
Fax: 44 207 8397830
Email: info@mallgalleries.com
Website: http://www.mallgalleries.org.uk
Founded: 1824
Members: 107
Contact: Briony Chaplin
Description: Professional artists. Organises art exhibitions of sculpture, watercolours, oils, drawings and prints, etc; most work is for sale at annual exhibit.
Publication: Catalog
Publication title: Annual Exhibition Catalogue. Advertisements.
Meetings/Conventions: - annual specialty show - Exhibits.

Royal Society of British Sculptors

108 Old Brompton Rd., London, SW7 3RA, England, UK
Tel: 44 207 3735554
Fax: 44 207 3703721
Email: info@rbs.org.uk
Website: http://www.rbs.org.uk
Founded: 1904
Members: 430
Staff: 5
Contact: Claire Foster
Fee: £125
Membership Type: International Associate
Description: Professional working sculptors. Aims to promote and advance the art of sculpture. Works to ensure the continued widespread debate on contemporary sculpture and promote the pursuit of excellence in the artform. Offers advice on technical, aesthetic and legal matters concerning the production of sculpture.

Advocates good fair practice in the commissioning and exhibition of work.
Library Subject: sculpture
Library Type: by appointment only
Meetings/Conventions: - annual general assembly - Exhibits. London UK

Royal Society of Chemistry
RSC

Burlington House, Piccadilly, London, W1J 0BA, England, UK
Tel: 44 20 74378656
Fax: 44 20 74378883
Email: rsc@rsc.org
Website: http://www.rsc.org
Founded: 1841
Members: 46000
Staff: 330
Contact: Julie Franklin
Description: Chemists and interested persons in most countries of the world. Fosters the growth and application of chemistry by disseminating information. Establishes standards of qualification and conduct for the profession. Seeks to serve the public in an advisory and consultative capacity in matters relating to science and chemistry; monitors developments in chemistry. Encourages communication and cooperation between higher education and industry; offers career guidance and continuing education courses; funds small research projects. Maintains the Benevolent Fund, which helps members, former members, and their dependents who are in need of aid and the Corday-Morgan Memorial Fund, which enables members to travel to developing countries to lecture and exchange information. Organizes symposia, conferences, scientific meetings, and exhibitions. Provides Schools Publications Service, offering subscriptions for schools in Canada, England, Ireland, and the United States. Compiles statistics; sponsors competitions.
Library Subject: chemistry
Library Type: reference
Formerly: Absorbed, Society for Analytical Chemistry
Publication: Annual Report
Publication title: Analytical Atomic Spectroscopy
Second publication: Journal
Publication title: Chemical Society Reviews

Royal Society of Literature

Somerset House, Strand, London, WC2R 1LA, England, UK
Tel: 44 20 78454676
Fax: 44 20 78454679
Email: info@rslit.org
Website: http://www.rslit.org
Founded: 1820
Members: 860
Staff: 3
Contact: Maggie Fergusson
Fee: £30
Description: Individuals interested in literature. Sustains all that is best in English letters, and encourages a catholic appreciation of literature. Lectures and poetry readings take place monthly.
Meetings/Conventions: - monthly lecture - Exhibits.

Royal Society of Literature of the United Kingdom
RSL

Strand, London, WC2R 1LA, England, UK
Tel: 44 20 78454676
Fax: 44 20 78454679

Email: info@rslit.org
Website: http://www.rslit.org
Founded: 1820
Members: 876
Staff: 3
Contact: Maggie Fergusson, Sec.
Fee: £30
Description: Encourages and sustains excellence in English letters; supports various literary causes.

Royal Society of Marine Artists
RSMA

c/o Federation of British Artists
17 Carlton House Terrace, London, SW1Y 5BD, England, UK
Tel: 44 207 9306844
Fax: 44 207 8397830
Email: info@mallgalleries.com
Website: http://www.mallgalleries.org.uk
Founded: 1945
Members: 45
Contact: Briony Chaplin
Description: Professional marine artists. Organises the exhibition of original works of art by marine artists; sales and commissions of marine art; educates the public in marine art through exhibitions.
Publication: Catalog
Publication title: Exhibition Catalogue. Advertisements.
Meetings/Conventions: - annual - Exhibits.

Royal Society of Medicine

1 Wimpole St., London, W1G 0AE, England, UK
Tel: 44 207 2902900
Fax: 44 207 2902992
Email: joanna.rose@rsm.ac.uk
Website: http://www.rsm.ac.uk
Founded: 1805
Members: 18000
Staff: 150
Contact: Dr. Anne Grocock, Exec.Dir.
Fee: £273
Description: Doctors, dentists, vets and lay members with interest in medicine.
Library Subject: medicine
Library Type: reference
Publication title: The AIDS Letter
Second publication: Journal
Publication title: International Journal of STD and AIDS
Meetings/Conventions: - periodic conference

Royal Society of Miniature Painters, Sculptors and Gravers

1 Knapp Cottages, Wyke, Gillingham, SP8 4NQ, England, UK
Tel: 44 1747 825718
Fax: 44 1747 826835
Email: hendersons@dial.pipex.com
Website: http://www.royal-miniature-society.org.uk
Founded: 1895
Members: 150
Staff: 1
Contact: Pamela Henderson, Exec. Sec.
Description: Associate Membership: candidates must have 5 works accepted 2 years running. Three years later they are eligible for election to full membership with six accepted works in election year. The Council may invite to membership in special circumstances. Aims

to achieve an ever higher standard in the long-established fine art of miniature work and to present this for the instruction and enjoyment of the public.
Publication: Catalog

Royal Society of Musicians of Great Britain
RSMGB

10 Stratford Pl., London, W1C 1BA, England, UK
Tel: 44 207 6296137
Fax: 44 207 6296137
Website: http://www.ianpartridge.pwp.blueyonder.co.uk/rsminfo.html
Founded: 1738
Members: 1200
Staff: 2
Contact: Maggie Gibb, Sec.
Fee: £5
Description: Provides immediate and vital aid for professional musicians and their families in distress due to accident, illness or old age.
Library Subject: Musical history and biography
Library Type: reference
Formerly: Absorbed, Royal Society of Female Musicians
Publication: Book
Publication title: History of the Royal Society of Musicians, 1738-1988
Second publication: Book
Publication title: Members of the Royal Society of Musicians, 1738-1984
Meetings/Conventions: - monthly meeting

Royal Society of Painter-Printmakers

Bankside Gallery, 48 Hopton St., Blackfriars, London, SE1 9JH, England, UK
Tel: 44 20 9287521
Fax: 44 20 9282820
Email: bankside@freeuk.com
Founded: 1880
Members: 150
Staff: 5
Contact:
Fee: £138
Membership Type: ordinary
Description: Artists, etchers, and engravers united to further the development of printmaking processes. Encourages public appreciation of prints; provides a forum for the presentation of original etchings and engravings. Organizes educational programs.
Publication: Magazine
Publication title: Bankside Bulletin. Advertisements.
Meetings/Conventions: - annual meeting - Exhibits.

Royal Society of Portrait Painters
RP

17 Carlton House Terrace, London, SW1Y 5BD, England, UK
Tel: 44 207 9306844
Fax: 44 207 8397830
Email: info@mallgalleries.com
Website: http://www.mallgalleries.org.uk
Founded: 1891
Members: 41
Contact: Briony Chaplin, Press Off.

Description: Professional portrait painters. Organises the exhibition and commissioning of portraits; educates the public in portraiture through exhibitions. Some work sold at annual exhibition.
Publication: Catalog
Meetings/Conventions: - annual specialty show - Exhibits.

Royal Society of Tropical Medicine and Hygiene RSTMH

Manson House, 26 Portland Pl., London, W1B 1EY, England, UK
Tel: 44 207 5802127
Fax: 44 207 4361389
Email: mail@rstmh.org
Website: http://www.rstmh.org/
Founded: 1907
Members: 3000
Staff: 4
Contact: C.R. Guest, Admin.
Fee: £85
Membership Type: medical and veterinary practitioners and scientists
Description: Medical and veterinary practititioners, scientists, and interested others representing 88 countries. Promotes health and seeks to advance the study, control, and prevention of tropical diseases in humans and animals. Encourages information exchange and facilitates discussion.
Publication title: Bulletin of Tropical Medicine & International Health
Second publication: Journal
Publication title: Transactions of the Royal Society of Tropical Medicine and Hygiene. Advertisements.
Meetings/Conventions: lecture

Royal Statistical Society

12 Errol St., London, EC1Y 8LX, England, UK
Tel: 44 207 6388998
Fax: 44 207 6143905
Email: rss@rss.org.uk
Website: http://www.rss.org.uk
Founded: 1834
Members: 6000
Staff: 15
Contact: I.J. Goddard, Exec.Sec.
Fee: £35
Membership Type: fellow
Description: Statisticians. Promotes and protects the professional interests of members; encourages study among statisticians into the proper use of statistical techniques for the solution of practical problems. Advocates the training of persons in the principles of statistics so that statistics may be applied to problems of administration and research in industry, commerce, government, and all fields of applied science. Works to develop a syllabus of study in statistics and to ensure that students proficient in statistical theory also acquire adequate practical experience. Grants qualification for statisticians through the administration of an annual examination given worldwide; organizes seminars and courses.
Library Type: reference
Publication: Journal
Publication title: Journal of the Royal Statistical Society
Second publication: Newsletter
Publication title: RSS News. Advertisements.
Meetings/Conventions: - annual conference - Exhibits. Hasselt-Diepenbeek Belgium

Royal Surgical Aid Society

47 Great Russell St., London, WC1B 3PB, England, UK
Tel: 44 2076374577
Fax: 44 2073236878
Email: enquiries@agecare.org.uk
Website: http://www.agecare.org.uk
Founded: 1862
Members: 17
Staff: 300
Description: Seeks to improve the care and well being of older people who are physically frail or suffering from dementia, through a combination of continuous development of good practice in it's own homes, seeking pre-eminence in education and training, supporting research and innovation, providing awards for excellence, and continuing in the exchange of knowledge and ideas.

Royal Television Society

Holborn Hall, 100 Grays Inn Rd., London, WC1X 8AL, England, UK
Tel: 44 207 4301000
Fax: 44 207 4300924
Email: info@rts.org.uk
Website: http://www.rts.org.uk
Founded: 1927
Members: 3603
Staff: 12
Contact: Simon Albury, CEO
Fee: £75
Description: From entire spectrum of the broadcasting industry including studio services, programme making, engineering, design, journalism and management. A central independent forum for the discussion of the art, science and politics of television. Organizes training courses, and lectures for the television industry. Also has 15 regional centres with their own programmes of lectures and functions.
Meetings/Conventions: - periodic conference

Royal Town Planning Institute

41 Botolph Ln., London, EC3R 8DL, England, UK
Tel: 44 207 9299494
Fax: 44 207 9299490
Email: online@rtpi.org.uk
Website: http://www.rtpi.org.uk
Founded: 1914
Members: 18000
Contact: Michael Napier
Description: Professional town planners in local government, private practice, central government, teaching and commerce. Exists to advance the science and art of town planning for the benefit of the public. It helps maintain high standards of professional education and training and promotes its members' expertise and competence. It also provides a national voice for the profession and runs a free planning aid service.
Publication title: Planning

Royal Watercolour Society RWS

Bankside Gallery, 48 Hopton St., Blackfriars, London, SE1 9JH, England, UK
Tel: 44 171 9287521
Fax: 44 171 9282820
Email: re&rws@banksidegallery.demon.co.uk
Founded: 1804
Members: 80

Staff: 4
Contact: Judy Dixey, Dir.
Fee: £219
Description: Supports watercolor artists in order to make their works known to the public. Works to increase appreciation of watercolors through exhibitions. Sponsors the Adopt a Picture Campaign, which provides funding for preservation and restoration of the RWS Diploma collection. Maintains permanent collection of works of present and past members. Organizes educational events including art days, demonstrations, studio visits, lectures, guided tours and international open painting competition for water-based media.
Library Subject: watercolour and works of art on paper
Library Type: open to the public
Publication: Bulletin
Publication title: Bankside Bulletin. Advertisements.
Meetings/Conventions: - semiannual - Exhibits.

Runnymede Trust
RT

The London Fruit & Wool Exchange, Ste. 106, Brushfield St., London, E1 6EP, England, UK
Tel: 44 20 7377 9222
Fax: 44 20 7377 6622
Email: info@runnymedetrust.org
Website: http://www.runnymedetrust.org
Founded: 1968
Staff: 9
Contact: Michelynn Lafleche, Dir.
Description: Seeks to eliminate all aspects of racism and discrimination in Great Britain and Europe. Conducts research and disseminates information on issues of race and immigration.
Library Subject: race relations and ethnic issues in England
Library Type: reference
Publication: Bulletin
Publication title: Runnymede Bulletin

Rural Crafts Association

Heights Cottage, Brook Rd., Wormley, Godalming, GU8 5UA, England, UK
Tel: 44 1428 682292
Fax: 44 1428 685969
Email: ruralcraftsassociation@btinternet.com
Website: http://www.craftsforchristmas.co.uk
Founded: 1970
Members: 600
Staff: 8
Contact: Trevor Sears
Fee: £82.25
Description: Mostly full time professional craftsmen and women who sell their work at the 50 shows a year the Association organises. Encourages men and women to make and sell their work and skills, to uphold the quality of work and to provide a vigorous forum for the sale of members' work, at a cost they can afford. Advisory service for crafts development and marketing for foreign governments.
Publication: Bulletins. Advertisements.

Rural Design and Building Association

c/o ATSS House
Station Rd. E, Stowmarket, IP14 1RQ, England, UK
Tel: 44 144 9676049
Fax: 44 144 9770028
Email: secretary@rdba.org.uk
Website: http://www.rdba.org.uk

Founded: 1956
Members: 3004
Staff: 2
Contact: Mr. Tony Hutchinson, Sec.
Fee: £220
Membership Type: corporate
Fee: £110
Membership Type: college
Description: Has the detailed knowledge of the foundation and environmental requirements of modern agricultural buildings, together with the breadth of expertise in their siting, planning, design and construction.
Publication: Journal
Publication title: Countryside Building. Advertisements.
Meetings/Conventions: Spring Conference - annual conference - Exhibits.

Ruskin Society of London

351 Woodstock Rd., Oxford, OX2 7NX, England, UK
Tel: 44 1865 310987
Fax: 44 1865 240448
Founded: 1985
Members: 40
Staff: 2
Contact: O. Forbes-Madden, Hon. Sec.
Fee: £15
Membership Type: member
Description: Promotes interest in John Ruskin through study and appreciation. An annual journal is produced.
Publication: Journal
Publication title: The Ruskin Gazette
Publication title: Ruskin Recalled
Meetings/Conventions: - semiannual lecture London UK

Russo-British Chamber of Commerce in Britian

42 Southwark St., London, SE1 1UN, England, UK
Tel: 44 207 4031706
Fax: 44 207 4031245
Email: mail@rbcc.co.uk
Website: http://www.rbcc.com
Founded: 1916
Members: 500
Staff: 15
Contact: David Cant
Description: Promotes business and commerce.
Publication: Journal
Publication title: MON. Advertisements.

Safety Assessment Federation

Nutmeg House, 60 Gainsford St. Butlers, Butlers Wharf, London, SE1 2NY, England, UK
Tel: 44 20 74030987
Fax: 44 20 74030137
Email: info@safed.co.uk
Website: http://www.safed.co.uk
Founded: 1995
Members: 17
Staff: 4
Contact: Richard Morgan, Tech.Dir.
Description: Represents the interests of companies that undertake the independent safety inspection and certification of machinery plant and equipment.
Publication title: Fact sheets

Safety Equipment Distributors Association

74 Chester Rd., Birmingham, B36 7BU, England, UK
Tel: 44 121 7767474
Fax: 44 121 7767605
Website: http://www.safetycentral.org
Contact: G.K. Edwards
Description: Safety equipment distributors.

Sail Training Association
STA

2a The Hard, Portsmouth, PO1 3PT, England, UK
Tel: 44 23 92832055
Fax: 44 23 92815769
Email: tallships@sta.org.uk
Website: http://www.sta.org.uk
Founded: 1956
Members: 2000
Staff: 12
Contact: Mrs. Christine Law, CEO
Fee: £30
Description: Aims to give young people aged 16 to 24 the opportunity of living and working together with other young people from all nationalities and backgrounds, facing real-life challenges to be found on board the two new tall ships, Stavros S. Niarchos and Prince William, promoting team building and personal development. Offers two-week voyages covering 1,000 miles and visiting foreign ports. Adult voyages offer similar opportunities to those ages 18-69.
Publication: Newspaper
Publication title: Aloft. Advertisements.
Publication title: Tall Ships News
Meetings/Conventions: International Tall Ships - annual conference - Exhibits.

Sailing Barge Association

c/o Frank Morris
PO Box 5191, Bournemouth, BH1 3WZ, England, UK
Tel: 44 1202 552582
Email: sba@ffbs.co.uk
Website: http://www.sailingbargeassociation.co.uk
Contact: F.P. Morris, Sec.

Saintpaulia and Houseplant Society

33 Church Rd., Newbury Park, Ilford, IG2 7ET, England, UK
Tel: 44 20 85903710
Founded: 1956
Members: 550
Contact: Mrs. F.B.F. Dunningham, Sec., Tres.
Fee: £7
Membership Type: individual
Description: Promotes the growing of houseplants. Conducts competitions, distribution scheme, and outings.
Library Subject: houseplants
Library Type: lending
Publication: Bulletin
Publication title: Success with Houseplants. Advertisements.
Meetings/Conventions: meeting

SALs Project

Springfield Complex, Squire Ln., Bradford, BD8 6RA, England, UK
Tel: 44 1274 548379
Fax: 44 1274 484346
Description: Individuals and organizations. Promotes community development and redevelopment, focusing on maintenance and improvement of transportation infrastructure in urban areas. Cooperates with local government agencies to devise public community development strategies.

Salt Manufacturers Association

PO Box 125, Kendall, Cumbria, LA8 8XA, England, UK
Tel: 44 1539 568005
Fax: 44 1539 568999
Email: salt@saltinfo.com
Website: http://www.saltinfo.com
Founded: 1970
Members: 6
Description: Promotes the consideration and discussion of all questions affecting the manufacture and use of salt, including its effects on health and the environment. Provides a focal point in the industry for the provision of information for and discussions with outside organisations.
Publication title: Facts on Salt

Salters' Company

Salters' Hall, Fore St., London, EC2Y 5DE, England, UK
Tel: 44 171 5885216
Fax: 44 171 6383679
Email: company@salters.co.uk
Website: http://www.salters.co.uk
Founded: 1394
Members: 300
Staff: 18
Contact: Col. Michael Barneby, Clerk
Description: Salters.
Publication: Newsletter
Publication title: Salters' Newsletter

Salters' Institute

Salters' Hall, 4 Fore St., London, EC2Y 5DE, England, UK
Tel: 44 20 76285962
Fax: 44 20 76383679
Email: institute@salters.co.uk
Website: http://www.saltersinstitute.co.uk
Founded: 1918
Staff: 6
Contact: Mrs. Audrey Strong, Institute Mgr.
Description: Aims to promote the appreciation of chemistry and related sciences among the young, and to encourage careers in the teaching of chemistry and in the UK chemical and allied industries.
Publication: Annual Report
Meetings/Conventions: Salters Teachers Conference - annual conference - Exhibits.

Salvage Association

37-39 Lime St., 5th Fl., London, EC3M 7AY, England, UK
Tel: 44 207 2349120
Fax: 44 207 6230439
Email: salvage@wreckage.org
Website: http://www.wreckage.org
Founded: 1856
Members: 80
Staff: 150
Contact: R.E. Padgett, Chief Exec.
Description: Underwriters at Lloyd's and marine insurance companies at the IUA of London. Maintains marine surveying offices in strategic locations, staffed by experienced marine and nautical surveyors, ready to act immediately in the event of collisions,

strandings, sinkings, salvage, wreck removal, and machinery investigations.
Publication: Directory
Publication title: International
Second publication: Newsletter
Publication title: Salvage Lines

Salvation Army Home League - England
SAHL

c/o Gen. John Gowans
101 Queen Victoria St., London, EC4 4EP, England, UK
Tel: 44 20 73320101
Founded: 1907
Members: 390627
Contact: Commissioner Gisele Gowans, Pres.
Description: Women over the age of 16 from 108 countries. Provides for education, fellowship, service, and worship.

Salvation Army Medical Fellowship
SAMF

c/o Gen. Paul Rader
101 Queen Victoria St., London, EC4P 4EP, England, UK
Tel: 44 171 3320101
Founded: 1943
Members: 10648
Staff: 80
Contact: Commissioner Kay F. Rader, World Pres.
Fee: £10
Membership Type: Full
Fee: £2
Membership Type: Students and retired persons
Description: Purpose is to support members of the International Headquarters of the Salvation Army involved in the field of medicine, particularly those involved in nursing.
Meetings/Conventions: - annual conference UK

Salvation Army UK and Ireland

101 Newington Causeway, London, SE1 6BN, England, UK
Tel: 44 20 73674500
Fax: 44 20 73674728
Email: thg@salvationarmy.org.uk
Website: http://www.salvationarmy.org.uk
Founded: 1865
Members: 46524
Staff: 15
Contact: Major Roger Batt, Territorial Youth Secretary
Description: Encourages Christian ideals and good citizenship among young people.
Publication: Magazine
Publication title: Forum. Advertisements.
Meetings/Conventions: Youth Rally - annual

Samaritans - England

The Upper Mill, Kingston Rd., Ewell, KT17 2AF, England, UK
Tel: 44 20 83948300
Fax: 44 20 83948301
Email: admin@samaritans.org
Website: http://www.samaritans.org
Founded: 1953
Members: 18300
Staff: 60
Contact: Simon Armson, CEO

Description: A nationwide charity providing confidential, emotional support to anyone in crisis, 24 hours a day, 365 days a year. Not a religious or political organization.
Publication title: Educational Materials
Publication title: Samaritan News
Meetings/Conventions: - annual conference

Sand and Gravel Association

1 Bramber Ct., Bramber Rd., London, W14 9PB, England, UK
Tel: 44 171 3818778
Fax: 44 171 3818770
Founded: 1930
Members: 75
Staff: 7
Contact: T.A. Macintyre
Description: Companies engaged in the extraction of sand and gravel from the land and beneath the sea. Represents the interests of member companies. Provides advisory services on minerals planning, technical standards, environmental legislation, public relations and industrial relations. Committed to high environmental standards and aims to achieve this objective through the management of an environmental code of practice.
Publication: Annual Report
Second publication: Bulletin

Satellite and Cable Broadcasters Group

64 West End, Northwold, Thetford, IP26 5LG, England, UK
Tel: 44 1366 728795
Fax: 44 1366 727411
Email: scbg.melwes@care4free.net
Founded: 1983
Members: 17
Staff: 2
Contact: Mark Elwes
Description: Companies providing a channel for satellite and/or cable television, or who have advanced plans. Provides members with the opportunity to discuss matters of mutual interest, and to negotiate when necessary with Government, EC, ITC etc.

SATRA Technology Centre
SATRA

SATRA House, Rockingham Rd., Kettering, NN16 9JH, England, UK
Tel: 44 1536 410000
Fax: 44 1536 410626
Email: info@satra.co.uk
Website: http://www.satra.co.uk/
Founded: 1919
Members: 1200
Staff: 180
Contact: Dr. R.E. Whittaker, Chief Exec.
Description: Manufacturers, retailers, materials and machinery suppliers, and other companies of the footwear and clothing industry, including furniture, PPE and fabric care. Promotes and facilitates competitiveness among members and offers training courses on aspects of footwear production. Compiles statistics. Carries out research.
Library Subject: Footwear production, materials science, adhesion, polymer science, and statistics
Library Type: reference
Formerly: British Boot, Shoe and Allied Trades Research Association
Publication: Newsletter

Publication title: Footwear Business International. Advertisements.
Second publication: Bulletin
Publication title: SATRA Bulletin
Meetings/Conventions: - periodic seminar

Save the Children - UK
SC UK

c/o Public Enquiry Unit
17 Grove Lane, London, SE5 8RD, England, UK
Tel: 44 20 77162268
Fax: 44 20 77032278
Email: enquiries@scfuk.org.uk
Website: http://www.savethechildren.org.uk
Founded: 1919
Staff: 3500
Contact: Dinusha Perera
Description: Works in over 65 countries including the UK. Provides emergency relief and long-term development and prevention work to help children, their families, and communities to be self-sufficient. Part of the International Save the Children Alliance.
Library Subject: work of Save the Children and related issues
Library Type: reference
Publication: Newsletter
Publication title: World's Children

Save the Children United Kingdom

17 Grove Ln., London, SE5 8RD, England, UK
Tel: 44 20 77035400
Fax: 44 20 77032278
Email: enquiries@scfuk.org.uk
Website: http://www.savethechildren.org.uk
Founded: 1919
Staff: 917
Description: Emergency relief runs alongside long-term development and prevention work to help children, families and communities to be self-sufficient. Learns from the reality of children's lives and campaigns for solutions to the problems they face. Is committed to making a reality of the rights of children.
Publication: Catalog

School and Group Travel Association
SAGTA

Katepwa House, Ashfield Park Ave., Ross-On-Wye, HR9 5AX, England, UK
Tel: 44 1989 567690
Fax: 44 1989 567676
Email: sagra@assocmanagemene.co.uk
Founded: 1970
Members: 140
Staff: 2
Contact: Gill Hinton, Sec. to the Assoc.
Description: Travel companies that organize trips for school and youth groups; youth organizations; educational institutions and authorities in the United Kingdom. Monitors educational travel; draws up codes of safety and good conduct. Promotes exchange and cooperation among members. Has membership for places of educational interest which welcome school and youth groups, including stately homes, zoos, steam railways, and museums. Organizes conferences; offers information and advisory service.
Publication: Booklet
Publication title: Code of Conduct
Second publication: Newsletter
Publication title: News
Meetings/Conventions: - annual conference - Exhibits. France

School Journey Association

48 Cavendish Rd., London, SW12 0DG, England, UK
Tel: 44 208 6756636
Fax: 44 208 6738763
Email: sja.demon@co.uk
Founded: 1911
Members: 2029
Staff: 7
Contact: Julia Coakley, Office Mgr.
Fee: £5
Membership Type: affiliated school
Description: Individual members form the Council which is responsible for the Association, which is managed by a Board of Management, assisted by some Tour Secretaries. Corporate members are those schools who use services. Assists schools with travel (UK and Europe), travel insurance; it runs two school hotels in London (Clapham) and runs language courses at Easter. All tours are educational and oriented towards the classroom situation including National Curriculum.
Formerly: Educational Travel Ltd.
Publication: Brochure
Publication title: SJA Tours. Advertisements.
Second publication: Newsletters
Meetings/Conventions: - monthly board meeting

School Library Association
SLA

Unit 2, Lotmead Business Village, Lotmead Farm, Wanborough, Swindon, SN4 0UY, England, UK
Tel: 44 1793 791787
Fax: 44 1793 791786
Email: info@sla.org.uk
Website: http://www.SLA.org.uk
Founded: 1937
Members: 3600
Staff: 6
Contact: Kathy Lemaire, Ch.Exec.
Fee: £45
Description: Schools, colleges, public library services, publishers, and individuals in the UK and overseas. Promotes the development of primary and secondary school libraries. Contributes to and reports on projects in education and librarianship. Works to assist in the development of training for school library work. Maintains advisory and information service. Lobbies for central role of the school library as essential in today's Information Society.
Publication: Bibliographies
Publication title: Books of Children's Fiction to Enjoy
Publication title: Guidelines
Meetings/Conventions: Annual Weekend Conference - annual conference - Exhibits. Leicester UK

Schools Music Association

71 Margaret Rd., New Barnet, Barnet, EN4 9NT, England, UK
Tel: 44 20 84406919
Fax: 44 20 84406919
Email: contact@schoolsmusic.org.uk
Website: http://www.schoolsmusic.org.uk
Founded: 1938
Members: 400
Contact: Maxwell Pryce
Fee: £35
Membership Type: individual
Fee: £40
Membership Type: corporate

Description: Teachers - primary, secondary, special, instrumental; lecturers and student teachers; inspectors, advisers, consultants; LEAs, local SMAs and Festivals; schools, colleges, music centres, libraries; the music trade -publishers, manufacturers, music. shops. Promotes music education by providing opportunities for its members to learn about, discuss and evaluate developments in music education; organizing national and regional weekend conferences, day courses and workshops; providing opportunities for children to perform at major venues, such as the Royal Festival Hall; maintaining close contact with other organizations.
Publication: Bulletin. Advertisements.
Second publication: Annual Report
Meetings/Conventions: - annual conference - Exhibits.

Science Council

76 Portland Pl., London, WIB 1NT, England, UK
Tel: 44 207 4704830
Fax: 44 207 74707937
Email: enquiries@sciencecouncil.org
Website: http://www.sciencecouncil.org
Founded: 1969
Members: 20
Staff: 2
Contact: Dr. Sarah Ball, Dir.
Description: Professional science bodies. Represents the views or acts on behalf of its members in dealing with all those bodies that use the services of professionally qualified scientists and technologists, or who require advice on science and technology. Also encourages and assists the adoption of common policies by its members.
Formerly: Council of Science and Technology Institutes

Science Fiction Foundation
SFF

University of Liverpool Library, PO Box 123, Liverpool, L69 3DA, England, UK
Tel: 44 151 7943142
Fax: 44 151 7942681
Email: asawyer@liverpool.ac.uk
Website: http://www.liv.ac.uk/~asawyers/sf_info.html
Founded: 1971
Contact: Andy Sawyer, Admin.
Description: Promotes the study of science fiction in education.
Library Subject: Science fiction allied topics
Library Type: reference
Publication: Journal
Publication title: Foundation: The Review of Science Fiction. Advertisements.
Meetings/Conventions: - periodic conference

Scientific Committee on Antarctic Research
SCAR

Scott Polar Research Inst., Lensfield Rd., Cambridge, CB2 1ER, England, UK
Tel: 44 1223 362061
Fax: 44 1223 336550
Email: info@scar.org
Website: http://www.scar.org
Founded: 1958
Members: 32
Staff: 2
Contact: Dr. P.D. Clarkson, Exec.Sec.
Description: A committee of the International Council of Scientific Unions. National organizations actively engaged in Antarctic research.

Initiates, promotes, and coordinates, scientific research in the Antarctic and provides scientific advice to the Antarctic Treaty system.
Publication: Report
Publication title: Biological Investigations of Marine Antarctic Systems and Stocks
Second publication: Bulletin
Publication title: SCAR Bulletin
Meetings/Conventions: SCAR Delegates Meeting - biennial meeting

Scientific Exploration Society
SES

Motcombe, Shaftesbury, SP7 9PB, England, UK
Tel: 44 1747 853353
Fax: 44 1747 851351
Founded: 1969
Description: Encourages scientifically orientated expeditions.

Scoliosis Association
SAUK

2 Ivebury Ct., 323-327 Latimer Rd., London, W10 6RA, England, UK
Tel: 44 20 89645343
Fax: 44 20 89645343
Email: sauk@sauk.org.uk
Website: http://www.sauk.org.uk
Founded: 1981
Members: 3000
Staff: 5
Contact: Pauline Grey
Description: Individuals affected by scoliosis; their parents and families. Seeks to increase knowledge and understanding of scoliosis (a lateral curvature of the spine) and emphasize the importance of early detection. Encourages contact between members; disseminates information to members and the public.
Publication title: A Twist of Fate
Second publication: Newsletter
Publication title: Newsletter
Meetings/Conventions: - semiannual regional meeting

Scope

6 Market Rd., London, N7 9PW, England, UK
Tel: 44 20 76197100
Email: cphelpline@scope.org.uk
Website: http://www.scope.org.uk
Description: People with cerebral palsy, their families, and carers in England and Wales. Promotes equality for disabled people. Provides residential, job help, and education services for people with cerebral palsy; carries out research into issues affecting disabled people.
Publication: Newspaper
Publication title: Disability Now

Scottish Church History Society
SCHS

39 Southside Rd., Inverness, 1V2 4XA, England, UK
Tel: 44 1463 231140
Fax: 44 1463 230537
Founded: 1922
Members: 293
Contact: Rev. Peter H. Donald, Hon.Sec. & Treas.
Fee: £15
Fee: £32

Description: Libraries, historians, and interested individuals in 18 countries. Promotes the study of Scottish ecclesiastical history. Organizes symposia.
Publication: Journal
Publication title: Records of the Scottish Church History Society
Publication title: Syllabus and Membership List
Meetings/Conventions: - bimonthly meeting

Scottish Pipers' Association

Glenfarg St., St. Georges Cross, Glasgow, , England, UK
Tel: 44 141 9462137
Founded: 1920
Members: 125
Staff: 0
Contact:
Fee: £25
Membership Type: Life
Fee: £5
Description: Anyone who is interested in piping may apply for membership. Concerned with the study and practice of the music of the great highland bagpipe, the banding together of the pipers of Scotland, and the fostering of the spirit of comradeship amongst them.
Meetings/Conventions: - monthly Glasgow

Scottish Text Society

c/o Dr. N. Royan
School of English, University of Nottingham, University Park, Nottingham, NG7 2RD, England, UK
Tel: 44 115 9515922
Fax: 44 115 9515922
Email: sts@atsarts.gla.ac.uk
Website: http://www.scottishtextsociety.org
Founded: 1882
Members: 154
Staff: 1
Contact: Dr. Nicola Royan, Ed.Sec.
Fee: £20
Membership Type: individual
Fee: £30
Membership Type: institutional
Description: Aims to further the study and teaching of Scottish literature, its language and history, in particular by publishing editions of original texts.
Library Type: not open to the public
Publication title: Annual Volume

Scout Association
SA

Bury Rd., Chingford, E4 7QW, England, UK
Tel: 44 20 84337100
Fax: 44 20 84337103
Email: info.centre@scout.org.uk
Website: http://www.scoutbase.org.uk/
Founded: 1907
Members: 500000
Staff: 210
Contact: John Fogg, Dir. of Commun.
Fee: £8.3
Description: Organization for Scouts in the United Kingdom. Promotes scouting and its ideals among youth.
Publication: Magazine
Publication title: Scouting Magazine. Advertisements.

Screen Advertising World Association
SAWA

c/o Pearl & Dean, 3 Waterhouse Sq., 138-142 Holborn, London, EC1N 2NY, England, UK
Tel: 44 207 8821100
Fax: 44 207 8821111
Email: rob.cooksey@pearlanddean.com
Website: http://www.sawa.com
Founded: 1952
Staff: 1
Contact: Rob Cooksey
Description: All cinema (screen) contractors. To promote and develop cinema screen advertising on an international basis.

Screen Printing Association U.K.
SPA

Association House, 7a West St., Reigate, RH2 9BL, England, UK
Tel: 44 1737 240792
Fax: 44 1737 240770
Email: info@spauk.co.uk
Website: http://www.spauk.co.uk
Founded: 1934
Members: 220
Staff: 2
Contact: Michael Turner, Dir.
Description: Producers, suppliers, and trade houses involved in the screen printing and digital printing industry. Promotes the screen printing industry in the United Kingdom; represents members' interests. Fosters technical exchange among members; disseminates information. Conducts educational programs; maintains apprenticeship project. Bestows awards; provides placement service.
Formerly: Display Producers and Screen Printers Association
Meetings/Conventions: - quadrennial trade show - Exhibits.

Sea Cadet Association
SCA

202 Lambeth Rd., London, SE1 7JF, England, UK
Tel: 44 207 9288978
Fax: 44 207 9288978
Email: awilson@sea-cadets.org
Founded: 1995
Members: 850
Staff: 113
Contact: Mr. A.J. Wilson, Company Sec.
Fee: £12
Description: Charity and Company limited by guarantee. Exists to jointly sponser the Sea Cadet Corps, which seeks to develop leadership qualities in youth through sports and boating activities. Offers research and educational programs for cadets (boys and girls ages 10 to 18, enrolled in program) and leaders. Sponsors internal competitions.
Formerly: Navy League
Publication: Newspaper
Publication title: Navy News
Meetings/Conventions: - annual convention

Sea Cadet Corps
SCC

c/o Sea Cadets Assn.
202 Lambeth Rd., London, SE1 7JF, England, UK
Tel: 44 20 79288978
Fax: 44 20 79288914
Email: info@sea-cadets.org
Website: http://www.sea-cadets.org
Founded: 1899
Members: 20000
Staff: 60
Contact: Commodore R.M. Parker
Description: Boys and girls (ages 12-18) and their instructors interested in the British Royal Navy, Royal Marines, Merchant Navy, and naval and marine practices in general. Seeks to promote development of character, leadership, self respect, and devotion to duty. Promotes services to community. Offers courses in general seamanship, boatwork mechanical and electrical engineering, and other subjects. Offers ship training and opportunities to work with British Royal Navy.
Formerly: Absorbed, Girls' Nautical Training Corps
Publication: Newspaper
Publication title: Navy News - Sea Cadet Edition
Meetings/Conventions: - annual convention

Seabird Group
SG

c/o BTO
The Nunnery, Thetford, 1P24 2PU, England, UK
Tel: 44 1842 750050
Fax: 44 1842 750030
Email: info@bto.org
Website: http://www.bto.org
Founded: 1966
Members: 250
Contact: Dr. Chris Wernham
Fee: £10
Membership Type: regular
Fee: £9
Membership Type: direct debit
Description: Amateur and professional ornithologists interested in seabirds. Seeks to promote knowledge of seabird biology, conservation, and ecology. Disseminates information; organizes and coordinates research activities.
Publication: Journal
Publication title: Atlantic Seabird
Second publication: Newsletter
Publication title: Seabird Group Newsletter
Meetings/Conventions: - triennial conference

Secondary Heads Association

130 Regent Rd., Leicester, LE1 7PG, England, UK
Tel: 44 116 2991122
Fax: 44 116 2991123
Email: info@sha.org.uk
Website: http://www.sha.org.uk
Founded: 1977
Members: 10000
Staff: 20
Contact: John Dunford, Gen.Sec.
Description: Principals, heads, deputies, assistant heads and senior teachers in secondary schools and colleges.
Publication: Magazine

Publication title: Headlines
Second publication: Journal
Publication title: SHA-Penned
Meetings/Conventions: - annual conference - Exhibits.

Securities and Futures Authority

25 The North Colonnade, Canary Wharf, London, E14 5HS, England, UK
Tel: 44 207 6761000
Fax: 44 207 6761099
Founded: 1991
Members: 1400
Staff: 260
Contact: David Jones
Description: Investment businesses that deal on the organized City markets eg stockbrokers, market makers, investment banks, futures dealers and brokers. The regulatory body for dealers and advisers in securities, bonds, financial futures and options commoditiy futures and corporate finance.
Publication: Book
Publication title: Rule Book
Second publication: Annual Report

Security Systems and Alarms Inspection Board
SSAIB

131 Bedford St., North Shields, NE29 6LA, England, UK
Tel: 44 191 2963242
Fax: 44 191 2962667
Email: ssaib@ssaib.co.uk
Website: http://www.ssaib.org/
Founded: 1994
Description: Promotes and encourages high standards of service and ethics in the security industry.

Selden Society

Mile End Rd., London, E1 4NS, England, UK
Tel: 44 20 78825136
Fax: 44 20 89818733
Email: selden-society@qmw.ac.uk
Website: http://www.selden-society.qmw.ac.uk
Founded: 1887
Description: Promotes the history of English law.

Self Storage Association

42 Heath St., Tamworth, B79 7JH, England, UK
Tel: 44 1827 52337
Fax: 44 1827 310827
Email: admin@ssauk.com
Website: http://www.ssauk.com
Founded: 1987
Members: 100
Contact: Michael P. Skelding
Description: Encourages members, of the Self Storage Industry, to operate their storage facilities within a suggested Code of Ethics. Promotes the industry to general public. Encourages prospective self-storage operators to carry out a full research of the Industry before opening their facilities. Promotes sound legislative proposals affecting the industry. Preserves high standards of conduct in their members and in the industry.
Library Subject: self storage
Library Type: not open to the public

Semiconductor Businesses Association

66 Hill Grove, Huddersfield, HD3 3TL, England, UK
Tel: 44 1484 656865
Fax: 44 1208 370916
Email: secretary@semiconductor.org
Website: http://www.semiconductor.org
Founded: 1992
Members: 30
Staff: 2
Contact: Ted Pritchard, Sec.
Description: Individuals working in microelectronic design, fabrication, and testing in the United Kingdom.

SENSE

11-13 Clifton Terrace, Finsbury Park, London, N4 3SR, England, UK
Tel: 44 20 72727774
Fax: 44 20 72726012
Email: enquiries@sense.org.uk
Website: http://www.sense.org.uk
Founded: 1955
Members: 650
Staff: 2000
Contact: Emma Clark, Web and Info.Officer
Fee: £10
Membership Type: individual
Description: Families, professionals and interested individuals. To provide services for deafblind people, their families, carers and the professionals with whom they work. Campaigns for legislative support for deafblind people.
Library Subject: deafblind issues, associated disabilities
Library Type: not open to the public
Formerly: National Deafblind and Rubella Association
Publication title: Publications list
Second publication: Magazine
Publication title: Talking Sense. Advertisements.
Meetings/Conventions: - periodic

Sewing Machine Trade Association

PO Box 123, Banberry, OX12 6WB, England, UK
Tel: 44 1295 738726
Fax: 44 1295 738275
Email: info@sewingmachine.org.uk
Website: http://www.sewingmachine.org.uk
Founded: 1939
Members: 397
Contact: A. Spencer-Bolland
Description: Promotes the sewing machine trade and industry.

Shakespeare Birthplace Trust
SBT

The Shakespeare Centre, Henley St., Stratford-Upon-Avon, CV37 6QW, England, UK
Tel: 44 1789 204016
Fax: 44 1789 296083
Email: reception@shakespeare.org.uk
Website: http://www.shakespeare.org.uk
Founded: 1847
Staff: 220
Contact: Roger Pringle, Dir.
Description: Purposes are: to honor William Shakespeare (1564-1616); to maintain Shakespeare's birthplace and other properties associated with Shakespeare; to further knowledge of Shakespeare's life and works. Maintains study center, museum, and records office.

Offers special educational services to schools and colleges. Produces a range of publications on Shakespeare and Stratford upon Avon.
Library Subject: Shakespeare, theater history, and drama, including archives of Royal Shakespeare Company
Library Type: reference
Publication title: Shakespeare Houses

Shakespeare Birthplace Trust
ISA

The Shakespeare Centre, Henley St., Stratford-Upon-Avon, CV37 6QW, England, UK
Tel: 44 1789 204016
Fax: 44 1789 296083
Email: isa@intershake.demon.co.uk; reception@shakespeare.org.uk
Website: http://www.shakespeare.org.uk
Founded: 1973
Members: 650
Staff: 1
Contact: Dr. Catherine Alexander, Exec.Sec.-Treas.
Fee: £15
Membership Type: individual
Fee: £15
Membership Type: individual
Description: College and university instructors and interested individuals; national Shakespeare societies and specialist libraries. Gathers and disseminates information on Shakespearean research, publications, translations, and performances. Maintains and circulates diary of future performances, conferences, graduate courses and opportunities for graduate work, and educational experiments relating to Shakespeare's works.
Library Type: reference
Publication title: Congress Proceedings
Publication title: Occasional Papers. Advertisements.
Meetings/Conventions: World Shakespeare Congress - quinquennial conference

Shaw Society
BSS

c/o Barbara Smoker
51 Farmfield Rd., Downham, Bromley, BR1 4NF, England, UK
Tel: 44 208 6973619
Fax: 44 208 6973619
Email: anthnyellis@aol.com
Founded: 1941
Members: 250
Contact: Barbara Smoker, Hon.Sec.
Fee: £15
Membership Type: individuals and libraries
Fee: £30
Description: Students, scholars, and other interested persons; universities, libraries, and institutes in 8 countries. Promotes the study of the life and work of Bernard Shaw (1856-1950).
Publication: Journal
Publication title: Shavian
Second publication: Newsletter
Publication title: Shaw Society Newsletter
Meetings/Conventions: - monthly meeting London UK

Sheffield Chamber of Commerce and Industry

Albion House, Savile St., Sheffield, S4 7UD, England, UK
Tel: 44 114 2018888
Fax: 44 114 2720950
Email: info@scci.org.uk

Website: http://www.scci.org.uk
Members: 1320
Staff: 60
Contact: Nigel Tomlinson, Chief Exec.
Description: Promotes business and commerce.

Shellfish Association of Great Britain

Fishmonger's Hall, London Bridge, London, EC4R 9EL, England, UK
Tel: 44 207 2838305
Fax: 44 207 9291389
Email: sagb@shellfish.org.uk
Website: http://www.shellfish.org.uk
Founded: 1903
Members: 360
Staff: 4
Contact: Dr. Peter Hunt, Dir.
Description: Cultivators, processors in the Shellfish Industry. The main representative trade association for the shellfish industry, SAGB liaises direct with Governments, Local Authorities, Members of Parliament, other bodies in the fishing industry, and is a market-orientated trade association Embassies and other commercial groups overseas use SAGB as the contact point for developing new shellfish markets.
Publication: Proceedings

Shepway Chamber of Commerce and Industry

Shepway Business Center, Shearway Business Pk., Shearway Rd., Folkestone, CT19 4RH, England, UK
Tel: 44 1303 270022
Fax: 44 1303 270476
Email: info@shepwaybc.co.uk
Website: http://www.shepwaybc.co.uk/docs/chamber.htm
Contact: John Barber
Description: Promotes business and commerce.

Shingles Support Society

c/o Marian Nicholson, Dir.
41 North Rd., London, N7 9DP, England, UK
Tel: 44 20 76079661
Email: marian@herpes.org.uk
Website: http://www.herpes.org.uk
Founded: 1985
Staff: 2
Contact: Marian Nicholson, Dir.
Description: Individuals suffering from post-herpetic neuralgia and their families. Offers advice on self-help for post-herpetic neuralgia which can follow shingles. Provides information for primary care doctors by a consultant neurologist regarding drug treatment with dosage information.
Library Type: open to the public

Shipbuilders and Shiprepairers Association

Marine House, Meadlake Pl., Thorpe Lea Rd., Egham, TW20 8BF, England, UK
Tel: 44 1784 223770
Fax: 44 1784 223775
Email: office@ssa.org.uk
Website: http://www.ssa.org.uk
Founded: 1989
Members: 55
Staff: 7
Contact: Nick Granger
Description: UK private sector shipbuilding and ship repair companies and marine specialists. Monitors developments in health and safety and environmental matters as they affect members' interests. Provides a focal point for collaboration on technical matters including developments in the 'International Maritime Organisation' (IMO). Sponsors collaborative research projects for the industry.
Publication: Membership Directory
Second publication: Newsletter

Shop and Display Equipment Association
SDEA

24 Croydon Rd., Caterham, CR3 6YR, England, UK
Tel: 44 1883 348911
Fax: 44 1883 343435
Email: enquiries@sdea.co.uk
Website: http://www.sdea.co.uk
Founded: 1947
Members: 227
Staff: 5
Contact: Lawrence Cutler, Dir.
Description: Suppliers of retail store fittings and equipment in the United Kingdom. Promotes the use of display equipment by retailers in the United Kingdom.
Publication: Directory
Publication title: SDEA Directory of Shopfittings and Display. Advertisements.

Showmen's Guild of Great Britain

151-A King St., Drighlington, BD11 1EJ, England, UK
Tel: 44 113 2853341
Fax: 44 113 2853329
Email: denise@sggbyork.freeserve.co.uk
Website: http://www.showmensguild.com/
Founded: 1889
Members: 4500
Staff: 3
Contact: K. Miller, Gen.Sec.
Description: Individuals over the age of 18 who own and operate or propose to own and operate fairground equipment. To secure the combination and organisation of all travelling showmen who regularly attend and carry on business at fairs and showgrounds and to regulate the conduct of all members.

Shropshire Archaeological and Historical Society
SAHS

Habberley, Pontesbury, SY5 0SQ, England, UK
Tel: 44 1743 790531
Email: jlwestcott@aol.com
Founded: 1877

Shropshire Chamber of Commerce, Training and Entrerprise

Trevithick House, Stafford Park 4, Telford, Newport, TF3 3BA, England, UK
Tel: 44 195 2208200
Fax: 44 195 2208208
Email: enquiries@shropshire-chamber.co.uk
Website: http://www.shropshire-chamber.co.uk
Members: 1365
Staff: 70
Contact: M Lowe, Pres.
Description: Promotes business and commerce.

Sight Savers International - England

Grosvenor Hall, Bolnore Rd., Haywards Heath, RH16 4BX, England, UK
Tel: 44 1444 446600
Fax: 44 1444 446688
Email: information@sightsavers.org
Founded: 1950
Members: 30
Staff: 88
Contact: Richard Porter, Exec.Dir.
Description: Works to prevent and cure blindness and also to provide education and rehabilitation for blind people in economically developing countries. Concentrates on comprehensive eye services which link the sectors together. Cooperates with indigenous government agencies and local leadership to develop and implement vision care programs. Conducts leadership development and educational programs to make projects sustainable using local resources and expertise.
Library Subject: eye care, education, rehabilitation, development, and voluntary sector
Library Type: by appointment only
Publication: Newsletter
Publication title: Sight Savers News

Silica and Moulding Sands Association

156 Buckingham Palace Rd., London, SW1W 9TR, England, UK
Tel: 44 2077 308194
Fax: 44 2077 304355
Email: kirby.samsa@qpa.org
Website: http://www.qpa.org
Founded: 1941
Members: 10
Staff: 2
Contact: Dr. C.E. Kirby, Dir.
Description: Producers and processors of industrial (silica) and moulding sands and associated products. Concerned with the promotion of the silica sand industry and its relationship with government departments, local authorities and the public, to ensure the continuity of essential supplies of indigenous industrial silica sands in the interests of consumer industries.

Silk Association of Great Britain
SAGB

5 Portland Pl., London, W1N 3AA, England, UK
Tel: 44 171 6367788
Fax: 44 171 6367515
Email: sagb@dial.pipex.com
Website: http://www.silk.org.uk
Founded: 1970
Members: 40
Staff: 1
Contact: A. Mansell, Sec.
Description: Trade associations and individuals. Promotes the use of silk. Offers educational services.
Formerly: Silk Group of Silk and Man-Made Fibre Users Association
Publication: Newsletter
Publication title: Serica
Meetings/Conventions: - annual meeting

Simplified Spelling Society

4 Valletta Way, Wellesbourne, CV35 9TB, England, UK
Tel: 44 1789 842112
Email: j.gledhill@coventry.ac.uk
Website: http://www.spellingsociety.org
Founded: 1908
Members: 130
Staff: 1
Contact: John Gledhill, Sec.
Fee: £30
Description: To encourage the serious study of spelling; promotes literacy through modernization of English spelling.
Publication: Journal
Publication title: Journal of the Simplified Spelling Society
Meetings/Conventions: - quarterly meeting

Simultaneous Interpretation Equipment Suppliers Association

c/o M & R Communications Ltd., 7 Bell Industrial Estate, 50 Cunnington St., London, W4 5HB, England, UK
Tel: 44 20 89954714
Fax: 44 20 89955136
Email: office@m-rcom.com
Founded: 1974
Members: 7
Contact: Nigel Palmer
Description: Manufacturers or suppliers of simultaneous interpretation equipment for multilingual conferences for sale or short or long term rental.

Single Ply Roofing Association

The Building Centre, 26 Store St., London, WC1E 7BT, England, UK
Tel: 44 115 9144445
Fax: 44 115 9749827
Email: enquiries@spra.co.uk
Website: http://www.spra.co.uk
Founded: 1978
Members: 63
Staff: 1
Contact: Jim Hooker, Sec.
Description: Manufacturers and contractors of single ply roofing membrane. Promotes the benefits of single ply roofing, and the development of technical guidelines and codes of practice for the application of single layer roofing membranes.
Publication title: Technical Information Sheets

Sir Arthur Sullivan Society

c/o Stephen H. Turnbull, Sec.
8 Westacres, Middleton St. George, Darlington, DL2 1LJ, England, UK
Tel: 44 1325 332557
Fax: 44 1388 603695
Email: shturnbull@aol.com
Website: http://www.sirarthursullivansociety.co.uk
Founded: 1977
Members: 450
Contact: Stephen H. Turnbull, Sec.
Fee: £50
Membership Type: individual overseas
Fee: £15
Membership Type: individual England
Description: Aims to advance the knowledge of the public in and promote the performance of the music of Arthur Sullivan (1842-1900).
Library Subject: life and music of Arthur Sullivan
Library Type: reference
Publication: Magazine. Advertisements.
Meetings/Conventions: - annual festival

Sixth Form Colleges' Association

c/o APVIC Secretariat
10 Lombard St., London, EC3V 9AT, England, UK
Tel: 44 181 3980077
Fax: 44 181 3987037
Members: 107
Staff: 1
Contact: Barbara Longford
Description: Reserves and upholds the interests and ethos of the sixth form colleges.
Meetings/Conventions: - semiannual conference

Skillshare International

126 New Walk, Leicester, LE1 7JA, England, UK
Tel: 44 116 2541862
Fax: 44 116 2542614
Email: info@skillshare.org
Website: http://www.skillshare.org
Contact: Dr. Cliff Alum, Dir.
Description: Works for sustainable development in partnership with the people and communities of Africa and Asia. Shares skills, facilitates organisational effectiveness, and supports organisational growth.
Formerly: Absorbed, Action Health - England

Skillshare International - United Kingdom

126 New Walk, Leicester, LE1 7JA, England, UK
Tel: 44 116 2541862
Fax: 44 116 2542614
Email: info@skillshare.org
Website: http://www.skillshare.org
Founded: 1990
Staff: 30
Contact: Rebecca Watson
Description: Individuals interested in global economic and community development; development organizations. Promotes more effective development through provision of volunteer support. Trains and places volunteers with development projects; provides technical and administrative assistance to local development initiatives; conducts vocational training courses to enhance local self-sufficiency in areas undergoing development.

Small Electrical Appliance Marketing Association

Orbital House, 85 Croydon Rd., Caterham, CR3 6PD, England, UK
Tel: 44 1883 334496
Fax: 44 1883 334490
Email: seama@admin.co.uk
Founded: 1982
Members: 11
Contact: Tim Faithfull
Description: Manufacturers and importers of small electrical appliances. Members represent 80% of the UK market. Products include irons, kettles, toasters, food preparation, electrical personal care etc. Offers a forum for the principal suppliers to the UK small electrical appliance market. Main activities include the provision of trade figures (members only), lobbying Government on key issues, support of service dealer network and annual trade dinner.

Small Landlords Association

78 Tachbrook St., London, SW1V 2NA, England, UK
Tel: 44 20 78282445
Fax: 44 20 78282446
Email: mail@landlords.org.uk
Website: http://www.landlords.org.uk
Founded: 1973
Members: 4500
Staff: 4
Contact: G.J. Hardwick, Sec.
Description: Private landlords of residential property in the United Kingdom. Exists to protect and promote the interests of landlords in the private rented sector. Contact is maintained with government, local authorities and the media in representing those interests. Members benefit from advice and guidance on all matters relating to their residential lettings.
Publication: Journal
Publication title: Residential Renting. Advertisements.
Second publication: Newsletter
Publication title: SLA Newsletter. Advertisements.

Snail Centre

72 High St., Ketton, Stamford, PE9 3TE, England, UK
Tel: 44 1780 722031
Fax: 44 1780 720226
Email: webmaster@snail-centre.co.uk
Website: http://www.snail-centre.co.uk/index.htm
Founded: 1986
Members: 300
Staff: 4
Contact: Martin Downes
Description: Snail farmers world wide. Research into the production and farming of edible snails; training courses; information services. Acts as central purchasing agency for overseas snail farmers, currently involved in over 30 countries.
Publication title: Cookery Book
Publication title: Induction Pack
Meetings/Conventions: - semiannual seminar - Exhibits.

Social Care Association

Thornton House, Hook Rd., Surbiton, KT6 5AN, England, UK
Tel: 44 208 3971411
Fax: 44 208 3971436
Email: web@scaed.demon.co.uk
Website: http://www.socialcareassoc.com
Founded: 1949
Members: 4100
Staff: 7
Contact: Steve Lee, Membership Administrator
Description: Those involved in social care at all levels.

Social History Society
SHS

Furness College, Bailrigg, Lancaster, LA1 4YG, England, UK
Tel: 44 1524 592605
Fax: 44 1524 846102
Email: l.persson@lancaster.ac.uk
Website: http://sochist.ntu.ac.uk/
Founded: 1976
Members: 700
Staff: 1
Contact: Linda Persson, Admin.Sec.
Fee: £15
Membership Type: institutions waged
Fee: £10
Membership Type: retired, unwaged
Description: All people interested in Social History. Aims to keep people abreast with current work/developments in Social History.
Publication: Bulletin

Publication title: Social History Society. Advertisements.
Meetings/Conventions: Cultures & Sub-Cultures: Rethinking Histories of Culture - annual conference - Exhibits.

Social Policy Association

Department of Policy Studies, University of Lincoln, Brayford Pool, Lincoln, LN6 7TS, England, UK
Tel: 44 1522 882000
Fax: 44 1522 886033
Email: cbochel@lincoln.ac.uk
Website: http://www.social-policy.com
Founded: 1966
Members: 580
Contact: Dr. Catherine Bochel, Sec.
Description: Social policy academics, researchers, policy-makers, policy officers, research officers and others with an interest in social policy. To encourage teaching, research and scholarship in social policy and administration; to represent its membership to government and other relevant policy-making bodies.
Publication: Proceedings
Publication title: Conference
Second publication: Journal
Publication title: Journal of Social Policy
Meetings/Conventions: - annual conference - Exhibits. Teesside UK

Social Research Association

PO Box 33660, London, N16 6WE, England, UK
Tel: 44 207 8805684
Fax: 44 207 8805684
Email: admin@the-sra.org.uk
Website: http://www.the-sra.org.uk
Founded: 1978
Members: 700
Staff: 1
Contact: Suzanna Cohen, Admin. Office
Fee: £45
Membership Type: individual
Description: Membership open to anyone interested or involved in social research. It includes social researchers in central and local government, higher education, market research and other organisations as well as freelance consultants. Aims to provide a forum for discussion and communication about social research activity in all areas of employment; to encourage the development of social research methodology, standards of work and codes of practice and to review and monitor the organisation and funding of social research.
Publication: Book
Publication title: Commissioning Social Research: A Good Practice Guide, 2nd Ed.
Second publication: Directory
Publication title: Directory of Members. Advertisements.
Meetings/Conventions: Improving the Quality of Social Research - annual conference London UK

Socialist Business Values Association
SBUA

6 Southgate Green, Bury St., Edmunds, Suffolk, IP33 2BL, England, UK
Tel: 44 1284 754123
Email: arenabooks@netscapeonline.co.uk
Founded: 1987
Staff: 3
Contact: Robert Corfe
Fee: £25

Membership Type: individual or corporate
Description: Corporate: All businesses in the private sector, especially firms that are independent of groups, but also subsidiaries of corporations wishing to operate their enterprises for longer term ends. Individual: Executives at all levels in company. Structures, shopfloor employees, and interested members of the general public. To promote UK-based productivity, predominantly manufacturing, primarily through advocating changes to the funding methods for industry and encouraging state intervention in promoting exports. To lobby all parliamentary, industrial, trades union and other groups, in fighting for import substitution in all spheres of materials and products.
Library Subject: social sciences
Library Type: not open to the public
Publication: Booklets

Socialist International
SI

Maritime House, Old Town, Clapman, London, SW4 0JW, England, UK
Tel: 44 207 6274449
Fax: 44 207 7204448
Email: secretariat@socialistinternational.org
Website: http://www.socialistinternational.org
Founded: 1951
Contact: Luis Ayala, Sec.Gen.
Description: Socialist, democratic socialist, and labor parties worldwide.
Publication: Newsletter
Publication title: Socialist Affairs
Meetings/Conventions: - biennial congress

Socialist International Women
SIW

Maritime House, Old Town, London, SW4 0JW, England, UK
Tel: 44 20 76274449
Fax: 44 20 77204448
Email: socintwomen@gn.apc.org
Website: http://www.socintwomen.org
Founded: 1907
Members: 130
Contact: Marlene Haas, Sec.Gen.
Description: Promotes action programmes to combat sex discrimination. Works for human rights, development, and peace.
Formerly: Women's Conference of the Socialist International
Publication title: Women and Politics
Meetings/Conventions: - triennial congress

Socialist Party
SPGB

PO Box 24697, London, E11 14D, England, UK
Tel: 44 208 9888777
Fax: 44 208 9888787
Email: contact@socialistparty.org.uk
Founded: 1904
Members: 600
Contact: Janet Carter, Gen.Sec.
Fee: £36
Description: Seeks to establish a world social system based on human need instead of private or state profit. Propagates non-market socialist ideas, including common ownership and democratic control of all productive resources and means of distribution.
Library Subject: Labor and social history.

Library Type: by appointment only
Formerly: Absorbed, World Socialist Party - Ireland
Publication: Pamphlet
Publication title: Ecology and Socialism, Ireland - Past, Present, and Future
Publication title: The Market System Must Go! - Why Reformism Doesn't Work
Meetings/Conventions: - semiannual conference

Society for Advanced Legal Studies

Charles Clore House, 17 Russell Sq., London, WC1B 5DR, England, UK
Tel: 44 20 78625800
Fax: 44 20 78625850
Email: sals@sas.ac.uk
Website: http://ials.sas.ac.uk
Founded: 1997
Members: 1000
Staff: 2
Contact: Prof. Barry A.K. Rider, Chm.
Fee: £75
Fee: £600
Description: Scholars, practitioners and those involved in the administration of justice from the UK and around the world.

Society for Advancement of Games and Simulation in Education and Training
SAGSET

11 Lloyd St., Ryton, NE40 4DJ, England, UK
Tel: 44 191 4132262
Fax: 44 191 4132262
Email: peter@j-walsh.freeserve.co.uk
Website: http://www.sagset.org
Founded: 1970
Description: Encourages and supports the development of gaming, simulation and other forms of active learning in all aspects of education.

Society for All Artists
SAA

c/o John Hope-Hawkins
PO Box 50, Newark, NG23 5GY, England, UK
Tel: 44 1949 844050
Fax: 44 1949 844051
Email: info@saa.co.uk
Website: http://www.saa.co.uk
Founded: 1992
Members: 16285
Staff: 2
Contact: John Hope-Hawkins, Chm.
Fee: £17.5
Membership Type: standard
Fee: £29.5
Membership Type: silver
Description: Promotes the interests of artists. Provides art tuition, step-by-step demonstrations, and free insurance for paintings.
Publication: Catalog
Publication title: SAA Home Shopping

Society for Anglo-Chinese Understanding
SACU

16 Portland St., Cheltenham, Gloucestershire, GL52 2PB, England, UK
Tel: 44 1253 894582
Fax: 44 1242 221274
Email: info@sacu.org
Website: http://www.sacu.org
Founded: 1965
Members: 700
Contact: Jane Hadley, Chair
Description: Individuals in Great Britain interested in promoting friendship and understanding between Great Britain and the People's Republic of China. Disseminates information on all aspects of contemporary China. Organizes Chinese language classes, cultural events, workshops, lectures, and seminars. Offers resources to schools.
Library Subject: Chinese art, language, history, and customs.
Library Type: reference
Publication title: Annual Report
Second publication: Magazine
Publication title: China in Focus. Advertisements.
Meetings/Conventions: - annual meeting

Society for Animal Welfare in Israel
SAWI

The Old School, Brewhouse Hill, Wheathampstead, St. Albans, AL4 8AN, England, UK
Tel: 44 1707 658202
Fax: 44 1707 649279
Founded: 1958
Members: 300
Staff: 1
Contact: Mr. D. Davidson, Sec.
Description: Operates under the trusteeship of the Universities Federation for Animal Welfare. Raises funds in the United Kingdom to support animal protection and welfare societies in Israel.

Society for Applied Microbiology
SFAM

c/o Lynne Boshier
The Blore Tower, Harpur Centre, Bedford, MK40 1TQ, England, UK
Tel: 44 1234 326661
Fax: 44 1234 326678
Email: info@sfam.org.uk
Website: http://www.sfam.org.uk
Founded: 1931
Members: 1700
Staff: 2
Contact: Lynne Boshier, Events/Off.Mgr.
Fee: £50
Membership Type: full member
Description: Individuals involved in the study of microbiology. Purpose is to promote and advance the study of microbiology, particularly bacteriology, in its application to agriculture, industry, and the environment. Topics of study include genetic manipulation, microbial spoilage of fermented beverages, plant cleaning, preservatives in the food, pharmaceutical, and environmental industries, safety cabinets, and water management.
Formerly: Society for Applied Bacteriology
Publication: Journal
Publication title: Environmental Microbiology

Second publication: Journal
Publication title: Journal of Applied Microbiology
Meetings/Conventions: meeting - Exhibits.

Society for Applied Philosophy
SAP

Malet St., London, WC1E 7HU, England, UK
Tel: 44 20 76368000
Email: sap@sas.ac.uk
Website: http://www.sas.ac.uk/philosophy/sap/
Founded: 1982

Society for Army Historical Research

c/o Hon. Sec., National Army Museum
Royal Hospital Rd., London, SW3 4HT, England, UK
Founded: 1921
Members: 1000
Staff: 6
Contact: G.J. Evelyn, Hon. Sec.
Description: Fosters an interest in and research into the history and traditions of the British army and of the land forces of the Empire, the Dominions, and colonies and the Commonwealth. Publishes a quarterly journal. Conducts lecture series.

Society for Cardiological Science and Technology

British Cardiac Society
9 Fitzroy Sq., London, W1P 5AH, England, UK
Tel: 44 20 73833887
Email: graham.tate@leedsth.nhs.uk
Website: http://www.scst.org.uk
Founded: 1948
Members: 1000
Contact: Graham Tate
Description: Persons whom the Council of the Society consider to be qualified to practice cardiography, technical cardiology and allied subjects. Aims to advance for the public benefit the science and practice of cardiography, technical cardiology and allied subjects by the promotion of improved standards of education and training and of research work therein and by making the results of such study and research available to practitioners and the general public.
Publication title: SCST Update. Advertisements.
Meetings/Conventions: - semiannual meeting - Exhibits.

Society for Companion Animal Studies
SCAS

The Blue Cross, Shilton Rd., Burford, OX18 4PF, England, UK
Tel: 44 1993 825597
Fax: 44 1993 825598
Email: info@scas.org.uk
Website: http://www.scas.org.uk
Founded: 1979
Members: 350
Contact: Anne Docherty, Dir.
Fee: £50
Membership Type: charity members
Fee: £25
Membership Type: members
Description: Academics, physicians, psychologists, veterinarians, and laypersons in 13 countries interested in the study of the relationship between people and companion animals. Examines the effects animals have on the emotional and physical well being of individuals. Studies and disseminates results on the benefits companion animals bring to the clients of health and social care professionals. Conducts surveys and research projects.
Library Subject: human-animal interaction
Library Type: reference
Publication: Booklet
Publication title: Death of an Animal Friend
Publication title: Guidelines for the Introduction of Pets in Nursing Homes and Other Institutions
Meetings/Conventions: Humans and Animals: A Timeless Relationship international conference

Society for Computers and Law
SCL

10 Hurle Crescent, Clifton, Bristol, BS8 2TA, England, UK
Tel: 44 1179 237393
Fax: 44 1179 239305
Email: enquiries@scl.org
Website: http://www.scl.org
Founded: 1973
Members: 2700
Staff: 2
Contact: Ruth Baker, Gen.Mgr.
Fee: £50
Membership Type: individual
Description: Academics, computer scientists, lawyers, librarians, and individuals in local government (2700) in 34 countries. Promotes the use of high technology in law for the benefit of lawyers as well as the public. Objectives are to: study the use of computers in legal research and practice; advance education in the implications of computers applied to the law; promote the development of legal computer systems and legal information retrieval systems, monitoring their performance on behalf of the public and the legal profession. Collaborates with other organizations holding similar objectives.
Publication: Magazine
Publication title: Computers and Law. Advertisements.
Second publication: Proceedings
Publication title: Conference Proceedings
Meetings/Conventions: - semiannual conference - Exhibits.

Society for Cooperation in Russian and Soviet Studies

c/o Jean S.F. Turner
320 Brixton Rd., London, SW9 6AB, England, UK
Tel: 44 20 72742282
Fax: 44 20 72743230
Email: ruslibrary@scrss.org.uk
Founded: 1924
Members: 900
Staff: 2
Contact: Jean Turner, Hon.Sec.
Fee: £15
Membership Type: full in London
Fee: £10
Membership Type: unwaged in London
Description: Promotes research, historical and visual records of the F.S.U. Publishes annual Russian information guide, regular newsletters and digests to members.
Library Subject: Russia, Soviet Union
Library Type: lending
Publication: Newsletter
Publication title: SCR Information Digest
Second publication: Directory
Publication title: SCR Russian Information Guide. Advertisements.

Society for Court Studies

PO Box 14057, London, N5 1WF, England, UK
Tel: 44 20 75039903
Fax: 44 20 75039876
Email: scs@wpp.globalnet.co.uk
Founded: 1995

Society for Earthquake and Civil Engineering Dynamics

c/o Institution of Civil Engineers
1 Great George St., Westminster, London, SW1P 3AA, England, UK
Tel: 44 20 72227722
Fax: 44 20 77991325
Email: secretary@seced.org.uk
Website: http://www.seced.org.uk
Members: 320
Staff: 1
Contact: Eunice Waddell
Fee: £24
Membership Type: individual
Fee: £10
Membership Type: student
Description: Those interested in the advancement of knowledge in the fields of earthquake engineering and civil engineering dynamics. Holds monthly evening meetings and annual conferences.
Publication title: Mallet-Milne Lecture
Second publication: Directory
Publication title: SECED
Meetings/Conventions: Informal Discussion - monthly seminar London UK

Society for Economic Analysis
SEAL

Lyncombe Vale Rd., Bath, BA2 4LP, England, UK
Tel: 44 1225 422196
Email: ccit@ssa.bristol.ac.uk
Founded: 1933

Society for Education in Film and Television
SEFT

63 Old Compton St., London, W1V 5PM, England, UK
Tel: 44 20 77345455
Founded: 1950

Society for Endocrinology

17/18 The Courtyard, Woodlands, Bradley Stoke, Bristol, BS32 4NQ, England, UK
Tel: 44 1454 642200
Fax: 44 1454 642222
Email: info@endocrinology.org
Website: http://www.endocrinology.org
Founded: 1939
Members: 2000
Staff: 23
Contact: Julie Cragg
Fee: £58
Membership Type: ordinary
Fee: £20
Membership Type: junior
Description: Clinicians and scientists working within the field of hormones and hormone related disease. Undertakes scientific/ medical publishing, conferences (including commercial exhibitions) and training courses.
Publication: Journal
Publication title: Endocrine-Related Cancer
Second publication: Journal
Publication title: European Journal of Endocrinology
Meetings/Conventions: Society for Endocrinology Meeting - annual conference London UK

Society for Existential Analysis

BM Existential, London, WC1N 3XX, England, UK
Tel: 44 7000 473337
Fax: 44 20 75380050
Email: info@existentialanalysis.co.uk
Website: http://www.go.to/existentialanalysis
Founded: 1988
Description: Provides a forum for the expression of views and the exchange of ideas amongst those interested in the analysis of existence, from philosophical and psychological perspective.

Society for Experimental Biology
SEB

Burlington House, Piccadilly, London, W1V 0LQ, England, UK
Tel: 44 20 74398732
Fax: 44 20 72874786
Email: seb@sebiology.org
Website: http://www.sebiology.org
Founded: 1923
Members: 2400
Staff: 4
Contact: Prof. J.M.N. Lakin, Ch.Exec.
Fee: £30
Membership Type: Full
Fee: £8
Membership Type: Postgraduate student
Description: Experimental biologists, postgraduate, students; universities; scientific institutions. Disseminates information on recent advances in experimental biological research. Promotes research and discussion.
Library Subject: biological sciences
Library Type: not open to the public
Publication: Journal
Publication title: Journal of Experimental Botany
Meetings/Conventions: - annual meeting Southampton UK

Society for French Studies
SFS

Egham Hill, Egham, TW20 0EX, England, UK
Tel: 44 1784 443254
Fax: 44 1784 437520
Founded: 1947

Society for General Microbiology
SGM

Marlborough House, Basingstoke Rd., Spencers Wood, Reading, RG7 1AG, England, UK
Tel: 44 1189 881800
Fax: 44 1189 885656
Email: admin@sgm.ac.uk
Website: http://www.sgm.ac.uk
Founded: 1945

Members: 5500
Staff: 32
Contact: Prof. R.S.S. Fraser, Exec.Sec.
Fee: £43
Membership Type: general
Fee: £74
Membership Type: United States
Description: Individuals interested in microbiology; students. Works to advance the study of general microbiology. Research interests include bacteria, viruses, micro-fungi, protozoa, and microscopic algae. Holds the biennial Marjory Stephenson Lecture and the biennial Fred Griffith and Colworth Lectures in alternating years, and the Fleming Lecture each year.
Publication: Journal
Publication title: International Journal of Systematic and Evolutionary Microbiology. Advertisements.
Second publication: Journal
Publication title: Journal of General Virology

Society for Italic Handwriting
SIH

205 Dyas Ave., Great Barr, Birmingham, B42 1HN, England, UK
Tel: 44 121 3580032
Fax: 44 121 3580032
Email: nickthenibs@netscapeonline.co.uk
Founded: 1952
Members: 1000
Staff: 1
Contact: Nicholas Caulkin, Sec.
Fee: £15
Description: Individuals in 30 countries. Promotes the practice of italic script. Offers handwriting consultation service for members; sponsors workshops and competitions.
Library Type: reference
Publication: Newsletter
Publication title: Writing Matters
Meetings/Conventions: - annual meeting - Exhibits. London UK

Society for Latin American Studies

Blackwell Publishers Journals
PO Box 1269, Oxford, OX4 1JD, England, UK
Tel: 44 1865 245957
Fax: 44 1865 381374
Email: membershipservices@blackwellpublishers.co.uk
Website: http://www.slas.org.uk/

Society for Libyan Studies
SLS

c/o Insititute of Archaeology
31-34 Gordon Sq., London, WC1H 0PY, England, UK
Website: http://www.britac3.britac.ac.uk/institutes/libya/index.html
Founded: 1969
Members: 330
Contact: Mrs. S.K. Strong, Gen.Sec.
Fee: £20
Membership Type: corporate or individual
Description: Institutions (140) and individuals (190) interested in the study of Libya. Promotes academic research in all subjects concerning Libya. Current concentration of support is in archaeology. Sponsors British archaeological expeditions to Libya; conducts periodic colloquia and lectures. Maintains multilingual collection of books, pamphlets, and offprints.
Library Subject: archaeology, history, geology, geography of Libya

Library Type: not open to the public
Publication: Book
Publication title: Excavations at Sabratha
Publication title: Farming the Desert, Vols. I-II, The UNESCO Libyan Valleys Archaeological Survey
Meetings/Conventions: - quarterly lecture London UK

Society for Lincolnshire History and Archaeology
SLHA

Steep Hill, Lincoln, LN2 1LS, England, UK
Tel: 44 1522 521337
Founded: 1974

Society for Low Temperature Biology
SLTB

c/o Inst. of Biology
20-22 Queensberry Pl., London, SW7 2DZ, England, UK
Tel: 44 1582 743729
Fax: 44 1582 743701
Website: http://www.sltb.info/
Founded: 1964
Members: 250
Contact: Dr. Paul Lynch, Gen.Sec.
Fee: £15
Description: Scientists and others in 24 countries interested in the effects of low temperatures on living things; firms manufacturing equipment for such studies. Goals are to foster study in low temperature biology and the application of cryobiology in medicine, agriculture and industry for the general good of the community.
Publication: Newsletter
Publication title: Newsletter. Advertisements.
Meetings/Conventions: - semiannual conference - Exhibits.

Society for Medicines Research
SMR

c/o Ms. Lilian Attar
Triangle House, Broomhill Rd., London, SW18 4HX, England, UK
Tel: 44 208 8752431
Fax: 44 208 8752434
Email: secretariat@socmr.org
Website: http://www.socmr.org
Founded: 1966
Members: 526
Staff: 1
Contact: Lilian Attar
Fee: £25
Description: Researchers at academic institutions and in the pharmaceutical industry; other concerned individuals. Promotes advancement in the field of medicinal education and research in order to provide the public with proper information on drug usage for relief of sickness.
Formerly: Society for Drug Research
Publication title: Proceedings
Second publication: Newsletter
Meetings/Conventions: - quarterly conference

Society for Medieval Archaeology

c/o Richard Hall
York Archaeology Trust, Cromwell House, 13 Ogleforth, York, YO1 7FG, England, UK
Tel: 44 1904 663000
Fax: 44 1904 663024
Email: rhall@yorkarchaeology.co.uk
Website: http://www.socmedarch.org
Founded: 1957
Members: 1500
Contact: Dr. Andrew Reynolds, Hon.Sec.
Description: Promotes the study of archaeology in the medieval period.

Society for Mucopolysaccharide Diseases
MPS

46 Woodside Rd., Amersham, HP6 6RU, England, UK
Tel: 44 1494 434156
Fax: 44 1494 434252
Email: mps@mpssociety.co.uk
Website: http://www.mpssociety.co.uk
Founded: 1982
Members: 1000
Staff: 11
Contact: Christine Lavery, Dir.
Fee: £25
Membership Type: outside U.K.
Description: Acts as a support group for individuals and their families worldwide afflicted with Mucopolysaccharide and related diseases. (MPS diseases, known individually as Hurler, Scheie, Hunter, Sanfilippo, Morquio, Maroteaux-Lamy, and Sly, and associated diseases called mucolipidosis, Fucosidosis, Mannosidosis, Fabry and Sialic Acid Disease, are genetic diseases. Children born with MPS are unable to produce certain enzymes necessary for appropriate metabolism to take place; consequently complex sugars become stored in connective tissues, causing progressive damage, including physical and mental handicaps. In many cases, MPS patients die before reaching adulthood.) Encourages public awareness of MPS diseases and the international transmission of medical knowledge and techniques. Raises funds to further MPS research and arranges for MPS families to assist in research such as carrier testing and biochemical diagnosis. Accepts donations to provide individual advocacy for MPS families. Sponsors research program on the natural history of MPS and the psychosocial problems of MPS children.
Publication: Report
Publication title: Conference Reports
Second publication: Report
Publication title: 21 Years of Bone Marrow Transplant
Meetings/Conventions: Parent and Professional Conference - annual conference - Exhibits. Alton UK

Society for Name Studies in Britain and Ireland

c/o Miss J. Scherr
School of Medical Sciences, University Walk, University of Bristol, Bristol, BS8 1TD, England, UK
Tel: 44 117 9287946
Email: j.scherr@bristol.ac.uk
Website: http://www.snsbi.org
Founded: 1991
Members: 190
Contact: Jennifer Scherr, Hon.Sec.
Fee: £15
Membership Type: personal and institutional
Fee: £5
Membership Type: student
Description: Professional scholars in name studies, philology, history, linguistics, etc, plus many individuals engaged in private study and research into place-names. Research into place names and personal names of Britain and Ireland.
Formerly: Council for Name Studies in Great Britain and Ireland
Publication: Journal
Publication title: NOMINA
Meetings/Conventions: - annual conference - Exhibits.

Society for Nautical Research
SNR

Stowell House, New Pond Hill, Cross in Hand, Heath Field, TN21 0LX, England, UK
Website: http://www.snr.org
Founded: 1910
Members: 2000
Staff: 2
Contact: MPJ Garvey, Sec.
Fee: £32
Description: Libraries, maritime organizations, and individuals. Encourages research into nautical antiquities, current and historical seafaring and shipbuilding, the language and customs of the sea, and other subjects of nautical interest. Assists in archaeological expeditions and caretaking of historic ships; provides funds to the National Maritime Museum for the purchase of prints and drawings. Is preparing a nautical dictionary. Conducts lectures.
Publication: Journal
Publication title: Mariner's Mirror. Advertisements.
Second publication: Newsletter
Publication title: Newsletter of the Society
Meetings/Conventions: HMS Victory Luncheon - annual meeting

Society for Post-Medieval Archaeology

c/o Department of Archaeology
University of York, The Kings Manor, York, Y01 7EP, England, UK
Tel: 44 191 4821037
Email: kfg103@york.ac.uk
Website: http://www.spma.org.uk
Founded: 1967
Members: 900
Contact: Dr. David Cranstone, Hon.Sec.
Fee: £20
Membership Type: Individual
Description: Professional archaeologists, historians, university libraries, institutions and interested individuals in 13 countries. Promotes the study of archaeology in the post-medieval period. Encourages the preservation of sites of archaeological importance, buildings, and artifacts. Strives to educate the public through the dissemination of information. Promotes archaeological research.
Publication: Journal
Publication title: Post Medieval Archaeology
Publication title: Post Medieval Newsletter
Meetings/Conventions: - semiannual conference

Society for Producers and Composers of Applied Music

Birchwood Hall, Storridge, Malvern, WR13 5EZ, England, UK
Tel: 44 906 8950908
Fax: 44 1886 884204
Email: bfromer@netcomuk.co.uk
Website: http://www.pcam.co.uk

Founded: 1982
Members: 80
Staff: 1
Contact: Bob Fromer, Admin.
Fee: £85
Membership Type: first year and small trader
Description: Music production companies or individuals who produce and/or compose music for commercials, television programmes and audio-visual media generally. Aims to improve and regularise practices and conditions for the production of music in advertising, television and audio-visual media; to improve technical standards and practices in music production for these purposes and to increase the profile of music production companies within the advertising and television industries.
Formerly: Society of Producers of Advertising Music, Society of Producers of Applied Music
Publication: Newsletter
Publication title: The Bugle
Second publication: Directory
Meetings/Conventions: - periodic meeting

Society for Promotion of Educational Reform through Teacher Training
SPERTTT

9-12 Barrett St., London, W1M 6DE, England, UK
Tel: 44 20 74864771
Founded: 1969

Society for Psychical Research

49 Marloes Rd., London, W8 6LA, England, UK
Tel: 44 20 79378984
Fax: 44 20 79378984
Website: http://www.spr.ac.uk
Founded: 1882
Members: 1000
Staff: 3
Contact: Peter Johnson
Fee: £38
Membership Type: associate member
Fee: £14
Membership Type: student
Description: Advances the understanding of events and abilities commonly described as psychic or paranormal without prejudice and in a scientific manner.
Library Type: lending
Publication: Journal
Publication title: Journal of SPR
Publication title: Paranormal Review
Meetings/Conventions: - annual conference

Society for Psychosomatic Research

Horseferry Rd., London, SW1P 2AP, England, UK
Founded: 1955

Society for Radiological Protection

76 Portland Pl., London, W1B 1NT, England, UK
Tel: 44 1364 644487
Fax: 44 1364 644492
Email: admin@srp-uk.org
Website: http://www.srp-uk.org
Founded: 1963
Members: 1264
Contact: Tony Bandle, Chairman

Description: Open to those engaged professionally in radiation protection or allied fields for at least 3 years, age 25 or over and normally with a degree or equivalent. Aids in the development of scientific, technological, medical and legal aspects of radiological protection, including nuclear safety, and to promote and improve radiological protection as a profession. The Society achieves its objectives by meetings, publications and conferences with emphasis on subjects contributing to knowledge and practice of radiological protection.
Publication: Journal
Publication title: Journal of Radiological Protection

Society for Renaissance Studies

35 Winchester Ave., Cranham, Oxford, RM14 3LP, England, UK
Tel: 44 1865 270999
Fax: 44 1865 270970
Email: srs@carelton.fsnet.co.uk
Website: http://www.sas.ac.uk/srs
Founded: 1967

Society for Research in the Psychology of Music and Music Education

c/o Prof. Graham Welch
University of Sheffield, Institute of Education, 20 Bedfordway, London, WC1H 0AL, England, UK
Tel: 44 114 2667234
Fax: 44 114 2668053
Members: 612
Contact: Prof. Graham Welch, Chm.
Description: Music educators and academics working in music departments, psychology departments, education departments and schools, and music teachers. To promote and disseminate research in the psychology of music and music education, and to explore the relationships between these two areas and with other related disciplines and practices, such as music therapy.
Library Subject: psychology of music, music education
Library Type: open to the public
Publication: Journal
Publication title: Psychology of Music

Society for Research into Higher Education
SRHE

3 Devonshire St., London, W1N 2BA, England, UK
Tel: 44 20 76372766
Fax: 44 20 76372781
Email: srheoffice@srhe.ac.uk
Website: http://www.srhe.ac.uk
Founded: 1964

Society for Research into Hydrocephalus and Spina Bifida
SRHSB

c/o Dr. Terry Cubitt
Alton Health Centre, Alton, GU34 2QX, England, UK
Tel: 44 1420 542542
Fax: 44 1420 549466
Email: srhsb@doctors.org.uk
Website: http://www.srhsb.org
Founded: 1957
Members: 284
Contact: Miss Carole A. Sobkowiak, Hon.Sec.
Fee: £60

Membership Type: ordinary
Fee: £30
Membership Type: senior
Description: Nursing, psychology, social work, scientific, and medical professionals from 29 countries with a common interest in hydrocephalus (an abnormal accumulation of fluid in the cranium) and spina bifida (a defect in the closing of the bony spinal canal). Object is to advance education and research on hydrocephalus and spina bifida. Brings together members to aid them in their endeavors to prevent, cure, and alleviate the conditions.
Publication: Journal
Publication title: European Journal of Pediatric Surgery
Meetings/Conventions: - annual - Exhibits. Dublin Ireland

Society for Screen-Based Learning
SSBL

9 Bridge St., Tadcaster, LS24 9AW, England, UK
Tel: 44 1937 530520
Fax: 44 1937 530520
Email: josie.key@learningonscreen.u-net.com
Website: http://www.learningonscreen.org.uk
Founded: 1968
Members: 220
Staff: 1
Contact: Josie Key, Admin.
Description: Schools, colleges, polytechnics, universities, local education authorities, hospitals, industries, television companies, and individuals in 9 countries. Promotes the use of television and video for educational purposes; encourages careers in educational television; organizes training programs.
Formerly: Educational Television Media Association
Publication: Newsletter
Publication title: Newsletter
Second publication: Membership Directory
Meetings/Conventions: - annual conference

Society for Social Medicine

c/o Ms. Angela Rowe
Population Health Group, School of Medicine, Health, Policy & Practice, University of East Angela, Norwich, NR4 7TJ, England, UK
Tel: 44 20 76791732
Fax: 44 20 78130280
Email: a.rowe@uea.ac.uk
Website: http://www.socsocmed.org.uk/
Founded: 1957

Society for South Asian Studies
SSAS

c/o The British Academy
10 Carlton House Ter., London, SW1Y 5AH, England, UK
Email: asianstudies28@hotmail.com
Website: http://www.britac.ac.uk/institutes/SSAS/index.html
Founded: 1972
Members: 230
Contact: Mrs. A.M. Howell
Fee: £25
Description: Academic institutions, libraries, museums, and scholars interested in South Asia. Promotes the study of South Asian culture. Finances and fieldwork and provides grants and fellowships.
Publication: Journal
Publication title: South Asian Studies
Second publication: Report
Meetings/Conventions: convention

Society for Storytelling

c/o Mrs. Tina Bilbe
PO Box 2344, Reading, RG6 7FG, England, UK
Tel: 44 118 9351381
Email: sfs@fairbruk.co.uk
Website: http://www.sfs.org
Founded: 1993
Members: 520
Contact: Tina Bilbe, Sec.
Description: Aims to provide a network for everyone interested in the exchange of knowledge regarding the art of storytelling. Provides information, increase public awareness, promotes exploration, advise and develop contacts, nationally and internationally, formally and informally.
Library Subject: oral storytelling, folktales
Library Type: reference
Publication: Magazine
Publication title: Storylines. Advertisements.
Meetings/Conventions: The Gathering - annual general assembly London UK

Society for the Advancement of Anaesthesia in Dentistry
SAAD

53 Wimpole St., London, W10 8YH, England, UK
Tel: 44 207 9351656
Fax: 44 1246 208729
Email: saaduk@freeuk.com
Website: http://www.saaduk.org
Founded: 1957
Members: 2100
Staff: 1
Contact: Dr. C. Holden, Pres.
Description: Dentists and physicians interested in dental anesthesia. Seeks to advance pain and anxiety control in dentistry. Offers courses on intravenous techniques and relative analgesia.
Library Subject: Dental anasthesia and related topics.
Library Type: reference
Publication: Book
Publication title: Dental Sedation and Anaesthesia
Publication title: SAAD Digest

Society for the Advancement of Games and Simulations for Education and Training

c/o Mr. Peter Walsh
11 Lloyd St., Ryton, NE40 4DJ, England, UK
Tel: 44 1914132262
Fax: 44 1914132262
Email: peter@j-walsh.freeserv.co.uk
Website: http://www.sagset.org
Founded: 1970
Members: 150
Contact: Peter Walsh, Admin.
Fee: £55
Membership Type: institutional
Fee: £33
Membership Type: individual
Description: Promotes learning.
Library Subject: gaming, simulations
Library Type: open to the public
Formerly: Society for Interactive Learning
Meetings/Conventions: conference

Society for the Autistically Handicapped
SFTAH

199-205 Blandford Ave., Kettering, NN16 9AT, England, UK
Tel: 44 1536 523274
Fax: 44 1536 523274
Email: autism@rmplc.co.uk
Website: http://www.autismuk.com
Description: Seeks to increase awareness of autism. Works to improve quality of life for people with autism.
Publication: Newsletter

Society for the Development of Techniques in Industrial Marketing
SDTIM

9 Aston Rd., Nuneaton, CV11 5EL, England, UK
Founded: 1967

Society for the History of Alchemy and Chemistry
SHAC

24 Kayemoor Rd., Sutton, SM2 5HT, England, UK
Tel: 44 20 86427437
Email: n.g.coley@surrey28.freeserve.co.uk
Website: http://www.open.ac.uk/arts/hst/shac/shac.htm
Founded: 1937
Members: 260
Contact: Dr. N.G. Coley, Hon.Treas.
Fee: £12
Membership Type: postgraduate student
Fee: £24
Membership Type: personal
Description: Subscribers to the society's journal, Ambix. Encourages exchange among members.
Publication: Journal
Publication title: Ambix. Advertisements.
Meetings/Conventions: - semiannual conference London UK

Society for the History of Natural History
SHNH

c/o K.M. Way
The Natural History Museum, Cromwell Rd., London, SW7 5BD, England, UK
Tel: 44 20 79425186
Fax: 44 20 79425054
Email: kmw@nhm.ac.uk
Website: http://www.shnh.org
Founded: 1936
Members: 650
Contact: K.M. Way, Hon.Sec.
Fee: £25
Fee: £50
Description: Archivists, bibliographers, book collectors, natural science historians, librarians, museum personnel, and university lecturers and professors. Provides a forum for the exchange of ideas and information on the history of botany, geology, and zoology and on artistic and literary expressions of the natural sciences.
Formerly: Society for the Bibliography of Natural History
Publication: Journal
Publication title: Archives of Natural History
Publication title: Member's Handbook
Meetings/Conventions: - periodic meeting

Society for the Promotion of Byzantine Studies

c/o Fiona Nicks
48 Hugh Allen Cres., Marston, Oxford, OX3 0HN, England, UK
Tel: 44 1332 764305
Email: fionanicks@kci.ac.uk
Website: http://www.byzantium.ac.uk
Founded: 1983
Members: 430
Staff: 1
Contact: Fiona Nicks, Sec.
Fee: £40
Membership Type: ordinary
Fee: £20
Membership Type: student
Description: Promotes Byzantine studies.
Publication: Bulletin
Publication title: Bulletin of British Byzantine Studies. Advertisements.
Meetings/Conventions: - annual symposium

Society for the Promotion of Hellenic Studies
SPHS

Senate House, Malet St., London, WC1E 7HU, England, UK
Tel: 44 20 78628730
Fax: 44 20 78628731
Email: hellenic@sas.ac.uk
Website: http://www.sas.ac.uk/icls/hellenic/
Founded: 1879
Members: 3500
Staff: 1
Contact: Russell Shone, Exec.Sec.
Fee: £36
Membership Type: Individual
Fee: £55
Membership Type: Institution
Description: Archaeologists, classicists, educators, numismatists, libraries, and museums worldwide. Promotes the study of the Greek language, literature, history, and art in the ancient, Byzantine, and modern periods. Maintains library jointly with the Society for the Promotion of Roman Studies.
Library Subject: classical studies
Library Type: reference
Publication: Journal
Publication title: Archaeological Reports. Advertisements.
Second publication: Journal
Publication title: Journal of Hellenic Studies. Advertisements.
Meetings/Conventions: - quarterly lecture

Society for the Promotion of New Music
SPNM

4th Fl., 18-20 Southwark St., London, SE1 1TJ, England, UK
Tel: 44 20 74071640
Fax: 44 20 74036545
Email: spnm@spnm.org.uk
Website: http://www.spnm.org.uk
Founded: 1943
Members: 1400
Staff: 4
Contact: Jo-Anne Naish, Administrator
Fee: £18
Membership Type: Individual
Fee: £5
Membership Type: Students

Description: Advocates new music in Britain including contemporary jazz, classical, popular, music written for film, dance, and other media. Provides concerts, workshops, education projects, and collaborations.
Publication: Brochure
Publication title: Composers
Second publication: Magazine
Publication title: New Notes. Advertisements.
Meetings/Conventions: Concerts

Society for the Promotion of Roman Studies
SPRS

c/o Senate House
Malet St., London, WC1E 7HU, England, UK
Tel: 44 207 8628727
Fax: 44 207 8628728
Email: romansoc@sas.ac.uk
Website: http://www.sas.ac.uk/icls/roman/
Founded: 1910
Members: 4000
Staff: 3
Contact: Helen M. Cockle, Sec.
Fee: £36
Membership Type: Individual
Fee: £45
Membership Type: Institutional
Description: Academies, academic libraries, archaeologists, and classicists in over 40 countries interested in the archaeology, art, literature, and history of Italy and the Roman Empire until the year 700 A.D. Assists the British School in Rome, Italy.
Library Subject: Operated jointly with the Society for the Promotion of Hellenic Studies and the Institute of Classical Studies of the University of London. Covers all aspects of classical antiquity
Library Type: reference
Publication: Journal
Publication title: Britannia. Advertisements.
Second publication: Journal
Publication title: Journal of Roman Studies
Meetings/Conventions: - periodic lecture

Society for the Protection of Ancient Buildings
SPAB

37 Spital Sq., London, E1 6DY, England, UK
Tel: 44 207 3771644
Fax: 44 207 2475296
Email: info@spab.org.uk
Website: http://www.spab.org.uk
Founded: 1877
Members: 7500
Staff: 14
Contact: Philip Venning, Sec.
Fee: £30
Description: Individuals united to preserve and protect ancient buildings. Gives advice and technical assistance on treatment and repair of old structures. Investigates proposals that place historic buildings in jeopardy. Sponsors courses and training programs on the conservation of buildings.
Library Subject: SPAB cases dating back to 1877
Library Type: by appointment only
Publication: Newsletter
Publication title: Newsletter
Second publication: Pamphlets
Publication title: SPAB Technical Information
Meetings/Conventions: - annual convention

Society for the Protection of Animals Abroad
SPANA

14 John St., London, WC1N 2EB, England, UK
Tel: 44 20 78313999
Fax: 44 20 78315999
Email: hq@spana.org
Website: http://www.spana.org
Founded: 1923
Staff: 12
Contact: Mr. J.F. Hulme, Chief Exec.
Fee: £20
Membership Type: ordinary members
Description: Charitable organization providing treatment for sick and injured working animals in many developing countries around the world. Maintains animal refuges and mobile clinics. Offers training for veterinary surgeons and an education program for children and animal owners.
Formerly: Society for the Protection of Animals in North Africa
Publication: Newsletter
Publication title: SPANA Bulletin. Advertisements.
Second publication: Newsletter
Publication title: SPANA News
Meetings/Conventions: Friends Meeting - annual meeting

Society for the Protection of Unborn Children
SPUC

5-6 St. Matthew St., London, SW1P 2JT, England, UK
Tel: 44 20 72225845
Fax: 44 20 72220630
Email: information@spuc.org.uk
Website: http://www.spuc.org.uk
Founded: 1967
Members: 48000
Staff: 40
Contact: John Smeaton, Natl.Dir.
Fee: £100
Membership Type: life
Description: Education and lobbying on right to life (abortion, embryo abuse, euthanasia, population control). Promotes alternatives to abortion. Provides support and assistance to those suffering post abortion syndrome. Finances research into population disability, pre-natal development.
Library Subject: abortion, embryo experimentation, I.V.F., population control, euthanasia
Library Type: by appointment only
Publication: Newspaper
Publication title: Pro-Life Times
Second publication: Book
Publication title: SPUC Evangelicals Love Your Unborn Neighbour
Meetings/Conventions: - annual conference

Society for the Responsible Use of Resources in Agriculture and on the Land

c/o Brig H J Hickman
Chester House 12 Hillbury Rd., Alderholt, Fordingbridge, SP6 3BQ, England, UK
Tel: 44 1425 652035
Founded: 1983
Staff: 1
Contact: Brig H John Hickman, Dir.
Fee: £15
Membership Type: ordinary
Fee: £500

Membership Type: corporate
Description: Promotes policy studies on farming, food, and countryside.
Publication title: Briefing

Society for the Study of Addiction to Alcohol and Other Drugs
SSA

c/o Alex Schardy, Membership Admin., 4 Windsor Walk, London, SE5 8AF, England, UK
Tel: 44 20 78480841
Fax: 44 20 77035787
Email: membership@addiction-ssa.org
Website: http://www.addiction-ssa.org
Founded: 1884
Members: 410
Staff: 4
Contact: Dr. R.E. Kendell, Pres.
Fee: £75
Description: Medical and allied health professionals seeking to stimulate scientific study of alcohol and drug addiction. Conducts research and educational programs.
Library Subject: Biographical.
Library Type: reference
Publication: Journal
Publication title: Addiction. Advertisements.
Second publication: Monographs
Meetings/Conventions: - annual convention - Exhibits.

Society for the Study of Human Biology
SSHB

c/o Dr. Alan Dangour
Public Health Nutrition Unit, Dept. of Epidemology and Population Health, London School of Hygiene and Tropical Medicine, 49-51 Bedford Sq., London, WC1B 3DP, England, UK
Tel: 44 207 2994688
Fax: 44 207 2994666
Email: alan.dangour@lshtm.ac.uk
Website: http://www-staff.lboro.ac.uk/~hungn/sshb.htm
Founded: 1958
Members: 400
Contact: Dr. Alan Dangour
Fee: £40
Membership Type: full, student, retired
Description: Professional human biologists in 45 countries. Purpose is to advance the study of the biology of human populations in all aspects, including human variability and genetics, human adaptability and ecology, and human evolution.
Publication: Journal
Publication title: Annals of Human Biology. Advertisements.
Second publication: Proceedings
Publication title: Annual Symposia
Meetings/Conventions: - annual symposium

Society for the Study of Labour History
SSLH

University of North Umbria, Department of Historical and Critical Studies, Lipman Bldg., Newcastle upon Tyne, NE1 8ST, England, UK
Tel: 44 191 2273193
Fax: 44 191 2274630
Website: http://facstaff.uww.edu/sslh/home.html
Founded: 1960

Members: 1000
Contact: Dr. Joan Hugman, Sec.
Fee: £18
Membership Type: Individual
Fee: £20
Membership Type: Institution
Description: Teachers, students, and others in 40 countries interested in the study, research, and teaching of labor history. Works to preserve labor archives. Provides the opportunity for researchers to publish papers of their recent work.
Publication: Journal
Publication title: Labour History Review: The Bulletin of the Society for the Study of Labour History. Advertisements.
Meetings/Conventions: - periodic conference - Exhibits.

Society for the Study of Medieval Languages and Literature
SSMLL

c/o Dr. D.G. Pattison
Magdalen College, Oxford, OX1 4AU, England, UK
Tel: 44 1865 276087
Fax: 44 1865 276087
Website: http://www.mod-langs.ox.ac.uk/ssmll/index.html
Founded: 1932
Members: 180
Contact: Dr. D.G. Pattison
Fee: £16
Membership Type: full member
Fee: £32
Membership Type: full member
Description: Scholars, students, and others interested in medieval languages and literature. Encourages research in medieval literature and history, and medieval languages and linguistics, including Romance, Germanic, Latin, and English languages.
Publication: Journal
Publication title: Medium Aevum. Advertisements.
Second publication: Monograph
Publication title: Medium Aevum Monographs

Society for the Study of Normal Psychology

151 Talgarth Rd., London, W14, England, UK
Tel: 44 20 87489338
Fax: 44 20 85630551
Email: colethouse@clara.net
Website: http://www.studysociety.net
Members: 270
Staff: 5
Contact:
Fee: £50
Library Type: not open to the public
Publication: Newsletter
Publication title: Contact
Second publication: Books

Society for Theatre Research
STR

c/o Theatre Museum
1E Tavistock St., London, WC2E 7PR, England, UK
Email: e.cottis@btinternet.com
Website: http://www.str.org.uk
Founded: 1948
Members: 750

Contact: Eileen Cottis, Hon.Sec.
Fee: £27
Membership Type: individual
Fee: £30
Membership Type: individual overseas
Description: University and college departments of drama, libraries, theatre professionals, theatre scholars, and other individuals. Purpose is to encourage research into the history and technique of the British theatre. Has established or helped to establish: the International Federation for Theatre Research; and the British Theatre Museum. Holds William Poel Festival. Sponsors periodic lecture in memory of Edward Gordon Craig (1872-1966), English actor, stage designer, and producer.
Publication title: Research Book
Second publication: Journal
Publication title: Theatre Notebook. Advertisements.
Meetings/Conventions: - annual meeting London UK

Society for Underwater Technology
SUT

80 Coleman St., London, EC2R 5BJ, England, UK
Tel: 44 20 73822601
Fax: 44 20 73822684
Email: ian.gallett@sut.org
Website: http://www.sut.org.uk
Founded: 1966
Members: 1600
Staff: 6
Contact: I.N.L. Gallett, Exec.Sec.
Fee: £55
Membership Type: member
Fee: £37
Membership Type: associate
Description: A multi-disciplinary learned society of individuals and organizations with a common interest in underwater technology, ocean science and offshore engineering, with members in more than 40 countries including engineers, scientists, other professionals, and students from industry, universities and government organizations.
Formerly: Absorbed, Engineering Committee on Oceanic Resources
Publication: Proceedings
Publication title: Advances in Ocean Science and Offshore Engineering
Second publication: Newsletter
Publication title: SUT News
Meetings/Conventions: - semiannual conference

Society for Veterinary Epidemiology and Preventive Medicine
SVEPM

PO Box 236, Early Gate, Reading, RG6 6AT, England, UK
Tel: 44 118 9264888
Fax: 44 118 9262431
Email: a.d.paterson@reading.ac.uk
Founded: 1982

Society of Academic and Research Surgery

Royal College of Surgeons of England, 35-43 Lincoln's Inn Fields, London, WC2A 3PE, England, UK
Tel: 44 207 8696640
Fax: 44 207 8696644
Email: smitchell@rcseng.ac.uk
Website: http://www.surgicalresearchsociety.org.uk

Members: 547
Contact: Helen Binks
Description: Surgeons. To provide for the interchange of information about research related to surgery and surgical disease.
Publication: Journal
Publication title: British Journal of Surgery
Meetings/Conventions: - semiannual

Society of All Cargo Correspondents

Freight Transport Buyer, 69-77 Paul St., London, EC2A 4LQ, England, UK
Tel: 44 207 5531681
Fax: 44 207 5531941
Founded: 1979
Members: 70
Contact: Emma Murray, Chair
Fee: £25
Membership Type: staff journalist
Fee: £20
Membership Type: freelance journalist
Description: Journalists who write about all modes of freight transport (air, road, rail, sea, express). Aims to facilitate communication between the freight industry and journalists who write about it.
Publication: Booklet
Publication title: The SACC Contacts Book
Meetings/Conventions: Press Evening - monthly London UK

Society of Antiquaries of London
SA

Burlington House, Piccadilly, London, W1J 0BE, England, UK
Tel: 44 207 4797080
Fax: 44 207 2876967
Email: admin@sal.org.uk
Website: http://www.sal.org.uk
Founded: 1707
Members: 2000
Staff: 12
Contact: David Morgan Evans, Gen.Sec.
Fee: £116
Description: Archaeologists, art historians, architectural historians, and historians united for the encouragement, advancement and furtherance of the study and knowledge of the antiquaries of the U.K. and other countries. Operates museum. Serves as a forum for discussion among members.
Library Subject: history, art history, archaeology
Library Type: reference
Publication: Journal
Publication title: Antiquaries Journal
Publication title: Archaeologia
Meetings/Conventions: - weekly meeting

Society of Antiquaries of Newcastle-upon-Tyne

Castle Garth, Newcastle upon Tyne, NE1 1RQ, England, UK
Tel: 44 191 2615390
Email: admin@newcastle-antiquaries.org.uk
Website: http://www.newcastle-antiquaries.org.uk
Founded: 1813
Members: 800
Staff: 5
Contact: Sarah Walters, Membership Sec.
Fee: £25

Description: Promotes the study, investigation, description and preservation of antiquities and historical records in the historic counties of Northumberland and Durham and the city and county of Newcastle upon Tyne.
Library Subject: history, archeology
Library Type: by appointment only
Publication: Journal
Publication title: Archaeologia Aeliana

Society of Apothecaries of London

Apothecaries Hall, Black Friars Ln., London, EC4V 6EJ, England, UK
Tel: 44 207 2361189
Fax: 44 207 3293177
Email: clerk@apothecaries.org
Website: http://www.apothecaries.org
Founded: 1617
Members: 1700
Staff: 16
Contact: R.J. Stringer, Clerk
Description: Members of the medical profession. Functions as City of London Livery Company and medical examining body.

Society of Archer-Antiquaries
SAA

36 Myrtledene Rd., Abbeywood, London, SE2 0EZ, England, UK
Tel: 44 181 3113416
Email: edhart@btopenworld.co.uk
Founded: 1956
Members: 400
Staff: 1
Contact: Edward Hart, Hon.Sec.
Fee: £15
Membership Type: individual/corporate/family
Description: Individuals, archery clubs, universities, libraries, museums, and firms in 14 countries who are interested in the history and development of the bow. Studies matters relating to the history of archery and the development of the bow and arrow in all parts of the world from prehistoric times to the present day. Maintains museum of archery equipment.
Library Subject: archery
Library Type: by appointment only
Publication: Journal
Publication title: A Guide to the Crossbow
Second publication: Newsletter
Publication title: Arrowhead
Meetings/Conventions: Annual Shoot - annual meeting - Exhibits.

Society of Archivists

Prioryfield House, 20 Canon St., Taunton, TA1 1SW, England, UK
Tel: 44 1823 327030
Fax: 44 1823 371719
Email: offman@archives.org.uk
Website: http://www.archives.org.uk
Founded: 1947
Members: 1700
Staff: 5
Contact: P.S. Cleary
Fee: £10
Membership Type: student
Fee: £200
Membership Type: international affiliate
Description: Members include archivists, records managers and conservators in central and local government, universities, charities

and the business sector. Aims to promote the care and preservation of archives, the better administration of archive repositories, to advance the training of members and to encourage relevant research and publication.
Library Subject: archives, archive conservation, records management
Library Type: open to the public
Publication: Journal
Publication title: Journal of the Society of Archivists
Second publication: Newsletter
Publication title: Society of Archivists Newsletter
Meetings/Conventions: - annual conference - Exhibits.

Society of Assistants Teaching in Preparatory Schools

Marlborough House School, High St., Hawkhurst, TN18 4PY, England, UK
Tel: 44 1580 752954
Fax: 44 1580 752954
Email: erad@dial.pipex.com
Website: http://www.satips.org.uk
Founded: 1952
Members: 800
Staff: 1
Contact: E. R. Andrew Davis, Sec.
Fee: £21
Membership Type: individual
Fee: £115
Membership Type: school
Description: Preparatory schools and individual preparatory school teachers. Provides support for staff in prep schools; advances independent education, encourages the interchange of ideas, circulates relevant information. Holds conferences, sporting activities, festivals and competitions.
Publication: Magazine
Publication title: Prep School. Advertisements.
Meetings/Conventions: - annual conference

Society of Authors - England
SOA

84 Drayton Gardens, London, SW10 9SB, England, UK
Tel: 44 20 73736642
Fax: 44 20 73735768
Email: info@societyofauthors.org
Website: http://www.societyofauthors.org
Founded: 1884
Members: 7000
Staff: 12
Contact: Emma Boniwell, Membership Sec.
Fee: £75
Description: Trade union for professional writers. Benefits include individual contract advice and advice on all of the business aspects of writing. Works for improved terms and conditions between authors and publishers. Also lobbies government authorities for legislation which will enhance conditions for writers.
Publication: Journal
Publication title: Author. Advertisements.
Publication title: Guides
Meetings/Conventions: - periodic conference

Society of Bookbinders

c/o Phillipa J.C. Harvey
Plaster Hill House, Churt, Farnham, GU10 2QT, England, UK
Email: secretary@societyofbookbinders.com
Website: http://www.societyofbookbinders.com
Founded: 1974
Members: 650
Contact: Phillipa J.C. Harvey, Natl.Sec.
Fee: £32
Membership Type: UK-Full
Fee: £65
Membership Type: UK-Corporate
Description: Represents the interests of bookbinders, book collectors and conservators, and provides a forum for the exchange of information thus promoting the highest standards of bookbinding both nationally and internationally. Activities include a biennial conference and frequent lectures and demonstrations. Regional programs throughout the country.
Library Type: open to the public
Publication: Journal
Publication title: Bookbinder. Advertisements.
Second publication: Newsletter
Publication title: National
Meetings/Conventions: - annual conference

Society of British Aerospace Companies
SBAC

Duxbury House, 60 Pretty France, Victoria, London, SW1H 9EU, England, UK
Tel: 44 207 2271000
Fax: 44 207 2271067
Email: post@sbac.co.uk
Website: http://www.sbac.co.uk
Founded: 1916
Members: 180
Staff: 55
Contact: Lindsey Hart, Mgr.
Description: Membership covers a cross-section of the aerospace industry in the areas of airframes, aero-engines, guided weapons and satellites. Seeks to improve the competitive performance of all United Kingdom aerospace companies by promoting communication between companies, the industry, and the government. Organizes the biennial Farnborough International exhibitions and flying displays.
Library Type: by appointment only
Meetings/Conventions: Farnborough International - biennial trade show - Exhibits. Farnborough UK

Society of British Gas Industries

36 Holly Walk, Leamington Spa, CV32 4LY, England, UK
Tel: 44 1926 334357
Fax: 44 1926 450459
Email: mail@sbgi.org.uk
Website: http://www.sbgi.org.uk
Founded: 1905
Members: 180
Staff: 12
Contact: John Stiggers, Dir.
Description: Companies involved in all aspects of the gas industry, including shipping, supplying, transportation, pipe laying, distribution engineering, metering, utilization and installation and service. Representing the interests of contractors and suppliers of gas plant, gas appliances and equipment.
Publication: Journal
Publication title: Gas Business. Advertisements.

Second publication: Directory
Publication title: Products and Services. Advertisements.
Meetings/Conventions: - annual meeting

Society of British Neurological Surgeons
SBNS

Oxford Rd., Manchester, M13 9WL, England, UK
Fax: 44 161 2764567
Founded: 1926

Society of British Water and Wastewater Industries

38 Holly Walk, Leamington Spa, CV32 4LY, England, UK
Tel: 44 1926 831530
Fax: 44 1926 831931
Email: hq@sbwwi.co.uk
Website: http://www.sbwwi.co.uk
Founded: 1986
Members: 76
Staff: 3
Contact: Carol Hickman
Description: Trade Association. Covers the interests of contractors and manufacturers of pipeline equipment, metering systems, instrumentation and controls. Members meet regularly to discuss developments in the water industry and the effects of legislation and standards. Acts as a forum for discussions with water companies and other bodies associated with the industry. Represented on CEN, ISO and national standards committees.
Formerly: Society of British Water Industries
Publication: Annual Report
Second publication: Directory
Meetings/Conventions: - quarterly meeting

Society of Business Economists
SBE

11 Bay Tree Walk, Watford, WD17 4RX, England, UK
Tel: 44 1923 237287
Email: admin@sbe.co.uk
Website: http://www.sbe.co.uk
Founded: 1953
Members: 650
Contact: Marian Marshall, Exec.Sec.
Fee: £65
Membership Type: individual
Description: Economists in 14 countries working in commerce, finance, and industry.
Publication: Journal
Publication title: Business Economist. Advertisements.
Meetings/Conventions: - annual conference

Society of Cable Telecommunication Engineers

Fulton House Business Centre, Fulton Rd., Wembley Park, Middlesex, HA9 0TF, England, UK
Tel: 44 20 8902 8998
Fax: 44 20 8903 8719
Email: office@scte.org.uk
Website: http://www.scte.org.uk
Founded: 1945
Members: 1200
Staff: 3
Contact: Mrs. Beverley Allgood, Sec.
Description: Those engaged in some branch of engineering directly or indirectly concerned with the design, development, manufacture

and employment of materials and components used by the cable telecommunications industry.
Formerly: Society of Cable Television Engineers
Publication title: Cable Telecommunications Engineering
Second publication: Yearbook
Meetings/Conventions: - quarterly lecture

Society of Cardiothoracic Surgeons of Great Britain and Ireland
35-43 Lincoln's Inn Fields, London, WC2A 3PE, England, UK
Tel: 44 207 8696893
Fax: 44 207 8696890
Email: sctsadmin@scts.org
Website: http://www.scts.org
Founded: 1933
Members: 561
Staff: 1
Contact: Isabelle Ferner, Society Admin.
Description: Cardiac and thoracic surgeons. Concerned with the study of cardiothoracic disease.
Publication: Bulletin. Advertisements.
Meetings/Conventions: - annual conference - Exhibits.

Society of Chemical Industry
SCI, 14-15 Belgrave Sq., London, SW1X 8PS, England, UK

Tel: 44 20 75981500
Fax: 44 20 75981545
Email: secretariat@soci.org
Website: http://www.soci.org
Founded: 1881
Members: 7000
Staff: 50
Contact: Mr. Richard Denyer, Gen.Sec.
Fee: £5
Membership Type: student
Fee: £21
Membership Type: individual aged 29 or younger
Description: Interdisciplinary network connecting industry, research, and consumer affairs at all levels throughout the world. Provides opportunities for forward-looking people in the process and materials technologies, energy, water, agriculture, food, pharmaceuticals, construction, and environmental protection areas to exchange ideas and gain new perspectives on markets, technologies, strategies, and people.
Formerly: Society of Chemical Industry
Publication: Magazine
Publication title: Chemistry and Industry. Advertisements.
Second publication: Journal
Publication title: Journal of Chemical Technology and Biotechnology (incorporating Clean Technology)

Society of Chief Librarians in England and Wales
c/o Catherine Blanshard
The Town Hall, The Headrow, Leeds, LS1 3AD, England, UK
Tel: 44 113 2478330
Fax: 44 113 2478331
Email: Catherine.Blanshard@leeds.gov.uk
Founded: 1996
Members: 122
Contact: Catherine Blanshard, Sec.
Fee: £80

Description: Chief Librarians of the public library authorities in England and Wales. Aims to promote and facilitate consultation, discussion, and exchange of views on matters relating to public libraries in England and Wales; to present advice to the local authority associations, to the Department of Culture, Media, and Sport, the Welsh office and to other bodies involved or interested in the provision of libraries and information in England and Wales.
Formerly: Federation of Local Authority Chief Librarians

Society of Chief Quantity Surveyors
Rycote Pl., 30-38 Cambridge St., Aylesbury, HP20 1RS, England, UK
Tel: 44 1296 339954
Fax: 44 1296 338514
Email: therise@nsrmanagement.co.uk
Website: http://www.scqs.org.uk
Founded: 1974
Members: 250
Staff: 1
Contact: Therese Quinn
Fee: £45
Membership Type: member
Fee: £30
Membership Type: associate
Description: Open to all quantity surveyors employed in senior quantity surveying posts of the public sector within the United Kingdom and extends to all those who, prior to promotion, held such a post and retain responsibility for quantity surveying within the public sector. Promotes discussion on professional, administrative, technical and other matters affecting the membership and affords advice to members in the execution of their duties; arranges annual conference, seminars and the interchange and publication of reports and information collated by members of the Society on Quantity Surveying and related subjects.
Publication: Magazine
Publication title: SCQS Newsletter
Meetings/Conventions: - annual meeting

Society of Chiropodists and Podiatrists
1 Fellmongers Path, Tower Bridge Rd., London, SE1 3LY, England, UK
Tel: 44 207 2348620
Fax: 44 207 2348621
Email: enq@scpod.org
Website: http://www.feetforlife.org
Founded: 1945
Members: 7800
Staff: 20
Contact: Hilary De Lyon, CEO
Fee: £188
Description: State registered chiropodists. The principal activities are to fulfill both a pre-registration and post-registration education function, to act as a trade union for its members employed in the National Health Service, to monitor the professional and ethical conduct and standards of its members, to publish professional journals, and to fulfil a public relations role.
Publication: Journal
Publication title: The Journal of British Podiatric Medicine. Advertisements.
Second publication: Journal
Publication title: Podiatry Now
Meetings/Conventions: - annual conference

Society of Clerks of Valuation Tribunals

Premier House, 1st Fl., W Wing, 36-48 Queen St., Horsham, RH13 5AD, England, UK
Tel: 44 1403 243785
Fax: 44 1403 261414
Email: alexandra.beeching@vto.gsx.gov.uk
Founded: 1950
Contact: Mrs. A.A.M. Beeching
Description: Clerks of valuation tribunals.
Formerly: Society of Clerks of Valuation and Community Charge Tribunals

Society of College, National and University Libraries

102 Euston St., London, NW1 2HA, England, UK
Tel: 44 207 3870317
Fax: 44 207 3833197
Email: info@sconul.ac.uk
Website: http://www.sconul.ac.uk
Founded: 1950
Members: 156
Staff: 3
Contact: Toby Bainton, Sec.
Description: Works to improve the quality and extend the influence of the university and national libraries of the United Kingdom and Ireland. Promotes the science and practice of librarianship. Discusses, develops, and recommends policies for the efficient operation of higher education and national libraries. Fosters cooperations between libraries, and seeks to avoid duplication of efforts.
Formerly: Standing Conference of National and University Libraries
Publication: Journal
Publication title: SCONUL Annual Library Statistics

Society of Computing and Technology in Anaesthesia
SCATA

c/o Associates of Anaesthesia
21 Portland Pl., London, W1B 1PY, England, UK
Website: http://www.scata.org.uk
Founded: 1990
Members: 340
Description: Anesthesiology associations in Europe concerned with coding, standards for medical devices, and development of medical information technology.
Publication: Newsletter
Publication title: SAN

Society of Construction Law

67 Newbury St., Wantage, OX12 8DJ, England, UK
Tel: 44 1235 770606
Fax: 44 1235 770580
Email: admin@scl.org.uk
Website: http://www.scl.org.uk
Founded: 1981
Members: 1200
Contact: Helen Garthwaite, Sec.
Fee: £50
Membership Type: admission
Fee: £65
Description: Barristers, solicitors, architects, surveyors, engineers and other construction professionals. Concerned with education, study, research and dissemination of knowledge of construction law and related subjects.

Library Subject: construction law and related subjects
Library Type: open to the public
Meetings/Conventions: - monthly lecture

Society of Consulting Marine Engineers and Ship Surveyors

202 Lambeth Rd., London, SE1 7JW, England, UK
Tel: 44 207 2610869
Fax: 44 207 2610871
Email: sec@scmshq.org
Website: http://www.scmshq.org
Founded: 1920
Members: 500
Staff: 1
Contact: Paul Owen, Sec.
Description: Consulting marine engineers and ship surveyors. Provides a central organisation for those engaged in a consultative or similar capacity in technical maritime affairs.
Publication title: Marine Technical Consultancy
Second publication: Newsletter
Publication title: NewsLink. Advertisements.

Society of Cosmetic Scientists
SCS

G.T. House, 24/26 Rothesay Rd., Luton, LU1 1QX, England, UK
Tel: 44 1582 726661
Fax: 44 1582 405217
Email: ifscc.scs@btinternet.com
Website: http://www.scs.org.uk
Founded: 1948
Members: 1100
Staff: 2
Contact: Mrs. Lorna Weston, Gen.Sec.
Fee: £40
Membership Type: member
Fee: £36
Membership Type: associate
Description: Scientists and technologists in the cosmetic industry. Works to advance the science of cosmetics and toiletries. Encourages education and research in cosmetics. Offers professional training programs.
Publication: Journal
Publication title: International Journal of Cosmetic Science. Advertisements.
Second publication: Newsletter
Publication title: SCS Newsletter
Meetings/Conventions: - annual symposium

Society of County and Regional Public Relations Officers

7 Greenlands, South Rd., Taunton, TA1 3EB, England, UK
Tel: 44 1823 251604
Contact: Gene Wonnacott, Sec.
Description: County and regional public relations officers.

Society of County Treasurers

c/o Somerset County Council
Financial Planning Team, County Treasurer's Dept., County Hall, Taunton, TA1 4DY, England, UK
Tel: 44 1823 356021
Fax: 44 1823 356937
Email: trichens@somerset.gov.uk

Website: http://www.sctnet.org.uk
Members: 36
Contact: Jon Pittam, Pres.
Fee: £40
Membership Type: Personal
Fee: £40
Membership Type: Family
Description: Treasurers of all County Councils in England. Established for the discussion of financial, management and other matters affecting local government generally, and county councils in particular and for the representation of the views of the Society on such matters.

Society of Craftsmen
29 Church St., Hereford, HR1 2LR, England, UK
Tel: 44 1432 266049
Founded: 1965
Contact: Mrs. C. Bulmer, Hon.Sec.
Description: Craftsmen, producing work to sell in the society's shop. To promote craftsmen and to encourage the continuation of craft work.

Society of Dairy Technology
PO Box 97, Bicester, OX27 7AB, England, UK
Tel: 44 1869 345838
Fax: 44 1869 345838
Email: socdt@btinternet.com
Website: http://www.sdt.org
Founded: 1943
Members: 600
Staff: 1
Contact: Dr. A.C. O'Sullivan, Exec.Dir.
Fee: £58
Membership Type: full
Fee: £29
Membership Type: retired
Description: Members from all sectors of the dairy and food industry - producers, suppliers, consultants, technicians, students, academics, researchers. Provides a means for disseminating knowledge and application of dairy technology across the dairy and food industry. It is a focal point of reference for all matters concerning dairy science and technology. Meetings and conferences of international calibre are organised and technical education and training is encouraged and provided.
Publication: Journal
Publication title: International Journal of Dairy Technology. Advertisements.
Meetings/Conventions: Aspects of Responsible Dairy Processing - semiannual symposium

Society of Designer Craftsmen
SDC
24 Rivington St., London, EC2A 3DU, England, UK
Tel: 44 207 7393663
Fax: 44 207 7393663
Email: info@societyofdesignercraftsmen.org.ukwww.SocietyofDesignerCraftsmen.org.uk
Founded: 1888
Members: 800
Contact: Alicia Merrett, Hon.Sec.
Fee: £55
Membership Type: fellows
Fee: £45
Membership Type: individual members

Description: Qualified, full-time designer-craftsmen. Seeks to establish the professional status of craftsmen and designers and increase members' awareness of users of their products. Fosters and exhibits British craftsmanship; provides up-to-date information on leading craftsmen. Assists graduates trying to establish their own workshops. Maintains slide library depicting members' works.
Publication: Magazine
Publication title: The Designer Craftsman
Publication title: Members' Newssheet
Meetings/Conventions: Designer Crafts - annual trade show - Exhibits.

Society of District Council Treasurers
PO Box 1, College Heath Rd., MildenHall, Bury St. Edmunds, 1P28 7UZ, England, UK
Tel: 44 1638 719701
Founded: 1974
Members: 256
Contact: Ray Bolton, Hon.Sec.
Fee: £40
Membership Type: full
Description: District Council Treasurers. Provide financial and technical advice and support to members in the furtherance of local government services.
Formerly: Association of District Council Treasurers
Meetings/Conventions: - periodic general assembly

Society of Dyers and Colourists - England
SDC
PO Box 244, Perkin House, 82 Grattan Rd., Bradford, BD1 2JB, England, UK
Tel: 44 1274 725138
Fax: 44 1274 392888
Email: secretariat@sdc.org.uk
Website: http://www.sdc.org.uk
Founded: 1884
Members: 2500
Staff: 30
Contact: Kenneth M. McGhee, Gen.Sec. & CEO
Fee: £65
Description: Dyers and colorists involved in industry and education. Promotes the advancement of science and technology concerning color through meetings, publications, technical work, and educational activities. Maintains museum. Administers professional examinations.
Publication title: Journal of the Society of Dyers and Colourists. Advertisements.
Publication title: Review of Progress in Coloration and Related Topics
Meetings/Conventions: - biennial conference - Exhibits.

Society of Editors
University Centre, Granta Pl., Cambridge, CB2 1RU, England, UK
Tel: 44 1223 304080
Fax: 44 1223 304090
Email: info@societyofeditors.org
Website: http://www.societyofeditors.org
Founded: 1946
Members: 500
Staff: 2
Contact: Bob Satchwell, Dir.
Fee: £230
Description: Editors, deputy editors and senior editorial executives of national, regional and local newspapers, magazines and broadcasting

organizations, journalism education, and media law. Seeks to defend and promote the independence of editors as an essential bulwark of media freedom. Fosters better education and training for journalists and monitors legislation for potential threats to media freedom.
Formerly: Formed by Merger of, Guild of Editors and Association of British Editors
Publication: Newsletter
Publication title: Briefing
Meetings/Conventions: - annual conference - Exhibits.

Society of Electrical and Mechanical Engineers Serving Local Government
SCEME

1 Lenfield Ave., Maidstone, ME14 5DU, England, UK
Tel: 44 1622 208631
Email: tamswelle@cableinet.co.uk
Founded: 1951
Members: 77
Contact: Mr. Charles Tanswell, Sec.
Fee: £40
Membership Type: member
Fee: £40
Membership Type: associate
Description: Provides a forum to discuss and promote mechanical and electrical engineering matters relating to Local Government Authorities and members of the Society in the U.K.

Society of Engineers

Guinea Wiggs, Nayland, Colchester, CO6 4NF, England, UK
Tel: 44 1206 263332
Fax: 44 1206 262624
Email: secretary@society-of-engineers.org.uk
Website: http://www.society-of-engineers.org.uk
Founded: 1854
Members: 858
Staff: 1
Contact: Mrs. L.C.A. Wright, Ch.Exec.
Description: Well qualified professional engineers from all the major disciplines. Aims to promote the interests of professional engineers, maintain liaison with government bodies, publish engineering information, holds meetings and lectures.
Publication title: Engineering World. Advertisements.

Society of Environmental Engineers

The Manor House, High St., Buntingford, SG9 9AB, England, UK
Tel: 44 1763 271209
Fax: 44 1763 273255
Email: office@environmental.org.uk
Website: http://www.environmental.org.uk
Founded: 1959
Members: 765
Contact: Sir John Mason, Pres.
Description: Members drawn from many engineering disciplines. Provides a forum for the sharing of knowledge and expertise in environmental engineering and control over a wide field. Activities include technical mettings, training and education, symposia, exhibitions, workshops and confernces.
Publication: Journal
Publication title: Environmental Engineering
Second publication: Newsletter

Society of Equestrian Artists

63 Gordon Close, Knowle Green, Staines, TW18 1AP, England, UK
Tel: 44 709 2018712
Email: enquiries@equestrianartists.co.uk
Website: http://www.equestrianartists.co.uk
Founded: 1978
Members: 400
Contact: Corinne Bickford, Sec.
Fee: £15
Description: Exists to encourage the study of equine art and, by mutual assistance between members, to promote a standard of excellence in its practice worthy of the subject's importance in British artistic tradition. The society is a registered charity and currently holds an annual exhibition and workshops throughout the country.
Publication: Newsletter. Advertisements.

Society of European Sonographers
SEUS

36 Portland Pl., London, W1N 3DG, England, UK
Tel: 44 20 78157911
Fax: 44 20 78158099
Email: chudlet@sbu.ac.uk

Society of Feed Technologists

156 Oxford Rd., Reading, , England, UK
Tel: 44 1734 595458

Society of Floristry

6 Carroll Ave., Dorset, Ferndown, BH22 8BP, England, UK
Tel: 44 870 2410432
Fax: 44 120 2855520
Email: info@societyoffloristry.org
Website: http://www.societyoffloristry.org
Founded: 1951
Members: 1000
Contact: Angela Vokalek, Sec.
Description: Professional florists and those in the floristry trade.
Publication title: Focal Point. Advertisements.

Society of Food Hygiene Technology

PO Box 37, Lymington, SO41 9WL, England, UK
Tel: 44 1590 671979
Fax: 44 1590 671359
Email: admin@sofht.co.uk
Website: http://www.sofht.co.uk
Founded: 1979
Members: 800
Staff: 2
Contact: Mrs. H.A. Hyde
Fee: £20
Membership Type: associate
Fee: £55
Membership Type: individual
Description: Membership open to those involved in food hygiene, throughout the commercial food chain. To promote the production, distribution and sale of safe and wholesome food by: communication within the industry on all matters related to hygiene; encouraging training of personnel and providing an informal advisory service.
Publication: Magazine
Publication title: SOFHT Focus. Advertisements.
Meetings/Conventions: - annual luncheon London UK

Society of Garden Designers

Katepwa House, Ashfield Park Ave., Ross-On-Wye, HR9 5AX, England, UK
Tel: 44 1989 566695
Fax: 44 1989 507676
Email: sgd@assocmanagement.co.uk
Website: http://www.society-of-garden-designers.co.uk
Founded: 1981
Members: 1100
Staff: 1
Contact: Gill Hinton, Admin.
Fee: £47
Membership Type: corresponding
Fee: £58
Membership Type: affiliate
Description: Full members/Fellows have exhibited highest professional standards of garden design; Corresponding members may be practising designers, students or interested in the subject. Emphasis is placed on the excellence of work and the Code of Practice is designed to protect the interests of clients and members alike.
Library Subject: garden design
Library Type: open to the public
Publication: Journal
Publication title: Garden Design Journal. Advertisements.
Meetings/Conventions: - semiannual seminar - Exhibits.

Society of Glass Technology
SGT

Don Valley House, Savile St. East, Sheffield, S4 7UQ, England, UK
Tel: 44 114 2634455
Fax: 44 114 2634411
Email: info@sgt.org
Website: http://www.sgt.org
Founded: 1916
Members: 1100
Staff: 5
Contact: David Moore
Fee: £60
Description: Associations and individuals interested in glass. Promotes the study of glass technology. Maintains 5 technical committees.
Library Subject: Joint Library of Glass Technology
Library Type: reference
Publication: Journal
Publication title: Glass Technology. Advertisements.
Publication title: Physics and Chemistry of Glasses
Meetings/Conventions: Glass Opportunities - annual conference

Society of Headmasters and Headmistresses of Independent Schools
SHMIS

Celedston, Rhosesmor Rd., Halkyn, Holywell, CH8 8DL, England, UK
Tel: 44 352 781102
Fax: 44 352 781102
Email: gensec@shmis.org.uk
Website: http://www.shmis.org.uk
Founded: 1961
Members: 95
Staff: 2
Contact: I.D. Cleland, Gen.Sec.

Description: Heads of smaller independent secondary schools. The promotion of independent education; support of Heads in their work and sharing of ideas and problems.

Society of Health and Beauty Therapists

77 New Bond St, London, W1Y 9DB, England, UK
Tel: 44 20 74933321
Founded: 1962

Society of Homeopaths

4a Artizan Rd., Northampton, NN1 4HU, England, UK
Tel: 44 1604 621400
Fax: 44 1604 622622
Email: info@homeopathy-soh.org
Website: http://www.homeopathy-soh.org
Founded: 1978
Members: 2706
Staff: 9
Contact: Mary Clarke
Description: Professional homeopaths on the Society's register. Aims to develop and maintain high standards for the practise of homeopathy and to promote public awareness of homeopathy. It also supports the establishment of education and training in homeopathy.
Publication: Journal
Publication title: The Homoeopath Journal. Advertisements.
Publication title: Register of Professional Homoeopaths
Meetings/Conventions: - annual conference - Exhibits.

Society of Hospital Linen Service and Laundry Managers

c/o Paul Gibson, Chairman
Bolton Hospitals NHS Trust, Bolton, BL4 0JR, England, UK
Tel: 44 1204 390613
Fax: 44 1204 390693
Email: paul.gibson@boltonh-tr.nwest.nhs.uk
Website: http://www.linenmanager.co.uk
Founded: 1951
Members: 80
Contact: G. Nixon, Natl.Chm.
Description: NHS staff employed in linen services management or indirectly involved in linen services.
Library Type: not open to the public
Meetings/Conventions: - annual seminar - Exhibits.

Society of Independent Brewers
SIB

PO Box 101, Thirsk, Y07 4WA, England, UK
Tel: 44 20 83559583
Fax: 44 20 83559087
Email: peter@siba.co.uk
Website: http://www.siba.co.uk
Founded: 1980
Members: 240
Contact: Peter Haydon
Description: Independent brewers and breweries. Seeks to obtain a sliding-scale tax exemption for breweries in the United Kingdom. Represents members' collective commercial interests; conducts lobbying and promotional activities; facilitates communication and cooperation among members.

Society of Independent Roundabout Proprietors

c/o Mr. John Carter
Carter's Yard, White Waltham, Maidenhead, SL6 3LW, England, UK
Tel: 44 860 284447
Founded: 1985
Members: 100
Contact: John Carter, Chm.
Fee: £20
Membership Type: member
Description: Independent showmen who own vintage fairground equipment. Represents members' interests to the government.

Society of Indexers
SI

Blades Enterprise Centre, John St., Sheffield, S2 4SU, England, UK
Tel: 44 114 2922350
Fax: 44 114 2922351
Email: admin@indexers.org.uk
Website: http://www.indexers.org.uk
Founded: 1957
Members: 950
Staff: 1
Contact: Wendy Burrow, Admin.
Fee: £60
Membership Type: individual in U.K. and Europe
Fee: £75
Membership Type: individual outside Europe
Description: Persons in 21 countries interested in all types of indexing, particularly of books and periodicals. Institutional membership open to publishers, universities and colleges, firms, and other organizations concerned with or interested in indexing. Promotes high standards of indexing and works to develop indexing techniques. Maintains list of persons willing and qualified to undertake indexing work for authors, editors, and publishers; acts as advisory body on the qualifications and remuneration of indexers. Conducts discussions on various aspects of indexing. Organizes training course on principles of indexing.
Library Subject: indexing
Library Type: not open to the public
Publication title: Indexers Available
Meetings/Conventions: Society of Indexers Conference - annual meeting

Society of Industrial Emergency Services Officers

The Oaks, Thames Lane, Cricklade, Wiltshire, SN6 6BH, England, UK
Tel: 44 1793 759225
Email: sec@sieso.org.uk
Website: http://www.sieso.org.uk
Founded: 1953
Members: 450
Contact: Derek F. Heathcote, Sec.
Fee: £20
Membership Type: ordinary
Description: Members come from industry, commerce, regulatory agencies, government, emergency services, health authorities, voluntary aid societies and the media. Aims to share experiences, ideas and practices for improving the prevention of and the planning and management of responses to industrial emergencies. Provides opportunities for discussion on the avoidance and mitigation of the effects of major incidents, by identifying good practice in industry and by liaising with central and local government and the U.K. regulatory bodies.
Publication: Magazine
Publication title: Industrial Safety Management. Advertisements.
Meetings/Conventions: conference

Society of Industrial Furnace Engineers

c/o Peat, Marwick, Mitchell and Co.
301 Glossop Rd., PO Box 121, Sheffield, S10 2HN, England, UK
Description: Industrial furnace engineers.

Society of Information Technology Management

PO Box 121, Northampton, NN4 6TG, England, UK
Tel: 44 1604 674800
Fax: 44 1604 674800
Email: bobg@socitm.gov.uk
Website: http://www.socitm.gov.uk
Founded: 1985
Members: 1500
Staff: 10
Contact: Bob Griffith, Sec.
Fee: £75
Membership Type: full
Description: IS/IT Managers in Local Government and the Public Sector. The professional organization for local government officers responsible for recommending corporate information technology policy. Provides a focal point for local government IT; produces standards of good practice.
Library Subject: IT management
Library Type: reference
Publication: Report
Publication title: IT Trends
Second publication: Newsletter
Publication title: SOCITM Newsletter
Meetings/Conventions: - semiannual conference - Exhibits.

Society of International Gas Tanker and Terminal Operators
SIGTTO

17 St. Helen's Place, London, EC3A 6DG, England, UK
Tel: 44 207 6281124
Fax: 44 207 6283163
Email: secretariat@sigtto.org
Website: http://www.sigtto.org
Founded: 1979
Members: 101
Staff: 6
Contact: John Gyles
Description: Companies from 27 countries operating natural and petroleum gas tankers. Promotes the safe operation of gas tankers and terminals. Represents members' interests before the International Maritime Organization.
Library Type: reference
Publication: Books
Second publication: Papers
Meetings/Conventions: - annual meeting

Society of International Treasurers
SIT

2 Tereslake Green, Westbury-On-Trym, Bristol, BS10 6LT, England, UK
Tel: 44 117 9508019
Fax: 44 117 9508019
Email: mail@socintrs.com
Website: http://www.socintrs.com
Founded: 1977
Members: 200

Staff: 1
Contact: Geoffrey Jones, Dir.Gen.
Description: Individuals in 15 countries involved in corporate treasury management within major multinational corporations, excluding financial service corps.
Meetings/Conventions: - annual conference

Society of Laundry Engineers and Allied Trades

Ste. 7, Southernhay, 207 Hook Rd., Chessinton, Chessington, KT9 1HJ, England, UK
Tel: 44 208 3912266
Fax: 44 208 3914466
Email: admin@sleat.co.uk
Website: http://sleat.co.uk
Founded: 1908
Members: 35
Contact: David M. Hart, CEO
Fee: £235
Membership Type: associate
Description: Suppliers of machinery, equipment and consumables to the laundry and dry cleaning trade. Support and sponsorship of trade exhibitions; monitoring of safety and specification standards and publications. Promotion of interests of supply trade in liaison activities with user organizations.

Society of Legal Scholars in the United Kingdom and Ireland

c/o Prof. Nick Wikeley
Faculty of Law, University of Southampton, Highfield, Southampton, SO17 1BJ, England, UK
Tel: 44 2380 593416
Fax: 44 2380 593024
Email: njw@soton.ac.uk
Website: http://www.ukcle.ac.uk/SPTL
Founded: 1908
Members: 2500
Staff: 1
Contact: Prof. Nick Wikeley, Hon.Sec.
Fee: £30
Membership Type: ordinary
Description: Individuals involved in legal research and the teaching of law at degree level or above in universities and other institutions; legal firms; chambers; other bodies.
Formerly: Society of Public Teachers of Law
Publication title: Directory of Members
Publication title: Legal Studies
Meetings/Conventions: - annual conference - Exhibits. Oxford UK

Society of Leisure and Entertainment Consultants and Publishers
SOLECAP

1 Sandringham Close, Sandringham Park, Tarleton, Preston, PR4 6UZ, England, UK
Tel: 44 1772 816046
Founded: 1991
Members: 32
Staff: 1
Contact: J.B.A. Sharples, Dir.
Fee: £25
Membership Type: member/individual
Fee: £50
Membership Type: affiliate/commercial

Description: Consultants and publishers working in the field of leisure, ie entertainment, recreation, tourism, hotels and catering, marketing, publicity. Affiliate membership is offered to commercial and corporate firms and organisations working in these fields. Represents, supports and provides a meeting area for consultants, publishers, corporate and commercial organizations in the whole field of leisure.
Formerly: Society of Leisure Consultants and Publishers
Publication: Newsletter
Publication title: SOLCAP News. Advertisements.
Meetings/Conventions: - annual conference

Society of Licensed Victuallers

Heatherley, London Rd., Ascot, Berkshire, SL5 8DR, England, UK
Tel: 44 1344 884440
Fax: 44 1344 884703
Email: info@slv-online.org.uk
Website: http://www.slv-online.org.uk
Founded: 1793
Members: 20000
Staff: 250
Contact: Colin Wheeler, Chief Exec.
Fee: £40
Membership Type: life
Description: Qualification for membership is as follows:- Under 60 years of age, hold or jointly hold, a full on-licence. Provides regular financial assistance from Society funds for elderly, sick or needy members, monetary grants to relieve temporary difficulties, burial grants, care and education for children at the Licensed Victuallers' Schools and a voice in the management of the Society's news magazine The Licensee and Morning Advertiser.
Publication title: The Licensee and Morning Advertiser. Advertisements.

Society of Local Authority Chief Executives and Senior Managers

Hope House, 45 Great Peter St., London, SW1P 3LT, England, UK
Tel: 44 845 6010649
Fax: 44 151 4433932
Email: hope.house@soalce.org.uk
Website: http://www.solace.org.uk
Founded: 1974
Members: 950
Staff: 8
Contact: James Hehir, Pres.
Description: Serving local authority chief executives and senior managers. Provides an authoritative voice on all of the subject matters of local government and in embracing all types of local authority in the UK, it is able to speak for the whole of local government.
Meetings/Conventions: - annual conference

Society of Local Council Clerks

1 The Crescent, Taunton, TA1 4EA, England, UK
Tel: 44 1823 253646
Fax: 44 1949 837444
Email: admin@slcc.co.uk
Website: http://www.slcc.co.uk
Founded: 1972
Members: 2486
Staff: 1
Contact: Mike Elliot, Sec.
Description: Clerks to parish and town councils in England and Wales. Serves local authority staff at parish and town council level of local government.

Publication: Magazine
Publication title: The Clerk. Advertisements.
Meetings/Conventions: - annual conference - Exhibits.

Society of London Art Dealers

91 Jermyn St., London, SW1Y 6JB, England, UK
Tel: 44 20 79306137
Fax: 44 20 73210685
Email: office@slad.org.uk
Website: http://www.slad.org.uk
Founded: 1932
Members: 100
Staff: 2
Contact: Christopher Battiscombe
Description: Art dealers who have been in business for at least 3 years in the Greater London area. Promotes and protects the good name and interests of the fine art trade and enhances public confidence in responsible art dealing. Members must have a proven reputation in their field and have signed an undertaking to observe standards of fair and honest dealing.
Publication: Membership Directory

Society of London Theatre

32 Rose St., London, WC2E 9ET, England, UK
Tel: 44 207 5576700
Fax: 44 207 5576799
Email: enquiries@solttma.co.uk
Website: http://www.officiallondontheatre.co.uk
Founded: 1908
Members: 95
Staff: 20
Contact: Richard Pulford, Ch.Exec.
Description: The Society comprises managers and proprietors of theatres and producers of shows in the West End of London; both the commercial and subsidised sectors are represented. Negotiates minimum rates of pay and conditions of employment with the theatrical unions: British Actors Equity (covering performers, stage management, directors and designers), BECTU (theatre staff including technicians) and the Musicians' Union (musicians). An arbitration and conciliation service is provided for disputes between managers and artists through the Society's partnership with Equity in the London Theatre Council.
Publication title: London Theatre Guide
Second publication: Manual
Publication title: Travel Trade Manual

Society of Maritime Industries

4th Fl., 30 Great Guildford St., London, SE1 0HS, England, UK
Tel: 44 20 7928 9199
Fax: 44 20 79286599
Email: ce@bmec.org.uk
Website: http://www.maritimeindustries.org
Founded: 1966
Members: 200
Staff: 10
Contact: John C. Murray, Ch.Exec.
Description: Member companies supply equipment for all types of ships, for the offshore oil and gas industry and for pollution control. Acts as a collective voice of the marine equipment industry, liaising with and lobbying government in the interests of equipment suppliers for the benefit of international trade.
Formerly: British Marine Equipment Council
Publication: Directory

Society of Master Shoe Repairers

St. Crispin's House, Station Rd., Desborough, Kettering, NN14 2SA, England, UK
Tel: 44 1536 760374
Fax: 44 1536 762348
Website: http://www.somsr.com
Founded: 1963
Members: 350
Contact: Frank Scrivener, Chm.
Fee: £72
Description: Shoe repairers. Trade association for shoe repairers throughout the UK.
Formerly: Absorbed, British Shoe Repair Association
Publication: Journal
Publication title: Shoe Service. Advertisements.

Society of Metaphysicians
S of M

Archers' Ct., Stonestile Ln., The Ridge, Hastings, TN35 4PG, England, UK
Tel: 44 1424 751577
Fax: 44 1424 722387
Email: newmeta@btinternet.com
Website: http://www.metaphysicians.org.uk
Founded: 1944
Members: 2800
Staff: 5
Contact: Dr. John J. Williamson, Pres.
Fee: £80
Membership Type: registered student, associate, graduate, member, fellow in Great Britain
Fee: £100
Membership Type: registered student, associate, graduate, member, fellow in Europe or the United States
Description: Persons in 17 countries who are skilled in neometaphysics; meet formal university qualifications in science and philosophy; are practically skilled in the parapsychological, paraphysical, and intuitive sciences; or are skilled in business and social arts. Seeks to create a new metaphysical system designed to optimize knowledge. Encourages members to develop personal parapsychological ability. Sponsors formalized research groups on international bases for parapsychology, paraphysics, social business, spiritual science, and its applications. Promotes a functional view of spiritual science through the media as the key to social harmony. Conducts meetings, discussions, research with workshop services, book sales, manufacturing and occult equipment sales, and correspondence courses. Research includes inquiries into aura phenomena, bio-energetics, psycho-kinetics, ESP, all psychic phenomena, and ultra-dimensional phenomena. Awards certificates in parapsychology and paraphysics upon satisfactory completion of examinations. Compiles statistics; offers placement services.
Library Type: reference
Publication: Journal
Publication title: Borderline Science Series (Paraphysics)
Publication title: Esoteric Series
Meetings/Conventions: - annual meeting - Exhibits.

Society of Miniaturists

Briargate, 2 The Brambles, Ilkley, LS29 9DH, England, UK
Fax: 44 1943 603753
Founded: 1895
Members: 60
Contact: Margaret Simpson, Dir.

Description: Dedicated artists who paint in the traditional manner in miniature form - one sixth actual size maximum outside measurement 3 plus inches by 4 plus inches. Aims to promote the traditional, ancient and precise art of miniature painting that goes back many centuries.
Publication: Catalog
Publication title: Catalogue

Society of Motor Manufacturers and Traders SMMT

Forbes House, Halkin St., London, SW1X 7DS, England, UK
Tel: 44 207 2357000
Fax: 44 207 2357112
Email: smmt@smmt.co.uk
Website: http://www.smmt.co.uk
Founded: 1902
Members: 800
Staff: 140
Contact: C. Macgowan, CEO
Description: Manufacturers and importers of cars, garage equipment, public service and commercial vehicles, and related equipment. Promotes the interests of the motor industry. Runs industry forum to improve quality and supply chain links in the U.K. automotive industry. Compiles statistics.
Publication: Bulletin
Publication title: Overseas Bulletin
Publication title: Press and PR Guide
Meetings/Conventions: Auto One - biennial trade show

Society of Municipal Treasurers

Washway Rd., PO Box 10, Sale, M33 7AL, England, UK
Tel: 44 121 5693500
Fax: 44 121 5693515
Founded: 1974
Staff: 100
Contact: E. Gamble, Hon.Sec.
Fee: £32
Description: Metropolitan treasurers.
Meetings/Conventions: - annual board meeting

Society of Museum Archaeologists

c/o Amanda Loaring
West Berkshire Heritage Service, The Wharf, Newbury, RG14 5AS, England, UK
Tel: 44 1635 30511
Fax: 44 1635 38535
Email: aloaring@westberks.gov.uk
Website: http://www.socmusarch.org.uk
Founded: 1976
Members: 300
Contact: Mr. David Allen
Description: Museum-based archaeologists. To promote museum involvement in all aspects of archaeology, and to emphasise the unique role of museums within the essential unity of the archaeological profession.
Publication: Proceedings
Publication title: The Museum Archaeologist
Second publication: Newsletter
Publication title: Museum Archaeologist's News
Meetings/Conventions: - annual conference

Society of Numismatic Artists and Designers

c/o Jane McAdam-Freud
116 Wendover, Thurlow St., London, SE17 2UE, England, UK
Founded: 1990
Members: 20
Contact: Jane McAdam-Freud, Sec.
Fee: £20
Membership Type: associates
Fee: £25
Membership Type: fellow
Description: Maintains high standards in coin and medal design among professional artists. Aims to meet and share ideas and information on artistic techniques and professional expertise.

Society of Nursery Nursing SNN

40 Archdale Rd., East Dulwich, London, SE22 9HJ, England, UK
Tel: 44 208 6930555
Fax: 44 208 6930555
Email: snn@totalise.co.uk
Founded: 1991
Members: 1500
Staff: 2
Contact: Dr. R.A. Herbert-Blankson, Sec.
Fee: £40
Membership Type: fellow
Fee: £35
Membership Type: associate
Description: Nursing managers, nursing administrators and nurses, nursery teachers, school nurses, nannies, and other workers and employers with an interest in the education, health and welfare of children from birth to five years of age. Seeks to establish professional standards and a uniform code of ethics within the field; works to enhance the professional standing of members. Gathers and disseminates information to inform legislative debate concerning child health issues. Conducts examinations and educational programs and maintains speakers' bureau.
Library Subject: nursery nursing
Library Type: not open to the public
Formerly: Society of Nursery Nursing Administrators
Publication: Newsletter
Publication title: Nursery Nursing Administrator. Advertisements.
Meetings/Conventions: - periodic board meeting

Society of Occupational Medicine

6 St. Andrew's Pl., Regent's Park, London, NW1 4LB, England, UK
Tel: 44 207 4862641
Fax: 44 207 4860028
Email: admin@som.org.uk
Website: http://www.som.org.uk/
Founded: 1935
Members: 2000
Staff: 5
Description: Doctors working in occupational medicine. Many of the members have specialist qualifications in occupational medicine but others may be family practitioners connected with or holding part-time appointments in the specialty. Concerned with protecting the health of people at work and the prevention and management of occupational diseases and injuries. Seeks to interest and inform members through publications and scientific meetings, organised regionally and nationally. Stimulates research and education in occupational medicine and actively liaises with professional organisations relevant to occupational health.
Publication: Newsletter

Publication title: Newsletter Periodical
Second publication: Journal
Publication title: Occupational Medicine Journal

Society of Operations Engineers
SOE

22 Greencoat Pl., London, SW1P 1PR, England, UK
Tel: 44 20 76301111
Fax: 44 20 76306677
Email: soe@soe.org.uk
Founded: 1944
Members: 22000
Staff: 27
Contact: P.J.G. Corp, Chief Exec.
Description: Promotes safe, efficient, and environmentally sustainable operations engineering to the benefits of society. Seeks to improve professional education, training and competence and ethics. Represents members' interests.
Formerly: Formed by Merger of, Institution of Plant Engineers
Publication: Journal
Publication title: The Plant Engineer
Publication title: Programme Booklet
Meetings/Conventions: - annual competition

Society of Parliamentary Agents

35 Great Peter St., London, SW1P 3LR, England, UK
Tel: 44 171 5935000
Fax: 44 171 5935199
Contact: P.M.C.F. Irving, Hon.Sec.
Description: Represents members' interests.

Society of Pension Consultants

Saint Bartholomew House, 92 Fleet St., London, EC4Y 1DG, England, UK
Tel: 44 207 3531688
Fax: 44 207 3539296
Email: john.mortimer@spc.uk.com
Website: http://www.spc.uk.com
Founded: 1958
Members: 138
Staff: 4
Contact: John Mortimer, Sec.
Description: Accountancy firms, actuaries, consultants, external pension administrators, independent trustees, investment houses, investment performance measurers, life offices and solicitors. Membership is corporate, which includes sole traders. Draws upon the knowledge and experience of members so as to contribute to legislation and other general developments affecting pension and related benefit provision. Maintains contact with a wide range of government departments and other groups, both in the UK and Europe.
Publication: Newsletter
Publication title: SPC News. Advertisements.
Meetings/Conventions: - monthly workshop

Society of Petroleum Engineers - London Office

Empire House, 4th Fl., 175 Piccadilly, London, W1J 9EN, England, UK
Tel: 44 207 4084466
Fax: 44 207 4082299
Email: spelon@spe.org
Website: http://www.spe.org
Members: 50000

Contact: Stephen A. Holditch, Pres.
Description: Petroleum engineers. Provides the means to collect, disseminate and exchange technical information concerning the development of oil and gas resources, subsurface fluid flow, and production of other materials through wellbores. Encourages members to maintain and improve their technical competence. Conducts educational programs.
Publication: Journal
Publication title: Journal of Petroleum Technology
Publication title: SPE Drilling & Completion
Meetings/Conventions: - annual conference - Exhibits.

Society of Pharmaceutical Medicine

20-22 Queensberry Place, London, SW7 2DZ, England, UK
Tel: 44 207 5818333
Fax: 44 207 5893606
Email: spm@iob.org
Website: http://www.socpharmed.org
Founded: 1987
Members: 120
Staff: 1
Contact: Amy Scales, Exec.Sec.
Fee: £45
Description: Open to all those involved within drug development - both in the pharmaceutical industry and also in academic/clinical medicine and the drug regulatory agencies. Aims to provide a focus for questions relating to the development of medicinal agents. This is promoted by the organisation of regular meetings and occasional workshops. Topics are wide ranging and collaboration with other societies is encouraged.
Publication: Journal
Publication title: Journal of Pharmaceutical Medicine
Meetings/Conventions: meeting

Society of Picture Researchers and Editors

455 Finchley Rd., London, NW3 0HN, England, UK
Tel: 44 171 4319886
Fax: 44 171 4319887
Founded: 1977
Members: 200
Contact: Emma Krikler, Gen.Sec.
Fee: £50
Membership Type: full
Fee: £40
Membership Type: intermediate
Description: Intermediate, up to 2 years full time picture research experience; Full, over 2 years full time picture research experience. Promotes the recognition of picture research as a profession, requiring particular skills and knowledge. Maintains professional standards and ethics within the profession.
Publication: Magazine
Publication title: SPREd

Society of Ploughmen

Quarry Farm, Loversall, Doncaster, DN11 9DH, England, UK
Tel: 44 1302 852469
Fax: 44 1302 859880
Email: info@ploughmen.co.uk
Website: http://www.ploughmen.co.uk
Founded: 1972
Members: 1052
Staff: 1
Contact:
Fee: £20

Membership Type: personal
Fee: £40
Membership Type: family
Description: Individual members and local ploughing societies throughout the UK. Organises the annual British National Ploughing Championships which are held in a different part of Great Britain each year. The Championships include modern tractor ploughing; vintage tractor ploughing and exhibitions; horse ploughing; trade stands and demonstrations; and country crafts.
Publication: Newsletter
Publication title: Society of Ploughmen Newsletter

Society of Practising Veterinary Surgeons
2 The Old Gunroom, Blagdon Estate, Seaton Burn, Newcastle upon Tyne, NE13 6DB, England, UK
Tel: 44 1670 789054
Fax: 44 1670 789359
Email: office@spvs.rog.uk
Website: http://www.spvs.org.uk
Description: Represents the interests of veterinary surgeons.

Society of Procurement Officers in Local Government
SOPO
c/o Peter Blanchard, Sec.
Gateshead Council, Stonehills, Pelaw, Gateshead, Tyne and Wear, NE10 0HW, England, UK
Tel: 44 191 4335940
Fax: 44 191 4950933
Email: peterblanchard@gateshead.gov.uk
Website: http://www.sopo.org
Founded: 1997
Members: 1250
Contact: Peter Blanchard, Sec.
Description: Promotes the strategic procurement function within local government in England, Wales, Scotland, and Northern Ireland. Represents members' interests and advises local government associations. Promotes professional development.
Formerly: Society of Purchasing Officers in Local Government
Meetings/Conventions: Annual Conference and AGM - annual conference - Exhibits. London

Society of Professional Engineers
Lutyenthouse, Billing Brook Rd., Northampton, NN3 8NW, England, UK
Tel: 44 1604 415729
Fax: 44 1604 415729
Founded: 1969
Members: 800
Staff: 1
Contact: David Gibson
Description: Well-qualified professional engineers from all the major engineering disciplines. Establishes and maintains a register that embraces all suitably qualified professional engineers of whatever discipline; protects and enhances the status of the professional engineer and promotes the concept of this title throughout the world and establishes and promotes the highest professional standards.
Publication: Newsletter
Publication title: The Professional Engineer. Advertisements.

Society of Protozoologists, British Section
Guy's Hospital Medical School, London, SE1 9RT, England, UK
Tel: 44 20 74077600
Founded: 1962

Society of Public Information Networks
SPIN
PO Box 2306, Chippenham, SN14 7WA, England, UK
Tel: 44 1249 783702
Fax: 44 1249 783702
Email: info@spin.org.uk
Website: http://www.spin.org.uk/
Founded: 1988
Members: 200
Contact: Lin O'Keefe
Fee: £125
Membership Type: local authority in the United Kingdom
Fee: £175
Membership Type: local authority in Europe
Description: Local government authorities, health agencies, libraries and museums, corporations, and public sector and nonprofit organizations maintaining public information services. Seeks to increase and ease access to public information. Promotes adherence to high standards of ethics and practice in the collection and dissemination of public information. Represents the interests of public information networks and providers before government agencies and the public. Serves as a forum for public information providers wishing to make use of electronic publishing information (EPI) technologies. Supports research and development designed to improve EPI techniques and technologies.
Publication title: EPI Magazine
Meetings/Conventions: - annual conference - Exhibits.

Society of Recorder Players
c/o Bob Horsley
15 Palliser Rd., London, W14 9EB, England, UK
Tel: 44 20 73857321
Website: http://www.srp.org.uk
Founded: 1938
Members: 1700
Contact: Bob Horsley
Fee: £10
Description: Recorder players of all ages and abilities. To promote the education of the public in the study, practice and appreciation of the recorder and its repertoire.
Publication: Magazine
Publication title: The Recorder Magazine. Advertisements.
Publication title: Teacher's Guide to the Recorder
Meetings/Conventions: Ensemble Playing - annual conference - Exhibits.

Society of Registration Officers
c/o Register Office
Aspen House, 1st Fl., Temple St., Swindon, SN1 1SQ, England, UK
Tel: 44 1793 521734
Fax: 44 1793 433887
Founded: 1968
Members: 600
Contact: Karen Knapton
Description: Registration Officers in England and Wales. To improve the conditions and protect the interests of members and regulate the relations between members and between the Registrar General the Local Authorities and any other organisation. The Society also aims to

promote, safe-guard, maintain or improve the interests and status of registration officers and the registration service.
Publication: Newsletter
Publication title: Unity. Advertisements.
Meetings/Conventions: - annual conference

Society of Sales Marketing
SSM

40 Archdale Rd., East Dulwich, London, SE22 9HJ, England, UK
Tel: 44 208 6930555
Fax: 44 208 6930555
Email: ssam@totalise.co.uk
Founded: 1980
Members: 2500
Staff: 2
Contact: Dr. R.A. Herbert-Blankson, Chief Exec.
Fee: £25
Membership Type: graduate
Fee: £30
Membership Type: associate
Description: Professionals engaged in sales, sales management, marketing, retailing, and international trade. Works to enhance the professional standing of members, and to encourage the study of sales, international trade, and related subjects. Conducts professional examinations; compiles statistics; maintains speakers' bureau.
Library Subject: sales, international trade, marketing, and retailing
Library Type: not open to the public
Formerly: Society of Sales Management Administrators
Publication: Journal
Publication title: Sales Management Administrator. Advertisements.
Meetings/Conventions: - periodic board meeting

Society of Schoolmasters and Schoolmistresses

c/o Dr. L.I. Baggott
Queen Mary House, Manor Park Rd., Manor Park Rd., Chistlehurst, Chislehurst, BR7 5PY, England, UK
Tel: 44 20 84687997
Fax: 44 20 84687200
Email: sgbi@sgbi.freeserve.co.uk
Founded: 1798
Contact: Dr. L.I. Baggott, Actg.Sec.
Description: Provides relief as needed to masters and mistresses of all recognized schools, independent or maintained, and their dependants, provided that such persons have been in teaching for at least 10 years.
Formerly: Society of Schoolmasters

Society of Scribes and Illuminators
SSI

6 Queen Sq., London, WC1 3AR, England, UK
Tel: 44 15242 51534
Email: scribe@calligraphyonline.org
Website: http://www.calligraphyonline.org
Founded: 1921
Members: 700
Contact: Gillian Hazeldine, Hon.Sec.
Fee: £35
Membership Type: fellow
Fee: £27
Membership Type: lay
Description: Aims to advance the crafts of writing and illuminating. Members of the society are technically accomplished, with an

appreciation of historical models and an ability to adapt them to contemporary work.
Library Type: reference
Publication title: Calligrapher's Handbook
Second publication: Journal
Publication title: Journal
Meetings/Conventions: Lay Members' Exhibition show

Society of Shoe Fitters

c/o Mrs. Laura West
The Anchorage, 28 Admirals Walk, Hingham, Norfolk, NR9 4JL, England, UK
Tel: 44 1953851171
Fax: 44 1953851171
Website: http://www.shoefitters-uk.org
Founded: 1959
Members: 250
Staff: 1
Contact: Mrs. Laura West
Fee: £40
Membership Type: member
Description: Aims to recognize fitting qualification and training in shoe fitting, and assists the public in finding shoes to fit and foot health advice.
Library Type: not open to the public

Society of Teachers in Business Education
STBE

28 Norlands Crescent, Chislehurst, BR7 5RN, England, UK
Tel: 44 208 4023569
Email: editor@stbe.clara.co.uk
Website: http://www.stbe.net
Founded: 1907
Members: 1500
Staff: 3
Contact: Mrs. M.D. Drew, Ed.
Fee: £39
Membership Type: subscription
Description: Teachers of business secretarial courses at the secondary and postsecondary level in the United Kingdom. Provides support services to members. Sponsors educational programs.
Publication: Magazine
Publication title: Focus on Business Education
Second publication: Magazine
Publication title: Focus on Business Education and Focus Plus. Advertisements.
Meetings/Conventions: Business Education/Training - annual conference - Exhibits. UK

Society of Teachers of Speech and Drama

73 Berry Hill Rd., Mansfield, NG18 4RU, England, UK
Tel: 44 1623 627636
Email: ann.p.jones@btinternet.com
Website: http://www.stsd.org.uk
Founded: 1908
Members: 755
Staff: 8
Contact: Mrs. A. Jones, Sec.
Fee: £30
Membership Type: full, overseas, friend, student
Description: Members are involved in all branches of speech and drama work schools, colleges of further education and universities. They work in the professional and amateur theatre as producers,

directors and coaches. Some are involved with the disabled whilst. others teach communication and presentation skills in the business world. The Society aims to uphold a high standard of teaching and support those working in the field. Each region has a representative who is responsible for promoting the work of the Society. A Conference is held in London in February and during August in another region.
Library Subject: all aspects of speech, drama, theatre
Library Type: not open to the public
Publication: Magazine
Publication title: Speech and Drama. Advertisements.
Second publication: Newsletter
Meetings/Conventions: Around the World - annual conference Leicester UK

Society of Teachers of the Alexander Technique
STAT

Linton House, 1st Fl., 39-51 Highgate Rd., London, NW5 1RS, England, UK
Tel: 44 20 72843338
Fax: 44 20 74825434
Email: info@stat.org.uk
Website: http://www.stat.org.uk
Founded: 1958
Members: 1864
Staff: 3
Contact: Ms. Maria da Silva
Fee: £188
Membership Type: teaching
Fee: £50
Membership Type: world P.A.
Description: Teachers (1130), students (242) and others (492) in 24 countries. Works to maintain professional standards and gain wider recognition of the Alexander Technique (a means of posture re-education). Encourages research and communication among members.
Publication: Journal
Publication title: Alexander Journal
Second publication: Directory
Publication title: List of Teachers
Meetings/Conventions: - annual conference

Society of Technical Analysists
STA

Dean House, Vernham Dean, SP11 0LA, England, UK
Tel: 44 7000 710207
Fax: 44 7000 710208
Email: info@sta-uk.org
Website: http://sta-uk.org/
Contact: Adam Sorab, Chm.
Description: Works to promote use and understanding of technical analysis as an investment tool serving all members of the investment community.
Publication: Journal

Society of Technical Analysts

Dean House, Vernham Dean, SP11 0LA, England, UK
Tel: 44 7000 710207
Fax: 44 7000 710208
Email: info@sta-uk.org
Website: http://www.sta-uk.org
Founded: 1969

Society of Television Lighting Directors

c/o Stuart Gain, Sec.
Longwall, Crayburne, Kent, Betsham, DA13 9PB, England, UK
Tel: 44 1603 701162
Fax: 44 1474 834886
Email: chairman@stld.org.uk
Website: http://www.stld.org.uk/
Founded: 1974
Members: 642
Contact: Bernie Davis, Chair
Description: Those engaged in the direction and design, or whose occupation is directly associated with, the creative aspect of television lighting. A forum that stimulates a free exchange of ideas in all aspects of the television profession, including the techniques and design of new equipment. It has no union or political affiliations.
Publication title: Television Lighting

Society of Thoracic and Cardiovascular Surgeons of Great Britain and Ireland

Walsgrave Hospital, Conventry, CV2 2DX, England, UK
Tel: 44 24 76538936
Fax: 44 24 76538829
Founded: 1933

Society of Water Management

c/o Mill House
Tolson's Mill, Fazeley, Tamworth, B78 3QB, England, UK
Tel: 44 1827 289558
Fax: 44 1827 250408
Members: 500
Staff: 1
Contact: Sue Pipe
Description: From all disciplines of industry and commerce. Manufacturers, suppliers, users; anyone interested in the safe and economical use of water and safe disposal. Interests and activities extend to all uses of water in industry and commerce.
Formerly: Industrial Water Society
Publication: Handbook
Publication title: Risk Assessment
Second publication: Book
Publication title: Site Log Book for Water Services

Society of Wildlife Artists
SWLA

c/o Federation of British Artists
17 Carlton House Terrace, London, SW1Y 5BD, England, UK
Tel: 44 207 9306844
Fax: 44 207 8397830
Email: info@mallgalleries.com
Website: http://www.mallgalleries.org.uk
Founded: 1964
Members: 72
Contact: Briony Chaplin
Description: Professional wild life artists. Organises the exhibition of original works of art by wildlife artists; sales and commissions of wildlife art; educates the public in wildlife art through exhibitions. Most work for sale at annual exhibition.
Publication: Catalog
Publication title: Annual Exhibition Catalogue. Advertisements.
Meetings/Conventions: - annual specialty show - Exhibits.

Society of Women Artists
SWA

c/o Elizabeth Meek, Pres.
482 Merton Rd., London, SW18 5AE, England, UK
Tel: 44 20 88744751
Email: elizabethmeek@email.msn.com
Website: http://www.society-women-artists.org.uk
Founded: 1855
Members: 138
Contact: Elizabeth R. Meek, Pres.
Fee: £120
Membership Type: associate and member
Description: Upholds the tradition of fine art on behalf of women artists of today. Gives serious women artists an opportunity to exhibit.
Library Subject: artists and their work in the annual exhibitions from 1855-1996
Library Type: reference
Publication title: Catalogue of Exhibits at Annual Exhibition. Advertisements.
Meetings/Conventions: Exhibition - annual convention - Exhibits. London UK

Society of Women Writers and Journalists

Calvers Farm, Thelveton, Diss, IP21 4NG, England, UK
Email: zoe@zoeking.com
Website: http://www.swwj.co.uk
Founded: 1894
Members: 450
Contact: Jean Hawkes, Sec./Vice Chair
Fee: £30
Description: Professional writers/journalists/poets. Encourages literary achievement, upholding of professional standards and social contact with other writers. Activities include lunchtime meetings, discussions and seminars, manuscript advice service, competitions and visits.
Publication: Journal
Publication title: The Woman Writer

Society of Wood Engravers

3 W St., Oundle, Northamptonshire, PE8 4EJ, England, UK
Tel: 44 1832 275028
Email: g.waddington@dial.pipex.com
Website: http://www.woodengravers.co.uk
Founded: 1920
Members: 75
Contact: Geraldine Waddington, Gen.Sec.
Fee: £35
Membership Type: member
Fee: £25
Membership Type: subscriber
Description: Full members wood engravers, elected by committee, on merit after exhibiting with the SWE; subscribers, anyone interested in wood engraving including prospective members, galleries, collectors, etc. Encourages a growing interest in wood engraving by exhibiting in well-established, as well as little-known venues; setting up courses for new engravers, welcomes wood engravers overseas in annual travelling exhibitions.
Publication: Newsletter
Publication title: 'Multiples'
Second publication: Books

Society of Young Publishers

c/o Endeavor House
189 Shaftesbury Ave., London, WC2H 8TJ, England, UK
Tel: 44 171 8368911
Email: info@thesyp.org.uk
Website: http://www.thesyp.org.uk
Founded: 1949
Members: 320
Contact: Jonathan Ruppin, Chair
Description: People, principally under the age of 35, working or interested in publishing and allied fields. Provides a forum for all young people in publishing and allied sectors to learn more about the industry and make contacts. Meetings are held monthly, an Annual conference is held in November, and a yearly trip is made to another country.
Publication: Newsletter
Publication title: INPRINT
Second publication: Handbook
Publication title: Young Publisher's

Socio-Legal Studies Association
SLSA

c/o Sally Wheeler, Chair
Law Department, Birkbeck College, 16 Gower St., London, , England, UK
Tel: 44 20 76316500
Fax: 44 20 76316506
Email: wheeler@bbk.ac.uk
Website: http://www.ukc.ac.uk/slsa
Contact: Linda Mulcahy
Description: Provides forum for socio-legal scholars in the United Kingdom; promotes information exchange.
Publication: Newsletter
Second publication: Membership Directory
Meetings/Conventions: - annual conference

Soil Association
SA

c/o Bristol House
40-56 Victoria St., Bristol, BS1 6BY, England, UK
Tel: 44 117 9290661
Fax: 44 117 9252504
Email: info@soilassociation.org
Website: http://www.soilassociation.org
Founded: 1946
Members: 14000
Staff: 160
Contact: Tom de Pass
Fee: £24
Membership Type: ordinary
Fee: £30
Membership Type: outside UK
Description: Consumers, farmers, foresters, and agricultural and forestry researchers; food and timber companies. Promotes organic farming and sustainable forestry and researches the links between environment and health. Provides information to the public and health authorities. Licenses organic processors, producers, retailers, and wholesalers, and sustainable forestry and timber manufacturers.
Library Subject: organic food and farming
Library Type: reference
Publication: Report
Publication title: Food & Farming Report

Second publication: Journal
Publication title: Living Earth. Advertisements.
Meetings/Conventions: - biennial conference England

Solar Energy Society
c/o School of Technology
Oxford Brookes University, Headington Campus, Gipsy Ln., Oxford,
OX3 0BP, England, UK
Tel: 44 1865484367
Fax: 44 1865484263
Email: uk-ises@brookes.ac.ukwww.thesolarline.com
Founded: 1974
Members: 300
Staff: 2
Contact: Mrs. C. Buckle
Fee: £47
Membership Type: national
Fee: £90
Membership Type: international
Description: Promotes the use of solar energy.
Publication title: Solar News
Meetings/Conventions: conference Loughborough UK

Solar Trade Association
STA
c/o National Energy Centre
Davy Ave., Knowlhill, Milton Keynes, MK5 8NG, England, UK
Tel: 44 1908 442290
Fax: 44 870 529194
Email: enquiries@solartradeassociation.org.uk
Website: http://www.solartradeassociation.org.uk
Founded: 1978
Members: 27
Staff: 1
Contact: Christine Ballard, Oper.Mgr.
Description: Companies dealing with solar energy appliances and
systems. Raises standards within the solar industry and promotes a
greater understanding by public and media of the advantages of solar
energy use. Has a Code of Practice to control members activities;
runs an arbitration service and acts as a centre for information about
solar energy.
Publication title: Solar Energy - What's In It For Me
Second publication: Directory

Solicitors Family Law Association
PO Box 302, Orpington, BR6 8QX, England, UK
Tel: 44 1689 850227
Fax: 44 1689 855833
Email: sfla@btinternet.com
Website: http://www.sfla.co.uk/
Founded: 1982
Members: 5000
Contact: Jane Craig, Chair
Description: Solicitors engaged in the practice of family law. Seeks to
reduce the distress and anger that can arise when family relationships
break down and insure that members handle their cases so as to
allow all the parties involved to preserve their dignity and reach
agreement without conflict. Maintains and enforces a Code of Practice
for family law practitioners; participates in legal reform initiatives;
produces and distributes guidelines for effective family law practice.

Solid Fuel Association
7 Swanwick Court, Alfreton, DE55 7AS, England, UK
Tel: 44 1773 835400
Fax: 44 1773 834351
Email: sfa@solidfuel.co.uk
Website: http://www.solidfuel.co.uk
Founded: 1994
Members: 35
Staff: 5
Contact: Mrs. J. Heginbotham, Chief Exec.
Description: Companies involved in mining coal, manufacturing or
importing fuels or distributing fuels. Concerned with the promotion of
the use of solid fuels and solid fuel appliances for domestic heating
throughout Great Britain. Provides support services for users and
specifiers.
Publication: Magazine
Publication title: The Complete Guide to Solid Fuel Heating

Solids Handling and Processing Association
SHAPA
20 Elizabeth Dr., Oadby, Leicester, LE2 4RD, England, UK
Tel: 44 116 2713704
Fax: 44 116 2713704
Email: shapaltd@aol.com
Website: http://www.shapa.co.uk
Founded: 1980
Members: 104
Staff: 1
Contact: John Whitehead, Gen.Sec.
Fee: £375
Membership Type: full
Fee: £280
Membership Type: associate
Description: Manufacturers of equipment and systems used in the
handling and processing of particulate solids.
Publication: Directory
Publication title: Product Directory
Meetings/Conventions: - quarterly meeting - Exhibits. Lichfield UK

Solvents Industry Association
Magnolia House, Bromley Rd., Frating, Colchester, CO7 7DR,
England, UK
Tel: 44 1206 252268
Fax: 44 1206 252268
Email: len@sia-uk.org.uk
Website: http://www.sia-uk.org.uk
Founded: 1973
Members: 24
Staff: 1
Contact: Mr. L.B. Christodoulides
Fee: £1150
Membership Type: ordinary
Description: Producers and distributors of solvents. Aims to provide
information, advice and services within the industry on technical,
environmental and legal matters and to assist governments,
authorities and other bodies in the promotion of environmental, health
and safety and quality measures. To co-operate with authorities and
institutes, support or oppose legislation affecting the interests of the
industry.

Somerset Chamber of Commerce and Industry

c/o Dr. Stephanie Berry, Ch.Exec.
Powers Chamber, Bath Pl., Taunton, TA1 4ER, England, UK
Tel: 44 1823 321231
Fax: 44 1823 323525
Email: manager@somerset_chamber.co.uk
Website: http://www.somerset-chamber.co.uk/
Founded: 1994
Members: 260
Staff: 3
Contact: Dr. Stephanie Berry, Business Development Mgr.
Description: Promotes business and commerce.
Publication: Newsletter

Sonic Arts Network
SAN

Jerwood Space, 171 Union St., London, SE1 0LN, England, UK
Tel: 44 207 9287337
Fax: 44 207 9287338
Email: phil@sonicartsnetwork.org
Website: http://www.sonicartsnetwork.org
Founded: 1979
Members: 400
Staff: 3
Contact: Phil Hallett, Sr.Admin.
Fee: £20
Membership Type: ordinary
Fee: £10
Membership Type: student
Description: Promotes experimental approaches to sound and the ways in which new technology is transforming the nature and practice of music. Works as a performance, information and education resource; aims to raise awareness and innovation of new approaches to sonic art by commissioning, encouraging and promoting new work.
Library Subject: Electroacoustic music
Library Type: reference
Publication: Newsletter
Publication title: Diffusion. Advertisements.
Second publication: Journal
Publication title: Electro-Acoustic Music
Meetings/Conventions: - bimonthly meeting - Exhibits.

Soroptimist International
SI

87 Glisson Rd., Cambridge, CB1 2HG, England, UK
Tel: 44 1223 311833
Fax: 44 1223 467951
Email: sorophq@dial.pipex.com
Website: http://www.sorop.org
Founded: 1921
Members: 95000
Staff: 3
Contact: Irmeli Torssonen, Pres.
Description: Professional women. Works to uphold high standards of ethics and practice in business and the professions. Promotes respect for the civil and human rights of all individuals; seeks to enhance the economic and social status of women. Facilitates development of friendship and camaraderie among members; encourages voluntarism and the spirit of community service. Conducts research and educational programs; sponsors charitable activities; makes available children's services.
Library Subject: business, ethics, social service, women
Library Type: reference

Publication: Newsletter
Publication title: International Soroptimist
Meetings/Conventions: - quadrennial conference Sydney Australia

Soroptimist International of Great Britain and Ireland
SIGBI

127 Wellington Rd., South Stockport, SK1 3TS, England, UK
Tel: 44 161 4807686
Fax: 44 161 4776152
Email: hq@soroptimist.prestel.co.uk
Website: http://www.soroptimist-gbi.org
Founded: 1921
Members: 12600
Staff: 5
Contact: Gina Coad, Fed.Admin.
Description: Individuals in 30 countries involved in elevating the status of women. Promotes human rights, goodwill, peace, and international understanding. Regional group of Soroptimist International (see separate entry). Promotes charitable programs.
Formerly: Soroptimist Federation of Great Britain and Ireland
Publication: Directory
Publication title: Directory
Second publication: Magazine
Publication title: The Soroptimist. Advertisements.
Meetings/Conventions: - annual conference - Exhibits.

SOS Sahel International - UK

1 Tolpuddle St., London, N1 0XT, England, UK
Tel: 44 20 78379129
Fax: 44 20 78370856
Email: mail@sahel.org.uk
Founded: 1982
Members: 50
Staff: 220
Contact: Duncan Fulton, Dir.
Description: Works in rural areas of the Sahel in sub-Saharan Africa. Supports community initiatives that focus on conservation of natural resources and sustainable agriculture and development. Implements long-term projects in Sudan, Ethiopia, Eritrea, Kenya, Mali and Niger.
Library Type: by appointment only
Publication: Report
Publication title: Annual Report
Second publication: Book
Publication title: At the Desert's Edge: Oral Histories from the Sahel
Meetings/Conventions: - annual meeting - Exhibits.

South Cheshire Chamber

Enterprise House, Wistaston Rd. Business Center, Wistaston Rd., Crewe, CW2 7RP, England, UK
Tel: 44 1270 504700
Fax: 44 1270 504701
Email: info@sccci.co.ukwww.southchesirechamber.co.uk
Members: 448
Staff: 15
Contact: John Dunning, Ch.Exec.
Description: Promotes business and commerce.

Southern Brick Federation

c/o M C Hayward
Woodside House, Winkfield, Windsor, SL4 2DX, England, UK
Tel: 44 1344 885651
Fax: 44 1344 890129
Email: melvynhayward@brick.org.uk
Founded: 1965
Members: 13
Contact: M C Hayward, Sec.
Description: Clay brick makers. Seeks to protect the interests of brick makers in the south of England.

Southern Derbyshire Chamber of Commerce, Training and Enterprise

Innovation House, Riverside Park, Raynesway, Derby, DE21 7BF, England, UK
Tel: 44 1332 548000
Fax: 44 1332 548088
Email: info@sdchamber.co.uk
Website: http://www.sdchamber.co.uk
Members: 1400
Staff: 142
Contact: George Tansley, Chief Exec.
Description: Promotes business and commerce.

Southhampton and Fareham Chamber of Commerce and Industry

c/o Bugle House
53 Bugle St., Southampton, SO14 2LF, England, UK
Tel: 44 23 80223541
Fax: 44 23 80227426
Email: info@soton-chamber.co.uk
Website: http://www.soton-chamber.co.uk
Members: 1550
Staff: 29
Contact: Michelle Cummins
Description: Promotes business and commerce.

Spanish Chamber of Commerce in Great Britain

126 Wigmore St., London, W1U 3RZ, England, UK
Tel: 44 20 70099070
Fax: 44 20 70099088
Email: info@spanishchamber.co.uk
Website: http://www.spanishchamber.co.uk
Contact: Jose Fernandez Bragado
Description: Promotes business and commerce.

Speakability

1 Royal St., London, SE1 7LL, England, UK
Tel: 44 207 2619572
Fax: 44 207 9289542
Email: speakability@speakability.org.uk
Website: http://www.speakability.org.uk
Founded: 1980
Members: 1500
Staff: 9
Contact: Charlotte Painter
Fee: £25
Membership Type: member outside UK
Description: People with dysphasia (acquired language disorder), their friends and families, professionals working in the field. Works to raise awareness and understanding of dysphasia, offers help and advice through booklets and telephone helpline, membership scheme and newsletter, lectures and conferences. Professional backup and advocacy. Presses for improved provision of services; local branches, and self help groups are being developed across the country.
Formerly: Action for Dysphasic Adults
Publication title: Dysphasia Matters: A Medical Teaching Pack
Second publication: Booklets
Publication title: How to Help
Meetings/Conventions: - annual conference - Exhibits.

Specialist Access Engineering and Maintenance Association

56/64 Leonard St., Construction House, London, EC2A 4JX, England, UK
Tel: 44 207 6085098
Fax: 44 207 6085081
Staff: 1
Contact: Robin James
Description: Suspended access equipment manufacturers.
Formerly: Suspended Access Equipment Manufacturers' Association
Publication: Membership Directory
Publication title: Directory of Members

Spinal Injuries Association
SIA

76 St. James's Ln., London, N10 3DF, England, UK
Tel: 44 20 84442121
Fax: 44 20 84443761
Email: sia@spinal.co.uk
Website: http://www.spinal.co.uk
Founded: 1974
Members: 6500
Staff: 25
Contact: Paul Smith, Exec.Dir.
Description: National organisation for individuals with spinal cord injuries. Provides assistance through: an information service that answers member queries on all aspects of daily living including specialist holiday and travel information; a personal assistance service which provides short term, emergency cover; a solicitors referral scheme, a counseling service; publications and bi-monthly newsletter.
Publication: Booklets
Publication title: Sexuality Booklets
Publication title: Spinal Cord Injuries: Guidance for General Practitioners

Spohr Society of Great Britain

c/o C. H. Tutt
123 Mount View Rd., Sheffield, S8 8PJ, England, UK
Tel: 44 114 2585420
Email: chtutt@yahoo.co.uk
Founded: 1969
Members: 72
Contact: K. Warsop, Ch.
Fee: £5
Membership Type: UK
Fee: £6
Membership Type: other EU
Description: Promotes the performance and recording of the music of Louis Spohr (1784-1859). Assists with research into Spohr's life and works.
Publication: Newsletter
Publication title: Spohr Journal
Second publication: Newsletter
Meetings/Conventions: - annual meeting Warwick UK

Sports Writers' Association of Great Britain

c/o Sport England
External Affairs Unit, 166 Upper Woburn Pl., London, WC1H 0QP, England, UK
Tel: 44 207 2731789
Fax: 44 207 3830273
Founded: 1948
Members: 550
Contact: Trevor Bond, Sec.
Fee: £23.5
Membership Type: within London
Fee: £35.25
Membership Type: outside London
Description: All professional sports journalists with newspapers, magazines, television and radio, plus freelancers, photographers and cartoonists.
Publication: Bulletin
Meetings/Conventions: meeting

Sprayed Concrete Association
SCA

99 West St., Farnham, GU9 7EN, England, UK
Tel: 44 1252 739153
Fax: 44 1252 739140
Email: info@associationhouse.org.uk
Website: http://www.sca.org.uk
Founded: 1976
Members: 54
Contact: John G. Fairley, Sec.
Description: Contractors and manufacturers of sprayed concrete. Promotes high standards in the application of sprayed concrete; supplies technical guidance to assist engineers, consultants, and specifiers working in the industry.
Publication: Directory
Publication title: Directory of Members
Second publication: Book
Publication title: Introduction to Sprayed Concrete
Meetings/Conventions: - periodic seminar

Sri Lanka Project
SLP

c/o British Refugee Council
3 Bondway, London, SW8 1SJ, England, UK
Tel: 44 71 8203000
Fax: 44 71 8203107
Email: slproject@refugeecouncil.org.uk
Website: http://brcslproject.gn.apc.org
Founded: 1987
Contact: Margaret Lally, Actg.Ch.Exec.
Description: Promotes and facilitates provision of humanitarian assistance to displaced and dispossessed people in Sri Lanka. Maintains liaison and seeks to coordinate efforts of a network of nongovernmental relief and development organizations with programs in Sri Lanka. Gathers and disseminates to Sri Lankan refugees in Europe and North America information about political events in their home areas.
Library Subject: Sri Lankan refugees
Library Type: reference
Publication: Newsletter
Publication title: Sri Lanka Monitor

St. Albans International Organ Festival

c/o Ken Chaproniere, Gen. Mgr.
PO Box 80, St. Albans, AL3 4HR, England, UK
Tel: 44 1727 844765
Fax: 44 1727 844765
Email: info@organfestival.com
Website: http://www.organfestival.com
Founded: 1963
Members: 500
Staff: 2
Contact: Ken Chaproniere, Gen.Mgr.
Fee: £16
Membership Type: regular individual
Fee: £24
Membership Type: regular joint
Description: Musicians, musicologists, and others interested in the study of the organ and organ music of the baroque, romantic, and 20th century styles. Promotes exchange and cooperation between members in 28 countries. Sponsors the Biennial International Organ Festival encompassing organ competitions (interpretation and improvisation) and entertainment including recitals, concerts, lectures, comedy, jazz, and folk music. Holds organ, choral, vocal, orchestral, and instrumental performances. Produces children's events. Organizes master classes. I.O.F. Society owns its own organ to promote student interest in and study of baroque organ music and performance.
Publication: Brochures
Publication title: Festival and Competition Brochure. Advertisements.
Publication title: Information and Application Form for Organ Competitions
Meetings/Conventions: - biennial festival - Exhibits. St. Albans UK

St. Helens Chamber of Commerce, Training and Enterprise

Technology Campus, 7 Waterside Ct., St. Helens, WA9 1UE, England, UK
Tel: 44 1744 742000
Fax: 44 1744 742001
Email: info@sthelenschamber.com
Website: http://www.sthelenschamber.com
Members: 570
Staff: 90
Contact: Kath Boullen, Chief Exec.
Description: Promotes business and commerce.

Stage Management Association

47 Bermondsey St., London, SE1 3XT, England, UK
Tel: 44 207 4036655
Fax: 44 207 3786170
Email: admin@stagemanagementassociation.co.uk
Website: http://www.stagemanagementassociation.co.uk
Founded: 1954
Members: 550
Staff: 1
Description: Working members of stage management in theatre and television. Helps with finding jobs, keeping members in touch and representation on the Council of Equity and with other bodies.
Publication: Booklet
Publication title: Stage management: A Career Guide

Standing Conference of Atlantic Organisations SCAO

Atlantic House, 8A Lower Grosvenor Pl., London, SW1W 0EN, England, UK
Tel: 44 207 8281012
Fax: 44 207 8281014
Founded: 1974
Members: 20
Contact: Dr. Peter Corterier, Chm.
Fee: £50
Membership Type: corporate
Fee: £20
Membership Type: individual
Description: Principal activity is its annual conference which is held at NATO Headquarters or in an Atlantic Alliance or Partnership for Peace country on an issue of transatlantic concern. It aims to provide an interchange of information between non-governmental organizations working in the field of Atlantic Affairs.
Publication: Directory
Publication title: Directory of Atlantic Organisations
Second publication: Newsletter
Publication title: Newsletter of Atlantic Organisations
Meetings/Conventions: - annual conference

Standing Conference of Principals

c/o Woburn House
20 Tavistock Sq., 3rd Fl., London, WC1H 9HB, England, UK
Tel: 44 207 3877711
Fax: 44 207 3877712
Email: info@scop.ac.uk
Website: http://www.scop.ac.uk
Founded: 1978
Members: 37
Staff: 5
Contact: P. Ambrose, Exec.Sec.
Description: Eligible membership is available to heads of institutions with over 55% HE. Associate membership is at the discretion of the Council of Management. Exists to further the interests of these members in dialogue with Government and other bodies and in providing other services to its members. Its primary function is to provide a forum in which the executive Heads of the institutions are able to consider and take action on matters of common concern. Through its corporate voice, it has an impact on national planning and debate concerning higher education.
Publication: Pamphlet
Publication title: Higher Destinations - Go To College

Standing Conference of Women's Organizations

2 South Dale, Penketh, Warrington, WA5 2AD, England, UK
Tel: 44 1925 495278
Fax: 44 1925 722043
Email: jillblock@southdale2.demon.co.uk
Founded: 1942
Members: 1500
Staff: 1
Contact: Jill Block, Sec.
Description: Representatives of local women's organizations. Fosters cooperation among women's groups. Works to further progress towards common objectives concerning women's issues.
Library Subject: transport, health, education, employment
Library Type: reference
Publication title: Golden Jubilee Commemorative Book
Publication title: Health Day Manual
Meetings/Conventions: - annual conference

Standing Conference on Library Materials on Africa SCOLMA

c/o Librarian
Commonwealth Secretariat, Marlborough House, Pall Mall, London, SW1Y 5HX, England, UK
Tel: 44 207 7476164
Fax: 44 207 7476168
Email: scolma@hotmail.com
Website: http://www.soas.ac.uk/scolma/
Founded: 1962
Members: 70
Contact: David Blake, Sec.
Fee: £23
Membership Type: institution
Description: Promotes the acquisition of library materials on Africa through a cooperative acquisition scheme between member libraries. Conducts bibliographical projects. Sponsors seminars.
Publication: Journal
Publication title: African Research and Documentation. Advertisements.
Second publication: Directory
Publication title: Directory of Libraries and Special Collections on Africa
Meetings/Conventions: - annual conference

Statistics Users' Council

c/o Mr. Ian Maclean
Lancaster House, More Lane, Esher, KT10 8AP, England, UK
Tel: 44 1372463121
Fax: 44 1372469847
Email: ian@worldtradestats.com
Founded: 1970
Members: 2000
Description: Aims to provide a forum at which users of statistics can meet, exchange views, and liaison with the Government Statistical Service on points of mutual interests.

Statute Law Society

c/o Institute of Advanced Legal Studies
17 Russell Sq., Charles Clore House, London, WC1B 5DR, England, UK
Tel: 44 207 3232978
Email: info@ila-hq.org
Founded: 1968
Members: 155
Contact: Juliet Fussell, Sec.
Description: For improving the form and manner in which statutes and delegated legislation are expressed, produced and published.

Steam Plough Club

c/o Mr. John Billard
Old Station House, Twyford, Reading, RG10 9NA, England, UK
Tel: 44 118 9340381
Website: http://www.steamploughclub.org.uk
Founded: 1966
Members: 480
Contact: John Billard, Sec.
Fee: £12
Membership Type: ordinary
Fee: £5
Membership Type: senior citizen
Description: Encourages and expands interest in steam cultivation. Ensures that proper place in history of British agricultural engineering.

Provides for the exchange of ideas and material to allow for steam ploughing engines and implements to be kept in the best possible working order for future generations to use and enjoy. Provides education, practical training, experience and competition for members in order to produce the best possible land work using steam ploughing engines and implements. Arranges meetings and visits to allow members to keep in touch. Maintains records and produces films to show the past and present history of steam cultivation.
Library Type: reference

Steel Construction Institute
SCI

Silwood Park, Ascot, SL5 7QN, England, UK
Tel: 44 1344 623345
Fax: 44 1344 622944
Email: reception@steel-sci.com
Website: http://www.steel-sci.org
Founded: 1986
Members: 850
Staff: 70
Contact: Sarah Houghton, Mktg.Mgr.
Description: Engineers, fabricators, architects, developers. All disciplines involved in the steel construction industry. Promotes and develops the proper and effective use of steel in construction. A range of technical publications result from industry led research projects and educational courses and seminars complement these. Advisory service for members.
Library Subject: specialist steel
Library Type: not open to the public
Publication: Magazine
Publication title: New Steel Construction. Advertisements.
Publication title: Technical publications

Steel Window Association

The Building Centre, 26 Store St., London, WC1E 7BT, England, UK
Tel: 44 20 7637 3571
Fax: 44 20 7637 3572
Email: info@steel-window-association.co.uk
Website: http://www.steel-window-association.co.uk
Founded: 1967
Members: 25
Staff: 2
Contact: Ms. J. Turner, Dir.
Description: Represents the majority of UK steel window manufacturers and supports member companies with a wide range of product development, market research and promotional activities. Also offers a technical advice service and free literature distribution is available to specifiers.
Publication title: Specifier's Guide to Steel Windows

Stephenson Locomotive Society

c/o Mr. Brian F. Gilliam
25 Regency Close, Chigwell, IG7 5NY, England, UK
Tel: 44 2085011210
Email: briangilliam@beeb.net
Website: http://www.stephensonloco.fsbusiness.co.uk
Founded: 1909
Members: 680
Contact: Mr. Brian F. Gilliam, Gen.Sec.
Fee: £23
Membership Type: uk full
Fee: £18
Membership Type: under 25's

Description: Aims to study the operation and history of railways, particularly locomotives and rolling stock.
Library Subject: railways and locomotives
Library Type: reference
Publication: Journal
Publication title: Journal of the Stephenson Locomotive Society. Advertisements.

STEPS: Association for People with Lower Limb Abnormalities

c/o Ms. Sue Banton
Lower Ground Floor, Lymm Court, 11 Eagle Brow, Lymm, WA13 0LP, England, UK
Tel: 44 671 7170044
Fax: 44 671 7170045
Email: info@steps-charity.org.uk
Website: http://www.steps-charity.org.uk
Founded: 1980
Members: 2000
Staff: 4
Contact: Mrs. Sue Banton, Dir.
Description: Provides information and support for families of children with lower limb abnormalities. Objectives are to put families in touch with one another, develops a network of local contacts providing support, help and advise and to gather and exchange information with parents and health professionals.
Library Type: reference

Stereoscopic Society
SS

36 Silverthorn Dr., Hemel Hempstead, HP3 8BX, England, UK
Tel: 44 1442 258805
Fax: 44 1442 250266
Email: info@stereoscopy.net
Website: http://www.stereoscopicsociety.org.uk
Founded: 1893
Members: 700
Contact: Mrs. Sue Makinson, Gen.Sec.
Fee: £18
Membership Type: full and family, Jan-Dec
Description: Individuals, mainly in the U.K., who are interested in the production of stereoscopic photographs. (Stereoscopy is the study of three dimensional imagery.) Seeks to advance stereoscopic photography by circulating prints or transparencies through the mail. Organizes meetings to encourage exchange of ideas and technical advice. Maintains small collection of books and stereoscopic production items. Computer group
Library Subject: all aspects of 3-D photography
Library Type: reference
Publication: Journal
Publication title: Journal of 3-D Imaging. Advertisements.
Second publication: Handbook
Publication title: Photographing in 3D
Meetings/Conventions: - annual convention - Exhibits. Harrogate UK

Stillbirth and Neonatal Death Society
SANDS

28 Portland Pl., London, W1B 1L4, England, UK
Tel: 44 171 4367940
Fax: 44 171 4363715
Email: support@uk-sands.org
Founded: 1978

Contact: Penni Thorne, Chm.
Fee: £15
Description: Offers support groups to parents who have experienced pregnancy loss, stillbirth, or neonatal death. Aims to increase understanding and awareness of the feelings and needs of bereaved parents within the health professions and general public.
Publication: Book
Publication title: A Dignified Ending
Second publication: Book
Publication title: Pregnancy Loss and the Death of a Baby: Guidelines for Professionals (1995)

Stilton Cheese Makers' Association
3 Imperial Studios, Imperial Rd., London, SW6 3AG, England, UK
Tel: 44 207 4045575
Fax: 44 207 6106007
Email: historicblue@stiltoncheese.com
Website: http://www.stiltoncheese.com
Founded: 1936
Members: 5
Contact: Jane Baersleman
Description: Stilton cheese makers. To protect registered certification trade mark Stilton throughout the world; maintain the high quality of the product; and promote the sale of Stilton cheeses, primarily in the UK and the USA.

Stockport Chamber of Commerce and Industry
Stockport Business Centre, 1 St. Peter's Sq., Stockport, SK1 1NN, England, UK
Tel: 44 161 4743780
Fax: 44 161 4760138
Email: info@stockportchamber.co.uk
Website: http://www.stockportchamber.com
Contact: M Makin
Description: Promotes business and commerce.

Storage and Handling Equipment Distributors' Association
Heathcote House, 136 HAgley Rd., Birmingham, B16 9PN, England, UK
Tel: 44 121 4544141
Fax: 44 121 4544949
Email: enquiries@sheda.org.uk
Website: http://www.sheda.org.uk
Founded: 1978
Contact: Phil Howe, Pres.
Description: Members include stockists, designers and installers.

Strategic Planning Society
SPS
Unit LFG 7, The Leathermarket, Weston St., London, SE1 3ER, England, UK
Tel: 44 207 0911310
Fax: 44 207 0911319
Email: enquiries@sps.org.uk
Website: http://www.sps.org.uk
Founded: 1967
Members: 4000
Staff: 6
Contact: Martin Whitehill, Chm.
Fee: £80
Membership Type: individual

Description: Corporations, educational institutions, and small companies and firms; executives, planners, government officials, and interested individuals. Promotes strategic planning in private, public, and governmental organizations. Seeks to: create and maintain networks for decision makers and planners; develop improved techniques for strategic planning; provide resources of knowledge and experience to aid businesses with planning problems; address political, economic, and social issues facing planners. Has established special interest and regional groups. Maintains speakers' bureau.
Publication: Journal
Publication title: Long Range Planning
Second publication: Magazine
Publication title: Strategy
Meetings/Conventions: Planning Directors' Strategy Forum - periodic

Stroke Association
240 City Rd., London, EC1V 2PR, England, UK
Tel: 44 20 75660300
Fax: 44 20 74902686
Website: http://www.stroke.org.uk
Founded: 1899

Study for the Promotion of Byzantine Studies
SPBS
19 Purcell Rd., Oxford, OX3 0HN, England, UK
Tel: 44 1865 244536
Email: Fiona.nicks@kcl.ac.uk
Website: http://www.byzantium.ac.uk
Founded: 1983
Members: 430
Staff: 1
Contact: Dr. Fiona Nicks
Fee: £40
Fee: £20
Membership Type: student
Publication: Journal
Publication title: Bulletin of British Byzantine Studies. Advertisements.
Meetings/Conventions: - annual symposium

Suffolk Chamber of Commerce
Felaw Maltings, South Kiln, 42 Felaw St., PO Box 293, Ipswich, IP2 8SZ, England, UK
Tel: 44 1473 680600
Fax: 44 1473 603888
Email: info@suffolkchamber.co.uk
Website: http://www.suffolknetwork.co.uk
Founded: 1884
Members: 1300
Staff: 16
Contact: Bob Feltwell, Chief Exec.
Description: Promotes business and commerce.

Sugar Association of London
Forum House, 15-18 Lime St., London, EC3M 7AQ, England, UK
Tel: 44 207 6261745
Fax: 44 207 2833831
Email: moond@sugar-assoc.co.uk
Founded: 1882
Members: 120
Staff: 12
Contact: D.G. Moon

Fee: £500
Description: Firms, companies or organisations which have a continuing interest in trading raw sugar. The supervision of weighing and sampling of raw sugar cargoes and the provision of contract rules for the international raw sugar trade. The provision of arbitrators for the settlement of disputes by commercial arbitration; to protect the interests of members and the international raw sugar trade in general.
Library Subject: rules and regulations for cane and beet sugar
Library Type: open to the public
Publication: Brochure
Meetings/Conventions: - periodic meeting

Sugar Bureau

Duncan House, Dolphin Sq., London, SW1V 3PW, England, UK
Tel: 44 207 8289465
Fax: 44 207 8215393
Email: info@sugar-bureau.co.uk
Founded: 1964
Members: 4
Staff: 10
Contact: Dr. Richard Cottrell, Dir.
Description: Companies supplying sugar in the UK. Develops and communicates scientific facts about sugar to health professionals, universities, consumers, and the media. Offers technical and consumer information. Represents members' commercial and public relations interests.
Publication title: Dental Digest
Second publication: Bulletin
Publication title: Nutrition in Practice

Sugar Traders Association of the United Kingdom

c/o C. Czarnikow Sugar, Ltd.
24 Chiswell St., London, EC1Y 4SG, England, UK
Tel: 44 20 79726631
Fax: 44 20 79726699
Email: dclark@czarnikow.com
Website: http://www.sugartraders.co.uk
Founded: 1952
Members: 12
Contact: D.F. Clark, Hon.Sec.
Description: Firms and companies in the UK who are recognized traders in and have a continuing interest in the import or marketing of sugar and associations representing sugar interests.

Supply Chain Knowledge Centre

Centre for Logistics and Transportation, Cranfield School of Management, Bedford, MK43 0AL, England, UK
Tel: 44 1234 754931
Fax: 44 1234 754930
Email: sckc@cranfield.ac.uk
Website: http://www.logisticsweb.co.uk
Founded: 1970
Members: 250
Staff: 12
Contact: Hilary Keeble, Mgr.
Description: All SIC categories. Consultancy in all aspects of logistics, short courses throughout year, library and information services, conferences.
Library Subject: logistics, supply chain management
Library Type: not open to the public
Formerly: National Materials Handling Centre
Publication title: International Logistics Abstracts
Second publication: Journal
Publication title: Supply Chain Practice

Surface Engineering Association

c/o Federation House
10 Vyse St., Birmingham, B18 6LT, England, UK
Tel: 44 121 2371123
Fax: 44 121 2371124
Email: info@sea.org.uk
Website: http://www.sea.org.uk
Founded: 1887
Members: 450
Staff: 4
Contact: David Elliott, Gen.Mgr.
Description: Companies which provide surface finishing services, supplies, equipment, and finishing departments of manufacturing companies. Also surface finishing consultants. Aims to raise the awareness in designers, regulators and customers of the importance of surface finishing industry. Companies also supply paint and powder finishes, as well as heat treatment services.
Library Subject: surface engineering
Library Type: not open to the public
Formerly: Formed by Merger of, Metal Finishing Association
Publication: Newsletter
Publication title: Sea News. Advertisements.
Second publication: Newsletter
Publication title: Watch Word

Surrey Chambers of Commerce

5th Floor Hollywood House, Church Street East, Woking, GU21 IHJ, England, UK
Tel: 44 1483 726655
Fax: 44 1483 740217
Email: info@surrey-chambers.co.uk
Members: 1451
Staff: 22
Contact: Chris Peers, Chief Exec.
Description: Promotes business and commerce.

Surtees Society

c/o Honorary Sec.
43 North Bailey, Durham, DH1 3EX, England, UK
Tel: 44 191 3742004
Fax: 44 191 3744754
Email: surtees.society@durham.ac.uk
Website: http://www.surteessociety.org.uk
Founded: 1834
Members: 227
Contact: Lynda Rollason, Hon.Sec.
Description: Promotes the advancement of public education in the region that constitutes the ancient kingdom of Northumbria in northeast England through the transcription, editing, translating, and publication of original historical documents.
Meetings/Conventions: - annual general assembly

SURVIVAL

6 Charterhouse Bldgs., London, EC1M 7ET, England, UK
Tel: 44 20 76878700
Fax: 44 20 76878701
Email: info@survival-international.org
Website: http://www.survival-international.org
Founded: 1969
Members: 20000
Staff: 30
Contact: Stephen Corry, Dir.Gen.
Fee: £16
Membership Type: individual

Fee: £25
Membership Type: family
Description: Worldwide organisation that supports tribal peoples. Stands for their right to decide their own future, and helps them protect their lands, lives, and human rights. Works through campaigns and education that focus on urgent situations and tend to deal with on the least contacted and so most vulnerable peoples. Currently working on about 80 cases in 34 countries around the world. Produces books and teaching packs; provides lessons in schools; organizes public talks; and arranges exhibitions. Aims to inform the public about tribal peoples, opposing racism by demonstrating that they are far from primitive. Distributes materials in more than 70 countries. Supports projects in health and land rights for indigenous groups in areas such as Argentina, Australia, Botswana, Brazil, Canada, India, Indonesia, Kenya, Paraguay, Russia, the Philippines, and Venezuela. Provides films, slide shows, radio projects, publications, and photographic exhibitions for display in colleges, libraries, schools, teachers' centers, and at conferences and meetings.
Library Subject: Indigenous peoples, development, and human rights
Library Type: not open to the public
Formerly: Primitive Peoples Fund
Publication: Catalog
Publication title: Tribale
Second publication: Bulletin
Publication title: Urgent Action Bulletin

Sussex Chamber of Commerce and Enterprise

Greenacre Ct., Station Rd., Burgess Hill, RH15 9DS, England, UK
Tel: 44 1444 259259
Fax: 44 1444 259190
Email: info@sussexenterprise.co.uk
Website: http://www.sussexenterprise.co.uk
Members: 2114
Staff: 154
Contact: Ken Caldwell, CEO
Description: Promotes business and commerce.

Swale Chamber of Commerce and Enterprise

Swale Business Ctr., Swale House, East St., Sittingbourne, ME10 3HT, England, UK
Contact: John Clark
Description: Promotes business and commerce.

Swedenborg Society

20/21 Bloomsbury Way, London, WC1A 2TH, England, UK
Tel: 44 20 74057986
Fax: 44 20 78315848
Email: swed.soc@netmatters.co.uk
Website: http://www.swedenborg.org.uk
Founded: 1810
Members: 815
Staff: 5
Contact: Richard Lines, Sec.
Fee: £5
Membership Type: member
Fee: £50
Membership Type: life
Description: Individuals interested in Emanuel Swedenborg's writings. Promotes the printing and publishing of the works of Swedenborg into various languages, including English, most European languages, and some Asian and African languages. Provides free grants of Swedenborg's works to public libraries.

Library Subject: Swedenborg, his writings, collateral works, followers, and groups
Library Type: lending
Publication: Journal
Publication title: Journal of the Swedenborg Society
Second publication: Newsletter
Publication title: Things Heard and Seen
Meetings/Conventions: meeting

Swedish-English Literary Translators' Association SELTA

14 Grennell Close, Sutton, SM1 3LU, England, UK
Tel: 44 20 86418176
Fax: 44 20 86418176
Website: http://www.swedishbookreview.com/se.html
Founded: 1982
Members: 50
Contact: Tom Geddes, Hon.Sec.
Fee: £15
Membership Type: full
Fee: £13
Membership Type: associate
Description: Swedish-English translators. Promotes publication of Swedish literature in English. Represents the interests of translators. Gathers and disseminates information.
Publication: Journal
Publication title: Swedish Book Review. Advertisements.
Meetings/Conventions: - semiannual meeting London UK

Swimming Pool and Allied Trades Association

SPATA House, 1a Junction Rd., Andover, SP10 3QT, England, UK
Tel: 44 1264 356210
Fax: 44 1264 332628
Email: admin@spata.co.uk
Website: http://www.spata.co.uk
Founded: 1961
Members: 200
Staff: 2
Contact: Alan Stokes, Pres.
Description: Swimming pool installers, retail suppliers, trade suppliers, manufacturers, and companies associated with the swimming pool industry. Sets the standards for the industry and ensures that these standards are maintained. SPATA is recognised as being the authoritative body and maintains contact with Government Departments and all public and professional organizations concerned in any way with swimming.
Publication title: Spata Standards Vols 1-5
Meetings/Conventions: Spatex - annual

Swindon Chamber of Commerce

1 Cricklade Ct., Old Town, Swindon, SN1 3EY, England, UK
Tel: 44 1793 642225
Fax: 44 1793 521165
Email: info@swindonchamber.co.uk
Website: http://www.swindonchamber.co.uk
Founded: 1894
Members: 805
Staff: 8
Contact: Dennis Grant, Chief Exec.
Description: Promotes business and commerce.

Systematics Association

c/o Dr. Zofia Lawrence
CABI Bioscience UK Centre, Bakeham Lane, Egham, TW20 9TY,
England, UK
Tel: 44 1491 829080
Fax: 44 1491 829100
Email: z.lawrence@cabi.org
Website: http://www.systass.org
Founded: 1937
Members: 600
Staff: 7
Contact: Prof. C.J. Humphries, Pres.
Fee: £20
Membership Type: full
Fee: £16
Membership Type: student
Description: Aims to provide a forum for discussing systematic
problems and integrated new information from genetics, ecology and
other specific fields into concepts and activities.
Publication: Newsletter

Tableware Distributors Association

Kennerley Works, 161 Buxton Rd., Stockport, SK2 6EQ, England, UK
Tel: 44 161 4836256
Members: 34
Contact: Dr. Cedric Thomas
Description: Manufacturers/distributors of tableware, cutlery, glass or
other items associated with table tops, in the United Kingdom.
Represents the views of its membership on matters related to the
tableware industry in the UK and acts as a channel of information
flowing between member manufacturers, importers, distributors and to
assist in this process by means of meetings, newsletters, publicity and
conferences.
Publication: Newsletter
Publication title: Newsletter

Talking Newspaper Association of the United Kingdom

10 Browning Rd., Heathfield, TN21 8DB, England, UK
Tel: 44 1435 866102
Fax: 44 1435 865422
Email: info@tnauk.org.uk
Website: http://www.tnauk.org.uk
Founded: 1974
Members: 18000
Staff: 30
Contact: Tim McDonald, CEO
Fee: £30
Membership Type: domestic
Fee: £45
Membership Type: abroad
Description: Records newspapers and magazine on audio tape,
computer disk, or CD-ROM for visually impaired persons.
Publication: Magazine
Publication title: Talking Newspaper News. Advertisements.
Meetings/Conventions: - annual meeting - Exhibits.

Tamil Information Centre
TIC

720 Romford Rd., London, E12 6BT, England, UK
Tel: 44 208 5146390
Fax: 44 208 5140164
Email: tamilinfo@compuserve.com

Website: http://www.tamilinfo.org
Founded: 1996
Staff: 2
Contact: V. Varadakumar
Description: Individuals with an interest in the Tamil people of Sri
Lanka. Seeks to increase public awareness of the history, culture, and
political position of the Tamil people. Facilitates cultural exchanges;
sponsors research and educational programs; serves as a
clearinghouse on the Tamil people. Monitors allegations of the abuse
of the human rights of Tamil people by Sri Lankan authorities;
provides relief and assistance to Tamil refugees fleeing political
turmoil in Sri Lanka.
Library Subject: tamil speaking people of Sri Lanka
Library Type: open to the public

Tattoo Club of Great Britain

389 Cowley Rd., Oxford, OX4 2BS, England, UK
Tel: 44 1865 716877
Fax: 44 1865 775610
Email: tcgb@tattoo.co.uk
Website: http://www.tattoo.co.uk
Founded: 1975
Members: 100
Staff: 1
Contact: Lionel Titchener
Fee: £10
Membership Type: professional tattoo artist
Description: Professionally registered tattoo artists working in
accordance with Miscellaneous Provisions Act 1982. Aims to promote
registered professional tattoo artists and to encourage clients to go to
professionals not amateurs. Discourages tattooing of hands, face and
neck. Has tattoo studio incorporating the Tattoo History Museum.
Library Subject: tattoo history and memorabilia
Library Type: open to the public
Formerly: British Tattoo Artists Federation
Publication title: Tattoo International

Tavistock Institute

30 Tabernacle St., London, EC2A 4UE, England, UK
Tel: 44 20 74170407
Fax: 44 20 74170566
Email: central.admin@tavinstitute.org
Website: http://www.tavinstitute.org
Founded: 1947
Members: 120
Staff: 30
Contact: Debbie Sorkin, Sec.
Description: Aims to encompass the study of human relations in
conditions of well-being, conflict and change in the community, the
work group and the larger organizations, together with the promotion
of the effectiveness of individuals and organizations.
Publication title: Annual Review
Second publication: Journal
Publication title: Human Relations
Meetings/Conventions: - annual conference

TE Lawrence Society

PO Box 728, Oxford, OX2 6YP, England, UK
Email: info@telawrencesociety.org
Website: http://www.telsociety.org
Founded: 1985
Members: 600
Contact: Ms. Suzanne Fox, Sec.
Fee: £18

Membership Type: in U.K.
Fee: £23
Membership Type: overseas
Description: Seeks to advance the education of the public in the life and work of Thomas Edward Lawrence, to promote research into his life and work.
Library Subject: history, biographies, literature
Library Type: reference
Publication: Newsletter
Publication title: The T.E. Lawrence Society Newsletter
Second publication: Journal
Publication title: Journal of the T.E. Lawrence Society
Meetings/Conventions: - biennial conference - Exhibits. Oxford UK

Tea Council

9, The Courtyard, Gowan Ave., Fulham, London, SW6 6RH, England, UK
Tel: 44 207 3717787
Fax: 44 207 3717958
Email: tea@teacouncil.co.uk
Website: http://www.teacouncil.co.uk
Founded: 1967
Members: 50
Staff: 4
Contact: William Gorman, Exec.Dir.
Description: Generic promotion of tea and tea drinking in UK, on behalf of tea producing countries and UK tea companies.
Publication: Annual Report
Publication title: Annual Report
Publication title: Guild of Tea Shops Guide

Teaching Aids at Low Cost
TALC

PO Box 49, St. Albans, AL1 5TX, England, UK
Tel: 44 1727 853869
Fax: 44 1727 846852
Email: talc@talcuk.org
Website: http://www.talcuk.org
Founded: 1966
Staff: 11
Contact: David Chandler, GM
Description: Distributes low-cost books, health and medical slides, and teaching aids worldwide in order to help improve standards of health care worldwide.
Publication: Newsletter
Second publication: Booklets
Meetings/Conventions: - annual general assembly

Tearfund
TF

100 Church Rd., Teddington, TW11 8QE, England, UK
Tel: 44 20 89779144
Fax: 44 20 89433594
Email: enquiry@tearfund.org
Website: http://www.tearfund.org
Founded: 1968
Staff: 270
Contact: Doug Balfour, Gen.Dir.
Description: Religious organizations providing relief and development services worldwide. Promotes appropriate and sustainable development; seeks to ensure respect for the human rights of indigenous peoples in developing areas. Provides support and assistance to church-based development and relief projects; publicizes human rights abuses; makes available services to refugees and other displaced persons.
Publication: Magazine
Publication title: Teartimes

Telecommunications Heritage Group

PO Box 561, South Croydon, CR2 6YL, England, UK
Tel: 44 870 3212887
Fax: 44 870 3212889
Email: membership@thg.org.uk
Website: http://www.thg.org.uk
Founded: 1986
Members: 450
Staff: 5
Contact: Andrew Emmerson, Founder Pres.
Fee: £10
Membership Type: individual and concession
Description: Promotes the study, collection, and preservation of telecommunications equipment. Works to preserve both individual articles and entire networks intact.
Library Subject: telephones, telegraphs, and associated apparatus and their histories
Library Type: not open to the public
Publication: Journal
Publication title: Telecommunications Heritage Group Journal. Advertisements.
Second publication: Newsletter
Publication title: Telecommunications Heritage News
Meetings/Conventions: - annual conference - Exhibits.

Telecommunications Industry Association

Douglas House, 32-34 Simpson Rd., Fenny Stratford, Bletchley, Milton Keynes, MK1 1BA, England, UK
Tel: 44 1908 645000
Fax: 44 1908 632263
Email: info@tia.org.uk
Website: http://www.tia.org.uk
Founded: 1984
Members: 400
Staff: 6
Contact: Alan P. Cobb, Dir.Gen.
Description: Dealers/installers; cable system suppliers; maintainers; voice manufacturers; data manufacturers; network operators; pre-owned equipment suppliers; telecommunications consultancies; test equipment manufacturers.
Publication title: TIA Link

Telecommunications Users' Association

c/o Woodgate Studios
2-8 Games Rd., Barnet, EN4 9HN, England, UK
Tel: 44 20 84498844
Fax: 44 20 84474901
Email: tua@dial.pipex.com
Website: http://www.tua.co.uk
Founded: 1965
Members: 1200
Staff: 6
Contact: Steve Thorpe
Fee: £220
Membership Type: standard
Description: Multinational corporations, medium to small businesses, professional practices. Aims to ensure that the public telecoms operators and other service suppliers become more responsive to

user needs. TUA consults with Government, European Commission and the regulatory authorities regarding liberalisation issues and consumer protection. Also offers direct services to members: consultancy, information services, training in telecommunications and corporate management. Sponsors members Helpline training and seminar programme and various workshops.
Library Subject: telecoms, historic
Publication title: eFactline
Second publication: Magazine
Publication title: INfocus

Telework Association
TCA

Freepost CV2312, Wren, Nailsworth, Kenilworth, CV8 2BR, England, UK
Tel: 44 2476 696986
Fax: 44 1453 836174
Email: tca@ruralnet.org.uk
Website: http://www.tca.org.uk
Members: 2300
Staff: 2
Contact: Alan Denbigh, Exec.Dir.
Fee: £39.5
Description: Individuals (teleworkers) working from home supported by technology, people running centres supporting home based teleworkers, regional development agencies, companies introducing teleworking schemes. Concerned with the improvement in employment, training and services for people living in rural areas and the development of local economies through the use of IT and telecommunications including share facilities in local centers.
Library Subject: teleworking, telecottages, and telecentres
Library Type: not open to the public
Publication: Magazine
Publication title: Teleworker Magazine. Advertisements.
Second publication: Book
Publication title: Teleworking Handbook
Meetings/Conventions: - annual - Exhibits.

Teligen
EF

Watermans Park, High St., Brentford, TW8 0BB, England, UK
Tel: 44 208 2635200
Fax: 44 208 2635222
Email: garryr@teligen.com
Website: http://www.teligen.com
Founded: 1976
Members: 17
Staff: 10
Contact: Marek Vaygelt, Mgr.
Description: A key information provider to both telcos and the international user marketplace.
Publication: Book
Publication title: T-Guide Tariffs

Tenant Farmers' Association
TFA

7 Brewery Ct., Theale, Reading, RG7 5AJ, England, UK
Tel: 44 118 9306130
Fax: 44 118 9303424
Email: tfa@tenant-farmers.org.uk
Website: http://www.tenant-farmers.org.uk
Founded: 1981

Members: 4000
Staff: 5
Contact: George Dunn, Chief Exec.
Fee: £250
Membership Type: ordinary
Description: Tenant Farmers in Great Britain and Wales requiring professional advice and guidance on landlord - tenancy matters. Aims to promote the landlord - tenant system and seeks to create a fair environment in which the tenant farmer can flourish commercially without unsustainable rents and stifling restrictions.
Publication: Pamphlet
Publication title: Briefing Notes
Second publication: Magazine
Publication title: TFA News. Advertisements.
Meetings/Conventions: conference - Exhibits.

Tennyson Society
TS

c/o Lincoln Central Library
Free School Lane, Lincoln, LN2 1EZ, England, UK
Tel: 44 1522 552862
Fax: 44 1522 552858
Email: linnet@lincolnshire.gov.uk
Website: http://www.tennysonsociety.org.uk
Founded: 1960
Members: 500
Contact: Kathleen Jefferson, Hon.Sec.
Fee: £8
Membership Type: personal
Fee: £10
Membership Type: family
Description: Individuals, libraries, universities, schools, and colleges seeking to promote the study and understanding of the life and works of Alfred, Lord Tennyson (1809-92), poet laureate of England from 1850 to 1892. Sponsors lectures, dinners, pilgrimages, annual memorial service and wreath-laying ceremony.
Library Subject: life and works of Alfred Lord Tennyson
Library Type: by appointment only
Publication title: Annual Report
Second publication: Papers
Publication title: List of Publications
Meetings/Conventions: - periodic conference

Tetrapyrrole Discussion Group
TG

c/o Dr. D.I. Vernon
University of Leeds, Dept. of Biochemistry and Molecular Biology, Leeds, LS2 9JT, England, UK
Tel: 44 113 2333143
Fax: 44 113 2333017
Email: d.i.vernon@leeds.ac.uk
Website: http://www.bmb.leeds.ac.uk/tpdg
Founded: 1976
Members: 95
Contact: Dr. D.I. Vernon
Description: Individuals interested in the tetrapyrrole group of chemicals, which includes components of hemoglobin, chlorophylls, vitamin B12, and bile pigments. Facilitates exchange of information among members.
Meetings/Conventions: - annual meeting

Textile Finishers' Association

Merrydale House, Roysdale Way, Bradford, BD4 6SB, England, UK
Tel: 44 1274 652207
Fax: 44 1274 682293
Email: cbwt@legend.co.uk
Founded: 1989
Members: 34
Staff: 4
Contact: John Lambert
Fee: £350
Membership Type: subscription
Description: Full members, textile finishing companies; Assoc Members, companies supply the textile finishing industry. Concerned with political and commercial representation - Whitehall & Brussels; gives advice to members on legislation and health and safety, environment, energy, standards and other problems.
Library Type: not open to the public

Textile Institute
TI

St. James's Bldgs., 1st Fl., Oxford St., Manchester, M1 6FQ, England, UK
Tel: 44 161 2371188
Fax: 44 161 2361991
Email: runsworth@textileinst.org.uk
Website: http://www.texi.org/
Founded: 1910
Members: 7000
Staff: 19
Contact: Terry Hennessey, Dir.Gen.
Fee: £95
Membership Type: individual
Fee: £550
Membership Type: company patron
Description: Companies and individuals in 100 countries involved in management, science, technology, design, information transfer, and marketing of textiles including clothing and footwear. Promotes interests of the textile industry worldwide; serves professional interests of members; confers qualifications and recognizes achievements in research, application of ideas, education, business, and public affairs. Maintains Textile Institute Information Service to collect information relating to textile industrial and economic conditions in different countries and economic sectors.
Library Subject: textiles
Library Type: by appointment only
Publication: Journal
Publication title: Journal of the Textile Institute

Textile Recycling Association

c/o Heather Stewart
16 High St., Brampton, Huntingdon, PE28 4TU, England, UK
Tel: 44 1480 455249
Fax: 44 1480 453680
Email: tra@britmetrec.org.uk
Website: http://www.textile-recycling.org.uk
Members: 42
Contact: Heather Stewart, Sec.
Fee: £800
Membership Type: corporate, 26 or more employees
Fee: £550
Membership Type: corporate, 11 to 25 employees
Description: Textile recyclers/reclaimers and wiping cloth manufacturers.
Formerly: Reclamation Association

Publication: Booklet
Publication title: Recyclatex Booklet for Schools
Meetings/Conventions: - annual conference

Textile Services Association

7 Churchill Ct., 58 Station Rd., North Harrow, Harrow, HA2 7SA, England, UK
Tel: 44 208 8637755
Fax: 44 208 8612115
Email: tsa@tsa-uk.org
Website: http://www.tsa-uk.org
Founded: 1886
Members: 600
Staff: 5
Contact: Murray Simpson, Ch.Exec.
Description: Members are companies involved in laundry, dry cleaning and textile rental. Gives advice to members on health and safety matters, industrial relations and environmental and trade protection matters through its various publications and member Bulletins.
Publication title: Health, Safety & Environment Guidelines
Second publication: Pamphlets

Textile Society for the Study of Art, Design and History

c/o Lyn Broster
Charlesbye Farm, Greetby Hill, Ormskirk, L39 2DT, England, UK
Tel: 44 1101 4320419
Email: sblack@lcf.linst.ac.uk
Website: http://www.textilesociety.org.uk
Founded: 1982
Members: 400
Contact: Kirstie Buckland, Sec.
Fee: £15
Membership Type: individual
Fee: £20
Membership Type: household
Description: Aims to unite scholars, designers, teachers, practitioners, artists, collectors, and others interested in the study of textile art, design, and history. Conducts an educational program with visits to exhibitions and lectures.
Publication: Journal
Publication title: TEXT
Meetings/Conventions: - annual conference

Thalidomide Society

c/o Ms. Vivien Kerr
19 Central Ave., Pinner, HA5 5BT, England, UK
Tel: 44 20 88685309
Fax: 44 20 88685309
Email: info@thalsoc.demon.co.uk
Founded: 1962
Members: 330
Staff: 1
Contact: Vivien Kerr, CON
Fee: £5
Membership Type: thalidomide
Description: Provides support, advice and information to thalidomide and similarly disabled people living in the U.K.

Thames Valley Chamber of Commerce

Commerce House, 2-6 Bath Rd., Slough, SL1 3SB, England, UK
Tel: 44 1753 870500
Fax: 44 1753 524644
Email: central@thamesvalleychamber.co.uk
Website: http://www.thamesvalleychamber.co.uk
Members: 3200
Staff: 42
Contact: Jean Charmack, Pres.
Description: Promotes business and commerce.

Thanet and East Kent Chamber of Commerce

Kent Innovation Centre, Millennium Way, Thanet Reach Business Park, Broadstairs, CT10 2QQ, England, UK
Tel: 44 1843 609289
Fax: 44 1843 609291
Email: admin@kmcoc.org.uk
Website: http://www.kmcoc.org.uk
Founded: 2000
Members: 900
Staff: 7
Contact: Anne Peeks
Description: Promotes business and commerce.
Publication: Newsletter
Publication title: Chamber Newsletter

The European-Atlantic Movement
TEAM

ROVINJ, Bakehill Ave., Bradford, BD2 3JT, England, UK
Tel: 44 1274 780756
Founded: 1958
Members: 200
Contact: Alan J. Thornton, Hon.Sec.
Fee: £10
Membership Type: ordinary
Description: Individuals and institutions. Promotes increased awareness of European, trans-Atlantic, and world affairs, particularly among young people and educators. Gathers and disseminates information on European and Atlantic public policies and international issues; organizes study tours; sponsors educational programs.
Meetings/Conventions: - periodic conference

The Eyecare Trust

PO Box 131, Market Rasen, LN8 5TS, England, UK
Tel: 44 1673 857847
Fax: 44 1673 857696
Email: eis@btinternet.com
Founded: 1993
Staff: 1
Contact: Tara Burghardt, Membership & Admin.Sec.
Description: Individual optometrists and dispensing opticians, multiples, manufacturing and importing companies, who subscribe voluntarily to fund the EIS's public relations work. Concerned with the generic promotion of eyecare services and products available from professionally qualified, registered UK optical practitioners.
Formerly: Eyecare Information Service

The Library Association

7 Ridgmount St., London, WC1E 7AE, England, UK
Tel: 44 20 72550500
Fax: 44 20 72550501
Email: info@la-hq.org.uk
Website: http://www.la-hq.org.uk/

Founded: 1877
Members: 24000
Staff: 70
Contact: Bob McKee, CEO
Description: Information specialists, librarians and consultants working in the field of librarianship and information services. The main UK body for library and information professionals, concerned with education, training and standards of practice.
Publication: Journal
Publication title: Library Association Record. Advertisements.
Second publication: Directory
Publication title: Library Association Yearbook
Meetings/Conventions: - biennial conference - Exhibits.

The Sports Industries Federation
TSIF

Federation House, National Agricultural Centre, Stoneleigh Park, Warwick, CV8 2RF, England, UK
Tel: 44 8708 709399
Fax: 44 2476 414990
Email: admin@sportslife.org.uk
Website: http://www.sportslife.org.uk
Founded: 1918
Members: 650
Staff: 11
Contact: David Pomfret, Chief Exec.
Description: Manufacturers of sporting goods and clothing. Serves as a forum for discussion of industry issues among members; represents members' interests before government agencies and international organizations. Promotes export of members' products; works to increase public participation in athletics.
Publication: Newsletter
Publication title: Sportslife. Advertisements.
Meetings/Conventions: Eurogolf - annual trade show - Exhibits.

The Survey Association

Marine House, Meadlake Pl., Thorpe Lea Rd., Egham, TW20 8BF, England, UK
Tel: 44 1784 223760
Fax: 44 1784 223775
Email: office@tsa-uk.org.uk
Website: http://www.tsa-uk.org.uk
Founded: 1979
Members: 79
Staff: 3
Contact: N.W. Granger
Description: Private sector firms engaged in all aspects of surveying; land, photogrammetric, aerial and hydrographic. Offers its members a comprehensive and professional service providing general and company specific advice, support and information on training, marketing, and health and safety, environmental matters etc. Monitors changes in UK and European Commission laws affecting the industry and issues guidance on the interpretation and application of legislation.
Publication: Membership Directory

The Tile Association

Forum Court, 83 Copers Cope Rd., Beckenham, BR3 1NR, England, UK
Tel: 44 208 6630946
Fax: 44 208 6630949
Email: info@tiles.org.uk
Website: http://www.tiles.org.uk

Founded: 2000
Members: 575
Contact: Lesley Reid
Description: Open to tile distributors, contractors and manufacturers of ceramic tile and related products, ceramic tile retailers and agents. Aims to achieve professional regulation in the ceramic tile industry; to provide training and information; to be the voice of the industry; to give technical advice and help; and to strengthen relationships with related bodies in the tile industry.
Formerly: National Association of Tile Distributors

The Vermiculite Association
TVA

Whitegate Acre, Metheringham Fen, Lincoln, LN4 3AL, England, UK
Tel: 44 1526 323990
Fax: 44 1526 323181
Email: tva@vermiculite.org
Website: http://www.vermiculite.org
Founded: 1947
Members: 60
Contact: Thorkil Krag, Pres.
Description: Miners, producers, and processors of vermiculite and vermiculite products. Sponsors research and testing programs in development of new uses and specifications for vermiculite in various fields such as acoustical tile, concrete loosefill and plastic, horticulture, and steel. Produces pictures illustrating production and preparation of vermiculite aggregate to job application.
Publication title: Letter
Meetings/Conventions: - annual meeting

The Work Foundation

c/o Peter Runge House
3 Carlton House Terrace, London, SW1Y 5DG, England, UK
Tel: 44 870 4792000
Fax: 44 870 4792222
Email: cutomercentre@theworkfoundation.com
Website: http://www.theworkfoundation.com
Founded: 1918
Members: 12000
Staff: 95
Contact: Will Hutton, Chief Exec.
Description: Works to improve the quality and productivity of U.K. work life, offers clients innovative solutions through research, consultancy, leadership and coaching programs.
Formerly: Industrial Society
Publication: Annual Report
Publication title: Annual Report
Publication title: Briefing Plus

Theatre Arts Society
TAS

Charing Cross Rd., London, WC2 0DA, England, UK
Tel: 44 20 78362671
Founded: 1969

Theatregoers' Club of Great Britain

47-51 Gt. Suffolk St., Harling House, London, SE1 OBS, England, UK
Tel: 44 207 4504040
Fax: 44 207 4504041
Email: info@theatregoers.co.uk
Website: http://www.theatregoers.co.uk
Founded: 1978

Members: 21100
Staff: 24
Contact: Susan Hampshire, Pres.
Fee: £27
Membership Type: single
Fee: £33
Membership Type: joint
Description: Theatrelovers who enjoy the convenience of quality theatre visits by coach, with convenient boarding points in their local area. Operates quality coach excursions taking members to a wide variety of shows and venues. Members are also offered a programme of social events, also arts based holidays around the UK and the world. The club also services corporate groups and incoming tours.
Publication: Magazine
Publication title: Stagecoach

Theosophical Society in England

50 Gloucester Place, London, W1U 8EA, England, UK
Tel: 44 20 79359261
Fax: 44 20 79359543
Email: theosophical@freenetname.co.uk
Website: http://www.theosophical-society.org.uk
Founded: 1875
Members: 1000
Staff: 4
Contact: Colin Price, Pres.
Fee: £33
Membership Type: subscription
Description: Aims to form a nucleus of the universal brotherhood of humanity without distinction or race, creed, sex, caste or color. Seeks to encourage the study of comparative religion, philosophy and science. Seeks to investigate unexplained laws of nature and the powers latent in man.
Library Subject: theosophy, psychic world, religion, philosophy, mysticism, science, modern civilization and culture, literature and fiction, health and healing, folklore and mythology, arts, yoga, ancient civilizations, western occultism, psychology and parapsychology, a
Library Type: lending
Publication: Journal
Publication title: Insight. Advertisements.
Meetings/Conventions: - annual conference

Thermal Insulation Contractors Association

TICA House, Allington Way, Yarm Rd. Business Park, Darlington, DL1 4QB, England, UK
Tel: 44 1325 466704
Fax: 44 1325 487691
Email: enquiries@tica-acad.co.uk
Website: http://www.tica-acad.co.uk
Founded: 1957
Members: 218
Staff: 15
Contact: George Iredale, Gen.Mgr.
Description: Represents the interests of thermal insulation contractors involved in various aspects of industrial insulation including power stations, oil refineries, chemical plants, on and off shore marine, fire protection, acoustics and asbestos removal and H & V in schools, hospitals and offices. Acts as joint signatory with the GMB and TGWU to the Thermal Insulating Industry's National Agreement.
Publication: Magazine
Publication title: Academy. Advertisements.

Thermal Insulation Manufacturers and Suppliers Association
TIMSA

99 West St., Farnham, GU9 7EN, England, UK
Tel: 44 1252 739154
Fax: 44 1252 739140
Email: info@associationhouse.org.uk
Website: http://www.timsa.org.uk/
Members: 36
Staff: 4
Contact: John G. Fairley
Publication: Handbook
Publication title: Thermal Insulation Handbook

Thermal Spraying and Surface Engineering Association

18 Hammerton Way, Wellesbourne, Warwick, CV35 9NT, England, UK
Tel: 44 1789 842822
Fax: 44 1789 842229
Email: thermal.sprayers@btinternet.com
Website: http://www.tssea.co.uk
Members: 100
Contact: I. Hoff, Sec.
Description: Companies worldwide involved in the metal coatings industry.
Formerly: Association of Metal Sprayers
Publication: Membership Directory
Publication title: Coatings Quarterly
Meetings/Conventions: - annual conference

Third World Foundation
TWF

2a Virginia Rd., Thornton Heath, CR7 8EG, England, UK
Tel: 44 208 7650550
Founded: 1978
Members: 3
Staff: 1
Contact: Mr. M.I. Hasan
Description: Seeks to aid the poor and deprived in their educational, medical and social needs in the Third World.
Meetings/Conventions: - annual conference

Thomas Hardy Society
THS

PO Box 1438, Dorchester, DT1 1YH, England, UK
Tel: 44 1305 251501
Fax: 44 1305 251501
Email: info@hardysociety.org
Website: http://www.hardysociety.org
Founded: 1968
Members: 1475
Contact: Olive Blackburn, Hon.Sec.
Fee: £18
Membership Type: UK
Fee: £23
Membership Type: overseas
Description: Individuals in 20 countries interested in the writings, life, and times of English novelist and poet Thomas Hardy (1840-1928). Serves to honor the memory of Hardy and to encourage the study and appreciation of his life and works.

Formerly: Thomas Hardy Festival Society
Publication: Journal
Publication title: Thomas Hardy Journal. Advertisements.
Second publication: Books
Meetings/Conventions: - biennial conference

Thomas Lovell Beddoes Society

c/o Mr. John Lovell Beddoes
11 Laund Nook, Belper, DE56 1GY, England, UK
Tel: 44 1773 828066
Fax: 44 1773 828066
Email: john@beddoes.demon.co.uk
Founded: 1994
Members: 100
Contact: John Lovell Beddoes, Chm.
Fee: £5
Membership Type: individual
Fee: £8
Membership Type: joint
Description: Aims to research Beddoes' life, times and work and encourage relevant publications. Aims to further the reading and appreciation of his works by a wider public. Aims to produce one Newsletter a year. Provides a liaise with other groups and organizations. Plans events to further the aims.
Library Subject: life and times of Thomas Lovell Beddoes
Library Type: not open to the public
Publication: Newsletter
Publication title: Thomas Lovell Beddoes Society Newsletter. Advertisements.
Meetings/Conventions: - annual meeting

Thomas Merton Society of Great Britain and Ireland

18 Colby Rd., Upper Norwood, London, SE19 1HA, England, UK
Tel: 44 207 9151445
Email: ucylpmp@ucl.ac.uk
Contact: Dr. Paul M. Pearson
Description: Admirers of American author Thomas Merton. Promotes appreciation Merton's contributions to the literature of spirituality, social criticism, and theology. Encourages study and research into Merton's writings; assists in the designing of undergraduate and graduate courses covering Merton and his works. Conducts educational programs; maintains speakers' bureau.

Thomas Paine Society - United Kingdom
TPS

43 Eugene Gardens, Nottingham, NG2 3LF, England, UK
Tel: 44 115 9860010
Founded: 1963
Members: 500
Contact: Robert Morrell, Hon.Sec.
Fee: £5
Membership Type: student or unwaged
Fee: £12
Membership Type: in U.K.
Description: Individuals in 22 countries interested in political philosopher and author Thomas Paine (1737-1809). Promotes the life and career of Paine and encourages the study and publication of his works. Does critical analyses of the author's treatises and books. Aids students and researchers. Organizes lectures and exhibitions; stimulates debate on contemporary issues.
Library Subject: Thomas Paine's life and works and the 18th century, early 19th century periods and other radicals
Library Type: reference

Publication: Journal
Publication title: Journal of Radical History. Advertisements.
Second publication: Newsletter
Publication title: TPS Echo
Meetings/Conventions: Eric Paine Memorial Lecture - annual lecture

Thoroughbred Breeders' Association

Stanstead House, The Avenue, Newmarket, CB8 9AA, England, UK
Tel: 44 1638 661321
Fax: 44 1638 665621
Email: info@tbassoc.co.uk
Website: http://www.thoroughbredbreedersassociation.co.uk
Founded: 1917
Members: 2700
Staff: 8
Contact: Gavin Pritchard-Gordon, Exec.Dir.
Description: Breeders of thoroughbred horses, and others involved or interested in the bloodstock industry. Encourages by means of the provision of educational or research facilities or otherwise the science of producing and improving the thoroughbred horse in Great Britain.
Library Subject: thoroughbred breeding and racing
Library Type: not open to the public
Publication title: The Pacemaker and Thoroughbred Breeder. Advertisements.

Three Counties Cider and Perry Association
3CC&PA

c/o Jean Howell
Kittles, Much Marcle, Ledbury, HR8 2NT, England, UK
Tel: 44 1531 660691
Email: j.nowell@ukonline.co.uk
Founded: 1993
Members: 60
Contact: Jean Nowell
Fee: £15
Membership Type: full
Fee: £12
Membership Type: associate
Description: Makers of cider or perry, particularly smaller makers and growers, from the three counties of Herefordshire, Worcestershire, and Gloucestershire. Furthers the image of the small cider and perry maker. Promotes the sharing of experiences and techniques, and represents members' interests with local and national government.
Publication: Newsletter
Publication title: 3CC&PA. Advertisements.
Meetings/Conventions: - quarterly meeting

Thyroid Eye Disease
TED

Solstice, Sea Road, Winchelsea Beach, Winchelsea, TN36 4LH, England, UK
Tel: 44 179 7222338
Email: tedassn@eclipse.co.uk
Founded: 1989
Members: 700
Staff: 1
Contact: Claire Hodger
Fee: £5
Description: Endocrinologists, ophthalmologists, radiologists, and other health care professionals; people with thyroid eye disease and their families. Seeks to advance the diagnosis and treatment of thyroid eye disease. Promotes increased awareness of thyroid eye disease in the medical community. Provides information, care, and support to people with thyroid eye disease; provides financial assistance to thyroid eye disease research. Maintains medical helpline.
Publication: Newsletter
Second publication: Bulletin

Tibet Relief Fund of the United Kingdom

Tower House, 139 Fonthill Rd., London, N4 3HF, England, UK
Tel: 44 207 2721414
Fax: 44 207 2721410
Email: members@tibet-society.org.uk
Website: http://www.tibetsociety.com
Founded: 1959
Members: 2000
Staff: 3
Contact: Alan Clements, Co-Ch.
Fee: £20
Membership Type: individual
Fee: £32
Membership Type: outside UK
Description: Assists Tibetan refugees to achieve a sustainable life in exile. Offers educational and training programs. Provides assistance to social and economic development programs for people within Tibet.
Library Subject: Tibetan culture and politics
Library Type: reference
Publication: Journal
Publication title: Tibet Alive
Meetings/Conventions: - annual general assembly - Exhibits.

Tilling Society

c/o Cynthia Reavell
5 Friars Bank, Guestling, Hastings, TN35 4EJ, England, UK
Fax: 44 1424 813237
Email: society@tilling.org.uk
Website: http://www.tilling.org.uk/society
Founded: 1982
Members: 500
Contact: Cynthia Reavell, Sec.
Fee: £8
Membership Type: renewing member
Fee: £10
Membership Type: renewing member outside U.K.
Description: Literary enthusiasts in 15 countries. Promotes enjoyment of the works of satirical English novelist Edward Frederic Benson (1867-1940). Encourages exchange of news and information, discussion, and speculation.
Library Type: reference
Publication: Book
Publication title: E.F. Benson as Mayor of Rye, 1934-1937: Reports from the Sussex Express
Second publication: Newsletter
Publication title: Tilling Society Newsletter
Meetings/Conventions: Tilling Get-Together - annual luncheon - Exhibits.

Timber Decking Association
TDA

CIRCE Bldg., Wheldon Rd., Castleford, WF10 2JT, England, UK
Tel: 44 1977 712718
Email: info@tda.org.uk
Website: http://www.tda.org.uk
Description: Committed to helping homeowners and design professionals source high quality and performance timber decks.

Publication: Brochure
Publication title: An Introduction to Creating Quality Decks
Second publication: Handbook
Publication title: Timber Decking Manual

Timber Research and Development Association and Trada Technology
TRADA

Chiltern House, Stocking Ln., Hughenden Valley, High Wycombe, HP14 4ND, England, UK
Tel: 44 1494 569600
Fax: 44 1494 565487
Email: information@trada.co.uk
Website: http://www.trada.co.uk
Founded: 1934
Members: 1200
Staff: 120
Contact: Jeremy Vibert, Information Centre Mgr.
Description: Timber importers, manufacturers, construction companies, architects, structural engineers, surveyors, and interested others from 38 countries. Promotes appropriate and economical use of timber and wood panels in the construction and packaging industries. Works in research and development in order to ensure that timber is used in the most efficient manner possible. Disseminates information to manufacturers and specifiers on topics such as surface finishes for wood, adhesives, and wood-based sheet materials. Advises members on European and international standards. Offers building design, consultancy, and structural appraisal services. Conducts product evaluations and mechanical tests for stress and fire resistance. Organizes professional training courses on subjects including visual stress grading, timber trade sales, and quality assurance services.
Formerly: Timber Development Association
Publication: Newsletter
Publication title: Trada Update
Second publication: Magazine
Publication title: Trada Viewpoint
Meetings/Conventions: - annual meeting

Timber Trade Federation

Clareville House, 26/27 Oxendon St., London, SW1Y 4EL, England, UK
Tel: 44 207 8391891
Fax: 44 207 9300094
Email: ttf@ttf.co.uk
Website: http://www.ttf.co.uk
Founded: 1892
Members: 500
Staff: 11
Contact: Jean Rennie, Deputy Dir. General
Description: Timber agents, importers and merchants. To create the best conditions in the market place for its members to trade. To promote timber as a building material and its potential for other uses.
Publication title: Statistical Information
Second publication: Brochures

Timber Trade Training Association

Ste. 4, Cornwall House, Station Road, Princes Risborough, HP27 9DN, England, UK
Tel: 44 1844 342064
Fax: 44 1844 342069
Founded: 1982
Members: 450
Staff: 4
Contact: G.J. Payne, Gen.Mgr.
Description: Timber importers and merchants. Training association for timber merchants.
Publication: Newsletter
Publication title: Training Matters Newsletter
Second publication: Brochure

Tin Plate Workers Alias Wireworkers' Company

66 Westbury Rd., New Malden, KT3 5AS, England, UK
Tel: 44 20 89496467
Fax: 44 20 87158398
Email: clerk@tinplateworkers.co.uk
Website: http://www.tinplateworkers.co.uk
Founded: 1670
Members: 250
Staff: 1
Contact: Michael Henderson-Begg, Clerk
Fee: £100
Description: Tin plate and wire workers. Works to increase contact within the industries. Pursues and develops educational and charitable activities.

Tin Technology

Unit 3, Curo Park, Frogmore, St. Albans, AL2 2DD, England, UK
Tel: 44 870 4584242
Fax: 44 870 4584273
Email: david.bishop@tintechnology.com
Website: http://www.tintechnology.com/index.htm
Contact: David Bishop, Dir.
Description: Individuals and organizations. Promotes development of new technologies in all scientific and commercial fields. Serves as a clearinghouse on emerging technologies; facilitates exchange of information among members.

Tin Technology
ITRI

Unit 3, Curo Park, Frogmore, St. Albans, AL2 2DD, England, UK
Tel: 44 870 4584242
Fax: 44 870 4584273
Email: david.bishop@tintechnology.com
Website: http://www.itri.co.uk
Founded: 1932
Staff: 40
Contact: David Bishop, Managing Dir.
Description: Develops tin uses based on scientific and technical study of tin, its alloys and compounds, and industrial processes that use tin or may provide future markets. Works to improve existing products and processes and to assist consumers in resolving technical difficulties and problems relating to tin. Participates in exhibitions and trade fairs; conducts practical demonstrations of tin-using processes.
Library Subject: Tin, tin alloys, compounds, coatings, and properties and uses.
Library Type: reference
Formerly: International Tin Research Council
Publication: Magazine
Publication title: Focus on Tin
Second publication: Annual Report

Tobacco Manufacturers Association

55 Tufton St., London, SW1P 3QL, England, UK
Tel: 44 20 75440100
Fax: 44 20 75440117
Email: information@the-tma.org.uk
Website: http://www.the-tma.org.uk/
Founded: 1978
Members: 5
Staff: 10
Contact: Gill Silverman, Media & Info.Mgr.
Description: Represents the interests of the UK tobacco manufacturers. Represents the industry as a whole and does not promote particular brands or products. It provides factual information on smoking.
Publication title: Briefing Cards
Second publication: Newsletter
Publication title: TMA Briefing

Tolkien Society - England
TS

c/o Trevor Reynolds
65 Wentworth Cres., Ashvale, Aldershot, GU12 5LF, England, UK
Tel: 44 1252 692432
Fax: 44 8700 525569
Email: tolksoc@tolkiensociety.org
Founded: 1969
Members: 1025
Contact: Christine Crawshaw, Chm.
Fee: £2
Membership Type: individuals under the age of 16 in the U.K.
Fee: £3
Membership Type: individuals under the age of 16 outside the U.K.
Description: Individuals in 30 countries interested in J.R.R. Tolkien (1892-1973), English scholar and author of fiction noted for its cogent use of fantasy. Promotes appreciation and study of Tolkien's works, particularly The Lord of the Rings.
Library Subject: Tolkien's life and work.
Library Type: reference
Publication: Bulletin
Publication title: Amon Hen. Advertisements.
Second publication: Journal
Publication title: Mallorn
Meetings/Conventions: - annual seminar

Tool and Trades History Society
TATHS

Barrow Mead Cottage, Rush Hill, Bath, BA2 2QP, England, UK
Tel: 44 1225 837031
Fax: 44 1225 855470
Email: taths@recstools.co.uk
Founded: 1983
Members: 5500
Contact: Mrs. Jane Rees, Chm.
Fee: £21
Membership Type: U.K.
Fee: £21
Membership Type: International
Description: Craft and tool collectors, historians of pre-industrial technology, antiquarians, archaeologists, museums, museum officials, libraries, and craft teachers in Europe, Australia, and North America. Promotes awareness and understanding of hand tools and the skills and techniques exercised by those who used them. Bestows awards.
Publication: Catalog

Publication title: James Isaac & John Fossell
Second publication: Monograph
Publication title: The Tool Chest of Benjamin Seaten
Meetings/Conventions: - annual conference - Exhibits.

Tools for Self Reliance
TFSR

Netley Marsh, Southampton, SO40 7GY, England, UK
Tel: 44 2380 869697
Fax: 44 2380 868544
Email: info@tfsr.org
Website: http://www.tfsr.org
Founded: 1979
Members: 300
Staff: 9
Contact: Jan Kidd, CEO
Description: Enables artisans in developing countries to better participate in the development of themselves and their communities. Works with local partner organisations to provide tools and skills training, and by raising awareness in the UK of the causes of poverty. Supports partner organisations in Ghana, Mozambique, Nicaragua, Sierra Leone, Tanzania, Uganda, and Zimbabwe. *VNU
Publication: Newsletter
Publication title: Forging Links
Meetings/Conventions: - annual conference - Exhibits.

Tornado and Storm Research Organisation
TORRO

Brookes University, Oxford, , England, UK
Email: ray.peverall@torro.org.uk
Website: http://www.torro.org.uk/
Founded: 1974
Members: 400
Contact: Prof. D.M. Elsom
Description: Meterologists, meteorological researchers, and weather observers worldwide. Seeks to advance scientific understanding of tornados and storms, particularly as they effect the United Kingdom. Gathers and disseminates information on tornados and storms; conducts visits to tornado touch down sites; undertakes climatological research.
Publication: Journal
Publication title: Journal of Meteorology
Meetings/Conventions: - semiannual conference

Tourism Society

1-2 Queen Victoria Ter., Sovereign Ct., London, E1W 3HA, England, UK
Tel: 44 207 4882789
Fax: 44 207 4889148
Email: tour.soc@btinternet.com
Website: http://www.tourismsociety.org
Founded: 1977
Members: 1050
Staff: 3
Contact: Adrian Clark, Admin.Dir.
Description: Professionals in all sectors of travel and tourism industry. Multi-sectoral membership organisation founded to encourage professionalism in tourism and to enhance the status of those working in the industry. Organises discussion meetings.
Meetings/Conventions: - annual conference - Exhibits.

Town and Country Planning Association

17 Carlton House Terr., London, SW1Y 5AS, England, UK
Tel: 44 207 9308903
Fax: 44 207 9303280
Email: tcpa@tcpa.org.uk
Website: http://www.tcpa.org.uk
Founded: 1899
Members: 1000
Staff: 10
Contact: Nancy Easter Garcia
Description: Promotes the art and science of urban, rural, and environmental planning with a particular focus on community empowerment and public participation in policy making.
Publication: Newsletter
Publication title: Planning Bulletin
Second publication: Journal
Publication title: Town and Country Planning
Meetings/Conventions: - annual general assembly

Trade Marks Patents and Designs Federation

63-66 Hatton Garden, London, EC1N 8LE, England, UK
Tel: 44 20 72423923
Fax: 44 20 72423924
Email: admin@tmpdf.org.uk
Founded: 1920
Members: 75
Staff: 2
Contact: P. Rau, Admin.
Fee: £3000
Membership Type: voting
Fee: £1000
Membership Type: committee
Description: Industrial and commercial companies with interests in intellectual property. Aims to promote and secure co-operation amongst traders in all matters relating to trade marks, patents, designs and other intellectual property rights; through considering developments in intellectual property, expressing views and trying to influence decisions and holding open conferences.
Publication: Newsletter
Publication title: INPACT
Publication title: Trends & Events
Meetings/Conventions: - annual luncheon

Trade Union International Research and Education Group
TUIREG

Ruskin College, Walton St., Oxford, OX1 2HE, England, UK
Tel: 44 1865 554599
Fax: 44 1865 511313
Email: tuireg@ruskin.ac.uk
Founded: 1976
Members: 28
Staff: 3
Contact: Jimmy Browne, Dir.
Description: Resource center promoting worker education and research on international issues affecting trade union members. Seeks to increase understanding and support of international initiatives conducted in the interests of workers by trade unions, government bodies, and international organizations. Facilitates discussion of global issues to promote solidarity and understanding among workers worldwide. Conducts courses in trade unionism and international development in Africa, Palestine, Bangladesh, and the United Kingdom; undertakes research projects; makes available teacher's aids including audiovisual programs and course notes.

Library Type: reference
Publication: Report
Publication title: International Solidarity Pack
Second publication: Newsletter
Publication title: Sponsor Newsletter. Advertisements.
Meetings/Conventions: - annual seminar

Trades Union Congress - England
TUC

Congress House, Great Russell St., London, WC1B 3LS, England, UK
Tel: 44 20 76364030
Fax: 44 20 76360632
Email: info@tuc.org.uk
Website: http://www.tuc.org.uk
Founded: 1868
Members: 6816971
Staff: 280
Contact: J. Monks, Gen.Sec.
Description: Trade unions in the United Kingdom. Maintains the TUC Educational Trust, offering courses to union staff and members, and the TUC National Education Centre, a residential college available for use by trade unions. Operates TUC Aid to provide charitable relief to famine, disaster, and poverty victims in Africa, Asia, and Latin America.
Publication: Directory
Publication title: TUC Directory
Second publication: Papers
Meetings/Conventions: - annual congress - Exhibits.

Trades Union Congress - Women's Committee

Congress House, Great Russel1 St., London, WC1B 3LS, England, UK
Tel: 44 20 76364030
Fax: 44 171 4671333
Email: info@tuc.org.uk
Website: http://www.tuc.org.uk
Founded: 1868
Members: 3000000
Staff: 140
Contact: Kay Carberry, Head, Equal Rights Dept.
Description: Promotes the interests of women workers within the trade union movement. Publicational available upon request.
Meetings/Conventions: TUC Women's Conference - annual conference - Exhibits.

Trading Standards Institute
TSI

3-5 Hadleigh Business Centre, 351 London Rd., Hadleigh, Benfleet, SS7 2BT, England, UK
Tel: 44 870 8729000
Fax: 44 870 8729025
Email: institute@tsi.org.uk
Website: http://www.tradingstandards.gov.uk
Founded: 1890
Members: 2500
Staff: 33
Description: Trading standards officers and organisations/companies with an interest in consumer protection and other related issues. Represents the views of its professional officers in promoting fair trading for the consumer and legitimate trader to their mutual benefit.
Library Subject: trading standards and related subjects

Library Type: not open to the public
Formerly: Institute of Trading Standards Administration
Publication: Journal
Publication title: Trading Standards Review. Advertisements.
Meetings/Conventions: - annual conference - Exhibits.

Traidcraft
Kingsway, Gateshead, NE11 0NE, England, UK
Tel: 44 191 4910591
Fax: 44 191 4976562
Email: comms@traidcraft.co.uk
Website: http://www.traidcraft.co.uk
Contact: Catharine Howe
Description: Promotes fair trade between industrialized countries and businesses located in economically developing areas. Works with institutions in developing areas to enable locally based businesses to enter global markets on an equitable basis.
Publication: Catalog
Publication title: Mail Order Catalogue

Tramway and Light Railway Society
c/o Mr. H.J. Leach
6 The Woodlands, Brightlingsea, Colchester, CO7 0RY, England, UK
Tel: 44 1206 304411
Founded: 1938
Members: 1000
Contact: Mr. H.J. Leach, Sec.
Publication title: Tramfare

Transform Program
TP
14 Dufferin St., London, EC1Y 8PD, England, UK
Tel: 44 171 4265820
Fax: 44 171 2511315
Founded: 1994
Contact: Graham Thom
Description: Management personnel working for development organizations with projects in Africa. Promotes effective administration of African development programs. Provides management and training assistance to nongovernmental organizations in Africa.

Transparency International - UK
TI(UK)
Tower Bldg., 2nd Fl., 11 York Rd., London, SE1 7NX, England, UK
Tel: 44 20 79810345
Fax: 44 20 79810346
Email: info@transparency.org.uk
Website: http://www.transparency.org.uk
Founded: 1993
Members: 200
Staff: 3
Contact: Laurence Cockcroft, Chm.
Fee: £35
Membership Type: individual
Fee: £250
Membership Type: corporate
Description: Corporations, organizations, and individuals interested in reducing corruption in international business transactions. Seeks to: raise public awareness of anticorruption measures; influence legislation regulating international business transactions. Formulates standards of integrity to govern international business dealings; maintains network of businesses agreeing to adhere to these

standards. Conducts anticorruption programs. Undertakes research and educational activities.
Meetings/Conventions: - monthly meeting

Transport and General Workers Union
TGWU
Transport House, 128 Theobald's Rd., London, WC1X 8TN, England, UK
Tel: 44 207 6112500
Fax: 44 207 6112555
Founded: 1933
Members: 1200000
Staff: 200
Contact: Bill Morris, Gen.Sec.
Fee: £1.95
Description: Transport workers, dockers, craftsmen, asphalt workers, and semi-skilled laborers in the United Kingdom. Provides union services; represents members' interests.
Library Subject: trade unionism and industrial relations
Library Type: not open to the public

Transport Association
c/o Peter Acton Associates
185 Great Tattenhams, Epsom Downs, KT18 5RA, England, UK
Tel: 44 1737 362232
Fax: 44 1737 352323
Email: support@trans-assoc.co.uk
Website: http://www.trans-assoc.org.uk
Founded: 1955
Members: 60
Contact: Mr. Peter Acton, Sec.
Description: Haulage contractors. Self help association - repairs, refuelling, return loads - meet regularly to discuss matters of interest.

Travel Trust Association
Parkway House, Albion House, 3rd Fl., Chertsey Rd., Woking, GU21 1BE, England, UK
Tel: 44 870 8890577
Fax: 44 148 3730746
Email: info@traveltrust.co.uk
Website: http://www.traveltrust.co.uk/
Description: Travelers and businesses whose employees travel frequently. Seeks to provide low-cost travel insurance to participants. Operates trust account to provide fidelity insurance to individual travelers.

Tree Council
51 Catherine Pl., London, SW1E 3DY, England, UK
Tel: 44 207 8289928
Fax: 44 207 8289060
Email: info@treecouncil.org.uk
Website: http://www.treecouncil.org.uk
Founded: 1974
Members: 186
Staff: 4
Contact: Pauline Buchanan Black, Dir.
Description: National organization concerned with trees. Aims to improve the environment in town and country by promoting the planting and conservation of trees and woods throughout the UK; to disseminate knowledge about trees and their management and to act as a forum for organizations concerned with trees, to identify national problems and to provide initiatives for cooperation.
Publication: Magazine
Publication title: Tree News

Triangles

3 Whitehall Ct., Ste. 54, London, SW1A 2EF, England, UK
Tel: 44 20 78394512
Fax: 44 20 78395575
Email: london@lucistrust.org
Website: http://www.triangles.org/triangles/
Founded: 1937
Contact: Mark Salzedo
Description: Persons of all faiths united to use the power of thought and prayer to establish harmonious human relations, to spread goodwill and understanding, and to strengthen and support practical and constructive action benefiting humanity. Members form groups of 3 persons (triangles) who spend a few minutes daily linking in thought with one another, not necessarily at the same time. They then say The Great Invocation - a world prayer, and visualise love and light flowing into human consciousness. Members of the triangle need not be in the same geographic locality.
Publication title: Energy Follows Thought
Publication title: Energy of Light
Meetings/Conventions: Day of World Invocation - annual

Tropical Biology Association

c/o Ms. Rosie Trevelyan
Dept. of Zoology, University of Cambridge, Downing St., Cambridge, CB2 3EJ, England, UK
Tel: 44 1223336619
Fax: 44 1223336619
Email: tba@zoo.com.ac.uk
Website: http://www.zoo.cam.ac.uk/tba
Founded: 1994
Members: 37
Staff: 6
Contact: Dr. R. Trevelyan, Dir.
Fee: £550
Membership Type: institutional
Description: Aims to meet the challenge of biodiversity conservation by establishing an informed, well-motivated community of tropical biologists both in Europe and in tropical countries.
Publication: Newsletter
Publication title: TBA Newsletter

Tropical Forest Resource Group
TFRG

2 Webbs Barn Cottage, Witney Rd., Kingston Bagpuize, Abingdon, OX13 5AN, England, UK
Tel: 44 1865 820935
Fax: 44 871 2209682
Email: alan.pottinger@tfrg.co.uk
Website: http://www.tfrg.co.uk
Founded: 1992
Members: 9
Staff: 3
Contact: Alan Pottinger, Coor.
Fee: £500
Membership Type: fee paying forestry organizations
Description: Organizations, universities, research institutes, private companies, and government agencies seeking to inform development project and policy developers in areas of forest management and conservation. Gathers and disseminates information on subjects including national and regional forest planning, land and soil evaluation, economic and social system assessments, and biomass energy resource management. Conducts educational and training programs. Initiates and coordinates responses to charitable public and private organizations worldwide.
Meetings/Conventions: Current Methods in Tropical Forestry - periodic seminar

Tropical Growers' Association
TGA

9 Dane Pk., Bishop's Stortford, CM23 2PR, England, UK
Tel: 44 1279 656763
Fax: 44 207 7099174
Email: tga@airt.dircon.co.uk
Founded: 1907
Members: 70
Staff: 1
Contact: Mr. P.D. Gatland, Dir.
Fee: £15
Membership Type: Individual
Fee: £50
Membership Type: Company
Description: Individuals and companies in 30 countries interested in cultivating tropical trees or plants including rubber, oil palm, cocoa, and coconut. Organizes seminars; compiles statistics.

Tropical Health and Education Trust
THET

24 Eversholt St., London, NW1 1AD, England, UK
Tel: 44 20 76798127
Fax: 44 20 76798190
Email: vpthet1@aol.com
Website: http://www.thet.org
Founded: 1989
Staff: 6
Contact: Sarah Adams
Description: Medical training institutions specializing in tropical medicine. Seeks to advance the study, teaching, and practice of tropical medicine. Serves as a liaison linking medical education institutions in Europe and the developing world; sponsors research and educational programs.
Publication: Annual Report
Publication title: THET Annual Review
Meetings/Conventions: - annual meeting

Tuberous Sclerosis Association

c/o Mrs. Janet Medcalf
PO Box 9644, Bromsgrove, B61 0FP, England, UK
Tel: 44 1527 871898
Fax: 44 1527 579452
Email: support@tuberous-sclerosis.org
Website: http://www.tuberous-sclerosis.org
Founded: 1977
Members: 1450
Staff: 5
Contact: Janet Medcalf
Description: Supports families and individuals affected by tuberous sclerosis. Raises awareness of the condition and to educate professionals, sufferers and the general public.
Library Subject: tuberous sclerosis
Library Type: reference

Tun Abdul Razak Research Centre

Brickendonbury, Hertford, SG13 8NL, England, UK
Tel: 44 1992 584966
Fax: 44 1992 554837
Email: general@tarrc.co.uk
Website: http://www.tarrc.co.uk
Founded: 1938
Staff: 92
Contact: A.J. Tinker, Dir.
Description: Conducts research on the technological development, processing, and uses of rubber. Provides and supports technical and consulting services to rubber manufacturers.
Library Subject: Rubber and polymer science.
Library Type: not open to the public
Formerly: Malaysian Rubber Producers' Research Association
Publication: Report
Publication title: Engineering Design with Natural Rubber
Second publication: Report
Publication title: Market for Condoms

Turkish-British Chamber of Commerce

Bury House, 33 Bury St., St. James, London, SW14 6AV, England, UK
Tel: 44 207 3210999
Fax: 44 207 3210989
Email: memlink@tbcci.demon.co.uk
Contact: Barry Thorne
Description: Promotes business and commerce.

Turner Society
TS

BCM Box Turner, London, WC1N 3XX, England, UK
Website: http://www.turnersociety.org.uk
Founded: 1975
Members: 400
Contact: Eric Shanes, Chm.
Fee: £15
Membership Type: in UK individual
Fee: £8
Membership Type: additional members at same address
Description: Art collectors, scholars, and individuals worldwide interested in the work of J.M.W. Turner; libraries and galleries. Works to further appreciation and study of Turner (1775-1851).
Publication: Journal
Publication title: Turner Society News. Advertisements.
Meetings/Conventions: - annual general assembly

Twentieth Century Society

70 Cowcross St., London, EC1M 6EJ, England, UK
Tel: 44 20 72503857
Email: coordinator@c20society.demon.co.uk
Website: http://www.c20society.org.uk
Founded: 1979
Members: 1800
Staff: 5
Contact:
Fee: £28
Membership Type: ordinary
Fee: £42
Membership Type: joint
Description: Works toward the protection of British architecture and design after 1914.

TWI

Granta Park, Great Abington, Cambridge, CB1 6AL, England, UK
Tel: 44 1223 891162
Fax: 44 1223 892588
Email: twi@twi.co.uk
Website: http://www.twi.co.uk/j32k/index.xtp
Founded: 1946
Members: 7600
Staff: 450
Contact: David Mikeown, Mktg.Mgr.
Description: Individuals and companies using welding and joining technology or supplying equipment and consumables for welding and joining processes. Activities cover all aspects of welding and joining technology and materials engineering.
Library Subject: welding, international welding standards, welding materials and equipment
Library Type: not open to the public
Publication: Journal
Publication title: Bulletin
Publication title: Connect

TWIN

1 Curtain Rd., London, EC2A 3LT, England, UK
Tel: 44 20 73751221
Fax: 44 20 73751337
Email: info@twin.org.uk
Founded: 1985
Staff: 18
Contact: Jessica Eugene
Description: Trade Development NGO, working with organizations and cooperatives of small scale farmers and artisans in the Third World. Facilitates trade and technology exchange; provides technical, marketing, and quality control assistance. Operates information service for Third World trade organizations; conducts training seminars on finance, technology, and trade. training seminars on finance, technology, and trade. finance, technology, and trade.
Library Subject: Third World development, business, marketing, fair trade
Library Type: by appointment only
Formerly: Third World Information Network
Publication: Book
Publication title: Tropical Commodities and Their Markets
Meetings/Conventions: - biennial conference

Twins and Multiple Births Association

2 The Willows, Gardner Rd., Guilford, Surrey, GUI 4PG, England, UK
Tel: 44 870 7703305
Fax: 44 870 7703303
Email: enquiries@tambahq.org.uk
Website: http://www.tamba.org.uk
Founded: 1978
Members: 5500
Staff: 11
Contact:
Fee: £20
Description: Parents with multiple birth children. Seeks to provide information and mutual support networks for families including multiple birth children; promotes increased understanding of the unique health and social needs of multiple birth children and their families. Gathers and disseminates information on multiple birth children; makes available specialist support services to members; serves as liaison linking members to local twins clubs; encourages research on the unique health, social, and educational needs of multiple birth children. Provides discounts on children's clothing and

other supplies to members. Represents the interests of families with multiple birth children before government agencies and the media.
Library Type: not open to the public
Publication: Magazine
Publication title: Twins, Triplets, and More. Advertisements.
Meetings/Conventions: - periodic conference

Twist Drill and Reamer Association

c/o Institute of Spring Technology
Henry St., Sheffield, S3 7EQ, England, UK
Tel: 44 114 2789143
Fax: 44 114 2726344
Email: info@britishtools.com
Contact: Mr. J.R. Markham
Description: Manufacturers of twist drills and reamers.

U.K. Irrigation Association

c/o Silsoe College
Cranfield University, Silsoe, Bedford, MK45 4DT, England, UK
Tel: 44 1525 635127
Fax: 44 1525 754537
Email: enquiries@ukia.org
Website: http://www.ukia.org
Founded: 1980
Members: 300
Staff: 1
Contact: Melvyn Kay, Exec.Sec.
Fee: £40
Membership Type: individual
Description: Anyone interested in UK irrigation, particularly farmers and growers including manufacturers and suppliers of equipment, advisers, consultants, contractors, members of water authorities, trainers and researchers. Aims to promote interest in, and a better understanding of, all aspects of irrigation in the UK, through courses, open days, conferences and specialist meetings.
Publication: Journal
Publication title: Irrigation News. Advertisements.
Second publication: Newsletter
Publication title: U.K. Irrigation Association Newsletter
Meetings/Conventions: - annual conference

UK Apitherapy Society

37 Cecil Rd., Cheshunt, EN8 8TN, England, UK
Tel: 44 1992 622645
Fax: 44 1992 622645
Email: peter.pebadale@virgin.net
Website: http://freespace.virgin.net/peter.pebadale/pages/UK_Api_-Society.htm
Founded: 1996
Contact: Sue Claydon, Co-Sec.
Description: Promotes the safe use of bee venom, whereby test stings are given before therapy begins.
Meetings/Conventions: lecture

UK Association of Frozen Food Producers

1 Green St., London, W1K 6RG, England, UK
Tel: 44 20 76290655
Fax: 44 20 74999095
Email: ukaffp@ukaffp.org.uk
Description: Represents frozen food manufacturers in the United Kingdom.

UK Cleaning Products Industry Association

1st Fl Ste., Century House, High St., Tattenhall, Cheshire, CH3 9RJ, England, UK
Tel: 44 1829 770055
Fax: 44 1829 770101
Email: ukcpi@ukcpi.org
Website: http://www.sdia.org.uk
Founded: 1939
Members: 70
Staff: 3
Contact: Dr. Andrew Williams, Dir.Gen.
Description: Companies engaged in the soap and detergent industry in the UK. Concerned with health and safety, consumer safety and environmental issues (excluding competitive issues). Actively involved with government, EC commission, consumer and environmental organisation's, retail trade, academic institutions and the media.
Formerly: Soap and Detergent Industry Association
Publication title: SDIA News

UK Fashion Exports

5 Portland Pl., London, W1B 1PW, England, UK
Tel: 44 207 6365577
Fax: 44 207 6367848
Email: info@ukfe.sportlandplace.org.uk
Website: http://www.ukfashionexports.com
Founded: 1983
Members: 800
Staff: 7
Contact: Paul Alger, Exec.Dir.
Description: UK manufacturers, designers and wholesale suppliers of British-made apparel of all kinds including fashion accessories; associate members supplying various services related to the trade. To promote increased sales abroad of British apparel by means of promotional events (e.g. exhibitions, trade missions) information to UK manufacturers and overseas buyers or agents.
Library Subject: industry, export
Library Type: not open to the public
Publication: Newsletter
Publication title: The Exporter. Advertisements.
Second publication: Directory
Publication title: Fashion Buyer's Guide to Britain

UK Industrial Vision Association
UKIVA

PO Box 25, Royston, SG8 6TL, England, UK
Tel: 44 1763 261419
Fax: 44 1763 261961
Email: info@ukiva.org
Website: http://www.ukiva.org/
Founded: 1992
Members: 46
Staff: 2
Contact: Don Braggins, Admin.
Fee: £800
Membership Type: world
Description: Manufacturers of vision technologies and other industrial concerns making use of vision technology. Seeks to advance vision technologies and the manufacturing processes used to produce them. Represents members before labor and trade organizations, government agencies, and the public; gathers and disseminates information on vision technologies and their manufacture.

UK Public Health Association
UKPHA

Holborn Gate, 7th Fl., 330 High Holborn, London, WC1A 7BA, England, UK
Tel: 44 8700 101932
Fax: 44 207 4000122
Email: info@ukpha.org.uk
Website: http://www.ukpha.org.uk/
Description: Committed to promoting the development of public health policy at all levels of government, across all sectors, and to support those working in public health both professionally or in a voluntary capacity.
Publication: Newsletter

UK Society of Investment Professionals

21 Ironmonger Lane, London, EC2V 8EY, England, UK
Tel: 44 207 7963000
Fax: 44 207 7963333
Email: uksipstaff@uksip.org
Website: http://www.uksip.org
Founded: 1955
Members: 4400
Staff: 10
Contact: Sir David Dobson, Chief Exec.
Fee: £180
Membership Type: regular, affiliate, companion, student
Description: Investment analysts and fund managers. Acts as the professional body for members of the investment community applying formal analytical skills to research, portfolio management and related activities.
Library Subject: investment fund management
Library Type: not open to the public
Formerly: Institute of Investment Management and Research
Publication: Journal
Publication title: Professional Investor. Advertisements.
Meetings/Conventions: seminar - Exhibits.

UK Steel Association

Broadway House, Tothill St., London, SW1H 9NQ, England, UK
Tel: 44 20 2227777
Fax: 44 20 2223531
Email: enquiries@uksteel.org.uk
Website: http://www.uksteel.org.uk
Founded: 1967
Members: 40
Staff: 20
Contact: David Rea, Sec.Gen.
Description: Trade association for the steel industry in the United Kingdom. Represents the industry to policy and opinion farmers; promotes the industry and the importance of steel to the public; provides information and services to members.
Formerly: British Independent Steel Producers Association
Publication title: Annual Report
Second publication: Membership Directory
Publication title: Member Companies List

UK Timber Frame Association

14 Kinnerton Place S., London, SW1X 8EH, England, UK
Tel: 44 207 2353364
Email: office@timber-frame.org
Website: http://www.timber-frame.org
Founded: 1983
Members: 40
Staff: 5
Contact: David Scott, Technical Dir.
Description: Membership ranges from complete design and build package companies, through to manufacturers of ancillary products, and other trade associations.
Formerly: Formed by Merger of, Timber Frame Industry Association and Timber and Brick Consortium

UK Web Design Association
UKWDA

Fareham Enterprise Centre, Hackett Way, Fareham, PO14 1TH, England, UK
Email: info@ukwda.org
Website: http://www.ukwda.org/
Description: Works to promote and encourage industry standards within the British Web design sector.

UNA International Service
UNAIS

Hunter House, Ste. 3A, 57 Goodramgate, York, YO1 2LS, England, UK
Tel: 44 1904 647799
Email: unais-uk@geoz.poptel.org.uk
Website: http://www.internationalservice.org.uk
Founded: 1953
Contact: Madrine Kamya
Description: Individuals aged 21 or older with an interest in global development. Promotes sustainable and locally administered economic and social development worldwide. Encourages international and intercultural exchange. Provides volunteer assistance to development programs.

Union for the International Language Ido

24 Nunn St., Leek, ST13 8EA, England, UK
Tel: 44 1538 381491
Founded: 1908
Contact: David Weston, Sec.
Description: Representatives in over 12 countries united to promote the learning and use of the international language Ido (pronounced EE-DOH) and to recommend its universal adoption as a second language to be taught in schools throughout the world. The union proposes that Ido should serve as an auxiliary language so that persons throughout the world will have a language in common. According to the union, Ido is a modernized and improved version of Esperanto and its vocabulary is based on the main European languages, including English, French, German, Italian, Russian, and Spanish. Maintains IDO Book Service.
Publication title: Dictionaries
Second publication: Magazine
Publication title: Progreso
Meetings/Conventions: - biennial international conference

Union of Shop, Distributive and Allied Workers
USDAW

188 Wilmslow Rd., Fallowfield, Manchester, M14 6LJ, England, UK
Tel: 44 161 2242804
Fax: 44 161 2572566
Email: enquiries@usdaw.org.uk
Website: http://www.usdaw.org.uk
Founded: 1947
Members: 320000

Staff: 400
Contact: Sir Bill Connor, Gen.Sec.
Fee: £1.39
Description: Shopworkers in the distributive and allied trades. To improve the terms and conditions and to protect the interests of members. To promote equal opportunities and equal treatment for all members and oppose discrimination on grounds of sex, race, ethnic origin, disability, sexual orientation or religion.
Publication: Magazine
Publication title: Agenda: Magazine for Activists
Second publication: Magazine
Publication title: ARENA. Advertisements.
Meetings/Conventions: - annual meeting - Exhibits.

UNISON

1 Mabledon Pl., London, WC1H 9AJ, England, UK
Tel: 44 845 3550845
Fax: 44 171 3876692
Email: direct@unison.co.uk
Website: http://www.unison.org.uk
Founded: 1993
Members: 1400000
Staff: 1200
Contact: Dave Prentis, Gen.Sec.
Description: Organizes those employed within areas which provide services to the public whether in public, private or voluntary sectors of the economy; to improve their pay and conditions of service and to seek to protect their rights. Provides a range of member directed services.
Publication: Journal
Publication title: Unison Journal. Advertisements.
Publication title: Unison Week
Meetings/Conventions: - annual conference - Exhibits.

Unitas Malacologica
UM

c/o Dr. Peter Mordan
The Natural History Museum, Cromwell Rd., London, SW7 5BD, England, UK
Email: pbm@nhm.ac.uk
Founded: 1962
Members: 300
Contact: Dr. Peter Mordan, Sec.
Description: Malacologists (zoologists specializing in the study of mollusks) in 47 countries who are members of museums and scientific institutions; interested individuals and institutions. Furthers the worldwide study of mollusks.
Publication: Newsletter
Publication title: UM Newsletter
Meetings/Conventions: International Congress Malacology - triennial congress - Exhibits.

United Kingdom Agricultural Supply Trade Association

21 Arlington St., London, SW1A 1RN, England, UK
Tel: 44 207 45959100
Fax: 44 207 45959150
Email: enquiries@ukasta.org.uk
Website: http://www.ukasta.org.uk
Founded: 1977
Members: 370
Staff: 15
Contact: J.W. Reed, CEO

Description: Traders in, manufacturers, distributors, processors or brokers of agricultural commodities i.e. grain, pulse, seeds, feeding stuffs, fertilizers, chemicals (agriculture and horticulture). Concerned with achieving the most favourable economic and political conditions possible for members; assisting members to realise their maximum business potential by offering them timely, accurate and concise information; enhancing public understanding of modern farm and food industry methods with particular reference to the products and practices of member companies.
Meetings/Conventions: - annual conference

United Kingdom Association for European Law

King's College, Strand, London, WC2R 2LS, England, UK
Tel: 44 207 7229746
Fax: 44 207 7229746
Email: eva.evans@kcl.ac.uk
Founded: 1974
Members: 320
Staff: 1
Contact: Eva Evans, Admin.
Description: Promotes European law in the United Kingdom.
Meetings/Conventions: conference

United Kingdom Association of Professional Engineers

Hayes Court, West Common Rd., Bromley, BR2 7AU, England, UK
Tel: 44 20 84627755
Fax: 44 20 83158234
Email: info@ukape.org.uk
Website: http://www.ukape.org.uk
Founded: 1969
Members: 2000
Staff: 3
Contact: John Kearney, Natl.Pres.
Fee: £10
Membership Type: professional engineers
Description: Professional engineers who are chartered. Trade union established to promote the interests and status of engineers and the engineering industry. Upholds a code of conduct and maintains professional standards within the industry.
Publication: Newsletter

United Kingdom Automatic Control Council

c/o Institution of Electrical Engineers
Michael Faraday House, 6 Hills Way, Stevenage, SG1 2AY, England, UK
Tel: 44 1438 765632
Fax: 44 1438 767305
Email: ahardy@iee.org.uk
Website: http://www.shef.ac.uk/acse/ukacc/
Founded: 1957
Members: 3
Staff: 1
Contact: Miss S. Curwen
Fee: £700
Membership Type: corporate
Fee: £350
Membership Type: associate
Description: National member organisation of the International Federation of Automatic Control (IFAC). Seeks to act as an effective link between the UK and the international control communities, and to provide a focus for IFAC-related activities. Member institutions include: Institution of Electrical Engineers; Institute of Measurement

and Control; Institution of Mechanical Engineers; and the Royal Aeronautical Society.
Meetings/Conventions: workshop

United Kingdom Bartenders Guild
36 Granville Rd., Blackpool, FY1 3NP, England, UK
Tel: 44 1253 295534
Fax: 44 1253 295534
Email: ukbgmalc@aol.com
Founded: 1933
Members: 1000
Staff: 1
Contact: Malcolm Greenall
Description: Bartenders and hotel and trade representatives. Non sectarian, non political, non union association which is run by bartenders, for bartenders whose primary function is the advancement of the bartending profession.
Publication: Newsletter
Publication title: Bartender International. Advertisements.

United Kingdom Cast Stone Association
UKCSA
Century House, Telford Ave., Crowthorne, RG45 6YS, England, UK
Tel: 44 1604 405666
Fax: 44 1604 405666
Email: info@ukcsa.co.uk
Website: http://www.ukcsa.co.uk
Founded: 1990
Members: 51
Contact: Neil Sparrow, Sec.
Description: Trade association of UK companies manufacturing cast stone to the strict technical specification laid down by the UKCSA, and companies in trades associated with the cast stone industry, whose mission statement is to encourage excellence in the manufacture of cast stone by the members and to increase the awareness and usage of the product.
Publication: Newsletter
Publication title: The Tablet
Meetings/Conventions: - semiannual general assembly

United Kingdom Committee of International Water Association
UKCIWA
c/o R.G. Ainsworth
Lower Common House, The Avenue, Bucklebury, Berkshire, RG7 6NS, England, UK
Tel: 44 118 9712489
Email: r.ainsworth@btinternet.com
Founded: 1965
Members: 35
Contact: R.G. Ainsworth, Sec.
Fee: £450
Description: Representatives from government agencies and departments, universities and research organizations, manufacturers and suppliers of water treatment equipment, water service companies, and regulatory agencies. Promotes Water Association activities.
Formerly: UK National Committee of the International Association on Water Pollution Research and Control
Publication: Newsletter
Meetings/Conventions: - annual seminar

United Kingdom Council for Psychotherapy
167-169 Great Portland St., London, W1N 5PF, England, UK
Tel: 44 20 74363002
Fax: 44 20 74363013
Email: ukcp@psychotherapy.org.uk
Website: http://www.psychotherapy.org.uk
Founded: 1989
Members: 79
Staff: 6
Contact: James Pollard, Chair
Fee: £400
Membership Type: organisational
Description: Psychotherapy organisations. The protection of the public by the promotion of appropriate standards for training, research, education and the practice of psychotherapy and by the dissemination of information. The publication of a register of psychotherapists. Liaison with Government and the European Commission as necessary.
Publication: Directory
Publication title: Directory of Member Organisations
Publication title: National Register of Psychotherapists
Meetings/Conventions: - annual conference

United Kingdom Credit Insurance Brokers' Committee
Biiba House, 14 Bevis Marks, London, EC3A 7NT, England, UK
Tel: 44 20 76239043
Fax: 44 20 76269676
Founded: 1978
Members: 2000
Staff: 20
Contact: Geraldine Wright
Description: Insurance and investment brokers.

United Kingdom Dance and Drama Federation
UKDDF
c/o Gloria Harrison
18 Ashbourne Grove, Hanley, Stoke-On-Trent, ST1 5QW, England, UK
Tel: 44 1782 257820
Email: u.k.dance.drama.fed@cwctv.net
Website: http://www.dtol.ndirect.co.uk/ukddf.htm
Founded: 1989
Contact: Gloria Harrison, Pres.
Description: Offers dance performance and teacher training. Provides a full syllabus and medal awards system to qualified teachers.
Library Subject: ballet, tap, acrobatic, modern stage, drama
Library Type: reference
Publication: Newsletter

United Kingdom dBase Users Group
3 Marlborough Rise, Camberley, GU15 2ED, England, UK
Tel: 44 1276 691338
Fax: 44 1276 691338
Founded: 1983
Members: 130
Contact: Dr. Marshall
Description: Software developers using dBase for Windows or dBase for DOS. Concerned with the exchange of information and ideas through seminars and a newsletter.
Publication: Newsletter
Publication title: Newsletter dBug

United Kingdom Education and Research Networking Association
UKERNA

Atlas Centre, Chilton, Didcot, OX11 0QS, England, UK
Tel: 44 1235 822200
Fax: 44 1235 822399
Website: http://www.ukerna.ac.uk/
Description: Committed to research, development and provision of advanced electronic communication facilities for community and industry, thus facilitating the extension of many classes of trade through community links with industry.

United Kingdom Egg Producers Association
UKEP

Kings House, Maunsel Rd., North Newton, Bridgwater, Somerset, TA7 0BP, England, UK
Tel: 44 1278 661280
Fax: 44 1278 661009
Email: chicken-doctor@demon.co.uk
Founded: 1972
Contact: David Spackman, Sec.
Description: Independent egg producers. Acts as a pressure group to protect the interests of all independent egg producers.
Publication: Newsletter
Publication title: UKEPRA News. Advertisements.

United Kingdom Environmental Law Association

Honeycroft House, Pangbourne Rd., Upper Basildon, Berkshire, RG8 8LP, England, UK
Tel: 44 1491 671184
Fax: 44 1491 671631
Email: cbth_ukela@yahoo.co.uk
Website: http://www.ukela.org
Founded: 1987
Members: 1000
Staff: 1
Contact: Dr. Christina Hill
Fee: £85
Membership Type: corporate
Fee: £35
Membership Type: individual
Description: Barristers, advocates, writers to the signet, solicitors, legal executives and academic lawyers, industry and environmental consultants and those interested in the development and practice of UK and EU environmental law. Aims to promote the enhancement and conservation of the environment and to advance the education of the public in all matters relating to the development, teaching, application and practice of law relating to the environment; encourage collaboration between those interested and concerned with environmental law.
Formerly: Environmental Law Association
Publication title: Environmental Law. Advertisements.
Meetings/Conventions: - annual conference - Exhibits.

United Kingdom Environmental Mutagen Society
UKEMS

c/o Dr. Anthony Lynch
GlaxoSmithKline R&D, Park Road, Ware, SG12 0DP, England, UK
Tel: 44 1920 883745
Fax: 44 1920 882679
Email: anthony_m_lynch@gsk.com
Website: http://www.swan.ac.uk/cget/newuk1.htm

Founded: 1977
Members: 250
Contact: Anthony Lynch, Treas./Membership Sec.
Fee: £20
Membership Type: full
Description: Section of the European Environmental Mutagen Society (see separate entry). Individuals working in or interested in environmental mutagenesis. Promotes research and education in environmental mutagenesis. Offers professional training; sponsors workshops.
Publication: Newsletter
Publication title: Mutagenesis. Advertisements.
Second publication: Newsletter
Publication title: Newsletter
Meetings/Conventions: - annual conference - Exhibits.

United Kingdom Forum for Organisational Health

43 Pemberton Rd., East Molesey, KT8 9LG, England, UK
Tel: 44 208 9793344
Fax: 44 171 2220211
Email: m@manolias.freeserve.co.uk
Founded: 1965
Members: 60
Contact: Mrs. M. Manolias
Fee: £40
Description: Professionals who share a common interest in the healthy development of organisations and includes occupational health physicians and nurses, researchers, counsellors, personnel managers, general managers and occupational psychologists. Concerned with the development and maintenance of the psychosocial health of organisations and of the individual within the workplace. Believes that people are the most critical resource in any organisation, supports humanisation of the the workplace and recognition of ways in which individual creativity and growth contribute to organisational effectiveness.
Publication: Newsletter
Meetings/Conventions: - monthly meeting

United Kingdom Home Care Association

42B Banstead Rd., Carshalton Beeches, SM5 3NW, England, UK
Tel: 44 20 82881551
Fax: 44 20 82881550
Email: enquiries@ukhca.co.uk
Website: http://www.ukhca.co.uk
Founded: 1988
Members: 1300
Staff: 10
Contact: Lucianne Sawyer, Exec.Com.Pres.
Fee: £310
Description: Represents independent home care organizations providing home care and nursing care to people in their own homes. Identifies and promotes the highest standards of home care.
Library Subject: home care
Library Type: not open to the public
Publication: Handbook
Publication title: Home Care Workers Handbook
Second publication: Newsletter
Publication title: The Homecarer
Meetings/Conventions: conference

United Kingdom Housekeepers Association

Flat 7, 14-15 Molyneux St., London, W1H 5HU, England, UK
Fax: 44 207 7247378
Email: marc@ukha.co.uk

Website: http://www.ukha.co.uk
Founded: 1985
Members: 800
Contact: Mrs. Lynn K.D. Yambao
Fee: £30
Membership Type: full
Fee: £75
Membership Type: associate
Description: Head housekeepers, domestic services managers or their equivalent and their deputies. Lecturers in housekeeping and domestic services and those linked with the housekeeping aspect of further or higher education. Associate and student membership is also available. Aims to improve the professional status of housekeepers, to promote housekeeping as a career and to provide a forum for the exchange of information and ideas.
Publication: Magazine
Publication title: Housekeeping Today
Meetings/Conventions: - annual conference - Exhibits. London UK

United Kingdom Industrial Space Committee

c/o Secretariat
PO Box 14, Wisbech, PE13 1JZ, England, UK
Tel: 44 1945 464975
Fax: 44 1945 461988
Email: hicks.ukisc@btinternet.com
Website: http://www.ukspace.com
Founded: 1975
Members: 40
Staff: 3
Contact: Alan Hicks
Description: The British space industry and employees. As the trade association of the British space industry, UKISC represents over three-quarters of the total turnover (1.2m) and employees (6000) of the industry. It represents the collective interests of members in increasing space and space-related business, and their share of the market, in accordance with the constitutions of its sponsor-associations SBAC and FEI.
Publication: Brochure
Second publication: Papers
Meetings/Conventions: - bimonthly meeting

United Kingdom Industrial Vision Association

53-57 High St., Kingston Upon Thames, KT1 1LQ, England, UK
Tel: 44 20 85477153
Fax: 44 1763 261961
Email: info@ukiva.org
Website: http://www.ukiva.org
Founded: 1992
Members: 60
Staff: 2
Contact: Don Braggins, Dir.
Fee: £650
Membership Type: member
Description: Suppliers of industrial vision systems. Seeks to promote the use of vision technology by manufacturers in the United Kingdom. Encourages information exchange among members. Works to enhance international marketing efforts.
Publication: Brochure
Publication title: Guide to Machine Vision
Second publication: Membership Directory
Meetings/Conventions: - annual conference - Exhibits.

United Kingdom Institute for Conservation of Historic and Artistic Works

109 The Chandlery, 50 Westminster Bridge Rd., London, SE1 7QY, England, UK
Tel: 44 20 77218721
Fax: 44 20 77218722
Email: iukic@ukic.org.uk
Website: http://www.ukic.org.uk/
Founded: 1979
Members: 1600
Staff: 4
Contact: Mrs. D. Copley, Office Admin.
Description: Professional conservators and restorers who are engaged in practical conservation or whose main occupation is concerned with conservation (e.g. lecturers, managers, conservation scientists). Seeks to promote the highest standards of conservation by encouraging education, study and research in any relevant branches of practice or science and supporting efforts to increase proficiency. Assists in the dissemination of technical and professional information relating to the field of conservation.
Publication title: Conservation News. Advertisements.
Publication title: The Conservator

United Kingdom Jute Goods Association

33 Haynes Park Ct., Slewins Close, Hornchurch, RM11 2DE, England, UK
Tel: 44 1708 453000
Fax: 44 1708 453010
Founded: 1909
Members: 45
Staff: 1
Contact: P.W. Rosamond, Gen.Sec.
Description: Those engaged in the jute goods trade on their own behalf or as members of a firm or as directors or employees. Aims to promote, support and protect the interests of the trade in jute goods, both new and second hand. Regulates the conduct of such trade and promotes fair and honourable practices.

United Kingdom Maritime Pilots' Association

Transport House, 128 Theobald's Rd., London, WC1X 8TH, England, UK
Tel: 44 20 76112571
Fax: 44 20 76112745
Email: ukmpa@tqwu.org.uk
Website: http://www.ukmpa.org
Founded: 1884
Members: 520
Staff: 1
Contact: Davina Connor, Sec.
Description: Marine pilots (maritime navigation). Active in all relevant matters to promote the profession and the welfare of its members.
Formerly: UK Pilots Association
Publication: Magazine
Publication title: The Pilot. Advertisements.
Meetings/Conventions: - annual conference - Exhibits. Liverpool UK

United Kingdom Offshore Operators' Association

2nd Fl., 232-242 Vauxhall Bridge Rd., London, SW1V 1AU, England, UK
Tel: 44 207 8022400
Fax: 44 207 8022401
Email: info@ukooa.co.uk
Website: http://www.oilandgas.org.uk/ukooa
Contact: James May, Dir.Gen.

Description: Offshore operators in the United Kingdom.

United Kingdom Online User Group
UKOLUG

The Old Chapel, Walden, West Burton, Leyburn, DL8 4LE, England, UK
Tel: 44 1969 663749
Fax: 44 1969 663749
Email: cabaker@ukolug.org.uk
Website: http://www.ukolug.org.uk
Founded: 1978
Members: 1100
Contact: Christine A. Baker, Admin.
Fee: £20
Membership Type: Personal
Fee: £90
Membership Type: Institutional
Description: Promotes familiarity with all aspects of online information retrieval including international online information systems, CD-ROMs and Internet resources.
Publication: Newsletter
Publication title: UKOLOG Newsletter. Advertisements.
Meetings/Conventions: - biennial conference

United Kingdom Onshore Operators Group
UKOOG

63 Duke St., London, W1K 5NS, England, UK
Tel: 44 20 76295709
Fax: 44 20 73553704
Email: ukoog@oilmanuk.com
Founded: 1986
Members: 10
Staff: 5
Contact: H.M. Boyd, Sec.
Fee: £15
Description: Licensed under UK landward to explore for and produce oil and natural gas including coalbed methane. Provides a forum in which representatives of the oil industry discuss matters relating to the exploration and drill of oil and natural gas, including natural gas in coal seams. Represents the interest of the UK onshore oil and gas industry in negotiations with the Government and other national and international authorities and organizations.
Library Subject: U.K. onshore oil and gas
Library Type: not open to the public
Publication title: UKOOG Guide to Legislation
Second publication: Handbook
Publication title: UKOOG Well Contingency
Meetings/Conventions: - quarterly

United Kingdom Petroleum Industry Association

9 Kingsway, London, WC2B 6XF, England, UK
Tel: 44 207 2400289
Fax: 44 207 3793102
Email: info@ukpia.com
Website: http://www.ukpia.com
Founded: 1978
Members: 9
Staff: 5
Contact: Malcolm Webb, Dir.Gen.
Description: Major oil supply companies with refining interests in the UK or Europe. Trade Association representing the supply, refining and distribution (downstream) sectors of the oil industry, in communication with government, industrial and commercial associations, the media and the public.
Publication: Newsletter
Publication title: Ukpia News

United Kingdom Reading Association

Unit 6, 1st Fl., The Maltings, Green Drift, Royston, SG8 5DB, England, UK
Tel: 44 1763 241188
Fax: 44 1763 243785
Email: admin@ukra.org
Website: http://www.ukra.org
Founded: 1963
Members: 764
Staff: 2
Contact: Lyn Overall, Gen.Sec.
Fee: £28
Membership Type: individual, U.K.
Fee: £36
Membership Type: school, U.K.
Description: Open to all interested in teaching of reading and language. Members are mainly teachers and teacher-educators/researchers. Covering the promotion and use of reading, language and communication.
Publication: Papers
Publication title: Journal of Research in Reading
Second publication: Papers
Publication title: Language and Literary News
Meetings/Conventions: - annual conference - Exhibits. Cambridge UK

United Kingdom Science Park Association
UKSPA

Aston Science Park, Love Ln., Birmingham, B7 4BJ, England, UK
Tel: 44 121 2503500
Fax: 44 121 3335852
Email: admin.ukspa@btconnect.com
Website: http://www.ukspa.org.uk/
Founded: 1984
Members: 63
Staff: 3
Contact: Paul Wright, Ch.Exec.
Description: Committed to supporting and encouraging the startup, incubation and development of innovation led, high growth, knowledge-based businesses. Provides opportunity for larger and international businesses to develop specific and close interactions with a particular centre of knowledge creation for mutual benefit.

United Kingdom Society for Trenchless Technology

PO Box 88, Department of Civil and Construction Engineering, Sackville St., Manchester, M60 1QD, England, UK
Tel: 44 1612004608
Fax: 44 1612004608
Email: ukstt@umist.ac.uk
Founded: 1993
Members: 312
Staff: 2
Contact: Ian Vickridge
Fee: £35
Membership Type: corporate
Description: Promotes the use of trenchless technology for utilities. Conducts research; disseminates information.

Library Subject: trenchless technology, utilities
Library Type: by appointment only
Meetings/Conventions: - annual dinner

United Kingdom Spring Manufacturers Association
Henry St., Sheffield, S3 7EQ, England, UK
Founded: 1997
Members: 100
Staff: 2
Contact: Mr. A. Hooper, Chief Exec.
Description: Trade association for manufacturers of springs in England. Represents members' interests.
Publication: Newsletter

United Kingdom Tea Association
UKTA
6 Catherine St., London, WC2B 5JJ, England, UK
Tel: 44 20 74207113
Fax: 44 20 78360580
Email: ddemenezes@fdf.org.uk
Members: 40
Contact: David de Menezes, Sec.
Description: Coordinates the tea industry in the United Kingdom.

United Kingdom Vineyards Association
Church Rd., Bruisyard, Saxmundham, IP17 2EF, England, UK
Tel: 44 1728 638080
Fax: 44 1728 638442
Founded: 1967
Members: 400
Staff: 1
Contact: I.H. Berwick, Gen.Sec.
Description: Membership is through 5 affiliated regional associations. Maintains close contacts with various government departments and other national and European bodies. It is the principal focus for media contact on matters concerning the industry and provides an information service to the public, students and the wine trade and press. Promotes quality English and Welsh wine.
Formerly: English Vineyards Association
Publication title: The Grape Press

United Kingdom Warehousing Association
UKWA
Walter House, 418-422 Strand, London, WC2R 0PT, England, UK
Tel: 44 20 78365522
Fax: 44 20 73796904
Email: dg@ukwa.org.uk
Website: http://www.ukwa.org.uk
Founded: 1944
Members: 650
Staff: 5
Contact: Mr. R.J. Williams, Dir.Gen.
Fee: £300
Membership Type: associate & corporate
Description: Companies providing public warehousing facilities for their customers. Represents member companies who, between them, operate around 800 million square feet of public warehousing space throughout the U.K. It aims to promote high quality storage conditions and a high level of customer service within the sector, to represent the view of its members to Government departments, trade and official organizations.
Publication: Membership Directory

Publication title: UKWA Directory of Members' Services. Advertisements.
Second publication: Newsletter
Publication title: Warehouse
Meetings/Conventions: - annual conference

United Kingdom Weighing Federation
Brooke House, 4 The Lakes, Bedford Rd., Northampton, NN4 7YD, England, UK
Tel: 44 1604 622023
Fax: 44 1604 631252
Email: ukwf@brookehouse.co.uk
Website: http://ukwf.org.uk
Members: 100
Contact: Mrs. D. Webb, Gen.Sec.
Description: Manufacturers, distributors, service/repair companies, systems and component suppliers. Legal metrology; miscellaneous membership services covering commercial and import activities.
Publication: Newsletter
Publication title: Weighlog
Meetings/Conventions: - annual conference

United Kingdom-Ireland Controlled Release Society
UKICRS
c/o Dr. Rupi Pannu
AstraZeneca R&D Charnwood, Bakewell Rd., Loughborough, LE11 5RH, England, UK
Tel: 44 1509 645019
Fax: 44 1509 645546
Email: rupi.pannu@astrazeneca.com
Website: http://www.pharmweb.net/pwmirror/pw9/ukcrs/pharm-web91.html
Founded: 1998
Contact: Dr. Rupi Pannu
Description: Dedicated to the advancement of the science and technology controlling the release and delivery of active agents. Research focuses on controlled release encompassing agriculture, veterinary, food, and cosmetic sciences.
Meetings/Conventions: meeting

United Nations Association of Great Britain and Northern Ireland
UNA-UK
3 Whitehall Ct., London, SW1A 2EL, England, UK
Tel: 44 207 9302931
Fax: 44 207 9305893
Email: info@una-uk.org
Website: http://www.una-uk.org
Founded: 1945
Members: 7000
Staff: 18
Contact: Malcolm Harper
Fee: £5
Membership Type: individual
Fee: £20
Membership Type: corporate
Description: Interested individuals, nationwide network of branches. Seeks to strengthen the role of the United Nations in global affairs through international cooperation. Acts as a forum for discussion of nonviolent conflict resolution, human rights, environment and development. Conducts educational and charitable programs. Maintains a speakers' bureau.
Library Type: reference

Publication: Newsletter
Publication title: New World. Advertisements.
Meetings/Conventions: - annual conference

United Road Transport Union
URTU

76 High Ln., Chorlton, Manchester, M21 9EF, England, UK
Fax: 44 161 8610976
Email: info@urtu.com
Website: http://www.urtu.com
Founded: 1890
Members: 16874
Staff: 30
Contact: Robert Monks
Description: Road haulage and distribution.
Publication: Magazine
Publication title: Wheels. Advertisements.

Universities Association for Continuing Education

c/o University of Cambridge
Board of Continuing Education, Madingley Hall, Madingley,
Cambridge, CB3 8AQ, England, UK
Tel: 44 1954 280279
Fax: 44 1954 280200
Email: mer1000@cam.ac.uk
Website: http://www.uace.org.uk
Founded: 1947
Members: 240
Staff: 2
Contact: Dr. Michael Richardson, Sec.
Fee: £500
Membership Type: institutional
Description: Open to all UK universities and higher education institutions with international membership for overseas universities and associate membership for professional bodies. Provides a forum for the interchange of information on university continuing education and lifelong learning. Its Council promotes all aspect of university continuing education. It encourages and conducts research on this subject and facilitates the dissemination of results to the general public and interested organisations.
Publication: Papers
Publication title: Conference
Publication title: Education Document
Meetings/Conventions: - annual conference

Universities Council for the Education of Teachers

58 Gordon Sq., London, WC1H 0NT, England, UK
Tel: 44 207 5808000
Fax: 44 207 3230577
Email: m.russell@ioe.ac.uk
Website: http://www.ucet.ac.uk
Founded: 1967
Members: 92
Staff: 5
Contact: Mary Russell
Description: All universities and university-sector colleges in the UK involved in the education of teachers. Acts as a national forum for the discussion of all matters relating to education of teachers and the study of education in universities. It contributes to the formulation of policy in these fields and makes representations to and collaborates with other groups in the UK with similar interests.
Library Type: open to the public
Publication title: University Courses in Education Open to Students

from Overseas
Second publication: Annual Report
Meetings/Conventions: - annual conference - Exhibits.

Universities Federation for Animal Welfare
UFAW

The Old School, Brewhouse Hill, Wheathampstead, St. Albans, AL4 8AN, England, UK
Tel: 44 1582 831818
Fax: 44 1582 831414
Email: scioff@ufaw.org.uk
Website: http://www.ufaw.org.uk
Founded: 1926
Members: 2500
Staff: 10
Contact: Mr. D. Davidson
Description: Individuals united to promote the humane treatment and handling of animals in the United Kingdom and internationally. Seeks to: improve the well-being of all animals; reduce the infliction of pain or duress on animals; ensure that when animals are killed, they are killed humanely. Promotes animal welfare as a scientific value. Provides advice on animal management and care methods. Evaluates British legislation on the treatment of animals. Conducts research; organizes lectures.
Library Type: reference
Publication: Journal
Publication title: Animal Welfare. Advertisements.
Second publication: Newsletter
Publication title: Newsletter
Meetings/Conventions: - periodic symposium

Universities U.K.

Woburn House, 20 Tavistock Square, London, WC1H 9HQ, England, UK
Tel: 44 20 74194111
Fax: 44 20 73888649
Email: info@universitiesuk.ac.uk
Website: http://www.universitiesuk.ac.uk
Founded: 1918
Members: 120
Staff: 50
Contact: Diana Warwick, Chief Exec.
Description: Members are executive heads of all the universities in the UK. Promotes, encourages and develops the university sector of higher education in the United Kingdom.
Library Subject: higher education, legislation, government, parliamentary and universities
Library Type: by appointment only
Formerly: Committee for Vice-Chancellors and Principals
Publication: Newsletter
Publication title: CVCP News

University and College Lecturers' Union
NATFHE

27 Britannia St., London, WC1X 9JP, England, UK
Tel: 44 171 8373636
Fax: 44 171 8374403
Email: hq@natfne.org.uk
Website: http://www.natfhe.org.uk
Founded: 1976
Members: 66000

Staff: 100
Contact: Paula Lanning
Description: Lecturers, tutors and research assistants in England, Wales and Northern Ireland working in colleges of further education, in universities and higher education institutes; agricultural education, adult education centers and penal education. establishments. Works for top quality post-school education and training. The expansion of educational opportunities is a key priority. Influences national education policy making, provides support for members in their professional development, and works for decent pay and conditions for staff.
Publication: Journal
Publication title: The Journal of Further and Higher Education
Publication title: The Lecturer
Meetings/Conventions: - annual conference - Exhibits.

University Association for Contemporary European Studies
UACES

King's College, Strand, London, WC2R 2LS, England, UK
Tel: 44 20 72400206
Fax: 44 20 78362350
Email: admin@uaces.org
Website: http://www.uaces.org/
Founded: 1970
Members: 850
Contact: Susan Jones, Exec.Dir.
Fee: £25
Membership Type: individual
Fee: £10
Membership Type: associate (student)
Description: Provides a forum for debate and a clearing house for information about European affairs. Directly involved in promoting research and establishing teaching and research networks. Brings together academics involved in researching and teaching on Europe with practitioners active in European affairs. Encourages people from all disciplines to become involved.
Publication: Journal
Publication title: Journal of Common Market Studies
Second publication: Newsletter
Publication title: UACES News
Meetings/Conventions: - periodic conference

Urania Trust

12 Warrington Spur, Old Windsor, Slough, SL4 2NF, England, UK
Tel: 44 17 53851107
Fax: 44 171 7006479
Email: uraniatrust@ntlworld.com
Website: http://www.uraniatrust.org
Founded: 1971
Members: 2000
Staff: 16
Contact: Dawn Roffe, Admin.
Fee: £8
Membership Type: ordinary
Fee: £14
Membership Type: postal
Description: Anyone interested in man's relationship with the cosmos. An educational charity sponsoring any activities which explore man's relationship with the cosmos eg philosophy, astrology, astronomy etc.
Library Subject: astrology and related arts, astronomy
Library Type: open to the public

Publication title: Guide to Astrology in Europe and the UK. Advertisements.
Publication title: Yearbook of Worldwide Astrology
Meetings/Conventions: - weekly lecture London UK

Urostomy Association of Great Britain and Ireland

c/o Angela Cooke
Buckland, Beaumont Park, Dunbar, CM3 4DE, England, UK
Tel: 44 1245 224294
Fax: 44 1245 227569
Email: ua@centraloffice.fsnet.co.uk
Website: http://www.uagbi.org/
Founded: 1971
Contact: Angela Cooke, Natl.Sec.
Description: Works to assist people who will undergo or have undergone surgery which results in a urinary diversion; assists caregivers in the rehabilitation process for the ostomate; improve quality of life for urostomates and their caregivers; undertakes research to enhance life for members.

Variety and Light Entertainments Council of Great Britain

56 Keynes House, Dolphin Sq., London, SW1V 3NA, England, UK
Tel: 44 207 8340515
Fax: 44 207 8210261
Email: info@equity.org.uk
Contact: Christine Payne
Description: Covering performers, managers and agents in the light, live entertainments business.

Vegan Society - England
VS

7 Battle Rd., St. Leonards-on-Sea, TN37 7AA, England, UK
Tel: 44 1424 427393
Fax: 44 1424 717064
Email: info@vegansociety.com
Website: http://www.vegansociety.com
Founded: 1944
Members: 4000
Staff: 7
Contact: Catriona Toms, Info.Off.
Fee: £21
Membership Type: individual
Description: Educational charity providing information on all aspects of veganism, which is a way of living which seeks to exclude, as far as possible, all forms of exploitation of, and cruelty to animals for food, clothing, or any other purpose. Promotes animal-free living for the benefit of people, animals and the environment. Provides information to the media, health care professionals, schools, caterers and the public.
Library Subject: vegan/vegetarian food, cooking, nutrition, ethics, animal rights, environment, medicine
Library Type: open to the public
Publication: Book
Publication title: The Animal-Free Shopper. Advertisements.
Second publication: Journal
Publication title: The Vegan. Advertisements.
Meetings/Conventions: - annual meeting - Exhibits.

Vegetarian Society of the United Kingdom

Parkdale, Dunham Rd., Altrincham, WA14 4QG, England, UK
Tel: 44 161 9252000
Fax: 44 161 9269182

Email: info@vegsoc.org
Website: http://www.vegsoc.org
Founded: 1846
Members: 22000
Staff: 25
Contact: Tina Fox, Chief Exec.
Fee: £21
Membership Type: adult
Fee: £16
Membership Type: underaged
Description: Aims to increase vegetarianism in order to save animals, benefit human health and protect the environment and world food resources. Runs a cookery school, sells books, information sheets, teachers materials and has leaflets available free of charge.
Library Subject: vegetarianism
Library Type: by appointment only
Publication title: The Vegetarian
Meetings/Conventions: National Vegetarian Week - annual

Vehicle Builders and Repairers Association
VBRA

Belmont House, 102 Finkle Ln., Gildersome, Leeds, LS27 7TW, England, UK
Tel: 44 113 2538333
Fax: 44 113 2530496
Email: vbra@vbra.co.uk
Website: http://www.vbra.co.uk
Founded: 1914
Members: 1200
Staff: 19
Contact: Ron Nicholson, Dir.Gen.
Description: Car body accident repair centres and commercial vehicle bodybuilders in the United Kingdom. Promotes members' interests.
Publication: Directory
Publication title: Industry Yearbook. Advertisements.
Meetings/Conventions: Business Forum - annual

Veterinary Association for Arbitration and Jurisprudence
VAAJ

c/o John Penfold
Hunters Spinney, Stow-on-the-Wold, Gloucester, GL54 1LD, England, UK
Tel: 44 1451 831567
Fax: 44 1451 831545
Email: vaaj@aol.com
Website: http://www.vaaj.co.uk
Founded: 1994
Members: 100
Contact: John Penfold, Sec.
Fee: £25
Membership Type: individual
Description: Veterinary surgeons, students, and lawyers. Aims to promote and assist dispute resolution by all means. Offers training in all aspects of dispute resolution.

Veterinary History Society

c/o The Royal Veterinary College
Royal College St., London, NW1 0TU, England, UK
Website: http://www.rvc.ac.uk/Guests/VetHistSoc/vhs.htm
Founded: 1962

Contact: John Clewlow, Editor
Description: Veterinarians and other interested individuals. Fosters all aspects of veterinary history.
Publication: Journal
Publication title: Veterinary History
Meetings/Conventions: - quarterly meeting

Victim Support

c/o Cranmer House
39 Brixton Rd., London, SW9 6DZ, England, UK
Tel: 44 20 77359166
Fax: 44 20 75825712
Email: contact@victimsupport.org.uk
Website: http://www.victimsupport.com
Founded: 1979
Members: 300
Staff: 1014
Contact: Dame Helen Reeves, Chf.Exec.
Description: All affiliated member schemes must adhere to the nationally agreed Code of Practice. Trained volunteers offer information, practical help and emotional support to victims of crime ranging from burglary to the murder of a relative. Service offered by home visit, or by the Witness Service at Crown Court centers and in a growing number of magistrates' courts. Aims to raise awareness of the effects of crime and the rights of victims.
Library Subject: victim's issues
Library Type: not open to the public
Formerly: National Association of Victims Support Schemes
Publication: Magazine
Publication title: Victim Support
Second publication: Pamphlets
Meetings/Conventions: - periodic conference

Victoria League for Commonwealth Friendship

55 Leinster Sq., London, W2 4PW, England, UK
Tel: 44 207 2432633
Fax: 44 207 2292994
Founded: 1901
Members: 300
Staff: 5
Contact: J.M.W. Allan, Gen.Sec.
Description: Individuals and organizations. Promotes good fellowship among the peoples of the British Commonwealth. Conducts educational, cultural, and exchange programs.
Publication: Newsletter
Publication title: The Victorial League Newsletter
Meetings/Conventions: - annual general assembly

Victorian Military Society
VMS

PO Box 58377, Newbury, RG14 7FJ, England, UK
Tel: 44 1483 856080
Email: ry003e5671@blueyonder.co.uk
Website: http://www.vms.org.uk
Founded: 1974
Members: 1000
Contact: Ralph Moore-Morris, Hon.Sec.
Fee: £17
Membership Type: individual and some museums
Description: Military historians, and enthusiasts; military museums and organizations. Aims to foster interest in the military history of the Victorian period, emphasizing the armies of the British Empire

between 1837 and 1914. Conducts historical research. Sponsors competitions and special publications.
Publication: Journal
Publication title: Soldiers of the Queen. Advertisements.
Publication title: Soldiers Small Book
Meetings/Conventions: - annual meeting - Exhibits.

Victorian Society

1 Priory Gardens, Bedford Park, London, W4 1TT, England, UK
Email: admin@victorian-society.org.uk
Website: http://www.victorian-Society.org.uk
Founded: 1958
Members: 3500
Staff: 6
Contact: R. Seedhouse
Description: Prevents the needless demolition of Victorian and Edwardian buildings of architectural interest; promotes public understanding and appreciation of the architecture and decorative arts of the period.
Publication: Magazine
Publication title: The Victorian. Advertisements.
Meetings/Conventions: - weekly meeting

Viking Society for Northern Research

Department of Scandinavian Studies, Gower St., University Coll. London, London, WC1E 6BT, England, UK
Tel: 44 20 76797176
Fax: 44 20 76797755
Email: s.rust@ucl.ac.uk
Website: http://www.nott.ac.uk/~aezjj/homepage.html
Founded: 1892
Members: 650
Contact: Prof. M.P. Barnes, Exec. Officer
Fee: £15
Description: Individuals and libraries of institutions in 23 countries. Promotes interest in the literature and antiquities of the Scandinavian North. Gives lectures; conducts seminars. Sponsors book auctions.
Library Type: reference
Formerly: Viking Club
Publication title: Dorothea Coke Memorial Lectures
Publication title: The Saga-Book
Meetings/Conventions: - periodic symposium

Vinegar Brewers' Federation

Castle House, Ste. 13, 25, Castlereagh St., London, W1H 5YR, England, UK
Tel: 44 171 7232083
Fax: 44 171 7245055
Members: 6
Contact: Walter J. Anzer, Sec.
Description: Vinegar Brewers. Protects the interests of the vinegar brewing industry.

Viola d'Amore Society of Great Britain
VDS

4 Constable Rd., Felixstone, IP11 7HH, England, UK
Tel: 44 1923 290339
Founded: 1965
Members: 30
Staff: 3
Contact: Ian White, Dir.

Description: Aim is to foster interest in the viola d'amore and its music. Supports contemporary composers. Sponsors concerts and publications of viola d'amore music.
Library Subject: Viola d'Amore music, history
Library Type: not open to the public
Publication: Newsletter
Publication title: Newsletter
Second publication: Books
Publication title: 60 Editions of 18th Century Viola d'Amore Music
Meetings/Conventions: Concerts show - Exhibits.

Violet Needham Society

c/o Mr. Richard H A Cheffins
19 Ashburnham Place, London, SE10 8TZ, England, UK
Tel: 44 2086924562
Founded: 1985
Members: 260
Contact: Hilary Clare, Chm.
Fee: £8
Membership Type: personal, U.K. & Europe
Fee: £8
Membership Type: corporate, U.K. & Europe
Description: Aims to foster appreciation of the works of Violet Needham, of other children's authors of that period (the 1940's to 50's) and of Ruritanian fiction.
Library Subject: works by or about Violet Needham
Library Type: lending
Publication: Journal
Publication title: Souvenir
Meetings/Conventions: - periodic conference Forest Row UK

Violet Society

PO Box 18, Market Drayton, TF9 2WD, England, UK
Email: violetsociety@sweetviolets.com
Website: http://www.sweetviolets.com
Description: Individuals interested in the Violets. Disseminates information on the Violet genus.

Virgil Society
VS

1 Lancaster Ave., West Norwood, London, SE27 9EL, England, UK
Tel: 44 208 7615615
Founded: 1943
Members: 200
Contact: M.M. Willcock, Exec.Off.
Fee: £10
Description: Individuals and institutions in 7 countries united for the promotion and study of literature written by the Roman poet Virgil (70-19 B.C.).
Publication: Journal
Meetings/Conventions: - quarterly lecture

Visit Britain
BTA

Thames Tower, Black's Rd., London, W6 9EL, England, UK
Tel: 44 20 88469000
Fax: 44 20 84630302
Email: tradehelpdesk@bta.org.uk
Website: http://www.britishtouristauthority.org
Founded: 1969
Staff: 450
Contact: Vaughan James, Hd., Mkt. & Trade Rel.

Description: Promotes the value of inbound tourism to Britain to generate additional tourism revenue throughout Britain. Provides impartial tourism information and gathers essential market intelligence for the UK tourism industry.
Publication: Newsletter
Publication title: Inbound
Meetings/Conventions: World Travel Market - annual trade show - Exhibits.

Vitreous Enamel Services
VEA

c/o C. Taylor, Sec.Gen.
12 Wharton St., Sherdley Road Industrial Estate, St. Helens, WA9 5AA, England, UK
Tel: 44 1744 737274
Fax: 44 1744 739404
Email: enquiries@vitreous-enamel.com
Website: http://www.vitreous-enamel.com
Contact: C. Taylor, Sec.Gen.
Description: Companies in the vitreous enamel and allied industries. Promote the use of vitreous enamel in all its many uses. Works closely with the IVE, the professional institute of the industry.

Voice of the Listener and Viewer

101 King's Dr., Gravesend, DA12 5BQ, England, UK
Tel: 44 1474 352835
Fax: 44 1474 351112
Email: vlv@btinternet.com
Website: http://www.vlv.org.uk
Founded: 1984
Members: 2520
Staff: 6
Contact: Jocelyn Hay, Hon.Chm.
Fee: £17.5
Membership Type: individual in the United Kingdom
Fee: £57.5
Membership Type: individual outside the United Kingdom
Description: Individuals united to support public service broadcasting in the United Kingdom. Seeks to ensure the maintenance of high standards, independence, and diversity of broadcasting. Offers educational trust program; conducts research programs. Maintains speakers' bureau. Provides a forum for communication and exchange among those interested in broadcasting.
Library Subject: Broadcasting issues.
Library Type: reference
Formerly: Voice of the Listener
Publication: Newsletter
Publication title: Newsletter. Advertisements.
Meetings/Conventions: - semiannual conference - Exhibits.

Voluntary Euthanasia Society
VES

13 Prince of Wales Ter., London, W8 5PG, England, UK
Tel: 44 20 79378721
Fax: 44 20 73762648
Email: info@ves.org.uk
Website: http://www.ves.org.uk/
Founded: 1935
Contact:
Fee: £15
Membership Type: single
Fee: £22
Membership Type: joint (two people at same address)

Description: Doctors, lawyers and clergymen dedicated to legalizing euthanasia for competent adults suffering from terminal illnesses wanting to die.

Voluntary Service Overseas - England
VSO

317 Putney Bridge Rd., London, SW15 2PN, England, UK
Tel: 44 208 7807200
Fax: 44 208 7807300
Email: enquiry@vso.org.uk
Website: http://www.vso.org.uk/
Founded: 1958
Members: 40000
Staff: 298
Contact: David Green, Dir.
Description: Volunteers working in over 59 countries in Africa, Asia, the Caribbean, and the Pacific. Recruits volunteers for assignments where they assist in the development and increased self-sufficiency of the poor. Operates educational programs on health and nutrition, conservation of natural resources, and operation of small business. Seeks, through the development of human skills, to bring about international understanding and a more equal distribution of the world's resources.
Publication title: Orbit
Second publication: Report
Meetings/Conventions: - annual meeting

Volunteer Service Overseas - United Kingdom
VSOUK

317 Putney Bridge Rd., Putney, London, SW15 2PN, England, UK
Tel: 44 20 87807200
Fax: 44 20 87807300
Email: enquiry@vso.org.uk
Website: http://www.vso.org.uk
Founded: 1958
Members: 1700
Contact: Rachel Bartlett
Description: International development agency that works through volunteers in 74 countries worldwide. Enables people aged 17-70 to share their skills and expertise with communities and organizations across the developing world. Aims to make a difference in tackling disadvantage by helping people realize their potential.
Publication: Magazine
Publication title: Orbit

Vulval Pain Society

PO Box 514, Slough, SL1 2BP, England, UK
Website: http://www.vul-pain.dircon.co.uk
Founded: 1996
Members: 500
Staff: 3
Contact: David Nunns
Fee: £10
Description: Provides information and support to women who suffer from Vulval pain and discomfort.
Library Type: not open to the public
Meetings/Conventions: meeting

Wallcovering Manufacturers Association of Great Britain

James House, Bridge St., Leatherhead, KT22 7EP, England, UK
Tel: 44 1372 360660
Fax: 44 1372 376069
Email: alison.brown@bcf.co.uk
Founded: 1965
Members: 35
Staff: 2
Contact: Mrs. A. Brown
Fee: £3000
Membership Type: full (manufactures)
Fee: £375
Membership Type: associate (suppliers)
Description: Trade Association for UK manufacturers and suppliers. Promotes the interests of the wall covering manufacturing industry. Provides a forum for discussion on environmental, technical, and commercial issues.
Meetings/Conventions: meeting

Walmsley Society

c/o Mr. Fred W Lane
April Cottage, 1 Brand Rd., Hampden Park, Eastbourne, BN22 9PX, England, UK
Tel: 44 1323 506447
Email: walmsley@mabarra.cloughf9.co.uk
Website: http://www.haughshw.demon.co.uk/walmsoc.htm
Founded: 1985
Members: 200
Contact: Dr. Sean Walmsley, Pres.
Fee: £9
Membership Type: standard
Fee: £10
Membership Type: standard
Description: Promotes and encourages an appreciation of the literary and artistic heritage left to us by Leo and James Ulric Walmsley.
Library Subject: Walmsley topics
Library Type: not open to the public
Publication: Journal

Walpole Society

Department of Prints and Drawings, The British Museum, London, WC1B 3DG, England, UK
Tel: 44 20 73238408
Email: dkesley@supaher.com
Website: http://www.walpolesociety.org.uk
Founded: 1911
Members: 590
Contact: D. Kealey, Membership Sec.
Fee: £70
Membership Type: personal
Fee: £90
Membership Type: corporate
Description: Exists to publish archival and other material relating to the history of the arts in Great Britain. The organization has published 65 volumes.

War on Want
WOW

Fenner Brockway House, 37-39 Great Guildford St., London, SE1 0ES, England, UK
Tel: 44 207 6201111
Fax: 44 207 2619291
Email: mailroom@waronwant.org
Website: http://www.waronwant.org
Founded: 1952
Members: 8000
Staff: 14
Contact: Louise Richards, Exec.Dir.
Fee: £15
Membership Type: waged
Fee: £20
Membership Type: household
Description: Campaigns against the root causes of global poverty; provides funding for projects in developing countries.
Library Type: not open to the public
Publication title: Annual Review
Second publication: Magazine
Publication title: Upfront. Advertisements.
Meetings/Conventions: - annual convention London UK

War Resisters' International
WRI

5 Caledonian Rd., London, N1 9DX, England, UK
Tel: 44 207 2784040
Fax: 44 207 2780444
Email: office@wri-irg.org
Website: http://www.wri-irg.org
Founded: 1921
Members: 150000
Staff: 2
Description: Pacifist organization of individuals and movements participating in war resistance and peace activities in 35 countries. Disseminates information on training for nonviolent action and the problems of violent and nonviolent revolutionary change. Acts as information and coordinating center for conscientious objectors.
Library Subject: Peace and nonviolence.
Library Type: reference
Publication title: Broken Rifle
Second publication: Magazine
Publication title: Peace News. Advertisements.
Meetings/Conventions: - triennial meeting

Warrington Chamber of Commerce and Industry

International Business Centre, Delta Crescent, Westbrook, Warrington, WA5 7WQ, England, UK
Tel: 44 1925 715150
Fax: 44 1925 715159
Email: info@warrington-chamber.co.uk
Website: http://www.warrington-chamber.co.uk
Founded: 1876
Contact: Colin Daniels, Chief Exec.
Description: Promotes business and commerce.

Water Jetting Association

17 St. Judith's Ln., Sawtry, Huntingdon, PE28 5XE, England, UK
Tel: 44 1487 834034
Website: http://www.waterjetting.org.uk
Founded: 1980
Members: 140
Staff: 1
Contact: N.G. Allen
Fee: £300
Membership Type: voting

Description: Contractors and manufacturers of high pressure water jetting equipment. Promotes the safe use of jet cutting technology and represents the interests of members.
Formerly: Association of High Pressure Water Jetting Contractors
Publication: Manual
Publication title: Code of Practice for Safe Use of High Pressure Water Training Manual and Operator Pack for Jet Cutting Training
Second publication: Magazine
Publication title: Pressure Points. Advertisements.
Meetings/Conventions: - annual conference - Exhibits.

Water Services Association of England and Wales
1 Queen Anne's Gate, London, SW1H 9BT, England, UK
Tel: 44 171 9574567
Fax: 44 171 3441866
Founded: 1989
Members: 9
Staff: 30
Contact: Sue Tabb
Description: Water and sewerage companies (9) in England and Wales. Promotes and protects the common interests of member companies in dealings with the UK Government, the European Union and other regulatory authorities.
Publication: Magazine
Publication title: Water Bulletin
Publication title: Water Facts

Water UK
1 Queen Anne's Gate, London, SW1H 9BT, England, UK
Tel: 44 171 2220644
Fax: 44 171 2223366
Email: info@water.org.uk
Founded: 1885
Members: 18
Staff: 8
Contact: Mr. M. Waddington
Description: Water supply companies. Exists to represent, promote and protect the common interests of members and to provide a forum within which members can consider and discuss matters of mutual interest and concern.
Formerly: Water Companies Association
Publication title: Water News
Publication title: WCA Fact Sheets

Wax Chandlers' Company
Wax Chandlers' Hall, Gresham St., London, EC2V 7AD, England, UK
Tel: 44 207 6063591
Fax: 44 207 6005462
Email: info@waxchandlershall.co.uk
Website: http://www.waxchandlershall.co.uk
Founded: 1484
Members: 140
Staff: 3
Contact: Richard Percival, Clerk
Description: City of London Livery Company with 130 liverymen (members). Social and charitable activities. Represents members' interests.

Weavers' Company
Saddlers' House, Gutter Lane, London, EC2V 6BR, England, UK
Tel: 44 171 6061155
Fax: 44 171 6061119
Founded: 1130

Members: 150
Staff: 4
Contact: Mrs. F. Newcombe, Clerk
Description: City of London Livery Company. Charitable activities associated with textile education, the provision of sheltered homes for the elderly and other diverse charitable activities.
Publication title: The London Weavers' Company from 12th to 16th C
Publication title: The London Weavers' Company 1600 to 1970

Web Offset Newspaper Association
c/o The Newspaper Society
74-77 Great Russell St., London, WC1B 3DA, England, UK
Tel: 44 207 6367014
Fax: 44 207 6315119
Email: ns@newspapersoc.org.uk
Founded: 1964
Members: 100
Staff: 1
Contact: Gary Cullum
Description: Newspaper publishers and printers. Provides a forum for discussion of production and technical topics.
Meetings/Conventions: - periodic seminar

Welding Manufacturers' Association
Westminster Tower, 3 Albert Embankment, London, SE1 7SL, England, UK
Tel: 44 20 77933041
Fax: 44 20 75828020
Email: wma@beama.org.uk
Website: http://www.wma.uk.com
Contact: Clive Betts, Dir.
Description: Welding manufacturers.

Well Drillers Association
12 Alder Way, Bromsgrove, Worcestershire, B60 1AJ, England, UK
Tel: 44 1527 876706
Fax: 44 1527 876706
Email: mail@welldrillers.org.uk
Website: http://www.welldrillers.org.uk
Members: 17
Contact: Malcolm Gamble
Description: Membership is by application and acceptance by a majority of the members meeting and is available to all bona fide drilling contractors.

West Africa Committee
WAC
2 Vincent St., London, SW1P 4LD, England, UK
Tel: 44 20 78285544
Fax: 44 20 7828525
Founded: 1956
Members: 180
Staff: 5
Contact: Brigadier G.G. Blakely, Advisor
Description: Firms and companies located outside West Africa with substantial commercial interests in the areas countries. Seeks to aid and stimulate the economic development of West African countries. Represents overseas private sector operators considering operations in West Africa that are mutually beneficial to the operator and country involved. Represents members' interests before governmental bodies. Provides information to members on economic and political developments in West African countries.

Publication title: Country Reports
Second publication: Bulletin
Publication title: Nigerian Bulletin
Meetings/Conventions: - monthly meeting London UK

West Kent Chamber of Commerce and Industry
West Kent Business Ctr., Riverwalk, Tonbridge, TN9 1DT, England, UK
Tel: 44 1732 366653
Fax: 44 1732 363776
Email: info@wkcci.com
Website: http://www.wkcci.com
Founded: 1858
Members: 500
Staff: 5
Contact: Jackie Matthias, Chief Exec.
Description: Promotes business and commerce.
Publication: Newsletter
Publication title: Echo Chamber. Advertisements.
Meetings/Conventions: - monthly workshop

Wheelwrights' Company
Ember House, 35-37 Creek Rd., East Molesey, KT8 9BE, England, UK
Tel: 44 20 89415404
Fax: 44 20 89795934
Email: enquiries@wheelwrights.org
Website: http://www.wheelwrights.org
Founded: 1670
Members: 206
Staff: 2
Contact: P.J.C. Crouch, Clerk
Description: Wheelwrights.

Whitebred Shorthorn Association
c/o Mrs. Rosemary Mitchinson
High Green Hill Kirkcambeck, Brampton, CA8 2BL, England, UK
Tel: 44 169 7748228
Email: rosie@whitebredshorthorn.com
Website: http://www.whitebredshorthorn.com
Founded: 1962
Members: 80
Staff: 1
Contact: Rosie Mitchinson, Breed Sec.
Fee: £5
Membership Type: full
Description: Promotes breeding and herd book registers of Whitebred Shorthorn Cattle.

Wholesale Confectionery and Tobacco Alliance
Hope Cottage Stoneyfields, Farnham, GU9 8DU, England, UK
Tel: 44 1252 727769
Fax: 44 1252 727779
Founded: 1902
Members: 240
Contact: J.B. Bowden
Description: Promotes the wholesale confectionery and tobacco industry.
Publication: Book
Publication title: The Wholesale Confectionery and Tobacco Alliance Year Book. Advertisements.
Meetings/Conventions: - biennial trade show - Exhibits.

Wholesale Markets Brokers' Association
c/o Mr. Michael Beales
Cable House No. 54-62, New Broad St., London, EC2M 1ST, England, UK
Tel: 44 20 78272800
Fax: 44 20 78272590
Email: wmba@wmba.org.uk
Website: http://www.vmba.org.uk
Founded: 1994
Members: 10
Staff: 2
Contact: Mr. MCP Beales, Chm.
Description: Anyone interested in knitting. Aims to preserve the best of the old while exploring the new in knitting. Promotes members' interests.

Wigan Borough Chamber of Commerce
Wigan Investment Centre, Waterside Dr., Wigan, WN3 5BA, England, UK
Tel: 44 194 2705705
Fax: 44 194 2705272
Email: chamberinfo@wbp.org.uk
Website: http://www.wbp.org.uk
Members: 1015
Staff: 131
Contact: Richard Bindless, CEO
Description: Promotes business and commerce.

Wildfowl and Wetlands Trust
WWT
Slimbridge, Gloucester, GL2 7BT, England, UK
Tel: 44 1453 891900
Fax: 44 1453 890827
Email: enquiries@wwt.org.uk
Website: http://www.wwt.org.uk
Founded: 1946
Members: 100000
Staff: 340
Contact: Tony Richardson, Mgr.Dir.
Fee: £11
Membership Type: junior
Fee: £19
Membership Type: senior citizen
Description: Individuals with an interest in wetlands and their wildlife. Promotes preservation of wetlands and protection of animals that frequent them. Conducts breeding programs to increase threatened wetland waterfowl populations; provides winter refuge for threatened wetland waterfowl; manages and restores wetland habitats; maintains network of conservation and environmental education centers. Makes available educational and social opportunities to members; sponsors children's services; conducts research.
Library Subject: conservation, wetlands, waterfowl
Library Type: by appointment only
Formerly: The Wildfowl Trust
Publication: Journal
Publication title: Wildfowl
Second publication: Magazine
Publication title: Wildfowl Wetlands. Advertisements.
Meetings/Conventions: - annual conference

Wildlife Trusts
WT

The Kiln, Waterside, Mather Rd., Newark, NG24 4BR, England, UK
Tel: 44 1636 677711
Fax: 44 1636 670001
Email: info@wildlife-trusts.cix.co.uk
Website: http://www.wildlifetrust.org.uk
Founded: 1912
Members: 320000
Staff: 60
Contact: David Bellamy, Pres.
Description: Wildlife trusts comprising 320,000 individuals in the U.K. Cares for 2,000 nature reserves and protect wildlife in the United Kingdom; experiment with conservation management techniques; disseminate information; advise government departments; provide national catalog of sites. Offers children's services and educational programs. Serves as umbrella organization and works in conjunction with the Urban Wildlife Partnership.
Formerly: Society for the Promotion of Nature Reserves
Meetings/Conventions: - biennial conference - Exhibits.

Wilkie Collins Society

c/o Mr. Paul Lewis
4 Earnest Gardens, London, W4 3QU, England, UK
Email: paul@paullewis.co.uk
Website: http://www.deadline.demon.co.uk/wilkie/wcs/publications.htm
Founded: 1980
Members: 125
Contact: Andrew Gasson, Chm.
Fee: £9
Membership Type: europe
Fee: £15
Membership Type: worldwide
Description: Promotes members' interests.
Publication: Journal
Publication title: Wilkie Collins Society Journal
Second publication: Newsletter

William Barnes Society

58 Mellstock Ave., Dorchester, DT1 2BQ, England, UK
Tel: 44 1305 265358
Website: http://www.thomashardy.co.uk/william_barnes.htm
Founded: 1983
Members: 200
Contact: Mr. A. Barrett, Chm.
Fee: £8
Membership Type: single
Fee: £10
Membership Type: joint
Description: Exists to enable its members to share fellowship and pleasure in the life and work of William Barnes.
Publication: Newsletter

William Cobbett Society
WCS

10 Grenehurst Way, Petersfield, GU31 4AZ, England, UK
Tel: 44 1252 715094
Website: http://www.hants.gov.uk/istcclr/cch05450.html
Founded: 1976
Members: 160
Contact: Molly Townsend, Membership Sec.
Fee: £8

Description: Individuals or associations interested in the life and works of William Cobbett (1763-1835), English journalist and essayist. Maintains 100 volume collection of works on or by William Cobbett. Sponsors annual memorial lecture and rural re-ride by motor coach.
Library Subject: Cobbett's Political Register
Library Type: open to the public
Publication: Journal
Publication title: Cobbett's New Register. Advertisements.
Meetings/Conventions: Memorial Lecture and Rerun of Rural Ride - annual meeting

William Herschel Society

19 New King St., Bath, BA1 2BL, England, UK
Tel: 44 1225 311342
Email: efring@lineone.net
Website: http://www.williamherschel.org
Founded: 1979
Members: 500
Contact: Prof. Francies Ring, Chm.
Fee: £10
Membership Type: Europe member
Fee: £15
Membership Type: member
Description: Researches and publicizes the life and works of William Herschel and his family.
Library Subject: history of astronomy, science music 18th century
Library Type: reference
Publication title: Speculum
Meetings/Conventions: - semiannual lecture

William Morris Society
WMS

Kelmscott House, 26 Upper Mall, Hammersmith, London, W6 9TA, England, UK
Tel: 44 208 7413735
Fax: 44 208 7485207
Email: william.morris@care4free.net
Website: http://www.morrissociety.org
Founded: 1956
Members: 2000
Staff: 1
Contact: Helen Elletson, Curator
Fee: £13.5
Membership Type: Individual
Description: Persons from 24 countries interested in the life and works of William Morris (1834-96), English poet, writer, craftsman, designer, printer, and socialist. Objective is to deepen understanding and to stimulate a wider appreciation of Morris and his work. Arranges study courses; encourages the republication of Morris' works and the continued manufacture of his wallpaper and textile designs. Sponsors exhibitions, lectures, and visits to places relevant to Morris' life and works. Maintains collection of Morris' original designs.
Library Subject: Morrisian and allied subjects
Library Type: reference
Publication: Journal
Publication title: William Morris Society Journal. Advertisements.

Wine and Spirit Association
WSA

Five Kings House, 1 Queen St. Pl., London, EC4R 1XX, England, UK
Tel: 44 207 2485377
Fax: 44 207 4890322

Email: info@wsa.org.uk
Website: http://www.wsa.org.uk
Founded: 1824
Members: 250
Staff: 7
Contact: Quentin Rappoport, Dir.
Fee: £480
Description: Represents Importers, Shippers' and Wholesalers of wine and spirit and products derived from them. Also represents English and Welsh wine growers and producers of British wine. Represents and promotes the interests of those who trade in wine and/or spirit and of those whose livelihood depends upon that trade. Enquiry service available to subscribing member companies
Library Type: not open to the public
Formerly: Wine and Spirit Association of Great Britain and Northern Ireland
Publication: Book
Publication title: Checklists

Winged Fellowship Trust

Angel House, 20-32 Pentonville Rd., London, N1 9XD, England, UK
Tel: 44 207 8332594
Fax: 44 207 2780370
Email: admin@wft.org.uk
Website: http://www.wft.org.uk
Founded: 1963
Staff: 280
Contact: Elizabeth Van Krinks, Volunteer Mgr.
Description: Volunteers required to provide respite care for physically disabled persons in England. Organizes holidays for disabled individuals at five regional centers operated by the Trust.
Publication: Brochure
Publication title: Volunteer Information Brochure

Wire and Wire Rope Employers' Association

6 Brome Way, Spital, Wirral, CH63 9ND, England, UK
Tel: 44 151 3461566
Fax: 44 131 3341848
Founded: 1974
Members: 34
Staff: 2
Contact: Gordon Capper
Description: UK manufacturers of ferrous wire and wire rope. Covers all employment - related subjects, with particular emphasis on industrial relations. It provides the Chairman and Employers' Panel of the Joint Industrial Council for the Wire and Wire Rope Industries.

Wirral Chamber of Commerce and Industry

Egerton House, 2 Tower Rd., Birkenhead, L41 1FN, England, UK
Tel: 44 51 6506913
Fax: 44 51 6500440
Contact: Lord Leverhulme, Pres.
Description: Promotes business and commerce.

Wolverhampton Chamber of Commerce Training and Enterprise

Pendeford Business Park, Wobaston Rd., Wolverhampton, WV9 5HA, England, UK
Tel: 44 1902 445500
Fax: 44 1902 445200
Email: timlan@wton-chamber.co.uk
Members: 1120
Staff: 100
Contact: Tim Lannon
Description: Promotes business and commerce.

Womankind Worldwide
WW

32-37 Cowper St., London, EC2A 4AW, England, UK
Tel: 44 20 75495700
Fax: 44 20 75495701
Email: info@womankind.org.uk
Website: http://www.womankind.org
Founded: 1989
Staff: 18
Description: Promotes, supports, and funds women's initiatives in developing countries. Seeks to create a more peaceful society through the equal participation of women in determining values, directions and governance of society at all levels.
Library Subject: conditions of women in different countries
Library Type: reference
Publication: Journal
Publication title: Annual Review
Second publication: Newsletter
Meetings/Conventions: White Ribbon Day - annual conference - Exhibits.

Women and Manual Trades
WAMT

52-54 Featherstone St., London, EC1Y 8RT, England, UK
Tel: 44 207 2519192
Fax: 44 207 2519193
Email: info@wamt.org
Website: http://www.wamt.org
Founded: 1975
Members: 200
Staff: 5
Contact: Rose Sharp
Description: Encourages women and girls to pursue careers in the skilled trades of the construction industry. Provides information and advice to women working in the trades. Offers advice on areas of work, self-employment, and developing skills. Conducts self-employment classes including courses on business plans, tax, insurance, book keeping, self assessment, pricing and estimating, and health and safety.
Library Subject: resources for self-employed women
Library Type: by appointment only
Formerly: Women and Manual Trades
Publication: Book
Publication title: Crossing the Border
Second publication: Video
Publication title: If I Had a Hammer
Meetings/Conventions: conference - Exhibits.

Women in Banking and Finance

43 Keswick Rd., West Wickham, BR4 9AS, England, UK
Tel: 44 20 87776902
Fax: 44 20 87777064
Email: admin@wibf.org.uk
Website: http://www.wibf.org.uk
Founded: 1980
Members: 700
Staff: 1
Contact: Pandora Omaset, Chair

Fee: £40
Membership Type: full
Description: Works for the advancement of the role of women in the banking and finance industry in England. Encourages networking; disseminates information.
Formerly: Women in Banking
Publication: Newsletter
Publication title: In Focus. Advertisements.
Meetings/Conventions: - monthly meeting

Women in Film and Television - United Kingdom
WFTV

6 Langley St., London, WC2H 9JA, England, UK
Tel: 44 207 2404875
Fax: 44 207 3791625
Email: info@wftv.org.uk
Website: http://www.wftv.org.uk
Founded: 1990
Members: 800
Staff: 2
Contact: Jane Cussons, Ch.Exec.
Fee: £98
Description: Women with a minimum of one year's work in the film and television industry. Provides information and professional support to members. Offers educational programs. Protects the interests of women in the film and television industry; promotes equal opportunities for members within the industry. Organizes events at major markets and festivals.
Publication: Newsletter
Publication title: Events Diary

Women in Management
WIM

45 Beech St., 5th Fl., London, EC2Y 8AO, England, UK
Tel: 44 171 3829978
Fax: 44 171 3829979
Founded: 1969
Members: 1400
Contact: Lynn Smith, Chair
Fee: £46
Description: Supports the advencement of women in management careers. Encourages the development of management knowledge among women, offering training seminars and activities. Provides a forum for the exchange of information related to management.
Publication: Newsletter

Women in Physics Group

c/o Institute of Physics
76 Portland Place, London, W1B 1NT, England, UK
Tel: 44 207 4704800
Fax: 44 207 4704848
Email: wipg@amarks.co.uk
Website: http://www.groups.iop.org/WP
Founded: 1985
Members: 2000
Contact: Dr. A. Jones, Chief Exec. & Mng.Dir.
Fee: £2
Description: Open to all female members (including student members) of institute of Physics. Strives to increase the number of girls studying physics and to raise the status of professional women physicists. Promotes physics as a viable career choice for women in Britian. Encourages networking among members. Bestow awards. Disseminates information.

Formerly: Women in Physics
Publication: Booklet
Publication title: A Career Break Kit for Physicists
Second publication: Booklet
Publication title: Professional Training for Women
Meetings/Conventions: - annual meeting

Women in Publishing

c/o Publishers Association
78 Salop Rd., London, E17 7HT, England, UK
Tel: 44 7985 792542
Email: info@wipub.org.uk
Website: http://www.wipub.org.uk
Founded: 1979
Members: 700
Contact:
Fee: £20
Description: Supports the advancement of women in the publishing industry. Provides a forum for networking and mutual support among women publishers and editors. Assists training and career development efforts.
Publication: Newsletter
Publication title: WiPlash. Advertisements.
Meetings/Conventions: - monthly meeting

Women into Science and Engineering
WISE

Dartmouth St., London, SW1H 9BP, England, UK
Fax: 44 207 2278401
Email: wisecampaign@emta.org.uk
Founded: 1984
Staff: 3
Contact: Mrs. Marie-Noelle Barton, Natl.Mgr.
Description: Provides support for women employed in engineering fields; encourages students, teachers, and career advisers to help increase the number of women entering engineering professions. Organizes conventions and group discussions.
Library Subject: Career and course information and research publications
Library Type: reference
Publication: Magazine
Publication title: Women in Science and Engineering
Meetings/Conventions: - periodic convention - Exhibits.

Women Living Under Muslim Laws

PO Box 28445, London, N19 5NZ, England, UK
Email: run@gn.apc.org
Website: http://www.wluml.org
Founded: 1992
Description: International network that provides information, solidarity, and support for all women whose lives are shaped, conditioned, or governed by laws and customs said to derive from Islam. Aims to increase the autonomy of women by supporting the local struggles of women from within Muslim countries and communities and linking them with feminist and progressive groups at large; facilitating interaction, exchanges, and contacts and providing information as well as a channel of communication.
Publication: Report
Publication title: War Crimes Against Women of ex-Yugoslavia

Women Members Network of the Royal Society of Chemistry

c/o Royal Society of Chemistry
Burlington House, Piccadilly, London, W1J 0BA, England, UK
Tel: 44 20 74403312
Fax: 44 20 74378883
Email: franklinj@rsc.org
Contact: Julie Franklin
Description: Organizes social and professional events for women members of the Royal Society of Chemistry.
Library Subject: women in chemistry, science
Library Type: not open to the public

Women Returners Network
WRN

100 Park Village East, London, NW1 3SR, England, UK
Tel: 44 171 4682290
Fax: 44 171 3800123
Founded: 1984
Members: 350
Contact: Ruth Michaels, Pres.
Description: Women professionals. Promotes the re-entry of women into the labor force. Disseminates information, advice, and support to women returning to work. Offers job placement assistance. Encourages the development of flexible employment and educational programs for women with families. Engages in networking on local, national, and international levels.
Publication: Booklet
Publication title: Country Choices for Women
Second publication: Newsletter
Publication title: Return
Meetings/Conventions: meeting

Women Welcome Women World Wide
WWWWW

88 Easton St., High Wycombe, HP11 1LT, England, UK
Tel: 44 1494 465441
Fax: 44 1494 465441
Website: http://www.womenwelcomewomen.org.uk
Founded: 1984
Members: 3400
Staff: 4
Contact: Frances Alexander
Fee: £25
Membership Type: sterling
Description: Women of all ages interested in international cultural exchange. Fosters international friendship among women from different countries. Encourages members' travel excursions and visits with other members.
Publication: Directory
Publication title: WWWWW Newsletter
Second publication: Newsletter
Meetings/Conventions: International Women's Day - periodic meeting London UK

Women Working Worldwide
WWW

MMU Manton Bldg., Rosamond St. W., Manchester, M15 6LL, England, UK
Tel: 44 161 2471760
Fax: 44 161 247 6333
Email: info@women-ww.org

Website: http://www.poptel.org.uk/women-ww
Founded: 1983
Members: 12
Contact: Angela Hale
Description: Promotes the interest of women employed in the work force in the United Kingdom. Encourages the improvement of employment, wages, and working conditions for women workers. Supports women employees through information exchange, international networking, and public education. Focuses efforts on industries that employ large numbers of women, such as clothing, textiles, and electronics. Conducts research and educational programs on health and safety issues, and employment legislation.
Publication: Book
Publication title: Common Interests: Women Organising in Global Electronics
Second publication: Book
Publication title: Labour Behind the Label
Meetings/Conventions: - annual meeting - Exhibits.

Women's Campaign for Soviet Jewry

One to One, Pannell House, 779/781 Pinchley Road, London, NW11 8DN, England, UK
Tel: 44 181 4587147
Fax: 44 181 4589971
Founded: 1970
Members: 5000
Contact: Margaret Rigal, Co-Chwm.
Description: Human rights groups, members of the media and parliament, trade unionists, religious bodies, and concerned individuals in 16 countries. Seeks to call attention to the treatment accorded to Jews in the Commonwealth of Independent States who are imprisoned or persecuted for having tried to obtain permission to emigrate or for having observed religious or cultural conventions. Furthers public awareness of such injustices; exerts pressure on members of parliament and influential organizations; stages demonstrations and petition drives. Offers assistance to Jews immigrating to Israel. Provides speakers; holds seminars. Offers children's services; maintains charitable program. Compiles statistics. Organises treks in Israel, Egypt and Jordan to raise funds for the disadvantaged among the new immigrant families.
Library Subject: Soviet Jewish prisoners of conscience and refusenik families
Library Type: reference
Publication: Newsletter
Publication title: Newsletter
Second publication: Bulletin
Publication title: 35's Circular
Meetings/Conventions: - annual conference

Women's Engineering Society

22 Old Queen Anne St., London, SW1H 9HP, England, UK
Tel: 44 20 72331974
Email: info@wes.org.uk
Website: http://www.wes.org.uk
Founded: 1920
Members: 797
Staff: 1
Contact: Cathy MacGillivray, Sec.
Description: From all disciplines of engineering and are professionals, incorporated and technicians. Includes students and juniors still at school and has associates who are not themselves women engineers, but are interested in what they are doing. Promotes awareness of engineering as the prime creator of wealth in society, and the contribution women can make to it; promotes the education and training of women engineers; ensures that women

engineers can influence the process of policy formation and decision making in government and other organizations.
Publication: Magazine
Publication title: The Woman Engineer. Advertisements.
Meetings/Conventions: - annual conference - Exhibits.

Women's Environmental Network

PO Box 30626, London, E1 1TZ, England, UK
Tel: 44 20 74819004
Fax: 44 20 74819144
Email: info@wen.org.uk
Website: http://www.wen.org.uk/
Founded: 1988
Members: 2000
Staff: 7
Contact: Ann Link, Coord.
Fee: £15
Membership Type: waged
Fee: £30
Membership Type: overseas
Description: UK national membership charity working to educate, inform, and empower women and men who care about the environment. Campaigns and provides info on waste prevention, real (cloth) nappies (diapers), health, sanitary protection, and local organic food.
Publication: Handbook
Publication title: Stop Talking Rubbish! A Guide to Greening a Social Space
Second publication: Newsletter
Publication title: WEN News. Advertisements.
Meetings/Conventions: - periodic meeting

Women's Farm and Garden Association WFGA

175 Gloucester St., Cirencester, GL7 2DP, England, UK
Tel: 44 1285 658339
Fax: 44 1285 642356
Email: admin@wfga.fsbusiness.co.uk
Founded: 1899
Members: 550
Staff: 4
Contact: Patricia McHugh
Fee: £15
Membership Type: ordinary
Description: Women working in agriculture and horticulture in England. Promotes members' interests. Offers training programs, garden tours and workshops.
Publication: Book
Publication title: The Hidden Workforce
Second publication: Book
Publication title: Women Rule the Plot
Meetings/Conventions: - annual conference

Women's Food and Farming Union WFU

National Agricultural Centre, Stoneleigh Park, Warwickshire, CV8 2LZ, England, UK
Tel: 44 24 76693171
Fax: 44 24 76693181
Email: admin@wfu.org.uk
Website: http://www.wfu.org.uk
Founded: 1979

Members: 2000
Staff: 2
Contact: Sue Archer, Natl.Sec.
Fee: £32
Fee: £32
Membership Type: Women
Description: Farmers' wives, women farmers, and others engaged in agriculture and food production industries. Promotes farm produce and food manufactured in the UK. Encourages farmers and growers to improve marketing techniques. Lobbies against unfair competition.
Library Subject: agriculture and horticulture
Library Type: open to the public
Publication title: Annual Review. Advertisements.
Second publication: Video
Publication title: Through the Farm Gate
Meetings/Conventions: - annual meeting - Exhibits. London

Women's Food and Farming Union

c/o National Rural Enterprise Centre
National Agricultural Centre, Stoneleigh Park, Warwick, CV8 2LZ, England, UK
Tel: 44 24 76693171
Fax: 44 24 76693181
Email: admin@wfu.org
Website: http://www.wfu.org.uk
Founded: 1979
Members: 1000
Contact: Janet Godfrey, Pres.
Fee: £30
Membership Type: member
Fee: £100
Membership Type: business
Description: Promotes British produce. Seeks to link women producers with consumers.

Women's Health

52 Featherstone St., London, EC1Y 8RT, England, UK
Tel: 44 20 72516333
Fax: 44 20 72504152
Email: womenshealth@pop3.poptel.org.uk
Website: http://www.womenshealthlondon.org.uk
Founded: 1982
Members: 250
Staff: 10
Contact: Ingrid Smit
Description: Women's health information organization in the UK. Works to empower women to make informed decisions about health and reproductive issues. Promotes a pro-choice perspective on women's health issues, including abortion. Informs women of their reproductive rights; provides information about women's health issues. Develops and promotes a feminist perspective of women's health and reproductive rights.
Library Subject: women's health
Library Type: reference
Publication: Newsletter
Publication title: Women's Health
Second publication: Newsletter

Women's National Commission
WNC

Cabinet Office, 1st Fl., 35 Great Smith St., London, SW1P 3BQ, England, UK
Tel: 44 207 2762555
Fax: 44 207 2762563
Email: wnc@cabinet-office.x.gsi.gov.uk
Website: http://www.thewnc.org.uk
Founded: 1969
Members: 200
Staff: 7
Contact: Janet Veitch, Dir.
Description: Individaul Women in the United Kingdom, and women's sections of major political parties; trade unions; religious groups; professional organizations; other groups representative of women. Seeks to ensure by all possible means that the informed opinions of women are given their due weight in the deliberations of Government. Addresses such issues as: caring for the elderly; violence against women; social security; women and public appointments; women returners. Conducts studies and submits results and views to the Minister for women and other government bodies.
Library Subject: Women's social and economic status
Library Type: not open to the public
Publication title: Annual Report
Second publication: Directory
Publication title: Directory of Women's Organisations in United Kingdom

Women's Royal Voluntary Service
WRVS

c/o Milton Hill House
Milton Hill, Steventon, Abingdon, OX13 6AD, England, UK
Tel: 44 1235 442900
Fax: 44 1235 861166
Email: enquiries@wrvs.org.uk
Website: http://www.wrvs.org.uk
Founded: 1938
Members: 120000
Contact: Suzanne Riley, Head & PR
Description: WRVS is among Britain's largest and most active volunteering organisation. In parmushy with public and private sectors, it is committed to pondling a high standard of care and assistance that will be of value to these in need within their local communities.

Wood Wool Slab Manufacturers Association

26 Store St., London, WC1E 7BT, England, UK
Tel: 44 171 3233770
Fax: 44 171 3230307
Email: 101326.2660@compuserve.com
Founded: 1946
Members: 1
Staff: 1
Contact: Richard H. Toms
Description: Promotes the use of wood wool cement slabs - chiefly in building; defines and develops standards and methods of use and is the focal point for information and technical assistance to specifiers and users. Generally represents manufacturers interests.
Publication title: Wood Wool Cement Building Slabs

Woodworkers', Builder's and Miscellaneous Tools Association

c/o Institute of Spring Technology
Henry St., Sheffield, S3 7EQ, England, UK
Tel: 44 114 2789143
Fax: 44 114 2726344
Email: jrm@britishtools.com
Contact: J.R. Markham, Sec.
Publication: Directory
Publication title: British Tools Directory

Woodworking Machinery Suppliers Association
WMSA

The Counting House, Sir Richard Arkwright's Cromford Mill, Mill Lane, Cromford, Derbyshire, DE4 3RQ, England, UK
Tel: 44 1629 826998
Fax: 44 1629 826997
Email: info@wmsa.org.uk
Website: http://www.wmsa.org.uk
Founded: 1984
Members: 90
Staff: 1
Contact: Doug Shopland, Chairman
Description: UK trade association representing established suppliers of woodworking machinery, tooling, and dust extraction equipment, engaged in the manufacture and import of products. Aims to provide a high standard of service and reliability. Sponsors biennial Woodmex Exhibition in Birmingham, England.
Publication: Directory
Publication title: Directory of British Manufactured Woodworking and Sawmill Machinery and Equipment
Second publication: Directory
Publication title: Directory of Members Buyers Guide

Woolmens' Company

Hollands, Hedsor Rd., Bourne End, SL8 5EE, England, UK
Tel: 44 1628 850363
Contact: Frank Allen, Clerk
Description: Woolmen.

Workers' Educational Association

17 Victoria Park Sq., Temple House, London, E2 9PB, England, UK
Tel: 44 208 9831515
Fax: 44 208 9834840
Email: national@wea.org.uk
Website: http://www.wea.org.uk
Founded: 1903
Members: 150000
Staff: 300
Contact: Robert Lochrie, Gen.Sec.
Description: People requiring adult educational opportunities. Promotes adult education. Stimulates interest in adult education, particularly the needs of the educationally, socially, and financially disadvantaged. Provides programme and courses.
Publication title: Cutting Edges
Second publication: Magazine
Publication title: Reportback. Advertisements.
Meetings/Conventions: - biennial conference - Exhibits.

World Arabian Horse Organization
WAHO

North Farm, 2 Trenchard Road, Stanton Fitzwarren, Swindon, SN6 7RZ, England, UK
Tel: 44 1793 766877
Fax: 44 1793 766711
Email: waho@compuserve.com
Website: http://www.waho.org
Founded: 1970
Members: 2000
Staff: 1
Contact: Katrina Murray, Exec.Sec.
Fee: £20
Membership Type: individual or associate
Fee: £200
Membership Type: lifetime
Description: National registries (62) and individuals (2000) interested in Arabian horses. Promotes the welfare and survival of the Arabian horse; encourages uniform terminology, definitions, and procedures. Acquires and disseminates information regarding the Arabian horse worldwide.
Library Subject: on Arabian horses.
Library Type: by appointment only
Publication title: Account of Biennial WAHO Conferences
Publication title: Membership Directory
Meetings/Conventions: conference Warsaw Poland

World Association for Christian Communication

357 Kennington Ln., London, SE11 5QY, England, UK
Tel: 44 20 75829139
Fax: 44 20 77350340
Email: wacc@wacc.org.uk
Website: http://www.wacc.org.uk
Founded: 1975
Members: 800
Staff: 20
Contact: Rev. R.N. Naylor
Fee: £100
Membership Type: corporate
Fee: £30
Membership Type: personal
Description: Seeks to promote human dignity, justice and peace through freedom of expression and the democratization of communication. Provides professional guidance on communication policies and interprets developments in and consequences of global communication methods. Works towards the empowerment of women and assists the training of Christian communicators.
Library Subject: media in developing countries
Library Type: open to the public
Publication: Newsletter
Publication title: Action
Second publication: Journal
Publication title: Media Development
Meetings/Conventions: - periodic conference

World Association of Detectives
WAD

PO Box 333, Brough, HU15 1XL, England, UK
Tel: 44 1482 665577
Fax: 44 870 8310957
Email: wad@wad.net
Website: http://www.wad.net
Founded: 1925

Members: 850
Staff: 3
Contact: Richard D. Jacques-Turner, Exec.Dir.
Fee: £150
Description: Executives of private investigation and security agencies. Promotes high ethical practices and seeks to imbue members with attitudes of efficiency and responsibility. Provides members with referral work.
Formerly: Formed by Merger of, World Association of Detectives
Publication: Magazine
Publication title: WAD News. Advertisements.
Second publication: Membership Directory
Meetings/Conventions: - annual board meeting

World Association of Girl Guides and Girl Scouts
WAGGGS

Olave Centre, 12c Lyndhurst Rd., London, NW3 5PQ, England, UK
Tel: 44 20 77941181
Fax: 44 20 74313764
Email: wagggs@wagggsworld.org
Website: http://www.wagggsworld.org
Founded: 1928
Members: 140
Staff: 80
Contact: Kirsty Gray, Chm.
Description: National organizations representing in excess of 10,000,000 girls and young women. Promotes unity of purpose and common understanding in the fundamental principles of the Girl Guide and Girl Scout movement throughout the world; encourages friendship and mutual understanding among girls and young women of all nations. Holds training sessions at world centers. Conducts charitable programs through community development projects. At the cutting edge of issues affecting girls and young women.
Library Type: reference
Publication: Book
Publication title: Challenging Movement
Second publication: Newsletter
Publication title: Our World News
Meetings/Conventions: - triennial international conference - Exhibits.

World Association of Professional Investigators
WAPI

Chesam Executive Centre, Chesam House, 150 Regent St., London, W1B 5SJ, England, UK
Tel: 44 20 74644646
Fax: 44 20 74644647
Email: enquiries@wapi.com
Description: Works to promote and uphold the image and status of investigation as an international profession; provides educational facilities and resources.

World Association of Wildlife Veterinarians
WAWV

Regents Park, London, NW1 4RY, England, UK
Tel: 44 171 4496668
Fax: 44 171 5861457
Email: t.sainsbury@ioz.ac.uk
Website: http://wildvet.home.com
Founded: 1990
Description: Coordinates and exchanges information on wildlife; promotes international meetings and seminars.

World Bureau of Metal Statistics
WBMS

27-A High St., Ware, SG12 9BA, England, UK
Tel: 44 1920 461274
Fax: 44 1920 464258
Email: wbms@dircon.co.uk
Website: http://www.world-bureau.com
Founded: 1946
Members: 20
Staff: 7
Contact: S.M. Eales, Gen.Mgr.
Description: Collects and disseminates current, accurate statistics on metal production, consumption, stocks, and international trade.
Publication title: Surveys on Minor Metals
Second publication: Bulletin
Publication title: World Metal Statistics

World Cancer Research Fund
WCRF

105 Park St., London, W1Y 3FB, England, UK
Tel: 44 20 73434200
Fax: 44 20 73434201
Founded: 1990
Description: Promotes research into cancer prevention.

World Coal Institute
WCI

Ground Fl., Cambridge House, 180 Upper Richmond Rd., Putney, London, SW15 2SH, England, UK
Tel: 44 20 82466611
Fax: 44 20 82466622
Email: info@wci-coal.com
Website: http://www.wci-coal.com
Contact: Malcolm Keay, CEO
Description: Coal producers and coal consumers worldwide. Promotes the merits and importance of coal as the single largest source of fuel for the generation of electricity and the manufacture of the world's steel. Provides a voice for the coal industry in international policy debates on energy and the environment; works to improve public awareness; encourages the efficient use of coal to reduce the impact of coal on the environment.
Publication: Book
Publication title: Coal - Power for Progress

World Confederation for Physical Therapy
WCPT

46-48 Grosvenor Gardens, London, SW1W 0EB, England, UK
Tel: 44 207 8819234
Fax: 44 207 8819239
Email: info@wcpt.org
Website: http://www.wcpt.org
Founded: 1951
Members: 83
Staff: 2
Contact: Ms. B.J. Myers, Sec.Gen.
Fee: £70
Description: Confederation of 83 national associations representing physical therapists around the world supported mainly by subscriptions from its member organizations. Works to improve global health by: representing physical therapy and physical therapists internationally, collaborating with international and national organisations, encouraging high standards of physical therapy research, education and practice, and supporting communications of WCPT.
Library Type: not open to the public
Publication title: Annual Report
Second publication: Reports
Publication title: Key Notes: Opinion Papers on a Variety of Professional Matters
Meetings/Conventions: - quadrennial international conference - Exhibits. Barcelona Spain

World Dance and Dance Sport Council
WDDSC

Terpsichore House, 240 Merton Rd., South Wimbledon, London, SW19 1EQ, England, UK
Tel: 44 208 5450085
Fax: 44 208 5450225
Email: secretary@british-dance-council.org
Website: http://www.wddsc.com
Founded: 1950
Members: 52
Staff: 1
Contact: Mrs. P. Hines
Fee: £1000
Membership Type: professional dance organizations
Description: National dance organizations. Seeks to popularize dancing as a social pastime and sport. Works to standardize international rules for teaching and judging. Promotes Annual world championships in ballroom and Latin dancing; encourages organization of area competitions. Sponsors meetings and seminars.
Formerly: International Council of Ballroom Dancing
Publication title: WDDSC Rules
Publication title: WDDSC Statutes
Meetings/Conventions: - annual congress Blackpool UK

World Development Movement
WDM

25 Beehive Pl., London, SW9 7QR, England, UK
Tel: 44 207 7376215
Fax: 44 207 2748232
Email: wdm@wdm.org.uk
Website: http://www.wdm.org.uk
Founded: 1970
Members: 7500
Staff: 25
Contact: Barry Coates, Dir.
Fee: £16
Fee: £25
Description: Achieves justice for the world's poorest people through campaigns that tackle the fundamental causes of poverty. Tries to change policies of governments, businesses and banks in wealthy countries and the international agencies that they control. Goal is to create the conditions that will enable the world's poorest people to achieve equitable and sustainable development. Current campaigns call for: fair trade with the Third World, including controls on multinational companies; an end to government support for the arms trade; cancellation of Third World debts; and for aid to reach the poorest.
Publication: Magazine
Publication title: WDM in Action. Advertisements.
Second publication: Report

World Disarmament Campaign
WDC

145-47 Blythe St., London, E2 5LN, England, UK
Tel: 44 20 77292523
Founded: 1980
Members: 500
Contact: Dr. Frank Barnaby, Co-Chair
Fee: £10
Description: Churches, colleges, individuals, local peace groups, and unions. Seeks to abolish both nuclear and conventional weapons leading to complete disarmament; promotes the transfer of military expenditure to end world poverty.
Publication title: World Disarm!. Advertisements.
Second publication: Pamphlets
Meetings/Conventions: - annual conference London UK

World Education Fellowship
WEF

58 Dickens Rise, Chigwell, IG7 6NY, England, UK
Tel: 44 20 82817122
Fax: 44 20 82817122
Email: 106465.1075@compuserve.com
Founded: 1921

World Energy Council - England
WEC

5th Fl., Regency House, 1-4 Warwick St., London, W1B 5LT, England, UK
Tel: 44 207 7345996
Fax: 44 207 7345926
Email: info@worldenergy.org
Website: http://www.worldenergy.org
Founded: 1924
Members: 94
Staff: 15
Contact: G. Doucet, Sec.Gen.
Description: Energy ministries, fuel and power corporations, engineering industries, universities, research organizations, and manufacturers in 91 countries involved in the production, supply, and study of energy resources. Promotes the development and peaceful use of energy resources by considering: potential resources and all means of production, transportation, and utilization; energy consumption in its overall relationship to the growth of economic activity in the area; and the social and environmental aspects of energy supply and utilization. Specific topics include worldwide survey of energy resources, national energy data profiles, and energy terminology. Maintains 8 technical and topical study committees.
Library Type: not open to the public
Formerly: World Power Conference
Publication title: Survey of Energy Resources
Meetings/Conventions: - triennial congress - Exhibits. Sydney NSW Australia

World Federation of Neurology
WFN

12 Chandos St., London, W1G 9DR, England, UK
Tel: 44 207 3234011
Fax: 44 207 3234012
Email: kimurakyoto@aol.com
Founded: 1955
Members: 23000

Staff: 2
Contact: Dr. Jun kimura, Pres.
Fee: £5
Description: Neurologists and neuroscientists dedicated to improving the care of neurological patients and to preventing diseases of the nervous system. Disseminates information in the field of neurology. Organizes research groups on disease topics; compiles statistics. Maintains speakers' bureau. Conducts educational and research programs.
Library Type: reference
Publication title: Journal of Neurological Sciences. Advertisements.
Publication title: World Neurology
Meetings/Conventions: World Congress of Neurology - quadrennial - Exhibits.

World Federation of Personnel Management Associations
WFPMA

c/o Chartered Institute of Personnel and Developmet, CIPD House, Camp Rd., Wimbledon, London, SW19 4UX, England, UK
Tel: 44 20 89719000
Fax: 44 20 82633333
Email: cipd@cipd.co.uk
Website: http://www.wfpma.com
Founded: 1976
Members: 6
Contact: Geoff Armstrong, Sec.
Description: Members are: Asian Pacific Federation of Personnel Management; European Association for Personnel Management;Institute of Personnel Management/Southern Africa; Interamerican Federation of Personnel administration; North African Association of Formation and Personnel Managers; Society for Human Resource Management. Seeks to improve professional personnel management and its role in employing organizations; assists in the establishment of personnel management associations worldwide. Maintains contact with and facilitates the exchange of information among member associations; provides representation before world organizations.
Publication: Directory
Publication title: WFPMA Informational Guide
Meetings/Conventions: - annual congress

World Federation of Societies of Anaesthesiologists
WFSA

WFSA Office, Level 7, Imperial House, 15-19 Kingsway, London, WC2B 6TH, England, UK
Tel: 44 20 78365652
Fax: 44 20 78365616
Email: info@wfsa-office.org
Website: http://www.anaesthesiologists.org
Founded: 1955
Members: 108
Staff: 1
Contact: Dr. A.A.E. Meursing, Sec.
Fee: £125
Membership Type: practicing anesthesiologist
Description: Societies of anesthesiologists. Objectives are to: promote research in anesthesiology; disseminate scientific information; encourage the establishment of safety measures including equipment standardization; recommend suitable standards for training in anesthesiology.
Publication: Newsletter

Publication title: WFSA Newsletter
Meetings/Conventions: World Congress of Anaesthesiologists - quadrennial congress Paris France

World Federation of Surgical Oncology Societies WFSOS

1 Wimpole St., London, W1M 8AE, England, UK
Tel: 44 20 72902968
Fax: 44 20 72902989
Email: sarah.caruey@roysocmed.ac.uk
Description: Promotes surgical oncology internationally; encourages and assists the formation of surgical oncology societies.

World Jewish Relief

The Forum, 74-80 Camden St., London, NW1 0EG, England, UK
Tel: 44 207 6911771
Fax: 44 207 6911780
Email: info@wjr.org.uk
Website: http://www.tolife.org.uk
Founded: 1933
Contact: Vivienne Lewis
Description: Individuals and organizations united to help Jewish people worldwide. Provides financial, medical, and educational assistance to Jews in Eastern European, Middle-Eastern, African, and Asian countries. Contributes food and clothing as well as medical and housing facilities to needy. Participates in retrieval of records of refugees who fled Europe.
Formerly: Absorbed, Czechoslovakian Jewish Aid Trust
Meetings/Conventions: - annual convention

World Nuclear Association

Bowater House West, 12th Fl., 114 Knightsbridge, London, SW1X 7LJ, England, UK
Tel: 44 20 72250303
Fax: 44 20 72250308
Email: wna@world-nuclear.org
Website: http://www.world-nuclear.org
Founded: 1975
Members: 100
Staff: 12
Description: Producers, processors, traders, consumers, electrical utilities with nuclear programs and government agencies in 30 countries, and other organizations whose work is related to uranium and the nuclear fuel cycle. Promotes the development of uranium for peaceful purposes and as a component of world energy supplies. Provides a forum for the exchange of information; conducts research concerning global requirements, resources, productive capacity of uranium, and conditions governing international nuclear trade.
Library Subject: all aspects of the nuclear field
Library Type: open to the public
Publication title: Data Cards
Second publication: Books
Meetings/Conventions: - annual meeting London UK

World Organization for Early Childhood Education

The Chiltern College, 15 Peppard, Reading Rd., Reading, RG4 8JZ, England, UK
Tel: 44 1189 471847
Fax: 44 1189 343260
Email: omep-us@crc.uiuc.edu
Founded: 1948
Staff: 2
Contact: Audrey Curtis, Pres.

Description: Organizations and individuals in 72 countries concerned with the health, education, and welfare of children. Promotes greater understanding of children from birth to age 8. Facilitates international exchange of research experience and knowledge on topics including child psychology, toys and play materials, living conditions of families with young children, preschool education and care, and other issues in education. Members promote research on early childhood education, conduct surveys of nursery schools and teacher training, and encourage parent education. Maintains speakers' bureau; conducts seminars and forums.
Publication: Newsletter
Publication title: Directory of Officers and Members
Second publication: Journal
Publication title: International Journal of Early Childhood Education. Advertisements.
Meetings/Conventions: - triennial congress - Exhibits.

World ORT

ORT House, 126 Albert St., London, NW1 7NE, England, UK
Tel: 44 207 4468500
Fax: 44 207 4468650
Email: wo@ort.org
Website: http://www.ort.org
Founded: 1880
Members: 120300
Staff: 13000
Contact: Robert Singer, Dir.Gen.
Description: Volunteer committees, women's groups, and professional groups in 46 countries. Aims to develop industrial and agricultural computer skills among Jews and others in an effort to help individuals become economically self-sufficient. Promotes the highest standards of production and improvement of the economy in affiliated countries. Provides vocational and technical training in schools in 46 countries; collaborates with various governments in sponsoring programs of technical assistance in developing nations; offers apprenticeship opportunities and placement services. Organizes apprenticeship programs.
Publication: Newsletter
Publication title: Front Line News
Publication title: ORTdata
Meetings/Conventions: board meeting

World Petroleum Congresses - A Forum for Petroleum Science, Technology, Economics, and Management WPC

1 Duchess St., 4th Fl., Ste. 1, London, W1N 3DE, England, UK
Tel: 44 20 76374958
Fax: 44 20 76374965
Email: pierce@world-petroleum.org
Website: http://www.world-petroleum.org
Founded: 1933
Members: 59
Staff: 15
Contact: Dr. Pierce Riemer, Dir.Gen.
Description: National committees. Advances petroleum science and technology and the study of economic, financial, and management issues in the petroleum industry.
Library Subject: petroleum
Library Type: open to the public
Publication: Newsletter
Publication title: Newsletter

647

Publication title: Proceedings of the World Petroleum Congress
Meetings/Conventions: - triennial congress - Exhibits. Johannesburg Republic of South Africa

World Pheasant Association
WPA

7-9 Shafesbury St., Hants, Fordingbridge, SP6 1JF, England, UK
Tel: 44 1425 657129
Fax: 44 1425 658053
Email: office@pheasant.org.uk
Website: http://www.pheasant.org.uk/
Founded: 1975
Members: 1850
Staff: 3
Contact: Gillian Court, Admin.
Fee: £20
Description: Individuals and institutions from 35 countries dedicated to the conservation, development, promotion, and support of pheasants and other galliformes (game birds), including currasows, francolins, grouse, guineafowl, megapodes, partridges, quail, and wild turkeys. Advocates the adoption of a coordinated policy for preservation and aviculture to save 48 species of pheasants, a third of which are in danger of extinction. Seeks to increase public awareness, understanding, and appreciation of nature and, in particular, gallinaceous birds and their requirements for survival. Works to improve and ensure sound avicultural methods in countries of origin and elsewhere, especially where conservation of natural habitats is difficult and wild populations are threatened. Facilitates the establishment of reserve collections and buffer stocks of threatened or endangered species. Encourages habitat conservation and the support of national parks, reserves, and sanctuaries of importance to galliformes. Sponsors research projects in the wild, breeding experiments, and field surveys. Offers advice on matters regarding the aviculture, conservation, ecology, and protection of pheasants and related birds; provides members with access to pheasant collections and conservation areas worldwide.
Publication: Annual Report
Publication title: Annual Review. Advertisements.
Second publication: Newsletter
Publication title: WPA News
Meetings/Conventions: - annual convention

World Plumbing Council
WPC

c/o The Institute of Plumbing
64 Station Ln., Hornchurch, RM12 6NB, England, UK
Tel: 44 1708 472791
Fax: 44 1708 448987
Email: secretariat@worldplumbing.org
Website: http://www.worldplumbing.org/
Description: Strives to unite the world plumbing industry to safeguard and protect the environment and the health of nations; works to promote the image and standards of the plumbing industry.

World Ship Trust
WST

202 Lambeth Rd., London, SE1 7JW, England, UK
Tel: 44 171 3854267
Fax: 44 171 3854267
Website: http://www.worldshiptrust.org
Founded: 1979
Members: 420

Staff: 1
Contact: Monsieur Jacques Chauveau, Chm.
Fee: £30
Description: Individuals in 48 countries interested in the preservation of historic ships. Seeks to display historic ships. Locates historic ships in distress and initiates preservation projects. Compiles information on the latest techniques and methods of ship preservation. Maintains liaison with ship preservation organizations worldwide.
Library Type: reference
Publication: Book
Publication title: International Register of Historic Ships, Third edition
Second publication: Newsletter
Publication title: World Ship Review. Advertisements.
Meetings/Conventions: - periodic conference

World Society for the Protection of Animals - England
WSPA

89 Albert Embankment, London, SE1 7TP, England, UK
Tel: 44 207 5875000
Fax: 44 207 7930208
Email: wspa@wspa.org.uk
Website: http://www.wspa.org.uk
Founded: 1981
Members: 100000
Staff: 50
Contact: Andrew Dickson, Chief Exec.
Fee: £20
Membership Type: individual
Fee: £500
Membership Type: member organization
Description: National animal welfare societies in 70 countries whose membership comprises over 100,000 individuals. Purposes are: to undertake and promote the conservation and protection of animals worldwide; to study international and national legislation relating to animal welfare; to promote efforts for the protection of animals and the conservation of their environment; to prevent cruelty to animals and relieve their suffering. Operates Emergency Rescue Service.
Formerly: Absorbed, International Council Against Bullfighting
Publication: Journal
Publication title: Animals International
Meetings/Conventions: - biennial meeting - Exhibits.

World Sugar Research Organisation
WSRO

Science & Technology Centre, University of Reading, Earley Gate, Reading, RG6 6BZ, England, UK
Tel: 44 1189 9357000
Fax: 44 1189 9357301
Email: wsro@wsro.org
Website: http://www.wsro.org
Founded: 1978
Members: 76
Staff: 3
Contact: Dr. Riaz Khan, Dir.Gen.
Description: Sugar producers, refiners, and users; individuals interested in the sugar industry. Distributes information on sugar, nutrition and health and technical information related to sugar. Conducts symposia.
Formerly: Supersedes, International Sugar Research Foundation
Publication: Newsletter
Publication title: Abstracts

Second publication: Bulletin
Publication title: Bulletin
Meetings/Conventions: - annual conference

World Trade Centre London

6 Harbour Exchange Square, London, E14 9GE, England, UK
Tel: 44 20 79873456
Fax: 44 20 79873498
Email: enquiries@worldtradecentrelondon.com
Website: http://www.worldtradecentrelondon.com/
Members: 300
Staff: 8
Contact: Ms. Jean Peto, Amdin.
Description: Businesses, professionals, and interested individuals. Facilitates the development of national and international trade by providing traders and investors with information and advice on new markets and products. Organizes trade missions to World Trade Centers and facilitates contact with government agencies. Services offered include research and information gathering on trade opportunities, educational programs, and consumer and business assistance.

World Union of Free Romanians
WUFR

54-62 Regent St., London, W1R 5PJ, England, UK
Tel: 44 207 4394052
Fax: 44 207 4375908
Founded: 1984
Members: 8000
Staff: 6
Contact: Ion Ratiu, Pres.
Description: Romanian organizations; individuals working for liberty and democracy in Romania.
Library Subject: Romanian history and politics.
Library Type: reference
Publication: Newspaper
Publication title: Free Romanian. Advertisements.
Publication title: Libertate si Democratie in Romania
Meetings/Conventions: - triennial congress

World Union of Pythagorean Organizations
WUPO

17 Longfield, Lutton near Cornwood, Ivybridge, PL21 9SN, England, UK
Tel: 44 1752 837462
Founded: 1955
Members: 45
Staff: 2
Contact: Ronald J. Strong, Dir.
Description: Organizations made up of adherents to the ideas of the Greek mathematician and philosopher, Pythagoras. Seeks to unite all Pythagorean organizations for the purpose of interchanging information, sharing common goals, and promoting their studies of Pythagoras.
Library Subject: Pythagorean philosophy and science
Library Type: reference
Publication: Bulletin
Publication title: Bulletin
Second publication: Journal
Publication title: Journal
Meetings/Conventions: - quadrennial meeting - Exhibits.

World University Service - United Kingdom

14 Dufferin St., London, EC1Y 8PD, England, UK
Tel: 44 171 4265800
Fax: 44 171 2511314
Email: international@wusuk.org
Website: http://www.wusuk.org
Founded: 1920
Members: 400
Staff: 40
Contact: Cameron Bowles, Dir.
Fee: £25
Membership Type: individual
Description: Works with refugees in the UK to provide advice on educational issues. Cooperates with partner organizations in Africa, Latin America, and the Middle East to educate refugees and other marginalized groups.

World Vision United Kingdom
WVUK

599 Avebury Blvd., Milton Keynes, MK9 3PG, England, UK
Tel: 44 1908 841000
Fax: 44 1908 841001
Founded: 1979
Staff: 101
Contact: Charles Clayton, Exec.Dir.
Description: Individuals and organizations with an interest in global poverty and related issues. Seeks to improve the quality of life of people living in economically disadvantaged areas. Sponsors educational programs to raise public awareness of global poverty in the United Kingdom. Conducts programs in areas including maternal and child health, emergency relief, and training for development workers.

World War Two Railway Study Group

c/o Mr. Greg Martin
17 Balmoral Crescent, West Molesey, KT8 1QA, England, UK
Email: tcane@ww2rsg.vianw.co.uk
Founded: 1989
Members: 130
Contact: Greg Martin, Sec.
Fee: £14
Membership Type: ordinary
Fee: £11
Membership Type: age concession
Description: Documents all aspects of railways during World War Two and promotes interest in the subject. Publishes a journal that includes articles on European, US, USSR, and Middle East subjects.
Library Subject: railways, military
Library Type: not open to the public
Publication: Journal
Publication title: Bulletin. Advertisements.
Meetings/Conventions: - annual meeting

Worldaware

Echo House, Ullswater Crescent, Coulsdon, CR5 2HR, England, UK
Tel: 44 20 87632555
Fax: 44 20 87632888
Email: info@worldaware.org.uk
Website: http://www.worldaware.org.uk
Founded: 1977
Staff: 8
Contact: Angus Willson, Asst.Dir.

Description: Seeks to raise public awareness in the United Kingdom of world development issues, including the need for sustainable development and the interdependence of U.K. and developing countries. Works with governmental education agencies to create an accurate and balanced national curriculum covering development issues. Makes use of media to publicize development issues.
Formerly: Centre for World Development Education
Publication title: Annual Report
Publication title: Education Resources Catalog
Meetings/Conventions: - periodic luncheon

World's Poultry Science Association - UK
Woodlands, Bradfield St. Clare, Bury., St. Edmunds, IP30 OEQ, England, UK
Tel: 44 1284 386520
Fax: 44 1284 386520
Email: parsonsbury@hotmail.com
Website: http://www.wpsa-uk.com
Founded: 1946
Members: 335
Contact: Mr. J.A. Parsons, Sec.
Fee: £20
Membership Type: ordinary
Fee: £40
Membership Type: affiliate
Description: Individuals and companies associated with the poultry industry in the UK and abroad. The Branch is one of about 40 throughout the world. Promotes advancement of knowledge of poultry production; disseminates the knowledge throughout the world. Promotes congresses, conferences, symposia and seminars; co-operates with other international organizations in achieving these aims.
Publication: Proceedings
Publication title: Poultry Science Symposium
Second publication: Newsletter
Publication title: WPSA UK Branch Newsletter
Meetings/Conventions: - annual meeting

Worldwide Dragonfly Association
49 James Rd., Kidderminster, D41O 2TR, England, UK
Email: lindamaverill@aol.com
Website: http://powell.colgate.edu/wda/constitution_and_by-laws.htm
Founded: 1997
Members: 200
Contact: Linda Averill, Sec.
Fee: £30
Membership Type: single with journal
Fee: £13
Membership Type: single without journal
Description: Strives to advance public education and awareness through promotion of the study and conservation of dragonflies (Odonata) and their natural habitats worldwide.
Publication: Newsletter
Publication title: Agriion
Second publication: Journal
Publication title: International Journal of Odonatology
Meetings/Conventions: International Symposium on Odonatology - biennial symposium

Worldwide Opportunities on Organic Farms - UK WWOOF
PO Box 2675, Lewes, BN7 1RB, England, UK
Tel: 44 1273 476286
Fax: 44 1273 476286

Email: fran@wwoof.org
Website: http://www.wwoof.org.uk
Founded: 1971
Members: 10000
Staff: 1
Contact: Fran Whittle, Coordinator
Fee: £15
Description: Organizations placing volunteers on organic farms requiring assistance worldwide. Promotes organic farming; encourages voluntary farm work as an educational and cultural experience. Places volunteer farm workers with organic farms willing to provide room and board in exchange for labor. Conducts educational programs.
Formerly: Willing Workers on Organic Farms
Publication: Newsletter
Publication title: WWOOFNews. Advertisements.
Meetings/Conventions: - semiannual conference

Worshipful Company of Actuaries
81 Worrin Rd., Shenfield, Brentwood, Essex, CM15 8JN, England, UK
Tel: 44 1277 261110
Email: jill.evans@virgin.net
Founded: 1979
Members: 200
Contact: Ms. J. V. Evans, Clerk
Description: Actuaries. Promotes professional advancement of members. Conducts educational, charitable, and social activities.

Worshipful Company of Bakers
Bakers Hall, Harp Ln., London, EC3R 6DP, England, UK
Tel: 44 207 6232223
Fax: 44 207 6211924
Email: clerk@bakers.co.uk
Website: http://www.bakers.co.uk/
Contact: J. Tompkins, Clerk
Description: Bakers.

Worshipful Company of Framework Knitters
37 The Uplands, Whitegarth Chambers, Loughton, IG10 1NQ, England, UK
Tel: 44 208 5021964
Fax: 44 208 5025237
Email: clerk@frameworkknitters.co.uk
Website: http://www.frameworkknitters.co.uk
Founded: 1657
Members: 225
Staff: 1
Contact: H.W.H. Ellis, Clerk
Description: Liverymen of the Company who are freemen of the City of London and have interests in the knitting and textile industry. In acting as an ancient livery company of the City of London, the Company supports the city and the knitting industry. Its charities run almhouses for the elderly and poor of the industry and maintain education bursaries for students of the industry.
Publication title: Annual Review
Publication title: History of the Company

Worshipful Company of Glass Sellers of London
43 Aragon Ave., Thames Ditton, KT7 0PY, England, UK
Tel: 44 181 3985481
Founded: 1664

Members: 180
Contact: B.J. Rawles, Hon.Clerk
Description: Glass Sellers united to pursue excellence in the art, craft, science, and technology of glass. Conducts charitable activities.

Worshipful Company of Glaziers' and Painters of Glass

c/o Glaziers' Hall
9 Montague Close, London Bridge, London, SE1 9DD, England, UK
Tel: 44 20 74033300
Fax: 44 20 74036652
Email: info@worshipfulglaziers.com
Website: http://www.worshipfulglaziers.com
Founded: 1638
Members: 300
Staff: 2
Contact: D.W. Eking, Clerk
Fee: £270
Description: Glass painters and stained glass artists.
Library Subject: stained glass
Library Type: not open to the public

Worshipful Company of Grocers

c/o Grocers' Hall
Princes St., London, EC2R 8AD, England, UK
Tel: 44 207 6063113
Fax: 44 207 6003082
Email: sarah@grocershall.co.uk
Website: http://www.grocershall.co.uk
Founded: 1345
Members: 900
Staff: 23
Contact: S.G. Mattingley, Clerk
Description: Grocers.

Worshipful Company of Information Technologists

39A Bartholomew Close, London, EC1A 7JN, England, UK
Tel: 44 207 6001992
Fax: 44 207 6001991
Email: info@wcit.org.uk
Website: http://www.wcit.org.uk
Founded: 1992
Members: 580
Staff: 3
Contact: Mrs. Gillian Davies, Clerk
Description: Freeman and liverymen.

Worshipful Company of Musicians

75 Watling St., London, EC4M 9BJ, England, UK
Tel: 44 171 4891615
Fax: 44 171 4891614
Email: clerk@musicianslivery.co.uk
Founded: 1500
Members: 340
Staff: 2
Contact: S.F.N. Waley
Description: Musicians or those interested in music. Concerned with the performing arts, their education and promotion and the trades and crafts associated with them. It is dedicated to the pursuit and recognition of excellence.

Worshipful Company of Pattenmakers

PO Box 521, Sutton Valence, Medway, Maidstone, ME17 3SU, England, UK
Tel: 44 1622 842440
Fax: 44 1622 844429
Email: pattenmakers@ukcharity.com
Website: http://www.pattenmakers.co.uk
Founded: 1670
Members: 220
Contact: Lt. Col. R.W. Murfin, Clerk
Fee: £195
Membership Type: Freemen and Liverymen
Description: Pattenmakers.
Publication: Magazine
Publication title: The Pattenmaker Magazine
Meetings/Conventions: - quarterly meeting

Worshipful Company of Pewterers

Oat Lane, Pewterers' Hall, London, EC2V 7DE, England, UK
Tel: 44 207 6069363
Fax: 44 171 6003896
Email: clerk@pewterers.org.uk
Website: http://www.pewterers.org.uk
Founded: 1348
Members: 260
Staff: 5
Description: Promotes and supports the pewter industry through organizations such as the Association of British Pewter Craftsmen (ABPC) and the European Pewter Union (EPU). Serves as custodians of the past of pewter.
Library Subject: pewter
Library Type: reference
Publication: Newsletter
Publication title: Pewter Review
Meetings/Conventions: Pewter Live - annual - Exhibits. London UK

Worshipful Company of Scientific Instrument Makers

9 Montague Close, London Bridge, London, SE1 9DD, England, UK
Tel: 44 20 74074832
Fax: 44 20 74071565
Email: theclerk@wcsim.co.uk
Founded: 1955
Members: 235
Staff: 2
Contact: F.G. Everard, Clerk
Fee: £265
Membership Type: individual
Description: Private individuals working in or closely connected with the manufacture and development of scientific instruments in the UK. A City Livery Company, supporting the craft of instrumentation in the UK. This is mainly achieved through the granting of financial help to those studying this subject in higher education.

Worshipful Company of Scriveners of the City of London

HQS Wellington, Temple Stairs, Victoria Embankment, London, WC2R 2PN, England, UK
Tel: 44 207 2400529
Fax: 44 207 4970645
Email: clerk@scriveners.org.uk
Website: http://www.scriveners.org.uk
Founded: 1373

Members: 200
Contact: Andrew Hill, Clerk
Description: Public Notaries of the City of London and its environs, and others in legal and related professions, including calligraphy and heraldry. Has a statutory responsibility for regulating the Notarial Profession within its jurisdiction.

Worshipful Company of Shipwrights

Ironmongers' Hall, Barbican, London, EC2Y 8AA, England, UK
Tel: 44 207 6062376
Fax: 44 207 6008117
Email: clerk@shipwrights.co.uk
Website: http://www.shipwrights.co.uk
Founded: 1199
Members: 400
Staff: 2
Description: Members of the maritime trades and professions. A livery company of the City of London, whose liverymen are all professional men and women in the maritime world (shipping etc), devoted to charitable and educational work in that field.
Publication: Handbook
Publication title: Members' Handbook

Worshipful Company of Tobacco Pipe Makers' and Tobacco Blenders

Penwood, Penwood End, Hook Heath, Woking, Surrey, GU22 0JU, England, UK
Founded: 1954
Members: 200
Staff: 2
Contact: N.J. Hallings-Pott, Clerk
Fee: £200
Membership Type: ordinary
Description: Companies engaged in the tobacco and related industries. Conducts charitable, educational, and social activities.
Publication: Newsletter
Publication title: Pipeline
Meetings/Conventions: Court Meetings - quarterly meeting London UK

Worshipful Company of Vintners

Vintners' Hall, Upper Thames St., London, EC4V 3BG, England, UK
Tel: 44 20 72361863
Fax: 44 20 72368177
Website: http://www.heraldicmedia.com/site/info/livery/livcomps/comp011a.html
Contact: M. Smythe, Clerk
Description: Vintners.

Writers and Scholars Educational Trust
WSET

Lancaster House, 33 Islington High St., London, N1 9LH, England, UK
Tel: 44 20 72782313
Fax: 44 20 73296461
Founded: 1971
Members: 8500
Staff: 10
Description: Writers, scholars, journalists, teachers, artists, publishers, and human rights organizations who monitor and report on censorship worldwide. Collects timely information on writers, artists, and others who have been silenced through censorship, persecution, and other forms of repression or assassination. Conducts research

and provides funding for the Index on Censorship published by Writers and Scholars International (see separate entry). Operates library and documentation center of books, press cuttings, and graphics; offers lectures, talks, and advice to arts centers; provides newspaper, television, and radio reporters with background information. Formerly part of WSI; became a separate organization in 1974.
Library Subject: Censored writers
Library Type: reference

Writers' Guild of Great Britain
WGGB

15 Britannia St., London, WC1X 9JN, England, UK
Tel: 44 20 78330777
Fax: 44 20 78334777
Email: admin@writersguild.org.uk
Website: http://www.writersguild.org.uk/
Founded: 1959
Members: 2000
Staff: 6
Contact: Bernie Corbett, Gen.Sec.
Description: Trade union for professional freelance writers. Aims to negotiate minimum terms agreements in all of those areas upon which members base their contracts. Also protects members by lobbying at the Houses of Parliament and lobbying government organisations.
Formerly: Absorbed, Theatre Writers Union
Publication: Newsletter
Publication title: The Writers' Newsletter. Advertisements.

Writers in Prison Committee of International P.E.N.
WIPC

9/10 Charterhouse Bldgs., Goswell Rd., London, EC1M 7AT, England, UK
Tel: 44 207 2533226
Fax: 44 207 2535711
Email: intpen@gnapc.org
Website: http://www.internatpen.org
Founded: 1960
Members: 45
Staff: 3
Contact: Sara Whyatt, Dir.
Description: A committee of International P.E.N. Seeks to secure the release from prison, house arrest, or confinement in a psychiatric institution of writers, journalists, translators, and publishers worldwide who have been detained for their writings or opinions. Works to ensure that imprisoned writers are treated well and given prompt, fair trials. Conducts letter-writing campaigns directed at authorities responsible for the imprisonment of writers; sends delegations to visit imprisoned writers; encourages members to adopt an imprisoned writer, work for their release, and publish and distribute their works. Conducts research.
Library Type: lending
Publication: Newsletter
Publication title: Centre to Centre
Publication title: Writers in Prison Committee Report
Meetings/Conventions: - semiannual conference

WWF-UK

Panda House, Weyside Pk., Godalming, GU7 1XR, England, UK
Tel: 44 1483 426444
Fax: 44 1483 426409
Website: http://www.wwf.org.uk

Founded: 1961
Members: 200000
Staff: 300
Contact: Robert Napier, Dir.
Fee: £10
Membership Type: benefactor
Fee: £5
Membership Type: companion
Description: Strives to conserve the natural environment and ecological processes essential to life on earth. Encourages the use of renewable resources and sustainable development practices. Finances and supervises conservation projects.
Formerly: World Wildlife Fund
Publication: Newsletter
Publication title: WWF News

Yacht Brokers, Designers and Surveyors Association
YBDSA

Wheel House, Petersfield Rd., Whitehill, Bordon, GU35 9BU, England, UK
Tel: 44 1420 473862
Fax: 44 1420 488328
Email: info@ybdsa.co.uk
Website: http://www.ybdsa.co.uk
Founded: 1987
Members: 250
Staff: 4
Contact: Jane Gentry, Ch.Exec.
Fee: £250
Membership Type: affiliate, associate, full fellow, honorary, retired
Description: Yacht and small craft brokers, designers, and surveyors in 10 countries. Objectives are to: conduct and maintain standards of professional competence; agree on common forms of contract; arbitrate disputes; provide for discussion and exchange of information. Conducts teaching programs and workshops.
Library Subject: surveying, design, brokerage
Library Type: not open to the public
Formerly: Formed by Merger of, Yacht Brokers, Designers and Surveyors Association
Publication: Directory
Publication title: Membership Directory
Second publication: Papers
Publication title: Newsletter
Meetings/Conventions: Brokers Course - semiannual

Yacht Charter Association

Deacons Boatyard, Bursledon Bridge, Southampton, S031 8AZ, England, UK
Tel: 44 2380 407075
Fax: 44 2380 407076
Email: charter@yca.co.uk
Website: http://www.yca.co.uk
Founded: 1960
Members: 80
Staff: 2
Contact: Michael Brown
Fee: £125
Membership Type: charter companies
Fee: £115
Description: British companies/operators chartering out yachts to the public in UK and abroad who observe YCA safety standards. Protects the public by imposing safety standards and code of practice to cover charter yachts in the UK. Liaises with the Department of Transport to improve legislation.
Library Subject: worldwide yacht charters
Library Type: not open to the public
Publication: Booklet
Publication title: Guide to Charter. Advertisements.
Meetings/Conventions: Committee Meeting - quarterly Southampton UK

Yacht Harbour Association

Evegate Park Barn, Smeeth, Ashford, TN25 6SX, England, UK
Tel: 44 1303 814434
Fax: 44 1303 814364
Email: slambert@britishmarine.co.uk
Website: http://yachtharbourassociation.com
Founded: 1975
Members: 220
Staff: 1
Contact: Sue Lambert
Description: Operators, professionals, equipment suppliers overseas and UK. Concerned with the development of coastal and inland boating facilities.
Publication title: Code of Practice for the Construction and Operation of Marinas and Yacht Harbours

Yachting Journalists' Association

Booker's Yard, The Street, Walberton, Arundel, West Sussex, BN18 0PF, England, UK
Tel: 44 1243 555561
Fax: 44 1243 555562
Email: ppl@mistral.co.uk
Founded: 1969
Members: 268
Staff: 1
Contact: Barry Pickthall, Hon.Sec.
Fee: £30
Membership Type: personal
Description: Specialist writers, radio and television presenters, photographers and illustrators with a knowledge of every aspect of yachting and boating. Exists to further the interest of yachting, sail and power in all its forms and to promote the interests of its members.
Publication: Handbook
Publication title: YJA Handbook. Advertisements.
Meetings/Conventions: - annual general assembly

York and North Yorkshire Chamber of Commerce and Industry

20 George Hudson St., York, YO1 1LP, England, UK
Tel: 44 904 629513
Fax: 44 904 630985
Email: info@yorkchamberco.uk
Members: 610
Staff: 5
Contact: Len Cruddas, Ch.Exec.
Description: Promotes business and commerce.

Young Women's Christian Association - Great Britain
YWCA - GB

Clarendon House, 52 Cornmarket St., Oxford, OX1 3EJ, England, UK
Tel: 44 1865 304200
Fax: 44 1865 204805

Email: info@ywca-gb.org.uk
Website: http://www.ywca-gb.org.uk
Founded: 1855
Staff: 250
Contact: Dorrie Gasser, Assistant to Chief Executive
Fee: £7
Description: Aims to be a force for change for women who are facing discrimination and inequalities of all kinds. Objectives are to enable young women facing disadvantage to identify and realize their full potential, to influence public policy in order to achieve equality and social justice for young women, and to provide opportunities for participation in a world-wide women's movement.
Publication: Magazine
Publication title: Annual Review
Meetings/Conventions: - annual conference

Youth Hostels Association - England and Wales

Trevelyan House, Dimple Rd., Matlock, DE4 3YH, England, UK
Tel: 44 1629 592600
Fax: 44 1629 592702
Email: customerservices@yha.org.uk
Website: http://www.yha.org.uk
Founded: 1930
Members: 300000
Staff: 600
Contact: Roger Clarke, Chief Exec.
Fee: £6
Membership Type: individuals under 18 years of age
Fee: £12
Membership Type: individuals over 18 years of age
Description: Provides inexpensive accomodations for travelers worldwide. Welcomes individuals and groups of people. Facilities at some youth hostels for educational groups. Has 238 Youth Hostels in England and Wales.
Formerly: Youth Hostels Association - England
Publication: Annual Report
Publication title: Guide
Second publication: Magazine
Publication title: Triangle. Advertisements.

Zoological Society of London

Regent's Park, London, NW1 4RY, England, UK
Tel: 44 20 77223333
Fax: 44 20 75865743
Website: http://www.zsl.org
Founded: 1826
Members: 40000
Staff: 350
Description: Fellows of the Learned Society; Friends of London Zoo; Friends of Whipsnade. To promote the worldwide conservation of animal species and their habitats by stimulating public awareness and concern through the presentation of living collections, by relevant research including captive breeding and by direct action in the field.
Library Subject: zoology, conservation, animal husbandry, and taxonomy
Library Type: open to the public
Publication: Yearbook
Publication title: International Zoo Yearbook
Second publication: Journal
Publication title: Journal of Zoology
Meetings/Conventions: Scientific Meeting - monthly

NORTHERN IRELAND

Action Cancer

1 Marlborough Park, Belfast, BT9 6XS, Northern Ireland, UK
Tel: 44 2890 803344
Fax: 44 2890 803356
Email: info@actioncancer.org
Website: http://www.actioncancer.org
Founded: 1973
Staff: 42
Contact: Louise Wardle Hunter
Description: Works to heighten awareness of the importance of early cancer detection. Offers breast and cervical cancer screening services for women, and testicular and prostatic screening services for men. Provides counselling for cancer patients, families, and friends. Maintains research lab. Disseminates information.
Publication: Magazine
Publication title: Action Cancer News Update
Second publication: Annual Report
Meetings/Conventions: - annual seminar

Action on Smoking and Health - Ireland
ASH-NI

5 Northumberland Rd., Dublin BT9 6DX, Northern Ireland, Ireland
Tel: 44 353 2310500
Fax: 44 353 2310555
Email: admin@irishcancer.ie
Website: http://www.ash.ie
Founded: 1970
Staff: 40
Contact: Ms. Arlene Spiers, Chief Exec.
Description: Supports cancer research/prevention and care. Individuals united to disseminate information on the dangers of smoking. Seeks to establish smoke-free public areas and help those addicted to smoking. Works with medical and health groups in support of its aims. Support groups for cancer patients and families, nurses in cancer centres and units, patient advocacy.

Alliance Party of Northern Ireland
APNI

88 University St., Belfast, BT7 1HE, Northern Ireland, UK
Tel: 44 2890 324274
Fax: 44 2890 333147
Email: alliance@allianceparty.org
Website: http://www.allianceparty.org
Founded: 1970
Members: 3000
Staff: 6
Contact: Stephen Farry, Gen.Sec.
Description: Cross-community party in Northern Ireland dedicated to a non-sectarian society.
Publication: Newsletter
Publication title: Alliance News
Second publication: Booklet
Publication title: Governing With Consent
Meetings/Conventions: - annual conference - Exhibits.

Amalgamated Transport and General Workers Union Women's Committee

Transport House, 102 High St., Belfast, BT1 2OL, Northern Ireland, UK
Tel: 44 1232 232381
Fax: 44 1232 240133
Contact: Fiona Marshall

Description: Represents the interests of women members in the Amalgamated Transport and General Workers Union. Liaises with women's organizations to develop the active involvement of women in society.

Association for Medical Deans in Europe
AMDE

Grosvenor Rd., Belfast, BT12 6HJ, Northern Ireland, UK
Tel: 44 28 90240503
Fax: 44 28 90240899
Founded: 1979

Association of Landscape Contractors of Ireland

c/o Mrs. Lyn Reagney
22 Summerhill Park, Bangor, BT20 5QQ, Northern Ireland, UK
Email: secretary@alci.org.uk
Website: http://www.alci.org.uk
Founded: 1971
Members: 120
Contact: Debbie Eve, Sec.
Description: Represents and supports landscape contractors in Ireland.

Breast Cancer Support Service - Northern Ireland

c/o Ulster Cancer Foundation
40-42 Eglantine Ave., Belfast, BT9 6DX, Northern Ireland, UK
Tel: 44 2890 663281
Fax: 44 2890 660081
Email: info@ulstercancer.org
Website: http://www.ulstercancer.co.uk
Founded: 1974
Staff: 50
Contact: Eileen Creery
Description: Promotes awareness of breast care and early detection of breast cancer. Supports the rehabilitation of women who have breast cancer and breast surgery.
Library Type: open to the public
Formerly: Breast Care and Mastectomy Support Service
Publication: Booklet
Publication title: Coping with Breast Cancer
Meetings/Conventions: Support Group Meetings - monthly

Carers Northern Ireland

11 Lower Crescent, Belfast, BT7 1NR, Northern Ireland, UK
Tel: 44 28 90439843
Fax: 44 28 90329299
Email: info@carersni.org
Staff: 5
Contact: Helen Ferguson, Dir.
Description: Individuals and organizations involved in caring. Seeks to raise the awareness of the needs of carers. Works with all levels of government and society to inform, support and advise.

Construction Employers' Federation

143 Malone Rd., Belfast, BT9 6SU, Northern Ireland, UK
Tel: 44 28 90877143
Fax: 44 28 90877155
Email: mail@cefni.co.uk
Website: http://www.cefni.co.uk
Founded: 1945
Members: 500
Staff: 20
Contact: J.R. Armstrong, Asst.Dir.

Description: Employers in the NI Construction Industry. Protects and promotes the interests of member firms in the NI construction industry.
Library Subject: law and construction
Library Type: not open to the public
Publication: Annual Report
Second publication: Bulletin

Eating Disorders Northern Ireland
78 Glengoland Pk., Belfast, BT17 0JB, Northern Ireland, UK
Tel: 44 2890 621627
Founded: 1992
Members: 20
Staff: 1
Contact: Ann McCann, Chair
Description: Support group for carers and sufferers of anorexia and other eating disorders. Disseminates information.
Library Subject: eating disorders
Library Type: reference

Equality Commission of Northern Ireland
EOCNI
Equality House, 7-9 Shaftesbury Sq., Belfast, BT2 7DP, Northern Ireland, UK
Tel: 44 2890 500600
Fax: 44 2890 331544
Email: information@equalityni.org
Website: http://www.equalityni.org
Founded: 1998
Staff: 143
Contact: I. Kingston
Description: Values and promotes respect for diversity, aims to eliminate unlawful discrimination and achieve equality and opportunity for all.
Library Subject: employment and society issues for women
Library Type: open to the public
Formerly: Equal Opportunities Commission - Northern Ireland
Meetings/Conventions: - annual conference

European Contact Dermatitis Society
ECDS
Grosvenor Rd., Belfast, BT12 6BA, Northern Ireland, UK
Tel: 44 28 90240503

Federation of the Retail Licensed Trade
91 University St., Belfast, BT7 1HP, Northern Ireland, UK
Tel: 44 28 90327578
Fax: 44 28 90327578
Founded: 1872
Members: 1200
Staff: 5
Contact: Nicola Jamison, Gen.Sec.
Fee: £95
Description: Trade protection and development.
Publication: Magazine
Publication title: Catering and Licensing Review. Advertisements.

Federation of Women's Institutes of Northern Ireland
209/211 Upper Lisburn Rd., Belfast, BT10 0LL, Northern Ireland, UK
Tel: 44 2890 301506
Fax: 44 2890 431127
Email: womensinstitute.ni@talk21
Founded: 1932
Members: 9000
Staff: 3
Description: Umbrella organization of institutes studying women and women's issues. Promotes and supports the interests of women of Northern Ireland.
Publication: Magazine
Publication title: Ulster Countrywoman. Advertisements.

Fermanagh Women's Network
FWN
52 Forthill St., Enniskillen, BT74 6AJ, Northern Ireland, UK
Tel: 44 2866 328998
Fax: 44 2866 323355
Email: fwn@compuserve.com
Founded: 1992
Members: 25
Staff: 3
Contact: Fidelma Carolan, Coordinator
Fee: £10
Membership Type: associate
Fee: £20
Membership Type: full
Description: Individuals and organizations. Seeks to advance the legal, social, and economic status of women; promotes increased attention to women's health concerns. Operates network of local women's associations; conducts lobbying and advocacy activities to insure public policies promoting gender equity.
Library Subject: Women, rural development
Library Type: reference

General Council of the Bar of Northern Ireland
Royal Courts of Justice, Chichester St., Belfast, BT1 3JZ, Northern Ireland, UK
Tel: 44 2890 562349
Fax: 44 2890 562350
Email: chief.executive@barcouncil-ni.org.uk
Website: http://www.barcouncil-ni.org.uk
Description: Professional body representing all Barristers in Northern Ireland.

Ileostomy and Internal Pouch Support Group
Peverill House, 1-5 Mill Rd., Ballyclare, BT39 9DR, Northern Ireland, UK
Tel: 44 28 93344043
Fax: 44 289 3324606
Email: info@the-ia.org.uk
Website: http://www.ileostomypouch.demon.co.uk
Founded: 1956
Members: 9636
Staff: 1
Contact: Anne Demick, Natl.Sec.
Description: To help people who have had or are about to have their colon removed, to return to a fully active and normal life as soon as possible. The activities of IA include hospital and home visiting,

members' meetings, equipment exhibitions, medical research, stoma-care clinics, advisory services, lectures and demonstrations.
Publication: Journal
Publication title: IA Journal

Institute of Chartered Accountants in Ireland
11 Donegall Sq. South, Belfast, BT1 5JE, Northern Ireland, UK
Tel: 44 2890 321600
Fax: 44 2890 230071
Email: ca@icai.ie
Website: http://www.icai.ie/contact.htm
Contact: Mary Armstrong, Admin.
Description: Chartered accountants in Ireland.

International Association of Neuromuscular Neurologists
Queen's University, Belfast, BT7 1NN, Northern Ireland, UK

International Society for Diagnostic Quantitative Pathology
ISDQP
Grosvenor Rd., Belfast, BT12 6BL, Northern Ireland, UK
Tel: 44 1232 263115
Fax: 44 1232 233643
Email: p.hamilton@qub.ac.uk
Founded: 1994
Description: Furthers the development and application of quantitative methodology in pathological research, practice and education.

International Society for Eighteenth-Century Studies
ISECS
c/o Simon Davies
School of Languages, Literatures and Arts, The Queen's University, Belfast, BT7 1NN, Northern Ireland, UK
Tel: 44 1865 284600
Fax: 44 1865 284610
Email: ab@c18.org
Website: http://www.c18.org/so/
Founded: 1963
Members: 9000
Contact: Simon Davies, Sec.Gen.
Description: Individuals interested in 18th century culture; libraries, associations, and institutes concerned with 18th century studies are corporate members. Objectives are to promote growth, development, and cooperation in studies and research related to the 18th century and to advance communication and circulation of information.
Publication: Newsletter
Meetings/Conventions: - quadrennial congress Los Angeles California United States

Irish Linen Guild
5C The Square, Hillsborough, BT26 6AG, Northern Ireland, UK
Tel: 44 2892 689999
Fax: 44 2892 689968
Email: info@irishlinen.co.uk
Website: http://www.irishlinen.co.uk
Founded: 1928
Members: 26
Staff: 3
Contact: Miss Cathy Martin, Mktg.Mgr.

Description: Members are drawn from all stages of the linen manufacturing process from spinning and weaving to finishing and converting. Membership is open to companies producing or converting 100% linen which is both woven and finished in Ireland. Promotes the image of Irish linen in national and international markets. This is done by advertising campaigns, working closely with national and international trade and consumer press, exhibiting at relevant textile trade fairs, providing p-o-s material, in-store promotions and training sessions.
Publication: Newsletter
Publication title: Cutting Edge. Advertisements.
Publication title: The Gift of Irish Linen
Meetings/Conventions: - annual

Irish Moiled Cattle Society
c/o Glenn Speer, Sec.
Countryside Services Ltd., 97 May Rd., Dungannon, BT71 7DX, Northern Ireland, UK
Tel: 44 2887 789770
Fax: 44 2890 371231
Email: irishmoiled@ufuhq.com
Founded: 1926
Contact: Glenn Speer, Sec.
Description: Committed to development and improvement of the moiled cattle breed; introduced a DNA testing program to ensure validity of pedigrees and integrity of the breed gene pool.

Law Society of Northern Ireland
98 Victoria St., Belfast, BT1 3JZ, Northern Ireland, UK
Tel: 44 28 90231614
Fax: 44 28 90232606
Founded: 1922

Londonderry Chamber of Commerce
Chamber of Commerce House, 1 St. Solumb's Ct., Londonderry, BT48 6PT, Northern Ireland, UK
Description: Promotes commerce and industry in Londonderry, Northern Irealnd.

National Association for Educational Guidance for Adults
PO Box 459, Belfast, BT2 8YA, Northern Ireland, UK
Tel: 44 2890 271509
Fax: 44 2890 271507
Email: admin@naega.org.uk
Website: http://www.naega.org.uk
Founded: 1982
Members: 1000
Contact: Penny Thei, Sec.
Fee: £180
Membership Type: corporate
Fee: £35
Membership Type: personal
Description: Members include individuals and corporations who are involved in adult guidance for lifelong learning. Aims to promote the formation and development of lifelong learning guidance for adults. Promotes high standards of practice. Established to provide a focus for the growing field of lifelong learning guidance for adults. Organizes conferences, seminars and staff development events. Provides a forum for news, views and debate through the Association Newsletter. Undertakes occasional publications on topical and relevant subjects.

Offers advice to its membership and acts as an information point for general inquiries.
Publication: Magazine
Publication title: News and Views
Meetings/Conventions: - annual conference

National Board for Nursing, Midwifery and Health Visiting for Northern Ireland

Centre House, 79 Chichester St., Belfast, BT1 4JE, Northern Ireland, UK
Tel: 44 28 9023 8152
Fax: 44 28 9033 3298
Email: enquiries@nbni.n-i.nhs.uk
Founded: 1979
Members: 9
Staff: 30
Contact: Lorraine Andrews, Sec.
Description: Non-executive members appointed by the Head of Department of Health and Social Services for Northern Ireland, executive members ie the Chief Executive, and Director of Finance & Administration of the National Board. The majority of members are registered nurses, midwives or health visitors. To approve institutions in relation to provision of training courses for nurses, midwives and health visitors which meet Central Council standards; to collaborate with Council in the promotion of improved training methods; and such other functions as the Head of the Department of Health may by order prescribe.
Publication: Annual Report
Second publication: Papers
Meetings/Conventions: - annual conference - Exhibits.

Northern Ireland Association for Mental Health

80 University St., Beacon House, Belfast, BT7 1HE, Northern Ireland, UK
Tel: 44 28 90328474
Fax: 44 28 90232940
Founded: 1959
Members: 280
Staff: 145
Contact: Pauline Rainey, Education Ofcr.
Fee: £10
Description: Promotes dignity, choice, integration and participation for those with mental health needs living in the community. Aims to offer services of the highest standard to people with mental health needs; inform and educate the public about mental health; and press for high standards in the provision of mental health services.
Publication title: Mental Health Matters. Advertisements.

Northern Ireland Bankers' Association

17-25 College Sq. E., Stokes House, Belfast, BT1 6DE, Northern Ireland, UK
Tel: 44 28 90327551
Fax: 44 28 90331449
Members: 4
Staff: 3
Contact: Bill McAlister
Description: Retail banks in Northern Ireland. Represents Northern Ireland banks to government, academics and the public. It operates as a forum for matters which must be dealt with collectively such as fraud attitudes to new legislation, maintaining clearing rules and statistics.

Northern Ireland Bat Group

c/o Mrs. L. Rendle
Zoology Department, Ulster Museum, Botanic Gardens, Belfast, BT9 5AB, Northern Ireland, UK
Tel: 44 28 90383144
Fax: 44 1232 383103
Email: lynne.rendle.um@nics.gov.uk
Founded: 1985
Members: 50
Contact: Mrs. L. Rendle
Fee: £10
Description: Coordinates bat conservation and research activities in Northern Ireland. Sponsors public education programs to encourage protection of bats and their roosting sites.

Northern Ireland Chamber of Commerce and Industry

22 Great Victoria St., Belfast, BT2 7BJ, Northern Ireland, UK
Tel: 44 28 90244113
Fax: 44 28 90247024
Email: mail@northernirelandchamber.com
Website: http://www.nicci.co.uk
Members: 1200
Staff: 11
Contact: John Stringer, Chief Exec.
Description: Promotes business and commerce.

Northern Ireland Chest Heart and Stroke Association

21 Dublin Rd., Belfast, BT2 7HB, Northern Ireland, UK
Tel: 44 28 90320184
Fax: 44 28 90333487
Website: http://www.nichsa.com
Founded: 1946
Staff: 106
Contact: Andrew Dougal, CEO
Description: Promotes the prevention of, and alleviate the suffering resulting from chest, heart, and stroke illnesses in Northern Ireland. Supports rehabilitation facilities; offers subsidized vacations for families affected by these diseases; provides nebulizers for asthmatic children and adults; provides help and advice; provides grants for people with low incomes; funds research.

Northern Ireland Committee

c/o Irish Congress of Trade Unions
3 Wellington Park, Belfast, BT9 6DJ, Northern Ireland, UK
Tel: 44 1232 681726
Fax: 44 1232 681726
Email: nic@ictu.iol.ie
Founded: 1944
Members: 32
Staff: 7
Contact: Tom Gillen, Acting NI Officer
Description: Umbrella organization for trade unions in Northern Ireland. Promotes women's enhanced status in the work place and community. Collaborates with community organizations on matters of common concern
Formerly: Formed by Merger of, ICTU Women's Committee
Meetings/Conventions: - biennial conference

Northern Ireland Countryside Staff Association

c/o Jenny Fuller
Peatlands Park, Dungannon, BT71 6NW, Northern Ireland, UK
Tel: 44 2838851102
Fax: 44 35338851821
Email: nicsa@yahoo.co.uk
Website: http://www.nicsa.co.uk
Founded: 1980
Members: 70
Contact: Jenny Fuller, Chairperson
Fee: £12
Description: Aims to promote and encourage a high standard of professionalism amongst members. Aims to assist the development of communication and the interchange of ideas both within the Association and with other bodies. Encourages and co-ordinates training for the membership.

Northern Ireland Deer Society

9 Mount Shalgus, Randalstown, Antrim, BT41 3LE, Northern Ireland, UK
Tel: 44 289 4472626
Email: jmac9@btinternet.com
Founded: 1970
Members: 50
Contact: John McCurdy, Chm.
Fee: £15
Membership Type: ordinary
Description: Conserves deer and their habitats.

Northern Ireland Federation of Housing Associations
NIFHA

38 Hill St., Belfast, BT1 2LB, Northern Ireland, UK
Tel: 44 28 90230446
Fax: 44 28 90238057
Email: info@nifha.org
Website: http://www.nifha.org
Founded: 1976
Members: 45
Staff: 5
Contact: Chris Williamson, Dir.
Description: Represents and promotes housing associations in Northern Ireland. Provides affordable housing for the benefit of the community.

Northern Ireland Food and Drink Association
NIFDA

Quay Gate House, 15 Scrabo St., Belfast, BT5 4BD, Northern Ireland, UK
Tel: 44 28 90452424
Fax: 44 28 90453373
Email: mbell@nifda.co.uk
Website: http://www.nifda.co.uk
Founded: 1996
Contact: Michael Bell, Dir.
Description: Companies involved in all sectors of the food and drink industry. Represents and promotes member interests to improve the competitiveness of the industry in Northern Ireland.

Northern Ireland Gay Rights Association
NIGRA

PO Box 44, Belfast, BT1 1SH, Northern Ireland, UK
Tel: 44 2890 665257
Fax: 44 2890 664111
Email: nigra@dnet.co.uk
Founded: 1975
Contact: P.A. MagLochlainn, Pres.
Description: Promotes gay rights in Northern Ireland.
Library Subject: gay community in Northern Ireland
Library Type: lending

Northern Ireland Grain Trade Association

Cuinne an Chaireil, 27 BerwickView, Moira, BT67 0SX, Northern Ireland, UK
Tel: 44 28 92611044
Fax: 44 28 92611979
Email: doris@leenanpr.demon.co.uk
Website: http://www.nifda.co.uk/company_details.asp?memID=88
Contact: Doris Lennan, Sec.

Northern Ireland Hotels Federation

Midland Bldg., Whitla St., Belfast, BT15 1JP, Northern Ireland, UK
Tel: 44 28 90351110
Fax: 44 28 90351509
Email: office@nihf.co.uk
Website: http://www.nihf.co.uk
Founded: 1922
Members: 170
Staff: 2
Contact: John Stuart, Off.Dir.
Description: Hotel, guesthouse and trade members. Represents fee paying members in discussion with government, tourist boards, other representative bodies. Co-ordinates information and advisory function for members.
Formerly: Northern Ireland Hotels and Caterers Association
Publication: Newsletter
Publication title: Hotplate

Northern Ireland Human Rights Commission
NIHRC

Temple Court, 39 North St., Belfast, BT1 1NA, Northern Ireland, UK
Tel: 44 28 9024 3987
Fax: 44 28 9024 7844
Email: info@nihrc.org
Website: http://www.nihrc.org/
Founded: 1992
Contact: Betsy Swart
Description: Aims to educate Americans about human rights violations in Northern Ireland. Sponsors an annual fact-finding delegation to Northern Ireland to investigate abuses. Compiles statistics; conducts educational programs.
Library Subject: human rights in Northern Ireland
Library Type: open to the public
Publication title: Truth to Power

Northern Ireland Local Government Association

123 York St., Belfast, BT15 1AB, Northern Ireland, UK
Tel: 44 2890 249286
Fax: 44 2890 233328
Email: susan.alani@btclick.com
Founded: 2001

Members: 26
Staff: 2
Contact: Heather Moorhead, Chief Exec.
Description: Open to all district councils in Northern Ireland. Promotes and protects the interests of district councils.
Formerly: Association of Local Authorities of Nothern Ireland
Publication title: Councillor's Handbook
Meetings/Conventions: - bimonthly general assembly

Northern Ireland Master Painters' Association

16 The Square, Ballygowan, Newtownards, BT23 6HU, Northern Ireland, UK
Tel: 44 1238 528384
Founded: 1922
Members: 85
Contact: Edwards Marks
Description: To raise the standards of their members and for the public.

Northern Ireland Meat Exporters Association
NIMEA

24 Ballydown Rd., Banbridge, BT32 3RP, Northern Ireland, UK
Tel: 44 28 40626338
Fax: 44 28 40626083
Email: enquiries@nimea.co.uk
Website: http://www.nimea.co.uk
Description: Major beef and lamb EC approved slaughtering and cutting companies. Promotes the interests of meat processors and exporters in Northern Ireland.

Northern Ireland Mixed Marriage Association
NIMMA

28 Bedford St., Belfast, BT2 7FE, Northern Ireland, UK
Tel: 44 28 90235444
Fax: 44 28 90434544
Email: nimma@nireland.com
Website: http://www.nimma.org.uk
Founded: 1974
Members: 70
Staff: 2
Contact: Philomena McQuillan
Description: Seeks to provide mutual help and support for people involved in or about to be involved in mixed marriages in Northern Ireland.
Publication: Newsletter
Publication title: NIMMA Update
Meetings/Conventions: - annual conference

Northern Ireland Ploughing Association
NIPA

475 Antrim Rd., Belfast, BT15 3DA, Northern Ireland, UK
Tel: 44 1232 370222
Fax: 44 1232 370739
Email: adair@upuhq.com
Founded: 1938
Members: 100
Staff: 3
Contact: R. Adair, Sec.
Fee: £15
Membership Type: by nomination
Fee: £20

Membership Type: voluntary
Description: Ploughmen. Seeks to maintain high standards in the ancient art of ploughing. Promotes friendship and understanding among ploughmen.
Publication: Booklet
Publication title: Match Program. Advertisements.
Meetings/Conventions: International Ploughing Match - annual - Exhibits.

Northern Ireland Public Service Alliance
NIPSA

54 Wellington Park, Belfast, BT9 6DP, Northern Ireland, UK
Tel: 44 28 90661831
Fax: 44 28 90665847
Email: info@nipsa.org.uk
Website: http://www.nipsa.org.uk/
Founded: 1974
Members: 35000
Staff: 51
Contact: James McCusker, Gen.Sec.
Description: Civil and public servants in Northern Ireland. Promotes and protects members' interests. Acts as a liaison between members and their employers. Offers legal assistance; sponsors courses.
Library Type: reference
Formerly: Absorbed, Civil Service Group
Publication: Report
Publication title: NIPSA Annual Report
Publication title: NIPSA News
Meetings/Conventions: - annual conference - Exhibits.

Northern Ireland Textiles and Apparel Association

5C The Square, Hillsborough, BT26 6AG, Northern Ireland, UK
Tel: 44 28 9268 9999
Fax: 44 28 9268 9968
Email: info@nita.co.uk
Website: http://www.nita.co.uk
Founded: 1993
Members: 50
Staff: 5
Contact: Mrs. Linda MacHugh, Dir.
Description: Companies in the Northern Ireland textiles and apparel sector representing 19,000 employees. Represents and lobbies on behalf of the Northern Ireland textiles and apparel industry.
Publication: Newsletter. Advertisements.
Meetings/Conventions: - annual conference - Exhibits.

Northern Ireland Training Council Association
NITCA

4B Weavers Court, Linfield Rd., Belfast, BT12 5GH, Northern Ireland, UK
Tel: 44 28 90244202
Fax: 44 28 90438638
Email: nitca@dnet.co.uk
Founded: 1995
Members: 32
Staff: 1
Contact: Ms. Sheree Totton
Description: Influences programs and policies of government. Coordinates linkages with national and international institutions and organizations; provides support and services to individual training councils; enhances people development culture and its contribution towards improving business competitiveness.

Northern Ireland Women's European Platform
NIWEP

58 Howard St., Belfast, BT1 6PJ, Northern Ireland, UK
Tel: 44 2890 339916
Fax: 44 2890 339917
Email: niwep@btconnect.com
Website: http://www.niwep.org
Founded: 1989
Members: 60
Staff: 2
Contact: Marian Laverty, Admin.
Fee: £30
Description: Organizations representing 40,000 women in Northern Ireland. Promotes gender equity; represents women's organizations before national and international agencies.
Library Subject: health, education, employment, childcare, equal opportunities, social issues, violence against women
Library Type: open to the public
Publication: Journal
Publication title: Northern Ireland Political Women and the Press
Meetings/Conventions: - semimonthly general assembly

Parents and Professionals and Autism Northern Ireland
PAPA

Donald House, Knockbracken Healthcare Park, Saintfield Rd., Belfast, BT8 8BH, Northern Ireland, UK
Tel: 44 28 90401729
Fax: 44 28 90403467
Email: info@autismni.org
Website: http://www.autismni.org
Founded: 1989
Members: 400
Staff: 6
Contact: Arlene Cassidy, Dir.
Fee: £15
Description: Established by parents of autistic children and professionals that are concerned with autism in Northern Ireland. Seeks to ensure that people within the autistic spectrum and their caregivers have access to appropriate services, enabling people with autism to be valued members of their community. Provides resources, information, and advice on autism; encourages research and training; works in partnership with a range of voluntary, private, and statutory agencies; works to increase public awareness of autism.
Library Subject: autism
Library Type: open to the public
Publication: Newsletter
Publication title: Contact
Meetings/Conventions: - annual conference

Pharmaceutical Society of Northern Ireland

73 University St., Belfast, BT7 1HL, Northern Ireland, UK
Tel: 44 2890 326927
Fax: 44 2890 439919
Email: chief.exec@psni.org.uk
Founded: 1925
Members: 1707
Staff: 3
Contact: Mrs. S. Maltby, Chief Exec.
Description: Registered pharmacists. Acts as a professional and registration body for pharmacists and pharmacies in Northern Ireland.

Railway Preservation Society of Ireland
RPSI

PO Box 171, Larne, BT40 1UU, Northern Ireland, UK
Tel: 44 28 28260803
Fax: 44 28 28260803
Email: rpsitrains@hotmail.com
Website: http://www.rpsi-online.org
Founded: 1964
Members: 1050
Contact: Paul McCann, Hon.Sec.
Fee: £20
Membership Type: adult
Fee: £10
Membership Type: junior
Description: Individuals working to promote interest in the railways of Ireland and their history. Promotes exchange of railway experience and knowledge among members. Seeks to restore, maintain, and operate vintage steam locomotives and rolling stock on the main lines of Ireland.
Publication: Magazine
Publication title: Five Foot Three. Advertisements.

Royal Society of Ulster Architects
RSUA

2 Mount Charles, Belfast, BT7 1NZ, Northern Ireland, UK
Tel: 44 28 90323760
Fax: 44 28 90237313
Founded: 1901

Royal Ulster Agricultural Society
RUAS

Balmoral, Belfast, BT9 6GW, Northern Ireland, UK
Tel: 44 28 90665225
Fax: 44 28 90661264
Email: general@kingshall.co.uk
Founded: 1826

Social Democratic and Labour Party
SDLP

121 Ormeau Rd., Belfast, BT7 1SH, Northern Ireland, UK
Tel: 44 28 90247700
Fax: 44 28 90236699
Email: sdlp@indigo.ie
Website: http://www.sdlp.ie
Founded: 1970
Staff: 7
Contact: Gerry Cosgrove, Gen.Sec.
Fee: £5
Membership Type: Individual/Associate
Description: Political party in Northern Ireland. Advocates European unity; encourages cooperation between Catholics and Protestants in Ireland; promotes social justice and human rights.
Publication: Newsletter
Publication title: SDLP Newsheet
Meetings/Conventions: - annual conference

The HIV Support Centre/AIDS Helpline

7 James St. S., Belfast, BT2 8DN, Northern Ireland, UK
Tel: 44 28 90249268
Fax: 44 28 90329845
Email: admin@aidshelpline.org.uk

Website: http://www.aidshelpline.org.uk
Founded: 1985
Members: 48
Staff: 6
Contact: G. Campbell, Dir.
Fee: £10
Membership Type: individual
Description: Makes available counselors to offer advice to those affected by AIDS. Offers home support. Conducts preventative education and a outreach programs. Promotes fundraising. Provides a range of complementary therapies freephone helpline, health enquiries, advice line.
Library Subject: HIV/AIDS
Library Type: open to the public

Ulster Archaeological Society

c/o The Hon. Secretary
Department of Archaeology and Ethnography, Ulster Museum, Botanic Gardens, Belfast, BT9 5AB, Northern Ireland, UK
Tel: 44 2890383051
Email: arcethno.um@nics.gov.uk
Website: http://journals.eecs.qub.ac.uk/uas/journals.html
Founded: 1935
Members: 250
Contact: Ken Pullin, Hon.Sec.
Fee: £30
Membership Type: individual
Fee: £10
Membership Type: retired
Description: Aims to promote and provide a forum for the interest in local archaeology and history, through lectures, fieldtrips and its annual publication, the Ulster Journal of Archaeology.
Publication: Journal
Publication title: Ulster Journal of Archaeology

Ulster Architectural Heritage Society

c/o Miss. Joan Kinch
66 Donegall Pass, Belfast, BT7 1BU, Northern Ireland, UK
Tel: 44 2890550213
Fax: 44 2890550214
Email: info@uahs.co.uk
Website: http://www.uahs.co.uk
Founded: 1967
Members: 1200
Staff: 3
Contact: Peter O'Marlow, Chm.
Fee: £14
Membership Type: annual
Fee: £20
Membership Type: joint
Description: Promotes members interests.

Ulster Cancer Foundation
UCF

40-42 Eglantine Ave., Belfast, BT9 6DX, Northern Ireland, UK
Tel: 44 28 90663281
Fax: 44 28 90660081
Email: info@ulstercancer.org
Website: http://www.ulstercancer.org
Founded: 1970
Staff: 40
Contact: Arlene Spiers, Chief Exec.

Description: Encourages and facilitates research on cancer and its prevention and early diagnosis. Seeks to help patients and their families cope with cancer. Works for new and better treatments for cancer, helps people reduce their risk of developing the disease. Conducts educational programs including clinics and training sessions for health care professionals; makes available children's services; sponsors competitions and bestows awards. Compiles statistics.
Library Type: reference
Publication: Book
Publication title: Cancer Control in Practice
Second publication: Book
Publication title: Cancer Education and Care in the Workplace
Meetings/Conventions: - periodic conference

Ulster Chemists' Association

c/o Andrea Grattan
73 University St., Belfast, BT7 1HL, Northern Ireland, UK
Tel: 44 2890320787
Fax: 44 2890313737
Members: 470
Contact: Fiona Martz, Pres.
Description: Promotes chemists in Northern Ireland.

Ulster Farmers' Union

475 Antrim Rd., Belfast, BT15 3DA, Northern Ireland, UK
Tel: 44 2890 370222
Fax: 44 2890 371231
Email: info@ufuhq.com
Website: http://www.ufuni.org
Founded: 1918
Members: 12500
Staff: 71
Contact: John Gilliand, Pres.
Description: Full membership is limited to persons actively engaged in farming, representatives of companies actively engaged in farming and retired farmers. To defend rights and promote interest of members; to seek to secure for members a fair return from their investment in agriculture; to stimulate social, educational, cultural and recreational activities in rural areas.
Publication title: UFU Diary
Second publication: Bulletin
Publication title: UFU News

Ulster Folk and Transport Museum

Cultra Manor, Holywood, BT18 0EU, Northern Ireland, UK
Tel: 44 28 90428428
Fax: 44 28 90428728
Email: jontybell@talk21.com
Founded: 1956
Members: 100
Contact:
Fee: £10
Membership Type: individual
Fee: £14
Membership Type: individual
Description: Aims to further and support the study of the history and culture of Ulster.
Formerly: Ulster Folk Life Society

Ulster Society of Organists and Choirmasters

16 Malone Hill Park, Belfast, BT9 6RD, Northern Ireland, UK
Tel: 44 28 90669273
Email: amaclaughlin@uk2.net
Website: http://dnausers.d-n-a.net/dnetzMNU/usoc/

Founded: 1918
Members: 175
Staff: 3
Contact: David Drinkell, Hon.Sec.
Fee: £17.5
Membership Type: ordinary
Fee: £10
Membership Type: student
Description: Church musicians of all denominations. Promotes: high standards in the selection and performance of church music; professional advancement of members; wider public interest in organ and choral music. Facilitates communication among members; sponsors social and educational activities.
Publication: Newsletter
Meetings/Conventions: - monthly meeting

Ulster Teachers' Union
UTU

94 Malone Rd., Belfast, BT9 5HP, Northern Ireland, UK
Tel: 44 28 90662216
Fax: 44 28 90663055
Email: office@utu.edu
Website: http://www.utu.edu/home.html
Founded: 1919
Members: 6000
Staff: 10
Contact: Ray Calvin, Gen.Sec.
Fee: £100
Membership Type: teachers
Description: Teachers and other educational personnel. Promotes effective primary and secondary education. Works to enhance the professional status of members. Represents members' interests before government agencies, school administrative bodies, and the public.
Library Subject: education service
Library Type: reference
Publication: Newspaper
Publication title: UTU News. Advertisements.
Meetings/Conventions: - annual conference

Ulster-Scots Language Society
USLS

24 Thornhill Park, Belfast, BT5 7AR, Northern Ireland, UK
Tel: 44 28 90655121
Founded: 1992
Description: Promotes knowledge and use of Ulster-Scots language and cultural traditions.

Visitor Attractions Association of Northern Ireland
VAANI

St. Anne's Ct., 59 N. St., Belfast, BT1 1NB, Northern Ireland, UK
Tel: 44 28 90246609
Founded: 1995
Members: 90
Description: Owners, operators, administrators, and other personnel of museums, country parks, heritage centers, and open farms. Promotes and advances tourism in Northern Ireland. Supports and assists attractions in improving product development and presentation and marketing.

Women in Alliance

88 University St., Belfast, BT7 1HE, Northern Ireland, UK
Tel: 44 1232 324274
Fax: 44 1232 333147
Founded: 1989
Members: 184
Contact: Eilcen Bell
Description: Political organization for women in Northern Ireland; branch of the Alliance Party of Northern Ireland.
Meetings/Conventions: Women in Politics - bimonthly conference

Women Together
WT

62 Lisburn Rd., Belfast, BT9 6AF, Northern Ireland, UK
Tel: 44 1232 315100
Fax: 44 1232 314864
Founded: 1970
Members: 300
Staff: 2
Contact: Anne Carr, Coordinator
Fee: £5
Membership Type: full
Description: Women united to advance peace and reconciliation. Promotes peaceful resolution of religious and political issues facing Northern Ireland. Seeks to create a pluralistic society where there is a mutual understanding and respect for cultural diversity. Provides support to victims of sectarian violence; sponsors cultural exchanges; conducts social and educational programs.
Library Subject: Peace, reconciliation, women's issues
Library Type: not open to the public
Publication: Brochure
Publication title: Women Together for Peace
Second publication: Newsletter
Meetings/Conventions: - periodic seminar

Women's Education Project-Worker's Educational Association

23 Market St., Enniskillen, BT74 7DS, Northern Ireland, UK
Tel: 44 2866 326914
Fax: 44 2866 327994
Email: eithne.mcnulty@wea-ni.com
Founded: 1910
Members: 130
Staff: 33
Contact: Eithne McNulty
Fee: £15
Membership Type: full
Description: Promotes women's education in Northern Ireland. Conducts day, evening, and weekend classes on women's issues. Provides tutor training.
Library Subject: community development, women's education, voluntary sector, WEA publications
Library Type: not open to the public
Publication: Reports

Women's Information Group

6 Mount Charles, Belfast, BT7 1NZ, Northern Ireland, UK
Tel: 44 2890 244119
Fax: 44 2890 244119
Email: women@infogroup.club24.co.uk
Founded: 1980
Members: 2500

Staff: 2
Contact: Kathleen Feenan
Description: An umbrella organization for women's groups in Northern Ireland. Provides an opportunity for women's organizations to meet and exchange experiences. Disseminates information.
Publication: Newsletter
Publication title: Women's Information Newsletter
Meetings/Conventions: Information Days - monthly

Young Alliance

88 University St., Belfast, BT7 1HE, Northern Ireland, UK
Tel: 44 2890 324274
Fax: 44 2890 33147
Email: alliance@allianceparty.org
Founded: 1970
Members: 100
Staff: 6
Contact: Chris Pilkington, Gen.Sec.
Description: Political organization for youth in Northern Ireland; branch of the Alliance Party of Northern Ireland.
Publication: Magazine
Publication title: The Other Line. Advertisements.
Meetings/Conventions: - monthly executive committee meeting

Zoological Society of Northern Ireland

33 Saratoga Av, Newtownards, BT23 4BO, Northern Ireland, UK
Founded: 1963

SCOTLAND

1745 Association

c/o Ms. C.W.H. Aikman
Ferry Cottage, Corran, Ardgour, Fort William, PH33 7AA, Scotland, UK
Tel: 44 1855 841306
Founded: 1946
Members: 300
Contact: Ms. C.W.H. Aikman, Sec.
Fee: £10
Description: Individuals in 10 countries interested in Jacobite history, particularly the 1745 Jacobite rising and its aftermath. (Led by Prince Charles Edward Stuart (1720-1788), the grandson of King James II, the Jacobite rising was an attempt to regain the throne of Great Britain, which was lost by the House of Stuart after the revolution of 1688 and acceded to William and Mary. The forces of Prince Charles were defeated at Culloden, Apr. 16, 1746).
Publication: Journal
Publication title: The Jacobite
Meetings/Conventions: - annual meeting UK

Aberdeen and Grampian Chamber of Commerce

21 Geoge St., Aberdeen, AB25 1XA, Scotland, UK
Tel: 44 1224 620621
Fax: 44 1224 645777
Email: amanda.harvie@agcc.co.uk
Members: 1700
Staff: 30
Contact: Amanda Harvie, Chief Exec.
Description: Supports and promotes the interests of business and commerce in northeastern Scotland.

Aberdeen Formation Evaluation Society
AFES

c/o John Owens, Pres.
Shell UK Exploration & Production, 1 Altens Farm Rd., Nigg, Aberdeen, AB9 3FY, Scotland, UK
Website: http://www.afes.org.uk/
Contact: John Owens, Pres.
Description: Dedicated to the promotion for the public benefit, education and knowledge in the scientific and technical aspects of formation evaluation, including reservoir characteristics of exposures from a geological and petrophysical perspective. Conducts career talks and a field trip to the Fife coast.
Meetings/Conventions: - monthly meeting

Aberdeen Geological Society

c/o Department of Geology & Petroleum Geology
University of Aberdeen, Meston Bldg., King's College, Aberdeen, AB24 3UE, Scotland, UK
Website: http://www.abdn.ac.uk/~gmi265/ags/ags.htm
Description: Amateur geologists, academics, students and professional geologists promoting the study of geology; conducts field trips to exotic geological locations around Scotland.
Meetings/Conventions: Christmas Party - annual party

Aberdeen-Angus Cattle Society
AACS

6 King's Pl., Perth, PH2 8AD, Scotland, UK
Tel: 44 1738 622477
Fax: 44 1738 636436
Email: info@aberdeen-angus.co.uk
Website: http://www.aberdeen-angus.com
Founded: 1879

Members: 1800
Staff: 7
Contact: Ron McHattie, Chief Exec.
Description: Breeders of Aberdeen-Angus cattle in Great Britain and Ireland. Promotes the breed; maintains pedigree records.
Publication title: Aberdeen-Angus Review. Advertisements.

Action by Christians Against Torture - England
ACAT

c/o Quex Road Methodist Church
40 Albert Rd., Saltash, PL12 4EB, Scotland, UK
Tel: 44 1752 849821
Fax: 44 1752 848921
Email: lois@acat-uk.freeserve.co.uk
Founded: 1984
Members: 500
Staff: 1
Contact: Lois Stamelis, Dir.
Fee: £15
Membership Type: Individual
Fee: £40
Membership Type: Group
Description: Christians and human rights activists in the United Kingdom working to abolish the practice of torture in all countries through letter writing, prayer, and education on the circumstances in which torture can occur. Works closely with related organizations in other countries.
Library Subject: Human rights
Library Type: reference
Publication: Newsletter
Publication title: ACAT Mailing
Meetings/Conventions: - annual conference - Exhibits.

Advocates for Animals

10 Queensferry St., Edinburgh, EH2 4PG, Scotland, UK
Tel: 44 131 2256039
Fax: 44 131 2206377
Email: info@advocatesforanimals.org
Website: http://www.advocatesforanimals.org.uk
Founded: 1912
Members: 10000
Staff: 5
Contact: Les Ward, Dir.
Fee: £8
Membership Type: regular
Fee: £5
Membership Type: unwaged
Description: Seeks to protect animals from cruelty and prevent of the infliction of suffering, the abolition of vivisection.
Library Subject: all animal subjects
Library Type: open to the public
Publication title: Annual Pictorial Review

Age Concern Scotland
ACS

113 Rose St., Edinburgh, EH2 3DT, Scotland, UK
Tel: 44 131 2203345
Fax: 44 131 2202779
Email: enquiries@acscot.org.uk
Website: http://www.ageconcernscotland.org.uk
Founded: 1943
Members: 500

Staff: 74
Description: Works to make the lives of older people in Scotland more secure, comfortable, dignified and enjoyable.
Library Subject: all topics concerning older people
Library Type: reference
Publication: Newsletter
Publication title: Adage
Second publication: Brochures
Meetings/Conventions: - annual convention - Exhibits.

Alcohol Focus Scotland

166 Buchanan St., Glasgow, G1 2LW, Scotland, UK
Tel: 44 141 3339677
Fax: 44 141 3331606
Email: jacklaw@alcohol-focus-scotland.org.uk
Website: http://www.alcohol-focus-scotland.org.uk
Founded: 1973
Staff: 14
Contact: Mr. Jack Law, Chief Exec.
Description: Seeks to reduce the level of alcohol abuse in Scotland. Conducts educational and training programs for health care professionals and therapists working with people who abuse alcohol; serves as a clearinghouse on alcohol abuse programs and services. Participates in charitable activities; compiles statistics.
Library Subject: alcohol, substance abuse counseling therapies
Library Type: reference
Formerly: Scottish Council on Alcohol
Publication: Newsletter
Publication title: Alcohol Update
Second publication: Annual Report
Publication title: Alcohol Focus Annual Report
Meetings/Conventions: - periodic board meeting

Alexander Thomson Society

1 Moray Place, Strathbungo, Glasgow, G41 2AQ, Scotland, UK
Tel: 44 141 4233747
Founded: 1991
Members: 400
Contact: Gavin Stamp, Chmn.
Fee: £10
Membership Type: ordinary
Description: Promotes and protects the work of the architect Alexander Thomson

Alzheimer Scotland-Action on Dementia
ASAD

22 Drumsheugh Gardens, Edinburgh, EH3 7RN, Scotland, UK
Tel: 44 131 2431453
Fax: 44 131 2431450
Email: alzheimer@alzscot.org
Website: http://www.alzscot.org
Founded: 1994
Members: 2100
Staff: 700
Contact: Jim Jackson, Chief Exec.
Fee: £15
Membership Type: individual
Fee: £20
Membership Type: group
Description: Works to help individuals with dementia and their carers in Scotland.
Publication: Newsletter
Publication title: Dementia in Scotland

Amnesty International - United Kingdom Scottish Office

6 Castle St., Edinburgh, EH2 3AT, Scotland, UK
Tel: 44 131 4666200
Fax: 44 131 4666201
Email: scotland@smanesty.org.uk
Website: http://www.amnesty.org.uk
Founded: 1992
Members: 15000
Staff: 3
Description: National branch of Amnesty International. Works to promote and defend human rights.

Applied Arts Scotland

6 Darnaway St., Edinburgh, EH3 6BG, Scotland, UK
Tel: 44 7890 376007
Website: http://appliedartsscotland.org.uk
Founded: 1992
Members: 300
Contact: Jenny Antonio
Fee: £25
Description: Craftspeople, galleries, organizations, local authorities and supporters of the applied arts. Formed to support and promote the applied arts in Scotland. Organizes exhibitions, workshops and members' events, and runs a commissioning register and information resource.
Publication: Bulletin
Publication title: Bulletin

Architectural Heritage Society of Scotland

33 Barony St., Edinburgh, EH3 6NX, Scotland, UK
Tel: 44 131 5570019
Fax: 44 131 5550047
Email: administrator@ahss.org.uk
Website: http://www.ahss.org.uk
Founded: 1959
Members: 1450
Staff: 2
Contact: Pauline Robinson
Description: People interested in historical buildings, architects. Concerned with the study and protection of Scottish architecture.
Formerly: Scottish Georgian Society
Publication: Journal
Publication title: Architectural Heritage
Second publication: Magazine

ASH Scotland

8 Frederick St., Edinburgh, EH2 2HB, Scotland, UK
Tel: 44 131 2254725
Fax: 44 131 2206604
Email: ashscotland@ashscotland.org.uk
Website: http://www.ashscotland.org.uk
Founded: 1973
Staff: 10
Contact: Maureen Moore, Ch.Exec.
Fee: £20
Description: National organisation dedicated to campaigning for a tobacco-free Scotland. Aims to: keep the tobacco issue on the public agenda; promote non-smoking as the norm; contribute to the reduction in the uptake of smoking; support stop smoking initiatives.
Library Subject: smoking and health, tobacco and society
Library Type: reference
Formerly: Scottish Committee Action on Smoking and Health

Publication: Newsletter
Publication title: Unfiltered News
Meetings/Conventions: - annual meeting

Associated Scottish Life Offices
ASLO

c/o Scottish Widows
69 Morrison St., Edinburgh, EH3 8BW, Scotland, UK
Fax: 44 1786 450427
Founded: 1848
Members: 7
Contact: G. Spence, Sec.
Description: Chief executives of Scottish life insurance companies. Represents members' interests in presentations on life assurance and related issues.

Association for Heritage Interpretation
AHI

c/o Administrator
Cruachan, Tayinloan, Tarbert, PA29 6XF, Scotland, UK
Tel: 44 1583 441114
Fax: 44 1583 441114
Email: admin@heritageinterpretation.org.uk
Website: http://www.heritageinterpretation.org.uk
Founded: 1975
Members: 600
Staff: 1
Contact: Michael H. Glen, Admin.
Fee: £75
Membership Type: full
Fee: £45
Membership Type: associate
Description: Encourages excellence in the presentation and management of UK's natural and cultural environments through promoting excellence in interpretation and raising interpretation as a profession.
Publication: Journal
Publication title: Interpretation Journal. Advertisements.
Meetings/Conventions: - annual conference Manchester UK

Association for International Cancer Research
AICR

Madras House, South St., North Haugh, St. Andrews, KY16 9EH, Scotland, UK
Tel: 44 1334 477910
Fax: 44 1334 478667
Email: jane.wilson@aicr.org.uk
Website: http://www.aicr.org.uk/
Founded: 1979
Members: 14
Staff: 4
Contact: Dr. C. Thomson, Chm.
Description: Funds cancer research. Disseminates research results.
Publication title: Progress
Meetings/Conventions: - periodic symposium

Association for Low Flow Anaesthesia

c/o Dr. Mike Logan
Department of Anaesthesia, Royal Infirmary of Edinburgh, Edinburgh, EH3 9YW, Scotland, UK
Tel: 44 131 5363652
Fax: 44 131 5363672

Email: mikel@srv1.med.ed.ac.uk
Website: http://www.alfanaes.freeserve.co.uk/alfa-1.htm
Founded: 1995
Contact: Dr. Mike Logan, Sec.
Description: Promotes the use and understanding of methods of inhalational anesthesia involving recirculation of exhaled gases and reduced fresh gas input. Fosters continuing education for anesthesiologists. Conducts research.

Association for Management Education and Training in Scotland

Cottrell Bldg., University of Stirling, Stirling, FK9 4LD, Scotland, UK
Tel: 44 1786 450906
Fax: 44 1786 465070
Founded: 1989
Members: 20
Staff: 1
Contact: Prof. Frank Pignatelli
Description: Providers and users of management education, training and development from across the spectrum of institutions, professional, corporate and government bodies. Provides a forum for discussion for providers and users of management education training and development in Scotland. Aims to get a balanced approach and a major objective is to recruit members from Scottish industry.
Publication title: MBA Factsheet

Association for Medical Education in Europe
AMEE

Centre for Medical Education, University of Dundee, Tay Park House, 484 Perth Rd., Dundee, DD2 1LR, Scotland, UK
Tel: 44 1382 631953
Fax: 44 1382 645748
Email: amee@dundee.ac.uk
Website: http://www.amee.org
Contact: Mrs. Pat Lilley, Admin.
Fee: £32
Membership Type: student
Fee: £42
Membership Type: individual
Description: Medical schools, educators, and students. Seeks to advance medical scholarship and practice. Serves as a clearinghouse on medical education; encourages communication and cooperation among members; sponsors research programs and continuing professional development courses.
Publication: Journal
Publication title: Medical Teacher. Advertisements.
Meetings/Conventions: Standards and Medical Education at a Time of Change - annual conference - Exhibits.

Association for Scottish Literary Studies
ASLS

c/o Department of Scottish History
9 University Gardens, University of Glasgow, Glasgow, G12 8QH, Scotland, UK
Tel: 44 141 3305309
Fax: 44 141 3305309
Email: d.jones@scothist.arts.gla.ac.uk
Website: http://www.asls.org.uk
Founded: 1970
Members: 800
Staff: 2
Contact: Duncan Jones
Fee: £34

Membership Type: individuals
Fee: £63
Membership Type: corporate
Description: Academics, teachers, writers, and other individuals in 22 countries interested in Scottish language and literature. Publishes books, journals, and study guides to promote the study, teaching, and writing of Scottish language and literature. Offers school, regional, and international conferences on all aspects of Scottish language and literature.
Publication title: New Writing Scotland. Advertisements.
Second publication: Newsletter
Publication title: Scotlit
Meetings/Conventions: - annual conference

Association for the Protection of Rural Scotland
APRS

Gladstone's Land, 3rd Fl., 483 Lawnmarket, Edinburgh, EH1 2NT, Scotland, UK
Tel: 44 131 2257012
Fax: 44 131 2256592
Email: aprs@aprs.org.uk
Website: http://www.aprs.org.uk
Founded: 1926
Members: 983
Staff: 3
Contact: Joan Geddes, Dir.
Description: Seeks to protect Scotland's countryside and to promote ideas for its care and improvement by means of constructive proposals, careful research and active involvement in the maintenance of landscape features.
Library Subject: Local authority development plans, countryside issues, planning
Library Type: open to the public
Publication: Newsletter
Publication title: APRS Newsletter. Advertisements.
Publication title: Costs and Benefits: The Role of Community Councils as Statutory Consultant for planning applications (June 1996) (No copyright)
Meetings/Conventions: - annual conference - Exhibits. UK

Association for the Study of Medical Education
ASME

12 Queen St., Edinburgh, EH2 1JE, Scotland, UK
Tel: 44 131 2259111
Fax: 44 131 2259444
Email: info@asme.org.uk
Website: http://www.asme.org.uk
Founded: 1957
Members: 970
Staff: 3
Contact: Nicky Pender, Off.Mgr.
Fee: £15
Membership Type: student
Fee: £60
Membership Type: non-clinical/training grade
Description: Individuals engaged in medical education at the undergraduate, postgraduate, and continuing professional development levels. Promotes knowledge and expertise in medical education. Facilitates information exchange and the establishment of formal networks linking members; serves as a forum for the debate of issues impacting the field of medical education.
Publication: Newsletter
Publication title: ASME Bulletin

Second publication: Journal
Publication title: Journal of Medical Education
Meetings/Conventions: - periodic meeting

Association in Scotland to Research Into Astronautics
ASTRA

c/o Duncan A. Lunan
Flat 65, Darliada Block, 56 Blythswood Ct., Anderston, Glasgow, G2 7PE, Scotland, UK
Tel: 44 141 2217658
Email: astra@dlunan.freeserve.co.uk
Website: http://www.astra.org.uk
Founded: 1953
Members: 100
Contact: Duncan A. Lunan, Treas.
Fee: £15
Membership Type: adult
Fee: £5
Membership Type: junior (under 18)
Description: Amateur and professional scientists from 9 countries active in the field of space research. Promotes, stimulates, and conducts space research. Engages in amateur astronomy and practical research such as waverider aerodynamics; operates public observatory in Airdrie, Scotland. Sponsors discussion projects as a basis for books on different aspects of space exploration; conducts scientific exhibitions and model rocketry for young members.
Library Subject: Exhibition material, space photos, astronomy and astronautic history.
Library Type: reference
Formerly: Scottish Branch of the British Interplanetary Society
Publication: Journal
Publication title: ASGARD. Advertisements.
Publication title: Newsletter/Programme
Meetings/Conventions: - periodic competition

Association of Arts Centres in Scotland
AACS

50 Forest Rd., Aberdeen, AB2 4BP, Scotland, UK
Tel: 44 1224 37115
Founded: 1970

Association of Bakery Ingredients Manufacturers

4A Torphichen St., Edinburgh, EH3 8JQ, Scotland, UK
Tel: 44 131 2299415
Fax: 44 131 2299407
Email: abim@abim.org.uk
Website: http://www.abim.org.uk
Founded: 1917
Members: 21
Staff: 3
Contact: Flora A. McLean, Exec.Sec.
Description: Promotes and represents members' interest in relation to European technical and legislative matters affecting the bakery ingredients manufacturing industry.

Association of Chief Police Officers in Scotland

c/o William Rae, Chief Constable, Strathclyde Police
Police Headquarters, 173 Pitt St., Glasgow, G2 4JS, Scotland, UK
Tel: 44 141 5322052
Fax: 44 141 5322058
Email: contactus@acpos.police.uk

Website: http://www.scottish.police.uk/main/acpos/acpos.htm
Contact: William Rae, Hon.Sec.
Description: Scottish police officers.

Association of Directors of Education in Scotland
ADES

c/o Children's Services
Stirling Council, Viewforth, Stirling, FK8 2ET, Scotland, UK
Fax: 44 1786 442782
Email: jeyesg@stirling.gov.uk
Founded: 1920
Members: 243
Contact: Mr. Gordon Jeyes, Gen.Sec.
Fee: £20
Description: Educational administrators in Scotland. Provides a forum for information exchange among members. Advises local and national governmental bodies on educational issues. Sponsors in-service training programs.
Publication: Directory
Publication title: Directory of Members
Second publication: Book
Publication title: The First Twenty-Five Years - 1920-1945
Meetings/Conventions: - annual conference UK

Association of European Metal Sink Manufacturers
AEMSM

Savoy Tower, 77 Renfrew St., 11th Fl., Glasgow, G2 3BZ, Scotland, UK
Tel: 44 141 3320826
Fax: 44 141 3325788
Email: aemsm@metcom.org.uk
Website: http://www.metcom.org.uk/memdetails/aemsm.htm
Founded: 1977
Members: 12
Staff: 2
Contact: F. Cruickshanks, Sec.
Fee: £940
Membership Type: full
Description: Metal sink manufacturers in 9 countries. Defends industry interests in dealings with governmental and other regulatory agencies.
Formerly: COFEB
Meetings/Conventions: - semiannual meeting

Association of Multiple Sclerosis Therapy Centres - Scotland
AMSTCS

MS Therapy Centre, 1 Burnett Rd., Inverness, IV1 1FT, Scotland, UK
Tel: 44 1463 240365
Founded: 1992
Members: 12
Staff: 40
Contact: Dr. Colin Webster
Fee: £200
Description: Multiple sclerosis therapy centers. Seeks to advance the treatment of multiple sclerosis; promotes an improved quality of life for people with multiple sclerosis and their families. Facilitates communication and cooperation among members; conducts research and educational programs; participates in charitable activities; compiles statistics.

Association of Planning Supervisors

16 Rutland Sq., Edinburgh, EH1 2BB, Scotland, UK
Tel: 44 131 2219959
Fax: 44 131 2210061
Email: info@aps.org.uk
Website: http://www.aps.org.uk
Founded: 1995
Members: 5000
Staff: 5
Contact: Brian B. Law, Chief Exec.
Fee: £85
Membership Type: ordinary
Fee: £180
Membership Type: corporate
Description: Across all disciplines within the construction industry subject to the CDM Regulations 1994. Aims to provide a centre of expertise and forum for information and research exchange for all those undertaking duties as Planning Supervisors under the CDM (Construction, Design & Management) Regulations 1994.
Publication title: Form of Appointment
Publication title: Model Health and Safety File
Meetings/Conventions: - annual meeting - Exhibits.

Association of Police Surgeons

1 Tennant Ave., College Milton South, East Kilbride, Glasgow, G74 5NA, Scotland, UK
Tel: 44 1355 244101
Email: aps@glasconf.demon.co.uk
Website: http://www.apsweb.org.uk
Founded: 1951
Members: 1050
Staff: 1
Contact: Dr. M.A. Knight
Description: Members are medical practitioners who regularly assist or advise the police in medical or forensic cases. To promote the best interests of police surgeons; advancement of medico legal knowledge in all its aspects; liaison between appointed police surgeons and other medical practitioners; practical and theoretical study of the subject by lectures, discussions, correspondence and any other means.

Association of Registrars of Scotland

77 Bank St., Alexandria, G83 OL3, Scotland, UK
Tel: 44 1389 608980
Fax: 44 1389 608982
Founded: 1865
Members: 230
Contact: E.A. Kilgour
Description: Practising Registrars of Births Deaths & Marriages, etc. Concerned with the dissemination of profession information, the consideration of questions arising in the practice of registration of births deaths and marriages and generally, the mutual benefit of Registrars and Assistant Registrars in Scotland.
Publication: Newsletter
Publication title: Informant

Association of Scottish Shellfish Growers

Mountview, Ardvasar, Isle of Skye, IV45 8RU, Scotland, UK
Tel: 44 147 1844324
Fax: 44 147 1844324
Email: 101723.1376@compuserve.com
Founded: 1981
Members: 65
Staff: 2
Contact: Doug McLeod, Chm.

Fee: £175
Membership Type: ordinary/associate
Description: Farmers of scallops, oysters and mussels in Scottish waters. Promotes and safeguards the interests of the shellfish cultivation industry in Scotland by acting as its voice in discussions with government, statutory bodies and the voluntary sector. Also seeks to raise the profile of the industry and to develop markets for shellfish growers.
Publication: Newsletter
Publication title: The Grower. Advertisements.
Meetings/Conventions: - annual conference

Association of Scottish Visitor Attractions
ASVA

Argyll's Lodging, Castle Wynd, Stirling, FK8 1EG, Scotland, UK
Tel: 44 1786 475152
Fax: 44 1786 474288
Email: info@asva.co.uk
Website: http://www.asva.co.uk
Founded: 1989
Members: 500
Staff: 3
Contact: Eva McDiarmid
Description: Visitor attractions companies and individuals interested in visitor attractions and suppliers of goods and services to visitor attractions. Represents the visitor attraction industry in Scotland. It aims to improve the quality and performance of existing attractions and inform the development of new ones, to promote attractions in a more effective way; develops staff and management skills through conferences, regular communication and the provision of a development helpline as well as on-site visits.
Publication: Newsletter
Publication title: ASVA News

Association of University Teachers - Scotland

6 Castle St., Edinburgh, EH2 3AT, Scotland, UK
Tel: 44 131 2266694
Fax: 44 131 2262066
Website: http://www.aut.org.uk/scotland
Members: 6500
Contact: T. McConnell, Pres.
Description: University academic and related staff. Acts as a trade union and professional association.
Publication: Bulletin
Publication title: AUT Bulletin
Publication title: AUT Update

Association of Veterinary Teachers and Research Workers

Department of Veterinary Pathology, Glasgow University Veterinary School, Bearsden Rd., Glasgow, G61 1QH, Scotland, UK
Tel: 44 141 3305783
Fax: 44 141 3305602
Email: a.williams@vet.gla.ac.uk
Website: http://www.avtrw.org
Founded: 1946
Members: 800
Contact: Dr. A. Williams, Hon.Sec.
Fee: £25
Description: Individuals engaged primarily in veterinary teaching and research in UK and Eire. To further contact between research workers and teachers in animal research; promote and influence veterinary

education; provide for and maintain the technical excellence of veterinary teaching and research.
Publication: Proceedings
Publication title: AVT and RW Annual Conference. Advertisements.
Second publication: Proceedings
Meetings/Conventions: - annual conference - Exhibits.

Bluefaced Leicester Sheep Breeders Association

Regent House, Bank St., Annan, DG12 6AA, Scotland, UK
Tel: 44 1461 206900
Fax: 44 1461 206903
Email: info@blueleicester.co.uk
Website: http://www.blueleicester.co.uk
Founded: 1962
Members: 1700
Staff: 2
Contact: Fiona Sloan, Sec.
Fee: £25
Description: Encourages the breeding and maintaining the purity of the Bluefaced Leicester sheep. Maintains registry of pure bred progeny of the Bluefaced Leicester sheep.
Library Type: reference
Publication: Magazine
Publication title: Looking Ahead

BMIF - Scotland

c/o Mike Balforth
Westgate, Dunoon, PA23 7UA, Scotland, UK
Tel: 44 1369 870251
Fax: 44 1369 870251
Email: bmif-s@clydemarinepress.co.uk
Members: 55
Staff: 1
Contact: Mike Balmforth, Sec./Admin.
Description: Members of the marine industry in Scotland who are members of the British Marine Industries Association.
Formerly: Scottish Marine Industries Association
Meetings/Conventions: - annual conference

Boiler and Radiator Manufacturers Association
BARMA

Savory Tower, 11th Fl., 77 Renfrew St., Glasgow, G2 3BZ, Scotland, UK
Tel: 44 141 3320826
Fax: 44 141 3325788
Email: fcruickshanks@metcom.org.uk
Website: http://www.metcom.org.uk
Founded: 1949
Members: 8
Contact: Fiona Cruickshanks, Sec.
Description: The major UK manufacturers of domestic and commercial/industrial boilers and steel radiators.

Botanical Society of Scotland
BSS

Inverleith Row, Edinburgh, EH3 5LR, Scotland, UK
Tel: 44 131 5527171
Fax: 44 131 2482901
Founded: 1836

British Artist Blacksmiths Association

c/o Phil Johnson
111 Main St., Ratho, Newbridge, Midlothian, EH28 8RS, Scotland, UK
Tel: 44 131 3331300
Fax: 44 131 3333354
Email: phil@rathobyres.demon.co.uk
Website: http://www.baba.org.uk
Founded: 1978
Members: 700
Contact: Phil Johnson, Mem.Sec.
Fee: £50
Membership Type: full
Fee: £25
Membership Type: concessionary student
Description: Mainly working blacksmiths/metalworkers specializing in pieces which are both utility and artistic. Members come from all parts of the UK, mainland Europe, USA, Australia and New Zealand. To encourage the hand skills associated with the hot working of metals, and to foster an appreciation of art blacksmith work among potential customers. To this end organizes exhibitions of members' work and working, social gatherings in many parts of the UK.
Publication: Magazine
Publication title: British Blacksmith. Advertisements.
Second publication: Pamphlet
Publication title: Working with an Artist Blacksmith
Meetings/Conventions: - annual general assembly - Exhibits.

British Association for Canadian Studies

21 George Sq., Edinburgh, EH8 9LD, Scotland, UK
Tel: 44 131 6621117
Fax: 44 131 6621118
Email: jodie.robson@ed.ac.uk
Website: http://www.canadian-studies.net
Founded: 1975
Members: 500
Staff: 1
Contact: Jodie Robson
Fee: £20
Membership Type: individual
Fee: £30
Membership Type: institutional
Description: Provides a forum for Canadian Studies in the UK.
Library Subject: Canadian studies
Library Type: reference
Meetings/Conventions: - annual conference Leeds UK

British Association of Academic Phoneticians

Department of English Language, The University, Glasgow, G12 8QQ, Scotland, UK
Tel: 44 141 3304596
Email: m.macmahon@englang.arts.gla.ac.uk
Website: http://www.phon.ucl.ac.uk/home/baap/
Founded: 1950
Members: 150
Contact: Prof. M MacMahon, Hon.Sec.
Description: Seeks to further the academic study of phonetics.
Library Subject: phonetics
Library Type: reference

British Association of Friends of Museums

c/o Carol Bunbury
Fonthill Cottages, Lewannick, Launceston, PL15 7QE, Scotland, UK
Tel: 44 1566 782440
Email: carolbunbury@waitrose.com

Website: http://www.bafm.org.uk
Founded: 1973
Members: 554
Contact: Ann Heeley, Sec.
Fee: £15
Membership Type: individual
Description: Groups of Friends of museums, libraries, art galleries, archives, and other institutions preserving the United Kingdom's cultural heritage. Acts as an umbrella and supports all Friends Groupings around the United Kingdom sharing news, advice, help and good practices. Offers rewarding volunteer activities. Provides a start up guide.
Publication: Handbook
Publication title: Handbook For Friends
Second publication: Handbook
Publication title: Handbook for Heritage Volunteer Managers & Administrators & Charter
Meetings/Conventions: - annual conference

British Association of Prosthetists and Orthotists BAPO

Sir James Clark Bldg., Abbey Mills Business Centre, Paisley, PA1 1TJ, Scotland, UK
Tel: 44 141 5617217
Fax: 44 141 5617218
Email: admin@bapo.com
Website: http://www.bapo.com
Contact: June Burgess, Admin.
Description: Orthotists and prosthetists. Seeks to protect the prosthetic and orthotic profession with regard to its status and interests. Encourages high standards of ethics and practice among members; conducts continuing professional education and training programs; serves as a clearinghouse on orthotics and prosthetics; provides advice and assistance to members.
Publication: Magazine
Publication title: BAPOMAG
Meetings/Conventions: - annual conference

British Box and Packaging Association

64 High St., Kirkintilloch, Glasgow, G66 1PR, Scotland, UK
Tel: 44 141 7777272
Fax: 44 141 7777747
Email: boxpackaging@aol.com
Website: http://www.boxpackaging.org.uk
Members: 100
Staff: 2
Contact: Susan Hunter, Sec.
Description: Represents members' interests.
Formerly: Absorbed, Packaging Distributors Association
Meetings/Conventions: - annual conference

British Christmas Tree Growers Association

18 Cluny Pl., Edinburgh, EH1O 4RL, Scotland, UK
Tel: 44 131 4470499
Fax: 44 131 4476443
Email: rogermhay@btinternet.com
Website: http://www.christmastree.org.uk
Founded: 1980
Members: 350
Staff: 1
Contact: Roger Hay
Fee: £100
Membership Type: full

Description: Christmas tree growers. (Landowners, farmers, small holders) Associate members, nurserymen, wholesalers etc. Aims to ensure that British growers produce top quality trees. Carries out market research, assists and co-ordinates marketing and reviews prospects. Represents the interests of British growers, advises on the growing and care of Christmas trees and organises Open Days, Symposiums and overseas visits.
Publication: Newsletter
Publication title: Christmas Tree Newsletter

British Crystallographic Association

c/o Northern Networking
1 Tennant Ave., College Milton S, East Kilbride, Glasgow, G74 5NA, Scotland, UK
Tel: 44 1355 244966
Fax: 44 1355 249959
Email: bca@glasconf.demon.co.uk
Website: http://bca.cryst.bbk.ac.uk/BCA/welcome.htm
Founded: 1982
Members: 800
Contact:
Fee: £15
Description: Crystallographers in universities, research establishments, and industry, with interests in the field of molecular biology, chemistry, physics, mineralogy, materials science, etc. To advance the science of crystallography.
Publication title: Crystallography News. Advertisements.

British Disposable Products Association

64 High St., Kirkintilloch, Glasgow, G66 1PR, Scotland, UK
Tel: 44 141 7777272
Fax: 44 141 7777747
Email: npcorg@aol.com
Website: http://www.bdpa.co.uk
Members: 20
Staff: 2
Contact: Ms. S. Hunter, Sec.
Description: Manufacturers, stockists, distributors and importers of catering disposables.

British Medical Laser Association
BMLA

Ninewells Hospital and Medical School, Dundee, DD1 9SY, Scotland, UK
Tel: 44 1382 632240
Fax: 44 1382 646047
Email: h.moseley@dundee.ac.uk
Website: http://www.bmla.co.uk/
Founded: 1983

British Psychodrama Association

Flat 1/1, 105 Hyndland Rd., Glasgow, G12 9JD, Scotland, UK
Tel: 44 141 3390141
Website: http://www.psychodrama.org.uk
Founded: 1984
Members: 250
Contact: James Scanlan, Admin.
Fee: £43
Membership Type: in Europe
Fee: £48
Membership Type: international
Description: Promotes the use of psychodrama and sociodrama as a creative and effective approach to working with a wide range of people in a variety of different settings. Psychodrama, sociometry, and group psychotherapy developed from the work of Jacob Levy Moreno (1889-1974).
Library Subject: psychodrama, sociodrama
Library Type: reference
Publication: Journal
Second publication: Bulletin
Meetings/Conventions: - annual conference

British Society for Oral Medicine

c/o Dr. David Felix
Glasgow Dental Hospital and School, Glasgow, G2 3JE, Scotland, UK
Tel: 44 114 2717956
Fax: 44 114 2717894
Website: http://www.oralmedicine.uk.com
Founded: 1967

British Society of Animal Science
BSAS

PO Box 3, Midlothian, Penicuik, EH26 0RZ, Scotland, UK
Tel: 44 131 4454508
Fax: 44 131 5353120
Email: bsas@ed.sac.ac.uk
Website: http://www.bsas.org.uk
Founded: 1943
Members: 1000
Staff: 4
Contact: Mr. M.A. Steele, Gen.Sec.
Fee: £58
Membership Type: individual
Fee: £28
Membership Type: student
Description: Individuals concerned with animal production. Provides opportunities for information exchange among members relating to animals and animal products.
Publication: Journal
Publication title: Animal Science
Publication title: Proceedings
Meetings/Conventions: - periodic meeting

British Society of Gerontology
BSG

c/o Prof. Mary Gilhooly
Centre of Gerontology & Health Studies, University of Paisley, Paisley, PA1 2BE, Scotland, UK
Tel: 44 141 8483771
Email: m.gilhooly@paisley.ac.uk
Website: http://www.britishgerontology.org
Contact: Prof. Mary Gilhooly, Pres.
Fee: £69
Membership Type: UK waged & ASO
Fee: £44
Membership Type: UK concessionary & ASO
Description: Promotes understanding of human aging and later life through research and communication in order to improve quality of life in old age.
Publication title: Ageing and Society
Meetings/Conventions: - annual conference

British Society of Psychosomatic Obstetrics, Gynaecology and Andrology

c/o Dr. Ian Allen
Wishaw General Hospital, 50 Netherton St., Wishaw, ML2 ODP, Scotland, UK
Email: kenbidgood@bspoga.org
Website: http://www.bspoga.ukgateway.net/
Founded: 1988
Description: Promotes the study of psychobiological and psychosocial, ethical and cross-cultural problems in the fields of obstetrics and gynaecology, women's health and reproductive health; facilitates the dissemination of new information in these fields.
Publication: Journal
Publication title: Journal of Psychosomatic Obstetrics and Gynecology
Meetings/Conventions: Women's Health: Psyche and Soma congress Edinburgh UK

British Society of Soil Science
BSSS

c/o Dr. Jim Gauld, Cunningham Bldg., Crabie Buckler, Macauly Institute, Aberdeen, AB15 8QH, Scotland, UK
Tel: 44 1224 498200
Fax: 44 1224 208065
Email: j.gauld@macaulay.ac.uk
Website: http://www.soils.org.uk
Founded: 1947
Members: 1000
Staff: 1
Contact: Jim Gauld, Sec.
Fee: £50
Description: Individuals in 48 countries interested in advancing the study of soil science. Encourages exchange of information.
Publication: Journal
Publication title: European Journal of Soil Science
Second publication: Newsletter
Publication title: Soil Use and Management
Meetings/Conventions: - semiannual conference

Brittle Bone Society

30 Guthrie St., Dundee, DD1 5BS, Scotland, UK
Tel: 44 1382 204446
Fax: 44 1382 206771
Email: bbs@brittlebone.org
Website: http://www.brittlebone.org
Founded: 1972
Members: 2000
Staff: 5
Contact: Raymond Lawrie, Chief Exec.
Fee: £10
Membership Type: full
Description: Supports research into osteogenesis imperfecta and related conditions. Supplies or identifies alternative sources of accurate information on genetics and other medical issues associated with OI.
Publication: Newsletter
Meetings/Conventions: - annual conference - Exhibits.

Call Centre Association

Strathclyde House 6, Elmbank St., Glasgow, G2 4PF, Scotland, UK
Tel: 44 141 5649010
Fax: 44 141 5649011
Email: cca@cca.org.uk
Website: http://www.cca.org.uk
Founded: 1996
Members: 490
Staff: 9
Contact: Anne Marie Forsyth
Fee: £700
Membership Type: corporate
Fee: £1000
Membership Type: consultation
Description: Provides a platform for member companies to communicate with each other via an independent industry body.
Library Subject: call and contact, e-commerce, technology, staffing
Library Type: not open to the public

Celtic Film and Television Association

1 Bowmount Gardens, Glasgow, G12 9LR, Scotland, UK
Tel: 44 141 3424947
Founded: 1981
Members: 262
Staff: 1
Contact: Frances Hendron
Description: Film and programme makers working in the Celtic countries; particular emphasis is given to productions in the indigenous languages. Promotes film and programme making in the Celtic countries and about Celtic countries. Promotes the education and training of skills relevant to production and encourages co-operation between members.
Publication: Newsletter

Centre for Women's Health

6 Sandyford Pl., Sauchiehall St., Glasgow, G3 7NB, Scotland, UK
Tel: 44 141 2116700
Fax: 44 141 2116702
Email: cwh@glacomen.scot.nhs.uk
Website: http://www.sandyford.org
Founded: 1994
Description: Seeks to promote women's health. Offers counseling services and groups for women. Provides a training center and meeting place. Conducts studies on the quality of existing women's health services. Disseminates information and provides an extensive information an library service and links to health service and local authority prevision.
Library Subject: health and well-being for men and women
Library Type: open to the public

Charles Rennie Mackintosh Society
CRMS

Queen's Cross Church, 870 Garscube Rd., Glasgow, G20 7EL, Scotland, UK
Tel: 44 141 9466600
Fax: 44 141 9452321
Email: info@crmsociety.com
Website: http://www.crmsociety.com
Founded: 1973
Members: 1500
Staff: 3
Contact: Stuart Robertson, Dir.
Fee: £27
Membership Type: ordinary
Fee: £50
Membership Type: student
Description: Individuals in 29 countries united to foster interest in the art and architecture of Charles Rennie Mackintosh (1868-1928),

Scottish architect, artist, and designer. Objectives are to: conserve and improve the condition of buildings and artifacts designed by Mackintosh; develop an interest in his works. Society is currently restoring Queens Cross Church in Glasgow, Scotland, the only church designed by Mackintosh that was built. Conducts lectures and tours.
Library Subject: architecture, art, and general design
Library Type: reference
Publication: Newsletter
Publication title: CRM Society Newsletter
Meetings/Conventions: - periodic conference - Exhibits.

Chart and Nautical Instrument Trade Association
Dalmore House, 310 Saint Vincent St., Glasgow, G2 5QR, Scotland, UK
Tel: 44 141 2288000
Fax: 44 141 2288310
Email: cnita@biggartbaillie.co.uk
Website: http://www.cnita.co.uk
Founded: 1918
Contact: Biggart Baillie, Sec.
Description: Represents members' interests.
Formerly: British Nautical Instrument Trade Association

Chartered Institute of Bankers - Scotland
38b Drumsheugh Gardens, Edinburgh, EH3 7SW, Scotland, UK
Tel: 44 131 4737777
Fax: 44 131 4737788
Email: info@ciobs.org.uk
Website: http://www.ciobs.org.uk
Founded: 1875
Members: 13000
Staff: 24
Contact: Prof. C.W. Munn, Chief Exec.
Fee: £50
Membership Type: personal
Description: Students and qualified members from the financial services sector. A professional, educational body for those employed in the financial services sector. The Institute publishes a wide range of study materials.
Library Subject: banking, finance, and economics
Library Type: not open to the public
Publication: Magazine
Publication title: The Scottish Banker. Advertisements.
Meetings/Conventions: - annual conference

Chartered Institute of Library and Information Professionals in Scotland
CILIPS
Scottish Centre for Information and Library Services, Brandon Gate, 1st Fl., Block C, Hamilton, ML3 7AU, Scotland, UK
Tel: 44 1698 458888
Fax: 44 1698 283170
Email: cilips@slainte.org.uk
Founded: 1908
Members: 2500
Staff: 3
Contact: Elaine Fulton, Dir.
Description: Individuals active in library and information industries. Promotes libraries and librarianship in Scotland. Seeks to: improve library services and the qualifications and status of librarians; strengthen the role of library services in the community. Represents members' interests; offers advice on salary levels, trade unions, and

working conditions. Disseminates information on recent developments in library science; organizes weekend schools.
Formerly: Scottish Library Association
Publication title: Scottish Libraries. Advertisements.
Publication title: Scottish library and Information Resources
Meetings/Conventions: - annual conference - Exhibits.

Children in Scotland
Princes House, 5 Shandwick Place, Edinburgh, EH2 4RG, Scotland, UK
Tel: 44 131 2288484
Fax: 44 131 2288585
Email: info@childreninscotland.org.uk
Website: http://www.childreninscotland.org.uk
Founded: 1983
Members: 320
Staff: 17
Contact: Cathie MacDonald, Office Mgr.
Description: The united voice of over 300 voluntary, statutory and professional organisations and individuals working with children and their families throughout Scotland. Involved in fair policy development for children. Offers a wide range of courses, seminars,and workshops; established Scotland-wide networks on specific policy areas regarding children, special needs, and HIV.
Formerly: Scottish Child and Family Alliance
Publication: Newsletter
Publication title: Children in Scotland Newsletter. Advertisements.
Meetings/Conventions: - annual conference

Clarsach Society
CS
c/o Alistair Cockburn
22 Durham Rd. S., Edinburgh, EH15 3PD, Scotland, UK
Tel: 44 131 6698972
Fax: 44 131 6200904
Email: arco@globalnet.co.uk
Website: http://www.clarsachsociety.co.uk
Founded: 1931
Members: 950
Staff: 2
Contact: Alistair Cockburn, Admn.
Fee: £15
Membership Type: Adult
Fee: £20
Membership Type: Family
Description: Promotes and encourages the playing of the clarsach (Scottish harp). Collects music; organizes performances; sponsors competitions. Holds concerts and festivals.
Library Subject: Harps and harp music of Scotland.
Library Type: lending
Publication: Journal
Publication title: Annual Report
Publication title: Harp Music Folios
Meetings/Conventions: Harp Festival - annual festival Edinburgh UK

Committee of Scottish Clearing Bankers
38 Drumsheugh Gardens, Edinburgh, EH3 7SW, Scotland, UK
Tel: 44 131 4737770
Fax: 44 131 4737799
Email: info@scotbanks.org.uk
Members: 4
Staff: 4
Contact: Gordon Fenton, Sec.
Description: Trade association of Scottish clearing banks.

Computer-Aided Learning in Veterinary Education
CLIVE

c/o Royal School of Veterinary Studies
University of Edinburgh, Summerhall, Edinburgh, EH9 1QH, Scotland, UK
Tel: 44 131 6506113
Fax: 44 131 6506576
Email: clive@ed.ac.uk
Website: http://www.clive.ed.ac.uk/
Description: Veterinary schools working to make computer-assisted learning an established part of veterinary undergraduate education.

Confederation of European Bath Manufacturers
COFEB

Savoy Tower, Glasgow, G2 3BZ, Scotland, UK
Tel: 44 141 3320826
Fax: 44 141 3325788
Email: fcruickshanks@metcom.org.uk
Website: http://www.metcom.org.uk/memdetails/cofeb.htm
Members: 25
Contact: F. Cruickshanks
Description: Manufacturer of baths in 11 countries. Promotes interests of the industry and the organization's members.
Meetings/Conventions: - annual conference

Consortium of European Research Libraries
CERL

National Library of Scotland, George IV Bridge, Edinburgh, EH1 1EW, Scotland, UK
Tel: 44 131 2264531
Fax: 44 131 2206662
Contact: Dr. Ann Matheson
Description: Research libraries. Promotes excellence in the practice of research librarianship; seeks to ensure free flow of scholarly information. Facilitates communication and cooperation among members; sponsors continuing professional development courses for research librarians.

Convention of Scottish Local Authorities
COSLA

Rosebery House, 9 Haymarket Terr., Edinburgh, EH12 5XZ, Scotland, UK
Tel: 44 131 4749200
Fax: 44 131 4749292
Email: enquiries@cosla.gov.uk
Website: http://www.cosla.gov.uk
Founded: 1975
Members: 29
Staff: 35
Contact: Rory Maur, Ch.Exec.
Description: Local authorities in Scotland. Considers legislation before Parliament; represents the interests of local authorities to the central government. Disseminates information on local government in Scotland. Serves as an employers' association for member councils; advises on salaries and conditions of service; assists in negotiations. Offers training courses.
Publication: Directory
Publication title: Scottish Local Government
Meetings/Conventions: - annual conference - Exhibits.

Costume Society of Scotland

LA Links Gardens, Edinburgh, EH3 7PX, Scotland, UK
Tel: 44 131 5551829
Email: annie.scanlan@drummond.edin.sch.uk
Founded: 1967
Members: 91
Contact: Mrs. A.W. Scanlon, Sec.
Fee: £10
Membership Type: ordinary, institution
Fee: £10
Membership Type: student
Description: Promotes members' interests.
Library Subject: historic and contemporary costume jewelry
Library Type: lending

Council for Scottish Archaeology
CSA

c/o National Museums of Scotland
Chambers St., Edinburgh, EH1 1JF, Scotland, UK
Tel: 44 131 2474119
Fax: 44 131 2474126
Email: csa@nms.ac.uk
Website: http://www.britarch.ac.uk/csa
Founded: 1943
Members: 1000
Staff: 9
Contact: David Lynn, Dir.
Fee: £20
Membership Type: individual
Fee: £86
Membership Type: group
Description: Individuals (900) and organizations (100) including museums and public archeological and historic preservation associations. Promotes increased public awareness of Scottish archeological heritage; encourages identification and preservation of archeological sites. Lobbies for improved public policies governing the preservation of archeological and historic sites; conducts research and educational programs; serves as liaison linking members and organizations pursuing similar goals. Maintains office at the Royal Museum in Edinburgh.
Publication: Journal
Publication title: Discovery and Excavation in Scotland. Advertisements.
Second publication: Newsletter
Publication title: Scottish Archaeological News. Advertisements.
Meetings/Conventions: Archaeological Research in Progress - annual conference

Couple Counselling Scotland
CCS

18 York Pl., Edinburgh, EH1 3EP, Scotland, UK
Tel: 44 131 5589669
Fax: 44 131 5566596
Email: enquiries@couplecounselling.org
Website: http://www.couplecounselling.org
Founded: 1948
Members: 600
Staff: 14
Contact: Mrs. Hilary Campbell, Ch.Exec.
Fee: £50
Membership Type: local services, individual
Description: Offers counseling services to couples in intimate personal relationships. Trains volunteers as counselors. Also provides

specialized training in psychosexual and divorce/separation counseling; and provides psychosexual therapy.
Formerly: Marriage Counselling Scotland
Publication: Papers
Publication title: Marriage Now. Advertisements.
Meetings/Conventions: - annual conference

Dalriada Celtic Heritage Trust

Taigh Arainn, Glenartney Hotel, Brodick, Isle of Arran, KA27 8BN, Scotland, UK
Tel: 44 1770 302532
Fax: 44 1770 302979
Email: dalriada@dalriada.co.uk
Website: http://www.dalriada.co.uk
Founded: 1986
Members: 300
Contact: Sammy Mcskimming
Fee: £10
Membership Type: inside the United Kingdom
Fee: £12
Membership Type: inside Europe
Description: Promotes increased awareness of Celtic culture, beliefs, and traditions. Encourages study of Celtic history; conducts research.
Publication: Directory
Publication title: Celtic Pages - A Directory of Celtic Resources in Europe. Advertisements.
Second publication: Booklet
Publication title: Trees of the Celtic Alphabet

Disability Scotland
DS

5 Shandwick Pl., Edinburgh, EH2 4RG, Scotland, UK
Tel: 44 131 2298632
Fax: 44 131 2295168
Email: disability.scotland@virgin.net
Website: http://www.dis_scot.gcal.ac.uk
Founded: 1982
Members: 200
Staff: 30
Contact: Kirsten Ferguson, Mgr.
Description: Individuals and organizations. Promotes legal and social equality for people with disabilities. Represents the interests of people with disabilities before government agencies, medical organizations, and the public; cooperates with public officials to draft policies encouraging the full inclusion of people with disabilities in society. Participates in charitable activities.
Library Subject: disability, public policy
Library Type: by appointment only
Publication: Newsletter
Publication title: Disability News
Second publication: Journal
Meetings/Conventions: - biennial conference

District Courts Association

Civic Centre, Motherwell, ML1 1TW, Scotland, UK
Tel: 44 1698 302273
Fax: 44 1698 302339
Email: district-courts@giv.uk
Website: http://www.district-courts.org.uk
Contact: Phyllis M. Hands, Hon.Sec.
Fee: £350
Description: Consults on and discusses all matters affecting the operation of the district courts in Scotland.

Dundee and Tayside Chamber of Commerce and Industry

Chamber of Commerce Buildings, Panmure St., Dundee, DD1 1ED, Scotland, UK
Tel: 44 1382 228545
Fax: 44 1382 228441
Email: webmaster@dundeechamber.co.uk
Website: http://www.dundeechamber.co.uk
Members: 870
Staff: 32
Contact: Mervyn Rolfe, Chief Exec.
Description: Promotes business and commerce.

Economic History Society

c/o Dept. of Economic & Social History
University of Glasgow, 4 University Gardens, Glasgow, G12 8QQ, Scotland, UK
Tel: 44 141 3304662
Fax: 44 141 3304889
Email: ehsocsec@arts.gla.ac.uk
Website: http://www.ehs.org.uk
Founded: 1926
Members: 1700
Contact: Prof. R.H. Trainor, Hon.Sec.
Fee: £21
Membership Type: individual
Fee: £64
Membership Type: UK/group
Description: Economic Historians. Concerned with the promotion of study of, and publication in, economic history.
Publication: Journal
Publication title: The Economic History Review. Advertisements.
Second publication: Newsletter
Meetings/Conventions: - annual conference - Exhibits. Durham UK

Edinburgh Architectural Association
EAA

15 Rutland Sq., Edinburgh, EH1 2BE, Scotland, UK
Tel: 44 131 2297545
Fax: 44 131 2282188
Email: mail@e-a-a.org.uk
Website: http://www.edarch.demon.co.uk
Founded: 1858

Edinburgh Bibliographical Society
EBS

c/o National Library of Scotland
George IV Bridge, Edinburgh, EH1 1EW, Scotland, UK
Tel: 44 131 2264531
Fax: 44 131 4662807
Email: m.simpson@ed.ac.uk
Founded: 1890

Edinburgh Chamber of Commerce and Enterprise

27 Melville St., Edinburgh, EH3 7JF, Scotland, UK
Tel: 44 131 4777000
Fax: 44 131 4777002
Email: information@ecce.org
Website: http://www.ecce.org
Members: 1300
Staff: 60
Contact: Peter Stillwell, Chief Exec.
Description: Promotes business and commerce.

Edinburgh Geological Society

c/o British Geological Survey
West Mains Rd., Edinburgh, EH9 3LA, Scotland, UK
Tel: 44 131 6671000
Fax: 44 131 6682683
Founded: 1834

Edinburgh Mathematical Society
EMS

James Clerk Maxwell Bldg., Mayfield Rd., Edinburgh, EH9 3JZ,
Scotland, UK
Email: edmathsoc@maths.ed.ac.uk
Website: http://www.maths.ed.ac.uk/~ems/
Founded: 1883
Contact: Tony Gilbert, Sec.
Description: Mathematicians employed by Scottish universities.
Promotes the mutual improvement of its members in the
mathematical sciences, pure and applied. Facilitates cooperation and
exchange of information among members; conducts research and
educational programs. Provides support and assistance to schools
offering mathematics courses and mathematics education programs
operating in developing countries.
Library Subject: mathematics
Library Type: reference
Publication: Journal
Publication title: Proceedings
Meetings/Conventions: meeting

Educational Institute of Scotland

46 Moray Pl., Edinburgh, EH3 6BH, Scotland, UK
Tel: 44 131 2256244
Fax: 44 131 2203151
Email: enquiries@eis.org.uk
Website: http://www.eis.org.uk
Founded: 1847
Members: 54663
Contact: Ronald A. Smith, Gen.Sec.
Description: Represents teachers and lecturers in nursery, primary,
secondary, further and higher education in Scotland. Promotes sound
learning and the interests and welfare of teachers and lecturers
throughout Scotland. Disseminates information to members.
Publication: Magazine
Publication title: The Scottish Educational Journal. Advertisements.
Meetings/Conventions: - annual meeting Perth UK

ENABLE

7 Buchanan St., 6th Fl., Glasgow, G1 3HL, Scotland, UK
Tel: 44 141 2264541
Fax: 44 141 2044398
Email: enable@enable.org
Website: http://www.enable.org.uk
Founded: 1954
Members: 4000
Staff: 334
Contact: Norman Dunning, Dir.
Fee: £15
Membership Type: Individual
Fee: £50
Membership Type: group
Description: Campaigns for better rights and services for individuals
with learning disabilities and their families in Scotland. Provides
national information service, legal service and local advocacy projects.
Offers jobs, training, respite and short breaks, day services, supported
living, housing and support for individuals with profound learning
disabilities in different regions of Scotland.
Library Subject: learning disabilities
Library Type: by appointment only
Formerly: Scottish Association for Parents of Handicapped Children
Publication: Newsletter
Publication title: Newslink. Advertisements.
Second publication: Books
Meetings/Conventions: - annual conference - Exhibits. UK

Engender

18 York Pl., Edinburgh, EH1 3EP, Scotland, UK
Tel: 44 131 5589596
Email: engender@engender.org.uk
Website: http://www.engender.org.uk
Founded: 1992
Members: 300
Staff: 4
Contact: Jackie Purves, Admin.
Description: An information, research and networking organisation
for women in Scotland. Works with other groups locally and
internationally to improve women's lives and increase women's power
and influence. Provides political skills training courses for women's
groups so they can lobby and campaign more effectively.
Library Subject: gender issues
Library Type: open to the public
Formerly: The Scottish Women's Foundation
Publication: Newsletter
Publication title: Engender
Meetings/Conventions: Women into Politics - annual conference -
Exhibits.

Environmental and Technical Association for the Paper Sack Industry
ETAPSI

c/o Susan Hunter
64 High St., Kirkintilloch, Glasgow, G66 1PR, Scotland, UK
Tel: 44 141 7777272
Fax: 44 141 7777747
Email: etapsnpc@aol.com
Website: http://www.papersacks.org.uk
Founded: 1991
Members: 8
Staff: 2
Contact: Susan Hunter
Description: Producers of paper stock. Seeks to reduce the
environmental impact of paper stock manufacturing. Facilitates
exchange of information among members; sponsors environmental
and technical research; maintains speakers' bureau; compiles
statistics.
Publication: Brochure
Meetings/Conventions: - periodic board meeting

Epilepsy Action Scotland
EAS

48 Govan Rd., Glasgow, G51 1JL, Scotland, UK
Tel: 44 141 4274911
Fax: 44 141 4191709
Email: enquiries@epilepsyscotland.org.uk
Website: http://www.epilepsyscotland.org.uk
Founded: 1954
Members: 600

Staff: 31
Contact: Hilary Mounfield, Chief Exec.
Fee: £10
Membership Type: personal
Fee: £25
Membership Type: professional
Description: Works to enable people with epilepsy to maximize their choices in life; lobbies for better services to meet local needs and campaigns against the stigma of epilepsy by raising public awareness. to members.
Library Subject: epilepsy
Library Type: reference
Formerly: Epilepsy Association of Scotland
Publication: Newsletter
Publication title: Epilepsy News. Advertisements.
Second publication: Booklets
Meetings/Conventions: - annual conference

European Brain Injury Consortium
EBIC

c/o University Department of Neurosurgery
Institute of Neurological Science, Southern General Hospital, Glasgow, G51 4TF, Scotland, UK
Tel: 44 141 2012031
Website: http://homepages.ed.ac.uk/gdm/EBIC/
Description: Promotes research aimed at improving the outcome of patients with acute brain injury. Fosters research.

European Business History Association
EBHA

Centre for Business History, University of Glasgow, 4 University Gardens, Glasgow, G12 8QQ, Scotland, UK
Tel: 44 141 3306890
Fax: 44 141 3304889
Email: g.g.jones@rdg.ac.uk
Website: http://www.rdg.ac.uk/EBHA/
Founded: 1994
Description: Promotes research on all aspects of European business and management history.

European Centre for Occupational Health, Safety and the Environment

c/o Dr. Charles Woolfson, Dir.
Faculty of Social Sciences, Lilybank House, University of Glasgow, Glasgow, G1N 8RT, Scotland, UK
Tel: 44 141 3304665
Fax: 44 141 3304665
Email: ecohse@socsci.gla.ac.uk
Website: http://www.gla.ac.uk/ecohse/
Contact: Dr. Charles Woolfson, Dir.
Description: Promotes the exchange of academic, policy and practitioner experience in the fields of industrial relations and workplace health, safety and the environment.
Meetings/Conventions: - annual symposium

European Confederation of Laboratory Medicine
ECLM

Milngavie, Glasgow, G62 8AW, Scotland, UK
Tel: 44 141 9564573
Fax: 44 141 5639421
Email: robert.rowan@virgin.net

Website: http://www.inserm.fr
Founded: 1993
Description: Promotes the application of laboratory medicine to the provision of health services; supports European congresses of laboratory medicine and regional congresses and meetings of European scope and interest.

European Design Education Network
EDEN

120 Bothwell St., Glasgow, G2 7JP, Scotland, UK

European Dystonia Federation

69 East King St., Helensburgh, G84 7RE, Scotland, UK
Tel: 44 143 6678799
Fax: 44 143 6678799
Email: sec@dystonia-europe.org
Website: http://www.dystonia-europe.org
Founded: 1993
Members: 19
Staff: 1
Contact: Mr. Alistair Newton, Exec.Dir.
Description: National dystonia patient support groups of individual countries in Europe.
Publication: Newsletter
Meetings/Conventions: - annual general assembly

European Educational Research Association
EERA

c/o Professional Development Unit
76 Southbrae Dr., University of Strathclyde, Faculty of Education, Glasgow, G13 1PP, Scotland, UK
Tel: 44 141 9503772
Fax: 44 141 9503210
Email: eera@strath.ac.uk
Website: http://www.eera.ac.uk/
Founded: 1994
Description: Promotes educational research and coordinates research efforts concerning educational issues within Europe.

European Environmental Mutagen Society
EEMS

10 Gloucester Place, Edinburgh, EH3 6EF, Scotland, UK
Tel: 44 131 2258282

European Flexible Intermediate Bulk Container Association

140 Camphill Rd., Broughty Ferry, Dundee, DD5 2NF, Scotland, UK
Tel: 44 1382 480049
Fax: 44 1382 480130
Email: efibca@aspects.net
Website: http://www.efibca.com
Founded: 1983
Members: 46
Staff: 1
Contact: H.M. Speirs
Fee: £1300
Membership Type: full
Fee: £1100
Membership Type: associate
Description: Full members are European manufacturers of FIBCs; distributor members are European agents/distributors of full members;

associate members are European suppliers to the FIBC industry; affiliate members are companies involved in FIBCs operating outwith Europe. Aims to promote the trade and to protect and advance the interests of the Association and of its members. Promotes the establishment of standards and codes of practice for the trade. Specific sectors are standards, testing and certification, labelling, quality assurance, environmental and handling issues. Affiliate members are FIBC manufacturers, FIBC agents/distributors and suppliers to the FIBC industry based outwith Europe.
Publication: Booklet
Publication title: Recommendations for Handling FIBCS
Meetings/Conventions: conference - Exhibits.

European Flexible Intermediate Bulk Container Association

140 Camphill Rd., Broughty Ferry, Dundee, DD5 2NF, Scotland, UK
Tel: 44 1382 480049
Fax: 44 1382 480130
Email: efibca@aspects.net
Website: http://www.efibca.com
Founded: 1983
Members: 46
Staff: 1
Contact: H.M. Speirs
Fee: £1300
Membership Type: full
Fee: £1100
Membership Type: associate
Description: Full members are European manufacturers of FIBCs; distributor members are European agents/distributors of full members; associate members are European suppliers to the FIBC industry; affiliate members are companies involved in FIBCs operating outwith Europe. Aims to promote the trade and to protect and advance the interests of the Association and of its members. Promotes the establishment of standards and codes of practice for the trade. Specific sectors are standards, testing and certification, labelling, quality assurance, environmental and handling issues. Affiliate members are FIBC manufacturers, FIBC agents/distributors and suppliers to the FIBC industry based outwith Europe.
Publication: Booklet
Publication title: Recommendations for Handling FIBCS
Meetings/Conventions: conference - Exhibits.

European Society for Ecological Economics ESEE

c/o Claudia Carter
SERP, The Macaulay Institute, Craigie Buckler, Aberdeen, AB15 8QH, Scotland, UK
Tel: 44 1224 498200
Fax: 44 1224 498205
Email: c.carter@macaulay.ac.uk
Website: http://www.euroecolecon.org
Founded: 1987
Contact: Claudia Carter, Sec.
Description: Fosters transdisciplinary discourse and research among the social and natural sciences regarding problems of nature and the environment. Provides a European network for activities in ecological economics. Produces and disseminates information on policies for sustainability globally, nationally, and locally. Promotes education, graduate research and research funding in ecological economics.
Publication: Newsletter
Publication title: ESEE Newsletter
Meetings/Conventions: European Applications in Ecological Economics - biennial conference

European Society for Mass Spectrometry

West Mains Rd., Edinburgh, EH9 3JJ, Scotland, UK
Tel: 44 131 6504710
Fax: 44 131 6506453
Email: John.Monaghan@ed.ac.uk
Website: http://www.bmb.leeds.ac.uk/esms/
Founded: 1994

European Society of Biochemical Pharmacology ESBP

c/o Dr. Brian Burchell
University of Dundee, Department of Biochem. Med., Ninewells Medical School, Dundee, DD1 9SY, Scotland, UK
Tel: 44 1382 632164
Fax: 44 1382 633952
Email: b.burchell@dundee.ac.uk
Website: http://www.geocities.com/ResearchTriangle/4787/welcome.htm
Contact: Dr. Brian Burchell, Pres.
Description: Researchers at academic institutions and in the pharmaceutical industry. Promotes advancements in the field of pharmacology.

European Society of Veterinary Virology

c/o Moredun Research Institute
Pentlands Science Park, Bush Loan., Edinburgh, EH2 6OPZ, Scotland, UK
Tel: 44 131 4455111
Fax: 44 131 4456111
Email: nettp@mri.sari.ac.uk
Website: http://www.ploufragan.afssa.fr/esvv/fee_member.html
Founded: 1985
Members: 250
Contact: Dr. P. Nettleton, Sec.
Fee: £50
Membership Type: full
Fee: £340
Membership Type: institute
Description: Researchers and teachers in veterinary virology. Seeks to further progress in veterinary virology. Fosters communication and exchange between members.
Publication: Newsletter
Meetings/Conventions: - triennial congress St. Malo France

European Theological Libraries

c/o Dr. Penelope Hall
5 Swanston Cres., Edinburgh, EH10 7BS, Scotland, UK
Tel: 44 131 4451691
Email: prjhall@aol.com
Founded: 1961
Members: 21
Contact: Dr. Penelope Hall, Sec.
Fee: £200
Description: National associations of theological libraries. Promotes international cooperation among theological libraries; assists theological libraries in developing countries.
Formerly: International Council of Associations of Theological Libraries
Publication: Newsletter
Publication title: BETH Newsletter
Meetings/Conventions: - annual general assembly Brixen Italy

European Underwater and BaroMedical Society
EUBS

Benview, Prospect Terrace, Port Elphinstone, Inverurie, AB51 3UN, Scotland, UK
Tel: 44 1467 620408
Fax: 44 1467 620408
Email: secretary@eubs.org
Website: http://www.eubs.org
Members: 390
Contact: Mrs. Angela Randell, Membership Sec.
Fee: £20
Membership Type: full
Fee: £10
Membership Type: undergraduate
Description: Professionals and students interested in undersea medicine and related fields. Provides a forum for scientific communication among those interested in undersea medicine; encourages cooperation with related scientific disciplines. Strives to improve the safety of underwater activities by providing expert advice and educational programs; promotes undersea medicine. Holds workshops on topics concerning medical aspects of diving.
Publication title: Long Term Neurological Consequences of Deep Diving
Second publication: Newsletter
Publication title: Newsletter. Advertisements.
Meetings/Conventions: - annual congress - Exhibits.

EXIT

17 Hart St., Edinburgh, EH1 3RN, Scotland, UK
Tel: 44 131 5564404
Email: exit@euthanasia.org
Website: http://www.euthanasia.org
Founded: 1980
Contact: Chris Docker, Dir.
Description: Aims to make dying with dignity an option available to anyone, to protect patients and doctors alike in upholding the humanity of dying well, to seek legal reform, where necessary, and to introduce safeguards regarding voluntary euthanasia.
Formerly: Voluntary Euthanasia Society of Scotland

Faculty of Actuaries

Maclaurin House, 18 Dublin St., Edinburgh, EH1 3PP, Scotland, UK
Tel: 44 131 2401300
Fax: 44 131 2401313
Email: faculty@actuaries.org.uk
Website: http://www.actuaries.org.uk
Founded: 1856
Members: 1870
Staff: 10
Contact: Jeremy Guford, Chair
Description: Aims to develop the role and enhance the reputation of the actuarial profession on providing expert and relevant solutions to financial and business problems especially those involving uncertain future events.
Library Subject: actuarial science, pensions, insurance, mortality, probability statistics, investment
Library Type: reference
Publication: Journal
Publication title: British Actuarial Journal
Publication title: Manual of the Actuarial Practice

Faculty of Advocates

c/o Advocates Library
Parliament House, Edinburgh, EH1 1RF, Scotland, UK
Tel: 44 131 2265071
Fax: 44 131 2253642
Email: ros.murray@advocates.org.uk
Website: http://www.advocates.org.uk
Founded: 1532
Members: 698
Contact: Mr. Eugene P. Creally, Clerk of Faculty
Description: All members of the Scottish Bar. Concerned with the provision of specialist advocacy before Courts, Tribunals, Inquiries, Arbitrations and similar bodies; the provision of legal advice on both litigious and non litigious matters.

Fairbridge in Scotland
FS

57 Albion Rd., Edinburgh, EH7 5Q2, Scotland, UK
Tel: 44 131 4752303
Fax: 44 131 4752312
Founded: 1984
Description: Educators, counselors, and others working with troubled youth. Seeks to provide educational and training opportunities to young people who have left the public educational system due to homelessness, drug abuse, or criminal activity. Provides counseling, support groups, and educational and training programs in personal, social, and life skills to troubled youth. Participates in charitable activities.

Family Mediation Scotland

18 York Place, Edinburgh, EH1 3EP, Scotland, UK
Tel: 44 131 5589898
Fax: 44 131 5589831
Email: info@familymediationscotland.org.uk
Website: http://www.familymediationscotland.org.uk
Founded: 1987
Members: 12
Staff: 10
Contact:
Fee: £80
Membership Type: affiliated family mediation services only
Description: Promotes the availability of family mediation services in Scotland. Works to maintain high standards for the qualifications and accreditation of mediators.
Library Subject: divorce/separation and the impact of divorce
Library Type: not open to the public
Formerly: Scottish Association of Family Conciliation Services
Publication title: Annual Report. Advertisements.
Second publication: Videos
Publication title: Training Video for Volunteers
Meetings/Conventions: - annual conference - Exhibits. Edinburgh UK

FEDORA - European Forum for Student Guidance

c/o Margaret Dane, Ch.Exec., AGCAS
25 Thomson Rd., Currie, EH14 5HT, Scotland, UK
Tel: 44 131 4669170
Fax: 44 131 4492771
Email: margaret.dane@agcas.org.uk
Website: http://www.fedora.eu.org
Founded: 1988
Members: 500
Contact: Margaret Dane, Pres.

Description: Student advisors in higher education. Collaborates with other organizations involved in university student guidance, within and outside the European Union. Promotes professional training; participates in activities relating to educational guidance.
Publication: Newsletter
Publication title: FEDORA Newsletter
Meetings/Conventions: - triennial congress Odense Denmark

Fife Chamber of Commerce and Enterprise
Wemyssfield House, Wemyssfield, Kirkcaldy, KY1 1XN, Scotland, UK
Tel: 44 159 2201932
Fax: 44 159 2641187
Email: lauriemethven@fifechamber.co.uk
Website: http://www.fifechamber.co.uk
Founded: 1825
Members: 350
Staff: 6
Contact: Laurie Methven
Description: Facilitates business opportunities and offers business representation information and advice.
Formerly: Fife Chamber of Commerce and Industry

Findhorn Foundation
The Park, Findhorn, Forres, IV36 3TZ, Scotland, UK
Tel: 44 1309 690311
Fax: 44 1309 691301
Email: enquiries@findhorn.org
Website: http://www.findhorn.org
Founded: 1962
Members: 150
Contact: Richard Coates
Description: International spiritual community. While holding no formal doctrine or creed, the foundation believes that humanity is involved in an evolutionary expansion of consciousness which is creating new patterns of civilization and a planetary culture infused with spiritual values. Serves as a center for spiritual and holistic education.
Publication: Pamphlet
Publication title: The Findhorn Foundation: Celebrating the Divinity Within All Life
Second publication: Brochure
Publication title: The Findhorn Foundation Guest Programme

Forestry and Timber Association
5 Dublin St. Lane S, Edinburgh, EH1 3PX, Scotland, UK
Tel: 44 131 5387111
Fax: 44 131 5387222
Email: info@forestryandtimber.org
Website: http://www.forestryandtimber.org
Founded: 1959
Members: 2300
Staff: 5
Contact: Chris Inglis, Exec.Dir.
Fee: £50
Membership Type: Individual
Fee: £194
Membership Type: Company
Description: Woodland owners, forestry contractors, managers, and consultants; manufacturers and suppliers of equipment; nurseries and others who earn their living through forestry. It endeavors to promote and contribute to the future of employment in the home-based forest industry. Represents members' interests to government, statutory bodies and other organizations, as well as to Europe through the Union of European Foresters. Provides support and information

services; makes recommendations and comments on issues such as health and safety and forest policy. Through the Education and Provident Funds (reg. charity), small discretionary grants are available to members of more than one year, for assistance in education and training; or in cases of hardship (respectively). International visits and exchanges are arranged worldwide.
Formerly: Formed by Merger of, Association of Professional Foresters and Timber Growers Association
Publication: Catalogs
Publication title: Exhibition. Advertisements.
Second publication: Newsletter
Publication title: News. Advertisements.
Meetings/Conventions: APF International Forestry Machinery Exhibition - biennial trade show - Exhibits.

Forestry Industry Council of Great Britain
c/o Stirling Business Centre
Well Green Pl., Stirling, FK8 20Z, Scotland, UK
Tel: 44 1786 473717
Fax: 44 1786 473731
Founded: 1987
Members: 60
Staff: 2
Contact: Alasdair McGregor
Description: Membership consists of enterprises, organisations and professional associations within the private sector of the forestry industry, and encompasses activities from silvicultural research to the commercial processing of timber. Aims to draw together all strands of the forestry industry, thus speaking as a single, united voice on those issues facing us today and in the future.
Formerly: Formed by Merger of, Forestry Industry Committee of Great Britain
Publication title: Beyond 2000
Second publication: Yearbook
Publication title: The Forestry Industry Year Book

Friends of the Earth - Scotland
Bonnington Mill, 72 Newhaven Rd., Edinburgh, EH6 5QG, Scotland, UK
Tel: 44 131 5549977
Fax: 44 131 5548656
Email: enquiries@foe-scotland.org.uk
Website: http://www.foe-scotland.org.uk
Founded: 1978
Members: 4500
Staff: 14
Contact: Kevin Dunion, Dir.
Fee: £20
Membership Type: waged
Fee: £10
Membership Type: unwaged
Description: Individuals campaigning for Environmental justice.
Library Subject: environmental topics
Library Type: not open to the public
Publication: Newsletter
Publication title: What On Earth. Advertisements.
Second publication: Booklet
Meetings/Conventions: - annual meeting - Exhibits.

Gaelic Pre-School Council
GPSC

53 Church St., Inverness, IV1 1DR, Scotland, UK
Tel: 44 1463 225469
Fax: 44 1463 716943
Email: info@cnsa.scotnet.co.uk
Founded: 1982
Members: 2000
Staff: 10
Contact: Fionnnlagh M. Macheold, CEO
Fee: £10
Membership Type: individual or regional group
Fee: £20
Membership Type: associate
Description: Individuals and organizations. Promotes availability of Gaelic language preschool facilities. Conducts continuing professional development programs for personnel of Gaelic preschool programs; makes avaialable children's services.
Library Subject: preschooling, bilingualism
Library Type: by appointment only
Publication: Newsletter
Publication title: CNSA Mun Chairt
Meetings/Conventions: - periodic board meeting

Galloway Cattle Society of Great Britain and Ireland

c/o A.J. McDonald
15 New Market St., Castle Douglas, DG7 1HY, Scotland, UK
Tel: 44 1556 502753
Fax: 44 1556 502753
Website: http://www.galloway-world.org/ukgal/intro.htm
Founded: 1877
Members: 560
Staff: 2
Contact: Alex McDonald, Sec.
Description: Aims to maintain the purity of the breed of cattle known as Calloway Cattle and to promote the breeding of these cattle.
Publication: Journal
Publication title: The Galloway Journal

General Teaching Council for Scotland
GTCS

Clerwood House, 96 Clermiston Rd., Edinburgh, EH12 6UT, Scotland, UK
Tel: 44 131 3146000
Fax: 44 131 3146001
Email: gtcs@gtcs.org.uk
Website: http://www.gtcs.org.uk
Founded: 1966
Members: 78000
Staff: 36
Contact: Irene Hunter, Sec.
Fee: £30
Description: Members of the profession of registered teachers in Scotland. Registration is a statutory requirement for teaching in education authority schools in Scotland. Keeps standards of teacher education and fitness to teach under review. Makes recommendations when necessary to Scotland's First Minister. Maintains a register of teachers eligible to teach in education authority and self-governing schools in Scotland. Oversees the probationary service of new entrants to the profession.
Publication: Newsletter
Publication title: Teaching Scotland
Second publication: Pamphlets

Genetics Society

c/o Jayne Richards
Roslin Bio Centre, Roslin, EH25 9PS, Scotland, UK
Tel: 44 131 5274472
Fax: 41 131 4400434
Email: mail@genetics.org.uk
Website: http://www.genetics.org.uk
Founded: 1919
Members: 2300
Staff: 2
Contact: Miss Jayne Richards
Fee: £25
Membership Type: full
Fee: £15
Membership Type: postgraduate student
Description: Individuals with an interest in genetical research, or in the practical breeding of plants and animals. Promotes the study of the mechanisms of inheritance.
Publication: Journal
Publication title: Genes & Development
Meetings/Conventions: - annual meeting - Exhibits.

Geological Society of Glasgow

Gregory Bldg., University of Glasgow, Glasgow, G12 8QQ, Scotland, UK
Tel: 44 141 3304816
Email: gsgmemsec@postmaster.co.uk
Website: http://www.geologyglasgow.org.uk/
Founded: 1858
Members: 450
Contact: Dr. Iain Allison, Hon.Sec.
Fee: £16
Membership Type: ordinary
Description: Dedicated to promoting understanding of geology, the science of the Earth, especially the study of geology in Scotland.

Girlguiding Scotland

16 Coates Crescent, Edinburgh, EH3 7AH, Scotland, UK
Tel: 44 131 2264511
Fax: 44 131 2204828
Founded: 1910
Members: 67000
Staff: 50
Contact: Sally Pitches
Description: Girls aged 5 to 18; adult leaders. Promotes healthy physical and social development of girls and young women. Conducts social, educational, and recreational activities, with an emphasis on camping and other outdoor pursuits.
Library Subject: scouting
Library Type: by appointment only
Formerly: Guide Association Scotland
Publication: Newsletter
Meetings/Conventions: - weekly meeting

Girls' Brigade International Council

Challenge House, 29 Canal St., Glasgow, G4 0AD, Scotland, UK
Tel: 44 141 3329696
Fax: 44 141 3329696
Email: hq@gbic.org
Website: http://www.gbic.org
Founded: 1893
Members: 150000
Staff: 1
Contact: Jill Clarke, Pres.

Fee: £34
Membership Type: girls
Description: Local groups of girls age 5 and older in 61 countries that are affiliated with a church or mission of a Christian denomination. Helps girls become followers of the Lord Jesus Christ and to find true enrichment of life through reverence, self-control, and a sense of responsibility. Provides activities designed to help members attain physical, mental, and spiritual maturity. Encourages girls to express what they learn through practical service to home, community, and church. Conducts quinquennial girls' international camp. Offers regional training courses for officers and young leaders; sponsors fundraising drives and competitions.
Publication title: Annual Report
Meetings/Conventions: - annual meeting

Glasgow Archaeological Society
G.A.S.

15 Brackenbrae Rd., Bishopbriggs, Glasgow, G64 2BS, Scotland, UK
Tel: 44 141 7721096
Email: primrose@orvean.u-net.com
Founded: 1856

Glasgow Chamber of Commerce

30 George Square, Glasgow, G2 1EQ, Scotland, UK
Tel: 44 141 5722121
Fax: 44 141 2212336
Email: chamber@glasgowchamber.org
Website: http://www.glasgowchamber.org
Founded: 1783
Members: 1985
Staff: 28
Contact: Duncan Tamvanill, Chief Exec.
Description: Promotes business and commerce.
Publication: Journal. Advertisements.

Glasgow Mathematical Association
GMA

University Gardens, Glasgow, G12 8QW, Scotland, UK
Tel: 44 141 3305176
Fax: 44 141 3304111
Email: fhg@maths.gla.ac.uk/links/gma
Founded: 1927

Glasgow Natural History Society

Kelvingrove, Glasgow, G3 8AG, Scotland, UK
Tel: 44 141 2872660
Email: RichardWeddle@lineone.net
Website: http://www.gnhs.freeuk.com
Founded: 1851

Glasgow Obstetrical and Gynaecological Society

Royal Maternity Hospital, Glasgow, G4 0NA, Scotland, UK
Tel: 44 141 5522435
Founded: 1886

Glasgow Women's Aid

30 Bell St., 4th Fl., Glasgow, GL 1LG, Scotland, UK
Tel: 44 141 5532022
Fax: 44 141 5530592
Founded: 1974

Staff: 18
Description: Offers support, information, and temporary accommodations for women, and their children, who are physically, emotionally, or sexually abused. Disseminates information on law and housing. Encourages women to determine their own futures. Conducts community education programs.
Library Subject: women, children, domestic abuse
Library Type: reference
Meetings/Conventions: - annual general assembly

Guild of Taxidermists

c/o Glasgow Museum & Art Gallery
Kelvingrove, Glasgow, G3 8AG, Scotland, UK
Tel: 44 141 2872671
Fax: 44 141 2872690
Email: duncan.ferguson@cls.glasgow.gov.uk
Website: http://www.taxidermy.org.uk
Founded: 1976
Members: 200
Contact: Duncan Ferguson
Fee: £21
Membership Type: standing order
Fee: £25
Description: Amateur, museum, commercial taxidermists and individuals interested in the subject from historical side. Represents the interests of taxidermists to government bodies.
Publication: Journal
Meetings/Conventions: conference Loughborough UK

Headteachers' Association of Scotland

c/o University of Strathclyde
Jordanhill Campus, Southbrae Dr., Glasgow, G13 1PP, Scotland, UK
Tel: 44 141 9503298
Fax: 44 141 9503434
Email: head.teachers@strath.ac.uk
Website: http://www.ahts.org/teachersform.htm
Founded: 1936
Members: 500
Staff: 2
Contact: George Ross, Gen.Sec.
Fee: £237
Membership Type: ordinary
Fee: £15
Membership Type: associate
Description: Headteachers, deputy and assistant headteachers of secondary schools in Scotland. Aims to safeguard and promote the interests of headteachers, depute headteachers and assistant headteachers in Scottish secondary schools and to promote education, particularly secondary education in Scotland.
Formerly: Association of Head Teachers in Scotland
Publication: Magazine
Publication title: Scottish Headlines. Advertisements.

Helping Offenders Prisoners and their Families
HOPF

18 Stevenson St., Glasgow, G40 2ST, Scotland, UK
Tel: 44 141 5520229
Fax: 44 141 5521991
Email: hope.organisation@virgin.net
Founded: 1990
Members: 160
Staff: 6
Contact: Frank Gallagher

Description: Prison visitors and other individuals with an interest in the rehabilitation of criminal offenders. Promotes increased outside contact for incarcerated individuals. Provides training to prison visitors; makes available support and services to the families of incarcerated individuals.
Library Subject: prison visitation; criminal offenders, rehabilitation
Library Type: reference
Publication: Newsletter. Advertisements.
Meetings/Conventions: - semiannual conference - Exhibits.

Herring Buyers Association

226 Queensferry Rd., Edinburgh, EH4 2BP, Scotland, UK
Tel: 44 131 3311222
Fax: 44 131 3314646
Founded: 1976
Members: 142
Staff: 2
Contact: E. Leedham
Description: All UK buyers and processors of pelagic fish (herring and mackerel). Looks after the interests of buyers and processors of pelagic fish throughout the UK.

Highland Cattle Society

c/o A.H.G. Wilson
59 Drumlanrig St., Thornhill, DG3 5LY, Scotland, UK
Tel: 44 1848331866
Fax: 44 1848331183
Email: info@highlandcattlesociety.com
Website: http://www.highlandcattlesociety.com
Founded: 1884
Members: 1200
Staff: 3
Contact: Hamish Wilson, Sec.
Description: Promotes the breeding of highland cattle in Scotland.

Implanted Defibrillator Association of Scotland
IDAS

10 Selkirk Ave., Paisley, PA2 8JF, Scotland, UK
Tel: 44 1505 813995
Email: hanheart@aol.comwww.hermit1960.pwp.blueyonder.co.uk
Founded: 1994
Members: 104
Contact: Mike Hanley, Sec.
Fee: £10
Membership Type: full
Description: Individuals with implanted defibrillating devices and their families. Promotes and improved quality of life for people with implanted defibrillators. Sponsors support groups for members; advocates on behalf of members before medical organizations and the public; conducts educational programs; participates in charitable activities.
Publication: Newsletter
Publication title: Vital Spark
Meetings/Conventions: - quarterly board meeting

Infection Control Nurses' Association

Freepost, Drumcross Hall, Bathgate, EH48 4BR, Scotland, UK
Tel: 44 1506 811077
Fax: 44 1506 811477
Email: info@fitwise.co.uk
Website: http://www.icna.co.uk
Founded: 1969
Members: 1079

Staff: 1
Contact: Lyn J. Parker, Hon.Sec.
Fee: £50
Membership Type: full
Fee: £40
Membership Type: associate
Description: Infection control nurses and allied professionals. Concerned with the education of public and health care staff in infection.
Publication: Journal
Publication title: British Journal of Infection Control. Advertisements.
Meetings/Conventions: - annual conference - Exhibits.

Institute of Chartered Accountants of Scotland

21 Haymarket Yards, Edinburgh, EH12 5BH, Scotland, UK
Tel: 44 131 3470100
Fax: 44 131 3470105
Email: enquiries@icas.org.uk
Website: http://www.icas.org.uk
Founded: 1854
Members: 14000
Staff: 105
Contact: Peter W. Johnston, Chief Exec.
Description: Chartered accountants. Provides the following: accountancy services, education, business courses, information technology services, computer consultancy, business publishing, printing, information service. Authorized to grant permits under the Insolvency Act 1986, authorisation under the Financial Services Act 1986 for Investment Business and Registration under the Companies Act 1989.
Publication: Magazine
Publication title: CA Magazine. Advertisements.
Second publication: Newsletter
Publication title: CA News

Institute of Chartered Foresters
ICF

7A St. Colme St., Edinburgh, EH3 6AA, Scotland, UK
Tel: 44 131 2252705
Fax: 44 131 2206128
Email: icf@charteredforesters.org
Website: http://www.charteredforesters.org
Founded: 1925
Members: 1200
Staff: 4
Contact: Mrs. M.W. Dick, Exec.Dir. & Sec.
Fee: £197
Membership Type: fellow
Fee: £145
Membership Type: ordinary
Description: The representative body of the forestry profession both nationally and internationally. Aims to maintain and improve the standards of practice and understanding of forestry, and to promote the professional status of foresters in the UK. All members are bound by a code of ethics and professional practice.
Library Type: not open to the public
Formerly: Institute of Foresters
Publication: Journal
Publication title: Forestry Journal. Advertisements.
Second publication: Newsletter
Publication title: ICF News
Meetings/Conventions: - annual conference - Exhibits.

Institute of Licensed Trade Stock Auditors
ILTSA

7 Comely Bank Pl., Edinburgh, EH4 1DT, Scotland, UK
Tel: 44 131 3152600
Fax: 44 131 3154346
Email: secretary@iltsa.org.uk
Website: http://www.iltsa.co.uk/
Founded: 1953
Members: 450
Staff: 12
Contact: Bruce Thompson, Sec.
Fee: £50
Membership Type: student
Fee: £90
Membership Type: associate
Description: Stocktakers in the United Kingdom. Represents members' interests.
Library Subject: licensed trade and stocktaking
Library Type: open to the public
Publication: Magazine
Publication title: The Stocktaker. Advertisements.
Second publication: Book
Publication title: Taking Stock
Meetings/Conventions: - annual conference

Institute of Occupational Medicine
IOM

8 Roxburgh Pl., Edinburgh, EH8 9SU, Scotland, UK
Tel: 44 131 6675131
Fax: 44 131 6670136
Email: info@iomhq.org.uk
Website: http://www.iom-world.org
Founded: 1969
Staff: 90
Contact: R.J. Aitken, Dir. of Research Development
Description: Major independent centre of scientific excellence in the fields of occupational and environmental health, hygiene and safety. We aim to provide quality research, consultancy and training to help ensure that peoples health is not damaged by conditions at work or in the environment.
Library Subject: occupational medicine, health, safety, hygiene, toxicology, environmental health and ergonomics
Library Type: not open to the public
Publication title: COSHH - A Helpful Guide
Publication title: COSHH - Making an Assessment

Institute of Professional Soil Scientists

Macaulay Land Use Research Institute, Craigiebuckler, Aberdeen, AB15 8QH, Scotland, UK
Tel: 44 1224 318611
Fax: 44 1224 208065
Email: admin@soilscientist.org
Website: http://www.soilscientist.org
Founded: 1991
Members: 200
Staff: 1
Contact: Jim Gauld, Admin.
Fee: £60
Membership Type: fellow
Fee: £50
Membership Type: member
Description: Professional soil scientists and associated disciplines operating as private consultants or as employees working in a variety

of organizations and fields of work. Aims to advance the practice of soil science and allied disciplines within industry and the environment. Members offer services covering soil survey and evaluation; agricultural, horticultural and forestry extension; environmental monitoring, protection and management; soil and water management; research and development; education; overseas assignments and expert witness. Prescribes professional standards and advances the scientific/technical competence of members. Provides an authoritative voice on all matters of interest to its members and the profession.
Publication: Directory
Publication title: IPSS Directory
Second publication: Newsletter
Publication title: IPSS Newsletter
Meetings/Conventions: - annual conference - Exhibits.

Institution of Engineers amd Shipbuilders in Scotland

Clydeport Bldg., 16 Robertson St, Glasgow, G2 8DS, Scotland, UK
Tel: 44 141 2212698
Founded: 1857

International Association for Biological Oceanography
IABO

Scottish Association for Marine Sciences (SAMS), PO Box 3, Oban, Argyll, Isle of Coll, PA34 4AD, Scotland, UK
Founded: 1966
Members: 25
Contact: Prof. Matthews, Pres.
Description: Seeks to provide and improve contact between biological oceanographers and oceanographic bodies in 30 countries. Participates in cooperative programs such as the Joint Oceanography Assembly and the International Southern Ocean Studies. Sponsors and cosponsors working groups in cooperation with the Scientific Committee on Oceanic Research and the United Nations Educational, Scientific, and Cultural Organization on topics concerning theoretical ecology, deep sea ecology, phytoplankton, benthic communities, and nutrient cycles. Conducts training courses on traditional understanding and management of coastal zones, coastal lagoons, mangrove ecology and management, and the ecology of tropical island coastal zones.
Publication: Newsletter
Publication title: IABO Newsletter
Publication title: Proceedings of IABO
Meetings/Conventions: International Coelenterate Conference - annual

International Association of Margaret Morris Method
IAMMM

PO Box 1525, Garelochhead, Helensburgh, G84 0AF, Scotland, UK
Tel: 44 1436 810215
Email: mmm@cosmic.org.uk
Founded: 1910
Members: 5450
Staff: 2
Contact: Jim Hastie, Admin.
Description: Individuals, groups, and junior members in 15 countries who are instructors or students of the Margaret Morris Method of Movement. Promotes a form of dance and movement created by Margaret Morris (1891-1980), English dancer and teacher. (The MMM technique combines aesthetics of dance with healthful and recreational aspects.) Advocates implementation of MMM in activities

such as: physical education programs; athletic and sports training; recreational and professional dance instruction; exercise programs for the elderly and handicapped; and postnatal and postoperative care. Provides instruction on a series of 300 exercises graded in order of difficulty and proficiency of performance, with each grade containing movement sequences designed to develop mobility, strength, and coordination in specific parts of the body. MMM techniques include: adapting exercises to suit various therapeutic, recreational, and physical education objectives; incorporating free movement improvisation and composition; employing music or percussion rhythms as accompaniment; and incorporating controlled breathing exercises. Offers courses in Danscript, a method of movement notation evolved by Margaret Morris. Conducts examinations for instructors.
Library Subject: Registry of MMM instructors worldwide.
Library Type: reference
Publication title: Textbooks
Second publication: Magazine
Meetings/Conventions: - annual meeting

International Association of Music Libraries, Archives and Documentation Centres - United Kingdom and Ireland

Music Library, Edinburgh City Libraries, 9 George IV Bridge, Edinburgh, EH1 1EG, Scotland, UK
Tel: 44 131 2428050
Fax: 44 131 2428009
Email: pbbaxter@hotmail.com
Website: http://www.iaml-uk.org
Founded: 1953
Members: 300
Contact: Peter Baxter, Gen.Sec.
Description: Members working in or have an interest in music librarianship. Committees and project groups look at specific concerns, such as education, cataloging, trade and copyright.
Publication: Journal
Publication title: BRIO. Advertisements.
Second publication: Newsletter
Publication title: Newsletter
Meetings/Conventions: Study Weekend - annual

International Centre for Island Technology
ICIT

The Old Academy, Back Rd., Stromness, KW16 3AW, Scotland, UK
Tel: 44 1856 850605
Fax: 44 1856 851349
Email: icit@hw.ac.uk
Website: http://www.icit.demon.co.uk
Founded: 1989
Description: Carries out advanced research, post-graduate training and consultancy in marine resource management and related issues.

International Centre for Mathematical Sciences
ICMS

14 India St., Edinburgh, EH3 6EZ, Scotland, UK
Tel: 44 131 2201777
Fax: 44 131 2201053
Email: icms@math.ed.ac.uk
Website: http://www.ma.hw.ac.uk/icms

International Committee on Taxonomy of Viruses
ICTV

Scottish Crop Research Institute, Virology Div., Invergowrie, Dundee, DD2 5DA, Scotland, UK
Tel: 44 382562731
Fax: 44 382562426
Email: mmayo@scri.sari.ac.uk
Website: http://www.ncbi.nlm.nih.gov/ICTV/
Founded: 1966
Members: 120
Contact: Dr. Mike A. Mayo, Sec.
Description: A committee of the Virology Division of the International Union of Microbiological Societies. Seeks to develop a standard, internationally-accepted system of virus classification and nomenclature.
Publication: Book
Publication title: ICTV Reports
Meetings/Conventions: - triennial congress - Exhibits. San Francisco California United States

International Council of Masonry Engineering for Developing Countries
ICMEDC

Crew Bldg., King's Bldg., West Mains Rd., Edinburgh, EH9 6HD, Scotland, UK
Tel: 44 131 4470364
Fax: 44 131 6679238
Email: braj.sinha@ed.ac.uk
Founded: 1984
Contact: Prof. B.P. Sinha, Exec. Officer
Description: Educational and research institutions, members of the brick and construction industries, and interested others. Promotes the development of the masonry industry by conducting educational activities; encourages the study of masonry design and construction in scientific training programs for those involved in all aspects of the construction industry. Advocates academic, professional, and industrial exchange and cooperative research projects among developed and developing countries.
Library Subject: structural masonry
Library Type: open to the public
Publication title: Proceedings of International Seminar
Publication title: Proceedings of Sixth International Seminar on Structural Masonry
Meetings/Conventions: International Seminar on Structural Masonry for Developing Countries - biennial conference - Exhibits. Montevideo Uruguay

International Federation for Research in Women's History

Department of Modern History, University of Glasgow, Glasgow, G12 8QQ, Scotland, UK
Tel: 44 141 3304513
Fax: 44 141 3305000
Founded: 1990
Contact: Dr. Mary O'Dowd, Pres.
Description: Promotes research into women's history worldwide. Fosters communication among members.
Publication: Newsletter
Meetings/Conventions: - periodic conference

International P.E.N. - Scottish Centre

126 W Princes St., Glasgow, G4 9DB, Scotland, UK
Email: info@scottishpen.org
Website: http://www.scottishpen.org
Founded: 1927
Members: 250
Contact: Simon Berry, Pres.
Fee: £20
Description: Writers and editors united to: encourage and support writing in Scotland, encourage and support among countries; provide for the unhampered transmission of thought within and between nations; combat the suppression of freedom of expression; oppose arbitrary censorship and the evils which often accompany a free press, such as deceptive publication and deliberate falsifications for political or personal gain.
Meetings/Conventions: - quarterly meeting

International Society for Prosthetics and Orthotics
ISPO

131 St. James Rd., Glasgow, G4 OLS, Scotland, UK
Tel: 44 141 5524049
Fax: 44 141 5521283
Email: l.mclachlan@strath.ac.uk
Founded: 1970

International Society for Teacher Education

c/o Janet Powney, Sec.Gen.
19 Eglington Cres., Edinburgh, EH12 5BY, Scotland, UK
Fax: 44 1315 562454
Email: janet.powney@virgin.net
Website: http://teachernet.hkbu.edu.hk/
Founded: 1981
Members: 400
Contact: Janet Powney, Sec.Gen.
Fee: £50
Membership Type: must attend one international seminar
Description: Seeks to stimulate improvement in the teacher education particularly professional school personnel worldwide. Fosters critical analysis and dissemination of ideas from research and innovative practices in teacher education.
Publication: Newsletter
Publication title: ISTE Newsletter
Second publication: Journal
Publication title: Journal of the International Society for Teacher Education
Meetings/Conventions: - annual seminar Hong Kong People's Republic of China

International Society of Electrocardiology
ISE

c/o Prof. Peter W. Macfarlane
University Department of Medical Cardiology, Royal Infirmary, 10 Alexandra Parade, Glasgow, G31 2ER, Scotland, UK
Tel: 44 141 2114724
Fax: 44 141 5526114
Email: peter.w.macfarlane@clinmed.gla.ac.uk
Website: http://www.electrocardiology.net
Founded: 1994
Members: 300
Contact: Prof. Peter W. Macfarlane, Sec.
Fee: £25
Membership Type: life

Description: Researchers and physicians in 25 countries in cardiovascular physiology and pathology, cardiology, biomathematics, biophysics, and computer science who are interested in electrocardiology. Sponsors International Congress on Electrocardiology to develop professional programs.
Publication: Journal
Publication title: Proceedings
Meetings/Conventions: International Congress on Electrocardiology - annual congress - Exhibits. Helsinki Finland

International Union of Pharmacology
IUPHAR

c/o Prof. P.M. Vanhoutte
University of Strathclyde, 204 George St., Glasgow, G1 1XW, Scotland, UK
Email: vanhoutt@servier.fr
Founded: 1966
Members: 52
Contact: Paul M. Vanhoutte, Sec.Gen.
Description: National and international societies in pharmacology and related disciplines representing approximately 30,000 individuals. Purpose is to promote cooperation between pharmacological societies and encourage free international exchange of ideas and research. Acts as a forum for participation between related scientific bodies. Works to standardize the use of drugs worldwide and rationally define the receptors and ion channels on which they act.
Publication title: Congress Proceedings
Publication title: Directory of IUPHAR
Meetings/Conventions: - quadrennial congress - Exhibits.

International Voluntary Service - Scotland
IVS

7 Upper Bow, Edinburgh, EH1 2JN, Scotland, UK
Tel: 44 131 2266722
Fax: 44 131 2266723
Email: ivs@ivsgbscot.demon.co.uk
Website: http://www.ivsgbn.demon.co.uk
Founded: 1931
Members: 920
Staff: 1
Contact: Jackie Purves, Prog.Mgr.
Description: Individuals dedicated to increasing international understanding through voluntary service. Brings together volunteers from different countries to work on short term development projects in communities throughout Eastern and Western Europe (inc. the former Soviet bloc), U.S.A., Australia, Japan, and some North African countries. Organizes a variety of projects fulfilling specific development needs. Assistance provided has included: helping refugees and ecology projects; services for children and the disabled.
Publication title: Annual Review. Advertisements.
Publication title: International Voluntary Projects

International Well Control Forum
IWCF

Inchbraoch House, South Quay, Montrose, DD10 9UA, Scotland, UK
Tel: 44 1674 678120
Fax: 44 1674 678125
Email: admin@iwcf.org
Website: http://www.iwcf.org
Founded: 1992
Members: 130

Staff: 17
Contact: Michael Cummins
Description: Companies or persons employed in the oil industry with an interest in the development of well control skills. Develops and administers well control examination programmes for personnel employed in oil well drilling and well intervention operations.

Justice and Peace Scotland
J & P

65 Bath St., Glasgow, G2 2BX, Scotland, UK
Tel: 44 141 3330238
Fax: 44 141 3330238
Email: justice.peace@virgin.net
Founded: 1979
Members: 1200
Staff: 3
Contact: Tim Duffy, Sec.
Description: Scottish division of the European Justice and Peace Commissions. Monitors human rights issues throughout the world and cooperates with other national commissions to campaign against human rights violations and work toward peace and disarmament and social justice.
Library Subject: social justice, peace, development, spiritual
Library Type: open to the public
Formerly: Scotish Catholic Justice and Peace Commission
Publication: Magazine
Publication title: Justice and Peace. Advertisements.
Meetings/Conventions: - annual conference - Exhibits.

Law Society of Scotland

26 Drumsheugh Gardens, Edinburgh, EH3 7YR, Scotland, UK
Tel: 44 131 2267411
Fax: 44 131 2252934
Email: lawscot@lawscot.org.uk
Website: http://www.lawscot.org.uk
Founded: 1949
Members: 9000
Staff: 103
Contact: Douglas R. Mill, Chief Exec./Sec.
Fee: £350
Membership Type: members holding or not holding practising certificates
Description: Scottish solicitors. Statutory duties to promote the profession of Scottish solicitors and the interests of the public in relation to that profession. Activities include legal education, client relations, law reform, practice development, and international law.
Publication: Report
Publication title: Annual Report
Second publication: Journal
Publication title: Journal of the Law Society of Scotland. Advertisements.
Meetings/Conventions: - annual conference - Exhibits.

Learning and Teaching Scotland

Gardyne Rd., Dundee, DD5 1NY, Scotland, UK
Tel: 44 1382 443600
Fax: 44 1382 443645
Email: enquiries@ltscotland.com
Website: http://www.ltscotland.com
Founded: 1975

Staff: 94
Contact: Tegwen R. Wallace, Information Officer
Description: Promotes learning through technology.
Formerly: Formed by Merger of, Scottish Consultative Council on the Curriculum and Scottish Council for Education Technology

Learning and Teaching Scotland

Gardyne Rd., Dundee, DD5 1NY, Scotland, UK
Tel: 44 1382 443600
Fax: 44 1382 443645
Email: enquiries@ltscotland.com
Website: http://www.ltscotland.com
Founded: 1975
Staff: 94
Contact: Tegwen R. Wallace, Information Officer
Description: Promotes learning through technology.
Formerly: Formed by Merger of, Scottish Consultative Council on the Curriculum and Scottish Council for Education Technology

Lighthouse Society of Great Britain

Gravesend Cottage, Cornwall, Torpoint, PL11 2LX, Scotland, UK
Email: k.trethewey@btinternet.com
Website: http://www.lsgb.co.uk
Founded: 1992
Members: 500
Staff: 1
Contact: Dr. K.R. Trethewey, Sec.
Description: Private citizens. Acts as the focus for information about lighthouses of England, Wales, Scotland, Channel Islands and Ireland. Maintains a database of structures and keepers; disseminates information, encourages preservation and publishes material from the archive.
Library Subject: lighthouse history & lighthouse keeper information
Library Type: not open to the public
Publication title: Lighthouse Encyclopedia

Malt Distillers Association of Scotland

1 North St., Elgin, IV30 1UA, Scotland, UK
Tel: 44 1343 544077
Fax: 44 1343 548523
Email: mdas@grigor-young.co.uk
Founded: 1874
Members: 22
Contact: W.P. Mennie
Description: Producers of malt whisky or are owners of malt distilleries. Aims to increase the friendly interchange of ideas amongst themselves, the removal of all obstructions to the proper carrying on of their business not only as regards improvement in the Excise Laws but also for the making of new arrangements as to the customs of Sales which would put both buyer and seller on a more equitable footing and ensure a uniformity of practice. Also assists in such matters as wages negotiations, environmental, animal feeds, health and safety, technical and educational.
Publication: Bulletin
Meetings/Conventions: Management Committee Meeting - semiannual

Marine Biological Association of the United Kingdom
MBAUK

The Laboratory, Citadel Hill, Plymouth, PL1 2PB, Scotland, UK
Tel: 44 1752 633207
Fax: 44 1752 633102

Email: sec@mba.ac.uk
Website: http://www.mba.ac.uk
Founded: 1884
Members: 1200
Staff: 40
Contact: Prof. Stephen J. Hawkins, Dir.
Fee: £12
Membership Type: student
Fee: £25
Membership Type: student with journal
Description: Marine biologists, botanists, and scientists. Encourages cooperation among members; disseminates information on latest research; studies living resources of the seas. Assists cooperative research programs; organizes scientific meetings.
Library Subject: marine sciences
Library Type: reference
Publication: Journal
Publication title: Journal of the Marine Biological Association. Advertisements.
Second publication: Newsletter
Publication title: MBA Newsletter

Money Advice Scotland
MAS

Pentagon Centre, Ste. 306, 36 Washington St., Glasgow, G3 8AZ, Scotland, UK
Tel: 44 141 5720237
Fax: 44 141 5720517
Email: moneyadv@globalnet.co.uk
Website: http://www.moneyadvicescotland.org.uk
Founded: 1989
Members: 120
Staff: 7
Contact: Yvonne Gallacher, Chief Exec.
Fee: £5
Membership Type: unwaged individual or unfunded group
Fee: £15
Membership Type: waged individual
Description: Individuals, organizations, companies, and public agencies involved in the provision debt counseling services. Promotes availability of money management advice to people of all economic strata; seeks to insure effectiveness of financial planning and debt counseling services. Represents members' interests; facilitates communication and cooperation among members; conducts training programs for financial planning counselors.
Library Subject: financial planning, debt counseling
Library Type: by appointment only
Publication: Journal
Publication title: Money Advice Scotland Journal
Meetings/Conventions: - quarterly board meeting

National Advisory Service for Parents of Children with Stomas
NASPCS

c/o John Malcolm, Pres.
51 Anderson Dr., Valley View Park, Darvel, KA17 ODE, Scotland, UK
Tel: 44 1560 322024
Email: john@stoma.freeserve.co.uk
Founded: 1988
Members: 650
Contact: John Malcolm, Chm./National Organizer
Description: Parents of children suffering from serious bladder and bowel disorders. Provides an information service for parents on the practical day-to-day management of all aspects of coping with a child who has undergone a colostomy, ileostomy, or urostomy and provides advice on the incontinence often encountered with bowel and bladder problems.
Formerly: National Association for Support of Parents with Children with Stomas

National Association for Mental After-care in Residential Care Homes

Silverwells House, 1 Old Mill Rd., Bothwell, Glasgow, G71 8AY, Scotland, UK
Tel: 44 1698 852771
Fax: 44 1698 854712
Email: silverwellshouse@btinternet.com
Contact: I Strachan
Fee: £60
Membership Type: corporate
Fee: £20
Membership Type: associate
Description: Promotes services for people with mental health problems. Provides help and advice.

National Association of Youth Orchestras
NAYO

Central Hall, West Tollcross, Edinburgh, EH3 9BP, Scotland, UK
Tel: 44 131 2211927
Fax: 44 131 2292921
Email: admin@nayo.org.uk
Website: http://www.nayo.org.uk
Founded: 1961
Members: 330
Staff: 3
Contact: Carol Main, Dir.
Fee: £50
Membership Type: patron
Fee: £60
Membership Type: individual orchestra
Description: Youth orchestras. Represents members' collective interests; fosters development of young musicians; facilitates exchange of ideas and information among members. Organizes annual European Youth Music Week, held alternately in Britain and Germany, enabling young musicians to play modern compositions not normally included in concert programs. Annual Festival of British Youth Orchestras in Edinburgh and Glasgow, in August, concurrent with Edinburgh Festival, with guests from abroad.
Library Subject: music
Library Type: not open to the public
Publication: Directory
Publication title: Directory of Youth & Student Orchestras
Second publication: Bulletin
Publication title: Full Orchestra. Advertisements.

National Metal Trades Federation

11th Fl., Savoy Tower, 77 Renfrew St., Glasgow, G2 3BZ, Scotland, UK
Tel: 44 141 3320826
Fax: 44 141 3325788
Email: alex.shaw@nmtf.org.uk
Founded: 1912
Members: 42
Contact: Alex Shaw, Sec.
Description: Promotes metal trades.
Publication: Newsletter

National Trust for Scotland
NTS

Wemyss House, 28 Charlotte Sq., Edinburgh, EH2 4ET, Scotland, UK
Tel: 44 131 2439300
Fax: 44 131 2439301
Email: membership@nts.org.uk
Website: http://www.nts.org.uk
Founded: 1931
Members: 28000
Staff: 400
Contact: Julia Downes
Description: Individuals and organizations with an interest in Scottish history and countryside conservation. Promotes preservation and restoration of historic sites. Provides voluntary assistance to site maintenance, restoration, and preservation projects; sponsors educational programs; participates in charitable activities. Runs conservation working holidays for volunteers over 16 from March to October.
Publication: Directory
Publication title: Guide to Properties
Second publication: Magazine
Publication title: Scotland in Trust

North Atlantic Salmon Conservation Organization
NASCO

11 Rutland Sq., Edinburgh, EH1 2AS, Scotland, UK
Tel: 44 131 2282551
Fax: 44 131 2284384
Email: hq@nasco.int
Website: http://www.nasco.int
Founded: 1984
Members: 7
Staff: 4
Contact: Dr. M.L. Windsor, Sec.
Description: Promotes the conservation, restoration, enhancement, and rational management of salmon stocks in the North Atlantic, taking into account the best available scientific evidence.
Publication: Report
Publication title: Annual Report of the Council
Second publication: Report
Publication title: Annual Reports of the Regional Commissions
Meetings/Conventions: - annual meeting

Ocean Youth Trust Scotland
OYTS

24 Blythswood Sq., Glasgow, G2 4QS, Scotland, UK
Tel: 44 141 3005511
Fax: 44 141 3005701
Email: office@oytscotland.org.uk
Website: http://www.oytscotland.org.uk
Founded: 1972
Members: 180
Staff: 4
Contact: Jethro Jeffery, Gen.Mgr.
Fee: £15
Description: Youths; adult leaders. Promotes healthy physical and social development of young people through the spirit of adventure under sail. Conducts sailing trips; sponsors educational programs.
Formerly: Ocean Youth Club Scotland
Publication: Magazine
Publication title: Scotmates. Advertisements.
Meetings/Conventions: - annual board meeting - Exhibits.

Offshore Contractors Association

58 Queens Rd., Aberdeen, AB15 4YE, Scotland, UK
Tel: 44 1224 326070
Fax: 44 1224 326071
Email: admin@oca-online.co.uk
Website: http://www.oca-online.co.uk
Founded: 1984
Members: 60
Staff: 4
Contact: Bill Murray, Chief Exec.
Fee: £540
Membership Type: associate
Fee: £5000
Membership Type: member
Description: Offshore contractors.
Publication: Newsletter
Publication title: Guidance Notes of Good Contracting Practice Within the Oil & Gas Industry: Hand/Arm Vibration Syndrome
Publication title: Guidance Notes of Good Contracting Practice Within the Oil & Gas Industry: Pressure Testing
Meetings/Conventions: - annual seminar

One Parent Families Scotland

13 Gayfield Sq., Edinburgh, EH1 3NX, Scotland, UK
Tel: 44 131 5563899
Fax: 44 131 5577899
Email: info@opfs.org.uk
Website: http://www.opfs.org.uk
Founded: 1944
Members: 300
Staff: 71
Contact: Sue Robertson, Director
Fee: £5
Membership Type: Individual
Fee: £20
Membership Type: Organization
Description: Provides support, information, and counseling services to single parents. Also organizes conferences and workshops and offers training to agencies which help single parents.
Library Subject: Finances, housing, childcare and divorce.
Library Type: open to the public
Formerly: Scottish Council for the Unmarried Mother and Her Child
Publication title: Lone Parent Rights Guide
Publication title: Money for Lone Parent Full-Time Students in Higher Education

Paisley and District Chamber of Commerce

Bute Ct., 2 Andrews Drive, Glasgow Airport, Paisley, PA3 2SW, Scotland, UK
Email: paisley_chamber@baa.co.uk
Members: 465
Staff: 10
Contact: Liz Cameron, Chief Exec.
Description: Promotes business and commerce.

Polish Society

Ashcroft House, Chalton Rd., Bridge of Allan, Stirlingshire, FK9 4EF, Scotland, UK
Tel: 44 1786 832793
Email: p.d.stachura@stir.ac.uk
Founded: 1996
Members: 30
Staff: 3
Contact: Prof. Peter D. Stachura, Chm.

Fee: £15
Membership Type: full
Description: Aims to provide a forum for Polish history, culture and contemporary affairs.
Library Subject: polish history
Library Type: reference
Publication: Newsletter
Publication title: Polish Society Newsletter. Advertisements.

Poverty Alliance
PA

162 Buchanan St., Glasgow, G1 2LL, Scotland, UK
Tel: 44 141 3530440
Fax: 44 141 3530686
Email: admin@povertyalliance.org
Website: http://www.povertyalliance.org
Founded: 1990
Members: 100
Staff: 20
Contact: Damian Killeen, Dir.
Fee: £500
Membership Type: ordinary
Fee: £200
Membership Type: associate
Description: Local authorities, health boards, enterprise, and voluntary organizations working to alleviate poverty. Seeks to combat poverty through collaborative action by members. Develops partnerships and encourages cooperation among members; conducts educational programs to raise public awareness of poverty and related issues; empowers people in poverty to improve their own quality of life.
Publication: Newsletter
Publication title: Alliance News

Primate Society of Great Britain

St. Andrew's University, St. Andrews, KY16 9JU, Scotland, UK
Tel: 44 1334 467174
Email: info@psgb.org
Website: http://www.psgb.org
Founded: 1967

Procurators Fiscals Office

87A Graham St., Airdrie, ML6 6DE, Scotland, UK
Tel: 44 1236 747027
Fax: 44 1236 747677
Founded: 1930
Members: 190
Contact: Jennifer Sloan, Sec.
Description: All members are qualified lawyers in Scotland and, as established civil servants, are employed as full-time public prosecutors. A staff association, membership of which is voluntary, representing the interests of the public prosecutors in Scotland.
Formerly: Procurators Fiscal Society

Project Trust
PT

The Hebridean Centre Ballyhough, Argyll, Isle of Coll, PA78 6TE, Scotland, UK
Tel: 44 1879 230444
Fax: 44 1879 230357
Email: info@projecttrust.org.uk
Website: http://www.projecttrust.org.uk

Founded: 1968
Staff: 14
Contact: Nicholas Maclean-Bristol, Dir.
Description: Individuals between 17 and 19 years old. Seeks to develop responsibility and self-reliance in youth through volunteer work in Third World countries. Participants work as teachers' aides, assist in care of deprived and mentally handicapped children, and work in hospitals. Organizes training courses for volunteers; conducts annual debriefing course.
Publication title: Annual Report
Publication title: Project Post
Meetings/Conventions: - periodic workshop - Exhibits.

Quality Meat Scotland

c/o Rural Centre - West Mains
Ingliston, Edinburgh, EH28 8NZ, Scotland, UK
Tel: 44 131 4724040
Fax: 44 131 4724038
Email: info@qmscotland.co.uk
Founded: 1974
Staff: 14
Contact: Jim Walker, Chm.
Description: Scotch livestock producers and marketers. Works on behalf of Scottish livestock farmers in the home and export markets to promote Scotch beef, lamb and pork with and through the wholesale, catering and retail sectors of the meat industry.
Formerly: Scotch Quality Beef and Lamb Association

Ronald Stevenson Society

3 Chamberlain Rd., Edinburgh, EH10 4DL, Scotland, UK
Fax: 44 131 2299298
Email: info@rssoc.org.uk
Website: http://www.rssoc.org.uk
Founded: 1993
Members: 125
Staff: 3
Contact: I.E. Colquhoun, Hon.Sec.
Fee: £30
Membership Type: ordinary
Fee: £15
Description: Aims to publish the music of Ronald Stevenson and to promote and publish performances and recordings of the music.
Library Subject: music of Ronald Stevenson
Library Type: reference
Publication: Newsletter
Publication title: Ronald Stevenson Society Newsletter
Meetings/Conventions: - annual workshop

Royal College of Physicians and Surgeons of Glasgow

232-242 St. Vincent St., Glasgow, G2 5RJ, Scotland, UK
Tel: 44 141 2216072
Fax: 44 141 2211804
Website: http://www.rcpsglasg.ac.uk
Founded: 1599
Members: 7060
Staff: 46
Contact: Prof. A. Ross Lorimer, Pres.
Fee: £240
Description: Physicians, surgeons, and dentists. Conducts educational and training programs.
Library Subject: medicine, surgery

Library Type: reference
Publication: Annual Report
Meetings/Conventions: - periodic lecture

Royal College of Physicians of Edinburgh
RCPE

9 Queen St, Edinburgh, EH2 1JQ, Scotland, UK
Tel: 44 131 2257324
Fax: 44 131 2203939
Email: president@rcpe.ac.uk
Website: http://www.rcpe.ac.uk
Founded: 1681

Royal College of Surgeons of Edinburgh

Nicolson St., Edinburgh, EH8 9DW, Scotland, UK
Tel: 44 131 5271600
Fax: 44 131 5576406
Email: mail@rcsed.ac.uk
Website: http://www.rcsed.ac.uk
Founded: 1505
Description: Promotes the education, training and examination, the raising of standards in surgical practice.

Royal Environmental Health Institute of Scotland

3 Manor Place, Edinburgh, EH3 7DH, Scotland, UK
Tel: 44 131 2256999
Fax: 44 131 2253993
Email: rehis@rehis.org.uk
Website: http://www.royal-environmental-health.org.uk
Founded: 1983
Members: 1100
Staff: 8
Contact: John Frater, Sec.
Fee: £77
Membership Type: full/associate
Description: Persons interested or engaged in any aspect of environmental health.
Library Type: open to the public
Publication: Journal
Publication title: Environmental Health Scotland

Royal Highland and Agricultural Society of Scotland

Royal Highland Centre, Ingliston, Edinburgh, EH28 8NF, Scotland, UK
Tel: 44 131 3356200
Fax: 44 131 3335236
Email: info@rhass.org.uk
Website: http://www.rhass.org.uk
Founded: 1784
Members: 13500
Staff: 35
Contact: G. Barwick, Sec.
Fee: £120
Membership Type: junior term
Fee: £360
Membership Type: 10-year term
Description: Membership is open to everyone interested in the society and its work to promote the land-based and allied industries of Scotland, and create a wider public understanding of the management of the land and rural resources.
Library Type: open to the public
Publication: Magazine

Publication title: The Review. Advertisements.
Second publication: Catalog
Publication title: Royal Highland Show
Meetings/Conventions: The Royal Highland Show - annual - Exhibits. Edinburgh UK

Royal Highland Education Trust

Royal Highland Centre, Ingliston, Edinburgh, EH28 8NF, Scotland, UK
Tel: 44 131 3356227
Fax: 44 131 3335236
Email: rhet@rhass.org.uk
Website: http://www.rhet.rhass.org.uk
Founded: 1999
Members: 108
Staff: 3
Contact: Jane Methven, Education Mgr.
Fee: £15
Membership Type: individual
Fee: £250
Membership Type: corporate
Description: Individuals, organizations, and corporations. Promotes increased understanding of farming and rural development issues. Serves as a clearinghouse for information on farming, rural development, and country life. Conducts educational programs; provides teaching aids to food and agricultural education courses; maintains educational center.
Library Subject: Scottish agriculture
Library Type: by appointment only
Formerly: Scottish Farm and Countryside Educational Trust
Publication: Booklets
Publication title: Agriculture and the Rural Environment in the United Kingdom. Advertisements.
Meetings/Conventions: - periodic board meeting - Exhibits.

Royal Incorporation of Architects in Scotland

15 Rutland Sq., Edinburgh, EH1 2BE, Scotland, UK
Tel: 44 131 2297545
Fax: 44 131 2282188
Email: info@rias.org.uk
Website: http://www.rias.org.uk
Founded: 1916
Members: 3800
Staff: 26
Contact: Sebastian Tombs, Sec./Treas.
Fee: £126
Membership Type: associate
Fee: £189
Membership Type: fellow
Description: Professional body for around 3000 chartered architect members in Scotland working from 800 private and public across the country. Has charitable status and offers a wide range of services and products for architects, students of architecture, construction industry professionals, and those interested in the built environment and the design process.
Library Subject: Scottish architecture
Library Type: by appointment only
Publication title: Architecture Guides to Scotland
Publication title: The Chartered Architect
Meetings/Conventions: - annual convention - Exhibits.

Royal Medical Society

Student Centre, 5/5 Bristol Sq., Edinburgh, EH8 9AL, Scotland, UK
Tel: 44 131 6502672
Fax: 44 131 6502672

Email: royalmedsoc@btinternet.com
Website: http://www.royalmedical.co.uk
Founded: 1737
Members: 2500
Staff: 1
Contact: Mrs. E. Singh, Sec.
Description: Mainly medical students. Fellows and Life Members are medical graduates. An educational charity for medical students, run by medical students.
Publication title: Res Medica

Royal Philosophical Society of Glasgow
c/o Hutchesons' Trust Office
21 Beaton Rd., Glasgow, G41 2NW, Scotland, UK
Tel: 44 141 4334484
Fax: 44 141 3304112
Email: info@royalphil.org
Website: http://www.royalphil.org
Founded: 1802
Members: 420
Staff: 1
Contact: Ephraim Borowski, Pres.
Fee: £15
Membership Type: full
Fee: £10
Membership Type: concessions
Description: Seeks to aid the study, advancement, and development of the physical, natural, mental and moral sciences; the arts of design, with their applications; and to promote the diffusion of scientific knowledge. Holds public lectures.
Library Type: by appointment only

Royal Scottish Academy of Painting, Sculpture and Architecture
The Mound, Edinburgh, EH2 2EL, Scotland, UK
Tel: 44 131 2256671
Fax: 44 131 2252349
Founded: 1826

Royal Scottish Country Dance Society
RSCDS
12 Coates Crescent, Edinburgh, EH3 7AF, Scotland, UK
Tel: 44 131 2253854
Fax: 44 131 2257783
Email: info@rscdsh.org
Website: http://www.rscds.org
Founded: 1923
Members: 21000
Staff: 5
Contact: Elspeth Gray
Description: Works to preserve the form and style of Scottish country dance. Conducts research on the history of country dance. Operates a summer training school; maintains a certification program for teachers of country dance.
Publication: Books
Meetings/Conventions: Summer School - annual

Royal Scottish Forestry Society
RSFS
c/o Andrew G. Little
Hagg-on-Esk, Canonbie, DG14 0XE, Scotland, UK
Tel: 44 13873 71518
Fax: 44 13873 71418
Email: rsfs@ednet.co.uk
Website: http://www.rsfs.org
Founded: 1854
Members: 1200
Staff: 1
Contact: Andrew G. Little, Admin.Dir.
Fee: £6
Membership Type: Student
Fee: £38
Description: Individuals concerned with the advancement of forestry in Scotland. Fosters cooperation between industry professionals and conservationists. Encourages tree planting nationwide. Organizes excursions to sawmills and factories as well as parks and gardens. Sponsors education and training programs. Arranges forestry exhibits.
Library Subject: Forestry.
Library Type: reference
Publication: Journal
Publication title: Scottish Forestry. Advertisements.
Meetings/Conventions: Spring Excursion - annual - Exhibits.

Royal Scottish Geographical Society
Graham Hills Bldg., 40 George St., Glasgow, G1 1QE, Scotland, UK
Tel: 44 141 5523330
Fax: 44 141 5523331
Email: rsgs@strath.ac.uk
Website: http://www.geo.ed.ac.uk/rsgs/
Founded: 1884
Members: 2200
Staff: 6
Contact: Dr. David M. Munro, Dir.
Fee: £60
Membership Type: ordinary
Fee: £36
Membership Type: single
Description: Academic geographers and lay members interested in travel and travel lectures. Aims to further the science of geography, stimulate research into the nature and causes of change in human and physical environments on Earth and disseminate knowledge of these changes and their possible consequences.
Library Subject: geography, travel, environment
Library Type: reference
Formerly: RSGS
Publication: Newsletter
Publication title: Geogscot. Advertisements.
Second publication: Journal
Publication title: Scottish Geographical Journal

Royal Society of Edinburgh
RSE
22-26 George St., Edinburgh, EH2 2PQ, Scotland, UK
Tel: 44 131 2405000
Fax: 44 131 2405024
Email: rse@royalsoced.org.uk
Website: http://www.royalsoced.org.uk
Founded: 1783
Members: 1300

Staff: 25
Contact: Dr. William Duncan, Exec.Sec.
Description: Organizes events and promotes links between academia and industry.
Library Type: open to the public
Publication: Journal
Publication title: Proceedings of the Royal Society of Edinburgh: Mathematics
Second publication: Journal
Publication title: Transactions of RSE: Earth Sciences
Meetings/Conventions: meeting

Royal Zoological Society of Scotland
RZSS

Murrayfield, Edinburgh, EH12 6TS, Scotland, UK
Tel: 44 131 3349171
Fax: 44 131 3164050
Email: info@edinburghzoo.org.uk
Website: http://www.edinburghzoo.org.uk
Founded: 1913
Members: 13000
Staff: 150
Contact: David Windmill, Dir.
Fee: £30
Membership Type: Adult
Fee: £48
Membership Type: Joint
Description: Individuals; companies, schools, and outdoor groups in Scotland. Enhances knowledge of and interest in animal life. Provides environmental education programs. Conducts conservation breeding programs at Edinburgh Zoo and Highland Wildlife Park, Kincraig Inverness-shire.
Publication: Magazine
Publication title: Ark File
Publication title: Guide Book
Meetings/Conventions: - annual general assembly Edinburgh UK

Saltire Society

9 Fountain Close, 22 High St., Edinburgh, EH1 1TF, Scotland, UK
Tel: 44 131 5561836
Fax: 44 131 5571675
Email: saltire@saltire.org.uk
Website: http://www.saltiresociety.org.uk
Founded: 1936
Members: 1445
Staff: 2
Contact: Kathleen Munro
Fee: £15
Membership Type: regular
Fee: £5
Membership Type: student
Description: All individuals and organizations who support the aims of the Society. Seeks to preserve all that is best in Scotland and Scottish tradition and to encourage every new development which can strengthen and enrich the country's cultural life.
Publication: Catalog
Second publication: Books

Sargent Cancer Care for Children
SCCC

Mercantile Chambers, 5th Fl, 53 Bothwell St., Glasgow, G2 6TS, Scotland, UK
Tel: 44 1415 725700
Fax: 44 1415 725701
Website: http://www.sargent.org/
Founded: 1969
Contact: Morag McIntosh, Natl. Organizer
Description: Provides care for children and young adults experiencing cancer and their families; works closely within the hospital multi-disciplinary team. The Malcolm Sargent House, Prestwick, provides supported short breaks for families year round.
Publication: Brochures
Second publication: Annual Report

Scotch Whisky Association

20 Atholl Crescent, Edinburgh, EH3 8HF, Scotland, UK
Tel: 44 131 2229202
Fax: 44 131 2229237
Email: contact@swa.org.uk
Website: http://www.scotch-whisky.org.uk
Founded: 1943
Members: 66
Staff: 38
Contact: Hugh Morison, Chief Exec.
Description: Distillers, blenders, brokers and bottlers of Scotch Whisky. The protection and promotion of Scotch Whisky at home and abroad.
Publication title: Distilleries Which Welcome Visitors
Second publication: Booklet
Publication title: Scotch Whisky Questions and Answers

ScotlandIS

Livingston Software Innovation Centre, 1 Michaelson Sq., Kirkton Campus, Livingston, EH54 7DP, Scotland, UK
Tel: 44 1506 472200
Fax: 44 1506 472209
Email: info@scotlandis.com
Website: http://www.scotlandis.com
Founded: 1985
Members: 350
Staff: 8
Contact: Polly Purvis, Exec.Dir.
Description: Represents the ICT industry involved in developing software, interactive media, e-commerce, and the Internet in Scotland.
Formerly: Scotland Softwared Federation

Scots Language Society
SLS

A.K. Bell Library, Perth, PH2 8EP, Scotland, UK
Tel: 44 1738 440199
Fax: 44 1738 477010
Website: http://www.lallans.co.uk
Founded: 1972

Scottish Agricultural Arbiters' Association

c/o Malcom S. Steel, Sec.
Princes Exchange, 1 Earl Grey St., Edinburgh, EH3 9EE, Scotland, UK
Tel: 44 131 2288111
Fax: 44 131 2288118
Email: enquiries@turcanconnell.com
Founded: 1924
Members: 250
Contact: Malcolm Strang Steel, Sec.
Fee: £25
Description: Persons interested in agricultural arbitration and valuation.

Scottish Agricultural Organisation Society

The Rural Centre, West Mains, Ingliston, Newbridge, EH28 8NZ, Scotland, UK
Tel: 44 131 4724100
Fax: 44 131 4724101
Email: saos@saos.co.uk
Website: http://www.saos.co.uk
Founded: 1905
Members: 85
Staff: 9
Contact: Eunice Mole
Description: Co-operative Societies - Agricultural. Consultancy, advisory, representative, training services.
Publication: Annual Report
Meetings/Conventions: - annual conference

Scottish Amateur Music Association

c/o Margaret W. Simpson
18 Craigton Crescent, Alva, Alva, FK12 5DS, Scotland, UK
Tel: 44 1259 760249
Email: secretary@sama.org.uk
Website: http://www.sama.org.uk
Founded: 1956
Contact: Miss Margaret W. Simpson, Hon.Sec.
Publication title: Gentle Jacobite
Meetings/Conventions: - annual

Scottish and Northern Ireland Plumbing Employers' Federation
SNIPEF

2 Walker St., Edinburgh, EH3 7LB, Scotland, UK
Tel: 44 131 2252255
Fax: 44 131 2267638
Email: info@snipef.org
Website: http://www.snipef.org
Founded: 1923
Members: 900
Staff: 26
Contact: Alan McIntosh, Pres.
Description: Trade association for plumbing and heating firms.
Publication title: Plumb Heat

Scottish Arts Council
SAC

c/o Giulio Romano
12 Manor Place, Edinburgh, EH3 7DD, Scotland, UK
Tel: 44 131 2266051
Fax: 44 131 2259833
Email: help.desk@scottisharts.org.uk
Website: http://www.sac.org.uk
Founded: 1946
Members: 16
Staff: 100
Contact: Giulio Romano
Description: Seeks to develop and improve the knowledge, understanding, and practice of the arts and increase their accessibility to the public. Sponsors traveling art exhibitions to areas without galleries. Subsidizes art associations and music clubs. Awards fellowships to artists in different fields. Offers general advisory service.
Library Subject: arts management
Library Type: reference
Publication: Directory
Publication title: Information Directory: A Guide to Information, Advice and Services from the Scottish Arts Council
Second publication: Annual Report
Meetings/Conventions: meeting

Scottish Asian Action Committee
SAAC

39 Napiershall St., Glasgow, G20 6EZ, Scotland, UK
Tel: 44 141 3410025
Fax: 44 141 3410020
Email: secretary@saac.freeserve.co.uk
Founded: 1983
Members: 29
Staff: 3
Contact: Rajender Aggarwal
Description: Individuals and organizations with an interest in the Asian community in Scotland. Promotes respect for the human and civil rights of Asians living in Scotland; works to eradicate racism and discrimination. Serves as a clearinghouse on the Asian community; provides support and assistance to organizations combatting racism; participates in charitable activities.
Library Subject: Asians in Scotland
Library Type: reference
Publication: Newsletter

Scottish Assessors Association

PO Box 467, Chesser House, 500 Gorgie Rd., Edinburgh, EH11 3YJ, Scotland, UK
Tel: 44 1224 664330
Email: lvob@callnetuk.com
Founded: 1856
Members: 60
Contact: John A. Cardwell, Pres.
Description: 14 assessor members, plus ordinary members (deputies or assistant directors). To encourage its members to exchange ideas regarding their statutory duties, to record results of discussions; to promote uniformity in the operation of valuation, electoral registration and council tax legislation. To act as a consultative and advisory body.

Scottish Association for Building Education and Training

c/o Mr. Tom Connelly
1 Wingate Pl., Main St., Kippen, Stirling, FK8 3DW, Scotland, UK
Tel: 44 1786 840331
Founded: 1951
Members: 15
Contact: Tom Connelly, Treas.

Description: Colleges, companies and individuals interested in building education and training. Runs an annual lecture on the subject of training in building, or related topics. Promotes interest in education and training in the building sphere.

Scottish Association for Marine Science

c/o Dunstaffnage Marine Laboratory, Argyll, Oban, PA37 1QA, Scotland, UK
Tel: 44 1631 559000
Fax: 44 1631 559001
Email: mail@dml.ac.uk
Website: http://www.sams.ac.uk
Founded: 1914
Members: 507
Staff: 100
Contact: Dr.Prof. Graham Shimmield, Dir.
Description: Marine scientists and others interested in marine science, primarily in Scotland, but also a substantial number in other parts of the UK and overseas. Promotes and conducts research and education in marine science, particularly on issues relevant to Scotland. Encourages new marine research; develops a wide range of activities, including scientific meetings in different parts of Scotland and a programme for schools. Offers a BSC Marine Science degree course.
Publication: Proceedings
Publication title: Symposium
Second publication: Annual Report

Scottish Association for Mental Health

Cumbrae House, 15 Carlton Ct., Glasgow, G5 9JP, Scotland, UK
Tel: 44 141 5687000
Fax: 44 141 5687001
Email: enquire@samh.org.uk
Website: http://www.samh.org.uk
Founded: 1923
Members: 239
Staff: 381
Contact: Shona Barcus, Dir.
Fee: £15
Membership Type: individual
Fee: £100
Membership Type: organisational
Description: Health Boards, Regional Councils, District Councils, Psychiatric Hospitals, local and regional voluntary organisations, Trade Unions, Professional Bodies Universities, individuals, local associations for mental health. Campaigns for better hospital and community services; seeks to increase understanding of mental distress; provides direct services to people who have suffered from mental health problems, namely supported accommodation and training for employment on projects all over Scotland. Information, training and a development consultancy are also offered to local groups, professionals and affiliated local mental health associations.
Library Subject: mental health
Library Type: by appointment only
Publication: Newsletter
Publication title: Mental Health Matters

Scottish Association for Public Transport

11 Queens Crescent, Glasgow, G4 9BL, Scotland, UK
Email: thstsg@aol.com
Founded: 1972
Members: 140
Contact: Alastair Reid, Sec.
Fee: £12

Membership Type: individual
Description: Campaigns for improved public passenger transport and the shift from lorries to rail and water-borne freight as part of sustainable, integrated, and inclusive transport policies for UK and Scotland.
Publication: Newsletter
Second publication: Papers

Scottish Association of Family History Societies

51/3 Mortonhall Rd., Edinburgh, EH9 2HN, Scotland, UK
Tel: 44 131 667 0437
Fax: 44 131 667 0437
Email: ajmacleo@aol.com
Website: http://www.safhs.org.uk
Contact: Alan J.L. Macleod
Description: Acts as the parent body for Scottish history societies.

Scottish Association of Geography Teachers

University of Strathclyde, Jordanhill Campus, Glasgow, G13 1PP, Scotland, UK
Tel: 44 1506 843211
Fax: 44 1506 848082
Email: alan.doherty@virgin.net
Website: http://www.geocities.com/sagtweb
Founded: 1970
Members: 800
Contact: Alan Doherty, Pres.
Fee: £20
Membership Type: full
Description: Mainly teachers of Geography in Scottish schools: also College lecturers and University staff concerned with Geography. Aims to further the teaching of geography in Scotland; to support teachers in developing new courses (through publications, Annual Conference (Oct.) and Annual Field Excursion (June)). Also responds to proposals/publications related to geography, eg by Scottish Qualifications Authority. Comments annually to SQA re-examinations.
Publication: Journal
Publication title: SAGT. Advertisements.
Publication title: SGN (Scottish Geographical News)
Meetings/Conventions: - annual conference - Exhibits.

Scottish Association of Health Councils

24 A Palmerston Place, Edinburgh, EH12 5AL, Scotland, UK
Tel: 44 131 2204101
Fax: 44 131 2204108
Email: admin1@sahc.sol.co.uk
Website: http://www.show.scot.nhs.uk/sahc
Founded: 1977
Members: 15
Staff: 3
Contact: John Wright, Dir.
Description: Membership is open to all 15 health councils in Scotland. Provides information, training resources and development of public participation to all health related matters. The organization is the focal point between Local Health Councils, the Scottish Executive and Health Department and other national organizations, SAHC is voluntary and funded by LHC's subscriptions.
Library Subject: health, NHS, patients issues
Library Type: reference
Publication: Papers
Meetings/Conventions: - annual conference

Scottish Association of Master Bakers

Atholl House, 4 Torphichen St., Edinburgh, EH3 8JQ, Scotland, UK
Tel: 44 131 2291401
Fax: 44 131 2298239
Email: master.bakers@samb.co.uk
Website: http://www.samb.co.uk
Founded: 1891
Members: 550
Staff: 11
Contact: Kirk Hunter, Chief Exec.
Description: Bakers and manufacturers of bakery equipment and supplies in Scotland. Promotes the baked goods industry in Scotland. Protects members' interests.
Publication title: A History of the Baking Trade in Scotland
Publication title: 100 Years of the Scottish Association of Master Bakers
Meetings/Conventions: - annual conference - Exhibits.

Scottish Association of Young Farmers' Clubs
SAYFC

c/o Ms. Fiona Bain
Young Farmers' Centre, Ingliston, Edinburgh, EH28 8NE, Scotland, UK
Tel: 44 131 3332445
Fax: 44 131 3332488
Email: fiona@sayfc.org
Website: http://www.sayfc.org
Founded: 1938
Members: 5000
Contact: Marie A. Wornin, Coord.
Description: Individuals aged 14-26 who are interested in agriculture. Works to further the cultural education of youth; fosters knowledge and appreciation of country life. Encourages good citizenship and efficiency in agriculture. Seeks to make rural life more attractive to youth by providing social and recreational opportunities. Cooperates with colleges of agriculture, education authorities, and other organizations; promotes the formation of new clubs and international understanding through contact with similar organizations worldwide. Participates in international exchange programs with Australia, Canada, other European countries, New Zealand, and the United States. Promotes technical education through competitions, skills tests, leadership training, and discussion meetings. Sponsors seminars; organizes rallies and regional conferences. Offers pesticide application testing service. Sponsors competitions.
Publication title: Annual Report
Publication title: Area Handbooks
Meetings/Conventions: - annual UK

Scottish Beekeepers' Association

c/o Fraser Sim
27 Moss Rd., Tain, IV19 1HH, Scotland, UK
Tel: 44 1862 894204
Email: fesim@tesco.net
Website: http://www.scottishbeekeepers.org.uk/
Members: 1600
Contact: Una Robertson, Pres.
Fee: £15
Membership Type: full, foreign, family, association, free exchange
Description: Represents Scottish beekeepers at the national and international level.
Library Subject: beekeeping
Library Type: not open to the public
Publication: Magazine
Publication title: The Scottish Beekeeper. Advertisements.
Meetings/Conventions: meeting

Scottish Building

Carron Grange, Carrongrange Ave., Stenhousemuir, Larbert, FK5 3BQ, Scotland, UK
Tel: 44 1324 555550
Fax: 44 1324 555551
Email: info@scottish-building.co.uk
Website: http://www.scottish-building.co.uk
Founded: 1895
Members: 1600
Staff: 22
Contact: Mr. S.C. Patten, Chief Exec.
Description: Employers in all sectors of the construction and building industry. Is the major employers' organization for the building industry in Scotland. It negotiates conditions of service, administers apprenticeship training, negotiates standard forms of contract and provides a wide range of other services designed to assist member firms in the conduct of their businesses.
Publication: Annual Report. Advertisements.
Second publication: Directory

Scottish Building Contractors Association
SBCA

4 Woodside Place, Glasgow, G3 7QP, Scotland, UK
Tel: 44 141 3535050
Fax: 44 1221 3322
Email: smith@sbca.foreserve.co.uk
Founded: 1869
Members: 40
Contact: N.J. Smith, Sec.
Description: Building contractors in Scotland.

Scottish Building Employers' Federation

Scottish Bldg. Headquarters, Carron Grange, Carrongrange Ave., Stenhousemuir, FK5 3BQ, Scotland, UK
Tel: 44 1324 555550
Fax: 44 1324 555551
Email: info@scottish-building.co.uk
Website: http://www.scottish-building.co.uk/
Members: 20
Description: Promotes the Scottish building industry; works to ensure the industry recruits, trains and retains a skilled workforce; maintains and develops standards and quality in the building industry.

Scottish Catholic International Aid Fund
SCIAF

9 Park Circus, Glasgow, G3 6BE, Scotland, UK
Tel: 44 141 3545555
Fax: 44 141 3545533
Email: sciaf@sciaf.org.uk
Website: http://www.sciaf.org.uk
Contact: Paul Chitnis, Exec.Dir.
Description: Seeks to ensure that international development benefits the economically disadvantaged worldwide. Provides financial, technical, and voluntary support to emergency relief and community development projects in Africa, Asia, and Latin America.

Scottish Centre for Studies in School Administration

Moray House Institute of Education, Holyrood Rd., Edinburgh, EH8 8AQ, Scotland, UK
Tel: 44 131 5586179
Fax: 44 131 5573458

Founded: 1972
Staff: 3
Contact: A. Cumming, Dir.
Description: To provide training programmes for headteachers and other senior staff in Scottish schools.

Scottish Childminding Association

7 Melville Terr., Ste. 3, Stirling, FK8 2ND, Scotland, UK
Tel: 44 1786 445377
Fax: 44 1786 449062
Website: http://www.childminding.org/
Description: Promotes childminding as a quality childcare service. Works to inform childminders, parents, employers, local authorities and central government about good practice in childminding and ways to attain this.

Scottish Churches Housing Agency

28 Albany St., Edinburgh, EH1 3QH, Scotland, UK
Tel: 44 131 4774500
Fax: 44 131 4772710
Email: scotchho@ednet.co.uk
Website: http://www.churches-housing.org
Founded: 1993
Members: 1700
Staff: 3
Contact: Alastair Cameron, Coord.
Description: Churches. Supports the work of churches in Scotland; seeks to end homelessness in Scotland. Provides advice and other support to local groups through community development approach to homelessness. Represents churches' views on homelessness to government. Promotes Homelessness Sunday in Scotland.
Library Subject: housing, homelessness, poverty
Library Type: by appointment only
Publication: Pamphlet
Publication title: Homelessness in Scotland - Facts and Figures
Second publication: Newsletter
Publication title: Our Homeless Neighbor
Meetings/Conventions: - bimonthly board meeting

Scottish Committee of Optometrists

7 Queens Bldgs., Queensferry Rd., Rosyth, St. Andrews, KY11 2RA, Scotland, UK
Tel: 44 383 419444
Fax: 44 383 416778
Email: secretarysco@aol.com
Founded: 1935
Members: 760
Staff: 1
Contact: David S. Hutton, Sec.-Treas.
Description: All optometrists in Scotland. Represents interests of independent optometrists in Scotland.
Publication: Newsletter
Publication title: Look North. Advertisements.
Meetings/Conventions: - biennial conference - Exhibits. Stirling UK

Scottish Community Care Forum
SCCF

c/o Sheena Munro, Exec.Dir.
Highland Community Care Forum, Highland House, 20 Longman Rd., Inverness, IV1 1RY, Scotland, UK
Tel: 44 146 3718817
Email: info@sccfonline.org.uk
Website: http://www.sccfonline.org.uk

Founded: 1993
Members: 47
Staff: 2
Contact: Jennifer Flueckiger, Development Officer
Fee: £20
Membership Type: affiliate
Description: Community care providers and organizations. Seeks to improve delivery and availability of community care and volunteer programs and services. Facilitates collaboration between users and providers of community care and related services; works to insure effective planning and practice among community care initiatives.
Library Subject: Community care
Library Type: by appointment only
Publication: Newsletter
Publication title: Community Care Update
Meetings/Conventions: - annual conference

Scottish Consumer Council
SCC

Royal Exchange House, 100 Queen St., Glasgow, G1 3DN, Scotland, UK
Tel: 44 141 2265261
Fax: 44 141 2210731
Email: mevans@scotconsumer.org.uk
Website: http://www.scotconsumer.org.uk/
Founded: 1975
Description: Promotes the interests of Scottish consumers, with particular regard to those who experience disadvantage in society. Carries out research into consumer issues and concerns, informs policymakers about concerns and issues, influences policy and decision-making processes, raises public awareness to consumers.

Scottish Consumer Credit Association

105 North High St., East Lothian, Musselburgh, EH21 6JE, Scotland, UK
Tel: 44 131 6652261
Contact: Liz Brody

Scottish Corn Trade Association

77/2 Hanover St., Edinburgh, EH2 1EE, Scotland, UK
Tel: 44 131 2257773
Fax: 44 131 2264448
Founded: 1964
Members: 60
Contact: Nigel Cook
Fee: £100
Description: Traders in grain produce.
Meetings/Conventions: - annual dinner

Scottish Council for Development and Industry
SCDI

23 Chester St., Edinburgh, EH3 7ET, Scotland, UK
Tel: 44 131 2257911
Fax: 44 131 2202116
Email: enquiries@scdi.org.uk
Website: http://www.sedi.org.uk/
Founded: 1931
Members: 1100
Staff: 25
Description: Works to strengthen Scotland's competitiveness; lobbies for government polices that encourage sustainable economic growth.
Publication: Bulletin

Publication title: Indicator
Publication title: Pointer
Meetings/Conventions: The Forum - annual conference

Scottish Council for International Arbitration

c/o James M. Arnott
Albany House, 58 Albany St., Edinburgh, EH1 3QR, Scotland, UK
Tel: 44 131 5571545
Fax: 44 131 5258651
Email: jim.arnott@simpmar.com
Website: http://www.scia.co.uk/
Founded: 1987
Members: 311
Contact: J.M. Arnott, Dir./Sec.
Description: Those interested in promoting international arbitration in Scotland. To administer international arbitrations in Scotland and arbitration as a method of resolving disputes.
Publication: Brochure

Scottish Council for Postgraduate Medical and Dental Education
SCPMDE

Hanover Bldg., 2nd Fl., 66 Rose St., Edinburgh, EH2 2NN, Scotland, UK
Tel: 44 131 2254365
Fax: 44 131 2255891
Email: enquiries@scpmde.scot.nhs.uk
Website: http://www.show.scot.nhs.uk/scpmde/
Contact: Dr. Graham Buckley, Exec.Dir.
Description: Directs, supports and commissions postgraduate studies in medical and dental education for approximately 4,700 doctors, dentists and clinical psychologists.

Scottish Council for Research in Education

61 Dublin St., Edinburgh, EH3 6NL, Scotland, UK
Tel: 44 131 5572944
Fax: 44 131 5569454
Email: scre.info@scre.ac.uk
Website: http://www.scre.ac.uk
Founded: 1928
Members: 26
Staff: 33
Contact: Dr. Valerie Wilson, Dir.
Description: Promotes the use and understanding of educational research throughout Scotland. It works to make teachers, administrators, researchers, parents, all these concerned with education aware of research ideas, findings and applications through a range of publications and meetings and through its information services.
Publication: Newsletter
Publication title: Research in Education
Second publication: Report
Publication title: Research Report

Scottish Council for Single Homeless
SCSH

Wellgate House, 200 Cowgate, Edinburgh, EH1 1NQ, Scotland, UK
Tel: 44 131 2264382
Fax: 44 131 2254382
Email: enquiries@scsh.demon.co.uk
Website: http://www.scsh.co.uk/
Contact: Robert Aldridge, Dir.

Description: Individuals and organizations. Promotes increased public awareness of the causes, nature and extent of single homelessness. Seeks to identify methods of preventing and alleviating homelessness. Gathers and disseminates information on single homelessness; advises policy makers and social workers on homelessness and related issues; serves as a forum for the public discussion of homelessness and its causes. Conducts research; collaborates in the implementation of policies designed to prevent and alleviate homelessness.

Scottish Council for Voluntary Organisations

Mansfield Traquair Centre, 15 Mansfield Pl., Edinburgh, EH3 6BB, Scotland, UK
Tel: 44 131 5563882
Fax: 44 131 5560279
Email: enquiries@svco.org.uk
Website: http://www.scvo.org.uk
Founded: 1943
Members: 1200
Staff: 140
Contact: Martin Sime, Ch.Exec.
Description: Includes Scotland's major voluntary sector bodies. National co-ordinating body for the voluntary sector in Scotland. In addition to representing and supporting the interests of the voluntary sector at national level, provides a wide range of services to locally based groups.

Scottish Council of Independent Schools
SCIS

21 Melville St., Edinburgh, EH3 7PE, Scotland, UK
Tel: 44 131 2202106
Fax: 44 131 2258594
Email: information@scis.org.uk
Website: http://www.scis.org.uk/
Description: Promotes and supports the contributions made by independent schools to education in Scotland.
Publication: Handbook

Scottish Council on Deafness
SCoD

Clerwood House, 96 Clermiston Rd., Edinburgh, EH12 6UT, Scotland, UK
Tel: 44 131 3146075
Fax: 44 131 3146077
Email: admin@scod.org.uk
Website: http://www.scod.org.uk/
Description: Committed to addressing the needs of deaf, deafened, deafblind and hard of hearing individuals, their families and caregivers, and the professionals working with them. Works to improve the quality of life for all deaf people in Scotland.

Scottish Council on Human Bioethics
SCHB

200 Bath St., Glasgow, G2 4HG, Scotland, UK
Tel: 44 7092 365757
Fax: 44 7092 365765
Email: secretary@schb.org.uk
Website: http://www.schb.org.uk/
Founded: 1997
Contact: Dr. George L. Chalmers, Pres.
Description: Doctors, lawyers, psychologists, ethicists and other professionals from disciplines associated with medical ethics whose

principles are set out in the United Nations Universal Declaration of Human Rights. Works to collect and evaluate evidence and information relating to ethical issues to inform public debate; assist legislators, fellow professionals and other interested parties with ethical analysis and comment on issues; respond appropriately to the media.

Scottish Daily Newspaper Society

48 Palmerston Place, Edinburgh, EH12 5DE, Scotland, UK
Tel: 44 131 2204353
Fax: 44 131 2204344
Email: info@sdns.org.uk
Founded: 1915
Members: 7
Staff: 1
Contact: J.B. Raeburn, Dir.
Description: Promotes and represents the interests of the publishers of Scottish daily and Sunday newspapers.

Scottish Dairy Association

46 Underwood Rd., Paisley, PA3 1TL, Scotland, UK
Tel: 44 141 8480009
Email: admin@scotdairy.org.uk
Website: http://www.efr.hw.ac.uk/SDA/welcome.html
Founded: 1988
Members: 50
Staff: 4
Contact: Kirk Hunter
Description: Dairy companies active in the Scottish market. Promotes advancement of members' interests. Facilitates communication and cooperation among members; conducts promotional activities.
Publication: Book
Publication title: History of Scottish Cheesemaking
Second publication: Newsletter
Publication title: SDA News
Meetings/Conventions: Scottish Dairy Conference - annual conference

Scottish Dance Teacher's Alliance
SDTA

101 Park Rd., Glasgow, G4 9JE, Scotland, UK
Tel: 44 141 3398944
Fax: 44 141 3574994
Email: alliance@mcmail.com
Founded: 1934
Members: 1600
Staff: 2
Contact: S. McDonald, Pres.
Description: Professional dance teachers, worldwide, who have passed an entrance examination. Seeks to: promote and encourage Scottish dance in all forms, particularly ballroom, ballet, Highland, theatre, rock 'n' roll, disco, and baton twirling; ensure that members are familiar with currently accepted techniques and principles; provide members with counsel and advice regarding the profession.
Library Subject: text and examination syllabus
Library Type: reference
Publication: Newsletter. Advertisements.
Meetings/Conventions: - annual meeting

Scottish Dancesport
SADA

93 Hillfoot Dr., Bearsden, Glasgow, G61 3QG, Scotland, UK
Tel: 44 141 5632001
Fax: 44 141 5632001
Founded: 1945
Members: 3000
Staff: 1
Contact: Margo Fraser, Gen.Sec/Admin.
Description: Individuals with an interest in competitive dancing as a means of exercise and recreation. Promotes participation in dance programs, particularly those involving ballroom dancing; selects dance teams to participate in international dancing competitions.
Publication: Newsletter. Advertisements.
Meetings/Conventions: - annual general assembly - Exhibits.

Scottish Ecological Design Association

PO Box 14167, Tranent, East Lothian, EH33 2YG, Scotland, UK
Email: info@sedanet.org
Website: http://www.sedanet.org
Founded: 1991
Members: 250
Staff: 1
Contact: Richard Atkiss, Sec.
Fee: £20
Membership Type: individual
Fee: £100
Membership Type: corporation
Description: Open to all involved or interested in the design of the environment. Seeks to promote ecologically responsible design of products, environments and communities; awareness of ecological design and choice; interdisciplinary contacts; ecological principles in education and the training of designers; research and evaluation of materials, products and services.
Library Subject: ecological design
Library Type: not open to the public
Publication: Newsletter
Publication title: SEDA Magazine. Advertisements.
Meetings/Conventions: - monthly meeting - Exhibits.

Scottish Economic Society

Department of Economics, University of Glasgow, Glasgow, G12 8RT, Scotland, UK
Tel: 44 141 3305534
Email: f.g.hay@socsci.gla.ac.uk
Founded: 1897
Members: 160
Contact: F.G. Hay, Sec.
Fee: £25
Membership Type: individual
Fee: £15
Membership Type: student
Description: Aims to advance the study and teaching of economics on the widest basis in accordance with the Scottish traditions of political economy inspired by Adam Smith and to provide a forum for the discussion of Scottish economic problems and the relationship to the political and social life in Scotland.

Scottish Education and Action for Development
SEAD

167-171 Dundee ST., Edinburgh, EH11 1BY, Scotland, UK
Tel: 44 131 4772780
Fax: 44 131 4772781

Email: information@sead.org.uk
Founded: 1978
Members: 800
Staff: 9
Contact: Fiona Sinclair, Dir.
Description: Researches and campaigns for world development from a Scottish perspective. Encourages networking and exchange of information among members. Conducts educational programs.
Publication title: Living in the Real World: The International Role for Scotland's Parliament
Second publication: Newsletter
Publication title: SEAD News
Meetings/Conventions: - annual meeting

Scottish Engineering

105 West George St., Glasgow, G2 1QL, Scotland, UK
Tel: 44 141 2213281
Fax: 44 141 2041202
Email: consult@scottishengineering.org.uk
Website: http://www.scottishengineering.org.uk
Founded: 1860
Members: 370
Staff: 18
Contact: E.J.P. Smith
Description: Engineering employers - traditional heavy mechanical to micro electronics. Largest manufacturing employers' organization in Scotland. Strong representational role in dealings with central Government, European Commission, Scottish Office and Scottish Enterprise. Comprehensive employee relations service, employment law and industrial tribunal management, health and safety and training including supervisor development courses. Quarterly Review of Scottish Engineering industry undertaken.
Publication title: Fortnightly Briefings
Second publication: Booklets

Scottish Enterprise Energy Group

10 Queens Road, Aberdeen, AB15 4ZT, Scotland, UK
Tel: 44 1224 626310
Fax: 44 1224 627006
Email: energy.info@scotent.co.uk
Website: http://www.se-energy.co.uk
Description: Aims to improve competitiveness and diversification of companies in the oil and gas industry in Scotland. Works with small to medium sized enterprises in Scotland to enable them to respond positively to changes in markets and technology, thereby enabling them to compete internationally.

Scottish Esperanto Association

47 Airbles Crescent, Motherwell, ML1 3AP, Scotland, UK
Tel: 44 1698 263199
Fax: 44 8453 340429
Email: david@bisset100.freeserve.co.uk
Website: http://www.skotlando.org
Founded: 1903
Members: 100
Contact: David W. Bisset, Hon.Sec.
Fee: £6
Membership Type: member
Fee: £2
Membership Type: child
Description: Promotes the international language Esperanto in Scotland; aims to increase the language fluency of the membership; aims to encourage the members to use Esperanto internationally.
Library Subject: Esperanto, language problem

Library Type: lending
Publication: Magazine
Publication title: Esperanto En Skotlando. Advertisements.
Second publication: Magazine
Publication title: Scottish Esperanto Bulletin

Scottish Federation of Housing Associations

38 York Place, Edinburgh, EH1 3HU, Scotland, UK
Tel: 44 131 5565777
Fax: 44 131 5576028
Email: sfha@sfha.co.uk
Website: http://www.sfha.co.uk
Founded: 1989
Members: 350
Staff: 45
Contact: David Orr, Ch.Exec.
Description: Represents housing associations and cooperatives in negotiations on housing policy with government and other bodies, as well as campaigning on their behalf.
Library Type: by appointment only
Publication: Magazine
Publication title: Federation Focus. Advertisements.

Scottish Federation of Meat Traders Association

8-10 Needless Rd., Perth, PH2 0JW, Scotland, UK
Tel: 44 1738 637472
Fax: 44 1738 441059
Email: enquiries@sfmta.co.uk
Website: http://www.sfmta.co.uk/index?/CATEGORY2=5-Members
Contact: Robert Booden
Description: Meat trader associations in Scotland.

Scottish Field Studies Association

Kindrogan Field Centre, Enochdhu by Blairgowrie, Perth, PH10 7PG, Scotland, UK
Tel: 44 125 0881286
Fax: 44 125 0881433
Email: kindrogan@btinternet.com
Website: http://www.kindrogan.com
Founded: 1963
Members: 250
Staff: 25
Contact:
Fee: £10
Membership Type: ordinary
Fee: £12
Membership Type: family
Description: Biologists, botanists, zoologists, ecologists, and other natural scientists with an interest in field studies of wildlife and wildlife behavior in Scotland. Facilitates communication and exchange of information among members; works to educate schools and the general public and to protect and conserve wild flora and fauna and their habitats. Offers courses in the natural environment.
Library Subject: history and natural history
Library Type: reference
Publication: Newsletter
Publication title: Members Newsletter

Scottish Fishermen's Federation

14 Regent Quay, Aberdeen, AB11 5AE, Scotland, UK
Tel: 44 1224 582583
Fax: 44 1224 574958
Email: sff@sff.co.uk

Website: http://www.sff.co.uk
Founded: 1973
Staff: 6
Contact: Roger Allan
Description: Associations of fishing vessel owners/share fishermen. Aims to promote and protect the interests of fishing vessel owners/ share fishermen engaged in the Scottish fishing industry, through contact with government, parliament, the EU and the media.
Publication: Yearbook
Publication title: Official Yearbook and Diary

Scottish Food and Drink Federation
SFDF

4a Torphichen St., Edinburgh, EH3 8JQ, Scotland, UK
Tel: 44 131 2299415
Fax: 44 131 2299407
Email: sfdf@sfdf.org.uk
Website: http://www.sfdf.org.uk/
Description: Works to promote the interests of the food and drink manufacturing industry in Scotland, including issues related to legislation, economics, social or political.

Scottish Further Education Funding Council
SFEFC

Donaldson House, 97 Haymarket Terr., Edinburgh, EH12 5HD, Scotland, UK
Tel: 44 131 3136500
Email: info@sfc.ac.uk
Website: http://www.sfefc.ac.uk
Founded: 1999
Staff: 100
Description: Promotes further education in Scotland; responsibilities include the funding for Scotland's further education colleges, monitoring the financial health of the sector, promoting innovation, offering guidance to colleges.

Scottish Gaelic Texts Society
SGTS

King's College, Aberdeen, AB24 3UB, Scotland, UK
Tel: 44 1224 272544
Fax: 44 1224 272562
Email: r.a.v.cox@abdn.ac.uk
Founded: 1934

Scottish Grocers' Federation

222-224 Queensferry Rd., Edinburgh, EH4 2BN, Scotland, UK
Tel: 44 131 3433300
Fax: 44 131 3436147
Email: scotgrocersfed@compuserve.com
Founded: 1918
Members: 580
Staff: 44
Contact: Caroline MacKay, Admin.
Fee: £100
Membership Type: gold
Description: Retail grocers but not multiples or co-ops. Represents retail independent grocers and provides services such as buying, training, VAT, insurance etc.

Scottish Gypsy Traveller Association
SGTA

31 Guthrie St., Edinburgh, EH1 1JG, Scotland, UK
Tel: 44 131 6506314
Fax: 44 131 6506328
Founded: 1993
Members: 200
Staff: 2
Contact: Florence Garabedian
Description: Individuals and organizations with an interest in the Romany people. Seeks to insure the right of the Romany people to travel freely withing Scotland. Promotes appreciation of Romany history and culture. Lobbies for legislation beneficial to the Romany people; advocates on behalf of the Romany people before government agencies, educational authorities, industrial organizations, and the public. Conducts educational programs.
Meetings/Conventions: - biennial conference

Scottish Higher Education Funding Council
SHEFC

Donaldson House, 97 Haymarket Terr., Edinburgh, EH12 5HD, Scotland, UK
Tel: 44 131 3136500
Email: info@sfc.ac.uk
Website: http://www.shefc.ac.uk
Description: Promotes and supports developments and innovations to benefit the Scottish higher education system.

Scottish History Society
SHS

c/o Department of Scottish History
University of Edinburgh, 17 Buccleuch Pl., Edinburgh, EH8 9LN, Scotland, UK
Tel: 44 131 6504035
Fax: 44 131 6504042
Email: steve.boardman@ed.ac.uk
Founded: 1886
Members: 700
Contact: Dr. Steve Boardman, Hon.Sec.
Description: Individuals (505) and libraries (195) interested in Scottish history. Seeks to print previously unpublished documents illustrative of the history of Scotland.
Meetings/Conventions: - annual convention

Scottish Homing Union

231a Low Waters Rd., Hamilton, ML3 7QN, Scotland, UK
Tel: 44 1698 286983
Founded: 1900
Members: 6750
Staff: 2
Contact: A. Shearer, Sec.
Description: Keepers and trainers of homing pigeons (racing). The provision of uniform rules and regulations for the ringing and registration of racing pigeons as to the ownership and transfer of same for the conduct of races and shows.

Scottish Human Rights Centre
SHRC

146 Holland St., Glasgow, G2 4NG, Scotland, UK
Tel: 44 141 3325960
Fax: 44 141 3325309

Email: info@scottishhumanrightscentre.org.uk
Website: http://www.scottishhumanrightscentre.org.uk
Founded: 1970
Members: 380
Staff: 3
Contact:
Fee: £20
Membership Type: couple
Fee: £15
Membership Type: individual
Description: We aim to promote human rights in Scotland through Advice and Information, Research, Scrutiny of Legislation, Monitoring the application of International Human Rights treaties in Scotland.
Library Subject: human rights
Library Type: reference
Formerly: Scottish Council for Civil Liberties
Publication: Newsletter
Publication title: Rights. Advertisements.

Scottish Industrial Heritage Society
SSIA

Abbotsinch Rd., Grangemouth, FK3 9UX, Scotland, UK
Founded: 1984

Scottish Inland Waterways Association

1 Craiglockhart Crescent, Edinburgh, EH14 1EZ, Scotland, UK
Tel: 44 131 4432533
Founded: 1947
Members: 25
Contact: G A Hunter, Sec.
Description: Coordinates the Canal Societies in Scotland. Ensures the canals in Scotland are maintained in good order.

Scottish Institute for Crop Research
SSCR

Invergowrie, Dundee, DD2 5DA, Scotland, UK
Tel: 44 1382 562731
Fax: 44 1382 562426
Email: l.Kelly@scri.sari.ac.uk
Website: http://www.scri.sari.ac.uk
Founded: 1981
Description: Provides a link between the Scottish Crop Research Institute and farmers, processors and other interested bodies.

Scottish Institute of Reflexology
SIR

110 Easterhouse Rd., Flt 1/2, Glasgow, G34 9RG, Scotland, UK
Tel: 44 141 7730018
Email: mmreflex@aol.com
Website: http://www.scottishreflexology.org
Founded: 1987
Members: 430
Contact: Elizabeth Hale, Pres.
Description: Works to promote, monitor and maintain professional standards among reflexologists; aims to advance acceptance of reflexology as an alternative treatment; provides training courses.
Meetings/Conventions: meeting

Scottish Joint Industry Board for the Electrical Contracting Industry

Bush House, Bush Estate, Midlothian, EH26 0SB, Scotland, UK
Tel: 44 131 4455577
Fax: 44 131 4455548
Email: admin@select.org.uk
Website: http://www.select.org.uk/index.htm
Founded: 1969
Members: 750
Staff: 30
Contact: M.D. Goodwin, Dir.
Description: Membership is divided into two classes - employer and employee. Each employer and employee must be engaged in the electrical contracting industry and accepts to observe and to comply with decisions, regulations, agreements and the national working. rules made by the national board. Provides a base for stable industrial relations to regulate and control employment and productive capacity within the industry and the level of skill and proficiency, safety, wages and welfare of persons concerned in the industry.
Library Subject: employment legislation
Library Type: not open to the public
Publication: Annual Report. Advertisements.
Meetings/Conventions: - annual conference - Exhibits.

Scottish Landowners' Federation

Stuart House, Eskmills Business Park, Musselburgh, EH21 7PB, Scotland, UK
Tel: 44 131 6535400
Fax: 44 131 6535401
Email: slfinfo@slf.org.uk
Website: http://www.slf.org.uk
Founded: 1906
Members: 3600
Staff: 12
Contact: Dr. Maurice Hankey, Dir.
Description: Ordinary membership for those who own 4 hectares or more; associate membership and business membership. Representing owners of rural land in Scotland.
Publication title: Landowning in Scotland

Scottish Language Dictionaries

27 George Sq., Edinburgh, EH8 9LD, Scotland, UK
Tel: 44 131 6504149
Fax: 44 131 6504149
Email: mail@snda.org.uk
Website: http://www.snda.org.uk
Founded: 1929
Description: Deals with the research on Scots language and publication of the results.

Scottish Law Agents Society

11 Parliament Sq., Edinburgh, EH1 1RF, Scotland, UK
Tel: 44 131 2255051
Fax: 44 131 2255051
Email: secretary@slas.co.uk
Website: http://www.slas.co.uk
Founded: 1884
Members: 1800
Staff: 2
Contact: Mrs. Janice Webster, Sec.
Fee: £60
Membership Type: full
Fee: £35
Membership Type: retired

Description: Represents the interests of solicitors in Scotland.
Library Subject: legal
Library Type: reference
Publication: Book
Publication title: Memorandum
Publication title: Scottish Law Gazette
Meetings/Conventions: - periodic seminar

Scottish Licensed Trade Association

10 Walker St., Edinburgh, EH3 7LA, Scotland, UK
Tel: 44 131 2255169
Fax: 44 131 2204057
Founded: 1880
Members: 4500
Staff: 5
Contact: Colin A. Wilkinson, Sec.
Description: Licensees of hotels, public houses, off-sale. A federation of regional and local associations throughout Scotland. It is the recognised body for the Licensed Trade in Scotland and is consulted by Government departments, national boards, press, radio and television, and other authorities when the interests of the trade are under consideration.
Publication: Yearbook
Publication title: The Scottish Licensee

Scottish Local Authority Network of Physical Education

Fife Council Education Service, Woodend Rd., Cardenden, Fife, KY5 0NE, Scotland, UK
Tel: 44 1592 414600
Fax: 44 1592 414641
Email: david.maiden@fife.gov.uk
Founded: 1999
Members: 90
Contact: David Maiden, Education Adv.
Fee: £50
Membership Type: local authority corporate
Description: To ensure that physical education makes its full contribution to formal and informal education and the health and well-being of the community. Also to promote the continuing development and advancement of the teaching profession in the field of physical education.
Formerly: Scottish Association Advisers of Physical Education

Scottish Low Pay Unit
SLPU

94 Duke St., Ste. 30, Ladywell, Glasgow, G4 0UW, Scotland, UK
Tel: 44 141 5525922
Fax: 44 141 5528377
Email: unit@scotlpu.org.uk
Website: http://www.scotlpu.org.uk
Founded: 1989
Staff: 6
Contact: John Wilson
Description: Seeks to improve the quality of life of individuals working in jobs with low pay. Provides information on topics including wages, employment, and benefit rights to people working in jobs with low pay; conducts legal training programs for people counseling low-pay workers. Conducts research; compiles statistics.
Library Subject: employment, poverty, wages and benefits
Library Type: by appointment only

Publication: Journal
Publication title: Employment Backup. Advertisements.
Second publication: Books
Meetings/Conventions: - periodic conference

Scottish Master Wrights and Builders Association

98 West George St., Glasgow, G2 1PJ, Scotland, UK
Tel: 44 141 3331679
Fax: 44 141 3331675
Founded: 1885
Members: 49
Staff: 1
Contact: John F. Lindsay
Description: Joiners and builders. Helps members and promotes the building industry.
Publication: Bulletin

Scottish Microbiological Society

c/o Dr. Simon Burton
University of Strathclyde, Royal College, Department of Bioscience and Biotechnology, University Bldg., Glasgow, G1 1XW, Scotland, UK
Email: s.a.q.burton@strath.ac.uk
Website: http://www.starth.ac.uk/Departments/BioSci/sms1.htm
Contact: Dr. Simon Burton, Sec.
Description: Provides a scientific and social forum for exchange of ideas and knowledge among microbiologists in Scotland.
Publication: Newsletter
Meetings/Conventions: - periodic symposium

Scottish Military Historical Society
SMHS

4 Hillside Cottages, Glenboig, ML5 2QY, Scotland, UK
Founded: 1967

Scottish Milk Records Association

c/o Milk Marketing Board
46 Underwood Rd., Paisley, PA3 1TJ, Scotland, UK
Tel: 44 141 8480404

Scottish Motor Neurone Disease Association

76 Firhill Rd., Glasgow, G20 7BA, Scotland, UK
Tel: 44 141 9451077
Fax: 44 141 9452578
Email: info@scotmnd.sol.co.uk
Website: http://www.scotmnd.org.uk
Founded: 1981
Members: 500
Staff: 8
Contact: Craig Stockton, CEO
Fee: £8
Fee: £40
Membership Type: life
Description: Promotes interest in motor neurone disease (MND) research among medical and scientific communities and the public in Scotland. Offers care and support services to MND patients in Scotland, and their families. Offers an information centre, equipment loan centre, organizes study days for health professionals.
Library Subject: Motor neurone disease, palliative care, bereavement, carers
Library Type: lending
Publication: Newsletter
Publication title: Aware. Advertisements.
Meetings/Conventions: - annual conference

Scottish Motor Trade Association

3 Palmerston Pl., Edinburgh, EH12 5AF, Scotland, UK
Tel: 44 131 2253643
Fax: 44 131 2200446
Email: info@smta.co.uk
Website: http://www.smta.co.uk
Founded: 1903
Members: 950
Staff: 11
Contact: Douglas Roberton, Ch.Exec.
Description: Motor dealers. To protect and promote Scottish retail motor dealers.

Scottish Museums Council

County House, 20-22 Torphichen St., Edinburgh, EH3 8JB, Scotland, UK
Tel: 44 131 2297465
Fax: 44 131 2292728
Email: inform@scottishmuseums.org.uk
Website: http://www.scottishmuseums.org.uk
Founded: 1964
Members: 320
Staff: 30
Contact: Jane Ryder, Dir.
Description: Museums or governing bodies of museums throughout Scotland: includes Local Authorities, Universities, and many independent charitable trusts. Aims to improve the quality of museum and gallery provision in Scotland. Seeks to do this by representing the interests of museums and providing a wide range of services to its membership.
Library Subject: museums, museology, conservation, interpretation
Library Type: by appointment only
Publication: Newsletter
Publication title: Tak Tent
Meetings/Conventions: seminar

Scottish National Blood Transfusion Association SNBTA

2 Otterburn Park, Edinburgh, EH14 1JX, Scotland, UK
Tel: 44 131 4437636
Founded: 1940
Members: 250000
Contact: William Mack, Sec.-Treas.
Description: Blood donors. Promotes donation of blood; seeks to insure a reliable and safe supply of blood and plasma for use in medical transfusions. Represents the interests of blood and bone marrow donors before medical organizations and government agencies; provides support and assistance to the Scottish National Blood Transfusion Service; consults with medical organizations to improve blood donation and transfusion techniques. Maintains speakers' bureau.
Publication: Annual Report
Publication title: Annual Report and Statement of Accounts
Meetings/Conventions: SNBTA Executive Committee - quarterly board meeting UK

Scottish National Federation for the Welfare of the Blind

Thomas Herd House, 10/12 Ward Rd., Dundee, DD1 1LX, Scotland, UK
Tel: 44 1307 460359
Fax: 44 1307 460359
Email: snfwb@dsvip.co.uk

Founded: 1917
Members: 63
Staff: 1
Contact: John Duncan, Honorary Sec.-Treas.
Description: Parent body for numerous charities and local authorities in Scotland concerned with the welfare of blind and partially sighted people. Provides information on social work, education, and employment services.
Publication: Annual Report
Meetings/Conventions: conference

Scottish National Party

107 McDonald Rd., Edinburgh, EH7 4NW, Scotland, UK
Tel: 44 131 5258900
Fax: 44 131 5258901
Email: snp.hq@snp.org
Website: http://www.snp.org
Founded: 1934
Staff: 40
Contact: Stewart Hosie, Sec.
Fee: £10
Description: National political party. Seeks the independence of Scotland within the European Union.
Library Subject: Scottish politics, self government, SNP history
Publication: Magazine
Publication title: Snapshot. Advertisements.
Meetings/Conventions: - annual convention - Exhibits. Inverness UK

Scottish National Party - Women's Forum

107 MacDonald Rd., Edinburgh, EH7 4NW, Scotland, UK
Tel: 44 131 5258900
Fax: 44 131 5258901
Email: snp.hq@snp.org
Website: http://www.snp.org
Founded: 1987
Contact: John Swinney, Natl. Convener
Description: Women members of the Scottish National Party. Ensures that women's issues are addressed within the party platform.
Meetings/Conventions: Women's Forum - annual workshop

Scottish Natural Heritage SNH

12 Hope Terrace, Edinburgh, EH9 2AS, Scotland, UK
Tel: 44 131 4474784
Fax: 44 131 4472277
Email: enquiries@snh.gov.uk
Website: http://213.121.208.4/
Founded: 1992
Staff: 650
Contact: Dr. John Markland, Chair
Description: Promotes wildlife conservation and wise land use in Scotland. Selects, establishes, and manages wildlife and marine reserves; designates sites of special scientific interest; supports and conducts conservation research. Conducts educational programs; seeks to increase public awareness of the dangers posed to wildlife by loss of habitat.
Library Type: by appointment only
Publication: Magazine
Publication title: Scotlands Natural Heritage

Scottish Neuroscience Group
SNG

St. Andrews University, St. Andrews, KY16 8LB, Scotland, UK
Tel: 44 1334 463458
Fax: 44 1334 463443
Founded: 1971

Scottish Newspaper Publishers Association
SNPA

48 Palmerston Pl., Edinburgh, EH12 5DE, Scotland, UK
Tel: 44 131 2204353
Fax: 44 131 2204344
Email: info@snpa.org.uk
Website: http://www.snpa.org.uk
Members: 16
Staff: 7
Contact: J.B. Raeburn, Dir.
Description: Publishers of weekly newspapers. Concerned with industrial relations, education and training and representational work including self regulation of the press.
Meetings/Conventions: - annual conference

Scottish Official Board of Highland Dancing

Heritage House, 32 Grange Loan, Edinburgh, EH9 2NR, Scotland, UK
Tel: 44 131 6683965
Fax: 44 131 6620404
Email: admin@scottishhighlanddancing.org
Website: http://www.highlanddancing.org/
Founded: 1950
Members: 30
Staff: 1
Contact: Marjory Rowan
Description: Teaching associations, independent members, competition organiser members, associations with an interest, either professional or otherwise, in highland dancing. To promote fairplay in both competition and judging, standardize highland dancing throughout the world and, as the world governing body, co-ordinate highland dancing on an international level.
Publication title: Highland Dancing
Publication title: Sailors Hornpipe/Irish Jig

Scottish Ornithologists' Club
SOC

21 Regent Terrace, Edinburgh, EH7 5BT, Scotland, UK
Tel: 44 131 5566042
Fax: 44 131 5589947
Founded: 1936

Scottish Out of School Care Network
SOSCN

6th Fl., Fleming House, 134 Renfrew St., Glasgow, G3 6ST, Scotland, UK
Tel: 44 141 3311301
Fax: 44 141 3321206
Email: info@soscn.org
Website: http://www.soscn.org
Founded: 1991
Members: 400
Staff: 8
Contact: Irene Audain, Dir.
Fee: £100

Membership Type: statutory body
Fee: £40
Membership Type: voluntary organization
Description: Organizations and agencies engaged in out-of-school child care. Promotes increased availability of affordable, quality child care. Establishes partnerships among members and between members and other organizations pursuing similar goals. Works to increase awareness of child care issues. Conducts research; makes available information about children's services; compiles statistics.
Library Subject: child care
Library Type: by appointment only
Publication: Newsletter
Publication title: Connections. Advertisements.
Meetings/Conventions: - annual conference - Exhibits.

Scottish Parent-Teacher Council

53 George St., Edinburgh, EH2 2HT, Scotland, UK
Tel: 44 131 2261917
Fax: 44 131 2264378
Email: sptc@sol.co.uk
Website: http://www.sol.co.uk/s/spt
Founded: 1948
Members: 1040
Staff: 3
Contact: Lynda Grant, Admin.
Fee: £52
Membership Type: for large schools
Description: Parent and teacher groups. Promotes quality primary and secondary education. Facilitates communication and cooperation among members.
Publication: Newsletter
Publication title: Backchat
Meetings/Conventions: - annual conference

Scottish Pelagic Fishermen's Association

1 Frithside St., Fraserburgh, AB43 9AR, Scotland, UK
Tel: 44 1346 510714
Fax: 44 1346 510614
Email: spfaltd@btinternet.com
Founded: 1932
Members: 50
Staff: 1
Contact: Derek Duthie, Sec.
Description: Pelagic fishermen vessel owners. Pelagic species are usually herring, mackerel and sprats. Represents the interests of Scottish pelagic fishermen.
Publication: Newsletter
Publication title: Pelagic News. Advertisements.
Meetings/Conventions: - quarterly board meeting Aberdeen UK

Scottish Pensions Association
SPA

54A Fountainbridge, Edinburgh, EH3 9PT, Scotland, UK
Tel: 44 131 2291886
Fax: 44 131 2291886
Email: spa@tinyworld.co.uk
Founded: 1937
Members: 10000
Staff: 3
Contact: Mr. John C. Wilson, Pres.
Description: Pensioners and those interested in issues affecting older peoples' lives, rights, and welfare. Aims to improve the quality of life for older people and urges that the State Pension should rise

annually in line with prices or average earnings. Provides opportunities for members to gain a voice on the key issues affecting older people.
Library Type: reference

Scottish Personnel Services

105 West George St., Glasgow, G2 1QL, Scotland, UK
Tel: 44 141 2214224
Fax: 44 141 2041202
Email: consult@scottishengineering.org.uk
Founded: 1988
Members: 36
Staff: 18
Contact: E.J.P. Smith
Description: Non-engineering manufacturing companies eg food processing, distillers, rubber. The non-engineering commercial arm of the employers' organization Scottish Engineering. Comprehensive employee relations service; employment law and industrial tribunal management; health and safety training including supervisor development courses; personnel policies and procedures; personnel services available too on consultancy basis.
Publication: Booklets
Publication title: Advisory

Scottish Pharmaceutical Federation

135 Wellington St., Glasgow, G2 2XD, Scotland, UK
Tel: 44 141 2211235
Fax: 44 141 2265047
Email: spf@npanet.co.uk
Website: http://www.npa.co.uk
Founded: 1919
Members: 1050
Staff: 1
Contact: F.E.J. McCrossin, Sec.
Description: Independent retail pharmacists in Scotland. Provides legal representation, general insurance, professional indemnity cover, staff training, clearing house and information services for Scotland.
Publication: Newsletter

Scottish Pharmaceutical General Council

42 Queen St., Edinburgh, EH2 3NH, Scotland, UK
Tel: 44 131 4677766
Fax: 44 131 4677767
Email: enquiries@spgc.org.uk
Website: http://www.spgc.org.uk
Founded: 1913
Staff: 8
Description: Body recognised by Secretary of State for Scotland as representing the interests of the general body of chemist contractors in Scotland. Concerned with all NHS matters which affect retail pharmacy in Scotland.

Scottish Plant Owners Association
SPOA

302 St. Vincent Pl., Glasgow, G2 5RZ, Scotland, UK
Tel: 44 141 2483434
Fax: 44 141 2211226
Email: info@spoa.org.uk
Website: http://www.spoa.org.uk
Founded: 1952
Members: 255
Contact: Graham Bell, Sec.
Fee: £140

Description: Companies involved in the hiring out of plant and machinery. Aims to protect and further the interests of plant owners on all matters affecting plant ownership and plant usage; advises and offers guidance on terms and conditions relating to the hiring and taking on hire of plant.
Publication: Handbook
Publication title: Handbook and Schedule of Rates. Advertisements.
Meetings/Conventions: - monthly executive committee meeting

Scottish Plastering and Drylining Association

222 Queensferry Rd., Edinburgh, EH4 2BN, Scotland, UK
Tel: 44 131 3433300
Contact: Alan McKinney
Description: Master plasterers.
Formerly: Scottish Master Plasterers' Association

Scottish Police Federation

5 Woodside Pl., Glasgow, G3 7QF, Scotland, UK
Tel: 44 141 3325234
Fax: 44 141 3312436
Email: jmcdonald@scottishpolicefederation.org.uk
Website: http://www.spf.org.uk
Founded: 1919
Members: 15000
Contact: James McDonald
Description: Police in Scotland.

Scottish Pre-School Play Association

14 Elliot Pl., Glasgow, G3 8EP, Scotland, UK
Tel: 44 141 2214148
Fax: 44 141 2216043
Founded: 1967
Members: 1924
Staff: 56
Contact: Mrs. Ruby Sullivan, Sec.
Fee: £35
Description: Playgroups, toddler groups under fives groups and interested organisations. Serves the needs of approx. 2000 member playgroups and toddler groups in Scotland through a network of area teams; training courses covering child development, the value of play, committee and group work are held throughout the country. Distance learning courses are available for fieldworkers and playworkers.
Library Subject: child development, play and recreation, social issues, education, administration
Library Type: open to the public
Publication: Magazine
Publication title: First Five. Advertisements.
Meetings/Conventions: - annual conference - Exhibits. UK

Scottish Print Employers Federation
SPEF

48 Palmerston Pl., Edinburgh, EH12 5DE, Scotland, UK
Tel: 44 131 2204353
Fax: 44 131 2204344
Email: info@spef.org.uk
Website: http://www.spef.org.uk
Founded: 1910
Members: 200
Staff: 9
Contact: J.B. Raeburn, Dir.
Description: Promotes the printing industry in Scotland. to increase the accessibility of Scottish printers to individuals and companies in need of printing services. Represents the interests of Scottish printers.

Formerly: Society of Master Printers of Scotland
Publication: Directory
Publication title: Scottish Print Directory
Meetings/Conventions: - biennial conference

Scottish Publishers Association
Scottish Book Centre, 137 Dundee St., Edinburgh, EH11 1BG, Scotland, UK
Tel: 44 131 2286866
Fax: 44 131 2283220
Email: enquiries@scottishbooks.org
Website: http://www.scottishbooks.org
Founded: 1973
Members: 85
Staff: 5
Contact: Liz Small
Description: Aims to help Scottish publishers to conduct their businesses in a professional manner, to market their output to the widest possible readership within Scotland, the UK and overseas, and to encourage the development of a literary culture in Scotland.
Publication: Directory
Publication title: Directory of Publishing in Scotland. Advertisements.

Scottish Qualifications Authority
Hanover House, 24 Douglas St., Glasgow, G2 7NQ, Scotland, UK
Fax: 44 141 2422244
Email: helpdesk@sqa.org.uk
Website: http://www.sqa.org.uk
Founded: 1997
Staff: 500
Contact: David Fraser, Chief Exec.
Description: Responsible for developing, awarding and accrediting most qualifications in Scotland.
Library Subject: vocational education
Library Type: reference
Formerly: Scottish Vocational Education Council

Scottish Railway Preservation Society
The Station, Union St., West Lothian, Bo'ness, EH51 9AQ, Scotland, UK
Tel: 44 1506 825855
Fax: 44 1506 828766
Email: railway@srps.org.uk
Founded: 1961
Members: 1400
Staff: 3
Contact:
Fee: £14
Membership Type: ordinary
Fee: £9
Membership Type: pensioner
Description: An educational charity established to preserve, restore, display, and interpret Scotland's railway heritage. Owns and operates the Bo'ness and Kinneil Railway, the Scottish Railway Exhibition, and SRPS Railtours.
Library Subject: society records, Scottish railway history
Library Type: reference
Publication: Magazine
Publication title: Blastpipe
Meetings/Conventions: - monthly meeting

Scottish Refugee Council
SRC
5 Cadogan Sq., 170 Blythswood Ct., Glasgow, G2 7PH, Scotland, UK
Tel: 44 141 2489799
Fax: 44 141 2432499
Website: http://www.scottishrefugeecouncil.org.uk/
Founded: 1985
Description: Provides advice and assistance to individuals forced to leave their country and seek protection in Scotland; dedicated to refugee and asylum issues.

Scottish Rock Garden Club
PO Box 14063, Edinburgh, EH10 4YE, Scotland, UK
Email: enquiries@srgc.org.uk
Website: http://www.srgc.org.uk
Founded: 1933
Members: 4225
Contact: Eileen Goodall, Sec.
Fee: £15
Membership Type: single
Fee: £18
Membership Type: family
Description: Promotes interests of members.
Library Subject: alpine and rock plants-systematics and cultivation
Library Type: not open to the public

Scottish Salmon Smokers Association
163c Cargo Terminal, Turnhouse Rd., Edinburgh, EH12 0AL, Scotland, UK
Tel: 44 131 3177329
Fax: 44 131 3177196
Founded: 1986
Members: 40
Staff: 1
Contact: Norman Maclean, Sec.
Description: Administer the quality approval scheme, run the PR and promotional work and represent the industry to UK and EC governments. Also to promote the sale of Scottish smoked salmon, and to maintain and to improve its quality in all markets; to collect and disseminate industry statistics.

Scottish Screen
249 W George St., 2nd Fl., Glasgow, G2 4QE, Scotland, UK
Tel: 44 141 3021700
Fax: 44 141 3021778
Email: info@scottishscreen.com
Website: http://www.scottishscreen.com
Founded: 1997
Members: 15
Staff: 35
Contact: Isabella Edgar, Info.Ofcr.
Description: Funded by H.M. Government via the Scottish office. Promotes moving image culture throughout Scotland. This is achieved through funding, the regional film theatre network film societies etc., through media education activities and industry development. Also encompasses the Scottish Film & Television Archive.
Library Subject: information about Scottish film and T.V.
Library Type: open to the public
Formerly: Scottish Film Council
Publication: Newsletter
Publication title: Rough Cuts
Second publication: Books
Meetings/Conventions: - periodic meeting

Scottish Secondary Teachers' Association

15 Dundas St., Edinburgh, EH3 6QG, Scotland, UK
Tel: 44 131 5565919
Fax: 44 131 5561419
Email: info@ssta.org.uk
Website: http://www.ssta.org.uk
Founded: 1944
Members: 8500
Staff: 8
Contact: David Eaglesham, Gen.Sec.
Description: Scottish secondary teachers trade union. Represents and negotiates on behalf of Scottish secondary teachers in professional matters. It is recognised by all employing local authorities and by the Scottish Executive Education Department.
Publication: Bulletin
Second publication: Journal

Scottish Society for Autism

Hilton House, Alloa Business Park, Whins Rd., Alloa, FK10 3SA, Scotland, UK
Tel: 44 1259 720044
Fax: 44 1259 720051
Email: liddell@autism-in-scotland.org.uk
Website: http://www.autism-in-scotland.org.uk
Members: 600
Staff: 430
Contact: Donald Liddell, CEO
Description: Families affected by autism, Asperger syndrome, or related communication disorders, as well as professionals and caregivers in the field. Works to deliver a comprehensive range of expertise in care, support, and education for people with autism, their families, and caregivers in Scotland. Operates community houses, respite care centers, and schools; provides family support visits and other community support services.

Scottish Society for Conservation and Restoration

Chantstoun, Tartraven, Bathgate Hills, West Lothian, EH48 4NP, Scotland, UK
Tel: 44 1506 811777
Fax: 44 1506 811888
Email: admin@sscr.demon.co.uk
Website: http://www.sscr.demon.co.uk
Founded: 1978
Members: 400
Staff: 1
Contact: Ms. Jane Dahnsjo, Chm.
Fee: £35
Membership Type: full in U.K.
Fee: £30
Membership Type: associate in U.K.
Description: Individuals or institutions concerned with conservation and restoration of Scotland's historic, scientific and artistic material, including conservators, restorers, architects curators, archaeologists, historians and students. Exists to promote the conservation and restoration of Scotland's historic, scientific and artistic material. It seeks to maintain and improve standards by providing a forum for all those concerned with these objectives.
Library Type: by appointment only
Publication: Journal
Publication title: SSCR. Advertisements.
Meetings/Conventions: - biennial conference - Exhibits.

Scottish Society for Contamination Control S2C2

c/o Administrator
James Watt Bldg., Glasgow University, Glasgow, G12 8QQ, Scotland, UK
Tel: 44 141 3303699
Fax: 44 141 3303501
Email: admin@s2c2.co.uk
Website: http://www.s2c2.co.uk
Members: 1000
Description: Individuals and corporations with an interest in cleanrooms. Seeks to improve the design, maintenance, and function of facilities to contain biological contaminants. Represents members before national and international standards committees; serves as a clearinghouse on cleanrooms and related technologies, products, and services. Conducts educational courses.
Publication: Newsletter
Second publication: Directory
Meetings/Conventions: - periodic meeting

Scottish Society for Northern Studies SSNS

27 George Sq., Edinburgh, EH8 9LD, Scotland, UK
Tel: 44 131 6504162
Fax: 44 131 6504163
Founded: 1967
Description: Promotes knowledge and study of all aspects of Scandinavian culture.

Scottish Society for Psychical Research

Bishopbriggs, Glasgow, G64 3AX, Scotland, UK
Tel: 44 141 7724588

Scottish Society for the Prevention of Cruelty to Animals

Braehead Mains, 603 Queensferry Rd., Edinburgh, EH4 6EA, Scotland, UK
Tel: 44 131 3390222
Fax: 44 131 3394777
Email: enquiries@scottishspca.org
Website: http://www.scottishspca.org
Founded: 1839
Members: 5000
Staff: 250
Contact: Diana Allen, Dir.
Fee: £275
Membership Type: life
Fee: £25
Membership Type: joint
Description: Committed to the prevention of cruelty to animals; promotes kindness and humanity in their treatment. Inspectors respond to 130,000 calls for help annually, supported by 13 Animal Welfare Centers; provides information to schools to prevent cruelty from an early age; lobbies for improved legislation to provide greater protection for animals.

Scottish Society of the History of Medicine

74 Glasgow Rd., Perth, PH2 0PG, Scotland, UK
Tel: 44 1738 624493
Fax: 44 1738 624493
Email: jdmac74@aol.com
Founded: 1948

Members: 200
Contact: Dr. A.R. Butler, Sec.
Fee: £10
Membership Type: member
Description: Aims to further the general history of medicine with particular attention to Scottish medicine.
Publication: Proceedings
Publication title: Report of Proceedings

Scottish Spina Bifida Association
SSBA

190 Queensferry Rd., Edinburgh, EH4 2BW, Scotland, UK
Tel: 44 131 3320743
Fax: 44 131 3433651
Email: gail@ssba.org.uk
Website: http://www.ssba.org.uk
Founded: 1965
Members: 3000
Staff: 6
Contact: Andrew H.D. Wynd, Chief Exec.
Description: Seeks to increase public awareness and understanding of individuals with Spina Bifida/Hydrocephalus and allied disorders. Aims to secure provision for their special needs and those of their families.

Scottish Textiles

Apex House, 99 Market Terrace, Edinburgh, EH12 5DH, Scotland, UK
Tel: 44 131 3134000
Fax: 44 131 3134231
Email: sta@scotnet.co.uk
Website: http://www.scottish-textiles.co.uk
Founded: 1993
Members: 144
Staff: 3
Contact: R.A. Chlopas
Description: Companies manufacturing and selling products made in Scotland within the textile industry.
Publication: Newsletter
Publication title: Scottish Textile Association

Scottish Timber Trade Association

c/o STA Secretariat David Sulman
John Player Bldg., Office 14, Stirling Enterprise Park, Springbank Rd., Stirling, FK7 7RP, Scotland, UK
Tel: 44 1786 451623
Fax: 44 1786 473112
Email: mail@stta.org.uk
Website: http://www.stta.org.uk
Members: 37
Contact: David J. Sulman, Sec.
Description: Timber importers, merchants, sawmillers, agents and brokers. Represents the interests of Scottish Members of the Timber Trade Federation. It performs an educational role by ensuring its members are updated on relevant timber and trade matters.

Scottish Tourist Board
STB

23 Ravelston Terr., Edinburgh, EH4 3EV, Scotland, UK
Tel: 44 131 3322433
Fax: 44 131 3431513
Email: conventionbureau@stb.gov.uk
Website: http://www.visitscotland.com

Founded: 1969
Members: 140
Contact: Dr. Brian Hay, Head of Research
Description: Promotes and develops tourism in Scotland. Conducts research program. Maintains speakers' bureau. Compiles statistics.
Library Subject: tourism
Library Type: reference
Publication title: Annual Report
Publication title: The Conference and Exhibition Market in Scotland

Scottish Tree Trust

30 Edgemont St., Glasgow, G41 3EL, Scotland, UK
Tel: 44 141 6492462
Founded: 1982
Members: 30
Staff: 2
Contact: Greer Hart, Pres.
Description: Individuals united to preserve the forests of Scotland. Conducts conservation and reforestation programs; provides support and assistance to other groups with similar goals. Operates a system of annual, international youth exchanges with Eastern Europe to further species conservation.
Publication: Newsletter
Meetings/Conventions: - annual general assembly

Scottish Urban Archaeological Trust
SUAT

55 S Methven St., Perth, PH1 5NX, Scotland, UK
Tel: 44 1738 622393
Fax: 44 1738 631626
Email: director@suat.demon.co.uk
Website: http://www.suat.demon.co.uk
Founded: 1982
Members: 20
Staff: 11
Contact: David Bowler, Dir.
Description: Archeologists and other individuals with an interest in the urban heritage and architecture of Scotland. Promotes preservation of historic buildings; encourages increased public awareness of urban archeology and the development of Scottish towns. Conducts research and educational programs.
Meetings/Conventions: - quarterly board meeting

Scottish Wild Land Group
SWLG

8 Hartington Pl., Edinburgh, EH10 4LE, Scotland, UK
Email: enquiries@swlg.org.uk
Website: http://www.swlg.org.uk
Founded: 1982
Members: 500
Contact: Alistair Cant, Coordinator
Fee: £2
Membership Type: junior or senior citizen
Fee: £10
Membership Type: ordinary
Description: Individuals interested in the protection of Scottish flora and fauna and their habitats. Promotes preservation and restoration of Scottish wild lands. Coordinates activities of conservation, environmental protection, and sustainable development organizations; conducts educational programs to raise public awareness of

conservation issues; lobbies for legislation and policies supporting conservation initiatives.
Publication: Magazine
Publication title: Wild Land News
Meetings/Conventions: - annual meeting Perth UK

Scottish Wildlife Trust
SWT

Cramond Glebe Rd., Edinburgh, EH4 6NS, Scotland, UK
Tel: 44 131 3127765
Fax: 44 131 3128705
Founded: 1964

Scottish Women's Aid

Norton Park, 57 Albion Rd., Edinburgh, EH7 5QY, Scotland, UK
Tel: 44 131 4752372
Fax: 44 131 4752384
Email: swa@swa-1.demon.co.uk
Website: http://www.scottishwomensaid.co.uk
Founded: 1976
Members: 39
Staff: 10
Description: National office of 39 Local women's aid groups. Offers information, counselling and support services, and refuge to abused women and their children. Monitors legislation to ensure that abused women's rights and well-being are protected. Campaigns to effect changes in legislation and societal attitudes to domestic violence.
Library Subject: domestic violence, abuse of women and children, refuge housing, legal issues, training resources, research
Library Type: not open to the public
Publication title: Scottish Women's Aid Newsletter
Second publication: Video
Meetings/Conventions: SWA External Conference - periodic conference

Scottish Women's Rural Institutes

42 Heriot Row, Edinburgh, EH3 6ES, Scotland, UK
Tel: 44 131 2251724
Fax: 44 131 2258129
Email: swri@swri.demon.co.uk
Website: http://www.swri.org.uk
Founded: 1917
Members: 25000
Staff: 9
Contact: Mrs. A. Peacock, Gen.Sec.
Fee: £5
Description: Promotes the interests of women living in rural areas in Scotland. Offers educational and recreational activities to women residing in the country or interested in country living. Encourages home-grown food production, home industry, and craftsmanship. Addresses issues of family welfare and community matters. Works to preserve the traditions of rural Scotland. Promotes peaceful living and understanding.
Publication: Magazine
Publication title: Scottish Home and Country. Advertisements.

Scottish Young Conservatives

83 Princes St., Edinburgh, EH2 2ER, Scotland, UK
Tel: 44 131 2476890
Fax: 44 131 2476891
Email: scottishycs@aol.com
Website: http://www.syc.tories.org.uk
Founded: 1963

Members: 1500
Staff: 1
Contact: Simon Turner, Dir.
Description: Political organization for youth in Scotland. Organizes campaigns; disseminates information.
Formerly: Young Unionists
Publication: Magazine
Publication title: Blue Moves. Advertisements.
Meetings/Conventions: - annual conference - Exhibits.

Sector SKills Alliance Scotland

28 Castle St., Edinburgh, EH2 3HT, Scotland, UK
Tel: 44 131 2267726
Fax: 44 131 2206431
Email: admin@ssascot.org.uk
Website: http://www.ssascot.org.uk
Description: Works to assist in the development of a competitive Scotland; provides focus for information exchange, development and promotion of Scottish workforce to improve skills.
Formerly: Scottish Council of National Training Organisations

SELECT

The Walled Garden, Bush Estate, Midlothian, EH26 0SB, Scotland, UK
Tel: 44 131 4455577
Fax: 44 131 4455548
Email: admin@select.org.uk
Website: http://www.select.org.uk
Founded: 1900
Members: 500
Staff: 30
Contact: M.D. Goodwin, Mng.Dir.
Description: Members of the Association range from large multi-national contractors to one man businesses. Through a comprehensive package of services to membership covering industrial relations, training, contractual and legal, technical and marketing, members are kept up to date on all issues and therefore fully qualified in every respect to carry out work ranging from large site installations to an extra socket in a kitchen.
Formerly: Electrical Contractors Association of Scotland
Publication: Magazine
Publication title: Cabletalk. Advertisements.
Second publication: Membership Directory. Advertisements.
Meetings/Conventions: - annual conference - Exhibits.

Shetland Knitwear Trades Association

175a Commercial St., Lerwick, ZE1 OHX, Scotland, UK
Tel: 44 1595 695631
Fax: 44 1595 695628
Email: skta@zetnet.co.uk
Website: http://www.zetnet.co.uk/skta
Contact: Lorna Graham, Mktg. Officer
Description: Producers of Shetland wool sweaters and their agents in Europe and the United States. Promotes the sale of Shetland wool sweaters. Provides contact information for members.
Publication: Membership Directory
Publication title: Buyer's Guide to the Real Shetland Knitwear

Shetland Salmon Farmers' Association

Shetland Seafood Centre, Stewart Bldg., Lerwick, Shetland, ZE1 0LL, Scotland, UK
Tel: 44 1595 695579
Fax: 44 1595 694494
Email: ssfa@fishuk.net

Website: http://www.fishuk.net/ssfa/index.htm
Founded: 1984
Members: 50
Staff: 3
Contact: David Sandison, Gen.Mgr.
Description: Salmon farmers. Liaises with local and central government agencies and the EC; arranges marketing and promotion, and training. Gives advice to members.

Society for the Protection of Unborn Children - Scotland
SPUC

5 St. Vincent Pl., Glasgow, G1 2DH, Scotland, UK
Tel: 44 141 2212094
Fax: 44 141 2482105
Email: spucscot@cwcom.net
Founded: 1967
Members: 5400
Staff: 7
Contact: Ian Murray, Dir.
Fee: £10
Membership Type: ordinary
Description: Individuals and organizations opposed to abortion. Seeks to protect what the group feels are the rights of the unborn; opposes voluntary euthanasia. Conducts educational and charitable programs; maintains speakers' bureau; compiles statistics.
Library Subject: abortion, rights of the unborn
Library Type: by appointment only
Publication: Journal
Publication title: Human Function
Meetings/Conventions: - quarterly conference

Society for the Social History of Medicine
SSHM

Department of History, Meston Walk, King's College, University of Aberdeen, Aberdeen, AB24 3FX, Scotland, UK
Tel: 44 1224 272456
Fax: 44 1224 272203
Email: h.l.diack@abdn.ac.uk
Website: http://www.sshm.org/
Founded: 1969
Members: 800
Contact: Dr. Lesley Diack, Hon. Sec.
Fee: £25
Membership Type: personal
Fee: £17
Membership Type: student
Description: Professionals and interested amateurs in medical, historical, sociological, and related disciplines. Promotes the study of the social history of medicine as it relates to patients, doctors, disease, and health. Topics of interest include national health service, mental handicaps, occupational health, general practice, and health and town planning.
Publication title: Membership List
Second publication: Journal
Publication title: Social History of Medicine. Advertisements.
Meetings/Conventions: - 3/year conference - Exhibits.

Society of Antiquaries of Scotland

c/o Royal Museum
c/o Royal Museum, Chambers St., Edinburgh, EH1 1JF, Scotland, UK
Tel: 44 131 2474115
Fax: 44 131 2474163
Email: f.ashmore@nms.ac.uk
Website: http://www.socantscot.org
Founded: 1780
Members: 3600
Staff: 5
Contact: Mrs. Fionna Ashmore, Dir.
Fee: £25
Membership Type: by election only
Description: Individuals interested in the study of antiquities and the history of Scotland through archaeological research. Encourages greater interest and scholarship in Scottish history and archaeology; provides financial assistance for research, excavation, and publication. Assisted the establishment of the National Museum of Antiquities of Scotland containing collections of artifacts, manuscripts, and books. Organizes discussions and excursions. Arranges for visiting scholars through the Lindsay-Fischer lectureship.
Library Subject: archaeology and history
Library Type: reference
Publication title: Monographs
Publication title: Proceedings
Meetings/Conventions: Rhind Lectures - annual lecture

Society of Architectural Historians of Great Britain
SAHGB

Flat 4, 23 London St., London, EH3 6LY, Scotland, UK
Email: secretary@sahgb.org.uk
Website: http://www.sahgb.org.uk
Founded: 1956
Members: 1300
Contact: Andrew Martindale, Hon.Sec.
Publication: Journal
Publication title: Architectural History

Society of Border Leicester Sheep Breeders

c/o Nesta D. Todd
St. Boswells, Melrose Borders, TD6 9ES, Scotland, UK
Tel: 44 1835824207
Email: info@borderleicesters.co.uk
Website: http://www.borderleicesters.co.uk
Founded: 1896
Members: 235
Staff: 1
Contact: Nesta D. Todd, Sec.
Fee: £15
Membership Type: full
Description: Aims to encourage the breeding of Border Leicester Sheep and the maintenance of the purity of the breed by the publication of a book.
Library Subject: border leicester
Library Type: by appointment only

Society of Cartographers
SUC

University of Glasgow, Glasgow, G12 8QQ, Scotland, UK
Tel: 44 141 3398855
Fax: 44 141 3304894
Founded: 1964

Society of Health Education and Health Promotion Specialists
SHEPS

c/o Sheffield Health
64 Terregles Ave., Glasgow, G41 4LX, Scotland, UK
Tel: 44 114 2711305
Fax: 44 114 2711318
Email: frances.cunning@sheffield-ha.nhs.uk
Website: http://www.hj-web.co.uk/sheps/
Founded: 1980
Members: 500
Contact: Frances Cunning, Chm.
Fee: £30
Membership Type: full
Fee: £15
Membership Type: associate
Description: Provides a voice for health promotion theory and practice within the broader context of public health.
Formerly: Society of Health Education and Promotion Specialists

Society of Scottish Artists

c/o Susan Cornish, Sec.
4 Barony St., Edinburgh, EH3 6PE, Scotland, UK
Tel: 44 131 5572354
Website: http://www.s-s-a.org
Founded: 1891
Members: 370
Staff: 1
Contact: Susan Cornish, Sec.
Fee: £5
Membership Type: association
Fee: £40
Membership Type: ordinary/professional
Description: Professional artists (elected), lay membership - open to anyone with interest in the visual arts. Aims to encourage interest in contemporary art; to show the work of young artists alongside work of more established artists, in the Annual Exhibition and smaller exhibitions throughout Scotland and Europe.
Library Subject: SSA
Library Type: reference
Publication: Catalog
Publication title: Annual Exhibition. Advertisements.
Second publication: Book
Publication title: Centenary

Society of Solicitors in the Supreme Courts of Scotland

11 Parliament Sq., Edinburgh, EH1 1RF, Scotland, UK
Tel: 44 131 2256268
Fax: 44 131 2252270
Email: enquiries@ssclibrary.co.uk
Website: http://www.ssclibrary.co.uk
Founded: 1784
Members: 300
Staff: 1
Contact: Ian L.S. Balfour, Sec.
Description: All Scottish solicitors practising in Scotland or elsewhere in the world. The Society forms part of the College of Justices in Scotland. Concerned with maintaining standards of practice particularly in the Scottish Courts; with giving assistance or encouragement to members; with supporting the law of Scotland and the affairs of the Scottish nation.
Library Subject: professional law

Library Type: reference
Publication: Papers
Meetings/Conventions: - biennial lecture

Society of Sports Therapists

c/o Graham N. Smith
45c Carrick St., Glasgow, G2 8PJ, Scotland, UK
Tel: 44 141 2213660
Fax: 44 141 2211525
Email: admin@society-of-sports-therapists.org
Website: http://www.society-of-sports-therapists.org
Founded: 1990
Members: 1500
Contact: Graham N. Smith, Chm.
Fee: £28
Membership Type: affiliate
Description: Open to anyone over the age of 18 years who has successfully completed a course in sports therapy and satisfies the criteria for membership of the Society. Aims to provide a professional body for sports therapists which will educate, monitor and legislate on all matters pertaining to sports therapy.

Society of West Highland and Island Historical Research

Breachachadh Castle, Isle of Coll, PA78 6TB, Scotland, UK
Tel: 44 1879 230444
Fax: 44 1879 230357
Email: swhihr@networld.com
Founded: 1972
Members: 160
Staff: 2
Contact: Nicholas Maclean-Bristol, Chmn.
Fee: £35
Membership Type: subscription
Description: Aims to encourage research into the history of the West Highlands of Scotland, and to make the results available to the public in an attractive format.

Society of Writers to Her Majesty's Signet

Parliament Sq., Edinburgh, EH1 1RF, Scotland, UK
Tel: 44 131 2254923
Fax: 44 131 2204016
Founded: 1594

St. Andrews Institute for Middle East Studies
IMES

School of History, St. Andrews, KY16 9AJ, Scotland, UK
Email: arabic@st-and.ac.uk
Website: http://www.st-and.ac.uk/institutes/mideast/Institute.html
Founded: 1994

Stair Society

c/o Thomas H. Drysdale
Saltire Ct., 20 Castle Terrace, Edinburgh, EH1 2ET, Scotland, UK
Tel: 44 131 2289900
Fax: 44 131 2281222
Email: mail.desk@shepwedd.co.uk
Founded: 1934
Members: 500
Contact: Dr. John Cairns, Chm.
Fee: £16
Membership Type: individual

Fee: £20
Membership Type: institution
Description: Promotes members' interests.

Stepping Stones for Families
55 Renfrew St., Glasgow, G2 3BD, Scotland, UK
Tel: 44 141 3312828
Fax: 44 141 3311991
Founded: 1988
Members: 82
Staff: 28
Contact: Isobel Lawson, Dir.
Fee: £1
Membership Type: individual
Fee: £15
Membership Type: associate or group
Description: Seeks to empower families with young children and young adults living in economically disadvantaged areas. Maintains network of family centers; operates poverty project; provides training and consulting services to families other agencies and groups.
Library Subject: families, children, poverty
Library Type: not open to the public
Formerly: Stepping Stones in Scotland
Publication: Report
Publication title: A Study of Volunteering
Second publication: Booklet
Publication title: Effective Volunteering
Meetings/Conventions: - annual meeting UK

Tartans of Scotland
c/o Keith G.A. Lumsden, Dir.
Scottish Tartans World Register, The Glack, Dunkeld, PH8 0ER, Scotland, UK
Tel: 44 1350 728849
Fax: 44 1350 728849
Email: info@startans.scotland.net
Website: http://www.tartans.scotland.net
Founded: 1963
Members: 500
Staff: 2
Contact: K E Lumsden, Admin.
Description: Persons in 16 countries interested in preserving the heritage of Scottish tartans and highland dress. Conducts research into the identification of tartans, particularly the relation of clan and tartan to surnames. Maintains 2 museums and collections of books, manuscripts, paintings, drawings, and photographs of tartans and historic highland dress. Maintains register of tartans. Offers authentication service. Awards fellowships. Organizes school visits.
Library Subject: history of tartan dress
Library Type: by appointment only
Formerly: Scottish Tartans Society

Technical Advisors Group
TAG
County House, 12/13 Sussex St., Plymouth, PL1 2HR, Scotland, UK
Tel: 44 1752 213665
Fax: 44 1752 222678
Email: royf@rfconsultancy.co.uk
Website: http://www.t-a-g.org.uk
Founded: 1978
Members: 500
Staff: 4
Contact: Roy Fairclough, Sec.

Fee: £95
Membership Type: regular
Fee: £75
Membership Type: associate
Description: Chief technical officers working with governmental and nongovernmental organizations on technical aspects of community and urban development and service provision. Disseminates information on community development projects and services.
Formerly: Formed by Merger of, Association of London Burough Engineers and Surveyors
Publication: Magazine
Publication title: TAG Bulletin. Advertisements.
Meetings/Conventions: Presidential Conference - annual seminar - Exhibits.

Tenovus - Scotland
TS
234 St. Vincent St., Glasgow, G2 5RJ, Scotland, UK
Tel: 44 141 2216268
Fax: 44 1292 311433
Email: gen.sec@talk21.com
Website: http://www.tenovus-scotland.org.uk
Founded: 1967
Staff: 4
Contact: Edward Read, Gen.Sec.
Description: Individuals and organizations. Promotes advancement of medical research projects undertaken by Scottish hospitals and university medical schools. Provides financial support and other assistance to medical research programs. Conducts fundraising activities.
Publication: Newsletter
Second publication: Brochure
Meetings/Conventions: - periodic board meeting

Tourette Syndrome (UK) Association
PO Box 26149, Dunfermline, KY12 8YU, Scotland, UK
Tel: 44 1383 629600
Fax: 44 1383 629609
Email: enquiries@tsa.org.uk
Website: http://www.tsa.org.uk
Founded: 1981
Members: 995
Staff: 3
Contact: Ann Gosling, Exec.Dir.
Fee: £20
Membership Type: membership
Description: Dedicated to providing support, education, and public awareness to the neurological disorder Gilles de la Tourette Syndrome; promotes medical research into Tourette Syndome.

Toxoplasmosis Trust
TTT
Edgebrook House, 13 E Feltes Ave., Edinburgh, EH4, Scotland, UK
Tel: 44 131 3325589
Email: info@toxo.org.uk
Founded: 1989
Members: 5000
Staff: 5
Contact: Christine Asbury, Dir.
Fee: £24
Description: Aims to raise awareness of toxoplasmosis among health professionals and the general public. (Taxoplasmosis is a parasitic infection, which, if caught during pregnancy, can cause damage to the

unborn baby.) Provides information and support to those affected by or concerned about taxoplasmosis.
Library Type: not open to the public
Publication title: Toxoplasmosis and Lambing: How to Avoid an Unnecessary Risk
Publication title: Toxoplasmosis in Pregnancy: Avoid Unnecessary Risk

Venture Scotland
VS

Norton Park, 57 Albion Rd., Edinburgh, EH7 5QY, Scotland, UK
Tel: 44 131 4752395
Fax: 44 131 4752396
Email: hq@venturescotland.force9.co.uk
Website: http://www.venturescotland.org.uk
Founded: 1987
Members: 130
Staff: 3
Contact: Peter Johnson, Dir.
Fee: £5
Membership Type: ordinary
Description: Participants in Bothy Ventures conducted by the organization. Promotes personal social and spiritual growth through participation in recreational outdoor activities; seeks to develop cooperation among members. Conducts ventures during which participants engage in activities such as raft building, mountain walking, and conservation and environmental protection projects. Conducts woodcraft education and training programs; participates in charitable activities.
Library Subject: adventure education
Library Type: not open to the public
Publication: Newsletter
Publication title: The Buchaille
Second publication: Newsletter
Publication title: Cairn
Meetings/Conventions: Fringe Sunday - annual meeting - Exhibits. Edinburgh UK

Volunteer Development - Scotland

Stirling Enterprise Park, Stirling, FK7 7RP, Scotland, UK
Tel: 44 1786 479593
Fax: 44 1786 449285
Email: information@vds.org.uk
Website: http://www.vds.org.uk
Founded: 1996
Contact: George Thomson, CEO
Fee: £15
Membership Type: general
Description: Management personnel overseeing voluntary activities. Promotes the professional advancement of members. Represents members' professional and economic interests; establishes standards of practice for managers of volunteers; serves as a clearinghouse on voluntary programs and volunteer management. Conducts research and educational programs; compiles statistics.
Publication: Newsletter
Publication title: SAVM Newsletter
Meetings/Conventions: - annual conference Stirling UK

Wholesale Grocers Association of Scotland

30 MacDonald Pl., Edinburgh, EH7 4NH, Scotland, UK
Tel: 44 131 5568753
Contact: Ms. C. Salmon, Exec.Sec.
Description: Wholesale grocers in Scotland.

Women's Leadership Forum
MAS

9 Edwin St., Glasgow, G51 1ND, Scotland, UK
Tel: 44 141 4276698
Email: meningitis@scotland.co.uk
Founded: 1991
Contact: E. McKiernan
Description: Women supporting the public policies of the Democratic Party. Promotes increased participation by women in the Party; seeks to advance the electoral prospects of Democratic candidates. Conducts educational and fundraising activities; works to influence Party positions on issues of interest to women. Assists in the formation of grass roots organizations of Democratic women.
Publication: Brochures
Meetings/Conventions: - monthly support group meeting

Women's Support Project

Granite House, 31 Stockwell St., Glasgow, G1 4RZ, Scotland, UK
Tel: 44 141 5522221
Fax: 44 141 5521876
Email: info@wsproject.demon.co.uk
Founded: 1983
Staff: 4
Contact: Jan Macleod, Dev. Worker
Description: Offers emotional and material support to women and children who are survivors of abuse. Administers training courses for organizations. Organizes discussion and support groups for women. Offers self-defense classes for women. Conducts research.
Library Subject: male violence against women and children.
Library Type: lending
Publication: Report
Publication title: Is There a Correlation Between Child Sexual Abuse & Domestic Violence:An Exploratory Study of Links Between Child Social Abuse and Domestic Violence
Publication title: Making Us Visible - Abuse of Women in Rural Areas

Woven Wire Association

c/o United Wire, Ltd.
Granton Park Ave., Edinburgh, EH5 1HT, Scotland, UK
Tel: 44 131 5526241
Fax: 44 131 5528462
Founded: 1930
Members: 5
Contact: Mrs. S.M. Sharp, Sec.
Description: Wire cloth manufacturers operating in the UK. Provides technical information and standards for the woven wire cloth industry.

YouthLink Scotland

Rosebery House, 9 Haymarket Terr., Edinburgh, EH12 5EZ, Scotland, UK
Tel: 44 131 3132488
Fax: 44 131 3136800
Email: info@youthlink.co.uk
Website: http://www.youthlink.co.uk
Founded: 1942
Members: 50
Staff: 30
Contact: Simon Jaquet, Chief Exec.
Fee: £350
Description: Group involved primarily with the support and development of young people in Scotland. Supports member organizations; advocates for member organizations, develops, along

with member organizations alternative methods and approaches to youth work, and promotes voluntary youth work, identifying and speaking up on issues regarding young people.
Library Subject: youth issues
Library Type: open to the public
Formerly: Scottish Standing Conference of Voluntary Youth Organisations
Publication title: Partners Briefing
Publication title: Youth Work and the Creative Arts
Meetings/Conventions: - annual general assembly UK

Zoological Society of Glasgow and West of Scotland

Glasgow Zoopark
Calderpark Uddingston, Glasgow, G71 7RZ, Scotland, UK
Tel: 44 141 7711185
Fax: 44 141 7712615
Email: roger@glasgowzoopark.fsnet.co.uk
Website: http://www.glasgowzoo.co.uk
Founded: 1936

WALES

Academi - Yr Academi Gymreig

3rd Fl., Mount Stuart House, Mount Stuart Sq., Cardiff, CF10 SFQ, Wales, UK
Tel: 44 29 20472266
Fax: 44 29 20492930
Email: post@academi.org
Website: http://www.academi.org
Founded: 1968
Members: 1500
Staff: 7
Contact: Peter Finch, Chief Exec.
Fee: £15
Membership Type: full
Description: Fellow - an honorary position; member - open by invitation to those who are deemed to have made a contribution to literature of Wales; associates - open to all interested in the Academy's work. The Yr Academi Gymreig, the national society of the writers of Wales, exists in order to promote literature in Wales.
Publication: Journal
Publication title: A470
Meetings/Conventions: - annual conference

Arts Council of Wales
ACW

9 Museum Pl., Cardiff, CF10 3NX, Wales, UK
Tel: 44 29 20376500
Fax: 44 29 20221447
Email: info@artswales.org.uk
Website: http://www.artswales.org.uk/language.htm
Founded: 1967
Members: 18
Staff: 80
Contact: Angela Blackburn, Commun.Off.
Description: Promotes development and appreciation of the arts in Wales; works to make the arts more accessible to the public; makes recommendations to government and other bodies on issues affecting the arts. Provides financial and other assistance to arts programs.
Publication: Newsletter
Publication title: Crefft/Craft

Asparagus Growers Association

133 Eastgate, Louth, LN11 9QG, Wales, UK
Tel: 44 1507 602427
Fax: 44 1507 600689
Email: crop.association@pvga.co.uk
Website: http://www.british-asparagus.co.uk
Founded: 1970
Members: 110
Contact: Mrs. Jayne A. Dyas
Description: Growers of asparagus. Provides help to UK asparagus growers both in growing and marketing.

Association for Applied Hypnosis
AAH

21B High Holme Rd., Louth, LN11 0EX, Wales, UK
Tel: 44 1507 607336
Website: http://www.fetq.org
Founded: 1980

Association for Environment Conscious Building

PO Box 32, Llandysul, SA44 52A, Wales, UK
Tel: 44 1559 370908

Email: admin@aecb.net
Website: http://www.aecb.net
Founded: 1989
Members: 1300
Staff: 1
Contact: Sally Hall, Chm.
Description: Building companies, developers, architects, local authorities, consultants etc. To generate more environmental awareness with the building and construction industry and to encourage greener building.
Library Type: by appointment only
Publication title: Building for a Future
Second publication: Directory
Publication title: Real Green Building Book

Association for Neuro-Linguistic Programming

PO Box 5, Haverfordwest, SA63 4YA, Wales, UK
Tel: 44 870 7871978
Fax: 44 870 8704970
Email: admin@anlp.org
Website: http://www.anlp.org
Founded: 1986
Members: 960
Staff: 1
Contact: Derek Jackson, Chair
Fee: £60
Membership Type: full, associate, professional full
Description: Provides methods and models on how people think.

Association of Independent Tobacco Specialists

14 Wyndham Arcade, Mill Lane, Cardiff, CF10 1FJ, Wales, UK
Tel: 44 29 20233443
Founded: 1976
Members: 126
Staff: 8
Contact: D.C. Higgins
Description: Group of independent retail tobacco specialists. Aims to keep the retail tobacconist in the high street.
Publication: Catalog
Publication title: Exhibition Catalogue
Publication title: Tobacco Index

Association of Master Upholsterers and Soft Furnishers

102A Commercial St., Newport, NP20 1LU, Wales, UK
Tel: 44 1633215454
Fax: 44 1633244488
Email: amu@easynet.co.uk
Website: http://www.upholsterers.co.uk
Founded: 1947
Members: 700
Contact: Andrew Vipond, Chair
Description: Craft upholsterers, upholstered furniture manufacturers, chair frame manufacturers, soft furnishing retailers, contractors, and others associated with the craft of upholstery.

Association of National Park Authorities

126 Bute St., Cardiff, CF10 5LE, Wales, UK
Tel: 44 29 20499966
Fax: 44 29 20499980
Email: enquiries@anpa.gov.ukwww.anpa.gov.uk
Founded: 1992
Members: 12

Staff: 6
Contact: Martin Fitton
Fee: £14000
Membership Type: authorities
Description: Chairmen of the 11 National Parks in England and Wales. Represents national parks in dealings with government and campaigns on their behalf nationally and internationally.
Formerly: Association of National Parks
Publication title: Annual Review
Meetings/Conventions: - annual general assembly

Association of Tank and Cistern Manufacturers
ATCM

22 Grange Park, St. Arvans, Chepstow, NP16 6EA, Wales, UK
Tel: 44 1291 623634
Email: info@atcmtanks.org.uk
Website: http://www.atcmtanks.org.uk
Founded: 1967
Members: 13
Staff: 2
Contact: I. McCrone, Chairman/Sec.
Fee: £1200
Description: Manufacturers of tanks and cisterns in a variety of materials including thermoplastics, grp and metal products. Generally promoting good practice concerning the manufacture and installation of tanks and cisterns. Primarily for water storage.
Library Subject: international & European water regulations and standards
Library Type: not open to the public
Publication: Newsletter
Publication title: ATCM News Update
Meetings/Conventions: - 3/year meeting

Association of University Radiation Protection Officers
AURPO

Heath Park, Dept. of Medical Physics and Engineering, University Hospital of Wales, Cardiff, CF4 4XW, Wales, UK
Tel: 44 29 20742003
Fax: 44 29 20742012
Founded: 1962

Badger Face Welsh Mountain Sheep Society

Hafan, 2 Tynlon, Tregarth, Bangor, LL57 4BB, Wales, UK
Tel: 44 1248 601380
Fax: 44 1248 601380
Email: 113776.3373@compuserve.com
Website: http://www.stockmaster.co.uk/site/flockmaster/sheep/badger_face/intro.htm
Founded: 1976
Members: 230
Contact: Mrs. M. Pritchard
Fee: £10
Membership Type: adult
Fee: £5
Membership Type: junior
Description: Promotes the breeding and improvement of the Badger Face Welsh Mountain Sheep.
Publication: Newsletter
Meetings/Conventions: Builth Wells, Powys UK

Balwen Welsh Mountain Sheep Society

Tyrmynydd, Llanddeilo, SA19 7LP, Wales, UK
Tel: 44 1558 822652
Description: Promotes members' interests.

Battery Vehicle Society
BVS

26 College Glade, Caerlon, Newport, NP18 3TB, Wales, UK
Tel: 44 1258 455470
Website: http://www.bvs.org.uk
Founded: 1973

British Housewives League

c/o Mrs. Mary Blakey, Pres.
Birchfield House, Mounton Rd., Chepston, Monmouth, NP16 5BS, Wales, UK
Tel: 44 129 1621748
Website: http://www.housewives.freeuk.com
Founded: 1945
Contact: Mrs. L.M. Riley, Sec.
Fee: £12
Description: Works to provide women with a voice in social issues. Encourages development of personality in accordance with Christian tradition. Acts politically to defend traditional values of family, nation and democracy.
Publication: Journal
Publication title: The Lantern
Second publication: Papers
Publication title: Lantern Lectures
Meetings/Conventions: - semiannual meeting - Exhibits.

British Leafy Salads Association

133 Eastgate, Louth, LN11 9QG, Wales, UK
Tel: 44 1507 602427
Fax: 44 1507 607165
Email: crop.associationsprograma.co.uk
Website: http://www.iceberg-lettuce.co.uk
Founded: 1986
Members: 24
Staff: 1
Contact: Mrs. Jayne A. Dyas
Description: Marketing information and bulk purchasing.
Formerly: British Iceberg Growers' Association

British Palomino Society

Penrhiwllan, Llandysul, Ceredigion, Llandysul, SA44 5NZ, Wales, UK
Tel: 44 1239 851387
Fax: 44 1239 851040
Email: britpal@lineone.net
Website: http://www.britishpalominosociety.co.uk
Members: 551
Staff: 1
Contact: Leonard Bigley, Chm.
Fee: £30
Membership Type: regular
Fee: £18
Membership Type: junior
Description: Promotes the advancement of Palominos and their breeding.
Publication: Magazine
Publication title: Palomino. Advertisements.
Meetings/Conventions: Championship Show - annual show

British Society for Allergy, Environmental and Nutritional Medicine
BSAENM

PO Box 7, Knighton, LD7 1WT, Wales, UK
Tel: 44 1547 550378
Fax: 44 1547 550339
Founded: 1981

British Society for Research on Ageing
BSRA

PO Box 2316, Cardiff, CF23 5YY, Wales, UK
Tel: 44 29 20744847
Fax: 44 29 20744276
Email: info@bsra.org.uk
Website: http://www.bsra.org.uk
Founded: 1945
Members: 150
Contact: Dr. David Kipling, Hon.Sec.
Fee: £20
Description: Biological scientists and clinicians involved in the study of aging. Promotes knowledge of the biology of aging and effective treatment of age-related diseases. Works to increase public awareness of the aging process. Sponsors annual postgraduate award competition.
Publication: Newsletter
Publication title: Lifespan
Second publication: Newsletter
Publication title: Newsletter
Meetings/Conventions: - annual convention

British Society of Rheology

University of Wales, Department of Mathematics, Aberystwyth, Ceredigion, SY23 6BZ, Wales, UK
Tel: 44 131 4495111
Fax: 44 131 4513161
Email: p.f.g.banfill@hw.ac.uk
Website: http://www.bsr.org.uk
Founded: 1940
Members: 600
Contact: Prof. Phil Banfill, Hon.Sec.
Fee: £25
Description: Anyone interested in rheology whether theoretical, experimental, manufacture of instruments - generally scientists in academia and industry. The promotion of science and dissemination of knowledge in areas of pure and applied rheology. Conference/seminars are usually held twice a year.
Library Type: open to the public
Publication title: Rheology Abstracts
Second publication: Bulletin. Advertisements.
Meetings/Conventions: - annual meeting

Campaign for the Protection of Rural Wales
CPRW

Ty Gwyn, 31 High St., Welshpool, SY21 7YD, Wales, UK
Tel: 44 1938 552525
Fax: 44 1938 552741
Email: info@cprw.org.uk
Website: http://www.cprw.org.uk
Founded: 1928
Members: 4000
Staff: 7
Contact: Mr. Merfyn Williams, Dir.

Fee: £15
Fee: £20
Membership Type: outside of wales
Description: Rural conservationists in Wales. Opposes industrial and real estate developments that would diminish the natural landscape of the countryside of Wales. Monitors European Economic Community policies cooperatively with the European Environmental Bureau. Examines government proposals and legislative efforts to encourage environmental protection.
Library Type: reference
Formerly: Council for the Protection of Rural Wales
Publication title: Annual Report
Publication title: Rural Wales
Meetings/Conventions: - periodic conference

Cardiff Chamber of Commerce

Ste. 1, 2nd Fl., St. David's House, Wood St., Cardiff, CF10 IES, Wales, UK
Tel: 44 29 20348280
Fax: 44 29 20377653
Email: enquiries@cardiffchamber.co.uk
Website: http://www.cardiffchamber.co.uk
Members: 1300
Staff: 25
Contact: Helen Conway, Chief Exec.
Description: Promotes business and commerce.

Centre for Alternative Technology, Machynlleth, SY20 9AZ, Wales, UK

Tel: 44 1654 705950
Fax: 44 1654 702782
Email: info@cat.org.uk
Website: http://www.cat.org.uk
Founded: 1974
Members: 5500
Staff: 130
Contact: Charlotte Cosserat, Info.Off.
Fee: £21
Membership Type: association overseas
Description: Promotes sustainability, including renewable energy, environmental building, energy efficiency, alternative sewage and wastewater treatment, and organic growing. Provides visitor center, courses, consultancy, and educational facilities.
Library Subject: sustainable technologies
Library Type: not open to the public
Publication: Magazine
Publication title: Clean Slate. Advertisements.
Second publication: Booklets
Publication title: New Futures Series
Meetings/Conventions: - annual conference

Commission for Local Administration in Wales

Derwen House, Court Rd., Bridgend, CF31 1BN, Wales, UK
Tel: 44 1656 661325
Fax: 44 1656 673279
Email: enquiries@ombudsman-wales.org
Website: http://www.ombudsman-wales.org
Founded: 1974
Members: 2
Staff: 18
Contact: Elwyn Moseley, Commissioner
Description: Concerned with considering, and where appropriate investigating, complaints of maladministration made against local

authorities in Wales; also works with concerns regarding allegations that members of local authorities in Wales have breached Authorities' Code of Conduct for members.
Publication: Annual Report
Publication title: Commission for Local Administration in Wales
Second publication: Pamphlet
Publication title: The Local Government Ombudsman for Wales

Conference of University Teachers of German in Great Britain and Ireland

c/o Prof. Rhys W. Williams, Pres.
Dept. of German, University of Wales, Singleton Park, Swansea, SA2 8PP, Wales, UK
Email: r.w.williams@swan.ac.uk
Website: http://www.cutg.ac.uk
Contact: E.J. Boa, Pres.
Fee: £25
Membership Type: full or part-time teachers
Fee: £10
Membership Type: post-graduates
Description: Represents members interests.
Meetings/Conventions: - annual meeting - Exhibits.

Construction Industry Trade Alliance
CITA

PO Box 56, Llanelli, SA14 6YN, Wales, UK
Tel: 44 8700 664404
Fax: 44 8700 664405
Email: enquiries@cita.co.uk
Website: http://www.cita.co.uk
Description: Builders, roofing contractors, painters and decorators, plumbers, electricians, and other building industry contractors and workers. Promotes the interests of the building trade in Britain.

Countryside Council for Wales

Maes y Ffynnon, Penrhosgarnedd, Ffordd Penrhos, Bangor, LL57 2DN, Wales, UK
Tel: 44 1248 385500
Fax: 44 1248 355782
Email: enquiries@ccw.gov.uk
Website: http://www.ccw.gov.uk
Founded: 1991
Members: 12
Staff: 500
Contact: Roger Thomas, Ch.Exec.
Description: Advises government agencies on sustaining natural beauty, wildlife, and the opportunity for outdoor enjoyment throughout Wales and its inshore waters. Cooperates with similar organizations in England and Scotland and at the international level.
Library Type: open to the public

Federation of Colleges and Associations of Economic Sciences Professionals in Central America and Panama

Tenovus Bldg, Heath Park, Cardiff, CF4 4XX, Wales, UK
Tel: 44 12222 744245
Fax: 44 12222 752642
Founded: 1980
Description: Promotes the development of economic sciences; supports the scientific, cultural, and material progress of professionals in the field.

Fencing Contractors Association

Warren Rd., Trellech, Monmouth, NP25 4PQ, Wales, UK
Tel: 44 7000 560722
Fax: 44 1600 860614
Email: info@fencingcontractors.org
Website: http://www.fencingcontractors.org
Founded: 1942
Members: 180
Staff: 3
Contact: Wendy Baker, Ch.Exec.
Description: Trade association for the fencing industry, including contractors, suppliers and manufacturers.
Publication: Newsletter
Publication title: FCA News Update
Second publication: Membership Directory

Guild of Welsh Lamb and Beef Supplies

PO Box 8, Gorseland, North Rd., Aberystwuth, Ceredigion, Llandysul, SY23 2WB, Wales, UK
Tel: 44 1970 624011
Fax: 44 1970 624049
Email: wlbp@wfsagri.net
Founded: 1990
Members: 16
Contact: Melfyn Ellis, Chm.
Description: Represents working committees and groups of the Welsh lamb and beef abattoirs and processing plants.

Historical Metallurgy Society
HMS

c/o Peter Hutchison
22 Easterfield Dr., Southgate, Swansea, SA3 2DB, Wales, UK
Tel: 44 1792 233223
Email: hon-sec@hist-met.org
Website: http://hist-met.org
Founded: 1962
Members: 700
Contact: Peter Hutchison, Hon.Gen.Sec.
Fee: £15
Membership Type: ordinary
Description: International organization of institutions, families, individuals, academies, libraries, museums, university departments, and archaeological and other societies. Encourages and records the preservation and study of all aspects of metallurgical history including: the extraction of ores and minerals; the melting and working of metals; the examination and analysis of metal artifacts; the preservation of archaeological and historical sites and objects.
Library Subject: out of date metallurgy
Library Type: open to the public
Publication: Journal
Publication title: Historical Metallurgy
Second publication: Newsletter
Publication title: HMS News
Meetings/Conventions: - annual conference - Exhibits.

Horticultural Export Bureau
HEB

133 Eastgate, Louth, LN11 9QG, Wales, UK
Tel: 44 1507 601919
Fax: 44 1507 600101
Email: nicola.watkins@heb.org.uk
Website: http://www.heb.org.uk

Founded: 1996
Members: 5
Staff: 2
Contact: Nicola Watkins
Fee: £3500
Membership Type: full member
Description: Strives to promote British fresh produce and develop export opportunities for British growers.
Formerly: Quality British Celery Association

Industrial Tyre Association

The Nook, 25 Cambridge St., Barry, CF62 6PJ, Wales, UK
Tel: 44 1446 700951
Founded: 1977
Members: 6
Contact: R.N. Peake, Sec.
Description: Manufacturers of industrial tyres and distributors of recognised brand industrial tyres. Aims for closer co-operation in the industrial tyre industry, exchange of information and furtherance of matters appertaining to the industry.
Formerly: British Industrial Tyre Manufacturers Association
Publication: Manual
Publication title: Guidelines on Industrial Tyres
Meetings/Conventions: - quarterly meeting

International Bee Research Association
IBRA

18 North Rd., Cardiff, CF1O 3DY, Wales, UK
Tel: 44 29 20372409
Fax: 44 29 20665522
Email: mail@ibra.org.uk
Website: http://www.ibra.org.uk
Founded: 1949
Members: 800
Staff: 6
Contact: Dr. Richard Jones, Dir.
Fee: £67
Membership Type: individual
Fee: £265
Membership Type: corporate
Description: Individuals, beekeeping societies, and research organizations in 130 countries. Promotes and coordinates bee research work and research on pollination. Provides worldwide information service through publications, correspondence, and journals. Aids beekeepers and promotes beekeeping as a sustainable activity in developing countries.
Library Subject: bees, beekeeping, bee products, and pollination
Library Type: reference
Publication: Journal
Publication title: Apicultural Abstracts. Advertisements.
Publication title: Bee World
Meetings/Conventions: IBRA Conference on Tropical Bees - quadrennial conference - Exhibits. Ribeiro Preto Brazil

International Fossil Algae Association

Cardiff University, Cardiff, CF1 3YE, Wales, UK
Tel: 44 29 20874329
Email: Riding@cardiff.ac.uk
Website: http://members.tripod.com/bruno.granier/index.html
Contact: Dr. Robert Riding
Description: Research and collaboration on fossil algae.
Meetings/Conventions: - biennial conference Granada Spain

International Institute of Peace Studies and Global Philosophy

Camlad House, Tarden, Powys, SY21 8NZ, Wales, UK
Tel: 44 1938 580319
Email: iipsgp@educationaid.net
Website: http://www.educationaid.net
Founded: 1991
Members: 100
Staff: 4
Contact: Dr. T. Daffern
Description: Promotes peace, education, interfaith, dialogue, comparative philosophy, educational research, and academic work.
Library Subject: education
Library Type: not open to the public
Publication: Journal
Publication title: The Muses Journal
Meetings/Conventions: symposium

International League for the Protection of Cetaceans
ILPC

4 Upper House Farm, Crickhowell, Machynlleth, NP8 1BZ, Wales, UK
Tel: 44 1873 812388
Fax: 44 1873 812389
Email: sidneyholt@aol.com
Founded: 1980
Staff: 2
Contact: Dr. Sidney Holt, Exec.Dir.
Description: Works for conservation and protection of whales and dolphins, worldwide.
Library Subject: cetacean biology, fisheries management, environmental issues, antarctic and southern ocean studies
Library Type: not open to the public
Publication: Papers
Publication title: Occasional papers

International Polychaetology Association

Cathays Park, Cardiff, CF1 3NP, Wales, UK
Email: andrew.mackie@nmgw.ac.uk
Website: http://www.biodiversity.uno.edu/~worms/ipa-intr.html
Founded: 1986

International Society of Radiographers and Radiological Technologists
ISRRT

143 Bryn Pinwydden, Pentzoyn, Cardiff, CF23 7DG, Wales, UK
Tel: 44 2920 735038
Fax: 44 2920 540551
Email: isrrt.yule@btopenworld.com
Website: http://www.isrrt.org
Founded: 1959
Members: 78
Staff: 1
Contact: Dr. A. Yule, Sec.Gen.
Fee: £500
Membership Type: corporate
Fee: £6
Membership Type: associate
Description: National radiographic societies and other organizations having radiographers as members. Objectives are to: advance the science and practice of radiography, radiotherapy, and allied subjects by promoting improved standards of training and research in technical

aspects of radiation medicine and protection; make results of research and experience available to practitioners; raise funds to further these objectives. Compiles statistics and maintains museum. Has established educational trust fund. Conducts teachers' seminars.
Library Subject: Radiation medicine technology
Library Type: reference
Formerly: International Society of Radiographers and Radiological Technicians
Publication: Proceedings
Publication title: Health and Safety Manual
Publication title: Quality Control Handbook
Meetings/Conventions: - biennial meeting - Exhibits. Hong Kong People's Republic of China

Leek Growers Association

133 Eastgate, Louth, LN11 9QG, Wales, UK
Tel: 44 1507 602427
Fax: 44 1507 600689
Email: crop.association@pvga.co.uk
Website: http://www.british-leeks.co.uk
Founded: 1980
Members: 12
Contact: Mrs. Jayne A. Dyas
Description: Marketing information.

Local Authority Recycling Advisory Committee LARAC

c/o Directorate of Environment Tourism and Leisure
PO Box 28, Knighton, LD8 2WA, Wales, UK
Tel: 44 1544 267860
Fax: 44 1544 267860
Email: larac@btinternet.com
Website: http://www.larac.org.uk
Founded: 1985
Members: 355
Contact: Colin Kirkby, Natl.Admin.
Fee: £125
Membership Type: local authority
Description: Exchanges information on waste reduction within local government and with other organisations; provides expert response to national, European and private sector recycling initiatives; assists others with technical information and advice to promote best practice; produces training and educational materials and publications on waste reduction and recycling.
Publication: Newsletter
Publication title: Dialogue. Advertisements.
Meetings/Conventions: - annual conference - Exhibits.

National Playing Fields Association NPFAS

2 Queen St., Cardiff, CF10 2BU, Wales, UK
Tel: 44 29 20353030
Fax: 44 29 20353039
Email: cymru@npfa.co.ukwww.npfa.co.uk
Founded: 1929
Members: 350
Staff: 2
Contact: Rhodri Edwards, Dev.Off.
Description: Individuals and organizations with an interest in public recreational space. Seeks to protect and preserve playing fields and recreational spaces. Provides assistance to agencies and organizations maintaining playing fields; conducts charitable programs.
Publication: Annual Report

Newport and Gwent Chamber of Commerce and Industry

Unit 30, Enterprise Way, Newport, NP20 2AQ, Wales, UK
Tel: 44 1633 222664
Fax: 44 1633 222301
Email: info@ngb2b.co.uk
Website: http://www.ngb2b.co.uk
Founded: 1870
Members: 350
Staff: 5
Contact: Kerys Sheppard, Business Development Exec.
Description: Chamber of commerce promoting business and commerce.
Publication: Newsletter
Publication title: Chamber Chat. Advertisements.

Palaeontological Association

c/o Dr. T.J. Palmer
Institute of Earth Sciences, University of Wales-Aberstywyth, Aberystwyth, SY23 3DB, Wales, UK
Tel: 44 1970 627107
Fax: 44 1970 622659
Email: palass@palass.org
Website: http://www.palass.org
Founded: 1957
Members: 1350
Staff: 2
Contact: Dr. T.J. Palmer, Exec.Off.
Fee: £50
Membership Type: ordinary
Fee: £18
Membership Type: student
Description: Professional and amateur palaeontologists. Covers topics from macropalaeontology, micropalaeontology, palaeobotany, vertebrate palaeotology, palaeoecology and biostratigraphy. Activities include up to two thematic review seminars each year and an annual conference, held in December, where a broad range of research is presented. Field trips to sites of palaeontological interest are led both within Britain and Europe.
Publication: Journal
Publication title: Palaeontology

Personal Safety Association

32 Cheam Place, Cardiff, CF14 5DD, Wales, UK
Tel: 44 29 20752508
Email: mark@ppts.co.uk
Founded: 1995
Contact: Mark Hewett, Chief Exec.
Description: Provides advice, instruction, and professional network for instructors and advisors in occupations such as Personal Safety, Conflict Management, Health and Safety, Law Enforcement, and Personal Security.
Library Subject: personal safety, health and safety, personal security, conflict management, stress management
Library Type: open to the public

Pizza, Pasta and Italian Food Association

Picton House, Lower Church St., Chepstow, NP16 5XT, Wales, UK
Tel: 44 1291 628970
Email: admin@papa.org.uk
Website: http://www.papa.org.uk
Founded: 1977
Members: 2300

Staff: 6
Contact: Jim Winship, Dir.
Description: Suppliers to the pizza, pasta, and italian food industries, including manufacturers, restaurants, pizzerias, pizza chains, distributors etc. Aims to set and maintain standards throughout the manufacturing, supply and service industries, in order to promote the reputation and growth of pizza, pasta, and italian food products. It also encourages the interchange of knowledge amongst PAPA members to their mutual interest.
Formerly: Pizza Association
Publication title: Pizza, Pasta, and Italian Food Magazine. Advertisements.
Meetings/Conventions: - periodic meeting

Plaid Cymru - The Party of Wales
18 Park Grove, Cardiff, CF10 3BN, Wales, UK
Tel: 44 29 20646000
Fax: 44 29 20646001
Email: post@plaidcymru.org
Website: http://www.plaidcymru.org
Founded: 1925
Members: 10000
Staff: 10
Contact: Dr. Meleri Evans
Fee: £18
Membership Type: waged individual
Fee: £6
Membership Type: unwaged individual
Description: Political party in Wales. Advocates self-government for Wales.
Formerly: Welsh National Party
Publication: Magazine
Publication title: CYMRU. Advertisements.
Second publication: Bulletin
Publication title: Gweithlen/Worksheet. Advertisements.
Meetings/Conventions: - annual conference - Exhibits. Cardiff UK

Pre-Eclamptic Society
c/o Dawn James
Rhianfa, Carmel, Caernarfon, LL54 7RL, Wales, UK
Tel: 44 1286 882685
Email: dawnjames@clara.co.uk
Website: http://www.dawnjames.clara.net
Founded: 1981
Members: 500
Contact: Dawn James
Fee: £10
Membership Type: members in UK
Fee: £15
Membership Type: overseas members
Description: Provides self help and support groups for those suffering or having suffered from pre-eclampsia.
Library Subject: pre-eclampsia, pregnancy nutrition
Library Type: lending

Processed Vegetable Growers Association
133 Eastgate, Louth, LN11 9QG, Wales, UK
Tel: 44 1507 602427
Fax: 44 1507 600689
Email: postbox@pvga.co.uk
Website: http://www.peas.org
Founded: 1969
Members: 1165

Staff: 8
Contact: Martin Riggall, Chief Exec.
Description: Growers of vegetables for processing.

Royal Welsh Agricultural Society
LLanelwedd, Builth Wells, LD2 3SY, Wales, UK
Tel: 44 1982 553683
Fax: 44 1982 553563
Email: requests@rwas.co.uk
Website: http://www.rwas.co.uk
Founded: 1904
Description: Promotes agriculture, horticulture, and forestry in Wales.

Schizophrenia Association of Great Britain
International Schizophrenia Centre, Bryn Hyfryd, The Crescent, Bangor, LL57 2AG, Wales, UK
Tel: 44 1248 354048
Fax: 44 1248 353659
Email: info@sagb.co.uk
Website: http://www.sagb.co.uk
Founded: 1970
Members: 3000
Staff: 5
Contact: Mrs. Gwynneth Hemmings, Dir.
Fee: £5
Description: Provides information about schizophrenia for patients and families to increase understanding of the illness.
Library Subject: schizophrenia
Library Type: by appointment only
Publication: Newsletter

Shooters' Rights Association
c/o Richard Law, Sec.
PO Box 3, Cardigan, Ceredigion, Llandysul, SA43 1BN, Wales, UK
Tel: 44 1239 698607
Fax: 44 1239 698614
Email: richardlaw@btinternet.com
Founded: 1984
Members: 4000
Staff: 4
Contact: Richard Law, Sec.
Fee: £24
Membership Type: full
Fee: £25
Membership Type: associate (via club)
Description: Gun owners and enthusiasts. Interests include the legal implication of firearms ownership where such ownership is currently or may become the subject of legislative controls. Provides legal costs insurance and legal advice to support members' continued possession of firearms within the law.
Library Subject: firearms, UK firearms law, court decisions
Library Type: reference

Society for Anaerobic Microbiology
Heath Park, Cardiff, CF4 4XW, Wales, UK
Tel: 44 29 20742378
Email: brazier@cardiff.ac.uk
Founded: 1975

Society for Folk Life Studies
c/o The Museum of Welsh Life
St. Fagans, Cardiff, CF5 6XB, Wales, UK
Tel: 44 2530 510851

Email: mared.sutherland@nmgw.ac.uk
Website: http://www.folklife.org.uk
Founded: 1961
Description: Deals with the interdisciplinary study of regional cultures and traditions within the British isles.

Society for the Study of Inborn Errors of Metabolism
SSIEM

c/o Department of Child Health
University Hospital of Wales, Heath Park, Cardiff, South Glamorgan, S1O 2TH, Wales, UK
Tel: 44 29 2074 6322
Fax: 44 29 2074 6322
Email: graham.shortland@uhw-tr.wales.nhs.uk
Website: http://www.ssiem.org.uk
Founded: 1962
Members: 1000
Contact: Graham Shortland, Treas.
Description: Biochemists, dietitians, pediatricians, pathologists, geneticists, and interested individuals in 41 countries. Purpose is to foster study of inherited metabolic disease diagnosis and treatment. Promotes exchange of ideas through meetings and publications.
Publication: Journal
Publication title: Journal of Inherited Metabolic Diseases
Publication title: Membership Handbook
Meetings/Conventions: - annual symposium - Exhibits.

Society of Leather Technologists and Chemists

Grooms Cottage, Bosherston, Pembroke, SA71 5DN, Wales, UK
Tel: 44 1646 661436
Fax: 44 1646 661436
Email: office@sltc.org
Website: http://www.sltc.org
Founded: 1897
Members: 600
Contact: J.M.V. Williams, Membership Sec.
Fee: £35
Description: People working in the leather-producing industry (tanneries) as technologists and chemists (analysts and production control) and associated industries (shoe and leathergoods). Technical staff in chemical supply industry selling to the. leather industry. Chemistry and technology of leather production - histology of skins and protein chemistry particularly collagen; tanning materials; vegetable and synthetic tannins, inorganic materials based on chromium, aluminum, zirconium, titanium; dyestuffs; pigments; polymers for surface coating. Tannery waste treatment; recycling and energy conservation; machines. Physical and chemical testing of leather.
Publication: Journal
Publication title: Journal of the Society of Leather Technologists and Chemists (JSLTC). Advertisements.
Meetings/Conventions: - annual conference Nottingham UK

Socio-Legal Studies Association

PO Box 427, Cardiff, CF10 3XJ, Wales, UK
Tel: 44 29 20874000
Fax: 44 29 20874097
Email: mumfordac@cardiff.ac.uk
Founded: 1989

Sustainable Alliance

Unit 1, Dyfi Eco Parc, Powys, Machynlleth, SY20 8AX, Wales, UK
Tel: 44 1654 705020
Fax: 44 1654 703000
Email: sustainable@gn.apc.org
Founded: 1997
Members: 35
Staff: 1
Contact: Dr. E. Carter, Co-ordinator
Description: Development charity providing specialists in small scale industrial development. Promotes and facilitates establishment of commercial partnerships to create and transfer technologies appropriate for international development. Makes available project management, technical, and training support to development initiatives in areas including technology transfer, alternative energy, manufacturing, financial services, and product development.

Swansea Museum
RISW

Victoria Rd., Swansea, SA1 1SN, Wales, UK
Tel: 44 1792 653763
Fax: 44 1792 652585
Email: swansea.museum@swansea.gov.uk
Website: http://www.swansea.gov.uk/culture/Museums/swansea.htm
Founded: 1835
Members: 350
Contact: Jennifer Sabine, Hon.Sec.
Fee: £6
Description: Dedicated to the cultivation and advancement of the various branches of natural history, as well as the local history of the town and neighborhood, the extension and encouragement of literature and fine arts, and the general diffusion of knowledge of South Wales.
Publication: Journal
Publication title: Minerva: The Journal of Swansea History
Meetings/Conventions: - annual lecture

Talyllyn Railway Preservation Society

c/o Mr. John S. Robinson
Wharf Station, Tywyn, LL36 9EY, Wales, UK
Tel: 44 1654 710472
Fax: 44 1654 711755
Email: secretary@talyllyn.co.uk
Website: http://www.talyllyn.co.uk
Founded: 1950
Members: 3800
Contact: John S. Robinson, Hon.Sec.
Fee: £500
Membership Type: life
Fee: £20
Membership Type: adult
Description: Preserves the Talyllyn (narrow-gauge steam-operated) railway by voluntary work, financial assistance and publicity.
Publication: Magazine
Publication title: Talyllyn News. Advertisements.
Meetings/Conventions: - annual general assembly Tywyn UK

Thomson Foundation

37 Park Pl., Cardiff, CF10 3BB, Wales, UK
Tel: 44 29 20353060
Fax: 44 29 20353061
Email: enquiries@thomfound.co.uk
Website: http://www.thomsonfoundation.co.uk
Founded: 1962

Contact: Gareth Price, Dir.
Description: Promotes excellence in journalism and broadcasting. Conducts educational programs and training courses for journalists and broadcasting technicians, particularly those working in central and eastern Europe. Maintains global network of freelance consultants; gathers and disseminates information on journalism, broadcasting, and media technologies; makes available financial aid and other assistance to individuals wishing to participate in training programs.
Publication: Magazine
Publication title: SCOPE
Meetings/Conventions: - periodic seminar

United Kingdom Environmental Mutagen Society
UKEMS

Singleton Park, Swansea, SA2 8PP, Wales, UK
Email: pjenkinson@safepharm.co.uk
Website: http://www.ukems.org.uk
Founded: 1977
Contact: Dr. P. Jenkinson
Fee: £20

Wales Assembly of Women

The Coach House, Glanmorlais, Kidwelly, SA17 5AW, Wales, UK
Tel: 44 1267 267428
Email: mairstephens@btconnect.com
Founded: 1984
Members: 200
Contact: Mair Stephens
Fee: £10
Membership Type: Individual
Fee: £20
Membership Type: Institutional
Description: Organizations and individuals in Wales. Seeks increased educational opportunity for women. Encourages women to ulitize their talents to full potential and to participate in local, national, and international issues.
Publication: Newsletter
Publication title: Conference Reports
Second publication: Pamphlets
Publication title: Conference Reports
Meetings/Conventions: - semiannual conference - Exhibits. UK

Wales Baltic Society

45 Village Farm, Bonvilston, Cardiff, CF5 6TY, Wales, UK
Founded: 1991
Members: 70
Contact: Rite Price, Sec.
Fee: £6
Membership Type: individual
Fee: £9
Membership Type: couples
Description: Promotes friendly links between the people of Wales and the people of the Baltic countries. Supports the continuing independence of the Baltic States. Conducts research, education and publicity to increase awareness about the Baltic countries.

Wales Chamber of Commerce and Industry

57 Bute St., 1st Fl., Cardiff, CF1 6AJ, Wales, UK
Tel: 44 29 20481648
Fax: 44 29 20489785
Contact: Mrs. M. E. Owen, Chief Exec.
Description: Businesses and trade organizations. Promotes increased international trade and tourism. Gathers and disseminates information; conducts promotional activities; represents members' interests.

Wales Craft Council
WCC

Henfaes Lane, Welshpool, SY21 7BE, Wales, UK
Tel: 44 1938 555313
Fax: 44 1938 556237
Email: crefft.cymru@btinternet.com
Website: http://www.walescraftcouncil.co.uk
Founded: 1977
Members: 165
Staff: 3
Contact: Helen Francis
Fee: £59
Membership Type: including V.A.T.
Description: Craft and giftware show organisers. Promotes increased demand for Welsh craft items. Publicizes Welsh crafts; gathers and disseminates industry information.
Library Subject: business, arts & crafts
Library Type: not open to the public
Publication: Catalog
Publication title: Trade Fair Catalogue. Advertisements.
Meetings/Conventions: Wales Fair - annual trade show

Wales Young Farmers' Clubs

Wales Young Farmers' Clubs Centre, Llanelwedd, Builth Wells, LD2 3NJ, Wales, UK
Tel: 44 1982 553502
Fax: 44 1982 552979
Email: information@yfc-wales.org.uk
Website: http://www.yfc-wales.org.uk
Founded: 1930
Members: 5500
Staff: 6
Contact: Meinir Wigley, Chm.
Description: Voluntary youth organization. Offers educational, training, and social programs for rural young people. Works to raise environmental awareness.
Publication: Magazine
Publication title: CYFFRO
Meetings/Conventions: - annual general assembly

Welsh Amateur Dance Sport Association
WADSA

Bryngoleu House, Bedlinog, CF46 6RY, Wales, UK
Tel: 44 1443 710588
Email: chrisrog@supanet.com
Contact: Christine Rogers, Gen.Sec.
Fee: £7
Membership Type: associate
Fee: £13
Membership Type: full
Description: Amateur dancing organizations, dance instructors, and individuals with an interest in competitive dancing as a means of exercise and recreation. Promotes participation in dance programs, particularly those involving ballroom dancing; selects dance teams to participate in international dancing competitions.

Welsh Amateur Music Federation

15 Mount Stuart Sq., Cardiff, CF10 5DP, Wales, UK
Tel: 44 29 20465700
Fax: 44 29 20462733
Email: wamf@tycerdd.org
Website: http://www.tycerdd.org
Founded: 1969

Members: 25000
Staff: 3
Contact: Keith Griffin, Dir.
Fee: £40
Membership Type: general
Description: Support, advice offered to affiliated amateur music promoting societies throughout Wales, representing some 25,000 performers.
Library Type: lending
Publication: Newsletter

Welsh Centre for International Affairs
WCIA

Temple of Peace, Cathays Park, Cardiff, CF10 3AP, Wales, UK
Tel: 44 29 20228549
Fax: 44 29 20640333
Email: centre@wcia.org.uk
Website: http://www.wcia.org.uk
Founded: 1973
Members: 225
Staff: 10
Contact: S. Thomas, Dir.
Fee: £20
Description: Welsh institutions including local government agencies, universities, churches, and the media. Fosters a sense of loyalty and obligation to the global community among the people of Wales. Conducts international volunteer and service programs; conducts citizenship education courses for young people.
Library Subject: history, international relations
Library Type: reference
Publication title: Annual Report. Advertisements.
Publication title: The UN at Fifty: The Welsh Contribution 1995
Meetings/Conventions: Anniversary Lecture - annual convention

Welsh Engineers and Founders Association

PO Box 360, Swansea, SA1 6DY, Wales, UK
Tel: 44 1792 472837
Founded: 1945
Members: 16
Staff: 1
Contact: Mrs. M.W. Davies
Description: Engineering foundry works within the West Glamorgan/ Dyfed area. Employers Association concerned with the settlement of annual wage claim, arbitrator of disputes at work. Informs member firms of changes in law etc.

Welsh Language Society

Penroc, Marine Terrace, Aberystwyth, SY23 2AZ, Wales, UK
Tel: 44 1970 624501
Fax: 44 1970 627122
Founded: 1962

Welsh Liberal Democrats
WLD

Bay View House, Cardiff Bay, Cardiff, CF10 5AD, Wales, UK
Tel: 44 29 20313400
Fax: 44 29 20313401
Email: ldwales@cix.co.uk
Website: http://demrhyddcymru.org.uk
Members: 4000
Staff: 2
Contact: Judi Lewis, Party Mgr.

Description: Political party in Wales. Conducts campaigns; disseminates information.
Formerly: Formed by Merger of, Welsh Liberal Party
Publication: Bulletin
Publication title: Bulletin
Second publication: Directory
Publication title: Directory
Meetings/Conventions: - semiannual conference - Exhibits.

Welsh Library Association
WLA

DILS, Llanbadarn Fawr, Aberystwyth, SY23 3AS, Wales, UK
Tel: 44 1970 622174
Fax: 44 1970 622190
Email: hle@aber.ac.uk
Website: http://www.dils.aber.ac.uk/holi/wla/wla.htm
Contact: Andrew Green, Pres.
Description: Librarians and information managers. Promotes professional development and advocates the role of high quality library and information services. Develops and promotes industry guidelines.

Welsh Mountain Sheep Society-Pedigree Section

c/o Meurig Voyle
Erw Myrddin, 52 Ffordd Celyn, Denbigh, St. Asaph, LL16 5UU, Wales, UK
Tel: 44 1745 814289
Contact: Mr. Meurig Voyle, Sec.
Fee: £10
Description: Seeks to promote improvement of sheep breeding through documentation of ram lambs and ewe lambs into the yearly flock book, flock competition, and promotion of prizes at shows and sales.
Library Subject: periodical statements to members, show and sale catalogue
Library Type: reference
Meetings/Conventions: - annual show

Welsh Music Guild

9 Brown St., Ferndale, CF43 4SF, Wales, UK
Tel: 44 1443 730383
Email: guild.info@ntlworld.com
Website: http://www.welshmusic.org.uk
Founded: 1955
Members: 200
Contact: John H. Lewis, Hon.Sec.
Fee: £15
Membership Type: regular
Description: Individuals in 10 countries united to promote the composition and performance of works by Welsh composers. Acts as source of information about Welsh music.
Library Subject: Welsh music
Library Type: reference
Formerly: Guild for the Promotion of Welsh Music
Publication title: Catalogue of Contemporary Welsh Music. Advertisements.
Second publication: Journal
Publication title: Welsh Music
Meetings/Conventions: - annual convention

Welsh Pony and Cob Society

c/o Mrs. S. Evelyn Jones
6 Chalybeate St., Aberystwyth, Ceredigion, Llandysul, SY23 1HP,
Wales, UK
Tel: 44 1970 617501
Fax: 44 1970 625401
Email: secretary@wpcs.uk.com
Website: http://www.wpcs.uk.com
Founded: 1901
Members: 7140
Staff: 13
Contact: Mrs. S. Evelyn Jones
Fee: £45
Membership Type: annual
Description: Owners, breeders, and admirers of Welsh ponies and
cobs. Records the breeding details of Welsh ponies and cobs and
seeks to improve the breed and promote its excellence.
Library Subject: Welsh ponies, cobs
Library Type: open to the public
Publication: Journal
Publication title: Stud Book
Meetings/Conventions: - annual meeting

Welsh Secondary Schools Association

124 Walter Rd., Swansea, SA1 5RF, Wales, UK
Tel: 44 1792 455933
Fax: 44 1792 455944
Email: wssa@supanet.com
Founded: 1895
Members: 829
Staff: 2
Contact: H.G.L. Clement, Sec.
Description: Head and deputies of secondary schools of Wales.
Aims to serve the maintenance and further development of effective
secondary education in Wales.
Publication: Journal
Publication title: Pulse
Publication title: Review
Meetings/Conventions: convention

Welsh Women's Aid

38-48 Crwys Rd., Cardiff, CF2 4NN, Wales, UK
Tel: 44 29 20390874
Fax: 44 29 20390878
Email: wwa.cardiff@tesco.net
Founded: 1978
Members: 32
Staff: 13
Contact: Gail Allen
Description: Advocates for the welfare of abused women in Wales.
Offers shelter to women and their children fleeing domestic violence.
Encourages women to be self-reliant and confident in building their
futures. Provides counseling services to women and children. Raises
awareness of abused women and domestic violence among the
public, media, police, courts, social services, etc. List of publications
available upon request.
Library Subject: Domestic violence.
Library Type: not open to the public
Publication: Annual Report
Second publication: Pamphlets
Meetings/Conventions: - annual conference - Exhibits.

West Wales Chamber of Commerce
WWCC

1st floor, Creswell Buildings, 1 Burrows Pl., Swansea, SA1 1SW,
Wales, UK
Tel: 44 1792 653297
Fax: 44 1792 648345
Email: info@westwaleschamber.co.uk
Website: http://www.westwaleschamber.co.uk
Contact: Lyn Harries
Description: Promotes business and commerce.

Alphabetical Index

Subject Index

Apparel

Apparel Knitting and Textiles Alliance, 68
Association of Button Merchants, 91
Association of Suppliers to the British Clothing Industry, 118
British Branded Hosiery Group, 156
British Clothing Industry Association, 160
British Fashion Council, 170
British Glove Association, 173
British Hat Guild, 175
British Menswear Guild, 187
Federation of Clothing Designers and Executives, 308
Haberdashers' Company, 338
International Apparel Federation, 388
International Fur Trade Federation, 409
Merchant Taylors' Company, 462
Northern Ireland Textiles and Apparel Association, 662
Shetland Knitwear Trades Association, 715
UK Fashion Exports, 622
Worshipful Company of Pattenmakers, 651

Appraisers

Academy of Experts, 51

Appropriate Technology

Appropriate Technology ASIA, 68
APT Enterprise Development, 69
Centre for Alternative Technology, 725
Intermediate Technology Development Group, 386

Aquaculture

Association of Scottish Shellfish Growers, 673
Shetland Salmon Farmers' Association, 715

Arachnology

British Arachnological Society, 141

Arbitration and Mediation

British and Irish Ombudsman Association, 140
Chartered Institute of Arbitrators, 225
Scottish Agricultural Arbiters' Association, 699
Scottish Council for International Arbitration, 703
Veterinary Association for Arbitration and Jurisprudence, 632

Archaeology

Archaeology Abroad, 69
Association for Environmental Archaeology, 76
Association of Roman Archaeology, 115
Bristol Industrial Archaeological Society, 136
British Aviation Archaeological Council, 154
Cornwall Archaeological Society, 255
Council for British Archaeology, 256
Council for British Archaeology, 256
Council for British Archaeology, 257
Council for British Archaeology, 257
Council for Independent Archaeology, 257
Council for Scottish Archaeology, 679
Egypt Exploration Society, 274
Exeter Industrial Archaeology Group, 303
Glasgow Archaeological Society, 687
Greater London Industrial Archaeology Society, 333
Hunter Archaeological Society, 348

Institute of Field Archaeologists, 365
International Fossil Algae Association, 727
London and Middlesex Archaeological Society, 450
Nautical Archaeology Society, 501
Royal Archaeological Institute, 546
Shropshire Archaeological and Historical Society, 568
Society for Medieval Archaeology, 576
Society for Post-Medieval Archaeology, 576
Society of Antiquaries of Scotland, 716
Society of Museum Archaeologists, 593
Ulster Archaeological Society, 664

Architectural Education

Architectural Association of Ireland, 4
Ulster Architectural Heritage Society, 664

Architecture

Alexander Thomson Society, 670
Architects in Industry and Commerce, 69
Architects Registration Board, 70
Architecture and Surveying Institute, 70
Association of Building Engineers, 90
Association of Consultant Architects, 96
British Institute of Architectural Technologists, 179
Cathedral Architects Association, 221
Commonwealth Association of Architects, 239
Edinburgh Architectural Association, 680
Energy Research Group, 13
European Council for the Village and Small Town, 290
European Intelligent Building Group, 294
Royal Incorporation of Architects in Scotland, 696
Royal Institute of British Architects, 551
Royal Institute of British Architects - Women Architects' Group, 551
Royal Society of Ulster Architects, 663
Rural Design and Building Association, 560
Society of Architectural Historians of Great Britain, 716
Twentieth Century Society, 621
Victorian Society, 633

Archives

Association of Chief Archivists in Local Government, 93
Association of Commonwealth Archivists and Records Managers, 95
British Record Society, 196
British Records Association, 196
Business Archives Council, 216
Irish Society for Archives, 32
Society of Archivists, 583
Society of Archivists - Ireland, 45

Art

Art Libraries Society of United Kingdom, 71
Art Through Touch, 71
Association of Art and Antique Dealers, 84
British Antique Dealers' Association, 140
British Art Medal Society, 141
British Origami Society, 191
Contemporary Art Society, 254
Creative Activity for Everyone, 11
Fine Art Trade Guild, 315
Friends of the Royal Watercolour Society and Royal Society of Painter-Printmakers, 323
International Confederation of Art Dealers, 399
New English Art Club, 502

Chemical Engineering

Chemicals

Coins

Colleges and Universities

Color

Commercial Law

Commodities

Communications

Community Development

Community Service

Composers

Computer Science

Computer Software

Computer Users

Computers

Cosmetology

British Association of Beauty Therapy and Cosmetology, 147
Hairdressing Council, 338
Hairdressing Employers' Association, 339
Hairdressing Manufacturers' and Wholesalers' Association, 339
International Federation of Societies of Cosmetic Chemists, 407
National Hairdressers' Federation, 492
Society of Cosmetic Scientists, 586

Costumes

Costume Society of Scotland, 679

Counseling

Association of Careers Advisers in Colleges Offering Higher
    Education, 92
Association of Graduate Careers Advisory Services, 102
FEDORA - European Forum for Student Guidance, 684
Institute of Career Guidance, 360
International Association for Educational and Vocational
    Guidance, 389
Irish Association for Counselling and Therapy, 22
ISCO Careerscope, 432
National Association of Careers and Guidance Teachers, 475
PTO, 533

Crafts

Association of British Pewter Craftsmen, 88
British Stickmakers Guild, 207
Craft Potters Association of Great Britain, 261
Crafts Council, 261
Embroiderers' Guild, 276
Guild of Glass Engravers, 336
Guild of Taxidermists, 687
Lace Guild, 439
Quilters' Guild of the British Isles, 535
Rural Crafts Association, 560
Society of Craftsmen, 587
Society of Designer Craftsmen, 587
Society of Miniaturists, 592
Wales Craft Council, 731

Craniofacial Abnormalities

International Association of Craniofacial Identification, 392

Credit

Credit Protection Association, 261
Irish Institute of Credit Management, 29

Credit Unions

Council of Mortgage Lenders, 259

Crime

ICC Commercial Crime Services, 349
ICC International Maritime Bureau, 349
Victim Support, 632

Criminal Justice

Helping Offenders Prisoners and their Families, 687
Howard League for Penal Reform, 347
NACRO, 470

National Association of Prison Visitors, 481
National Association of Probation Officers, 481
Penal Reform International, 515
Probation Boards' Association, 528

Criminology

British Society of Criminology, 204

Critical Care

Intensive Care Society, 386

Cryogenics

British Cryoengineering Society, 163
Society for Low Temperature Biology, 575

Crystallography

British Association of Crystal Growth, 148
British Crystallographic Association, 676
International Union of Crystallography, 429

Cultural Exchange

Experiment in International Living - Ireland, 15

Curriculum

Qualifications and Curriculum Authority, 534

Cytology

British Society for Clinical Cytology, 200

Dairies

British Sheep Dairying Association, 199
Royal Association of British Dairy Farmers, 546
Stilton Cheese Makers' Association, 605

Dairy Products

Association of Cheese Processors, 93
Dairy Council - United Kingdom, 263
Dairy Industry Association, 263
Ice Cream Alliance, 349
National Dairymen's Association, 487
Scottish Dairy Association, 704
Scottish Milk Records Association, 708

Dance

Ballroom Dancers Federation, 126
Benesh Institute, 130
British Ballet Organization, 154
British Dance Council, 164
English Amateur Dancesport Association, 279
Imperial Society of Teachers of Dancing, 350
International Association of Margaret Morris Method, 689
International Dance Teachers' Association, 402
Laban Guild, 439
London Swing Dance Society, 452
Royal Academy of Dance, 544
Royal Scottish Country Dance Society, 697
Scottish Dance Teacher's Alliance, 704
Scottish Dancesport, 704
Scottish Official Board of Highland Dancing, 710

Engines

English

Entertainment

Entomology

Environment

Environmental Health

Environmental Law

Enzymology

Epidemiology

Food

Food and Drugs

Food Equipment

Food Service

Footwear

Forensic Medicine

Forensic Sciences

Forensics

Forest Industries

Forestry

Foundries

Fragrances

History

Home Care

Home Study

Homeless

Homeopathy

Horses

Hydrology

British Hydrological Society, 178

Hypertension

British Hypertension Society, 178
International Society for the Study of Hypertension in Pregnancy, 423

Hypnosis

Association for Applied Hypnosis, 723
Association of Qualified Curative Hypnotherapists, 114
British Society of Experimental and Clinical Hypnosis, 205
British Society of Hypnotherapists, 205
British Society of Medical and Dental Hypnosis, 205
European College of Hypnotherapy, 288
Hypnotherapy Association, 349

Imaging Media

UK Industrial Vision Association, 622

Immigration

Immigration Advisory Service, 350
Joint Council for the Welfare of Immigrants, 436
National Coalition of Anti-Deportation Campaigns, 486

Immunology

British Society for Immunology, 201
Primary Immunodeficiency Association, 527

Impotence

Impotence Association, 350

Incontinence

International Continence Society, 400

Indigenous Peoples

PARTIZANS, 514
SURVIVAL, 606

Industrial Design

Design Council, 265

Industrial Equipment

Association of British Mining Equipment Companies, 87
Association of Loading and Elevating Equipment Manufacturers, 108
Association of Manufacturers of Power Generating Systems, 109
Automated Material Handling Systems Association, 123
Ball and Roller Bearing Manufacturers Association, 126
Boiler and Radiator Manufacturers Association, 674
British Abrasives Federation, 136
British Combustion Equipment Manufacturers Association, 160
British Fluid Power Distributors Association, 171
British Industrial Furnace Constructors Association, 179
British Mechanical Power Transmission Association, 186
British National Committee for Electroheat, 189
British Pump Manufacturers Association, 196
British Textile Machinery Association, 208
British Turned-Parts Manufacturers Association, 210
British Valve and Actuator Manufacturers Association, 211

Cleaning and Hygiene Suppliers' Association, 235
Construction Equipment Association, 253
European Committee of Manufacturers of Compressors, Vacuum Pumps, and Pneumatic Tools, 289
European Control Manufacturers Association, 290
European Cutting Tools Association, 291
European Resin Manufacturers' Association, 297
Federation of Drum Reconditioners, 309
Forecourt Equipment Federation, 319
Foundry Equipment and Supplies Association, 321
Gauge and Tool Makers' Association, 326
Industrial Cleaning Machine Manufacturers' Association, 354
International Powered Access Federation, 417
Lift and Escalator Industry Association, 446
Lifting Equipment Engineers Association, 446
Manufacturers of Domestic Unvented Systems, 456
Manufacturing Technologies Association, 456
Metalforming Machinery Makers' Association, 462
Milling Cutter and Toolbit Association, 464
Pattern, Model, and Mould Manufacturers Association, 515
Picon, 519
Pressure Gauge and Dial Thermometer Association, 527
Pump Distributors Association, 534
Scottish Plant Owners Association, 711
Sewing Machine Trade Association, 567
Society of Laundry Engineers and Allied Trades, 591
Solids Handling and Processing Association, 599
Specialist Access Engineering and Maintenance Association, 601
TWI, 621
Twist Drill and Reamer Association, 622
United Kingdom Weighing Federation, 629
Water Jetting Association, 635
Welding Manufacturers' Association, 636
Woodworking Machinery Suppliers Association, 643

Industrial Workers

Manufacturing Science Finance, 456
National Union of Knitwear, Footwear and Apparel Trades, 500
National Union of Lock and Metal Workers, 500

Infants

Association of Breastfeeding Mothers, 85
Baby Milk Action, 125
Foundation for the Study of Infant Deaths, 320

Infectious Diseases

Herpes Viruses Association, 343

info@britishtools.com

British Engineers' Cutting Tools Association, 168

Information Management

Association for Information Management, 77
Association of European Document Exchanges, 100
British Urban and Regional Information Systems Associations, 211
CIMTECH, 232
European Information Association, 294
Institute for the Management of Information Systems, 357
International Records Management Trust, 418
Learning Information Network Association, 442
Records Management Society of Great Britain, 537
Society of Information Technology Management, 590
Society of Public Information Networks, 595

Information Processing

Irish Internet Association, 29

Instructional Media

British Universities Film and Video Council, 210
Concord Video and Film Council, 248
Society for Screen-Based Learning, 578

Insurance

150 Association, 51
Associated Scottish Life Offices, 671
Association of Average Adjusters, 85
Association of British Insurers, 87
Association of Consulting Actuaries, 96
Association of European Cooperative and Mutual Insurers, 100
Association of Insurance and Risk Managers, 105
Association of Insurance and Risk Managers, 105
Association of Insurance and Risk Managers, 105
Association of Insurance and Risk Managers, 105
Aviation Insurance Offices' Association, 125
British Health Care Association, 175
British Insurance Broker's Association, 182
British Insurance Law Association, 182
Chartered Institute of Loss Adjusters, 226
Chartered Insurance Institute, 228
European Actuarial Consultative Group, 283
Faculty of Actuaries, 684
Institute of Actuaries - United Kingdom, 357
Institute of Insurance Brokers, 368
Institute of Public Loss Assessors, 375
Institute of Risk Management, 376
Insurance Institute of Ireland, 20
Insurance Institute of London, 385
International Association for Insurance Law - United Kingdom, 389
International Association of Engineering Insurers, 392
International Cooperative and Mutual Insurance Federation, 400
International Credit Insurance and Surety Association, 401
International Underwriting Association of London, 428
International Union of Aviation Insurers, 428
International Union of Credit and Investment Insurers/ The Berne Union, 429
Irish Brokers Association, 24
Irish Insurance Federation, 29
Life Insurance Association, 446
LIMRA Europe, 447
Lloyd's Aviation Underwriters' Association, 449
Lloyd's Motor Underwriters' Association, 449
Loss Prevention Council, 452
Non-Marine Association, 504
Travel Trust Association, 619
United Kingdom Credit Insurance Brokers' Committee, 625
Worshipful Company of Actuaries, 650

Intellectual Property

Anti-Counterfeiting Group, 67
British Copyright Council, 162
Chartered Institute of Patent Agents, 227
Copyright Licensing Agency, 255
ICC Counterfeiting Intelligence Bureau, 349
Institute of International Licensing Practitioners, 368
Institute of Trade Mark Attorneys, 378
Irish Music Rights Organisation, 30
Licensing Executives Society - Britain and Ireland, 445

Mechanical-Copyright Protection Society, 459
Performing Right Society, 516
Trade Marks Patents and Designs Federation, 618

Intelligence

Association of European Trade Mark Owners, 100
British Brands Group, 156
MARQUES - Association of European Trademark Owners, 458

Intercultural

Anglo-Chilean Society, 66
Association for Cultural Exchange, 75
British Coalition for East Timor, 160
Indian Volunteers for Community Service, 353
London Welsh Association, 452
New Zealand Ireland Association, 40
Society for Anglo-Chinese Understanding, 572
Women Welcome Women World Wide, 641

Interdisciplinary Studies

Africa-Europe Group for Interdisciplinary Studies, 56

Interior Design

Access Flooring Association, 52
Association of Interior Specialists, 105
British Carpet Manufacturers Association, 157
British Contract Furnishing Association, 162
British Resilient Flooring Manufacturers Association, 197
Contract Flooring Association, 254
European Academy of Design, 283
Home Decoration Retailer's Association, 345
Interior Decorators and Designers Association, 386
National Association of Shopfitters, 482
Painting and Decorating Association of Great Britain, 512
Wallcovering Manufacturers Association of Great Britain, 635
Wax Chandlers' Company, 636

Internal Medicine

European Federation of Internal Medicine, 292

International Cooperation

Caribbean Council for Europe, 220
Commonwealth Secretariat, 245

International Development

ABANTU for Development, 51
Africa Now, 56
African Foundation for Development, 57
Agency for Cooperation and Research in Development, 58
Banana Link, 127
British Overseas NGOs for Development, 192
Catholic Institute for International Relations, 221
Comhlamh, 10
Commonwealth Foundation, 241
Commonwealth Fund for Technical Co-Operation, 241
Department for International Development, 265
European Movement - Ireland, 14
Fourth World Educational and Research Association Trust, 321
Institute for African Alternatives - England, 355
Institute for Development Policy and Management, 356
International Institute for Environment and Development, 411

Lupus Erythematosus

European Lupus Erythematosus Federation, 295

Maintenance

Association Building Cleaning Direct Service Providers, 74
Association of Domestic Management, 98
British Cleaning Council, 160
British Council of Maintenance Associations, 163
British Institute of Cleaning Science, 179
British Institute of Facilities Management, 180
Cleaning and Support Services Association, 235
Domestic Appliance Service Association, 269
Home Laundering Consultative Council, 345
National Association of Chimney Sweeps, 475
Society of Hospital Linen Service and Laundry Managers, 589

Malacology

International Association for Malacology, 389
Unitas Malacologica, 624

Management

Association for Project Management, 79
Association of British Certification Bodies, 85
Association of Business Executives, 90
Association of Directors of European Centres for Plastics, 98
Association of MBA's, 109
Council for Hospitality Management Education, 257
European Association for Personnel Management, 285
European Strategic Planning Federation, 301
Institute of Administrative Management, 357
Institute of Commercial Management, 361
Institute of Directors - England, 363
Institute of Leadership and Management, 368
Institute of Management, 370
Institute of Management Consultancy, 370
Institute of Management Services, 370
Institute of Management Specialists, 370
Interim Management Association, 386
Irish Institute of Purchasing and Materials Management, 29
Irish Management Institute International, 30
Management Consultancies Association, 455
Production Managers Association, 529
Professional Business and Technical Management, 530
Strategic Planning Society, 605
Transform Program, 619
Women in Management, 640
World Federation of Personnel Management Associations, 646

Managers

Federated Union of Managerial and Professional Officers, 307

Manufacturing

Association of Rooflight Manufacturers, 116
European Association of Fibre Drum Manufacturers, 286
Federation of British Engineers' Tool Manufacturers, 308
Fibre Bonded Carpet Manufacturers' Association, 314
Gasket Cutters Association, 326
Institute for Manufacturing, 356
Polymer Machinery Manufacturers and Distributors Association, 523
Pressure Sensitive Manufacturers Association, 527
Production Engineering Research Association, 529

Socialist Business Values Association, 571
United Kingdom Industrial Vision Association, 627
United Kingdom Spring Manufacturers Association, 629

Marine

Association for the History of the Northern Seas, 81
Association of Brokers and Yacht Agents, 89
Association of Canoe Trades, 91
British and International Sailors Society, 139
British Marine Life Study Society, 185
Captain Cook Society, 219
Challenger Society for Marine Science, 224
Commercial Boat Operators Association, 238
Historical Diving Society, 344
Inland Waterways Association of Ireland, 19
Institute of Estuarine and Coastal Studies, 364
International Bunker Industry Association, 396
International Centre for Island Technology, 690
International Society for Reef Studies, 422
Marine Biological Association of the United Kingdom, 692
Marine Society, 457
National Federation of Fishermen's Organisations, 490
Nautical Campus, 501
Royal National Lifeboat Institution - Ireland, 44
Scottish Association for Marine Science, 700
Society for Nautical Research, 576
World Ship Trust, 648

Marine Biology

International Polychaetology Association, 727

Marine Industries

Association of British Sailmakers, 88
Baltic Exchange, 127
BMIF - Scotland, 674
British Marine Federation, 185
British Naval Equipment Association, 189
British Ports Association, 194
British Tugowners' Association, 210
Chamber of Shipping, 224
Chart and Nautical Instrument Trade Association, 678
European Tugowners Association, 302
Federation of National Associations of Shipbrokers and Agents, 311
Honourable Company of Master Mariners, 346
Institute of Chartered Shipbrokers - England, 360
International Association for Marine Electronics Companies, 389
International Association of Classification Societies, 391
International Association of Dry Cargo Shipowners, 392
International Association of Maritime Institutions, 392
International Chamber of Shipping, 397
International Council of Marine Industry Associations, 400
International Federation of Shipmasters' Associations, 407
International Harbour Masters' Association, 410
International Marine Contractors Association, 413
International Maritime Industries Forum, 413
International Maritime Pilots Association, 414
International Ship Electrical and Engineering Service Association, 419
International Ship Suppliers Association, 420
International Shipping Federation, 420
Irish Chamber of Shipping, 25
Sailing Barge Association, 561
Salvage Association, 561
Shipbuilders and Shiprepairers Association, 568
Society of International Gas Tanker and Terminal Operators, 590

Musculoskeletal Disorders

Museums

Mushrooms

Music

Mycology

Nutrition

British Dietetic Association, 165
British Nutrition Foundation, 190
Coeliac Society of the United Kingdom, 236
Irish Nutrition and Dietetic Institute, 31
Nutrition Society, 506

Nuts

British Peanut Council, 192
Combined Edible Nut Trade Association, 237

Obesity

International Association for the Study of Obesity, 390

Obstetrics and Gynecology

Association of Radical Midwives, 114
Association of Supervisors of Midwives, 117
British Society of Gynaecological Endoscopy, 205
British Society of Psychosomatic Obstetrics, Gynaecology and
    Andrology, 677
Glasgow Obstetrical and Gynaecological Society, 687
Independent Midwives Association, 352
International Federation of Gynecology and Obstetrics, 405
International Society of Ultrasound in Obstetrics and Gynecology, 425
Maternity Alliance, 459
Midwives Information and Resource Service, 463
Miscarriage Association, 465
National Endometriosis Society, 488
Premenstrual Society, 526
Royal College of Midwives, 547
Royal College of Obstetricians and Gynaecologists, 547

Occupational Medicine

British Occupational Hygiene Society, 190
Faculty of Occupational Medicine, 304
Institute of Occupational Medicine, 689
International Society for the Study of Tension in Performance, 423
Irish Society of Occupational Medicine, 33
Occupational and Environmental Diseases Association, 506
Society of Occupational Medicine, 593

Occupational Safety and Health

European Centre for Occupational Health, Safety and the
    Environment, 682

Oceanography

Estuarine and Coastal Sciences Association, 282
International Association for Biological Oceanography, 689
Permanent Service for Mean Sea Level, 517
Society for Underwater Technology, 582

Office Equipment

British Office Supplies and Services Federation, 190
Letter File Manufacturers Association, 444

Oils and Fats

British Essential Oils Association, 169
Federation of Oils, Seeds, and Fats Associations, 311
International Fish Meal and Fish Oil Organization, 408
Margarine and Spreads Association, 456

Oncology

European Society for Psychosocial Oncology, 299
Irish Association for Nurses in Oncology, 22

Operations Research

Institute of Logistics and Transport, 369
Operational Research Society - United Kingdom, 508

Ophthalmology

Applied Vision Association, 68
British Orthoptic Society, 191
British Retinitis Pigmentosa Society, 197
European Contact Lens Society of Ophthalmologists, 290
European Opthalmological Society, 295
European Society for Cataract and Refractive Surgeons, 14
Institute of Ophthalmology, 372
International Color Vision Society, 398
International Glaucoma Association, 409
International Orthoptic Association, 416
International Society for Clinical Electrophysiology of Vision, 421
National Pro-Life Religious Council, 39
Royal College of Ophthalmologists, 547
Thyroid Eye Disease, 615

Opticianry

Association of British Dispensing Opticians, 86
Benevolent Fund of the College of Optometrists, 130
Federation of Manufacturing Opticians, 310
General Optical Council, 328
International Opticians Association, 415
Optical Frame Importers' and Manufacturers Association, 508
Optra Exhibits UK, 508

Optometry

American Academy of Optometry - British Chapter, 64
Association of Optometrists, 111
British Association of Behavioral Optometrists, 147
College of Optometrists, 237
European Council of Optics and Optometry, 291
European Glaucoma Society, 294
Orthoptic and Binocular Vision Association, 510
Scottish Committee of Optometrists, 702
The Eyecare Trust, 612

Oral and Maxillofacial Surgery

British Association of Oral and Maxillofacial Surgeons of England, 150
European Association for Cranio-Maxillo-Facial Surgery, 284

Organic Farming

Henry Doubleday Research Association, 342
Irish Organic Farmers and Growers Association, 31
Permaculture Association, 517
Soil Association, 598

Organization Development

European Group for Organization Studies, 294

Ornithology

Avicultural Society, 125
British Ornithologists' Union, 191

Pathology

Association of Clinical Pathologists, 94
British Society of Toxicological Pathologists, 206
Clinical Pathology Accreditation, 236
International Association of Oral Pathologists, 392
International Society for Diagnostic Quantitative Pathology, 659
Pathological Society of Great Britain and Ireland, 515
Royal College of Pathologists - United Kingdom, 548

Pattern Recognition

International Association for Pattern Recognition, 389

Peace

Action from Ireland, 3
Campaign for the Accountability of American Bases, 218
International Institute of Peace Studies and Global Philosophy, 727
Irish Peace Council, 31
Mothers for Peace - U.K., 466
Pax Christi - Great Britain, 515
Pax Christi - Ireland, 41
Peace Pledge Union, 515
Pensioners for Peace International, 516
Quaker Peace and Social Witness, 534
Women Together, 665

Pedestrians

Federation of European Pedestrian Associations, 310
Living Streets, 448

Pediatrics

British Association of Paediatric Surgeons, 151
European Society for Paediatric Infectious Diseases, 298
Neonatal Society, 501
Royal College of Paediatrics and Child Health, 548

Pensions

Institute of Payroll and Pensions Management, 373
Irish Association of Pension Funds, 23
National Association of Pension Funds, 480
Pensions Management Institute, 516
Society of Pension Consultants, 594

Performing Arts

Association of British Jazz Musicians, 87
Equity, 281
Film Artistes Association, 314
International Federation of Actors, 403
OISTAT Centre of Great Britain, 507
Variety and Light Entertainments Council of Great Britain, 631

Perinatology

British Association of Perinatal Medicine, 151

Pest Control

British Pest Control Association, 192
CABI Bioscience, 217

Petroleum

Association for Petroleum and Explosives Administration, 78

Association of British Oil Industries, 87
British Drilling Association, 166
British Lubricants Federation, 184
British Rig Owners' Association, 198
Federation of Petroleum Suppliers, 311
Frontier (Society for Environmental Exploration - United
    Kingdom), 323
Institute of Petroleum, 373
International Petroleum Exchange of London, 416
International Petroleum Marketing Association, 417
International Well Control Forum, 691
NOF, 504
Offshore Contractors Association, 694
Oil Companies International Marine Forum, 506
Oil Firing Technical Association for the Petroleum Industry, 507
Oil Industry International Exploration and Production Forum, 507
Petroleum Exploration Society of Great Britain, 518
Pigging Products and Services Association, 519
Pipeline Industries Guild, 520
Production Engineering Association, 529
Society of Petroleum Engineers - London Office, 594
United Kingdom Offshore Operators' Association, 627
United Kingdom Petroleum Industry Association, 628
Well Drillers Association, 636
World Petroleum Congresses - A Forum for Petroleum Science,
    Technology, Economics, and Management, 647

Pets

Pet Care Trust, 517
Pet Food Manufacturers' Association, 518

Pharmaceuticals

Association of Information Officers in the Pharmaceutical
    Industry, 104
Association of the British Pharmaceutical Industry, 119
British Association of Pharmaceutical Physicians, 151
British Association of Pharmaceutical Wholesalers, 151
British Society for the History of Pharmacy, 203
European Committee on Radiopharmaceuticals, 289
Institute of Clinical Research, 361
Institute of Pharmacy Management International, 373
Irish Pharmaceutical Healthcare Association, 31
National Pharmaceutical Association, 496
Pharmaceutical Society of Ireland, 41
Proprietary Association of Great Britain, 531
Society of Pharmaceutical Medicine, 594

Pharmacy

British Association for Psychopharmacology, 145
British Pharmacological Society, 192
Commonwealth Pharmaceutical Association, 244
European Society of Biochemical Pharmacology, 683
International Union of Pharmacology, 691
National Association of Women Pharmacists, 483
Pharmaceutical Society of Northern Ireland, 663
Royal Pharmaceutical Society of Great Britain, 554
Scottish Pharmaceutical Federation, 711
Scottish Pharmaceutical General Council, 711
Society for Medicines Research, 575
Society of Apothecaries of London, 583

Phenomena

British UFO Research Association, 210
Cheirological Society, 229

Philanthropy

Association of Charity Officers, 92

Philosophy

Aristotelian Society, 70
International Society for Utilitarian Studies, 423
Royal Institute of Philosophy, 552
Royal Philosophical Society of Glasgow, 697
Society for Applied Philosophy, 573
Society of Metaphysicians, 592
Theosophical Society in England, 613
University Philosophical Society, 47
Urania Trust, 631
World Union of Pythagorean Organizations, 649

Phobias

National Phobics Society, 496

Photogrammetry

International Society for Photogrammetry and Remote Sensing, 422
Remote Sensing and Photogrammetry Society, 539

Photography

Affiliation of Honourable Photographers, 56
Association of Photographers, 112
British Institute of Professional Photography, 182
British Photographic Imaging Association, 193
Bureau of Freelance Photographers, 215
Centre for Photographic Conservation, 223
Disabled Photographers' Society, 268
European Society for the History of Photography, 299
Guild of British Camera Technicians, 335
Guild of Wedding Photographers, 338
International Committee for the Science of Photography, 399
Master Photographers Association, 458
Monaghan Photographic Society, 37
Photo Imaging Council, 518
Professional Photographic Laboratories Association, 531
Royal Photographic Society of Great Britain, 555
Society of Picture Researchers and Editors, 594
Stereoscopic Society, 604

Physical Education

British Association of Advisers and Lecturers in Physical Education, 145
Fitness League, 317
Physical Education Association of Ireland, 41
Physical Education Association of the United Kingdom, 519
Scottish Local Authority Network of Physical Education, 708

Physical Fitness

Fitness Industry Association, 317
National Register of Personal Trainers, 497

Physical Science

Association of Physical Scientists in Medicine, 6

Physicians

Association of Operating Department Practitioners, 111
Association of Police Surgeons, 673

Association of Surgeons of Great Britain and Ireland, 118
Hospital Doctors' Association, 346
International Federation of Practitioners of Natural Therapeutics, 406
Medical Women's Federation, 461
Royal College of Physicians, 548
Royal College of Physicians and Surgeons of Glasgow, 695
Royal College of Physicians of Edinburgh, 696
Royal College of Physicians of Ireland, 43

Physics

British Electrophoresis Society, 167
British Society of Rheology, 725
British Vacuum Council, 211
European Neutron Scattering Association, 295
Institute of Physics, 373
Institute of Physics and Engineering in Medicine, 374
International Society for General Relativity and Gravitation, 421
Royal Irish Academy - National Committee for Physics, 43

Physiology

Federation of European Societies of Plant Physiology, 310
International Union of Physiological Sciences, 429
Physiological Society - UK, 519

Pipes

International Tube Association, 427

Planning

European Council of Town Planners, 291

Plastics

British Independent Plastic Extruders' Association, 178
British Laminated Fabricators Association, 184
British Plastics Federation, 194
European Plasticised PVC Film Manufacturers' Association, 296
Packaging and Industrial Films Association, 511
Plastics Historical Society, 520
Plastics Machinery Distributors Association, 521

Plumbing

Bathroom Manufacturers Association, 128
World Plumbing Council, 648

Podiatry

Society of Chiropodists and Podiatrists, 585

Poetry

English Poetry and Song Society, 280
Poetry Society, 522

Polar Studies

British Polarological Research Society, 194
Scientific Committee on Antarctic Research, 564

Polio

Polio Fellowship of Ireland, 42

Political Action

300 Group, 51
Association for the Reduction of Aircraft Noise, 82
European Movement, 295
Liberal International, 444
Liberal International, 444

Political Federations

International Democrat Union, 402
International Young Democrat Union, 431
Liberal International, 444
Liberal International, 444
Socialist International, 571

Political Parties

Alliance Party of Northern Ireland, 657
Conservative Party Central Office, 252
EMILY'S List, 276
Labour Party - Britain, 439
Labour Party - Ireland, 35
Labour Party Women's Organisation - NEC Women's Committee, 439
Labour Women's Network, 439
Plaid Cymru - The Party of Wales, 729
Scottish National Party, 709
Scottish National Party - Women's Forum, 709
Social Democratic and Labour Party, 663
Socialist Party, 571
Welsh Liberal Democrats, 732

Political Reform

Nicaragua Solidarity Campaign, 503
World Union of Free Romanians, 649

Political Science

Association for the Study of German Politics, 82
European Consortium for Political Research, 289
Political Studies Association, 523
Political Studies Association of Ireland, 42

Politics

Politics Association, 523
Women's Leadership Forum, 719

Pollution Control

Advisory Committee on Protection of the Sea, 55
British Oil Spill Control Association, 190
British Water, 212
International Oil Pollution Compensation Funds, 415
International Petroleum Industry Environmental Conservation Association, 417
International Society for the Prevention of Water Pollution, 423
International Tanker Owners Pollution Federation, 426
International Union of Air Pollution Prevention and Environmental Protection Associations, 428
International Water Association, 430
Joint Group of Experts on the Scientific Aspects of Marine Environmental Protection, 436
Offshore Pollution Liability Association, 506
Photographic Waste Management Association, 518
United Kingdom Committee of International Water Association, 625

Population

ALL Party Parliamentary Group on Population, Development and Reproductive Health, 61
Population Concern, 524

Postal Service

Mail Users' Association, 454
Postwatch, 525

Postcards

Great Britain Postcard Club, 332

Poultry

British Egg Industry Council, 167
British Poultry Council, 194
European Union of Wholesale with Eggs, Egg-Products, Poultry and Game, 302
International Egg Commission, 402
National Association of Poultry Suppliers, 480
United Kingdom Egg Producers Association, 626
World's Poultry Science Association - UK, 650

Poverty

Africa Resources Trust, 56
Find Your Feet, 315
Poverty Alliance, 695
Scottish Education and Action for Development, 704
War on Want, 635
World Vision United Kingdom, 649

Press

Association of American Correspondents in London, 84
Association of Golf Writers, 101
Association of Newspaper and Magazine Wholesalers, 111
Association of Regional City Editors, 115
British Guild of Travel Writers, 174
Chartered Institute of Journalists, 226
Circle of Wine Writers, 233
Commonwealth Journalists Association, 242
Commonwealth Journalists Association - United Kingdom, 242
Commonwealth Press Union - United Kingdom, 244
Council of Photographic News Agencies, 260
European Association of Science Editors, 286
Foreign Press Association in London, 319
Gemini News Service, 326
Guild of Agricultural Journalists, 334
Guild of Agricultural Journalists - Ireland, 17
Guild of Motoring Writers, 337
Hockey Writers' Club, 345
Independent Schools Council Information Service, 353
Institute of Scientific and Technical Communicators, 377
Media Society, 460
National Association of Press Agencies, 480
National Council for the Training of Journalists, 486
National Union of Journalists - England, 500
Overseas Press and Media Association, 511
Press Complaints Commission, 527
Regional Newspapers Association of Ireland, 42
Reuter Foundation, 542
Society of All Cargo Correspondents, 582
Society of Women Writers and Journalists, 598
Sports Writers' Association of Great Britain, 602

Primates

Primate Society of Great Britain, 695

Professionals

Federation of Professional Association, 312

Professions

Association of Management and Professional Staffs, 109
Prospect, 532

Professors

International Association of University Professors of English, 394

Programming Languages

Association of Logic Programming, 108

Property Rights

Country Land and Business Association, 260

Psychiatry

Association for Child Psychology and Psychiatry, 74
Institute of Psychiatry, 374
Institute of Social Psychiatry, 377
International Balint Federation, 395
Royal College of Psychiatrists, 548

Psychoanalysis

British Psychoanalytical Society, 195
British Psychoanalytical Society, 195
British Psychoanalytical Society, 195
British Psychoanalytical Society, 195
European Federation for Pscyhoanalytic Psychotherapy, 292
European Psycho-Analytical Federation, 296
International Psychoanalytical Association, 418
International Psychoanalytical Association Trust, 418
Irish Psycho-Analytical Association, 31

Psychology

Association for Teaching Psychology, 81
Association for Therapeutic Philosophy, 83
Association of Humanistic Psychology Practitioners, 102
Association of Humanistic Psychology Practitioners, 103
Association of Humanistic Psychology Practitioners, 102
Association of Humanistic Psychology Practitioners, 103
British Psychological Society, 195
European Society for Cognitive Psychology, 298
European Society for Communicative Psychotherapy, 298
European Society for Developmental Psychology, 298
Experimental Psychology Society, 303
International Association for the Psychology of Food and Nutrition, 390
Play Therapy International, 521
Psychological Society Ireland, 42
Society for Multivariate Experimental Psychology, 45
Society for the Study of Normal Psychology, 581

Psychopathology

European Association for Integrative Psychotherapy, 284

Psychosomatic Medicine

International College of Psychosomatic Medicine, 398
Society for Psychosomatic Research, 577

Psychotherapy

Association for Group and Individual Psychotherapy, 77
Association of Child Psychotherapists, 93
British Association for Behavioural and Cognitive Psychotherapies, 142
British Association of Psychotherapists, 152
General Hypnotherapy Register, 328
Group-Analytic Society, 334
Guild of Psychotherapists, 337
Institute of Group Analysis, 366
Institute of Psychosexual Medicine, 375
International Association for Forensic Psychotherapy, 389
London Association of Primal Psychotherapists, 450
National College of Hypnosis and Psychotherapy, 486
National Register of Hypnotherapists and Psychotherapists, 497
United Kingdom Council for Psychotherapy, 625

Public Administration

British Council, 162
Institute of Public Administration, 20

Public Finance

Society of County Treasurers, 586
Society of Municipal Treasurers, 593

Public Health

Association of Community Health Councils for England and Wales, 95
Association of Port Health Authorities, 113
British Fluoridation Society, 171
Faculty of Public Health Medicine, 304
Healthlink Worldwide, 341
Mental Health Media, 462
Royal Institute of Public Health, 552
Royal Institute of Public Health, 552
Royal Institute of Public Health, 552
Royal Institute of Public Health, 552
Royal Society for the Promotion of Health, 556
Scottish Association of Health Councils, 700
UK Public Health Association, 623

Public Policy

Economic and Social Research Institute, 13
European Policy Forum, 296
Social Policy Association, 571

Public Relations

European Public Relations Confederation, 296
European Sponsorship Consultants Association, 301
Institute of Public Relations, 375
International Communications Consultancy Organization, 399
International Public Relations Association, 418
Public Relations Consultants Association, 533
Publicity Club of London, 533
Society of County and Regional Public Relations Officers, 586

Public Speaking

Association of Speakers Clubs, 117
British Professional Toastmasters' Authority, 195
Guild of Professional After Dinner Speakers, 337
Royal Guild of Toastmasters, 550

Public Transit

Scottish Association for Public Transport, 700

Publishing

Association of Circulation Executives, 93
Association of Learned and Professional Society Publishers, 107
Association of Little Presses, 107
Association of Publishing Agencies, 114
Association of Subscription Agents and Intermediaries, 117
Authors' Licensing and Collecting Society, 123
Book Packagers Association, 134
Commonwealth Hansard Editors Association, 242
Council of Academic and Professional Publishers, 259
Directory and Database Publishers Association, 267
Educational Publishers Council, 274
English Westerners Society, 280
Guild of Food Writers, 336
Independent Publishers Guild, 352
International Federation of the Periodical Press, 407
Irish Book Publishers' Association, 23
Music Publishers Association, 469
Newspaper Publishers Association, 503
Newspaper Society, 503
Periodical Publishers Association, 517
Periodical Publishers Association of Ireland, 41
Publishers Association, 533
Publishers Licensing Society, 533
Publishers Publicity Circle, 534
Scottish Daily Newspaper Society, 704
Scottish Newspaper Publishers Association, 710
Scottish Publishers Association, 712
Society of Bookbinders, 584
Society of Editors, 587
Society of Young Publishers, 598
Web Offset Newspaper Association, 636
Women in Publishing, 640
Writers' Guild of Great Britain, 652
Yachting Journalists' Association, 653

Purchasing

Chartered Institute of Purchasing and Supply, 227

Quality Assurance

British Association for Research Quality Assurance, 145

Quality Control

Institute of Quality Assurance, 375

Radiation

Association for Radiation Research, 79
Association of University Radiation Protection Officers, 724
Society for Radiological Protection, 577

Radio

Association of Independent Radio Stations, 6
Commerical Radio Companies Association, 238

Radiology

British Institute of Radiology, 182
European Society of Urogenital Radiology, 301
Royal College of Radiologists, 549

Railroads

Electric Railway Society, 275
Highland Railway Society, 343
Locomotive and Carriage Institution, 450
Permanent Way Institution, 517
Railway Canal Historical Society, 536
Railway Correspondence and Travel Society, 536
Railway Development Society, 536
Railway Industry Association, 536
Stephenson Locomotive Society, 604
Talyllyn Railway Preservation Society, 730
Tramway and Light Railway Society, 619
World War Two Railway Study Group, 649

Real Estate

Association of Chief Estate Surveyors and Property Managers in
    Local Government, 93
Association of Relocation Agents, 115
Association of Residential Letting Agents, 115
Association of Residential Managing Agents, 115
Association of Valuers of Licensed Property, 121
British Property Federation, 195
European Real Estate Society, 14
Federation of Overseas Property Developers Agents and
    Consultants, 311
Incorporated Society of Valuers and Auctioneers, 352
Land Institute, 440
Property Consultants Society, 531
Scottish Assessors Association, 699
Scottish Landowners' Federation, 707
Small Landlords Association, 570

Recordings

Association of Professional Recording Services, 113
British Phonographic Industry, 193
International Federation of the Phonographic Industry - England, 408
Music Producers Guild, 469

Recreation

Airline Sports and Cultural Association, 60
Institute of Leisure and Amenity Management, 369
Institute of Sport and Recreation Management, 377

Recreational Vehicles

National Caravan Council, 484

Refugees

European Council on Refugees and Exiles, 291
Ockenden International - England, 506
Scottish Refugee Council, 712
Sri Lanka Project, 602

Safety

Association of Industrial Road Safety Officers, 104
British Safety Council, 198
Choice in Personal Safety, 231
Christian Road Safety Association, 231
Guild of Experienced Motorists, 335
Institute of Road Safety Officers, 376
Institution of Occupational Safety and Health, 384
International Institute of Risk and Safety Management, 412
Local Authority Road Safety Officers' Association, 449
National Safety Council of Ireland, 39
Personal Safety Association, 728
Personal Safety Manufacturers Association, 517
Photoluminescent Safety Products Association, 518
Road Operators' Safety Council, 543
Royal Society for the Prevention of Accidents, 556
Safety Assessment Federation, 560
Safety Equipment Distributors Association, 561
Society of Industrial Emergency Services Officers, 590

Sales

Direct Selling Association - United Kingdom, 267
Society of Sales Marketing, 596

Scalp

Institute of Trichologists, 379

Scandinavian

Scottish Society for Northern Studies, 713
Viking Society for Northern Research, 633

Schools

Association of Business Schools, 91
Scottish Council of Independent Schools, 703

Science

Associates for Research into the Science of Enjoyment, 74
Association for Astronomy Education, 74
Association for Science Education, 80
Association for Women in Science and Engineering, 83
Association of Consulting Scientists, 96
BA, 125
Commonwealth Science Council, 245
Institute for Scientific Information - Europe, Middle East, and
    Africa, 357
Institute of Science Technology, 377
Institute of Surface Science and Technology, 378
Royal Institution of Great Britain, 553
Science Council, 564
Scientific Exploration Society, 564
Women in Physics Group, 640

Science Fiction

British Science Fiction Association, 198
Science Fiction Foundation, 564

Scientific Products

Association of British Steriliser Manufacturers, 88
Association of X-ray Equipment Manufacturers, 122
BAREMA, 128

BLWA - Association of the Laboratory Supply Industry, 133
British Civil Engineering Test Equipment Manufacturers
    Association, 160
Worshipful Company of Scientific Instrument Makers, 651

Scottish

1745 Association, 669
Saltire Society, 698
Scots Language Society, 698
Scottish Esperanto Association, 705
Scottish Gaelic Texts Society, 706
Scottish Text Society, 565
Society of West Highland and Island Historical Research, 717
Tartans of Scotland, 718

Scouting

Boys' Brigade, 135
Girl Guiding UK, 330
Girlguiding Scotland, 686
Girls' Brigade International Council, 686
Guide Association UK, 334
Irish Girl Guides, 28
Scout Association, 565
Scouting Ireland CSI, 44
World Association of Girl Guides and Girl Scouts, 644

Sculpture

Public Monuments and Sculpture Association, 533
Sculptors' Society of Ireland, 44

Seamen

International Committee on Seafarer's Welfare Office, 399
Mission to Seafarers, 465
Royal Sailors' Rests, 555

Securities

European Association of Securities Dealers, 286
Financial Services Authority, 315
Futures and Options Association, 324
Gilt Edged Market Makers Association, 330
International Primary Market Association, 417
International Securities Market Association - London, 419
National Association of Steel Stockholders, 482
ProShare (United Kingdom), 532
Securities and Futures Authority, 566

Security

Association of European Manufacturers of Fire and Intruder Alarm
    Systems, 100
Association of Security Consultants, 116
British American Security Information Council, 139
British Security Industry Association, 199
International Institute of Security, 412
International Professional Security Association - England, 418
Irish Security Industry Association, 32
Master Locksmiths Association, 458
National Security Inspectorate, 497
Security Systems and Alarms Inspection Board, 566

Seed

British Association of Seed Analysts, 152
British Sugar Beet Seed Producers Association, 207

Sonography

British Medical Ultrasound Society, 187
European Federation of Societies for Ultrasound in Medicine and Biology, 293
Society of European Sonographers, 588

Soviet Union

Society for Cooperation in Russian and Soviet Studies, 573

Space

Mars Society, 458

Spanish

Association of Hispanists of Great Britain and Ireland, 102

Special Education

European Association for Special Education, 285

Spectroscopy

European Society for Mass Spectrometry, 683

Speech

Irish Stammering Association, 34

Speech and Hearing

AFASIC - Overcoming Speech Impairments, 55
British Stammering Association, 207
British Tinnitus Association, 208
Royal College of Speech and Language Therapists, 549
Society of Teachers of Speech and Drama, 596
Speakability, 601

Speleology

British Cave Research Association, 158
National Caving Association, 485

Spinal Injury

Association for Spina Bifida and Hydrocephalus, 81
International Spinal Cord Society, 425
Jennifer Trust for Spinal Muscular Atrophy, 434
Scoliosis Association, 564
Society for Research into Hydrocephalus and Spina Bifida, 577
Spinal Injuries Action Association, 46
Spinal Injuries Association, 601

Sporting Goods

Association of Cycle Traders, 98
Bicycle Association of Great Britain, 131
European Fishing Tackle Trade Association, 293
Lightweight Cycle Manufacturers' Association, 447
Outdoor Industries Association, 510
The Sports Industries Federation, 612

Sports

International Society of Biomechanics in Sports, 424
International Sports Engineering Association, 425

Sports Medicine

British Association of Sport and Medicine, 153
Irish Sports Medicine Association, 34

Sri Lanka

Tamil Information Centre, 608

Standards

British Measurement and Testing Association, 186
British Standards Institution, 207
European Cooperation in Legal Metrology, 290
Institute of Measurement and Control, 371
National Standards Authority of Ireland, 39

Stationery

Envelope Makers' and Manufacturing Stationers' Association, 280
Greeting Card Association, 333

Statistics

Association of Football Statisticians, 101
Organisation of Professional Users of Statistics, 509
Royal Statistical Society, 559
Statistical and Social Inquiry Society of Ireland, 46
Statistics Users' Council, 603

Steam Engines

Steam Plough Club, 603

Stone

Institute of Quarrying - England, 375
Master Carvers Association, 458
National Federation of Terrazzo Marble and Mosaic Specialists, 491
Natural Slate Quarries Association, 501
United Kingdom Cast Stone Association, 625

Storytelling

Folklore of Ireland Society, 16
Society for Storytelling, 578

Stress

Association of Stress Consultants, 117
Association of Stress Therapists, 117

Stroke

Stroke Association, 605

Students

National Union of Students - United Kingdom, 501
Union of Students in Ireland, 47

Substance Abuse

Al-Anon Family Groups - United Kingdom and Eire, 60
Alcohol Focus Scotland, 670
Alcoholics Anonymous - England, 60
DrugScope, 271
European Association for the Treatment of Addiction - U.K., 285
National Association of Alcohol and Drug Abuse Counsellors, 474

Institute of Export, 365
Irish Exporters Association, 26
Middle East Association, 463
Military Heraldry Society, 463
National Guild of Master Craftsmen, 39
Trading Standards Institute, 618
Traidcraft, 619
World Trade Centre London, 649

Trainers

Northern Ireland Training Council Association, 662
Sector SKills Alliance Scotland, 715

Translation

Association of Translation Companies, 120
Institute of Translation and Interpreting, 379
Simultaneous Interpretation Equipment Suppliers Association, 569
Swedish-English Literary Translators' Association, 607

Transplantation

British Transplantation Society, 209

Transportation

Associated Society of Locomotive Engineers and Firemen, 74
Association for European Transport, 76
Association for Road Traffic Safety and Management, 80
Association of British Drivers, 86
Association of Local Bus Company Managers, 108
British Institute of Traffic Education Research, 182
British International Freight Association, 183
British Parking Association, 192
British Road Federation, 198
British Tunnelling Society, 210
Chartered Institute of Logistics Transport, 226
Community Transport Association, 247
Confederation of Passenger Transport - UK, 251
Freight Transport Association, 322
Heavy Transport Association, 342
Institute of Highway Incorporated Engineers, 367
Institute of Transport Administration, 379
Institution of Highways and Transportation, 383
International Transport Workers' Federation, 427
Licensed Taxi Drivers Association, 445
Light Rail Transit Association, 446
London Transport Users Committee, 452
National Federation of Bus Users, 489
National Taxicab Association, 499
National Union of Marine, Aviation and Shipping Transport Officers, 500
National Union of Rail, Maritime and Transport Workers, 501
Passenger Shipping Association, 514
Road Haulage Association, 543
Services, Industrial Professional and Technical Union, 44
Society of Operations Engineers, 594
Transport and General Workers Union, 619
Transport Association, 619
United Road Transport Union, 630
Wheelwrights' Company, 637

Trauma

European Wound Management Association, 303

Travel

Association for the Study of Travel in Egypt and the Near East, 83
Association of British Travel Agents, 89
Association of Independent Tour Operators, 104
Association of National Tourist in the UK, 111
Association of Scottish Visitor Attractions, 674
British Activity Holiday Association, 137
European Business Travel Association, 287
Federation of Tour Operators, 312
Hong Kong Tourist Association - London, 346
Institute of Travel and Tourism, 379
International Federation of Tour Operators, 408
International Youth Hostel Federation, 431
Irish Youth Hostel Association, 35
School and Group Travel Association, 563
School Journey Association, 563
Scottish Tourist Board, 714
Tourism Society, 617
Youth Hostels Association - England and Wales, 654

Travel Services

Irish Travel Agents Association, 34

Trees and Shrubs

European Arboricultural Council, 283
International Dendrology Society, 402
Irish Christmas Tree Growers, 25

Tropical Medicine

International Federation for Tropical Medicine, 403
Royal Society of Tropical Medicine and Hygiene, 559

Tropical Studies

International Institute of Tropical Agriculture, 412

Undersea Medicine

European Underwater and BaroMedical Society, 684

Unions

Amalgamated Transport and General Workers Union Women's Committee, 657
Commonwealth Trade Union Council, 246
Federation of Managerial Professional and General Associations, 310
General Federation of Trade Unions, 328
Northern Ireland Committee, 660
Trades Union Congress - England, 618
Trades Union Congress - Women's Committee, 618

United Nations

United Nations Association of Great Britain and Northern Ireland, 629

Urban Affairs

Association of Town Centre Management, 119
London Society, 451
Town and Country Planning Association, 618

Urology

Association for Continence Advice, 75
British Association of Urological Surgeons of England, 154

Zoological Gardens

Federation of Zoological Gardens of Great Britain and Ireland, 313
Zoological Society of London, 654

Zoology

Association for the Study of Animal Behaviour, 82
Association of British Wild Animal Keepers, 89
International Commission on Zoological Nomenclature, 398
International Society for Anthrozoology, 420
Mammal Society, 455
North of England Zoological Society, 504
Royal Zoological Society of Scotland, 698
Society of Protozoologists, British Section, 595
Zoological Society of Glasgow and West of Scotland, 720
Zoological Society of Ireland, 48
Zoological Society of Northern Ireland, 666

Acronym Index